Leaders & the Leadership Process

Readings, Self-Assessments & Applications

Leaders & the Leadership Process

Readings, Self-Assessments & Applications

Fifth Edition

Jon L. Pierce

John W. Newstrom

Boston   Burr Ridge, IL   Dubuque, IA   Madison, WI   New York   San Francisco   St. Louis
Bangkok   Bogotá   Caracas   Kuala Lumpur   Lisbon   London   Madrid   Mexico City
Milan   Montreal   New Delhi   Santiago   Seoul   Singapore   Sydney   Taipei   Toronto

McGraw-Hill
Irwin

LEADERS & THE LEADERSHIP PROCESS:
READINGS, SELF-ASSESSMENTS & APPLICATIONS

Published by McGraw-Hill/Irwin, a business unit of The McGraw-Hill Companies, Inc., 1221 Avenue of the Americas, New York, NY, 10020. Copyright © 2008, 2006, 2003, 2000, 1995 by The McGraw-Hill Companies, Inc. All rights reserved. No part of this publication may be reproduced or distributed in any form or by any means, or stored in a database or retrieval system, without the prior written consent of The McGraw-Hill Companies, Inc., including, but not limited to, in any network or other electronic storage or transmission, or broadcast for distance learning.

Some ancillaries, including electronic and print components, may not be available to customers outside the United States.

This book is printed on acid-free paper.

3 4 5 6 7 8 9 0 QPD/QPD 0 9

ISBN 978-0-07-353028-4
MHID 0-07-353028-X

Editorial director: *Brent Gordon*
Publisher: *Paul Ducham*
Managing developmental editor: *Laura Hurst Spell*
Editorial assistant: *Sara Knox Hunter*
Associate marketing manager: *Kelly Odom*
Project manager: *Dana M. Pauley*
Lead production supervisor: *Michael R. McCormick*
Senior designer: *Cara David*
Lead media project manager: *Cathy L. Tepper*
Cover design: *George Kokkonas*
Typeface: *10/12 New Century Schoolbook*
Compositor: *International Typesetting and Composition*
Printer: *Quebecor World Dubuque Inc.*

Library of Congress Cataloging-in-Publication Data

Leaders & the leadership process: readings, self-assessments & applications / [edited by] Jon L. Pierce, John W. Newstrom.—5th ed.
    p. cm.
    Includes bibliographical references and index.
    ISBN 13: 978-0-07-353028-4 (alk. paper)
    ISBN 10: 0-07-353028-X (alk. paper)
    1. Leadership. 2. Leadership—Case studies. 3. Leadership—Problems, exercises, etc.
I. Pierce, Jon L. (Jon Lepley). II. Newstrom, John W. III. Title: Leaders and the leadership process.
HM1261.L413 2008
303.3'4—dc22   2007036792

About the Editors

Jon L. Pierce is a Morse-Alumni Distinguished Professor of Management and Organization in the Labovitz School of Business and Economics at the University of Minnesota Duluth (UMD). He received his Ph.D. in management and organizational studies at the University of Wisconsin–Madison. He is the author of more than 70 papers that have been published or presented at various professional conferences. His publications have appeared in the *Academy of Management Journal, Academy of Management Review, Journal of Management, Journal of Organizational Behavior, Journal of Applied Behavioral Science, Journal of Social Psychology, Journal of Occupational and Organizational Psychology, Organizational Dynamics, Organizational Behavior and Human Decision Processes, Personnel Psychology,* and *Review of General Psychology.* His research interests focus on the psychology of work and organization in general, with an emphasis on the effects of employee ownership systems, work, and social system design. Much of his recent work is oriented around psychological ownership and organization-based self-esteem. He was a visiting scholar in the Department of Psychology at the University of Waikato in New Zealand. He has served on the editorial review board for the *Academy of Management Journal, Personnel Psychology, Journal of Management,* and *Scandinavian Management Journal.* He is the coauthor of seven books—*Management, Managing, Management and Organizational Behavior: An Integrated Perspective,* and along with John W. Newstrom, *Alternative Work Schedules, Windows into Management, The Manager's Bookshelf: A Mosaic of Contemporary Views,* and *Leaders and the Leadership Process.* Along with Randall B. Dunham he was the recipient of the Yoder-Heneman Personnel Research Award for their alternative work schedule research. In 2000 he was inducted into the *Academy of Management Journal's* Hall of Fame; in 2005 he received UMD's prestigious award for excellence in research. Dr. Pierce may be contacted at jpierce@d.umn.edu.

John W. Newstrom is a Morse-Alumni Distinguished Teaching Professor Emeritus of Management in the Labovitz School of Business and Economics at the University of Minnesota Duluth, where he taught for 28 years. Prior to that, he completed his doctoral degree in management and industrial relations at the University of Minnesota and then taught at Arizona State University for several years. His work has appeared in publications such as *Academy of Management Executive, Personnel Psychology, California Management Review, Journal of Management, Academy of Management Journal, Business Horizons,* and the *Journal of Management Development.* He has served as an editorial reviewer for the *Academy of Management Review, Academy of Management Journal, Academy of Management Executive, Human Resource Development Quarterly, Advanced Management Journal,* and the *Journal of Management Development.* He is the author or coauthor of 40 books in various editions, including *Organizational Behavior: Human Behavior at Work* (twelfth edition), *Supervision* (ninth edition), *Transfer of Training* (with Mary Broad), *Leading with Laughter* (with Robert C. Ford), and *The Big Book of Team Building Games* (with Ed Scannell). He is a member of the University of Minnesota's Academy of Distinguished Teachers and has served on the boards of directors for several nonprofit organizations. He has also actively served as a seminar leader for leadership development programs around the country and as a consultant to many others. One of his current interests lies in helping managers create and sustain a fun work environment for their employees. Dr. Newstrom can be contacted at jnewstro@d.umn.edu.

Dedication

To the founders of the university (the University of Wisconsin and the University of Minnesota, our respective alma maters), to those who support its existence, and to those who have worked to sustain the academic freedom that makes the university a place where there can be a "continuous and fearless sifting and winnowing by which truth can be found,"[1] a place where free thought and expression are encouraged, and a place dedicated to intellectual growth and development of others.

Jon L. Pierce

John W. Newstrom

[1] University of Wisconsin Board of Regents 1894.

Preface

THE BOOK: LEADERS AND THE LEADERSHIP PROCESS

Several years ago the management and organization faculty at the University of Minnesota Duluth decided that the undergraduate curriculum needed a course in leadership. Claims that many of our organizations were overmanaged and underled and that the crisis facing American organizations was in large part a function of bad management and inept leadership led us to believe that it was important for our students to explore the subject of leadership in greater depth and to begin thinking about and looking at themselves within the leadership context. A course in leadership might serve as an important catalyst in fulfilling this objective. Today two decades later, this course remains one of the most popular within our management major, as personal, professional, and intellectual interest in leaders and leadership remains alive and well. A romantic notion for leaders (and heroes) is still intact.

As part of the design process for the first edition of this book—a design that has guided the subsequent editions—we consulted several leadership scholars around the country, asking for assistance with the construction of a reading list for our new course. We informed these individuals of our decision to conduct an undergraduate seminar in leadership and asked them to help identify important material from the leadership literature. After compiling this list, we offered our first course. During the past two decades, this course has been offered on numerous occasions and continually refined.

Mary Fischer, John Weimeister, and Bill Schoof of Austen Press encouraged us to take our undergraduate course materials in leadership and put them into book form. Their interest in our leadership class led to the creation of this book and its first editions.

PURPOSE OF THE BOOK

Few management and organization topics have generated as much interest and research activity as leadership. Fads in the corporate world find their roots in practitioners' fancies for and belief in quick fixes for organizational woes and consultants' desires to make a quick buck. Thus, the corporate desire to search continually for "new bottles for old wine," coupled with academicians' inclinations to study and think about what inspires them, creates all the ingredients for a short-lived interest in leaders and the leadership process. However, this has not been the case. Instead, widespread interest in leadership has spanned more than eight decades, with significant historical roots stemming from the works of many ancient Greek, Roman, Chinese, and Egyptian philosophers.

Thousands of pages in academic books and journals have been devoted to the topic of leadership. During the past several years, the popular press has published and sold millions of copies of several dozen books written on the topic of leaders and leadership. Organizations frantically search for the magical leader who can pull the firm together and place it back on the competitive path. We frequently hear stories about important historical leaders; we attribute organizational successes and failures to the things that our leaders did or failed to do; and at the national level we commonly resurrect dreams of the way it was when certain charismatic leaders were at the nation's helm. *Time* magazine and CBS on occasion offer segments on leaders and revolutionary individuals, portraying such individuals as Mao Zedong, Ho Chi Minh, Margaret Thatcher, Winston Churchill, Joseph Stalin, Margaret Sanger, Ronald Reagan, and Franklin and Eleanor Roosevelt.

A strong interest in leadership is evident. Our university, along with a large number of other institutions of higher education, has in recent years instituted courses in leadership. During the past half-dozen years, we have witnessed the publication of several academic textbooks devoted to the topic of leadership. This is testimony to the popularity and presumed importance of leadership.

This book's development reflects that interest and the obvious need for a greater number of individuals to take the issue of organizational leadership more seriously. *The primary purpose of this book is to serve as a catalyst for the student of leadership's thinking and dialogue about leaders and the leadership process.* This book is intended to give the student a feel for the breadth and richness of this study. This set of readings aims to provide the student with a sense of the complexity associated with organizational leadership, as well as an important understanding of some of the pieces that serve to define this complex mosaic called leadership.

Selection of readings for inclusion in *Leaders and the Leadership Process* has been guided by several operating principles. First, we recognize the fact that the leadership literature is extremely voluminous and that the typical leadership course is one academic term in length. Therefore, we have sought to create a book of readings that provides a glimpse of the leadership literature from the beginning of its study to the current period. The articles included here provide the reader with the opportunity to look into the major leadership themes (e.g., leader traits, leader behavior, situational leadership, followers, charismatic and transformational leadership). Second, we have chosen to limit this set of readings to those that have appeared in the scientific literature, as opposed to the popular press. These selections will give students a substantive foundation for their further study of and reflections on leadership. Finally, as instructors of a course in leadership, we have included readings that we feel are teachable. Our primary test for inclusion consisted of these questions: Does the reading provide our students with insight into this complex phenomenon? Are the ideas presented comprehensible for upper-level undergraduate students? Is the reading capable of generating a provocative dialogue among students? Do the authors provide students with "take aways"—useful ideas, observations, and insights—that they can carry away from the article and employ in subsequent readings and conversations and use to inform their leadership decisions.

THE LEADERSHIP CONTEXT

The concept of leadership has been employed within different contexts and at different levels of analysis (e.g., self-leadership, small group leadership, organizational leadership, national leadership, leadership of the free world). As editors of this book of readings, we hope that the readings contained in *Leaders and the Leadership Process* will accomplish two objectives. First, while this collection of readings is not a cookbook that tells you how to lead successfully, the writings of the scholars represented in this collection can be used to inform your thinking about and understanding of leadership, as well as to guide the leadership decisions that you will have the occasion to make when you are called upon to lead. Second, we strive to assist you in understanding leadership within the small group (team) context. We are confident that at one time or another, you will be called upon to lead in a small group (team) setting, and we trust that the leadership literature to which you will be exposed in this collection will aid you in understanding the concept of leadership within the small group (team) setting and will provide you with a knowledge base so that you will be able to practice evidence-based leadership.

With regard to this second objective, it is evident that during the past few decades we have witnessed an increase in the organizational use of work teams. Teams have slowly and quietly revolutionized how people perform work and how organizations are structured. Teams are virtually everywhere—on the production floor, in the boardroom, in the office of the president, and at virtually every level between the very top and bottom of the organization. Not only are teams everywhere, there is a myriad of different *types* of teams—production and service teams, self-directed work teams, parallel teams, cross-functional teams, cross-level teams, task teams, quality control circles, joint labor–management teams, executive teams, action teams, negotiation teams, advice and involvement teams, and on and on.

Work teams arose from the human resource movement and the belief that employee involvement, collaborative efforts, and the synergies created through group cohesiveness and involvement increase organizational efficiency and effectiveness. As people became more productive, personal and group experiences of accomplishment became a source of increased job satisfaction, increased commitment, and motivation to sustain the very success that brought satisfaction.

Social psychologists and small group scholars commonly define a *group* as two or more interdependent individuals who interact with one another to achieve a commonly held objective. Groups are seen as living, self-regulating systems that sense and interact with their environment. The term *team* has a long history as a part of our sports vocabulary—the University of Wisconsin (Badger) football team, the Johns Hopkins (Blue Jays) lacrosse team, the Duke (Blue Devils) basketball team, and the University of Minnesota Duluth (Bulldog) hockey team. Within the workplace, the use of the concept of teams (work teams) is relatively new. While Procter & Gamble pioneered the contemporary use of teams in North America in the 1960s, work done at London's Tavistock Institute of Human Relations after World War II demonstrated the importance of cohesive and self-regulating work teams, giving rise to the emergence of sociotechnical systems theory.

Today many organizations have created teams. Anecdotal reports suggest that the vast majority of the Fortune 100 companies use work teams. For many, the terms *team* and *group* are used interchangeably. For those who make a distinction, all teams are groups, but not all groups are teams. *A team is a group of two or more people joined in cooperative activity for work or play.* Team members not only interact with each other, they also perceive themselves as a team, have a common goal, share responsibility for outcomes, see themselves and are seen by others as a social system, and endeavor, often strenuously, to attain that goal.[1] Attaining the goal results in a collective feeling of accomplishment, which further strengthens the team's emotional and intellectual bond. The primary distinguishing characteristics of teams, then, are the intensity with which team members work together, their emotional and interpersonal bonding, and the overriding pursuit of a collectively shared goal—their *esprit de corps*. The degree of 'bondedness' may be seen as a primary criterion which distinguishes groups from teams. Groups do not exhibit the cohesiveness, either emotionally or socially, that teams do. This bondedness is part of what makes the team work well.

As noted above, there is a myriad of different types of teams. One useful typology identifies several different types of work teams based on their level (degree) of self-management. For example, there are manager-led teams, self-managing teams, self-designing teams, and self-governing teams. In the first type mentioned, the team is headed by a manager, whose responsibility is to plan, organize, direct, and control the team's task performance. The self-managing team has a manager who assumes responsibility for planning (i.e., goal setting) and organizing, while team members take on responsibilities associated with

---

[1] M.E. Shaw, *Group Dynamics: The Psychology of Small Group Behavior,* 3rd ed. (New York: McGraw-Hill, 1981).

directing, controlling, and task performance. The self-designing team also has a manager whose task is to set goals and the overall direction for the team, while the team members assume responsibility for organizing, directing, controlling, and task performance. In the self-governing team, all the team management responsibilities (e.g., planning, organizing, directing, and controlling) and task performance are borne by the team members. It is in such groups that leaders may emerge (see Chapter 5), and on a few occasions the groups manage to sustain themselves as a leaderless group via the central leadership role provided by substitutes for leadership (see Chapter 12). It is not at all unusual to witness the emergence of a leader and leader-provided leadership in each of the four team contexts.

Self-managed work teams typically find themselves embedded within the context of larger organization. As a result each team finds itself surrounded by the presence of an organizational hierarchy to which it is accountable. At least in their early stages, yet throughout their entire lives, virtually all self-managed work teams will be exposed to what is referred to as *vertical leadership*—leadership coming from a person formally appointed to play a leadership role within and for the team—leadership that is projected downward on one's followers.

With a team's maturity, horizontal leadership commonly emerges. *Horizontal leadership* is defined as leadership that is shared by team members. According to Pearce (2004) "shared leadership entails a simultaneous, ongoing, mutual influence process within a team" (p. 48).[2] The sharing of leadership among team members, in the face of an emergent leader or in a truly leaderless group, is likely to be commonplace when the team's vertical leader is characterized by a passive/democratic empowered leadership style.

Throughout this set of readings there will be the occasional reference to commanders, supervisors, managers, dictators, and presidents. In spite of that fact, it is toward the development of an understanding of leadership within the work group (team) context that this collection of readings is intended and toward which we hope to channel your thinking.

WHAT THE BOOK IS AND IS NOT

This book of readings cannot provide the reader with thorough and complete coverage of the leadership literature. During the past eight decades, those leadership scholars who have chosen to observe, study, think, and write about leadership have produced literally thousands of pages of theory and empirical observation. For obvious reasons, this text provides but a sampling of this literature.

While this book does touch on many of the major themes that have characterized the work done in the realm of leadership, many important authors and contributions could not be included. These omissions are not intended to downplay the importance of the scholarship that they have given to our understanding of this very important topic.

While this book does include some of the classic and seminal articles on leadership, many classical pieces could not be included. Once again, the omissions are not intended to suggest that these works are less important than the pieces we ultimately chose to include.

THE LEADERSHIP MOSAIC

Before we embark on our study of leadership, we would like to share a metaphor with you. The metaphor is that of a mosaic. Your authors live and work at the University of Minnesota in Duluth, Minnesota, a community located along the north shore of Lake Superior. On the city's boardwalk there are many beautiful

---

[2] C.L. Pearce. The future of leadership: Combining vertical and shared leadership to transform knowledge work. *Academy of Management Executive,* 18, 1 (2004), pp. 47–57.

views of the "big lake" (Lake Gitchi Gummi, as named by the Native Americans who lived in this part of the world) and the hilled city rising several hundred feet above the lake and named after the explorer Daniel Greysolon Sieur du-Luth.

As you walk along Duluth's boardwalk, you come upon an extremely large, blue and white mosaic that depicts many scenes from the city's long maritime history. This mosaic is made up of literally thousands and thousands of 1 by 1 inch tile squares.

As we worked to prepare our school's leadership class and to select the readings for this book, we were confronted by an extremely rich, complex, and extensive literature. This is a literature whose history dates back to the early 1900s, a literature given to us by those who have led and those who have followed, a literature given to us by a number of philosophers, and a literature that has stemmed from the careful and systematic application of the scientific method. Not only have there been hundreds of books written about leadership, there have also been thousands and thousands of journal pages devoted to an exploration of the concept and its myriad themes.

The study of leadership that you are about to embark on reminds us of a mosaic. There are dozens and dozens of concepts, perspectives, themes, hypotheses, and theories. Each represents a small piece of the overall leadership mosaic. It is impossible to see and therefore appreciate the mosaic that captures images of the tall ships and whale-back boats that once sailed Lake Superior by looking at a single tile. In a similar way, you will not come to understand leadership by reading the work of a single author or by becoming familiar with a single concept, definition of leadership, or one of the many midrange leadership theories.

We invite you to read carefully the many authors who share with us their views and observations on leadership. No one singularly paints a full and complete picture for us. We encourage you to examine the concepts, propositions, perspectives, and theories one at a time; then use each as a tile for the construction of your own leadership mosaic. We hope this will be a challenging as well as a fun and personally enriching task.

THE BOOK'S ORGANIZATION

Part One: Readings: The Conceptual and Empirical Leadership Literature

Part One presents readings and self-assessments that are focused on various aspects of leaders and the leadership process. Part Two contains a set of applications. Part One, divided into 15 chapters, presents a set of readings that will help students understand leaders and the leadership process. The majority of the readings are taken from academic journals. Our editing has streamlined several readings by removing complex sections, thus making the material more reader-friendly and appropriate for diverse audiences.

- Chapter 1 looks at the definition of leadership, suggests that leadership is a process, and provides some insight into the role played by leaders.

- Chapter 2 inquires about the leader–follower relationship. Fairness, trust, and ethical behavior are three important dimensions that define this relationship.

- Chapter 3 suggests that effective leaders are individuals who possess the "right stuff." The traits associated with effective leadership are reviewed.

- Chapter 4 continues the theme of leader traits and looks specifically at the role of sex and gender in the leadership equation.

- Chapter 5 asks the question, How do people come to be leaders? The dynamics associated with leader emergence are explored.

- Chapter 6 builds on the suggestion that leadership is an influence process. The bases of power and forms of influence that leaders use to move followers are examined.

- Chapter 7 explores the suggestion that effective leadership is in part a function of what leaders do. The behaviors that can be used to describe effective leadership are examined.

- Chapter 8 suggests that different situations call for different leader behaviors. One leadership style simply does not serve all individuals (followers), nor does it serve all situations within which leaders and their followers find themselves embedded.

- Chapter 9 continues the theme that "it all depends upon the situation," or "every situation is different." This chapter asks if leadership style and effectiveness are bound by cultural dissimilarities.

- Chapter 10 reinforces the notion that the follower plays a powerful role in the leadership process. The follower is not a passive part of the leadership formula and, in fact, the attributes and behaviors of the follower frequently serve to shape the leadership process.

- Chapter 11 explores the long-standing interest in participative leadership. Issues surrounding the theoretical reasons for the use of participative leadership and insight into the relationship between participation and leader effectiveness are explored.

- Chapter 12 suggests that there are substitutes for leadership. While it is easy to conclude that leadership is always necessary, the readings in this chapter suggest that there are situational factors that can serve as substitutes for, neutralizers of, and enhancers of leaders and their behaviors.

- Chapters 13 and 14 provide insight into the nature and character of the charismatic and the transformational leaders—leadership styles that today's business world appears to be frantically searching for.

- Chapter 15 asks us to recognize that leadership is not always a positive force. The readings in this chapter suggest that there are a number of potentially dysfunctional aspects associated with leadership.

- The Epilogue asks this seemingly strange question, Does leadership really make a difference? You are asked to reflect upon two propositions: *Point:* Leadership does *not* make a difference; it is simply the product of a societal love affair and romantic notions that surround leaders. *Counterpoint:* Leadership *does* make a difference in the level of organizational performance; it is not simply a socially constructed organizational reality.

- Finally, Appendix A presents a tuitorial which is intended to assist the students in their reading of the three different types of scientific literature (i.e., empirical studies, literature reviews, and theory/conceptual) appearing in this book of readings.

Self-Assessments

Many of the chapters include self-assessment exercises, which give readers the opportunity to profile themselves along several different dimensions associated with leaders and the leadership process. These self-assessments provide readers with an opportunity to take a look at themselves and further understand how they fit within the realm of this complex mosaic of leadership.

We encourage you to be brutally honest with yourself as you complete your self-assessments. Unless you are, the results will lack validity as a basis for self-improvement. You might even consider asking one person or more (who know you well) to fill out the same forms (focused on you) to provide you with additional useful perspectives for triangulation in comparison with your own self-portrait.

You are encouraged to use the grid that follows the preface to record your score on each of the self-assessments and interpret your score as it relates to you as a leader.

Part Two: Beyond the Theory and Empiricism and into the Practice of Leadership

Part Two provides readers with additional opportunities to explore leaders and the leadership process. This section of the book is intended to move students beyond the theory of leadership and closer to the world of practice and application.

To facilitate students' ability to apply their understanding of the leadership literature and work on the development of analytical and problem-solving skills, we have included several case studies and exercises. We firmly believe that active learning contributes more to the overall learning process than passive learning. We therefore encourage students to read, think about, discuss, debate, observe, experiment with, analyze, and solve issues that define leadership and the leadership process. The cases and exercises are intended to supplement the conceptual material and help readers come to understand leaders and the leadership process more fully.

A LEADERSHIP DIARY—REFLECTIONS UPON LEADERSHIP

We would like to encourage you to keep a *leadership diary* in which you record your experiences, your reactions, your reflections, and your interpretations of specific leadership events and transactions.

The day-to-day world that we live in is a giant leadership laboratory; leaders and the leadership process surround us. Take advantage of this laboratory by observing and attempting to interpret its various events. Use the concepts and models to which you are being exposed through this set of readings.

A portion of your leadership diary should contain reflections entitled "Coming to Understand Leadership Transactions." From the perspective of self-guided learning, you are encouraged to observe and reflect upon several leadership transactions. Take notes and record them in your leadership diary. Specifically, we encourage you to identify a leadership event or transaction that you have experienced. These events may be situations that you passively observed unfold in which leadership was exercised, events in which you held a leadership role, and/or transactions during which you were actively and personally exposed to someone else exercising leadership.

In addition to describing the event, *interpret* this experience by framing it within the context of the leadership literature that you are examining this academic term. (For example, based upon Bass's approaches to the definition of leadership, how do you see leadership unfolding? Based upon French and Raven's sources of power framework, what power base was operating, how, and why? Based upon trait theory, what leader attributes were at work, and why do you think so? Based upon Hollander's work, how did this person emerge as the group's leader? What were the dynamics and processes that were at play?

YOUR LEADERSHIP REFLECTIONS

Now that we have spent nearly a decade conducting undergraduate seminars on leaders and the leadership process, two observations stand out. First, students quite naturally seem to focus their attention on successful (effective) leaders, ignoring those leaders or leadership practices that lead to failure. Second, there is a strong reliance on isolated and personal experiences to define reality. Leadership, after all, is something that we have all encountered. Leadership is one topic in the university curriculum on which virtually every student has opinions before taking the course and reading this set of readings.

With regard to these two observations, we offer two suggestions with the hope that they will guide your leadership reflections. Relating to our first observation, we comment on the use of the method of differences. Related to our second observation, we comment on a role for personal experiences.

The first suggestion relates to the use of the *method of differences* as opposed to the *method of extremes*. In this case the method of extremes refers to that tendency to focus almost exclusively upon the successful leaders (e.g., Ghandi, Martin Luther King, Jesus Christ, Adolph Hitler) or on the unsuccessful leaders even though they are often the less-interesting ("sexy") topic. Borrowing the thoughts of a friend and former colleague, the late Professor Larry L. Cummings (Carlson Professor of Organizational Behavior, University of Minnesota), we note that the method of differences would require us to study the conditions that gave rise to successful leadership, and to contrast those leaders with leaders that were not successful. The method of differences is likely to lead to observations that are much less dramatic and much less exciting, but it is much more likely to lead to observations that are more generalizable across leadership situations, as well as being generative in terms of ideas for further inquiry.

The method of extremes (i.e., looking only at the most successful leaders) does not lead to a diagnostic frame of mind. It does not lead to a frame of mind that questions why something happened, under what conditions it happened, or under what conditions it would not happen. The method of differences is much more likely to lead to the discovery of the conditional nature of knowledge and the conditional nature of prescriptions.

The second observation relates to the role of direct and personal experiences as a teacher. There are many ways (e.g., faith; intuition; the words of attractive, trusted, and respected others; direct and vicarious experiences; and science) through which we come to know that which we know. Because experiences are direct and personal, our experiences tend to be one of our most powerful teachers. While there are many problems associated with learning from personal experience (e.g., we are biased observers of our own behaviors, one's experience is quite simply that—in all likelihood it is one of many, and it may not be very representative of its universe), there is a powerful role for your personal experiences to play in your study of leadership.

McGill University management professor Henry Mintzberg recently observed that learning is most interesting and powerful when formalized knowledge (i.e., well-developed concepts, theories, and scientific-based observations) and lived experiences connect. It is our hope that this can be accomplished through your thoughtful reflection and the dialogue that you have with your professors and fellow students.

Self-Assessment Summary Record

Instructions: You are encouraged to record each of your self-assessment scores below. Accompanying each score you should also provide a brief interpretation of what that score means to you and/or an action plan for change. You might find it interesting to return to this self-assessment in one, three, and five years to monitor changes (or consistency) in your profile.

You might also consider preparing additional commentary for each self-assessment score that portrays (a) how you will behaviorally *demonstrate* that particular dimension (e.g., self-confidence, or various influence tactics), and (b) what your personal *plan for self-improvement* on that dimension will be.

Self-confidence (Generalized self-efficacy)
Score: _____
Personal meaning/Interpretation: _____

Leader-member exchange
Score: _____
Personal meaning/Interpretation: _____

Justice

Procedural justice
Score: _____
Personal meaning/Interpretation: _____

Distributive justice
Score: _____
Personal meaning/Interpretation: _____

Interpersonal justice
Score: _____
Personal meaning/Interpretation: _____

Informational justice
Score: _____
Personal meaning/Interpretation: _____

Trust in leadership
Score: _____
Personal meaning/Interpretation: _____

Job affect

Positive job affect
Score: _____
Personal meaning/Interpretation: _____

High positive job affect
Score: _____
Personal meaning/Interpretation: _____

Negative job affect
Score: _____
Personal meaning/Interpretation: _____

High negative job affect
Score: _____
Personal meaning/Interpretation: _____

Motivation to lead
Score: _____
Personal meaning/Interpretation: _____

Masculinity–Femininity

    Masculinity

        Score: _____

        Personal meaning/Interpretation: _____

    Femininity

        Score: _____

        Personal meaning/Interpretation: _____

    Androgyny

        Score: _____

        Personal meaning/Interpretation: _____

Self-monitoring

    Score: _____

    Personal meaning/Interpretation: _____

Emotional intelligence

    Overall (global) score: _____

    Personal meaning/Interpretation: _____

    Perception, appraisal, and expression of emotions

        Score: _____

        Personal meaning/Interpretation: _____

    Emotional facilitation of thinking

        Score: _____

        Personal meaning/Interpretation: _____

    Understanding and analyzing emotions and employing emotional knowledge

        Score: _____

        Personal meaning/Interpretation: _____

    Reflective regulation

        Score: _____

        Personal meaning/Interpretation: _____

Influence tactics

    Rational persuasion

        Score: _____

        Personal meaning/Interpretation: _____

    Pressure

        Score: _____

        Personal meaning/Interpretation: _____

    Upward appeal

        Score: _____

        Personal meaning/Interpretation: _____

    Exchange

        Score: _____

        Personal meaning/Interpretation: _____

    Ingratiation

        Score: _____

        Personal meaning/Interpretation: _____

    Coalition

        Score: _____

        Personal meaning/Interpretation: _____

Inspirational appeal

Score: _____

Personal meaning/Interpretation: _____

Consultation

Score: _____

Personal meaning/Interpretation: _____

Personal power profile

Reward power

Score: _____

Personal meaning/Interpretation: _____

Coercive power

Score: _____

Personal meaning/Interpretation: _____

Legitimate power

Score: _____

Personal meaning/Interpretation: _____

Referent power

Score: _____

Personal meaning/Interpretation: _____

Expert power

Score: _____

Personal meaning/Interpretation: _____

Michigan Organizational Assessment

Personal support

Score: _____

Personal meaning/Interpretation: _____

Goal emphasis

Score: _____

Personal meaning/Interpretation: _____

Work facilitation

Score: _____

Personal meaning/Interpretation: _____

Initiating structure and consideration

Consideration behavior

Score: _____

Personal meaning/Interpretation: _____

Initiating structure behavior

Score: _____

Personal meaning/Interpretation: _____

Least Preferred Co-worker (LPC)

Score: _____

Personal meaning/Interpretation: _____

Need for leadership

Score: _____

Personal meaning/Interpretation: _____

Individualism–Collectivism

Score: _____

Personal meaning/Interpretation: _____

Participatory leadership attitudes

Overall Score: _____

Personal meaning/Interpretation: _____

Person's capacity

Score: _____

Personal meaning/Interpretation: _____

Information sharing

Score: _____

Personal meaning/Interpretation: _____

Participation

Score: _____

Personal meaning/Interpretation: _____

Supervisory control

Score: _____

Personal meaning/Interpretation: _____

Substitutes for leadership

Ability, experience, training, and knowledge

Score: _____

Personal meaning/Interpretation: _____

Professional orientation

Score: _____

Personal meaning/Interpretation: _____

Indifference toward organizational rewards

Score: _____

Personal meaning/Interpretation: _____

Unambiguous, routine, and methodologically invariant tasks

Score: _____

Personal meaning/Interpretation: _____

Task-provided feedback concerning accomplishments

Score: _____

Personal meaning/Interpretation: _____

Intrinsically satisfying tasks

Score: _____

Personal meaning/Interpretation: _____

Organizational formalization

Score: _____

Personal meaning/Interpretation: _____

Organizational inflexibility

Score: _____

Personal meaning/Interpretation: _____

Advisory and staff functions

Score: _____

Personal meaning/Interpretation: _____

Closely knit, cohesive, interdependent work group

Score: _____

Personal meaning/Interpretation: _____

Rewards not within the leader's control

Score: _____

Personal meaning/Interpretation: _____

Spatial distance between superior and subordinate

Score: _____

Personal meaning/Interpretation: _____

Subordinate need for independence

Score: _____

Personal meaning/Interpretation: _____

Group cohesiveness

Score: _____

Personal meaning/Interpretation: _____

Organization-based self-esteem

Score: _____

Personal meaning/Interpretation: _____

Transformational leadership

Articulate vision

Score: _____

Personal meaning/Interpretation: _____

Role model

Score: _____

Personal meaning/Interpretation: _____

Foster goal acceptance

Score: _____

Personal meaning/Interpretation: _____

Performance expectations

Score: _____

Personal meaning/Interpretation: _____

Individual support

Score: _____

Personal meaning/Interpretation: _____

Intellectual stimulation

Score: _____

Personal meaning/Interpretation: _____

Transactional leader behaviors

Score: _____

Personal meaning/Interpretation: _____

Machiavellianism

Score: _____

Personal meaning/Interpretation: _____

Acknowledgments

There are many individuals whom we would like to acknowledge for their role in assisting us with the creation of this book. First, many organization scholars have worked hard at developing the theory of leadership and providing scientific observations of leaders and the leadership process. We thank them for providing us with an understanding of and insight into this very important organizational phenomenon.

Initial guidance was provided by Robert J. House, Craig Lundberg, Jerry Hunt, Chet Schreisheim, Warren Bennis, Henry P. Sims Jr., Peter Frost, Jane M. Howell, Alan C. Filley, Charles C. Manz, Kimberly Boal, Larry L. Cummings, and Bernard M. Bass. Each provided us with ideas pertaining to important pieces of leadership literature, case studies, and exercises, that could be employed to help communicate the many lessons of leadership.

Following the first edition several individuals, including Anne Cummings, Larry Cummings, Alice Eagly, Edwin Hollander, Brian P. Niehoff, Albert A. Vicere, Jennifer Mencl, Greg Emery, Donald Maier, Gerald Thomas, James Gelah, Dean Frear, Morgan McCall, and Martin Schatz, reviewed, critiqued, and offered very helpful suggestions that aided us in strengthening the breadth, inclusiveness, thoroughness, and quality of our edited work. We want to say "thank you" for your assistance.

A special form of recognition must go to the undergraduate and graduate students who took the leadership course from us here at the University of Minnesota Duluth. Your passionate interest in leadership and the understanding of leaders and the leadership process that you derived from this set of readings encouraged us to assemble this book. Consequently, other students can now benefit from this interesting collection of materials taken from the leadership literature.

We benefited greatly from the many hours of assistance that we received from Andi Pesola and Connie Johnson here at the University of Minnesota Duluth. Andi and Connie provided help with the myriad tasks associated with the preparation of our manuscript, and their patience and ever-willingness to help is appreciated.

We would like to extend our appreciation to Mary Fischer and Bill Schoof of Austen Press. We sincerely appreciate your encouragement, which led to the creation and publication of this book. Finally, we would like to thank John Weimeister for his encouragement and assistance in bringing about the birth and subsequent editions of this book.

Jon L. Pierce

John W. Newstrom

Contents in Brief

Table of Contents

Prologue

Your journey into the study of leadership starts with two very different readings. The first essay, entitled "The Language of Science: A Lens for Understanding the Organizational Sciences Literature," by Jon L. Pierce and Geoffrey G. Bell, is designed to introduce you to the language commonly employed by those who write about the science of leadership. The authors of many of the articles in this book of readings assume you understand the concepts and the language used in science. Pierce and Bell will provide you with a working understanding of the language of science. The second essay takes us into the leadership literature by examining one of the many classics from which leadership lessons can be learned.

The language of science aside, when assembling this book of readings, we found ourselves asking, where should a systematic study of leadership begin? The contemporary study of leaders and the leadership process finds its most recent roots stemming from social psychology, sociology, psychology, and organizational behavior. Several noted group and organizational scholars, among them Kurt Lewin, Ronald Lippitt, Ralph White, J. Dowd, Ralph Stogdill, Edwin Fleishman, and G. Spiller, launched their inquiries into leadership during the 1930s and 1940s, yet many other leadership studies were published during the earlier part of the 1900s.

It is possible however, to start the study of leadership by turning to the classics. Homer's *Iliad* and *Odyssey* provide detailed biographies of great leaders. Plutarch's *Lives* provides insight into what makes great leaders act the way that they do, while Sophocles's plays *Ajax* and *Antigone* depict the psychology of leadership. Shakespeare, in *Othello,* provides a look into the role of intuition and in *King Lear,* provides clues into the difference that leadership makes by examining the role of succession. *The Republic,* by Plato, examines and expresses reservations about democratic management and leadership, while John Stuart Mill, in his essay *On Liberty,* constructs his arguments for participative management.[1]

Fred A. Kramer (1992), author of the second reading, launches our study of leadership with his "Perspectives on Leadership from Homer's *Odyssey.*" We concur with his conclusion that "each of us should evaluate our own journey into self-awareness and self-understanding." We believe you will find many important and contemporary leader attributes that Kramer believes are exemplified in Homer's *Odyssey;* among them are self-confidence, integrity, vision, curiosity, creativity, the management of meaning and trust, and humility.[2] Throughout this collection of readings you will see a return to the importance of many of these aspects of leadership. We hope that the wide variety of readings and other materials in this collection will stimulate you to begin that search into your understanding of leaders and the leadership process. We invite you to study the classic, recent, and emerging perspectives on leadership and reflect on their implications for you, organizations, and our rapidly emerging global community.

Before reading Kramer's article, we again encourage you to start your own leadership diary. Record, daily, your emerging reflections and observations of leaders and acts of leadership that surround you. In addition and as a part of your diary, record your scores and reflections from each of the self-assessment exercises throughout your book, the first of which appears on the next page.

---

[1] For the reader interested in the "classic touch" to the subject of leadership, we recommend John K. Clemens and Douglas F. Mayer's *The Classic Touch: Lessons in Leadership from Homer to Hemingway* (Homewood, IL: Dow Jones–Irwin, 1987).

[2] J. Andrew Morris, C. M. Brotherridge, and J. C. Urbanski offer us an interesting essay on the role of humility and leadership—"Bringing humility to leadership: Antecedents and consequences of leader humility"—appearing in *Human Relations,* 2005, 58, 1323–1350.

Self-Assessment

Self-confidence: Generalized Self-efficacy

This is the first of several self-assessment exercises that you will complete as you read *Leaders and the Leadership Process*. This self-assessment highlights one of Homer's leadership lessons—the importance of self-confidence. As you will see, Chapter 3 ("Leaders and the Role of Personal Traits") also emphasizes the importance of self-confidence as a part of leader emergence and leader effectiveness. We encourage you to return to this particular self-assessment in conjunction with your reading and reflect upon the material in Chapter 3 and the question, Who is a leader and what are his/her distinguishing personal traits?

Instructions: For each of the following statements, indicate the degree to which you *agree* or *disagree* with the statement.

	Strongly Disagree	Disagree	Slightly Disagree	Neither Agree nor Disagree	Slightly Agree	Agree	Strongly Agree
1. When I make plans, I am certain I can make them work.	1	2	3	4	5	6	7
2. One of my problems is that I cannot get down to work when I should.	1	2	3	4	5	6	7
3. If I can't do a job the first time, I keep trying until I can.	1	2	3	4	5	6	7
4. When I set important goals for myself, I rarely achieve them.	1	2	3	4	5	6	7
5. I give up on things before completing them.	1	2	3	4	5	6	7
6. I avoid facing difficulties.	1	2	3	4	5	6	7
7. If something looks too complicated, I will not even bother to try it.	1	2	3	4	5	6	7
8. When I have something unpleasant to do, I stick to it until I finish it.	1	2	3	4	5	6	7
9. When I decide to do something, I go right to work on it.	1	2	3	4	5	6	7
10. When trying to learn something new, I soon give up if I am not initially successful.	1	2	3	4	5	6	7
11. When unexpected problems occur, I don't handle them well.	1	2	3	4	5	6	7
12. I avoid trying to learn new things when they look too difficult for me.	1	2	3	4	5	6	7
13. Failure just makes me try harder.	1	2	3	4	5	6	7
14. I feel insecure about my ability to do things.	1	2	3	4	5	6	7
15. I am a self-reliant person.	1	2	3	4	5	6	7
16. I give up easily.	1	2	3	4	5	6	7
17. I do not seem capable of dealing with most problems that come up in life.	1	2	3	4	5	6	7

Scoring: Subtract each of your scores to questions 2, 4, 5, 6, 7, 10, 11, 12, 14, 16, and 17 from 8. Next, employing your adjusted scores, sum your score for each of the 17 questions, then divide by 17, and enter your score here: _____.

Interpretation: Mowday (1979) notes that self-confidence can be viewed as a belief in one's ability to successfully influence an outcome—that is, a belief that one's efforts can produce results.[1] Thus, it might be suggested that an individual with high self-confidence possesses a strong generalized self-efficacy. Homer (in the *Odyssey*) suggests to us that self-confidence (i.e., a belief in one's self) is a precursor to strong and effective leadership. In addition, it is suggested that Mentor's sense of confidence and vision was contagious, empowering Telemachus to become, himself, an effective leader. The higher your score the stronger your expressed sense of generalized self-efficacy, and the lower your score the weaker the assessment of your generalized self-efficacy. A score of 6 or greater would reflect a strong sense of self-efficacy—confidence that one believes that one has the capacity to succeed when confronted with achievement situations in general. A score of 2 or less would suggest a weak sense of self-efficacy—possessing doubt as to one's capacity to succeed when confronted with achievement situations.

Source: M. Sherer, J. E. Maddux, B. Mercadante, S. Prentice-Dunn, B. Jacobs, and R. W. Rogers, "The Self-efficacy Scale: Construction and Validation," *Psychological Reports* 53 (1982), pp. 899–902. Reprinted with permission.

[1] R. T. Mowday, "Leader Characteristics, Self-confidence, and Methods of Upward Influence in Organizational Decision Making," *Academy of Management Journal* 22 (1979), pp. 709–725.

Reading 1

The Language of Science

A Lens for Understanding the Organizational Sciences Literature

Jon L. Pierce and Geoffrey G. Bell
University of Minnesota Duluth

Psychologist William James (1890) observed that we live in a world of "blooming, buzzing confusion" (p. 480), and each of us works to make personal sense of that which surrounds us. As a part of this process, it is important that each of us come to understand the ways that we come to know the habits of the mind[1] that we have acquired which influence our knowing, and the means by which we can improve upon the processes of adding to our storehouse of knowledge.

Much like in the practice of medicine, there exists today a body of knowledge that can be employed to inform your thinking, aid your decision making, and guide your managerial and leadership actions. 'Evidence-based' management and leadership practices (cf. Pfeffer & Sutton, 2006; Rousseau, 2006) can become a part of your repertoire only if you are capable of accessing, reading, and understanding the evidence that is revealed through the scientific literature. Herein lies the focus of this essay. It is our intention to provide you with the keys to unlock that door. Familiarity with the content of this essay will enable you to access the body of evidence that is scientifically derived, thereby enhancing your ability to engage in evidence-based management and the leadership of others.

There are three different types of scientific literature awaiting your access and use, and to which you will be exposed as a student of leadership, management, and the organizational sciences. First, there are articles that report *empirical evidence*. These articles present research findings of studies conducted by the author. This research unfolds in the field (i.e., in real-world organizations) or in the research laboratory. These types of articles are likely to be the most challenging to read and comprehend, simply because they employ a language particular to the application of the canons of the scientific method (e.g., variables, conceptual relationships, research design, statistics, empirical observations, internal and external validity). This essay is intended to make you more comfortable with this language, and to equip you with a lens that can aid your thinking and understanding of the evidence-based literature. Second, there are articles that present a *theory*. A theory is a generalized explanation (i.e., something akin to a story) of some phenomenon that provides us with insight into that phenomenon—why and when it exists, what it is related to, and what effects it produces. Third, there are articles that are *literature reviews*. In these articles the author systematically attempts to summarize the theory and accumulated empirical work that has focused on a particular phenomenon. The purpose of literature reviews is to provide a current, up-to-date summary of an existing body of knowledge. These reviews can be of two types. The vast majority of the published literature reviews reflect the author's reading and summarization of the literature. Starting during the decade of the 1990s the use of a statistical technique called "meta-analysis" has been employed to provide a more objective summarization of the existing empirically based research findings. Meta-analyses take into consideration the sample sizes employed in the different investigations, as well as statistical observations (e.g., correlation coefficients) among the studied variables. On the basis of statistical analyses of these empirical findings, the author draws conclusions about a body of knowledge. Knowing how to read each of these pieces of literature is important, since they can be a bit overwhelming. To assist you in this activity, we encourage you to look at the contents of Appendix A, "Reading the Scientific Literature: A Tutorial," appearing at the end of Part One of this book of readings. There you are provided with a simple user's guide to aid your reading and understanding of the three different types of scientific (academic) literature.

---

[1] A recurrent, often unconscious pattern of behavior that reflects an inclination of the mind's operation, such as exaggeration, cynicism, indecision, and fantasy.

THE GENESIS OF OUR BELIEFS

We come to our beliefs and knowledge by many different means. While this essay will focus on science as a way of knowing, it is important to recognize that (a) science is not the *only* way of knowing, (b) there are many questions for which science is an inadequate (poor) teacher, (c) for many questions science may well be the most objective teacher, and (d) for many it is one of the least understood and most feared teacher[s]. Our beliefs find their genesis in direct and personal experiences (probably the most powerful teacher for the majority of us), vicarious experiences (i.e., indirect experiences; experiences that a person has that emanate from observations of the direct experiences of others), socially provided information (i.e., verbal persuasion; the opinions, attitudes, and information passed along to us by others), faith (i.e., a belief that stems from trust or a strong and underlying desire that something is true), intuition (i.e., the instantaneous apprehension or knowing of something; the sudden appearance of a belief in one's consciousness arrived at without prior conscious thought; a state of awareness arrived at by feeling, rather than through logical and conscious analysis), logical verification (i.e., reasoning; the weaving together of disparate pieces of information, opinions, and beliefs to arrive at an emergent belief), and science.

It is important that we recognize the limitations to each of these ways of knowing, so that safeguards can be put into place and employed. The biggest threats to each of the first six ways of knowing are subjectivity and the tendency to develop a habit of the mind, such as the overreliance upon one's direct and personal experiences as one's teacher, without the simultaneous understanding of its limitations.

SCIENCE AS A WAY OF KNOWING

Science is a way through which we come to know, one that is poorly understood, yet key to our ability to engage in evidence-based management and leadership practices. The word *science* gets employed in at least three different ways and possibly in different contexts. First, there is a *dynamic* view of science, which envisions it as an activity or process. As a process, science consists of an application of the scientific method (i.e., the application of theory to guide inquiry; the use of measurement or manipulation; and an assessment of relationships under controlled, objective, and systematic conditions).[2] According to McMullin (1987), it is "the ensemble of activities of the scientist in pursuit of his [her] goal of scientific observation and understanding" (p. 3). Second, there is a *static* view of science. In this context, the word *science* refers to a body of knowledge, a collection of propositions (McMullin, 1987, p. 3) that has been created through the application of the scientific method. The third view of science is *heuristic*. The heuristic view is focused on the purpose of science. According to the heuristic perspective, the purpose underlying science is the creation of a body of knowledge to explain what is, to understand why, to comprehend how things got that way, and to predict what will happen in the future. The main goals of science are explanation and prediction—understanding what happens and why it happens (Salmon, 1987).

From a contextual perspective, it is important to note that science (e.g., the dynamic search to distinguish what *is* from what *seems to be*) in the natural sciences is somewhat distinct from science in the social sciences. Flyvbjerg (2001, p. 5) observes that the "social sciences have not had the type of theoretical and methodological success that the natural sciences have," while MacIntyre (1981) notes that unlike achievements in the natural sciences, the social sciences are completely devoid of the discovery of lawlike generalizations. Whether it is the natural or social sciences, the goal of science is to discover or reveal the unknown through objective, controlled, and systematic research. Science ultimately seeks to make available a body of knowledge arrived at through a means other than an expression of personal opinion while guided, to varying degrees, by the canons of the scientific method.

In the remainder of this essay we will provide a road map (i.e., a user's guide) for the employment of science as a way of knowing. More specifically, we aim to introduce you to several different concepts that are employed in science in general and in many lectures and readings to which you will be exposed as a student of the organizational sciences.

---

[2] In this context, "controlled" means that the researcher attempts to rule out those forces that would render the results of the study noncredible; "objective" means that there is a reliance upon measurement and the use of data for one's observations and upon which to render one's conclusions, as opposed to personal observation and judgment; and "systematic" means that there is a logical progression from the beginning to the end of the process of knowledge creation.

THE TWO LEVELS OF SCIENCE

In this discussion of science, we will expose you, the reader, to both the *language* of science and the basic *elements* of the scientific paradigm. We provide a framework that can be used to aid you in your understanding of information that is presented to you as stemming from—and/or that can be interpreted through—the canons of the scientific method.

Science unfolds at two levels—conceptual and operational. There exists a tight and reciprocal relationship between theory operating at the conceptual level and research (scientific inquiry) operating at the operational level. Theory is constructed from research (observations from the real world) and serves to guide future and further scientific inquiry. It is through this interactive process that a body of knowledge is built, much like the construction of a brick wall—one brick at a time, each brick building upon and adding to that which has been laid before. We now examine in turn the conceptual and operational levels of science.

THE CONCEPTUAL LEVEL OF SCIENCE

The conceptual level of science works with constructs, conceptual definitions, conceptual relationships, and theory. A *construct* refers to any concept employed in science which has properties that vary. For example, job satisfaction is a construct that is frequently employed as part of the micro-organizational behavior literature. People display varying degrees (levels) of job satisfaction—some people are job dissatisfied, some display low levels of job satisfaction, others are moderately satisfied, while some are extremely job satisfied.

A *conceptual definition* is the formal meaning given to each construct. This parallels the idea of a dictionary, which employs words to express the meaning of each word it contains. Conceptual definitions are useful because they allow us to converse in a standard way about constructs. For example, Locke (1976) defined job satisfaction as a positive, pleasurable emotional state that stems from a person's evaluation of his or her job and its capacity to facilitate the attainment of one's job values. It is not uncommon for students of organizations to experience different authors defining a construct differently, or using different terms to refer to the same phenomenon. Thus, it is important to have a firm grasp on the conceptual definition for the constructs employed.

A *conceptual relationship* represents the articulation of the type of relationship [(e.g., causal or covariational), and direction (i.e., positive or negative)] that is believed to exist between two or more constructs. For example, if we were to tell you that there is a positive and causal relationship between job satisfaction and the frequency of a person's acts of good organizational citizenship, that would be an illustration of a conceptual relationship. The two constructs employed here are job satisfaction and acts of good organizational citizenship. The type of relationship (i.e., direction) that is expressed is a positive one—meaning that as the strength of job satisfaction increases, so too does the frequency of that person's acts of good organizational citizenship. The relationship is also said to be causal in nature, whereby job satisfaction is positioned as a cause (stimulus, antecedent) of those acts of citizenship.

Finally, theory plays a critical role at the conceptual level of science. A *theory* is a generalized explanation of the nature and character of the relations among a set of interrelated constructs. A theory consists of the definitions and propositions that present a systematic view of some phenomenon by specifying relations among constructs with the purpose of explaining and predicting the phenomenon.

More specifically, a theory seeks to explain what a particular phenomenon is and to answer the questions how and/or why something is. A theory may be as simple (i.e., a *narrow theory*) as a detailed discussion that provides insight into the nature and character of the relationship between two constructs (e.g., X and Y). A theory may also be much more complex. There are many *mid-range theories* that connect several constructs (e.g., X, Y, Z, U, V, W) and/or join several narrow theories, and are accompanied by the story that explains the nature and character (i.e., the who, what, when, where, how, and why) of their relationship. Finally, there is *grand theory*, which seeks to explain the totality of some phenomenon. A grand theory of work motivation would explain what it is, as well as when and for whom it exists, while providing insight into how it comes into being, and its causes and its consequences. As of today, there are many narrow and mid-range theories yet virtually no grand theories in organizational studies.

To illustrate: Homans' (1961) theory of distributive justice (a theory of motivation) provides us with partial insight into both the cause and consequences of job satisfaction (dissatisfaction). He states in his theory that people are motivated to achieve fairness when they are engaged in exchange relationships. Fairness is defined as the perception that there is a balance in the exchange that takes place. Fairness or unfairness is experienced when an individual looks at the outcomes received and the inputs given in an exchange. When the outcome-to-input ratio is perceived to be equal to 1, the exchange relationship is judged as fair, satisfaction in the exchange relationship is experienced, and the individual will be motivated to repeat that exchange again in the future—a way that hedonistic people seek to maintain satisfaction. When the outcome-to-input ratio is greater or less than 1, unfairness is perceived to exist. The lack of fairness is said to produce dissonance, feelings of dissatisfaction with the exchange, and a motivation to take corrective action by modifying the outcomes and/or inputs to future exchanges. Note that this illustration is an attempt to explain the relationship between a limited set of constructs (e.g., outcomes from an exchange, inputs into an exchange, positive and negative feelings—satisfaction and dissatisfaction—with the exchange, dissonance and tension, motivation, and corrective behavior).

According to Dubin (1976, p. 26), "theory tries to make sense out of the observable world by ordering the relationships among elements that constitute the theorist's focus of attention in the real world." Theory has an important role to play in our understanding of that world. Social psychologist Kurt Lewin expressed it well when he stated that "nothing is so practical as a good theory" (Lewin, 1945, p. 129). Building upon Lewin's (1945) statement, Van de Ven (1989) suggests that "good theory is practical precisely because it advances knowledge in a scientific discipline, guides research toward crucial questions, and enlightens" (Van de Ven, 1989, p. 486). Several scholars (e.g., Klein and Zedeck, 2004; Kuhn, 1987) provide us with insight into what constitutes a good theory. Good theory, according to Klein and Zedeck (2004), (1) offers *novel insights*—it provides a "sense of discovery and illumination;" (2) is *interesting*—it is more than a ho-hum documentation of the obvious; (3) is *focused and cohesive*—"good theory illuminates and clarifies, often by organizing, and thus simplifying, a set of previously unorganized and scattered observations," and it "renders real-world processes and phenomena clear and coherent by simplifying and structuring our inchoate understanding of them. This is only possible if the theory itself is clear and coherent" (p. 932). They go on to note that good theory (4) is *grounded in the*

relevant literature, but offers more than a review or integration of that literature; and (5) presents *clearly defined constructs* and offers clear, thorough, and thoughtful *explanations of how and why the constructs in the model are linked*—"If clearly defined constructs are the building blocks of good theory, then thorough and thoughtful propositions linking the constructs—explaining what constructs lead to what, when, how, and why—provide the mortar" (p. 932). Finally, they indicate that good theory (6) is *testable*—the constructs are clear and precise; how the constructs are to be measured and how key ideas are to be tested are clearly articulated;[3] (7) in many fields, has *practical implications* [for example, good organization theory is theory that can be used to address organizational problems (e.g., the causes and consequences of job satisfaction)]; and (8) is *well-written*—the work presents a clear and logical flow, while it is simultaneously "clear, focused and interesting" (p. 933).

Application of the criteria presented by Klein and Zedeck (2004) reveals that not all theory (or espoused theory) is good theory. For example, many purported theories are not testable, are not well grounded in the relevant literature, nor do they offer a clear explanation for what constructs lead to what, when, how, and why. It also is apparent that many people use the term *theory* loosely and inappropriately (e.g., What is your theory on why so many hurricanes have hit the Gulf states over the past several years?), as they make reference to a personal opinion rather than offering observations that are grounded in sound scientific inquiry.

Maslow's (1943) popular theory of human motivation may fail the test of good theory (Hall & Nougaim, 1968; Lawler & Suttle, 1972). While it offers an appealing, intuitively logical, interesting explanation of human motivated behavior, the theory as articulated does not appear to be testable. For example, Maslow failed to provide sufficient insight into many different facets of his theory, such as when and where food and water satisfies a physiological as opposed to a safety need, when growth and development fulfill the esteem as opposed to the self-actualization need, where the divide is between the social and self-esteem needs. He failed to provide an exact conceptual definition of self-actualization. These are only a few of the questions, challenges, and controversies

---

[3] There is a distinction between *testable* and *tested*. Good theory is capable of being tested regardless of whether or not it has been tested.

that have surrounded this popular theory of human motivation, leading to the question, Is the need hierarchy theory a good theory, or is it Maslow's informed, insightful, and philosophical view on human motivation?

Theories provide the basis for research questions and hypotheses. *Research questions* inquire about the relationship between two or more constructs. (For example, Is there a positive relationship between pay level and subsequent levels of performance?) Researchers routinely seek to answer such questions by testing research hypotheses. A *hypothesis* provides the best possible answer to the question at the time that it is posed. Thus, a hypothesis is a testable statement that expresses what the nature and direction of the relationship is between two or more variables. (For example: There is a positive relationship between pay level and subsequent levels of performance.)

THE OPERATIONAL LEVEL OF SCIENCE

The second level at which science unfolds is the operational level. The operational level is where research is conducted. At this level the researcher seeks to explore, provide evidence in support of (or to refute) the conceptual relationship (or theory) that she is interested in understanding. For the purpose of differentiating the substantive level at which a conversation is unfolding, the language employed at this level of science is different from that employed at the conceptual level (which employs such words as *constructs, conceptual definitions, conceptual relationships*, and *theory*). At the operational level in science we deal with such terms as *empiricism, variables, operational definitions, measurement and manipulation*, and *empirical relationships*.

Empiricism and empirical research are terms frequently employed within the context of the conduct of research. Schwab (1999) observes that "empirical research can help obtain evidence of the veracity of expected causal relationships" (p. 4) as they are expressed at the conceptual level. He goes on to state that "empirical research addresses expected relationships, through the systematic study of relationships between scores obtained from cases or measures" (p. 4). As suggested by these comments, empirical research consists of an examination of expected relationships, through the systematic observation (i.e., measurement and/or manipulation) of the constructs embedded in the hypothesis being tested.

At the operational level of science the term *variable* is substituted for the term *construct*. Thus, a *variable* is simply a construct manifested at the operational level of science, and as such, it too has properties that vary. There are several different properties that can characterize a variable—it can be dichotomous, discrete, continuous, ordinal, or ratio in nature.

An *operational definition* refers to how a variable is actually *measured* (observed) or *manipulated* (experimented with) when research is being conducted. The operational definition for a variable should reflect the conceptual definition that has been given to the construct. For example, Kunin (1955) developed, and Dunham and Herman (1975) expanded, the Faces Scale (see Figure 1) as an operational definition for the measurement of job satisfaction, which has been conceptually defined as the positive emotional feelings (i.e., positive affect) that are produced as a result of one's appraisal of one's job.

Flexible working hours have been conceptually defined as a work schedule arrangement that permits employees to exercise an element of discretion

FIGURE 1
The Faces Scale

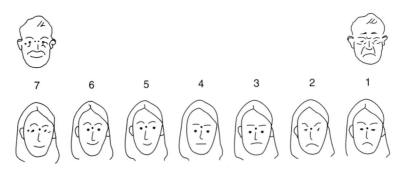

7   6   5   4   3   2   1

The male faces as illustrated here were originally developed by T. Kunin (1955) as reported in *Personnel Psychology*, 8:65–78. Two of the faces appear here for illustrative purposes. The matching female faces were created by R. B. Dunham and J. B. Herman and published in the *Journal of Applied Psychology*, 60:629–631, copyright 1975 by the American Psychological Association. Reprinted with permission of the authors.

in choosing their time of work (Pierce & Newstrom, 1982). A researcher studying the job satisfaction effects of work scheduling might hypothesize a positive and causal relationship between the amount of work scheduling discretion and the level of job satisfaction (a conceptual relationship). To test this hypothesized (conceptual) relationship, the researcher might take a group of employees and move them from a fixed work schedule (e.g., 8 a.m. to 5 p.m. Monday through Friday) and put them on a flexible working hour arrangement, where the employee can choose to start each working day anytime between 6 a.m. and 9 a.m. The implemented work schedule (a manipulation) would be the operational definition given to the conceptual definition for flexible working hours. The Faces Scale, illustrated earlier, could be employed to assess (measure) job satisfaction while the employees are working under each of the two schedules.

Not everyone employs the same conceptual definition for a particular construct. Job satisfaction, for example, has been conceptually defined as the affective (feeling) component of an attitude reflecting how one's job makes one feel (Kunin, 1955; Weiss, Dawis, England, & Loftquist, 1967). It has also been conceptually defined as simply "the overall evaluation one has towards one's job (Weiss & Cropanzano, 1996, p. 65). In addition, people doing research (e.g., students, managers, scientists) often create their own variable measures.[4] The use of different measures to capture an underlying construct may generate a very different perspective on that construct. For example, periodic national surveys of worker job satisfaction have frequently employed the following operational definition: If you were to do it all over again, would you have the same job? (Leatherman, 2000). This assumes, correctly or incorrectly, that an answer of "yes" implies job satisfaction and "no" signals job dissatisfaction. The operational definition employed in the national survey is very different (e.g., in terms of meaning, and possibly in terms of results generated) from that revealed by the Faces Scale we presented earlier. Because of this, it is important for you to understand both the conceptual and operational definitions if you truly want to understand what is being communicated.

---

[4] It is extremely difficult to develop and validate a research tool (i.e., demonstrate that a research tool measures what it purports to measure). Consequently, we strongly encourage students and anyone else conducting research to employ existing research measures, as opposed to developing their own. The use of existing instruments also makes available normative data with which students and others can compare their findings.

Finally, an *empirical relationship* refers to a relationship that has been identified through research. As previously noted, Schwab (1999) suggested that an empirical relationship is revealed by measurement taken on the variables being studied and the interconnection between them. If a researcher's data reveal a correlation of .45 between job satisfaction and acts of good organizational citizenship, this observation is an example of an empirical relationship. In the flexible working hours study, if the researcher were to observe a significant increase in the level of job satisfaction (e.g., mean satisfaction on the Faces Scale changing from 3.1 to 5.0) as workers were moved from a schedule with no discretion to a schedule with substantial discretion, this observation would reflect an empirical relationship. Assuming that work scheduling flexibility is one cause of job satisfaction, this empirical relationship would provide *evidence in support of* (i.e., it is a relationship that must exist if the flexible working hours cause job satisfaction), yet *not proof of* a causal connection between the two variables, where flexibility is the cause and job satisfaction is the effect produced.

We can learn about organizations, management, leadership, and organizational behavior in many different ways. Among some of the *types of research* are (1) *setting-based strategies* in which research is carried out either in the field or in the laboratory; (2) *time-based strategies,* in which each variable is measured at a single point in time (i.e., cross-sectional studies), or the research is carried out across time (i.e., longitudinal studies); (3) *purpose-based strategies,* wherein research is conducted with the specialized purpose of validating a research instrument (i.e., validation research) or to address real relationships (i.e., substantive research) among variables; (4) *"type of"* data-based strategies, which are characterized by the production of quantitative data (e.g., in the measurement of job satisfaction with the Faces Scale) or qualitative data (e.g., illustrated by an employee's recounting of work incidents that resulted in feelings of job dissatisfaction that persisted over a long period of time); (5) *"source of"* data-based strategies, wherein researchers measure or manipulate the variables under investigation (i.e., primary data) or wherein the data to be worked with is collected from existing (archival) sources (e.g., last year's employee pay and performance information) commonly referred to as secondary data; and (6) *technique-based strategies* such as case studies, surveys, field studies, experimental studies, and aggregate quantitative literature reviews (e.g., meta-analyses). The seventh and final strategy is one that is based upon *researcher control*. Typically, this research method is characterized by one of three different designs, namely, (a) the true (pure) experimental design, in which the researcher exercises control over who is studied, who is exposed to the manipulation, and what the independent variable is; (b) quasi-experimental design, wherein the researcher studies a naturally occurring event (e.g., organizational downsizing) or manipulates the independent variable (e.g., introduces a compressed workweek schedule) with virtually no control over who is involved in the study and without random assignment of the study participants to either the control or experimental groups; and finally, (c) low or no control correlational (non- or preexperimental) design, in which the researcher measures the variables under consideration.

THE DEVELOPMENT OF THE SCIENTIFIC BODY OF KNOWLEDGE: THEORY AND EMPIRICISM

As previously noted, theory has an important role to play in our understanding of the world. First, a good theory should *summarize what is known* about the phenomenon in question. A good theory is a generalized explanation that integrates what has been previously learned through empirical research guided by the canons (principles) of the scientific method. Second, theory is intended to *guide further inquiry* into a particular phenomenon, so as to advance, deepen, and strengthen our understanding of that phenomenon. Klein and Zedeck (2004) offer the following comments on the linkage between the conceptual (theory) and operational (empirical) levels of science:

> Theories provide meaning. They allow us to understand and interpret data. Theories specify which variables are important and for what reason, describe and explain the relationships that link the variables, and identify the boundary conditions under which variables should or should not be related (Campbell, 1990). Theories help identify and define problems, prescribe a means for evaluating or solving the problems, and facilitate responses to new problems. They permit generalizations beyond the immediate sample and provide a basis for making predictions. Theory tells us *why* [emphasis added] something occurs, not simply *what* occurs. Research in the absence of theory is often trivial—a technical feat more likely to yield confusion and boredom than insight. In contrast, research that is guided by

theory, or that develops theory, generates understanding and excitement. (p. 931)

Thus, the systematic observations of phenomena (events, incidents) provide the grist out of which theory is constructed. Commonly, theory in the behavioral and social sciences derives from authors' combining observations from the existing literature, experience, and rational and creative thought. Theory can be constructed either deductively or inductively. In deduction, general ideas and observations are honed, resulting in the articulation of very specific stories of cause-and-effect relationships. Alternatively, some scholars in the social and behavioral sciences employ induction; they work from a specific in-depth case or group of cases (cf. Eisenhardt, 1989) and/or personal observations (cf. Gersick, 1992) to build a theory. Without regard for how (i.e., the processes employed) a theory was constructed, theory is intended to provide us with hypotheses that can be tested through empirical (i.e., controlled, objective, systematic) research, the results of which are intended to modify the current theory. This modified theory once again becomes the guiding light for further testing, giving rise to subsequent theory modification. It is through this iterative (repetitious, cyclic) process that a body of knowledge, insight into and understanding of phenomena, emerges. Since there are few, if any, grand theories that explain 100 percent of the variance in some phenomenon (e.g., the totality of work motivation), many people show a tendency to judge a theory as incomplete (deficient) and dismiss it too readily. The sophisticated consumer of information, on the other hand, recognizes that theories are works in progress, and that there are good narrow and mid-range theories that can aid our understanding of a small part of complex and multidimensional phenomena. For example, Homans' (1961) theory of distributive justice provides good insight into a small, but significant part of human motivation.

It is this dynamic interplay between empiricism conducted at the operational level and theory construction and refinement at the conceptual level that generates advances in our understanding. At any time, a theory, assuming that it is a good theory, informs our most current understanding of a particular phenomenon.

TYPES OF RELATIONSHIPS

Science at both the conceptual and operational levels is largely about developing an understanding of different phenomena (e.g., the meaning of job satisfaction, the causes and consequences of this state). As such, science involves developing an understanding of relationships among phenomena. In this section we explore the word *relationship* because it is an important part of science.

Relationship means simply that two or more things are associated, connected, or tied to one another. For example, each of us has a relationship with our parents, in that we are connected or tied together. As is readily apparent, there are many different types of relationships (e.g., friendship, parental, contractual, causal). As should be evident, even though it is often confused, two phenomena can be similar in appearance and strongly related and still not be the same phenomenon (e.g., identical twins). In science we also deal with different types of relationships; as previously noted, conceptual relationships are expressed in our theories, and empirical relationships are revealed in our research.

A relationship between two variables can be either *covariational* or *causal* in nature. In a related manner, there are two different types of *predictive* relationships. At the outset a predictive relationship is simply one in which the appearance of one variable (e.g., X at time 1), with varying degrees of certainty, expresses what will happen to another variable (e.g., Y at time 2). For example, farmers can predict the rising of the sun with the crow of the rooster. In this instance, the presence of X (rooster crowing) enables the prediction of Y sun rising even though X is *not* the cause of Y. (While this example illustrates a covariational relationship across time, such a relationship may also occur at a single point in time.) The two variables have a relationship in that they appear to or do co-vary with one another. It is also possible for X to be the cause (i.e., determinant) of Y. In this case X precedes the emergence of Y, and X is capable of predicting the emergence of Y.

From the perspective of *direction* (sign), relationships can be positive or negative. A positive relationship means simply that as the value of one variable increases, so too does the value of the second. A negative relationship, on the other hand, means that as the value of one variable increases, the value of the second variable declines. It is also possible that there is *no* systematic (or predictable) relationship between the value of one variable relative to the value of a second. A positive and a negative relationship between two variables (e.g., X and Y) can occur under conditions wherein X is the cause of Y, and when X is merely a covariate (not a cause) of Y.

Relationships between two or more variables are further understood by the *strength* of that relationship. In the simplest of terms, the strength of a relationship can be revealed by the size of the correlation coefficient between two variables, or the percent of variance in one variable that can be predicted (accounted for) by knowledge of a second variable. Correlationally, the strength of relationship ranges from .00 to 1.00 (with a plus or minus revealing the direction (sign) of the relationship between the two variables). Two variables with a correlated relationship of .00 means no systematic relationship and/or 0 percent of the variance in one variable can be predicted (explained; accounted for) at this time by the second variable. A correlated relationship of 1.00 means that there is a systematic relationship between the two variables and that 100 percent of the variance in one variable can be explained by knowledge of the second variable. This conversion from the correlated value to the percent of variance is found by taking the squared value of the correlation coefficient. A correlation coefficient of .60 between two variables (e.g., job satisfaction and acts of organizational citizenship) means that 36 percent of the variance (r^2, or $.60 \times .60 = 36$ percent) of one variable (e.g., acts of citizenship) can be accounted for by the second (e.g., job satisfaction).

The *shape* of the relationship reveals the pattern of change in one variable relative to the pattern (amount) of change in the second variable. Relationships, therefore, can be linear or curvilinear in nature. A linear relationship (i.e., one characterized by a straight line) is one for which there is a constant and proportionate increase or decrease in the value between two variables. For example, there may be a linear relationship between education and salary, such that every year of education after high school increases the mean salary of an employee by 5 percent. That would indicate that the employee with a typical four-year undergraduate degree could expect to earn about 20 percent more than an average high school graduate. A curvilinear relationship means that the relationship between two variables takes the shape of a curve (e.g., monotonic, U-shaped, inverted U-shaped) rather than a straight line. For example, it is often simplistically assumed that employee performance decreases as stress increases. This assumption is only partially correct, since the relationship is best represented by an inverted U-shaped (curvilinear) relationship. Research evidence reveals that stress initially raises an individual's arousal level, causing a person to be more attentive to job demands and thus perform more effectively. At a critical point, however, additional increases in stress, and thus one's arousal level, make the person less capable of coping, and performance subsequently drops (McGrath, 1976).

Finally, there are *variable-based* relationships. To understand the different variable-based relationships, it will be helpful to first understand the different types of variables. Among the most common variables employed in science are the *independent* variable (i.e., the cause, antecedent, or predictor), the *dependent* variable (i.e., the effect, consequence, criterion, outcome, unit of analysis), the *moderating* variable (i.e., the situation, contingency; the "yes, but" or "I can think of the exception" variable), the *intervening* (also known as the mediating) variable (i.e., the one that comes in between two other variables, such as one coming in between the independent and dependent variables), and the *extraneous* variable (i.e., a variable that lies outside the specified conceptual relationship yet potentially plays a meaningful, though an unrecognized, role[5]). While there are other types of variables (e.g., control, nuisance, and suppressor), those that have been identified and defined are the primary ones.

We cannot provide a listing of variables as independent, dependent, moderating, intervening, and extraneous within a discipline. The only way to type a variable is by its placement within the causal chain, and this can be revealed by the placement of the corresponding construct in the conceptual relationship that is being explored. Consider the following two research questions: (1) Is there a positive and causal relationship between pay level and subsequent levels of performance? and (2) Is there a positive and causal relationship between the level of an individual's performance and his or her subsequent level of pay? In the first question, pay level is positioned as the independent variable (i.e., the cause, predictor, or antecedent) and performance, as the dependent variable (i.e., the effect, consequence, criterion, outcome, unit of analysis). The second research question reverses their order. Thus, the variable's type is determined by the research question that is being asked, or the placement of its parallel construct in the conceptual relationship.

The first type of variable-based relationship is the *independent–dependent variable relationship*, which is frequently referred to as a main effect

---

[5] For example, consider the lightning–thunder relationship. Lightning is often thought to cause thunder. In fact, there is an extraneous variable that belongs in the consideration of that relationship. It is believed that both are caused by electrical discharge in the atmosphere.

FIGURE 2 Independent–Dependent Variable Relationships

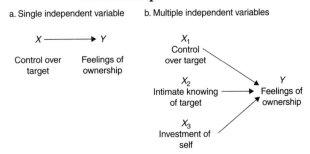

a. Single independent variable

b. Multiple independent variables

relationship. In causal language it depicts the effect (i.e., main effect) produced on the dependent variable by the independent variable. In non-causal (i.e., covariation or correlational) language it means that the independent variable is a predictor of the dependent variable. Visually, this relationship when modeled looks like Figure 2a, where X (control) is the independent and Y (feelings of ownership) is the dependent variable. Independent–dependent variable relationships may have one or more independent (predictor) variables (see Figure 2b). For example, Pierce, Kostova, and Dirks (2003) proposed that feelings of organizational ownership (Y) find their origin in control over that target of ownership (X_1), intimate knowing of the target of ownership (X_2), and an investment of the self (X_3) into the target of ownership.

A *reciprocal relationship* is one in which two variables influence one another in what might be considered a back-and-forth influence relationship. For example, it is possible that the amount that an employee is paid positively affects the level of that employee's performance, which in turn positively impacts the amount that the employee is subsequently paid.

Consider the following statement: It is currently thought that formal employee ownership as an organizational arrangement impacts employee organizational commitment by working through the employee's psychological experiences of ownership (Pierce, Rubenfeld, & Morgan, 1991). This statement suggests that the relationship between employee ownership as an organizational arrangement and organizational commitment is mediated by psychological ownership. As illustrated in Figure 3, we have a *mediated relationship* (also referred to as an intervening variable relationship), wherein psychological ownership lies in the path between employee ownership as an organizational arrangement and organizational commitment. As previously noted, an intervening variable is one that comes in between two other variables of interest.

FIGURE 3   Fully Mediated Relationship

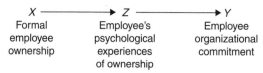

Figure 3 illustrates the mediated relationship such that X is the independent variable, Y is the dependent variable, and Z is the intervening (mediating) variable. In the model illustrated in the figure, the variable Z is positioned in between variables X and Y. Interpreting this relationship, we note the following: (a) there is a significant relationship between X and Y, (b) there is a significant relationship between X and Z, (c) there is a significant relationship between Z and Y, (d) X affects Y by working *through* the effect that X has on Z, and (e) when the effects of Z are accounted for in Y, there is no longer any meaningful relationship between X and Y, since *all* of X's effects on Y have been accounted for by the fact that X works on (affects) Y through its effects on Z. In other words, the path between X and Y is through Z; thus, X can have a relationship with Y only through its (i.e., X's) relationship with Z and Z's relationship with Y. Under this condition we have *full mediation*.

Figure 4 illustrates *partial (part) mediation*. If and when X (i.e., the independent variable) works on Y (i.e., the dependent variable), both directly and in part (indirectly) through Z (i.e., the intervening variable), it is said that we have partial (part) mediation; that is, only part of the relationship between the independent and dependent variables stems from the influence that the independent variable has upon the dependent variable by working through the intervening variable (an *indirect effect*), and part of its effect is *direct* (i.e., a main effect). For example, work environment control affects organizational citizenship behavior both directly and through its effects on feelings of ownership which, in part, stem from work environment control.

Next, we have the *moderated relationship* (also referred to as the moderating variable relationship). Recall that the moderating variable is a situational or conditional variable. Quite simply, the moderating variable changes the nature (e.g., direction, strength) of the relationship between two other variables. If someone were to say that job complexity causes job satisfaction for some employees and dissatisfaction for others, we have an expression of a moderated relationship. The relationship between job complexity (X) and job satisfaction (Y) is positive for some employees and negative for others; note that the relationship between X and Y went from positive to negative (a change in the sign of the relationship occurred). A moderator may also change the strength of the relationship such that it could have also gone from strong positive (or strong negative) to weak positive (or weak negative) with only its strength changing. What has not been revealed in this statement is exactly what individual difference variable (i.e., a personal characteristic, such as age, education, and need motivation, that can be used to differentiate people) gave rise to the change in relationship depicted. Until that variable is known (identified), we have an extraneous variable at work (i.e., one not yet identified in the expressed conceptual relationship). In our example, when further research reveals that the strength of the employee's growth needs (W) is the "culprit," we will have identified the moderating variable. The moderating variable relationship is modeled in Figure 5 and revealed by the following expression: Job complexity leads to job satisfaction for employees who are motivated by their growth needs, and much less so for those employees with weak growth need motivation.

Note that the moderating variable is working on the relationship between X and Y, and not directly on either variable X or Y. This reveals that there is an *interaction* effect between X and W. The two working in combination account for the impact (effect) on Y. (An interactive or joint effect means that there is an outcome that is created when two or more things are simultaneously present that would not be there otherwise.)

FIGURE 4   Partially Mediated Relationship

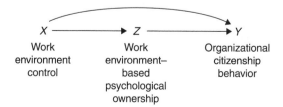

FIGURE 5   Moderated Relationship

Finally, there is the *spurious relationship*. The spurious relationship is a false, nongenuine, or illegitimate relationship—a causal relationship that appears to exist between two variables, but one that does not exist in reality. Consider the following hypothetical example (cf. Stone, 1978): A researcher is interested in the relationship between coffee consumption and heart disease. Research gets conducted in an organization involving employees from different levels in the organizational hierarchy (i.e., shop-floor and lower-level supervisory personnel, middle and upper-level managers). A significant empirical relationship ($r = .46, p < .01$) is observed between the two variables, leading the author to argue that coffee consumption appears to cause heart disease. Upon closer inspection of the study from which those findings were reported, it was observed that job level is positively related to (a) coffee availability and coffee consumption, and simultaneously to (b) job-induced stress and heart disease. This produced the researcher's observation of a positive relationship between coffee consumption and heart disease and the suggestion that there is a causal relationship between the two variables. Instead, coffee consumption and heart disease are spuriously related, since both variables were caused by job level. There are many interesting examples of the spurious relationship. A few years ago, a Wall Street "theory" arose suggesting that the length of women's skirts was related to the emergence of a bullish or a bearish market (www.investopedia.com/s/skirtlength theory.asp). More specifically, the observation was made that when women's skirt lengths shortened (lengthened), the stock market became bullish (bearish). While the two variables may be correlated with one another, rising and falling skirt lengths do not cause the market to rise and fall. The relationship is a false relationship, one that may exist because both variables have a common driver (e.g., when consumer confidence and excitement is high, skirt length may shorten and investors become active, and when there is fear and gloom in the economy skirt length may lengthen and investors become bearish).

There are many other types of relationships, such as the biased relationship, noise relationship, multiple main effect relationship, combined moderated and mediated relationship, and suppressor variable relationship. Many of them build upon and integrate the variables that were previously discussed, as well as the three basic relationships, namely, the independent-dependent, mediated, and moderated relationships.

THREATS AND LIMITATIONS TO SCIENCE AS A WAY OF KNOWING

Just as not all opinions are sound, not all beliefs are true, not all experiences are representative of their population, and not all observations of one's personal experiences or those of others are without bias, we also know that not all science is good science. There are threats and limitations to the beliefs that we have arrived at through *all* ways of knowing. Knowing through science is no exception; it too is vulnerable to a variety of threats. In this section, we comment briefly on the role of the participants in the scientific process (the passionately interested and the disinterested participants) and on two issues that pertain to scientific validity—flawed data and flawed conclusions.

INTERESTED AND DISINTERESTED PARTICIPANTS

Just like a reliance on personal and vicarious experiences, socially provided information, faith, intuition, and reasoning, science may be limited by *subjectivity*. Researchers are not always disinterested parties. Many of them will try to sell you on the correctness or soundness of their ideas, hypotheses, and theories. There is always a story to tell, one that details the relationships under investigation (e.g., the argument presented to justify the hypothesized linkage between the constructs of interest). The second story reflects the researcher's interpretation of his or her research findings (i.e., the story that interprets observed support for one's hypotheses, or the one that offers speculation as to why the observations were other than what was expected).

The interested (disinterested) participant may not be the researcher, but those who are financially supporting the research. The sophisticated consumer of information is sensitive to who is the funding source for the research conducted: What are their interests, and what control do they exercise over the research and/or the findings? Increasingly, the funding for research generated by the nation's universities is coming from private interests (e.g., corporations, politically leaning think tanks), as opposed to impartial agencies who are interested in basic research and the advancement of the frontiers of knowledge for the benefit of society. Consumer beware!

THE SCIENTIFIC PROCESS

In terms of the scientific process, there are two major threats to science as a way of knowing that we focus on in this section. These threats stem from (a) flawed measurement and/or manipulation, and (b) contaminated findings. The measures employed by a researcher must measure the intended variables; otherwise we will be unable to draw any meaningful conclusions that pertain to those variables and their underlying constructs. In addition, the researcher needs to exercise sufficient control over the conduct of his or her study so that competing explanations for what was found can be eliminated. Without such control it would be virtually impossible to address the true relationship between constructs.

Understanding flawed measurement (manipulation) and contaminated findings requires that you first understand the meaning of the word *validity* and its different uses. In the scientific world, the words *validity* and *reliability* differ from their common usage, and within the realm of science, there are two different uses of the term valid—valid data and valid findings.

Flawed observations (bad data)   To have credible (valid) findings, the data (i.e., scores, observations) that derive from measurement must be credible (valid). The instrument that is employed to measure a variable must measure that variable and nothing else. That is, the instrument should be neither contaminated nor deficient. A *contaminated* measure is one that purports to measure *X*, while it simultaneously measures, at least in part, something else. A *deficient* measure is one that measures only part of what it is that it purports to measure, leaving part of the construct unassessed. A measurement instrument is said to be *construct valid* when it measures what it purports to measure—nothing more and nothing less. If a measure is construct valid, the operational definition and the conceptual definition reflect and correspond with one another.

Reliability is often confused with the words *valid* and *validity*. Reliability means consistent and predictable. A measure needs to be reliable for it to be valid and for it to give us valid data. Thus, reliability becomes a necessary condition for validity even though it is not a sufficient condition. More specifically, it is possible for a measure to be reliable yet not valid, while all valid measures are reliable. Consider the following illustration: Get on and off your bathroom scale several times, without adding or subtracting what you are carrying onto and off the scale. Do the readings match? If each reading is 125 pounds, we would conclude that the scale is reliable; that is, it gives you a consistent (predictable) reading. If you actually weigh 125 pounds, the reliable assessment is an accurate

assessment providing evidence in support of its measurement validity. If, however, you weigh more (or less) than 125 pounds, the assessment is reliable, but deficient and lacking validity.

Flawed conclusions   To have valid research findings, we must start with construct valid measures on all the variables that are specified in the conceptual relationship (or research question). Thus, construct validity is a necessary, but not a sufficient, condition to having valid empirical findings (i.e., a valid observation). The two primary threats or challenges to valid research findings are internal and external validity.

Internal validity simply asks whether there are rival explanations for the observed (empirical) relationship. In the study of flexible working hours mentioned above, the researcher observed a decrease in symptoms of physical and psychological stress following the conversion from the fixed working hour arrangement to the flexible working hour arrangement. This study was conducted over a six-month period of time between the first and last assessment of stress symptoms, and a five-month period of time elapsed after the implementation of the work schedule change and the second assessment of the stress symptoms. The claim stemming from this study was that the implementation of the flexible working hours resulted in a decrease in stress symptoms. The study's author reasoned that the employees had more flexibility in the morning, enabling them to deal with delays in arriving at work due to inclement weather, oversleeping, dealing with sick children, and so on, which resulted in lower levels of stress when they arrived and while at work. When considering the internal validity of this study, we ask, Are there rival explanations for the decrease in stress? The presence of viable alternative explanations for the observed change in the level of stress would call into question claims of internal validity. For example, research environmental threats such as the researcher's control over the research environment could affect the observed outcomes. In addition, between group effects (e.g., selection of which individuals or groups are to be studied and their pre-existing condition could influence the observed outcome) and longitudinal (across-time) effects, such as historical (outside events) and subject maturation that simultaneously occurred with the manipulation of the flexible hours) could also affect the observed outcomes (Schwab, 1999). Without any viable alternative explanation for the observed effect, the researcher would likely claim that the study's findings appear to be internally valid.

The *external validity* question inquires about the generalizability of the research findings. Are the findings unique to the study that was conducted? If the research findings are generalizable (extendable, applicable) to other settings, to another time and place, to a different sample of study participants, then the test of external validity has been achieved. A study conducted on telemarketers, which finds no adverse stress-related effects of a 12-hour workday is unlikely to yield results that can be applied to people who are air traffic controllers at the world's busiest airports because these two jobs may be vastly different in terms of the burden of responsibility associated with the lives of others. In this case, the study is said to have constrained (limited) external validity (generalizability). Uniqueness in terms of the cases studied, when the study was conducted, and/or where the study was conducted can constrain a study's external validity.

STUDY DESIGN

Not all research investigations are equally efficacious. As previously noted, some research is conducted in the laboratory and some in the field (i.e., the real world). Field studies generally possess greater external validity, while laboratory studies allow the researcher to exercise more of the control needed for internal validity. Some research is experimental (i.e., conducted under conditions in which the independent variable is manipulated and subjects are randomly assigned to the different study conditions), while other studies are simply correlational in nature (e.g., performed such that both the independent and dependent variables are measured). Only in true experimentally designed studies are we capable of observing (and proving) causality and ascertaining the direction of the causal arrow. The results stemming from correlational studies (e.g., a cross-sectional examination of the relationship between a measurement of job satisfaction with the Faces Scale and a peer report on the frequency of a co-worker's acts of good organizational citizenship) can be employed to infer causality, but never prove a cause-and-effect relationship. Many of the studies conducted in the organizational sciences (including management and leadership) have employed the correlational design. In view of the fact that we cannot prove cause and effect through this design, it is appropriate to ask about the value of observations that stem from this type of study. We are of the opinion that the strength and value of findings produced by the popular correlational field study stem from (a) the soundness of the the-

ory being tested, (b) the validity of the data collected, (c) their real-world setting, (d) observations that confirm the hypothesized relationships, and (e) replication, replication, replication—observing the same relationships time and again, across multiple settings.

CONCLUSION

Why is all of this important? Every day, whether in the student center, on the evening news, from a favorite subscription, on the Internet, in class, or at a favorite pub, students are bombarded by many different assertions, presented to them by many different people, and reflecting many different ways of knowing. Students and all other consumers of information who unthinkingly accept all of these as true may come to be highly misinformed and as a consequence, experience a variety of negative outcomes. However, applying the canons of the scientific method as a lens to examine such assertions, and relying on the principles of the scientific method to expand one's own knowing wherever possible, will help generate a more well-informed platform upon which to understand and navigate through life's experiences.

For centuries, it was believed that management and leadership were arts and that successful managers and leaders were those who had the personal experience and an intuitive sense for the decisions that needed to be made and the actions to be taken. During the last century, starting with managers and management consultants such as Frederick W. Taylor, Chester Barnard, Frank and Lillian Gilbreth, and the managers at Western Electric's Hawthorne plant in Chicago, Illinois, science (e.g., data collection, measurement, experimentation) became an increasingly defining character of management and leadership. Today, there exists a vast amount of research-based evidence that can be used to inform our understanding of organizations, groups (teams), and the people who make them a functioning reality. As such, the practice of management and the exercise of leadership is capable of being much more than a reliance upon faith, intuition, and personal and vicarious experiences. There is an important role for science to play—first, in your education and later, in guiding your management and leadership practices.

The practice of medicine is evidence-based. There isn't one of us who wants our physician to diagnose our health problems and to prescribe cures without a thorough understanding of the latest advances in health care. The best and most advanced evidence-based clinical care is what all of us want for the care and treatment of our grandparents, parents, other relatives, and friends. After nearly a century of research carried out in and by major corporations and the nation's research universities, there exists an opportunity for you to engage in evidence-based management and leadership. To do so, however, you will need (a) to be willing to expose yourself to that literature, (b) to be able to read and interpret its presentation, (c) to be able to suspend judgment until you understand what a study is saying to you, (d) to possess the ability to think critically about what is being reported, and (e) to be insightful in terms of how to apply these findings within your unique situation.

This essay was written to aid you in this journey, with the profound hope that your education will be evidence based and that you will practice evidence-based management and exercise evidence-based leadership. It is our hope that this essay will help make your reading and ultimate understanding of the organizational sciences literature easier, more enjoyable, and more fruitful.

References

Campbell, J. P. 1990. The role of theory in industrial and organizational psychology. In M. Dunnette (Ed.), *Handbook of Industrial and Organizational Psychology,* (pp. 39–74). Palo Alto, CA: Consulting Psychologists Press.

Dubin, R. 1976. Theory building in applied areas. In M. Dunnette (Ed.), *Handbook of Industrial and Organizational Psychology,* (pp. 17–39). Chicago: Rand McNally.

Dunham, R. B., & Herman, J. B. 1975. Development of a female faces scale for measuring job satisfaction. *Journal of Applied Psychology,* 60, 629–631.

Eisenhardt, K. M. 1989. Building theories from case study research. *Academy of Management Review,* 14, 532–550.

Flyvberg, B. 2001. *Making social science matter: Why social inquiry fails and how it can succeed again.* Cambridge, UK: Cambridge University Press.

Gersick, C. J. 1992. Time and transition in my work on teams: Looking back on a new model of group development. In P. Frost & R. Stablein (Eds.), *Doing exemplary research,* (pp. 52–64). London: Sage.

Hall, D. T., & Nougaim, K. E. 1968. An examination of Maslow's need hierarchy in an organizational setting. *Organizational Behavior and Human Performance,* 3, 12–35.

Homans, G. C. 1961. *Social behavior: Its elementary forms.* New York: Harcourt, Brace & World.

James, W. 1890/1918. *Principles of psychology.* New York: Holt.

Klein, K. J., & Zedeck, S. 2004. Theory in applied psychology: Lessons (re)learned. *Journal of Applied Psychology,* 87, 931–933.

Kuhn, T. 1987. The function of dogma in scientific research. In J. A. Kourany (Ed.), *Scientific knowledge: Basic issues in the philosophy of science,* (pp. 253–265). Belmont CA: Wadsworth.

Kunin, T. 1955. The construction of a new type of attitude measure. *Personnel Psychology,* 8, 65–78.

Lawler, E. E., III, & Suttle, J. L. 1972. A causal correlational test of the need hierarchy concept. *Organizational Behavior and Human Performance,* 7, 265–287.

Leatherman, C. 2000. Despite their gripes, professors are generally pleased with careers, poll finds. *The Chronicle of Higher Education,* March 3, 2000, 419.

Lewin, K. 1945. The Research Center for Group Dynamics at Massachusetts Institute of Technology. *Sociometry,* 8(2), 126–136.

Locke, E. A. 1976. The nature and causes of job satisfaction. In M. Dunnette (Ed.), *Handbook of Industrial and Organizational Psychology,* (pp. 1297–1350). Chicago: Rand McNally.

MacIntyre, A. 1981. *After virtue: A study in moral theory.* Notre Dame, IN: University of Notre Dame Press.

Maslow, A. H. 1943. A theory of human motivation. *Psychological Bulletin,* 50, 370–396.

McGrath, J. E. 1976. Stress and behavior in organizations. In M. Dunnette (Ed.), *Handbook of Industrial and Organizational Psychology,* (pp. 1351–1395). Chicago: Rand McNally.

McMullin, E. 1987. Alternative approaches to the philosophy of science. In J. A. Kourany (Ed.), *Scientific knowledge: Basic issues in the philosophy of science,* (pp. 3–19). Belmont, CA: Wadsworth.

Pfeffer, J., & Sutton, R. I. 2006. Evidence-based management. *Harvard Business Review,* 84 (July/August), 7/8, p. 184.

Pierce, J. L., Kostova, T., & Dirks, K. T. 2003. The state of psychological ownership: Integrating and extending a century of research. *Review of General Psychology,* 7(1), 84–107.

Pierce, J. L., & Newstrom, J. W. 1982. Employee responses to flexible work schedules: An inter-organization, inter-system comparison. *Journal of Management,* 8(1), 9–25.

Pierce, J. L., Rubenfeld, S., & Morgan, S. 1991. Employee ownership: A conceptual model of process and effects. *Academy of Management Review,* 16, 121–144.

Rousseau, D. M. 2006. Is there such a thing as "evidence-based management"? *Academy of Management Review,* 31, 256–269.

Salmon, W. C. 1987. Why ask, "Why?" An inquiry concerning scientific explanation. In J. A. Kourany (Ed.),

Scientific knowledge: Basic issues in the philosophy of science, (pp. 51–64). Belmont, CA: Wadsworth.

Schwab, D. P. 1999. *Research methods for organizational sciences.* Mahwah, NJ: Lawrence Erlbaum.

Stone, E. 1978. *Research methods in organizational behavior.* Santa Monica, CA: Goodyear.

Van de Ven, A. H. 1989. Nothing is quite so practical as a good theory. *Academy of Management Review*, 14, 486–489.

Weiss, D. J., Dawis, R. V., England, G. W., & Loftquist, L. H. 1967. *The manual for the Minnesota Satisfaction Questionnaire.* Minneapolis, MN: University of Minnesota Industrial Relations Center.

Weiss, H. M., & Cropanzano, R. 1996. Affective events theory: A theoretical discussion of the structure, causes and consequences of affective experiences at work. In B. M. Staw & L. L. Cummings (Eds.), *Research in Organizational Behavior,* (pp. 1–74). Greenwich, CT: JAI Press.

Reading 2

Perspectives on Leadership from Homer's *Odyssey*

Fred A. Kramer
University of Massachusetts–Amherst

Business and public-administration education and practice can be a harrowing experience. As Warren Bennis has suggested, "The more our work makes us specialists, the more we must strive to remain or become generalists in other matters, to perceive the interconnections among science, esthetics, and ethics, to avoid becoming lopsided. All of humanity's pursuits are connected, after all, and we remain ignorant of those connections at our peril."[1] Classic works of literature can help us overcome parochial tendencies, so we can better deal with our immediate problems and look beyond them.

Homer's epic poem, the *Odyssey*, illuminates truths that have value today. Many of us may look back to our high-school introduction to the *Odyssey* and recall a series of stories that may surface from the mists of our memories. Maybe our memories of the *Odyssey* support Edgar Allen Poe's view of epic poems. To Poe, epic was "the art of being dull in verse."[2] But the *Odyssey* need not be dull if read by more mature minds than the average teenager's. It may even be relevant. Surely modern leaders are not going to confront a Cyclops in a cave or see some of our trusted lieutenants turned into swine by the magical powers of Circe. But on some level, similar things happen in the course of coping with administrative demands today.

There are two levels on which the modern manager who aspires to improve his or her leadership abilities may engage the story of Odysseus. The deeper level is the intensely personal psychological journey toward self-awareness and self-development. As Cedric H. Whitman suggests, "The nature of myth, or folk tale, is to reflect in external form the psyche's subconscious exploration of itself and its experience."[3] In the changing environment of modern business and government, leaders are expected to embark on journeys into the unknown. Perhaps the successful completion of these journeys depends on notions of self-discovery similar to the ones that Odysseus went through.

To deal with this personal level of the *Odyssey,* one must read the tales and reflect deeply on how Homer's metaphors enhance one's personal growth.

On another level, however, one can reinterpret the stories that we first encountered in high school with a special relevance to management or leadership problems. The purpose of this paper is to show the relevance of some of Homer's insights into management with the hope that some readers will be inspired to read more of Homer to develop the arguments on a deeper, more personal level. We will see that many of Homer's key insights on leadership and management are relevant today, but, more important, we will see that thinking metaphorically can enhance our own development.

The *Odyssey* is, in part, the story of one man's adventures after the Trojan War. After the successful sack of Troy, Odysseus embarked with several ships and many followers to return to his native Ithaca, off the western coast of the Peloponesian peninsula. In what should have been a fairly standard trip—there was the usual side trip to sack and pillage Lauchachia en route just to keep certain that standard operating procedures honed by years of planning and maneuvers remained in good order—Odysseus incurred the wrath of Poseidon, the god of earth and sea. Despite Odysseus's efforts to meet his goal on time and within budget, events beyond his control intervened. Instead of a few weeks, Odysseus was gone for 10 more years.

During this time, his wife, Penelope, steadfastly remained loyal to him. Although pursued by several dozen suitors from all over the Greek world, she remained virtuous. She also was faced with some budgetary difficulties. In the manner of the times, the suitors who wanted to replace Odysseus in Penelope's bed as well as lay claim to Odysseus's kingdom hung around the palace drinking and feasting—at Penelope's expense. This drain on Ithaca's coffers did not escape the gods. Athena, in particular, took pity on Penelope and

Source: Edited and reprinted with permission from *Business and the Contemporary World* (Summer 1992), pp. 168–173. Copyright John Wiley & Sons, Inc. Reprinted with permission of John Wiley & Sons, Inc.

At the time this article was written, Fred A. Kramer was a professor of political science and director of the MPA Program at the University of Massachusetts—Amherst. He is the author of *Dynamics of Public Bureaucracy* and a variety of articles that have appeared in professional journals.

successfully argued that the gods should allow Odysseus to return. As part of her plan, she told Telemachus, Odysseus's son, who was a baby when Odysseus went off to war but who was not full grown, to outfit a ship and go looking for his father.

Fed up with the actions of the suitors, who had virtually taken over his father's palace, Telemachus embarked on what he felt would be an impossible mission. He was helped in this effort by the man Odysseus left behind to look after the palace and grounds, Mentor. Athena assumed Mentor's appearance and accompanied Telemachus on the journey. Along the way, "Mentor" gave him encouragement—the encouragement that he needed to develop into a fully functioning, responsible adult. Telemachus was relieved to be doing something. He was a man of action even though he perceived that the odds were against him.

Like all good mentors, Athena imbued Telemachus with a sense of responsibility. In seeking to master his challenging assignment, Telemachus discovered his inner strength. The babbling teenager became an articulate, courageous adult who impressed others with his leadership potential. With his mentor's help and support, Telemachus gained confidence and achieved a degree of success that he had not previously thought possible. In short, under a mentor's guidance, Telemachus showed leadership qualities similar to those his father had displayed during the Trojan War.

Mentor meets each of the leadership criteria suggested by a current observer of leadership problems, Warren Bennis. In *Why Leaders Can't Lead,* Bennis suggests four "competencies" that leaders must show. These are: management of attention through vision; management of meaning through communication; management of trust through reliability and constancy; and management of self through knowing one's skills and deploying them effectively.[4]

The first three competencies are closely related. To Bennis, having a vision is absolutely essential to leadership. The leader's vision provides a focus and sets the agenda for the organization. Having a clear vision brings about confidence in the followers. To engender confidence in the followers, the leader must be able to communicate that vision. A leader organizes meaning for the members of the organization. "Leadership creates a new audience for its ideas because it alters the shape of understanding by transmitting information in such a way that it 'fixes' and secures tradition. Leadership, by communicating meaning, creates a commonwealth of learning, and that, in turn, is what effective organizations are."[5] The management of trust implies accountability, predictability, and reliability and is based on the kinds of positions that a leader takes.[6] These positions are based on the leader's vision for the organization, which must be clear, attractive, and attainable. According to Bennis and Burt Nanus, his collaborator on an earlier book, vision and position stand in the same relationship to each other as do thought and action.[7]

The management of self is another order of skill—one that may have to precede the others. Deployment of self is based largely on positive self-regard. To Bennis, positive self-regard is not "narcissistic character." Instead, leaders know their worth; they trust themselves without letting their ego or image get in the way.[8] They do this in several ways. First, they recognize their strengths and compensate for their weaknesses. Second, they nurture their own skills with discipline by working on and developing their own talents. And third, leaders have the capacity to discern the fit between their perceived skills and what the job requires. According to Bennis and Nanus, the self-regard that leaders show is "contagious." It empowers subordinates throughout the organization to bring their own skills to bear on issues that affect the organization within the context of the leader's vision.[9]

In the *Odyssey,* Mentor provides a vision—Telemachus must search for his father. Mentor communicates that vision clearly and takes positions that indicate to Telemachus that he, in fact, can succeed in his task. This is possible because, as one of the immortals (remember that Mentor was really Athena, Zeus's daughter), Mentor had a strong sense of self. What is more important for us, however, is the impact that Mentor has on Telemachus. Mentor's sense of confidence and vision was contagious. This confidence and vision empowered Telemachus to become a leader in his own right.

Not only did Athena get the gods' consent to serve as mentor and protector of Telemachus in his search for his father, but she convinced Zeus to intervene directly with Calypso, the beautiful nymph, who had kept Odysseus prisoner on her island for seven years. Even though Calypso was disappointed at the prospect of losing Odysseus, she helped him build and stock a raft for his sea journey back to Ithaca. All was smooth sailing for Odysseus until his old Nemesis, Poseidon, spotted his raft. Poseidon had not been a party to the gods' discussion about Odysseus. Athena had broached the idea of allowing Odysseus to return to Ithaca at a meeting that took place on Olympus while Poseidon was finishing up a project in Ethiopia. Even though the gods had made a decision regarding the Odysseus matter, Poseidon felt that his interests had not been adequately treated in the deliberations. Upon spotting Odysseus, the "mighty Earthshaker" waved his trident to start an incredible storm. Unanticipated changes in the political environment can upset stated goals.

With some supernatural help, Odysseus managed to swim to shore in the land of the Phaeacians. The Phaeacians were a neutral, peace loving, seafaring people. Because the ruler, Alcinous, claimed to be a direct descendent of Poseidon, Odysseus wisely did not relate the story of his adventures. Initially Odysseus was mistakenly thought to be an immortal, but, without revealing his identity, he convinced his host that he was just an ordinary guy who wanted to get home. Although Odysseus struck a modest, humble pose, he was goaded into participating in some athletic games. Naturally, the self-effacing stranger beat his adversaries at their own games. But Odysseus was a gracious winner, and Alcinous agreed to help him get back to Ithaca. Odysseus, at this point, shows virtually all the aspects that Bennis attributes to leaders.[10] He shows integrity, dedication, magnanimity, humility, and creativity. No wonder he was mistaken for an immortal.

At a feast that preceded his departure, Odysseus, upon hearing a song about his exploits during the Trojan War, broke into tears and admitted that he was the long-suffering subject of the bard's song. He then related his story, which is a metaphoric journey into self-awareness—a journey essential for all leaders.

A brief recapitulation of a few stories will show how interesting and relevant Odysseus's adventures are for today's managers. Odysseus had an early encounter in the land of the lotus-eaters. The lotus-eaters were a peaceful people. They were different from Odysseus and his men, who were the aggressive sackers of cities. What made the lotus-eaters so different was their food—lotus flowers. Bread and meat were the staples of Odysseus and his band. The lotus flowers induced a feeling of well-being in anyone who ate them. Odysseus discovered this when some of his men who were sent out to serve as ambassadors to these people accepted some lotus flower snacks. Perhaps they should have just said, "No." The effect of their tasting the lotus was to deflect them from group goals. One taste and they lost sight of the objective of returning to Ithaca and desired only to "go native"—to stay happily in the land of the lotus-eaters. Odysseus exercised a classical Theory X management technique to cope with this insubor-

dination. He ordered these men dragged back to the ships by force and kept under tight control until the effects of the lotus flowers dissipated. We can interpret this action as a solely managerial, as opposed to a leadership, response. There is no attempt to broaden vision or incorporate new goals or learn from new experiences. Dragging those spaced-out comrades back to the boat was efficient, but was it really the right thing to do?

After the interlude with the lotus-eaters, Odysseus and his band rowed on to the land of the Cyclopes, who are described as having had no stable laws, and, by implication, no lawyers. Odysseus, like many modern public and business leaders, was curious as to how such a system could operate. He and a group of 12 followers set off to explore the environment. Their curiosity drew them to the care of Polyphemus, the one-eyed giant who imprisoned them. Of course, the monster did take a couple of men for dinner and breakfast, summarily dashing their heads on the rocks in the cave and devouring them. Clearly Odysseus's leadership was put to the test.

Analyzing the situation and the materials available to him, Odysseus developed a plan while the monster was out tending his flocks of sheep and goats. Essentially it entailed getting the Cyclops drunk and poking his eye out with a burning stake while he slept under the influence of some fortified wine, which Odysseus just happened to have brought with him. While Odysseus gave Polyphemus the wine, he referred to himself as "Nobody." Odysseus, evidently, had a passion for anonymity. This ruse had immediate benefits for Odysseus, because the monster agreed that he would eat Nobody last. Carrying out the plan was dangerous, but Odysseus rallied his men and they successfully blinded Polyphemus.

The pain of the blinding, however, woke the giant and he called for his fellow Cyclopes, who gathered at the mouth of his cave. Polyphemus told his fellows, "Nobody is murdering me by craft." They were puzzled. "If nobody harms you . . . ," they responded before going about their own business. Odysseus managed to get his men out of the angry monster's cave and back to the ships.

Once aboard his ship, Odysseus could not refrain from deriding the blind, miserable monster. Far from keeping in the background and practicing anonymity, Odysseus boasted of his cleverness. Despite the wise words of those in his crew who advised him to keep quiet and get on with the journey, Odysseus continued to make fun of the blinded Cyclops and told Polyphemus his name. Even a vanquished foe may have some power resources that can be brought to bear on future issues. In Polyphemus's case, he prayed to his father Poseidon to make life difficult for Odysseus. His prayers were answered, but perhaps Odysseus became a better person, and leader, because of the trials set up by Poseidon.

This story brings out some leadership attributes of Odysseus as well as some drawbacks. Bennis would applaud the curiosity and vision that took Odysseus and his band to the cave. Although Bennis sees a difference between leadership and problem solving, the clever way in which Odysseus leads his men to freedom is a positive aspect of leadership potential. Once back on his ship, however, Odysseus shows us that he is not really a true leader yet. His boasting almost brings disaster immediately. Surely there is little of the magnanimity and humility that Bennis found in some modern leaders.

The adventures of Odysseus go on and on. The story of this journey becomes increasingly metaphorical at ever-deepening levels until he reaches a state of self-awareness that is a key to successful leadership. But we need not get into all the details of Odysseus's adventures on his eventual return to Ithaca and reunion with his wife and son. There are enough interesting stories—the sailors breaking into the bag of winds while Odysseus slept, the dilemma of Scylla and Charybdis, the Sirens' song, and many more—to keep a modern manager engaged with the plot so that he or she may encounter the deeper metaphors that might inspire more creative thinking. If one reacquaints oneself with the rich metaphors of the epic, one will think. One will grow.

Public and business leaders should be beyond literal thinking. Although they certainly have to be concerned with real-world problems, perhaps the solutions to these problems can be found through more creative responses than are routinely tried in both the public and private sectors.

Rosabeth Moss Kanter has admonished her readers to "think across boundaries."[11] A fundamental challenge to leaders in this turbulent world is to expand their own, and others', thinking. They must also engage in integrative, holistic thinking. As Kanter puts it:

> To see problems and opportunities integratively is to see them as wholes related to larger wholes, rather than dividing information and experience into discrete bits assigned to distinct, separate categories that never touch one another. Blurring the boundaries and challenging the categories permit new possibilities to emerge, like twisting a kaleidoscope to see the endless patterns that can be created from the same set of fragments.[12]

Think of that metaphor of the kaleidoscope. Those are the same fragments. They have simply been rearranged. Can we train our minds to rearrange the fragments that we work with in business and public-policy problems?

The modern reader generally sees myths to be misconceptions or lies. Indeed, Bennis and Nanus present several leadership "myths" and then dispel them.[13] Myth to Homer, however, is a metaphor for the truth. The teachings about leadership that come from Homer are distilled from myths as metaphors. From these metaphors we find that such attributes as vision, dedication, communication, delegation, openness, creativity, magnanimity, and integrity are important components of leadership. But most important, Homer teaches us that a person should grow and develop. A person should learn from experience.

The main lesson of the *Odyssey* is that each of us should undertake our own journeys into self-awareness and self-understanding. By so doing we can develop our own leadership potential if we so choose. Although Homer does not tell us exactly how to go about our search for self-understanding, a deep reflection on his metaphors might illuminate that search for some people because thinking metaphorically can help us see things in new ways.

Notes

1 Warren Bennis, *Why Leaders Can't Lead* (San Francisco: Jossey-Bass, 1989), 119.

2 Quoted in Cedric H. Whitman, *Homer and the Heroic Tradition* (Cambridge, MA: Harvard University Press, 1958), 15.

3 Ibid., 297.

4 Bennis, 19–21.

5 Warren Bennis and Burt Nanus, *Leaders: The Strategies for Taking Charge* (New York: Harper & Row, 1985), 42.

6 Ibid., 43.

7 Ibid., 154.

8 Bennis, 57–58.

9 Bennis and Nanus, 58–60.

10 Bennis, 118–20.

11 Rosabeth Moss Kanter, "Thinking Across Boundaries," *Harvard Business Review* 68 (November–December 1990), 9.

12 Ibid.

13 Bennis and Nanus, 222–25.

Readings: The Conceptual and Empirical Leadership Literature

Introduction
to Leadership

This journey through the leadership literature starts with a set of readings that helps define leadership. On the surface, leadership would appear to have a simple definition. In fact, arriving at a definition is difficult because of the variety of ways that leadership has been envisioned, and because of the complexity brought on by its multiple dimensions. This chapter is intended to start us on our journey in search of an understanding of leaders and the leadership process.

At the outset it is important to recognize that the study of leadership started with the assumption that it was a phenomenon embedded in the leader, as opposed to within the follower and/or the relationship that brings and holds them together. As will be seen in many of our readings, especially in the first reading, where the concept and definition of leadership are explored, emphasis is from the perspective of the leader—his or her role, personality, behavior, influence, and guidance. The leadership literature is largely leader centered.

In the first reading in this chapter, Jon L. Pierce and John W. Newstrom provide a perspective on the meaning of leadership. The ancient Greeks, Egyptians, and Chinese tended to focus on some of the key qualities possessed by the leader. For example, Taoism suggests that leaders need to act such that others come to believe that their success is due to their own efforts and not that of the leaders. As Lao Tzu said: "A leader is best when people barely know he exists, Not so good when people obey and acclaim him, Worse when they despise him. But of a good leader, who talks little, When his task is done, his aim fulfilled, They will all say, We did it ourselves."[1] The Greeks believed that leaders possessed justice and judgment, wisdom and counsel, shrewdness and cunning, and valor and activism.

Drawing upon the Egyptians, Bernard Bass (1990) suggests that the leadership context consists of the leader and follower.[2] He goes on to note that there are nearly as many definitions given to leadership as there have been authors who have written about the concept. Based upon an extensive review of the leadership literature, Bass provides us with an overview to the meaning of leadership by organizing the myriad of definitions around 13 different approaches. Pierce and Newstrom provide an overview of Bass's review. Among some of the interesting concepts that have been linked to the definition of leadership has been its role as "the focus of group processes, as a personality attribute, as the art of inducing compliance, as an exercise of influence, as a particular kind of act, as a form of persuasion, as a power relation, as an instrument in the attainment of goals, as an effect of interaction, as a differentiated role, and as the initiation of structure" (Bass, 1990, 20). To these many roles, many contemporary writers are

---

[1] www.brainingquote.com/quotes/authors/l/lao-tzu.html
[2] Bernard Bass, "Concepts of Leadership," in *Bass & Stogdill's Handbook of Leadership* (New York: Free Press, 1990), pp. 13–20.

suggesting that leaders also coach, facilitate, and nurture. Finally, Pierce and Newstrom comment upon several alternative perspectives (e.g., self, symbolic, team, and organizational) on the leadership concept.

According to Albert Murphy (1941), the author of the second reading, leadership is not a psychological phenomenon (something embedded in the traits of the individual); instead, leadership is essentially *sociological* in nature. Situations in which people find themselves create needs, and it is the nature of these demands that serves to define the type of leadership needed and thus who will lead. Leadership, according to Murphy, is said to be a function of the whole situation and not something that resides in a person. Murphy views leadership as a function of an interaction between the person and the situation, where the situation consists of the follower(s) and the context confronting them. $L = f$ [(Person) (Group) (Context)].

Also suggesting that leadership is a sociological phenomenon are comments made by University of Washington's leadership scholar Fred Fiedler. In a recent interview in celebration of the fortieth anniversary of Cornell University's publication of the *Administrative Science Quarterly,* Fiedler said that "the most important lesson we have learned over the past 40 years is probably that the leadership of groups and organizations is a highly complex interaction between an individual and the social and task environment. Leadership is an ongoing transaction between a person in a position of authority and the social environment."[3]

Leadership, when viewed from a sociological perspective, is framed as an interplay and relationship between two or more actors (i.e., leader and followers) within a particular context. This interplay and relationship between the situation, and the needs that it creates for people and the individual are defined as the leadership process, and it is this process that serves to define who the leader is, group effectiveness, future group (social) needs, and once again, who serves as the group's next leader. Thus, the leadership process is fluid and not static in nature.

Edwin P. Hollander and James W. Julian (1969), in the third reading, provide us with insight into several dimensions of leadership. Among their observations is that leadership is a process, an influence relationship, a leader–follower transaction, a differentiated role, an element of the situation in which the follower finds him/herself, and an exchange relationship.

Today, in the popular world of leadership, the word *vision* is at center stage. The country and many organizations find themselves suffering from a leadership void. As a consequence there is a search for those who have a vision that can unite people in the social system, providing them with a sense of purpose, unity, and a common direction. The third selection in this opening chapter provides a perspective on the leadership phenomenon of *vision*.

Linda Smircich and Gareth Morgan (1982) define the phenomenon of leadership from the perspective of what it is that leaders do for the groups that they are a part of. *Leaders,* according to Smircich and Morgan, *assign meaning to events for others.* Some individuals emerge as leaders because they "frame experience in a way that provides a viable basis for action" (258). They are individuals who are capable of taking ambiguous situations, interpreting these situations, and framing for the follower an understanding of the situation and what needs to be done to move forward. Smircich and Morgan reinforce Murphy's notion that leadership is a sociological process that is characterized by an interplay between the leader, the followers, and their common situation (context). Finally, their work implies a power and dependency relationship. Followers surrender their power to interpret and define reality, while simultaneously granting this power to someone else. A later chapter of this book takes a closer look at the role of power and influence as a part of the leadership process.

[3] Fred E. Fiedler, "Research on Leadership Selection and Training: One View of the Future," *Administrative Science Quarterly* 41 (1996), pp. 241–251.

An implicit message derived from this set of readings is that leadership can sometimes be differentiated from management and headship. Leadership therefore has been cast as either a *formal* role, wherein someone is a group's designated leader, or an *informal* role, as in the case of an emergent leader arising from a set of dynamics that are transpiring between members of a group and the context within which they are embedded. For those interested in pursuing the manager/leader distinction further, we encourage you to read the following: "What Leaders Really Do," by John P. Kotter, appearing in the *Harvard Business Review* (May–June 1990), pp. 103–111; and "The Manager's Job: Folklore and Fact," by Henry Mintzberg, also appearing in the *Harvard Business Review* (July–August 1975), pp. 49–61. Platitudes regarding the differences between manager and leader, such as "managers manage things and leaders lead people," and "managers do things right and leaders do the right things" serve very little useful purpose and are often misleading. In fact, there are differences *and* a commonality between leadership and managing. Quite simply, differences between the concepts of leader (leadership) and manager (managing) can be found in their respective definitions, the process or path by which one comes to the position, the source and type of power frequently employed, the base of respective legitimacy, how the position or role is maintained and lost, and the fact that the substance of the connection between leader and follower differs from that between a manager and subordinate or employee. That said, there is often an overlap between the two concepts. To be an outstanding manager often necessitates being a good leader, and to be an outstanding leader requires one to be good at decision making, planning, organizing, directing, and controlling—the essence of managing.

Figure 1.1 provides a visual and conceptual framework around which you can organize your understanding of leadership and the leadership process. The leadership process can be envisioned as a complex and dynamic exchange. There are five key components involved in this schematic portrayal (i.e., leader, followers, the context [or situations], the leadership process, and the resulting by-products) that can be employed to articulate the meaning of leadership and the leadership process:

• The *leader* is the person who takes charge and guides the performance or activity.

• The *followers* are people who perform under the guidance and instructions of a leader.

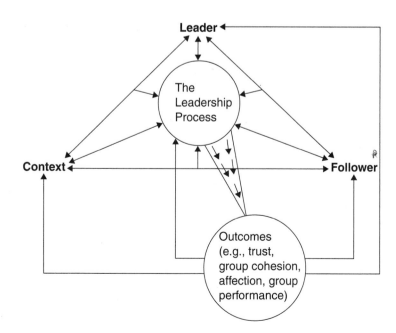

FIGURE 1.1
The Leadership Process

Source: R. B. Dunham and J. L. Pierce, *Management* (Glenview, IL: Scott, Foresman, 1989), p. 556.

- The *context* is the situation—formal or informal, social or work, dynamic or static, emergency or routine, complex or simple, and so on—surrounding a leader–follower relationship.

- The *process* reflects that which is embedded in the act of leadership. Process is multidimensional in nature and consists of leading and following, as well as the assumption and surrender of power to define the situation, the provision of guidance toward goal attainment, exchanges, and the building of relationships (e.g., trust, respect, working).

- *Outcomes* can include nearly anything arising from interplay between the leader, follower, and situation (context), such as respect for an able leader's decisions, goal attainment, customer satisfaction, high-quality products, or animosity resulting from a punitive leader's actions.

The leadership process is both interactive and dynamic. Leaders influence followers, followers influence leaders, and all parties are influenced by the context in which the exchange takes place. In turn, the outcomes that stem from a leader–follower exchange can influence future interactions because they may produce a change in the context, in the followers, and/or in the leader.

According to this model, understanding of leadership and the leadership process necessitates developing an understanding of the leader, the followers, the context, the processes (e.g., the influence process whereby follower → leader; situation → follower; situation → leader; leader → situation; leader → follower), and the resulting consequences. The figure reveals that leadership (according to Murphy, 1941) is a sociological phenomenon and that it is dynamic (fluid) in nature. As suggested by Murphy (1941), Hollander and Julian (1969), and Smircich and Morgan (1982), leadership is a social influence relationship, interactive between two or more people dependent upon one another for the attainment of certain mutual goals, bound together within a group situation. *Leadership is a dynamic and working relationship, built over time, involving an exchange between leader and follower in which leadership is a resource embedded in the situation, providing direction for goal attainment.*

Reading 3

On the Meaning of Leadership

Jon L. Pierce and John W. Newstrom
University of Minnesota Duluth

Leaders and leadership permeate the context of contemporary society, in much the same way that they have throughout the history of civilization. Mythical characters, such as those in Homer's *Odyssey* and *Iliad,* have been used to portray great leaders and great feats of leadership, as well as to carry messages of leader character to succeeding generations. In Homer's *Odyssey,* for example, we learn about the importance of self-confidence in successful leadership.

In addition to the leadership lessons in the Latin, Greek, and Roman classics, Chinese classics from as early as the sixth century B.C. illustrate an interest in leaders and feats of leadership. Confucian writings emphasized the importance of setting a moral example and using rewards and punishment as leadership tools for molding moral behavior. In addition, Taoism emphasized that effective leaders maintain a low profile and work through others:

> A leader is best, When people barely know he [she] exists, Not so good when people obey him [her], Worse when they despise him [her]. But of a good leader, who talks little, When his [her] task is done, his aim fulfilled, They will say: We did it ourselves.

Stories from the Old and New Testaments provide more recent evidence of a long-standing interest in leadership. The book of Exodus, for example, presents an interesting story about the leadership challenges confronting Moses in his attempt to lead the Israelites out of Egypt.

Scholars writing during the twentieth century maintained this long-standing interest in leaders and the leadership process. During the twentieth century, there were few, if any, organizational concepts that received as much scholarly attention for as long a period of time as the concept of leadership. Stogdill's review of the leadership literature, published in 1948, examined studies of leadership dating back to 1904. He cited more than 100 authors who provided insight into the nature of leaders and their personality traits. In 1974, he published a second review of 163 studies which were published between 1949 and 1970. Today there are jour-

nals, such as *Leadership Quarterly, Leadership, Leadership and Organizational & Studies,* and the *Journal of Leadership Studies,* that focus exclusively on leadership. In addition, each of the major management and organization journals (e.g., *Academy of Management Journal, Academy of Management Review, Journal of Applied Psychology, Journal of Management, Journal of Organizational Behavior,* and *Administrative Science Quarterly*) routinely publish leadership articles, and virtually every organizational behavior and management textbook devotes a chapter to the topic. Finally, the last three decades have witnessed the publication of dozens of popular leadership books (e.g., Covey's *The 7 Habits of Highly Effective People,* Bennis's *Why Leaders Can't Lead,* Peter Dean's *Leadership for Everyone,* and Daft and Lengel's *Fusion Leadership*), which are sold in most of the major airports in North America, online (e.g., Amazon.com), and in major bookstores (e.g., Borders and B. Dalton). Many of these books have sold literally thousands upon thousands of copies.

Scholars interested in leadership have approached the development of an understanding of leadership from a variety of perspectives, starting with the "Great Person Theory of Leadership," which posited that great leaders, such as Julius Caesar, Joan of Arc, Catherine II the Great, Napoleon, Mao Tsetung, Winston Churchill, and Franklin Delano Roosevelt, were born with a set of personal qualities that destined them to be great leaders. Much of the leadership scholarship conducted during the first half of the twentieth century was focused on the identification of the personal traits (attributes) that characterized those individuals who emerged as leaders and those who came to be highly effective leaders. Following the study of leaders and personal traits, the focus turned to a variety of themes, such as leader behaviors, the conditions under which certain leader behaviors were effective, the nature of the relationship between leaders and followers, and the forms of influence that were associated with effective leadership. During the first part of the twenty-first century, leadership scholars have demonstrated a strong interest in charismatic and transformational leadership.

Source: Prepared for a previous edition and revised for the 5th edition.

In this reading for *Leaders and the Leadership Process,* we will address the question, What does the concept of leadership mean? We recommend that you read an outstanding piece on the "Concepts of Leadership" by Bernard M. Bass (Chapter 1 in *Bass & Stogdill's Handbook of Leadership: Theory, Research, and Management Applications*). Bass provides a detailed review of the diversity of perspectives that have been taken by scholars as they have attempted to wrestle with the leadership phenomenon.

ON THE MEANING OF LEADERSHIP

A review of the leadership literature quickly reveals that there are multiple definitions that have been given to the leadership construct. This diversity of definitions reveals, in part, the complexity of the construct. Some authors have chosen to treat leadership as a psychological phenomenon (i.e., the leader is a person who possesses certain desirable personality and demographic traits), while others see it as a sociological phenomenon (i.e., the leader is the result of a confluence of a person, a group, and the needs arising from a situation faced by each). To use an analogy, those taking this position suggest that to understand a marriage, you cannot focus simply on the wife (husband), but instead, you need to study the wife, the husband, their relationship, and the context within which it is embedded.

Bass (1990), in the introductory chapter to *Bass & Stogdill's Handbook of Leadership,* focuses on the concept of leadership. He suggests that there are several different approaches to the definition. Specifically, he identifies the following:

- *Leadership as a focus of group processes.* This set of definitions positions the leader as the hub, nucleus, and/or pivotal point for group activity, as might be illustrated with Chapin's (1924) definition of leadership as "a point of polarization for group cooperation."

- *Leadership as personality and its effects.* This set of definitions tends to define leadership in terms of the personality attributes or the strength of character of the leader her- or himself. Of leadership, Bernard (1926) said: "Any person who is more than ordinarily efficient in carrying psychosocial stimuli to others and is thus effective in conditioning collective responses may be called a leader."

- *Leadership as an act or behavior.* A tradition in leadership research focused upon the acts of leadership, attempting to answer the question, What do leaders do? This set of definitions can be illustrated by Shartle's (1956) suggestion that the act of leadership is "one which results in others acting or responding in a shared direction."

- *Leadership as an instrument of goal achievement.* This set of definitions ascribes an instrumental value to the act of leadership. A leader, according to Cowley (1928), "is a person who has a program and is moving toward an objective with his group in a definite manner," while Davis (1942) defines leadership as "the principal dynamic force that motivates and coordinates the organization in the accomplishment of its objectives."

- *Leadership as an emerging effect of interaction.* A set of definitions of leadership cast it as an "effect or outgrowth" of group interaction. It is not seen as the "cause" of group action, but something which emerges as a result of interactions within and among members of the group. Bogardus (1929) suggests that it is a social process "which causes a number of people to set out toward an old goal with new zest or a new goal with hopeful courage."

- *Leadership as a differentiated role.* Emerging out of role theory and its perspective that members of social systems occupy different roles that are needed to advance the system, leadership is but one of several well-defined, needed, and differentiated roles. Different members of a social system (group) might be seen as making different contributions to the attainment of the group's goals. These roles, according to Sherif and Sherif (1956) come to be defined in terms of stable expectations that group members develop for themselves and other members of the group. From this perspective, leadership might be seen as that role which integrates the other roles to advance the cause of the social system.

- *Leadership as the initiation of structure.* A continuation of the role theme to the definition of leadership, those who view leadership as the initiation of structure see a unique role as defining leadership. Stogdill (1959) took this approach, when he defined leadership as "the initiation and maintenance of structure in expectation and interaction." This approach is often coupled with leadership as a behavior with initiating structure serving as one of the central behaviors.

Several approaches to the definition of leadership revolve around such concepts as influence, power, and securing compliance. For example:

- *Leadership as the art of inducing compliance.* This set of definitions tends to cast leadership in terms of the molding of the group around the will, intentions, and/or wishes of the leader. Leadership is, therefore, cast from an induction-compliance perspective, and influence is exercised from a single direction—leader to follower—without regard to the follower's wishes. Allport's (1924) definition of leadership as "personal social control" and Bundel's (1930) definition of leadership as "the art of inducing others to do what one wants them to do" are illustrative of the inducing compliance approach to the definition of leadership.

- *Leadership as the exercise of influence.* A set of definitions of leadership appears to employ the concept of influence as separate and distinct from dominance, control, or the forcing of compliance. Such definitions might range from Gandhi's emphasis upon leading by example (he states: "Clean examples have a curious method of multiplying themselves"), to the statement "follow me" (cf. Bass, 1990), to attempts to move others through speech and the communication process (cf. Tannenbaum, Weschler, & Massarik, 1961), to the movement of others through the production of an effect on followers' perceptions (cf. Ferris & Rowland, 1981). Some of the definitions simply employ the word *influencing,* such as Tannenbaum et al.'s (1961) suggestion that leadership is "interpersonal influence," and Tead's (1935) observation that it is "the activity of influencing people to cooperate toward some goal which they come to find desirable."

- *Leadership as a form of persuasion.* Some definitions of leadership reflect the movement of others through strongly held convictions and/or reason. A former U.S. president, Dwight Eisenhower, built his definition of leadership around the concept of persuasion. For Eisenhower, "leadership is the ability to decide what is to be done, and to get others to want to do it" (cf. Larson, 1968, p. 21). Lippmann (1922) employed the same conceptualization: "the final test of a leader is that he leaves behind him in other men the conviction and the will to carry on."

- *Leadership as a power relationship.* This set of definitions focuses on the key role played by

power. French and Raven (1959) defined leadership from the perspective of the differences in power relationships among members of a group. Similarly, Janda (1960) saw leadership in terms of a "group member's perception that another group member has the right to prescribe behavior patterns for the former regarding his activity as a member of a particular group."

Finally, Bass (1990) observes that there are a number of conceptualizations of leadership that employ a combination of elements. Leadership as a combination of elements was illustrated by Dupuy and Dupuy (1959), who make reference to obedience, confidence, respect, and loyal cooperation in their definition.

Bass (1990) employs the following definition of leadership in *Bass and Stogdill's Handbook of Leadership:*

> Leadership is an interaction between two or more members of a group that often involves a structuring or restructuring of the situation and the perceptions and expectations of the members. (p. 19)

He goes on to suggest that leaders are "agents of change," "persons whose acts affect other people more than other people's acts affect them," and that "leadership occurs when one group member modifies the motivation or competencies of others in the group" (pp. 19–20).

Joseph Rost (1991) in *Leadership for the Twenty-First Century* reviewed 221 definitions of leadership, which emphasizes the point that there are many definitions. After reviewing many of the different definitions of leadership, Ciculla (1995) notes that "one can detect a family resemblance between the different definitions. All of them talk about leadership as some kind of process, act, or influence that in some way gets people to do something" (p. 12). She suggests that if the authors of these 221 definitions were assembled in a room, each would understand one another and they would be able to understand the individual who spoke of leadership as the process of influencing the movement of a group toward the attainment of a particular outcome. The major differences, Ciculla notes, are to be found in aspects of the relationship that exist between the leader and follower and in terms of how leaders get people to do things.

Yukl (1998), commenting upon the variety of definitions of leadership, states: "The differences are not just a case of scholarly nitpicking. They reflect deep disagreement about identification of leaders and leadership processes" (p. 3). We, too, have come to believe that it is unlikely that there will ever be a single definition. The complexity of the phenomenon, the fact that it manifests itself in so many different ways in so many different contexts, and the different purposes to which it gets put call for a variety of defining features. Nevertheless, it appears to us that most students of leadership see it as *a sociological phenomenon (a process) involving the intentional exercise of influence exercised by one person over one or more other individuals, in an effort to guide activities toward the attainment of some mutual goal, a goal that requires interdependent action among members of the group.* While we too adopt the notion that leadership is a social (interpersonal) influence process in the pursuit of a common goal, the various other definitions of leadership provide us with valuable insight into important aspects of the leadership phenomenon.

ALTERNATIVE CONCEPTUALIZATIONS

Part of the difficulty and confusion that is associated with attaching meaning to the concept of leadership stems from the fact that there are a variety of non–mutually exclusive categories to which the concept has been employed. First, from a *levels of analysis* perspective, reference to leadership has been made at the community level (e.g., United Nations, nation-state, state/province, city, township), at the industry level (e.g., Boeing leading the aerospace industry into the twenty-first century), and at the organization level (e.g., Mulally's leadership of Ford), at the small group–work team level, dyadically, and on self-leadership. Leaders (and leadership) are also commonly approached from a *stylistic* perspective, with references made to autocratic, democratic, servant (i.e., providing a service to others; cf. Robert Greenleaf, 1977), people- and task-oriented, and laissez-faire leadership. From a *thematic,* or issues, perspective, we routinely hear, for example, the free world, strategic, ethics, and campaign finance reform leadership. The term *leadership* has also been employed from the perspective of *where the leader comes from,* such that we have designated and emergent leaders, formal and informal leaders, and vertical and horizontal leaders. Finally, we occasionally make reference here to coleadership (i.e., team leadership wherein two or more people simultaneously serve as leader), symbolic leadership (i.e., the institutalization of symbols as the tools of leadership, such as

the leadership provided in absentia by Buddha, Jesus Christ, Muhammad), and strategic leadership. Adding to the confusion is the fact that the terms *management* and *leadership* are often used interchangeably. Going hand in hand with this notion, leadership studies are often conducted in organizations in which managers are treated as leaders and subordinates are treated as followers, and the student of this literature is left wondering how much of the variance in the observed outcomes (e.g., motivation, satisfaction, performance, citizenship behaviors) is a function of the manager–subordinate vis-à-vis the leader–follower relationship.

While each of these perspectives and uses of the term is a legitimate use of the leadership construct, each reflects a conceptualization different from that which traditionally has been employed. Each of these alternative perspectives on the concept of leadership is different from that which is focused on by this collection of readings. Throughout the remainder of this set of readings, leadership will be seen as a sociological phenomenon, arising out of and operating within a group context. The term *leadership* will generally be cast as a dynamic (fluid), interactive, working relationship between a leader and one or more followers, operating within the framework of a group context for the accomplishment of some collective goal. Efforts to address self, coleadership, strategic, symbolic, organizational, and nation leadership will not be undertaken in this collection of readings.

EMERGING ROLES

Finally, several of the readings in this collection will provide insight into the role and meaning of leadership by answering the question, What do leaders do? Smircich and Morgan (1982), in the last reading in this chapter, for example, suggest that leaders provide meaning by framing reality for others, and Stogdill (1948) suggests that leaders orchestrate group activity.

Some contemporary writers suggest that there may be a new role for leaders in organizations of the twenty-first century. Manz and Sims (1991), for example, talk about *SuperLeadership.* This type of leader will represent the transformation from the "follow me" leader to the leader who engages in leading others to lead themselves and thus the attainment of self-leadership.

Senge (1990) suggests that accompanying the emergence of the learning organization, a new leadership role emerges. The role of the leader of a learning organization will be that of designer, teacher, and steward. This new leader role brings with it the need for a new set of leadership skills and tools of leadership.

We also note that an increasing number of management gurus are suggesting that many of today's organizations are "overmanaged and underled." Increasingly, organizations are modifying the role of yesterday's manager, changing the role to that of a leader charged with the responsibility to gain follower recognition and acceptance, and to become a facilitator and orchestrator of group activity, while also serving as coach and cheerleader. It is feasible that many of these roles (e.g., servant, teacher, coach, cheerleader) will become a common part of the conceptualization of leader and leadership as the twenty-first century unfolds further.

References

Allport, F. H. (1924). *Social Psychology*. Boston: Houghton Mifflin.

Bass, B. M. (1990). "Concepts of Leadership" (Chapter 1). *Bass & Stogdill's Handbook of Leadership: Theory, Research, & Managerial Applications* (3rd edition). New York: Free Press.

Bernard, L. L. (1926). *An Introduction to Social Psychology*. New York: Holt.

Bogardus, E. S. (1929). "Leadership and Attitudes." *Sociology and Social Research* 13, pp. 377–387.

Bundel, C. M. (1930). "Is Leadership Losing Its Importance?" *Infantry Journal* 36, pp. 339–349.

Chapin, F. S. (1924). "Leadership and Group Activity." *Journal of Applied Psychology* 8, pp. 141–145.

Ciculla, J. B. (1995). "Leadership Ethics: Mapping the Territory." *Business Ethics Quarterly* 5, 1, pp. 5–28.

Cowley, W. H. (1928). "Three distinctions in the study of leaders." *Journal of Abnormal and Social Psychology* 23, 144–157.

Davis, R. C. (1942). *The Fundamentals of Top Management*. New York: Harper.

Dupuy, R. E., & Dupuy, T. N. (1959). *Brave Men and Great Captains*. New York: Harper & Row.

Ferris, G. R., & Rowland, K. M. (1981). "Leadership, Job Perceptions, and Influence: A Conceptual Integration." *Human Relations* 34, pp. 1069–1077.

French, J. R. P., Jr., & Raven, B. (1959). "The Bases of Social Power." In D. Cartwright (ed.), *Studies in Social Power*. Ann Arbor, MI: Institute for Social Research, University of Michigan.

Greenleaf, R. K. (1977). *Servant Leadership*. New York: Paulist Press.

Janda, K. F. (1960). "Towards the Explication of the Concept of Leadership in Terms of the Concept of Power." *Human Relations* 13, pp. 345–363.

Larson, A. (1968). *Eisenhower: The President Nobody Knew*. New York: Popular Library.

Lippmann, W. (1922). *Public Opinion*. New York: Harcourt Brace.

Manz, C. C., & Sims, H. J., Jr. (1991). "SuperLeadership: Beyond the Myth of Heroic Leadership." *Organizational Dynamics* 32, p. 1.

Rost, J. (1991). *Leadership for the Twenty-First Century*. New York: Praeger.

Senge, P. M. (1990). "The Leader's New Work: Building Learning Organizations." *Sloan Management Review* 32, p. 1.

Shartle, C. L. (1956). *Executive Performance and Leadership*. Englewood Cliffs, NJ: Prentice-Hall.

Sherif, M., & Sherif, C. W. (1956). *An Outline of Social Psychology*. New York: Harper.

Smircich, L., & Morgan, G. (1982). "Leadership: The Management of Meaning." *Journal of Applied Behavioral Science* 18, 3, pp. 257–273.

Stogdill, R. M. (1948). "Personal Factors Associated with Leadership: A Survey of the Literature." *Journal of Psychology* 28, pp. 35–71.

Stogdill, R. M. (1959). *Individual Behavior and Group Achievement*. New York: Oxford University Press.

Tannenbaum, R., Weschler, I. R., & Massarik, F. (1961). *Leadership and Organization*. New York: McGraw-Hill.

Tead, O. (1935). *The Art of Leadership*. New York: McGraw-Hill.

Yukl, G. (1998). *Leadership in Organizations*. Englewood Cliffs, NJ: Prentice-Hall.

Reading 4

A Study of the Leadership Process

Albert J. Murphy
New York University

A fault of most leadership studies is emphasis upon the "individual" rather than upon the individual as a factor in a social situation. Such studies seek to determine the qualities of a person which distinguish him as a leader. They imply that these somehow can be abstracted. Difficulties immediately appear. It is discovered that leadership takes protean forms, that it is unstable, that the qualities necessary at one time are unnecessary at other times, that leaders rise and fall as situations change, that the same individual alternates between leading and following. Consequently, leadership becomes a slippery, ill-defined concept. These are commonplaces, but in spite of them, the authors usually fail to sense the root difficulty, viz., the inadequacy of the personality concept as a means of understanding the problem. Leadership is not a psychologically simple concept.

Leadership study calls for a situational approach; this is fundamentally sociological, not psychological. Leadership does not reside in a person. It is a function of the whole situation. The situation calls for certain types of action; the leader does not inject leadership but is the instrumental factor through which the situation is brought to a solution. The emphasis in the title of this paper is not on "leadership qualities" but on the "leadership process." The word *process* calls attention to the interplay of factors in a total situation. The situation is fundamental and in all cases makes the leader. This is obvious in everyday life and in history. The Hitlers and the Mussolinis are made by situations, and they can be understood only in terms of those situations. Their characteristics are indicative of the times in which they live and the situations of which they are a part. Groups do not act because they have leaders, but they secure leaders to help them to act. In other words, the leader meets a critical need just as a dentist meets a critical need. We go to a dentist because we have a toothache, not the other way around. Skills and abilities of all kinds have a functional relation to the needs of the situation, and these needs are always primary. Leadership comes into being when an individual meets certain social needs, when he releases in the social situation of which he is a part certain ideas and tendencies which are accepted by the group because they indicate solutions of needs which are dimly sensed. Leadership is best understood when it is looked at impersonally as that quality of a complex situation which, when lifted into a place of prominence, composes its conflicts and creates a new and more desirable situation.

The concept of process is important also in that it calls attention to the fluidity of the leadership situation. Leadership is not a static thing; it is an immutable aspect of personality. Many of the components of leadership, such as self-confidence and the confidence of the group, which are so essential, change with the situation. The self-confidence of a work leader or of a boys' gang leader usually disappears as soon as these individuals are put into a parlor. Ascendance, also a leadership component, increases when training is given in handling the materials of a situation. While leadership, self-confidence, ascendancy, and other so-called traits and attitudes, apparently carry over from one situation to another, it is only because the situations have practically identical elements. They are not fixed qualities of a person in any sense, nor are they fixed in the relation of two people, but are functions of a three-cornered relation—between the persons concerned and the job. Shyness often becomes dominance when the situation includes elements in which the individual's skill counts. So-called traits are names of processes; they are fluid; in no strict sense are they "attached" to anybody as "innate" or "acquired" characteristics. While studies of leadership make it appear that leaders usually have certain characteristics which combine under the term leadership ability, this generalization is misleading. Such factors as knowledge, forcefulness, tone of voice, and size are effective components in the solution of many social situations and are, therefore, generally regarded as leadership qualities, especially in unorganized group situations like gangs, but the variety of possible factors is endless. Leadership qualities, so called, vary indefinitely as the needs of groups vary indefinitely.

Source: Edited and reprinted with permission from *American Sociological Review* 6 (1941), pp. 674–687.

A few illustrations will make it obvious that the choice of leaders is dictated by group needs. A group lost in the woods would immediately follow the man who, no matter what his personal qualities, had a knowledge of the woods and the way out. A social group whose needs are conviviality and the pleasant interplay of personalities will be most stimulated by a person who is lively and sociable. The leader of an organization which integrates the functions of other organizations will be a person through whom the leadership drives of others may function; such a person becomes a leader through releasing, channelizing, and integrating the abilities of others. A discussion group leader will be self-effacing, tolerant, critical, and interested in the contributions of others. In the case of the group in the woods, personality, height, weight, and voice count for nothing: The only qualification is a knowledge of the way out. In the case of the social gathering, a personality characterized by pleasing vivacity is of major importance. In the third case, the essential characteristic of the leader is ability to release the activities and ambitions of others in a way which will promote the interest of all the groups concerned; in this case, height, weight, and voice would be irrelevant and forcefulness might even be disastrous. In the case of the discussion group, where leadership is of a highly integrative type, dominance and self-assertiveness, usually thought of as leadership traits, would be fatal. When the great variety of possible groups is considered, leadership appears clearly as a function of the situation. When the situation is simple, as in the case of the group lost in the woods, the demands on leadership are simple, but in complex situations the demands on leadership are multiple.

In order to bring out the meaning of leadership in terms of the situational processes, we may take a case from the study of leaders in work camps. In response to the request that members of work crews describe the characteristics of leaders whom they regarded as successful, the men mentioned things like these: he gets the work done; he explains things to you and doesn't yell at you; he plays no favorites but treats all men alike; he isn't so easy that you can step all over him; he watches out for the safety of the men in his crew.

These are modes of behavior. They are called for by the situation and are, in fact, responses to it. The young men who mentioned these desirable activities were not thinking of traits. So-called traits are derived by grouping these activities which are responses to the situation under classificatory labels or trait names. The first activity,

"He gets the work done," is called the trait of efficiency. The second is called reasonableness; the third is called justice; the fourth is called strictness; the fifth, carefulness. Obviously, the leader is reacting to a total situation which embraces these elements as well as others. The qualities mentioned are simply names for types of activity which meet the needs of a group, which incorporate and make effective the important factors of the situation, emotional and otherwise. The group takes pride in doing a reasonable amount of work; it desires reasonable explanations; it desires fair play in work assignments; it appreciates the need of necessary strictness; it appreciates care for its safety. Does the leader have these traits? The abstractions mentioned and imputed to the leader as qualities are really descriptions of what most of the members of the work gang desire. The names of the appropriate activities are imputed to him as his characteristics. In short, what has happened is this: (1) the group has certain needs, practical and emotional; (2) the leader responds to the situation as a whole with appropriate activities; (3) those responses are classified and labeled with trait names; (4) these names which are abstractions and summational fictions are imputed to the leader as causal psychological entities.

Confusion in the study of leadership results from endowing abstractions with reality and imputing character qualities to the person who brings the element of control into the situation. We have failed to see the leadership process as an interplay of forces, as an integrative activity. Of course, when types of a leader's integrative activities become habitual, we may call them traits provided we understand that they are activities, and we may try to develop them because these habits of conduct are useful in a large number of situations.

In summary, leadership is the process of securing direction in social activity which otherwise would be blind and disorderly. Leadership activities are resultants of the interplay of the factors which emerge out of a situation and reenter it as controls. Emphasis on so-called traits of personality, which have been shown to be hypostatized summational fictions, therefore, gives way to a study of the integrative factors in the situation. The personality does not stand alone but is a changing element in a total situation. The situation is a concept embracing many elements: the leader with his abilities and drives, the group (including potential leaders), material resources, viewpoints, desires, and needs, and a condition of readiness for leadership. This situational whole is a continuous series of influences and changes. Relativity characterizes every factor. Leading alternates with following. Solutions are new stages in the situation preparing the way for other solutions which in turn call for new types of leadership to secure new ends. Leadership may be defined as *that element in a group situation which, when made conscious and controlling, brings about a new situation that is more satisfying to the group as a whole.* . . .

Reading 5

Contemporary Trends in the Analysis of Leadership Processes

Edwin P. Hollander and James W. Julian
State University of New York at Buffalo

The history of leadership research is a fitful one. Certainly as much as, and perhaps more than, other social phenomena, conceptions and inquiry about leadership have shifted about. The psychological study of leadership in this century began with a primary focus on the personality characteristics which made a person a leader. But the yield from this approach was fairly meager and often confused, as Stogdill (1948) and Mann (1959), among others, documented in their surveys of this literature. In the 1930s, Kurt Lewin and his coworkers (Lewin, Lippitt, & White, 1939) turned attention to the "social climates" created by several styles of leadership, that is, authoritarian, democratic, or laissez-faire. Together with developments in the sociometric study of leader–follower relations (e.g., Jennings, 1943), this work marked a significant break with the past.

Two residues left by Lewin's approach fed importantly into later efforts, even with the limited nature of the original study. One was the concern with "leader style," which still persists, especially in the work on administrative or managerial leadership (see, e.g., McGregor, 1960, 1966; Preston & Heintz, 1949). The other was the movement toward a view of the differential contexts of leadership, ultimately evolving into the situational approach which took firm hold of the field by the 1950s (cf. Gouldner, 1950).

For the most part, the situational movement was spurred by the growing recognition that there were specialized demands made upon leadership, depending upon the nature of the group task and other aspects of the situation. Clearly, a deficiency in the older approach was its acceptance of "leader" as a relatively homogeneous role, independent of the variations in leader–follower relationships across situations. The disordered state in which the trait approach left the study of leadership was amply revealed by Stogdill in his 1948 survey, which marked a point of departure for the developing situational emphasis. The publication in 1949 of Hemphill's *Situational Factors in*

Source: Edited and reprinted with permission of *Psychological Bulletin* 71, 5 (1969), pp. 387–397. Copyright (1969) American Psychological Association.

Leadership contributed a further push in this direction.

The main focus of the situational approach was the study of leaders in different settings, defined especially in terms of different group tasks and group structure. Mainly, though not entirely, through laboratory experimentation, such matters as the continuity in leadership across situations with variable tasks was studied (e.g., Carter, Haythorn, Meirowitz, & Lanzetta, 1951; Carter & Nixon, 1949; Gibb, 1947). The findings of this research substantially supported the contention that who became a leader depended in some degree upon the nature of the task. With this movement, however, there came a corresponding de-emphasis on the personality characteristics of leaders or other group members. . . .

Within the present era, characterized by a greater sensitivity to the social processes of interaction and exchange, it becomes clearer that the two research emphases represented by the trait and situational approaches afforded a far too glib view of reality. Indeed, in a true sense, neither approach ever represented its own philosophical underpinning very well, and each resulted in a caricature. The purpose here is to attempt a rectification of the distortion that these traditions represented, and to point out the increasing signs of movement toward a fuller analysis of leadership as a social influence process, and not as a fixed state of being.

AN OVERVIEW

By way of beginning, it seems useful to make a number of observations to serve as an overview. First, several general points which grow out of current research and thought on leadership are established. Thereafter, some of the directions in which these developments appear to be heading are indicated, as well as those areas which require further attention.

One overriding impression conveyed by surveying the literature of the 1960s, in contrast to the preceding two decades, is the redirection of interest in leadership toward processes such as power and authority relationships (e.g., Blau, 1964; Emerson, 1962; Janda, 1960; Raven, 1965). The tendency now is to attach far greater significance to the interrelationship between the leader, the followers, and the situation (see, e.g., Fiedler, 1964, 1965, 1967; Hollander, 1964; Hollander & Julian, 1968; Steiner, 1964). In consequence, the problem of studying leadership and understanding these relationships is recognized as a more formidable one than was earlier supposed (cf. Cartwright & Zander, 1968). Several of the particulars which signalize this changing emphasis may be summarized under four points, as follows:

1. An early element of confusion in the study of *leadership* was the failure to distinguish it as a process from the *leader* as a person who occupies a central role in that process. Leadership constitutes an influence relationship between two, or usually more, persons who depend upon one another for the attainment of certain mutual goals within a group situation. This situation not only involves the task but also comprises the group's size, structure, resources, and history, among other variables.

2. This relationship between leader and led is built *over time,* and involves an exchange or *transaction* between leaders and followers in which the leader both gives something and gets something. The leader provides a *resource* in terms of adequate role behavior directed toward the group's goal attainment, and in return receives greater influence associated with status, recognition, and esteem. These contribute to his "legitimacy" in making influence assertions, and in having them accepted.

3. There are differential tasks or functions attached to being a leader. While the image of the leader frequently follows Hemphill's (1961) view of one who "initiates structure," the leader is expected to function too as a mediator within the group, as a group spokesman outside it, and very often also as the decision maker who sets goals and priorities. Personality characteristics which may fit a person to be a leader are determined by the perceptions held by followers, in the sense of the particular role expectancies and satisfactions, rather than by the traits measured via personality scale scores.

4. Despite the persisting view that leadership traits do not generalize across situations, leader effectiveness can and should be studied as it bears on the group's achievement of desired outputs (see Katz & Kahn, 1966). An approach to the study of leader effectiveness as a feature of the group's success, in system terms, offers a clear alternative to the older concern with what the leader did do or did not do.

A richer, more interactive conception of leadership processes would entertain these considerations as points of departure for further study. Some evidence for a trend toward this development is considered in what follows.

WHITHER THE "SITUATIONAL APPROACH"?

What was the essential thrust of the situational approach, after all? Mainly, it was to recognize that the qualities of the leader were variously elicited, valued, and reacted to as a function of differential group settings and their demands. Hemphill (1949a) capped the point in saying "there are no absolute leaders, since successful leadership must always take into account the specific requirements imposed by the nature of the group which is to be led, requirements as diverse in nature and degree as are the organizations in which persons band together" [p. 225].

Though leadership events were seen as outcomes of a relationship that implicates the leader, the led, and their shared situation, studies conducted within the situational approach usually left the *process* of leadership unattended. . . .

But even more importantly, the situational view made it appear that the leader and the situation were quite separate. Though they may be separable for analytic purposes, they also impinge on one another in the perceptions of followers. Thus, the leader, from the follower's vantage point, is an element in the situation, and one who shapes it as well. As an active agent of influence he communicates to other group members by his words and his actions, implying demands which are reacted to in turn. In exercising influence, therefore, the leader may set the stage and create expectations regarding what he should do and what he will do. Rather than standing apart from the leader, the situation perceived to exist may be his creation.

It is now possible to see that the trait and situational approaches merely emphasize parts of a process which are by no means separable. One kind of melding of the trait and situational approaches, for example, is found in the work of Fiedler. His essential point, sustained by an extensive program of research (see 1958, 1964, 1965, 1967), is that the leader's effectiveness in the group depends upon the structural properties of the group and the situation, including interpersonal perceptions of both leader and led. He finds, for example, that the willingness of group members to be influenced by the leader is conditioned by leader characteristics, but that the quality and direction of this influence is contingent on the group relations and task structure (1967). This work will be discussed further in due course. . . .

A leader, therefore, sets the basis for relationships within the group, and thereby can affect outcomes. As Hemphill (1961) suggested, the leader initiates structure. But more than just structure in a concrete sense, he affects the process which occurs within that structure. Along with other neglected aspects of process in the study of leadership is the goal-setting activity of the leader. Its importance appears considerable, though few studies give it attention. In one of these, involving discussion groups, Burke (1966) found that the leader's failure to provide goal orientations within the group led to antagonism, tension, and absenteeism. This effect was most acute when there was clear agreement within the group regarding who was to act as the leader. Though such expectations about the leader undoubtedly are pervasive in groups studied in research on leadership, they are noted only infrequently.

LEGITIMACY AND SOCIAL EXCHANGE IN LEADERSHIP

Among the more substantial features of the leader's role is his perceived legitimacy—how he attains it and sustains it. One way to understand the process by which the leader's role is legitimated is to view it as an exchange of rewards operating to signalize the acceptance of his position and influence.

In social exchange terms, the person in the role of leader who fulfills expectations and achieves group goals provides rewards for others which are reciprocated in the form of status, esteem, and heightened influence. Because leadership embodies a two-way influence relationship, recipients of influence assertions may respond by asserting influence in return, that is, by making demands on the leader. The very sustenance of the relationship depends upon some yielding to influence on both sides. As Homans (1961) put it, "Influence over others is purchased at the price of allowing one's self to be influenced by others" [p. 286]. To be influential, authority depends upon esteem, he said. By granting esteem itself, or symbolic manifestations of it, one may in turn activate leadership, in terms of a person taking on the leader role. . . .

The "idiosyncrasy credit" concept (Hollander, 1958) suggests that a person's potential to be influential arises out of the positive dispositions others hold toward him. In simplest terms, competence in helping the group achieve its goals, and early conformity to its normative expectations for members provide the potential for acting as a leader and being perceived as such. Then, assertions of influence which were not tolerated before are more likely to be acceptable. This concept applies in an especially important way to leadership succession, since it affords the basis for understanding how a new leader becomes legitimized in the perceptions of his peers. Further work on succession phenomena appears, in general, to be another area of fruitful study. There are many intriguing issues here, such as the question of the relative importance in legitimacy of factors such as "knowledge" and "office," in Max Weber's terms, which deserve further consideration (see, e.g., Evan & Zelditch, 1961). . . .

EFFECTIVENESS OF THE LEADER

By now it is clear that an entire interpersonal system is implicated in answering the question of the leader's effectiveness. The leader is not effective merely by being influential, without regard to the processes at work and the ends achieved. Stressing this point, Selznick (1957) said that, "far more than the capacity to mobilize personal support . . . (or) the maintenance of equilibrium through the routine solution of everyday problems," the leader's function is "to define the ends of group existence, to design an enterprise distinctively adapted to these ends, and to see that the design becomes a living reality" [p. 37].

As Katz and Kahn (1966) observed, any group operates with a set of resources to produce certain outputs. Within this system, an interchange of inputs for outputs occurs, and this is facilitated by leadership functions which, among other things, direct the enterprise. The leader's contribution and its consequences vary with system demands, in terms of what Selznick referred to as "distinctive competence." Taken by itself, therefore, the typical conception of leadership as one person directing others can be misleading, as already indicated. Though the leader provides a valued resource, the group's resources are not the leader's alone. Together, such resources provide the basis for functions fulfilled in the successful attainment of group goals, or, in other terms, group outputs.

Given the fact that a group must work within the set of available resources, its effectiveness is gauged in several ways. Stogdill (1959), for one, distinguished these in terms of the group's performance, integration, and member satisfaction as group outputs of a leadership process involving the use of the group's resources. Thus, the leader and his characteristics constitute a set of resources contributing to the effective utilization of other resources. A person who occupies the central role of leader has the task of contributing to this enterprise, within the circumstances broadly confronting the group. . . .

IDENTIFICATION WITH THE LEADER

For any leader, the factors of favorability and effectiveness depend upon the perceptions of followers. Their identification with him implicates significant psychological ties which may affect materially his ability to be influential. Yet the study of identification is passé in leadership research. Though there is a recurring theme in the literature of social science, harking back to Weber (see 1947), about the so-called charismatic leader, this quality has a history of imprecise usage; furthermore, its tie with identification processes is by no means clear. Putting the study of the sources and consequences of identification with the leader on a stronger footing seems overdue and entirely feasible.

Several lines of work in social psychology appear to converge on identification processes. The distinction made by Kelman (1961) regarding identification, internalization, and compliance, for example, has obvious relevance to the relationship between the leader and his followers. This typology might be applied to the further investigation of leadership processes. The work of Sears (1960) and of Bandura and Walters (1963), concerning the identification of children with adult models, also has implications for such study.

One point which is clear, though the dynamics require far more attention, is that the followers' identification with their leader can provide them with social reality, in the sense of a shared outlook. . . .

SOME CONCLUSIONS AND IMPLICATIONS

The present selective review and discussion touches upon a range of potential issues for the further study of leadership. The discussion is by no means exhaustive in providing details beyond noting suggestive developments. It is evident, however, that a new set of conceptions about leadership is beginning to emerge after a period of relative quiescence. . . .

Then, too, there is a need to consider the two-way nature of the influence process, with greater attention paid to the expectations of followers within the system. As reiterated here, the key to an understanding of leadership rests in seeing it as an influence process, involving an implicit exchange relationship over time.

No less important as a general point is the need for a greater recognition of the system represented by the group and its enterprise. This recognition provides a vehicle by which to surmount the misleading dichotomy of the leader and the situation which so long has prevailed. By adopting a systems approach, the leader, the led, and the situation defined broadly are seen as interdependent inputs variously engaged toward the production of desired outputs.

Some release is needed from the highly static, positional view of leadership if we are to analyze its processes. A focus on leadership maintenance has weighted the balance against a more thorough probe of emerging leadership and succession phenomena. Investigators should be more aware of their choice and the differential implications, as between emerging and ongoing leadership. In this regard, the significance of the legitimacy of leadership, its sources, and effects requires greater attention in future investigations.

In studying the effectiveness of the leader, more emphasis should be placed on the outcomes for the total system, including the fulfillment of expectations held by followers. The long-standing overconcern with outcome, often stated only in terms of the leader's ability to influence, should yield to a richer conception of relationships geared to mutual goals. Not irrelevantly, the perception of the leader held by followers, including their identification with him, needs closer scrutiny. In this way, one may approach a recognition of stylistic elements allowing given persons to be effective leaders.

Finally, it seems plain that research on task oriented groups must attend more to the organizational frameworks within which these groups are imbedded. Whether these frameworks are industrial, educational, governmental, or whatever, they are implicated in such crucial matters as goal-setting, legitimacy of authority, and leader succession. Though not always explicit, it is the organizational context which recruits and engages members in particular kinds of tasks, role relationships, and the rewards of participation. This context deserves more explicitness in attempts at understanding leadership processes.

References

Anderson, L. R., & Fiedler, F. E. The effect of participatory and supervisory leadership on group creativity. *Journal of Applied Psychology,* 1964, 48, 227–236.

Bandura, A., & Walters, R. H. *Social learning and personality development.* New York: Holt, Rinehart & Winston, 1963.

Banta, T. J., & Nelson, C. Experimental analysis of resource location in problem-solving groups. *Sociometry,* 1964, 27, 488–501.

Bavelas, A. Leadership: Man and function. *Administrative Science Quarterly,* 1960, 4, 491–498.

Bavelas, A., Hastorf, A. H., Gross, A. E., & Kite, W. R. Experiments on the alteration of group structure. *Journal of Experimental Social Psychology,* 1965, 1, 55–70.

Berkowitz, L. Personality and group position. *Sociometry,* 1956, 19, 210–222.

Blau, P. *Exchange and power in social life.* New York: Wiley, 1964.

Brown, J. F. *Psychology and the social order.* New York: McGraw-Hill, 1936.

Burke, P. J. Authority relations and descriptive behavior in small discussion groups. *Sociometry,* 1966, 29, 237–250.

Carter, L. F., Haythorn, W., Meirowitz, B., & Lanzetta, J. The relation of categorizations and ratings in the observation of group behavior. *Human Relations,* 1951, 4, 239–253.

Carter, L. F., & Nixon, M. An investigation of the relationship between four criteria of leadership ability for three different tasks. *Journal of Psychology,* 1949, 27, 245–261.

Cartwright, D. C., & Zander, A. (eds.) *Group dynamics: Research and theory.* (3rd ed.) New York: Harper & Row, 1968.

Clifford, C., & Cohen, T. S. The relationship between leadership and personality attributes perceived by followers. *Journal of Social Psychology,* 1964, 64, 57–64.

Cohen, A. M., & Bennis, W. G. Continuity of leadership in communication networks. *Human Relations,* 1961, 14, 351–367.

Dittes, J. E., & Kelley, H. H. Effects of different conditions of acceptance upon conformity to group norms. *Journal of Abnormal and Social Psychology,* 1956, 53, 100–107.

Dubno, P. Leadership, group effectiveness, and speed of decision. *Journal of Social Psychology,* 1965, 65, 351–360.

Emerson, R. M. Power-dependence relations. *American Sociological Review,* 1962, 27, 31–41.

Evan, W. M., & Zelditch, M. A laboratory experiment on bureaucratic authority. *American Sociological Review,* 1961, 26, 883–893.

Fiedler, F. E. *Leader attitudes and group effectiveness.* Urbana: University of Illinois Press, 1958.

Fiedler, F. E. A contingency model of leadership effectiveness. In L. Berkowitz (ed.), *Advances in experimental social psychology.* Vol. 1. New York: Academic Press, 1964.

Fiedler, F. E. The contingency model: A theory of leadership effectiveness. In H. Proshansky & B. Seidenberg (eds.), *Basic studies in social psychology.* New York: Holt, Rinehart & Winston, 1965.

Fiedler, F. E. The effect of leadership and cultural heterogeneity on group performance: A test of a contingency model. *Journal of Experimental Social Psychology,* 1966, 2, 237–264.

Fiedler, F. E. *A theory of leadership effectiveness.* New York: McGraw-Hill, 1967.

Freud, S. *Group psychology and the analysis of the ego.* London & Vienna: International Psychoanalytic Press, 1922.

Gibb, C. A. The principles and traits of leadership. *Journal of Abnormal and Social Psychology,* 1947, 42, 267–284.

Goldman, M., & Fraas, L. A. The effects of leader selection on group performance. *Sociometry,* 1965, 28, 82–88.

Gordon, L. V., & Medland, F. F. Leadership aspiration and leadership ability. *Psychological Reports,* 1965, 17, 388–390.

Gouldner, A. W. (ed.) *Studies in leadership.* New York: Harper, 1950.

Haythorn, W., Couch, A., Haefner, D., Langham, P., & Carter, L. F. The effects of varying combinations of authoritarian and equalitarian leaders and followers. *Journal of Abnormal and Social Psychology,* 1956, 53, 210–219.

Hemphill, J. K. The leader and his group. *Education Research Bulletin,* 1949, 28, 225–229, 245–246. (a)

Hemphill, J. K. *Situational factors in leadership.* Columbus: Ohio State University, Bureau of Educational Research, 1949. (b)

Hemphill, J. K. Why people attempt to lead. In L. Petrullo & B. M. Bass (eds.), *Leadership and interpersonal behavior.* New York: Holt, Rinehart & Winston, 1961.

Hollander, E. P. Authoritarianism and leadership choice in a military setting. *Journal of Abnormal and Social Psychology,* 1954, 49, 365–370.

Hollander, E. P. Conformity, status, and idiosyncrasy credit. *Psychological Review,* 1958, 65, 117–127.

Hollander, E. P. Competence and conformity in the acceptance of influence. *Journal of Abnormal and Social Psychology,* 1960, 61, 365–369.

Hollander, E. P. Emergent leadership and social influence. In L. Petrullo & B. M. Bass (eds.), *Leadership and interpersonal behavior.* New York: Holt, Rinehart & Winston, 1961.

Hollander, E. P. The "pull" of international issues in the 1962 election. In S. B. Withey (Chm.), Voter attitudes and the war–peace issue. Symposium presented at the American Psychological Association, Philadelphia, August 1963.

Hollander, E. P. *Leaders, groups, and influence.* New York: Oxford University Press, 1964.

Hollander, E. P., & Julian, J. W. Leadership. In E. F. Borgatta & W. W. Lambert (eds.), *Handbook of personality theory and research.* Chicago: Rand McNally, 1968.

Homans, G. C. *Social behavior: Its elementary forms.* New York: Harcourt, Brace & World, 1961.

Hunt, J. McV. Traditional personality theory in the light of recent evidence. *American Scientist,* 1965, 53, 80–96.

Janda, K. F. Towards the explication of the concept of leadership in terms of the concept of power. *Human Relations,* 1960, 13, 345–363.

Jennings, H. H. *Leadership and isolation.* New York: Longmans, 1943.

Julian, J. W., & Hollander, E. P. A study of some role dimensions of leader–follower relations. Technical Report No. 3, April 1966, State University of New York at Buffalo, Department of Psychology, Contract 4679, Office of Naval Research.

Julian, J. W., Hollander, E. P., & Regula, C. R. Endorsement of the group spokesman as a function of his source of authority, competence, and success. *Journal of Personality and Social Psychology,* 1969, 11, 42–49.

Katz, D., & Kahn, R. *The social psychology of organizations.* New York: Wiley, 1966.

Kelman, H. C. Processes of opinion change. *Public Opinion Quarterly,* 1961, 25, 57–78.

Kirkhart, R. O. Minority group identification and group leadership. *Journal of Social Psychology,* 1963, 59, 111–117.

Lewin, K., Lippitt, R., & White, R. K. Patterns of aggressive behavior in experimentally created "social climates." *Journal of Social Psychology,* 1939, 10, 271–299.

Maier, N. R., & Hoffman, L. R. Acceptance and quality of solutions as related to leader's attitudes toward disagreement in group problem solving. *Journal of Applied Behavioral Science,* 1965, 1, 373–386.

Mann, R. D. A review of the relationships between personality and performance in small groups. *Psychological Bulletin,* 1959, 56, 241–270.

Marak, G. E. The evolution of leadership structure. *Sociometry,* 1964, 27, 174–182.

McGrath, J. E., & Altman, I. *Small group research: A critique and synthesis of the field.* New York: Holt, Rinehart & Winston, 1966.

McGregor, D. *The human side of enterprise.* New York: McGraw-Hill, 1960.

McGregor, D. *Leadership and motivation.* (Essays edited by W. G. Bennis & E. H. Schein.) Cambridge, Mass.: M.I.T. Press, 1966.

Nelson, P. D. Similarities and differences among leaders and followers. *Journal of Social Psychology,* 1964, 63, 161–167.

Pepinsky, P. N., Hemphill, J. K., & Shevitz, R. N. Attempts to lead, group productivity, and morale under conditions of acceptance and rejection. *Journal of Abnormal and Social Psychology,* 1958, 57, 47–54.

Preston, M. G., & Heintz, R. K. Effects of participatory versus supervisory leadership on group judgment. *Journal of Abnormal and Social Psychology,* 1949, 44, 345–355.

Pryer, M. W., Flint, A. W., & Bass, B. M. Group effectiveness and consistency of leadership. *Sociometry,* 1962, 25, 391–397.

Raven, B. Social influence and power. In I. D. Steiner & M. Fishbein (eds.), *Current studies in social psychology.* New York: Holt, Rinehart & Winston, 1965.

Riecken, H. W. The effect of talkativeness on ability to influence group solutions to problems. *Sociometry,* 1958, 21, 309–321.

Rosen, S., Levinger, G., & Lippitt, R. Perceived sources of social power. *Journal of Abnormal and Social Psychology,* 1961, 62, 439–441.

Rudraswamy, V. An investigation of the relationship between perceptions of status and leadership attempts. *Journal of the Indian Academy of Applied Psychology,* 1964, 1, 12–19.

Scodell, A., & Mussen, P. Social perception of authoritarians and nonauthoritarians. *Journal of Abnormal and Social Psychology,* 1953, 48, 181–184.

Sears, R. R. The 1958 summer research project on identification. *Journal of Nursery Education,* 1960, 16, (2).

Secord, P. F., & Beckman, C. W. Personality theory and the problem of stability and change in individual behavior: An interpersonal approach. *Psychological Review,* 1961, 68, 21–33.

Selznick, P. *Leadership in administration.* Evanston; Ill.: Row, Peterson, 1957.

Shaw, M. E. A comparison of two types of leadership in various communication nets. *Journal of Abnormal and Social Psychology,* 1955, 50, 127–134.

Shaw, M. E., & Blum, J. M. Effects of leadership style upon group performance as a function of task structure. *Journal of Personality and Social Psychology,* 1966, 3, 238–242.

Slater, P. E., & Bennis, W. G. Democracy is inevitable. *Harvard Business Review,* 1964, 42(2), 51–59.

Steiner, I. Group dynamics. *Annual Review of Psychology,* 1964, 15, 421–446.

Stogdill, R. M. Personal factors associated with leadership: A survey of the literature. *Journal of Psychology,* 1948, 25, 35–71.

Stogdill, R. M. *Individual behavior and group achievement.* New York: Oxford University Press, 1959.

Weber, M. *The theory of social and economic organization.* (Trans. and ed. by T. Parsons & A. M. Henderson.) New York: Oxford University Press, 1947.

Zoep, S. M., & Oakes, W. I. Reinforcement of leadership behavior in group discussion. *Journal of Experimental Social Psychology,* 1967, 3, 310–370.

Reading 6

Leadership: The Management of Meaning

Linda Smircich
University of Massachusetts–Amherst

Gareth Morgan
York University

The concept of leadership permeates and structures the theory and practice of organizations and hence the way we shape and understand the nature of organized action, and its possibilities. In fact, the concept and practice of leadership, and variant forms of direction and control, are so powerfully ingrained into popular thought that the absence of leadership is often seen as an absence of organization. Many organizations are paralyzed by situations in which people appeal for direction, feeling immobilized and disorganized by the sense that they are not being led. Yet other organizations are plagued by the opposite situation characterized in organizational vernacular as one of "all chiefs, no Indians"—the situation where the majority aspire to lead and few to follow. Thus, successful acts of organization are often seen to rest in the synchrony between the initiation of action and the appeal for direction; between the actions of leaders and the receptivity and responsiveness of followers. . . .

THE PHENOMENON OF LEADERSHIP

Leadership is realized in the process whereby one or more individuals succeeds in attempting to frame and define the reality of others. Indeed, leadership situations may be conceived as those in which there exists an *obligation* or a perceived *right* on the part of certain individuals to define the reality of others.

This process is most evident in unstructured group situations where leadership emerges in a natural and spontaneous manner. After periods of interaction, unstructured leaderless groups typically evolve common modes of interpretation and shared understandings of experience that allow them to develop into a social organization (Bennis

Source: Edited and reprinted with permission from NTL Institute, "Leadership: The Management of Meaning" by L. Smircich and G. Morgan, pp. 257–273, *Journal of Applied Behavioral Science* 18, 3, copyright 1982.

& Shepard, 1965). Individuals in groups that evolve this way attribute leadership to those members who structure experience in meaningful ways. Certain individuals, as a result of personal inclination or the emergent expectations of others, find themselves adopting or being obliged to take a leadership role by virtue of the part they play in the definition of the situation. They emerge as leaders because of their role in framing experience in a way that provides a viable basis for action, e.g., by mobilizing meaning, articulating and defining what has previously remained implicit or unsaid, by inventing images and meanings that provide a focus for new attention, and by consolidating, confronting, or changing prevailing wisdom (Peters, 1978; Pondy, 1976). Through these diverse means, individual actions can frame and change situations, and in so doing enact a system of shared meaning that provides a basis for organized action. The leader exists as a formal leader only when he or she achieves a situation in which an obligation, expectation, or right to frame experience is presumed, or offered and accepted by others.

Leadership, like other social phenomena, is socially constructed through interaction (Berger & Luckmann, 1966), emerging as a result of the constructions and actions of both leaders and led. It involves a complicity or process of negotiation through which certain individuals, implicitly or explicitly, surrender their power to define the nature of their experience to others. Indeed, leadership depends on the existence of individuals willing, as a result of inclination or pressure, to surrender, at least in part, the powers to shape and define their own reality. If a group situation embodies competing definitions of reality, strongly held, no clear pattern of leadership evolves. Often, such situations are characterized by struggles among those who aspire to define the situation. Such groups remain loosely coupled networks of interaction, with members often feeling that they are "disorganized" because they do not share a common way of making sense of their experience.

Leadership lies in large part in generating a point of reference, against which a feeling of organization and direction can emerge. While in certain circumstances the leader's image of reality may be hegemonic, as in the case of charismatic or totalitarian leaders who mesmerize their followers, this is by no means always the case. For the phenomenon of leadership in being interactive is by nature dialectical. It is shaped through the interaction of at least two points of reference, i.e., of leaders and of led.

This dialectic is often the source of powerful internal tensions within leadership situations. These manifest themselves in the conflicting definitions of those who aspire to define reality and in the fact that while the leader of a group may forge a unified pattern of meaning, that very same pattern often provides a point of reference for the negation of leadership (Sennett, 1980). While individuals may look to a leader to frame and concretize their reality, they may also react against, reject, or change the reality thus defined. While leadership often emerges as a result of expectations projected on the emergent leader by the led, the surrender of power involved provides the basis for negation of the situation thus created. Much of the tension in leadership situations stems from this source. Although leaders draw their power from their ability to define the reality of others, their inability to control completely provides seeds of disorganization in the organization of meaning they provide.

The emergence of leadership in unstructured situations thus points toward at least four important aspects of leadership as a phenomenon. First, leadership is essentially a social process defined through interaction. Second, leadership involves a process of defining reality in ways that are sensible to the led. Third, leadership involves a dependency relationship in which individuals surrender their powers to interpret and define reality to others.[1] Fourth, the emergence of formal leadership roles represents an additional stage of institutionalization, in which rights and obligations to define the nature of experience and activity are recognized and formalized.

LEADERSHIP IN FORMALIZED SETTINGS

The main distinguishing feature of formal organization is that the way in which experience is to be structured and defined is built into a stock of taken-for-granted meanings, or "typifications" in use (Schutz, 1967) that underlie the everyday definition and reality of the organization. In particular,

a formal organization is premised upon shared meanings that define roles and authority relationships that institutionalize a pattern of leadership. In essence, formal organization truncates the leadership process observed in natural settings, concretizing its characteristics as a mode of social organization into sets of predetermined roles, relationships, and practices, providing a blueprint of how the experience of organizational members is to be structured.

Roles, for example, institutionalize the interactions and definitions that shape the reality of organizational life. Rules, conventions, and work practices present ready-made typifications through which experience is to be made sensible. Authority relationships legitimize the pattern of dependency relations that characterize the process of leadership, specifying who is to define organizational reality, and in what circumstances. Authority relationships institutionalize a hierarchical pattern of interaction in which certain individuals are expected to define the experience of others—to lead, and others to have their experience defined—to follow. So powerful is this process of institutionalized leadership and the expectation that someone has the right and obligation to define reality, that leaders are held to account if they do not lead "effectively." . . .

LEADERSHIP AS THE MANAGEMENT OF MEANING

A focus on the way meaning in organized settings is created, sustained, and changed provides a powerful means of understanding the fundamental nature of leadership as a social process. In understanding the way leadership actions attempt to shape and interpret situations to guide organizational members into a common interpretation of reality, we are able to understand how leadership works to create an important foundation for organized activity. This process can be most easily conceptualized in terms of a relationship between figure and ground. Leadership action involves a moving figure—a flow of actions and utterances (i.e., what leaders do) within the context of a moving ground—the actions, utterances, and general flow of experience that constitute the situation being managed. Leadership as a phenomenon is identifiable within its wider context as a form of action that seeks to shape its context.

Leadership works by influencing the relationship between figure and ground, and hence the meaning and definition of the context as a whole. The actions and utterances of leaders guide the attention of those involved in a situation in ways that are consciously or unconsciously designed to shape the meaning of the situation. The actions and utterances draw attention to particular aspects of the overall flow of experience, transforming what may be complex and ambiguous into something more discrete and vested with a specific pattern of meaning. This is what Schutz (1967) has referred to as a "bracketing" of experience, and Goffman (1974) as a "framing" of experience, and Bateson (1972) and Weick (1979) as the "punctuation of contexts." The actions and utterances of leaders frame and shape the context of action in such a way that the members of that context are able to use the meaning thus created as a point of reference for their own action and understanding of the situation.

This process can be represented schematically in terms of the model presented in Figure 1. When leaders act, they punctuate contexts in ways that provide a focus for the creation of meaning. Their action isolates an element of experience, which can be interpreted in terms of the context in which it is set. Indeed, its meaning is embedded in its relationship with its context. Consider, for example, the simple situation in which someone in a leadership role loses his or her temper over the failure of an employee to complete a job on time. For the leader this action embodies a meaning that links the event to context in a significant way—e.g., "This employee has been asking for a reprimand for a long time"; "This was an important job"; "This office is falling apart." For the employees in the office, the event may be interpreted in similar terms, or a range of different constructions placed upon the situation—e.g., "Don't worry about it; he always loses his temper from time to time"; "She's been under pressure lately because of problems at home."

The leader's action may generate a variety of interpretations that set the basis for meaningful action. It may serve to redefine the context into a situation where the meeting of deadlines assumes greater significance, or merely serves as a brief interruption in daily routine, soon forgotten. As discussed earlier, organized situations are often characterized by complex patterns of meaning, based on rival interpretations of the situation. Different members may make sense of situations with the aid of different interpretive schemes, establishing "counterrealities," a source of tension in the group situation that may set the basis for change of an innovative or disintegrative kind. These counterrealities underwrite much of the political activities within organizations, typified by the leader's loyal lieutenants—the "yes men" accepting and reinforcing the leader's definition of the situation and the "rebels" or "out" groups forging and sustaining alternative views.

Effective leadership depends upon the extent to which the leader's definition of the situation (e.g., "People in this office are not working hard enough") serves as a basis for action by others. It is in this sense that effective leadership rests heavily on the framing of the experience of others, so that action can be guided by common conceptions as to what should occur. The key challenge for a leader is to manage meaning in such a way that individuals orient themselves to the achievement of desirable ends. In this endeavor the use of language, ritual, drama, stories, myths, and symbolic construction of all kinds may play an important role (Pfeffer, 1981; Pondy, Frost, Morgan & Dandridge, 1982; Smircich, 1982). They constitute important tools in the management of meaning. Through words and images, symbolic actions and gestures, leaders can structure attention and evoke patterns of meaning that give them considerable control over the situation being managed. These tools can be used to forge particular kinds of figure–ground relations that serve to create appropriate modes of organized action. Leadership rests as much in these symbolic modes of action as in those instrumental modes of management, direction, and control that define the substance of the leader's formal organizational role. . . .

FIGURE 1 Leadership: A Figure–Ground Relationship Which Creates Figure–Ground Relationships

Framing Experience	⟶ Interpretation	⟶ Meaning and Action
Leadership action creates a focus of attention within the ongoing stream of experience which characterizes the total situation. Such action "brackets" and "frames" an element of experience for interpretation and meaningful action.	The action assumes significance, i.e., is interpreted within its wider context. The leader has a specific figure–ground relation in mind in engaging in action; other members of the situation construct their own interpretation of this action.	Action is grounded in the interpretive process which links figure and ground.

IMPLICATIONS FOR THE THEORY AND PRACTICE OF CONTEMPORARY ORGANIZATION

. . . Leaders symbolize the organized situation in which they lead. Their actions and utterances project and shape imagery in the minds of the led, which is influential one way or another in shaping actions within the setting as a whole. This is not to deny the importance of the voluntary nature of the enactments and sense-making activities initiated by members of the situation being managed. Rather, it is to recognize and emphasize the special and important position accorded to the leader's view of the situation in the frame of reference of others. Leaders, by nature of their leadership role, are provided with a distinctive opportunity to influence the sense making of others. Our case study illustrates the importance of the leader recognizing the nature of his or her influence and managing the meaning of situations in a constructive way. At a minimum this involves that he or she (a) attempt to deal with the equivocality that permeates many interactive situations; (b) attend to the interpretive schemes of those involved; and (c) embody, through use of appropriate language, rituals, and other forms of symbolic discourse, the meanings and values conducive to desired modes of organized action. A focus on leadership as the management of meaning encourages us to develop a theory for the practice of leadership in which these three generalizations are accorded a central role.

Our analysis also draws attention to the role of power as a defining feature of the leadership process. We see the way the power relations embedded in a leadership role oblige others to take particular note of the sense-making activities emanating from that role. We have characterized this in terms of a dependency relation between leaders and led, in which the leader's sense-making activities assume priority over the sense-making activities of others.

The existence of leadership depends on and fosters this dependency, for insofar as the leader is expected to define the situation, others are expected to surrender that right. As we have noted, leadership as a phenomenon depends upon the existence of people who are prepared to surrender their ability to define their reality to others. Situations of formal leadership institutionalize this pattern into a system of rights and obligations whereby the leader has the prerogative to define reality, and the led to accept that definition as a frame of reference for orienting their own activity.

Organized action in formal settings constitutes a process of enactment and sense making on the part of those involved, but one shaped in important ways by the power relations embedded in the situation as a whole. Leadership and the organizational forms to which it gives rise enact a reality that expresses a power relationship. An understanding of the power relationship embedded in all enactment processes is thus fundamental for understanding the nature of organization as an enacted social form, for enactments express power relationships.

Thus our analysis of the leadership process tells us much about the nature of organization as a hierarchical phenomenon. Most patterns of formal organization institutionalize the emergent characteristics of leadership into roles, rules, and relations that give tangible and enduring form to relationships between leaders and led. Our analysis of leadership as a social phenomenon based on interaction, sense making, and dependency implies a view of much modern organization in which these factors are seen as defining features. To see leadership as the management of meaning is to see organizations as networks of managed meanings, resulting from those interactive processes through which people have sought to make sense of situations.

This view of leadership and organization provides a framework for reconsidering the way leadership has been treated in organizational research. By viewing leadership as a relationship between traits, roles, and behaviors and the situations in which they are found, or as a transactional process involving the exchange of rewards and influence, most leadership research has focused upon the dynamics and surface features of leadership as a tangible social process. The way leadership as a phenomenon involves the structuring and transformation of reality has with notable exceptions (e.g., Burns, 1978), been ignored, or at best approached tangentially. The focus on the exchange of influence and rewards has rarely penetrated to reveal the way these processes are embedded in, and reflect a deeper structure of, power-based meaning and action. Leadership is not simply a process of acting or behaving, or a process of manipulating rewards. It is a process of power-based reality construction and needs to be understood in these terms.

The concept of leadership is a central building block of the conventional wisdom of organization and management. For the most part the idea that good organization embodies effective leadership practice passes unquestioned. Our analysis here leads us to question this wisdom and points toward the unintended consequences that leadership situations often generate.

The most important of these stem from the dependency relations that arise when individuals surrender their power and control over the definition of reality to others. Leaders may create situations in which individuals are crippled by purposelessness and inaction when left to guide efforts on their own account. Leadership may actually work against the development of self-responsibility, self-initiative, and self-control, in a manner that parallels Argyris's (1957) analysis of the way the characteristics of bureaucratic organization block potentialities for full human development. These blocks arise whenever leadership actions divert individuals from the process of defining and taking responsibility for their own action and experience.

Leadership situations may generate a condition of "trained inaction" in the led, a variant form of Veblen's (1904) "trained incapacity," observed by Merton (1968) as a dominant characteristic of the bureaucratic personality. . . .

The conventional wisdom that organization and leadership are by definition intertwined has structured the way we see and judge alternative modes of organized action. Approaching this subject from a perspective that treats organization as a phenomenon based on the management of meaning, we can begin to see and understand the importance of developing and encouraging alternative means through which organized action can be generated and sustained.

Note

1. A minor qualification is appropriate here in that certain charismatic leaders may inspire others to restructure their reality in creative ways. The dependency relation is evident, however, in that the individual takes the charismatic leader as a point of reference in this process.

References

Argyris, C. *Personality and organization.* New York: Harper, 1957.

Barnard, C. *The functions of the executive.* Cambridge, Mass.: Harvard University Press, 1938.

Bateson, G. *Steps to an ecology of mind.* New York: Ballantine Books, 1972.

Bennis, W. G., & Shepard, H. A. A theory of group development. *Human Relations,* 1965, 9, 415–457.

Berger, P., & Luckmann, T. *The social construction of reality.* New York: Anchor Books, 1966.

Bogdan, R., & Taylor, S. J. *Introduction to qualitative methods.* New York: Wiley, 1975.

Burns, J. M. *Leadership.* New York: Harper & Row, 1978.

Emery, F. E., & Trist, E. L. *Towards a social ecology.* Harmondsworth., U.K.: Penguin, 1973.

Fiedler, F. E. *A theory of leadership effectiveness.* New York: McGraw-Hill, 1967.

Goffman, E. *Frame analysis.* New York: Harper Colophon Books, 1974.

Jacobs, T. O. *Leadership and exchange in formal organizations.* Alexandria, Va.: Human Resources Organization, 1971.

Katz, D., & Kahn, R. L. *The social psychology of organizations.* New York: Wiley, 1966.

Mann, R. D. A review of the relationships between personality and performance in small groups. *Psychological Bulletin,* 1959, 56, 241–270.

Merton, R. K. *Social theory and social structure* (enlarged ed.). New York: Free Press, 1968.

Mintzberg, H. *The nature of managerial work.* Englewood Cliffs, N.J.: Prentice-Hall, 1973.

Peters, T. J. Symbols, patterns and settings: An optimistic case for getting things done. *Organizational Dynamics,* 1978, 3–22.

Pfeffer, J. Management as symbolic action: The creation and maintenance of organizational paradigms. *Research in Organizational Behavior,* 1981, 3, 1–52.

Pondy, L. R. Leadership is a language game. In M. McCall & M. Lombardo (eds.), *Leadership: Where else can we go?* Durham, N.C.: Duke University Press, 1976.

Pondy, L. R., Frost, P., Morgan, G., & Dandridge, T. (eds.). *Organizational symbolism.* Greenwich, Conn.: JAI Press, 1982.

Quinn, J. B. *Strategies for change.* New York: Irwin, 1980.

Roethlisberger, F. J., & Dickson, W. J. *Management and the worker.* Cambridge, Mass.: Harvard University Press, 1939.

Schatzman, L., & Strauss, A. *Fieldwork.* Englewood Cliffs, N.J.: Prentice-Hall, 1973.

Schutz, A. *Collected papers I: The problem of social reality* (2nd ed.). The Hague: Martinus Nijhoff, 1967.

Selznick, P. *Leadership in administration.* New York: Harper & Row, 1957.

Sennett, R. *Authority.* New York: Knopf, 1980.

Smircich, L. Organizations as shared meanings. In Pondy, L. R., Frost, P., Morgan, G., & Dandridge, T. (eds.), *Organizational symbolism.* Greenwich, Conn.: JAI Press, 1982.

Stogdill, R. M. *Handbook of leadership: A survey of theory and research.* New York: Free Press, 1974.

Veblen, T. *The theory of business enterprise.* Clifton, N.J.: Augustus M. Kelly, 1975 (originally published 1904).

Weick, K. *The social psychology of organizing.* Reading, Mass.: Addison-Wesley, 1979.

The Leader–Follower Relationship

Fairness, Trust, and Ethical Behavior

In this chapter we continue to develop our exploration of the meaning of the concept of leadership. More specifically, the position is advanced here that leadership is a relational phenomenon.

After conducting an extensive review of the leadership literature in an attempt to gain insight into the role of personal traits, Ralph Stogdill in 1948 offered the observation that leadership is a *relationship*.[1] Specifically, he wrote that the findings from his literature review "suggest that leadership is not a matter of passive status, or of the mere possession of some combination of traits. It appears rather to be a *working relationship* [emphasis added] among members of a group, in which the leader acquires status through active participation and demonstration of his [her] capacity for carrying cooperative tasks through to completion" (p. 66).

The conceptualization of leadership as a relationship has been taken by a large number of leadership scholars. In the previous chapter, for example, Hollander and Julian (1969) and Smircich and Morgan (1982) suggested that leadership is a relationship that exists between the leader and follower. Also in the previous chapter, Smircich and Morgan (1982) noted that leadership is a power relationship, in that the followers surrender their power to define reality for themselves to someone else who now assumes the responsibility of providing meaning and direction to the situation. Hollander and Julian (1969) suggested that leadership is a relationship whose legitimacy and strength of the psychological tie is built over time.

The close connection between leader and follower manifests itself in a number of diverse ways. Leadership, in addition to being seen as a working relationship where two or more people in differentiated roles work to accomplish a goal held in common, is also often cast in terms of a power or influence relationship. We observed that Hollander and Julian (1969) see leadership as a "social influence process." Leadership, they note, "constitutes an influence relationship between two, or usually more, persons who depend upon one another for the attainment of certain mutual goals."[2]

In this chapter we continue to explore the central question raised in the last chapter: What does the concept of leadership mean? In this chapter we conceptualize

---

[1] R. M. Stogdill. "Personal Factors Associated with Leadership: A Survey of the Literature," *Journal of Psychology* 28 (1948), pp. 35–71.

[2] E. P. Hollander, & J. W. Julian. "Contemporary Trends in the Analysis of Leadership Processes," *Psychological Bulletin* 7, 5 (1969), pp. 387–397.

leadership as a *relationship*. The relationship (i.e., connection) that develops between a leader and follower is often complex and multidimensional in nature. It is filled with perception, cognition, affect, behavioral tendencies, and actual behavior. A full and complete examination of the concept of leadership from a relational perspective necessitates an exploration of each of these areas, a task well beyond the scope of this chapter. While there are many dimensions to a relationship (e.g., identification, loyalty, possessiveness, affect, commitment, attachment), three aspects of this relationship (i.e., *fairness, trust,* and *ethical behavior*) will be illuminated by the readings contained in this chapter. More specifically, the conceptualization of leadership as a relationship will be addressed through an examination of Leader–Member Exchange (LMX) theory, and an examination of the role played by follower experiences of organizational justice, trust, and ethical behavior.

Leadership viewed as a relationship should be seen as a connection that simultaneously manifests itself from the perspectives of both the leader and the follower. As noted by Hollander and Julian (1969) in Chapter 1, leadership is an exchange relationship. This social exchange consists of the leader's receipt of status, esteem, and heightened influence when he or she fulfills the expectations of and assists the group in the achievement of its goals. In similar fashion, Smircich and Morgan (1982) envision the leader receiving power to define and manage reality for his or her followers from those followers, in exchange for the guidance that the followers seek in their efforts to deal with the situational demands that they encounter.

We anticipate that a psychological relationship (attachment, tie) emerges between the leader and follower(s). There are a number of ways that this relationship can be visualized. Meyer and Allen (1997)[3] remind us that commitment can form around a number of different targets (e.g., organization, work group, union, career, manager or supervisor, leader). Commitment to one's leader, like organizational commitment, can take on three different forms. In general, commitment asks the question, Why do I maintain this relationship? *Affective* commitment represents an attachment that stems from wanting to be in the relationship because it produces positive emotion—it simply feels good. *Normative* commitment reflects a relationship that exists because one perceives that she or he ought to maintain the relationship. This connection exists because it is the right thing to do. *Continuance* commitment reflects a relationship that is based on need. The costs associated with leaving the relationship are too great, and as a consequence, the individual maintains his or her relationship with the target in question (e.g., the leader).

O'Reilly and Chatman (1986)[4] provide another useful way to think about the psychological tie and the strength of that connection between the leader and follower. At the weakest level this psychological tie is compliance in nature. Each party to the relationship is connected simply because the costs that they incur are offset by the benefits that are received. At a somewhat stronger level is a relationship that is based on identification. There is a pride in affiliation. One's personal identity is expressed and enhanced as a result of the relationship that the leader has with his or her followers, and that the follower has with the leader. An extremely strong psychological tie can be depicted by internalization and psychological ownership.[5] In the former case the goals and values of the group are the goals and values of the leader and follower. They attach and maintain that attachment because of the inherent value they place in the goals that they share and pursue in common. In the case of psychological ownership, the

---

[3] J. P. Meyer, & N. J. Allen, *Commitment in the Workplace: Theory, Research, and Application.* (Thousand Oaks, CA: Sage, 1997).

[4] C. O'Reilly, & J. Chatman, "Organizational Commitment and Psychological Attachment: The Effects of Compliance, Identification, and Internalization on Prosocial Behavior," *Journal of Applied Psychology* 71, (1986), pp. 492–499.

[5] J. L. Pierce, T. Kostova, & K. T. Dirks, "The State of Psychological Ownership: Integrating and Extending a Century of Research," *Review of General Psychology* 7, 1 (2003), pp. 84–107.

relationship between the leader and follower is highly integrated and possessive in nature. The leader feels as though the follower is "My follower," and the follower experiences the leader as "My leader."

One of the most extensive elaborations of leadership as a relationship is the Leader–Member Exchange (LMX) theory. Developed during the mid-1970s with subsequent articulations (cf. Dansereau, Graen, & Haga, 1975; Graen & Cashman, 1975; Graen, 1976; Graen & Uhl-Bien, 1995),[6] LMX describes how leaders, over time, develop different exchange relationships with their various followers.

A basic premise of LMX theory notes that *leaders develop separate exchange relationships with each of their followers.* Two very different types of relationships develop. One relationship that the leader develops is with a small group of followers that constitutes an in-group, while with the majority of the followers an out-group relationship emerges. Selection of those who will come to be a part of the leader's in-group is based, in large part, on personal compatibility, perceptions of subordinate competence, and dependability. This relationship identifies a trusted subset of one's followers, those with whom the leader has a very special relationship. With regard to the personal compatibility, Phillips and Bedeian (1994) observed a significant relationship between leader perceptions of leader–follower attitudinal similarity and the quality of the leader–member exchange relationship. This observation supports a basic tenet of LMX theory—attitudinal similarity is an important influence on leader-follower interactions, being a major cause of a successful and ongoing relationship. Phillips and Bedeian (1994) also observed a positive relationship between follower extroversion and the quality of the leader–member exchange relationship.[7] These two observations suggest that attributes of the follower play a role in shaping the nature of the relationship that develops between the leader and follower. (Chapter 10 provides additional insight into the follower as a part of the leadership equation.)

The relationships that develop between the leader and her or his followers vary in terms of the quality of their exchange relationship (e.g., How well does your leader understand your job problems and needs? Would your leader "bail you out" at his or her own expense?). The first self-assessment, presented near the end of these introductory comments to Chapter 2, provides you with the opportunity to assess the quality of your relationship with one of your leaders. According to the theory, the quality of the relationship that develops between a leader and a follower is predictive of the outcomes that will be attained (e.g., commitment, member satisfaction, member and group performance, member competence, and turnover intentions) and ultimately leader effectiveness.[8]

In addition to the quality of the relationship being different for in- and out-group followers, significant differences emerge in the exchanges that take place between the leader and followers, differences in terms of their roles, expectations, rights, and responsibilities. In-group members may be given more interesting and desirable task assignments, they are likely to be communicated with more frequently and completely, they are likely to participate more frequently and therefore exercise more

[6] G. Dansereau, G. B. Graen, & W. Haga, "The Role of Affect and Ability in Initial Exchange Quality Perceptions," *Group & Organization Management* 17 (1975), pp. 388–397; G. B. Graen, & J. Cashman. A Role-making Model of Leadership in Formal Organizations: A Developmental Approach," In J. G. Hunt & L. L. Larson (Eds.), *Leadership Frontiers* (pp. 143–166). Kent, OH: Kent State University Press, 1975; G. B. Graen. "Role-making Processes Within Complex Organizations," In M. D. Dunnette (Ed.), *Handbook of Industrial and Organizational Psychology,* (pp. 1201–1245). Chicago: Rand-McNally, 1976; G. B. Graen, & M. Uhl-Bien, "Relationship-based Approach to Leadership: Development of Leader–Member Exchange (LMX) Theory of Leadership over 25 Years: Applying a Multi-level Multi-domain Approach, *Leadership Quarterly* 6 (1995), pp. 219–247.

[7] A. S. Phillips, & A. G. Bedeian, "Leader–Follower Exchange Quality: The Role of Personal and Interpersonal Attributes, *Academy of Management Journal* 37 (1994), pp. 990–1001.

[8] For a recent review of the correlates of the quality of the leader–follower relationship literature, see: C. R. Gerstner, & D. V. Day. "Meta-analytic Review of Leader–Member Exchange Theory: Correlates and Construct Issues," *Journal of Applied Psychology* 82 (1997), pp. 827–844.

influence or control over group activities and receive more support and recognition, and their tangible rewards are often greater than that received by out-group members. There is a price to be paid for this differential in relationship, however. The leader commonly expects more from in-group members. They are often expected to work harder, make more sacrifices, assume greater risk, accept more responsibility, be more loyal and committed, and give more personal time to the satisfaction of the leader needs and to the attainment of the group's goals.

As shown by this brief overview of LMX theory, it is evident that the idea of leadership as a relationship can be extremely complex and multidimensional in nature. As illustrated in Figure 2.1, any attempt to understand leadership as a relationship identifies for us a number of domains (i.e., the leader, the follower, their relationship, and the context in which the leader, the follower(s), and their relationship is forged).

In the first reading, Terri A. Scandura employs Leader–Member Exchange (LMX) theory to explore one dimension of the leader–follower relationship. Scandura introduces us to the concept of organizational justice. She employs and expands LMX theory to explore the social comparison processes that operate within groups. The construct of organizational justice reflects the notion that group members engage in social comparisons, and one result of these comparisons is the experience of fairness—fairness, for example, in terms of the distribution of outcomes (e.g., rewards) among group members. The second self-assessment in this chapter provides you with an opportunity to reflect upon your experiences with organizational justice in one of your leader–follower relationships.

In the second reading, Kurt T. Dirks introduces us to another very important dimension of the leader–follower relationship—trust. (Before you read the article by Dirks, we encourage you to complete the third self-assessment in this introduction to Chapter 2.)

Dirks explored the relationship between leadership, trust, and team performance. Dirks studied this relationship inside 30 different basketball teams that are members of the National Collegiate Athletic Association. Dirks conceptualizes trust as "an expectation or belief that the team can rely on the leader's actions or words and that the leader has good intentions toward the team" (p. 1004). His work gives us the opportunity to reflect on several very important questions, among them: What is trust (distrust)? Where does it come from? Why is it important? What role does trust play in the leader–follower relationship? Is a high level of trust always important in the leader–follower relationship, or is it more important under some circumstances? What are the implications of the lack of trust in a leader–follower relationship?

FIGURE 2.1
Leadership
Domains

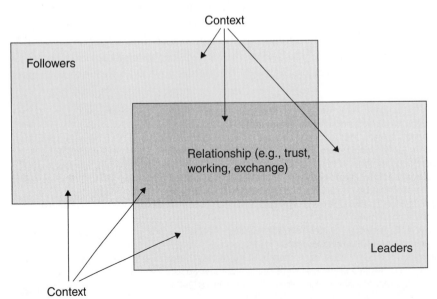

Leader–Member Exchange

Instructions: Think about a situation in which you are a follower (subordinate) in a group (team) situation, and for which you have a leader (manager, supervisor). Indicate the degree to which you *agree* or *disagree* with each of the following statements.

1 = Strongly disagree

2 = Disagree

3 = Slightly disagree

4 = Neither agree nor disagree

5 = Slightly agree

6 = Agree

7 = Strongly agree

1. I usually know where I stand with my leader.	1	2	3	4	5	6	7
2. My leader has enough confidence in me that he/she would defend and justify my decisions if I was not present to do so.	1	2	3	4	5	6	7
3. My working relationship with my leader is effective.	1	2	3	4	5	6	7
4. My leader understands my problems and needs.	1	2	3	4	5	6	7
5. I can count on my leader to "bail me out," even at his or her own expense, when I really need it.	1	2	3	4	5	6	7
6. My leader recognizes my potential.	1	2	3	4	5	6	7
7. Regardless of how much power my leader has built into his/her position, my leader would be personally inclined to use his/her power to help me solve problems in my work.	1	2	3	4	5	6	7

Scoring: Sum your answers to questions 1 through 7 and divide by 7.

My leader–member exchange relationship score is: _____.

Interpretation: A high score (6 and greater) suggests that you have a high-quality leader–member exchange relationship with your leader. A low score (2 or less) suggests that you have a low-quality leader–member exchange relationship with your leader. Recent research evidence (cf. Wayne, Shore, & Liden, 1997)[1] suggests that followers who experience a high-quality leader–member exchange relationship may help their leader by carrying out their required role activities and by engaging in good citizenship behaviors (i.e., going above and beyond expected role requirements) in exchange for the benefits provided by the leader in the exchange process.

Source: Reprinted with the permission of the author, T. A. Scandura: T. A. Scandura and G. B Graen, "Moderating Effects of Initial Leader–Member Exchange Status on the Effects of a Leadership Intervention," *Journal of Applied Psychology* 69 (1984), pp. 428–436.

[1] S. J. Wayne, S. M. Shore, and R. C. Liden, "Perceived Organizational Support and Leader–Member Exchange: A Social Exchange Perspective," *Academy of Management Journal* 40 (1997), pp. 92–111.

EXERCISE	**Justice**
Self-Assessment	

Instructions: The following set of questions ask that you think about one of your most recent class-based team assignments. As a normal part of your work as students your performance is evaluated and you are assigned a grade. This is typically the case even when you work on team (group) assignments.

The following questions refer to the *procedures used* to arrive at your grade. Employing the following response scale, please answer this first set of questions:

To a Small Extent 1 .... 2 .... 3 .... 4 .... 5 To a Large Extent

To what extent:

_____ 1. Have you been able to express your views and feelings during those procedures?

_____ 2. Have you had influence over the outcomes arrived at by those procedures?

_____ 3. Have those procedures been applied consistently?

_____ 4. Have those procedures been free of bias?

_____ 5. Have those procedures been based on accurate information?

_____ 6. Have you been able to appeal the outcome arrived at by those procedures?

_____ 7. Have those procedures upheld ethical and moral standards?

The following questions refer to your *grade*. Employing the same response scale (1 = to a small extent to 5 = to a large extent), please answer the following four questions.

To what extent:

_____ 8. Does your grade reflect the effort you have put into your work?

_____ 9. Is your grade appropriate for the work you have completed?

_____ 10. Does your grade reflect what you have contributed to the organization?

_____ 11. Is your grade justified, given your performance?

The following questions refer to how you were treated. Employing the same response scale (1 = to a small extent to 5 = to a large extent), please answer the following four questions.

To what extent:

_____ 12. Has s/he treated you in a polite manner?

_____ 13. Has s/he treated you with dignity?

_____ 14. Has s/he treated you with respect?

_____ 15. Has s/he refrained from improper remarks or comments?

The following questions refer to the way you were communicated with. Employing the same response scale (1 = to a small extent to 5 = to a large extent), please answer the following five questions.

To what extent:

_____ 16. Has s/he been candid in his/her communications with you?

_____ 17. Has s/she explained the procedures thoroughly?

_____ 18. Were his/her explanations regarding the procedures reasonable?

_____ 19. Has s/he communicated details in a timely manner?

_____ 20. Has s/he seemed to tailor his/her communications to individuals' specific needs?

Scoring: You will construct four scores, one for each set of questions.

Sum your score for questions 1 through 7, and divide by 7.

My procedural justice score is: _____

Now sum your score for questions 8 through 11, and divide by 4.

My distributive justice score is: _____

Next sum your scores for questions 12 through 15, and divide by 4.

My interpersonal justice score is: _____

Finally, sum your scores for questions 16 through 20, and divide by 5.

My informational justice score is: _____

Interpretation: The concept of "Organizational Justice" is concerned with the notion of "fairness" or "justice" within the context of an individual's relationship with an organization. Organizational justice has been conceptualized from a number of different dimensions (e.g., distributive justice, procedural justice, and interactional justice). Interactional justice is evident when decision makers treat people with respect and sensitivity. In addition, they attempt to explain thoroughly the rationale for the decisions that they make. Some justice scholars have broken interactional justice into two additional dimensions—interpersonal justice (I have been treated in a polite manner; I have been treated with dignity) and informational justice (s/he has been candid in his/her communication with me; s/he communicated with me in a timely manner).

The first set of questions and your first score reflects **procedural justice.** Procedural justice reflects experienced "fairness" in terms of the *procedures* that were employed to make a decision, such as the allocation of pay increases, promotions, and the assignment of grades. The higher your score, the greater the level of fairness or justice experienced. A score of 4 or greater suggests a high level of experienced fairness in the procedures employed to assign your grade. A score of 2 or less suggests that you experienced a lack of fairness (justice) in the way that the grading decision was made.

The second set of questions and your second score reflects **distributive justice.** Distributive justice reflects experienced "fairness" in terms of the *outcomes* that were administered, such as the size of the pay increase, the promotion (or lack of promotion), and the grade received. The higher your score, the greater the level of fairness or justice experienced. A score of 4 or greater suggests a high level of experienced fairness in the outcome received. A score of 2 or less suggests that you experienced the lack of fairness (justice) in the grade received.

The third and fourth set of questions reflect **interpersonal justice** and **informational justice.** These two dimensions of justice reflect experienced "fairness" in terms of how you were treated interpersonally and the manner in which you were communicated with. The higher your score, the greater the level of fairness or justice experienced. A score of 4 or greater suggests a high level of experienced fairness. A score of 2 or less suggests that you experienced the lack of fairness (justice) in the way you were personally treated and/or the way in which you were communicated with.

Source: J. A. Colquitt. On the dimensionality of organizational justice: A construct validation of a measure. *Journal of Applied Psychology* 86 (2000), p. 389. Copyright 2001. American Psychological Association, adapted with permission.

The ethics of leadership can be examined from a number of perspectives, among them "the moral character of the leader; the ethical legitimacy of the values embedded in the leader's vision, articulation, and program which followers either embrace or reject; and the morality of the processes of social ethical choice and action that the leaders and followers engage in and collectively pursue" (Bass & Steidlmeier, 1999, p. 182).[9] Reflection on Mahatma Gandhi contrasted with Osama bin Laden, or Mother Teresa contrasted with Saddam Hussein provides us with the opportunity to draw rich and interesting contrasts among these leaders along each of these three dimensions.

The third and final reading in this chapter invites us to think about the leader–follower relationship from the perspective of ethics. Over the past decade Michael Brown, Linda K. Treviño, and David A. Harrison have thought about leadership ethics, and they have conducted research and written extensively on the subject. In this reading they provide us with a definition of ethical leadership. Through the conduct of several field studies they report that ethical leadership is related to consideration behavior, honesty, trust in the leader, interactional fairness, socialized charismatic leadership, and abusive supervision. In addition, they observe that ethical leadership predicts ratings of leader effectiveness, follower satisfaction and dedication, and followers' willingness to report problems.

In closing, many times throughout your readings in *Leaders and the Leadership Process* you will have the occasion to think about leadership and followership from

[9] B. M. Bass, & P. Steidlmeier, "Ethics, Character, and Authentic Transformational Leadership Behavior," *Leadership Quarterly* 10 (1995), pp. 181–217.

EXERCISE	**Trust in Leadership**
Self-Assessment	**Instructions:** In responding to the following set of questions, please think about your team leader. To what extent do you *agree* or *disagree* with each of the following statements.

1 = Strongly disagree

2 = Disagree

3 = Slightly disagree

4 = Neither agree nor disagree

5 = Slightly agree

6 = Agree

7 = Strongly agree

_____ 1. Most team members trust and respect our leader.

_____ 2. I can talk freely to the team leader about difficulties I am having on the team and know that s/he will want to listen.

_____ 3. If I shared my problems with the team leader, I know s/he would respond constructively and caringly.

_____ 4. I have a sharing relationship with the team leader; I can freely share my ideas, feelings, and hopes with him/her.

_____ 5. I would feel a sense of loss if the team leader left to take a job elsewhere.

_____ 6. The team leader approaches his/her job with professionalism and dedication.

_____ 7. Given the team leader's past performance, I see no reason to doubt his/her competence.

_____ 8. I can rely upon the team leader not to make my job more difficult by poor coaching.

_____ 9. Others consider the team leader to be trustworthy.

Scoring: You now have a score of 1 to 7 for each question. Sum your scores across the 9 questions and divide by 9.

Interpretation: The higher your score, the more trust you place in your team leader. A score of 6 and greater reflects a very high level of trust. The lower your score, the less you trust your team leader. A score of 2 or less reflects a very low level of trust.

Source: K. T. Dirks. Trust in leadership and team performance: Evidence from NCAA basketball. *Journal of Applied Psychology* 85 (2000), p. 1012. Copyright 2000, American Psychological Association. Reprinted with permission along with an edited version of the Dirks 2000 article.

a relational perspective. It appears appropriate at this point to ask you if someone can become your leader without your *acceptance* of that relationship. It should be obvious that a boss, manager, supervisor, or president can move us in a particular direction by virtue of the formal position that he or she holds and its accompanying authority. To what extent are the people in any one of these roles simultaneously your leader, or do they only become your leader when you accept them in that role? If leadership is a relationship that one is a party to only by choice, then it is likely that such factors as trust, competence, role contributions, ethical behavior, and just acts play a critical role in forming and maintaining this relationship.

Reading 7

Rethinking Leader–Member Exchange

An Organizational Justice Perspective

Terri A. Scandura
University of Miami

INTRODUCTION

Relationships between leaders and members have been researched for over 25 years (Graen & Uhl-Bien, 1995), beginning with studies of the socialization of organizational newcomers indicating the importance of supervisors' attention to new role incumbents (Dansereau, Graen, & Haga, 1975). In these studies, some leaders treated their subordinates in different ways. Some were treated as "trusted assistants" (in-group members) and others as "hired hands" (out-group members) (Dansereau, Graen, & Haga, 1975). In-group members have better relationships with leaders and receive more work-related benefits in comparison to out-group members. This "Vertical Dyad Linkage" (VDL) concept includes characteristics of leaders, members, and the relationships between leaders and members (Dansereau, Yammarino, & Markham, 1995). This concept was later measured differently and labelled Leader–Member Exchange, or LMX (Graen, Liden, & Hoel, 1982a; Graen, Novak, & Sommerkamp, 1982b). LMX has recently been defined as the unique relationship-based social exchange between leaders and members (Graen & Uhl-Bien, 1995). However, this new emphasis on the relationship may obscure important exchange-based issues (including economic exchange such as performance ratings and pay increases) that take place in leader–member dyads. It is perhaps necessary to rethink the LMX concept, considering what constitutes "fair exchange in leadership" (Hollander, 1978, p. 71).

Dyadic relationships that emerge between leaders and followers in organizations are an important aspect of leadership theory and research (Bass, 1990; Graen & Uhl-Bien, 1995; Yukl, 1994). Moreover, measures of LMX have been related in some studies to a number of important outcome variables in organizational research including job satisfaction and performance ratings (Graen, Novak, & Sommerkamp, 1982b), turnover (Graen, Liden, & Hoel, 1982a; Ferris, 1985), subordinate decision influence (Scandura, Graen, & Novak, 1986), and career progress of managers (Wakabayashi & Graen, 1984; Scandura & Schriesheim, 1994). Yet, other studies do not find such conclusive evidence for the relationship between LMX and productivity (cf., Vecchio & Gobdel, 1984; Duarte, Goodson, & Klich, 1994) nor turnover (Vecchio, 1985). Such discrepancies in empirical studies conducted suggest that there might be mediator variables that account for some of the differences reported across studies of LMX. One possible explanation for discrepant findings across studies is the relationship between LMX and organizational justice, which delves into complex issues of the exchange aspect of LMX relationships. Yet, these issues have received scant theoretical and empirical attention in the LMX literature.

The purpose of this review is to extend LMX theory to consider issues of organizational justice. Despite numerous empirical investigations of LMX, some authors have commented that there has been limited theoretical development of the concept (Dansereau et al., 1995; Dienesch & Liden, 1986; Miner, 1980; Vecchio & Gobdel, 1984). It seems useful to re-examine some underlying assumptions in the literature on LMX, reintroducing relevant exchange theory concepts and treating LMX development from a justice perspective. This article briefly reviews the LMX literature and introduces relevant concepts from literature on organizational justice to reconcile some theoretical concerns regarding the usefulness of the model. Next, a model of the role of organizational justice in the formation of in-groups and out-groups is offered and new research propositions are developed.

REVIEW

WORK GROUP DIFFERENTIATION PROCESS

Dansereau et al. (1975) presented a descriptive model of how work groups become differentiated into in-groups and out-groups based upon the quality of leader–member relationships that emerge between immediate supervisors and members of work groups. Despite the clear indication that work group differentiation occurs (Graen & Cashman, 1975; Vecchio, 1997), the idea that some subordinates are treated better than others is inconsistent with norms of equality (cf., Kabanoff, 1991; Meindl, 1989). However, empirical research studies continue to document differences in the quality of relationships and more benefits for in-group members [cf. (Graen & Uhl-Bien, 1995) for review]. For example, Lagace, Castleberry and Ridnour (1993) found that in-group members (with higher quality LMX relationships) were higher on motivational factors and evaluations of their bosses and experienced less role-related stress (role overload, role insufficiency, role ambiguity and conflict). The literature has indicated, in some studies, that in-group members (i.e., those with higher quality LMX) receive more attention and support from the leader than out-group members (those with lower quality LMX) (cf., Graen et al., 1982b). Also, out-group members (with lower LMX) are more likely to file grievances (Cleyman, Jex, & Love, 1993). These results seem relevant to the concept of organizational justice since out-group members might see their leader as treating them unfairly. A careful review of the literature indicates that the LMX literature has referenced issues related to the fair treatment of members.

Dansereau, Alutto, and Yammarino (1984) presented a general model of exchange theory discussing the role of equity perceptions in the development of leader–member relationships. They defined investments as ". . . what one party gives to another party" (p. 98) and returns as ". . . what one party gets back from another" (p. 98). Their formulation suggests that investments trigger returns and vice versa and that, over time, stable patterns of exchange emerge between leaders and members, based on the ratios of investments to returns by both parties. Equity is thus maintained by changes in either what is invested or returned to attain an overall optimal level for both parties. Relationship development, over time, was proposed to be a function of these investment-return cycles.

As an illustrative example of the use of multiple levels of analysis in theory-building, Dansereau et al. (1984) then elaborated their model to include multiple-relationships which invokes the concept of social comparisons between work group members. Investment-return cycles were compared for two different hypothetical work group members, noting that equity can be maintained at different levels of investments and returns. Social comparison processes emerge as one member compares his/her investments and returns to a comparison other in the work group. However, as long as the leader attends to the appropriate level of returns for investments, feelings of inequity should not emerge for the member receiving lower returns. This theoretical example presented by Dansereau and his colleagues captures the complexity (and also the necessity) of examining issues of organizational justice in studies of LMX.

As noted by Graen and Scandura (1987), one of the requirements for the development of high quality leader–member exchanges in organizations is that ". . . each party must see the exchange as reasonably equitable or fair" (p. 182). Yet, current theoretical approaches may limit the potential of LMX theory, because they place too much emphasis on social exchange and do not develop aspects of economic exchange (Graen & Uhl-Bien, 1995). Both social and economic exchange should perhaps be given more weight in future studies. It seems that exchange can involve both social aspects (such as availability and support) and economic aspects (such as pay raises).

Most studies of work group differentiation into in-groups and out-groups are descriptive, and not intended to instruct managers on how to manage their work groups. This differs from prescriptive or normative theory where guidelines for managerial practice are developed. Without concerns for organizational justice, LMX may have limited contributions in terms of normative theory, because perceptions of organizational justice are necessary for the leadership process. From an organizational justice perspective, the LMX model might be criticized as reinforcing the special treatment of some work group members over others (Vecchio, 1997). Hence, supervisors may be reluctant to discuss the work group differentiation process; concern for organizational justice may explain lower variance in some supervisor reports of LMX (Scandura et al., 1986).

Lack of attention to theoretical concerns related to organizational justice have perhaps limited the theoretical development of LMX. Yet, the empirical literature on LMX is expanding (cf., Graen & Uhl-Bien, 1995). Several researchers have employed longitudinal research designs (cf., Liden, Wayne, & Stilwell, 1993), which have illuminated the development of LMX relationships over time. These studies support the premise that in-group members receive more benefits compared to out-group members, yet the question of whether or not this results in deprecation of team-level outcomes remains. This study reviews the literature on organizational justice to further explain the "fair exchange" aspect of LMX development (Dansereau et al., 1984; Graen & Scandura, 1987; Hollander, 1978) by revisiting important exchange-based issues in LMX (including economic exchange) that may be lost in current treatments of LMX as relationship-based and predominantly grounded in relationship-based social exchange (Graen & Uhl-Bien, 1995).

ORGANIZATIONAL JUSTICE: A BRIEF REVIEW OF RELEVANT CONCEPTS

Cropanzano and Folger (1991) present a two-component model of justice, which includes distributive and procedural forms of justice. Distributive justice is defined as the individual's perception that the outcomes that they receive are fair (Adams, 1965; Greenberg, 1990). Examples of distributive outcomes are pay increases, promotions, and challenging work assignments. Procedural justice is defined as an employee's perception that the procedures followed by the organization in determining who receives benefits are fair (Folger & Greenberg, 1985; Greenberg, 1987; Lind & Tyler, 1988). Examples of procedural justice are the degree of voice the person has in decision making and whether or not consistent rules are followed in making decisions.

Research on justice has indicated that a decision will be accepted by subordinates if procedural justice is followed, even if the distributive outcome is less than what an individual desires (Tyler, 1986). For example, a low pay raise would still be accepted if the organization's procedures of performance appraisal and rewards are seen as being followed in the determination of the raise. Also, communications about what is fair to organizational members, labelled interactional justice, has been proposed as a third aspect of justice at the workplace (Bies & Moag, 1986; Moorman, 1991). Interactional justice involves the manner in which organizational justice is communicated by supervisors to followers. Moorman (1991) demonstrated that distributive, procedural, and interactional justice are correlated, but distinct aspects of organizational justice. Following this conceptualization, organizational justice is defined as distributive, procedural, and interactional justice.

Members of work groups often interpret the behavior of their immediate supervisor in terms of organizational justice. Studies of procedural and distributive justice indicate that leaders who are perceived as procedurally fair are rated favorably by subordinates even when resource allocation is unequal (Folger & Konovsky, 1989; Tyler, 1986; Tyler, 1989; Tyler & Caine, 1981: Tyler & Lind, 1992). Organizational justice has implications for LMX theory since the focus of LMX is on the development of differentiated (in-group/out-group) leader–member relationships.

Despite suggestions by Hollander (1978), Dansereau et al. (1984) and Graen and Scandura (1987) that equity matters for LMX development, the issue has received little empirical attention. Notable exceptions are studies by Vecchio, Griffeth, and Hom (1986) and Manogran, Stauffer, and Conlon (1994). These studies suggest LMX is significantly related to perceptions of organizational justice by subordinates. Vecchio et al. (1986) showed a relationship between LMX and distributive justice. Those who had high quality relationships with their immediate supervisor viewed the workplace as being more fair than those with low quality relationships with their boss. Manogran et al. (1994) showed positive and significant correlations between LMX and procedural and interactional justice, in addition to distributive justice, using measures developed by Moorman (1991). These empirical findings are intriguing, yet it is unclear whether the correlations reported between LMX and organizational justice variables reflect that organizational justice is a tangential outcome to the LMX process or a more central element in the development of LMX relationships. A theoretical framework is needed to further elucidate the role of organizational justice in the LMX development process.

LMX AND ORGANIZATIONAL JUSTICE

Hollander (1978) noted that a "psychological contract" (p. 73) emerges between leaders and followers that depends upon expectations and actions of both parties to the dyad. He noted that equitable treatment of subordinates is often one of the most valued behaviors of a leader, since social comparison processes are so fundamental to human nature (Festinger, 1957). Hollander's (1978) treatment of leadership and exchange focused mostly on issues of distributive justice, ensuring that reward distribution is fair. Meindl (1989) contrasted equity with parity, noting that equity refers to ". . . entitlement based on relative contributions" (p. 254). He also noted that the most frequently used alternative to equity is parity (also referred to as equality). Yet, equal distribution of rewards would not totally avoid inequity perceptions, since those whose investments are high might feel that they are not receiving appropriate (i.e., higher) levels of returns in comparison to others (Dansereau et al., 1984). Equal reward distribution may harm those who are the hardest workers in the group.

Now we come to the crux of the argument: can we have work group differentiation and organizational justice as well? LMX and work group differentiation may be perceived very differently, based upon whether norms of equity or parity (equality) are operating in the leader's decisions regarding allocation of work group resources. Viewing LMX from an organizational justice perspective expands the model, in that LMX must be viewed as a system of interdependent relationships rather than as a set of independent dyads (Graen & Scandura, 1987). Social comparison processes operate at the unit, team, or network level. Although it makes the model more complex, justice in LMX is a theoretically rich framework through which the distribution of benefits (both economic and social) within the LMX process may be studied. Understanding role development within complex systems of interlocked roles necessitates incorporation of multiple levels of analysis (Dansereau et al., 1984). For example, social comparison processes between work group members (i.e., between dyads) must be addressed. At the group level of analysis, we must also consider the interdependencies between subordinate and subordinate in addition to leader–member interdependencies.

The differentiation process of in-groups and out-groups is not discrepant with the concept of organizational justice. Procedural justice suggests that as long as a leader is perceived as fair by all work unit members (fair procedures for allocating rewards are followed), then a fair exchange of inputs to rewards might be maintained for all members of the work unit. Also, interactional justice seems to play a role in members' perceptions of the reasons for reward distribution in the work group as these are communicated to them by the leader.

In the development of work group perceptions of organizational justice, it is necessary to consider whether fair procedures are followed (procedural justice) and how this is communicated to members (interactional justice). Although it makes the model more complex, viewing LMX through a broad justice perspective (distributive, procedural, and interactional) provides a rich theoretical framework from which some interesting and non-obvious hypotheses can be generated. First, distributive justice enables us to understand how leaders distribute both economic and social benefits. Second, procedural justice and interactional justice provide an understanding as to how employees in the in-group and the out-group react to the distribution of benefits.

Figure 1 suggests how organizational justice issues may affect the LMX development process over time. This time-based model suggests the points at which organizational justice concepts become relevant to the development of LMX and performance (other possible outcomes will be discussed later). Time in this model specifically refers to the tenure of the leader–member relationship. Once leader and member begin to interact, a process unfolds which results in the differentiation of the member into an in-group or an out-group member.

Role Specification

Early in the LMX development process, leaders send roles to members and members respond to these sets of expectations. Specifically, the leader specifies the tasks to be performed by the member. Issues of organizational justice may emerge in this early phase, since the leader and member are essentially strangers and levels of trust are probably low (Graen & Uhl-Bien, 1995). Distributive justice may become a concern, for example, if a member is asked to perform a task that he/she feels is beyond the formal job description. The member may feel that his/her level of compensation is too low for the task

FIGURE 1
The Role of Organizational Justice in In-Group/Out-Group Differentiation

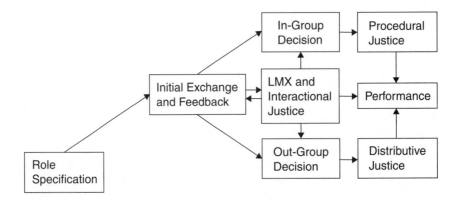
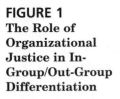

and that they are being asked to perform work that is more appropriate to a higher job classification. This involves issues of procedural justice, because if the member's perceptions are correct, then the formal procedures of the organization for assigning work have been violated. These early perceptions of roles develop into patterns of initial exchange as the member provides feedback to the leader regarding whether or not roles are accepted.

Initial Exchange and Feedback

As the leader makes requests and the member responds, the leader begins to form a perception of the member based upon his/her responses to requests. Dansereau et al. (1984) referred to these exchange patterns as investment-return cycles. In the above example in which the leader asks the member to perform an extra-role behavior (i.e., a task that is outside of the formal job description), the member can provide different forms of feedback to the leader. In response to the request the member can (a) complete the task without questions, but expect a reward (a distributive justice response), (b) not do the task or do it poorly because it is not in the job description and he/she is not compensated for it (another variation on the distributive justice theme), (c) file a grievance because the leader has asked for an inappropriate task for his/her level (a procedural justice response), or (d) ask the leader for an explanation regarding why he/she has been asked to perform the task (an interactional justice response). These responses have clear implications for the next step, which is the emergence of a leader–member relationship of either an in-group or out-group type. It is important to note that this decision is not necessarily the sole judgment of the leader; it is, in part, based upon the feedback provided to the leader by the member. As Vecchio (1997) notes, some group members may want to be in the out-group. Some members may not want to invest extra effort in their work, and out-group status is perceived as equitable.

LMX and Interactional Justice

Aspects of interactional justice such as honesty (Bies & Moag, 1986) are important in the development of LMX. In Figure 1, LMX and interactional justice are included in the same box because they represent aspects of the leader–member relationship. The leader must be consistent, and not hide things from members—even those with low LMX. This is critical to the process of LMX development,

since the first test of the leader by the member will often be his/her honesty in dealing with the member. For example, if the leader promises a reward, the leader must come through or else the member may perceive the leader as dishonest. Interactional justice pervades the LMX-organizational justice process because communication is such an integral part of LMX relationships (Fairhurst & Chandler, 1989; Schiemann, 1977) and the construction of meaning regarding what constitutes fair exchange (Sias & Jablin, 1995).

While interactional justice is a distinct concept from LMX, it is expected that they will be positively and significantly correlated (Manogran et al., 1994). LMX and interactional justice are variables that measure aspects of the quality of the leader–member relationship. Based upon the quality of the relationship that emerges, a decision is made regarding each member's in-group/out-group status in the work group, as shown in Figure 1. This process is described in detail by Vecchio (1997):

> The boss tries out each new employee by offering small but challenging assignments. The subordinate's reaction to these additional responsibilities is then closely watched. If the employee reacts negatively (by saying, "It's not *my* job") or positively (by replying, "I'm happy to help"), then a cycle of trust or distrust is begun. In short, supervisors learn quickly who is reliable and who is not. (p. 275)

In this manner, members in a work group are sorted into in-group or out-group members.

It is important to note that LMX and interactional justice are measured along a continuum (Dienesch & Liden, 1986), and some work group members' status may therefore be ambiguous (maybe in-group or out-group). As depicted in Figure 1, the LMX and interactional justice process have not yet resulted in an in-group or out-group decision, and the exchange and feedback processes continue (this is shown as recursive arrows between the initial exchange and feedback box and the LMX/interactional justice box).

In-Group/Out-Group Decisions

Dansereau et al. (1975) presented a descriptive model of how units become differentiated into in-groups and out-groups based upon the degree of negotiating latitude offered by the immediate supervisor to members of their work groups. From a distributive justice perspective, LMX is equity based. From procedural and interactional justice perspectives, in-groups and out-groups may peacefully coexist, if the leader maintains fairness in procedures and interactions with all work group members (Tyler, 1986). Research has indicated that if a leader is procedurally fair, his/her resource allocation decisions will be accepted by all work group members, even the out-group (Tyler & Caine, 1981).

In-group members are more likely to understand procedural justice issues due to the higher quality LMX and communication with supervisors. In-group members perform at higher levels, based upon perceptions that their leader is being procedurally just and explains decisions (interactional justice). Out-group members may be more likely to focus on distributive justice and perform at the level that is appropriate to the rewards they receive based upon the formal employment agreement (Graen & Scandura, 1987). This does not mean that procedural justice is irrelevant for out-group members, however, because their performance may be more related to reward distribution (distributive justice).

Performance and Other Outcomes

Since LMX has been linked to a number of outcome variables in organizational research [cf. (Graen & Uhl-Bien)], it can be expected that job satisfaction, organizational commitment, and extra-role behavior (such as organizational citizenship) would have similar relationships to organizational justice. Also, decision influence and delegation (Scandura et al., 1986; Schriesheim, Neider, & Scandura, 1998) would be outcomes of the LMX-organizational justice model. Also, absenteeism and turnover might be negatively related to LMX and organizational justice variables, since those who perceive their leader as being fair may be less likely to psychologically and/or physically withdraw from work. Role conflict and role ambiguity might be lower, since the process of why the work group has become differentiated might be better understood by work group members. For simplification, the model and research propositions refer to performance as an outcome. However, propositions with the additional outcome variables noted above as dependent variables can be tested as well. . . .

IMPLICATIONS FOR PRACTICE

Perceptions of organizational justice within work groups must be maintained throughout the LMX development process. For example, [in] a critical incident in which the leader or the member perceives the other's action as violating the norms that have emerged, justice may be questioned. The idea that attributions of leaders (or members) may bound the process of leader–member exchanges has been proposed by Dienesch and Liden (1986). For example, a leader may fail to come through on a promised reward (a distributive justice concern), without appropriately communicating the reasons to the member (interactional justice). Without communications about organizational justice, the member begins to question the leader's actions, which over time destroys the established norms of procedural justice. These perceptions may send the relationship back to the role-specification phase (see Figure 1).

A second implication of the model outlined in this review is that leaders should offer in-group relationships to all work group members initially. Also, out-group members should be re-tested periodically by the leader making offers of in-group roles. Work group differentiation should not be based on factors other than performance (such as race, sex, or handicap status). The assumption should be made that all members can become in-group members if given the opportunity to contribute to the work group and the research base on LMX supports this (Scandura & Graen, 1984). Thus, the leaders' offering of in-group tasks and benefits to all members has clear ethical (and perhaps legal) implications. Thus, the integration of organizational justice and LMX moves LMX theory in the direction of normative theory which provides clearer guidelines for leaders in the management of work groups. Access must be provided to the leadership process for all members and out-group status should be based upon members' decisions not to participate and/or performance and not other factors.

Failure to recognize the important role that organizational justice plays in LMX can help explain why some high quality LMXs disintegrate over time. Recognition of distributive, procedural, and interactional justice is necessary to maintain long-term LMX relationships. Key issues for future empirical study are attribution processes and interactional justice variables (such as perceptions of honesty) in the process of communicating justice issues to members (Lind & Lissak, 1985). Perceptions of justice may operate at multiple levels of analysis—both between unit members as they compare their inputs to rewards, but also within the dyad as individuals compare their current level of outcomes with previous outcomes from the LMX relationship (Dansereau et al., 1984; Klein et al., 1994).

Summary

Issues of organizational justice appear central to further refinement of the LMX model. A conceptual framework was offered in this review that integrates LMX and organizational justice theories. This framework highlighted some multiple level research propositions that might be pursued in future research on LMX and organizational justice. The empirical examination of some research questions regarding LMX and justice requires multiple levels of analysis perspective because a leader may have an overall approach to justice (between unit) and may also develop unique justice norms with members one-on-one through the LMX development process (within unit). Also, the collection of data from multiple perspectives to determine the degree of agreement between leaders and members is encouraged. The LMX model is perhaps one of the more promising developments in leadership research. Grounded in initial descriptive studies of work group differentiation (Dansereau et al., 1975), the model has been integrated with a number of other theories and variables in organizational research over the past 25 years (Graen & Uhl-Bien, 1995). Although the importance of equity was noted by some leadership theorists [cf. (Dansereau et al., 1984)], research on this aspect of LMX has been sparse. This review hopefully addresses this deficiency in the literature by further developing a conceptualization of LMX and organizational justice.

References

Adams, J. S. (1965). Inequity in social exchange. In L. Berkowitz (Ed.), *Advances in Experimental Social Psychology,* 2, 267–300.

Baron, R. B., & Kenny, D. A. (1986). The moderator-mediator variable distinction in social psychological research: Conceptual, strategic and statistical considerations. *Journal of Personality and Social Psychology,* 51, 1173–1182.

Bass, B. M. (1990). *Bass and Stogdill's handbook of leadership,* 3rd ed. New York, NY: Free Press.

Bies, R. J., & Moag, J. S. (1986). Interactional justice: Communication criteria of effectiveness. In R. J. Lewicki, B. H. Sheppard, & B. H. Bazerman (Eds.), *Negotiation in organizations,* 1, 43–55. Greenwich, CT: JAI Press.

Cleyman, K. L., Jex, S. M., & Love, K. G. (1993). *Employee grievances: An application of the leader–member exchange model.* Paper presented at the 9th Annual Meeting of the Society for Industrial and Organizational Psychology, Nashville, TN.

Cropanzano, R., & Folger, R. (1991). Procedural justice and worker motivation. In R. M. Steers and L. W. Porter (Eds.), *Motivation and work behavior.* New York. NY: McGraw-Hill.

Dansereau, F., Alutto, J. A., & Yammarino, F. J. (1984). *Theory testing in organizational behavior: The varient approach.* Englewood Cliffs, NJ: Prentice-Hall.

Dansereau, F., Graen, G., & Haga, W. J. (1975). A vertical dyad linkage approach to leadership within formal organizations: A longitudinal investigation of the role making process. *Organizational Behavior and Human Performance,* 13, 46–78.

Dansereau, F., Yammarino, F. J., & Markham, S. E. (1995). Leadership: The multiple-level approaches. *Leadership Quarterly,* 6, 97–109.

Dienesch, R. M., & Liden, R. C. (1986). Leader–member exchange model of leadership: A critique and further development. *Academy of Management Review,* 11, 618–634.

Duarte, N. T., Goodson, J. R., & Klich, N. R. (1994). Effects of dyadic quality and duration on performance appraisal. *Academy of Management Journal,* 37, 499–521.

Fairhurst, G. T., & Chandler, T. (1989). Social structure in leader–member interaction. *Communication Monographs,* 56, 215–239.

Ferris, G. R. (1985). Role of leadership in the employee withdrawal process: A constructive replication. *Journal of Applied Psychology,* 70, 777–781.

Festinger, L. (1957). *A theory of cognitive dissonance.* Evanston, IL: Row, Peterson.

Folger, R., & Greenberg, J. (1985). Procedural justice: An interpretive analysis of personnel systems. In K. Rowland & G. Ferris (Eds.), *Research in personnel and human resources management,* Vol. 3 (pp. 141–183). Greenwich, CT: JAI Press.

Folger, R., & Konovsky, M. A. (1989). Effects of procedural and distributive justice on reactions to pay raise decisions. *Academy of Management Journal,* 32, 115–130.

Graen, G., & Cashman, J. (1975). A role-making model of leadership in formal organizations: A developmental approach. In J. G. Hunt & L. L. Larson (Eds.), *Leaderships frontiers.* Kent, OH: Kent State University Press.

Graen, G., Ginsburgh, S., & Schiemann, W. (1977). Effects of linking-pin quality on the quality of working life of lower participants. *Administrative Science Quarterly,* 22, 491–504.

Graen, G., Liden, R., & Hoel, W. (1982a). Role of leadership in the employee withdrawal process. *Journal of Applied Psychology,* 67, 868–872.

Graen, G., Novak, M., & Sommerkamp, P. (1982b). The effects of leader–member exchange and job design on productivity and satisfaction: Testing a dual attachment model. *Organizational Behavior and Human Performance, 30,* 109–131.

Graen, G. B., & Scandura, T. A. (1986). A theory of dyadic career reality. In G. Ferris and K. Rowland (Eds.), *Research in Personnel and Human Resource Management,* 4, 147–181.

Graen, G. B., & Scandura, T. A. (1987). Toward a psychology of dyadic organizing. In L. L. Cummings, & B. Staw (Eds), *Research in Organizational Behavior,* 9, 175–208.

Graen, G. B., & Uhl-Bien, M. (1995). Relationship-based approach to leadership: Development of leader–member exchange (LMX) theory of leadership over 25 years: Applying a multi-level-multi-domain perspective. *Leadership Quarterly,* 6, 219–247.

Greenberg, J. (1987). A taxonomy of organizational justice theories. *Academy of Management Review,* 12, 9–22.

Greenberg, J. (1990). Organizational justice: Yesterday, today and tomorrow. *Journal of Management,* 16, 399–432.

Greenberg, J., & Folger, R. (1983). Procedural justice, participation, and the fair process effect in groups and organizations. In P. B. Paulus (Ed.), *Basic group processes* (pp. 235–256). New York, NY: Springer-Verlag.

Hollander, E. P. (1978). *Leadership dynamics: A practical guide to effective relationships.* New York, NY: Free Press.

Kabanoff, B. (1991). Equity, equality, power, and conflict. *Academy of Management Review,* 16, 416–441.

Klein, K. J., Dansereau, F., & Hall, R. J. (1994). Levels issues in theory development, data collection, and analysis. *Academy of Management Review,* 19, 195–229.

Lagace, R. R., Castleberry, S. B., & Ridnour, R. E. (1993). An exploratory salesforce study of the relationship between leader–member exchange and motivation, role stress, and manager evaluation. *Journal of Applied Business Research,* 9, 110–119.

Liden, R. C., Wayne, S. J., & Stilwell, D. (1993). A longitudinal study on the early development of leader–member exchanges. *Journal of Applied Psychology,* 78, 662–674.

Lind, E. A., & Lissak, R. I. (1985). Apparent impropriety and procedural fairness judgements. *Journal of Experimental Social Psychology,* 21, 19–29.

Lind, E. A., & Tyler, T. R. (1988). *The social psychology of procedural justice.* New York, NY: Plenum Press.

Manogran, P., Stauffer, J., & Conlon, E. J. (1994). *Leader–member exchange as a key mediating variable between employees' perceptions of fairness and organizational citizenship behavior.* National Academy of Management meeting proceedings, Dallas, TX.

Meindl, J. R. (1989). Managing to be fair: An exploration of values, motives, and leadership. *Administrative Science Quarterly,* 34, 252–276.

Miner, J. B. (1980). *Theories of organizational behavior.* Hinsdale, IL: Dryen Press.

Moorman, R. H. (1991). Relationship between organizational justice and organizational citizenship behavior: Do fairness perceptions influence employee citizenship? *Journal of Applied Psychology,* 76, 845–855.

Scandura, T. A., & Graen, G. B. (1984). Moderating effects of initial leader–member exchange status on the effects of a leadership intervention. *Journal of Applied Psychology,* 69, 428–436.

Scandura, T. A., Graen, G. B., & Novak, M. A. (1986). When managers decide not to decide autocratically: An investigation of leader–member exchange and decision influence. *Journal of Applied Psychology,* 71, 579–584.

Scandura, T. A., & Schriesheim, C. A. (1994). Leader–member exchange and supervisor career mentoring as complementary concepts in leadership research. *Academy of Management Journal,* 37, 1588–1602.

Schiemann, W. A. (1977). *Structural and interpersonal effects on patterns of managerial communications: A longitudinal investigation* (Ph.D. dissertation), University of Illinois, Urbana-Champaign, IL.

Schriesheim, C. A., Neider, L. L., & Scandura, T. A. (1998). A within- and between-groups analysis of leader–member exchange as a correlate of delegation and a moderator of delegation relationships with performance and satisfaction. *Academy of Management Journal,* 41, 298–318.

Sias, P. M., & Jablin, F. M. (1995). Differential superior-subordinate relations, perceptions of fairness, and coworker communication. *Human Communication Research,* 22, 5–38.

Tyler, T. R. (1986). The psychology of leadership evaluation. In H. W. Bierhoff, R. L. Cohen, & J. Greenberg (Eds.), *Justice in social relations.* New York. NY: Plenum.

Tyler, T. R. (1989). The psychology of procedural justice: A test of the group-value model. *Journal of Personality and Social Psychology,* 57, 830–838.

Tyler, T. R., & Caine, A. (1981). The role of distributive and procedural fairness in the endorsement of formal leaders. *Journal of Personality and Social Psychology,* 41, 643–655.

Tyler, T. R., & Lind, E. A. (1992). A relational model of authority in groups. In M. P. Zanna (Ed.), *Advances in experimental social psychology,* 25, 115–191.

Vecchio, R. P. (1985). Predicting employee turnover from leader–member exchange: A failure to replicate. *Academy of Management Journal,* 28, 478–485.

Vecchio, R. P. (1997). Are you in or out with your boss? In R. P. Vecchio (Ed.), *Leadership: Understanding the dynamics of power and influence in organizations.* Notre Dame, IN: University of Notre Dame Press.

Vecchio, R. P., & Gobdel, B. C. (1984). The vertical dyad linkage model of leadership: Problems and prospects. *Organizational Behavior and Human Performance, 34,* 5–20.

Vecchio, R. P., Griffith, R. W., & Hom, P. W. (1986). The predictive utility of the vertical dyad linkage approach. *Journal of Applied Psychology, 126,* 617–625.

Wakabayashi, M., & Graen, G. (1984). The Japanese career progress study: A 7-year follow up. *Journal of Applied Psychology,* 69, 603–614.

Yukl, G. (1994). *Leadership in organizations,* 3rd ed. Englewood Cliffs, NJ: Prentice-Hall.

Reading 8

Trust in Leadership and Team Performance
Evidence from NCAA Basketball

Kurt T. Dirks
Simon Fraser University

In the past 3 decades, research from several literatures in applied psychology, as well as writings in the popular press, has implied that a higher level of trust in a leader results in higher team (or organizational) performance (e.g., Bennis & Nanus, 1985; Fairholm, 1994; Golembiewski & McConkie, 1975; Kouzes & Posner, 1987; Likert, 1967; McGregor, 1967; Zand, 1972, 1997). This proposition has served as the basis for the claim that trust is an important variable in applied settings and therefore deserves further research. The proposition also provides a justification for the importance of management practices such as leadership development and team building.

Despite its importance for research and practice, the relationship between trust in leadership and team performance has been the subject of little empirical research. The purpose of this article is to address two specific issues. First, does trust in a leader affect team performance? At this point, there is no empirical evidence to directly substantiate the proposition that a higher level of trust in a leader results in higher team performance. It is dangerous to use this untested assumption as a basis for research and practice—particularly given that related studies on the main effects of trust in teammates on team performance have provided very inconsistent results (Dirks & Ferrin, in press). Second, this study explores a more complex and dynamic relationship between trust and team performance. Specifically, the study examines whether trust in leadership mediates the relationship between past and future team performance. This idea advances prior research that has focused on a unidirectional relationship (trust → team performance) by examining how trust is both an important product and a determinant of team performance.

In addressing the preceding issues, this research is intended to contribute to the growing literature on the role of trust in applied settings (Kramer, 1999), as well as to the more established literatures on leadership and group performance. Given the frequency of the use of teams in applied settings, understanding the role of trust in leadership within teams is particularly important for research and practice.

THEORY AND HYPOTHESES

TRUST

It is clear that trust has been defined in multiple ways in the literature. Although each researcher has used slight variations, most empirical studies seem to conceptualize and measure trust as an expectation or belief that one can rely on another person's actions and words and/or that the person has good intentions toward oneself (e.g., Cook & Wall, 1980; Cummings & Bromiley, 1996; Dirks, 1999; McAllister, 1995; Robinson, 1996). As Mayer, Davis, and Schoorman (1995) and Rousseau, Sitkin, Burt, and Camerer (1998) have noted, trust is most meaningful in situations in which one party is at risk or vulnerable to another party.

In this study, the focal referent of the belief or expectation is the leader of the team. Specifically, the study conceptualizes trust as an expectation or belief that the team can rely on the leader's actions or words and that the leader has good intentions toward the team. Trust in leadership is a meaningful concept in many teams, because the leader typically has the most formal power on the team (Bass, 1990), causing others to be vulnerable to him or her. As I discuss later, I also take into account the extent to which team members trust each other, because they are also vulnerable to each other, given their interdependence.

THE EFFECT OF TRUST IN LEADERSHIP ON TEAM PERFORMANCE

The idea that trust can have an important influence on team performance can be found in several literatures, as well as in management practices. In the early literature on organizational psychology, Argyris (1962), McGregor (1967), and Likert (1967) professed the significance of trust in leadership for effective teams and organizations. Consistent with these ideas, more current researchers studying trust have suggested that it is an important element of effective work groups (e.g., Golembiewski & McConkie, 1975; Larson & LaFasto, 1989). Other researchers have begun to examine empirically the effects of trust in leadership on workplace outcomes, including organizational citizenship behavior, information sharing, goal acceptance, and task performance (Oldham, 1975; O'Reilly & Roberts, 1974; Podsakoff, MacKenzie, Moorman, & Fetter, 1990; Rich, 1997). Multiple theories of leadership have also cited the critical role of trust. For example, theories have suggested that charismatic leaders build trust in their followers (Kirkpatrick & Locke, 1996; Shamir, Zakay, Breinen, & Popper, 1998), that integrity or trustworthiness is an important trait of leaders (Bass, 1990), that trust is a core basis of effective leadership (Bennis & Nanus, 1985; Fairholm, 1994; Zand, 1997), and that trust is central in subordinates' perceptions of effective leadership (Hogan, Curphy, & Hogan, 1994). Lastly, a number of management practices, such as leadership development programs, recognize the importance of trust to varying degrees (e.g., Conger, 1992; Peterson & Hicks, 1996). To date, however, the idea that a team's trust in its leader has a main effect on team performance has not yet directly been examined or validated empirically.

The studies previously cited share a common theory as to why trust in leadership is assumed to be an important determinant of team performance. In short, trust in leadership is important in that it allows the team to be willing to accept the leader's activities, goals, and decisions and work hard to achieve them. The leader's role typically involves a number of activities related to team performance, such as determining team member roles, distributing rewards and motivating employees, developing team members, and setting the team's goals and strategies. When the team feels that it cannot rely on the leader or that the leader does not have the team's interests at heart, team members are unlikely to carry out the roles specified by the leader or to work toward the performance-related objectives and strategies set by the leader. This makes it difficult for the team to work together effectively and perform at a high level.

Although elements of this idea can be found in several domains of leadership research, the literature on transformational and charismatic leadership provides perhaps the best case in point. Trust in leadership is cited as one means by which transformational leadership operates (Yukl, 1998).[1] Podsakoff et al. (1990) empirically examined how trust mediated the effect of transformational leadership on whether subordinates worked beyond role expectations. Other researchers have suggested that trust is important if followers are to accept the goals, beliefs, or vision of the leader (Bennis & Nanus, 1985; House, 1977). One might hypothesize that these effects are particularly important under conditions of perceived uncertainty (Waldman & Yammarino, 1999). For instance, under high levels of perceived uncertainty, trust in the leader may be crucial for getting individuals to buy into a common goal and work toward it as a unit. Given little trust in the leader, team members are unlikely to be willing to sacrifice their interests for the team or its goals in a context of uncertainty.

Hypothesis 1: Trust in leadership has a positive effect on team performance.

It is important to note that the effect of trust in leadership is distinct from the potential effect of another form of trust within a team that has received attention in the literature: trust in teammates (work partners). Prior empirical research examining the role of trust in teams has focused on the proposition that a higher level of trust between team members results in higher team performance (e.g., Dirks, 1999; Klimoski & Karol, 1976), although the results have been mixed (Dirks & Ferrin, in press). This proposition is built on the logic that trust increases the ability of group members to work together, which in turn increases team performance (Larson & LaFasto, 1989). Although the distinction between trust in the leader and trust in teammates is implicit in the literature, it has not been clarified, nor has it been used empirically. In this study, I empirically control for the potential effects of trust in team members when examining the impact of trust in leadership on team performance.

---

[1] The meaningful role of trust in transformational leadership is recognized by the conceptualization of the charismatic component (Bass, 1985) and its measurement (at least 3 of the 19 items in the charismatic component of the Multifactor Leadership Questionnaire are related to trust building). To the extent that the charismatic component does involve some trust-building behaviors, there exists indirect evidence of a relationship between trust in leadership and leader effectiveness or unit performance (see the results of the meta-analysis by Lowe, Kroeck, & Sivasubramaniam, 1996). Nevertheless, the qualities or behaviors of leaders are distinct from the outcomes (e.g., trust, motivation, identification) they produce. Several recent studies have provided evidence that it is useful to distinguish between behaviors of transformational or charismatic leaders and the level of trust that followers have in them (Kirkpatrick & Locke, 1996; Podsakoff et al., 1990; Shamir et al., 1998). Hence, the present study provides evidence relevant to, but not directly overlapping with, existing research on transformational leadership.

TRUST AS MEDIATING THE EFFECTS OF PAST PERFORMANCE ON FUTURE PERFORMANCE

The logic in the prior section, as well as in existing research, has been focused on a relationship between trust and team performance that is unidirectional—that is, trust affects team performance. In this section, I examine a more complex relationship between trust and team performance, whereby trust mediates the relationship between past and future team performance. Examining this connection may help advance understanding of trust from a simple unidirectional relationship to a more sophisticated and dynamic relationship. The foundation for this argument is derived by combining theories of trust with attributional theories of leadership.

The idea that trust has multidirectional relationships with other variables has a precedent in research that has theorized that trust is interrelated with risk-taking behaviors (Butler, 1995; Golembiewski & McConkie, 1975; Mayer et al., 1995). To date, however, research has not discussed such a relationship between trust and group performance. A multidirectional relationship between trust and performance may, however, be derived from Bhattacharya, Devinney, and Pillutla's (1998) proposition that trust involves expectations about outcomes associated with another party under uncertainty. From this definition, one can argue that expectations about future outcomes in situations of uncertainty are likely to be created by observing past outcomes produced by the party. In other words, observations of past outcomes (e.g., performance) are likely to shape those expectations, particularly in an uncertain environment.

Although the preceding idea helps explain why past performance of a team might influence trust, it does not speak to why the belief might be transferred to the leader. Attributional theories of leadership provide the explanation. According to Lord and Maher (1991), "people tend to assume that a major function of leaders is to produce good performance outcomes, and they infer leadership from knowledge of successful task or organizational performance" (p. 55). Studies have suggested that because of the ambiguity involved in team or organizational performance, individuals tend to make inferences about the leader on the basis of information about past performance (Lord & Maher, 1991; Meindl, Ehrlich, & Dukerich, 1985). Positive qualities tend to be inferred from high team performance, and negative qualities tend to be inferred from poor team performance (Staw, 1975).[2]

Hence, in the present case, the team would perceive a team's past performance and would be likely to attribute (correctly or incorrectly) that performance to the team's leader. After attributing the performance to the team's leader, team members may come to form expectations about team outcomes from those attributions—and hence may be more or less willing to trust the leader. Perceiving low performance may cause the team to expect low team performance in the future and make them unwilling to trust the leader and unwilling to "put themselves in the leader's hands." In contrast, perceiving high team performance in the past may cause the team to expect high team performance in the future and make them willing to trust the leader and put themselves in his or her hands. In summary, trust in the leader seems to be a viable cognitive process through which past performance is translated into future performance.

Hypothesis 2: Trust in leadership mediates the relationship between past team performance and future team performance.

METHOD

SAMPLE

I examine the previous questions using a sample of men's college basketball teams that are members of the National Collegiate Athletic Association (NCAA). Head coaches of teams were identified using the NCAA directory and were contacted either by mail or by telephone. Teams from Division I and Division III were contacted to obtain maximum variation in teams within the NCAA. Thirty-four teams originally agreed to participate by completing surveys; data were eventually received from 31 teams. One team was subsequently dropped from the analysis when it was determined that the coach was new, leaving a total of 30 teams (11 Division I and 19 Division III). The 30 teams are members of 12 different conferences located in the Midwestern and Western United States. In these 30 teams, 355 individuals completed surveys.

---

[2] Following the social information processing perspective (Salancik & Pfeffer, 1978), the process is likely to involve numerous social processes (discussion among team members) and symbols (e.g., ceremonies, newspaper articles), particularly in a team context that would foster a common perception on the team.

TABLE 1   Means, Standard Deviations, and Correlations for Study Variables

Variable	M	SD	1	2	3	4	5	6	7	8	9
1. Team performance$_{Future}$	0.59	0.23									
2. Trust$_{Leader}$	51.01	6.56	.57**	—							
3. Team performance$_{Prior}$	0.51	0.21	.62**	.60**	—						
4. Trust$_{Teammates}$	48.77	5.40	.37*	.64**	.23	—					
5. Team talent	0.15	0.11	.72**	.27	.54**	.24	—				
6. Coach record	0.45	0.18	.39*	.18	.44**	−.06	.26	—			
7. Experience	305.27	218.42	.19	−.11	−.08	−.14	.06	.71**	—		
8. Preconference	0.67	0.28	.41*	.10	.25	.13	.45*	−.05	.21	—	
9. Player tenure	2.14	0.42	.18	−.04	.08	.04	−.02	.36*	.50**	.16	—

Note: $N = 30$.
* $p < .05$. ** $p < .01$.

College basketball teams are an attractive setting, both empirically and theoretically, for studying the relationship between trust and team performance. Empirically, the setting provides a reliable and valid measure of team performance that is independent of team members' perceptions (which are the source of measure of trust). In addition, the setting provides access to reliable and objective measures of control variables. Lastly, each team operates under the same guidelines (NCAA rules) and has the same performance objectives. Because these issues typically present problems in collecting data on teams, the present sample is attractive. Theoretically, basketball teams provide a setting in which trust in the leader and trust in teammates are likely to be meaningful. Teams are highly vulnerable to the coach, because he or she controls many resources (e.g., playing time, key decisions) that are valuable to the team. In addition, given the interdependence on the team, basketball teams provide a setting in which players are highly vulnerable to each other. Lastly, there is significant uncertainty (actual and perceived) for players on important issues, including the likelihood that a coach can help a team win, the performance of one's own team and opposing teams throughout the season, and the amount of playing time one will receive. As I noted earlier, perceived vulnerability, interdependence, and uncertainty are likely to be important factors for trust in leadership.[3] . . .

[3] As a reviewer pointed out, although all teams face perceived uncertainty, vulnerability, and interdependence, there is likely to be some variation between teams. Although highly restricted, this variation may impact the relationship between trust and team performance.

RESULTS

Descriptive statistics are provided in Table 1. . . . The data provide support for Hypothesis 1. After controlling for several potential determinants of performance, trust in the coach had a significant effect on winning percentage ($\beta = .44, p < .05$).

Because trust had a significant effect on winning percentage, mediation can be examined. In the first two equations, the preconditions for mediation are fulfilled: Past performance does have a significant effect on trust ($\beta = .61, p < .01$) and an effect on winning percentage ($\beta = .44, p < .05$), after controlling for other variables. When trust was added in the third equation ($\beta = .44, p < .05$), the coefficient for past performance decreased in magnitude ($\beta = .20$) and became statistically insignificant. Hence, the pattern of results from these three equations provides support for trust mediating the relationship between past performance and future performance.

Trust in leadership and the control variables accounted for a substantial portion of the variance in team performance ($R^2_{adj} = .66$). Variables other than trust in leadership that demonstrated significant bivariate correlations with team performance include team talent, past team performance, preconference performance, coach record (but not coach experience), and trust in teammates.

DISCUSSION

Much of the current interest in trust arguably stems from its assumed (and relatively empirically unvalidated) impact on the performance of various social units. The present study examines the significance of trust by exploring potential relationships between trust in leadership and team performance. The study provides several noteworthy findings. First, the finding that trust in the leader has an effect on team performance has significance for theory and practice. This evidence validates an idea that is fundamental to theories of trust and leadership and provides a basis for management practices. Although prior research has focused on the effects of trust in leadership on various behaviors and attitudes, this is the first study to directly examine its effects on performance—arguably the most important criterion. The findings suggest that the effects of trust on team performance are not only important theoretically but also substantial in practical terms. For example, after I took into account a number of alternative determinants of team performance, trust in the coach accounted for a significant amount of variance ($\Delta R^2_{adj} = .07$). A qualitative examination of the data illustrates the substance of this difference. The 2 teams reporting the highest levels of trust in their coach early in the season excelled: 1 team was ranked as the Number 1 team in the nation for the latter part of the season, before being upset in the NCAA tournament, and the other team ended up playing in the championship game for the national title. In contrast, the team with the lowest level of trust in its coach won approximately 10% of its conference games, and the coach was fired at the end of the season.

The effect of trust in leadership is particularly interesting when compared with the effect of another frequently cited determinant of team performance—trust in teammates. Although the effect of trust in leadership was substantial and significant, trust in teammates was not significant after controlling for other variables, despite the fact that it was studied in a context that theoretically should have allowed both variables to be important. Although some may consider this to be surprising, they should note that other researchers have also found that trust in a partner does not have a main effect on the performance of the group or dyad (e.g., Dirks, 1999; Kimmel, Pruitt, Magenau, Konar-Goldband, & Carnevale, 1980). The relative importance of trust in these two different referents for group outcomes provides an interesting direction for future research. Researchers might, for example, examine whether the relative importance of trust in the leader versus trust in the team differs by the type of task the team performs. For instance, would the relative importance of the two referents differ if

the team was engaging in a problem-solving task (e.g., creating a new product or idea), as opposed to performing a physical task that requires carrying out a strategy (particularly in situations in which the leader champions the strategy)? To date, there is not enough research on trust to address this question.

The results of the current study provide initial evidence that trust in leadership is critical to team effectiveness in some situations. Building on the theory discussed earlier, one might speculate that trust in leadership is particularly important because the decisions are of great importance to the team and must be embraced by followers for the team to perform well. Exploratory interviews with coaches and players provide some tentative support for this idea. According to one coach, trust "allows players to be willing to accept their role, so that they can do what it takes to win" and to "be willing to do things that we ask of them that are unpleasant or hard but are necessary to win" (personal communication, April 1998). Likewise, a player commented that

> once we developed trust in Coach —, the progress we made increased tremendously because we were no longer asking questions or were apprehensive. Instead, we were buying in and believing that if we worked our hardest, we were going to get there. (personal communication, April 1998)[4]

Hence, trust in leadership allows the team members to suspend their questions, doubts, and personal motives and instead throw themselves into working toward team goals. Future research might explore these ideas empirically.

Whereas past research on trust has focused on the effects of trust on team performance, this study suggests that a more complex relationship may exist than has been previously theorized. Specifically, the study provides theory and evidence that trust mediates the relationship between past performance and future performance. This provides several interesting implications. One implication of this idea is that trust in the leader is not only a determinant of team performance but also a product of it. Although researchers have suggested that trust might have such a relationship with behaviors (e.g., Mayer et al., 1995), they have not yet examined theoretically, let alone empirically within a single study, this idea with regard to performance.

On the basis of the findings of the mediating role of trust, one might speculate that trust in a

---

[4] Personal communications are taken from interviews that were conducted with the promise of anonymity.

leader plays a crucial role in helping translate past performance of a team into future performance. Prior research by Hackman (1990) "found considerable evidence to support the dictum, that, over time the rich get richer and the poor get poorer" (p. 481). Whereas existing research on this topic appears to be focused on team efficacy (e.g., Lindsley, Brass, & Thomas, 1995), this study suggests that one of the reasons that the inertia in performance can be sustained is because performance affects the team's trust in its leader, which in turn affects team performance. For example, low levels of past performance may be translated into low levels of future performance, because the team does not trust the leader and is unwilling to accept his or her decisions, goals, and strategies. Future research might consider the significant role trust might play in this phenomenon.

The more complex relationship just noted was derived by combining theories from the trust and leadership literatures to explain why past performance influenced a team's trust in its leader. The data suggest that this effect was quite strong. This evidence suggests that researchers should consider trust as having the potential to be both an outcome and a determinant of organizational outcomes. The finding also suggests that future research on the determinants of trust in a leader clearly should take past performance of a relationship into account.

IMPLICATIONS FOR PRACTICE

The increasing use of work teams makes the findings of this study important for practice. This is particularly the case because much of the existing research on trust has been focused on individuals. Given some evidence that trust in leadership can affect team performance, one can begin to speculate about the implications for selecting, evaluating, training, and retaining leaders for teams. On the basis of the present study, trust, whatever its origins, appears be a valid criterion for these decisions, as it can have performance implications.

Given that trust is important, leaders may consider existing research on how trust can be built through their actions. For example, research suggests that leaders can build trust by engaging in transformational leadership behaviors such as role modeling (Podsakoff et al., 1990; Rich, 1997), by creating fair processes (Korsgaard, Schweiger, & Sapienza, 1995), and by allowing followers to participate in decision making (Magner, Welker, & Johnson, 1996).

Lastly, the data from this study highlight the fact that there are many determinants of team performance, of which trust is only one. For example, team talent appeared to be the single greatest determinant of team success in this sample. Clearly, leaders need to attend to many of these factors to create successful teams.

LIMITATIONS AND DIRECTIONS FOR FUTURE RESEARCH

This study has several limitations that provide opportunities for future research. First, the correlational design of the study does not completely rule out all plausible relationships between trust and team performance. For example, despite the statistical support for mediating the relationship between past performance and future performance and statistically controlling for other key constructs, the design cannot completely rule out the possibility that trust co-occurs with group performance, as opposed to affecting it directly. This idea needs to be ruled out using an experimental method.

Second, this study provides data from a single setting—men's college basketball teams. Although the teams in this sample share numerous attributes (e.g., performance objectives, ongoing relationships, existing roles and norms) common to most types of teams that are of interest to applied psychologists, it is important to highlight differentiating attributes. One of the most common attributes used to differentiate groups is their task (McGrath, 1984). The task of the teams in this sample primarily involved the execution of manual or psychomotor tasks, as opposed to intellective tasks. As McGrath (1984) noted, these type of tasks arguably constitute much of the work of groups in organizations but are often overlooked in research. A second factor to note is that I intentionally chose teams with hierarchical leader–member relations (i.e., "manager-led teams"—see Hackman, 1990) and high levels of interdependence to create high levels of actual vulnerability. Vulnerability is likely to help maximize the magnitude of the effects of trust; therefore, the magnitude of the effect in the present sample may be higher than in samples of less hierarchical teams. Even if the effect was smaller in other contexts, trust in leadership would, however, still be likely to be important, given the magnitude of the effect in the present study.

Lastly, as I discussed earlier, higher levels of perceived vulnerability (Rousseau et al., 1998) or perceived uncertainty (Waldman & Yammarino, 1999) may increase the impact of trust in leadership on team performance. Although they are not assessed in this study, these factors are likely to vary between teams for a variety of reasons (e.g., higher levels of player turnover, autocratic leadership styles). Future research directed at examining the potential moderating effect of perceived vulnerability and perceived uncertainty (and the factors creating them) may advance knowledge of the conditions under which trust in leadership is more or less critical to team success.

References

Argyris, C. (1962). *Interpersonal competence and organizational effectiveness.* Homewood, IL: Dorsey.

Baron, R. M., & Kenny, D. A. (1986). The moderator-mediator variable distinction in social psychological research: Conceptual, strategic, and statistical considerations. *Journal of Personality and Social Psychology,* 51, 1173–1182.

Bass, B. (1985). *Leadership and performance beyond expectations.* New York: Free Press.

Bass, B. (1990). *Bass & Stodgill's handbook of leadership.* New York: Free Press.

Bennis, W., & Nanus, B. (1985). *Leaders: The strategies for taking charge.* New York: Harper & Row.

Bhattacharya, R., Devinney, T., & Pillutla, M. (1998). A formal model of trust based on outcomes. *Academy of Management Review,* 23, 459–472.

Butler, J. K. (1995). Behaviors, trust, and goal achievement in a win–win negotiating role play. *Group & Organization Management,* 20, 486–501.

Conger, J. (1992). *Learning to lead: The art of transforming managers into leaders.* San Francisco: Jossey-Bass.

Cook, J., & Wall, T. (1980). New work attitude measures of trust, organizational commitment, and personal need fulfillment. *Journal of Occupational Psychology,* 53, 39–52.

Cummings, L., & Bromiley, P. (1996). The organizational trust inventory (OTI): Development and validation. In R. Kramer & T. Tyler (Eds.), *Trust in organizations* (pp. 302–330). Thousand Oaks, CA: Sage.

Dirks, K. T. (1999). The effects of interpersonal trust on work group performance. *Journal of Applied Psychology,* 84, 445–455.

Dirks, K. T., & Ferrin, D. L. (in press). The role of trust in organizational settings. *Organization Science.*

Fairholm, G. (1994). *Leadership and the culture of trust.* Westport, CT: Praeger.

Georgopolous, D. B. (1986). *Organizational structure, problem solving, and effectiveness.* San Francisco: Jossey-Bass.

Golembiewski, R., & McConkie, M. (1975). The centrality of interpersonal trust in group process. In C. Cooper (Ed.), *Theories of group process* (pp. 131–185). New York: Wiley.

Hackman, J. R. (Ed.). (1990). *Groups that work (and those that don't).* San Francisco: Jossey-Bass.

Hogan, R., Curphy, G., & Hogan, J. (1994). What we know about leadership: Effectiveness and personality. *American Psychologist,* 49, 493–504.

House, R. (1977). A 1976 theory of charismatic leadership. In J. Hunt & L. Larson (Eds.), *Leadership: The cutting edge* (pp. 189–207). Carbondale: Southern Illinois University Press.

James, L., Demaree, R., & Wolf, G. (1984). Estimating within-group interrater reliability with and without response bias. *Journal of Applied Psychology,* 69, 85–98.

Jehn, K., & Shah, P. (1997). Interpersonal relationships and task performance: An examination of mediating processes in friendship and acquaintance groups. *Journal of Personality and Social Psychology,* 72, 775–790.

Jones, M. (1974). Regressing group on individual effectiveness. *Organizational Behavior and Human Performance,* 11, 426–451.

Kimmel, M., Pruitt, D., Magenau, J., Konar-Goldband, E., & Carnevale, P. (1980). Effects of trust, aspiration, and gender on negotiation tactics. *Journal of Personality and Social Psychology,* 38, 9–22.

Kirkpatrick, S., & Locke, E. (1996). Direct and indirect effects of three core charismatic leadership components on performance and attitudes. *Journal of Applied Psychology,* 81, 36–51.

Klimoski, R. J., & Karol, B. L. (1976). The impact of trust on creative problem solving groups. *Journal of Applied Psychology,* 61, 630–633.

Korsgaard, M. A., Schweiger, D., & Sapienza, H. (1995). Building commitment, attachment, and trust in strategic decision-making teams: The role of procedural justice. *Academy of Management Journal,* 38, 60–84.

Kouzes, J., & Posner, B. (1987). *The leadership challenge: How to get extraordinary things done in organizations.* San Francisco: Jossey-Bass.

Kramer, R. (1999). Trust and distrust in organizations: Emerging perspectives, enduring questions. *Annual Review of Psychology,* 50, 569–598.

Larson, C., & LaFasto, F. (1989). *Teamwork.* Newbury Park, CA: Sage.

Likert, R. (1967). *The human organization.* New York: McGraw-Hill.

Lindsley, D., Brass, D., & Thomas, J. (1995). Efficacy-performance spirals: A multi-level perspective. *Academy of Management Review,* 20, 645–678.

Lord, R., & Maher, K. (1991). *Leadership and information processing: Linking perceptions and performance.* Boston: Unwin Hyman.

Lowe, K., Kroeck, K. G., & Sivasubramaniam, N. (1996). Effectiveness correlates of transformational and transactional leadership: A metaanalytic review of the MLQ literature. *Leadership Quarterly, 7,* 385–425.

Magner, N., Welker, R., & Johnson, G. (1996). The interactive effects of participation and outcome favorability on turnover intentions and evaluations of supervisors. *Journal of Occupational and Organizational Psychology, 69,* 135–143.

Mayer, R. C., Davis, J. H., & Schoorman, F. D. (1995). An integrative model of organizational trust. *Academy of Management Review, 20,* 709–734.

McAllister, D. (1995). Affect- and cognition-based trust as foundations for interpersonal cooperation in organizations. *Academy of Management Journal, 38,* 24–59.

McGrath, J. (1984). *Groups: Interaction and performance.* Englewood Cliffs, NJ: Prentice-Hall.

McGregor, D. (1967). *The professional manager.* New York: McGraw-Hill.

Meindl, J., Ehrlich, S., & Dukerich, J. (1985). The romance of leadership. *Administrative Science Quarterly, 30,* 78–102.

Neter, J., Wasserman, W., & Kunter, M. (1990). *Applied linear statistical models* (3rd ed.). Homewood, IL: Irwin.

Oldham, G. (1975). The impact of supervisory characteristics on goal acceptance. *Academy of Management Journal, 18,* 461–475.

O'Reilly, C. A., & Roberts, K. H. (1974). Information filtration in organizations: Three experiments. *Organizational Behavior and Human Performance, 11,* 253–265.

Peterson, D., & Hicks, M. D. (1996). *Leader as coach.* Minneapolis, MN: Personnel Decisions International.

Podsakoff, P., MacKenzie, S., Moorman, R., & Fetter, R. (1990). Transformational leader behaviors and their effects on followers' trust in leader, satisfaction, and organizational citizenship behaviors. *Leadership Quarterly, 1,* 107–142.

Pollock, T. (1998). *Risk, reputation, and interdependence in the market for initial public offerings: Embedded networks and the construction of organization value.* Unpublished doctoral dissertation, University of Illinois at Urbana–Champaign.

Rich, G. (1997). The sales manager as a role model: Effects of trust, job satisfaction, and performance of salespeople. *Journal of Academy of Marketing Science, 25,* 319–328.

Robinson, S. (1996). Trust and the breach of the psychological contract. *Administrative Science Quarterly, 41,* 574–599.

Rousseau, D. (1985). Issues of level in organizational research: Multi-level and cross-level perspectives. In L.L. Cummings & B. Staw (Eds.), *Research in organizational behavior* (pp. 1–37). Greenwich, CT: JAI Press.

Rousseau, D., Sitkin, S., Burt, R., & Camerer, C. (1998). Not so different after all: A cross-discipline view of trust. *Academy of Management Review, 23,* 387–392.

Salancik, G. J., & Pfeffer, J. (1978). A social information processing approach to job attitudes and task design. *Administrative Science Quarterly, 23,* 224–253.

Shamir, B., Zakay, E., Breinen, E., & Popper, M. (1998). Correlates of charismatic leader behavior in military units: Subordinates' attitudes, unit characteristics, and superiors' appraisals of leader performance. *Academy of Management Journal, 41,* 387–409.

Staw, B. (1975). Attribution of the 'causes' of performance: A general alternative interpretation of cross-sectional research on organizations. *Organizational Behavior and Human Performance, 13,* 414–432.

Waldman, D., & Yammarino, F. (1999). CEO charismatic leadership: Levels-of-management and levels-of-analysis effects. *Academy of Management Review, 24,* 266–285.

Yukl, G. (1998). *Leadership in organizations* (4th ed.). Upper Saddle River, NJ: Prentice Hall.

Zand, D. (1972). Trust and managerial problem solving. *Administrative Science Quarterly, 17,* 229–239.

Zand, D. (1997). *The leadership triad: Knowledge, trust, and power.* New York: Oxford University Press.

Reading 9

Ethical Leadership

A Social Learning Perspective for Construct Development and Testing

Michael E. Brown
Pennsylvania State University–Erie

Linda K. Treviño and David A. Harrison
Pennsylvania State University-University Park

Recent ethical scandals in business (Colvin, 2003, Mehta, 2003 and Revell, 2003) have raised important questions about the role of leadership in shaping ethical conduct. Most employees look outside themselves to significant others for ethical guidance (Kohlberg, 1969, and Treviño, 1986). Therefore, in the workplace, leaders should be a central source of such guidance. Yet, we know little about the ethical dimension of leadership. Most attention to this topic has relied upon a philosophical perspective, focusing on the question of how leaders *ought* to behave. But, even philosophers note that "it's remarkable that there has been little in the way of sustained and systematic treatment of the subject [ethical leadership] by scholars" (Ciulla, 1998, p. 3).

We propose to study ethical leadership from a descriptive perspective so that we can better understand what characterizes ethical leadership, and how it relates to other variables in its nomological network. Previous study of an ethical dimension of leadership has been embedded primarily within the transformational and charismatic leadership domains (Bass & Avolio, 2000), two styles of leadership that are distinct, yet conceptually similar enough that they are sometimes discussed as if they were interchangeable (Bono and Judge, 2003, Conger, 1999 and Shamir, 1999). We follow that convention in this research. The ethical dimension of leadership represents a small component that falls within the nexus of inspiring, stimulating and visionary leader behaviors that make up transformational and charismatic leadership. But, even this work on the ethical aspects of charismatic and transformational leadership has been mainly conceptual and has conveyed a normative perspective (i.e., Bass and Steidlmeier, 1999, Kanungo and Mendonca, 1996 and May et al., 2003).

Source: Edited and reprinted from *Organizational Behavior and Human Decision Processes*, 97:2, 117–135. Copyright 2005 with permission from Elsevier.

Qualitative, interview-based research has begun to explore ethical leadership from the perspective of organization members. Howell and Avolio (1992) differentiated between ethical and unethical charismatic leaders and Treviño, Brown, and Hartman (2003) asked interviewees to describe what they saw as the characteristics of ethical leaders. Yet, little has been done to systematically develop an ethical leadership construct necessary for testing theory about its origins and outcomes.

Therefore, our purpose is to lay the necessary conceptual and empirical groundwork that might advance knowledge about ethical leadership. Specifically, we: (a) review related literature; (b) propose social learning or social cognitive theory (Bandura, 1977 and Bandura, 1986) as a conceptual basis for understanding ethical leadership; (c) offer a formal, constitutive definition of ethical leadership; (d) develop a nomological network that specifies and explains its connections to other variables; (e) build and refine an instrument, the Ethical Leadership Scale (ELS), to measure the construct, estimate its psychometric properties, and provide evidence of its construct validity; and (f) demonstrate the utility of an ethical leadership construct by showing its ability to uniquely predict outcomes beyond other, related leadership dimensions.

ETHICAL LEADERSHIP IN PRIOR RESEARCH

Most reviews of the behavioral science (rather than philosophical) literature on leadership have given scant attention to its ethical dimensions (e.g., Bass, 1990 and House and Aditya, 1997). However, we have identified three constructs in organizational behavior (OB) that have the potential to overlap with ethical leadership, and we discuss their distinctions below.

ETHICAL LEADERSHIP AND TRANSFORMATIONAL/CHARISMATIC LEADERSHIP

Most attention to an ethical dimension of leadership has been embedded within the charismatic or transformational leadership paradigm. Burns (1978) said that "transforming" leaders inspire followers by aligning their own and their followers' value systems toward important moral principles. Bass and Avolio (1993) described four dimensions of transformational leadership—inspirational motivation, idealized influence, individualized consideration, and intellectual stimulation. Of these, the idealized influence dimension has been defined as having an ethical component. Idealized influence means that transformational leaders are "role models for followers to emulate" (Avolio, 1999, p. 43). They "can be counted on to do the right thing" and they demonstrate "high standards of ethical and moral conduct" (1999, p. 43).

Lending support to the proposed relationship between transformational leadership and high ethical standards, Turner, Barling, Epitropaki, Butcher, and Milner (2002) recently found that leader cognitive moral development is positively related to transformational leadership, but unrelated to transactional leadership, an influence process based on contingent reinforcement and characterized by management-by-exception (Avolio, 1999). Some have suggested that the compliance-based (Kelman, 1958) influence style associated with transactional leadership behavior is unethical. Kanungo and Mendonca (1996) noted that "the near destruction of the followers' self-esteem for the benefit of the leader makes the transactional influence process highly offensive to the dignity of people; therefore, it cannot be considered to be an ethical social influence process" (1996, p. 73).

Yet, these proposed relationships between transformational versus transactional leadership and ethical versus unethical leadership are not clear-cut. First, some have suggested that transformational and charismatic leaders can be unethical (Bass, 1985) if they are motivated by selfishness rather than altruism (Bass, 1998 Howell, 1988 and Howell and Avolio, 1992), and if they use power inappropriately (House and Aditya, 1997, and McClelland, 1975). Scholars now differentiate between socialized (ethical) and personalized (unethical) charismatic leaders (Howell Avolio, 1992) and authentic and pseudo-transformational leaders (Bass and Steidlmeier, 1999), suggesting that transformational (charismatic) and ethical leadership are not necessarily aligned. Further, Gini (1998) suggested that ethical leaders set clear standards and hold employees accountable for following them, which are cardinal features of transactional leadership. And, the relationship between cognitive moral development and transformational leadership found in Turner and colleagues' research (2002) was actually based on a measure of transformational leadership that included some transactional leadership behaviors. Finally, Treviño et al. (2003) found that ethical leaders use transactional type influence processes such as standard setting, performance appraisal, and rewards and punishments to hold followers accountable for ethical conduct, along with transformational leadership styles. Thus, at best, there is only partial overlap between transformational and ethical leadership. Ethical leaders likely use both transformational and transactional leadership approaches to influence followers' behavior. This assertion is also consistent with recent work that argues against the stark bipolarity between transactional and transformational styles (Kark, Shamir, and Chen, 2003).

ETHICAL LEADERSHIP AND LEADER HONESTY

Survey research frequently links perceived leadership effectiveness with leader honesty (i.e., truth-telling), integrity (i.e., principled behavior), or trustworthiness (i.e., can be trusted) (Den Hartog et al., 1999, Kouzes and Posner, 1993 and Posner and Schmidt, 1992). Honesty and integrity are seen as important components of a transformational leader's idealized influence (Avolio 1999 and Bass and Steidlmeier, 1999). On its face, then, it might appear that ethical leadership equates to such leader traits. But, Howell and Avolio (1992) found that honesty was only one of many characteristics that differentiated ethical and unethical charismatic leaders. Further, Treviño, Hartman, and Brown (2000) reported that traits such as honesty and trustworthiness contributed to only one aspect—what they termed the "moral person" aspect—of ethical leadership. They also found that ethical leadership involved a "moral manager" aspect that involved a number of visible behaviors that do not necessarily flow only from personal traits (e.g., sustained communication of an ethics message, holding followers accountable for ethical conduct). Therefore, although leader trustworthiness and honesty might contribute to ethical leadership, they are unlikely to be the same construct.

ETHICAL LEADERSHIP AND CONSIDERATE OR FAIR TREATMENT

Leaders are in a unique position to mete out justice because of their legitimate power, control of resources, and responsibility for important decisions about employees. Tyler argued that employee support of leaders is heavily based on fairness judgments, with people acting as "naive moral philosophers, judging the actions of leaders against abstract criteria of fairness" (1986, p. 309), and research has supported this relationship (Alexander and Ruderman, 1987, Folger and Konovsky, 1989, Tyler and Degoey, 1995 and Tyler et al., 1985). The closest alignment of fairness with supervisory leadership is likely in the notion of interactional fairness (Bies & Moag, 1986) and its focus on treating employees with dignity and respect. Further, supervisors have the opportunity to create a just work environment by making decisions that are perceived by employees to be fair. In addition, a consideration-oriented leadership style has long been associated with follower satisfaction and performance (Yukl, 2002). Therefore, it is reasonable to ask whether ethical leadership is simply demonstrated consideration or treatment with dignity and respect.

Treviño et al., 2000 and Treviño et al., 2003 found that leader behaviors reflecting a concern for people and fair treatment of employees contributed to perceptions of ethical leadership. Yet, other formulations of what might constitute ethical leadership go beyond fair treatment to include principled decision-making (Avolio, 1999), setting ethical expectations for followers (Treviño et al., 2003) and using rewards and punishments to hold followers accountable for ethical conduct (Gini, 1998 and Treviño et al., 2003). Thus, considerate and fair treatment of followers appears to overlap with ethical leadership, but not completely.

In sum, we find that ethical leadership is related to these other leader styles and characteristics, but that none of these (transformational/charismatic leadership, leader honesty, and leader considerate/fair treatment) is broad enough to encompass all that an ethical leader is seen to do. Each of these other constructs suffers from what might be termed a deficiency bias when it is equated with ethical leadership on its own (Schwab, 1980). Perhaps more important, this previous work has not provided a deductive theoretical basis for understanding ethical leadership and its outcomes. Hence, we propose one below that can best be understood within a social learning framework (Bandura, 1977 and Bandura, 1986).

ETHICAL LEADERSHIP AS SOCIAL LEARNING

Leadership involves influence (Yukl, 2002). A social learning perspective on ethical leadership proposes that leaders influence the ethical conduct of followers via modeling. The term modeling covers a broad range of psychological matching processes, including observational learning, imitation, and identification. According to Bandura (1986) virtually anything that can be learned via direct experience can also be learned by vicarious experience, via observing others' behavior and its consequences. This process seems particularly important when the behavioral target is ethical conduct in organizations. Employees can learn what behavior is expected, rewarded, and punished via role modeling. Leaders are an important and likely source of such modeling first by virtue of their assigned role, their status and success in the organization, and their power to affect the behavior and outcomes of others. High standing in a "prestige hierarchy" and the ability to control rewards both contribute to modeling effectiveness (Bandura, 1986, p. 207). And, previous research has demonstrated that models influence prosocial behavior (Bryan and Test, 1967 and Rosenhan and White, 1967).

A social learning perspective is consistent with some of the previous, but not yet integrated arguments about ethics and leadership. House (1977), Bass (1985), and Kouzes and Posner (1987) have all referred to role modeling as essential leader behavior. And, the idealized influence dimension of transformational leadership views transformational leaders as role models (Avolio, 1999, Avolio et al., 1999 and Kelman, 1958). Gini noted that the importance of ethics and role modeling goes as far back as Aristotle: "the spirit of morality . . . is awakened in the individual only through the witness and conduct of a moral person" (1998, p. 29).

ATTENTION TO THE LEADER AND LEADER BEHAVIORS

Effective role modeling requires attention to be focused on the model and the behavior being modeled (Wood & Bandura, 1989). Model attractiveness is an important means of channeling observer attention to the model. If leaders are to be seen as ethical leaders who can influence employee ethical conduct, they must be legitimate and credible ethical role models because employees may be cynical about ethical pronouncements coming from some organizational leaders, especially in a scandalous business climate.

We propose that leaders become attractive, credible, and legitimate as ethical role models in part by engaging in ongoing behaviors that are evaluated by followers as normatively appropriate, and that suggest altruistic (rather than selfish) motivation. Such behaviors include honesty, consideration of others, and fair treatment of employees (including respect and voice). Altruistically based motivation is consistent with the socialized influence processes that characterize ethical charismatic leaders (Howell and Avolio, 1992), and authentic transformational leaders (Bass and Steidlmeier, 1999). Finally, research has found that justice is particularly important to employee evaluations of organizational authorities in general (Alexander and Ruderman, 1987) and to role modeling in particular (Scandura, 1997). By engaging in transparent, fair, and caring actions, and by creating a fair working environment, the leader becomes a legitimate source of information about appropriate conduct, and a target of identification and emulation.

Second, effective modeling requires attention to the behavior being modeled. Employees are bombarded with messages of all kinds, from all directions. By virtue of their position in the hierarchy, leaders are generally observable and may be able to focus followers' attention on a particular message or behavior. But, privately or stoically carrying out ethical actions may be insufficient to focus attention on ethical conduct. Particularly in business settings, employees' attention may easily be distracted (e.g., toward messages about the bottom line). Treviño and colleagues (2003) found that ethical leaders gain followers' attention by making an ethics message salient enough to stand out in the organizational context. Thus, steering employees' attention to ethical standards by accentuating their importance through explicit communication seems crucial to ethical leadership as a social learning process.

People in organizations pay obviously close attention to behaviors that are rewarded and punished (Arvey and Jones, 1985, Kanfer, 1990 and Treviño, 1992). And, rewards and punishments contribute to modeling effectiveness by being socially salient. Social learning theory argues that consequences (rewards and punishments) facilitate learning in an anticipatory manner (Bandura, 1986). They inform individuals about the benefits of the modeled (ethical) behavior and the costs of inappropriate behavior. So, ethical leaders become social learning models by rewarding appropriate and disciplining inappropriate conduct (Gini, 1998 and Treviño et al., 2003) and by doing so in a way that is perceived to be fair. Therefore, another element of ethical leadership is the structuring of just work environments that mete out positive and negative outcomes for normatively appropriate versus normatively inappropriate behavior.

To summarize, we conceptualize ethical leadership in terms of social learning. Ethical leaders are models of ethical conduct who become the targets of identification and emulation for followers. For leaders to be perceived as ethical leaders and to influence ethics-related outcomes, they must be perceived as attractive, credible, and legitimate. They do this by engaging in behavior that is seen as normatively appropriate (e.g., openness and honesty) and motivated by altruism (e.g., treating employees fairly and considerately). Ethical leaders must also gain followers' attention to the ethics message by engaging in explicit ethics-related communication and by using reinforcement to support the ethics message.

A CONSTITUTIVE DEFINITION OF ETHICAL LEADERSHIP

We define ethical leadership here as *the demonstration of normatively appropriate conduct through personal actions and interpersonal relationships, and the promotion of such conduct to followers through two-way communication, reinforcement, and decision-making.* The first component of this constitutive definition, "demonstration of normatively appropriate conduct through personal actions and interpersonal relationships, . . ." suggests that those who are perceived to be ethical leaders model conduct that followers consider to be normatively appropriate (e.g., honesty, trustworthiness, fairness, and care), making the leader a legitimate and credible role model. The term "normatively appropriate" is deliberately vague because, beyond the generalities noted above, what is deemed appropriate behavior is somewhat context dependent. For example, in some cultures normatively appropriate behavior might include speaking out publicly against some organizational action; in other cultures, such public voice would be considered to be normatively inappropriate.

The next part of the definition, ". . . promotion of such conduct to followers through two-way communication, . . ." suggests that ethical leaders not only draw attention to ethics and make it salient in the social environment by explicitly talking to followers about it, but they also provide followers with voice, a procedurally or interpersonally just process (Bass and Steidlmeier, 1999 and Howell and Avolio, 1992). The ". . . reinforcement . . . " component of the definition implies that ethical leaders set ethical standards, reward ethical conduct and discipline those who don't follow the standards (Gini, 1998 and Treviño et al., 2003), contributing to vicarious learning. The final element of the definition related to "decision-making" reflects the fact that ethical leaders consider the ethical consequences of their decisions, and make principled and fair choices that can be observed and emulated by others (Bass and Avolio, 2000, Burns, 1978 and Howell and Avolio 1992). . . .

PROPOSED RELATIONSHIPS WITH LEADERSHIP STYLES AND CHARACTERISTICS

Consistent with our earlier theoretical arguments, we hypothesize that ethical leadership will be positively related to, but empirically distinguishable from, the ethical dimension of authentic transformational leadership (*idealized influence;* Bass and Avolio, 2000) and the relationship-oriented, *consideration* leadership style (Stogdill, 1963). As we previously noted, idealized influence is defined partly in terms of role modeling and demonstrating ethical values and should therefore partially overlap with ethical leadership. In addition, observational learning depends, at least in part, upon the provision of symbolic representations of the modeled behavior, including verbal construction. Therefore, transformational leaders contribute to observational learning about ethical values and ethical conduct by demonstrating ethical behavior and communicating with employees about conduct standards and values.

The consideration leadership style should also overlap with ethical leadership because both constructs are similar in their people orientation (Fleishman, 1969). Consideration-oriented leaders are nurturant in their relationships with employees. In social learning research, observers have been found to seek nurturant models over non-nurturant ones and to learn from them because nurturant models draw and hold observers' attention (Yussen and Levy, 1975). Yet, both idealized influence and consideration should also be distinguishable from ethical leadership given that ethical leadership incorporates a broader set of behaviors (e.g., communicating ethical standards), and, that idealized influence and consideration are comprised behaviors that are not necessarily associated with ethical leadership.

For similar reasons, we expect that ethical leadership will be positively related to *interactional fairness and trust in the leader*. An ethical leader's concern for the best interests of employees, openness to input, and fair decision making about matters important to employees are all consistent with a nurturant orientation and should result in the leader's attractiveness as a model and observers' attentiveness to the model's behavior. Also, benevolence is an important component of perceived trustworthiness. Benevolence "is the extent to which a trustee is believed to want to do good to a trustor, aside from an egocentric profit motive" (Mayer, Davis, and Schoorman, 1995, p. 718). This is substantively similar to the altruistic motive that is attributed to ethical leaders and to the nurturant orientation that is required of an attractive model. Therefore, we propose that ethical leadership will correlate positively with affective trust (trust based upon caring and concern).

By contrast, ethical leadership should be negatively related to *abusive supervision,* "the sustained display of hostile verbal and nonverbal behaviors" (Tepper, 2000, p. 178). Bass and Steidlmeier (1999) suggested that pseudo or unethical transformational leaders are often abusive and inconsiderate. Such an abusive leadership style is non-nurturant, uncharacteristic of effective role models, and contrasts sharply with the care and concern ethical leaders display.

We also expect that ethical leadership will be positively related to *leader honesty*. Honesty should be crucial to the legitimacy and attractiveness of a model (Bandura, 1986) and has frequently been linked with effective and ethical leadership (Avolio, 1999, Bass and Steidlmeier, 1999, Craig and Gustafson, 1998 and Treviño et al., 2003). However, because ethical leadership encompasses more than truth-telling, we expect that the overlap between ethical leadership and honesty will be incomplete; the two constructs will be positively correlated but be empirically distinguishable from one another.

Overall, we suggest that ethical leadership overlaps with, yet stands apart from the aforementioned constructs, most notably, the idealized influence dimension of transformational leadership. Both idealized influence and ethical leadership have their own unique content—idealized influence reflects inspirational/visionary leadership that is not necessary for ethical leadership (Treviño et al., 2003). Conversely, ethical leadership taps leader behavior that is not necessarily inspirational such as punishing misconduct, which is considered part of a transactional leadership style (Bass, 1985). In that regard, ethical leadership might even be considered to be mundane (e.g., steadfast, everyday adherence to standards of conduct) rather than visionary or transformational.

Similar to many leadership constructs, ethical leadership does not occupy a wholly unique conceptual space. As such, we do not expect it to be orthogonal to other elements of leadership. For example, ethical leaders are likely to be honest, considerate of their followers, fair in their decisions, use rewards and punishments to promote ethical conduct, and make decisions based on ethical values. All of these come together to characterize ethical leadership. But, none of these aspects, by themselves, constitutes all of what ethical leadership entails.

RELATIONSHIP WITH FOLLOWER ATTITUDES AND CONTEXTUAL PERFORMANCE

We predict that ethical leadership will be positively related to *employees' satisfaction with their leader*, ratings of *leader effectiveness, employees' willingness to give extra effort* (an aspect of contextual performance) and their *willingness to report problems to management*. First, employees should be more satisfied with a leader who disciplines wrongdoers (Treviño, 1992 and Treviño and Ball, 1992), treats followers fairly (Colquitt, Conlon, Wesson, Porter, and Ng, 2001) and considerately (Yukl, 2002), is trustworthy (Dirks and Ferrin, 2002), and exhibits transformational leadership behaviors (Lowe, Kroeck, and Sivasubramaniam, 1996). Supervisors have power over important employee decisions such as work assignments, performance evaluation, pay, and promotion. Employees should have more positive attitudes toward the leader making these decisions if that leader is seen as fair, considerate, and trustworthy (Dirks and Ferrin, 2002).

Theory and research also suggest that ethical leadership should be positively related to perceptions of leader effectiveness. Characteristics of ethical leaders (e.g., fairness, openness, and consideration) have long been considered important to perceived leader effectiveness (Yukl, 2002). Kanungo and Mendonca (1996) proposed that leaders motivated by altruism are perceived to be more effective compared to those who have a personalized power motive. Research suggests that honesty and integrity, important aspects of ethical leadership, are consistently associated with perceived leader effectiveness (Hogan, Curphy, and Hogan, 1994), even across cultures (Den Hartog

et al., 1999). Furthermore, leadership effectiveness has been related to authentic transformational leadership (Lowe et al., 1996) which has an ethical component. From a social learning perspective, ethical leaders are legitimate and attractive models who gain and hold followers' attention and can therefore influence them more effectively. Fair treatment of followers is an important source of legitimacy for ethical leaders (Tyler, 1986 and Tyler and Degoey, 1995) and that legitimacy contributes to a leader's ability [to] gain voluntary compliance and support for decisions, contributing to perceptions of leader effectiveness.

In addition, ethical leadership should promote going above and beyond the call of duty because when employees are treated fairly and well by a leader they trust, they are likely to think about their relationship with the leader and organization in terms of social exchange (Blau, 1964) rather than economic exchange and they are likely to reciprocate by helping the organization in a variety of ways (Organ, 1990). Thus, we propose that followers of an ethical leader will be willing to put extra effort into their work, or as Van Scotter and Motowidlo (1996) have termed it, job dedication. Bass (1985) proposed and research (Lowe et al., 1996) has supported a similar link involving transformational leadership. More frequent organizational citizenship and other extrarole behaviors have been associated with employee trust in the leader (Dirks and Ferrin, 2002, Konovsky and Pugh, 1994, Podsakoff et al., 2000), fair treatment from the leader (Pillai, Schriesheim, and Williams, 1999), and consideration-oriented leadership behaviors (Podsakoff et al., 2000).

Similarly, we propose that ethical leadership will be positively associated with *employees' willingness to report problems to the leader*. Reporting problems can be considered a type of extra-role behavior because it is generally not required (save for particular jobs such as auditing) and can be considered helpful to the organization. It also carries the risk of negative outcomes such as reprisal, but employees should be more likely to accept such a risk if they have confidence in the ethicality and trustworthiness of management (Brockner et al., 1997 and Mayer et al., 1995). Employees should be more willing to be the bearer of bad news to an ethical leader because they trust that the ethical leader will do the right thing, listen to their concerns and treat them fairly even if the bad news might be costly for the organization. . . .

DISCUSSION

Although much has been said about the importance of ethical leadership, the topic has received little systematic scholarly attention (Ciulla, 1998). And, an ethical leadership construct has not yet been precisely defined or adequately measured. Little theoretical or empirical work has been done to understand its theoretical base or its connection to related constructs and outcomes. Our research begins that work by using social learning as a theoretical foundation by developing an explicit, constitutive definition of the ethical leadership construct based upon prior theory and research and by demonstrating its relationship to and distinctiveness from other constructs.

We proposed that social learning theory provides a strong theoretical foundation for understanding ethical leadership. In order to be an ethical leader who can influence employee outcomes, the leader must be viewed as an attractive, credible, and legitimate role model who engages in normatively appropriate behavior and makes the ethics message salient. Follower perceptions of the leader's altruistic motivation and creation of a just work environment contribute to the attractiveness, credibility, and legitimacy of the role model. Explicit ethics-related communication and reinforcement contribute to the salience of the leader's ethics message. As an important first step, this research was focused primarily on the development of a constitutive definition, instrument development and demonstration of convergent, discriminant, and predictive validity. Additional research will be needed to specify the underlying theoretical processes in greater detail. . . .

As we predicted, ethical leadership is positively related to consideration behavior, interactional fairness, leader honesty, and the idealized influence dimension of transformational leadership (Bass and Avolio, 2000). Just as notably, confirmatory factor analysis found that it is distinct from those, partially overlapping, leadership constructs. Furthermore, ethical leadership is positively related to affective trust in the leader, and negatively related to abusive supervision. It is unrelated to rater demographics and perceived leader-subordinate similarity. Finally, it predicts an important combined criterion of outcomes—satisfaction with the leader, perceived leader effectiveness, job dedication (willing to give extra effort to one's job), and followers' willingness to report problems to management—beyond the effects of idealized influence, arguably the closest conceptual cousin to ethical leadership in the literature.

These many, consistent patterns of evidence provide support for the viability, coherence and potential importance of the ethical leadership construct in organizational behavior.

LIMITATIONS AND RESEARCH DIRECTIONS . . .

DEVELOPING OR PREDICTING ETHICAL LEADERSHIP AND ETHICAL LEADERSHIP OVER TIME

A limitation of these studies is their cross-sectional designs. Although those designs are consistent with the constitutive definition of ethical leadership, they do not allow complete tests of a temporally elaborated theory of ethical leadership. In such a theory, antecedent questions will need to be answered. Do individuals come to their organizations as ethical leaders or do organizations develop them? If they come as ethical leaders, can we predict ethical leadership based upon personality or other individual characteristics? Level of moral reasoning has been associated with transformational leadership (Turner et al., 2002) and therefore may also be associated with ethical leadership. Agreeableness (one of the Big Five personality dimensions) might be related to ethical leadership through the concern for people aspect of the construct. Individuals who are less conscientious are more careless, unreliable, and irresponsible (Digman, 1990 and McCrae and John, 1992). Thus, conscientious leaders may be more likely to be perceived as trustworthy because they behave dependably and consistently (McAllister, 1995 and Whitener et al., 1998). Finally, experience working in a highly ethical organization may contribute to ethical leadership characteristics that are carried with the leader from one organization to another.

If ethical leaders can be developed, how is this done? Is a particular type of training or intervention effective? Given the social learning perspective, we expect that role modeling (Bandura, 1977) or mentoring—pairing young managers with more senior leaders who have reputations for ethical leadership could be important in developing ethical leadership. Longitudinal designs will be required to answer these questions.

ETHICAL LEADERSHIP AT MULTIPLE LEVELS OF MANAGEMENT

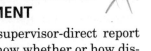

Our research focused on supervisor-direct report relationships. We do not know whether or how distance from the leader would influence employees' ratings of ethical leadership. Most lower-level employees in large organizations rarely see or interact with senior managers and must make inferences about the attributes of such leaders based upon available information rather than direct experience (Lord and Maher, 1991). Thus, perceptions of executive ethical leadership may rely more upon public relations information or organizational outcomes (e.g., corporate malfeasance or philanthropy), and may be more open to image management than are perceptions of supervisory ethical leadership. Alternatively, it might be useful to know if employees' ratings of close and distant leaders' ethical leadership coincide—does ethical leadership cascade (Bass, Waldman, Avolio, and Bebb, 1987) from the top to influence perceptions of leaders throughout the organization? Lower level employees may be cynical (Dean, Brandes, and Dharwadkar, 1998) about the integrity of top managers, and consequently, rate senior managers lower compared to their ratings of their direct supervisors. Or, employees may have a rosy view of senior leaders (based upon effective image management) but view their direct supervisors more cynically in the harsh light of day-to-day interaction.

PREDICTING ADDITIONAL OUTCOMES

Our research contributes to understanding of ethical leadership by offering social learning as the key theoretical perspective in defining it. Social learning theory suggests that ethical leadership should influence employees' ethical conduct at work because ethical leaders are attractive and legitimate models who attract and hold followers' attention. In addition, they convey the importance of and role model ethical behavior, and they use the reward system to hold employees accountable. We demonstrated that employees whose supervisor is perceived to be an ethical leader are more willing to engage in proactive helpful behavior such as reporting problems to management. Future research should investigate whether unethical behaviors (such as employee theft, sabotage, lying to one's supervisor, etc.) are also reduced.

CIRCUMSTANCES INFLUENCING THE IMPORTANCE OF ETHICAL LEADERSHIP

We expect the importance of ethical leadership to depend, in part, on the job context and the outcome being predicted. For example, the more often employees' work involves ethical dilemmas, the more likely the ethical dimension of leadership will influence employee attitudes and conduct. Employees in boundary spanning positions are likely to encounter ethical ambiguity and values

conflicts more often than employees who are protected within the technical core of the organization (Thompson, 1967) and they will need more ethical guidance. Also, in situations where tasks are ill-defined, and standards of practice are not well established, the ethical guidance provided by leaders should be more important.

We also expect that in context in which the moral intensity (Jones, 1991) of ethical decisions is high, leaders will have greater opportunities to demonstrate—or not demonstrate—ethical leadership to their employees. These morally intense situations may lead to greater consensus in employee perceptions of ethical leadership because of the salience of ethical issues in that situation and the opportunity to observe a leader's actions in response.

CONCLUSION

Concerns about ethics and leadership have dominated recent headlines about business and shaken public confidence in many organizations. Now, more than ever, rigorous, systematic research on ethical leadership is needed. We have developed the ethical leadership construct to overcome some of the fractious nature of past treatments. By basing such a construct on a foundation of social learning theory, constructing a reliable and construct valid measure of it, and demonstrating its predictive validity, we hope to spur further study of ethical leadership, its antecedents and additional consequences. . . .

References

Alexander and Ruderman, 1987 S. Alexander and M. Ruderman, The role of procedural and distributive justice in organizational behavior, *Social Justice Research* 1 (1987) pp. 177–198.

Ambrose and Schminke, 1999 M. L. Ambrose and M. Schminke, Sex differences in business ethics: The importance of perceptions, *Journal of Managerial Issues* 11 (1999), pp. 454–474.

Arvey and Jones, 1985 R. D. Arvey and A. P. Jones, The use of discipline in organizational settings: A framework for future research. In. L. L. Cummings and B. M. Staw, Editors, *Research in organizational behavior* Vol. 7, JAI Press, Greenwich, CT (1985), pp. 367–408.

Ashford, 1989 S. J. Ashford, Self Assessments in organizations: A literature review and integrative model. In. L.L. Cummings and B.M. Staw, Editors, *Research in organizational behavior* Vol. 11, JAI Press, Greenwich, CT (1989), pp. 133–174.

Atwater et al., 1998 L. Atwater, C. Ostroff, F. Yammarino and J. Fleenor, Self-other agreement: Does it really matter?, *Personnel Psychology* 51 (1998), pp. 577–598.

Avolio, 1999 B. J. Avolio, Full leadership development: Building the vital forces in organizations, Sage, Thousand Oaks, CA (1999).

Avolio et al., 1999 B. J. Avolio, B.M. Bass and D. I. Jung, Re-examining the components of transformational and transactional leadership using the multifactor leadership questionnaire, *Journal of Occupational and Organizational Psychology* 72 (1999), pp. 441–462.

Bagozzi and Yi, 1988 R. P. Bagozzi and Y. Yi, On the evaluation of structural equation models, *Journal of the Academy of Ma0g Science* 16 (1988), pp. 74–94.

Bandura, 1977 A. Bandura, Social learning theory, Prentice-Hall, Englewood Cliffs, NJ (1977).

Bandura, 1986 A. Bandura, Social foundations of thought and action, Prentice-Hall, Englewood Cliffs, NJ (1986).

Bass, 1985 B. M. Bass, Leadership and performance beyond expectations, Free Press, New York (1985).

Bass, 1990 B. M. Bass, Bass & Stogdill's handbook of leadership, The Free Press, New York (1990).

Bass, 1998 B. M. Bass, Transformational leadership: Industrial, military and educational impact, Erlbaum, Mahwah, NJ (1998).

Bass and Avolio, 1993 B. M. Bass and B. J. Avolio, Improving organizational effectiveness through transformational leadership, Sage, Thousand Oaks, CA (1993).

Bass and Avolio, 2000 B. Bass and B. Avolio, Multifactor leadership questionnaire (2nd ed.), Mind Garden, Redwood City, CA (2000).

Bass and Steidlmeier, 1999 B. M. Bass and P. Steidlmeier, Ethics, character, and authentic transformational leadership behavior, *Leadership Quarterly* 10 (1999), pp. 181–218.

Bass et al., 1987 B. M. Bass, D. A. Waldman, B. J. Avolio and M. Bebb, Transformational leadership and the falling dominoes effect, *Group and Organization Studies* 12 (1987), pp. 73–87.

Bies and Moag, 1986 R. J. Bies and J. S. Moag, Interactional justice: Communication criteria of fairness. In: R. J. Lewicki, B. H. Sheppard and M. H. Bazerman, Editors, *Research on negotiations in organizations* Vol. 1, JAI Press, Greenwich, CT (1986), pp. 43–55.

Blau, 1964 P. M. Blau, Exchange and power in social life, Wiley, New York (1964).

Bliese et al., 2002 P. D. Bliese, R. R. Halverson and C. A. Schriesheim, Benchmarking multilevel methods in leadership: The articles, the models, the data set, *Leadership Quarterly* 13 (2002), pp. 3–14.

Bono and Judge, 2003 J. E. Bono and T. A. Judge, Self-concordance at work: Toward understanding the motivational effects of transformational leaders, *Academy of Management Journal* 46 (2003), pp. 554–571.

Brockner et al., 1997 J. Brockner, P. A. Siegel, J. P. Daly, T. Tyler and C. Martin, When trust matters: The moderating effect of outcome favorability, *Administrative Science Quarterly* 42 (1997), pp. 558–583.

Browne and Cudeck, 1993 M. W. Browne and R. Cudeck, Alternative ways of assessing model fit. In: K. A. Bollen and J. S. Long, Editors, *Testing structural equation models*, Sage, Thousand Oaks, CA (1993), pp. 136–162.

Bryan and Test, 1967 J. H. Bryan and M. A. Test, Models and helping: naturalistic studies in aiding behavior, *Journal of Personality and Social Psychology* 6 (1967), pp. 400–407.

Burns, 1978 J. M. Burns, Leadership, Harper Row, New York (1978).

Byrne, 1971 D. Byrne, The attraction paradigm, Academic Press, New York (1971).

Campbell, 1960 D. T. Campbell, Recommendations for APA test standards regarding construct, trait, or discriminant validity, *American Psychologist* 15 (1960), pp. 546–553.

Ciulla, 1998 J. Ciulla, Ethics, the heart of leadership, Quorum Books, Westport, CT (1998).

Colquitt et al., 2001 J. A. Colquitt, D. E. Conlon, M. J. Wesson, C.O.L.H. Porter and K. Y. Ng, Justice at the millennium: A meta-analytic review of 25 years of organizational justice research, *Journal of Applied Psychology* 86 (2001), pp. 425–445.

Colvin, 2003 Colvin, G. (2003), Corporate crooks are not all created equal, *Fortune, October;* 27, 64.

Conger, 1999 J. A. Conger, Charismatic and transformational leadership in organizations: An insider's perspective on these developing streams of research, *Leadership Quarterly* 10 (1999), pp. 145–179.

Craig and Gustafson, 1998 S. B. Craig and S. B. Gustafson, Perceived leader integrity scale: An instrument for assessing employee perceptions of leader integrity, *Leadership Quarterly* 9 (1998), pp. 127–145.

Dean et al., 1998 J. W. Dean, P. Brandes and R. Dharwadkar, Organizational cynicism, *Academy of Management Review* 23 (1998), pp. 341–352.

Den Hartog et al., 1999 D. N. Den Hartog, R. J. House, P. J. Hanges, S. A. Ruiz-Quintanilla and P. W. Dorfman *et al.*, Culturally specific and cross-culturally generalizable implicit leadership theories: Are attributes of charismatic/transformational leadership universally endorsed? *Leadership Quarterly* 10 (1999), pp. 219–256.

Digman, 1990 J. M. Digman, Personality structure: Emergence of the five-factor model, *Annual Review of Psychology* 41 (1990), pp. 417–440.

Dirks and Ferrin, 2002 K. T. Dirks and D. L. Ferrin, Trust in leadership: Meta-Analytic findings and implications for research and practice, *Journal of Applied Psychology* 87 (2002), pp. 611–628.

Edwards, 2003 J. R. Edwards, Construct development in organizational behavior research (2nd ed.). In. J. Greenberg, Editor, *Organizational behavior: The state of the science*, Erlbaum, Mahwah, NJ (2003), pp. 327–372.

Fabrigar et al., 1999 L.R. Fabrigar, D. T. Wegener, R. C. MacCallum and E. J. Strahan, Evaluation of the use of exploratory factor analysis in psychological research, *Psychological Methods* 4 (1999), pp. 272–299.

Fernandes and Randall, 1992 M. F. Fernandes and D. M. Randall, The nature of social desirability response effects in business ethics research, *Business Ethics Quarterly* 2 (1992), pp. 183–205.

Folger and Konovsky, 1989 R. Folger and M. A. Konovsky, Effects of procedural and distributive justice on reactions to pay raise decisions, *Academy of Management Journal* 32 (1989), pp. 115–130.

Fleishman, 1969 E. A. Fleishman, Manual for leadership opinion questionnaire, Science Research Associates, Chicago (1969).

Ghiselli et al., 1981 E. E. Ghiselli, J. P. Campbell and S. Zedeck, Measurement theory for the behavioral sciences, W.J. Freeman, San Francisco (1981).

Gini, 1998 A. Gini, Moral leadership and business ethics. In. J. B. Ciulla, Editor, *Ethics, the heart of leadership*, Quorum Books, Westport, CT (1998), pp. 27–45.

Harrison et al., 1996 D. A. Harrison, M. E. McLaughlin and T. M. Coalter, Context, cognition, and common method variance: Psychometric and verbal protocol evidence, *Organizational Behavior and Human Decision Processes* 68 (1996), pp. 246–261.

Harrison and Shaffer, 1994 D. A. Harrison and M. A. Shaffer, Comparative examinations of self reports and perceived absenteeism norms: Wading through Lake Wobegon, *Journal of Applied Psychology* 79 (1994), pp. 240–251.

Hinkin, 1998 T. R. Hinkin, A brief tutorial on the development of measures for use in questionnaires, *Organizational Research Methods* 1 (1998), pp. 104–121.

Hogan et al., 1994 R. Hogan, G. J. Curphy and J. Hogan, What we know about leadership: Effectiveness and personality, *American Psychologist* 49 (1994), pp. 493–504.

House, 1977 R. J. House, A 1976 theory of charismatic leadership. In. J. G. Hunt and L. L. Larson, Editors, *Leadership: The cutting edge*, Southern Illinois University Press, Carbondale, IL (1977), pp. 189–207.

House and Aditya, 1997 R. J. House and R. N. Aditya, The social scientific study of leadership: Quo vadis?, *Journal of Management* 23 (1997), pp. 409–473.

House et al., 1991 R. J. House, W. D. Spangler and J. Woycke, Personality and charisma in the US Presidency: A psychological theory of leader effectiveness, *Administrative Science Quarterly* 36 (1991), pp. 364–396.

Howell, 1988 J. M. Howell, Two faces of charisma: Socialized and personalized leadership in organizations. In. J. A. Conger and R. N. Kanungo, Editors, *Charismatic leadership*, Jossey-Bass, San Francisco. CA (1988), pp. 213–236.

Howell and Avolio; 1992 J. M. Howell and B. J. Avolio, The ethics of charismatic leadership: submission or liberation, *Academy of Management Executive* 6 (1992), pp. 43–54.

James et al., 1984 L. R. James, R. J. Demaree and G. Wolf, Estimating within-group interrater reliability with and without response bias, *Journal of Applied Psychology* 69 (1984), pp. 85–98.

Jones, 1991 T. M. Jones, Ethical decision making by individuals in organizations: An issue contingent model, *Academy of Management Review* 16 (1991), pp. 366–395.

Joreskog and Sorbom, 1993 K. G. Joreskog and D. Sorbom, LISREL R 8: Structural equation modeling with *SIMPLIS*™ command language, Scientific Software International Inc, Chicago, IL (1993).

Judge and Bono, 2000 T. A. Judge and J. E. Bono, Five-factor model of personality and transformational leadership, *Journal of Applied Psychology* 85 (2000), pp. 751–765.

Kanfer, 1990 R. Kanfer, Motivation theory and industrial and organizational psychology (2nd ed.). In. M. D. Dunnette and L. M. Hough, Editors, *Handbook of industrial and organizational psychology* Vol. 1, Consulting Psychologists Press, Palo Alto, CA (1990), pp. 75–170.

Kanungo and Mendonca, 1996 R. Kanungo and M. Mendonca, Ethical dimensions of leadership, Sage, Thousand Oaks, CA (1996).

Kark et al., 2003 R. Kark, B. Shamir and G. Chen, The two faces of transformational leadership: Empowerment and dependency, *Journal of Applied Psychology* 88 (2003), pp. 246–255.

Kelley, 1939 T. L. Kelley, Mental factors of no importance, *The Journal of Educational Psychology* 30 (1939), pp. 139–142.

Kelman, 1958 H. C. Kelman, Compliance, identification, and internalization: Three processes of attitude change, *Journal of Conflict Resolution* 2 (1958), pp. 51–56.

Kirchmeyer, 1995 C. Kirchmeyer, Demographic similarity to the work group: A longitudinal study of managers at the early career stage, *Journal of Organizational Behavior* 16 (1995), pp. 67–83.

Kohlberg, 1969 L. Kohlberg, State and sequence: The cognitive-development approach to socialization. In D. Goslin, Editor, *Handbook of socialization theory and research*, Rand-McNally, Chicago (1969), pp. 347–480.

Konovsky and Pugh, 1994 M. A. Konovsky and S. D. Pugh, Citizenship behavior and social exchange, *Academy of Management Journal* 37 (1994), pp. 656–669.

Kouzes and Posner, 1987 J. M. Kouzes and B. Z. Posner, The leadership challenge: How to get extraordinary things done in organizations, Jossey-Bass, San Francisco, CA (1987).

Kouzes and Posner, 1993 J. M. Kouzes and B. Z. Posner, Credibility: How leaders gain and lose it, why people demand it, Jossey-Bass, San Francisco, CA (1993).

Lord and Maher, 1991 R. G. Lord and K. J. Maher, Leadership and information processing: Linking perception and performance, Unwin-Hyman, Boston (1991).

Lowe et al., 1996 K. B. Lowe, K. G. Kroeck and N. Sivasubramaniam, Effectiveness correlates of transformational and transactional leadership: A meta-analytic review of the MLQ literature, *Leadership Quarterly* 7 (1996), pp. 385–425.

May et al., 2003 D. May, A. Y. L. Chan, T. D. Hodges and B. Avolio, Developing the moral component of authentic leadership, *Organizational Dynamics* 32 (2003), pp. 247–260.

Mayer et al., 1995 R. C. Mayer, J. H. Davis and F. D. Schoorman, An integrative model of organizational trust, *Academy of Management Review* 20 (1995), pp. 709–734.

McAllister, 1995 D. J. McAllister, Affect-and cognition-based trust as foundations for interpersonal cooperation in organizations, *Academy of Management Journal* 38 (1995), pp. 24–59.

McClelland, 1975 D. C. McClelland, Power: The inner experience, Irvington, New York (1975).

McCrae and John, 1992 R. R. McCrae and O. P. John, An introduction to the five-factor model and its applications, *Journal of Personality* 2 (1992), pp. 175–215.

Mehta, 2003 S. Mehta, MCI: Is being good good enough? *Fortune* 27 (2003), pp. 117–124.

Montanelli and Humphreys, 1976 R. G. Montanelli and L. G. Humphreys, Latent roots of random data correlation matrices with squared multiple correlations on the diagonal: A Monte Carlo study, *Psychometrika* 41 (1976), pp. 341–348.

O'Connor et al., 1995 J. A. O'Connor, M. D. Mumford, T. C. Clifton, T. E. Gessner and M. S. Connelly, Charismatic leaders and destructiveness: A historiometric study, *Leadership Quarterly* 6 (1995), pp. 529–555.

Organ, 1990 D. W. Organ, The motivational basis of organizational citizenship. In. L. L. Cummings and B. M. Staw, Editors, *Research in organizational behavior* Vol. 12, JAI Press, Greenwich, CT (1990), pp. 43–72.

Paulhus, 1991 D. L. Paulhus, Measurement and control of response bias. In. J. P. Robinson, P. R. Shaver and L. S. Wrightsman, Editors, *Measures of personality and social psychological attitudes,* Academic Press, San Diego, CA (1991), pp. 17–59.

Pillai et al., 1999 R. Pillai, C. A. Schriesheim and E. S. Williams, Fairness perceptions and trust as mediators for transformational and transactional leadership: A two-sample study, *Journal of Management* 25 (1999), pp. 897–933.

Podsakoff et al., 2000 P. M. Podsakoff, S. B. MacKenzie, J. B. Paine and D. G. Bachrach, Organizational citizenship behaviors: A critical review of the theoretical and empirical literature and suggestions for future research, *Journal of Management* 26 (2000), pp. 513–563.

Posner and Schmidt, 1992 B. Z. Posner and W. H. Schmidt, Values and the American manager: An update updated, *California Management Review* 34 (1992), pp. 80–94.

Revell, 2003 J, Revell, The fires that won't go out, *Fortune* 13 (2003), p. 139.

Rosenhan and White, 1967 D. Rosenhan and G. M. White, Observation and rehearsal as determinants of prosocial behavior, *Journal of Personality and Social Psychology* 5 (1967), pp. 423–431.

Scandura, 1997 T. A. Scandura, Mentoring and organizational justice: An empirical investigation, *Journal of Vocational Behavior* 51 (1997), pp. 58–69.

Schriesheim, 1979 C. A. Schriesheim, The similarity of individual-directed and group-directed leader behavior descriptions, *Academy of Management Journal* 22 (1979), pp. 345–355.

Schriesheim et al., 1995 C. A. Schriesheim, C. C. Cogliser and L. L. Neider, Is it "trustworthy". A multiple levels-of-analysis examination of an Ohio State leadership study with implications for future research, *Leadership Quarterly* 6 (1995), pp. 111–145.

Schriesheim et al., 1998 C. A. Schriesheim, C. C. Cogliser and L. L. Neider, Appendix: Measures and assessments for the Ohio State approach. In. F. Dansereau and F. J. Yammarino, Editors, *Leadership: The multiple-level approaches* Vol. A, JAI Press, Stanford, CT (1998), pp. 43–50.

Schriesheim et al., 1999 C.A. Schriesheim, C. C. Cogliser, T. A. Scandura, M. J. Lankau and K. J. Powers, An empirical comparison of approaches for quantitatively assessing the content adequacy of paper-and-pencil measurement instruments, *Organizational Research Methods* 2 (1999), pp. 140–156.

Schwab, 1980 D. P. Schwab, Construct validity in organizational behavior. In. L. L. Cummings and B. M. Staw, Editors, *Research in organizational behavior*, JAI Press, Greenwich, CT (1980), pp. 3–43.

Shamir, 1999 B. Shamir, Taming charisma for better understanding and greater usefulness, *Leadership Quarterly* 10 (1999), pp. 555–662.

Stogdill, 1963 R. M. Stogdill, Manual for the leader behavior description questionnaire—Form XII. Bureau of Business Research, Ohio State University, Columbus, OH (1963).

Tepper, 2000 B. J. Tepper, Consequences of abusive supervision, *Academy of Management Journal* 43 (2000), pp. 178–190.

Thompson, 1967 J. D. Thompson, *Organizations in action*, McGraw Hill, New York (1967).

Treviño, 1986 L. K. Treviño, Ethical decision making in organizations: A person-situation interactionist model, *Academy of Management Review* 11 (1986), pp. 601–617.

Treviño, 1992 L. K. Treviño, The social effects of punishment in organization: A justice perspective, *Academy of Management Review* 17 (1992), pp. 647–676.

Treviño and Ball, 1992 L. K. Treviño and G. A. Ball, The social implications of punishing unethical behavior: Observers' cognitive and affective reactions, *Journal of Management* 18 (1992), p. 4.

Treviño et al., 2003 L. K. Treviño, M. Brown and L. P. Hartman, A qualitative investigation of perceived executive ethical leadership: Perceptions from inside and outside the executive suite, *Human Relations* 55 (2003), pp. 5–37.

Treviño et al., 2000 L. K. Treviño L. P. Hartman and M. Brown, Moral person and moral manager: How executives develop a reputation for ethical leadership, *California Management Review* 42 (2000), pp. 128–142.

Treviño and Weaver, 2003 L. K. Treviño and G. R. Weaver, Managing ethics in business organizations: Social scientific perspectives, Stanford University Press, Stanford, CA (2003).

Turner et al., 2002 N. Turner, J. Barling, O. Epitropaki, V. Butcher and C. Milner, Transformational leadership and moral reasoning, *Journal of Applied Psychology* 87 (2002), pp. 304–311.

Tyler, 1986 T. R. Tyler, The psychology of leadership evaluation. In. H. W. Bierhoff, R. L. Cohen and J. Greenberg, Editors, *Justice in social relations*, Plenum, NY (1986).

Tyler and Degoey, 1995 T. R. Tyler and P. Degoey, Collective restraint in social dilemmas: Procedural justice and social identification effects on support for authorities, *Journal of Personality and Social Psychology* 69 (1995), pp. 482–497.

Tyler et al., 1985 T. R. Tyler, K. A. Rasinski and N. Spodick, Influence of voice on satisfaction with leaders: Exploring the meaning of process control, *Journal of Personality and Social Psychology* 48 (1985), pp. 72–81.

Van Scotter and Motowidlo, 1996 J. R. Van Scotter and S. J. Motowidlo, Interpersonal facilitation and job dedication as separate facets of contextual performance, *Journal of Applied Psychology* 81 (1996), pp. 525–531.

Whitener et al., 1998 E. M. Whitener, S. E. Brodt, M. A. Korsgaard and J. M. Werner, Managers as initiators of trust: An exchange relationship framework for understanding managerial trustworthy behavior, *Academy of Management Review* 23 (1998), pp. 513–530.

Wood and Bandura, 1989 R. Wood and A. Bandura, Social cognitive theory of organizational management, *Academy of Management Review* 14 (1989), pp. 361–384.

Wrightsman, 1991 L. S. Wrightsman, Interpersonal trust and attitudes toward human nature. In. J. P. Robinson, P. R. Shaver and L. S. Wrightsman, Editors, *Measures of personality and social psychological attitudes*, Academic Press, San Diego, CA (1991), pp. 373–412.

Yukl, 2002 G. A. Yukl, Leadership in organizations (5th ed.), Prentice Hall, Englewood Cliffs, NJ (2002).

Yussen and Levy, 1975 S.R. Yussen and V. M. Levy Jr., Effects of warm and neutral models on the attention of observational learners, *Journal of Experimental Child Psychology* 20 (1975), pp. 66–72.

Leaders and the Role of Personal Traits

At one time, "great person" theories of leadership were popular. It was commonly assumed that certain individuals, when born, were destined to lead. Julius Caesar, Joan of Arc, Catherine the Great, and Napoleon are cited as naturally great leaders, individuals supposedly born with a set of personal qualities that enabled them to emerge and be effective leaders.

Early in the twentieth century, students of leadership raised a critical question assumed by the great person theories. Do leaders tend to possess a common set of traits (e.g., physical, demographic, intellective, and personality characteristics) that equip them to be leaders? For some, leadership began to be seen as a psychological phenomenon, with individuals inherently possessing capacities, motives, and patterns of behavior that distinguished them from others (i.e., nonleaders). This view that the essence of leadership was lodged in the person led to a leader-centric approach to leadership that spanned more than the final half of the twentieth century.

Ralph Stogdill (1948) conducted an extensive review of the literature (covering most of the first four decades of the twentieth century) and attempted to identify and summarize the personal factors associated with leadership.[1] His review leaves us with a number of interesting observations. First, it reveals that a *large number of traits emerged* in different studies as descriptive of leaders. Some of these traits were educational, demographic, physical, and intellectual in nature while some pertained to status, skill, and energy. Second, *traits are an important part of the picture*, although each trait accounted for a small portion of the criterion variance. Third, *leadership is proactive versus passive* in nature and is a *working relationship* that includes the *orchestration of group activity*. The leader acquires leadership status through active participation and demonstration of the capacity to assist the group with task completion. Finally, Stogdill notes that while a leader's traits are important tools, the traits must fit with the situation. (This later observation did not take root, in any serious way, for nearly two decades.)

Among the important traits identified were the following:

- Capacity (intelligence, alertness, verbal facility, originality, judgment).

- Achievement (scholarship, knowledge, athletic accomplishments).

- Responsibility (dependability, initiative, persistence, aggressiveness, self-confidence, desire to excel).

- Participation (activity, sociability, cooperation, adaptability, humor).

- Status (socioeconomic position, popularity).

[1] R. M. Stogdill, "Personal Factors with Leadership: A Survey of the Literature," *Journal of Psychology* 28 (1948), pp. 35–71.

Stogdill's most consistent observation pertained to the relationship between intelligence and leadership (Lord, DeVader, & Alliger, 1986; Judge, Colbert, & Ilies, 2004).[2] Stogdill's (1948) literature review and the review conducted by Mann (1959)[3] produced the observation that there is a fairly strong relationship between an individual's personality and others' perceptions of him or her as a leader.

Stogdill's work also provided additional insight into the *process* of leadership. He suggested that leadership is a *relationship;* that it is associated with the attainment of group objectives, implying that leadership is an activity, consisting of movement and getting work accomplished; and that it is evolutionary and interactive in nature.

In 1974 Stogdill reviewed 163 studies published between 1949 and 1970 that provided additional insight into leader traits. This body of evidence reinforced the observations that he drew in 1948 and identified some additional traits and skills. Stogdill (1974) provided the following trait profile of the successful leader:

> The leader is characterized by a strong drive for responsibility and task completion, vigor and persistence in pursuit of goals, venturesomeness and originality in problem solving, drive to exercise initiative in social situations, self-confidence and sense of personal identity, willingness to accept consequences of decision and action, readiness to absorb interpersonal stress, willingness to tolerate frustration and delay, ability to influence other persons' behavior, and capacity to structure social interaction systems to the purpose at hand. (p. 81)[4]

Certain individuals (i.e., those possessing a unique configuration of personal factors—ideas, initiative, persistence, knowledge of how to get things done, responsibility, status—relative to the other members of the group) come to occupy a special position in the group. Through their orchestration of group activity (e.g., providing meaning, information, judgment, activity), they emerge as leaders, and in this capacity they continue to provide orchestration to group activities. Reference to the orchestration of group activity suggests that leadership can be seen as a *working relationship* among members of a group. Through this working and interactive process, the leader makes contributions that are important to the group, acquires a status within the group, and comes to fulfill a leadership role. Verbal fluency, popularity, cooperativeness, self-confidence, initiative, and persistence, for example, tend to contribute to the individual's emergence into this leadership role and subsequently tend to reinforce the person's legitimacy as the group's leader.

Stogdill also highlighted the importance of the situation. He notes that a person does not emerge as a leader simply by possessing these key traits. The pattern of traits possessed must achieve some semblance of fit with the situation in which the followers find themselves as well as the characteristics, goals, and activities of the followers. Thus, according to Stogdill, the person who is a leader in one group may not be a leader in the next situation.

There were problems with the early trait leadership studies. While many studies identified a set of traits that were associated with leader emergence and/or leader effectiveness, many of these findings failed to replicate in subsequent studies. By the late 1940s and early 1950s this observation led many leadership scholars to the belief that this search was futile. A review of more recent leadership

---

[2] R. G. Lord, C. L. DeVader, & G. M. Alliger, "A Meta-Analysis of the Relation Between Personality Traits and Leadership Perceptions: An Application of Validity Generalization Procedures," *Journal of Applied Psychology* 71, 3 (1986), pp. 402–410; T. A. Judge, A. E. Colbert, & R. Ilies, "Intelligence and Leadership: A Quantitative Review and Test of Theoretical Propositions," *Journal of Applied Psychology*, 89, 3 (2004), pp. 542–552.

[3] R. D. Mann, "A Review of the Relationships Between Personality and Performance in Small Groups," *Psychological Bulletin* 56 (1959), pp. 241–270.

[4] R. M. Stogdill, *Handbook of Leadership: A Survey of the Literature* (New York: Free Press, 1974).

studies, illustrated by the two readings in this chapter and in subsequent chapters, focuses on gender and charismatic leadership, revealing that trait theory is once again alive and well.

Additional problems seemed to plague these early investigations (cf. House & Aditya, 1997).[5] First, there was an absence of sound personality leadership theory to guide this research. As a result, researchers bounced from one personality trait to another, without any systematic guidance. Second, many of the research instruments that had been developed at the time to measure personality traits lacked sufficient validity, so they failed to produce sound data. Finally, there were many instances in which more than one measure had been developed to measure the same personality trait and these measures often produced very different results—once again raising questions about the validity of the data that were being collected and analyzed.

The last few decades of the twentieth century brought a better understanding of personality, the relationship between personality traits and behavior, and the conditions under which personality versus situational forces serve as the primary driver of human behavior. For example, the Big Five typology of personality, which emerged during the 1960s (cf. Tupes & Christal, 1961; Norman, 1963),[6] would later come to drive some of the leadership personality research. Scholars started to theorize, creating hypotheses that linked personality traits and leadership. For example, Dobbins, Long, Dedrick, & Clemons (1990)[7] hypothesized that people with a high self-monitoring personality (i.e., those who have the ability and motivation to read and respond to social cues) are more likely to engage in the behaviors that others find attractive in time of leadership need, and thus they are more likely to emerge as leaders than their low self-monitor counterparts. In 1973, Walter Mischel made the observation that personality expresses itself behaviorally more strongly in weak situations (i.e., weak situations are those that are unstructured, without rules and incentives to guide people's actions) as opposed to strong situations (i.e., situations in which there are strong behavioral norms and incentives that encourage some behaviors and discourage others).[8] As a consequence, traits are going to play a more prominent role in leader emergence and leader effectiveness in weak than in strong situations. In the light of such developments, the leader trait research that has been undertaken during the past two to three decades has produced more interesting and consistent results than that which was produced throughout the first two-thirds of the twentieth century.

In the early 1990s Edwin A. Locke and several of his students conducted an extensive review of the leadership trait literature, resulting in the publication of *The Essence of Leadership* (1991). Part of their work is summarized in the first reading in this chapter. Shelley A. Kirkpatrick and Edwin A. Locke (1991)[9] provide a contemporary answer to the question, Do leadership traits really matter?

According to Kirkpatrick and Locke, there is a set of traits that endow an individual with "the right stuff" to be an effective leader. These traits are important "preconditions" giving an individual the *potential* to be an effective leader. Possessing these traits, however, does not guarantee leadership success. Among

[5] R. J. House & R. N. Aditya. "The Social Scientific Study of Leadership: Quo Vadis". *Journal of Management* 23 (1997), pp. 409–473.
[6] E. C. Tupes & R. E. Christal, "Recurrent Personality Factors Based on Trait Ratings," Technical Report ASD-TR-61-97. (Lackland Air Force Base, TX: U. S. Air Force, 1961); W. T. Norman, "Toward an Adequate Taxonomy of Personality Attributes: Replicated Factor Structure in Peer Nomination Personality Ratings." *Journal of Abnormal Social Psychology* 66 (1963), pp. 574–583.
[7] G. H. Dobbins, W. S. Long, E. J, Dedrick, & T. C. Clemons, "The Role of Self-Monitoring and Gender on Leader Emergence: A Laboratory and Field Study," *Journal of Management* 16, 3 (1990), pp. 609–618.
[8] W. Mischel, "Toward a Cognitive Social Learning Reconceptualization of Personality," *Psychological Review* 80 (1973), pp. 252–283.
[9] Kirkpatrick & Locke (1991).

the key traits that appear to differentiate leaders from nonleaders, according to Kirkpatrick and Locke, are drive, the desire to lead, honesty and integrity, self-confidence, cognitive ability, and knowledge of the business. Several other traits identified as possible characteristics of effective leaders included charisma, creativity and originality, and flexibility and adaptiveness. According to Hooijberg (1996)[10] and House & Aditya (1997), leader behavior flexibility may be highly significant in terms of leader emergence and effectiveness when the leader operates in an unstable environment. In their article the authors provide us with insight into the meaning of and leadership role played by each of these attributes.

Energy and drive, as these traits characterize an individual's disposition, have been the focus of recent research. Evidence suggests that individuals whose personality can be characterized by *positive affectivity* (i.e., a positive mood state, high levels of energy and drive) tend to be more competent interpersonally and contribute more to group activities; therefore they are able to function more effectively in their leadership role.[11] By virtue of their energetic personalities, these individuals infuse excitement and energy into group activity. The first self-assessment presented at the end of this chapter opener provides you with an opportunity to profile your own level of positive and negative affectivity.

According to Kirkpatrick and Locke, people who possess these traits are more likely to engage in the behaviors associated with effective leadership. These traits help leaders acquire the necessary skills (i.e., capacities for action such as decision making and problem solving) needed for effective leadership. In addition, people with these traits have the ability to create vision, and they possess the capacity to design a strategy that leads to vision implementation (e.g., structure activities, motivate others, manage information, build teams, and promote change and innovation). Those who possess these traits are simply more likely to engage in the behaviors associated with effective leadership than individuals who are not endowed with these characteristics.

Kirkpatrick and Locke also note that knowledge, skills, and abilities (KSA) play an important role in understanding the leader as a person. The abilities to set goals, build teamwork, organize people, and make complex decisions are important KSAs. Many note that missing from this list is experience—something often presumed to be important. Speaking to the role of experience Fred Fiedler (1996) states that "experience . . . [has] been shown to be completely unrelated to leadership performance."[12] In support of this comment he notes that Abraham Lincoln and Harry Truman had virtually no leadership experience and they were significantly more successful presidents than Herbert Hoover and Franklin Pierce, two individuals who had extensive leadership experience.

Kirkpatrick and Locke note that the motivation to lead (e.g., How much do you like being in the position of group leader?) was an important precondition for an individual's assumption of the leadership role. Chan and Drasgow (2001) suggest that the motivation to lead may be multidimensional in nature. Some people may be motivated to lead simply because they *like* the role (affective-based motivation). Others may choose to lead out of a *sense of duty or responsibility*. Chan and Drasgow refer to this as the social/normative motive. Finally, they suggest that there is a *calculative dimension* to the motive. The calculative motive is based on the costs and benefits that are associated with the role. They note that "it is . . . possible that other people may only lead if they are not calculative about the costs of leading relative to the benefits (i.e., noncalculative [motive to lead]). The

[10] See R. Hooijberg, "A Multidirectional Approach Toward Leadership: An Extension of the Concept of Behavioral Complexity," *Human Relations* 49, 7 (1996), pp. 917–946.
[11] B. M. Staw & S. G. Barsade, "Affect and Managerial Performance: A Test of the Sadder-but-Wiser vs. Happier-and-Smarter Hypothesis," *Administrative Science Quarterly* 38 (1993), pp. 304–331.
[12] Fred E. Fiedler, "Research on Leadership Selection and Training: One View of the Future" (40th anniversary issue), *Administrative Science Quarterly* 41, 2 (1996), pp. 241–251.

reason for the noncalculative direction is that leadership usually involves certain responsibility or costs. Hence, the less calculative that one is about leading others, the less one would wish to avoid leadership roles" (p. 481).[13] Before proceeding with this chapter, turn to the self-assessment on p. 73 and consider your own motivation to lead.

Judge, Bono, Ilies, and Gerhardt (2002) provide us with another look at leader traits and leadership—emergence and performance. Prior to their work, Judge and his colleagues note that several previous literature reviews attempted to identify meaningful leader traits. Although there is some overlap in the traits identified (e.g., self-confidence, integrity, adjustment, sociability) there is a great deal of inconsistency. Part of this inconsistency in research findings suggests, as noted by Stogdill back in 1948, that the importance of some traits are situationally specific. Judge and his colleagues also note that some of this inconsistency may be due to the lack of standardization for the meaning and measurement of different traits, and more importantly, to the absence of a taxonomic structure for classifying and organizing the traits.

In recent years scholars interested in personality have come to believe that the Big Five personality taxonomy can be used to describe the most salient aspects of personality. Each of the Big Five personality dimensions (e.g., neuroticism, extraversion, openness to experience, agreeableness, and conscientiousness) captures several personality traits. Openness to experience, for example, represents imaginative, nonconforming, unconventional, and autonomous thinking, while extraversion suggests sociable, assertive, active behavior, and positive affect.

In the second reading in this chapter, Judge and his colleagues (2002) provide us with a recent meta-analysis of personality and leadership, employing the Big Five model. They note that "the five-factor model had a multiple correlation of .48 with leadership, indicating strong support for the leader trait perspective when traits are organized according to the five-factor model (p. 765)."[14]

Both the Kirkpatrick and Locke and the Judge, Bono, Ilis, and Gerhardt (2002) readings cause us to ask, From where do these traits stem? Do they provide support for the great person theory of leadership? Are leaders born or made? Arvey, Rotundo, Johnson, and McGue (2002) provide valuable insight into that question based on evidence that stems from the University of Minnesota Twin Studies.[15] Arvey and his colleagues note that prior to their work, there was only one other study (cf. Johnson, Vernon, McCarthy, Molson, Harris, & Jang, 1998)[16] that explored the genetic-leadership linkage. In that study they found that 48 to 59 percent of the variance in the transactional and transformational dimensions of leadership was associated with genetic factors. On the basis of the Minnesota Twin Studies, Arvey et al. (2002) note that identical (monozogotic) twins held significantly more leadership positions than had fraternal (dizogotic) twins. In addition they note that 39 percent of the variance in the leadership factor was accounted for by genetic (heritability) factors. They conclude that the question as to whether leaders are born or made is probably a red herring. They base this conclusion on the observation that while genetics accounts for a large and significant portion of the variance in leadership activity, *empirical evidence clearly establishes an important role for environmental factors.*

---

[13] K. Y. Chan & F. Drasgow, "Toward a Theory of Individual Differences and Leadership: Understanding the Motivation to Lead," *Journal of Applied Psychology* 86 (2001), pp. 481–498.

[14] T. A. Judge, J. E. Bono, R. Ilies, & M. W. Gerhardt, "Personality and Leadership: A Qualitative and Quantitative Review," *Journal of Applied Psychology* 87 (2002), pp. 765–780.

[15] R. Arvey, M. Rotundo, W. Johnson, & M. McGue, *Leaders Born or Made, or a Red Herring? The Determinants of Leadership: The Role of Genetic, Personality and Cognitive Factors* (Minneapolis: University of Minnesota, Industrial Relations Research Center Working Paper, 2002).

[16] A. M. Johnson, P. A. Veron, J. M. McCarthy, J. A., Harris, & K. J. Jang, "Nature vs Nurture: Are leaders born or made? A behavior genetic investigation of leadership style. *Twin Research,*" 1 (1998), pp. 216–223.

FIGURE 3.1
**The Leadership
Process: Leader
Traits**

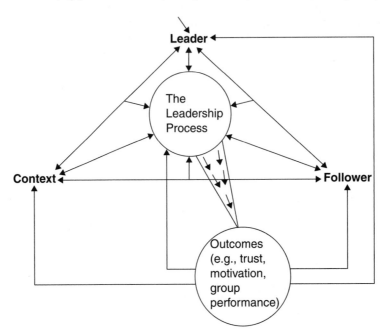

Returning to our leadership process model (see Figure 3.1), we see that the discussion of traits provides further insight into the leadership process through an expanded understanding of the leader.

Finally, it was Stodgill (1948) who suggested that leadership unfolds as a working relationship. Similarly, Kirkpatrick and Locke (1991) concluded that those with the key leadership traits are more likely to engage in the behaviors associated with leadership than those individuals who possess these traits to a lesser degree. These observations lead to a new question: What are the behaviors associated with leadership? The readings in Chapter 7 ask, What is it that effective leaders "do" as behaviors? What is leadership? Smircich and Morgan (1982), authors of Reading 6 (in Chapter 1), provided us with partial insight into those questions when they suggested leaders manage meaning and shape reality for others.

Job Affect

Instructions: For each of the following items, please indicate how you felt at work during the past week.

	Very Slightly or Not at All				Very Much
1. Active	1	2	3	4	5
2. Calm	1	2	3	4	5
3. Distressed	1	2	3	4	5
4. Sleepy	1	2	3	4	5
5. Strong	1	2	3	4	5
6. Excited	1	2	3	4	5
7. Scornful	1	2	3	4	5
8. Hostile	1	2	3	4	5
9. Enthusiastic	1	2	3	4	5
10. Dull	1	2	3	4	5
11. Fearful	1	2	3	4	5
12. Relaxed	1	2	3	4	5
13. Peppy	1	2	3	4	5
14. At rest	1	2	3	4	5
15. Nervous	1	2	3	4	5
16. Drowsy	1	2	3	4	5
17. Elated	1	2	3	4	5
18. Placid	1	2	3	4	5
19. Jittery	1	2	3	4	5
20. Sluggish	1	2	3	4	5

Scoring:

1. Subtract your response to each of the following items from 6: 2 (calm), 4 (sleepy), 10 (dull), 12 (relaxed), 14 (at rest), 16 (drowsy), 18 (placid), and 20 (sluggish).

2. *Positive job affect* is reflected with two scores, the first signaling general and positive affect and the second denoting "high positive affect."

   a. Positive job affect—Where appropriate, employing your adjusted response scores, sum your response scores to the following items: 1, 4, 5, 6, 9, 10, 13, 16, 17, and 20; divide by 10; and enter that score here _____.

   b. High positive job affect—Where appropriate, employing your adjusted response scores, sum your response scores to the following items: 1, 5, 6, 9, 13, and 17; divide by 6; and enter that score here _____.

3. *Negative job affect* is reflected with two scores, the first signaling general and negative affect and the second denoting "high negative affect."

   a. Negative job affect—Where appropriate, employing your adjusted response scores, sum your response scores to the following items: 2, 3, 7, 8, 11, 12, 14, 15, 18, and 19; divide by 10; and enter that score here _____.

   b. High negative job affect—Where appropriate, employing your adjusted response scores, sum your response scores to the following items: 3, 7, 8, 11, 15, and 19; divide by 6; and enter that score here _____.

Interpretation: The job affect test is designed to measure "mood at work"—that is, how people felt at work, while on the job, during the past week. A high score (4 and greater) implies a high level of affect (i.e., positive, negative, high positive, and high negative). A low score (2 or less) implies a low level of affect (i.e., positive, negative, high positive, and high negative).

Mood at work, as assessed here, is a state-based condition. As a state-based condition, people can express different moods, depending upon the state to which they are exposed.

Mood can, however, be relatively stable across emotional states (situations) and across time. It has been noted that some people have a "sunny" disposition—seeing the glass as almost full as opposed to almost empty. Others nearly always appear gloomy. Affectivity (to be distinguished

(Continued)

from affect as measured by this instrument) essentially reflects an individual's *pervasive mood.* Negative affectivity and high negative affectivity reflect negative emotionality. Those people are distressed, scornful, hostile, fearful, nervous, and jittery. Positive affectivity and high positive affectivity reflect positive emotionality. These individuals tend to feel active, excited, enthusiastic, peppy, and strong. Leaders who have strong positive affect (and/or affectivity) are characterized as possessing an air of confidence, competency, and optimism. They tend to transfer their energy to others and to be characterized as leaders of cohesive, productive work groups.

Source: M. J. Burke, A. P. Brief, J. M. George, L. Roberson, and J. Webster, Measuring Affect at Work: Confirmatory Analyses of Competing Mood Structures with Conceptual Linkage to Cortical Regulatory Systems, *Journal of Personality and Social Psychology* 57 (1989), pp. 1091–1102. Copyright 1989, American Psychological Association, adapted with permission of publisher and A. P. Brief.

Motivation to Lead

Instructions: These statements focus on your motivation to lead. For each of the following items indicate the degree to which you agree or disagree with the statement.

Strongly Disagree	Disagree	Slightly Disagree	Neither Agree nor Disagree	Slightly Agree	Agree	Strongly Agree
1	2	3	4	5	6	7

Item

1. Most of the time, I prefer being a leader rather than a follower when working in a group.
2. I am the type of person who is not interested to lead others.
3. I am definitely not a leader by nature.
4. I am the type of person who likes to be in charge of others.
5 I believe I can contribute more to a group if I am a follower rather than a leader.
6. I usually want to be the leader in the groups that I work in.
7. I am the type who would actively support a leader but prefers not to be appointed as leader.
8. I have a tendency to take charge in most groups or teams that I work in.
9. I am seldom reluctant to be the leader of a group.
10. I am only interested to lead a group if there are clear advantages for me.
11. I will never agree to lead if I cannot see any benefits from accepting that role.
12. I would only agree to be a group leader if I know I can benefit from that role.
13. I would agree to lead others even if there are no special rewards or benefits with that role.
14. I would want to know "what's in it for me" if I am going to agree to lead a group.
15. I never expect to get more privileges if I agree to lead a group.
16. If I agree to lead a group, I would never expect any advantages or special benefits.
17. I have more of my own problems to worry about than to be concerned about the rest of the group.
18. Leading others is really more of a dirty job rather than an honorable one.
19. I feel that I have a duty to lead others if I am asked.
20. I agree to lead whenever I am asked or nominated by the other members.
21. I was taught to believe in the value of leading others.
22. It is appropriate for people to accept leadership roles or positions when they are asked.
23. I have been taught that I should always volunteer to lead others if I can.
24. It is not right to decline leadership roles.
25. It is an honor and privilege to be asked to lead.
26. People should volunteer to lead rather than wait for others to ask or vote for them.
27. I would never agree to lead just because others voted for me.

Scoring: Sum your response to items 1 through 9 and divide by 9. This is your affective identity–based motivation-to-lead score. Record that number here ____. Next, sum your response to items 10 through 18 and divide by 9. This is your noncalculative–based motivation-to-lead score. Record that number here ____. Finally, sum your response to items 19 through 27 and divide that score by 9. Record that number here ____. This is your social normative–based motivation to lead score.

Interpretation: A score of 6 or above for each of the three motivation-to-lead dimensions indicates a strong motivation to lead based on that factor. A score of 2 or less indicates a weak motivation to lead based on the specified factor.

Source: K. Y. Chan and F. Drasgow, "Toward a Theory of Individual Differences and Leadership: Understanding the Motivation to Lead," *Journal of Applied Psychology* 86 (2001), p. 486. Reprinted with permission. Copyright American Psychological Association, 2001.

Reading 10

Leadership: Do Traits Matter?

S. A. Kirkpatrick and E. A. Locke
University of Maryland

Few issues have a more controversial history than leadership traits and characteristics. In the nineteenth and early twentieth centuries, "great man" leadership theories were highly popular. These theories asserted that leadership qualities were inherited, especially by people from the upper class. Great men were born, not made (in those days, virtually all business leaders were men). Today, great man theories are a popular foil for so-called superior models. To make the new models plausible, the "great men" are endowed with negative as well as positive traits. In a recent issue of the *Harvard Business Review,* for example, Slater and Bennis write,

> The passing years have . . . given the coup de grace to another force that has retarded democratization—the "great man" who with brilliance and farsightedness could preside with dictatorial powers as the head of a growing organization.[1]

Such great men, argue Slater and Bennis, become "outmoded" and dead hands on "the flexibility and growth of the organization." Under the new democratic model, they argue, "the individual *is* of relatively little significance."

Early in the twentieth century, the great man theories evolved into trait theories. ("Trait" is used broadly here to refer to people's general characteristics, including capacities, motives, or patterns of behavior.) Trait theories did not make assumptions about whether leadership traits were inherited or acquired. They simply asserted that leaders' characteristics are different from nonleaders'. Traits such as height, weight, and physique are heavily dependent on heredity, whereas others such as knowledge of the industry are dependent on experience and learning.

The trait view was brought into question during the mid-century when a prominent theorist, Ralph Stogdill, after a thorough review of the literature concluded that "a person does not become a leader by virtue of the possession of some combination of traits."[2] Stogdill believed this because

Source: Edited and reprinted with permission from *Academy of Management Executive* 5, 2 (1991), pp. 48–60.

the research showed that no traits were universally associated with effective leadership and that situational factors were also influential. For example, military leaders do not have traits identical to those of business leaders.

Since Stogdill's early review, trait theory has made a comeback, though in altered form. Recent research, using a variety of methods, has made it clear that successful leaders are not like other people. The evidence indicates that there are certain core traits which significantly contribute to business leaders' success.

Traits *alone,* however, are not sufficient for successful business leadership—they are only a precondition. Leaders who possess the requisite traits must take certain *actions* to be successful (e.g. formulating a vision, role modeling, setting goals). Possessing the appropriate traits only makes it more likely that such actions will be taken and be successful. After summarizing the core leadership traits, we will discuss these important actions and the managerial implications.

THE EVIDENCE: TRAITS DO MATTER

The evidence shows that traits do matter. Six traits on which leaders differ from nonleaders include drive, the desire to lead, honesty/integrity, self-confidence, cognitive ability, and knowledge of the business.[3]

DRIVE

The first trait is labeled "drive," which is not to be confused with physical need deprivation. We use the term to refer to a constellation of traits and motives reflecting a high-effort level. Five aspects of drive include achievement motivation, ambition, energy, tenacity, and initiative.

Achievement

Leaders have a relatively high desire for achievement. The need for achievement is an important motive among effective leaders and even more important among successful entrepreneurs. High achievers obtain satisfaction from successfully completing challenging tasks, attaining standards of excellence, and developing better ways of doing things. To work their way up to the top of the organization, leaders must have a desire to complete challenging assignments and projects. This also allows the leader to gain technical expertise, both through education and work experience, and to initiate and follow through with organizational changes. . . .

Ambition

Leaders are very ambitious about their work and careers and have a desire to get ahead. To advance, leaders actively take steps to demonstrate their drive and determination. Ambition impels leaders to set hard, challenging goals for themselves and their organizations. Walt Disney, founder of Walt Disney Productions, had a "dogged determination to succeed," and C. E. Woolman of Delta Air Lines had "inexhaustible ambition."

Effective leaders are more ambitious than nonleaders. In their 20-year study, psychologists Ann Howard and Douglas Bray found that among a sample of managers at AT&T, ambition, specifically the desire for advancement, was the strongest predictor of success 20 years later. . . .

Energy

To sustain a high achievement drive and get ahead, leaders must have a lot of energy. Working long, intense work weeks (and many weekends) for many years requires an individual to have physical, mental, and emotional vitality.

Leaders are more likely than nonleaders to have a high level of energy and stamina and to be generally active, lively, and often restless. Leaders have been characterized as "electric, vigorous, active, full of life" as well as possessing the "physical vitality to maintain a steadily productive work pace."[4] Even at age 70, Sam Walton, founder of Wal-Mart discount stores, still attended Wal-Mart's Saturday morning meeting, a whoop-it-up 7:30 A.M. sales pep rally for 300 managers.

The need for energy is even greater today than in the past, because more companies are expecting all employees, including executives, to spend more time on the road visiting the organization's other locations, customers, and suppliers.

Tenacity

Leaders are better at overcoming obstacles than nonleaders. They have the "capacity to work with distant objects in view" and have a "degree of strength of will or perseverance."[5] Leaders must

be tirelessly persistent in their activities and follow through with their programs. Most organizational change programs take several months to establish and can take many years before the benefits are seen. Leaders must have the drive to stick with these programs, and persistence is needed to ensure that changes are institutionalized. . . .

Persistence, of course, must be used intelligently. Dogged pursuit of an inappropriate strategy can ruin an organization. It is important to persist in the right things. But what are the right things? In today's business climate, they may include the following: satisfying the customer, growth, cost control, innovation, fast response time, and quality, or, in Tom Peters's terms, a constant striving to improve just about everything.

Initiative

Effective leaders are proactive. They make choices and take action that leads to change instead of just reacting to events or waiting for things to happen; that is, they show a high level of initiative. . . .

Instead of sitting "idly by or [waiting] for fate to smile upon them," leaders need to "challenge the process."

Leaders are achievement-oriented, ambitious, energetic, tenacious, and proactive. These same qualities, however, may result in a manager who tries to accomplish everything alone, thereby failing to develop subordinate commitment and responsibility. Effective leaders must not only be full of drive and ambition, they must *want to lead others*.

LEADERSHIP MOTIVATION

Studies show that leaders have a strong desire to lead. Leadership motivation involves the desire to influence and lead others and is often equated with the need for power. People with high leadership motivation think a lot about influencing other people, winning an argument, or being the greater authority. They prefer to be in a leadership rather than subordinate role. The willingness to assume responsibility, which seems to coincide with leadership motivation, is frequently found in leaders. . . .

Sears psychologist Jon Bentz describes successful Sears executives as those who have a "powerful competitive drive for a position of . . . authority . . . [and] the need to be recognized as men of influence."[6] Astronauts John Glenn and Frank Borman built political and business careers out of their early feats as space explorers, while other astronauts did not. Clearly, all astronauts possessed the same opportunities, but it was their personal makeup that caused Glenn and Borman to pursue their ambitions and take on leadership roles.

Psychologist Warren Bennis and colleague Burt Nanus state that power is a leader's currency, or the primary means through which the leader gets things done in the organization. A leader must want to gain the power to exercise influence over others. Also, power is an "expandable pie," not a fixed sum; effective leaders give power to others as a means of increasing their own power. Effective leaders do not see power as something that is competed for but rather as something that can be created and distributed to followers without detracting from their own power. . . .

A manager who was not as successful completed the sentence fragment "Taking orders . . ." with the ending "is easy, for it removes the danger of a bad decision."

Successful leaders must be willing to exercise power over subordinates, tell them what to do, and make appropriate use of positive and negative sanctions. Previous studies have shown inconsistent results regarding dominance as a leadership trait. According to Harvard psychologist David McClelland, this may be because there are two different types of dominance: a personalized power motive, or power lust, and a socialized power motive, or the desire to lead.[7]

Personalized Power Motive

Although a need for power is desirable, the leader's effectiveness depends on what is behind it. A leader with a personalized power motive seeks power as an end in itself. These individuals have little self-control, are often impulsive, and focus on collecting symbols of personal prestige. Acquiring power solely for the sake of dominating others may be based on profound self-doubt. The personalized power motive is concerned with domination of others and leads to dependent, submissive followers.

Socialized Power Motive

In contrast, a leader with a socialized power motive uses power as a means to achieve desired goals, or a vision. Its use is expressed as the ability to develop networks and coalitions, gain cooperation from others, resolve conflicts in a constructive manner, and use role modeling to influence others.

Individuals with a socialized power motive are more emotionally mature than those with a personalized power motive. They exercise power more for the benefit of the whole organization and are less likely to use it for manipulation. These leaders are also less defensive, more willing to take advice from experts, and have a longer-range view. They use their power to build up their organization and make it successful. The socialized power motive takes account of followers' needs and results in empowered, independent followers.

HONESTY AND INTEGRITY

Honesty and integrity are virtues in all individuals but have special significance for leaders. Without these qualities, leadership is undermined. Integrity is the correspondence between word and deed, and honesty refers to being truthful or nondeceitful. The two form the foundation of a trusting relationship between leader and followers.

In his comprehensive review of leadership, psychologist Bernard Bass found that student leaders were rated as more trustworthy and reliable in carrying out responsibilities than followers. Similarly, British organizational psychologists Charles Cox and Cary Cooper's "high flying" (successful) managers preferred to have an open style of management, where they truthfully informed workers about happenings in the company. Morgan McCall and Michael Lombardo of the Center for Creative Leadership found that managers who reached the top were more likely to follow the following formula: "I will do exactly what I say I will do when I say I will do it. If I change my mind, I will tell you well in advance so you will not be harmed by my actions."[8]

Successful leaders are open with their followers, but also discreet and do not violate confidences or carelessly divulge potentially harmful information. One subordinate in a study by Harvard's John Gabarro made the following remark about his new president: "He was so consistent in what he said and did, it was easy to trust him." Another subordinate remarked about an unsuccessful leader, "How can I rely on him if I can't count on him consistently?"[9]

Professors James Kouzes, Barry Posner, and W.H. Schmidt asked 1,500 managers "What values do you look for and admire in your supervisors?" Integrity (being truthful and trustworthy, and having character and conviction) was the most frequently mentioned characteristic. Kouzes and Posner conclude:

> Honesty is absolutely essential to leadership. After all, if we are willing to follow someone, whether it be into battle or into the boardroom, we first want to assure ourselves that the person is worthy of our trust. We want to know that he or she is being truthful, ethical, and principled. We want to be fully confident in the integrity of our leaders.

Effective leaders are credible, with excellent reputations, and high levels of integrity. The following description (from Gabarro's study) by one subordinate of his boss exemplifies the concept of integrity: "By integrity, I don't mean whether he'll rob a bank, or steal from the till. You don't work with people like that. It's whether you sense a person has some basic principles and is willing to stand by them."

Bennis and Nanus warn that today credibility is at a premium, especially since people are better informed, more cautious, and wary of authority and power. Leaders can gain trust by being predictable, consistent, and persistent and by making competent decisions. An honest leader may even be able to overcome lack of expertise, as a subordinate in Gabarro's study illustrates in the following description of his superior: "I don't like a lot of the things he does, but he's basically honest. He's a genuine article and you'll forgive a lot of things because of that. That goes a long way in how much I trust him."

SELF-CONFIDENCE

There are many reasons why a leader needs self-confidence. Being a leader is a very difficult job. A great deal of information must be gathered and processed. A constant series of problems must be solved and decisions made. Followers have to be convinced to pursue specific courses of action. Setbacks have to be overcome. Competing interests have to be satisfied. Risks have to be taken in the face of uncertainty. A person riddled with self-doubt would never be able to take the necessary actions nor command the respect of others.

Self-confidence plays an important role in decision making and in gaining others' trust. Obviously, if the leader is not sure of what decision to make, or expresses a high degree of doubt, then the followers are less likely to trust the leader and be committed to the vision.

Not only is the leader's self-confidence important, but so is others' perception of it. Often, leaders engage in impression management to bolster their image of competence; by projecting self-confidence they arouse followers' self-confidence. Self-confident leaders are also more likely to be assertive and decisive, which gains others' confidence in the decision. This is crucial for effective implementation of the decision. Even when the decision turns out to be a poor one, the self-confident leader admits the mistake and uses it as a learning opportunity, often building trust in the process. . . .

Emotional Stability

Self-confidence helps effective leaders remain even-tempered. They do get excited, such as when delivering an emotionally charged pep talk, but generally do not become angry or enraged. For the most part, as long as the employee did his/her homework, leaders remain composed upon hearing that an employee made a costly mistake. For example, at PepsiCo, an employee who makes a mistake is "safe . . . as long as it's a calculated risk."

Emotional stability is especially important when resolving interpersonal conflicts and when representing the organization. A top executive who impulsively flies off the handle will not foster as much trust and teamwork as an executive who retains emotional control. Describing a superior, one employee in Gabarro's study stated, "He's impulsive and I'm never sure when he'll change signals on me."

Researchers at the Center for Creative Leadership found that leaders are more likely to "derail" if they lack emotional stability and composure. Leaders who derail are less able to handle pressure and more prone to moodiness, angry outbursts, and inconsistent behavior, which undermines their interpersonal relationships with subordinates, peers, and superiors. In contrast, they found the successful leaders to be calm, confident, and predictable during crisis.

Psychologically hardy, self-confident individuals consider stressful events interesting, as opportunities for development, and believe that they can influence the outcome. K. Labich in *Fortune* magazine argued that "By demonstrating grace under pressure, the best leaders inspire those around them to stay calm and act intelligently."[10]

COGNITIVE ABILITY

Leaders must gather, integrate, and interpret enormous amounts of information. These demands are greater than ever today because of rapid technological change. Thus, it is not surprising that leaders need to be intelligent enough to formulate suitable strategies, solve problems, and make correct decisions.

Leaders have often been characterized as being intelligent, but not necessarily brilliant and as being conceptually skilled. Kotter states that a "keen mind" (i.e., strong analytical ability, good judgment, and the capacity to think strategically and multidimensionally) is necessary for effective leadership, and that leadership effectiveness requires "above average intelligence," rather than genius.

An individual's intelligence and the perception of his or her intelligence are two highly related factors. Professors Lord, DeVader, and Alliger concluded that "intelligence is a key characteristic in predicting leadership perceptions."[11] Howard and Bray found that cognitive ability predicted managerial success 20 years later in their AT&T study. Effective managers have been shown to display greater ability to reason both inductively and deductively than ineffective managers.

Intelligence may be a trait that followers look for in a leader. If someone is going to lead, followers want that person to be more capable in *some* respects than they are. Therefore, the follower's perception of cognitive ability in a leader is a source of authority in the leadership relationship.

KNOWLEDGE OF THE BUSINESS

Effective leaders have a high degree of knowledge about the company, industry, and technical matters. For example, Jack Welch, president of GE, has a PhD in engineering; George Hatsopolous of Thermo Electron Corporation, in the years preceding the OPEC boycott, had both the business knowledge of the impending need for energy-efficient appliances and the technical knowledge of thermodynamics to create more efficient gas furnaces. Technical expertise enables the leader to understand the concerns of subordinates regarding technical issues. Harvard Professor John Kotter argues that expertise is more important than formal education.

Effective leaders gather extensive information about the company and the industry. Most of the successful general managers studied by Harvard's Kotter spent their careers in the same industry, while less successful managers lacked industry-specific experiences. Although cognitive ability is needed to gain a thorough understanding of the business, formal education is not a requirement. Only 40 percent of the business leaders studied by Bennis and Nanus had business degrees. In-depth knowledge of the organization and industry allows effective leaders to make well-informed decisions and to understand the implications of those decisions.

OTHER TRAITS

Charisma, creativity/originality, and flexibility are three traits with less clear-cut evidence of their importance to leadership.[12] Effective leaders may have charisma; however, this trait may only be important for political leaders. Effective leaders also may be more creative than nonleaders, but there is no consistent research demonstrating

this. Flexibility or adaptiveness may be important traits for a leader in today's turbulent environment. Leaders must be able to make decisions and solve problems quickly and initiate and foster change.

There may be other important traits needed for effective leadership; however, we believe that the first six that we discussed are the core traits. . . .

MANAGEMENT IMPLICATIONS

Individuals can be *selected* either from outside the organization or from within non- or lower-managerial ranks based on their possession of traits that are less changeable or trainable. Cognitive ability (not to be confused with knowledge) is probably the least trainable of the six traits. Drive is fairly constant over time although it can change; it is observable in employees assuming they are given enough autonomy and responsibility to show what they can do. The desire to lead is more difficult to judge in new hires who may have had little opportunity for leadership early in life. It can be observed at lower levels of management and by observing people in assessment center exercises.

Two other traits can be developed through experience and *training*. Knowledge of the industry and technical knowledge come from formal training, job experience, and a mentally active approach toward new opportunities for learning. Planned job rotation can facilitate such growth. Self-confidence is both general and task-specific. People differ in their general confidence in mastering life's challenges, but task-specific self-confidence comes from mastering the various skills that leadership requires as well as the technical and strategic challenges of the industry. Such confidence parallels the individual's growth in knowledge.

Honesty does not require skill building; it is a virtue one achieves or rejects by choice. Organizations should look with extreme skepticism at any employee who behaves dishonestly or lacks integrity, and should certainly not reward dishonesty in any form, especially not with a promotion. The key role models for honest behavior are those at the top. On this issue, organizations get what they model, not what they preach.

CONCLUSIONS

Regardless of whether leaders are born or made or some combination of both, it is unequivocally clear that *leaders are not like other people*. Leaders do not have to be great men or women by being intellectual geniuses or omniscient prophets to succeed, but they do need to have the "right stuff," and this stuff is not equally present in all people. Leadership is a demanding, unrelenting job with enormous pressures and grave responsibilities. It would be a profound disservice to leaders to suggest that they are ordinary people who happened to be in the right place at the right time. Maybe the place matters, but it takes a special kind of person to master the challenges of opportunity. Let us not only give credit, but also use the knowledge we have to select and train our future leaders effectively. We believe that in the realm of leadership (and in every other realm), the individual *does* matter.

Notes

1. P. Slater and W. G. Bennis, "Democracy Is Inevitable," *Harvard Business Review,* Sept–Oct, 1990, 170 and 171. For a summary of trait theories, see R. M. Stogdill's *Handbook of Leadership* (New York: Free Press, 1974). For reviews and studies of leadership traits, see R. E. Boyatzis, *The Competent Manager* (New York: Wiley & Sons, 1982); C. J. Cox and C. L. Cooper, *High Flyers: An Anatomy of Managerial Success* (Oxford: Basil Blackwell); G. A. Yukl, *Leadership in Organizations* (Englewood Cliffs, NJ: Prentice Hall, 1989), Chapter 9.

2. R. M. Stogdill, "Personal Factors Associated with Leadership: A Survey of the Literature," *Journal of Psychology,* 1948, 25, 64.

3. See the following sources for evidence and further information concerning each trait: 1) drive: B. M. Bass's *Handbook of Leadership* (New York: The Free Press, 1990); K. G. Smith and J. K. Harrison, "In Search of Excellent Leaders" (in W. D. Guth's *The Handbook of Strategy,* New York: Warren, Gorham, & Lamont, 1986). 2) desire to lead: V. J. Bentz, "The Sears Experience in the Investigation Description, and Prediction of Executive Behavior," In F. R. Wickert and D. E. McFarland's *Measuring Executive Effectiveness* (New York: Appleton-Century-Crofts, 1967); J. B. Miner, "Twenty Years of Research on Role-Motivation Theory of Managerial Effectiveness," *Personnel Psychology,* 1978, 31, 739–760. 3) honesty/integrity: Bass, op cit.; W. G. Bennis and B. Nanus, *Leaders: The Strategies for Taking Charge* (New York: Harper & Row, 1985); J. M. Kouzes and B. Z. Posner, *The Leadership Challenge: How to Get Things Done in*

Organizations (San Francisco: Jossey-Bass); T. Peters, *Thriving on Chaos* (New York: Harper & Row, 1987); A. Rand, *For the New Intellectual* (New York: Signet, 1961). 4) self-confidence: Bass, op cit. and A. Bandura, *Social Foundations of Thought and Action: A Social Cognitive Theory* (Englewood Cliffs, NJ: Prentice-Hall). Psychological hardiness is discussed by S. R. Maddi and S. C. Kobasa, *The Hardy Executive: Health under Stress* (Chicago: Dorsey Professional Books, 1984); M. W. McCall, Jr., and M. M. Lombardo, *Off the Track: Why and How Successful Executives Get Derailed* (Technical Report No. 21, Greensboro, NC: Center for Creative Leadership, 1983). 5) cognitive ability: R. G. Lord, C. L. DeVader, and G. M. Alliger, "A Meta-Analysis of the Relation between Personality Traits and Leadership Perceptions: An Application of Validity Generalization Procedures," *Journal of Applied Psychology,* 1986; 61, 402–410; A. Howard and D. W. Bray, *Managerial Lives in Transition: Advancing Age and Changing Times* (New York: Guilford Press, 198). 6) knowledge of the business: Bennis and Nanus, op. cit.; J. P. Kotter, *The General Managers* (New York: MacMillan); Smith and Harrison, op. cit.

4. From Kouzes and Posner, op. cit., pp. 122 and V. J. Bentz, op. cit. The Sam Walton quote is from J. Huey, "Wal-Mart: Will It Take Over the World?" *Fortune,* January 30, 1989, 52–59.

5. From Bass, op. cit.

6. From Bentz, op. cit.

7. The distinction between a personalized and a socialized power motive is made by D. C. McClelland, "N-Achievement and Entrepreneurship: A Longitudinal Study," *Journal of Personality and Social Psychology,* 1965, 1, 389–392. These two power motives are discussed further by Kouzes and Posner, op. cit.

8. From McCall and Lombardo, op. cit.

9. From Gabarro, op. cit.

10. From K. Labich, "The Seven Keys to Business Leadership," *Fortune,* October 24, 1988, 58–66.

11. From Lord, DeVader, and Alliger, op. cit.

12. For research on charisma, see Bass, op. cit., and R. J. House, W. D. Spangler, and J. Woycke, "Personality and charisma in the U.S. presidency: A psychological theory of leadership effectiveness (Wharton School, University of Pennsylvania, 1989, unpublished manuscript), on creativity/originality, see Howard and Bray, op. cit., and A. Zaleznik, *The Managerial Mystique* (New York: Harper and Row, 1989); on flexibility, see Smith and Harrison, op. cit.

Reading 11

Personality and Leadership: A Qualitative and Quantitative Review

Timothy A. Judge
University of Florida

Remus Ilies
University of Florida

Joyce E. Bono
University of Minnesota

Megan W. Gerhardt
University of Iowa

The great Victorian era historian Thomas Carlyle commented that "the history of the world was the biography of great men" (Carlyle, 1907, p. 18). This "great man" hypothesis—that history is shaped by the forces of extraordinary leadership—gave rise to the trait theory of leadership. Like the great man theory, trait theory assumed that leadership depended on the personal qualities of the leader, but unlike the great man theory, it did not necessarily assume that leadership resided solely within the grasp of a few heroic men. Terman's (1904) study is perhaps the earliest on trait theory in applied psychology; other discussions of the trait approach appeared in applied psychology in the 1920s (e.g., Bowden, 1926; Kohs & Irle, 1920). Cowley (1931) summarized well the view of trait theorists in commenting that "the approach to the study of leadership has usually been and perhaps must always be through the study of traits" (p. 144).

Despite this venerable tradition, results of investigations relating personality traits to leadership have been inconsistent and often disappointing. Most reviews of the literature have concluded that the trait approach has fallen out of favor among leadership researchers. As Zaccaro, Foti, and Kenny (1991) noted, "trait explanations of leader emergence are generally regarded with little esteem by leadership theorists" (p. 308). The original source of skepticism with the trait approach is often attributed to Stogdill's (1948) influential review. Although Stogdill did find

some consistent relations, he concluded "The findings suggest that leadership is not a matter of passive status or of the mere possession of some combination of traits" (Stogdill, 1948, p. 66). As Bass (1990) noted, after Stogdill's (1948) review, "situation-specific analyses took over, in fact, dominating the field" (p. 59). Indeed, Hughes, Ginnett, and Curphy (1996) and Yukl and Van Fleet (1992) commented that any trait's effect on leadership behavior will depend on the situation. Even today, with the renewed interest in dispositional explanations of attitudes and behaviors, there remains pessimism about the relationship of personality variables to leadership. Conger and Kanungo (1998) described the trait approach as "too simplistic" (p. 38). House and Aditya (1997) concluded, "It appeared . . . that there were few, if any, universal traits associated with effective leadership. Consequently, there developed among the community of leadership scholars near consensus that the search for universal traits was futile" (p. 410).

Notwithstanding these stark assessments, all of the aforementioned reviews uncovered some traits that appeared to be related to leadership emergence or effectiveness. Table 1 provides the results of previous qualitative reviews of the leader trait perspective. . . .

Several aspects of the results in Table 1 are noteworthy. It is clear there is some overlap in the traits identified by the reviews. For example, self-confidence appears in all but two of the reviews, and other traits (adjustment, sociability, integrity) appear in multiple reviews. On the other hand, despite some agreement, the reviews are not overly consistent. C. R. Anderson and Schneier (1978)

TABLE 1   Past Qualitative Reviews of the Traits of Effective or Emergent Leaders

Daft (1999)	Stogdill (1948)	R. Hogan et al. (1994)	House & Aditya (1997)	Mann (1959)
Alertness	Dependability	Surgency	Achievement motivation	Adjustment
Originality, creativity	Sociability	Agreeableness	Prosocial influence motivation	Extraversion
Personal integrity	Initiative	Conscientiousness	Adjustment	Dominance
Self-confidence	Persistence	Emotional stability	Self-confidence	Masculinity
	Self-confidence			Conservatism
	Alertness			
	Cooperativeness			
	Adaptability			

Northouse (1997)	Bass (1990)	Yukl (1998)	Kirkpatrick & Locke (1991)	Yukl & Van Fleet (1992)
Self-confidence	Adjustment	Energy level and stress tolerance	Drive (achievement, ambition, energy, tenacity, initiative)	Emotional maturity
Determination	Adaptability	Self-confidence	Honesty/integrity	Integrity
Integrity	Aggressiveness	Internal locus of control	Self-confidence (emotional stability)	Self-confidence
Sociability	Alertness	Emotional maturity		High energy level
	Ascendance, dominance	Personal integrity		Stress tolerance
	Emotional balance, control	Socialized power motivation		
	Independence, nonconformity	Achievement orientation		
	Originality, creativity	Low need for affiliation		
	Integrity			
	Self-confidence			

commented, "These searches seemed to result in a myriad of characteristics, few of which recurred consistently across studies" (p. 690). For example, (a) masculinity emerged in two reviews (Mann, 1959; Stogdill, 1948) and is absent in all others, (b) dominance emerged as an important leadership trait in some reviews (e.g., Mann, 1959) but was absent in others, (c) four traits (persistence, initiative, responsibility, and insight) surfaced in Stogdill's (1948, 1974) reviews but were absent in all others, and (d) some traits appeared in only one review (e.g., alertness [Stogdill, 1948]; drive [Kirkpatrick & Locke, 1991]).

It is telling that, except for self-confidence, no trait emerged as related to leadership in a majority of these reviews.

Even when the same traits are included in these reviews, they are often assumed to be distinct and thus are labeled differently. For example, adjustment and self-confidence are indicators of the same construct—emotional stability (Hogan, Curphy, & Hogan, 1994)—yet were reviewed as distinct traits in two reviews (Mann, 1959; Stogdill, 1948). Similarly, persistence and determination are indicators of Conscientiousness (Costa, McCrae, & Dye, 1991) yet were studied separately as well (Northouse, 1997; Stogdill, 1948). One of the biggest problems in past research relating personality to leadership is the lack of a structure in describing personality, leading to a wide range of traits being investigated under different labels. As Hughes et al. (1996) noted, "the labeling dilemma made it almost impossible to find consistent relationships between personality and leadership even when they really existed" (p. 179). House and Aditya (1997) commented, "One problem with early trait research was that there was little empirically substantiated personality theory to guide the search for leadership traits" (p. 410). . . .

The purpose of the remainder of this article is to provide a quantitative review of the relationship between personality and leadership. One possible reason for the inconsistent and disappointing results from previous reviews is that, until recently, we have lacked a taxonomic structure for classifying and organizing traits. Accordingly, in this study we use the five-factor model of personality as an organizing framework to estimate relations between personality and leadership. Furthermore, we estimate relations involving multiple criteria. Lord et al. (1986) made a distinction between leadership emergence and leadership effectiveness. Accordingly, we estimate personality–leadership relations according to two criteria—leadership emergence and leader effectiveness. Finally, because there is much concern in personality research about whether broad or specific personality traits best predict criteria (Block, 1995; Hough, 1992), we also investigate the relative predictive power of broad versus specific measures of the Big Five traits. Before exploring relations between personality traits and leadership, we provide a brief review of the five-factor model and of the dimensionality of leadership.

FIVE-FACTOR MODEL OF PERSONALITY

Consensus is emerging that a five-factor model of personality (often termed the *Big Five*) can be used to describe the most salient aspects of personality (Goldberg, 1990). The first researchers to replicate the five-factor structure were Norman (1963) and Tupes and Christal (1961), who are generally credited with founding the five-factor model. The five-factor structure has been recaptured through analyses of trait adjectives in various languages, factor analytic studies of existing personality inventories, and decisions regarding the dimensionality of existing measures made by expert judges (McCrae & John, 1992). The cross cultural generalizability of the five-factor structure has been established through research in many countries (McCrae & Costa, 1997). Evidence indicates that the Big Five are heritable and stable over time (Costa & McCrae, 1988; Digman, 1989).

The dimensions comprising the five-factor model are Neuroticism, Extraversion, Openness to Experience, Agreeableness, and Conscientiousness. Neuroticism represents the tendency to exhibit poor emotional adjustment and experience negative affects, such as anxiety, insecurity, and hostility. Extraversion represents the tendency to be sociable, assertive, active and to experience positive affects, such as energy and zeal. Openness to Experience is the disposition to be imaginative, nonconforming, unconventional, and autonomous. Agreeableness is the tendency to be trusting, compliant, caring, and gentle. Conscientiousness is comprised of two related facets: achievement and dependability. . . .

LEADERSHIP CRITERIA

. . . . Conceptually, leadership effectiveness and emergence represent two levels of analysis. Leadership emergence is a within-group phenomenon, as evidenced by many early studies of leadership that were conducted in groups with no formal leader (see Mann's [1959] review)—that is, a leader emerged from within a group. In contrast, leadership effectiveness, as defined above, represents a between-groups phenomenon. Effectiveness refers to a leader's ability to influence his or her subordinates. Therefore, the individual being evaluated must first be a leader. Subsequent evaluation of that leader's effectiveness implies a comparison to the performance of other leaders, generally (by necessity) in different groups. Although leader emergence and leadership effectiveness are distinct in concept, in practice the criteria sometimes become blurred, particularly when measured perceptually (House & Podsakoff, 1994). Nonetheless, in the development of our hypotheses, we distinguish ratings of a leader's effectiveness from perceptions of leader emergence.

RELATIONSHIP OF BIG FIVE TRAITS TO LEADERSHIP

Below we consider possible linkages between personality and leadership. We organize this discussion according to each of the Big Five traits. We then consider overall relationships between the Big Five traits and leadership and the issue of the relationship of lower order personality constructs to leadership.

Neuroticism

Lord et al.'s (1986) meta-analysis revealed a corrected correlation of .24 between measures of adjustment and leadership perceptions on the basis of a relatively small number of studies cumulated in their analysis. This estimate, however, could not be distinguished from zero. Bass (1990), in his review, indicated that almost all studies on the relationship of self-confidence—indicating low Neuroticism—to leadership "were uniform in the positive direction of their findings" (p. 69). Hill and Ritchie (1977) suggested that self-esteem—another indicator of low Neuroticism (Eysenck, 1990)—is predictive of leadership: "It appears that there is convincing evidence for the inclusion of self-esteem as an important trait of both superior and subordinate in analyzing leadership effectiveness" (Hill & Ritchie, 1977, p. 499). Evidence also indicates that neurotic individuals are less likely to be perceived as leaders (R. Hogan et al., 1994). In light of this evidence and these arguments, we would expect that Neuroticism is negatively related to leader emergence and leadership effectiveness.

Extraversion

In Bass's (1990) review, results linking Extraversion to leadership were inconsistent. In early studies (those completed between 1904 and 1947), Extraversion was positively related to leadership in five studies and negatively related in three, and there was no relation in four. Other reviews, however, suggest that extraverts should be more likely to emerge as leaders in groups. Extraversion is strongly related to social leadership (Costa & McCrae, 1988) and, according to Watson and Clark (1997), to leader emergence in groups. R. Hogan et al. (1994) noted that Extraversion is related to being perceived as leaderlike. Extraverts tend to be energetic, lively people. Kirkpatrick and Locke (1991) commented, "Leaders are more likely than nonleaders to have a high level of energy and stamina and to be generally active, lively, and often restless" (p. 50). Adjectives used to describe individuals who emerged as leaders in leaderless group discussions included active, assertive, energetic, and not silent or withdrawn (Gough, 1988). These are the characteristics of extraverts. Indeed, Gough (1990) found that both of the major facets of Extraversion—dominance and sociability—were related to self and peer ratings of leadership. Considering this evidence, Extraversion should be positively related to both leader emergence and leadership effectiveness, although somewhat more strongly to leader emergence.

Openness

When Bass (1990) listed the traits that were the best correlates of leadership, originality—a clear hallmark of Openness—topped the list. Openness correlates with divergent thinking (McCrae, 1987) and is strongly related to both personality-based and behavioral measures of creativity (Feist, 1998; McCrae & Costa, 1997). Creativity appears to be an important skill of effective leaders. Creativity was one of the skills contained in Yukl's (1998) summary of the skills of leaders, which was based on Stogdill's (1974) earlier review. Research indicates that creativity is linked to effective leadership (see Sosik, Kahai, & Avolio, 1998), suggesting that open individuals are more likely to emerge as leaders and be effective leaders.

Agreeableness

Conceptually, the link between Agreeableness and leadership is ambiguous. On the one hand, cooperativeness tends to be related to leadership (Bass, 1990), and Zaccaro et al. (1991) found that interpersonal sensitivity was related to leadership. That altruism, tact, and sensitivity are hallmarks of an agreeable personality would suggest that leaders should be more agreeable. On the other hand, agreeable individuals are likely to be modest (Goldberg, 1990), and leaders tend not to be excessively modest (Bass, 1990, p. 70). Furthermore,

although it often is considered to be part of Extraversion (Watson & Clark, 1997), many scholars consider affiliation to be an indicator of Agreeableness (Piedmont, McCrae, & Costa, 1991). Need for affiliation appears to be negatively related to leadership (Yukl, 1998). These factors suggest that Agreeableness would be negatively related to leadership. In light of these conflicting justifications, the possible relationship between Agreeableness and leadership is ambiguous.

Conscientiousness

Bass (1990) commented, "Task competence results in attempts to lead that are more likely to result in success for the leader, effectiveness for the group, and reinforcement of the tendencies" (p. 109). We know that Conscientiousness is related to overall job performance (Barrick & Mount, 1991), and this suggests that Conscientiousness will be related to leader effectiveness. Furthermore, initiative and persistence are related to leadership. As Kirkpatrick and Locke (1991) noted, "leaders must be tirelessly persistent in their activities and follow through with their programs" (p. 51). Because conscientious individuals have more tenacity and persistence (Goldberg, 1990), we expect that conscientious individuals will be more effective leaders.

Overall Relationships

Similar to meta-analyses involving job performance in which various aspects of performance are combined into an overall estimate (e.g., Barrick & Mount, 1991), we investigated the relationship of the Big Five traits to leadership pooling across the leadership criteria (effectiveness and emergence). As noted earlier, conceptually, leadership effectiveness and emergence are distinct constructs. However, operationally, both are generally measured via ratings or observations of others, which means that both criteria represent individuals' perceptions of leadership. Because there is good reason to believe that Neuroticism, Extraversion, and Openness will be related to multiple leadership criteria, we believe that these traits will display significant (nonzero) relationships with leadership in the combined analysis.

RELEVANCE OF FACETS

One of the most prominent criticisms of the five factor model is that it provides too coarse a description of personality (Block, 1995; Hough, 1992). Although some researchers have argued for fewer than five traits (e.g., Eysenck, 1992), most personality psychologists who criticize the number of factors do so on the basis of too few factors. As Block (1995) noted, "for an adequate understanding of personality, it is necessary to think and measure more specifically than at this global level if behaviors and their mediating variables are to be sufficiently, incisively represented" (p. 208). In industrial–organizational psychology, the relative merits of broad versus specific traits (framed in terms of the bandwidth–fidelity issue) also have been debated with respect to the Big Five traits. Some researchers have argued in favor of traits more numerous or specific than the Big Five. Hough (1992) argued that the Big Five obscures important relations between traits and criteria. She concluded, "If prediction of life outcomes or criteria is important in evaluating personality taxonomies, the Big Five is an inadequate taxonomy of personality constructs" (Hough, 1992, p. 153). Conversely, Ones and Viswesvaran (1996) argued that "broader and richer personality traits will have higher predictive validity than narrower traits" (p. 622).

In accordance with the reasoning of the five-factor model critics, the Big Five traits may be too broad to predict the leadership criteria, thus potentially masking personality–leadership relations. For example, the two main facets of Extraversion—dominance and sociability (referred to by Hogan [e.g., R. Hogan et al., 1994] as ambition and sociability and by Hough, 1992, as potency and affiliation)—may correlate differently with leadership, and each has been investigated separately as predictors of leadership (Bass, 1990). Similarly, the two primary facets of Conscientiousness—achievement and dependability (Mount & Barrick, 1995a)—may display differential relations with leadership. Finally, evidence suggests that self-esteem and locus of control indicate the same factor as Neuroticism (Judge, Locke, Durham, & Kluger, 1998). In fact, Eysenck (1990) considered self-esteem to be a facet of Neuroticism. However, because these traits have usually been investigated separately rather than as facets of Neuroticism, it is important to determine their individual predictive validity. As Vickers (1995) noted, "no study has systematically sampled leadership relevant facets within the general personality domains" (p. 15). Because there are arguments on both sides of the issue, we investigated the relative predictive power of more specific facets of the Big Five traits with respect to (a) dominance and sociability, (b) achievement-orientation and dependability, and (c) self-esteem and locus of control.

METHOD

Literature Search

We conducted our search for studies on the personality–leadership relationship in two stages. In the first search, we entered the keywords *personality* and *leadership* and each of the Big Five traits and *leadership* in the PsycINFO database (1967–1998: at that time, PsycINFO did not contain studies prior to 1966). That search resulted in 998 studies. In addition to the electronic search, we also manually searched journals thought to be particularly relevant (e.g., *Leadership Quarterly*), as well as the most comprehensive reviews of the literature (Bass, 1990; Lord et al., 1986; Mann, 1959; Stogdill, 1974) to identify pre-1967 studies. After examining these abstracts, articles, and dissertations, it became clear that our search excluded some studies in which particular traits were included as keywords but *personality* was not. Accordingly, we searched the PsycINFO database (1887–1999) and used *leadership* and 48 additional traits (e.g., self-esteem, locus of control, modesty, and self-control) known to have been studied in relationship to leadership (Bass, 1990). In both searches, disordered populations were excluded from the searches, as were non-English articles. This search resulted in 1,447 abstracts, many of which we had previously examined (as a part of the original 998). In reviewing all of the abstracts, we eliminated studies in which reports of personality and leadership were not in reference to the same person (i.e., several studies reported a correlation between follower personality and leader behaviors), studies of leadership that were specific to a particularistic criterion (e.g., opinion leadership or fashion leadership), studies without data (e.g., literature reviews or theoretical works), and studies at the group or organizational level of analysis.

For the remaining 263 journal articles and 77 doctoral dissertations, we examined each study to determine whether it contained a personality measure for leaders, a criterion measure, and the data necessary to calculate a correlation between the two. Sixty studies (73 independent samples in all), containing 222 correlations that were classified into one or more of the five-factor traits, met these criteria. Additionally, 20 studies involving self-esteem or locus of control were coded, including two of the 60 five-factor model studies noted above. . . .

RESULTS

As noted earlier, because we believe emergence and effectiveness to be related but distinct criteria, we first conducted an overall analysis combining the two criteria. Results of the meta-analyses relating the Big Five traits to leadership are provided . . . , Extraversion ($\rho = .31$) was the strongest correlate of leadership. Conscientiousness ($\rho = .28$) and then Neuroticism and Openness to Experience ($\rho = -24$ and $\rho = .24$, respectively) displayed the next strongest correlations with leadership. Both the confidence and credibility intervals excluded zero for these traits, indicating that we can be confident that the relationship of four of the Big Five traits to leadership is distinguishable from zero across situations. Finally, Aggreeableness showed a relatively weak correlation with leadership ($\rho = .08$), although the confidence interval excluded zero. Across the five traits, 23.1% of the variance in the correlations was accounted for by statistical artifacts.

. . . . analyses linking the lower order personality traits to leadership. Four traits displayed moderately strong correlations with leadership—sociability, dominance, achievement, and dependability. However, all mean correlations are nonzero (the limits of the 95% CIs excluded zero). Furthermore, when one examines the credibility intervals, only for locus of control did it include zero. Thus, most of the lower order traits included in the analysis had nonzero effects on leadership. Results provided mixed support for differential validity of the lower order traits when compared with the higher order Big Five traits. Locus of control and self-esteem displayed lower correlations with leadership than did Neuroticism (see below), but the indicators of Extraversion (sociability and dominance) and Conscientiousness (achievement and dependability) were somewhat more strongly related to leadership compared with the overall effects. Thus, results for the so-called levels of analysis issue (Mount & Barrick, 1995a) were mixed. . . .

Table 4 displays the meta-analyzed correlations between the Big Five traits and the two leadership criteria. Across criteria, results reveal areas of

TABLE 4 **Relationship Between Big Five Traits and Leadership by Leadership Criteria**

Trait	Leader Emergence		Leadership Effectiveness	
	k	ρ	k	ρ
Neuroticism	30	−.24[a]	18	−.22[a,b]
Extraversion	37	.33[a,b]	23	.24[a,b]
Openness	20	.24[a,b]	17	.24[a,b]
Agreeableness	23	.05	19	.21[a]
Conscientiousness	17	.33[a,b]	18	.16[a]

Note. k = Number of correlations; ρ = estimated corrected correlation.
[a] 95% confidence interval excluding zero.
[b] 80% credibility interval excluding zero.

TABLE 5 **Relationship Between Big Five Traits and Leadership, by Study Setting**

Trait	Business		Government/ Military		Students	
	k	ρ	k	ρ	k	ρ
Neuroticism	9	−.15[a,b]	12	−.23[a]	27	−.27[a,b]
Extraversion	13	.25[a,b]	10	.16[a,b]	37	.40[a,b]
Openness	9	.23[a,b]	6	.06	22	.28[a,b]
Agreeableness	10	−.04	11	−.04	21	.18[a]
Conscientiousness	8	.05	6	.17[a,b]	21	.36[a,b]

Note. k = Number of correlations; ρ = estimated corrected correlation.
[a] 95% confidence interval excluding zero.
[b] 80% credibility interval excluding zero.

consistency and some inconsistencies in the relation of the traits to the criteria. Extraversion and Openness displayed nonzero correlations with both criteria, and most traits (except for Agreeableness and leader emergence) showed nonzero mean correlations with the leadership criteria. Only for Extraversion and Openness, however, did the credibility intervals exclude zero across the criteria. For Conscientiousness, the credibility interval excluded zero for leader emergence but not for leadership effectiveness. For Neuroticism, that pattern was reversed. For neither of the criteria did the credibility intervals for Agreeableness exclude zero.

Another analysis investigated the degree to which personality–leadership relations generalized across different study settings [see Table 5]. We divided the studies into three categories: (a) business—studies completed in business contexts, mostly those involving managers, supervisors, or executives: (b) government or military—studies of military officers or enlisted personnel, or students at military academies; studies of government employees (i.e., teachers, principals); studies of political leaders; (c) students—studies with elementary (10% of correlations), high school (22% of correlations), or college (68% of correlations) students, completed either in natural or laboratory situations. . . . Extraversion was the only trait that generalized across the three settings. Three other traits generalized across two of the three settings. Specifically, the credibility intervals for Neuroticism and Openness excluded zero in business and student settings (but not in military or government settings), whereas for Conscientiousness, the credibility intervals excluded zero in government or military and student settings. All traits were more strongly related to leadership in studies involving students.

Yukl and Van Fleet (1992) argued that leadership research has increasingly taken a holistic

TABLE 6   Regression of Leadership on Big Five Traits

Trait	Leadership Emergence			Leadership Effectiveness			Overall Analysis		
	β/R	SE	t	β/R	SE	t	β/R	SE	t
Neuroticism	−.09	.06	−1.67	−.10	.10	−1.04	−.10	.07	−1.54
Extraversion	.30	.05	5.90*	.18	.09	2.00*	.27	.06	4.30*
Openness	.21	.05	4.06*	.19	.09	2.10*	.21	.06	3.25*
Agreeableness	−.14	.05	−2.66*	.10	.10	1.07	−.09	.07	−1.41
Conscientiousness	.36	.05	6.88*	.12	.09	1.26	.29	.07	4.48*
Multiple R	.53	.05	10.86*	.39	.09	4.55*	.48	.06	8.03*

Note. With the exception of the multiple R estimates in the last row, all estimates in the β/R column are standardized regression coefficients. * $p < .01$.

approach to the study of leader traits (as opposed to focusing on each trait as a separate predictor). Accordingly, we sought to determine the multivariate relationship of the set of Big Five traits to leadership. Using J. E. Hunter's (1992) regression program, we regressed leadership on the Big Five traits. . . .

The regression results are provided in Table 6. As is shown in the table, two traits, Extraversion and Openness, were significantly predictive of leadership across the criteria. However, in two of the three regressions (emergence and overall), Conscientiousness had the highest standardized regression coefficient ($\beta = 36$ and $\beta = 29$, respectively). Neuroticism was not significantly predictive of any of the criteria, and Agreeableness was predictive of just one (emergence), in a negative direction. Perhaps the most meaningful statistics were the strong and significant multiple correlations ($R = .53$, $R = .39$, and $R = .48$ for emergence, effectiveness, and overall, respectively) between the traits and leadership.[4] . . .

DISCUSSION

In reviewing the literature on trait theories of leadership, Bass (1990) noted two pertinent questions: (a) What traits distinguish leaders from other people? and (b) What is the magnitude of those differences? Despite considerable research on this topic in the past century and a previous meta-analytic review (Lord et al., 1986), surprisingly little consensus has emerged in answering the two questions Bass posed in his review. Using the five-factor model as an organizing framework, we sought to answer these questions in a more definitive manner than what has been possible in the past.

[4] Ideally, we would have conducted a hierarchical moderator analysis wherein the type of criterion and study setting are nested within each of the Big Five traits. It was uncommon for studies of leadership emergence to be conducted in business settings and studies of leadership effectiveness to be conducted with student samples. As a result, in many cases there were too few correlations to conduct a fully hierarchical moderator analysis.

The relatively strong multiple correlation ($R = .39–.53$) between the Big Five traits and the leadership criteria suggest that the Big Five typology is a fruitful basis for examining the dispositional predictors of leadership. Given that many reviewers of the literature consider trait theory to be obsolete (Conger & Kanungo, 1998) or only applicable in certain situations (Yukl & Van Fleet, 1992), this is an important finding. Although other reviewers of the literature have argued in favor of trait theory (e.g., Kirkpatrick & Locke, 1991), this study—like Lord et al. (1986)—provides empirical data to substantiate this optimism. In addition to the comprehensiveness of our review, we believe that the primary reason for the more encouraging results is the use of the five-factor model as an organizing framework. As Kenny and Zaccaro (1983) noted, one reason past research failed to identify traits correlated with leadership is that many purportedly different traits were studied, with few of the same traits being investigated across studies. This points to one of the main benefits of the five-factor model. Digman (1989) noted,

> Many reviewers despaired at the lack of organization in the field of personality . . . a great majority —if not all—of our verbally based personality constructs can be housed somewhere within that [five-factor] structure, bringing an orderliness to a field long in need of one. (p. 196)

In using the five-factor model to organize these myriad traits, the present study sheds considerable light on the dispositional basis of leadership.

Turning to the specific traits, Extraversion emerged as the most consistent correlate of leadership. Not only was it the strongest correlate of leadership in the combined analysis, but it also displayed a nonzero effect in all analyses—when controlling for the other Big Five traits—and when broken down in the moderator analysis by criteria and sample type. Thus, these results suggest that Extraversion is the most important trait of leaders and effective leadership. As expected, results also confirmed that Extraversion was more strongly related to leader emergence than to leader effectiveness. If attempted leadership is more likely to result in leader emergence than it is in leadership effectiveness, the results for Extraversion make sense, as both sociable and dominant people are more likely to assert themselves in group situations.

After Extraversion, Conscientiousness and Openness to Experience were the strongest and most consistent correlates of leadership. Conscientiousness displayed the second strongest correlation with leadership and, in the multivariate analysis (by using the N-weighted correlations), was the strongest predictor of leadership in two of the three regressions. Conscientiousness was more strongly related to leader emergence than to leadership effectiveness; the organizing activities of conscientious individuals (e.g., note taking, facilitating processes) may allow such individuals to quickly emerge as leaders.

Of the Big Five traits, Openness to Experience is the most controversial and least understood. One of the problems is that, with a few exceptions, such as creativity and sociopolitical attitudes (cf. McCrae, 1996) [sic]. Openness has not been related to many applied criteria. Openness to Experience does appear to be related to leadership: In business settings, it—along with Extraversion—was the strongest dispositional correlate of leadership. Although the mean correlation for Neuroticism was distinguishable from zero, it failed to emerge as a significant predictor of leadership in the multivariate analysis, which was probably due to the fact that Neuroticism displays the highest average correlation with the other Big Five traits (Ones et al., 1996).

Overall, Agreeableness was the least relevant of the Big Five traits. However, this overall result is masked somewhat by differences in criteria and setting. There were two situations in which Agreeableness was related to leadership—when the criterion was effectiveness and with student samples. Because agreeable individuals tend to be passive and compliant, it makes sense they would be less likely to emerge as leaders. This was found to be particularly true in field studies (business and government or military settings) where the "conforming to others' wishes" (Graziano & Eisenberg, 1997, p. 796) nature of agreeable individuals may be most likely to evidence itself.

Results were equivocal as to whether the Big Five constructs or the lower order traits were better suited to predict leadership. In the cases of Extraversion, the facets were more predictive—

measures of dominance and sociability better predicted leadership than did overall measures of Extraversion. Thus, some support is provided for the relative merits of lower order traits, although two caveats should be kept in mind. First, the test is indirect as almost no studies included measures of both facets along with the five-factor constructs. Thus, it is possible that differences in validity are confounded with other study characteristics. Second, it was not possible to develop facets for every Big Five trait (e.g., Openness to Experience, Agreeableness). Future research should look into this issue further.

Results varied somewhat by criteria and study setting. The Big Five traits predicted leader emergence slightly better than they predicted leadership effectiveness, but the rank order of the traits' influence on leadership varied. For leader emergence, Extraversion and Conscientiousness displayed the strongest correlations; the relationship of Openness to Experience to leader emergence also generalized across studies. For leadership effectiveness, three traits (Neuroticism, Extraversion, and Openness) displayed correlations that generalized across studies, and whereas the correlations involving Agreeableness and Conscientiousness were more variable across studies, the mean correlations were nonzero and moderate in magnitude ($\rho = .21$ and $\rho = .16$, respectively).

The Big Five traits predicted student leadership better than leadership in government or military settings (business settings were somewhat in between). Personality may have better predicted student leadership because, in many of the studies that we reviewed, the situations were relatively unstructured with few rules or formally defined roles (e.g., leader emergence in teams of students in an introduction to psychology class or election of dormitory leaders of students in a residence hall). As House, Shane, and Herold (1996) noted, weak situations allow dispositional forces to be more powerful. By the same token, most individuals would consider government organizations to be relatively bureaucratic and military organizations to be rule oriented, which might suppress dispositional effects.

There is a second reason why the Big Five traits may have predicted leadership emergence and student leadership more strongly than they predicted leadership effectiveness and leadership in business, government, or the military. It is in student situations, where student participants in group exercises are being rated on the extent to which they emerged as leaders, that individuals' implicit leadership theories would be expected to have the greatest influence. Thus, it is possible that in both of these situations (students and leadership emergence) the relations we found between personality and leadership reflect, at least in part, individuals' naive conceptions of leadership.

Future Research

The results of this meta-analysis show that, overall, Extraversion, Conscientiousness, Openness, and Neuroticism are useful traits in relation to leadership. Collectively, the results provide support for the relevance of the five-factor model in leadership research. Previous research notwithstanding, however, we have a relatively poor idea of not only which traits are relevant, but why. Is Neuroticism negatively related to leadership because neurotic individuals are less likely to attempt leadership, because they are less inspirational, or because they have lower expectations of themselves or others? Similarly, Extraversion may be related to leadership because extraverts talk more, and talking is strongly related to emergent leadership (Bass, 1990). Alternatively, it may be that individuals implicitly expect leaders to be extraverted. Implicit views of leaders include aspects of both sociability ("out-going") and assertiveness ("aggressive," "forceful"; Lord et al., 1984), or extraverts could be better leaders due to their expressive nature or the contagion of their positive emotionality. Open individuals may be better leaders because they are more creative and are divergent thinkers, because they are risk takers, or because their tendencies for esoteric thinking and fantasy (McCrae, 1996) make them more likely to be visionary leaders. Agreeableness may be weakly correlated with leadership because it is both a hindrance (agreeable individuals tend to be passive and compliant; Graziano & Eisenberg, 1997) and a help (agreeable individuals are likeable and empathetic; Hogan & Hogan, 2000) to leaders. Finally, is Conscientiousness related to leadership because conscientious individuals have integrity and engender trust (R. Hogan et al., 1994); because they excel at process aspects of leadership, such as setting goals; or because they are more likely to have initiative and persist in the face of obstacles? Our study cannot address these process-oriented issues, but future research should attempt to explain the linkages between the Big Five traits and leadership.

We also believe there are many situational factors that may moderate the validity of personality in predicting leadership. The literature on various leadership theories provides suggestions for possible moderators of the effectiveness of leadership traits. For example, following from substitutes for leadership (Kerr & Jermier, 1978), Conscientiousness may be more related to leadership effectiveness when task structure is low, because with ill-defined tasks structure is needed to enhance followers' expectancies of successful goal completion. Similarly, leader Agreeableness should be less relevant for intrinsically satisfying tasks because the task itself provides positive feedback and encouragement. Finally, other aspects of Kerr and Jermier's (1978) theory may exert moderating effects, especially organizational inflexibility and spatial distance. Fiedler's LPC theory (Fiedler, 1971) might also provide relevant moderators. For example, a leader's personality might matter most when he or she has the ability to influence the group (high situational control).

Contributions and Limitations

. . . In sum, trait theories have had a curious history in leadership research. The perceived efficacy of the trait approach has waxed and waned throughout the past century. Nonetheless, progress has occurred, most notably through a prior meta analysis (Lord et al., 1986). We hope this study, although it raises questions as well as answers others, may help bring further order to this research area. Results in this study provide strong evidence in favor of the trait approach and suggest that we have come a long way since J. A. Murphy (1941) remarked, "Leadership does not reside in the person" (p. 674), and Jenkins (1947) concluded, "No single trait or group of characteristics has been isolated which sets off the leader from members of his group" (pp. 74–75). On the basis of the results presented in this study, future research should develop process models that illuminate the dispositional source of leadership.

References

References marked with an asterisk indicate studies included in the meta-analysis.

*Adams, J. (1984). Women at West Point: A three-year perspective. *Sex Roles,* 11, 525–541.

Anderson, C. R., & Schneier, C. E. (1978). Locus of control, leader behaviors and leader performance among management students. *Academy of Management Journal,* 21, 690–698.

Anderson, G., & Viswesvaran, C. (1998, April). *An update of the validity of personality scales in personnel selection: A meta-analysis of studies published after 1992.*

Paper presented at the 13th Annual Conference of the Society for Industrial and Organizational Psychology, Dallas, TX.

*Andrea, R. K., & Conway, J. A. (1982). Linear and curvilinear considerations of Machiavellianism and school leader effectiveness. *School Psychology International 3,* 203–212.

Armilla, J. (1967). Predicting self-assessed social leadership in a new culture with the MMPI. *Journal of Social Psychology, 73,* 219–225.

*Bahr. H. M., & Martin, T. K. (1983). "And thy neighbor thyself": Self-esteem and faith in people as correlates of religiosity and family solidarity among Middletown High School students. *Journal for the Scientific Study of Religion, 22,* 132–144.

Barrick, M. R., & Mount. M. K. (1991). The Big Five personality dimensions and job performance: A meta-analysis. *Personnel Psychology, 44,* 1–26.

*Bass, B. M. (1961). Some aspects of attempted, successful, and effective leadership. *Journal of Applied Psychology, 45,* 120–122.

Bass, B. M. (1990). *Bass and Stogdill's handbook of leadership.* New York: Free Press.

*Bass, B. M., McGehee, C. R., Hawkins, W. C., Young, P. C., & Gebel, A. S. (1953). Personality variables related to leaderless group discussion behavior. *Journal of Abnormal and Social Psychology, 48,* 120–129.

*Batlis, N. C., & Green, P. C. (1979). Leadership style emphasis and related personality attributes. *Psychological Reports, 44,* 587–592.

Bem, S. L. (1974). The measurement of psychological androgyny. *Journal of Consulting and Clinical Psychology, 42,* 155–162.

Benet-Martînez, V., & John, O. P. (1998). *Los Cinco Grandes* across cultures and ethnic groups: Multitrait-multimethod analyses of the Big Five in Spanish and English. *Journal of Personality and Social Psychology, 75,* 729–750.

*Bennett, A., & Derevensky, J. (1995). The medieval kingdom topology: Peer relations in kindergarten children. *Psychology in the Schools, 32,* 130–141.

Block, J. (1995). A contrarian view of the five-factor approach to personality description. *Psychological Bulletin, 117,* 187–215.

Bowden, A. O. (1926). A study of the personality of student leaders in the United States. *Journal of Abnormal and Social Psychology, 21,* 149–160.

*Brandstatter, H., & Farthofer, A. (1997). Personality in social influence across tasks and groups. *Small Group Research, 28,* 146–163.

Caprara, G. V., Barbaranelli, C., Borgogni, L., & Perugini, M. (1993). The "Big Five Questionnaire": A new questionnaire to assess the five factor model. *Personality and Individual Differences, 15,* 281–288.

Carlyle, T. (1907). *On heroes, hero-worship, and the heroic in history.* Boston: Houghton Mifflin.

*Carter, L., & Nixon, M. (1949). Ability, perceptual, personality, and interest factors associated with different criteria of leadership. *Journal of Psychology, 27,* 377–388.

Cattell, R. B., & Stice, G. F. (1957). *Handbook for the Sixteen Personality Factor Questionnaire.* Champaign, IL: Institute of Personality and Ability Testing.

*Chakraborti, P. K., Kundu, R., & Rao, J. (1983). Prediction of leadership traits of teachers from certain other personality variables. *Personality Study and Group Behaviour, 3,* 74–80.

*Charlier, P. J. (1977). *A study of the relationship between selected personal and interpersonal dimensions of elementary principals and their leadership behavior.* Unpublished doctoral dissertation, Temple University, Philadelphia.

*Chemers, M. M., Watson, C. B., & May, S. T. (2000). Dispositional affect and leadership effectiveness: A comparison of self-esteem, optimism, and efficacy. *Personality and Social Psychology Bulletin, 26,* 267–277.

*Christie, M. (1981). *A study of the relationship of locus of control and job satisfaction to leadership.* Unpublished doctoral dissertation, University of Maryland, College Park.

Conger, J. A., & Kanungo, R. N. (1998). *Charismatic leadership in organizations.* Thousand Oaks, CA: Sage.

Conway, J. M., & Huffcutt, A. I. (1997). Psychometric properties of multisource performance ratings: A meta-analysis of subordinate, supervisor, peer, and self- ratings. *Human Performance, 10,* 331–360.

Costa, P. T., Jr., & McCrae, R. R. (1988). Personality in adulthood: A six-year longitudinal study of self-reports and spouse ratings on the NEO Personality Inventory. *Journal of Personality and Social Psychology, 54,* 853–863.

Costa, P. T., Jr., & McCrae, R. R. (1992). *Revised NEO Personality Inventory (NEO-PI-R) and NEO Five-Factor (NEO-FFI) Inventory professional manual.* Odessa, FL: Psychological Assessment Resources.

Costa, P. T., Jr., McCrae, R. R., & Dye, D. A. (1991). Facet scales for agreeableness and conscientiousness: A revision of the NEO Personality Inventory. *Personality and Individual Differences, 12,* 887–898.

Cowley, W. H. (1931). Three distinctions in the study of leaders. *Journal of Abnormal and Social Psychology, 26,* 304–313.

Daft, R. L. (1999). *Leadership: Theory and practice.* Orlando, FL: Dryden Press.

*DeBolt, J. W., Liska, A. E., Love, W., & Stahlman, R. W. (1973). Status-role consequences of internal-external control of reinforcement. *Psychological Reports, 32,* 307–311.

*DeBolt, J. W., Liska, A. E., & Weng, B. R. (1976). Replications of association between internal locus of control and leadership in small groups. *Psychological Reports, 38,* 470.

DeNeve, K. M., & Cooper, H. (1998). The happy personality: A meta-analysis of 137 personality traits and subjective well-being. *Psychological Bulletin, 124,* 197–229.

Digman, J. M. (1989). Five robust trait dimensions: Development, stability, and utility. *Journal of Personality, 57,* 195–214.

*Doll, R. E., & Gunderson, E. K. (1970). The relative importance of selected behavioral characteristics of group members in an extreme environment. *Journal of Psychology, 75,* 231–237.

*Drake, R. M. (1944). A study of leadership. *Character and Personality, 12,* 285–289.

*EchoHawk, M., & Parsons, O. A. (1977). Leadership vs. behavioral problems and belief in personal control among American Indian youth. *Journal of Social Psychology, 102,* 47–54.

*Edwards, C. A. (1990). *Leadership, social networks, and personal attributes in school age girls.* Unpublished doctoral dissertation, University of North Carolina. Chapel Hill.

*Ellis, R. J. (1988). Self-monitoring and leadership emergence in groups. *Personal and Social Psychology Bulletin, 14,* 681–693.

Emrich. C. G. (1999). Context effects in leadership perception. *Personality and Social Psychology Bulletin, 25,* 991–1006.

Engle, E. M., & Lord, R. G. (1997). Implicit theories, self-schemas, and leader-member exchange. *Academy of Management Journal, 40,* 988–1010.

Eysenck, H. J. (1990). Biological dimensions of personality. In E. Pervin (Ed.), *Handbook of personality* (pp. 244–276). New York: Guilford Press.

Eysenck, H. J. (1992). Four ways five factors are *not* basic. *Personality and Individual Differences, 13,* 667–673.

Feist, G. J. (1998). A meta-analysis of personality in scientific and artistic creativity. *Personality and Social Psychology Bulletin, 2,* 290–309.

Fiedler, F. E. (1971). Validation and extension of the contingency model of leadership effectiveness: A review of empirical findings. *Psychological Bulletin, 76,* 128–148.

*Flemming, E. G. (1935). A factor analysis of the personality of high school leaders. *Journal of Applied Psychology, 5,* 596–605.

Friedman, H. S., Tucker, J. S., Schwartz, J. E., Martin, L. R., Tomlinson-Keasey, C., Wingard, D. L., & Criqui, M. H. (1995). Childhood conscientiousness and longevity: Health behaviors and cause of death. *Journal of Personality and Social Psychology, 68,* 696–703.

*George, E. I., & Abraham. P. A. (1966). A comparative study of leaders and non-leaders among pupils in secondary schools. *Journal of Psychological Researches, 10,* 116–120.

Goldberg, L. R. (1990). An alternative "description of personality": The Big-Five factor structure. *Journal of Personality and Social Psychology, 59,* 1216–1229.

Goldberg, L. R. (1999). A broad-bandwidth, public-domain, personality inventory measuring the lower-level facets of several five-factor models. In I. Mervielde, I. J. Deary, F. De Fruyt, & F. Ostendorf (Eds.), *Personality psychology in Europe* (Vol. 7, pp. 7–28). Tilburg, the Netherlands: Tilburg University Press.

*Gordon, L. V. (1951). Personal factors in leadership. *Journal of Social Psychology, 36,* 245–248.

Gough, H. G. (1957). *Manual for the California Psychological Inventory.* Palo Alto, CA: Consulting Psychologists Press.

Gough, H. G. (1988). *Manual for the California Psychological Inventory.* Palo Alto, CA: Consulting Psychologists Press.

*Gough, H. G. (1989). A leadership index on the California Psychological Inventory. *Journal of Counseling Psychology, 16,* 283–289.

Gough, H. G. (1990). Testing for leadership with the California Psychological Inventory. In K. E. Clark & M. B. Clark (Eds.), *Measures of leadership* (pp. 355–379). West Orange, NJ: Leadership Library of America.

*Gough, H. G., & Heilbrun, A. B., Jr. (1983). *The Adjective Check List manual—1983 edition.* Palo Alto, CA: Consulting Psychologists Press.

*Gough, H. G., Lazzari, R., Fioravanti, M., & Stracca, M. (1978). An Adjective Check List scale to predict military leadership. *Journal of Cross-Cultural Psychology, 9,* 381–401.

*Gowan, J. C. (1955). Relationship between leadership and personality measures. *Journal of Educational Research, 48,* 623–627.

Graziano, W. G., & Eisenberg, N. H. (1997). Agreeableness: A dimension of personality. In R. Hogan, J. Johnson, & S. Briggs (Eds.), *Handbook of personality psychology* (pp. 795–824). San Diego, CA: Academic Press.

*Greenwood, J. M., & McNamara, W. J. (1969). Leadership styles of structure and consideration and managerial effectiveness. *Personnel Psychology, 22,* 141–152.

*Hanawalt, N. G., & Richardson, H. M. (1944). Leadership as related to the Bernreuter personality measures: IV. An item analysis of responses of adult leaders and non-leaders. *Journal of Applied Psychology, 28,* 397–411.

*Hiers, J. M., & Heckel, R. V. (1977). Seating choice, leadership, and locus of control. *Journal of Social Psychology, 103,* 313–314.

Hill, N. C., & Ritchie, J. B. (1977). The effect of self-esteem on leadership and achievement: A paradigm and a review. *Group and Organization Studies, 2,* 491–503.

*Hogan, J. C. (1978). Personological dynamics of leadership. *Journal of Research in Personality, 12,* 390–395.

Hogan, R., Curphy, G. J., & Hogan, J. (1994). What we know about leadership: Effectiveness and personality. *American Psychologist, 49,* 493–504.

Hogan, R., & Hogan, J. (1995). *Hogan Personality Inventory manual* (2nd ed.). Tulsa, OK: Hogan Assessment Systems.

Hogan, R., & Hogan, J. (2000). *Leadership and sociopolitical intelligence.* Unpublished manuscript, University of Tulsa, OK.

*Hollander, E. P. (1954). Authoritarianism and leadership choice in a military setting. *Journal of Abnormal and Social Psychology, 49,* 365–370.

*Holmes, C. M., Sholley, B. K., & Walker, W. E. (1980). Leader, follower, and isolate personality patterns in Black and White emergent leadership groups. *Journal of Psychology, 105,* 41–46.

Hough, L. (1992). The "Big Five" personality variables—construct confusion: Description versus prediction. *Human Performance, 5,* 139–155.

Hough, L. M., Ones, D. S., & Viswesvaran, C. (1998, April). *Personality correlates of managerial performance constructs.* Paper presented at the 13th Annual Conference of the Society for Industrial and Organizational Psychology. Dallas, TX.

*Houltzman, W. H. (1952). Adjustment and leadership: A study of the Rorschach test. *Journal of Social Psychology, 36,* 179–189.

House, R. J., & Aditya, R. N. (1997). The social scientific study of leadership: Quo vadis? *Journal of Management, 23,* 409–473.

House, R. J., & Howell, J. M. (1992). Personality and charismatic leadership. *Leadership Quarterly, 3,* 81–108.

House, R. J., & Podsakoff, P. M. (1994). Leadership effectiveness. In J. Greenberg (Ed.), *Organizational behavior: The state of the science* (pp. 45–82). Hillsdale, NJ: Erlbaum.

House, R. J., Shane, S. A., & Herold, D. M. (1996). Rumors of the death of dispositional research are vastly exaggerated. *Academy of Management Review, 21,* 203–224.

*House, R. J., Spangler, W. D., & Woycke, J. (1991). Personality and charisma in the U.S. presidency: A psychological theory of leader effectiveness. *Administrative Science Quarterly, 36,* 364–396.

*Howell, J. M., & Avolio, B. J. (1993). Transformational leadership, transactional leadership, locus of control, and support for innovation: Key predictors of consolidated-business-unit performance. *Journal of Applied Psychology, 78,* 891–902.

Haffcutt, A. I., Roth, P. L., & McDaniel, M. A. (1996). A meta-analytic investigation of cognitive ability in employment interview evaluations: Moderating characteristics and implications for incremental validity. *Journal of Applied Psychology, 81,* 459–473.

*Huffty, J. E. (1979). *The relationship of personality types, leadership styles, and effectiveness with attitudes toward women in a selected group of public school superintendents.* Unpublished doctoral dissertation. East Texas State University, Commerce.

Hughes, R. L., Ginnett, R. C., & Curphy, G. J. (1996). *Leadership.* Boston: Irwin McGraw-Hill .

*Hunter, E. C., & Jordan, A. M. (1939). An analysis of qualities associated with leadership among college students. *Journal of Educational Psychology, 30,* 497–509.

Hunter, J. E. (1992). *REGRESS: A multiple regression program in BASICA.* East Lansing: Michigan State University, Department of Psychology.

Hunter, J. E., & Schmidt, F. L. (1990). *Methods of meta-analysis.* Newbury Park, CA: Sage Publications.

Hurtz, G. M., & Donovan, J. J. (2000). Personality and job performance: The Big Five revisited. *Journal of Applied Psychology, 85,* 869–879.

Jackson, D. N. (1967). *Personality Research Form manual.* Goshen, NY: Research Psychologists Press.

Jenkins, W. O. (1947). A review of leadership studies with particular reference to military problems. *Psychological Bulletin, 44,* 54–79.

*Johnson, A. L., Luthans. F., & Hennessey, H. W. (1984). The role of locus of control in leader influence behavior. *Personnel Psychology, 37,* 61–75.

*Judge, T. A. (2000a). [Leadership effectiveness in the 21st century]. Unpublished raw data.

*Judge, T. A. (2000b). [Transformational leadership in the Administrative Institute]. Unpublished raw data.

*Judge, T. A., & Bono, J. E. (2000). Five-factor model of personality and transformational leadership. *Journal of Applied Psychology, 85,* 751–765.

Judge, T. A., & Bono, J. E. (2001). Relationship of core self-evaluations traits—self-esteem, generalized self-efficacy, locus of control, and emotional stability—with job satisfaction and job performance: A meta-analysis. *Journal of Applied Psychology, 86,* 80–92.

*Judge, T. A., & Colbert, A. (2000a). [Personality and leadership among students in 6J:262, Leadership and Personal Development]. Unpublished raw data.

*Judge, T. A., & Colbert, A. (2000b). [Personality and leadership among students in 6J:262, Leadership and Personal Development—Muscatine, IA]. Unpublished raw data.

Judge, T. A., Higgins, C., Thoresen, C. J., & Barrick, M. R. (1999). The Big Five personality traits, general mental ability, and career success across the life span. *Personnel Psychology, 52,* 621–652.

Judge, T. A., Locke, E. A., Durham, C. C., & Kluger, A. N. (1998). Dispositional effects on job and life satisfaction: The role of core evaluations. *Journal of Applied Psychology, 83,* 17–34.

*Kalma, A. P., Visser, L., & Peeters, A. (1993). Sociable and aggressive dominance: Personality differences in leadership style? *Leadership Quarterly, 4,* 45–64.

*Karnes, F. A., Chauvin, J. C., & Trant, T. J. (1984). Leadership profiles as determined by the 16 PF scores of honors college students. *Psychological Reports, 55,* 615–616.

*Karnes, F. A., & D'Ilio, V. R. (1990). Correlations between personality and leadership concepts and skills as measured by the High School Personality Questionnaire and the Leadership Skills Inventory. *Psychological Reports, 66,* 851–856.

*Karnes, F. A., & McGinnis, J. C. (1996). Scores on indicators of leadership skills, locus of control, and self-actualization for student leaders in grades 6 to 10. *Psychological Reports, 78,* 1235–1240.

*Kendall, M. J. (1981). *The role of personality on leadership dimensions among United States Army adjutant general corps officers.* Unpublished doctoral dissertation, University of Southern California, Los Angeles, CA.

Kenny, D. A., & Zaccaro, S. J. (1983). An estimate of variance due to traits in leadership. *Journal of Applied Psychology, 68,* 678–685.

Kerr, S., & Jermier, J. M. (1978). Substitutes for leadership: Their meaning and measurement. *Organizational Behavior and Human Performance, 22,* 375–403.

Kirkpatrick, S. A., & Locke, E. A. (1991). Leadership: Do traits matter? *Academy of Management Executive, 5,* 48–60.

Kohs, S. C., & Irle, K. W. (1920). Prophesying army promotion. *Journal of Applied Psychology, 4,* 73–87.

*Kureshi, A., & Fatima, B. (1984). Power motive among student leaders and non-leaders: Testing the affective-arousal model. *Journal of Psychological Researchers, 28,* 21–24.

*Landau, E., & Weissler, K. (1990). Tracing leadership in gifted children. *Journal of Psychology, 125,* 681–688.

LePine, J. A., Hollenbeck, J. R., Ilgen, D. R., & Hedlund, J. (1997). Effects of individual differences on the performance of hierarchical decision-making teams: Much more than g. *Journal of Applied Psychology, 82,* 803–811.

*Linimon, D., Barron, W. L., & Falbo, T. (1984). Gender differences in perceptions of leadership. *Sex Roles, 11,* 1075–1089.

*Lonetto, R., & Williams, D. (1974). Personality, behavioural and output variables in a small group task situation: An examination of consensual leader and non-leader differences. *Canadian Journal of Behavioral Science, 6,* 59–74.

Lord, R. G. (1985). An information processing approach to social perception, leadership and behavior measurement in organizations. *Research in Organizational Behavior, 7,* 87–128.

Lord, R. G., De Vader, C. L., & Alliger, G. M. (1986). A meta-analysis of the relation between personality traits and leadership perceptions: An application of validity generalization procedures. *Journal of Applied Psychology, 71,* 402–410.

Lord, R. G., Foti, R. J., & De Vader, C. L. (1984). A test of leadership categorization theory: Internal structure, information processing, and leadership perceptions. *Organizational Behavior and Human Performance, 34,* 343–378.

*MacNitt, R. D. (1930). *Introversion and extroversion in the high school,* Unpublished doctoral dissertation, University of Michigan, Ann Arbor.

*Makiney, J. D., Marchioro, C. A., & Hall, R. J.(April, 1999). *Relations of leader perceptions to personality, leadership style and self schema.* Paper presented at 14th Annual Meeting of the Society for Industrial and Organizational Psychology, Atlanta, GA.

Mann, R. D. (1959). A review of the relationships between personality and performance in small groups. *Psychological Bulletin, 56,* 241–270.

McCrae, R. R. (1987). Creativity, divergent thinking, and openness to experience. *Journal of Personality and Social Psychology, 52,* 1258–1265.

McCrae, R. R. (1996). Social consequences of experiential openness. *Psychological Bulletin, 120,* 323–337.

McCrae, R. R., & Costa, P. T., Jr. (1997). Personality trait structure as a human universal. *American Psychologist, 52,* 509–516.

McCrae, R. R., & John, O. P. (1992). An introduction to the five-factor model and its applications. *Journal of Personality, 2,* 175–215.

*McCullough, P. M., Ashbridge, D., & Pegg, R. (1994). The effect of self-esteem, family structure, locus of control, and career goals on adolescent leadership behavior. *Adolescence, 29,* 605–614.

*Mills, C. J., & Bohannon, W. E. (1980). Personality characteristics of effective state police officers. *Journal of Applied Psychology, 65,* 680–684.

Mount, M. K., & Barrick, M. R. (1995a). The Big Five personality dimensions: Implications for research and practice in human resources management. *Research in Personnel and Human Resources Management, 13,* 153–200.

Mount, M. K., & Barrick, M. R. (1995b). *Manual for the Personal Characteristics Inventory.* Unpublished manuscript.

Murphy, J. A. (1941). A study of the leadership process. *American Sociological Review, 6,* 674–687.

Murphy, K. R., & DeShon, R. (2000). Interrater correlations do not estimate the reliability of job performance ratings. *Personnel Psychology, 53,* 873–900.

*Nath, M., & Seriven, G. (1981). Leadership and self-esteem in preschool children. *Child Psychiatry Quarterly,* 14, 138–141.

*Nelson, D. O. (1965). Leadership in sports. *Research Quarterly,* 37, 268–275.

*Nelson, P. D. (1964). Similarities and differences among leaders and followers. *Journal of Social Psychology,* 63, 161–167.

*Nichols, R. C., & Holland, J. L. (1963). Prediction of the first year college performance of high aptitude students. *Psychological Monographs,* 77, 1–29.

Norman, W. T. (1963). Toward an adequate taxonomy of personality attributes: Replicated factor structure in peer nomination personality ratings. *Journal of Abnormal Psychology,* 66, 574–583.

Northouse, P. G. (1997). *Leadership: Theory and practice.* Thousand Oaks, CA: Sage.

Offerman, L. R., Kennedy, J. K., & Wirtz, P. W. (1994). Implicit leadership theories: Content, structure, and generalizability. *Leadership Quarterly,* 5, 43–58.

Ones, D. S. (1993). *The construct validity of integrity tests.* Unpublished doctoral dissertation, University of Iowa, Iowa City.

Ones, D. S., & Viswesvaran, C. (1996). Bandwidth-fidelity dilemma in personality measurement for personnel selection. *Journal of Organizational Behavior,* 17, 609–626.

Ones, D. S., Viswesvaran, C., & Reiss, A. D. (1996). Role of social desirability in personality testing for personnel selection: The red herring. *Journal of Applied Psychology,* 81, 660–679.

*Palmer, W. J. (1974). Management effectiveness as a function of personality traits of the manager. *Personnel Psychology,* 27, 283–295.

Piedmont, R. L., McCrae, R. R., & Costa, P. T., Jr. (1991). Adjective check list scales and the five-factor model. *Journal of Personality and Social Psychology,* 60, 630–637.

*Richardson, H. M., & Hanawalt, N. G. (1943). Leadership as related to the Bernreuter Personality Measures: I. College leadership in extracurricular activities. *Journal of Social Psychology,* 27, 237–249.

*Richardson, H. M., & Hanawalt, N. G. (1952). Leadership as related to the Bernreuter Personality Measures: V. Leadership among adult women in social activities. *Journal of Social Psychology,* 36, 141–153.

Robertson, I. T., & Kinder, A. (1993). Personality and job competencies: The criterion-related validity of some personality variables. *Journal of Occupational and Organizational Psychology,* 66, 226–244.

*Robinson, W. A. (1980). *Influence of leader personality and compatibility of leader-follower personalities on the leadership effectiveness of male public secondary school principals in Louisiana.* Unpublished doctoral dissertation. Northwestern State University Natchitoches, LA.

*Rowland, K. M., & Scott, W. E. (1968). Psychological attributes of effective leadership in a formal organization. *Personnel Psychology,* 21, 365–377.

*Rueb, J. D. (1994). *Intelligence, dominance, masculinity–femininity, and self-monitoring: The use of traits in predicting leadership emergence in a military setting.* Unpublished doctoral dissertation. Virginia Polytechnic Institute and State University, Blacksburg.

*Russell, G. W. (1981). Conservatism, birth order, leadership, and the aggression of Canadian ice hockey players. *Perceptual and Motor Skills,* 55, 3–7.

*Rychlak, J. F. (1963). Personality correlates of leadership among first level managers. *Psychological Reports,* 12, 43–52.

Salgado, J. F. (1997). The five factor model of personality and job performance in the European Community. *Journal of Applied Psychology,* 82, 30–43.

Salgado, J. F. (1998). *Criterion validity of personality measures based and non-based on the five-factor model.* Paper presented at the 106th Annual Conference of the American Psychological Association, San Francisco, CA.

*Savelsbergh, M., & Staebler, B. (1995). Investigating leadership styles, personality preferences, and effective teacher consultation. *Journal of Educational and Psychological Consultation,* 6, 277–286.

Schmidt, F. L., & Hunter, J. E. (1996). Measurement error in psychological research: Lessons from 26 research scenarios. *Psychological Methods,* 1, 199–223.

*Sinha, D., & Kumar, P. (1966). A study of certain personality variables in student leadership. *Psychological Studies,* 11, 1–8.

*Smith, J. A., & Foti, R. J. (1998). A pattern approach to the study of leader emergence. *Leadership Quarterly,* 9, 147–160.

Sosik, J. J., Kahai, S. S., & Avolio, B. J. (1998). Transformational leadership and dimensions of creativity: Motivating idea generation in computer-mediated groups. *Creativity Research Journal,* 11, 111–121.

Stogdill, R. M. (1948). Personal factors associated with leadership: A survey of the literature. *Journal of Psychology,* 25, 35–71.

Stogdill, R. M. (1950). Leadership, membership and organization. *Psychological Bulletin,* 47, 1–14.

Stogdill, R. M. (1974). *Handbook of leadership.* New York: Free Press.

*Taggar, S., Hackett, R., & Saha, S. (1999). Leadership emergence in autonomous work teams: Antecedents and outcomes. *Personnel Psychology,* 52, 899–926.

Terman, L. M. (1904). A preliminary study in the psychology and pedagogy of leadership. *Journal of Genetic Psychology,* 11, 413–451.

Tett, R. P., Jackson, D. N., & Rothstein, M. (1991). Personality measures as predictors of job performance:

A meta-analytic review. *Personnel Psychology,* 44, 703–742.

*Tripathi, R. R., & Agrawal, A. (1978). The achievement motive in leaders and non-leaders: A role analysis. *Psychologia.* 21, 97–103.

Tupes, E. C., & Christal, R. E. (1961). *Recurrent personality factors based on trait ratings* (Technical Report ASD-TR-61-97). Lackland Air Force Base, TX: U.S. Air Force.

*Vanfossen, B. E., Jones, J. D., & Spade, J. Z. (1987). Curriculum tracking and status maintenance. *Sociology of Education,* 60, 104–122.

Vickers, R. R., Jr. (1995). *Using personality assessment for leadership selection.* (Report No. 95–16). San Diego, CA: Naval Health Research Center.

Viswesvaran, C., & Ones, D. S. (1995). Theory testing: Combining psychometric meta-analysis and structural equations modeling. *Personnel Psychology,* 48, 865–885.

Viswesvaran, C., Ones, D. S., & Schmidt, F. L., (1996). Comparative analysis of the reliability of job performance retings. *Journal of Applied Psychology,* 81, 557–574.

Watson, D., & Clark, L. A. (1997). Extraversion and its positive emotional core. In R. Hogan, J. A. Johnson, &
S. R. Briggs (Eds.), *Handbook of personality psychology* (pp. 767–793). San Diego, CA: Academic Press.

Whitener, E. M. (1990). Confusion of confidence intervals and credibility intervals in meta-analysis. *Journal of Applied Psychology,* 75, 315–321.

*Wunderley, L. J., Reddy, W. B., & Dember, W. N. (1998). Optimism and pessimism in business leaders. *Journal of Applied Social Psychology,* 28, 751–760.

*Yukelson, D., Weinberg, R., Richardson, P., & Jackson, A. (1983). Interpersonal attraction and leadership within collegiate sport teams. *Journal of Sport Behavior,* 6, 28–36.

Yukl, G. (1998). *Leadership in organizations.* Upper Saddle River, NJ: Prentice Hall.

Yukl, G., & Van Fleet, D. D. (1992). Theory and research on leadership in organizations. In M. D. Dunnette & L. M. Hough (Eds.), *Handbook of industrial and organizational psychology* (Vol. 3, pp. 147–197). Palo Alto, CA: Consulting Psychologists Press.

*Zaccaro, S. J., Foti, R. J., & Kenny, D. A. (1991). Self-monitoring and trait-based variance in leadership: An investigation of leader flexibility across multiple group situations. *Journal of Applied Psychology.* 76, 308–315.

Leadership and the Role of Gender

The past three decades have been characterized by significant increases in the number of women in business and other professional careers such as law and medicine. Accompanying this trend has been an increase in the number of women occupying leadership positions as well as managerial (administrative) positions in work organizations.

In recent years, leadership scholars have attempted to address the issue of sex-based and gender role differences within the context of leadership. There has been an interest, for example, in the effects of sex and gender role in terms of leader emergence, leadership style, uses of power, and effectiveness.

In 1994 Russell L. Kent and Sherry E. Moss examined the effects of sex and gender role on leader emergence. They note that whereas prior research revealed that men were more likely to emerge as leaders than are women, the results from their study show that women are slightly more likely to emerge as leaders than are men. Stronger effects, however, were produced for gender role than for biologically based sex differences. *Individuals characterized by androgynous and/or masculine attributes were more likely to emerge as leaders than those with feminine attributes.* The self-assessment exercise appearing at the end of this chapter opener provides you with an opportunity to profile your gender characteristics.

In the first reading in this chapter, Amy B. Gershenoff and Roseanne J. Foti (2003) advance our understanding of the role of gender in leader emergence as they address the question, how do gender role and task type influence the perception of leadership by fellow group members? Gershenoff and Foti hypothesize that there will be an interaction between individual differences in gender role (i.e., masculinity, femininity, and androgyny) and the context (e.g., type of task) on leadership emergence. They report that in initiating-structure task conditions, masculine-intelligent and androgynous-intelligent individuals emerge more than feminine-intelligent individuals. Under consensus-building task conditions, feminine-intelligent individuals did *not* emerge as leaders more often than masculine-intelligent individuals, and partial support was found on behalf of the androgynous-intelligent individuals.

Alice H. Eagly and Blair T. Johnson (1990), in the second reading, review the arguments given for expecting an absence (and presence) of sex differences in leadership style. They also conduct a statistical (meta) analysis of a number of research studies that have attempted to address the question, Is there a difference in the leadership style of men and women? Although this study uncovers gender-related leadership style patterns, it is yet unclear whether the behaviors observed are primarily caused by different sex-based traits, perceived role requirements, or other task and environmental factors.

Speaking to the issue of effectiveness, Alice H. Eagly and her colleagues Steven J. Karau and Mona G. Makhijani conducted a statistical review of the gender and leader effectiveness literature.[1] They report that male and female leaders are equally effective. In addition, they report that men were more effective in roles that were defined in more masculine terms, and women were more effective in less masculine roles.

It is frequently assumed that if groups have both a maintenance (socioemotional) and task need, leaders who are androgynous may be more effective than those who are masculine or feminine in nature. This presumed positive androgynous-effectiveness relationship stems from the assumption that the individual's feminine side (empathetic, expressive) may enable him or her to assist the group as it deals with its maintenance needs, while his or her masculine side (instrumental, assertive) assists in addressing the group's task needs. Galen L. Baril and colleagues (Nancy Elbert, Sharon Mahar-Potter, and George C. Reavy) address the issue of leader effectiveness. Specifically, they pose the question, Is there a relationship between androgynousness and effectiveness? In the process they alert us to the fact that masculinity and femininity are not always neutral states, as they briefly recognize negative masculinity (egotism and hostility) and negative femininity (subservience and neurotic complaining).[2]

According to Baril et al. (1989) the relationship between gender and effectiveness is much more complex than that which is frequently hypothesized. Eagly, Karau, and Makhijani (1995) conducted a meta-analysis of the gender-effectiveness literature and offer several interesting conclusions. First, they note that in the aggregate, *male and female leaders are equally effective.* Second, this finding needs to be looked at more closely as *female and male leaders are not equally effective in every situation.* More specifically, female leaders do not fare well in those situations that are defined as masculine in nature (e.g., military), and men do worse than women in situations that are defined as less than masculine (or more feminine) in nature (e.g., educational, governmental, and social service organizations). Thus, they note that "if gender [was] entirely unimportant in organizations and groups, it would be irrelevant to leaders' effectiveness, and men and women would fare equally well as leaders throughout all types of organizations and groups" (p. 142). In view of these findings, men may well find themselves less effective as leaders in contexts defined in relatively feminine terms, and similarly, women may well be less effective in their leadership attempts in situations that are defined relatively in masculine terms.[3]

Returning to our leadership process model (see Figure 4.1), we can see that the discussion of gender, together with our discussion of traits presented in Chapter 3, provides further insight into the leadership process through an expanded understanding of "the leader."

In the next chapter, we will address the issue of leader emergence. Although we will not discuss the role of gender *per se* in that chapter, it will be important to keep in mind all that you have learned regarding the role of gender.

---

[1] A. H. Eagly, S. J. Karau, & M. G. Makhijani, "Gender and the Effectiveness of Leaders: A Meta-analysis," *Psychological Bulletin* 117 (1995), pp. 125–145.

[2] Baril, G. L., Elbert, N., Mahar-Potter, S., & Reavy, G. C. (1989). "Are Androgynous Managers Really More Effective?" *Group & Organization Management*, 14:2, 234–249.

[3] A. H. Eagly, S. J. Karau, & M. G. Makjijana, "Gender and the Effectiveness of Leaders: A Meta-analysis," *Psychological Bulletin* 117 (1995), pp. 125–145.

Sex, Gender (masculine, feminine androgynous attributes)

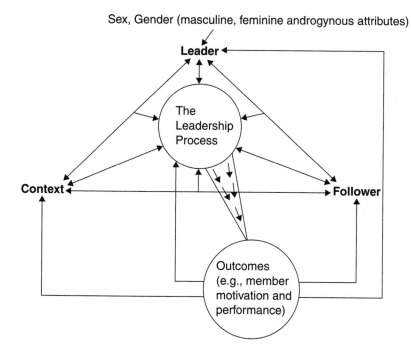

FIGURE 4.1
The Leadership
Process: Gender

EXERCISE	
Self-Assessment	**Masculinity–Femininity**

Instructions: Please indicate how well each of the characteristics presented below describes you.

	Never, or Almost Never True						Always, or Almost Always True
1. Defends own beliefs	1	2	3	4	5	6	(7)
2. Cheerful	1	2	3	4	5	6	(7)
3. Controlling	1	2	3	4	5	6	(7)
4. Affectionate	1	2	3	4	5	6	(7)
5. Assertive	1	2	3	4	5	(6)	7
6. Intuitive	1	2	3	4	5	(6)	7
7. Loyal	1	2	3	4	5	6	(7)
8. Analytical	1	2	3	4	5	(6)	7
9. Winning	1	2	3	4	5	6	(7)
10. Sympathetic	1	2	3	4	5	6	(7)
11. Willing to take risks	1	2	3	4	5	6	(7)
12. Empathic	1	2	3	4	5	6	(7)
13. Sensitive to the needs of others	1	2	3	4	5	6	(7)
14. Understanding	1	2	3	4	5	6	(7)
15. Rational	1	2	3	4	5	(6)	7
16. Makes decisions easily	1	2	3	4	5	(6)	7
17. Aggressive	1	2	3	4	5	6	(7)
18. Collaborative	1	2	3	4	5	6	(7)
19. Gullible	1	2	3	4	(5)	6	7
20. Competitive	1	2	3	4	5	(6)	7
21. Willing to take a stand	1	2	3	4	5	6	(7)
22. Gentle	1	2	3	4	5	6	(7)

Scoring: The Bem Sex-Role Inventory (BSRI) provides three (3) scores—masculinity, femininity, and androgyny. (What follows reflects a modification of the scoring instructions for the BSRI, employed here for the ease of in-class assessment and utilization.)

Masculinity consists of the following items: 1, 5, 8, 11, 16, 17, 20, and 21.
  Sum your response to each of these 8 items for your *masculinity* score.
  My masculinity score is __52__.

Femininity consists of the following items: 2, 4, 7, 10, 13, 14, 19, and 22.
  Sum your response to each of these 8 items for your *femininity* score.
  My femininity score is __54__.

The following are neutral items: 3, 6, 9, 12, 15, and 18. You do not need to sum your responses to these items.

Your *androgyny* score is the arithmetic difference between your masculinity score and your femininity score.
  My androgyny score is __2__.

Interpretation: The masculinity and femininity scores indicate the extent to which a person employs masculine and feminine personality characteristics as self-descriptive. Your scores do *not* have any known connection to your biological sex, nor are your scores intended to reflect something that is "right or wrong," "good or bad." Instead, masculinity is characterized by (*a*) a high score reflecting the endorsement of the masculine attributes, and (*b*) a low score reflecting the simultaneous rejection of the feminine attributes. Similarly, femininity is reflected by (*a*) a high score endorsing the feminine attributes as self-descriptive, and (*b*) a low score reflecting the simultaneous rejection of the masculine attributes. Finally, the closer the true androgyny score (without regard to sign) is to zero, the more the person is androgynous. Lower androgyny scores reflect the equal endorsement of both masculine and feminine attributes.

A person is "sex-typed"—masculine or feminine—to the extent that the difference score is large, and androgynous, to the extent that the difference score is low. Your masculinity and femininity scores may range from a low of 8 to a high of 56. Your difference scores can range from a low of 0 to a high of 48. The closer your difference score is to 0, the more your orientation is assessed as androgynous. The closer your difference score is to 48, the more you are assessed as endorsing either masculine or feminine attributes (the masculine versus feminine distinction is determined by the higher of the two masculine/feminine assessments). A difference score of 40 or greater might be seen as reflecting a strong masculine or feminine self-description, while a difference score of 8 or less might be seen as reflecting a strong androgynous self-description.

My sex-type orientation is _____.

Unlike many, who see masculinity and femininity as bipolar ends of a single dimension, such that a person is either masculine or feminine in orientation, Bem (1974) suggests that people can be androgynous. Androgynous individuals are both masculine and feminine in orientation—both assertive and yielding, both instrumental and expressive, dependent upon the situational appropriateness of a particular behavior. Bem's measure of "psychological androgyny" characterizes a person as either masculine, feminine, or androgynous as a function of one's endorsement of masculine and feminine personality characteristics as self-descriptive.

Kent and Moss (1994) reports on the effects of sex and gender role on leader emergence. Based upon their North American study conducted in the early 1990s, they report that "androgynous and masculine subjects were the most likely to emerge as leaders" (p.1335).

Source: The eight masculinity and eight femininity items are presented here for illustrative purposes. They are a subset of the full instrument. The response scale and scoring instructions are reflective of the procedure employed in the Bem Sex-Role Inventory to assess masculinity, femininity, and androgyny.

Reproduced by special permission of the Publisher, MIND GARDEN, Inc., Menlo Park, CA 94025, USA www.mindgarden.com, from the **Bem Sex Role Inventory** by Sandra Bem. Copyright 1978 by Consulting Psychologists Press, Inc. All rights reserved. Further reproduction is prohibited without the Publisher's written consent.

Original source: S. L. Bem (1974). The Measurement of Psychological Androgyny. *Journal of Consulting and Clinical Psychology* 42, 2, pp. 155–162.

Items 3, 6, 9, 12, 15, and 18 derive from M. Loden's (1985) description of characteristics which describe "masculine and feminine leadership." They were employed here as neutral items in our illustration of Bem's Sex-Role Inventory. M. Loden, *Feminine Leadership or How to Succeed in Business without Being One of the Boys.* New York: Random House, Inc.

Kent, R. L., & Moss, S. E., Effects of Sex and Gender Role on Leader Emergence. *Academy of Management Journal* 37 (1994), pp. 1335–1346.

Reading 12

Leader Emergence and Gender Roles in All-Female Groups

A Contextual Examination

Amy B. Gershenoff and Roseanne J. Foti
Virginia Polytechnic Institute and State University

Leadership emergence is a result of the consensual agreement in the perceptions of fellow group members that one individual is the leader in work groups in which a formal leader has not been assigned (Berdahl, 1996; Hall, Workman, & Marchioro, 1998). According to Lord and Maher (1991), group members' perception that one individual has emerged as the leader results as an outcome of individual differences, behaviors, and outcomes produced by the leader, and then perceived by followers as leader-like.

Research in small group leadership has focused on finding individual differences that predict leadership emergence. For example, the effect of sex on leadership emergence has been widely researched, but studies that have explored this relationship have found mixed results. Some research finds a sex difference, with a preference for male leadership (Carbonell, 1984; Fleischer & Chertkoff, 1986; Hegstrom & Griffith, 1992; Megargee, 1969). Other studies have failed to find a sex difference in the proportion of males and females that emerge as leaders (Anderson & Schneier, 1978; Hawkins, 1995; Kolb, 1997; Schneier & Bartol, 1980). A meta-analysis by Eagly and Karau (1991) revealed that the tendency for males to emerge as leaders was moderated by the type of leadership being studied (i.e., task-oriented or interpersonally oriented), gender orientation of the task (i.e., masculine or feminine), and the social complexity of the task. More recent research suggests that studying the effect of gender role, rather than sex, may be more fruitful in explaining these differences (Goktepe & Schneier, 1989; Kent & Moss, 1994; Moss & Kent, 1996). These researchers have found that leadership emergence is influenced more by gender role than sex. Thus, understanding the relationship between gender-role and leadership

perceptions may have important implications for the selection and evaluation of group leaders in organizations.

Although sex and gender role are correlated, gender role is not necessarily dictated by biological sex. Rather, gender is a distinct and culturally constructed phenomenon defined as the shared expectations of individuals based solely on socially identified sex (Eagly, 1987). Masculinity and femininity are often thought of as opposite ends of a continuum, but they are actually independent dimensions (Bem, 1974). As such, an individual of either sex can be masculine, feminine, or both (androgynous). Androgyny is associated with flexibility in behavior, such that androgynous individuals are able to adapt their behavior to be more masculine or feminine depending on what is appropriate. The current study seeks to examine the effect of gender role, rather than sex, on leadership emergence. To control for the effect of sex on emergence, all female participants were studied.

Aside from neglecting the influence of gender role on leadership emergence, the mixed support for the effect of sex on leadership emergence may be explained by the tasks used in studies of leadership emergence. Many of these studies examine leadership emergence on tasks that have a masculine-gender orientation. Because context provides clues about the appropriate type of leadership required for task performance, the masculine nature of these tasks may facilitate the emergence of male leaders. Empirical evidence suggests that the gender orientation of the task moderates the sex and leader emergence relationship (Carbonell, 1984; Eagly & Karau, 1991; Wentworth & Anderson, 1984). In addition, evidence from social psychological literature suggests that the relationship between gender role and leader emergence may be moderated by the gender orientation of the task type (Bem, 1975; Bem & Lenney, 1976). Although Hall et al. (1998) did not find support for the emergence of feminine leaders on a consideration task, these authors

Source: A. B. Gershenoff & R. J. Foti, "Leader Emergence and Gender Roles in All-Female Groups," from *Small Group Research*, Vol 34, No. 2, April 2003, 170–196. © 2003 Sage Publications. Edited and reprinted with permission from Sage Publications, Inc.

called for future research to examine other tasks that may allow for the emergence of feminine leaders. In the current study, the gender orientation of the task will be manipulated to reflect either an initiating-structure or a consensus-building context associated with masculine or feminine gender roles, respectively.

The purpose of this study is to examine the interaction of individual differences in gender role and context on leadership emergence. We are particularly interested in the effect of androgyny on leadership emergence across task types. In addition, in answer to a call by Lord and Emrich (2001) to study the variables associated with leadership from a more holistic perspective, gender role will be examined using a pattern approach, making the individual, not the variables, the unit of study.

GENDER AND LEADERSHIP

Gender-role theory (Eagly, 1987) states that people develop gender-role expectations for themselves and others based on their beliefs about what constitutes socially acceptable behavior for men and women (Eagly & Johnson, 1990; Eagly & Karau, 1991; Eagly, Makhijani, & Klonsky, 1992). Bem (1974) classified gender roles by identifying characteristics that are more valued for one sex or the other in American society. According to Bem, "masculinity has been associated with an instrumental orientation, a cognitive focus on 'getting the job done'; and femininity has been associated with an expressive orientation, an affective concern for the welfare of others" (p. 156).

Given the "getting the job done" perspective of masculine-gender-typed individuals, it is not surprising that studies of the effects of gender on leadership emergence consistently have found that masculine individuals tend to be identified as emergent leaders more often than feminine individuals (Goktepe & Schneier, 1989; Kent & Moss, 1994; Kolb, 1997; Moss & Kent, 1996; Powell & Butterfield, 1979). Although there is less of a linkage between femininity and the perception of leadership, Ross and Offermann (1997) found feminine attributes positively associated with transformational leadership. Transformational leaders can create drastic changes in organizations by engaging in behaviors that convey charisma, intellectual stimulation, and individualized consideration (Bass, 1985). This suggests that a link may exist between feminine traits and the perception of leadership.

As noted above, in addition to masculine and feminine gender roles, Bem (1974) also introduced the concept of the androgynous personality as endorsing high levels of both masculine and feminine behaviors and characteristics. Unlike sex-typed individuals, androgynous individuals, regardless of sex, displayed both "masculine" independence and "feminine" playfulness in different sex-typed contexts (Bem, 1975). Bem asserted that androgynous individuals are able to show flexibility in their behavior and adapt to situations that demand behavior that is stereotypically more appropriate for one sex or the other by displaying behaviors that are masculine, instrumental, and assertive as well as those that are feminine, expressive, and yielding. In addition, androgyny has been linked to a communication style of rhetorical reflection associated with a concern for what is appropriate for a given situation (House, Dallinger, & Kilgallen, 1998).

The few empirical studies that have examined the role of psychological androgyny and leadership emergence have generally supported a relationship between the two. In initially leaderless groups that allowed for only one emergent leader, Moss and Kent (1996) found that masculine personality types emerged most often, but when multiple emergent leaders were allowed, both masculine and androgynous group members emerged. Furthermore, Kent and Moss (1994) found that androgynous and masculine participants were most likely to emerge as the leader in gender-neutral task situations. Finally, Kolb (1997) replicated these findings in a classroom setting with students who worked in groups on gender-neutral projects over a 2-month period, suggesting that further exploration of the linkage between psychological androgyny and leadership emergence is warranted.

PATTERNS AND LEADERSHIP EMERGENCE

Previous research has examined the relationship between gender and leadership at the level of the individual variables. However, Lord and Emrich (2001) suggested that because patterns of individual differences in perceivers' implicit leadership theories contain important information beyond their specific elements for the prediction of emergence, it may be more useful for the effect of individual differences to be examined in an interactive, multivariate sense. A person approach (Magnusson, 1995) asserts that to understand human functioning, an individual's pattern of scores across a set of theoretically meaningful variables must be obtained. Of key importance is the interaction among the variables involved, in which the person, not individual difference variables, is the basic unit of observation. Individuals are clustered into homogenous groups on the basis of their pattern of scores across variables. Once the individuals have been classified into groups, these groups—and not the variables—become the focus of study.

The pattern approach has been useful in exploring a diverse array of research topics ranging from juvenile delinquency to career choice (Gibbs, 1982; Goeke, Tosi, & Eshbaugh, 1993; Tango & Uziuban, 1984). More specifically, this approach has also been a useful tool in the study of personality and leadership. McClelland and Boyatzis (1982) supported the hypothesis that the leadership motive pattern, which includes moderate to high need for power, low need for affiliation, and high activity inhibition, was related to managerial success for nontechnical managers after 8 and 16 years. Sorrentino and Field (1986) classified individuals according to their achievement-related and affiliation-related motives and placed them into 4-person work groups with each person varying on his or her combination of these traits. They found that over the course of 5 weeks, participants who were high on both of these variables scored the highest on two measures of leadership emergence and persons who were low on both variables scored the lowest. Finally, Smith and Foti (1998) classified participants based on their pattern of dominance, general self-efficacy, and intelligence and found that participants who were high on all three traits emerged significantly more often as leaders than participants who were low on all three traits.

In the current study, gender role will be examined using a pattern approach. In addition to masculinity and femininity, intelligence will be examined as a third variable in the pattern. The decision to include intelligence as a variable in the pattern was based on the consistent and robust relationship between intelligence and leadership perceptions (Lord, De Vader, & Alliger, 1986; Lord, Foti, & De Vader, 1984; Smith & Foti, 1998; Zaccaro, Foti, & Kenny, 1991). Therefore, individuals will be grouped based on their pattern of masculinity, femininity, and intelligence. The patterns to be compared are, masculine-intelligent (high masculinity, low femininity, high intelligence) (HLH), feminine-intelligent (low masculinity, high femininity, high intelligence) (LHH), and androgynous-intelligent (high masculinity, high femininity, high intelligence) (HHH). Because we are interested in comparing the emergence of individuals with these specific patterns, individuals with any other combination of these characteristics

were classified as having a mixed pattern (HHL, HLL, LHL, LLL, or LLH).

THE EFFECT OF TASK TYPE ON LEADERSHIP EMERGENCE

The type of task used in leadership emergence studies is critical because tasks provide information to leaders and followers indicating what kind of behaviors are appropriate in that particular situation (Lord & Emrich, 2001). Specifically, the perception of leadership may depend on whether the task demands that the leader have (a) masculine attributes and behaviors such as independence and initiating structure, with a focus on effective or efficient task completion; or (b) feminine attributes and behaviors such as friendliness and consideration, with a focus on maintaining good relationships with followers (Hall et al., 1998; Lord & Maher, 1991). Thus, it is likely that leadership emergence is not only a function of individual differences but also that different task types lead to different leadership outcomes.

Traditionally, differences in leadership emergence have been studied in masculine or "neutral" contexts such as required business course projects (Goktepe & Schneier, 1989; Kent & Moss, 1994; Luthar, 1996; Moss & Kent, 1996). However, studies in the social psychological literature have found differential effects of gender associated with different types of tasks (Bem, 1975; Bem & Lenney, 1976) and a positive effect for psychological androgyny across tasks. Thus, emergence is expected when leader gender is congruent with the gender orientation of the task type and androgynous individuals are expected to emerge across tasks due to flexibility in their behavior.

Despite the assertion that task type moderates the effect of gender on leadership emergence, some studies have found mixed results for the effect of femininity on female-oriented tasks (e.g., Eagly & Karau, 1991; Hall et al., 1998; Karakowsky & Seigel, 1999). These results may be due to the nature of the task used in these studies. For instance, the task used by Hall et al. (1998) was a consideration task in which participants were asked to brainstorm recommendations for dealing with children with AIDS, and the task used by Karakowsky and Seigel (1999) was a negotiation task that differed from the male-oriented task only in that participants negotiated sexual harassment issues rather than issues surrounding cars. Although they deal with sensitive female-oriented or social topics, these tasks may not be strong enough manipulations of feminine leadership behavior to lead to the perception of feminine participants as emergent leaders. Therefore, in the current study, an attempt was made to more powerfully manipulate the gender orientation of the task demands such that they require more masculine or more feminine leadership styles. The initiating-structure task chosen requires the group to be efficient and effective, whereas the consensus-building task requires the group to be more social and reach agreement. Thus, the gender orientation of these tasks was manipulated by using tasks associated with maximizing demands (to produce effectively and efficiently) associated with masculine leadership or optimizing demands (to come to agreement on the best possible solution) associated with feminine leadership (Huston-Comeaux & Kelly, 1996).

The differentiation between task types may lead to a preference for different types of leaders, indicating that depending on the nature of the situation, different gender-typed leadership behavior may be preferable. Moreover, it is possible that psychological androgyny is advantageous because it allows the individual to be flexible and emerge as a leader in situations that demand either masculine or feminine leadership. Based on gender-role congruency theory and Bem's (1974) conception of sex-role stereotyping and gender-role adaptability, we offer the following hypotheses:

> *Hypothesis 1:* Individuals possessing masculine-intelligent and androgynous-intelligent patterns will be rated and ranked higher on leadership than individuals possessing feminine-intelligent or mixed-personality patterns on initiating-structure tasks.

> *Hypothesis 2:* Individuals possessing feminine-intelligent and androgynous-intelligent patterns will be rated and ranked higher on leadership than individuals showing masculine-intelligent or mixed patterns on consensus-building tasks.

METHOD

PARTICIPANTS AND DESIGN

Participants included in the focal study were 200 undergraduate females. Initially, to screen a sufficient number of participants to fill the pattern conditions in the focal study, 601 individuals were asked to complete measures of masculinity and femininity (Bem Sex-Role Inventory) (Bem, 1974) and intelligence (Wonderlic Personnel Test) (Wonderlic, 1983). . . .

Individuals were classified into masculine-intelligent, feminine-intelligent, androgynous-intelligent, or mixed-personality patterns based on their scores on measures of three variables: masculinity, femininity, and intelligence (see Pattern Designations section below). Individuals participated in groups of 4. Each experimental group contained 1 masculine-intelligent member, 1 feminine-intelligent member, 1 androgynous-intelligent member, and 1 mixed-personality pattern member. . . .

PERSONALITY TRAIT MEASURES

The Bem Sex-Role Inventory (BSRI). The BSRI contains a masculinity scale, a femininity scale, and a social desirability scale, which contain 20 items each. Participants rated, on a 7-point scale, how well each of the personality characteristics described her. The scales range from 1 (*never or almost never true*) to 7 (*always or almost always true*). . . .

TASK CONDITIONS

Initiating-structure task. In this condition, participants engaged in a manufacturing game associated with a predominant leadership style of initiating structure. . . .

Consensus-building task. In this condition, participants engaged in a problem-solving task called "Lost in Summer Camp." This is a consensus-building task in which participants are told a story about several crises going on simultaneously at a summer camp and are asked rank order 10 items in order of importance. . . .

PROCEDURES

Each of the 50 groups contained a masculine-intelligent, feminine-intelligent, androgynous-intelligent, and mixed-personality pattern member. . . .

DEPENDENT MEASURES

General Leadership Impression (GLI). The GLI (Lord et al., 1984) was used to measure leadership emergence. This 5-item scale asks participants to rate the other members of the group on their contribution to the group's overall effectiveness on the activity. For example, 1 item asks, "If you had to choose a leader for a new task, how willing would you be to vote for this member as leader?". . . .

Leadership emergence was also measured by using a ranking measure identical to the one used by Smith and Foti (1998) in their study of patterns and leadership emergence. Group members ranked themselves and each other based on their preference for individuals as leaders. . . .

RESULTS

. . . Hypothesis 1 predicted that individuals possessing masculine-intelligent and androgynous-intelligent patterns would be rated and ranked higher on leadership than individuals possessing feminine-intelligent or mixed-personality patterns in the initiating-structure task condition. . . .

Hypothesis 2 predicted that individuals with feminine-intelligent and androgynous-intelligent patterns would be rated and ranked higher on leadership than individuals possessing masculine-intelligent or mixed-personality patterns in the consensus-building task condition. Hypothesis 1 was fully supported. . . . Hypothesis 2 was not supported for feminine-intelligent individuals, but partial support was found for the emergence of androgynous-intelligent individuals. Androgynous-intelligent individuals emerged as the leader more than mixed-pattern individuals but not more than masculine-intelligent individuals.

Given that intelligence has been shown to have a strong relationship with leader emergence, it is reasonable to suspect that intelligence alone, rather than in combination with masculinity and femininity, is responsible for the findings in this study. . . .

. . . the emergence scores gained by having high intelligence alone were not as high as having high intelligence in combination with high masculinity and low femininity in the masculine-intelligent pattern or having high intelligence in combination with high masculinity and high femininity in the androgynous-intelligent pattern.

. . . An inspection of the means and effect sizes suggests that having high intelligence alone did not lead to higher emergence scores than having the inclusive mixed pattern, and having high intelligence in combination with high masculinity and high femininity in the androgynous-intelligent pattern resulted in higher emergence scores than having high intelligence alone.

DISCUSSION

The current study contributes to an understanding of how gender roles affect leadership emergence in all-female leaderless work groups. We address the following research question: How do gender role and task type influence the perception of leadership by fellow group members? The hypotheses draw from the literature on gender-role congruency theory and Bem's conception of sex-role stereotypes (Bem, 1975) and predicted that individuals with personality patterns congruent with the gender orientation of the task type would emerge as leaders. A primary aim of this study was to examine the effect of gender-role adaptability on leadership perceptions by exploring the emergence of androgynous individuals across gender-oriented task conditions. The findings have important implications for how gender role influences the identification of leaders in organizations.

Perhaps the most interesting finding of this study is that possession of an androgynous-intelligent personality led to the perception of leadership in both the consensus-building and the initiating-structure task conditions, fully supporting Hypothesis 1 and partially supporting Hypothesis 2. Although an all-female sample was used in the present study, the finding that androgynous-intelligent individuals emerged is congruent with Kolb's (1997) finding that androgynous individuals were described as leaders with greater frequency than either feminine or undifferentiated individuals, and it extends this finding from the gender-neutral situation in her study to both the initiating-structure and consensus-building tasks studied in this research. This makes sense given Bem's (1974) argument that androgynous individuals, who have high levels of both masculine and feminine attributes (and high levels of intelligence in this study), are able to display behavioral flexibility and adapt to the demands of the situation.

The relationship between androgyny and leadership emergence has important implications for women in the workplace. This is especially true as women increasingly aspire to more male-stereotyped positions (Konrad, Ritchie, Lieb, & Corrigall, 2000). Recent research suggests that current conceptualizations of leadership are expanding to include both masculine and feminine characteristics (Diekman & Eagly, 2000; Moss & Kent, 1996). However, our findings suggest that femininity is simply tolerated when in conjunction with masculinity because high levels of femininity and intelligence only lead to leadership emergence when combined with high levels of masculinity in the androgynous-intelligent pattern. This suggests that women leaders move toward a more androgynous role by including masculine behaviors in addition to feminine behaviors in their leadership style. Although the inclusion of more masculine attributes violates gender norms, this may lead to positive leader outcomes if women combine increased masculinity with legitimacy (Kawakami, White, & Langer, 2000; Ridgeway,

2001). Furthermore, there is evidence that androgyny may be related to transformational leadership (Hall et al., 1998), and transformational leader behaviors as well as traditional transactional leader behaviors are essential to effective leadership (Bass, 1985, 1990).

Overall, masculine-intelligent and androgynous-intelligent individuals emerged as leaders, but feminine-intelligent individuals did not. Consistent with Hypothesis 1, masculine-intelligent individuals were rated and ranked higher on leadership than feminine-intelligent and mixed-pattern individuals in the initiating-structure task. However, contrary to Hypothesis 2, feminine-intelligent individuals did not emerge in the consensus-building task condition. This is consistent with Heilman, Block, Simon, and Martell's (1989) finding that stereotypes of women, in general, are far less consistent with descriptions of successful managers than are stereotypes of men in general. Feminine attributes may be inconsistent with followers' implicit leadership theories, whereas masculine attributes match followers' prototypes for leaders (Baumgardner, Lord, & Maher, 1991). In addition, it is possible that leadership situations, whether initiating structure or building consensus, are associated with masculine prototypes. Thus, asking individuals about leadership even on a more feminine task may activate a masculine prototype rather than a feminine one. . . .

Eagly and Karau's (1991) meta-analysis suggested that in accordance with gender-role theory, females are more likely to emerge as leaders in socially oriented groups. Hall et al. (1998) explained weak support for the hypothesized effect of the sex-role congruence of the task as potentially due to a lack of overlap between the behavioral demands of the tasks and the feminine characteristic of "consideration." To more thoroughly facilitate the feminine-oriented behavioral task demands in the current study, a consensus-building task was used that requires participants to come to agreement about an optimal solution (Huston-Comeaux & Kelly, 1996). Although the pilot study suggested that the task was perceived as building consensus, the consensus-building manipulation also may not have been "feminine" enough to support this theory. Because neither the consideration nor the consensus-building task manipulations produced a significant effect of a feminine leadership style, one wonders whether there exists a feminine task with any generalizability to organizational situations.

Due to the likelihood that social cohesion is more important to groups that have to maintain

themselves over time, feminine leadership attributes may be of greater value to these groups than to those groups that meet only once, like those in the present study (Carli & Eagly, 1999; Eagly & Karau, 1991). It is possible that the combination of characteristics in the masculine-intelligent personality pattern became salient to followers during the short amount of interaction time in this study's tasks, leading to initial perceptions of leadership, but these perceptions may not persist over time. Instead, feminine attributes such as nurturance and consideration may become more salient over several interactions and ultimately may be more instrumental in sustaining work groups.

The replication of other research on traits and leadership that have shown significant relationships between masculinity but not femininity and leadership ratings may also be due to a reliance on the BSRI (Bem, 1974) as the primary measure of gender role in these studies. The BSRI was developed based on males' and females' judgment of the social desirability of traits for men and women more than 25 years ago. Because perceptions of women have changed over time, the BSRI may no longer capture the characteristics that are currently socially desirable for women or men (Hoffman & Borders, 2001). Although we attempted to overcome this potential limitation by adding 5 additional items to the BSRI, the addition of these items did not change the way that participants were classified into patterns. However, additional modification to the BSRI may be beneficial in future studies of gender and leadership.

To determine whether intelligence alone was responsible for the emergence of masculine-intelligent- and androgynous-intelligent-pattern individuals, the hypothesis tests were repeated comparing these patterns to the LLH subset of mixed-pattern individuals. The expected patterns emerged more often than the LLH pattern in three of the six comparisons. One explanation for the failure of the expected pattern to emerge more than the LLH pattern in half of the comparisons is that the small sample size in the LLH pattern may have reduced the power to find significant differences in these tests. It is also important to recognize that even when the mean differences were not significant, the means for the masculine-intelligent pattern and the androgynous-intelligent pattern were still higher than the means for LLH pattern and the effect sizes were small to medium (Cohen, 1992). It is particularly interesting that androgynous-intelligent-pattern individuals emerged (both rating and ranking) more than LLH-pattern individuals in the consensus-building task condition because the comparison between the androgynous-intelligent pattern (HHH) and the LLH pattern compares the most extreme groups, providing the most stringent test.

These findings suggest that although intelligence is important for leadership emergence, it has more of an influence on leadership perceptions when in concert with masculinity (e.g., the masculine-intelligent pattern) or masculinity and femininity (e.g., the androgynous-intelligent pattern). In addition, the finding that masculinity is related to leadership emergence in both task conditions (consensus-building task: $r = .30$, $p < .01$; initiating-structure task: $r = .31$, $p < .01$) suggests that masculinity is also important for the perception of leadership. Furthermore, the finding that masculine-intelligent individuals emerged and feminine-intelligent individuals did not bolsters the argument that more than just intelligence is operating here. . . .

References

Anderson, C. R., & Schneier, C. E. (1978). Locus of control, leader behavior, and leader performance among management students. *Academy of Management Journal, 21,* 690–698.

Bass, B. M. (1985). *Leadership and performance beyond expectations.* New York: Free Press.

Bass, B. M. (1990). *Bass and Stogdill's handbook of leadership: A survey of theory and leadership.* New York: Free Press.

Baumgardner, T. L., Lord, R. G., & Maher, K. J. (1991) Perceptions of women in management. In R. G. Lord & K. J. Maher (Eds.), *Leadership and information processing: Linking perceptions and performance* (pp. 95–113). Boston: Unwin Hyman.

Bem, S. L. (1974). The measurement of psychological androgyny. *Journal of Consulting and Clinical Psychology, 42,* 155–162.

Bem, S. L. (1975). Sex-role adaptability: One consequence of psychological androgyny. *Journal of Personality and Social Psychology, 31,* 634–643.

Bem, S. L., & Lenney, E. (1976). Sex typing and the avoidance of cross-sex behavior. *Journal of Personality and Social Psychology, 33,* 48–54.

Berdahl, J. L. (1996). Gender and leadership in work groups: Six alternative models. *Leadership Quarterly, 7,* 20–40.

Carbonell, J. L. (1984). Sex roles and leadership revisited. *Journal of Applied Psychology, 69,* 44–49.

Carli, L. L., & Eagly, A. H. (1999). Gender effects on social influence and emergent leadership. In G. N.

Powell (Ed.), *Handbook of gender and work* (pp. 203–222). Thousand Oaks, CA: Sage.

Cohen, J. (1992). A power primer. *Psychological Bulletin, 112,* 155–159.

Davis, B. L., Skube, C. J., Hellervik, L. W., Gebelein, S. H., & Sheard, J. L. (1996). *Successful managers's handbook.* Minneapolis, MN: Personnel Decisions International.

Deal, J. J., & Stevenson, M. A. (1998). Perceptions of female and male managers in the 1990s: Plus ça change . . . *Sex Roles, 38,* 287–300.

Diekman, A. B., & Eagly, A. H. (2000). Stereotypes as dynamic constructs: Women and men of the past, present, and future. *Personality and Social Psychology Bulletin, 26,* 1171–1188.

Dodrill, C. B. (1981). An economical method for the evaluation of general intelligence in adults. *Journal of Consulting and Clinical Psychology, 49,* 668–673.

Dodrill, C. B. (1983). Long-term reliability of the Wonderlic Personnel Test, *Journal of Consulting and Clinical Psychology, 51,* 316–317.

Dodrill, C. B., & Warner, M. H. (1988). Further studies of the Wonderlic Personnel Text as a brief measure of intelligence. *Journal of Consulting and Clinical Psychology, 56,* 145–147.

Eagly, A. H. (1987). *Sex differences in social behavior: A social role interpretation.* Hillsdale, NJ: Lawrence Erlbaum.

Eagly, A. H., & Johnson, B. T. (1990). Gender and leadership style: A meta-analysis. *Psychological Bulletin, 2,* 233–256.

Eagly, A. H., & Karan, S. J. (1991). Gender and the emergence of leaders: A meta-analysis. *Journal of Personality and Social Psychology, 60,* 685–710.

Eagly, A. H., Makhijani, M. G., & Klonsky, B. G. (1992). Gender and the evaluation of leaders: A meta-analysis. *Psychological Bulletin, 111,* 3–22.

Fleischer, R. A., & Chertkoff, J. M. (1986). Effects of dominance and sex on leader selection in dyadic work groups. *Journal of Personality and Social Psychology, 50,* 94–99.

Gibbs, J. L. (1982). Personality patterns of delinquent females: Ethnic and sociocultural variations. *Journal of Clinical Psychology, 38,* 198–206.

Goeke, K. R., Tosi, D. J., & Eshbaugh, D. M. (1993), Personality patterns of male felons in a correctional halfway house setting: An MMPI typology analysis. *Journal of Clinical Psychology, 49,* 413–422.

Goktepe, J. R., & Schneier, C. E. (1989). Role of sex, gender roles, and attraction in predicting emergent leaders. *Journal of Applied Psychology, 74,* 165–167.

Hall, R. J., Workman, J. W., & Marchioro, C. A. (1998). Sex, task, and behavioral flexibility effects on leadership perceptions. *Organizational Behavior and Human Decision Processes, 74,* 1–32.

Hawkins, K. W. (1995). Effects of gender and communication content on leadership emergence in small task-oriented groups. *Small Group Research, 26,* 234–249.

Hegstrom, J. L., & Griffith, W. L. (1992). Dominance, sex, and leader emergence. *Sex Roles, 27,* 209–220.

Heilman, M. E., Block, C. J., Simon, M. C., & Martell, R. F. (1989). Has anything changed? Current characterizations of men, women, and managers. *Journal of Applied Psychology, 74,* 935–942.

Hoffman, R. M., & Borders, D. (2001). Twenty-five years after the Bem Sex Role Inventory: A reassessment and new issues regarding classification variability. *Measurement and Evaluation in Counseling and Development, 34,* 39–55.

House, A., Dallinger, J. M., & Kilgallen, D. (1998). Androgyny and rhetorical sensitivity: The connection of gender and communicator style. *Communication Reports, 11,* 11–20.

Huston-Comeaux, S. L., & Kelly, J. R. (1996). Sex differences in interaction style and group task performance: The process-performance relationship. *Journal of Social Behavior and Personality, 11,* 255–275.

Karakowsky, L., & Siegel, J. P. (1999). The effects of proportional representation and gender orientation of the task on emergent leadership in mixed-gender work groups. *Journal of Applied Psychology, 84,* 620–631.

Kawakami, C., White, J. B., & Langer, E. J. (2000). Mindful and masculine: Freeing women leaders from the constraints of gender roles. *Journal of Social Issues, 56,* 49–63.

Kent, R. L., & Moss, S. E. (1994). Effects of sex and gender role on leader emergence. *Academy of Management Journal, 37,* 1335–1346.

Kolb, J. A. (1997). Are we still stereotyping leadership? A look at gender and other predictors of leader emergence. *Small Group Research, 28,* 370–393.

Konrad, A. M., Ritchie, E., Jr., Lieb, P., & Corrigall, E. (2000). Sex differences and similarities in job attribute preferences: A meta-analysis. *Psychological Bulletin, 126,* 593–641.

Levene, H. (1960). Test of homogeneity of variances. In I. Olkin, S. Ghurye, W. Hoeffdiug, W. Madow, & H. Mann (Eds.), *Contributions to probability and statistics: Essays in honor of Harold Hotelling* (pp. 278–292). Palo Alto, CA: Stanford University Press.

Lord, R. G., Brown, D. J., & Harvey, J. L. (2001). System constraints on leadership perceptions, behavior, and influence: An example of connectionist level process. In M. A. Hogg & R. S. Tindale (Eds.), *Blackwell handbook of social psychology, Vol. 3: Group processes.* Oxford, UK: Basil Blackwell.

Lord, R. G., De Vader, C. L., & Alligen G. M. (1986). A meta-analysis of the relation between personality traits and leadership perceptions: An application of validity generalization procedures. *Journal of Applied Psychology, 71,* 402–410.

Lord, R. G., & Emrich, C. G. (2001). Thinking outside the box by looking inside the box: Extending the cognitive revolution in leadership research. *Leadership Quarterly, 11,* 551–579.

Lord, R. G., Foti, R. J., & De Vader, C. L. (1984). A test of leadership categorization theory: Internal structure, information processing, and leadership perceptions. *Organizational Behavior and Human Performance, 34,* 343–378.

Lord, R. G., & Maher, K. J. (1991). *Leadership and information processing: Linking perceptions and performance.* Boston: Unwin Hyman.

Lord, R. G., & Smith, W. G. (1998). Leadership and the changing nature of work performance. In D. R. Ilgen & E. D. Pulakos (Eds.), *The changing nature of work performance: Implications for staffing, personnel decisions, and development.* San Francisco: Jossey-Bass.

Luthar, H. K. (1996). Gender differences in evaluation of performance and leadership ability: Autocratic vs. democratic managers. *Sex Roles, 35,* 337–361.

Magnusson, D. (1995). Individual development: A holistic, integrated model. In P. Moen, G. L. Elder, Jr., & K. Luscher (Eds.), *Examining lives in context* (pp. 19–60). Washington, DC: American Psychological Association.

McClelland, D. C., & Boyatzis, R. E. (1982). Leadership motive pattern and long-term success in management. *Journal of Applied Psychology, 67,* 737–743.

McGrath, J. E. (1984). *Groups: Interaction and performance.* Englewood Cliffs, NJ: Prentice Hall.

Megargee, E. I. (1969). Influence of sex roles on the manifestation of leadership. *Journal of Applied Psychology, 53,* 377–382.

Moss, S. E., & Kent, R. L. (1996). Gender and gender-role categorization of emergent leaders: A critical review and comprehensive analysis. *Sex Roles, 35,* 79–96.

Motowidlo, S. J. (1981). A scoring procedure for sex-role orientation based on profile similarity indices. *Educational and Psychological Measurement, 41,* 735–745.

Powell, G. N., & Butterfield, D. A., (1979). Sex, attributions, and leadership: A brief review. *Psychological Reports, 51,* 1171–1174.

Ridgeway, C. L. (2001). Gender, status, and leadership. *Journal of Social Issues, 57,* 637–655.

Ross, S. M., & Offermann, L. R. (1997). Transformational leaders: Measurement of personality attributes and work group performance. *Personality and Social Psychology Bulletin, 10,* 1078–1086.

Schneier, C. E., & Bartol, K. M. (1980). Sex effects in emergent leadership. *Journal of Applied Psychology, 65,* 341–345.

Smith, J. A., & Foti, R. J. (1998). A pattern approach to the study of leadership emergence. *Leadership Quarterly, 9,* 147–160.

Sorrentino, R. M., & Field, N. (1986). Emergent leadership over time: The functional value of positive motivation. *Journal of Personality and Social Psychology, 50,* 1091–1099.

Spence, J. T., Helmreich, R. L., & Stapp, J. (1975). Ratings of self and peers on sex-role attributes and their relation to self-esteem and conceptions of masculinity and femininity. *Journal of Personality and Social Psychology, 32,* 29–39.

Tango, R. A., & Uziuban, C. U. (1984). The use of personality components in the interpretation of career indecision. *Journal of College Student Personnel, 25,* 509–512.

Wentworth, D. K., & Anderson, L. R. (1984). Emergent leadership as a function of sex and task type. *Sex Roles, 11,* 513–524.

Wonderlic, E. F. (1983). *Wonderlic Personnel Test Manual.* Northfield, IL: E. P. Wonderlic & Associates.

Zaccaro, S. J., Foti, R. J., & Kenny, D. A. (1991). Self-monitoring and trait-based variance in leadership: An investigation of leader flexibility across multiple group situations. *Journal of Applied Psychology, 76,* 308–315.

Zaccaro, S. J., Gilbert, J. A., Thor, K. K., & Mumford, M. D. (1991). Leadership and social intelligence: Linking social perceptiveness and behavioral flexibility to leader effectiveness. *Leadership Quarterly, 2,* 317–342.

Reading 13

Gender and Leadership Style

A Meta-analysis

Alice H. Eagly and Blair T. Johnson
Purdue University

In recent years many social scientists, management consultants, and other writers have addressed the topic of gender and leadership style. Some authors with extensive experience in organizations who write nontechnical books for management audiences and the general public have argued for the presence of sex differences in leadership style. For example, Loden (1985) maintained that there is a masculine mode of management characterized by qualities such as competitiveness, hierarchical authority, high control for the leader, and unemotional and analytic problem solving. Loden argued that women prefer and tend to behave in terms of an alternative feminine leadership model characterized by cooperativeness, collaboration of managers and subordinates, lower control for the leader, and problem solving based on intuition and empathy as well as rationality. Loden's writing echoes the androgynous manager theme developed earlier by Sargent (1981), who accepted the idea that women and men, including those who are managers in organizations, behave stereotypically to some extent. Sargent advocated that managers of each sex adopt "the best" of the other sex's qualities to become more effective, androgynous managers. In a somewhat different rendition of this sex-difference theme, Hennig and Jardin (1977) also acknowledged sex-differentiated managerial behavior, which they ascribed to personality traits acquired in early socialization, particularly through differing male and female resolutions of the Oedipus complex.

Source: Edited and reprinted with permission from *Psychological Bulletin* 108 (1990), 233–256. Copyright (1990) by the American Psychological Association. Author A. H. Eagly made some additional modifications to the original article for this student audience.

This research was supported by National Science Foundation Grants BNS–8605256 and BNS–8807495. Preliminary reports of this research were presented at the Annual Meetings of the Eastern Psychological Association, April 1988; the Midwestern Psychological Association, April 1988; the International Congress of Psychology, September 1988; and the American Psychological Association, August 1989. A table showing the effect sizes and study characteristics for each study included in the meta-analysis is available from the first author.

In contrast to these generalizations about gender-stereotypic leadership styles promulgated in books written primarily for practicing managers and the general public, social scientists have generally maintained that there are in fact no reliable differences in the ways that women and men lead. Although a few social scientists have acknowledged that there is some evidence for sex differences in leadership style among research participants who have not been selected for occupancy of leadership roles in natural settings (e.g., Brown, 1979; Hollander, 1985), most have agreed that women and men who occupy leadership roles in organizations do not differ (but see Shakeshaft, 1987, for a contrasting opinion). Illustrating this consensus among social scientists are the following representative statements summarizing research comparing the styles of female and male leaders: "The preponderance of available evidence is that no consistently clear pattern of differences can be discerned in the supervisory style of female as compared to male leaders" (Bass, 1981, p.499); "Contrary to notions about sex specialization in leadership styles, women leaders appear to behave in similar fashion to their male colleagues" (Nieva & Gutek, 1981, p.91); "There is as yet no research evidence that makes a case for sex differences in either leadership aptitude or style" (Kanter, 1977a, p.199); "In general, comparative research indicates that there are few differences in the leadership styles of female and male designated leaders" (Bartol & Martin, 1986, p. 278).

Underlying this divergence in the opinions voiced in popular and social scientific writings is the fact that authors in these two camps have based their conclusions on quite different kinds of data. Authors such as Loden (1985) who have written books for managers and the general public based their conclusions primarily on their own experience in organizations as well as on the impressions they gleaned from interviews with practicing managers. Social scientists typically based their conclusions on more formal studies of managerial behavior in which data were gathered via questionnaires or behavioral observations and then analyzed quantitatively. In view of these contrasting methods, it is tempting for social scientists to dismiss the generalizations that are based on personal experience and interviews and to accept as valid only those conclusions that stem from more formal empirical research on leadership. However, the generalizations that social scientists appear to have accepted in this area, which stem from reviews of empirical research (e.g., Bartol & Martin, 1986), are quite vulnerable to error because of the relatively informal methods by which reviewers have drawn conclusions from the available research. With only one exception,[1] these reviews were traditional, narrative reviews and, therefore, were not based on any clear rules about how one derives conclusions from research findings. Moreover, none of the existing reviews was based on more than a small proportion of the available studies. For example, both Bartol and Martin (1986) and Dobbins and Platz (1986) based their generalizations on eight studies that compared the leadership styles of men and women, yet we located 162 studies pertaining only to the four types of leadership style we included in our meta-analysis (see *Method*). Moreover, prior reviewers did not state the criteria by which they selected their small samples of studies. As we became aware of these selection problems and of the severe underuse of available research on gender and leadership style, we decided that a thorough survey of this domain was long overdue. Our meta-analysis thus provides a systematic, quantitative integration of the available research in which the leadership styles of men and women were compared and statistical analyses were performed on the resulting data.

THEORETICAL ANALYSIS OF SEX DIFFERENCES IN LEADERSHIP STYLES

Leaving aside the claims of both the social scientists and the management experts who have written about gender and leadership style, we face a topic of considerable complexity that we analyze from several perspectives. One of our perspectives takes into account existing knowledge about sex differences in social behaviors such as aggression, helping, and conformity as well as numerous nonverbal and communicative behaviors. Large numbers of laboratory and field studies have been performed on such behaviors, primarily by social psychologists, and in many of these studies female and male behavior has been compared. Quantitative reviews of this research

have established the presence rather than the absence of overall sex differences (see overviews by Eagly, 1987; Eagly & Wood, in press; Hall, 1984). These differences, although typically not large, tend to be comparable in magnitude to most other findings reported in social psychological research. On the average, sex appears to be a variable that has neither especially impactful nor especially weak effects on social behavior and that produces findings consistent with laypeople's ideas about how the sexes differ (see Eagly, 1987).

REASONS TO EXPECT THE ABSENCE OF SEX DIFFERENCES IN LEADERSHIP STYLE

Despite the gender-stereotypic findings generally produced in studies of social behavior, similar results would not necessarily be obtained for leaders and managers because of important differences between leadership research and typical research in social psychology. In particular, the majority of leadership studies have been performed in organizations. In contrast, most social psychological research has been carried out in experimental laboratories and to a lesser extent in field settings not embedded within organizations (e.g., on street corners). In such environments, subjects interact with strangers on a short-term basis, and the constraints of organizational and familial roles are generally minimal or absent. Consequently, there is often considerable ambiguity about how one should behave, and people may react in terms of quite global and readily observable attributes of themselves and others (e.g., sex, age, race, and general physical appearance). In situations of this type, gender roles, which are rules about how one should behave as a male or female, may provide more guidance than they otherwise would and thus produce gender-stereotypic behavior.

Behavior may be less stereotypic when women and men who occupy the same managerial role are compared because these organizational leadership roles, which typically are paid jobs, usually provide fairly clear guidelines about the conduct of behavior. Managers become socialized into their roles in the early stages of their experience in an organization (see Feldman, 1976; Graen, 1976; Terborg, 1977; Wanous, 1977). In addition, male and female managers have presumably been selected by organizations (and have selected themselves into these roles) according to the same set of organizationally relevant criteria, further decreasing the likelihood that the men and women who occupy these roles differ substantially in their style. Thus, reasonable assumptions about socialization into leadership roles and selection for these roles suggest that male and female leaders *who occupy the same organizational role* should differ very little. Managers of both sexes are presumably more concerned about managing effectively than about representing sex-differentiated features of societal gender roles.

This argument that organizational roles should override gender roles is consistent with Kanter's (1977a) structural interpretation of organizational behavior. Kanter argued that apparent sex differences in the behavior of organizational leaders are in fact a product of the differing structural positions of the sexes within organizations. Because women are more often in positions of little power or opportunity for advancement, they behave in ways that reflect their lack of power. Kanter's reasoning thus suggests that women and men who are equivalent in terms of status and power would behave similarly, even though sex differences may appear to be substantial when women and men are compared without control of their organizational status.

REASONS TO EXPECT THE PRESENCE OF SEX DIFFERENCES IN LEADERSHIP STYLE

Despite these reasons for arguing that differences between female and male organizational leaders should be minimal, other perspectives suggest that sex differences may be common, especially in some types of leadership research. As our reasoning has already implied, the social structural rationale for the absence of differences between occupants of the same managerial role within organizations is fully consistent with the presence of differences in leadership studies that compare women and men in other circumstances. In the leadership literature, there are two major types of studies that did not examine organizational leaders—namely, laboratory experiments, usually conducted with college students, and assessment studies, which we defined as research assessing the styles of people who were not selected for occupancy of leadership positions. Because the social structural rationale for the absence of differences between women and men in the same organizational role is not relevant to studies of these two types, sex-differentiated leadership styles are likely to be prevalent in such research, just as gender-stereotypic behavior is commonly found in social psychological research more generally.

There are, in addition, several reasons to suggest that male and female organizational leaders, even those who occupy the same positions, may

differ to some extent in their leadership style despite the structural forces for minimizing differences that we have already noted. One such reason acknowledges the possibility of ingrained sex differences in personality traits and behavioral tendencies, differences that are not nullified by organizational selection or socialization. For example, some psychologists have maintained that sex differences in adult social behavior are in part a product of biological influences such as the greater prenatal androgynization of males (e.g., Money & Ehrhardt, 1972). Other psychologists have emphasized the importance of childhood events that are different for the sexes such as experiences that occur in sex-segregated play groups in which girls and boys play in different styles and use different methods of influencing one another (Maccoby, 1988). Thus, it is possible that biological sex differences and sex-differentiated prior experiences cause men and women to be somewhat different kinds of people, even if they do occupy the same managerial role. It may not be possible to find men and women who are so nearly equivalent that trait-level differences disappear entirely, even though sex differences in the behavior of organizational leaders may be smaller than those in the general population. In particular, men and women may come to managerial roles with a somewhat different set of skills. Especially relevant is the evidence meta-analyses have provided for women's social skills: Women as a group, when compared with men as a group, can be described as friendly, pleasant, interested in other people, expressive, and socially sensitive (see Eagly, 1987; Hall, 1984). To the extent that such findings reflect ingrained sex differences that are not leveled by organizational selection or socialization, male and female managers may behave differently, despite structural forces toward sameness.

Another perspective suggesting that leader behavior may be somewhat sex differentiated in organizations postulates *gender-role spillover,* which is "a carryover into the workplace of gender-based expectations for behavior" (Gutek & Morasch, 1982, p. 58; see also Nieva & Gutek, 1981). The spillover concept suggests that gender roles may contaminate organizational roles to some extent and cause people to have different expectations for female and male managers. In support of this idea, Russell, Rush, and Herd (1988) found that university women described an effective female (vs. male) leader as exhibiting higher levels of both the interpersonally oriented and the task-oriented aspects of leadership (i.e., higher in consideration and initiation of structure, see discussion of these variables in next subsection).[2]

Consistent with the idea that gender roles spill over to organizational roles, several social scientists have claimed that female leaders and managers experience conflict between their gender role and their leadership role (see Bass, 1981; Bayes & Newton, 1978; Kruse & Wintermantel, 1986; O'Leary, 1974). This conflict arises for female leaders because the stereotype of manager and the normative expectations associated with being a good manager include more masculine than feminine qualities (see Powell, 1988). The idea that women are subjected to incompatible expectations from the managerial and the female role thus presumes that gender roles are important within organizations.

Another manifestation of the spillover of gender roles onto organizational roles is that people who hold positions in organizations tend to have negative attitudes about women occupying managerial roles. Reflecting the subordinate status of women in the society, numerous studies have shown that people are often reluctant to have a female supervisor and think that women are somewhat less qualified for leadership and that female managers would have negative effects on morale (see reviews by O'Leary, 1974; Riger & Galligan, 1980; Terborg, 1977). Because these attitudes and beliefs raise questions about women's competence, ability to lead, and potential for advancement, female managers often face a less supportive environment than male managers. Sex differences in leadership style might result from this aspect of gender-role spillover as well as from the other aspects we have noted.

Finally, some of the fine-grained features of the structural interpretation of organizational behavior suggest other possible sources of sex differences in the behavior of organizational leaders. One such consideration is that, as Kanter (1977b) pointed out, women in managerial roles often have the status of *token* because of their rarity in such positions. Thus, female managers commonly are members of a numerically small minority, whereas their male counterparts are members of a majority group. As Kanter and others argued, token status increases one's visibility (Taylor, Fiske, Etcoff, & Ruderman, 1978) and can have a number of negative implications for how one is perceived and treated, especially when the token is a woman (Crocker & McGraw, 1984; Ott, 1989; Yoder & Sinnett, 1985). In addition, even those female and male leaders who occupy the same organizational role may differ systematically in seniority, salary, the availability of mentoring and informal collegial support, and other characteristics that convey some of the subtleties of organizational status. Women, especially as relative newcomers in many managerial roles, tend to have less status in these ways, and this difference may be reflected in their behavior.

In summary, ingrained sex differences in traits and behavioral tendencies, a spillover of gender roles onto organizational roles, and subtle differences in the structural position of women and men could cause leadership behavior to be somewhat sex-differentiated even when occupants of the same organizational role are compared. Therefore, some evidence of sex differences in leadership style in organizational studies would not be surprising. Nonetheless, our reasoning that organizational roles are more important than gender roles led us to predict that differences between men and women occupying the same leadership role in organizations would be smaller than differences between men and women observed in other types of leadership research, namely laboratory experiments and assessment studies.

DESIGN OF THE META-ANALYSIS

TYPES OF LEADERSHIP STYLE

The fact that investigators have examined many facets of leadership style (see Bass, 1981) requires that reviewers decide which facets to include and how to organize them into types. In examining this issue, we found that the majority of the studies had assessed the extent to which leaders or managers were concerned with two aspects of their work. The first of these aspects we termed *task accomplishment* (or, for brevity, task style)— that is, organizing activities to perform assigned tasks. The second aspect we termed *maintenance of interpersonal relationships* (or, for brevity, interpersonal style)—that is, tending to the morale and welfare of the people in the setting.

This distinction between task and interpersonal styles was first represented in leadership research by Bales (1950), who proposed two categories of leaders, those with an orientation to task accomplishment and those with a socioemotional orientation indicative of concern for morale and relationships among group members. This distinction was developed further in the Ohio State studies on leadership (e.g., Halpin, 1957; Halpin & Winer, 1957; Hemphill & Coons, 1957; Stogdill, 1963). In this research, task orientation, labeled *initiation of structure,* included behavior such as having subordinates follow rules and procedures, maintaining high standards for performance, and making leader and subordinate roles explicit. Interpersonal orientation, labeled *consideration,* included behavior such as helping and doing favors for subordinates, looking out for their welfare, explaining procedures, and being friendly and available. Task and interpersonal orientations are typically regarded as separate, relatively orthogonal dimensions (e.g., in the Leader Behavior Description Questionnaire [LBDQ] constructed by the Ohio State researchers; Halpin & Winer, 1957). Less commonly, these orientations are treated as two ends of a single continuum (e.g., in the Least Preferred Co-Worker [LPC] instruments; Fiedler, 1967).[3]

Task and interpersonal styles in leadership research are obviously relevant to gender because of the stereotypes people have about sex differences in these aspects of behavior (see Ashmore, Del Boca, & Wohlers, 1986; Eagly & Steffen, 1984). Men are believed to be more self-assertive and motivated to master their environment (e.g., more aggressive, independent, self-sufficient, forceful, dominant). In contrast, women are believed to be more selfless and concerned with others (e.g., more kind, helpful, understanding, warm, sympathetic, aware of others' feelings). In research on gender, these two orientations have been labeled *masculine and feminine, instrumental and expressive,* and *agentic* and *communal.* Although the task and interpersonal dimensions studied in leadership research are not as broad as these very general tendencies examined in gender stereotype research, the ideas are quite similar. Therefore, leadership research provides an excellent opportunity to determine whether the behavior of leaders is gender stereotypic.

The only other aspect of leadership style studied frequently enough to allow us to represent it in our meta-analysis is the extent to which leaders (a) behave democratically and allow subordinates to participate in decision making, or (b) behave autocratically and discourage subordinates from participating in decision making.[4] The dimension of *democratic* versus *autocratic* leadership (or *participative* versus *directive* leadership) follows from early experimental studies of leadership style (e.g., Lewin & Lippitt, 1938) and has been developed since that time by a number of researchers (e.g., Likert, 1961; Vroom & Yetton, 1973). Although democratic versus autocratic style is a different (and narrower) aspect of leader behavior than task-oriented and interpersonally oriented styles (see Bass, 1981), the demo-

cratic–autocratic dimension also relates to gender stereotypes, because one component of the agentic or instrumental aspect of these stereotypes is that men are relatively dominant and controlling (i.e., more autocratic and directive than women).

METHODS OF ASSESSING LEADERSHIP STYLE

The diversity of the methods that have been used to assess style complicates the task of integrating research in this area. Moreover, a substantial methodological literature criticizes and compares these measures (see Bass, 1981). Because the methodological issues that have been raised remain largely unresolved by leadership researchers, we did not attempt to settle these issues in order to base our meta-analytic generalizations on only those measures that we or other investigators might regard as most valid. Instead, we included all measures that researchers regarded as assessing task-oriented and interpersonally oriented styles or autocratic versus democratic style. We coded our studies on a number of these measures' features, many of which may be regarded as having implications for the quality of the measures. For example, measures differed in how directly or indirectly they assessed leadership style; the most direct measures were based on observers' coding of ongoing leadership behavior, and the most indirect measures were based on leaders' responses to questionnaire measures of attitudes or personality. Representing such features in our coding scheme (see *Method*) allowed us to determine whether they covaried with sex differences in leadership style.

CONGENIALITY OF LEADERSHIP ROLES FOR MEN AND WOMEN

When we thought about gender in relation to the available studies of leadership style, we were struck by the variation in the extent to which the leadership roles investigated in this research (e.g., elementary school principal, nursing supervisor, military officer) would be perceived as congenial mainly for women or men. For leadership roles that are typically regarded as especially suitable for women, negative attitudes toward female leaders presumably would not be prevalent, nor would conflict between the female and the leader role be an issue. Presumably women would be under less pressure to adopt male-stereotypic styles of leadership in such positions.

To enable us to take account of the gender congeniality of leadership roles, we conducted a questionnaire study to obtain judgments of each role and analyzed these judgments to estimate the extent to which women or men were more interested in each role and believed themselves more competent to perform it. In addition, because people associate task-oriented qualities with men and interpersonally oriented qualities with women, we also determined the extent to which each role was judged to require each set of these gender-stereotypic qualities. These features of our meta-analysis allowed us to determine whether the ascription of gender-stereotypic qualities to leadership roles related to sex differences in the styles by which people carry out these roles.

PREDICTIONS FOR META-ANALYSIS

As we have already stated, our major prediction is that gender-stereotypic sex differences in leadership style are less pronounced in organizational studies comparing occupants of the same managerial role than in leadership studies of other types. Beyond this prediction, our purposes as reviewers are primarily descriptive and exploratory, even though other predictions might follow from the issues we have discussed. For example, if, as we suggested, female managers often face a less supportive environment than do male managers, these women might strive so hard to overcome antifemale prejudices that they behave counter-stereotypically as a result. Additional complexities enter if we reason that ratings of leaders' behavior could produce findings that are more stereotypic than those produced by measures grounded more firmly in behavior. Rather than set forth a series of speculative hypotheses that take these and other considerations into account, we prefer to present our review and to discuss such issues as they become relevant to interpreting our meta-analytic findings. . . .

SUMMARY OF METHOD[5]

The method used in this project was meta-analysis. The task of meta-analyzing requires the following steps: (a) locating relevant studies and deciding whether they are appropriate for inclusion, (b) coding the studies to represent their attributes, (c) computing effect sizes to represent the studies' findings, and (d) performing statistical analyses on the effect sizes. One type of statistical analysis in this meta-analysis consisted of averaging the effect sizes to determine what the overall findings were in the studies that had compared the leadership styles of men and women. A second type of analysis consisted of using the attributes of the

studies to predict the effect sizes; the point of these analyses was to find out if studies with different attributes produced different results.

Locating the studies was accomplished primarily by performing keyword searches in databases such as PsycINFO, *Dissertation Abstracts International,* and ABI/INFORM. Other studies were located by scrutinizing existing reviews in articles and books and searching through the reference lists of all of the studies that were located. We then developed decision rules for including studies, and many studies were excluded by them. For example, studies that assessed participants' *ideas* about ideal leadership styles were omitted because we were interested only in actual leadership style.

The coding of the studies was carried out by the two authors working independently. The results of their coding were then compared to assess inter-rater reliability and to catch any errors that either person made. Many features were coded, including characteristics of the report (e.g., publication date); type of study (organizational, assessment, or laboratory); level of leadership (line, middle, or higher); percentage of men among leaders and subordinates; and type of style assessed (interpersonal, task, interpersonal versus task, or democratic versus autocratic). It was also important to keep track of the identity of the raters whose data provided the measure of leadership style: The main variants were that people rated themselves, supervisors rated the leaders, subordinates rated the leaders, peers rated the leaders, or judges not related organizationally to the leaders rated the leaders. What was rated to produce a measure of leadership style also differed across the studies: The main types of ratings were responses to attitude or personality scales, responses to hypothetical leadership situations, presumed observation of a leader's behavior (e.g., subordinates rating how their supervisor typically behaved), and actual observation of a leader's behavior based on behaviors made available during the study itself.

Another important part of the method consisted of having student judges rate each leadership role that appeared in the studies of leadership style. These ratings provided an assessment of the perceived gender congeniality of the roles—that is, whether women or men would be more comfortable in the role and more attracted to it. The means of the ratings of the role were attached to each study in the meta-analytic data set as additional characteristics of the studies. These rated variables thus provided a numerical representation of the extent to which the role in each study was more congenial to men (e.g., military officer) or more congenial to women (e.g., nursing supervisor).

For this rating task, the student judges each received a questionnaire in which leadership roles were briefly described—for example, "principal of an elementary school," "manager in the communications division of a company," "director of intercollegiate athletics in a major university," and "leader of a laboratory group trying to decide which items to take along in order to survive in a desert." Ratings were made in response to the following questions: (a) How competent would you be as a [role description given]? (b) How interested would you be in becoming a [role description given]? (c) How interested would the *average woman* be in becoming a [role description given]? (d) How interested would the *average man* be in becoming a [role description given]? (e) How much *ability to cooperate and get along with other people* is needed to be an effective [role description given]? (f) How much *ability to direct and control people* is needed to be an effective [role description given]? For the competence and interest questions, role congeniality was represented by differencing the ratings of the male and female judges. The responses to the questions about the average woman and average man were analyzed by subtracting the average woman rating from the average man rating to yield a stereotypic sex difference. The question on cooperation and getting along with others and the question on directing and controlling were used separately to estimate how much interpersonal ability and task ability each leadership role was perceived to require.

The authors calculated an effect size for each study to represent the sex difference in leadership style. If more than one type of style was assessed, more than one effect size was computed. Each effect size consisted of the difference in the leadership style of the men and women on whatever measure was used, divided by the pooled standard deviation. A positive sign was given to stereotypic differences (i.e., women more interpersonally oriented, men more task-oriented, women more democratic and less autocratic), and a negative sign to counterstereotypic differences.

SUMMARY OF RESULTS

One component of the results consisted of a presentation of frequency distributions classifying the studies on all of the study characteristics, to display the kinds of studies that were typical or atypical of this research literature. This display showed, for example, that the majority of the studies were doctoral dissertations rather than journal articles, that most studies were organizational, that middle managers were usually examined, and that most leadership measures required people to rate themselves or subordinates to rate their supervisors. Also displayed in the results were the specific measures of leadership style used, many of which were standard, well-validated instruments.

Another component of the results consisted of averages of the effect sizes across all of the studies for each type of leadership style that had been studied. These mean sex differences showed little evidence that men and women differed in their interpersonal style or task style. However, on measures that assessed tendencies to be democratic versus autocratic or participative versus directive, men were more autocratic or directive than women, and women were more democratic or participative than men.

Because averaging effect sizes over all of the studies can obscure important results that are limited to subgroups of studies, we divided the studies into the three main types of studies that we had identified: organizational, assessment, and laboratory. We found that the absence of sex differences for task and interpersonal style that appeared in our analysis averaged over all of the studies was limited to the organizational studies. In contrast, in the laboratory studies, and to some extent in the assessment studies, men and women did have stereotypic styles, with men appearing more task-oriented and women more interpersonally oriented. However, the tendency for women to be more participative and democratic than men was intact in all three classes of studies, including the organizational. This sex difference on democratic–autocratic styles was thus quite robust. Yet, another analysis showed that in studies in which women were rare as leaders (i.e., they were numerical tokens), the tendency for them to be more participative and democratic than men eroded.

One of the most provocative findings showed the influence of the gender congeniality of the leadership roles. These are the variables that we constructed from judges' ratings of the roles. Gender congeniality influenced sex differences in task style. If the leadership role was more congenial to men than women, men were more task-oriented than women. If the role was more congenial to women than men, women were more task-oriented than men.

DISCUSSION

INTERPERSONAL AND TASK STYLES

Our major hypothesis was that stereotypic sex differences would be less pronounced in organizational studies than in assessment or laboratory studies. Indeed, this hypothesis was confirmed for both interpersonal and task styles. These findings support our arguments that the criteria organizations use for selecting managers and the forces they maintain for socializing managers into their roles minimize tendencies for the sexes to lead or manage in a stereotypic manner. Yet these data also suggest that people not selected or trained for leadership roles do manifest stereotypic leadership behavior when placed in these roles, as shown by the data from the assessment and the laboratory studies. Moreover, our claim that selection criteria lessen sex differences is strengthened by the finding that those few laboratory leaders who gained their positions through emergence did not manifest the stereotypic styles of laboratory leaders who were appointed. Evidently sex differences were leveled even by the implicit leader selection criteria of initially leaderless groups.

When we ignored whether the sex comparisons were from organizational, assessment, or laboratory studies, sex differences in interpersonal and task styles were quite small, with overall trends toward women being more concerned about both maintenance of interpersonal relationships and task accomplishment. In view of these trends, it is not surprising that measures placing interpersonal and task orientation on the ends of a single dimension produced no sex difference in any of the overall summaries. On such bipolar measures, the stereotypic interpersonal sex difference and the counterstereotypic task difference would cancel one another, resulting in no difference.

Given the variety of settings, roles, and measures encountered in this research, the sex comparisons for the task and interpersonal styles were expected to be inconsistent across the studies. Yet the removal of relatively small numbers of the effect sizes (10 percent to 13 percent) produced homogeneous sets of effect sizes consistent with description in terms of single means. This aspect of the findings lends some confidence to our statements that if we take the entire research literature into account, women's leadership styles emphasize both interpersonal relations and task accomplishment to a slightly greater extent than men's styles.

DEMOCRATIC VERSUS AUTOCRATIC STYLE

The strongest evidence we obtained for a sex difference in leadership style occurred on the tendency for women to adopt a more democratic or participative style and for men to adopt a more autocratic or directive style. Moreover, this sex difference did *not* become smaller in the organizational studies, as did the differences in the interpersonal and task styles. Although the overall mean weighted effect size ($d_+ = 0.22$) was not large, the mean became larger once outliers were removed ($d_+ = 0.27$), and 92 percent of the available comparisons went in the direction of more democratic behavior from women than men. Despite this impressive consistency in the direction of the sex difference, the effect sizes themselves were quite heterogeneous, requiring the removal of 22 percent to obtain a set that did not reject the hypothesis of homogeneity. Yet substantial inconsistency across the studies is not unexpected for this type of style in view of the tendency for investigators to construct unique measures and not to rely on standard instruments, as did most investigators of the other types of leadership style that we reviewed.

Our interpretation of the sex difference in the extent to which leaders behave democratically versus autocratically is necessarily speculative, but follows from some of the considerations that we presented early in this article (see *Reasons to Expect the Presence of Sex Differences in Leadership Style*). We thus argued that women and men recruited into leadership roles in organizations may not be equivalent in personality and behavioral tendencies, even though they satisfy the same selection criteria. In particular, we noted that women's social skills might enable them to perform managerial roles differently than men. Interpersonal behavior that is skillful (e.g., in terms of understanding others' feelings and intentions) should facilitate a managerial style that is democratic and participative. Making decisions in a collaborative style requires not only the soliciting of suggestions from one's peers and subordinates, but also the preservation of good relationships with them when evaluating and perhaps rejecting their ideas. The give-and-take of collaborative decision making introduces interpersonal complexity not encountered by leaders who behave in an autocratic or directive manner. This interpretation is supported by research showing that teachers who lacked social skills, as indexed by their relative inability to decode nonverbal cues, had more autocratic attitudes and were generally more dogmatic (Rosenthal, Hall, DiMatteo, Rogers, & Archer, 1979).

Another perspective on the democratic–autocratic sex difference acknowledges the attitudinal bias against female leaders that we considered in the beginning of the article. The skepticism that many people have expressed concerning women's capabilities in managerial and leadership roles may be exacerbated by any tendency for women in these roles to take charge in an especially authoritative manner. Placating subordinates and peers so that they accept a woman's leadership may to some extent require that she give them input into her decisions and allow some degree of control over these decisions. Moreover, to the extent that women leaders have internalized to some degree the culture's reservations about their capability for leadership, they may gain confidence as leaders by making collaborative decisions that they can determine are in line with their associates' expectations. Thus, proceeding in a participative and collaborative mode may enable many female leaders to win acceptance from others, gain self-confidence, and thereby be effective. Because men are not so constrained by attitudinal bias, they are freer to lead in an autocratic and nonparticipative manner should they so desire.[6]

THE IMPACT OF GENDER CONGENIALITY OF LEADERSHIP ROLES AND SEX DISTRIBUTION OF ROLE OCCUPANTS

Our findings suggested that leaders of each sex emphasized task accomplishment when they were in a leadership role regarded as congruent with their gender. Thus, only the sex differences in task style were significantly correlated with the tendency for the leadership roles to be regarded as more congenial for men or women, as indexed by our questionnaire respondents' judgments. Male leaders tended to be more task oriented than female leaders to the extent that a leadership role was more congenial to men; female leaders tended to be more task oriented than male leaders to the extent that a leadership role was more congenial to women. Furthermore, women tended to be more task oriented than men in leadership roles that are feminine in the sense that our respondents judged they require considerable interpersonal ability.[7]

These findings suggest that being out of role in gender-relevant terms has its costs for leaders in terms of some decline in their tendency to organize activities to accomplish relevant tasks. Because our meta-analytic data are not informative concerning the mediation of these effects, these provocative findings should be explored in primary research. Perhaps people who are out of role lack (or are perceived to lack) the skills necessary to organize the task-relevant aspects of their environment. Out-of-role leaders may be somewhat deficient in the knowledge and authority required to organize people and resources to accomplish task-relevant goals.

The extent to which leadership roles were male dominated numerically also related to sex differences in leadership style. Specifically, the tendencies for female leaders to be more interpersonally oriented and more democratic than male leaders weakened to the extent that a role was male dominated. Thus, when women were quite rare in leadership roles and therefore tended to have the status of token in organizations or groups, they abandoned stereotypically feminine styles characterized by concern for the morale and welfare of people in the work setting and consideration of these people's views when making decisions. These findings suggest that women may tend to lose authority if they adopt distinctively feminine styles of leadership in extremely male-dominated roles. Women who survive in such roles probably have to adopt the styles typical of male role occupants.

CONCLUSION

The view, widely accepted by social scientists expert on leadership, that women and men lead in the same way should be very substantially revised. Similarly, the view, proclaimed in some popular books on management, that female and male leaders have distinctive, gender-stereotypic styles also requires revision. Our quantitative review has established a more complex set of findings. Although these findings require further scrutiny before they should be taken as definitive, the agreement of these findings with our role theory framework substantiates our interpretation of them. Thus, consistent with research on sex differences in numerous social behaviors (Eagly, 1987; Hall, 1984), we have established that leadership style findings generated in experimental settings tend to be gender stereotypic. Indeed, these findings concur with the generalizations of those narrative reviewers who noted that male and female leaders often differ in laboratory experiments (Brown, 1979; Hollander, 1985). In such settings, people interact as strangers without the constraints of long-term role relationships. Gender roles are moderately important influences on behavior in such contexts and tend to produce gender-stereotypic behavior (see Eagly, 1987). In addition, somewhat smaller stereotypic sex differences were obtained in assessment studies, in which people not selected for leadership responded to instruments assessing their leadership styles. Because respondents not under the constraints of managerial roles completed questionnaires in these studies, some tendency for leadership styles to appear stereotypic was expected from the perspective of our social role framework.

When social behavior is regulated by other, less diffuse social roles, as it is in organizational settings, behavior should primarily reflect the influence of these other roles and therefore lose much of its gender-stereotypic character. Indeed, the findings of this meta-analysis for interpersonal and task styles support this logic. Nonetheless, women's leadership styles were more democratic than men's even in organizational settings. This sex difference may reflect underlying differences in female and male personality or skills (e.g., women's superior social skills) or subtle differences in the status of women and men who occupy the same organizational role. Deciding among the various causes that we have discussed would require primary research targeted to this issue.

The magnitude of the aggregate effect sizes we obtained in this meta-analysis deserves comment. When interpreting effect sizes, reviewers should take the methods of the studies into account, and, as Glass, McGaw, and Smith (1981) argued, they should avoid applying numerical guidelines to identify effect sizes as small or large. One feature of research on leadership style that is especially relevant to interpreting the magnitude of our aggregate effect sizes is that investigators face many barriers to achieving well-controlled studies. In organizational studies, the environments in which managers carry out their roles are quite diverse, even within a single organization. Because managers' leadership styles are evaluated either by themselves or by their associates, the various managers in a study are not necessarily evaluated by the same standard. Although more control of environmental influences can be achieved in laboratory studies of leadership (e.g., all leaders can be observed in a similar social setting), even these studies are relatively uncontrolled because each leader interacts with a unique group of followers. Counterbalancing the greater control of environmental factors in laboratory than organizational studies is the less rigorous selection of research participants for laboratory research and the resulting greater variability of leadership style within each sex. In general, uncontrolled variability in both organizational and laboratory studies of leadership would inflate the standard deviations that are the denominators of the effect sizes and thereby decrease the magnitude of these effect sizes. As a consequence, neither sex nor other variables would ordinarily produce large effect sizes in studies of leadership style. Therefore, we believe that effect sizes of the magnitude we obtained are considerably more consequential than effect sizes of the same magnitude obtained in more controlled forms of research.

Our review has not considered the extent to which the sex differences in leadership style that we have documented might produce differences in the effectiveness of leaders. Whether men or women are more effective leaders as a consequence of their differing styles is a complex question that could be addressed meta-analytically only by taking measures of group and organizational outcomes into account along with measures of leadership style. Because experts on leader effectiveness ordinarily maintain that the effectiveness of leadership styles is contingent on features of the group or organizational environment (e.g., Fiedler, 1967; Vroom & Yetton, 1973), we are unwilling to argue that women's relatively democratic and participative style is either an advantage or disadvantage. No doubt a relatively democratic style enhances a leader's effectiveness under some circumstances.[8] Nonetheless, we note that in recent years many management and organizational consultants have criticized traditional management practices for what they believe are overly hierarchical and rigidly bureaucratic forms (Foy, 1980; Heller & Van Til, 1986; Kanter, 1983; Naisbett, 1982; Ouchi, 1981; Peters & Waterman, 1982). Moreover, it is consistent with many feminist theorists' descriptions of hierarchy and domination (e.g., Elshtain, 1981; Miller, 1976) to argue that employment would be less alienating if forms of interaction in the workplace were less hierarchical and instead characterized by cooperation and collaboration between collegial groups of coworkers. Indeed, both consultants and feminists have advocated organizational change toward the more democratic and participative leadership styles that our meta-analysis suggests are more prevalent among women than men.

Notes

1. The one available quantitative review of sex differences in leadership style (Dobbins & Platz, 1986) unfortunately included studies with designs not suited for examining these differences. These inappropriate studies investigated bias in subjects' perceptions of leaders by equalizing the behavior of male and female leaders and varying only the leader's sex (Butterfield & Powell, 1981; Lee & Alvares, 1977). Because equivalence of male and female behavior was ensured in these studies, they cannot be regarded as assessing sex differences in leadership style.

2. Whereas the belief that effective female managers are especially concerned about relationships may reflect stereotypic beliefs about women in general, the belief that effective female managers are especially concerned about task accomplishment may reflect a more complex theory about women having to perform extremely well to succeed as managers.

3. Although the Least Preferred Co-Worker Scale has been given a variety of interpretations, the view that low-LPC people are task oriented and high-LPC people are relationship oriented seems to be the most widely accepted of these interpretations (see Rice, 1978).

4. Although Bass (1981) distinguished between (a) democratic versus autocratic leadership and (b) participative versus directive leadership, we treated these measures as a single class because we found this distinction difficult to maintain when categorizing measures. We refer to this single class as *democratic versus autocratic* style. Researchers have treated this style as a single, bipolar dimension because democratic and autocratic styles presumably are incompatible. In contrast, interpersonal and task styles apparently are not incompatible, as suggested by the preference of most researchers for treating these styles as separate, relatively orthogonal dimensions.

5. The "Summary of Method" and "Summary of Results" sections were prepared by Professor Alice Eagly exclusively for this edited version of the original publication. We sincerely appreciate her time, effort, and contribution to our work.

6. A subsequent meta-analysis by Eagly, Makhijani, and Klonsky (1990) showed that subjects evaluate autocratic behavior by female leaders more negatively than they evaluate the equivalent behavior by male leaders. An additional consideration in interpreting the democratic–autocratic sex difference is that measures of this type were based primarily on leaders' self-reports, and, at least for task and interpersonal styles, leaders' self-reports were more stereotypic than subordinates' reports on leaders (see *Results*). Thus, it is possible that the tendency for women to be more democratic than men was exaggerated somewhat by the reliance on leaders' self-reports in these studies. Yet, because the sex comparisons for the democratic versus autocratic style were more stereotypic than the subset of sex comparisons for the interpersonal and task styles that were based on self-reports, it is very unlikely that this methodological feature of the democratic–autocratic studies fully accounts for the sex difference in this type of style.

7. We explored whether a tendency for laboratory leadership roles to be more congenial for men might have contributed to the more stereotypic task styles found in laboratory (vs. organizational) studies. Indeed, our questionnaire respondents judged the laboratory (vs. organizational) roles as somewhat more congenial to men on the measures of sex differences in competence and interest and on the measure of stereotypic sex differences in interest (*ps* < .05 or smaller). In addition, the laboratory roles were judged to require less interpersonal ability than organizational roles but, contrary to the idea that the laboratory roles were relatively masculine, they were also judged to require less task ability (*ps* < .001). Thus, there was some degree of confounding between the type of study and the gender congeniality of the roles. Nonetheless, the significant relations between the congeniality measures and sex differences in task style remained significant when examined within the set of organizational studies.

8. Consistent with the position that effectiveness of leadership styles depends on a group's task and other considerations, Wood (1987) argued, based on her meta-analysis of sex differences in group performance, that women's distinctive style of social interaction facilitated group performance at tasks requiring positive social activities such as cooperation but lacked this facilitative effect for other types of tasks.

References

Alpren, M. (1954). The development and validation of an instrument used to ascertain a school principal's pattern of behavior (Doctoral dissertation, University of Florida). *Dissertation Abstracts International* 33, 1579A.

Arcy, J. A. B. (1980). Self-perceptions of leader behavior of male and female elementary school principals in selected school districts in the midwest United States (Doctoral dissertation, Iowa State University, 1979). *Dissertation Abstracts International* 40, 3638A.

Ashmore, R. D., Del Boca, F. K., & Wohlers, A. J. (1986). Gender stereotypes. In R. D. Ashmore & F. K. Del Boca (eds.), *The social psychology of female–male relations: A critical analysis of central concepts* (pp. 69–119). Orlando, FL: Academic Press.

Bales, R. F. (1950). *Interaction process analysis: A method for the study of small groups*. Reading, MA: Addison-Wesley.

Barone, F. J. (1982). A comparative study of Theory X–Theory Y attitudes among managers and OD agents. *Dissertation Abstracts International* 42, 4260A. (University Microfilms No. 82–07, 156).

Bartol, K. M., & Martin, D. C. (1986). Women and men in task groups. In R.D. Ashmore & F. K. Del Boca (eds.), *The social psychology of female–male relations: A critical analysis of central concepts* (pp. 259–310). Orlando, FL: Academic Press.

Bass, B. M. (1981). *Stogdill's handbook of leadership: A survey of theory and research* (rev. ed.). New York: Free Press.

Baugher, S. L. (1983). Sex-typed characteristics and leadership dimensions of vocational education administrators in a midwest region of the United States (Doctoral dissertation, University of Missouri–Columbia, 1982). *Dissertation Abstracts International* 44, 22A.

Bayes, M., & Newton, P. M. (1978). Women in authority: A sociopsychological analysis. *Journal of Applied Behavioral Science* 14, 7–20.

Birdsall, P. (1980). A comparative analysis of male and female managerial communication style in two organizations. *Journal of Vocational Behavior* 16, 183–196.

Blake, R. R., & Mouton, J. S. (1964). *The managerial grid*. Houston, TX: Gulf.

Blake, R. R., & Mouton, J. S. (1978). *The new managerial grid*. Houston, TX: Gulf.

Brown, S. M. (1979). Male versus female leaders: A comparison of empirical studies. *Sex Roles* 5, 595–611.

Butterfield, D. A., & Powell, G. N. (1981). Effect of group performance, leader sex, and rater sex on ratings of leader behavior. *Organizational Behavior and Human Performance* 28, 129–141.

Carli, L. L. (1989). Gender differences in interaction style and influence. *Journal of Personality and Social Psychology* 56, 565–576.

Coleman, D. G. (1979). *Barnard's effectiveness and efficiency applied to a leader style model*. Unpublished manuscript, Northeast Missouri State University, Kirksville, MO.

Crocker, J., & McGraw, K. M. (1984). What's good for the goose is not good for the gander: Solo status as an obstacle to occupational achievement for males and females. *American Behavioral Scientist* 27, 357–369.

Crudge, J. (1983). The effect of leadership styles on the rehabilitation training of student-workers (Doctoral dissertation, United States International University, 1982). *Dissertation Abstracts International* 43, 3300A.

Dobbins, G. H. (1986). Equity vs. equality: Sex differences in leadership. *Sex Roles* 15, 513–525.

Dobbins, G. H., Pence, E. C., Orban, J. A., & Sgro, J. A. (1983). The effects of sex of the leader and sex of the subordinate on the use of organizational control policy. *Organizational Behavior and Human Performance* 32, 325–343.

Dobbins, G. H., & Platz, S. J. (1986). Sex differences in leadership: How real are they? *Academy of Management Review* 11, 118–127.

Eagly, A. H. (1987). *Sex differences in social behavior: A social-role interpretation*. Hillsdale, NJ: Erlbaum.

Eagly, A. H., & Carli, L. L. (1981). Sex of researchers and sex-typed communications as determinants of sex differences in influence-ability: A meta-analysis of social influence studies. *Psychological Bulletin* 90, 1–20.

Eagly, A. H., Makhijani, M. G., & Klonsky, B. G. (1990). *Gender and the evaluation of leaders: A meta-analysis*. Manuscript submitted for publication.

Eagly, A. H., & Steffen, V. J. (1984). Gender stereotypes stem from the distribution of women and men into social roles. *Journal of Personality and Social Psychology* 46, 735–754.

Eagly, A. H., & Wood, W. (in press). Explaining sex differences in social behavior: A meta-analytic perspective. *Personality and Social Psychology Bulletin*.

Elshtain, J. (1981). *Public man, private woman: Women in social and political thought*. Princeton, NJ: Princeton University Press.

Feldman, D. C. (1976). A contingency theory of socialization. *Administrative Science Quarterly* 21, 433–452.

Fiedler, F. E. (1967). *A theory of leadership effectiveness*. New York: McGraw-Hill.

Fleishman, E. A. (1953). The management of leadership attitudes in industry. *Journal of Applied Psychology* 36, 153–158.

Fleishman, E. A. (1957). The Leadership Opinion Questionnaire. In R.M. Stogdill & A.E. Coons (eds.), *Leader behavior: Its description and measurement* (pp. 120–133). Columbus, OH: Bureau of Business Research, Ohio State University.

Fleishman, E. A. (1960). *Manual for the Leadership Opinion Questionnaire*. Chicago: Science Research Associates.

Fleishman, E. A. (1970). *Manual for the Supervisory Behavior Description Questionnaire*. Washington, DC: American Institutes for Research.

Foy, N. (1980). *The yin and yang of organizations*. New York: Morrow.

Ghiselli, E. E. (1964). *Theory of psychological measurement*. New York: McGraw-Hill.

Glass, G. V., McGaw, B., & Smith, M. L. (1981). *Meta-analysis in social research*. Beverly Hills, CA: Sage.

Graen, G. (1976). Role-making processes within complex organizations. In M.D. Dunnette (ed.), *Handbook of industrial and organizational psychology* (pp. 1201–1245). Chicago: Rand McNally.

Grobman, H., & Hines, V.A. (1956). What makes a good principal? *National Association of Secondary School Principals Bulletin* 40, 5–16.

Gupta, N., Jenkins, G. D., Jr., & Beehr, T. A. (1983). Employee gender, gender similarity, and supervisor-subordinate cross-evaluations. *Psychology of Women Quarterly* 8, 174–184.

Gustafson, L.C. (1982). The leadership role of the public elementary school media librarian as perceived by the principal and its relationship to the factors of the sex, educational background, and the work experience of the media librarian (Doctoral dissertation, University of Maryland). *Dissertation Abstracts International* 43, 2206A.

Gutek, B. A., & Morasch, B. (1982). Sex-ratios, sex-role spillover, and sexual harassment of women at work. *Journal of Social Issues* 38, 55–74.

Hall, A. H. (1983). The influence of a personal planning workshop on attitudes toward managerial style (Doctoral dissertation, University of Maryland, 1983). *Dissertation Abstracts International* 44, 2953A.

Hall, J. A. (1984). *Nonverbal sex differences: Communication accuracy and expressive style.* Baltimore, MD: Johns Hopkins University Press.

Halpin, A. W. (1957). *Manual for the Leader Behavior Description Questionnaire.* Columbus, OH: Bureau of Business Research, Ohio State University.

Halpin, A. W. (1966). *Theory and research in administration.* New York: Macmillan.

Halpin, A. W., & Winer, B. J. (1957). A factorial study of the leader behavior descriptions. In R. M. Stogdill & A. E. Coons (eds.), *Leader behavior: Its description and measurement* (pp. 39–51). Columbus, OH: Bureau of Business Research, Ohio State University.

Hedges, L. V. (1981). Distribution theory for Glass's estimator of effect size and related estimators. *Journal of Educational Statistics* 6, 107–128.

Hedges, L. V. (1982a). Fitting categorical models to effect sizes from a series of experiments. *Journal of Educational Statistics* 7, 119–137.

Hedges, L. V. (1982b). Fitting continuous models to effect size data. *Journal of Educational Statistics* 7, 245–270.

Hedges, L. V. (1987). How hard is hard science, how soft is soft science? The empirical cumulativeness of research. *American Psychologist* 42, 443–455.

Hedges, L. V., & Becker, B. J. (1986). Statistical methods in the meta-analysis of research on gender differences. In J. S. Hyde & M. C. Linn (eds.), *The psychology of gender: Advances through meta-analysis* (pp. 14–50). Baltimore, MD: Johns Hopkins University Press.

Hedges, L. V., & Olkin, I. (1985). *Statistical methods for meta-analysis.* Orlando, FL: Academic Press.

Heft, M., & Deni, R. (1984). Altering preferences for leadership style of men and women undergraduate residence advisors through leadership training. *Psychological Reports* 54, 463–466.

Heller, T., & Van Til, J. (1986). Leadership and followership: Some summary propositions. In T.Heller, J.Van Til, & L. A. Zurcher (eds.), *Contemporary studies in applied behavioral science: Vol. 4. Leaders and followers: Challenges for the future* (pp. 251–263). Greenwich, CT: JAI Press.

Hemphill, J. K., & Coons, A. E. (1957). Development of the Leader Behavior Description Questionnaire. In R.M. Stogdill & A. E. Coons (eds.), *Leader behavior: Its description and measurement* (pp. 6–38). Columbus, OH: Bureau of Business Research, Ohio State University.

Hennig, M., & Jardin, A. (1977). *The managerial woman.* New York: Anchor Press.

Hersey, P., & Blanchard, K. H. (1977). *Management of organizational behavior: Utilizing human resources* (3rd ed.). Englewood Cliffs, NJ: Prentice-Hall.

Hersey, P., & Blanchard, K. H. (1982). *Management of organizational behavior: Utilizing human resources* (4th ed.). Englewood Cliffs, NJ: Prentice-Hall.

Hollander, E. P. (1985). Leadership and power. In G.Lindzey & E. Aronson (eds.), *Handbook of social psychology* (3rd ed., Vol. 2, pp. 485–537). New York: Random House.

Hughes, H., Jr., Copeland, D. R., Ford, L. H., & Heidt, E. A. (1983). *Leadership and management education and training (LMET) course requirements for recruit company and "A" school instructors* (Tech. Rep. No.154, Report No. AD-A137306). Orlando, FL: Department of the Navy.

Hurst, A. G., Stein, K. B., Korchin, S. J., & Soskin, W.F. (1978). Leadership style determinants of cohesiveness in adolescent groups. *International Journal of Group Psychotherapy* 28, 263–277.

Jacoby, J., & Terborg, J. R. (1975). *Managerial Philosophies Scale.* Conroe, TX: Teleometrics International.

Kanter, R. M. (1977a). *Men and women of the corporation.* New York: Basic Books.

Kanter, R. M. (1977b). Some effects of proportions on group life: Skewed sex ratios and responses to token women. *American Journal of Sociology* 82, 965–990.

Kanter, R. M. (1983). *The change masters: Innovations for productivity in the American corporation.* New York: Simon and Schuster.

Koberg, C. S. (1985). Sex and situational influences on the use of power: A follow-up study. *Sex Roles* 13, 625–639.

Kruse, L., & Wintermantel, M. (1986). Leadership Ms.-qualified: I. The gender bias in everyday and scientific thinking. In C. F. Graumann & S. Moscovici (eds.), *Changing conceptions of leadership* (pp. 171–197). New York: Springer-Verlag.

Lanning, G. E., Jr. (1982). A study of relationships and differences between management styles and staff morale as perceived by personnel in the colleges of the Ventura County community district. *Dissertation Abstracts International* 43, 996A. (University Microfilms No. 82–20, 739).

Lee, D. M., & Alvares, K. M. (1977). Effects of sex on descriptions and evaluations of supervisory behavior in a simulated industrial setting. *Journal of Applied Psychology* 62, 405–410.

Lewin, K., & Lippitt, R. (1938). An experimental approach to the study of autocracy and democracy: A preliminary note. *Sociometry* 1, 292–300.

Likert, R. (1961). *New patterns of management.* New York: McGraw-Hill.

Loden, M. (1985). *Feminine leadership or how to succeed in business without being one of the boys.* New York: Times Books.

Maccoby, E. E. (1988). Gender as a social category. *Developmental Psychology* 24, 755–765.

Marnani, E. B. (1982). Comparison of preferred leadership styles, potential leadership effectiveness, and managerial attitudes among black and white, female and male management students (Doctoral dissertation, United States International University, 1981). *Dissertation Abstracts International* 43, 1271A.

Martinez, M. R. (1982). A comparative study on the relationship of self-perceptions of leadership styles between Chicano and Anglo teachers (Doctoral dissertation, Bowling Green State University). *Dissertation Abstracts International* 43, 766A.

McGregor, D. (1960). *The human side of enterprise.* New York: McGraw-Hill.

McNemar, Q. (1962). *Psychological statistics* (3rd ed.). New York: Wiley.

Miller, J. B. (1976). *Toward a new psychology of women.* Boston: Beacon Press.

Money, J., & Ehrhardt, A. A. (1972). *Man & woman, boy & girl.* Baltimore, MD: Johns Hopkins University Press.

Moore, S. F., Shaffer, L., Goodsell, D. A., & Baringoldz, G. (1983). Gender or situationally determined spoken language differences? The case of the leadership situation. *International Journal of Women's Studies* 6, 44–53.

Myers, M. S. (1970). *Every employee a manager.* New York: McGraw-Hill.

Naisbitt, J. (1982). *Megatrends: Ten new directions transforming our lives.* New York: Warner Books.

Nieva, V. F., & Gutek, B. A. (1981). *Women and work: A psychological perspective.* New York: Praeger.

O'Leary, V. E. (1974). Some attitudinal barriers to occupational aspirations in women. *Psychological Bulletin* 81, 809–826.

Ott, E. M. (1989). Effects of the male-female ratio at work: Policewomen and male nurses. *Psychology of Women Quarterly* 13, 41–57.

Ouchi, W. G. (1981). *Theory Z: How American business can meet the Japanese challenge.* Reading, MA: Addison-Wesley.

Peters, T. J., & Waterman, R. H., Jr. (1982). *In search of excellence: Lessons from America's best-run companies.* New York: Harper & Row.

Powell, G. N. (1988). *Women & men in management.* Newbury Park, CA: Sage.

Reddin, W. J., & Reddin, M. K. (1979). *Educational Administrative Style Diagnosis Test (EASDT).* Fredericton, New Brunswick, Canada: Organizational Tests.

Renwick, P. A. (1977). The effects of sex differences on the perception and management of superior–subordinate conflict: An exploratory study. *Organizational Behavior and Human Performance* 19, 403–415.

Rice, R. W. (1978). Construct validity of the Least Preferred Co-Worker score. *Psychological Bulletin* 85, 1199–1237.

Rice, R. W., Instone, D., & Adams, J. (1984). Leader sex, leader success, and leadership process: Two field studies. *Journal of Applied Psychology* 69, 12–31.

Riger, S., & Galligan, P. (1980). Women in management: An exploration of competing paradigms. *American Psychologist* 35, 902–910.

Rosenthal, R., Hall, J. A., DiMatteo, M. R., Rogers, P.L., & Archer, D. (1979). *Sensitivity to nonverbal communication: The PONS test.* Baltimore, MD: Johns Hopkins University Press.

Rosenthal, R., & Rubin, D. B. (1986). Meta-analytic procedures for combining studies with multiple effect sizes. *Psychological Bulletin* 99, 400–406.

Russell, J. E. A., Rush, M. C., & Herd, A. M. (1988). An exploration of women's expectations of effective male and female leadership. *Sex Roles* 18, 279–287.

Sargent, A. G. (1981). *The androgynous manager.* New York: Amacom.

Sargent, J. F., & Miller, G. R. (1971). Some differences in certain communication behaviors of autocratic and democratic group leaders. *Journal of Communication* 21, 233–252.

Shakeshaft, C. (1987). *Women in educational administration.* Newbury Park, CA: Sage.

Sirianni-Brantley, K. (1985). The effect of sex role orientation and training on leadership style (Doctoral dissertation, University of Florida, 1984). *Dissertation Abstracts International* 45, 3106B.

Stake, J. E. (1981). Promoting leadership behaviors in low performance–self-esteem women in task-oriented mixed-sex dyads. *Journal of Personality* 49, 401–414.

Stogdill, R. M. (1963). *Manual for the Leader Behavior Description Questionnaire-Form XII.* Columbus, OH: Bureau of Business Research, Ohio State University.

Stogdill, R. M., Goode, O. S., & Day, D. R. (1962). New leader behavior description subscales. *Journal of Psychology* 54, 259–269.

Tanner, J. R. (1982). Effects of leadership, climate and demographic factors on school effectiveness: An action research project in leadership development (Doctoral dissertation, Case Western Reserve University, 1981). *Dissertation Abstracts International* 43, 333A.

Taylor, S. E., Fiske, S. T., Etcoff, N., & Ruderman, A. (1978). The categorical and contextual bases of person memory and stereotyping. *Journal of Personality and Social Psychology* 36, 778–793.

Terborg, J. R. (1977). Women in management: A research review. *Journal of Applied Psychology* 62, 647–664.

Van Aken, E. W. (1954). An analysis of the methods of operation of principals to determine working patterns (Doctoral dissertation, University of Florida). *Dissertation Abstracts International* 14, 1983.

Vroom, V. H., & Yetton, P. W. (1973). *Leadership and decision-making*. Pittsburgh, PA: University of Pittsburgh Press.

Wanous, J. P. (1977). Organizational entry: Newcomers moving from outside to inside. *Psychological Bulletin* 84, 601–618.

Wood, W. (1987). Meta-analytic review of sex differences in group performance. *Psychological Bulletin* 102, 53–71.

Yoder, J. D., & Sinnett, L. M. (1985). It is all in the numbers? A case study of tokenism. *Psychology of Women Quarterly* 9, 413–418.

Leader Emergence
A Dynamic Process

In this chapter we ask the question, How do people become leaders? This question represents a continuation of the theme addressed in Chapter 3. There we learned that the "great person" theory of leadership, while not necessarily accurate in its literal suggestion that some people are born to lead, may have been accurate in suggesting that leaders are those individuals who generally possess "the right stuff." This right stuff, as Kirkpatrick and Locke (1991) refer to it, may help identify who will be an effective leader as well as who will emerge as "the" leader.

Scholars interested in the dynamics and processes that are associated with the emergence of a leader provide us with several different perspectives. Some have looked at forces residing outside the group and suggest that people often come to the position of leadership via direct appointment to the position (role) of leader. Others interested in the issue of leader emergence look to forces and dynamics that are at work within the group and the interactions that transpire among group members (Hollander, 1964).

As suggested in Chapter 3, "Leaders and the Role of Personal Traits," many scholars have examined the role played by attributes of the individual, such as personal attributes (cf. Kirkpatrick & Locke, 1991; Mann, 1959; Stogdill, 1948); sex and gender (cf. Kent & Moss, 1994); and the Big Five personality dimensions (cf. Judge, Ilies, Bono, & Gerhardt, 2000). During the decade of the 1990s many scholars focused on the personality trait of *self-monitoring* and its role in influencing leader emergence. Self-monitoring refers to the individual's ability and motivation to manage how she or he presents her or himself to others as a function of the reading of the social cues emitted by others. On the basis of their investigation, Dobbins, Long, Dedrick, and Clemons (1990), for example, concluded that high self-monitors are more "attentive to the attitudes, needs, and desires of group members" (p. 611) and as a consequence, they are more likely to exhibit the behaviors that will result in their emergence as leaders. (The first self-assessment appearing after this chapter opener gives you the chance to profile your self-monitoring personality.)

In recent years some literature has focused on *emotional intelligence* (i.e., "the ability to perceive emotions, to access and generate emotions to assist thought, to understand emotions and emotional knowledge, and to regulate emotions reflectively to promote emotional and intellectual growth" [Tapia, 2001, p. 353]),[1] and the role played by this individual attribute in leader emergence (cf. Wolff et al., 2002; George, 2000). The *Journal of Organizational Behavior* [26; 4 (2005), pp. 409–466] presents an interesting point–counterpoint discussion among several scholars (i.e., Paul E. Spector, Frank J. Landy, Edwin A. Locke, Jeffrey M. Conte, and Neal M. Ashkanasy and Catherine S. Daus) who don't necessarily see eye-to-eye on the legitimacy of the emotional intelligence construct, thereby calling into question its place in the leadership literature.

---

[1] M. Tapia, "Measuring Emotional Intelligence," *Psychological Reports* 88 (2001), pp. 353–364.

As an advocate, George (2000)[2] suggests that feelings (i.e., moods and emotions) play a critical role in the leadership process. She notes that moods and emotions affect the way people think, their motivation, the decisions that they make, and the behaviors they engage in. Building on these observations, George suggests that it is important to consider the role that feelings and emotions play in leadership, and therefore she focuses on the role played by emotional intelligence.

(The second self-assessment at the end of this chapter introduction provides you with the opportunity to examine your emotional intelligence.) George suggests that leader effectiveness is affected by the strength of the emotional intelligence possessed by the leader.

In addition, Steven B. Wolff, Anthony T. Pescosolido, and Venessa Urch Druskat (2002) suggest that emotional intelligence plays an important role in leader emergence, especially within the context of self-managing teams.[3]

Not all the scholarly interest in leader emergence has focused on forces at work within the individual (e.g., personality). Some scholars have attempted to look at group dynamics and leader emergence (cf. Hollander, 1961), while others have looked at forces associated with the accumulation and use of power within groups (cf. Salancik & Pfeffer, 1977). As, Figure 5.1 suggests, the forces that give rise to leadership do not reside totally in the leader.

Our earlier readings provided a glimpse into the dynamics and processes that are associated with leadership. Bass's (1990) reference to figureheads clearly suggests that in many organizational situations, people come to positions of leadership as a result of forces outside the group per se. These individuals can be referred to as "designated leaders." They are not the focus of this chapter. Our focus in Chapter 5 is on emergent processes and what we will refer to as "emergent leaders." This means that there are forces at work within the group that play a role in the leader-emergent process.

Murphy (1941) suggests that there are situational needs that call for certain knowledge, skills, and abilities. Emergent leadership results from an interaction between the situational needs for certain knowledge, skills, and abilities, and the individual's knowledge, skills, and abilities. Within this context, Smircich and Morgan (1982) point out that, as individuals confront ambiguous situations, certain individuals surrender their power to define reality to others and it is through this surrendering process that a leader emerges.

Stogdill (1948) and Kirkpatrick and Locke (1991) provide a similar perspective on leader emergence. Leadership is a relational process (i.e., a working relationship). As individuals and group members attempt to work with situational demands, individuals who possess certain traits are more likely to engage in efforts directed toward the orchestration of group activity. Simultaneously, group members are more likely to turn to (i.e., accept the orchestration attempts of) individuals possessing the right stuff (e.g., self-confidence, drive, trustability) as opposed to allowing themselves to be directed by individuals who are not endowed with the right mix of individual traits.

Hollander's (1961) *idiosyncrasy credit theory* provides insight into leader emergence.[4] According to the idiosyncrasy model, group members evaluate other members in terms of the degree to which they conform to expectations and help the group move toward goal attainment. The result of these evaluations serves to define an individual's status and role in the group. Group status is defined in

[2] J. M. George, "Emotions and Leadership: The Role of Emotional Intelligence," *Human Relations* 53, 8 (2000), pp. 1027–1055.

[3] S. B. Wolff, A. T. Pescosolide, & V. U. Druskat, "Emotional Intelligence as the Basic of Leader Language in Self-Managing Teams," *Leadership Quarterly* 13 (2002), pp. 505–522.

[4] E. P. Hollander, "Emergent Leadership and Social Influence." In L. Petrullo and J. C. Brengelmann, eds., *Leadership and Interpersonal Behavior* (New York: Holt, Rinehart & Winston, 1961), pp. 30–47.

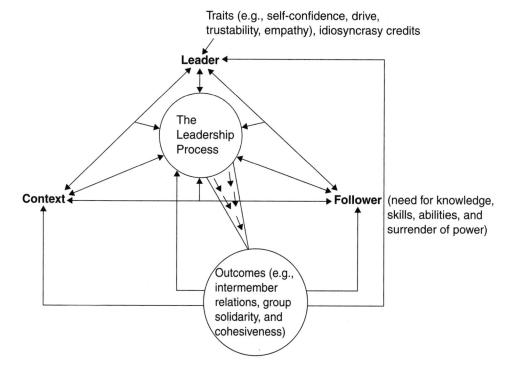

FIGURE 5.1
Leader Emergence

terms of idiosyncrasy credits, which represent the accumulation of positive impressions that others hold toward members of the group. These credits allow a group member to deviate from the group's norms of accepted behavior. For an individual to emerge as a group leader, he or she must deviate from expected member behavior and in the process, display behaviors that are unique and that are perceived as helping the group move toward the attainment of its goals.

Two of these behaviors, according to Bales (1950) and Hollander (1961) are task-focused and socioemotional.[5] The task-focused behaviors are directed toward alleviating team members' task accomplishment concerns. These behaviors are instrumental in guiding the group in the achievement of its goals. The socioemotional behaviors are directed toward alleviating the team's social concerns by building trust. These behaviors build intermember relations and assist in the building of group solidarity (i.e., group cohesiveness). To accomplish the latter set of group needs, *emergent leaders possess empathy*—that part of emotional intelligence which enables the emergent leader to be "socially perceptive and uniquely able to identify and understand unstated team needs" (Wolff, Pescosolido & Druskat (2002, p. 509).

The first reading in this chapter is by Hollander (1964). In this reading he provides us with some insight into social influence and emergent leadership. As suggested by Hollander's reference to idiosyncrasy credits and the emergence of a group leader, power does not automatically flow to just anyone, nor is one guaranteed that, once received, the power will be retained. In the second reading in this chapter, Salancik and Pfeffer (1977) provide an interesting insight into two questions—Who gets power, and how does a person hold on to it?[6] The answer to these two questions provides additional insight into who is the group's leader, as well as leader influence and the leadership process.

---

[5] R. F. Bales, *Interaction Process Analysis: A Method for the Study of Small Groups* (Chicago: University of Chicago Press, 1950); E. P. Hollander, "Emergent Leadership and Social Influence." In L. Petrullo and B. Bass, eds., *Leadership and Interpersonal Behavior* (New York: Holt, Rinehart & Winston, 1961), pp. 30–47.
[6] G. R. Salancik & J. Pfeffer, "Who Gets Power—And How They Hold On to It: A Strategic-Contingency Model of Power," *Organizational Dynamics* (Winter 1977), pp. 3–21.

Power—according to Salancik and Pfeffer—derives from activities rather than individuals, and *the power possessed by a leader is never absolute.* As the situation in which a leader and his or her followers are embedded changes, so too may the amount of power held by the leader change as well as the person in the leadership position.

As the situation facing a group of individuals (e.g., a project team, work group, organization) changes, so too do the critical issues facing the group. Power in social systems tends to flow to those individuals who possess the resources, especially if those resources that the group needs to solve its critical issues are scarce. The individual in a group, therefore, who is capable of contributing the scarce resources needed by the group to solve its most pressing problems tends to define leadership, the nature of the leader's power, and the amount of influence that he or she is capable of exercising.

At this juncture, we believe that it is worthwhile for you to think about and to discuss with other students of leadership whether there is such a thing as an appointed leader, or if all leaders must emerge from various dynamics at work within the group and the context within which the group is embedded. In similar fashion, we believe that it might be fruitful to consider how stepping up and going first (volunteering oneself) figures into leader emergence. For example, does standing up and going first make one a leader?

Drawing from the literature that you have read thus far, we make the following observation: There appear to be at least three different paths (see Figure 5.2) down which people travel that may eventually lead them to the position of leadership. First, there is the *appointment* path. Forces at work outside the group often place people into a formal position that gives them visibility and the opportunity to gain acceptance and to emerge as the group's leader. Second, there are *forces at work within the group and the working relationship* that connect group members and that may result in an individual's being accepted as the group's leader. It would appear that within the individual there is a motivation to lead at work that simultaneously collides with the group's willingness to accept that person's leadership acts. This second path is similar to Hollander's (1964) discussion of leader emergence in the first reading in this chapter and to Salancik and Pfeffer's (1977) thinking that appears in the second reading. The third path results from *forces within the individual* that propel him or her to step up and go first. Facing discomfort with the status quo or needing resolution to a pressing problem, for example, potentially provides the motivation for others to follow.

A person traveling down any one of these three paths can be met with an acceptance or a rejection of her or his leadership attempts. If the person is

FIGURE 5.2
Leader Emergence and Entrenchment

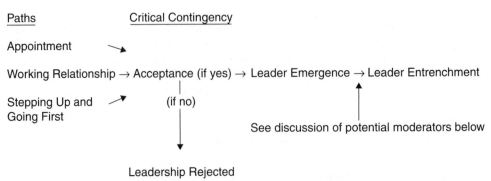

(Note: Even if leadership is rejected, an appointed leader may retain the position and positional power.)

accepted, we have leader emergence. On the basis of several of the readings that have appeared in the previous chapters, we note that if there is a fit among (a) the demands of the situation, (b) the emergent needs experienced by the followers, and (c) the personality, knowledge, skills, and abilities of the individual (Murphy, 1941, Reading 4), or a figure–ground match (Smircich & Morgan, 1982, Reading 6), leader acceptance and emergence are likely to transpire.

Finally, as illustrated in Figure 5.2, we encourage you to consider the notion of "leader entrenchment" (i.e., embeddedness in or solidification of the leadership position). The idea is quite simple and straightforward: Across time and situations individuals may be firmly embedded in the leadership role, while in other instances their role may be much more tenuous in nature. The degree (level) of entrenchment in the leader position is a function of many forces, each capable of affecting the likelihood that emergent leaders will become strongly embedded in their leadership role. (These forces are the moderators portrayed in Figure 5.2.) At the emergence stage the following forces have just started to develop, and as each develops to a greater extent an individual's entrenchment in the position of leader increases:

1. the quality of the leader-member exchange (LMX) is low and membership in both the in- and out-groups has just started to materialize (Scandura, 1999, Reading 7),

2. the strength of the psychological tie between the leader and follower is low to moderately strong (Hollander & Julian, 1969, Reading 5),

3. the amount of power surrendered is limited, and it has been surrendered tentatively (Smircich & Morgan, 1982, Reading 6),

4. the emergent leader has more idiosyncrasy credits than other group members (Hollander, 1964, Reading 14) yet that leader probably has not accumulated a large bank of credits,

5. the followers' trust in the leader is low to moderate as it too is just beginning to develop (Dirks, 2000, Reading 8),

6. the emergent leader probably does possess some scarce and critical resources (Salancik & Pfeffer, 1977, Reading 15),

7. the psychological contract between the leader and follower (i.e., expectations that both have constructed in their minds regarding their respective roles and relationships (cf. Rousseau, 1995) is just beginning to take shape, and

8. the emotional attachment that characterizes the leader-follower relationship (e.g., as reflected in the case of transformational and charismatic leadership) is, at best, in the early stages of development.

Each of these forces (i.e., moderating variables) can influence the degree to which leader entrenchment manifests itself after leader emergence.

D. M. Rousseau, *Psychological Contracts in Organizations: Understanding Written and Unwritten Agreements* (Thousand Oaks, CA: Sage, 1995).

EXERCISE	**Self-Monitoring**		
Self-Assessment	**Instructions:** The statements below concern your personal reaction to a number of different situations. No two statements are exactly alike, so consider each statement carefully before answering. If a statement is *True* or *Mostly True* as applied to you, circle the "T." If a statement is *False* or *Not Usually True* as applied to you, circle the "F." It is important that you answer as frankly and as honestly as you can.		

	True or Mostly True	False, or Not Usually True
1. I find it hard to imitate the behavior of other people.	T	F
2. My behavior is usually an expression of my true inner feelings, attitudes, and beliefs.	T	F
3. At parties and social gatherings, I do not attempt to do or say things that others will like.	T	F
4. I can only argue for ideas which I already believe.	T	F
5. I can make impromptu speeches even on topics about which I have almost no information.	T	F
6. I guess I put on a show to impress or entertain people.	T	F
7. When I am uncertain how to act in a social situation, I look to the behavior of others for cues.	T	F
8. I would probably make a good actor.	T	F
9. I rarely need the advice of my friends to choose movies, books, or music.	T	F
10. I sometimes appear to others to be experiencing deeper emotions than I actually am.	T	F
11. I laugh more when I watch a comedy with others than when alone.	T	F
12. In a group of people I am rarely the center of attention.	T	F
13. In different situations and with different people, I often act like very different persons.	T	F
14. I am not particularly good at making other people like me.	T	F
15. Even if I am not enjoying myself, I often pretend to be having a good time.	T	F
16. I'm not always the person I appear to be.	T	F
17. I would not change my opinions (or the way I do things) in order to please someone else or win their favor.	T	F
18. I have considered being an entertainer.	T	F
19. In order to get along and be liked, I tend to be what people expect me to be rather than anything else.	T	F
20. I have never been good at games like charades or improvisational acting.	T	F
21. I have trouble changing my behavior to suit different people and different situations.	T	F
22. At a party I let others keep the jokes and stories going.	T	F
23. I feel a bit awkward in company and do not show up quite so well as I should.	T	F
24. I can look anyone in the eye and tell a lie with a straight face (if for a right end).	T	F
25. I may deceive people by being friendly when I really dislike them.	T	F

Scoring: Assign yourself one (1) point if you answered True or Mostly True (i.e., you circled T) for each of the following questions: 5, 6, 7, 8, 10, 11, 13, 15, 16, 18, 19, 24, and 25, and assign yourself one (1) point if you answered False or Not Usually True (i.e., you circled F) for each of the following questions: 1, 2, 3, 4, 9, 12, 14, 17, 20, 21, 22, and 23.

My self-monitoring score is: _____.

Interpretation: Snyder (1974) provides the following description of the self-monitoring individual: "The self-monitoring individual is one who, out of a concern for social appropriateness, is particularly sensitive to the expression and self-presentation of others in social situations and uses these cues as guidelines for monitoring his (her) own self-presentation" (Snyder, 1974, p. 528). Your score on this self-assessment could range from zero (0) to twenty-five (25). The higher your score, the stronger your "self-monitoring" tendencies. A score of 20 and higher would be indicative of very strong self-monitoring, while a score of 5 or less would reflect extremely low self-monitoring.

Source: M. Snyder (1974). Self-monitoring of expressive behavior. *Journal of Personality and Social Psychology,* 30, no. 4, p. 531. Copyright 1974, American Psychological Association. Reprinted with permission.

Emotional Intelligence

Instructions: For each of the following questions, please indicate the degree to which each statement characterizes you.

For each item, assign yourself:

1. if—Never like me.
2. if—Occasionally like me.
3. if—Sometimes like me.
4. if—Frequently like me.
5. if—Always like me.

_____ 1. I sympathize with other people when they have problems.

_____ 2. I go out of my way to help someone in need.

_____ 3. Most people feel comfortable talking to me about their personal feelings.

_____ 4. People enjoy spending time with me.

_____ 5. It is easy for me to openly express warm and loving feelings toward others.

_____ 6. When someone is annoying me. I stop to think about the other person's situation rather than losing my temper.

_____ 7. In most cases I give people a second chance.

_____ 8. I think about how I can improve my relationships with those people with whom I don't get along.

_____ 9. I think why I don't like a person.

_____ 10. When someone makes me uncomfortable, I think why I am uncomfortable.

_____ 11. I can be assertive and forceful in situations where others are trying to take advantage of me.

_____ 12. I can delay gratification in pursuit of my goals.

_____ 13. When I am anxious about a challenge, I still can prepare for it.

_____ 14. I am able to stay motivated when things do not go well.

_____ 15. I keep myself focused on my goals.

_____ 16. Overt human suffering makes me feel uncomfortable.

_____ 17. Criticism is difficult for me to accept.

_____ 18. Having car trouble makes me feel stressed.

_____ 19. I lose control when I do not win in a sporting contest.

_____ 20. Traffic jams cause me to lose control.

Scoring: Sum your score for questions 1–5, and divide by 5.

My "perception, appraisal, and expression of emotions" score is: _____.

Sum your score for questions 6–10, and divide by 5.

My "emotional facilitation of thinking" score is: _____.

Sum your score for questions 11–15, and divide by 5.

My "understanding and analyzing emotions, and employing emotional knowledge" score is: _____.

For questions 17–20, reverse score each item by subtracting your score from 6. Next sum your new scores for these four questions, and add in your score to question 16, then divide by 5.

My "reflective regulation of emotions" score is: _____.

Finally, sum your four scores together and divide by 4.

My overall (global) emotional intelligence score is: _____.

Interpretation: Thorndike (1920) provided an intelligence framework that identified three types of intelligence—social, concrete, and abstract. Thorndike's conceptualization of social intelligence is the underpinning for the contemporary reference to emotional intelligence (EI).

(Continued)

EI "involves the ability to perceive emotions, to access and generate emotions to assist thought, to understand emotions and emotional knowledge, and to regulate emotions reflectively to promote emotional and intellectual growth" (Tapia, p. 353). This definition links intelligence and emotion and promotes the dual ideas that emotion can make thinking more intelligent and that one can think intelligently about emotions.

According to Tapia (pp. 354–355), your first score reflects your ability to appraise emotions in yourself and appraise emotions in others (empathy). The second score deals with emotions when thinking is prioritized by directing attention to important information. (Are your emotions sufficiently vivid and available so they can be used as aids to judgment and memory concerning feelings?) Your third score deals with your ability to label emotions and to understand complex feelings. Your fourth and final score concerns the ability to stay open to feelings (both those that are pleasant and unpleasant). Overall, the global scale for emotional intelligence attempts to assess the perception, assimilation, understanding, and management of emotion.

A high score on each of the four dimensions is reflective of a high level of emotional intelligence on that particular dimension. A score equal to or greater than 4 on each dimension and on the global assessment suggests a high level of emotional intelligence. A score equal to or less than 2 on each dimension and on the global assessment suggests a low level of emotional intelligence.

Sources: Reproduced with permission of author and publisher from: M. Tapia, Measuring Emotional Intelligence, *Psychological Reports,* 88 (2001), pp. 353–364. © Psychological Reports 2001. These 20 items reflect a subset of the Tapia (2001) and Tapia & Burry-Stock (1998) instrument for the measurement of emotional intelligence and are shown here to illustrate the measure and highlight the construct's meaning. Tapia and Burry-Stock's 41-item measure can be found in M. Tapia & J. Burry-Stock, 1998, *Emotional Intelligence Inventory,* Tuscaloosa, AL. The University of Alabama.

Reading 14

Emergent Leadership and Social Influence

E. P. Hollander
State University of New York at Buffalo

The term *leader* is used so broadly that it is best to define our use of it at the outset. In general, leader denotes an individual with a status that permits him to exercise influence over certain other individuals. Specifically, our concern is directed toward leaders deriving status from followers who may accord or withdraw it, in an essentially free interchange within a group context. Group consent is therefore a central feature in the leader–follower relationships touched on here, although this limitation does not mean that we will totally neglect the possible implications for all kinds of groups, from the simple dyad to the institutionally based formal group or society. . . .

STATUS IN GENERAL

There are different bases for status and different expectations regarding its operational features. These defy ready cataloguing, but in our usage here, *status* refers to the placement of an individual along a dimension, or in a hierarchy, by virtue of some criterion of value. To say that an individual has "status" does not describe an intrinsic attribute or a stable pattern of his behavior; rather it describes the relationship of that individual to certain others and their attendant behavior toward him. Interpersonal perception is a necessary part of this process.

Who perceives what about whom is of central importance not just in terms of the literal case, but also in terms of expectancies. The behavior of the object person is not seen just by itself; it is also effectively *matched* against a standard of expectation held by the perceiver. Before a status distinction can arise, therefore, two things must hold: an arousal of a socially conditioned expectancy, and a flow of information regarding the object person. The perceiver will have had some exposure to the perceived through direct experience or through secondary sources; this leads to a perceptual differentiation which underlies a shift in "behavior toward."

Source: Edited and reprinted with permission from E. P. Hollander, *Leaders, Groups, & Influence* (New York: Oxford Univ. Press, 1964).

Granting, as an example, that a millionaire possesses a fairly uniform degree of higher status in our society, he operates without it if, unshaven, unkempt, and unknown, he moves about among strangers. Even though an economic criterion and an expectancy already exist for a status distinction, the relevant information is absent. In this instance, the emergence of status is linked to one kind of standard, though a wide variety of others could apply (Hyman, 1942). What the relative impact of these will be resides in complex issues of value. In any case, status is not a sole and stable function of some given feature of social interaction between two particular individuals. Cross-pressures of time and place affect the balance.

If leaders occupy a given status relative to followers, this is one function of the way the former are at some moment perceived and reacted to by the latter. Gibb (1954, p. 915) has made the point this way: Followers subordinate themselves, not to an individual whom they perceive as utterly different, but to a member of their group who has superiority at this time and whom they perceive to be fundamentally the same as they are, and who may, at other times, be prepared to follow. Being a follower is not inconsistent with being a leader, in time. This begs the question of the persisting dichotomy, so some history may be useful here.

THE CHANGING APPROACH TO LEADERSHIP

The tradition of concern and controversy about leadership extends far back into the history of social philosophy. This was to stamp related empirical work with a decided bent toward enumerating qualities of the leader. While recent research has seen the leader displaced from this traditional position at center-stage, not very long ago it was typical to indulge in a quest for broad traits of leadership.

Though essentially a matter of emphasis, as in the work of Cowley (1931), traits were selected without regard for situational variants. Gradually a useful distinction between appointed leaders and those who emerged through the willing response of followers was recognized. This was partly a reaction to the burgeoning interest in informal groups with their self-generating status hierarchies, and partly a result of the accessibility of sociometric devices which provided means for studying the consensual choice patterns of various groups.

During this phase, popularity as a feature of group-emergent leadership was given disproportionate importance. Much of the earlier sociometric work equated choice as a roommate or study companion with choice as a leader, and several well-known and substantial studies gave credence to this presumed parity, though only within a limited context (for example, Jennings, 1943).

Eventually, both the trait and popularity emphases were subordinated to an approach which focused on the varying demands for leadership imposed by an immediate situation (Hemphill, 1949; Carter, Haythorn, Shriver, and Lanzetta, 1951). The literature survey by Stogdill (1948) on personal factors associated with leadership was quite decisive in pointing up the disordered state of the earlier viewpoint, which disregarded situations. It was not as though the situational view prevailed entirely, however; influential as it was, the literature reflected some dissent (Gibb, 1950; Bell and French, 1950). We have this appropriate comment by Gouldner (1950, p. 13):

> The group contexts of leadership must be specified if a formalism sterile of action utility is to be avoided. Leadership must be examined in specific kinds of situations, facing distinctive problems. The opposite shortcoming must also be detoured; in other words, the similarities among *some* leadership situations or problems must be emphasized. Failure to do so would enmesh our investigation in an infinite analysis of unique situations as devoid of practical potentiality as the formalist approach.

Still another refinement within the situational framework was an awareness that followers define a situation in responding to leadership; they are not passive creatures of a frozen social matrix. Of his research on the follower as an alert participant, F. H. Sanford (1950, p. 4) has said:

> There is some justification for regarding the follower as the most crucial factor in any leadership event and for arguing that research directed at the follower will eventually yield a handsome payoff. Not only is it the follower who accepts or rejects leadership, but it is the follower who *perceives* both the leader and the situation and who reacts in terms of what he perceives. And what he perceives may be, to an important degree,

a function of his own motivations, frames of reference, and "readinesses."

Thus, it is seen, several viewpoints have been held concerning leadership and followership: first, a search for characteristics of the leader on the supposition that there is some universality among these; second, a concern with group-emergent leadership where popularity among followers may be of significance; third, a focus upon situational factors that determine, or program, the demands made upon leadership and for leadership; and finally, an interest in the more subtle interplay of motives and perceptions between followers and their leaders.

If any current leaning is discernible, it seems to be toward a focus upon the interaction between individuals and its relation to influence assertion and acceptance. In this way, we are becoming more acute in noting how interpersonal perception affects and is affected by status differentiation, as shown, for example, in the work of Jones and deCharms (1957), Dittes and Kelley (1956), and the research reported here.

While it is true that two individuals may bear a stable relationship to one another in a given situation, the demands made upon them in a changing situation could reasonably alter their interpersonal behavior, assuming the necessary volitional conditions; being a leader or follower through the course of time or within a given group setting is not then a fixed state. The context for study consequently becomes more than the immediate situation in which interactions occur, since it includes the past interactions of the parties involved and their impressions of each other as well. The development of newer sociometric approaches has abetted this focus. . . .

SOME IMPLICATIONS OF EMERGENT STATUS

The findings amassed suggest that two things in particular are important in an individual's attainment of leadership. First, that he be seen as competent in the group's central task; and second, that broadly speaking he be perceived as a member of the group—what Brown (1936) has called "membership character."

Any group member is bound by certain expectancies—whether norms or roles—which prevail at a given time. To directly challenge these would very likely limit his upward mobility, unless a person were extremely competent and, what is more important, widely perceived as such. In most instances, adherence to the prevailing expectancies of the group is essential for the group member's acceptance. We are in effect speaking then of conformity, but not in the usual sense of fixed behavioral norms to which all group members are expected to display manifest allegiance. We conceive of conformity in terms of *group expectancies* which may be person-specific and fluid or more generally applicable and static. Thus, what may be perceived to be nonconforming behavior for one group member may not be so perceived for another. Moreover, this is a function of status accumulated from past interactions, and is taken up more fully where we present the construct *idiosyncrasy credit* to refer to status as a summative consequence of being perceived by others as contributing to the group's task and living up to expectancies applicable at any given time. These "credits" are in essence positively disposed impressions of a person held by others; operationally, they provide the basis for influence assertion and its acceptance. The apparent paradox that leaders are said to be at once innovators and also to be conformers to group norms may be seen therefore as a matter of sequence.

So long as the person does not lose credits by sharp breaks with a past record of competence and conformity to expectancies, he rises to a level of credit which permits deviation from, and even open challenge of, prevailing social patterns of the group. In attaining this level, however, the particular expectancies applicable to him will have undergone change, so that it may be less appropriate to behave in the same way.

Guided by this credit model, an experiment with problem-solving groups was conceived to test the effects upon influence acceptance produced by the nonconformity to procedural norms of a confederate of the experimenter who was very competent in the task.

The key manipulation in that experiment was nonconformity by the confederate, through various zones of five trials each, to procedures previously agreed upon by the group in a pretrial discussion. The 15 trials were considered as three zones—early, middle, and late—with the discussion taken to be part of the first zone. A group choice, whether by majority rule or otherwise (this determined by the group) was required for each trial, following the three minutes permitted for considering alternatives. At the conclusion of each trial, the experimenter announced the outcome, that is, a negative or positive sum of varying magnitudes representing funds won or lost.

Six treatments were used: nonconformity throughout; nonconformity for the first two zones;

for just the first zone alone; for the last two zones; for just the last zone alone; and not at all, as a control condition. Each subject was heard to report his recommended choice at least once during every one of the trials. Had it been *accepted* by the group as its own, the choice recommended by the confederate would have yielded the higher payoffs on all but four trials.

In the zones calling for nonconformity, the confederate violated procedures by speaking out of prescribed turn, by questioning the utility of majority rule, and by unsupported—but not harsh—challenges to the recommendations made by others. He manifested such behaviors on an approximate frequency of at least one per trial with a mean of two per trial considered optimum. Thus, he would break in with his choice immediately after an earlier respondent had spoken and before the next in sequence could do so; when there were periods of silence during a trial, he would observe aloud that maybe majority rule didn't work so well; and he would show a lack of enthusiasm for the choice offered by various others on the matter of basis.

The findings revealed the ongoing effect of task competence in increasing influence acceptance over time, seen in the rising means across zones. While current nonconformity does not yield a significant effect, past nonconformity does. In those groups where the confederate began nonconforming after the first zone, both his suggestions and nonconformity were accepted with minimal challenge; by the third zone, his suggestion that majority rule was faulty typically netted a rubber-stamping of his choice. Again, if he had already accrued credit, the pattern of interrupting people out of turn was simply imitated by others. However, where he exhibited nonconformity from the outset, quite opposite effects were elicited from the others, notably with comments of censure.

Summary

In this chapter we have considered variables yielding emergent status in terms of potential influence. It has been shown that social interaction gives rise to a kind of interpersonal assessment, and that this is made up of task-related elements and behaviors matched by the perceiver against some social standard, referred to here as an "expectancy."

Where an individual fulfills these conditions of competence and an adherence to group expectancies over time, he is said to have accumulated "idiosyncrasy credits" and, at some threshold, these credits permit innovation in the group as one evidence of social influence. Thus the task-competent follower who conforms to the common expectancies of the group at one stage may emerge as the leader at the next stage. Correspondingly, the leader who fails to fulfill the expectancies associated with his position of influence may lose credits among his followers and be replaced by one of them. Which person achieves and retains leadership will therefore depend upon the perceptions of others from ongoing social interaction.

References

Bell, G. B., & French, R. L. Consistency of individual leadership position in small groups of varying membership. *J. Abnorm. Soc. Psychol.*, 1950, 45, 764–767.

Brown, J. F. *Psychology and the social order.* New York: McGraw-Hill, 1936.

Carter, L. F., Haythorn, W., Shriver, B., & Lanzetta, J. The behavior of leaders and other group members. *J. Abnorm. Soc. Psychol.*, 1951, 46, 589–595.

Cowley, W. H. The traits of face-to-face leaders. *J. Abnorm. Soc. Psychol.*, 1931, 26, 304–313.

Dittes, J. E., & Kelley, H. H. Effects of different conditions of acceptance upon conformity to group norms. *J. Abnorm. Soc. Psychol.*, 1956, 53, 100–107.

Gibb, C. A. The sociometry of leadership in temporary groups. *Sociometry,* 1950, 13, 226–243.

Gibb, C. A. Leadership. In G. Lindzey (ed.), *Handbook of social psychology.* Vol. II. Cambridge, Mass.: Addison-Wesley, 1954.

Gouldner, A. W. (Ed.) *Studies in leadership.* New York: Harper, 1950.

Hemphill, J. K. *Situational factors in leadership.* Columbus: Ohio State Univer., 1949.

Hyman, H. H. The psychology of status. *Arch. Psychol.,* 1942, No. 269.

Jennings, H. H. *Leadership and isolation.* New York: Longmans, Green, 1943 (Rev. ed., 1950).

Jones, E. E., & deCharms, R. Changes in social perception as a function of the personal relevance of behavior. *Sociometry,* 1957, 20, 75–85.

Sanford, F. H. *Authoritarianism and leadership.* Philadelphia: Institute for Research in Human Relations, 1950.

Stogdill, R. M. Personal factors associated with leadership: A survey of the literature. *J. Psychol.,* 1948, 25, 37–51.

Reading 15

Who Gets Power—And How They Hold On to It

A Strategic-Contingency Model of Power

Gerald R. Salancik
University of Illinois

Jeffrey Pfeffer
University of California at Berkeley

Power is held by many people to be a dirty word or, as Warren Bennis has said, "It is the organization's last dirty secret."

This article will argue that traditional "political" power, far from being a dirty business, is, in its most naked form, one of the few mechanisms available for aligning an organization with its own reality. However, institutionalized forms of power—what we prefer to call the cleaner forms of power: authority, legitimization, centralized control, regulations, and the more modern "management information systems"—tend to buffer the organization from reality and obscure the demands of its environment. Most great states and institutions declined, not because they played politics, but because they failed to accommodate to the political realities they faced. Political processes, rather than being mechanisms for unfair and unjust allocations and appointments, tend toward the realistic resolution of conflicts among interests. And power, while it eludes definition, is easy enough to recognize by its consequences—the ability of those who possess power to bring about the outcomes they desire.

The model of power we advance is an elaboration of what has been called strategic-contingency theory, a view that sees power as something that accrues to organizational subunits (individuals, departments) that cope with critical organizational problems. Power is used by subunits, indeed, used by all who have it, to enhance their own survival through control of scarce critical resources, through the placement of allies in key positions, and through the definition of organizational problems and policies. . . .

WHAT IS ORGANIZATIONAL POWER?

You can walk into most organizations and ask without fear of being misunderstood, "Which are the powerful groups or people in this organization?" Although many organizational informants may be *unwilling* to tell you, it is unlikely they will be *unable* to tell you. Most people do not require explicit definitions to know what power is.

Power is simply the ability to get things done the way one wants them to be done. For a manager who wants an increased budget to launch a project that he thinks is important, his power is measured by his ability to get that budget. For an executive vice president who wants to be chairman, his power is evidenced by his advancement toward his goal. . . .

WHERE DOES ORGANIZATIONAL POWER COME FROM?

Earlier we stated that power helps organizations become aligned with their realities. This hopeful prospect follows from what we have dubbed the strategic-contingencies theory of organizational power. Briefly, those subunits most able to cope with the organization's critical problems and uncertainties acquire power. In its simplest form, the strategic-contingencies theory implies that when an organization faces a number of lawsuits that threaten its existence, the legal department will gain power and influence over organizational decisions. Somehow other organizational interest groups will recognize its critical importance and confer upon it a status and power never before enjoyed. This influence may extend beyond handling legal matters and into decisions about product design, advertising production, and so on. Such extensions undoubtedly would be accompanied by appropriate, or acceptable, verbal justifications. In time, the head of the legal department may become the head of the corporation, just as in times past the vice president for marketing had become the president when market shares were a worrisome problem and, before him, the chief engineer, who had made the production line run as smooth as silk.

Stated in this way, the strategic-contingencies theory of power paints an appealing picture of power. To the extent that power is determined by the critical uncertainties and problems facing the organization and, in turn, influences decisions in the organization, the organization is aligned with the realities it faces. In short, power facilitates the organization's adaptation to its environment—or its problems.

We can cite many illustrations of how influence derives from a subunit's ability to deal with critical contingencies. Michael Crozier described a French cigarette factory in which the maintenance engineers had a considerable say in the plantwide operation. After some probing he discovered that the group possessed the solution to one of the major problems faced by the company, that of troubleshooting the elaborate, expensive, and irrascible automated machines that kept breaking down and dumbfounding everyone else. It was the one problem that the plant manager could in no way control. . . .

The engineers' strategic role in coping with breakdowns afforded them a considerable say on plant decisions. Schedules and production quotas were set in consultation with them. And the plant manager, while formally their boss, accepted their decisions about personnel in their operation. His submission was to his credit, for without their cooperation he would have had an even more difficult time in running the plant. . . .

POWER SHARING IN ORGANIZATIONS

Power is shared in organizations; and it is shared out of necessity more than out of concern for principles of organizational development or participatory democracy. Power is shared because no one person controls all the desired activities in the organization. While the factory owner may hire people to operate his noisy machines, once hired they have some control over the use of the machinery. And thus they have power over him in the same way he has power over them. Who has more power over whom is a mooter point than that of recognizing the inherent nature of organizing as a sharing of power. . . .

Because power derives from activities rather than individuals, an individual's or subgroup's power is never absolute and derives ultimately from the context of the situation. The amount of power an individual has at any one time depends, not only on the activities he or she controls, but also on the existence of other persons or means by which the activities can be achieved and on those who determine what ends are desired and, hence, on what activities are desired and critical for the organization. One's own power always depends on other people for these two reasons. Other people, or groups or organizations, can determine the definition of what is a critical contingency for the organization and can also undercut the uniqueness of the individual's personal contribution to the critical contingencies of the organization.

Perhaps one can best appreciate how situationally dependent power is by examining how it is distributed. In most societies, power organizes around scarce and critical resources. Rarely does power organize around abundant resources. In the United States, a person doesn't become powerful because he or she can drive a car. There are simply too many others who can drive with equal facility. In certain villages in Mexico, on the other hand, a person with a car is accredited with enormous social status and plays a key role in the community. In addition to scarcity, power is also limited by the need for one's capacities in a social system. While a racer's ability to drive a car around a 90° turn at 80 mph may be sparsely distributed in a society, it is not likely to lend the driver much power in the society. The ability simply does not play a central role in the activities of the society.

The fact that power revolves around scarce and critical activities, of course, makes the control and organization of those activities a major battleground in struggles for power. Even relatively abundant or trivial resources can become the bases for power if one can organize and control their allocation and the definition of what is critical. Many occupational and professional groups attempt to do just this in modern economies. Lawyers organize themselves into associations, regulate the entrance requirements for novitiates, and then get laws passed specifying situations that require the services of an attorney. Workers had little power in the conduct of industrial affairs until they organized themselves into closed and controlled systems. In recent years, women and blacks have tried to define themselves as important and critical to the social system, using law to reify their status. . . .

THE CRITICAL CONTINGENCIES

The critical contingencies facing most organizations derive from the environmental context within which they operate. This determines the available needed resources and thus determines the problems to be dealt with. That power organizes around handling these problems suggests an important mechanism by which organizations keep in tune with their external environments. The strategic-contingencies model implies that subunits that contribute to the critical resources of the organization will gain influence in the organization. Their influence presumably is then used to bend the organization's activities to the contingencies that determine its resources. This idea may strike one as obvious. But its obviousness in no way diminishes its importance. Indeed, despite its obviousness, it escapes the notice of many organizational analysts and managers, who all too frequently think of the organization in terms of a descending pyramid, in which all the departments in one tier hold equal power and status. This presumption denies the reality that departments differ in the contributions they are believed to make to the overall organization's resources, as well as to the fact that some are more equal than others. . . .

THE IMPACT OF ORGANIZATIONAL POWER ON DECISION MAKING

. . . Will organizational decisions always reflect the distribution of power in the organization? Probably not. Using power for influence requires a certain expenditure of effort, time, and resources. Prudent and judicious persons are not likely to use their power needlessly or wastefully. And it is likely that power will be used to influence organizational decisions primarily under circumstances that both require and favor its use. We have examined three conditions that are likely to affect the use of power in organizations: scarcity, criticality, and uncertainty. The first suggests that subunits will try to exert influence when the resources of the organization are scarce. If there is an abundance of resources, then a particular department or a particular individual has little need to attempt influence. With little effort, he can get all he wants anyway.

The second condition, criticality, suggests that a subunit will attempt to influence decisions to obtain resources that are critical to its own survival and activities. Criticality implies that one would not waste effort, or risk being labeled obstinate, by fighting over trivial decisions affecting one's operations.

An office manager would probably balk less about a threatened cutback in copying machine usage than about a reduction in typing staff. An advertising department head would probably worry less about losing his lettering artist than his illustrator. Criticality is difficult to define because what is critical depends on people's beliefs about what is critical. Such beliefs may or may not be based on experience and knowledge and may or may not be agreed upon by all. Scarcity, for instance, may itself affect conceptions of criticality. When slack resources drop off, cutbacks have to be made—those "hard decisions," as congressmen and resplendent administrators like to call them. Managers then find themselves scrapping projects they once held dear.

The third condition that we believe affects the use of power is uncertainty: When individuals do not agree about what the organization should do or how to do it, power and other social processes will affect decisions. The reason for this is simply that, if there are no clear-cut criteria available for resolving conflicts of interest, then the only means for resolution is some form of social process, including power, status, social ties, or some arbitrary process like flipping a coin or drawing straws. Under conditions of uncertainty, the powerful manager can argue his case on any grounds and usually win it. Since there is no real consensus, other contestants are not likely to develop counterarguments or amass sufficient opposition. Moreover, because of his power and their need for access to the resources he controls, they are more likely to defer to his arguments.

Although the evidence is slight, we have found that power will influence the allocations of scarce and critical resources. In the analysis of power in the university, for instance, one of the most critical resources needed by departments is the general budget. First granted by the state legislature, the general budget is later allocated to individual departments by the university administration in response to requests from the department heads. Our analysis of the factors that contribute to a department getting more or less of this budget indicated that subunit power was the major predictor, overriding such factors as student demand for courses, national reputations of departments, or even the size of a department's faculty. Moreover, other research has shown that when the general budget has been cut back or held below previous uninflated levels, leading to monies becoming more scarce, budget allocations mirror departmental powers even more closely. . . .

CHANGING CONTINGENCIES AND ERODING POWER BASES

The critical contingencies facing the organization may change. When they do, it is reasonable to expect that the power of individuals and subgroups will change in turn. . . .

One implication of the idea that power shifts with changes in organizational environments is that the dominant coalition will tend to be that group that is most appropriate for the organization's environment, as also will the leaders of an organization. One can observe this historically in the top executives of industrial firms in the United States. Up until the early 1950s, many top corporations were headed by former production line managers or engineers who gained prominence because of their abilities to cope with the problems of production. Their success, however, only spelled their demise. As production became routinized and mechanized, the problem of most firms became one of selling all those goods they so efficiently produced. Marketing executives were more frequently found in corporate boardrooms. Success outdid itself again, for keeping markets and production steady and stable requires the kind of control that can only come from acquiring competitors and suppliers or the invention of more and more appealing products—ventures that typically require enormous amounts of capital. During the 1960s, financial executives assumed the seats of power. And they, too, will give way to others. Edging over the horizon are legal experts, as regulation and antitrust suits are becoming more and more frequent in the 1970s, suits that had their beginnings in the success of the expansion generated by prior executives. The more distant future, which is likely to be dominated by multinational corporations, may see former secretaries of state and their minions increasingly serving as corporate figureheads. . . .

IMPLICATIONS FOR THE MANAGEMENT OF POWER IN ORGANIZATIONS

While we could derive numerous implications from this discussion of power, our selection would have to depend largely on whether one wanted to increase one's power, decrease the power of others, or merely maintain one's position. More important, the real implications depend on the particulars of an organizational situation. To understand power in an organization one must begin by looking outside it—into the environment—for those groups that mediate the organization's outcomes but are not themselves within its control.

Instead of ending with homilies, we will end with a reversal of where we began. Power, rather than being the dirty business it is often made out to be, is probably one of the few mechanisms for reality testing in organizations. And the cleaner forms of power, the institutional forms, rather than having the virtues they are often credited with, can lead the organization to become out of touch. The real trick to managing power in organizations is to ensure somehow that leaders cannot be unaware of the realities of their environments and cannot avoid changing to deal with those realities. That, however, would be like designing the "self-liquidating organization," an unlikely event since anyone capable of designing such an instrument would be obviously in control of the liquidations.

Management would do well to devote more attention to determining the critical contingencies of their environments. For if you conclude, as we do, that the environment sets most of the structure influencing organizational outcomes and problems, and that power derives from the organization's activities that deal with those contingencies, then it is the environment that needs managing, not power. The first step is to construct an accurate model of the environment, a process that is quite difficult for most organizations. We have recently started a project to aid administrators in systematically understanding their environments. From this experience, we have learned that the most critical blockage to perceiving an organization's reality accurately is a failure to incorporate those with the relevant expertise into the process. Most organizations have the requisite experts on hand but they are positioned so that they can be comfortably ignored.

One conclusion you can, and probably should, derive from our discussion is that power—because of the way it develops and the way it is used—will always result in the organization suboptimizing its performance. However, to this grim absolute, we add a comforting caveat: If any criteria other than power were the basis for determining an organization's decisions, the results would be even worse.

References

The literature on power is at once both voluminous and frequently empty of content. Some is philosophical musing about the concept of power, while other writing contains popularized palliatives for acquiring and exercising influence. Machiavelli's *The Prince,* if read carefully, remains the single best prescriptive treatment of power and its use. Most social scientists have approached power descriptively, attempting to understand how it is acquired, how it is used, and what its effects are. Mayer Zald's edited collection *Power in Organizations* (Vanderbilt University Press, 1970) is one of the more useful sets of thoughts about power from a sociological perspective, while James Tedeschi's edited book, *The Social Influence Processes* (Aldine-Atherton, 1972), represents the social psychological approach to understanding power and influence. The strategic-contingencies approach, with its emphasis on the importance of uncertainty for understanding power in organizations, is described by David Hickson and his colleagues in "A Strategic Contingencies Theory of Intraorganizational Power" (*Administrative Science Quarterly,* December 1971, pp. 216–229).

Unfortunately, while many have written about power theoretically, there have been few empirical examinations of power and its use. Most of the work has taken the form of case studies. Michel Crozier's *The Bureaucratic Phenomenon* (University of Chicago Press, 1964) is important because it describes a group's source of power as control over critical activities and illustrates how power is not strictly derived from hierarchical position. J. Victor Baldridge's *Power and Conflict in the University* (John Wiley & Sons, 1971) and Andrew Pettigrew's study of computer purchase decisions in one English firm (*Politics of Organizational Decision-Making,* Tavistock, 1973) both present insights into the acquisition and use of power in specific instances. Our work has been more empirical and comparative, testing more explicitly the ideas presented in this article. The study of university decision making is reported in articles in the June 1974, pp. 135–151, and December 1974, pp. 453–473, issues of the *Administrative Science Quarterly,* the insurance firm study in J. G. Hunt and L. L. Larson's collection, *Leadership Frontiers* (Kent State University Press, 1975), and the study of hospital administrator succession will appear in 1977 in the *Academy of Management Journal.*

Leadership as an
Influence Process

As noted by the reference to Bass (1990) in Chapter 1, it has been common for leadership scholars to define leadership from the perspective of an exercise of influence (power) over others in the pursuit of goal attainment. Hollander (1964) and Smircich and Morgan (1982), for example, see leadership from the perspective of persons within a group setting who have the status that enables them to exercise influence over others to bring about a desired end. Smircich and Morgan also provide us with insight into the source of the leader's power: It is surrendered to them by their followers. From a variety of readings to which you will be exposed in *Leaders and the Leadership Process,* you will come to see that leaders, for example, frame reality, provide direction, initiate structure, facilitate, induce compliance, support, remove barriers, serve as role models, and control the behaviors of others. Each of these acts implies the exercise of influence (power) over others. This chapter asks several key questions: How do leaders *influence* others? How do leaders *move others to action* in a particular direction? What are their *sources of power?* Complete the first self-assessment exercise at the end of this introduction to profile your own preferred means of influence.

In response to the question of *how* leaders influence others, we note that there does not appear to be an agreed-upon taxonomy for the classification of the different types of power. Nonetheless, several scholars provide us with ways of thinking about the different modes of influence and their sources. Yukl and Tracey (1992),[1] for example, find that there are a number of influence tactics that leaders employ in their relationship with their followers. Among those that they have studied are ingratiation, exchange, personal appeal, coalition, pressure, legitimating, rational persuasion, inspirational appeal, and consultation. Their work provides insight into the effectiveness of these different tactics, highlighting the efficacy of rational persuasion, inspirational appeal, and consultation. Another classification scheme might differentiate position power (e.g., formalization, rewards, coercion), personal power (e.g., charisma, expertise, friendship), and political power (e.g., coalitions, cooperation). Finally, we note that French and Raven (1959) provide a taxonomy that has remained popular for half a century. The five sources of power that they identify are reward, coercive, expert, referent, and legitimate power.

The first reading in this chapter is John R. P. French and Bertram Raven's (1959) classic perspective on "the bases of social power." The authors identify the major types of power and articulate the source from which each type of power stems. According to French and Raven, *power* is the ability to exercise influence, and *influence* is the ability to bring about change (i.e., a "change in behavior, opinions, attitudes, goals, needs, values, and all other aspects of the

[1] G. Yukl & J. B. Tracey, "Consequences of Influence Tactics Used with Subordinates, Peers, and the Boss," *Journal of Applied Psychology* 77 (1992), pp. 525–535.

person's psychological field" [pp. 150–151]). Power, therefore, can be seen as the ability to induce change in one's environment.

The work of French and Raven suggests that part of the leadership process consists of the exercise of influence. *A leader's ability to influence others stems from his or her ability (or perceived ability) to exercise reward, coercive, referent, expert, and/or legitimate power.* The nature of each of these types of power is defined in their article. You read about leader emergence in the previous chapter. As a part of that discussion, it was suggested that many believe that people can come to the position of leadership through appointment and through emergence. As a part of the emergent process, Hollander (1964) provides us with insight into the role played by the accumulation of idiosyncrasy credits. From a power–influence perspective, Raven and French (1958)[2] conducted a laboratory experiment that has some interesting findings. Essentially, Raven and French observe that people who come to their position of leadership through internal group processes (e.g., being selected, elected, or turned to) have greater legitimacy (i.e., where legitimate power refers to the perceived right to the position) than those who arrive at the position of leader through appointment. They note that greater group support is associated with greater legitimacy, and those leaders without legitimate power not only had less influence over their followers, but also were less accepted personally.

It has been suggested that a leader's power base is not the simple sum of the various sources of power that he or she is capable of exercising. Instead, it appears as though there is a synergistic effect that stems from some combinations of power. For example, referent power, because it stems from a valued and respected person, tends to magnify the impact of other sources of power, especially legitimate, resource, and expert power. The opposite effect can also be produced. High coercive power may well dilute the impact of referent power. As might be suspected, therefore, not all forms of power are equally effective. Hinkin and Schriesheim (1990) find that "rationality" is the most commonly used influence tactic by effective leaders and that rationality is positively related to referent, expert, and legitimate power.[3] According to Podsakoff and Schriesheim's (1985) literature review, follower performance and satisfaction are commonly associated with the leader's use of expert and referent power, while at times the use of legitimate, reward, and coercive power has a negative relationship with these two dimensions of leader effectiveness. These results suggest that *effective leaders rely more on some forms of power than others.*[4] (You can develop your own power profile by completing the second self-assessment exercise at the end of this introduction to Chapter 6.)

According to sociologist Amitai Etzioni (1961), these observations are not surprising. He suggests that different forms of power produce different forms of compliance.[5] Coercive power commonly produces resistance, which eventually leads to alienation. Remunerative or reward power frequently produces an instrumental or calculative response. The level and type of subordinate compliance is based on the attractiveness of the benefits offered relative to the cost incurred. Finally, reliance upon rationality, moralistic appeal, expert and/or referent power frequently elicits follower commitment. As illustrated in Figure 6.1, it is this level or type of compliance that mediates the impact of a leader's power upon the group's performance, member performance, and follower satisfaction with the leader.

[2] B. H. Raven & J. R. P. French, "Group Support, Legitimate Power, and Social Influence," *Journal of Personality* 26 (1958), pp. 400–409.

[3] T. R. Hinkin & C. A. Schriesheim, "Relationships between Subordinate Perceptions of Supervisor Influence Tactics and Attributed Bases of Supervisory Power," *Human Relations* 43 (1990), pp. 221–237.

[4] P. M. Podsakoff & C. A. Schriesheim, "Field Studies of French and Raven's Bases of Power: Critique, Reanalysis, and Suggestions for Future Research," *Psychological Bulletin* 97 (1985), pp. 387–411.

[5] A. Etzioni, *A Comparative Analysis of Complex Organizations, on Power, Involvement, and Their Correlates* (New York: Free Press of Glencoe, 1961).

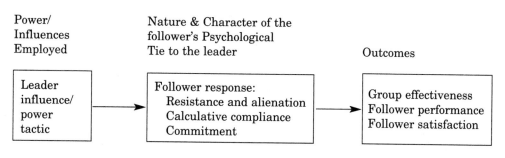

FIGURE 6.1
The Leader Power—Follower Response Relationship

As suggested by Hollander's (1961) idiosyncrasy credits theory, power does not automatically flow to just anyone, nor is one guaranteed that once one has power, one will be able to retain that power.[6] As the situation in which a leader and his or her followers are embedded changes, so too may the amount of power held by the leader as well as the person who holds the leadership position.

As illustrated in Figure 6.2, the work of Salancik and Pfeffer (1977) suggests that critical contingencies play a role in defining the situation facing the group, which in turn influences who the leader will be (critical contingencies → situation → leader) and in part defines and shapes the leader's power. Also playing a role in giving definition to "who the leader will be" is who controls scarce resources (scarce resource control → leader) that are critical to helping the group overcome its most pressing issues. French and Raven's work suggests that a person's ability to administer rewards and coercion, for example, enables him or her to serve as a leader and provides further insight into the leader–follower and the leader–situation relationships.

In the second, and final, reading in this chapter, our attention turns to the use of rewards and punishment (contingent and noncontingent) as an influence tactic commonly employed by leaders. Podsakoff and Todor (1985) look at the relationship between leader use of rewards and punishment and the effects on group cohesion, drive, and productivity. The heart of what is referred to as *transactional leadership* is the give-and-take relationship that exists between leader and follower. This is best portrayed by a leader's giving rewards for progress toward or for meeting goals. Similarly, leaders can threaten or impose penalties for failure. Therein lies a major part of the exchange relationship that characterizes transactional leadership.

Recently Podsakoff, along with his colleagues Bommer, Podsakoff, and MacKenzie (2006),[7] reexamine the effects associated with leader reward and punishment behavior. They report on the results of their meta-analytic review of 78 studies, including 118 independent samples, that focused on the effects that reward and punishment behavior have on follower perceptions, attitudes, and behaviors. While they report many interesting findings, we will provide a brief overview of some of their strongest observations as a way of highlighting the overall effects that are associated with the use of rewards and punishment (contingent and noncontingent) as a way of leading and moving one's followers.

First, the use of rewards and punishment was more effective when they were administered contingently (i.e., contingent positive reinforcement reflects the administration of rewards for employee performance, and contingent aversive

[6] E. P. Hollander, "Emergent Leadership and Social Influence." In L. Petrullo and J. C. Brengelmann, eds., *Leadership and Interpersonal Behavior* (New York: Holt, Rinehart & Winston, 1961), pp. 30–47.
[7] P. M. Podsakoff, W. H. Bommer, N. P. Podsakoff, & S. B. MacKenzie, "Relationships between Leader Reward and Punishment Behavior and Subordinate Attitudes, Perceptions, and Behavior: A Meta-analytic Review of Existing and New Research," *Organizational Behavior and Human Decision Processes* 99 (2006), pp. 113–142.

FIGURE 6.2
The Expanded
Leadership Process

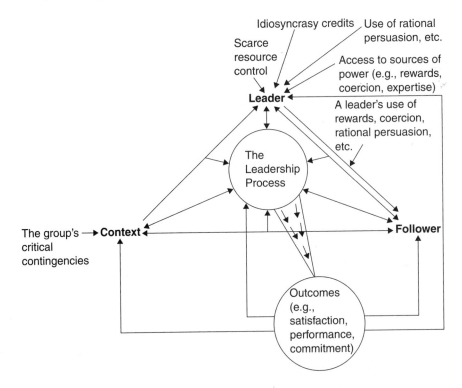

reinforcement is the leader's administration of some form of punishment for the lack of progress toward or the failure to attain an agreed-upon goal) as opposed to noncontingently (i.e., when reward or punishment is based on some other factor, such as need, seniority, or equality).

Second, two immediate and key effects associated with leader reward and punishing behaviors were those produced in terms of follower perceptions of justice and role ambiguity (i.e., when reward or punishment is administered contingently, there will be less role ambiguity and greater perceptions of fairness—distributive, procedural, and interactional justice). These two variables served as mediators of the leader behavior–follower attitude and behavior relationship.

Third, effort was positively related to contingent reward behavior, and there was a negative relationship with noncontingent punishment behavior. In addition, task and overall in-role performance was positively related to contingent reward behavior and had a negative relationship with noncontingent punishment behavior.

Fourth, Podsakoff and his colleagues provide us with insight into the relationship between reward and punishment behavior and follower satisfaction, trust, and commitment. The two strongest relationships with satisfaction are the positive relationship with contingent reward behavior and the negative relationship with noncontingent punishment behavior. Contingent reward behavior also has a positive relationship with followers' trust in their leader. Contingent reward and noncontingent punishment behavior have a positive and negative relationship, respectively, with organizational commitment.

In conclusion, the authors state that these results indicate that "the manner in which leaders administer rewards and punishment is a critical determinant of the effectiveness of these leader behaviors"; these findings "suggest that leaders need to be aware of the fact that the real key to providing praise and commendations to employees on the one hand, and reprimands and social disapproval to them on the other hand, is whether these events are administered contingently upon employee performance. In addition, these findings also suggest that leaders need to communicate to employees those specific behaviors that they feel merit their (the leaders') praise and social approval" (p. 135).

Influence Tactics

Instructions: The questions below ask you about the way in which you influence others. Read each statement carefully and indicate the degree to which you *agree* or *disagree* that this particular influence tactic is descriptive of your leadership style.

	Strongly Disagree	Disagree	Slightly Disagree	Neither Agree nor Disagree	Slightly Agree	Agree	Strongly Agree
1. I would confront my follower(s) and demand that requested actions be carried out promptly.	1	2	3	4	5	6	7
2. I would explain the reason for a request or proposal.	1	2	3	4	5	6	7
3. I would make reference to a higher authority in order to get a requested action carried out.	1	2	3	4	5	6	7
4. I would explain how the person would benefit from my proposal.	1	2	3	4	5	6	7
5. I would indicate that I would do a favor in return for their carrying out a requested action.	1	2	3	4	5	6	7
6. I would provide evidence that a proposal is feasible.	1	2	3	4	5	6	7
7. I would compliment people on their past accomplishments before asking them to do another task.	1	2	3	4	5	6	7
8. I would explain why my proposal is objectively better than competing ones.	1	2	3	4	5	6	7
9. I would get other people to provide evidence in support of a plan or proposal that I was attempting to carry out.	1	2	3	4	5	6	7
10. I would explain how likely problems or concerns should be handled.	1	2	3	4	5	6	7
11. I would describe a proposed task or project with enthusiasm and conviction to convey that it is important and worthwhile.	1	2	3	4	5	6	7
12. I would provide evidence that the requested action that I am proposing will lead to the successful completion of a task or project.	1	2	3	4	5	6	7
13. I would tell others what it is that I am trying to accomplish and ask if they know a good way to do it.	1	2	3	4	5	6	7

Scoring: This self-assessment is designed to reflect the extent to which the use of **rational persuasion** characterizes your leadership influence tactics. Sum your answers to questions 2, 4, 6, 8, 10, and 12 and divide by 6. This score reflects the extent to which you indicate that you rely on rational persuasion as a way of influencing others while in a leadership situation. The other questions ask about other forms of influence: pressure (1), upward appeal (3), exchange (5),

(continued)

ingratiation (7), coalition (9), inspirational appeal (11), and consultation (13). (See Yukl, Lepsinger, & Lucia [1993] for a preliminary report on the development and validation of the Influence Behavior Questionnaire. See K. Clark and M. Clark, eds., *The Impact of Leadership* [Greensboro, NC: Center for Creative Leadership] for guidance on the measurement of these other forms [e.g., pressure, upward appeal] of leader influence.)

My rational persuasion score is: _____.
My other influence tactic scores are:
  Pressure _____
  Upward appeal _____
  Exchange _____
  Ingratiation _____
  Coalition _____
  Inspirational appeal _____
  Consultation _____

Interpretation: A score of 6 and greater on *rational persuasion* implies that you strongly prefer to influence others by employing rationality. Several leadership scholars (cf., Hinkin & Schriesheim, 1990) have observed that rationality is one of the more commonly used influence tactics. Indirect evidence suggests that rationality, as a form of influence, is positively associated with two dimensions of leader effectiveness—follower performance and satisfaction. You are also provided with a glimpse into your propensity to employ pressure, upward appeal, exchange, ingratiation, coalition building, inspirational appeal, and consultation as a part of your "influence repertoire."

Sources: Items 2, 4, 6, 8, and 10 are patterned after items presented by G. Yukl, *Leadership in Organizations*, 4th edition (Englewood Cliffs, NJ: Prentice Hall), p. 219. The remaining items are patterned after items presented by G. Yukl and C. M. Falbe, "Influence Tactics and Objectives in Upward, Downward, and Lateral Influence Attempts," *Journal of Applied Psychology* 75, no. 2 (1990), p. 134.

Personal Power Profile

EXERCISE
Self-Assessment

Instructions: Below is a list of statements that may be used in describing behaviors that supervisors (leaders) in work organizations can direct toward their subordinates (followers). First, carefully read each descriptive statement, thinking in terms of *how you prefer to influence others.* Mark the number that most closely represents how you feel. Use the following numbers for your answers.

7 = Strongly agree
6 = Agree
5 = Slightly agree
4 = Neither agree nor disagree
3 = Slightly disagree
2 = Disagree
1 = Strongly disagree

To influence others, I would prefer to	Strongly Disagree	Disagree	Slightly Disagree	Neither Agree nor Disagree	Slightly Agree	Agree	Strongly Agree
1. Increase their pay level.	1	2	3	4	5	6	7
2. Make them feel valued.	1	2	3	4	5	6	7
3. Give undesirable job assignments.	1	2	3	4	5	6	7
4. Make them feel like I approve of them.	1	2	3	4	5	6	7
5. Make them feel that they have commitments to meet.	1	2	3	4	5	6	7
6. Make them feel personally accepted.	1	2	3	4	5	6	7
7. Make them feel important.	1	2	3	4	5	6	7
8. Give them good technical suggestions.	1	2	3	4	5	6	7
9. Make the work difficult for them.	1	2	3	4	5	6	7
10. Share my experience and/or training.	1	2	3	4	5	6	7
11. Make things unpleasant here.	1	2	3	4	5	6	7
12. Make being at work distasteful.	1	2	3	4	5	6	7
13. Influence their getting a pay increase.	1	2	3	4	5	6	7
14. Make them feel like they should satisfy their job requirements.	1	2	3	4	5	6	7
15. Provide them with sound job-related advice.	1	2	3	4	5	6	7
16. Provide them with special benefits.	1	2	3	4	5	6	7
17. Influence their getting a promotion.	1	2	3	4	5	6	7
18. Give them the feeling that they have responsibilities to fulfill.	1	2	3	4	5	6	7
19. Provide them with needed technical knowledge.	1	2	3	4	5	6	7
20. Make them recognize that they have tasks to accomplish.	1	2	3	4	5	6	7

Scoring: Using the grid below, insert your scores from the 20 questions and proceed as follows: *Reward power*—sum your responses to items 1, 13, 16, and 17 and divide by 4. *Coercive power*—sum your responses to items 3, 9, 11, and 12 and divide by 4. *Legitimate power*—sum your responses to questions 5, 14, 18, and 20 and divide by 4. *Referent power*—sum your responses to questions 2, 4, 6, and 7 and divide by 4. *Expert power*—sum your responses to questions 8, 10, 15, and 19 and divide by 4.

(continued)

Reward	Coercive	Legitimate	Referent	Expert
1_____	3_____	5_____	2_____	8_____
13_____	9_____	14_____	4_____	10_____
16_____	11_____	18_____	6_____	15_____
17_____	12_____	20_____	7_____	19_____
Total_____	_____	_____	_____	_____
Divide by 4_____	_____	_____	_____	_____

Interpretation: A high score (6 and greater) on any of the five dimensions of power implies that you prefer to influence others by employing that particular form of power. A low score (2 and less) implies that you prefer not to employ this particular form of power to influence others. This represents your power profile. Your overall power position is not reflected by the simple sum of the power derived from each of the five sources. Instead, some combinations of power are synergistic in nature—they are greater than the simple sum of their parts. For example, *referent power* tends to magnify the impact of other power sources because these other influence attempts are coming from a "respected" person. *Reward power* often increases the impact of referent power, because people generally tend to like those who give them things that they desire. Some power combinations tend to produce the opposite of synergistic effects, such that the total is less than the sum of the parts. Power dilution frequently accompanies the use of (or threatened use of) *coercive power*.

Source: Modified version of T. R. Hinkin and C. A. Schriesheim, "Development and Application of New Scales to Measure the French and Raven (1959) Bases of Social Power," *Journal of Applied Psychology* 74 (1989), pp. 561–567. Copyright 1989, American Psychological Association, adapted and printed with permission.

Reading 16

The Bases of Social Power

John R. P. French, Jr., and Bertram Raven
University of Michigan

The processes of power are pervasive, complex, and often disguised in our society. Accordingly, one finds in political science, in sociology, and in social psychology a variety of distinctions among different types of social power or among qualitatively different processes of social influence (1, 6, 14, 20, 23, 29, 30, 38, 41). Our main purpose is to identify the major types of power and to define them systematically so that we may compare them according to the changes which they produce and the other effects which accompany the use of power. The phenomena of power and influence involve a dyadic relation between two agents which may be viewed from two points of view: (a) What determines the behavior of the agent who exerts power? (b) What determines the reactions of the recipient of this behavior? We take this second point of view and formulate our theory in terms of the life space of P, the person upon whom power is exerted. In this way we hope to define basic concepts of power which will be adequate to explain many of the phenomena of social influence, including some which have been described in other less genotypic terms.

Recent empirical work, especially on small groups, has demonstrated the necessity of distinguishing different types of power in order to account for the different effects found in studies of social influence. Yet there is no doubt that more empirical knowledge will be needed to make final decisions concerning the necessary differentiations, but this knowledge will be obtained only by research based on some preliminary theoretical distinctions. We present such preliminary concepts and some of the hypotheses they suggest.

POWER, INFLUENCE, AND CHANGE

PSYCHOLOGICAL CHANGE

Since we shall define power in terms of influence, and influence in terms of psychological change, we begin with a discussion of change. We want to

Source: Edited and reprinted with permission from D. Cartwright, *Studies in Social Power* (Ann Arbor, MI: Institute for Social Research, University of Michigan, 1959), pp. 150–67.

define change at a level of generality which includes changes in behavior, opinions, attitudes, goals, needs, values, and all other aspects of the person's psychological field. We shall use the word *system* to refer to any such part of the life space. Following Lewin (26, p. 305), the state of a system at time 1 will be denoted $s_1(a)$.

Psychological change is defined as any alteration of the state of some system *a* over time. The amount of change is measured by the size of the difference between the states of the system *at* time 1 and at time 2: $ch(a) = s_2(a) - s_1(a)$.

Change in any psychological system may be conceptualized in terms of psychological forces. But it is important to note that the change must be coordinated to the resultant force of all the forces operating at the moment. Change in an opinion, for example, may be determined jointly by a driving force induced by another person, a restraining force corresponding to anchorage in a group opinion, and an own force stemming from the person's needs. . . .

THE BASES OF POWER

By the basis of power, we mean the relationship between O and P, which is the source of that power. It is rare that we can say with certainty that a given empirical case of power is limited to one source. Normally, the relation between O and P will be characterized by several qualitatively different variables which are bases of power (30, Chapter 11). Although there are undoubtedly many possible bases of power which may be distinguished, we shall here define five which seem especially common and important. These five bases of O's power are: (1) *reward power*, based on P's perception that O has the ability to mediate rewards for him; (2) *coercive power*, based on P's perception that O has the ability to mediate punishments for him; (3) *legitimate power*, based on the perception by P that O has a legitimate right to prescribe behavior for him; (4) *referent power*, based on P's identification with O; and (5) *expert power*, based on the perception that O has some special knowledge or expertness. . . .

REWARD POWER

Reward power is defined as power whose basis is the ability to reward. The strength of the reward power of O/P increases with the magnitude of the rewards which P perceives that O can mediate for him. Reward power depends on O's ability to administer positive valences and to remove or decrease negative valences. The strength of reward power also depends upon the probability that O can mediate the reward, as perceived by P. A common example of reward power is the addition of a piecework rate in the factory as an incentive to increase production.

The new state of the system induced by a promise of reward (for example the factory worker's increased level of production) will be highly dependent on O. Since O mediates the reward, he controls the probability that P will receive it. Thus P's new rate of production will be dependent on his subjective probability that O will reward him for conformity minus his subjective probability that O will reward him even if he returns to his old level. Both probabilities will be greatly affected by the level of observability of P's behavior. Incidentally, a piece rate often seems to have more effect on production than a merit rating system because it yields a higher probability of reward for conformity and a much lower probability of reward for nonconformity.

The utilization of actual rewards (instead of promises) by O will tend over time to increase the attraction of P toward O and therefore the referent power of O over P. As we shall note later, such referent power will permit O to induce changes which are relatively independent. Neither rewards nor promises will arouse resistance in P, provided P considers it legitimate for O to offer rewards.

The range of reward power is specific to those regions within which O can reward P for conforming. The use of rewards to change systems within the range of reward power tends to increase reward power by increasing the probability attached to future promises. However, unsuccessful attempts to exert reward power outside the range of power would tend to decrease the power; for example if O offers to reward P for performing an impossible act, this will reduce for P the probability of receiving future rewards promised by O.

COERCIVE POWER

Coercive power is similar to reward power in that it also involves O's ability to manipulate the attainment of valences. Coercive power of O/P stems from the expectation on the part of P that he will be punished by O if he fails to conform to the influence attempt. Thus negative valences will exist in given regions of P's life space, corresponding to the threatened punishment by O. The strength of coercive power depends on the magnitude of the negative valence of the threatened punishment multiplied by the perceived probability that P can avoid the punishment by conformity, i.e., the probability of punishment for nonconformity minus the probability of punishment for conformity (11). Just as an offer of a piece-rate bonus in a factory can serve as a basis for reward power, so the ability to fire a worker if he falls below a given level of production will result in coercive power.

Coercive power leads to dependent change also; and the degree of dependence varies with the level of observability of P's conformity. An excellent illustration of coercive power leading to dependent change is provided by a clothes presser in a factory observed by Coch and French (3). As her efficiency rating climbed above average for the group the other workers began to "scapegoat" her. That the resulting plateau in her production was not independent of the group was evident once she was removed from the presence of the other workers. Her production immediately climbed to new heights.[1]

At times, there is some difficulty in distinguishing between reward power and coercive power. Is the withholding of a reward really equivalent to a punishment? Is the withdrawal of punishment equivalent to a reward? The answer must be a psychological one—it depends upon the situation as it exists for P. But ordinarily we would answer these questions in the affirmative; for P, receiving a reward is a positive valence as is the relief of suffering. There is some evidence that conformity to group norms in order to gain acceptance (reward power) should be distinguished from conformity as a means of forestalling rejection (coercive power) (5).

The distinction between these two types of power is important because the dynamics are different. The concept of "sanctions" sometimes lumps the two together despite their opposite effects. While reward power may eventually result in an independent system, the effects of coercive power will continue to be dependent. Reward power will tend to increase the attraction of P toward O; coercive power will decrease this attraction (11, 12). The valence of the region of behavior will become more negative, acquiring some negative valence from the threatened punishment. The negative valence of punishment would also spread to other regions of the life space. Lewin (25) has pointed out this distinction between the effects of rewards and punishment. In the case of threatened punishment, there will be a resultant force on P to leave the field entirely. Thus, to achieve conformity, O must not only place a strong negative valence in certain regions through threat of punishment, but O must also introduce restraining forces, or other strong valences, so as to prevent P from withdrawing completely from O's range of coercive power. Otherwise the probability of receiving the punishment, if P does not conform, will be too low to be effective.

LEGITIMATE POWER

Legitimate power is probably the most complex of those treated here, embodying notions from the structural sociologist, the group-norm and role-oriented social psychologist, and the clinical psychologist.

There have been considerable investigation and speculation about socially prescribed behavior, particularly that which is specific to a given role or position. Linton (29) distinguishes group norms according to whether they are universals for everyone in the culture, alternatives (the individual having a choice as to whether or not to accept them), or specialties (specific to given positions). Whether we speak of internalized norms, role prescriptions and expectations (34), or internalized pressures (15), the fact remains that each individual sees certain regions toward which he should locomote, some regions toward which he should not locomote, and some regions toward which he may locomote if they are generally attractive for him. This applies to specific behaviors in which he may, should, or should not engage; it applies to certain attitudes or beliefs which he may, should, or should not hold. The feeling of "oughtness" may be an internalization from his parents, from his teachers, from his religion, or may have been logically developed from some idiosyncratic system of ethics. He will speak of such behaviors with expressions like "should," "ought to," or "has a right to." In many cases, the original source of the requirement is not recalled.

Though we have oversimplified such evaluations of behavior with a positive-neutral-negative trichotomy, the evaluation of behaviors by the person is really more one of degree. This dimension of evaluation, we shall call "legitimacy." Conceptually, we may think of legitimacy as a valence in a region which is induced by some internalized norm or value. This value has the same conceptual property as power, namely an ability to induce force fields (26, p. 40–41). It may or may not be correct that values (or the superego) are internalized parents, but at least they can set up force fields which have a phenomenal "oughtness" similar to a parent's prescription. Like a value, a need can also induce valences (i.e., force fields) in P's psychological environment, but these valences have more the phenomenal character of noxious or attractive properties of the object or activity. When a need induces a valence in P—for example, when a need makes an object attractive to P—this attraction applies to P but not to other persons. When a value induces a valence, on the other hand, it not only sets up forces on P to engage in the activity, but P may feel that all others ought to behave in the same way. Among other things, this evaluation applies to the legitimate right of some other individual or group to prescribe behavior or beliefs for a person even though the other cannot apply sanctions.

Legitimate power of O/P is here defined as that power which stems from internalized values in P which dictate that O has a legitimate right to influence P and that P has an obligation to accept this influence. We note that legitimate power is very similar to the notion of legitimacy of authority, which has long been explored by sociologists, particularly by Weber (42), and more recently by Goldhammer and Shils (14). However, legitimate power is not always a role relation: P may accept an induction from O simply because he had previously promised to help O and he values his word too much to break the promise. In all cases, the notion of legitimacy involves some sort of code or standard accepted by the individual by virtue of which the external agent can assert his power. We shall attempt to describe a few of these values here.

Bases for Legitimate Power

Cultural values constitute one common basis for the legitimate power of one individual over another. O has characteristics which are specified by the culture as giving him the right to prescribe behavior for P, who may not have these characteristics. These bases, which Weber (42) has called the authority of the "eternal yesterday," include some things as age, intelligence, caste, and physical characteristics. In some cultures, the aged are granted the right to prescribe behavior for others in practically all behavior areas. In most cultures, there are certain areas of behavior in which a person of one sex is granted the right to prescribe behavior for the other sex.

Acceptance of the social structure is another basis for legitimate power. If P accepts as right the social structure of his group, organization, or society, especially the social structure involving a hierarchy of authority, P will accept the legitimate authority of O who occupies a superior office in the hierarchy. Thus legitimate power in a formal organization is largely a relationship between offices rather than between persons. And the acceptance of an office as *right* is a basis for legitimate power—a judge has a right to levy fines; a foreman should assign work; a priest is justified in prescribing religious beliefs; and it is the management's prerogative to make certain decisions (10). However, legitimate power also involves the perceived right of the person to hold the office.

Designation by a legitimizing agent is a third basis for legitimate power. An influencer O may be seen as legitimate in prescribing behavior for P because he has been granted such power by a legitimizing agent whom P accepts. Thus, a department head may accept the authority of his vice president in a certain area because that authority has been specifically delegated by the president. An election is perhaps the most common example of a group's serving to legitimize the authority of one individual or office for other individuals in the group. The success of such legitimizing depends upon the acceptance of the legitimizing agent and procedure. In this case it depends ultimately on certain democratic values concerning election procedures. The election process is one of legitimizing a person's right to an office which already has a legitimate range of power associated with it.

Range of Legitimate Power of O/P

The areas in which legitimate power may be exercised are generally specified along with the designation of that power. A job description, for example, usually specifies supervisory activities and also designates the person to whom the jobholder is responsible for the duties described. Some bases for legitimate authority carry with them a very broad range. Culturally derived bases for legitimate power are often especially broad. It is not uncommon to find cultures in which a member of a given caste can legitimately prescribe behavior for all members of lower castes in practically all regions. More common, however, are instances of legitimate power where the range is specifically and narrowly prescribed. A sergeant in the army is given a specific set of regions within which he can legitimately prescribe behavior for his men.

The attempted use of legitimate power which is outside of the range of legitimate power will decrease the legitimate power of the authority

figure. Such use of power which is not legitimate will also decrease the attractiveness of O (11, 12, 36).

Legitimate Power and Influence

The new state of the system which results from legitimate power usually has high dependence on O though it may become independent. Here, however, the degree of dependence is not related to the level of observability. Since legitimate power is based on P's values, the source of the forces induced by O include both these internal values and O. O's induction serves to activate the values and to relate them to the system which is influenced, but thereafter the new state of the system may become directly dependent on the values with no mediation by O. Accordingly, this new state will be relatively stable and consistent across varying environmental situations, since P's values are more stable than his psychological environment.

We have used the term *legitimate* not only as a basis for the power of an agent, but also to describe the general behaviors of a person. Thus, the individual P may also consider the legitimacy of the attempts to use other types of power by O. In certain cases, P will consider that O has a legitimate right to threaten punishment for nonconformity; in other cases, such use of coercion would not be seen as legitimate. P might change in response to coercive power of O, but it will make a considerable difference in his attitude and conformity if O is not seen as having a legitimate right to use such coercion. In such cases, the attraction of P for O will be particularly diminished, and the influence attempt will arouse more resistance (11). Similarly the utilization of reward power may vary in legitimacy; the word *bribe,* for example, denotes an illegitimate reward.

REFERENT POWER

The referent power of O/P has its basis in the identification of P with O. By identification, we mean a feeling of oneness of P with O, or a desire for such an identity. If O is a person toward whom P is highly attracted, P will have a desire to become closely associated with O. If O is an attractive group, P will have a feeling of membership or a desire to join. If P is already closely associated with O, he will want to maintain this relationship (39, 41). P's identification with O can be established or maintained if P behaves, believes, and perceives as O does. Accordingly, O has the ability to influence P, even though P may be unaware of this referent power. A verbalization of such power by P might be, "I am like O, and therefore I shall behave or believe as O does," or "I want to be like O, and I will be more like O if I behave or believe as O does." The stronger the identification of P with O the greater the referent power of O/P.

Similar types of power have already been investigated under a number of different formulations. Festinger (7) points out that in an ambiguous situation, the individual seeks some sort of "social reality" and may adopt the cognitive structure of the individual or group with which he identifies. In such a case, the lack of clear structure may be threatening to the individual, and the agreement of his beliefs with those of a reference group will both satisfy his need for structure and give him added security through increased identification with his group (16, 19).

We must try to distinguish between referent power and other types of power which might be operative at the same time. If a member is attracted to a group and he conforms to its norms only because he fears ridicule or expulsion from the group for nonconformity, we would call this coercive power. On the other hand, if he conforms in order *to obtain praise* for conformity, it is a case of reward power. The basic criterion for distinguishing referent power from both coercive and reward power is the mediation of the punishment and the reward by O: To the extent that O mediates the sanctions (i.e., has means control over P), we are dealing with coercive and reward power; but to the extent that P avoids discomfort or gains satisfaction by conformity based on identification, regardless of O's responses, we are dealing with referent power. *Conformity with majority opinion* is sometimes based on a respect for the collective wisdom of the group, in which case it is expert power. It is important to distinguish these phenomena, all grouped together elsewhere as "pressures toward uniformity," since the type of change which occurs will be different for different bases of power.

The concepts of "reference group" (40) and "prestige suggestion" may be treated as instances of referent power. In this case, O, the prestigeful person or group, is valued by P; because P desires to be associated or identified with O, he will assume attitudes or beliefs held by O. Similarly a negative reference group which O dislikes and evaluates negatively may exert negative influence on P as a result of negative referent power.

It has been demonstrated that the power which we designate as referent power is especially great when P is attracted to O (2, 7, 8, 9, 13, 23, 30). In our terms, this would mean that the greater the attraction, the greater the identification, and consequently the greater the referent power. In some cases, attraction or prestige may have a specific basis, and the range of referent power will be limited accordingly: A group of campers may have great referent power over a member regarding campcraft, but considerably less effect on other regions (30). However, we hypothesize that the greater the attraction of P toward O, the broader the range of referent power of O/P.

The new state of a system produced by referent power may be dependent on or independent of O; but the degree of dependence is not affected by the level of observability to O (6, 23). In fact, P is often not consciously aware of the referent power which O exerts over him. There is probably a tendency for some of these dependent changes to become independent of O quite rapidly.

EXPERT POWER

The strength of the expert power of O/P varies with the extent of the knowledge or perception which P attributes to O within a given area. Probably P evaluates O's expertness in relation to his own knowledge as well as against an absolute standard. In any case expert power results in primary social influence on P's cognitive structure and probably not on other types of systems. Of course changes in the cognitive structure can change the direction of forces and hence of locomotion, but such a change of behavior is secondary social influence. Expert power has been demonstrated experimentally (8, 33). Accepting an attorney's advice in legal matters is a common example of expert influence; but there are many instances based on much less knowledge, such as the acceptance by a stranger of directions given by a native villager.

Expert power, where O need not be a member of P's group, is called "informational power" by Deutsch and Gerard (4). This type of expert power must be distinguished from influence based on the content of communication as described by Hovland et al. (17, 18, 23, 24). The influence of the content of a communication upon an opinion is presumably a secondary influence produced after the *primary* influence (i.e., the acceptance of the information). Since power is here defined in terms of the primary changes, the influence of the content on a related opinion is not a case of expert power as we have defined it, but the initial acceptance of the validity of the content does seem to be based on expert power or referent power. In other cases, however, so-called facts may be accepted as self-evident because they fit into P's cognitive structure; if this impersonal acceptance of the truth of the fact is independent of the more or less enduring relationship between O and P, then P's acceptance of the fact is not an actu-alization of expert power. Thus we distinguish between expert power based on the credibility of O and informational influence which is based on characteristics of the stimulus such as the logic of the argument or the "self-evident facts."

Wherever expert influence occurs, it seems to be necessary both for P to think that O knows and for P to trust that O is telling the truth (rather than trying to deceive him).

Expert power will produce a new cognitive structure which is initially relatively dependent on O, but informational influence will produce a more independent structure. The former is likely to become more independent with the passage of time. In both cases the degree of dependence on O is not affected by the level of observability.

The "sleeper effect" (18, 24) is an interesting case of a change in the degree of dependence of an opinion on O. An unreliable O (who probably had negative referent power but some positive expert power) presented "facts" which were accepted by the subjects and which would normally produce secondary influence on their opinions and beliefs. However, the negative referent power aroused resistance and resulted in negative social influ-ence on their beliefs (i.e., set up a force in the direction opposite to the influence attempt), so that there was little change in the subjects' opin-ions. With the passage of time, however, the sub-jects tended to forget the identity of the negative communicator faster than they forgot the contents of his communication, so there was a weakening of the negative referent influence and a consequent delayed positive change in the subjects' beliefs in the direction of the influence attempt ("sleeper effect"). Later, when the identity of the negative communicator was experimentally reinstated, these resisting forces were reinstated, and there was another negative change in belief in a direc-tion opposite to the influence attempt (24).

The range of expert power, we assume, is more delimited than that of referent power. Not only is it restricted to cognitive systems, but the expert is seen as having superior knowledge or ability in very specific areas, and his power will be limited to these areas, though some "halo effect" might occur. Recently, some of our renowned physical scientists have found quite painfully that their expert power in physical sciences does not extend to regions involving international politics. Indeed, there is some evidence that the attempted exer-tion of expert power outside of the range of expert power will reduce that expert power. An under-mining of confidence seems to take place.

Summary

We have distinguished five types of power: refer-ent power, expert power, reward power, coercive power, and legitimate power. These distinctions led to the following hypotheses.

1. For all five types, the stronger the basis of power, the greater the power.

2. For any type of power, the size of the range may vary greatly, but, in general, referent power will have the broadest range.

3. Any attempt to utilize power outside the range of power will tend to reduce the power.

4. A new state of a system produced by reward power or coercive power will be highly depend-ent on O, and the more observable P's confor-mity, the more dependent the state. For the other three types of power, the new state is usu-ally dependent, at least in the beginning, but in any case the level of observability has no effect on the degree of dependence.

5. Coercion results in decreased attraction of P toward O and high resistance; reward power results in increased attraction and low resis-tance.

6. The more legitimate the coercion, the less it will produce resistance and decreased attraction.

Note

1. Though the primary influence of coercive power is dependent, it often produces secondary changes which are independent. Brainwashing, for example, utilizes coercive power to produce many primary changes in the life space of the prisoner, but these dependent changes can lead to identification with the aggressor and hence to secondary changes in ideology which are independent.

References

[1] Asch, S. E. *Social psychology.* New York: Prentice-Hall, 1952.

[2] Back, K. W. Influence through social communication. *J. Abnorm. Soc. Psychol.,* 1951, 46, 9–23.

[3] Coch, L., & French, J. R. P., Jr. Overcoming resistance to change. *Hum. Relat.,* 1948, 1, 512–32.

[4] Deutsch, M., & Gerard, H. B. A study of normative and informational influences upon individual judgment. *J. Abnorm. Soc. Psychol.,* 1955, 51, 629–36.

[5] Dittes, J. E., & Kelley, H. H. Effects of different conditions of acceptance upon conformity to group norms. *J. Abnorm. Soc. Psychol.,* 1956, 53, 100–107.

[6] Festinger, L. An analysis of compliant behavior. In Sherif, M., & Wilson, M. O., (Eds.). *Group relations at the crossroads.* New York: Harper, 1953, 232–56.

[7] Festinger, L. Informal social communication. *Psychol. Rev.,* 1950, 57, 271–82.

[8] Festinger, L., Gerard, H. B., Hymovitch, B., Kelley, H. H., & Raven, B. H. The influence process in the presence of extreme deviates. *Hum. Relat.,* 1952, 5, 327–346.

[9] Festinger, L., Schacter, S., & Back, K. The operation of group standards. In Cartwright, D., & Zander, A. *Group dynamics: research and theory.* Evanston: Row, Peterson, 1953, 204–23.

[10] French, J. R. P., Jr., Israel, Joachim, & Ås Dagfinn. "Arbeidernes medvirkning i industribedriften. En eksperimentell under Økelse." Institute for Social Research, Oslo, Norway, 1957.

[11] French, J. R. P., Jr., Levinger, G., & Morrison, H. W. The legitimacy of coercive power. In preparation.

[12] French, J. R. P., Jr., & Raven, B. H. An experiment in legitimate and coercive power. In preparation.

[13] Gerard, H. B. The anchorage of opinions in face-to-face groups. *Hum. Relat.,* 1954, 7, 313–325.

[14] Goldhammer, H., & Shils, E. A. Types of power and status. *Amer. J. Sociol.,* 1939, 45, 171–178.

[15] Herbst, P. G. Analysis and measurement of a situation. *Hum. Relat.,* 1953, 2, 113–140.

[16] Hochbaum, G. M. Self-confidence and reactions to group pressures. *Amer. Soc. Rev.,* 1954, 19, 678–687.

[17] Hovland, C. I., Lumsdaine, A. A., & Sheffield, F. D. *Experiments on mass communication.* Princeton: Princeton Univer. Press, 1949.

[18] Hovland, C. I., & Weiss, W. The influence of source credibility on communication effectiveness. *Publ. Opin. Quart.,* 1951, 15, 635–650.

[19] Jackson, J. M., & Saltzstein, H. D. The effect of person–group relationships on conformity processes. *J. Abnorm. Soc. Psychol.,* 1958, 57, 17–24.

[20] Jahoda, M. Psychological issues in civil liberties. *Amer. Psychologist,* 1956, 11, 234–240.

[21] Katz, D., & Schank, R. L. *Social psychology.* New York: Wiley, 1938.

[22] Kelley, H. H., & Volkart, E. H. The resistance to change of group-anchored attitudes. *Amer. Soc. Rev.,* 1952, 17, 453–465.

[23] Kelman, H. Three processes of acceptance of social influence: compliance, identification and internalization. Paper read at the meeting of the American Psychological Association, August 1956.

[24] Kelman, H., & Hovland, C. I. "Reinstatement" of the communicator in delayed measurement of opinion change. *J. Abnorm. Soc. Psychol.,* 1953, 48, 327–335.

[25] Lewin, K. *Dynamic theory of personality.* New York: McGraw-Hill, 1935, 114–170.

[26] Lewin, K. *Field theory in social science.* New York: Harper, 1951.

[27] Lewin, K., Lippitt, R., & White, R. K. Patterns of aggressive behavior in experimentally created social climates. *J. Soc. Psychol.,* 1939, 10, 271–301.

[28] Lasswell, H. D., & Kaplan, A. *Power and society: A framework for political inquiry.* New Haven: Yale Univer. Press, 1950.

[29] Linton, R. *The cultural background of personality.* New York: Appleton-Century-Crofts, 1945.

[30] Lippitt, R., Polansky, N., Redl, F., & Rosen, S. The dynamics of power. *Hum. Relat.,* 1952, 5, 37–64.

[31] March, J. G. An introduction to the theory and measurement of influence. *Amer. Polit. Sci. Rev.,* 1955, 49, 431–451.

[32] Miller, J. G. Toward a general theory for the behavioral sciences. *Amer. Psychologist,* 1955, 10, 513–531.

[33] Moore, H. T. The comparative influence of majority and expert opinion. *Amer. J. Psychol.,* 1921, 32, 16–20.

[34] Newcomb, T. M. *Social psychology.* New York: Dryden, 1950.

[35] Raven, B. H. The effect of group pressures on opinion, perception, and communication. Unpublished doctoral dissertation, University of Michigan, 1953.

[36] Raven, B. H., & French, J. R. P., Jr. Group support, legitimate power, and social influence. *J. Person.,* 1958, 26, 400–409.

[37] Rommetveit, R. *Social norms and roles.* Minneapolis: Univer. Minnesota Press, 1953.

[38] Russell, B. *Power: A new social analysis.* New York: Norton, 1938.

[39] Stotland, E., Zander, A., Burnstein, E., Wolfe, D., & Natsoulas, T. Studies on the effects of identification. University of Michigan, Institute for Social Research. Forthcoming.

[40] Swanson, G. E., Newcomb, T. M., & Hartley, E. L. *Readings in social psychology.* New York: Henry Holt, 1952.

[41] Torrance, E. P., & Mason, R. Instructor effort to influence: An experimental evaluation of six approaches. Paper presented at USAF-NRC Symposium on Personnel, Training, and Human Engineering. Washington, DC, 1956.

[42] Weber, M. *The theory of social and economic organization.* Oxford: Oxford Univer. Press, 1947.

Reading 17

Relationships between Leader Reward and Punishment Behavior and Group Processes and Productivity

Philip M. Podsakoff
Indiana University

William D. Todor
Ohio State University

In a presentation at the Biennial Leadership Symposium, C. A. Schriesheim, Mowday and Stogdill (1979) argued strongly that greater consideration of group processes is necessary if our understanding of leadership effectiveness is to be facilitated.

C. A. Schriesheim et al. (1979) observed that there are several reasons why understanding the relationship between leaders and groups is important. First, leaders emerge from groups or are appointed to manage them and therefore must have a working knowledge of group processes in order to be effective. Leaders also play an important role in determining the goals of the groups they lead and in monitoring the social relationships of those groups. Finally, leaders are influenced by the groups they lead; and, to the extent that they understand the nature of this influence process, the better able they will be to change or modify their own behavior in an effective manner.

Despite the convincing arguments presented by C. A. Schriesheim et al. (1979) regarding the inclusion of groups into our analysis of leadership effectiveness, to our knowledge only two studies have been explicitly designed to analyze leader–subordinate interactions since the presentation was made. Both of these studies examined group processes within the context of a leader's instrumental and supportive behaviors. Greene and C. A. Schriesheim (1980) found both instrumental leader behavior (ILB) and supportive leader behavior (SLB) to positively influence group cohesion and arousal. In addition, they found that ILB had particularly strong effects on these group processes in large and newly formed groups while SLB exerted its greatest influence in small and newly formed groups. J. F. Schriesheim (1980) examined the moderating effects of group cohesiveness on

the relationships between instrumental and supportive leader behaviors and several subordinate criterion variables. She reported that group cohesiveness negatively moderated the relationships between ILB and subordinates' role clarity, satisfaction, and performance and positively moderated the relationship between SLB and these same criterion variables. In the discussion of her findings, Schriesheim concluded that "this study examined only one aspect of the primary work group. The results were encouraging and suggest that leadership research might benefit from more careful attention to the literature on groups" (J. F. Schriesheim, 1980, p. 191).

Given the theoretical importance C. A. Schriesheim et al. (1979) have accorded group processes in the determination of leader effectiveness and the empirical evidence reported by Greene and C. A. Schriesheim (1980) and J. F. Schriesheim (1980), it would appear that additional research designed to examine other forms of leader behavior that might be expected to be related to group criterion variables would be warranted. Two general classes of leader behavior that seem to be particularly relevant to group processes and productivity are leader reward and punishment behaviors.

There is a substantial amount of evidence which suggests that the way leaders administer individual rewards and punishments influences subordinates' performance and satisfaction (cf. Greene, 1976a; Hunt & Schuler, 1976; Podsakoff, 1982; Podsakoff, Todor, Grover, & Huber, 1984; Podsakoff, Todor, & Skov, 1982; Sims, 1977; Sims & Szilagyi, 1975; Szilagyi, 1980). The way rewards and punishments are administered to *groups* of individuals has also been shown to have a significant relationship with various group criterion variables, including group productivity (French, Brownell, Graziano, & Hartup, 1977; Rosenbaum, Moore, Cotton, Cook, Hieser, Shovar, & Gray, 1980), cohesiveness and interpersonal attraction among group members (see Bersheid & Walster,

Source: P. M. Podsakoff, W. D. Todor, *Journal of Management* 1985, 11, 1, 55–73. Copyright: Sage 1985. Edited and reprinted by permission of Sage Publications, Inc.

1978; Byrne, 1971; or Lott & Lott, 1965, for reviews), the amount of dysfunctional or inappropriate group member behaviors (Sulzbacher & Houser, 1970), and the amount of tutoring that takes place in a group (Hamblin, Hathaway, & Wodarski, 1971). What has been relatively neglected, however, is the effects that individual reward and punishment contingencies administered by a leader have upon group processes and productivity.

An analysis of the impact that individually administered rewards and punishments have upon group processes and productivity should prove to be of considerable interest to practicing managers and leaders. Several authors have noted that while particular reward and punishment contingencies may appear to have functional effects at the individual level, they may have just the opposite effects at the group level. Hardin (1968), for example, in his discussion of the "tragedy on the commons," noted the problems encountered in a small community when all the townspeople responded to individual reinforcement contingencies which eventually hurt the community as a whole. Schelling (1971) provided a number of similar examples of situations in which individuals acted rationally in order to increase their own outcomes, only to find that the overall result of their actions was a loss for the entire group of which they were members. And, in discussing the effects of monetary rewards in organizations, Lawler (1971) noted that even though individual incentive systems have generally positive effects on subordinates' performance, they sometimes lead to "soldiering" by group members (that is, pressure by group members to limit or restrict productivity to a particular level). Taking these findings into consideration, it is possible that even though leaders who administer rewards contingent upon performance have been generally found to have functional effects on individual levels of performance and satisfaction, such behavior by the leader may have unintended or dysfunctional effects on group processes or productivity. Leaders who administer contingent rewards, for example, may not only increase the motivation of their subordinates to perform, but also may increase the competitiveness of these individuals. Such competition, while not inherently bad, may prove dysfunctional if the tasks performed by the subordinates require cooperation. For, under these conditions, the competition developed among the subordinates may interfere with or disrupt the cooperation needed among the group members to perform effectively. Thus, it

makes practical sense to examine the effects of rewards administered by the leader not only on the individual, but also on the group.

The purpose of the research reported here is to examine the relationships between individually administered rewards and punishments and subordinates' perceptions of various group characteristics. In addition to productivity, Stogdill (1972) has identified group cohesiveness and drive as essential dimensions of organized groups. Stogdill (1972) defined group drive as "the degree of group arousal, motivation, freedom, enthusiasm, or esprit" and group cohesiveness as "the extent to which members reinforce each other's expectations regarding the value of maintaining the identity of the group" (p. 27). Because of the prominence assigned to group cohesiveness and drive by both Stogdill (1972) and Schriesheim et al. (1979), these group processes, along with group members' perceptions of their group's productivity, are considered in the present study. Consistent with the research of Hunt and Schuler (1976) and Podsakoff, Todor, and Skov (1982), the relationships between both contingent and noncontingent reward and punishment behaviors and the group criterion variables will be examined. Contingent rewards and punishments are those that are based on the performance of the subordinates. Leaders who administer contingent rewards provide praise, commendation, and acknowledgement to group members when they perform at high levels or improve their performance. Similarly, leaders who administer contingent punishment reprimand their subordinates when they perform poorly or at low levels. Noncontingent rewards and punishments, on the other hand, are those that are administered independently of subordinates' performance. Thus, a leader who utilizes noncontingent rewards (or punishments) administers them to group members who deserve them as well as to group members who do not deserve them.

BACKGROUND AND EXPECTATIONS

LEADER BEHAVIOR AND GROUP COHESIVENESS

Byrne and a colleague (Byrne, 1971, Byrne & Clore, 1970) have suggested that the interpersonal attraction we express toward other individuals is influenced by the rewards and punishments associated with those individuals. More specifically, Byrne has hypothesized that we like and/or are attracted to those individuals or groups in whose presence we receive rewards, but we dislike and are not attracted to those individuals or groups in whose presence we are punished. Numerous studies have been conducted in order to assess the effects that receiving rewards or punishments in the presence of other individuals or groups of individuals has upon a person's attitude toward those individuals or groups (cf. Byrne, 1971; Lott & Lott, 1965). In general, the results of these studies indicate that individuals are more attracted to groups with which they interact, or describe groups as more cohesive, when the individuals receive rewards in the presence of the group's members than when they receive no rewards or are punished.

The findings reported above should not be taken to suggest that all types of rewards and punishments have precisely the same effects on a group member's perception of group cohesiveness however. Several studies have demonstrated that the reinforcing potential of a stimulus event, and subsequently its effects on an individual's attitude, is influenced by the manner in which the stimulus is administered (cf. Hunt & Schuler, 1976; Keisler, 1966; Podsakoff, Barman, Todor, & Grover, 1982). Podsakoff, Barman, Todor, and Grover, for example, found that while there is a positive relationship between co-worker satisfaction and leader reward behavior when rewards are administered contingently by the leader, no such relationship existed when leaders administered rewards noncontingently. In addition, these researchers reported that while there is a negative relationship between leader noncontingent punishment behavior and subordinates' satisfaction with their co-workers, no such relationship existed between leader contingent punishment behavior and this criterion variable. Based on these findings, and assuming that co-worker satisfaction may serve as an indirect measure of group cohesiveness, we would expect that *while neither leader contingent punishment nor noncontingent reward behavior will be related to group members' perceptions of cohesion, leader contingent reward behavior will be positively related to perceptions of group cohesion and leader noncontingent punishment behavior will be negatively related to this criterion variable.*

LEADER BEHAVIOR AND GROUP DRIVE

Zander (1971) has suggested that group drive may be assessed by a group's aspiration level. Among other things, he views the group's aspiration level to be a function of individual group members' perceptions of the probability that the group will be able to achieve success and avoid failure. Leaders who allocate rewards and punishments contingently administer reinforcing and punitive events according to the performance levels of group members. Such behavior on the part of the leader would therefore be expected to increase group members' perceptions that by performing well in their tasks, they should be able to increase the rewards and decrease the punishments they receive. If this perception regarding the ability to obtain rewards and avoid punishments also generalizes to the group members' beliefs regarding the probability that the group they belong to will be able to increase its rewards and to avoid punishment, we would expect that both *leader contingent reward and contingent punishment behavior will be positively related to group members' perceptions of group drive.*

Leaders who allocate rewards and punishments noncontingently, on the other hand, administer reinforcing and punitive events independent of the performance levels of group members. Under such circumstances group members have an approximately equal probability of receiving rewards or punishments, regardless of how well or how poorly they perform their tasks. For these reasons, we would expect that both *leader noncontingent reward and noncontingent punishment behavior will not be related to group drive.*

LEADER BEHAVIOR AND GROUP PRODUCTIVITY

Of all the group criterion variables examined in this study, it is perhaps the most difficult to make specific predictions concerning group productivity. As noted earlier, several authors (e.g., Hardin, 1968; Lawler, 1971; Schelling, 1971) have provided examples of the potential dysfunctional consequences that may occur when members of a group are rewarded individually. These examples suggest that while individually administered contingencies may increase the motivation of individual group members, this motivation may be channeled into behavior which is counterproductive to the group as a whole. Stogdill (1972), however, has reported that group drive (or motivation) is generally positively related to group productivity, suggesting that leader behaviors which increase a group's drive will also increase a group's productivity. Moreover, Zander (1971) has noted that group drive may result in group productivity when group members are provided with accurate performance feedback. Leaders who administer rewards and punishments contingently provide feedback which is appropriate to the level of performance of group members. Leaders who administer rewards and punishments noncontingently, on the other hand, provide feedback to group members which is independent of their performance levels. Therefore, as in the case with group drive, we expect that *group members' perceptions of leader contingent reward and punishment behaviors will be positively related to their perceptions of group productivity, while perceptions of leader noncontingent reward and punishment behaviors will not be related to this criterion variable.*

ASSUMPTIONS UNDERLYING EXPECTATIONS

The preceding expectations regarding the relationships between leader reward and punishment behaviors and group cohesiveness, drive, and productivity are based on two basic assumptions. The first assumption is that the respondents in the present study are in functioning groups. Reitz (1981), among others, has indicated that there are four essential criteria that must be met to have a functioning group. These criteria are: (a) two or more people who (b) interact with each other or influence each others' behavior, (c) share a common goal, and (d) see themselves as a group. Respondents used in the present study were drawn from three different samples of state and local government bodies or agencies. Within these samples, all of the groups exceeded three people (range = 4 to 14), all had a common supervisor, and all of the group members were located in the same general proximity. While it was not possible to actually assess the absolute level of interaction that took place among the group members or the degree to which the group members saw themselves as a group, we feel it safe to assume that these conditions were generally met because (a) the close proximity of the majority of the group members would be expected to produce numerous interactions among them and because (b) the questions relating to the group processes measured in this study asked respondents to describe the group of individuals who report to the same immediate supervisor.

The second assumption regarding the nature of the groups in the present study is that generally no competition or work-flow interdependence exists among the group members. Several studies (see Johnson, Maruyama, Johnson, Nelson, & Skon, 1981, for a review of this literature) suggest that dysfunctional consequences may accrue in groups in which rewards are administered individualistically if the performance of the group

members is interdependently linked. The majority of the respondents sampled in the present study were clerical, administrative, or white-collar government employees who interact with each other in their jobs but whose work flow is not linked. Thus, interdependence was not seen as a general problem. Similarly, since these employees are paid either by salary or on an hourly basis according to their seniority or tenure (but not by their actual performance), little or no competition was also assumed. . . .

DISCUSSION AND CONCLUSIONS

The purpose of this study was twofold. The primary objective was to examine the relationships between leader reward and punishment behaviors and group drive, cohesiveness, and productivity. The findings of the study reported here provide little support for the proposition that leaders who administer evaluative rewards contingently at the individual level will have dysfunctional effects on group processes. Group cohesion, drive, and group productivity were all found to be positively related to leader contingent reward behavior. The positive relationship between CR [contingent reward behavior] and group cohesion may be explained by Byrne's (1971) interpersonal attraction model. However, other plausible explanations also exist. It is possible, for example, that leaders who administer evaluative rewards to group members according to their performance levels increase the group members' perceptions of equity, which subsequently increase their feelings of interpersonal attraction toward the group. An alternative explanation is that leaders who reward individuals appropriately also reward the group as a whole when it performs well or succeeds on a task. Several studies have shown that groups which receive rewards for their performance express more cohesion than groups which receive no rewards (cf. Lott & Lott, 1965).

The somewhat weaker support provided for the relationship between contingent reward behavior and group productivity than the support provided for either the relationship between CR and group cohesiveness or CR and group drive suggests that even though CR increases group drive and cohesiveness, these group processes are not always translated into improved levels of group performance. Greene (1976b) has suggested the possibility that group acceptance of organizational goals may serve to moderate the relationship between group cohesiveness and productivity. In a longitudinal field study he reported that group cohesiveness caused increases in the productivity of groups that accepted organizational goals but decreased the productivity of groups that did not accept organizational goals. Thus, one possible reason for the lower level of relationship between CR and group productivity is that organizational goals may have been accepted by some groups but not by other groups in the study.

Another plausible reason for the lower level of correspondence between contingent reward behavior and group productivity than between either CR and group drive or cohesiveness has to do with the nature of the tasks performed by the work groups. As noted earlier, results from several studies (cf. Cherrington, Reitz, & Scott, 1971; Miller & Hamblin, 1963; Rosenbaum et al., 1980; Scott & Cherrington, 1974) suggest that individually administered monetary rewards are more effective when the tasks subordinates perform are independent or nonadditive, whereas rewards based on group performance are more effective when tasks are additive or require cooperation. If these findings are applicable to social rewards such as the praise and commendations provided by leaders, it may mean that leaders who establish individualistic reward contingencies will positively affect the performance of groups that perform nonadditive tasks but will have no effect, or a negative effect, on the performance of groups which perform tasks which are interdependent or require cooperation. Despite the fact that it was assumed that no work-flow interdependence was present among the groups in this study, no explicit measure of these relationships was taken. Future research directed at analyzing the relationships between leader reward and punishment behaviors and group productivity should therefore consider the nature of the tasks performed by the subordinates.

Among the more interesting findings in this study were the generally consistent positive relationships between contingent punishment behavior and group drive and productivity (although the results between CP and drive are somewhat equivocal). The majority of research conducted to date suggests that contingent punishment is frequently not related to individual subordinate performance (cf. Sims, 1980); and in those instances in which it has been shown to be related, the relationship is often negative and the causal direction is reversed (cf. Greene, 1976a; Szilagyi, 1980). That is, the evidence suggests that it is decreases in employee performance that cause increases in the leader's use of contingent punishment and not vice versa. The results of the present study, however, do suggest that contingent punishment

behavior administered by the leader may have significant positive effects on group productivity. There are several possible reasons for this finding. First, we might speculate that leaders who use contingent punishment convey to the individual being punished as well as to the other group members, that their expectations were not met. This may lead to increased goal setting at either the individual or group level, both of which have been shown to influence the productivity of workers (cf. Locke, Cartledge, & Knerr, 1970; Zander, 1971). Second, we would expect that leaders who administer CP are perceived by most group members to be administering punishment to those who deserve it. Under these circumstances, the group members themselves may also encourage the poorly performing group co-worker to straighten up, or the group may take other forms of corrective action. Related to this is the fact that several behavioral scientists (Hamner & Organ, 1977; Scott & Podsakoff, 1982; Skinner, 1953; Solomon, 1964) have noted that the administration of punishment is often an emotional experience, not only for those being punished but also for the one administering the punishment as well. If group members find that when a leader punishes a poorly performing group member it decreases the likelihood that the leader will administer rewards to other group members for some time because the leader is too upset, the group may bring pressure to bear on the employee to improve performance. Finally, leaders who employ contingent punishment behavior not only identify what they consider dysfunctional or unproductive behavior for the individual being punished, but for other group members as well. In so doing, the leaders may clarify their expectations for all group members.

The results of this study with respect to noncontingent rewards also proved to be quite intriguing. For, while the relationship between NCR and the three group criterion variables measured in this study were nonsignificant before accounting for common method variance, all of these relationships were found to be significantly negative when same-source variance was removed. This finding contrasts with the generally positive relationships found between leader contingent reward behavior and these same criterion variables; it also suggests that it is not rewards alone which determine the relationships between the leader behaviors measured in this study and group processes, but it it how the rewards are administered that is important. This finding also suggests that, in general, the common method variance factor measured in this study served as a suppressor of the negative relationships between NCR and group cohesiveness, drive, and productivity.

Few significant relationships were found between leader noncontingent punishment behavior and the group criterion variables measured in this study when common method variance was partialled out. The one exception, the negative relationship between NCP and group drive, suggests that leaders who administer noncontingent punishment decrease the group's motivation to perform. This is consistent with the findings of research on individual behavior which demonstrates that uncontrollable aversive events decrease an individual's effort and often induce a feeling of helplessness (Seligman, 1975).

Taken as a whole, therefore, the results of our study indicate that leaders who administer evaluative rewards and punishments contingently will have a more functional effect not only on subordinate performance and satisfaction (cf. Hunt & Schuler, 1976; Podsakoff, 1982; Podsakoff, Todor, & Skov, 1982; Podsakoff, Todor, Grover, & Huber, 1984; Sims & Szilagyi, 1975) but also on group outcomes as well. This suggests that leaders will be more effective to the extent that they identify those classes of behavior which prove functional (or dysfunctional) to the organization as a whole and provide evaluative rewards (or punishments) for them accordingly. . . .

Of course, given the fact that the relationships reported in our study are relatively conservative (and cross-sectional in nature), additional research utilizing longitudinal and experimental designs is going to be necessary before unequivocal evidence regarding the relationships between leader reward and punishment behaviors and group processes can be obtained. Nevertheless, we do feel the results of our study are of considerable interest and do indicate a need to focus more attention on the effects that evaluative rewards administered on an individualistic basis by leaders have on group processes and productivity.

References

Bersheid, E., & Walster, E. H. (1978). *Interpersonal attraction* (2nd ed.), Reading, MA: Addison-Wesley.

Blau, P. M. (1964). *Exchange and power in social life.* New York: Wiley.

Bryne, D. (1971). *The attraction paradigm.* New York: Academic Press.

Bryne, D., & Clore, G. L. (1970). A reinforcement model of evaluative responses. *Personality, 1,* 103–128.

Cherrington, D. J., Reitz, H. J., & Scott, W. E. (1971). Effects of contingent and non-contingent rewards on the relationship between satisfaction and task performance. *Journal of Applied Psychology, 55,* 531–536.

Cohen, J., & Cohen, P. (1975). *Applied multiple regressional/correlation analysis for the behavioral sciences.* Hillsdale, NJ: Lawrence Erlbaum.

French, D. C., Brownell, C. A., Graziano, W. G., & Hartup, W. W. (1977). Effects of cooperative, competitive, and individualistic sets on performance in children's groups. *Journal of Experimental Child Psychology, 24,* 1–10.

Fulk, J., & Wendler, E. R. (1982). Dimensionality of leader-subordinate interactions: A path-goal investigation. *Organizational Behavior and Human Performance, 30,* 241–254.

Greene, C. N. (1976a). A longitudinal investigation of performance-reinforcing leader behavior and satisfaction and performance. In A. F. Sikula & R. L. Hilgert (Eds.), *Proceedings of the Midwest Academy of Management Meetings* (pp. 157–185).

Greene, C. N. (1976b, August). *Causal connections among cohesion, drive, goal acceptance and productivity in work groups.* Paper presented at the annual meeting of the Academy of Management, Kansas City, KS.

Greene, C. N., & Schriesheim, C. A. (1980). Leader-group interactions: A longitudinal field investigation. *Journal of Applied Psychology, 65,* 50–59.

Hamblin, R. I., Hathaway, C., & Wodarski, J. (1971). Group contingencies, peer tutoring and accelerating academic achievement. In E. A. Ramp & B. L. Hopkins (Eds.), *A new direction for education: Behavior analysis* (Vol. 1, pp. 276–290). Lawrence, KS: University of Kansas Press.

Hamner, W. C., & Organ, D. W. (1977). *Organizational behavior: An applied psychological approach.* Dallas, TX: Business Publications.

Hardin, G. (1968). The tragedy of the commons. *Science, 162,* 1243–1248.

Homans, G. C. (1974). *Social behavior. Its elementary forms* (Revised ed.). New York: Harcourt, Brace and World.

Hunt, J. G., & Schuler, R. S. (1976). *Leader reward and sanctions behavior in a public utility: What difference does it make?* Unpublished working paper, Southern Illinois University at Carbondale, Carbondale, IL.

Johnson, D. W., Maruyama, G., Johnson, R., Nelson, D., & Skon, L. (1981). Effects of cooperative, competitive and individualistic goal structures on achievement: A meta-analysis. *Psychological Bulletin, 89,* 47–62.

Keisler, S. B. (1966). The effects of perceived role requirements as reactions to favor doing. *Journal of Experimental Social Psychology, 2,* 298–310.

Lawler, E. E., III (1971). *Pay and organizational effectiveness: A psychological view.* New York: McGraw-Hill.

Locke, E. A., Cartledge, N., & Knerr, C. S. (1970). Studies of the relationship between satisfaction, goal-setting, and performance. *Organizational Behavior and Human Performance, 5*, 135–158.

Lott, A. J., & Lott, B. E. (1965). Group cohesiveness as interpersonal attraction: A review of relationships with antecedent and consequent variables. *Psychological Bulletin, 64*, 259–309.

McGinnies, E. (1970). *Social behavior: A functional analysis*. Boston: Houghton Mifflin.

Miller, L. K., & Hamblin, R. L. (1963). Interdependence, differential rewarding and productivity. *American Sociological Review, 28*, 768–778.

Podsakoff, P. M. (1982). Determinants of a supervisor's use of rewards and punishments: A literature review and suggestions for future research. *Organizational Behavior and Human Performance, 29*, 58–83.

Podsakoff, P. M., Barman, M. L., Todor, W. D., & Grover, R. A. (1982). Relationships between leader reward and punishment behaviors, role ambiguity and hospital pharmacists' satisfaction. In K. H. Chung (Ed.), *Proceedings of the 42nd Annual Meeting of the Academy of Management* (pp. 42–46).

Podsakoff, P. M., & Skov, R. (1980). [Leader reward and punishment behavior scales]. Unpublished research, Indiana University, Bloomington, IN.

Podsakoff, P. M., Todor, W. D., Grover, R. A., & Huber, V. L. (1984). Situational moderators of leader reward and punishment behavior: Fact or fiction? *Organizational Behavior and Human Performance, 34*, 21–63.

Podsakoff, P. M., Todor, W. D., & Skov, R. B. (1982). Effects of leader contingent and noncontingent reward and punishment behaviors on subordinate performance and satisfaction. *Academy of Management Journal, 25*, 810–821.

Reitz, H. J. (1981). *Behavior in organizations* (rev. ed.). Homewood, IL: Irwin.

Rosenbaum, M. E., Moore, D. L., Cotton, J. L., Cook, M. S., Hieser, R. A., Shovar, M. N., & Gray, M. J. (1980). Group productivity and process: Pure and mixed reward structure and task interdependence. *Journal of Personality and Social Psychology, 39*, 626–642.

Schelling, T. (1971). The ecology of micromotives. *Public Interest, 25*, 61–98.

Schriesheim, C. A., Mowday, R., & Stogdill, R. M. (1979). Crucial dimensions of leader-group interactions. In J. G. Hunt & L. L. Larson (Eds.), *Crosscurrents in leadership* (pp. 106–125). Carbondale, IL: Southern Illinois University Press.

Schriesheim, C. A. (1982). [Effects of group re-structuring on group processes and productivity]. Unpublished study.

Schriesheim, J. F. (1980). The social context of leader-subordinate relations: An investigation of the effects on group cohesiveness. *Journal of Applied Psychology, 65*, 183–194.

Scott, W. E., Jr., & Cherrington, D. J. (1974). Effects of competitive, cooperative, and individualistic reinforcement contingencies. *Journal of Personality and Social Psychology, 30*, 748–758.

Scott, W. E., & Podsakoff, P. M. (1982). Leadership, supervision and behavioral control: Perspectives from an experimental analysis. In L. Fredericksen (Ed.), *Handbook of Organizational Behavior Management* (pp. 39–69). New York: Wiley.

Seligman, M. E. P. (1975). *Helplessness: On depression, development, and death*. San Francisco: W. H. Freeman.

Sims, H. P., Jr. (1977). The leader as a manager of reinforcement contingencies: An empirical example and a model. In J. G. Hunt & L. L. Larson (Eds.), *Leadership, the cutting edge* (pp. 121–137). Carbondale, IL: Southern Illinois University Press.

Sims, H. P., Jr. (1980). Further thoughts on punishment in organizations. *Academy of Management Review, 5*, 133–138.

Sims, H. P., Jr, & Szilagyi, S. D. (1975). Leader reward behavior and subordinate satisfaction and performance. *Organizational Behavior and Human Performance, 14*, 426–438.

Skinner, B. F. (1953). *Science and human behavior*. New York: MacMillan.

Solomon, R. L. (1964). Punishment. *American Psychologist, 19*, 239–253.

Stogdill, R. M. (1965a). *Managers, employees, organizations: A study of 27 organizations*. Columbus, OH: Bureau of Business Research, Ohio State University.

Stogdill, R. M. (1965b). Manual for group dimensions descriptions. Columbus, OH: Bureau of Business Research, Ohio State University.

Stogdill, R. M. (1972). Group productivity, drive and cohesiveness. *Organizational Behavior and Human Performance, 8*, 26–43.

Sulzbacher, S. I., & Huser, J. E. (1970). A tactic to eliminate disruptive behaviors in the classroom: Group contingent consequences. In R. Ulrich, T. Stachnik, & J. Mabry (Eds.), *Control of Human Behavior* (Vol. 2, pp. 187–189). Glenview, IL: Scott, Foresman.

Szilagyi, A. D. (1980). Causal inferences between leader reward behavior and subordinate performance, absenteeism, and work satisfaction. *Journal of Occupational Psychology, 53*, 195–204.

Thibaut, J. W., & Kelley, H. H. (1959). *The social psychology of groups*. New York: Wiley.

Zander, A. (1971). *Motives and goals in groups*. New York: Academic Press.

Leadership and Leader Behaviors

The studies of leader traits reported in Chapter 3 successfully identify a number of personal attributes that endow an individual with the *potential* to emerge and to be a successful leader. However, while these are important traits, the characteristics that an individual possesses do not provide a complete picture of "who is the leader" and "who is the effective leader," nor an answer to the question, "What determines leadership success?" From his review of the trait literature, Ralph Stogdill (1948) suggests that leadership consists of movement and getting work accomplished. He notes that the leader–follower relationship could be seen as a *working relationship,* one in which the leader orchestrates group activity. Kirkpatrick and Locke (1991) also suggest that leadership can be seen as an *activity,* noting that people who possess a key set of traits are more likely to engage in the behaviors associated with leadership and effective leadership.

Following the inability to explain the totality of leadership and effective leadership by employing the traits that individuals carry with them into leadership situations, an interest in understanding what it is that effective leaders actually *do* emerged. Students of leadership continued their leader-centric approach, turning their attention to the *behaviors* that leaders engage in, and whether or not effective leadership was a function of the actual behaviors engaged in by leaders. David G. Bowers and Stanley E. Seashore (1966) define leadership as "organizationally useful behavior by one member of an organizational family toward another member or members of that same organizational family" (p. 240).

During the late 1940s, major research efforts looking into leader behavior were launched at the University of Michigan, The Ohio State University, and Harvard University. These initiatives resulted in the identification of a number of different leader behaviors and accompanying categorization schemes.

Some of the more popular typologies employed to categorize leader behavior now focused on the amount of control exercised (or closeness of supervision), employee versus job (task, production) orientation, as well as some very specific behaviors (e.g., communication, representation, fraternization, and organization[1]). Theoretically, it has been reasoned that leader behaviors have an impact on follower attitudes (e.g., satisfaction with the leader and the job), motivation, work-related behaviors (e.g., performance), and group properties (e.g., group cohesiveness), each of which ultimately has an impact on work group effectiveness.

According to House and Aditya (1997), the early research into leader behaviors was limited by many of the same problems (e.g., the lack of a theoretical anchoring and poor measurement) that characterized the trait research that preceded it. In spite of those limitations, valuable research was conducted at both The Ohio State Leadership Center and the University of Michigan's Institute for

[1] E. A. Fleishman, "The Description of Supervisory Behavior," *Journal of Applied Psychology* 37 (1953), pp. 1–6.

Social Research. The major contribution was the identification and detailed specification of two broad classes of leader behavior—task-oriented and person-oriented leader behaviors.

The first reading in this chapter, by Bowers and Seashore (1966), highlights the fact that the work conducted at the University of Michigan resulted in the identification of a number of different leader behaviors and leader behavior classification schemes. Four dimensions of leader behavior (i.e., support, interaction facilitation, goal emphasis, and work facilitation) emerged as "the basic structure of what one may term 'leadership'" (Bowers and Seashore, p. 247). (The self-assessments appearing at the end of this chapter introduction provide you with the opportunity to profile your own leadership style as it pertains to several important leader behaviors.) Accompanying their review of significant leader behaviors, Bowers and Seashore provide an interesting perspective on leadership. They note that effective work groups tend to require the presence of *each* of these four behaviors, yet they go on to note that *anyone* in a group may provide these behaviors and that they need not be directly infused into the group by the leader. The formal leader's role may be one of making sure that the necessary behaviors are present and in sufficient degree.

Under the direction of Ralph Stogdill, a group of researchers at The Ohio State University began an extensive and systematic study directed toward the identification of the behaviors that were associated with effective group performance. This work identifies several behaviors engaged in by leaders (e.g., integration, production emphasis, evaluation, domination, initiation), which eventually resulted in an almost exclusive focus on two specific leader behaviors—consideration and initiating structure behaviors.

An early study conducted by Andrew W. Halpin (1957) examines the role of the leader's initiating structure and consideration, and their relationship to leader effectiveness, the level of satisfaction of the leader's group members, and member ratings of confidence and proficiency, friendship and cooperation, and morale in association with their leader. While this study was conducted in a military context, similar findings have been observed in numerous other settings. Halpin's work highlights leader behavior as an important part of the leadership process, making a difference in terms of morale, satisfaction, and effectiveness.

In the second reading, Edwin A. Fleishman (1962) and his colleague Edwin F. Harris investigate the effect of leader initiating structure and consideration behavior on member grievances, turnover, and group effectiveness. Their findings reinforce Halpin's observations, suggesting the usefulness of employing these two behavioral dimensions in organization settings and across relatively divergent cultures (i.e., Japan, United States, and Israel).

Taken together, these studies provide a useful framework suggesting that leaders and leadership can be studied from the perspective of leader behaviors. In addition, their evidence suggests that what leaders do can make a difference. Meaningful effects of leader behavior have been found in the areas of employee behavior (e.g., grievances, turnover) and attitudes (e.g., satisfaction, morale, group culture), as well as assessments of leader performance and group effectiveness.

An overview of the leader behavior literature highlights the fact that the consequences associated with leader behaviors are not always consistent.[2] While consideration is commonly associated with follower satisfaction, the effects associated with initiating structure behavior are more volatile across situations. At times, initiating structure is positively associated with satisfaction, while at

---

[2] A. K. Korman, "Consideration, Initiating Structure, and Organizational Criteria—A Review," *Personnel Psychology* 19 (1966), pp. 349–361; S. Kerr and C. Schriesheim, "Consideration, Initiating Structure, and Organizational Criteria—An Update of Korman's 1966 Review," *Personnel Psychology* 27 (1974), pp. 555–568.

other times, its effects are negative. Although leader consideration behavior is seldom associated with positive performance effects, the relationship between initiating structure and performance produces a mixed picture. Sometimes the effects are positive, sometimes there are no meaningful relationships, and at other times the effects are, in fact, negative.

It has been argued on numerous occasions, especially by Robert R. Blake and Jane S. Mouton in the presentation of their *managerial grid*,[3] that leaders who simultaneously display high degrees of both structuring and consideration behavior (high–high) are likely to be the most effective in terms of follower satisfaction and performance. Larson, Hunt, and Osborn (1976), after reviewing the literature, conclude that the high–high paradigm is still open to question.[4] While consideration and initiating structure are positively related, they observe support for the high–high paradigm in only 4 of 14 samples that examined the interactive effects of consideration and structure on satisfaction. There was no support found for the high–high paradigm in terms of its prediction of performance. Larson and his colleagues note that in many situations, "models involving structure only or consideration only were found to predict satisfaction as well as the more complex models" (p. 628), reflecting the high–high paradigm.

In recent years, some scholars cast doubt on the importance of the Ohio State leadership behaviors (see House & Podsakoff, 1994).[5] The recent meta-analytic review by Judge, Piccolo, and Ilies[6] which focuses on the leader behaviors of consideration and initiating structure, led them to conclude that "both consideration and initiating structure have important main effects on numerous criteria that most would argue are fundamental indicators of effective leadership" (p. 44). They also note that these behaviors do not explain the totality of leader effectiveness, but they are "important pieces in the leadership puzzle" (p. 44).

The Fleishman and Harris (1962) study, reported in Reading 19, along with the results summarized here from Judge et al.'s (2004) review of the initiating structure and consideration literature, provides us with insight into the outcomes that are associated with these two leader behaviors. On the basis of their meta-analytic review of 130 studies, Judge and his colleagues find consideration and initiating structure to be significantly related to follower job and leader satisfaction, follower motivation, leader job performance, group–organization performance, and leader effectiveness. Consideration is more strongly related to satisfaction (job satisfaction and leader satisfaction), motivation, and leader effectiveness than is initiating structure. Initiating structure, on the other hand, is slightly more strongly related to follower and group performance than is consideration behavior. They also examine the relationship between the two leader behaviors. The average correlation is positive but is relatively weak ($r = .17$), and it is inconsistent. While in some studies the relationship between consideration and initiating structure is positive, it is zero or negative in 35 percent of the samples.

The final reading is by David De Cremer and Daan van Knippenberg. They remind us that leadership unfolds in a group context where two or more individuals pool their time, energy, ideas, and skills to pursue a common goal. Leader

[3] R. R. Blake & J. S. Mouton, *The Managerial Grid* (Houston: Gulf, 1964); *The New Managerial Grid* (Houston: Gulf, 1978); *The Versatile Manager: A Grid Profile* (Homewood, IL: Dow Jones–Irwin, 1980); "Management by Grid Principles or Situationalism: Which?" *Group & Organization Studies* 6, 4 (1981), pp. 439–455.
[4] L. L. Larson, J. G. Hunt, & R. N. Osborn, "The Great Hi-Hi Leader Behavior Myth: A Lesson from Occam's Razor," *Academy of Management Journal* 19 (1976), pp. 628–641.
[5] R. J. House & P. M. Podsakoff, "Leader Effectiveness." In J. Greenberg (ed.), *Organizational Behavior: The State of Science* (Hillsdale, NJ: Erlbaum, 1994), pp. 45–82.
[6] T. A. Judge, R. F. Piccolo, & R. Ilies, "The Forgotten Ones? The Validity of Consideration and Initiating Structure in Leadership Research," *Journal of Applied Psychology* 89 (2004), pp. 36–51.

and team effectiveness will, in part, be determined by the willingness of the followers to make the attainment of the common good and common goal a priority higher than their own personal priorities. An important leadership question quite simply asks—How? What can a leader do to get his or her followers to elevate their concern, to place as a high priority the common good and the goals that the group shares? De Cremer and van Knippenberg provide some insight into that question by focusing our attention on self-sacrificial leadership behavior (i.e., the willingness of a leader to incur personal costs to help achieve the overall goal).

Figure 7.1 provides a perspective on where leader behavior fits into the model of the leadership process. This set of readings suggests strongly that *leader behavior is important.* It provides additional insight into leadership and the leadership process. Leader behaviors reflect part of the process of leadership—goals are set, roadblocks are removed, people are provided encouragement—and at the same time, these behaviors have an impact on the attitudes, motivation, and behaviors of the members of the group.

The next chapter will address the question of how the different situations in which leaders and followers find themselves operating affect the style (behaviors) of the leader and the effects that are produced by these behaviors. Blake and Mouton suggest that there is a "one best style" of leadership that fits and works best in *all* situations (i.e., 9,9, or the team leader who simultaneously shows a strong regard for employees and a strong production emphasis). They envision a unique interaction that gets produced by the simultaneous display of a concern for people and production. By contrast, the readings presented in the next chapter will focus on situational demands and the shaping effects that these forces have on leader behaviors and leader effectiveness. Chapter 8, then, calls into question the argument that a single best model can be employed to define what it is that effective leaders do.

FIGURE 7.1
The Leadership Process: Leader Behaviors

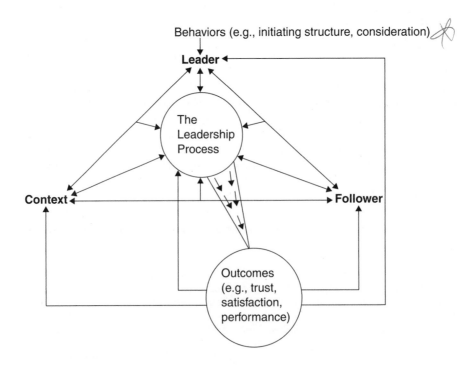

Leadership—Michigan Organizational Assessment

EXERCISE
Self-Assessment

Instructions: This self-assessment asks about your leadership behaviors. The following statements describe the way you as a supervisor/leader might perform your job. Please indicate whether or not you AGREE with each of the statements as a description of your leader behavior.

As a leader (supervisor/manager) I would:	Strongly Disagree	Disagree	Slightly Disagree	Neither Agree nor Disagree	Slightly Agree	Agree	Strongly Agree
1. Help subordinates with their personal problems.	1	2	3	4	5	6	7
2. Make sure subordinates have clear goals to achieve.	1	2	3	4	5	6	7
3. Keep people informed about the work which is being done.	1	2	3	4	5	6	7
4. Make sure subordinates know what has to be done.	1	2	3	4	5	6	7
5. Be concerned about them as people.	1	2	3	4	5	6	7
6. Make it clear how they should do their job.	1	2	3	4	5	6	7
7. Help them discover problems before they get too bad.	1	2	3	4	5	6	7
8. Feel each subordinate is important as an individual.	1	2	3	4	5	6	7
9. Help them solve work-related problems.	1	2	3	4	5	6	7

Scoring: *Personal support*—Sum your answers to items 1, 5, and 8, and then divide by 3. *Goal emphasis*—Sum your responses to items 2, 4, and 6, and divide by 3. *Work facilitation*—Sum your responses to items 3, 7, and 9, and divide by 3.

Record your scores here:
Personal support _____
Goal emphasis _____
Work facilitation _____

Interpretation: This profile identifies the extent to which you perceive yourself engaging in three different behaviors as you carry out your leadership role: (1) *support*—you would likely engage in behaviors that enhance someone else's feelings of personal worth and importance; (2) *goal emphasis*—you would likely engage in behaviors that stimulate an enthusiasm for meeting the group's goal or achieving excellent performance; and (3) *work facilitation*—you would likely engage in behaviors that help achieve goal attainment by such activities as scheduling, coordinating, planning, and by providing resources such as tools, materials, and technical knowledge. A score of 6 and higher suggests that your leadership style would be strong on that particular dimension of leader behavior. A score of 2 and less suggests that your leadership style would not likely be characterized by this particular dimension of leader behavior.

Source: Reprinted with permission from the Institute for Social Research, *Michigan Assessment of Organizations II* (Ann Arbor, MI: Institute for Social Research, 1975).

EXERCISE	Initiating Structure and Consideration
Self-Assessment	**Instructions:** The questions below ask about your personal leadership orientation. Each item describes a specific kind of behavior but does not ask you to judge whether the behavior is desirable or undesirable.

READ each item carefully.

THINK about how frequently you engage in the behavior described by the item.

DRAW A CIRCLE around one of the five numerical response codes (1, 2, 3, 4, 5) following each question, which reflects the frequency of this behavior.

As a leader I would:

1. Put suggestions made by people in the work group into operation.

Always	**Often**	**Occasionally**	**Seldom**	**Never**
1	2	3	4	5

2. Treat all people in the work group as your equal.

Always	**Often**	**Occasionally**	**Seldom**	**Never**
1	2	3	4	5

3. Back up what people under you do.

Always	**Often**	**Occasionally**	**Seldom**	**Never**
1	2	3	4	5

4. Reject suggestions for change.

Always	**Often**	**Occasionally**	**Seldom**	**Never**
1	2	3	4	5

5. Talk about how much should be done.

A Great Deal	**Fairly Much**	**To Some Degree**	**Comparatively Little**	**Not at All**
1	2	3	4	5

6. Assign people in the work group to particular tasks.

Always	**Often**	**Occasionally**	**Seldom**	**Never**
1	2	3	4	5

7. Offer new approaches to problems.

Often	**Fairly Often**	**Occasionally**	**Once in a While**	**Very Seldom**
1	2	3	4	5

8. Emphasize meeting the deadlines.

A Great Deal	**Fairly Much**	**To Some Degree**	**Comparatively Little**	**Not at All**
1	2	3	4	5

Scoring: *Consideration behavior*—Subtract your score to questions 1, 2, and 3 from 6. Next, sum your adjusted response to questions 1, 2, 3, and 4 and divide by 4.

Enter your Consideration score here _____.

Initiating Structure behavior—Subtract your score to questions 5, 6, 7, and 8 from 6. Next, sum your adjusted response to questions 5, 6, 7, and 8, and divide by 4.

Enter your Initiating Structure score here _____.

Interpretation: A high score (4 and greater) suggests a relatively strong orientation toward consideration-oriented behavior by you as a leader. A low score (2 and less) suggests a relatively weak consideration orientation.

A high score (4 and greater) suggests a relatively strong orientation toward initiating structure–oriented behavior by you as a leader. A low score (2 and less) suggests a relatively weak orientation toward initiation of structure behavior.

Source: Sample items from and reprinted with permission: Edwin A. Fleishman's *Leadership Opinion Questionnaire* (Copyright 1960, Science Research Associates, Inc., Chicago, IL).

Reading 18

Predicting Organizational Effectiveness with a Four-Factor Theory of Leadership

David G. Bowers and Stanley E. Seashore
University of Michigan

For centuries writers have been intrigued with the idea of specifying predictable relationships between what an organization's leader does and how the organization fares. In our own time, behavioral science has looked extensively at this question, yet incongruities and contradictory or unrelated findings seem to crowd the literature. It is the intent in this paper to locate and integrate the consistencies, to explore some neglected issues, and, finally, to generate and use a network of variables for predicting outcomes of organizational effectiveness.

Leadership has been studied informally by observing the lives of great men and formally by attempting to identify the personality traits of acknowledged leaders through assessment techniques. Review of the research literature from these studies, however, reveals few consistent findings.[1] Since the Second World War, research emphasis has shifted from a search for personality traits to a search for behavior that makes a difference in the performance or satisfaction of the followers. The conceptual scheme to be outlined here is an example of this approach.

In this paper, the primary concern is with leadership in businesses or industrial enterprises, usually termed "supervision" or "management," although most of the constructs of leadership to be used here apply equally well to social groups, clubs, and voluntary associations.

Work situations in business organizations in a technologically advanced society typically involve a comparatively small number of persons who receive direction from one person. This is the basic unit of industrial society and has been called the "organizational family."[2] In this modern organizational family, there is usually task interdependence and there is frequently social interdependence as well. The ideal is that of a group of people working effectively together toward the accomplishment of some common aim.

Source: Edited and reprinted with permission from *Administrative Science Quarterly* 2, no. 2 (1966), pp. 238–263 by permission of Administrative Science Quarterly 2. © Johnson Graduate School of Management, Cornell University.

This paper presents a review of the conceptual structure resulting from several programs of research in leadership practices, followed by a reconceptualization that attempts to take into consideration all of these earlier findings. In an attempt to assess the usefulness of the reconceptualization, it is then applied to leadership and effectiveness data from a recent study.

DIMENSIONS OF LEADERSHIP

It seems useful at the outset to isolate on a common-sense basis certain attributes of "leadership." First, the concept of leadership is meaningful only in the context of two or more people. Second, leadership consists of behavior; more specifically, it is behavior by one member of a group toward another member or members of the group, which advances some joint aim. Not all organizationally useful behavior in a work group is leadership; leadership behavior must be distinguished from the performance of noninterpersonal tasks that advance the goals of the organization. On a common-sense basis, then, leadership is organizationally useful behavior by one member of an organizational family toward another member or members of that same organizational family.

Defined in this manner, leadership amounts to a large aggregation of separate behaviors, which may be grouped or classified in a great variety of ways. Several classification systems from previous research have achieved considerable prominence and are briefly described here.

OHIO STATE LEADERSHIP STUDIES

In 1945, the Bureau of Business Research at Ohio State University undertook the construction of an instrument for describing leadership. From extended conversations and discussions among staff members who represented various disciplines, a list of nine dimensions or categories of leadership behavior were postulated. Descriptive statements were then written and assigned to one or another of the nine dimensions, and after further refinement, 150 of these were selected as representing these nine dimensions and were incorporated into the Leader Behavior Description Questionnaire.

Two factor analyses attempted to simplify its conceptual framework further. Hemphill and Coons[3] intercorrelated and factor-analyzed group mean scores for 11 dimensions for a sample composed largely of educational groups,[4] and obtained three orthogonal factors.

1. *Maintenance of membership character.* Behavior of a leader which allows him to be considered a "good fellow" by his subordinates; behavior which is socially agreeable to group members.

2. *Objective attainment behavior.* Behavior related to the output of the group: for example, taking positive action in establishing goals or objectives, structuring group activities in a way that members may work toward an objective, or serving as a representative of group accomplishment in relation to outside groups, agencies, forces, and so on.

3. *Group interaction facilitation behavior.* Behavior that structures communication among group members, encouraging pleasant group atmosphere and reducing conflicts among members.

Halpin and Winer[5] made an analysis using data collected from air-force crews, revising the original measuring instrument to adapt it to the respondent group. Only 130 items were used, with appropriate rewording, and the number of dimensions was reduced to eight. Treatment of the data indicated that five of the eight were sufficient for describing the entire roster, and the correlation of the 130 items with these five dimensions was regarded as a matrix of oblique factor loadings. These item loadings were then factor analyzed and the results rotated, producing four orthogonal factors.

1. *Consideration.* Behavior indicative of friendship, mutual trust, respect, and warmth.

2. *Initiating structure.* Behavior that organizes and defines relationships or roles and establishes well-defined patterns of organization, channels of communication, and ways of getting jobs done.

3. *Production emphasis.* Behavior which makes up a manner of motivating the group to greater activity by emphasizing the mission or job to be done.

4. *Sensitivity (social awareness).* Sensitivity of the leader to, and his awareness of, social interrelationships and pressures inside or outside the group.

The Halpin and Winer analysis has been the more widely known and used. Because the investigators dropped the third and fourth factors as accounting for too little common variance, "consideration" and "initiating structure" have become to some extent identified as "the Ohio State" dimensions of leadership.

EARLY SURVEY RESEARCH CENTER STUDIES

Concurrent with the Ohio State studies was a similar program of research in human relations at the University of Michigan Survey Research Center. Approaching the problem of leadership or supervisory style by locating clusters of characteristics which *(a)* correlated positively among themselves and *(b)* correlated with criteria of effectiveness, this program developed two concepts called "employee-orientation" and "production-orientation."[6]

Employee-orientation is described as behavior by a supervisor, which indicates that he feels that the "human relations" aspect of the job is quite important; and that he considers the employees as human beings of intrinsic importance, takes an interest in them, and accepts their individuality and personal needs. Production-orientation stresses production and the technical aspects of the job, with employees as means for getting work done; it seems to combine the Ohio State dimensions of initiating structure and production emphasis. Originally conceived to be opposite poles of the same continuum, employee-orientation and production-orientation were later reconceptualized,[7] on the basis of further data, as representing independent dimensions.

Katz and Kahn,[8] writing from a greater accumulation of findings, presented another conceptual scheme, with four dimensions of leadership.

1. *Differentiation of supervisory role.* Behavior by a leader that reflects greater emphasis upon activities of planning and performing specialized skilled tasks; spending a greater proportion of time in actual supervision, rather than performing the men's own tasks himself or absorption in impersonal paperwork.

2. *Closeness of supervision.* Behavior that delegates authority, checks upon subordinates less frequently, provides more general, less frequent instructions about the work, makes

greater allowance for individuals to perform in their own ways and at their own paces.

3. *Employee-orientation.* Behavior that gives major emphasis to a supportive personal relationship and that reflects a personal interest in subordinates; being more understanding, less punitive, easy to talk to, and willing to help groom employees for advancement.

4. *Group relationships.* Behavior by the leader that results in group cohesiveness, pride by subordinates in their work group, a feeling of membership in the group, and mutual help on the part of those subordinates.

Differentiation of supervisory role corresponds in part to what the Ohio State studies refer to as initiating structure or objective attainment behavior, and clearly derives from the earlier concept of production-orientation. Closeness of supervision, on the other hand, has something in common with maintenance of membership character, consideration, and employee-orientation, but also with objective attainment behavior, initiating structure, and production-orientation. Employee-orientation clearly corresponds to the earlier concept by the same name, while group relationships is to some extent similar to the interaction facilitation behavior and social sensitivity of the Ohio State studies.

In still another conceptualization, combining theory with review of empirical data, Kahn[9] postulated four supervisory functions.

1. *Providing direct need satisfaction.* Behavior by a leader, not conditional upon behavior of the employee, which provides direct satisfaction of the employee's ego and affiliative needs.

2. *Structuring the path to goal attainment.* Behavior that cues subordinates toward filling personal needs through attaining organizational goals.

3. *Enabling goal achievement.* Behavior that removes barriers to goal achievement, such as eliminating bottlenecks or planning.

4. *Modifying employee goals.* Behavior that influences the actual personal goals of subordinates in organizationally useful directions.

Direct need satisfaction clearly resembles consideration and employee-orientation; enabling goal achievement seems similar to initiating structure or objective attainment behavior; structuring the path to goal attainment and modifying employee goals are probably closer to the Ohio State production emphasis factor.

STUDIES AT THE RESEARCH CENTER FOR GROUP DYNAMICS

Cartwright and Zander,[10] at the Research Center for Group Dynamics, on the basis of accumulated findings, described leadership in terms of two sets of group functions.

1. *Group maintenance functions.* Behavior that keeps interpersonal relations pleasant, resolves disputes, provides encouragement, gives the minority a chance to be heard, stimulates self-direction, and increases interdependence among members.

2. *Goal achievement functions.* Behavior that initiates action, keeps members' attention on the goal, develops a procedural plan, evaluates the quality of work done, and makes expert information available.

These descriptive terms clearly refer to broader constructs than consideration or initiating structure. Group maintenance functions, for example, include what has been termed consideration, maintenance of membership character, or employee-orientation, but they also include functions concerned with relationships among group members not in formal authority positions. This concept is in some ways similar to group interaction facilitation behavior in the Ohio State factor analysis of Hemphill and Coons.[11] Goal achievement functions seem to encompass what the Ohio State studies referred to as initiating structure and production emphasis or objective attainment behavior, and what early Survey Research Center studies called production-orientation.

MANN'S THREE SKILLS

In subsequent work at the Survey Research Center built upon earlier findings, a recent classification, proposed by several writers and developed and operationalized by Floyd Mann,[12] treats leadership in terms of a trilogy of skills required of supervisors or managers. Although behaviors requiring particular skills and those skills themselves are not necessarily perfectly parallel, it seems reasonable to assume at least an approximate correspondence between the two. The three skills are:

1. *Human relations skill.* Ability and judgment in working with and through people, including knowledge of principles of human behavior, interpersonal relations, and human motivation.

2. *Technical skill.* Ability to use knowledge, methods, techniques, and equipment necessary for the performance of specific tasks.

3. *Administrative skill.* Ability to understand and act according to the objectives of the total organization, rather than only on the basis of the goals and needs of one's own immediate group. It includes planning, organizing the work, assigning the right tasks to the right people, inspecting, following up, and coordinating the work.

LIKERT'S NEW PATTERNS OF MANAGEMENT

Rensis Likert of the University of Michigan Institute for Social Research, building upon many of the findings of the Survey Research Center and the Research Center for Group Dynamics as well as upon his own early work in the same area for the Life Insurance Agency Management Association, describes five conditions for effective supervisory behavior.

1. *Principle of supportive relations.* The leadership and other processes of the organization must be such as to ensure a maximum probability that in his interactions and his relationships with the organization, each member will, in the light of his background, values, and expectations, view the experience as supportive, and as one that builds and maintains his sense of personal worth and importance.[13]

2. *Group methods of supervision.* Management will make full use of the potential capacities of its human resources only when each person in an organization is a member of one or more effectively functioning work groups that have a high degree of group loyalty, effective skills of interaction, and high performance goals.[14]

3. *High performance goals.* If a high level of performance is to be achieved, it appears to be necessary for a supervisor to be employee-centered, and at the same time to have high performance goals and a contagious enthusiasm as to the importance of achieving these goals.[15]

4. *Technical knowledge.* The (effective) leader has adequate competence to handle the technical problems faced by his group, or he sees that access to this technical knowledge is fully provided.[16]

5. *Coordinating, scheduling, planning.* The leader fully reflects and effectively represents the views, goals, values, and decisions of his group in those other groups where he is performing the function of linking his group to the rest of the organization. He brings to the group of which he is the leader the views, goals, and decisions of those other groups. In this way, he provides a linkage whereby communication and the exercise of influence can be performed in both directions.[17]

COMPARISON AND INTEGRATION

These various research programs and writings make it clear that a great deal of conceptual content is held in common. In fact, four dimensions emerge from these studies, which seem to comprise the basic structure of what one may term "leadership":

1. *Support.* Behavior that enhances someone else's feeling of personal worth and importance.

2. *Interaction facilitation.* Behavior that encourages members of the group to develop close, mutually satisfying relationships.

3. *Goal emphasis.* Behavior that stimulates an enthusiasm for meeting the group's goal or achieving excellent performance.

4. *Work facilitation.* Behavior that helps achieve goal attainment by such activities as scheduling, coordinating, planning, and by providing resources such as tools, materials, and technical knowledge.

This formulation is obviously very close, except in terminology, to that expressed by Rensis Likert and was, in fact, stimulated by it. Table 1 indicates how concepts from the various research programs relate to these four basic concepts of leadership. More important, however, is the fact that each of these four concepts appears, sometimes separately, sometimes in combination, in all but two (Katz, et al., 1950; Kahn, 1958) of the previous formulations listed. These four dimensions are not considered indivisible, but capable of further subdivision according to some regularity of occurrence in social situations or according to the conceptual preferences of investigators.

INDEPENDENCE OF LEADERSHIP AND POSITION

Traditional leadership research has focused upon the behavior of formally designated or recognized leaders. This is probably due, at least in part, to the historical influence of the hierarchical models

TABLE 1   Correspondence of Leadership Concepts of Different Investigators

Bowers and Seashore (1964)	Hemphill and Coons (1957)	Halpin and Winer (1957)	Katz et al. (1950)	Katz and Kahn (1951)		Kahn (1958)	Mann (1962)	Likert (1961)	Cartwright and Zander (1960)
Support	Maintenance of membership character	Consideration	Employee-orientation	Employee-orientation		Providing direct need satisfaction	Human relations skills	Principle of supportive relationships	Group maintenance functions
				Closeness of supervision					
Interaction facilitation	Group interaction facilitation behavior	Sensitivity		Group relationships				Group methods of supervision	
Goal emphasis	Objective attainment behavior	Production emphasis	Production-orientation		Structuring path to goal attainment		Administrative skills	High-performance goals	Goal-achievement functions
						Modifying employee goals			
Work facilitation		Initiating structure		Differentiation of supervisory role		Enabling goal achievement	Technical skills	Technical knowledge, planning, scheduling	
				Closeness of supervision					

of the church and the army. As a result, it has until recently been customary to study leadership either as an attribute of the person of someone who is authority-vested, or as an attribute of his behavior. More recently, attention has been paid to leadership in groups less formally structured, as illustrated by the work of Bass with leaderless group discussion, the work of Sherif, as well as some of the work of other researchers in the area of group dynamics.[18]

In the previous section, leadership was conceptualized in terms of four social-process functions, four kinds of behavior that must be present in work groups if they are to be effective. The performance of these functions was deliberately not limited to formally designated leaders. Instead, it was proposed that leadership, as described in terms of support, goal emphasis, work facilitation, and interaction facilitation, may be provided by anyone in a work group for anyone else in that work group. In this sense, leadership may be either "supervisory" or "mutual"; that is, a group's needs for support may be provided by a formally designated leader, by members for each other, or both; goals may be emphasized by the formal leader, by members to each other, or by both; and similarly for work facilitation and interaction facilitation.

This does not imply that formally designated leaders are unnecessary or superfluous, for there are both common-sense and theoretical reasons for believing that a formally acknowledged leader through his supervisory leadership behavior sets the pattern of the mutual leadership which subordinates supply each other.

LEADERSHIP AND ORGANIZATIONAL EFFECTIVENESS

Leadership in a work situation has been judged to be important because of its connection, to some extent assumed and to some extent demonstrated, to organizational effectiveness. Effectiveness, moreover, although it has been operationalized in a variety of ways, has often been assumed to be a unitary characteristic. These assumptions define a commonly accepted theorem that leadership (if not a unitary characteristic, then a limited roster of closely related ones) is always salutary in its effect and that it always enhances effectiveness. . . .

RESULTS

RELATION OF LEADERSHIP TO EFFECTIVENESS

Table 2 presents the correlation coefficients of leadership measures with measures of satisfaction.

TABLE 2 **Correlation of Leadership with Satisfactions**

Leadership Measure	Satisfaction with				
	Company	Fellow Agents	Job	Income	Manager
Peer					
Support	.03*	.68	.39	.29*	.47
Goal emphasis	.37	.77	.26*	.42	.62
Work facilitation	.29*	.68	.34	.51	.45
Interaction facilitation	.31	.72	.30*	.42	.55
Manager					
Support	.31	.65	.35	.45	.86
Goal emphasis	.11*	.71	.09*	.43	.31
Work facilitation	.31	.61	.24*	.36	.41
Interaction facilitation	.30*	.67	.10*	.53	.78

*All others significant beyond .05 level of confidence, 2-tail.

Table 3 presents similar correlations of leadership measures to performance factors. These data indicate first, that the incidence of significant relationships of leadership to effectiveness is well above the chance level. Of 40 satisfaction-leadership coefficients, 30 are significant beyond the 5 percent level of confidence. Of 56 performance-leadership coefficients, 13 are significant beyond the 5 percent level of confidence. Second, the significant coefficients are not uniformly distributed throughout the matrix; instead, certain effectiveness criteria (e.g., satisfaction with income) and certain leadership measures (e.g., peer work facilitation) have many significant relationships, whereas others have few or none (e.g., performance factor VI). Third, significant coefficients are as often found in relation to peer as to managerial leadership characteristics. . . .

RELATION OF PEER TO MANAGERIAL LEADERSHIP

Before assessing the adequacy of leadership as a predictor of effectiveness, it seems advisable to answer the question posed earlier about the relationship between peer and managerial leadership. There is a close relationship between all managerial characteristics, on the one hand, and all peer characteristics on the other. Following the same method as that used for effectiveness, it appears that the best predictor of peer support is managerial support; of peer goal emphasis, managerial interaction facilitation; of peer work facilitation, managerial interaction facilitation. With one exception, therefore, the best predictor of the peer characteristic is its managerial opposite number. Table 4 indicates that three predictions are improved by related managerial characteristics.

Assuming causation, one may say that if a manager wishes to increase the extent to which his subordinates support one another, he must increase his own support and his own emphasis upon goals. If he wishes to increase the extent to which his subordinates emphasize goals to one another, he must first increase his own facilitation

TABLE 3 **Correlation of Leadership with Performance Factors**

Leadership Measure	Performance Factor						
	I	II	III	IV	V	VI	VII
Peer							
Support	.26	−.02	−.27	−.21	.23	−.12	.27
Goal emphasis	.49*	−.05	−.45*	−.27	.15	.04	.04
Work facilitation	.33*	.14	−.41*	−.41*	.18	.00	.04
Interaction facilitation	.44*	−.13	−.44*	−.24	.11	.14	.05
Manager							
Support	.28	−.24	−.26	−.12	.25	.16	.10
Goal emphasis	.31*	.11	−.27	−.18	.41*	.03	−.19
Work facilitation	.43*	.13	−.37*	−.33*	.21	.16	−.12
Interaction facilitation	.42*	−.29	−.30	−.21	.13	.20	.01

*Significant beyond .05 level of confidence, 2-tail.

TABLE 4 Improvement of Prediction of Peer Leadership Characteristics by Addition of Other Managerial Leadership Characteristics

Peer Measure	Managerial Best Predictor	Other Managerial Measures Improving Prediction
Support	Support	Goal emphasis
Goal emphasis	Interaction facilitation	Goal emphasis
Work facilitation	Work facilitation	None
Interaction facilitation	Interaction facilitation	Work facilitation

of interaction and his emphasis upon goals. By increasing his facilitation of the work, he will increase the extent to which his subordinates do likewise, and if, in addition, he increases his facilitation of interaction, his subordinates will in turn facilitate interaction among themselves.

These data appear to confirm that there is in fact a significant and strong relationship between managerial and peer leadership characteristics. In general, the statement may be made that a forerunner of each peer variable is its managerial opposite number, and that substantial improvement is in most cases made by combining with this another managerial characteristic. . . .

Figure 1a presents the relationships of leadership and nonleadership variables to satisfaction with the company and with income. This diagram indicates that supportive managers make more satisfactory arrangements about the office expenses of their agents and that these arrangements, in part, lead to greater satisfaction with the company as a whole. In addition, as managers facilitate the interaction of their agents, the goals of the company and needs or aspirations of the people who work for it come to be more compatible, which also leads to satisfaction with the company and with income.

Figure 1b presents a similar chain of relationships to satisfaction with the job itself. This diagram is interpreted to mean that as agents facilitate the work for each other, less time is spent by agents in paperwork for specific clients. When this happens, when agents behave more supportively toward each other, and when the agents are, on the whole, higher in need for affiliation, there is greater job satisfaction. Figure 1c presents relationships to two criteria: satisfaction with fellow agents and volume of business. When agents emphasize goals among themselves, they become more satisfied with each other; and when this condition exists, an agency does a greater volume of business. Figure 1d shows very succinctly that agents are satisfied with their manager if he is supportive and knowledgeable. Figure 1e presents relationship to business costs in diagram form.

Earlier diagrams showed the network of relationships associated with satisfaction with the company and with the job; here, these two satisfaction states are associated with lower business costs. In addition, as agents facilitate the work for each other, they spend a smaller proportion of their time in miscellaneous activities. When this occurs, and when agents emphasize goals to one another, costs are also lower.

Figure 1f diagrams relationships to business growth. The relationships presented in this diagram are less reliable than those presented in earlier figures. They are, as a group, somewhat smaller in size than those found in relation to other criteria already described. With this caution in mind, however, they can be interpreted as follows: business growth is high when the agent force does *not* hold to a classical business ideology; when regional managers, by accepting the opinions and ideas of their agents, encourage professional development; and when managers reduce rivalries among agents by encouraging their interaction. Far from stressing growth attained by competitive effort, this paradigm presents a picture of growth through cooperative professionalism.

Two additional performance measures of effectiveness present one significant, reasonable "causal" relationship each: staff-clientele maturity is greater when agents have a higher level of aspiration, and more advanced underwriting occurs when agents have a higher level of education. Although significant correlations were presented earlier in relation to these two factors, the reasonable interpretation of them is that the leadership measures are either effects or coordinates, not causes, of these descriptive rather than evaluative performance factors.

That no reasonable, significant relationships to manpower turnover are to be found is extremely puzzling. In most investigations of the effect of social-psychological variables upon organizational behavior, it is assumed that performance measures which are more "person" than "production" oriented will show the highest relationships to questionnaire measurements. In the present case

FIGURE 1
Predicted Measures:
(a) Satisfaction with
Company and with
Income; (b)
Satisfaction with
Job; (c) Satisfaction
with Fellow Agents;
Business Volume;
(d) Satisfaction with
Manager; (e)
Business Costs; (f)
Business Growth

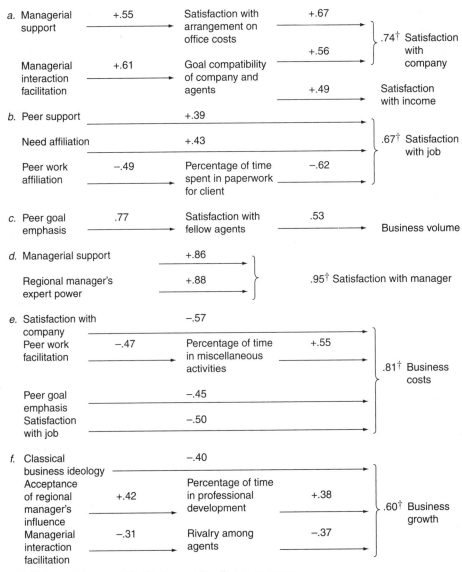

† Multiple correlation of variables listed against the effectiveness measure.

this assumption is not supported. No variations of analysis that were attempted produced any noticeable change. An attempt was made to assess curvilinear correlations, but no improvement over linear correlation resulted. It was also thought that the factorial measure of turnover might be too complicated and that a simpler measure of proportion of terminations might be more productive. This also produced no noticeable effect. Apparently, manpower turnover in this particular company or industry is related to forces in the individual, the environment, or perhaps the organizational situation not tapped by the questionnaire measurement used.

It is not surprising that no correlations are found with the regional manager's personal per-

formance. It is, as explained earlier, the weakest factor, and differs from the other factors in being descriptive of a single individual rather than of the agency as a whole. It may well be affected more by variables such as the regional manager's distance from retirement than by factors assessed here.

DISCUSSION AND CONCLUSIONS

To what extent have the data demonstrated the usefulness of the conceptualization presented at the beginning of this article? It seems reasonable to state the following:

1. Seven of the eight leadership characteristics outlined above in fact play some part in the

predictive model generated from the data; only peer interaction facilitation seems to play no unique role.

2. Both managerial and peer leadership characteristics seem important.

3. There are plausible relationships of managerial to peer leadership characteristics.

4. The model is not a simple one of managerial leadership leading to peer leadership, which in turn leads to outcomes separately; instead, different aspects of performance are associated with different leadership characteristics, and, in some cases, satisfaction outcomes seem related to performance outcomes.

5. Some effectiveness measures are related to causal factors other than those tapped in this instrument.

6. The ability to predict outcomes with the variables selected varies from .95 to .00.

7. The role of leadership characteristics in this prediction varies in importance from strong, direct relationships in some cases (e.g., satisfaction with manager) to indirect relationships (e.g., business volume) to no relationship (e.g., advanced underwriting).

8. Leadership, as conceived and operationalized here, is not adequate alone to predict effectiveness; instead, additional and, in some cases, intervening constructs must be included to improve prediction. These "other" constructs are of several distinct types:
   a. *Leadership-related.* Regional manager's expert power, regional manager's influence acceptance, and rivalry among agents.
   b. *Work Patterns.* Percentage of time in miscellaneous activities, in paperwork for clients, and in professional development.
   c. *Personal and Motivational.* Education, level of aspiration, need for affiliation, goal compatibility of individual and organization, and classical business ideology.

Notes

1. C. A. Gibb, "Leadership," in G. Lindzey, *Handbook of Social Psychology.* Cambridge, Mass.: Addison-Wesley Publishing Co., Inc. (1954), II, 877–917; R. M. Stogdill, Personal Factors Associated with Leadership: A Survey of the Literature, *Journal of Psychology,* 25 (1948), 35–71.

2. F. C. Mann, "Toward an Understanding of the Leadership Role in Formal Organization," in R. Dubin, G. C. Homans, F. C. Mann, and D. C. Miller, *Leadership and Productivity.* San Francisco, Calif.: Chandler Publishing Company (1965), pp. 68–103.

3. J. K. Hemphill and A. E. Coons, "Development of the Leader Behavior Description Questionnaire," in R. M. Stogdill and A. E. Coons (Eds.) *Leader Behavior: Its Description and Measurement.* Research Monograph No. 88, Columbus, Ohio: Bureau of Business Research, the Ohio State University (1957), pp. 6–38.

4. The 11 dimensions were made up of the original 9, one of which (communication) had been subdivided, plus an overall leadership evaluation.

5. A. W. Halpin and J. Winer, "A Factorial Study of the Leader Behavior Description Questionnaire," in R. M. Stogdill and A. E. Coons, *Leader Behavior, op. cit.,* pp. 39–51.

6. D. Katz, N. Maccoby, and Nancy C. Morse, *Productivity, Supervision, and Morale in an Office Situation.* Detroit, Mich.: The Darel Press, Inc. (1950); D. Katz, N. Maccoby, G. Gurin, and Lucretia G. Floor, *Productivity, Supervision, and Morale Among Railroad Workers.* Ann Arbor, Mich.: Survey Research Center (1951).

7. R. L. Kahn, The Prediction of Productivity, *Journal of Social Issues,* 12 (1956), 41–49.

8. D. Katz and R. L. Kahn, "Human Organization and Worker Motivation," in L. R. Tripp (Ed.), *Industrial Productivity.* Madison, Wisc.: Industrial Relations Research Association (1951), pp. 146–171.

9. R. L. Kahn, "Human Relations on the Shop Floor," in E. M. Hugh-Jones (Ed.), *Human Relations and Modern Management.* Amsterdam, Holland: North-Holland Publishing Co. (1958), pp. 43–74.

10. D. Cartwright and A. Zander, *Group Dynamics Research and Theory.* Evanston, Ill.: Row, Peterson & Co. (1960).

11. Hemphill and Coons, *op. cit.*

12. Mann, *op. cit.*

13. R. Likert, *New Patterns of Management.* New York: McGraw-Hill Book Co. (1961), p. 103.

14. *Ibid.,* p. 104.

15. *Ibid.,* p. 8.

16. *Ibid.,* p. 171.

17. *Ibid.,* p. 171.

18. B. M. Bass, *Leadership, Psychology, and Organizational Behavior.* New York: Harper & Bros. (1960); Cartwright and Zander, op. cit.; M. and Carolyn W. Sherif, *An Outline of Social Psychology.* New York: Harper & Bros. (1956).

Reading 19

Patterns of Leadership Behavior Related to Employee Grievances and Turnover

Edwin A. Fleishman
Yale University

Edwin F. Harris
Chrysler Corporation

This study investigates some relationships between the leader behavior of industrial supervisors and the behavior of their group members. It represents an extension of earlier studies carried out at the International Harvester Company, while the authors were with the Ohio State University Leadership Studies.

Briefly, these previous studies involved three primary phases which have been described elsewhere (Fleishman, 1951, 1953a, 1953b, 1953c; Fleishman, Harris & Burtt, 1955; Harris & Fleishman, 1955). In the initial phase, independent leadership patterns were defined and a variety of behavioral and attitude instruments were developed to measure them. This phase confirmed the usefulness of the constructs "Consideration" and "Structure" for describing leader behavior in industry.

Since the present study, as well as the previous work, focused on these two leadership patterns, it may be well to redefine them here:

Consideration includes behavior indicating mutual trust, respect, and a certain warmth and rapport between the supervisor and his group. This does not mean that this dimension reflects a superficial "pat-on-the-back," "first name calling" kind of human relations behavior. This dimension appears to emphasize a deeper concern for group members' needs and includes such behavior as allowing subordinates more participation in decision making and encouraging more two-way communication.

Structure includes behavior in which the supervisor organizes and defines group activities and his relation to the group. Thus, he defines the role he expects each member to assume, assigns tasks, plans ahead, establishes ways of getting things done, and pushes for production. This dimension seems to emphasize overt attempts to achieve organizational goals.

Since the dimensions are independent, a supervisor may score high on both dimensions, low on both, or high on one and low on the other.

The second phase of the original Harvester research utilized measures of these patterns to evaluate changes in foreman leadership attitudes and behavior resulting from a management training program. The amount of change was evaluated at three different times—once while the foremen were still in the training setting, again after they had returned to the plant environment, and still later in a "refresher" training course. The results showed that while still in the training situation there was a distinct increase in Consideration and an unexpected decrease in Structure attitudes. It was also found that leadership attitudes became more *dissimilar* rather than similar, despite the fact that all foremen had received the same training. Furthermore, when behavior and attitudes were evaluated back in the plant, the effects of the training largely disappeared. This pointed to the main finding, i.e., the overriding importance of the interaction of the training effects with certain aspects of the social setting in which the foremen had to operate in the plant. Most critical was the "leadership climate" supplied by the behavior and attitudes of the foreman's own boss. This was more related to the foreman's own Consideration and Structure behavior than was the fact that he had or had not received the leadership training.

The third phase may be termed the "criterion phase," in which the relationships between Consideration and Structure and indices of foremen proficiency were examined. One finding was that production supervisors rated high in "proficiency" by plant management turned out to have leadership patterns high in Structure and low in Consideration. (This relationship was accentuated in departments scoring high on a third variable, "perceived pressure of deadlines.") On the other hand, this same pattern of high Structure

Source: Edited and reprinted with permission from *Personnel Psychology* 15 (1962), pp.43–56. Copyright Blackwell Publishing.

and low Consideration was found to be related to high labor turnover, union grievances, worker absences and accidents, and low worker satisfaction. There was some indication that these relationships might differ in "nonproduction" departments. An interesting sidelight was that foremen with low Consideration *and* low Structure were more often bypassed by subordinates in the informal organizational structure. In any case, it was evident that "what is an effective supervisor" is a complex question, depending on the proficiency criterion emphasized, management values, type of work, and other situational variables.

The present study examines some of the questions left unanswered by this previous work.

PURPOSE

The present study focused on two main questions. First, what is the *form* of the relationship between leader behavior and indices of group behavior? Is it linear or curvilinear? As far as we know, no one has really examined this question. Rephrased, this question asks if there are critical levels of Consideration and/or Structure beyond which it does or does not make a difference in group behavior. Is an "average" amount of Structure better than a great deal or no Structure at all? Similarly, is there an optimum level of Consideration above and below which worker grievances and/or turnover rise sharply?

The second question concerns the interaction effects of different combinations of Consideration and Structure. Significant correlations have been found between each of these patterns and such indices as rated proficiency, grievances, turnover, departmental reputation, subordinate satisfactions, etc. (e.g., Fleishman, Harris & Burtt, 1955; Halpin, 1954; Hemphill, 1955; Stogdill & Coons, 1957). These studies present some evidence that scoring low on both dimensions is not desirable. They also indicate that some balance of Consideration and Structure may be optimal for satisfying both proficiency and morale criteria. The present study is a more intensive examination of possible optimum combinations of Consideration and Structure.

The present study investigates the relationships between foreman behavior and two primary indices of group behavior: labor grievances and employee turnover. Both of these may be considered as partial criteria of group effectiveness.

PROCEDURE

LEADER BEHAVIOR MEASURES

The study was conducted in a motor truck manufacturing plant. Fifty-seven production foremen and their work groups took part in the study. They represented such work operations as stamping, assembly, body assembly, body paint, machinery, and export. At least three workers, drawn randomly from each foreman's department, described the leader behavior of their foreman by means of the *Supervisory Behavior Description Questionnaire* (described elsewhere, Fleishman, 1953, 1957). Each questionnaire was scored on Consideration and Structure, and a mean Consideration score and a mean Structure score was computed for each foreman. The correlation between Consideration and Structure among foremen in this plant was found to be −.33. The correlation between these scales is usually around zero (Fleishman, 1957), but in this plant, foremen who are high in Structure are somewhat more likely to be seen as lower in Consideration and vice versa. However, the relationship is not high. . . .

RESULTS

LEADER BEHAVIOR AND GRIEVANCES

Figure 1 plots the average employee grievance rates for departments under foremen scoring at different levels of Consideration. From the curve fitted to these points, it can be seen clearly that the relationship between the foremen's behavior and grievances from their work groups is negative and curvilinear. For most of the range increased Consideration goes with reduced grievance rates. However, increased Consideration above a certain critical level (approximately 76 out of a possible 112) is not related to further decreases in grievances. Furthermore, the curve appears to be negatively accelerated. A given decrease in Consideration just below the critical point (76) is related to a small increase in grievances, but, as Consideration continues to drop, grievance rates rise sharply. Thus, a five-point drop on the Consideration scale, just below a score of 76, is related to a small grievance increase, but a five-point drop below 61 is related to a large rise in grievances. The correlation ratio (eta) represented by this curve is −.51.

Figure 2 plots grievances against the foremen's Structure scores. Here a similar curvilinear relationship is observed. In this case the correlation is positive (eta = .71). Below a certain level

FIGURE 1
**Relation between
Consideration and
Grievance Rates**

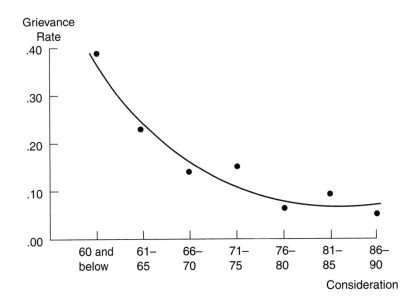

(approximately 36 out of a possible 80 on our scale), Structure is unrelated to grievances, but above this point increased Structure goes with increased grievances. Again we see that a given increase in Structure just above this critical level is accompanied by a small increase in grievances, but continued increases in Structure are associated with increasingly disproportionately large increases in grievances rates.

Both curves are hyperbolic rather than parabolic in form. Thus, it appears that for neither Consideration nor Structure is there an "optimum" point in the middle of the range below and above which grievances rise. Rather there seems to be a range within which increased Consideration or decreased Structure makes no difference. Of

course, when one reaches these levels, grievances are already at a very low level and not much improvement can be expected. However, the important point is that this low grievance level is reached before one gets to the extremely high end of the Consideration scale or to the extremely low end of the Structure scale. It is also clear that extremely high Structure and extremely low Consideration are most related to high grievances.

DIFFERENT COMBINATIONS OF CONSIDERATION AND STRUCTURE RELATED TO GRIEVANCES

The curves described establish that a general relationship exists between each of these leadership

FIGURE 2
**Relation between
Structure and
Grievance Rates**

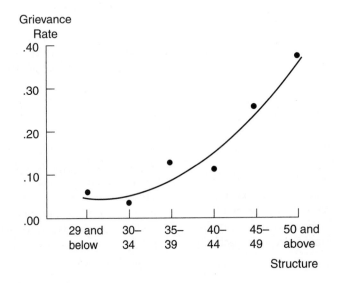

FIGURE 3 **Combinations of Consideration and Structure Related to Grievances**

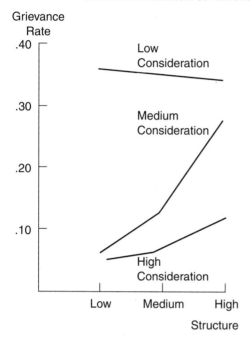

LEADER BEHAVIOR AND TURNOVER

Figures 4 and 5 plot the curves for the *Supervisory Behavior Description* scores of these foremen against the turnover criteria. Again, we see the curvilinear relationships. The correlation (eta) of Consideration and turnover is –.69; Structure and turnover correlate .63. As in the case with grievances, below a certain critical level of Consideration and above a certain level of Structure, turnover goes up. There is, however, an interesting difference in that the critical levels differ from those related to grievances. The flat portions of each of these curves are more extended and the rise in turnover beyond the point of inflection is steeper. The implication of this is quite sensible and indicates that "they gripe before they leave." In other words, a given increase in Structure (to approximately 39) or decrease in Consideration (to 66) may result in increased grievances, but not turnover. It takes higher Structure and lower Consideration before turnover occurs.

DIFFERENT COMBINATIONS OF CONSIDERATION AND STRUCTURE RELATED TO TURNOVER

Figure 6 plots the relation between Structure (low, medium, and high) and turnover for groups of foremen who were also either low, medium, or high on Consideration. As with grievances, the curves show that turnover is highest for the work groups whose foremen combine low Consideration with high Structure; however, the amount of Consideration is the dominant factor. The curves show that turnover is highest among those work groups whose foremen are low in Consideration, regardless of the amount of emphasis these same foremen show on Structure. There is little distinction between the work groups of foremen who show medium and high Consideration since both of these groups have low turnover among their workers. Furthermore, increased Structure does not seem related to increased turnover in these two groups.[1]

CONCLUSIONS

1. This study indicates that there are significant relationships between the leader behavior of foremen and the labor grievances and employee turnover in their work groups. In general, low

patterns and the frequency of employee grievances. But how do *different combinations* of Consideration and Structure relate to grievances? Some foremen score high on both dimensions, some score low on both, etc.

Figure 3 plots the relation between Structure (low, medium, and high) and grievances for groups of foremen who were either low, medium, or high on Consideration. The curves show that grievances occur most frequently among groups whose foremen are low in Consideration, regardless of the amount of emphasis on Structure. The most interesting finding relates to the curve for the high Consideration foremen. This curve suggests that, for the high Consideration foremen, Structure could be increased without any appreciable increase in grievances. However, the reverse is not true; that is, foremen who were low in Consideration could not reduce grievances by easing up on Structure. For foremen average on Consideration, grievances were lowest where Structure was lowest and increased in an almost linear fashion as Structure increased. These data show a definite interaction between Consideration and Structure. Apparently, high Consideration can compensate for high Structure. But low Structure will not offset low Consideration.

Before we speculate further about these relationships, let us examine the results with employee turnover.

[1] This, of course, is consistent with our earlier finding that for increased turnover it takes a bigger drop in Consideration and a bigger increase in Structure to make a difference. Thus, our high and medium Consideration groups separate for grievances, but overlap for turnover.

FIGURE 4
Relations between Consideration and Turnover Rates

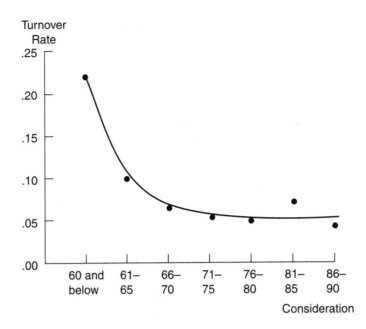

Consideration and high Structure go with high grievances and turnover.

2. There appear to be certain critical levels beyond which increased Consideration or decreased Structure have no effect on grievance or turnover rates. Similarly, grievances and turnover are shown to increase most markedly at the extreme ends of the Consideration (low end) and Structure (high end) scales. Thus, the relationship is curvilinear, not linear, and hyperbolic, not parabolic.

3. The critical points at which increased Structure and decreased Consideration begin to relate to group behavior are not the same for grievances and turnover. Increases in turnover do not occur until lower on the Consideration scale and higher on the Structure scale, as compared with increases in grievances. For example, if Consideration is steadily reduced, higher grievances appear before increased turnover occurs. It appears that there may be different "threshold levels" of Consideration and Structure related to grievances and turnover.

4. Other principal findings concern the interaction effects found between different combinations of Consideration and Structure. Taken in combination, Consideration is the dominant

FIGURE 5 **Relation between Structure and Turnover Rates**

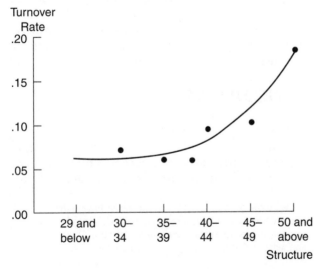

FIGURE 6 **Combination of Consideration and Structure Related to Turnover**

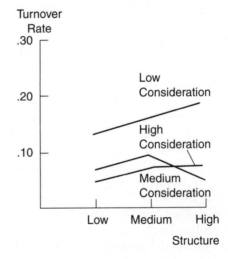

factor. For example, both grievances and turnover were highest in groups having low Consideration foremen, regardless of the degree of Structuring behavior shown by these same foremen.

5. Grievances and turnover were lowest for groups with foremen showing medium to high Consideration together with low Structure. However, one of the most important results is the finding that high Consideration foremen could increase Structure with very little increase in grievances and no increase in turnover. High Consideration foremen had relatively low grievances and turnover, regardless of the amount of Structuring engaged in.

Thus, with regard to grievances and turnover, leader behavior characterized by low Consideration is more critical than behavior characterized by high Structure. Apparently, foremen can compensate for high Structure by increased Consideration, but low Consideration foremen cannot compensate by decreasing their Structuring behavior.

One interpretation is that workers under foremen who establish a climate of mutual trust, rapport, and tolerance for two-way communication with their work groups are more likely to accept higher levels of Structure. This might be because they perceive this Structure differently from employees in "low Consideration" climates. Thus, under "low Consideration" climates, high Structure is seen as threatening and restrictive, but under "high Consideration" climates, this same Structure is seen as supportive and helpful. A related interpretation is that foremen who establish such an atmosphere can more easily solve the problems resulting from high Structure. Thus, *grievances* may be solved at this level before they get into the official records. Similarly, *turnover* may reflect escape from a problem situation which cannot be resolved in the absence of mutual trust and two-way communication. In support of this interpretation, we do have evidence that leaders high in Consideration are also better at predicting subordinates' responses to problems (Fleishman & Salter, 1961).

One has to be careful in making cause and effect inferences here. A possible limitation is that our descriptions of foremen behavior came from the workers themselves. Those workers with many grievances may view their foremen as low in Consideration simply because they have a lot of grievances. However, the descriptions of foreman behavior were obtained from workers drawn randomly from each foreman's group; the odds are against our receiving descriptions from very many workers contributing a disproportionate share of grievances. In the case of turnover, of course, our descriptions could not have been obtained from people who had left during the previous 11 months. Yet substantial correlations were obtained between foremen descriptions, supplied by currently employed workers, with the turnover rates of their work groups. Furthermore, we do have evidence that leader behavior over a year period tends to be quite stable. Test-retest correlations for Consideration, as well as for Structure, tend to be high even when different workers do the describing on the retest (Harris & Fleishman, 1955). Our present preference is to favor the interpretation that high turnover and grievances result, at least in part, from the leader behavior patterns described.

The nonlinear relations between leader behavior and our criteria of effectiveness have more general implications for leadership research. For one thing, it points up the need for a more careful examination of the *form* of such relationships before computing correlation coefficients. Some previously obtained correlations with leadership variables may be underestimates because of linearity assumptions. Similarly, some previous negative or contradictory results may be "explained" by the fact that (*a*) inappropriate coefficients were used or (*b*) these studies were dealing with only the flat portions of these curves. If, for example, all the foremen in our study had scored over 76 on Consideration and under 36 on Structure, we would have concluded that there was no relation between these leadership patterns and grievances and turnover. Perhaps in comparing one study with another, we need to specify the range of leader behavior involved in each study.

There is, of course, a need to explore similar relationships with other criteria. There is no assurance that similar curvilinear patterns and interaction effects will hold for other indices (e.g., group productivity). Even the direction of these relationships may vary with the criterion used. We have evidence (Fleishman, Harris & Burtt, 1955), for example, that Consideration and Structure may relate quite differently to another effectiveness criterion: management's perceptions of foremen proficiency. However, research along these lines may make it possible to specify the particular leadership patterns which most nearly "optimize" these various effectiveness criteria in industrial organizations.

References

Fleishman, E. A. *"Leadership Climate" and Supervisory Behavior.* Columbus, Ohio: Personnel Research Board, Ohio State University, 1951.

Fleishman, E. A. "Leadership Climate, Human Relations Training, and Supervisory Behavior." *Personnel Psychology,* VI (1953) 205–222. (a)

Fleishman, E. A. "The Description of Supervisory Behavior." *Journal of Applied Psychology,* XXXVII (1953) 1–6. (b).

Fleishman, E. A. "The Measurement of Leadership Attitudes in Industry." *Journal of Applied Psychology,* XXXVII (1953) 153–158. (c)

Fleishman, E. A. "A Leader Behavior Description for Industry." In Stogdill, R. M., and Coons, A. E. (Editors). *Leader Behavior: Its Description and Measurement.* Columbus, Ohio: Bureau of Business Research, 1957.

Fleishman, E. A., Harris, E. F., and Burtt, H. E. *Leadership and Supervision in Industry.* Columbus, Ohio: Bureau of Educational Research, Ohio State University, 1955.

Fleishman, E. A., and Salter, J. A. "The Relation between the Leader's Behavior and His Empathy toward Subordinates." *Advanced Management,* March, 1961, 18–20.

Harris, E. F., and Fleishman, E. A. "Human Relations Training and the Stability of Leadership Patterns." *Journal of Applied Psychology,* XXXIX (1955), 20–25.

Halpin, A. W. "The Leadership Behavior and Combat Performance of Airplane Commanders." *Journal of Abnormal and Social Psychology,* XLIX (1954), 19–22.

Hemphill, J. K. "Leadership Behavior Associated with the Administrative Reputation of College Departments." *Journal of Educational Psychology,* XLVI (1955), 385–401.

Stogdill, R. M., and Coons, A. E. (Editors). *Leader Behavior: Its Description and Measurement.* Columbus, Ohio: Bureau of Business Research, Ohio State University. 1957.

Reading 20

Leader Self-sacrifice and Leadership Effectiveness

The Moderating Role of Leader Self-confidence

David De Cremer
Tilburg University

Daan van Knippenberg
Erasmus University of Rotterdam

INTRODUCTION

Effective leadership plays an important role in influencing employees' willingness to exert themselves on the job and to cooperate towards collective goals. Indeed, "leadership involves persuading other people to set aside for a period of time their individual concerns and to pursue a common goal that is important for the responsibilities and welfare of a group" (Hogan, Curby, & Hogan, 1994, p. 493). Theories of charismatic and transformational leadership in particular have highlighted the importance of leadership being able to elicit favorable leadership perceptions, willingness to cooperate with the leader towards collective goals, and personal involvement in the job (e.g., Bass, 1985; Burns, 1978; Conger & Kanungo, 1987; House, 1977; Shamir, House, & Arthur, 1993). Because organizations are dependent on the willingness of their employees to cooperate towards collective goals and to get personally involved in the job (cf. Katz, 1964; Smith, Carroll, & Ashford, 1995), leadership may thus play a key role in organizational effectiveness. Accordingly, identifying leader's abilities to promote positive attitudes and behavior towards the job and the organization may be of great importance to the effective functioning of organizations (Dirks & Ferrin, 2002; Yukl, 1998). In the present study, we focus on the interactive effects of leader self-sacrifice and leader's display of self-confidence, two behaviors that may be considered exemplars of the kinds of behavior that have been advanced as effective in theories of charismatic and transformational leadership.

The effectiveness of leader self-sacrifice has recently attracted increasing attention from leadership researchers (e.g., Choi & Mai-Dalton, 1998

and Choi & Mai-Dalton, 1999; De Cremer, 2002; Yorges, Weiss, & Strickland, 1999), but to date relatively little is known about the potential moderators and mediators of the effects of leader self-sacrifice, and especially the possibility that the effectiveness of leader self-sacrifice may be contingent on other aspects of the leader's behavior has hardly received any attention. To address these issues, in the present study we tested the moderating effect of leader's display of self-confidence on the effects of self-sacrifice in a scenario experiment, a laboratory experiment, and a cross-sectional survey. In addition, we studied the role of collective identification as a mediating variable in the relationship between this interactive effect and leadership effectiveness.

SELF-SACRIFICE AND LEADERSHIP EFFECTIVENESS

Self-sacrifice indicates a person's willingness "to suffer the loss of types of things to maintain personal beliefs and values" (Yorges et al., 1999, p. 428), and has been noted to be a behavior observed among great leaders (Burns, 1978; cf. Conger & Kanungo, 1987). Through its extraordinary and unusual nature, and because it communicates the leader's commitment to the collective and its plight, leader self-sacrifice may elicit favorable leadership perceptions, including perceptions of charisma (Choi & Mai-Dalton, 1998 and Choi & Mai-Dalton, 1999; Conger & Kanungo, 1987; De Cremer, 2002; De Cremer & van Knippenberg, 2002; Shamir et al., 1993). Moreover, self-sacrifice is proposed to be related to criteria of leadership effectiveness such as follower organizational citizenship behavior and prosocial behavior (Choi & Mai-Dalton, 1998). The concept of self-sacrifice indicates that the leader is willing to incur personal costs (or run the risk of such costs) to serve the goals and mission of the group or organization (Conger & Kanungo, 1987; Shamir et al., 1993). If a leader is perceived to be

Source: Edited and reprinted from *Organizational Behavior and Human Decision Processes,* 95:2, 140–155, Copyright 2004, with permission from Elsevier.

self-sacrificing, perceptions of effectiveness and charisma, and cooperation are positively influenced (Choi & Mai-Dalton, 1999; Yorges et al., 1999). For example, Yorges et al. (1999) demonstrated that participants exposed to a self-sacrificing leader (vs. a self-benefiting leader) contributed more money to a charity fund. In a similar vein, Choi and Mai-Dalton (1999) showed that followers were most willing to reciprocate the behavior of a self-sacrificial leader, De Cremer (2002) showed that a self-sacrificial leader (vs. a self-benefiting leader) was more effective in motivating cooperative behavior in a public good dilemma, and van Knippenberg and van Knippenberg (in press) showed that leader self-sacrifice (vs. no self-sacrifice) motivated higher task performance.

Thus, these findings clearly suggest that self-sacrificial leadership is positively related to criteria of leadership effectiveness. One important psychological explanation for the fact that a self-sacrificial leader is able to motivate followers to go beyond their self-interest and to look to the welfare of the collective is that a self-sacrificing leader links followers' sense of identity to the organization and its mission and goals (cf. Lord, Brown, & Freiberg, 1999; Shamir et al., 1993). Leader self-sacrifice in pursuit of collective goals directs attention towards the collective and its goals and demonstrates the leader's commitment to the collective (Hogg & van Knippenberg, 2003; van Knippenberg & Hogg, 2003; van Knippenberg & van Knippenberg, in press). By exhibiting self-sacrificial behavior on behalf of the collective, the leader may thus identify the collective as a valued group, worthy of individuals' dedicated efforts. Both the salience of the collective identity and the suggestion that the collective is worthy of one's dedicated effort may promote identification with the collective among followers (Hogg & Abrams, 1988). By fostering collective identification, a self-sacrificing leader may thus shift the emphasis from the pursuit of solely the own interests to the pursuit of group or organizational interests—an argument that aligns well with analyses of organizational effectiveness and cooperation that accord an important role to identification and collective-oriented motivations (e.g., Ashforth & Mael, 1989; De Cremer & van Dijk, 2002; Dutton, Dukerich, & Harquail, 1994; Tyler, 1999; van Knippenberg, 2000).

Corroborating this line of reasoning, De Cremer and van Knippenberg (2002) found that collective identification mediated the interactive effect of leader self-sacrifice and procedural fairness on cooperative behavior. Following this line of rea-soning, we adopt the expectation that leader behavior that enhances, or attenuates, the effects of self-sacrifice on follower identification will moderate the effectiveness of leader self-sacrifice. Thus, this expectation implies that such moderating leader behavior variables will interact with self-sacrifice in influencing both mediating variables such as collective identification and dependent variables such as cooperation. We propose that leader's display of self-confidence is such a behavior.[1]

LEADER DISPLAY OF SELF-CONFIDENCE AS A MODERATOR

It is widely acknowledged that the effectiveness of specific leadership styles or behavior may be contingent on a host of personal, situational, and organizational characteristics (for reviews, see e.g., Bass, 1985; Yukl, 1998).

When it comes to the effectiveness of self-sacrifice and other leader behaviors that are proposed to be aspects of charismatic and transformational leadership, however, the possibility that the effectiveness of a particular leadership behavior may be contingent on other aspects of the leader's behavior has received far less attention (De Cremer & van Knippenberg, 2002; Kirkpatrick & Locke, 1996). In an attempt to break new ground for research in leadership effectiveness, in particular in the effectiveness of leader self-sacrifice, the present study therefore focuses on the hypothesis that the effectiveness of leader self-sacrifice is contingent on another aspect of the leader's behavior that has been proposed to be important to a leader's effectiveness, that is, leader's display of self-confidence (note that our analysis concerns public display of confidence as a leader *behavior* rather than confidence as an intrapersonal quality; cf. Conger & Kanungo, 1987).

Leader display of self-confidence has been identified in a number of theoretical analyses of charismatic leadership as an important factor in leadership effectiveness, and as an antecedent of attributions of charisma (e.g., Conger & Kanungo, 1987; House, 1977; Shamir et al., 1993), and observations from the field seem to corroborate this analysis (Conger, 1989; Khurana, 2002). By communicating the expectation of success, leader self-confidence may render the leader more attractive and charismatic, and motivate involvement in the job (cf. Bandura, 1986; Vroom, 1964). A leader's display of self-confidence may thus feed into the leader's effectiveness. There is, however, not only reason to expect that displays of self-confidence render a leader more effective, but also that the display of self-confidence enhances the relationship between leader self-sacrifice and follower identification.

Leaders' display of self-confidence in pursuit of collective goals communicates the likelihood or expectation of collective success. Group or organizational success is one of the main antecedents of collective identification (Ashforth & Mael, 1989; Dutton et al., 1994; Hogg & Abrams, 1988). Moreover, the impact of the perception that the collective is worthy of one's dedication (e.g., as a result of leader self-sacrifice) is enhanced by this message of expected collective success, because people typically do not only need to value a cause but also need to believe in its attainability to commit themselves to it (Hollenbeck & Klein, 1987; van Knippenberg, 2000). As such, these beliefs of collective value and expected collective success parallel the concept of valence and expectancy, respectively, in expectancy theory (Vroom, 1964), and, in addition, extend the logic of this theory to the process of motivating followers to be committed to a leader's cause. Thus, by complementing the message of the value of the collective and its goals with the expectation of collective success, leader's display of self-confidence may enhance the effect of leader self-sacrifice on collective identification, and consequently on leadership effectiveness as is evident in leadership perceptions, willingness to cooperate with the leader towards collective goals, and followers' involvement in the job. In other words, if either the value (self-sacrifice) or expectancy (self-confidence) is low, motivation to follow a leader's cause is dramatically undercut, and if both components are high, motivation is substantially enhanced, thus leading to an expected interaction (multiplicative relationships) between these components.

THE PRESENT RESEARCH

In sum then, we predict that leader self-sacrifice and leader self-confidence interact in determining leadership effectiveness and perceptions of charisma,[2] such that the effects of self-sacrifice and self-confidence are stronger in conjunction than on their own. Although the main focus of the present study was on this interaction effect, we also included hypotheses about the main effects of self-sacrifice and self-confidence, because there is only limited experimental evidence for the effects of self-sacrifice (De Cremer, 2002; De Cremer & van Knippenberg, 2002; van Knippenberg & van Knippenberg, in press; Yorges et al., 1999) and to our knowledge no experimental evidence pertaining to the effects of self-confidence. Testing these main effects is therefore valuable.

Hypothesis 1. Leader self-sacrifice is positively related to leadership effectiveness and perceptions of charisma.

Hypothesis 2. Leader self-confidence is positively related to leadership effectiveness and perceptions of charisma.

Hypothesis 3. Leader self-sacrifice and self-confidence interact, such that the effects of self-sacrifice on leadership effectiveness and perceptions of charisma are stronger when self-confidence is high rather than low.

Leadership research has been criticized for establishing relationships between leader behavior and effectiveness criteria without providing evidence of the process through which these effects come about (Hunt, 1999; Yukl, 1999). An important feature of the present study, then, is that it also focused on the process mediating the effects of leader self-sacrifice and self-confidence. As may be clear from the above, theoretical as well as empirical (i.e., De Cremer & van Knippenberg, 2002) considerations tie the interactive effect of leader self-sacrifice and display of self-confidence to follower identification (cf. Conger & Kanungo, 1998; Conger et al., 2000; Kark, Shamir, & Chen, 2003; Shamir et al., 1993; Shamir, Zakay, Breinin, & Popper, 1998; van Knippenberg & Hogg, 2003). We therefore propose that collective identification mediates the interactive effect of self-sacrifice and self-confidence on leadership effectiveness and perceptions of charisma.

Hypothesis 4. Leader self-sacrifice and self-confidence interact, such that the effects of self-sacrifice on collective identification are stronger when self-confidence is high rather than low.

Hypothesis 5. Collective identification mediates the interactive effect of leader self-sacrifice and self-confidence on leadership effectiveness and perceptions of charisma.

Evidence for causality in the relationship between leadership and effectiveness criteria is scarce. Given that reverse causality often provides a plausible alternative explanation for observed relationships between leadership and effectiveness criteria (i.e., perceived leader effectiveness leading to more charismatic leader ratings, cf. Kirkpatrick & Locke, 1996), the scarcity of experimental research is an important impediment to the development of leadership theories (Yukl, 1999). Accordingly, our hypotheses should preferably (also) be tested in controlled experiments.

However, this leaves open the question of whether the same processes may be observed in actual organizations. Therefore, we tested our main hypotheses in three different types of studies: A scenario experiment (Study 1), a laboratory experiment (Study 2), and a cross-sectional survey assessing perceptions of leadership in organizations (Study 3).

Both the scenario experiment and the lab experiment allowed us to draw conclusions concerning causality. They complemented each other in that the scenario experiment allowed us to maintain a higher degree of mundane realism than the lab experiment, whereas the lab experiment in contrast to the scenario allowed us to study people that were actually immersed in the leadership situation (i.e., yielding higher experimental realism). The field study provided a test of whether the interaction between leader self-sacrifice and leader self-confidence may also be obtained in a study of the perceptions of leadership in actual organizations. This combination of methods allowed us to benefit from the strengths of each method, and to compensate for the weaknesses of each method with the strengths of the other methods (Dipboye, 1990; cf. De Cremer & van Knippenberg, 2002). To further establish the robustness of the predicted interaction, each study focused on a different operationalization of leadership effectiveness following from our conceptualization of leadership effectiveness as the ability to engender positive perceptions of the leader, elicit the willingness to cooperate towards collective goals, and to involve followers in the job: Overall ratings of leadership effectiveness (Study 1), follower willingness to cooperate with the leader (Study 2), and follower job involvement (Study 3). In addition, both experimental studies were designed to provide a test of the mediational role of collective identification.

STUDY 1 . . .

DISCUSSION

Study 1 replicated earlier experimental findings that leader's self-sacrifice has a positive effect on perceptions of leadership effectiveness and leader charisma (Hypothesis 1; cf. De Cremer, 2002; De Cremer & van Knippenberg, 2002; van Knippenberg & van Knippenberg, in press; Yorges et al., 1999). Moreover, it provides the first experimental evidence that leader self-confidence affects perceptions of leadership effectiveness and leader charisma (Hypothesis 2). Of primary importance,

self-sacrifice and self-confidence had stronger effects in conjunction with each other (Hypotheses 3 and 4Hypotheses 3 and 4 [*sic*]). Also, the mediation analysis showed that this interactive effect on leadership effectiveness was mediated by collective identification (Hypothesis 5).

To our knowledge, this is the first demonstration of the interactive effect of self-sacrifice and self-confidence, and one of the first of the interactive effects of different aspects of leader behavior (cf. De Cremer & van Knippenberg, 2002), and an important aspect of Study 1 is that it allows us to establish causality in this relationship. However, Study 1 is a scenario study and therefore Study 2 aimed to extend these findings by manipulating the two leadership elements in a controlled laboratory setting, where we created ad hoc groups doing a group task with a leader appointed to regulate and monitor the outcomes of this task. This set-up allowed for an experimental test in which, in contrast to the scenario experiment, participants were actually immersed in the leadership situation. In addition, Study 2 also aimed to replicate the findings for the mediating role of collective identification and for perceptions of charisma from Study 1, thus determining the robustness of these findings.

STUDY 2 . . .

DISCUSSION

As in Study 1, the findings of Study 2 show that, in a controlled laboratory setting, leaders' self-sacrifice and self-confidence interact to affect cooperation with the leader. Both studies thus reveal strong causal evidence for the significant main effects of self-sacrifice and self-confidence and the interactive effect between these two leadership behaviors. Again, the mediational analysis showed that this interactive effect was mediated by collective identification.

Even so, an obvious question is whether this interactive effect may also be observed among employees working in actual organizational settings. Study 3 was designed to address that question by distributing surveys among participants from a wide variety of organizations. In Study 3, as a measure of leadership effectiveness we assessed job involvement. Effective leaders are proposed to link the job and the organization's mission to the self-concept of employees, and thus to heighten employee involvement in the job at hand (Conger & Kanungo, 1998; Shamir et al., 1993; cf. van Knippenberg & van Schie,

2000). Accordingly, we expected Hypotheses 1–3 to be supported for job involvement as an indicator of leadership

STUDY 3 . . .

DISCUSSION

The results of Study 3 show that the predicted interaction between self-sacrifice and self-confidence can also be found when tested among employees from a variety of organizations: Job involvement was strongest when the leader was evaluated as high in self-sacrifice and self-confidence. Combining the results of our survey with those of the two experimental studies provides us strong evidence for the hypotheses tested in both an external and internal valid manner.

GENERAL DISCUSSION

Self-sacrificial leadership has recently been championed as an effective form of leadership (Choi & Mai-Dalton, 1998 and Choi & Mai-Dalton, 1999; De Cremer, 2002; De Cremer & van Knippenberg, 2002; Yorges et al., 1999). Obviously, then, deeper insight in the conditions under which, and the mechanisms through which, self-sacrifice translates in effective leadership are crucial to our understanding of leadership effectiveness. The main findings of the present study concern the interaction between leader self-sacrifice and self-confidence. Consistent over studies, self-sacrifice and self-confidence had stronger effects in conjunction than on their own on leadership effectiveness and perceptions of charisma, and Studies 1 and 2 showed that this effect is mediated by collective identification. In the following paragraphs, we discuss the implications of these findings.

In view of the growing evidence that leader self-sacrifice contributes to leadership effectiveness, it is of obvious importance to identify contingencies of the effectiveness of self-sacrificial behavior—especially because self-sacrifice is, in principle, under the leader's volitional control and insights into the working of leader self-sacrifice may thus feed relatively easily into organizational practice. For this reason alone, then, identifying leader displays of self-confidence as a moderator of the effectiveness of self-sacrificial behavior would seem valuable. The contribution of identifying leader displays of self-confidence as a moderator goes beyond this point, however. As noted in the introduction, even though leadership research is sensitive to the contingencies of leadership effective-

ness, other leader behaviors have typically not been studied as moderators of the effectiveness of a particular leader behavior (Kirkpatrick & Locke, 1996). The present findings thus also point to the value of studying the interactive effects of different leader behaviors.

Of special interest in this respect is the fact that we focused on two leadership behaviors that are identified in the literature as elements of charismatic leadership (Choi & Mai-Dalton, 1998; Conger & Kanungo, 1987; House, 1977; Shamir et al., 1993; Yorges et al., 1999). Corroborating these analyses, our findings show that both leader behaviors lead to perceptions of charismatic leadership. More importantly, however, our findings show that both behaviors interact. As such, the present findings support Kirkpatrick and Locke's (1996) proposition that different aspects of charismatic leadership should interact in determining leadership effectiveness. Moreover, they provide the first evidence of such an interactive effects [*sic*] (Kirkpatrick & Locke, 1996, predicted an interaction, but only found main effects). Of course, based on the present findings we cannot conclude that other aspects of charismatic leadership interact as well, but the present findings do suggest that for charismatic leadership research in particular it might be worthwhile to pursue the possibility that different aspects of leader behavior interact in affecting leadership effectiveness.

Findings from Studies 1 and 2 showed that the interactive effect of leader self-sacrifice and self-confidence on leadership effectiveness and perceived charisma was mediated by follower collective identification (Hypotheses 4 and 5Hypotheses 4 and 5 [*sic*]), although in Study 2 mediation for charisma was only partial. The finding that support for Hypothesis 5 was more conclusive for leadership effectiveness than for perceptions of charisma may be attributable to the possibility that leadership effectiveness more than perceived charisma reflects leader influence on follower motivation, and collective identification is primarily proposed to underlie leadership effectiveness through its motivational effects (van Knippenberg & Hogg, 2003; cf. Shamir et al., 1993). These findings in support of Hypothesis 5 complement and extend the findings from De Cremer and van Knippenberg (2002), and provide support for theoretical analyses of leadership that argue for the important role of identification as mediating [*sic*] variable [*sic*] (e.g., Shamir et al., 1993; van Knippenberg & Hogg, 2003). Identifying identification as a mediating variable is important for several reasons. First, to date only a limited number of empirical studies have shown that leader behaviors are related to follower identification (Conger et al., 2000; De Cremer & van Knippenberg, 2002; Kark et al., 2003; Shamir et al., 1998), and only De Cremer and van Knippenberg and Kark et al. were able to demonstrate that identification mediated the effect of leader behavior on leadership effectiveness. The present findings thus add important new evidence for the role of identification. Second, leadership research has been criticized for providing little information about the possible mechanisms through which leader behavior influences followers (e.g., Dirks & Ferrin, 2002; Hunt, 1999; Podsakoff, MacKenzie, Paine, & Bachrach, 2000; Yukl, 1999). The finding that collective identification mediated the interactive effect of self-sacrifice and self-confidence thus is a step forward in uncovering the processes through which leadership affects followers (see also Lord et al., 1999).

Although leadership effects on identification provide an account for the interactive effect of leader sacrifice and confidence, the main effects of leader self-sacrifice and leader self-confidence were not mediated by identification. As we noted in'[1] a mediating role of identification does not preclude the role of other processes in translating leader self-sacrifice and self-confidence in follower responses to leadership (cf. Shamir et al., 1993), and indeed the main effects of sacrifice and confidence appear to be attributable to other processes. Following the reasoning outlined in the introduction, we may propose that the expectation of success communicated by leader self-confidence may affect not only identification, but also follower self-efficacy and collective efficacy. Both self-efficacy and collective efficacy may be expected to enhance the motivation for the leader's cause (cf. Shamir et al., 1993; Shea & Howell, 1999), and may thus underlie the main effect of self-confidence on leadership effectiveness and perceptions of charisma. Leader self-sacrifice similarly may be linked to other possible mediators in addition to identification. van Knippenberg and van Knippenberg (in press) argued and showed that leader self-sacrifice engenders trust in the leader's group-orientedness, which may lay a basis for self-sacrifice's effect on leadership effectiveness and perceptions of charisma. Future research will have to shed more light on the merits of these propositions. In contrast to the more common practice in leadership research to focus on only one mediating variable (e.g., De Cremer & van Knippenberg, 2002; Podsakoff et al., 1990; Shea & Howell, 1999), this would require assessing the role of multiple (potential) mediators simultaneously (e.g., Kark

et al., 2003), which would seem an important step in uncovering the processes underlying the effectiveness of (charismatic) leadership. In addition, this line of reasoning highlights the fact that our findings should be regarded as evidence in support of the role of collective identification and not in denial of the role of other processes.

In this respect, it is of particular interest that our theoretical analysis suggests that leader self-sacrifice and leader self-confidence interact because they affect collective identification through slightly different routes. Self-sacrifice is proposed to affect identification because it communicates that the collective is valuable and worthy of one's dedicated efforts; self-confidence is proposed to affect identification because it communicates perceived likelihood or expectation of collective success. This suggests, then, that the interactive effect of leader self-sacrifice and self-confidence on identification and leadership effectiveness derives from self-sacrifice's influence on the perceived value of the collective and self-confidence's influence on the expected success of the collective—that is, an interaction of perceived value of the collective and perceived successfulness of the collective analogous to the interaction articulated in expectancy theory (Vroom, 1964).'[5] . . .

In sum, then, we would conclude that the present study not only demonstrates the potential to advance our understanding of leadership effectiveness, and charismatic leadership in particular, by studying the interactive effects of different (charismatic) leader behaviors, but also illustrates the added value of studying leadership using multiple methods.

References

Aiken, L. S., and West, S. G., 1991. *Multiple regression: Testing and interpreting interactions*. Sage, New York.

Ashforth, B. E., and Mael, F., 1989. Social identity theory and the organization. *Academy of Management Review* 35, pp. 232–244.

Bandura, A., 1986. *Social foundations of thought and action: Social cognitive theory*. Prentice Hall, Englewood Cliffs, NJ.

Baron, R. M., and Kenny, D. A., 1986. The moderator–mediator variable distinction in social psychological research: Conceptual, strategic, and statistical considerations. *Journal of Personality and Social Psychology* 51, pp. 1173–1182.

Bass, B. M., 1985. *Leadership and performance beyond expectations*. Free Press, New York.

Brown, D. J., and Lord, R. G., 1999. The utility of experimental research in the study of transformational/charismatic leadership. *Leadership Quarterly* 10, pp. 531–539.

Burns, J. M., 1978. *Leadership*. Harper & Row, New York.

Choi, Y., and Mai-Dalton, R. R., 1998. On the leadership function of self-sacrifice. *Leadership Quarterly* **9**, pp. 475–501.

Choi, Y., and Mai-Dalton, R. R., 1999. The model of followers' responses to self-sacrificial leadership: An empirical test. *Leadership Quarterly* 10, pp. 397–421.

Conger, J. A., 1989. *The charismatic leader: Behind the mystique of exceptional leadership*. Jossey-Bass, San Francisco.

Conger, J. A., and Kanungo, R. N., 1987. Toward a behavioral theory of charismatic leadership in organizational settings. *Academy of Management Review* 12, pp. 637–647.

Conger, J. A., and Kanungo, R., 1998. *Charismatic leadership in organizations*. Sage, Thousand Oaks, CA.

Conger, J. A., Kanungo, R. N., and Menon, S. T., 2000. Charismatic leadership and follower effects. *Journal of Organizational Behavior* 21, pp. 747–767.

De Cremer, D., 2002. Charismatic leadership and cooperation in social dilemmas: A matter of transforming motives? *Journal of Applied Social Psychology* 32, pp. 997–1016.

De Cremer, D., and van Dijk, E., 2002. Reactions to group success and failure as a function of identification level: A test of the goal-transformation hypothesis in social dilemmas. *Journal of Experimental Social Psychology* 38, pp. 435–442.

De Cremer, D., and van Knippenberg, D., 2002. How do leaders promote cooperation: The effects of charisma and procedural fairness. *Journal of Applied Psychology* 87, pp. 858–866.

Dipboye, R. L., 1990. Laboratory vs. field research in industrial and organizational psychology. *International Review of Industrial and Organizational Psychology* 5, pp. 1–34.

Dirks, K. T., and Ferrin, D. L., 2002. Trust in leadership: Meta-analytic findings and implications for research and practice. *Journal of Applied Psychology* 87, pp. 611–628.

Dutton, J. E., Dukerich, J. M., and Harquail, C. V., 1994. Organizational images and member identification. *Administrative Science Quarterly* 39, pp. 239–263.

Evans, M. G., 1985. A Monte Carlo study of the effects of correlated method variance in moderated multiple regression analysis. *Organizational Behavior and Human Decision Processes* 36, pp. 305–323.

Hogan, R., Curby, G. J., and Hogan, J., 1994. What we know about leadership: Effectiveness and personality. *American Psychologist* 49, pp. 493–504.

Hogg, M. A., and Abrams, D., 1988. *Social identifications: A social psychology of intergroup relations and group processes*. Routledge, London.

Hogg, M. A., and van Knippenberg, D., 2003. Social identity and leadership processes in groups. *Advances in Experimental Social Psychology* 35, pp. 1–52.

Hollenbeck, J. R., and Klein, H. J., 1987. Goal commitment and the goal-setting process: Problems, prospects, and proposals for future research. *Journal of Applied Psychology* 72, pp. 212–220.

House, R. J., 1977. A 1976 theory of charismatic leadership. In Hunt, J. G., and Larson, L. L., Editors, 1977. *Leadership: The cutting edge*, Southern Illinois University Press, Carbondale, IL, pp. 189–207.

Hunt, J. G., 1999. Transformational/charismatic leadership's transformation of the field: An historical essay. *Leadership Quarterly* 10, pp. 129–144.

Kark, R., Shamir, B., and Chen, G., 2003. The two faces of transformational leadership: Empowerment and dependency. *Journal of Applied Psychology* 88, pp. 246–255.

Katz, D., 1964. The motivational basis of organizational behavior. *Behavioral Science* 9, pp. 131–146.

Khurana, R., 2002. The curse of the superstar. *Harvard Business Review*. September, pp. 60–66.

Kirkpatrick, S. A., and Locke, E. A., 1996. Direct and indirect effects of three core charismatic leadership components on performance and attitudes. *Journal of Applied Psychology* 81, pp. 36–51.

Lord, R. G., Brown, D. J., and Freiberg, S. J., 1999. Understanding the dynamics of leadership: The role of follower self-concepts in the leader/follower relationship. *Organizational Behavior and Human Decision Processes* 78, pp. 167–203.

Mook, D. G., 1983. In defense of external invalidity. *American Psychologists* 38, pp. 379–387.

Rice, R. W., Instone, D., and Adams, J., 1984. Leader sex, leader success, and leadership process: Two field studies. *Journal of Applied Psychology* 69, pp. 12–31.

Podsakoff, P. M., MacKenzie, S. B., Moorman, R. H., and Fetter, R., 1990. Transformational leader behaviors and their effects on followers' trust in leader, satisfaction, and organizational citizenship behaviors. *Leadership Quarterly* 1, pp. 107–142.

Podsakoff, P. M., MacKenzie, S. B., Paine, J. B., and Bachrach, D. G., 2000. Organizational citizenship behaviors: A critical review of the theoretical and empirical literature and suggestions for future research. *Journal of Management* 26, pp. 513–563.

Shamir, B., House, R. J., and Arthur, M. B., 1993. The motivational effects of charismatic leadership: A self-concept based concept. *Organizational Science* 4, pp. 577–594.

Shamir, B., Zakay, E., Breinin, E., and Popper, M., 1998. Correlates of charismatic leader behavior in military units: Subordinates' attitudes, unit characteristics, and superiors' appraisals of leader performance. *Academy of Management Journal* 41, pp. 387–409.

Shea, C. M., and Howell, J. M., 1999. Charismatic leadership and task feedback: A laboratory study of their effects on self-efficacy and task performance. *Leadership Quarterly* 10, pp. 375–396.

Smith, K. G., Carroll, S. J., and Ashford, S. J., 1995. Intra- and interorganizational cooperation: Toward a research agenda. *Academy of Management Journal* 38, pp. 7–23.

Sobel, M. E., 1982. Asymptotic confidence intervals for indirect effects in structural equation models. In Leinhardt, S., Editor, 1982. *Sociological methodology*, American Sociological Association, Washington DC, pp. 290–312.

Tyler, T. R., 1999. Why people cooperate with organizations: An identity-based perspective. *Research in Organizational Behavior* 21, pp. 201–246.

van Knippenberg, D., 2000. Work motivation and performance: A social identity perspective. *Applied Psychology: An International Review* 49, pp. 357–371.

van Knippenberg, D., and Hogg, M. A., 2003. A social identity model of leadership effectiveness in organizations. *Research in Organizational Behavior* 25, pp. 243–295.

van Knippenberg, B., and van Knippenberg, D. (in press). Leader self-sacrifice and leadership effectiveness: The moderating role of leader prototypicality. *Journal of Applied Psychology*.

van Knippenberg, D., and van Schie, E.C.M., 2000. Foci and correlates of organizational identification. *Journal of Occupational and Organizational Psychology* 73, pp. 137–147.

Vroom, V. H., 1964. *Work and Motivation.* Wiley, New York.

Yukl, G., 1998. *Leadership in organizations* (4th ed). Prentice Hall, Englewood Cliffs, NJ.

Yukl, G., 1999. An evaluation of conceptual weaknesses in transformational and charismatic leadership theories. *Leadership Quarterly* 10, pp. 285–305.

Yorges, S. L., Weiss, H. M., and Strickland, O. J., 1999. The effect of leader outcomes on influence, attributions, and perceptions of charisma. *Journal of Applied Psychology* 84, pp. 428–436.

Leadership and Situational Differences

Research into leader traits and now leader behaviors (i.e., initiating structure and consideration) failed to reveal strong relationships with indicators of leader effectiveness. Frustration with this failure prompted an examination of the role played by the context (i.e., the situation) in which leader behavior was embedded. Also playing a significant role prompting an examination of situational differences was Stogdill's (1948) suggestion that *the context creates a unique set of group needs,* which then calls for a different approach to leadership.[1]

We probe the issue of situational differences in this chapter. More specifically, we explore these three questions:

- Does the situation in which the leader and follower are embedded make a difference?

- What leader behaviors work and when?

- What is the process through which the situation produces its effects?

The importance of the situation has already been alluded to on numerous occasions through the first several chapters. Murphy (1941), for example, notes that situations in which people find themselves create needs, and it is the nature of those needs that defines the type of leadership that best serves the group. Accordingly, Murphy sees leadership as a function (interaction) of (a) what it is that an individual has to offer and (b) the nature of the demands placed on followers by the situation in which they are embedded. In a similar fashion, Stogdill (1948) suggests that leadership is a working relationship—one in which different contexts create a unique set of group needs, and a group's emerging leader is that individual who is capable of making meaningful contributions to the group.

Leaders, according to Smircich and Morgan (1982), are those individuals who are capable of taking an ambiguous situation and framing it in a meaningful and acceptable way for the followers. Smircich and Morgan also define leadership as a product of an interaction between the situation, the leader, and the followers.

In Salancik and Pfeffer's (1977) strategic contingencies model of leadership, the leader is a person who brings scarce resources to assist a group of individuals in overcoming a critical problem that they face. As the problems facing a group change, their leader may change because of his or her access to critical and scarce resources. Thus, Salancik and Pfeffer's work also serves to highlight the importance of the situation in defining leadership and the leadership process.

Chapter 7's overview of the leader behavior literature highlighted the fact that there are inconsistent relationships between the behaviors that leaders engage

[1] R. M. Stogdill, "Personal Factors Associated with Leadership: A Survey of the Literature". *The Journal of Psychology*, 28 (1948), pp. 35–71.

in and the effects of those behaviors on member attitudes, behavior, and group effectiveness. While these inconsistent observations (e.g., the relationship between initiating structure and performance is sometimes positive, while at other times there is no significant relationship, or the relationship is even negative in nature) can be frustrating, they underscore two very important facts. First, these behaviors (e.g., initiating structure and consideration) are *important* as witnessed by their occasionally significant relationship with follower attitudes and behavior. Second, the observation that these behaviors do not always produce significant and positive effects suggests that *something else is transpiring,* such that in one situation the particular leader behavior produces significant effects, and in another situation that behavior is relatively unimportant. The question that these observations raise is, What effects do situational differences produce in the leader–follower relationship?

Many decades ago Ralph Stogdill (1948) stated that "the qualities, characteristics, and skills required in a leader are determined to a large extent by the demands of the situation in which he [she] is to function as a leader" (p. 63). Chapter 8 provides an understanding of situational differences in the leadership process.

The simple theme of this chapter might well be "different strokes for different folks" and/or "different strokes for the same folks at different points in time." Put more directly, *as conditions change, so do the leadership needs that are created and the leader behaviors that will prove effective.* If team members know, for example, exactly what needs to be done, when, how, and why, it is unlikely that initiating structure will prove to be needed or to be effective if used. In contrast, when team members are operating under conditions of high levels of uncertainty—not knowing what the task is nor when or how to execute the task—a leader who is capable of initiating some structure should make a meaningful contribution.

Influenced by Stogdill's (1948, 1974)[2] reviews of the leader behavior literature and the emerging recognition of the importance of the leadership context, Steven Kerr, Chester A. Schriesheim, Charles J. Murphy, and Ralph M. Stogdill (1974), advance a number of situational propositions linking leader initiation of structure and consideration to leader effectiveness.[3] They note that accumulated evidence suggests that leader effectiveness is not always associated with those who behave in a highly considerate and structuring manner. Among some of the situational factors that influence the effectiveness of leader consideration and initiating structure behavior are, for example, time urgency, amount of physical danger, presence of external stress, degree of autonomy, degree of job scope, and importance and meaningfulness of work.

In recognition of the powerful role played by situational forces, several contingency theories have appeared in the leadership literature. Four of these theories have gained widespread visibility. They are the Path-Goal Theory of Leadership (House, 1971); Fiedler's (1957) Contingency Theory of Leadership; Hersey and Blanchard's (1982) Situational Leadership Theory, also known as the Life Cycle Theory; and the Decision Process Theory (Vroom &Yetton, 1973).[4]

Robert J. House (1971) contends that leader effectiveness is most appropriately examined in terms of the leader's *impact* on the performance of his or her followers.[5] In the first reading in this chapter, House and Terence R. Mitchell

---

[2] R. M. Stogdill, *Handbook of Leadership: A Survey of the Literature* (New York: Free Press, 1974).

[3] S. Kerr, C. A. Schriesheim, C. J. Murphy, & R. M. Stogdill, "Toward a Contingency Theory of Leadership Based upon the Consideration and Initiating Structure Literature," *Organizational Behavior and Human Performance* 12 (1974), pp. 62–82.

[4] See the following readings in this chapter: House and Mitchell (1974), Fiedler (1974), Hersey (1988), and Vroom (2000).

[5] R. J. House, "A Path-Goal Theory of Leader Effectiveness," *Administrative Science Quarterly* 16 (1971), pp. 321–338.

(1974) assert that a leader's behavior will be motivational and subsequently have an impact on the attitudes and performance behavior of the follower to the extent that it makes the satisfaction of a subordinate's needs contingent upon his or her performance. The strategic functions of a leader, according to House and Mitchell, consist of

> (1) recognizing and/or arousing subordinates' needs for outcomes over which the leader has some control, (2) increasing personal payoffs to subordinates for work-goal attainment, (3) making the path to those payoffs easier to travel by coaching and direction, (4) helping subordinates clarify expectancies, (5) reducing frustrating barriers, and (6) increasing the opportunities for personal satisfaction contingent on effective performance. (p. 229)

Characteristics of the follower and the situation in which the leader and follower are embedded tend to alter the nature of the leader–follower relationship. Thus, the effectiveness of a leader's behavior is a function of the influence that the leader exercises over the follower in interaction with attributes of the work environment.

According to House and Mitchell, there are four important dimensions to leader behavior—supportive (consideration), directive (initiating structure), participative, and achievement-oriented leadership—that are important under different situational (i.e., task-based) conditions. Their *path-goal model* addresses the leader's unique need to provide for follower satisfaction, motivation, and performance under four different task conditions: boring, ambiguous, unstructured, and lack of challenge. Role ambiguity, for example, calls for directive leadership to clarify the path to performance. The reduction of role ambiguity enables followers to see their way more clearly toward performance accomplishment. This role clarification, coupled with directive leadership, should prove to be motivating and satisfying for the followers, ultimately producing positive performance consequences.

While the current research evidence for the path-goal theory is somewhat mixed, several students of the theory contend that it has yet to be adequately tested. This is in part due to the complexity of the theory, and therefore the difficulty of designing and executing an adequate test.[6]

The second reading in this section presents Fred E. Fiedler's (1974) *contingency theory of leadership*. Fiedler argues that situations vary in the degree to which they are favorable to the leader. Some situations are simply more favorable for a leader than other situations. Three factors that have a major influence on situation favorability are *leader–member relations* (i.e., the quality of the relationship between the leader and followers, as might be reflected by the degree to which the group accepts the leader and member loyalty to the leader); *task structure* (i.e., the degree of structure of the task to be performed, as might be reflected by the presence of a clear and unambiguous goal and a well-defined procedure that details how to proceed); and *position power* (i.e., the leader's ability to influence the followers, as might be achieved through the exercise of legitimate, reward, coercive, expert, and/or referent power).

An important part of the leadership process, according to Fiedler, is the interaction of the leader's orientation toward others and the favorability of the leadership situation. Some leaders have a strong interpersonal orientation. These individuals need to develop and maintain close interpersonal relationships. Task accomplishment is of secondary importance and becomes important only after their relationship needs have been reasonably well satisfied. Other leaders have a strong task orientation. Their first motivational concern centers on task accomplishment, with the development of good

---

[6] R. J. House & P. M. Podsakoff, "Leadership Effectiveness." In L. Greenberg (ed.), *Organizational Behavior: The State of the Science* (Hillsdale, NJ: Erlbaum, 1994), pp. 45–82; C. A. Schriesheim & L. Neider, "Path-Goal Leadership Theory: The Long and Winding Road," *Leadership Quarterly* 7 (1996), pp. 317–321.

interpersonal relationships being a secondary interest. According to the contingency theory of leadership, leaders' motivational orientation toward others can be captured by the attitudes they express about their *least preferred co-worker (LPC)*. (The first self-assessment presented at the end of this chapter opener enables you to profile yourself according to your own least preferred co-worker.)

Leaders with a high LPC score tend to see their least preferred co-workers in fairly favorable terms. These leaders tend to be relationship-oriented, and they are most effective as leaders in situations of intermediate favorability. Leaders with a low LPC score are more task-oriented, and they tend to evaluate their least preferred co-worker fairly negatively. These individuals and their directive leadership styles tend to be associated with effective group performance under highly favorable and unfavorable situations.

Reviews of the major studies that have tested Fiedler's theory are generally supportive of the theory. While the theory has undergone very little modification since it was first introduced, some confusion remains as to exactly what it is that LPC is measuring. In recent years Fiedler has collapsed the eight cells of the original model into three—reflecting low, medium, and high control situations.[7] The low LPC (i.e., task-oriented) leader is seen as performing best under low and high control situations (previously referred to as low and high favorable situations), while the high LPC (i.e., relationship-oriented) leader performs best in moderate control situations.

Paul Hersey and Kenneth Blanchard's (1976) *situational leadership model* has received a high level of visibility among management practitioners. Their theory has also been referred to as the life cycle theory. House and Aditya (1997) write that the theory's emphasis on four evolving leadership styles (i.e., telling, selling, participating, and delegating) is "analogous to a parent–child relationship where the parent gradually relinquishes control as the child matures" (p. 423).

Hersey, as noted in Reading 3, tends to see both the situation facing the leader and follower, and the follower, as significant components of the context facing the leader and his or her choice as to the appropriate style of leadership. According to their situational theory of leadership, appropriate leader behavior is defined by (a) situational demands for direction (task behavior) and for socioemotional support (relationship behavior) and (b) the level of maturity of the follower or group relative to the task or objective that the leader is attempting to accomplish through the follower's efforts. Attempts to test and validate the theory have been limited and somewhat disappointing.[8]

It should be noted that there are inconsistent views as to whether or not there is "one best style" of leadership. Bass (1997) notes that there is very little empirical evidence that supports Hersey and Blanchard's (1969) model of situational leadership based on follower maturity. In addition, Bass (1997) notes that, after several hundred investigations, controversy still surrounds Fiedler's (1983) contingency theory. Contingencies do, however, provide important insight into leadership. Bass (1997) contends that evidence supports the notion that "better leaders integrate a task-oriented and a relations-oriented approach" (p. 132).[9] In addition, effective leaders also "demonstrate the ability to clarify the path to the goals" (p. 132).[10] Blake and Mouton (1981) advocate (in their managerial grid) that the "ideal" is a leader who exhibits high levels of task- and relationship-oriented behavior.[11] Several of the authors presented in this chapter, including Hersey

[7] R. J. House & R. N. Aditya, "The Social Scientific Study of Leadership: Quo Vadis?" *Journal of Management* 23, 3 (1997), pp. 409–473.

[8] C. L. Graeff, "Evolution of Situational Leadership Theory: A Critical Review," *Leadership Quarterly* 8 (1997), pp. 153–170; House & Aditya, 1997.

[9] Bernard Bass, "Does the Transactional-Transformational Leadership Paradigm Transcend Organizational and National Boundaries?" *American Psychologist* 52, 2 (1997), pp. 130–139.

[10] Ibid.

[11] R. R. Blake & J. S. Mouton, *The Versatile Manager: A Grid Profile* (Homewood, IL: Dow-Jones/Irwin, 1981).

and Blanchard, essentially argue that *any one of a number of different styles of leadership is effective, so long as it is appropriately matched with the task (situation) facing the group.*

Robert Hooijberg (1996) notes that the significant changes that have come about in organizations during the past couple of decades have given birth to a number of new roles (e.g., leading cross-functional teams). Hooijberg suggests that accompanying these changes is an increasing pressure on the leader to have a wide range of behaviors on which to call as needs arise. He proposes that *leaders with behavioral complexity will be more effective than those managers who are behaviorally restricted to a limited number of leadership functions.* Hooijberg's work parallels the implicit call for a leader to possess the ability to shift between supportive, directive, participative, and achievement-oriented leadership, as outlined in House and Mitchell's path-goal theory of leadership. In addition, Hooijberg's behavioral complexity construct runs counter to the assumption in Fiedler's work, which suggests that it may be easier to match the leader with the situation or reengineer the situation—since changing a person's leadership orientation is extremely difficult.

When Hersey and Blanchard talk about the follower's readiness (i.e., job readiness—the ability to perform the task at hand—and psychological readiness—the motivation and commitment to accomplish the task at hand), they hint at the notion of the follower's need for leadership. This concept was addressed by Reinout E. de Vries, Robert A. Roe, and Tharsi C. B. Taillieu when they suggest that the follower and his or her need for leadership play a critical role influencing the leader-outcome relationship. The need for leadership is defined in terms of the "extent to which an [individual] wishes the leader to facilitate the paths toward individual, group, and/or organizational goals" (p. 122).[12] A follower will be open to a person's attempt at leadership when it is perceived as instrumental to the achievement of the goals important to the follower. When this leadership attempt is experienced as an unwanted intervention, it is unlikely to be favorably received. The second self-assessment in this chapter provides you with an opportunity to profile your need for leadership.

The last reading in this chapter, "Leadership and the Decision-Making Process," could be presented here as a situation-based theory of leadership or as a reading that provides us with insight into participative leadership. Victor H. Vroom, from Yale University, and his associates have worked on the development of a model that addresses the use of participative decision making in the organizational context.[13] In this reading Vroom (2000) presents a framework that is designed to help managers decide *when* to use a participative style of leadership vis-a-vis an autocratic style, and the *amount* of subordinate involvement that should be employed in a variety of situations. Instead of adopting a style that is most comfortable, leaders should be flexible in their behavioral approach, analyze each leadership situation, and then select an approach that best fits the situation. This situationally driven decision tree model is designed to prescribe the best style of leadership for a given leadership situation. Vroom's work highlights the fact that *neither the autocratic nor participative style of leadership is universally the most appropriate.* It is important to note that Vroom's work has been cast as both a leadership and a decision-making model. His objective is to provide a framework that details the type of leader behavior and the amount of subordinate participation that should be employed in different types of situations.

[12] R. E. de Vries, R. A. Roe, & T. C. B. Tailieu, "Need for Leadership as a Moderator of the Relationships between Leadership and Individual Outcomes," *Leadership Quarterly* 13 (2002), pp. 121–137; R. Hooijberg, "A Multidirectional Approach Toward Leadership: An Extension of the Concept of Behavioral Complexity," *Human Relations,* 49, 7 (1996), pp. 917–946.
[13] V. H. Vroom & P. H. Yetton, *Leadership and Decision Making* (Pittsburgh, PA: University of Pittsburgh Press, 1973); V. H. Vroom & A. G. Jago, *The New Leadership* (New York: Prentice-Hall, 1973).

According to House and Aditya (1997), nine studies have empirically tested the work of Vroom and his colleagues. While there are limitations to the field and laboratory tests that have been conducted, there appears to be reasonable support for the model that stems from the field tests conducted to date.

Figure 8.1 highlights several important components that now contribute to the leadership mosaic. Situational conditions (i.e., attributes of the task being performed) and follower attributes (e.g., task frustration, experienced ambiguity, expertise, ability to exercise self-direction and self-control) interact with the leader, shaping what might be effective leadership behavior.

FIGURE 8.1 **The Leadership Process: Critical Contextual Factors**

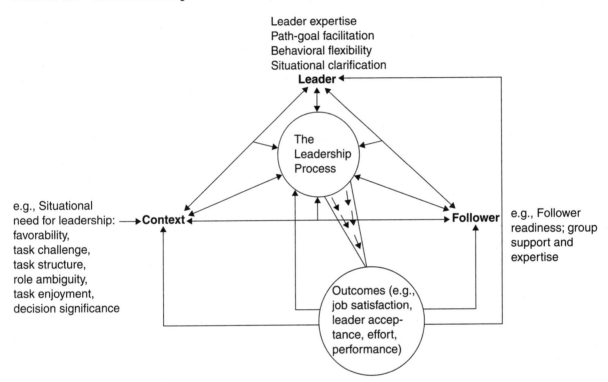

Least Preferred Co-worker (LPC)

Instructions: Think of the person with whom you can work least well. This may be someone you work with now or someone you knew in the past. It does not have to be the person you like least well, but it should be the person with whom you had the most difficulty in getting a job done. Describe this person as he or she appears to you, by circling a number for each scale.

EXERCISE
Self-Assessment

Pleasant	8	7	6	5	4	3	2	1	Unpleasant
Friendly	8	7	6	5	4	3	2	1	Unfriendly
Rejecting	1	2	3	4	5	6	7	8	Accepting
Helpful	8	7	6	5	4	3	2	1	Frustrating
Unenthusiastic	1	2	3	4	5	6	7	8	Enthusiastic
Tense	1	2	3	4	5	6	7	8	Relaxed
Distant	1	2	3	4	5	6	7	8	Close
Cold	1	2	3	4	5	6	7	8	Warm
Cooperative	8	7	6	5	4	3	2	1	Uncooperative
Supportive	8	7	6	5	4	3	2	1	Hostile
Boring	1	2	3	4	5	6	7	8	Interesting
Quarrelsome	1	2	3	4	5	6	7	8	Harmonious
Self-assured	8	7	6	5	4	3	2	1	Hesitant
Efficient	8	7	6	5	4	3	2	1	Inefficient
Gloomy	1	2	3	4	5	6	7	8	Cheerful
Open	8	7	6	5	4	3	2	1	Guarded

Scoring: Your LPC score is the sum of the answers to these 16 questions. A high score (greater than 64) reflects a relationship-orientation, while a low score (less than 57) signals a task-orientation. A score of 58 to 63 places you in the intermediate range.

Interpretation: According to Fiedler's work, a person with a high LPC tends to be relationship-oriented. These leaders generally tend to perform best under conditions of intermediate favorability. Leaders with a low LPC score are more task-oriented, and they tend to function best under conditions of high and low favorability. Work by John K. Kennedy, Jr., (1982) indicates that "the performance of middle LPC leaders is generally superior to that of the high and low LPC leaders. . . ." (p.1)[1]

Source: F. E. Fiedler and M. M. Chemers, *Leadership and Effective Management* (Glenview, IL: Scott, Foresman, 1974). Reprinted with permission.

[1] J. K. Kennedy, Jr., "Middle LPC Leaders and the Contingency Model of Leadership Effectiveness," *Organizational Behavior and Human Performance* 31 (1982), pp. 1–14.

EXERCISE
Self-Assessment

Need for Leadership

Instructions: Think of a task that you are currently working on that involves two or more other individuals. Please indicate on which of the following aspects you *personally* need the contribution of your leader (supervisor, boss, manager, or professor).

I need my leader to:

	Not At All	Not Much	Partly	Mainly	A Lot
1. Set goals.	1	2	3	4	5
2. Decide what work should be done.	1	2	3	4	5
3. Transfer knowledge.	1	2	3	4	5
4. Motivate me.	1	2	3	4	5
5. Coordinate, plan and organize my work.	1	2	3	4	5
6. Maintain external contacts.	1	2	3	4	5
7. Provide me with information.	1	2	3	4	5
8. Gear all activities of the team to one another.	1	2	3	4	5
9. Create a good team spirit.	1	2	3	4	5
10. Provide me with support.	1	2	3	4	5
11. Arrange things with higher-level management.	1	2	3	4	5
12. Handle conflicts.	1	2	3	4	5
13. Give work-related feedback.	1	2	3	4	5
14. Correct mistakes.	1	2	3	4	5
15. Help solve problems.	1	2	3	4	5
16. Recognize and reward contributions.	1	2	3	4	5
17. Inspire me.	1	2	3	4	5

Scoring: Sum your score to the 17 items and divide by 17.

Interpretation: If your score is 4 or greater you have a strong need for leadership on the task in question. If your score is 2 or less you have not expressed a need for leadership.

Source: R. E. de Vries, R. A. Roe, & T. C. B. Tailieu, 2002. "Need for Leadership as a Moderator of the Relationships between Leadership and Individual Outcomes," *Leadership Quarterly* 13 (2002), pp. 121–137. Copyright Elsevier Science 2002. Reprinted with permission from Elsevier.

Reading 21

Path-Goal Theory of Leadership

Robert J. House
University of Toronto

Terence R. Mitchell
University of Washington

An integrated body of conjecture by students of leadership, referred to as the "path-goal theory of leadership," is currently emerging. According to this theory, leaders are effective because of their impact on subordinates' motivation, ability to perform effectively, and satisfactions. The theory is called path-goal because its major concern is how the leader influences the subordinates' perceptions of their work goals, personal goals, and paths to goal attainment. The theory suggests that a leader's behavior is motivating or satisfying to the degree that the behavior increases subordinate goal attainment and clarifies the paths to these goals.

HISTORICAL FOUNDATIONS

The path-goal approach has its roots in a more general motivational theory called expectancy theory.[1] Briefly, expectancy theory states that an individual's attitudes (e.g., satisfaction with supervision or job satisfaction) or behavior (e.g., leader behavior or job effort) can be predicted from: (1) the degree to which the job, or behavior, is seen as leading to various outcomes (expectancy), and (2) the evaluation of these outcomes (valences). Thus, people are satisfied with their job if they think it leads to things that are highly valued, and they work hard if they believe that effort leads to things that are highly valued. This type of theoretical rationale can be used to predict a variety of phenomena related to leadership, such as why leaders behave the way they do, or how leader behavior influences subordinate motivation.[2]

This latter approach is the primary concern of this article. The implication for leadership is that subordinates are motivated by leader behavior to the extent that this behavior influences expectancies, e.g., goal paths and valences (goal attractiveness).

Several writers have advanced specific hypotheses concerning how the leader affects the paths and the goals of subordinates.[3] These writers focused on two issues: (1) how the leader affects subordinates' expectations that effort will lead to effective performance and valued rewards, and (2) how this expectation affects motivation to work hard and perform well.

While the state of theorizing about leadership in terms of subordinates' paths and goals is in its infancy, we believe it is promising for two reasons. First, it suggests effects of leader behavior that have not yet been investigated but which appear to be fruitful areas of inquiry. And, second, it suggests with some precision the situational factors on which the effects of leader behavior are contingent.

The initial theoretical work by Evans asserts that leaders will be effective by making rewards available to subordinates and by making these rewards contingent on the subordinates' accomplishment of specific goals.[4] Evans argued that one of the strategic functions of the leader is to clarify for subordinates the kind of behavior that leads to goal accomplishment and valued rewards. This function might be referred to as path clarification. Evans also argued that the leader increases the rewards available to subordinates by being supportive toward subordinates, i.e., by being concerned about their status, welfare, and comfort. Leader supportiveness is in itself a reward that the leader has at his or her disposal, and the judicious use of this reward increases the motivation of subordinates.

Evans studied the relationship between the behavior of leaders and the subordinates' expectations that effort leads to rewards and also studied the resulting impact on ratings of the subordinates' performance. He found that when subordinates viewed leaders as being supportive (considerate of their needs) and when these superiors provided directions and guidance to the subordinates, there was a positive relationship between leader behavior and subordinates' performance ratings.

Source: Edited and reprinted with permission from *Journal of Contemporary Business* (Autumn 1974), pp. 81–97.

However, leader behavior was only related to subordinates' performance when the leader's behavior also was related to the subordinates' expectations that their effort would result in desired rewards. Thus, Evans's findings suggest that the major impact of a leader on the performance of subordinates is clarifying the path to desired rewards and making such rewards contingent on effective performance.

Stimulated by this line of reasoning, House, and House and Dessler advanced a more complex theory of the effects of leader behavior on the motivation of subordinates.[5] The theory intends to explain the effects of four specific kinds of leader behavior on the following three subordinate attitudes or expectations: (1) the satisfaction of subordinates, (2) the subordinates' acceptance of the leader, and (3) the expectations of subordinates that effort will result in effective performance and that effective performance is the path to rewards. The four kinds of leader behavior included in the theory are: (1) directive leadership, (2) supportive leadership, (3) participative leadership, and (4) achievement-oriented leadership. Directive leadership is characterized by a leader who lets subordinates know what is expected of them, gives specific guidance as to what should be done and how it should be done, makes his or her part in the group understood, schedules work to be done, maintains definite standards of performance, and asks that group members follow standard rules and regulations. Supportive leadership is characterized by a friendly and approachable leader who shows concern for the status, well-being, and needs of subordinates. Such a leader does little things to make the work more pleasant, treats members as equals, and is friendly and approachable. Participative leadership is characterized by a leader who consults with subordinates, solicits their suggestions, and takes these suggestions seriously into consideration before making a decision. An achievement-oriented leader sets challenging goals, expects subordinates to perform at their highest level, continuously seeks improvement in performance, *and* shows a high degree of confidence that the subordinates will assume responsibility, put forth effort, and accomplish challenging goals. This kind of leader constantly emphasizes excellence in performance and simultaneously displays confidence that subordinates will meet high standards of excellence.

A number of studies suggest that these different leadership styles can be shown by the same leader in various situations.[6] For example, a leader may show directiveness toward subordinates in some instances and be participative or supportive in other instances.[7] Thus, the traditional method of characterizing a leader as either highly participative and supportive *or* highly directive is invalid; rather, it can be concluded that leaders vary in the particular fashion employed for supervising their subordinates. Also, the theory, in its present stage, is a tentative explanation of the effects of leader behavior—it is incomplete because it does not explain other kinds of leader behavior and does not explain the effects of the leader on factors other than subordinates' acceptance, satisfaction, and expectations. However, the theory is stated so that additional variables may be included in it as new knowledge is made available.

PATH-GOAL THEORY

GENERAL PROPOSITIONS

The first proposition of path-goal theory is that leader behavior is acceptable and satisfying to subordinates to the extent that the subordinates see such behavior as either an immediate source of satisfaction or as instrumental to future satisfaction.

The second proposition of this theory is that the leader's behavior will be motivational, i.e., increase effort, to the extent that (1) such behavior makes satisfaction of subordinates' needs contingent on effective performance, and (2) such behavior complements the environment of subordinates by providing the coaching, guidance, support, and rewards necessary for effective performance.

These two propositions suggest that the leader's strategic functions are to enhance subordinates' motivation to perform, satisfaction with the job, and acceptance of the leader. From previous research on expectancy theory of motivation, it can be inferred that the strategic functions of the leader consist of: (1) recognizing and/or arousing subordinates' needs for outcomes over which the leader has some control, (2) increasing personal payoffs to subordinates for work-goal attainment, (3) making the path to those payoffs easier to travel by coaching and direction, (4) helping subordinates clarify expectancies, (5) reducing frustrating barriers, and (6) increasing the opportunities for personal satisfaction contingent on effective performance.

Stated less formally, the motivational functions of the leader consist of increasing the number and kinds of personal payoffs to subordinates for work-goal attainment and making paths to these payoffs easier to travel by clarifying the paths, reducing road blocks and pitfalls, and increasing the opportunities for personal satisfaction en route.

CONTINGENCY FACTORS

Two classes of situational variables are asserted to be contingency factors. A contingency factor is a variable which moderates the relationship between two other variables such as leader behavior and subordinate satisfaction. For example, we might suggest that the degree of structure in the task moderates the relationship between leaders' directive behavior and subordinates' job satisfaction. Figure 1 shows how such a relationship might look. Thus, subordinates are satisfied with directive behavior in an unstructured task and are satisfied with nondirective behavior in a structured task. Therefore, we say that the relationship between leader directiveness and subordinate satisfaction is contingent upon the structure of the task.

The two contingency variables are (a) personal characteristics of the subordinates and (b) the environmental pressures and demands with which subordinates must cope in order to accomplish the work goals and to satisfy their needs. While other situational factors also may operate to determine the effects of leader behavior, they are not presently known.

With respect to the first class of contingency factors, the characteristics of subordinates, path-goal theory asserts that leader behavior will be acceptable to subordinates to the extent that the subordinates see such behavior as either an immediate source of satisfaction or as instrumental to future satisfaction. Subordinates' characteristics are

hypothesized to partially determine this perception. For example, Runyon[8] and Mitchell[9] show that the subordinate's source on a measure called Locus of Control moderates the relationship between participative leadership style and subordinate satisfaction. The Locus-of-Control measure reflects the degree to which an individual sees the environment as systematically responding to his or her behavior. People who believe that what happens to them occurs because of their behavior are called internals; people who believe that what happens to them occurs because of luck or chance are called externals. Mitchell's findings suggest that internals are more satisfied with a participative leadership style and externals are more satisfied with a directive style.

A second characteristic of subordinates on which the effects of leader behavior are contingent is subordinates' perception of their own ability with respect to their assigned tasks. The higher the degree of perceived ability relative to task demands, the less the subordinate will view leader directiveness and coaching behavior as acceptable. Where the subordinate's perceived ability is high, such behavior is likely to have little positive effect on the motivation of the subordinate and to be perceived as excessively close control. Thus, the acceptability of the leader's behavior is determined in part by the characteristics of the subordinates.

The second aspect of the situation, the environment of the subordinate, consists of those factors that are not within the control of the subordinate but which are important to need satisfaction or to ability to perform effectively. The theory asserts that effects of the leader's behavior on the psychological states of subordinates are contingent on other parts of the subordinates' environment that are relevant to subordinate motivation. Three broad classifications of contingency factors in the environment are: the subordinates' tasks, the formal authority system of the organization, and the primary work group.

Assessment of the environmental conditions makes it possible to predict the kind and amount of influence that specific leader behaviors will have on the motivation of subordinates. Any of the three environmental factors could act upon the subordinate in any of three ways: first, to serve as stimuli that motivate and direct the subordinate to perform necessary task operations; second, to constrain variability in behavior. Constraints may help the subordinate by clarifying expectancies that effort leads to rewards or by preventing the subordinates from experiencing conflict and confusion. Constraints also may be counterproductive

FIGURE 1 **Hypothetical Relationship between Directive Leadership and Subordinate Satisfaction with Task Structure as a Contingency Factor**

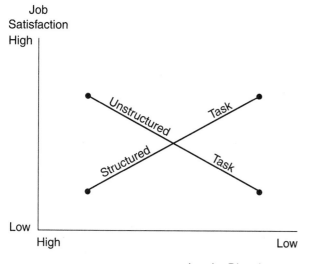

Leader Directiveness

to the extent that they restrict initiative or prevent increases in effort from being associated positively with rewards. Third, environmental factors may serve as rewards for achieving desired performance, e.g., it is possible for the subordinate to receive the necessary cues to do the job and the needed rewards for satisfaction from sources other than the leader, e.g., coworkers in the primary work group. Thus, the effect of the leader on subordinates' motivation will be a function of how deficient the environment is with respect to motivational stimuli, constraints, or rewards.

With respect to the environment, path-goal theory asserts that when goals and paths to desired goals are apparent because of the routine nature of the task, clear group norms, or objective controls of the formal authority systems, attempts by the leader to clarify paths and goals will be both redundant and seen by subordinates as imposing unnecessary, close control. Although such control may increase performance by preventing soldiering or malingering, it also will result in decreased satisfaction (see Figure 1). Also with respect to the work environment, the theory asserts that the more dissatisfying the task, the more the subordinates will resent leader behavior directed at increasing productivity or enforcing compliance to organizational rules and procedures.

Finally, with respect to environmental variables, the theory states that leader behavior will be motivational to the extent that it helps subordinates cope with environmental uncertainties, threats from others, or sources of frustration. Such leader behavior is predicted to increase subordinates' satisfaction with the job context and to be motivational to the extent that it increases the subordinates' expectations that their effort will lead to valued rewards.

These propositions and specification of situational contingencies provide a heuristic framework on which to base future research. Hopefully, this will lead to a more fully developed, explicitly formal theory of leadership.

Figure 2 presents a summary of the theory. It is hoped that these propositions, while admittedly tentative, will provide managers with some insights concerning the effects of their own leader behavior and that of others.

EMPIRICAL SUPPORT

The theory has been tested in a limited number of studies which have generated considerable empirical support for our ideas and also suggest areas in which the theory requires revision. A brief review of these studies follows.

LEADER DIRECTIVENESS

Leader directiveness has a positive correlation with satisfaction and expectancies of subordinates who are engaged in ambiguous tasks and has a negative correlation with satisfaction and expectancies of subordinates engaged in clear tasks. These findings were predicted by the theory and have been replicated in seven organizations. They suggest that when task demands are ambiguous or when the organization procedures, rules, and policies are not clear, a leader behaving in a directive manner complements the tasks and the organization by providing the necessary guidance and psychological structure for subordinates.[10] However, when task demands are clear to subordinates, leader directiveness is seen more as a hindrance. . . .

FIGURE 2 **Summary of Path-Goal Relationships**

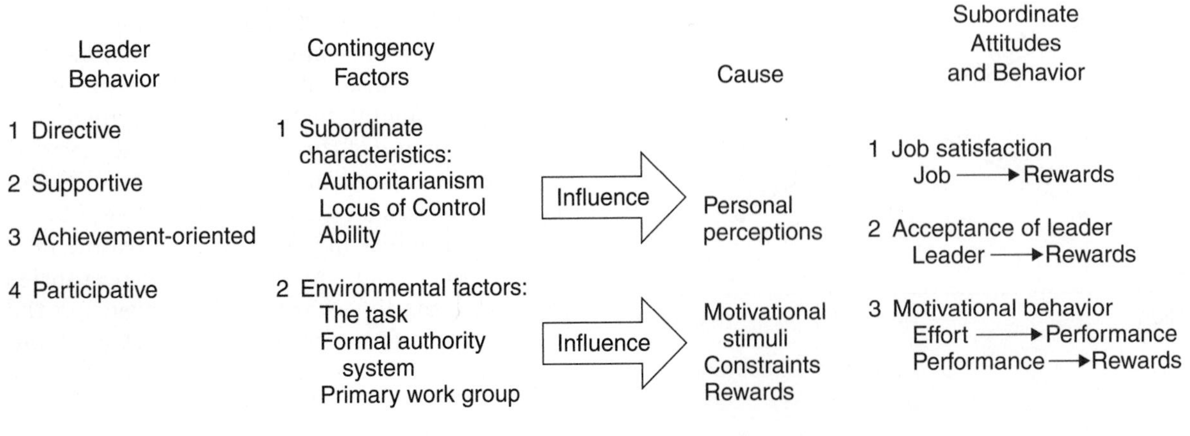

SUPPORTIVE LEADERSHIP

The theory hypothesizes that supportive leadership will have its most positive effect on subordinate satisfaction for subordinates who work on stressful, frustrating, or dissatisfying tasks. This hypothesis has been tested in 10 samples of employees,[11] and in only one of these studies was the hypothesis disconfirmed.[12] Despite some inconsistency in research on supportive leadership, the evidence is sufficiently positive to suggest that managers should be alert to the critical need for supportive leadership under conditions where tasks are dissatisfying, frustrating, or stressful to subordinates. . . .

ACHIEVEMENT-ORIENTED LEADERSHIP

The theory hypothesizes that achievement-oriented leadership will cause subordinates to strive for higher standards of performance and to have more confidence in the ability to meet challenging goals. A recent study by House, Valency, and Van der Krabben provides a partial test on this hypothesis among white-collar employees in service organizations.[13] For subordinates performing ambiguous, nonrepetitive tasks, they found a positive relationship between the amount of achievement orientation of the leader and subordinates' expectancy that their effort would result in effective performance. Stated less technically, for subordinates performing ambiguous, nonrepetitive tasks, the higher the achievement orientation of the leader, the more the subordinates were confident that their efforts would pay off in effective performance. For subordinates performing moderately unambiguous, repetitive tasks, there was no significant relationship between achievement-oriented leadership and subordinate expectancies that their effort would lead to effective performance. This finding held in four separate organizations.

Two plausible interpretations may be used to explain these data. First, people who select ambiguous, nonrepetitive tasks may be different in personality from those who select a repetitive job and may, therefore, be more responsive to an achievement-oriented leader. A second explanation is that achievement orientation only affects expectancies in ambiguous situations because there is more flexibility and autonomy in such tasks. Therefore, subordinates in such tasks are more likely to be able to change in response to such leadership style. Neither of the above interpretations have been tested to date; however, additional research is currently under way to investigate these relationships.

PARTICIPATIVE LEADERSHIP

In theorizing about the effects of participative leadership, it is necessary to ask about the specific characteristics of both the subordinates and their situation that would cause participative leadership to be viewed as satisfying and instrumental to effective performance.

Mitchell recently described at least four ways in which a participative leadership style would impact on subordinate attitudes and behavior as predicted by expectancy theory.[14] First, a participative climate should increase the clarity of organizational contingencies. Through participation in decision making, subordinates should learn what leads to what. From a path-goal viewpoint, participation would lead to greater clarity of the paths to various goals. A second impact of participation would be that subordinates, hopefully, should select goals they highly value. If one participates in decisions about various goals, it makes sense that this individual would select goals he or she wants. Thus, participation would increase the correspondence between organization and subordinate goals. Third, we can see how participation would increase the control the individual has over what happens on the job. If our motivation is higher (based on the preceding two points), then having greater autonomy and ability to carry out our intentions should lead to increased effort and performance. Finally, under a participative system, pressure towards high performance should come from sources other than the leader or the organization. More specifically, when people participate in the decision process, they become more ego-involved; the decisions made are in some part their own. Also, their peers know what is expected and the social pressure has a greater impact. Thus, motivation to perform well stems from internal and social factors as well as formal external ones.

A number of investigations prior to the above formulation supported the idea that participation appears to be helpful,[15] and Mitchell presents a number of recent studies that support the above four points.[16] However, it is also true that we would expect the relationship between a participative style and subordinate behavior to be moderated by both the personality characteristics of the subordinate and the situational demands. Studies by Tannenbaum and Allport and Vroom have shown that subordinates who prefer autonomy and self-control respond more positively to participative leadership in terms of both satisfaction and performance than subordinates who do not have such preferences.[17] Also, the studies mentioned by Runyon[18] and Mitchell[19] showed that subordinates who were external in orientation were less satisfied with a participative style of leadership than were internal subordinates.

House also has reviewed these studies in an attempt to explain the ways in which the situation or environment moderates the relationship between participation and subordinate attitudes and behavior.[20] His analysis suggests that where participative leadership is positively related to satisfaction, regardless of the predispositions of subordinates, the tasks of the subjects appear to be ambiguous and ego-involving. In the studies in which the subjects' personalities or predispositions moderate the effect of participative leadership, the tasks of the subjects are inferred to be highly routine and/or nonego-involving.

House reasoned from this analysis that the task may have an overriding effect on the relationship between leader participation and subordinate responses, and that individual predispositions or personality characteristics of subordinates may have an effect only under some tasks. It was assumed that when task demands are ambiguous, subordinates will have a need to reduce the ambiguity. Further, it was assumed that when task demands are ambiguous, participative problem solving between the leader and the subordinate will result in more effective decisions than when the task demands are unambiguous. Finally, it was assumed that when the subordinates are ego-involved in their tasks, they are more likely to want to have a say in the decisions that affect them. Given these assumptions, the following hypotheses were formulated to account for the conflicting findings reviewed above:

- When subjects are highly ego-involved in a decision or a task and the decision or task demands are ambiguous, participative leadership will have a positive effect on the satisfaction and motivation of the subordinate, regardless of the subordinate's predisposition toward self-control, authoritarianism, or need for independence.

- When subordinates are not ego-involved in their tasks and when task demands are clear, subordinates who are not authoritarian and who have high needs for independence and self-control will respond favorably to leader partici-

pation, and their opposite personality types will respond less favorably.

These hypotheses were derived on the basis of path-goal theorizing; i.e., the rationale guiding the analysis of prior studies was that both task characteristics and characteristics of subordinates interact to determine the effect of a specific kind of leader behavior on the satisfaction, expectancies, and performance of subordinates. To date, one major investigation has supported some of these predictions[21] in which personality variables, amount of participative leadership, task ambiguity, and job satisfaction were assessed for 324 employees of an industrial manufacturing organization. As expected, in nonrepetitive, ego-involving tasks, employees (regardless of their personality) were more satisfied under a participative style than a nonparticipative style. However, in repetitive tasks which were less ego-involving, the amount of authoritarianism of subordinates moderated the relationship between leadership style and satisfaction. Specifically, low authoritarian subordinates were *more satisfied* under a participative style. These findings are exactly as the theory would predict; thus, it has promise in reconciling a set of confusing and contradictory findings with respect to participative leadership.

Summary and Conclusions

We have attempted to describe what we believe is a useful theoretical framework for understanding the effect of leadership behavior on subordinate satisfaction and motivation. Most theorists today have moved away from the simplistic notions that all effective leaders have a certain set of personality traits or that the situation completely determines performance. Some researchers have presented rather complex attempts at matching certain types of leaders with certain types of situations, e.g., the articles written by Vroom and Fiedler. But, we believe that a path-goal approach goes one step further. It not only suggests what type of style may be most effective in a given situation—it also attempts to explain *why* it is most effective.

We are optimistic about the future outlook of leadership research. With the guidance of path-goal theorizing, future research is expected to unravel many confusing puzzles about the reasons for and effects of leader behavior that have, heretofore, not been solved. However, we add a word of caution: The theory, and the research on it, are relatively new to the literature of organizational behavior. Consequently, path-goal theory is offered more as a tool for directing research and stimulating insight than as a proven guide for managerial action.

Notes

1. T. R. Mitchell, "Expectancy Model of Job Satisfaction, Occupational Preference and Effort: A Theoretical, Methodological and Empirical Appraisal," *Psychological Bulletin* (1974, in press).

2. D. M. Nebeker and T. R. Mitchell, "Leader Behavior: An Expectancy Theory Approach," *Organizational Behavior and Human Performance,* Vol. 11 (1974), pp. 355–367.

3. M. G. Evans, "The Effects of Supervisory Behavior on the Path-Goal Relationship," *Organizational Behavior and Human Performance,* Vol. 55 (1970), pp. 277–298; T. H. Hammer and H. T. Dachler, "The Process of Supervision in the Context of Motivation Theory," Research Report No. 3 (University of Maryland, 1973); F. Dansereau, Jr., J. Cashman, and G. Graen, "Instrumentality Theory and Equity Theory as Complementary Approaches in Predicting the Relationship of Leadership and Turnover among Managers," *Organizational Behavior and Human Performance,* Vol. 10 (1973), pp. 184–200; R. J. House, "A Path-Goal Theory of Leader Effectiveness," *Administrative Science Quarterly,* Vol. 16, No. 3 (September 1971), pp. 321–338; T. R. Mitchell, "Motivation and Participation: An Integration," *Academy of Management Journal,* Vol. 16, No. 4 (1973), pp. 160–179; G. Graen, F. Dansereau, Jr., and T. Minami, "Dysfunctional Leadership Styles," *Organizational Behavior and Human Performance,* Vol. 7 (1972), pp. 216–236; "An Empirical Test of the Man-in-the-Middle Hypothesis among Executives in a Hierarchical Organization Employing a Unit Analysis," *Organizational Behavior and Human Performance,* Vol. 8 (1972), pp. 262–285; R. J. House and G. Dessler, "The Path-Goal Theory of Leadership: Some Post Hoc and A Priori Tests," to appear in J. G. Hunt, ed., *Contingency Approaches to Leadership* (Carbondale, Ill.: Southern Illinois University Press, 1974).

4. M. G. Evans, "Effects of Supervisory Behavior"; "Extensions of a Path-Goal Theory of Motivation," *Journal of Applied Psychology,* Vol. 59 (1974), pp. 172–178.

5. R. J. House, "A Path-Goal Theory"; R. J. House and G. Dessler, "Path-Goal Theory of Leadership."

6. R. J. House and G. Dessler, "Path-Goal Theory of Leadership"; R. M. Stogdill, *Managers, Employees, Organization* (Ohio State University, Bureau of Business Research, 1965); R. J. House, A. Valency, and R. Van der Krabben, "Some Tests and Extension of the Path-Goal Theory of Leadership" (in preparation).

7. W. A. Hill and D. Hughes, "Variations in Leader Behavior as a Function of Task Type," *Organizational Behavior and Human Performance* (1974, in press).

8. K. E. Runyon, "Some Interactions between Personality Variables and Management Styles," *Journal of Applied Psychology,* Vol. 57, No. 3 (1973), pp. 288–294; T. R. Mitchell, C. R. Smyser, and S. E. Weed, "Locus of Control: Supervision and Work Satisfaction," *Academy of Management Journal* (in press).

9. T. R. Mitchell, "Locus of Control."

10. R. J. House, "A Path-Goal Theory"; and G. Dessler, "Path-Goal Theory of Leadership"; A. D. Szilagyi and H. P. Sims, "An Exploration of the Path-Goal Theory of Leadership in a Health Care Environment," *Academy of Management Journal* (in press); J. D. Dermer, "Supervisory Behavior and Budget Motivation" (Cambridge, Mass.: unpublished, MIT, Sloan School of Management, 1974); R. W. Smetana, "The Relationship between Managerial Behavior and Subordinate Attitudes and Motivation: A Contribution to a Behavioral Theory of Leadership" (Ph.D. diss., Wayne State University, 1974).

11. R. J. House, "A Path-Goal Theory"; and G. Dessler, "Path-Goal Theory of Leadership"; A. D. Szilagyi and H. P. Sims, "Exploration of Path-Goal"; J. E. Stinson and T. W. Johnson, "The Path-Goal Theory of Leadership: A Partial Test and Suggested Refinement," *Proceedings* (Kent, Ohio: 7th Annual Conference of the Midwest Academy of Management, April 1974), pp. 18–36; R. S. Schuler, "A Path-Goal Theory of Leadership: An Empirical Investigation" (Ph.D. diss., Michigan State University, 1973); H. K. Downey, J. E. Sheridan, and J. W. Slocum, Jr., "Analysis of Relationships Among Leader Behavior, Subordinate Job Performance and Satisfaction: A Path-Goal Approach (unpublished mimeograph, 1974); S. E. Weed, T. R. Mitchell, and C. R. Smyser, "A Test of House's Path-Goal Theory of Leadership in an Organizational Setting" (paper presented at Western Psychological Assoc., 1974).

12. A. D. Szilagyi and H. P. Sims, "Exploration of Path-Goal."

13. R. J. House, A. Valency, and R. Van der Krabben, "Tests and Extensions of Path-Goal Theory of Leadership, II" (unpublished, in process).

14. T. R. Mitchell, "Motivation and Participation."

15. H. Tosi, "A Reexamination of Personality as a Determinant of the Effects of Participation," *Personnel Psychology,* Vol. 23 (1970), pp. 91–99; J. Sadler, "Leadership Style, Confidence in Management and Job Satisfaction," *Journal of Applied Behavioral Sciences,* Vol. 6 (1970), pp. 3–19; K. N. Wexley, J. P. Singh, and J. A. Yukl, "Subordinate Personality as a Moderator of the Effects of Participation in Three Types of Appraisal Interviews," *Journal of Applied Psychology,* Vol. 83 (1973), pp. 54–59.

16. T. R. Mitchell, "Motivation and Participation."

17. A. S. Tannenbaum and F. H. Allport, "Personality Structure and Group Structure: An Interpretive Study of Their Relationship through an Event-Structure Hypothesis," *Journal of Abnormal and Social Psychology,* Vol. 53 (1956), pp. 272–280; V. H. Vroom, "Some Personality Determinants of the Effects of Participation," *Journal of Abnormal and Social Psychology,* Vol. 59 (1959), pp. 322–327.

18. K. E. Runyon, "Some Interactions between Personality Variables and Management Styles," *Journal of Applied Psychology,* Vol. 57, No. 3 (1973), pp. 288–294.

19. T. R. Mitchell, C. R. Smyser, and S. E. Weed, "Locus of Control."

20. R. J. House, "Notes on the Path-Goal Theory of Leadership" (University of Toronto, Faculty of Management Studies, May 1974).

21. R. S. Schuler, "Leader Participation, Task-Structure and Subordinate Authoritarianism" (unpublished mimeograph, Cleveland State University, 1974).

Reading 22

How Do You Make Leaders More Effective? New Answers to an Old Puzzle

Fred E. Fiedler
University of Washington

Let's begin with a basic proposition: The organization that employs the leader is as responsible for his success or failure as the leader himself. Not that this is a new insight—far from it. Terman wrote in 1904 that leadership performance depends on the situation, as well as on the leader. Although this statement would not be questioned by anyone currently working in this area, it also has been widely ignored. Practically all formal training programs attempt to change the individual; many of them assume explicitly or implicitly that there is one style of leadership or one way of acting that will work best under all conditions. Most military academies, for example, attempt to mold the individual into a supposedly ideal leader personality. Others assume that the training should enable the individual to become more flexible or more sensitive to his environment so that he can adapt himself to it.

Before going further let's define a few terms. I will confine my discussion to *task groups* rather than the organization of which the group is a part. Furthermore, we will assume that anyone who is placed in a leadership position will have the requisite technical qualifications for the job. Just as the leader of a surgical team obviously has to have medical training, so a manager must know the essential administrative requirements of his job. We will here talk primarily about training *as a leader* rather than training as a specialist. The effectiveness of the leader will be defined in terms of how well his group or organization performs the primary tasks for which the group exists. We measure the effectiveness of a football coach by how many games his team wins and not by the character he builds, and the excellence of an orchestra conductor by how well his orchestra plays, not by the happiness of his musicians or his ability as a musicologist. Whether the musicians' job satisfaction or the conductor's musicological expertness

do, in fact, contribute to the orchestra's excellence is an interesting question in its own right, but it is not what people pay to hear. Likewise, the performance of a manager is here measured in terms of his department's or group's effectiveness in doing its assigned job. Whether the accomplishment of this job is to be measured after a week or after five years depends, of course, upon the assignment the organization gives the group, and the accomplishments the organization considers important.

When we think of improving leadership, we almost automatically think of training the individual. This training frequently involves giving the man a new perspective on his supervisory responsibilities by means of role playing, discussions, detailed instructions on how to behave toward subordinates, as well as instruction in the technical and administrative skills he will need in his job. A training program might last a few days, a few months, or as in the case of college programs and military academies, as long as four years. What is the hard evidence that this type of training actually increases organizational performance?

Empirical studies to evaluate the effectiveness of various leadership training programs, executive development, and supervisory workshops have been generally disappointing. Certainly, the two field experiments and two studies of ongoing organizations conducted by my associates and me failed to show that training increases organizational performance. . . .

I repeat that these findings are by no means unusual. Empirical studies to determine whether or not leadership training improves organizational performance have generally come up with negative findings. Newport, after surveying 121 large companies, concluded that not *one* of the companies had obtained any scientifically acceptable evidence that the leadership training for their middle management had actually improved performance.

T-group and sensitivity training, which has become fashionable in business and industry, has yielded similarly unsatisfactory results. Reviews of the literature by Campbell and Dunnette and by House found no convincing evidence that this type of training increased organizational effectiveness, and a well-known study at the International Harvester Company by Fleishman, Harris, and Burtt on the effects of supervisory training concluded that the effects of supervisory training in modifying behavior were very short-lived and did not improve performance.

EFFECT OF EXPERIENCE ON LEADERSHIP

Let us now ask whether supervisory experience improves performance. Actually, since leadership experience almost always involves on-the-job training, we are dealing with a closely related phenomenon.

Interestingly enough, the literature actually contains few, if any, studies which attempt to link leadership experience to organizational effectiveness. Yet, there seems to be a firmly held expectation that leadership experience makes a leader more effective. We simply have more trust in experienced leaders. We can infer this, for example, from the many regulations that require time in grade before promotion to the next higher level, as well as the many specifications of prior job in hiring executives for responsible positions.

We have . . . seen that the experienced petty officers and military academy officers did not perform more effectively than did the inexperienced enlisted men, nor did the more experienced officers or petty officers perform better than the less experienced.

In addition, we also analyzed data from various other groups and organizations. These included directors of research and development teams at a large physical research laboratory, foremen of craftshops, general foremen in a heavy machinery manufacturing company, managers of meat, and of grocery markets, in a large supermarket chain as well as post office supervisors and managers, and police sergeants. For all these managers we could obtain reliable performance ratings or objective group effectiveness criteria. None of the correlations was significant in the expected direction. The median correlation relating leadership experience to leadership performance for all groups and organizations was –.12—certainly not significant in the positive direction!

To summarize the findings, neither orthodox leadership training nor leadership experience nor sensitivity training appear to contribute across the board to group or organizational effectiveness. It is, therefore, imperative, first, that we ask why this might be so, and second that we consider alternative methods for improving leadership performance.

THE CONTINGENCY MODEL

The "Contingency Model," a recent theory of leadership, holds that the effectiveness of group performance is contingent upon (a) the leader's motivational pattern and (b) the degree to which the situation gives the leader power and influence. We have worked with a leadership motivation measure called the "Esteem for the Least Preferred Co-worker," or LPC for short. The subject is first asked to think of all the people with whom he has ever worked, and then given a simple scale on which he describes the one person in his life with whom he has been able to work *least well.* This "least preferred co-worker" may be someone he knows at the time or it may be someone he has known in the past. It does not have to be a member of his present work group.

In grossly oversimplified terms, the person who describes his least preferred co-worker in relatively favorable terms is basically motivated to have close interpersonal relations with others. By contrast, the person who rejects someone with whom he cannot work is basically motivated to accomplish or achieve on the task, and he derives satisfaction from being recognized as having performed well on the task. The task-motivated person thus uses the task to obtain a favorable position and good interpersonal relations.

CLASSIFYING LEADERSHIP SITUATIONS

The statement that some leaders perform better in one kind of situation while some leaders perform better in different situations is begging a question, "What kinds of situations are best suited for which type of leader?" In other words, how can we best classify groups if we wish to predict leadership performance?

We can approach this problem by assuming that leadership is essentially a work relationship involving power and influence. It is easier to be a leader when you have complete control than when your control is weak and dependent on the good will of others. It is easier to be the captain of a ship than the chairman of a volunteer group organized to settle a school busing dispute. The *job* may be more complex for the navy captain, but *being in the leadership role* is easier for him than for the committee chairman. It is, therefore, not unreasonable to classify situations in terms of how much power and influence the situation gives the leader. We call this "situational favorableness." One simple categorization of groups on their situational favorableness classifies leadership situations on the basis of three major dimensions:

1. *Leader–member relations.* Leaders presumably have more power and influence if they have a good relationship with their members than if they have a poor relationship with them, if they are liked, respected, trusted, than if they are not. Research has shown that this is by far the most important single dimension.

2. *Task structure.* Tasks or assignments that are highly structured, spelled out, or programmed give the leader more influence than tasks that are vague, nebulous, and unstructured. It is easier, for example, to be a leader whose task it is to set up a sales display according to clearly delineated steps than it is to be a chairman of a committee preparing a new sales campaign.

3. *Position power.* Leaders will have more power and influence if their position is vested with such prerogatives as being able to hire and fire, being able to discipline, to reprimand, and so on. Position power, as it is here used, is determined by how much power the leader has over his subordinates. If the janitor foreman can hire and fire, he has more position power in his own group than the chairman of a board of directors who, frequently, cannot hire or fire—or even reprimand his board members.

Using this classification method we can now roughly order groups as being high or low on each of these three dimensions. This gives us an eight-celled classification (Figure 1). This scheme postulates that it is easier to be a leader in groups that fall into Cell 1 since you are liked, have position

power, and have a structured task. It is somewhat more difficult in Cell 2 since you are liked, have a structured task, but little position power, and so on to groups in Cell 8 where the leader is not liked, has a vague, unstructured task, and little position power. A good example of Cell 8 would be the disliked chairman of the volunteer committee we mentioned before.

The critical question is, "What kind of leadership does each of these different group situations call for?" Figure 2 summarizes the results of 63 analyses based on a total of 454 separate groups. These included bomber and tank crews, antiaircraft artillery units, managements of consumer cooperative companies, boards of directors, open-hearth shops, basketball and surveying teams, and various groups involved in creative and problem-solving tasks.

The horizontal axis of the graph indicates the "situational favorableness," namely, the leader's control and influence as defined by the eight-fold classification shown in Figure 1. The vertical axis indicates the relationship between the leader's motivational pattern, as measured by the LPC score, and his group's performance. A median correlation above the midline shows that the relationship-motivated leaders tended to perform better than the task-motivated leaders. A correlation below the midline indicates that the task-motivated leaders performed better than the relationship-motivated leaders. Figure 3 shows the predictions that the model would make in each of the eight cells.

These findings have two important implications for our understanding of what makes leaders effective. First, Figure 2 tells us that the task-motivated leaders tend to perform better than relationship-motivated leaders in situations that are very favorable and in those that are unfavorable. Relationship-motivated leaders tend to perform better than task-motivated leaders in situations that are intermediate in favorableness. Hence, both the relationship- and the task-motivated leaders perform well under some

FIGURE 1 **Cells or "Octants"**

	Very Favorable			Intermediate in Favorableness			Unfavorable	
	1	2	3	4	5	6	7	8
Leader–member relations	Good	Good	Good	Good	Poor	Poor	Poor	Poor
Task structure	High	High	Low	Low	High	High	Low	Low
Position power	Strong	Weak	Strong	Weak	Strong	Weak	Strong	Weak

FIGURE 2
Relationship between Leader LPC and Group Performance

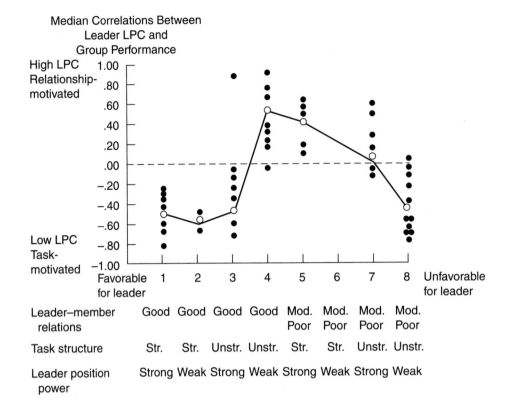

Median Correlations Between Leader LPC and Group Performance

Leader–member relations	Good	Good	Good	Good	Mod. Poor	Mod. Poor	Mod. Poor	Mod. Poor
Task structure	Str.	Str.	Unstr.	Unstr.	Str.	Str.	Unstr.	Unstr.
Leader position power	Strong	Weak	Strong	Weak	Strong	Weak	Strong	Weak

conditions and not under others. It is, therefore, not correct to speak of any person as generally a good leader or generally a poor leader. Rather, a leader may perform well in one situation but not in another. This is also borne out by the repeated findings that we cannot predict a leader's performance on the basis of his personality traits, or even by knowing how well he performed on a previous task unless that task was similar in situational favorableness.

Second, the graph on Figure 2 shows that the performance of a leader depends as much on the situational favorableness as it does on the individual in the leadership position. Hence, the organization can change leadership performance either by trying to change the individual's personality

and motivational pattern or by changing the favorableness of the leader's situation. As we shall see, this is really what training is all about.

Before we go further, we must ask how valid the Contingency Model is. How well does it predict in new situations? There have been at least 25 studies to date that have tested the theory. These validation studies included research on grocery and meat markets, a physical science laboratory, a machinery plant, a hospital, an electronics company, and teams of volunteer public health workers in Central America, as well as various experimentally assembled groups in the laboratory. Of particular importance is a large experiment that used cadets at West Point to test the entire eight cells of the model. This study almost completely

FIGURE 3   **Prediction of the Performance of Relationship- and Task-Motivated Leaders**

Relationship-motivated High LPC				Good	Good	Some-what better	Some-what better	
Task-motivated Low LPC	Good	Good	Good					Good
	1	2	3	4	5	6	7	8

reproduced the curve shown on Figure 2. In all studies that were recently reviewed, 35 of the 44 obtained correlations that were in the predicted direction—a finding that could have occurred by chance less than one time in 100. An exception is Cell 2, in which laboratory experiments—but not field studies—have yielded correlations showing the relationship-motivated leaders perform better than task-motivated leaders. . . .

TO TRAIN OR NOT TO TRAIN

What does all this mean for improving managerial performance, and how can we apply the findings that we have described?

In sum, if we want to improve leadership performance, we can either change the leader by training, or we can change his leadership situation. Common sense suggests that it is much easier to change various aspects of a man's job than to change the man. When we talk about leadership behavior, we are talking about fairly deeply ingrained personality factors and habits of interacting with others. These cannot be changed easily, either in a few hours or in a few days. In fact, as we have seen, not even four years of military academy and 5 to 17 years of subsequent experience enable a leader to perform significantly better on different tasks than someone that has had neither training nor experience.

We have seen that a leader's performance depends not only on his personality, but also on the organizational factors that determine the leader's control and influence—that is, the "situational favorableness." As we have shown, appropriate training and experience improve situational favorableness. Whether or not they improve performance depends upon the match between the leader's motivational pattern and the favorableness of the situation. This means that a training program that improves the leader's control and influence may benefit the relationship-motivated managers, but it will be detrimental to the task-motivated managers, or vice versa, depending upon the situation.

The idea that we can improve a leader's performance by increasing the favorableness of his situation is, of course, far from new. A poorly performing manager may be given more authority, more explicit instructions, more congenial coworkers in the hope that it will help him do a better job. Moreover, decreasing the favorableness of the situation in order to improve a manager's performance is also not quite as unusual as it might appear at first blush. If a man becomes bored, stale, or disinterested in his job, a frequent remedy is to transfer him to a more challenging job. As it turns out, "challenging" is just another way of saying that the job is less structured, has less position power, or requires working with difficult people. It is certainly well known that some men perform best under pressure and that they get into difficulty when life is too calm. These are the trouble shooters who are dispatched to branch offices or departments that need to be bailed out.

What, then, can an organization do to increase managerial performance? As a first step, it is necessary to determine which of the managers are task- and which are relationship-motivated. This can be accomplished by means of a short scale. Second, the organization needs to categorize carefully the situational favorableness of its managerial jobs. (Scales are available in Fiedler, F. E., *A Theory of Leadership Effectiveness,* McGraw-Hill, 1967.) Third, the organization can decide on a number of options in its management of executive personnel.

The least expensive and probably most efficient method is to develop a careful program of managerial rotation that moves some individuals from one job to another at a faster rate than it moves others. . . .

A second major option is management training. The problem here is whether to train only some people or all those who are eligible: Training a task-motivated manager who is accepted by his group and has a structured task is likely to improve his performance; training a relationship-motivated manager for the same job is likely to make him less effective. The organization would, therefore, be better off if it simply did not train relationship-motivated managers for these particular jobs. On the other hand, the relationship-motivated but not the task-motivated managers should be trained for jobs in which the situational favorableness is intermediate. . . .

CONCLUSION

As a consequence of our research, we have both discredited some old myths and learned some new lessons.

The old myths:

• That there is one best leadership style, or that there are leaders who excel under all circumstances.

- That some men are born leaders, and that neither training, experience, nor conditions can materially affect leadership skills.

The lessons, while more pedestrian and less dogmatic, are more useful. We know that people differ in how they respond to management situations. Furthermore, we know that almost every manager in an organization can perform effectively, providing that we place him in a situation that matches his personality, providing we know how to match his training and experience to the available jobs—and providing that we take the trouble.

Selected Bibliography

The interested reader may wish to consult Fiedler's *A Theory of Leadership Effectiveness* (McGraw-Hill, 1967), which presents a detailed summary of many of his studies as well as a fairly technical description of the theory. A more popular version of the theory is described in a *Harvard Business Review* article entitled, "Engineer the Job to Fit the Manager" (September 1965) and in *Psychology Today,* "Style or Circumstance: the Leadership Enigma" (March 1969). A more technical and extensive summary of the work on leadership training will appear shortly in a forthcoming issue of *Administrative Science Quarterly*.

Reading 23
Situational Leadership®

Paul Hersey
Center for Leadership Studies, Inc.

Situational Leadership is a practical model designed to help leaders be more effective in their interactions with people. It is based on an interplay among three factors:

1. The amount of guidance and direction a leader gives (similar to task behavior);

2. The amount of socio-emotional support a leader provides (similar to relationship behavior); and

3. The readiness level that followers exhibit in performing a specific task, function, or objective.

According to the Situational Leadership model, there is no one best style of leadership, or way to influence people. The style to be used depends on the readiness level of the people the leader is attempting to influence, as illustrated in Figure 1.

The model displays the interaction of two separate and distinct leadership orientations—task and relationships—appearing on the horizontal and vertical axes:

• *Task behavior* is defined as the extent to which the leader engages in spelling out the duties and responsibilities of an individual or group. These behaviors include telling people what to do, how to do it, when to do it, where to do it, and who is to do it. This is the guidance role of a leader.

• *Relationship behavior* is defined as the extent to which the leader engages in two-way or multi-way communication. The behaviors include listening, facilitating, and supportive behaviors.

The products of this interaction are four leadership styles, one in each of the quadrants shown in Figure 1. Each behavior is plotted from low to high on its axis. This produces four distinct styles:

• Style 1 (Tell): This style demonstrates high degrees of task behavior and low degrees of relationship behavior.

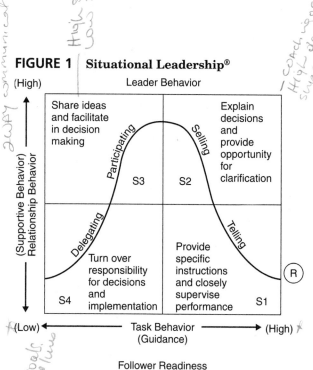

FIGURE 1 **Situational Leadership®**

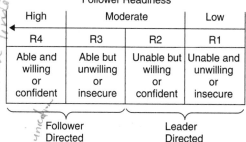

• Style 2 (Sell): This style is characterized by high amounts of both task and relationship behavior.

• Style 3 (Participate): This style uses high amounts of relationship behavior and low amounts of task behavior.

• Style 4 (Delegate): In this style, low amounts of both task and relationship behavior are used.

Any one of the four styles may prove effective in a given situation. The key (independent) variable that is believed to affect its success lies in the concept of *follower readiness*. This is the extent to which a follower has the ability and willingness to accomplish a specific task. In contrast to personal characteristics (such as traits, values, or age), readiness is a measure of how ready a person is to perform a specific task, function, assignment, or objective that a leader views as important.

In assessing (and developing) follower readiness, a leader must consider two separate components:

- *Ability* (job readiness) is the knowledge, experience, and skill that an individual or group brings to a particular task or activity.

- *Willingness* (psychological readiness) is the extent to which an individual or group has the confidence, commitment, and motivation to accomplish a specific task. These components are interactive; willingness affects not only the use of present ability, but the extent to which competence and ability will grow. Similarly, one's current ability may impact self-assessments of competence, commitment, and motivation.

The combination of low or high levels of ability and willingness produces a continuum of follower readiness. For the sake of discussion and analysis, this continuum can be divided into four levels, each representing a different combination:

- Readiness Level One (R1): The follower is both unable to do the task, and lacks commitment, confidence, and willingness.

- Readiness Level Two (R2): The follower is motivated to make an effort and would try if the leader was there to provide guidance, but lacks current ability to perform well.

- Readiness Level Three (R3): The follower has the capacity to perform the function requested, but is insecure, apprehensive, or unwilling to use that ability.

- Readiness Level Four (R4): The follower has the requisite ability to perform successfully, and also demonstrates the necessary commitment and confidence to do it.

The leader's challenge is to identify follower readiness and then match it with the appropriate leadership style called for by the model. For example, a follower or group at Readiness Level 1 requires a leader to *tell* the person what to do. Guiding, directing, and structuring the work environment are all appropriate. Readiness Level 2 (willing but unable) calls for a *selling* approach—providing answers to the questions of what, how, when, where, and who. Although selling focuses on explaining, persuading, and clarifying, it also opens up the possibility of dialogue for the follower to ask questions and receive clarification.

Readiness Level 3 calls for a *participating* style. The leader encourages an able person through supportive communication, and engages in collaborative, facilitating, or committing behaviors, while accenting both task and relationship orientations. Readiness Level 4 needs a *delegating* style. The follower or group is able, confident, and willing, and only needs the opportunity to perform. Although some relationship behavior is still needed, followers need to take responsibility for the objective and implement action on their own. The leader may wish to observe, stand by to respond to requests for assistance, and monitor results.

In addition to specifying the high-probability leadership style for various readiness levels, Situational Leadership also attempts to indicate the probability of success of the other three options for each situation. In order of preference, they appear as follows for each level of follower readiness:

- R1: S1, S2, S3, S4.

- R2: S2, S1, S3, S4.

- R3: S3, S2, S4, S1.

- R4: S4, S3, S2, S1.

The Situational Leadership model has been used in a large number of U.S. companies for several decades, and therefore has considerable face validity. It is a prescriptive approach that tells leaders how to assess their followers and how to respond to that assessment of follower readiness with one of the four defined styles. It is flexible, with no hard and fast rules. It is based on subjective probabilities of success from using each style, in hopes of improving the odds for a productive outcome. Finally, the Situational Leadership model also recognizes that other situational variables may be of equal or greater importance, such as a crisis, time pressures, or the unique nature of the work.

Reading 24

Leadership and the Decision-Making Process

Victor H. Vroom
Yale University

THE BURNS DECISION

Jim Burns is an emergency response manager in a large company, specializing in ecological control systems. His work runs the gamut from removal and disposal of toxic waste to cleaning up spills of oil and other contaminants. Typically, his firm works on contracts with organizations both public and private, but occasionally Jim is called upon to deal with situations not covered by existing contracts.

This morning Jim received a phone call from the police in a nearby town. They asked for his firm's assistance in dealing with an oil spill that threatened a nearby river. Jim drove to the site with four of his associates, and within an hour the team of five had obtained the following picture of what happened.

While filling an oil tanker, the driver had gone into the cab and had fallen asleep. Before it was noticed, 10,000 gallons of crude oil had escaped and begun making its way five miles downstream and was within four hours of reaching a wildlife sanctuary.

Although the potential for environmental damage is clear, the liability is not. The driver was an employee of a small subcontractor who was uninsured and who would be forced into bankruptcy, if deemed liable. The oil company contacted its insurance company, which denied any responsibility for claims that might be made against it. Representatives of the State Environmental Protection Agency and Department of Fish and Game were contacted, and they offered their moral support, but neither had the half million dollars Jim estimated would be necessary to contain and clean up the spill.

A decision must be made soon about whether to risk the company's money in a matter in which reimbursement, if any, may have to be decided by the courts. The decision is Jim's to make, and he is experienced in making the difficult judgments that are called for. Although conscientious, the members of his team lack this experience and are likely to look to him for direction. Nonetheless, they will have to carry out any action, and Jim has found that their involvement in decisions helps them to work together as a team.

Jim Burns' challenge raises two general issues relevant to solving problems and making decisions in organizations. The first issue involves determining what solution or decision should be adopted. In this case should Jim begin the cleanup or defer any action pending resolution of the liability issues? It is this facet of decision making that is the focus of most business school curricula and of the optimization models developed by management scientists. (To be sure, the nature of this particular problem complicates matters further by the introduction of a potential conflict between organization goals and broader social concerns.)

The second issue revolves around not *what* should be decided but *how* and with *whom* it should be decided. Should Jim decide himself, or should he involve the team in some way in determining what decision would be made? In this second issue, theories of decision making intersect with theories of leadership style.

LEADERSHIP STYLE

It is the latter perspective that has interested my colleagues and me and has become the focus of a large-scale program of research at Yale. We are interested in what happens between a leader and the leader's associates in decision-making situations. Our interest was inspired by an article by Bob Tannenbaum and Warren Schmidt. Their work distinguished seven different styles, varying in influence by the manager and the size of the area of freedom afforded subordinates.

Being a believer in parsimony, I have collapsed some of their alternatives, resulting in five styles that are labeled Decide, Consult Individually, Consult Group, Facilitate, and Delegate. Definitions of each of these styles were given to forty specialists in the field of organization development. The specialists were then asked to locate the styles on a 10-point scale, corresponding to the relative

EXHIBIT 1 **Vroom's Adaptation of Tannenbaum and Schmidt's Taxonomy**

0	**3**	**5**	**7**	**10**
Decide	**Consult Individually**	**Consult Group**	**Facilitate**	**Delegate**
You make the decision alone and either announce or "sell" it to the group. You may use your expertise in collecting information that you deem relevant to the problem from the group or others.	You present the problem to the group members individually, get their suggestions, and then make the decision.	You present the problem to the group members in a meeting, get their suggestions, and then make the decision.	You present the problem to the group in a meeting. You act as facilitator, defining the problem to be solved and the boundaries within which the decision must be made. Your objective is to get concurrence on a decision. Above all, you take care to ensure that your ideas are not given any greater weight than those of others simply because of your position.	You permit the group to make the decision within prescribed limits. The group undertakes the identification and diagnosis of the problem, developing alternative procedures for solving it, and deciding on one or more alternative solutions. While you play no direct role in the group's deliberations unless explicitly asked, your role is an important one behind the scenes, providing needed resources and encouragement.

Area of Freedom for Group

Influence by Leader

opportunities for influencing the decision that they were likely to provide to group or team members. The definitions of these five processes, adapted from Tannenbaum and Schmidt, and the mean-scale values assigned by the OD professionals, are shown in Exhibit 1.

This language for describing leadership styles can be used in two distinctly different ways. It can be the starting point for the development of a *normative* model that would help managers or leaders to select the style that best fits a given situation. Like our predecessors, we are convinced that each of the styles is appropriate to certain kinds of situations, and that an effective leader is one who explicitly tailors his or her style to demands of the immediate problem at hand.

The taxonomy of leadership styles in Exhibit 1 can also be used to describe what people do. A common vocabulary, independent of its normative uses, may be helpful in communication and setting of expectations between leaders and their colleagues. Furthermore, these concepts can be used

by social scientists in developing a descriptive model aimed at understanding how managers actually decide whether and when to share their decision-making power.

Over the last two decades, my colleagues and I at Yale have conducted a program of research designed to provide us with a normative model that can be used by managers in evaluating specific decisions that they face and in selecting the most effective leadership style of each. The result has been the development of an "expert system" that shows substantial promise in helping managers through the myriad of factors that need attention in deciding when and how to involve associates in making decisions. In addition, we have made progress in developing a descriptive model of what managers' decision-making practices actually do. Our studies, which now involve over 100,000 managers, have been aimed at understanding the factors that actually influence what managers do. Specifically, we have looked at such factors as organizational level, cultural influences, and the role of gender in leadership style. This article outlines the normative model first, and then examines our progress in understanding its similarities to, and differences from, what managers actually do.

TOWARD A NORMATIVE MODEL

DECISION QUALITY

Let us first examine what is at stake in the choice of how much and in what way to involve others in solving problems and making decisions. The first, and undoubtedly the most important, is the quality of the decision. Above all we want wise, well reasoned, and analytically sound decisions that are consistent with the goals to be achieved and with potentially available information about the consequences of alternative means of achieving them.

What happens to decision quality as one moves from the autocratic process to more participative processes? Undoubtedly the nature of the decision and its quality will change as we move across the scale. But will decision quality increase or decrease? A conservative answer, and one that we believe to be consistent with the available research evidence, is that the effects of participation on decision quality depend on certain observable features of the decision-making situation. It depends on where the relevant knowledge or expertise resides, that is, in the leader, in the group, or both. It depends on the goals of the potential participants, particularly on the extent to which group or team members support the organizational objectives embedded in the problem. Finally, the amount of synergy exhibited in team-based processes depends on the skills and abilities of team members in working together effectively in solving problems.

DECISION IMPLEMENTATION

Although the quality of the decision may be the most important component of its effectiveness, it is not the only component. Many high-quality decisions have been ineffective because they were not effectively implemented. The effectiveness with which a group or team implements a decision can be shown to depend on the extent to which they are committed to its success. Here the evidence is clearer and less equivocal. People do support what they help to build. Under a wide range of conditions, increasing participation leads to greater "buy-in," commitment to decisions, and motivation to implement them effectively. To be sure, there are some situations in which the motivational benefits

of greater commitment are nonexistent or irrelevant to implementation. Sometimes the team may not be playing a role in implementation; in other situations, the team may view the leader as the expert or as a person with the legitimate right to make the decision and, as a result, may fully support whatever decision the leader might make.

COSTS OF DECISION MAKING

Apart from considerations of decision quality and implementation, which determine the effectiveness of the decision, there are considerations of efficiency relevant to the decision process. Use of any decision-making process consumes resources. At the same time it can add to resources, albeit of a different kind. The resources consumed are costs and principally involve the time "used up" in the decision-making process. Increasing the amount of participation will increase the elapsed time to make the decision and, to an even greater degree, increase the number of hours consumed by the process. Both of these meanings of time constitute liabilities of participative leadership styles. Seeking consensus slows down the process and consumes substantially more hours than the directive or even consultative methods of decision making. The first of these costs, increasing the time interval between the occurrence of a problem and obtaining a solution, is most relevant in emergencies where a quick or immediate response is necessary. The second consideration, the hours consumed, is more generally relevant.

DEVELOPMENT

Potentially offsetting these costs are developmental benefits of increased participation. Moving from the autocratic to highly participative styles increases the potential value of the group or team to the organization in three ways: (1) It develops the knowledge and competence of individual members by providing them with opportunities to work through problems and decisions typically occurring at higher organizational levels. (2) It increases teamwork and collaboration by providing opportunities to solve problems as part of a team. (3) It increases identification with organizational goals by giving people "a voice" in making significant decisions in *their* organizations. These developmental benefits may be negligible when the decision lacks significance, that is, when the issue being decided is trivial and lacks consequences to the organization. Furthermore, the development benefits may be of negligible value if the group or team members have a nonexistent or tenuous future within the broader organization.

We term a style inefficient when it wastes time without a commensurate return in development. Conversely, it is efficient when it is used judiciously in precisely those situations in which sufficient developmental benefits are realized. It is interesting to note that costs (time) and development, the two components of efficiency, are realized at different points in time. The time costs are immediately realizable. The slowness of response and the number of hours consumed in a group meeting have immediate effects. In contrast, the growth and development of individuals and team may not pay off for a substantial period of time.

PUTTING IT ALL TOGETHER

So far our inquiry has led us to identify four outcomes of participation, each of which is contingent on one or more situational factors. To be useful to leaders, we must supplement our analysis with a suitable tool for synthesizing the effects that we have postulated. Exhibits 2 and 3 depict decision matrices that constitute such a tool. In Exhibit 2 we show the Time-Driven Model. It is short-term in its orientation, being concerned with making effective decisions with minimum cost. No value is placed on employee development.

In contrast, Exhibit 3 shows the Development-Driven Model. It may be thought of as a long-term model, because it is concerned with making effective decisions with maximum developmental consequences. No value is placed on time.

To use one of these two models, you must have a decision problem in mind that has two properties. First, it must fall within your area of freedom or discretion, that is, it must be up to you to decide. Second, there must be some identifiable group of others who are potential participants in the decision.

One enters the matrix at the left-hand side, at "Problem Statement." Arranged along the top of the matrix are seven situational factors, each of which may be present (H for high) or absent (L for low) in that problem. To obtain the recommended process, you first ascertain whether the decision to be made is a significant one. If so, you select H and answer the second question, concerning the importance of gaining commitment from the group. Continuing this procedure (avoiding the crossing of any horizontal line) will bring you to a recommended process. Sometimes a conclusive determination can be made based on as few as two factors (e.g., L, L); others require three (e.g., L, H, H), four

(e.g., H, H, H, H), or as many as seven factors (e.g., H, H, L, L, H, H, H).

Submitting the same problem to both the Time-Driven and Development-Driven Model can be instructive. Sometimes the two models yield identical recommendations. Where they differ, the Development-Driven Model recommends a higher level of participation. Occasionally, the difference may be greater than one position on the participation scale. For example, in the Jim Burns case with which this article began, the Time-Driven Model recommends Decide (H, H, H, H) and the Development-Driven Model recommends Consultation with the Group (H, H, H, H, L).

Although the situational factors that identify the columns in Exhibits 2 and 3 are sufficient for the experienced user of these matrices, a less experienced user may wish to refer to explanations of the situational factors in Exhibit 4. To practice using the models, read each of the four cases in Exhibit 5. Underneath each case, we have shown the recommended actions made by the two models, along with the path by which these recommended actions are obtained.

WHERE DID THE MODEL COME FROM?

The model is an outgrowth of 25 years of research on leadership and decision-making processes. We began by collecting cases from managers of successful and unsuccessful decisions and ascertaining which decision process they used on each. If the decisions were unsuccessful, we wanted to find out why, whether it could have been avoided, and if so, how. Our goal was to build a model that would maximize the frequency of successful decisions, while avoiding as many of the unsuccessful ones as possible. Early on, we were joined by social scientists operating in various parts of the world, which helped us to test our concepts. We were somewhat encouraged by the findings (based on six separate studies conducted in three different countries): decisions made in accordance with a decision tree on which we were working at the time were almost twice as likely to be successful as were decisions that were inconsistent with the model.

But these investigations also made it clear that we had a long way to go, so we continued our efforts to extend and refine our early work. Now we have developed a complex set of equations that show great promise in forecasting the consequences of participation on quality, implementation, cost, and

EXHIBIT 2
Time-Driven Model

Instructions: The matrix operates like a funnel. You start at the left with a specific decision problem in mind. The column headings denote situational factors which may or may not be present in that problem. You progress by selecting High or Low (H or L) for each relevant situational factor. Proceed down from the funnel judging only those situational factors for which a judgment is called for until you reach the recommended process.

Decision Significance	Importance of Commitment	Leader Expertise	Likelihood of Commitment	Group Support	Group Expertise	Team Competence	
H	H	H	H	-	-	-	Decide
			L	H	H	H	Delegate
						L	Consult (Group)
					L	-	Consult (Group)
				L	-	-	Consult (Group)
		L	H	H	H	H	Facilitate
						L	Consult (Individually)
					L	-	Consult (Individually)
				L	-	-	Consult (Individually)
			L	H	H	H	Facilitate
						L	Consult (Group)
					L	-	Consult (Group)
				L	-	-	Consult (Group)
	L	H	-	-	-	-	Decide
		L	-	H	H	H	Facilitate
						L	Consult (Individually)
					L	-	Consult (Individually)
				L	-	-	Consult (Individually)
L	H	-	H	-	-	-	Decide
			L	-	-	H	Delegate
						L	Facilitate
	L	-	-	-	-	-	Decide

P R O B L E M S T A T E M E N T

development. The decision matrices shown in Exhibits 2 and 3 are derived from the use of these equations and are the simplest way in which the implications of the model can be shown *on paper*. However, the full power of the model is better revealed in a computer program that allows much more complexity and precision whereas, at the same time, is easier to use. Contained on a CD-ROM, the program has a number of features not possible in a decision matrix. These include: (1) using eleven situational factors, rather than the seven shown in the matrices, (2) permitting five

EXHIBIT 3
Development-Driven Model

Decision Significance	Importance of Commitment	Leader Expertise	Likelihood of Commitment	Group Support	Group Expertise	Team Competence	
H	H	-	H	H	H	H	Delegate
				H	H	L	Facilitate
				H	L	-	Consult (Group)
				L	-	-	Consult (Group)
			L	H	H	H	Delegate
				H	H	L	Facilitate
				H	L	-	Facilitate
				L	-	-	Consult (Group)
	L	-	-	H	H	H	Delegate
				H	H	L	Facilitate
				H	L	-	Consult (Group)
				L	-	-	Consult (Group)
L	H	-	H	-	-	-	Decide
			L	-	-	-	Facilitate
	L	-	-	-	-	-	Decide

(left side of table labeled vertically: PROBLEM STATEMENT)

possible responses, corresponding to the degree to which situational factors are present, (3) incorporating the Value of Time and Value of Development as situational factors, rather than portraying them as separate matrices, and (4) guiding managers through the process of analyzing the situations they face with definitions, examples, and other sources of help.

We have found by observing managers' use of the model on problems they are currently facing on their jobs that the model's recommendations can be affected by the way in which the problem is framed. For example, if the problem is seen as a deficiency within the team, efforts to find a solution are less likely to be affected than if the problem is located in the situation. Accordingly, we have provided a

EXHIBIT 4   Situational Factors in the Normative Model

DECISION SIGNIFICANCE:	The significance of the decision to the success of the project or organization.
IMPORTANCE OF COMMITMENT:	The importance of team members' commitment to the decision.
LEADER'S EXPERTISE:	Your knowledge or expertise in relation to this problem.
LIKELIHOOD OF COMMITMENT:	The likelihood that the team would commit itself to a decision that you might make on your own.
GROUP SUPPORT FOR OBJECTIVES:	The degree to which the team supports the organization's objectives at stake in this problem.
GROUP EXPERTISE:	Team members' knowledge or expertise in relation to this problem.
TEAM COMPETENCE:	The ability of team members to work together in solving problems.

EXHIBIT 5   Applying the Matrices to the Sample Cases

Setting: Banking; Your Position: President & Chief Executive Officer	Setting: Repertory Theater; Your Position: Executive Director	Setting: Auto Parts Manufacturer; Your Position: Country Manager	Setting: Manufacturer of Internal Combustion Engines; Your Position: Project Manager
The bank examiners have just left, insisting that many of your commercial real estate loans be written off, thereby depleting already low capital. Along with many other banks in your region, your bank is in serious danger of being closed by the regulators. As the financial problems surfaced, many of the top executives left to pursue other interests, but fortunately, you were able to replace them with three highly competent younger managers. While they had no prior acquaintance with one another, each is a product of a fine training program with one of the money center banks in which they rotated through positions in each of the banking functions.

Your extensive experience in the industry leads you to the inevitable conclusion that the only hope is a two-pronged approach involving reduction of all but the most critical expenses and the sale of assets to other banks. The task must be accomplished quickly since further deterioration of the quality of the loan portfolio could result in a negative capital position forcing regulators to close the bank.

The strategy is clear to you, but you have many details that will need to be worked out. You believe that you know what information will be needed in order to get the bank on a course for future prosperity. You are fortunate in having three young executives to help | You are the executive director of a repertory theater affiliated with a major university. You are responsible for both financial and artistic direction of the theater. While you recognize that both of these responsibilities are important, you have focused your efforts where your own talents lie—on insuring the highest level of artistic quality to the theater's productions. Reporting to you is a group of four department heads responsible for production, marketing, development, and administration, along with an assistant dean who is responsible for the actors who are also students in the university. They are a talented set of individuals, and each is deeply committed to the theater and experienced in working together as a team.

Last week you received a comprehensive report from an independent consulting firm commissioned to examine the financial health of the theater. You were shocked by the major conclusion of the report. *"The expenses of operating the theater have been growing much more rapidly than income, and by year's end the theater will be operating in the red. Unless expenses can be reduced, the surplus will be consumed, and within five years the theater might have to be closed."*

You have distributed the report to your staff and are surprised at the variety of reactions that it has produced. Some dispute the | Your firm has just acquired a small manufacturer of spare auto parts in Southeast Asia. The recent collapse in the economies in this region made values very attractive. Your senior management decided to acquire a foothold in this region. It was less interested in the particular acquired firm, which produces parts for the local market, than it was in using it as a base from which to produce parts at reduced cost for the worldwide market.

When you arrived at your new assignment two weeks ago, you were somewhat surprised by the less than enthusiastic reception that you received from the current management. You attribute the obvious strain in working relations not only to linguistic and cultural differences but also to a deep-seated resentment to their new foreign owners. Your top management team seem to get along very well with one another, but the atmosphere changes when you step into the room.

Nonetheless, you will need their help in navigating your way through this unfamiliar environment. Your immediate need is to develop a plan for land acquisition on which to construct new manufacturing and warehouse facilities. You and your administrative assistant, who accompanied you from your previous assignment, should be able to carry out the plan, but its development would be hazardous without local knowledge. | Your firm has received a contract from one of the world's largest automobile manufacturers to produce an engine to power their "flagship" sports car. The engine is of Japanese design and is very complex not only by American but by world standards. As project manager, you have been involved in this venture from the outset, and you and your team of engineers have taken pride at the rave reviews the engine has received in the automotive press. Your firm had previously been known as a producer of outboard engines for marine use, and its image is now greatly enhanced as the manufacturer of the power plant of one of the world's fastest sports cars.

Your excitement at being a part of this project was dashed by a report of serious engine problems in cars delivered to customers. Seventeen owners of cars produced in the first month have experienced engine seizures—a circumstance which has caused the manufacturer to suspend sales, to put a halt to current production, and to notify owners of this year's production not to drive their cars! Needless to say, this situation is a disaster and unless solved immediately could expose your firm to extended litigation as well as terminate what had been a mutually beneficial relationship. As the person most informed about the |

(continued)

EXHIBIT 5 (*continued*)

you out. While they have had little or no experience in working together you know that each is dedicated to the survival of the bank. Like you, they know what needs to be done and how to do it.	report's conclusions criticizing its assumptions or methods. Others are more shaken, but even they seem divided about what steps ought to be taken and when. None of them or, in fact, anyone connected with the theater would want it to close. It has a long and important tradition both in the university and in its surrounding community.		engine, you have spent the last two weeks on the road inspecting several of the seized engines, the plant in which they are installed, and reviewing the practices in your own company's plant in which the engine is manufactured. As a result of this research, you have become convinced that the problem is due to operation of the engine at very high RPM's before it has warmed up to develop sufficient oil pressure. The solution would be to install an electronic control limiting engine RPM's until the engine has reached normal operating1 temperature.

ANALYSIS
TIME DRIVEN:
  H H H L H H L—CONSULT GROUP
DVPT DRIVEN:
  H H L H H L—FACILITATE
	ANALYSIS
	TIME DRIVEN:
	  H H L L H H H—FACILITATE
	DVPT DRIVEN:
	  H H L H H H—DELEGATE
		ANALYSIS
		TIME DRIVEN:
		  H L L L—CONSULT INDIVIDUALLY
		DVPT DRIVEN:
		  H L L—CONSULT GROUP
			ANALYSIS
			TIME DRIVEN:
			  H H H H—DECIDE
			DVPT DRIVEN:
			  H H H H L—CONSULT GROUP

help screen for "testing" a manager's framing of the problem, to make sure that it has been defined in a way that is likely to be productive. In addition, we have found in this rapidly changing world that groups defined by a common manager may not be the most effective for solution of organizational problems. Thus, the software provides a help screen called Team Formation, which provides advice on making up a group to solve a particular problem or make a particular decision.

WHAT DETERMINES MANAGERS' STYLES?

TOWARD A DESCRIPTIVE MODEL

To study managerial styles (as they are, rather than how our models say they should be), we have developed an innovative measuring device that we term a problem set. It consists of a set of 30 cases, each depicting a manager faced with a decision to make. Exhibit 5 gives examples of some of the shorter cases from a typical set. Cases are based on real situations. Each has been condensed to fit on a single page, providing information on the manager's role,

the organizational context, the decision that has to be made, the group of persons that the manager is considering involving, and so on.

The set of cases covers the whole gamut of managerial decisions. Titles include "Saving a Savings Bank," "Trimming Expense Accounts," "Relocating the Head Office," and so forth. However, the cases are not randomly selected. Rather, they vary with respect to the critical factors that the model deems highly relevant to choice of leadership style. Each of the factors contained in the decision matrices shown in Exhibits 2 and 3 is varied across the set of cases, and each is varied independently of each other factor. This latter feature, which statisticians refer to as a multifactorial experimental design, is most important, because it permits determining which of the relevant factors influences each individual manager, in what way, and to what degree. Thus, the problem set becomes a powerful diagnostic tool capable of revealing "the manager's model," that is, the way in which each individual manager responds to decision-making situations.

Although we originally developed the problem set as a research tool, we discovered early on that managers enjoyed and benefited from the experience of thinking through how they would deal with highly different situations, and attempting to make sense out of the different choices they made. To aid in the learning that was resulting from this measuring instrument, we have developed a Java-based computer program that could quickly analyze a manager's choices and produce a five-page individualized report comparing him or her with peers and with the models, both time-driven and development-driven. Furthermore, due to the power of the statistical design underlying the problem set, we are able to show each manager how his or her choices were influenced by each of the situational factors used in the decision matrices. Each manager's individualized analysis also shows how well his or her choices are likely to result in decisions that are (1) of high quality, (2) would be effectively implemented, (3) were economical in use of time, and (4) would have favorable developmental consequences on their team.

Here we will focus not on what *managers have learned* from having a mirror held up to them but rather what *we have learned from managers* about how they go about deciding when and where to share their decision-making power. In a world in which it is common to label managers with terms like autocratic or participative or Theory X or Theory Y, it was instructive to see that managers make different choices in different situations. In fact, it makes somewhat more sense to talk about autocratic and participative situations than autocratic or participative managers do. The differences in behavior among managers are about one-third of the size of the differences among situations.

Managers behave situationally. They adapt their behavior to the situations they face. Furthermore, the kinds of situations that evoke autocratic and participative styles are very similar to those in which the normative model would recommend such styles. Each of the seven situational factors shown at the top of Exhibits 2 and 3 affects the average manager in roughly the same way as they affect the behavior of the model. Managers make more participative choices on highly significant decisions, when they need the commitment of the group, when they lack the expertise, when the likelihood of commitment to *their* decision is low, when the group's expertise is high and when the group has a history of working together effectively.

But not all managers behave that way! Some are influenced by only one or two of these factors and seem to ignore the rest. Still others are affected by one of these factors, but in what we believe to be the wrong way. For example, one fifth of the U.S. managers that we have studied (and three quarters of all managers from Poland) are more likely to involve others in insignificant, trivial decisions.

One of the most important functions of the feedback is to draw each individual's attention to those aspects of the situation that they are overlooking. We should make it clear that the model not only responds to the seven situational factors, but also does so configurally. Thus, the effects of one factor depend on the level of certain other factors. For example, where the knowledge resides (in the leader or in the group or both or neither) has more effect on leadership style in highly significant decisions than in those of lesser significance.

Of great interest to us is the fact that managers also behave configurally. There is evidence in our data that managers attend to combinations of factors rather than being influenced by each factor separately. However, these effects are less strong among managers than in the model, suggesting that only a small number of managers behave that way or that, in the typical manager, the configural effects are small in relation to those that are linear.

We said earlier that the situational effects dwarfed the differences among individual managers. Although that statement is true, it does not imply that differences among managers in their typical or overall behavior are insignificant or inconsequential. If one averages the choices of a manager on the 30 cases, one obtains a mean score that reflects, on average, where he or she stands on the scale shown in Exhibit 1. We turn now to consider some of the things that we have found to correlate with differences in where people stand on our 10-point scale of participation.

The first factor is *when* people took the test! Our data have been collected over a 25-year period, and throughout most of that period we have observed an increase in the use of the more participative processes on that scale. Something seems to be producing a move toward higher involvement, more participation, greater empowerment, and more frequent use of teams over time. We do not know precisely what is producing this, but we suspect that it reflects changes in (1) the external environment of organizations (greater rates of change, greater complexity), (2) the flattening of the pyramid (greater spans of control resulting in difficulties in hierarchical control), (3) the growth of information technology, making it easier to get information closer to the occurrence of problems, and (4) the changing nature of the labor force (higher education, higher needs for independence, etc.). Of the demographic factors, the culture in which the organization functions accounts for the greatest variance.

High involvement managers are more likely to be found in countries with high per capita GNP, with a strong democratic tradition and with a highly educated work force.

We have also investigated gender differences and have found women managers to be significantly more participative than their male counterparts. Supporting this conclusion, we have found sizeable differences in the reactions to autocratic men and autocratic women managers. In general, being participative is valued by direct reports, but this is truer for women than for men. Participative men and women are equally valued, but autocratic males are strongly preferred to autocratic women.

A third demographic factor that correlates with leadership style as measured by our problem sets is level in the organization. In each organization that we have studied in depth, the higher the level in the organizational ladder, the more participative the manager. To be sure, we have never carried our investigation up to the level of the CEO, where we cannot rely on sample size and the law of large numbers to cancel out chance factors due to personality or to measurement.

We should point out that our findings are restricted to what managers say they would do on a standardized set of cases. Although managers have no incentive to lie (because it will only decrease the accuracy of the computer feedback that they alone will receive), we have no guard against self-deception. As a possible check on such tendencies, we have given the same problem sets to both the manager and to his or her direct reports. The latter are asked to describe how their manager would respond to each case. The result is striking. Virtually all managers are seen by their direct reports as closer to the left side of that scale than they see themselves. We have referred to this difference as the autocratic shift. We do not know whether the biases are in managers' conceptions of themselves, the perceptions of them held by their direct reports, or both.

CONCLUSION

Historically, the people dimension of management has been viewed as basically intuitive, clinical, and "touchy-feely." The kinds of analytical approaches that are customary in finance, operations, and to a lesser degree, strategy, have not been applied, or even viewed as applicable to issues of behavior. We have violated that norm and have sought to apply analytical methods to the development of better normative and descriptive tools for understanding leadership style. We will be the first to admit that our model is far from perfect. We ignore deliberately what style managers are "good at," what they are accustomed to practicing, and what they are encouraged to use in their "organizational culture." We do this because we believe that what worked in the past is not a guarantee of success in the future. We believe that leadership styles deserve a fresh look.

At Yale and in other environments, when I teach the model presented in this paper and provide people with computer feedback on their own leadership style, I stress that both are intended to stimulate reflection, and self-examination. They are not tools to be slavishly embraced and used in all decisions. I believe that much of the behavior that is currently driven by habits needs to be converted back into choices. The changing demands of today demand that we reexamine the styles we used in the past and reassess their appropriateness to today's environment.

Selected Bibliography

The original inspiration for this body of work may be found in an article written in the *Harvard Business Review* by Bob Tannenbaum and Warren Schmidt ("How to Choose a Leadership Pattern," *Harvard Business Review,* 1958, 99–101).

My initial work on leadership was done with Philip Yetton (*Leadership and Decision Making,* University of Pittsburgh Press: 1973). Subsequently I collaborated with Arthur G. Jago in writing *The New Leadership* (Prentice-Hall: 1988).

Those who wish to learn more about the specific findings cited, or the computer programs that are referred to in this article, may contact me at victor.vroom @yale.edu or at The Yale School of Management, 135 Prospect Street, P.O. Box 208200, New Haven, CT 06520-8200.

Leadership in the Cross-cultural Context

The vast majority of the contemporary scholarship directed toward leaders and the leadership process has been conducted in North America and Western Europe. Observing the volume of theory and research that has emerged around the concept of leadership over the past several decades led James R. Meindl and his colleagues (Sanford B. Ehrlich and Janet M. Dukerich, 1985)[1] to suggest that "we may have developed a highly romanticized, heroic view of leadership" (pp. 30–31). Leaders have come to occupy center stage in organizational life. We use leaders in our attempts to make sense of organizational behavior. They are seen as the key to organizational success and profitability, they are credited for organizational competitiveness, and they are the focus of blame in the face of organizational failure. This larger-than-life role ascribed to leaders and the Western romanticized affair with successful leaders raises questions as to how representative our understanding of leadership is across other cultures. That is, do leadership theory and research results generalize from one culture to the next?

Research into culture has generally addressed two questions. First, there has been an interest in whether or not there are significant leadership differences across cultures. Thus, it might be asked whether culture gives rise to leadership differences. The second question treats culture as a key contextual variable. A driving question in this stream of inquiry asks whether or not the effectiveness of leadership (e.g., leader behavior) is *culture-specific*.

It seems logical to ask, Why might culture make a leadership difference? *Culture*, according to Hofstede (1980), is defined as the collective programming of the mind that distinguishes the members of one human group from another. According to House, Wright, and Aditya (1997),[2] others have defined it as a system of meanings placed on events (Smith & Peterson, 1994);[3] a patterned way of thinking, feeling, and reacting (Kluckhohn, 1951);[4] and norms, roles, belief systems, and values that form meaningful wholes for an individual or group of people (Triandis, 1982).[5] Empirical evidence (e.g., Hofstede, 1993, 1980) reveals that different groups of people from around the world possess different values and belief systems.

---

[1] J. R. Meindl, S. B. Ehrlich, & J. M. Dukerich, "The Romance of Leadership," *Administrative Science Quarterly* 30 (1985), pp. 78–102.

[2] R. J. House, N. S. Wright, & R. N. Aditya, "Cross-cultural Research on Organizational Leadership: A Critical Analysis and a Proposed Theory." In P. C. Earley & E. Miriam (eds.), *New Perspectives on International Industrial/Organizational Psychology*. (San Francisco: The New Lexington Press/Jossey-Bass Publishers, 1997), pp. 535–625.

[3] P. B. Smith, & M. F. Peterson, *Leadership as Event Management: A Cross-cultural Survey Based on Managers from 25 Nations.* Paper presented at the meeting of the International Congress of Psychology, Madrid.

[4] C. Kluckhohn, "Culture and Behavior," *Handbook of Social Psychology* (1951), pp. 921–976.

[5] H. C. Triandis, "Review of Culture's Consequences: International Differences in Work-related Values." *Human Organization* 41 (1982), pp. 86–90.

Within the leadership context, cultural differences shape the beliefs, attitudes, opinions, preferences, and behaviors of those who lead and of those who make the decision to follow or not. As a consequence, "expected, accepted, and effective leadership varies by culture" (House & Aditya, 1997, p. 454). Cultural values tend to give rise to implicit theories of leadership (i.e., culturally based stereotypes, convictions, assumptions, beliefs, expectations that define, for example, *how* leaders are to act). For example, they might reflect what is expected of leaders in terms of their proactiveness versus reactiveness; their orientation toward vision, change, risk, direction; and the use of inducements (e.g., rewards, punishment, role modeling, position, rationality) to move others to action.

Reviews of the cross-culture leadership literature are provided by House, Wright, and Aditya (1997); Dorfman (1996),[6] which was updated by Dorfman (2003),[7] and Dickson, Den Hartog, and Mitchelson (2003).[8] In addition to their review of the literature, House and his colleagues (1997) provide us with a theory of cross-cultural leadership.

Geert Hofstede's (1993, 1980) work provides a useful framework for the identification and classification of cultural differences. Hofstede's work spans over two decades, involving more than 150,000 people and cutting across 60 countries.[9] He identifies five value dimensions that can be employed to explain differences in leadership (i.e., leader traits and behaviors) that might cut across cultures. These value frameworks (and the countries in which they are dominant) consist of:

- Individualism–Collectivism

Individualism is a mental set in which people see themselves first as individuals and believe their own interests and values take priority (Canada, Great Britain, and the United States).

Collectivism reflects the feeling that the group or society should receive top priority (Hong Kong, Greece, Japan, and Mexico).

The self-assessment appearing at the end of this chapter opener provides you with the opportunity to profile yourself in terms of your individualistic/collectivistic values (general guiding principles for behavior).

- Power Distance

Power distance reflects the extent to which members of a social system accept the notion that members have different levels of power.

High power distance suggests that leaders make decisions simply because they are the leaders (France, Japan, Spain, and Mexico).

Low power distance suggests that social system members do not automatically acknowledge the power of a hierarchy (Germany, Israel, Ireland, and the United States).

- Uncertainty Avoidance

Low uncertainty avoidance is reflected by people who accept the unknown and tolerate risk and unconventional behavior (Australia, Canada, and the United States).

[6] P. W. Dorfman, "International and Cross-cultural Leadership Research." In B. J. Punnett & O. Shenkar (eds.), *Handbook for International Management Research* (Oxford, UK: Blackwell, 1996), pp. 267–349.
[7] P. W. Dorfman, "International and Cross-cultural Leadership Research." In B. J. Punnett & O. Shenkar (eds.), *Handbook for International Management Research* (2nd ed.) (Ann Arbor: University of Michigan Press, 2003).
[8] M. W. Dickson, D. N. Den Hartog, & J. K. Mitchelson, "Research on Leadership in a Cross-cultural Context: Making Progress and Raising New Questions," *Leadership Quarterly* 14 (2003), pp. 729–768.
[9] G. Hofstede, *Cultural Consequences: International Differences in Work-related Values* (Beverly Hills, CA: Sage, 1980). See also *Organizational Dynamics* (Spring 1993), pp. 53–61, for an interview with G. Hofstede by R. Hodgetts.

High uncertainty avoidance is characterized by people who want predictable and certain futures (Argentina, Israel, Japan, and Italy).

- Masculinity–Femininity

Masculinity refers to an emphasis on assertiveness and the acquisition of money and material objects, coupled with a deemphasis on caring for others (Italy and Japan).

Femininity places an emphasis upon personal relationships, a concern for others, and a high quality of life (Denmark and Sweden).

- Time Orientation

Long-term orientation is characterized by a long-range perspective coupled with a concern for thrift and weak expectations for quick returns on investments (Pacific Rim countries).

Short-term orientation is characterized by demands for immediate results and a low propensity to save (Canada and the United States).

On the basis of their review of the cross-cultural leadership literature published since 1996 and their application of Hofstede cultural values framework, Dickson et al. (2003) offer the following observation:

> research shows that power distance in society has an impact on different aspects of leadership. People tend to prefer leadership that is more egalitarian when power distance is low. Where power distance is high, leaders tend to be less participative and more authoritarian and directive. Such directive leadership is also more effective in a high power distance context. In addition, a stronger emphasis on the use of rules and procedures is seen when power distance is high and people are more inclined to gain support from those in authority before carrying out new plans.

It would be useful for you as a student of leadership to think about and formulate your own hypotheses and rationale for the connection between each of the other values in Hofstede's framework, and leadership needs and styles.

In the first reading in this chapter, Peter W. Dorfman and his colleagues Jon P. Howell, Shozo Hibino, Jin K. Lee, Uday Tate, and Arnoldo Bautista (1997) look at commonalities and differences in effective leadership processes across a set of Western and Asian countries. Dorfman et al. find that three leader behaviors (i.e., supportive, contingent reward, and charismatic) appear across different cultural settings, while three behaviors (i.e., directive, participative, and contingent punishment) appear to be culturally specific in terms of their linkage with leader effectiveness. The effects of contingent punishment are unique in that this behavior has a desirable effect in only one of the Western countries (the United States) and in neither of the two Asian countries studied. Leaders who demonstrate supportive kindness and concern for followers are valued and effective in each of the countries studied. Leader contingent reward behavior is highly effective in the more collectivistic Asian cultures—as it often is in Western countries.

The second reading, by Hugo Zagorsek, Marko Jaklic, and Stanley J. Stough (2004), explores the impact of culture on leadership practices. The authors employ Hofstede's (1980) typology to explore whether or not effective Western leadership practices are effective in two countries that are both culturally and economically different from the United States. The five leadership practices examined are *challenging process, inspiring a shared vision, enabling others to act, modeling the way,* and *encouraging the heart*. At the conclusion of their investigation, Zagorsek and his colleagues note that "culture does matter. But its impact is not as strong as is commonly thought. Maybe the world is actually becoming a 'global village' after all" (p. 31). Their concluding comment is an interesting one, and one that runs counter to a normative view. It is also one that needs confirmation before it is automatically (blindly) accepted.

The readings in this and the preceding chapter sensitize us to the contextual factors with which leaders need to contend. Specifically, Hofstede (1993), Dorfman et al. (1997), and Zagorsek et al. (2004) alert us to the fact that *not all followers will have the same belief and value orientation.* These differences clearly have leader and leadership implications. Our earlier reading by Murphy (1941) suggests that leadership is a function of an interaction between the leader, the situation, and the follower. In the next chapter, we will focus on the follower in the leadership process. We will want to carry into those readings an understanding of the individual differences that are produced by cultures and differential belief or value systems.

Figure 9.1 adds to our evolving mosaic yet another significant component that adds to the complexity of the different contexts (situations) creating follower demands and demands upon the leader. The two readings in this chapter illuminate the importance of culture-imposed values, expectations, and demands.

FIGURE 9.1
The Leadership Process: Critical Contextual Factors

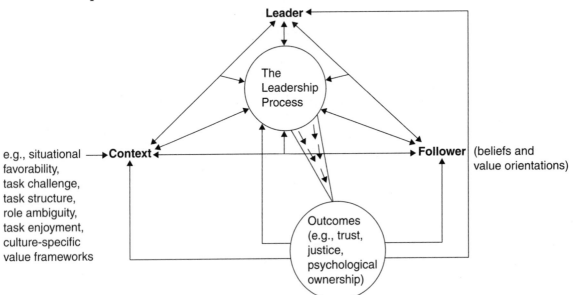

Individualism–Collectivism

Instructions: Different social groups (e.g., family, friends, colleagues, and strangers) surround us. Focus upon those individuals whom you consider to be *your colleagues* (e.g., team/group members, coworkers, classmates). Then consider each of the following 25 statements and indicate its degree of importance.

EXERCISE
Self-Assessment

	Not at All Important						Very Important
	0	1	2	3	4	5	6
How Important Is It:							
1. To comply with direct requests from your colleagues?	0	1	2	3	4	5	6
2. To maintain self-control toward your colleagues?	0	1	2	3	4	5	6
3. To maintain status differences between you and your colleagues?	0	1	2	3	4	5	6
4. To share credit for accomplishments of your colleagues?	0	1	2	3	4	5	6
5. To share blame for failures of your colleagues?	0	1	2	3	4	5	6
6. To respect and honor traditions and customs among your colleagues?	0	1	2	3	4	5	6
7. To be loyal to your colleagues?	0	1	2	3	4	5	6
8. To sacrifice your goals for your colleagues?	0	1	2	3	4	5	6
9. To sacrifice your possessions for your colleagues?	0	1	2	3	4	5	6
10. To respect elder colleagues?	0	1	2	3	4	5	6
11. To compromise your wishes to act together with your colleagues?	0	1	2	3	4	5	6
12. To maintain harmonious relationships among your colleagues?	0	1	2	3	4	5	6
13. To nurture or help your colleagues?	0	1	2	3	4	5	6
14. To maintain a stable environment (e.g., maintain the status quo) among your colleagues?	0	1	2	3	4	5	6
15. To accept your position or role among your colleagues?	0	1	2	3	4	5	6
16. To follow advice regarding major decisions from your colleagues?	0	1	2	3	4	5	6
17. To exhibit "correct" behaviors (i.e., proper manners and etiquette), regardless of how you really feel, toward your colleagues?	0	1	2	3	4	5	6
18. To exhibit "correct" emotions, regardless of how you really feel toward your colleagues?	0	1	2	3	4	5	6
19. To be like or similar to your colleagues?	0	1	2	3	4	5	6
20. To accept awards or recognition based only on age or position rather than merit from your colleagues?	0	1	2	3	4	5	6
21. To cooperate with your colleagues?	0	1	2	3	4	5	6
22. To communicate verbally with members of your colleagues?	0	1	2	3	4	5	6
23. To "save face" of the members of your colleagues?	0	1	2	3	4	5	6
24. To follow norms established by your colleagues?	0	1	2	3	4	5	6
25. To identify yourself as a member of your colleagues?	0	1	2	3	4	5	6

Scoring: Sum your answers to questions 1 through 25 and divide by 25. A low score (1 and less) reflects an individualistic orientation within this particular context. A high score (5 and greater) reflects a collectivistic orientation as it pertains to the set of colleagues upon whom you focused your attention.

My individualism/collectivism score is: _____

(continued)

Interpretation: Individualism–collectivism (IC) is one of the most popular dimensions employed by cross-cultural psychologists to explain and predict differences across cultures. At the cultural level of analysis, IC refers to the degree to which a culture "encourages, fosters, and facilitates the needs, wishes, desires, and values of an autonomous and unique self over those of a group" (Matsumoto et al., 1997, p. 744). Individuals within an individualistic culture tend to see themselves as separate and autonomous individuals, while their counterparts in a collectivistic culture see themselves as fundamentally connected to others. Individual needs and goals take precedence in individualistic cultures, whereas they are sacrificed to satisfy the needs of the group in a collectivistic culture.

It should be noted that many cross-cultural psychology scholars (e.g., Triandis, McCusker, and Hui, 1990)[1] have suggested that an individual's IC should manifest differently in different contexts. Thus, an individual could have a collectivistic orientation at home and with close friends (in-group) and an individualistic orientation within the work context (out-group).

Individualism/collectivism has been linked to a number of factors important to leader and group behavior. Earley (1989), for example, hypothesized and observed that social loafing (i.e., the reduced performance displayed by individuals when they act as a part of a group rather than when they are acting alone) is more likely to occur among individuals who hold individualistic rather than collectivistic beliefs.[2] "Social loafing should not appear in a collective society, however, since an individual is motivated by in-group goals rather than self-interest" (p. 568). Based upon these tendencies it might be hypothesized that leaders with collectivistic beliefs might be more likely to take an in-group self-orientation.

Source: D. Matsumoto, M. D. Weissman, K. Preston, B. R. Brown, and C. Kupperbausch, "Context-Specific Measurement of Individualism–Collectivism on the Individual Level: The Individualism–Collectivism Interpersonal Assessment Inventory," *Journal of Cross-Cultural Psychology* 28, no. 6 (1997), pp. 743–767. Copyright 1997, Sage Publications, Inc. Reprinted by permission of Sage Publications, Inc.

[1] H. C. Triandis, C. M. McCusker, & C. H. Hui. "Multi-Method Probes of Individualism and Collectivism." *Journal of Personality and Social Psychology* 59 (1990), pp. 1006–1020.
[2] P. C. Earley, "Social Loafing and Collectivism: A Comparison of the United States and the People's Republic of China," *Administrative Science Quarterly* 34 (1989), pp. 565–581.

Reading 25

Leadership in Western and Asian Countries: Commonalities and Differences in Effective Leadership Processes Across Cultures

Peter W. Dorfman
Jon P. Howell
New Mexico State University

Shozo Hibino
Chukyo University

Jin K. Lee
Korea University

Uday Tate
Southeastern Louisiana University

Arnoldo Bautista
Rural Development Directorship

INTRODUCTION

It has become an axiom among international researchers that effective management and leadership processes must reflect the culture in which they are found (Ayman, 1993; Smith & Peterson, 1988). Unique cultural characteristics such as language, beliefs, values, religion, and social organization are generally presumed to necessitate distinct leadership approaches in different groups of nations—popularly known as culture clusters (Hofstede, 1993; Jackofsky, Slocum, & McQuaid, 1988; Ronen & Shenkar, 1985; Triandis, 1993a). Researchers who adhere to this culture-specific position often cite the individualistic nature of the United States as support for the argument that leadership theories developed in the United States are limited in their applicability to different cultures (Adler, 1991; Hofstede, 1980, 1993; Smith & Peterson, 1988; Triandis, 1993b). Some recent writers have pointed out, however, that universal tendencies in leadership processes *also* exist—the culture universal position (Bass & Avolio, 1993; Dorfman & Ronen, 1991; Fahr, Podsakoff, & Cheng, 1987; Wakabayashi & Graen, 1984).

Bass (1990) has shown that both of these two perspectives—culture-specific versus culture-

universal—have demonstrated validity for practitioners and researchers alike. Construct development and research methods employed, however, often differ between those researchers who subscribe more to the culture-specific approach than those who acknowledge the possibility of culture universals. The culture-specific perspective, which is consistent with an "emic" or insider approach to construct development (Berry, 1980), reflects the view that certain leadership constructs and behaviors are likely to be unique to a given culture. In-depth emic studies that are culture-specific provide descriptively rich information about how leadership constructs are enacted in those cultures. In support of this position, Smith et al. (1989) found that the specific expression or enactment of basic leader functions of midlevel managers vary according to cultural constraints. At the executive level, research also indicates that successful CEOs often employ leadership styles consistent with society's cultural values (Jackofsky, Slocum, & McQuade, 1988).

The culture-universal position, in contrast, is consistent with an "etic" or outside imposed perspective that certain leadership constructs are comparable across cultures. In order to explore the universalist position, an etic methodology is employed whereby comparative studies are carried out among various cultures to empirically test potentially generalizable leadership hypotheses. In

Source: Edited and reprinted from *Leadership Quarterly* 8, 3, 233–274. Copyright 1997, with permission from Elsevier.

support of this "universalist" position, researchers have reported findings that show commonalities in leadership patterns across widely varying cultures. For instance, a literature review by Smith and Peterson (1988) showed the general leader behavior patterns of task- and relationship-oriented behaviors, which have been prominent in many U.S. leadership models, were effective in studies of collectivist cultures. *Our approach in this study employed both the emic and etic perspectives—emic culture-based predictions were developed regarding the incidence and impact of etic dimensions of leaders' behavior within a theoretically sound contingency model of leadership.* Thus the overall thrust of the research project reported here was to extend contingency theories of leadership to include national culture as an important situational variable.

LEADERSHIP THEORY

Until recently, the major focus of leadership research in the United States has been on contingency theories that have attempted to specify the organizational circumstances under which particular leader behavior patterns are most effective (cf., Fiedler & Garcia, 1987; Indvik, 1986; Vroom & Jago, 1988). A careful reading of the leadership literature and recent summaries demonstrates that much has been learned by contingency theory researchers (Fiedler & House, 1988; Indvik, 1986; Yukl & Van Fleet, 1992). These researchers have shown that situational factors play a critical role in determining when a particular leader behavior is most effective. Contingency leadership theories thus provide an appropriate theoretical framework for this study because they were designed primarily to test leadership impacts in different situations and contexts. The primary contextual variable in this study is national culture.

We attempted to avoid the universalist bias of simply testing a specific U.S.-made theory abroad (Boyacigiller & Adler, 1991). Instead, we chose two well-known contingency models—House's path-goal theory and Yukl's multiple linkage model—and we created a syncretic model of leadership based on these two theories. Behling and McFillan (1993) have described syncretic models as combining and integrating similarities among existing models. Admittedly, our syncretic model was developed within a "Western" context. Yet the leadership constructs employed in our model have been employed in leadership models by non-Western researchers (e.g., Misumi

& Peterson, 1985b; Sinha, 1980) and have been studied in some cross-cultural contexts (reviewed by Dorfman, 1996). Our objective at this stage was to develop a model with variables and processes that had sound theoretical and research bases as well as potentially wide application across cultures.

House's path-goal theory of leadership is a midrange theory designed to predict subordinates' motivation, satisfactions, and performance (House, 1971). In addition to an extensive research base in the United States (Indvik, 1988), it has been found useful in leadership research in different cultures (Al-Gattan, 1985; Dorfman & Howell, 1988). Yukl's multiple linkage model (1994) is a metatheory that is designed to predict work group performance. Although the complexity of the multiple linkage model makes it difficult to test in its entirety, it is probably the most comprehensive contingency theory developed to date (Yukl & Van Fleet, 1992). In addition to being carefully developed by excellent scholars, these two models possess several characteristics that make them attractive as the basis for a model of leadership behaviors in different cultures. First, both models include etic leader behaviors that can be identified and described in all the cultures studied. Second, the leader behaviors have been widely researched in the United States and to some degree in other cultures. Third, both models incorporate mediator variables to help track the causal impacts of leadership behaviors on outcomes. Fourth, these models systematically incorporate situational moderator variables in their predictions. A weakness of these and other contingency models is that they neglect to include culture as a key type of moderator variable. Figure 1 describes the syncretic leadership model used in this study. This model is briefly described, followed by a justification of the relationships depicted in the model.

Figure 1 shows the leadership process as a set of causal leader behavior variables that impact followers' job satisfaction and role ambiguity—representing mediators in this model. The mediators are the most immediate results of a leader's behavior. Organizational commitment and job performance are outcome variables in the model. Job satisfaction and role ambiguity are shown affecting organizational commitment (Williams & Hazer, 1986) as well as job performance. Although the satisfaction-performance relationship in the U.S. literature is not strong, recent meta-analysis research indicates that the relationship is positive,

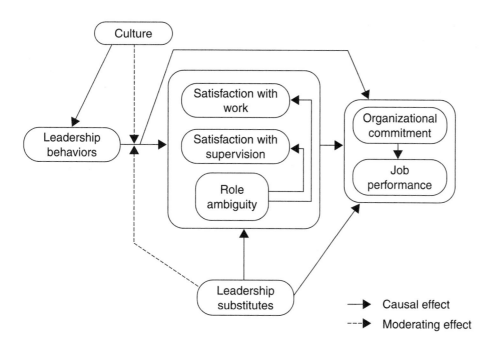

FIGURE 1
Theoretical Model of Leadership Processes

and when using the best satisfaction measures (e.g., Job Descriptive Index), correlations are approximately in the .30 range (Iaffaldano & Muchinsky, 1985; Ostroff, 1992).

To our knowledge, the link between satisfaction and performance has not been investigated systematically in non-Western countries. Job performance and commitment are also directly affected by leader behaviors (because this model does not attempt to include an exhaustive list of mediators). Finally, job performance is influenced by organizational commitment. Leadership substitutes moderate leadership effects and have direct effects on mediators and outcome variables. (We have chosen not to test for "substitutes for leadership" in this project because of the complexity of our study due to the multiplicity of data sets.) Culture is also an overall moderator of leadership effects and is shown to have a direct effect on the behaviors exhibited by leaders.

Viewing leader behaviors as causal variables is consistent with contingency leadership theories and most cross-cultural leadership research (Misumi & Peterson, 1985a, 1985b; Smith & Peterson, 1988). The actual leader behaviors used in this study are *directive, supportive, participative, contingent reward and punishment,* and *charismatic* behaviors. Each of these has shown potential importance in cross-cultural research, has been claimed by researchers to be universally important across cultures, and/or is used by managers and management trainers abroad (Al-Gattan, 1985; Ayman & Chemers, 1983; Bass & Avolio,

1993; Bass & Yokochi, 1991; Bond & Hwang, 1986; Dorfman, 1996; Dorfman & Ronen, 1991; Dorfman & Howell, 1988; Fahr, Podsakoff, & Cheng, 1987; House, 1991; Misumi & Peterson, 1985b; Sinha, 1980). Showing culture as a causal variable affecting the level of leader behaviors is consistent with existing models of cross-cultural management (Bass, 1990; Negandhi & Prasad, 1971), and its role as a moderator in Figure 1 is implicit in much cross-cultural leadership research (Misumi & Peterson, 1985b; Smith, Peterson, Bond, & Misumi, 1992). . . .

FIVE COUNTRIES

Five countries in the Asian-Pacific Basin were studied—Japan, South Korea, Taiwan, Mexico, and the United States. The five countries were chosen for two reasons. First, they are major players in a growing economic bloc called the Asian-Pacific Basin. Second, they represent considerable cultural variation on numerous dimensions such as individualism/collectivism, uncertainty avoidance, power distance, degree of industrialization, paternalism, and Eastern versus Western attitudes toward work and authority (Hofstede, 1991; Ronen & Shenkar, 1985). Our goal was to obtain two samples of respondents from North America (the United States and Mexico) and match these samples with the three major ethnic cultures in the Asian-Pacific Rim. Because of their cultural variation and the current interest in business issues in the Pacific Rim, we believe these cultures are theoretically and practically valuable contexts in which to test the transferability of general dimensions of leadership behavior.

LEADERSHIP IN JAPAN

Japan is the second largest trading partner with the United States, and it may be a unique culture within the Pacific Rim, being higher in masculinity and uncertainty avoidance and only medium on collectivism in comparison to South Korea and Taiwan (Dorfman & Howell, 1994; Hofstede, 1991). Confucianism in Japan requires respect and obedience to leaders who have historically responded with highly paternalistic attitudes toward their subordinates, expressed by *mendou* ("I think about you; I will take care of you"). Japanese organizations are extremely hierarchical and are rigidly organized (Chen, 1995), yet helping and caring for followers and being involved in their personal lives is expected of Japanese managers (Whitehall & Takezawa, 1968; Bass, Burger et al., 1979). The Japanese *sempai-kohai* mentor relationship system reinforces a close personal bond between supervisors and subordinates (Chen, 1995).

The ideal leadership model in Japan comes from early village leaders who were skillfully unassertive and who led by implicit consensus, nonverbal communication, and indirect discussions ("Too much talk was bad"). Japanese managers typically outline general objectives, make vague group assignments, and generally let subordinates use their own approaches to achieve overall objectives. The phrase *omakase* ("I trust you, you can do it") reflects this approach. Although only medium on collectivism, Asian scholars describe the Japanese as placing strong emphasis on group harmony and collective (not individual) responsibility (e.g., Hayashi, 1988). The Japanese tendency for collective decision making and extensive consultation through the ringi system of decision making is also well noted (Chen, 1995). We expect these complex forces to cause *supportive and participative* leadership to be highly impactful, and *directive* leadership to be impactful to some extent in Japan.

An emphasis by managers on equality of all group members also supports group harmony, which is usually considered more important than making money or overall productivity (Bass, 1990). Individuals are not singled out in Japan for praise or criticism ("The nail which sticks out gets pounded down"). Compliments and criticism are usually directed at the group; individual criticism is not conveyed openly, but may be directed at the individual after the workday is over. *Leader contingent punishment* behavior is therefore predicted to have no positive impact and may have a negative impact in Japan. However, since leader contingent reward behavior has been found impactful in other Asian cultures (Fahr et al., 1987) and since Japanese leaders do control recognition and symbolic exchanges with followers (often shown over long periods through promotions and/or added responsibilities), *leader contingent reward* behavior is predicted to have a positive impact on followers in Japan.

Charisma is important for top-level managers in Japan, who represent a symbol of respected authority and may be called "mini-emperors." The main functions of senior management in Japan include establishing an overall theme, developing strategy, and engaging in high-level external relations (Morgan & Morgan, 1991). Other managers in Japanese organizations are considered part of their group, not separate from the group as is often the case with charismatics. Japanese managers also do not view themselves as risk-takers, another characteristic often attributed to charismatic leaders (Bass, 1985). We therefore expect *charismatic leader behaviors* to have little or no impact in this Japanese sample of middle managers and professionals. Based on the considerations discussed above, we present the following hypothesis:

> **Hypothesis 1.** In Japan, directive, supportive, contingent reward and participative leader behaviors will positively affect mediators and/or outcome measures; contingent punishment will have no positive impact, and may have a negative impact on the same criteria. Charismatic leader behaviors will have no significant effects.

LEADERSHIP IN SOUTH KOREA

South Korea continues to develop rapidly and represents an important manufacturing competitor to the United States and Japan. Its high collectivism and medium/high uncertainty avoidance make it culturally akin to Taiwan (Dorfman & Howell, 1994; Hofstede, 1991). South Korea is perhaps more heavily influenced by Confucianism than other Asian countries. The Confucian code of ethical behavior includes maintenance of harmonious relationships and trust as the basis of business activities. A social order emphasizes respect and obedience to senior individuals, who, in turn, assume responsibility for the well being and future of the young. Absolute loyalty to the ruler (or company president) is required (Steers, Shin,

& Ungson, 1989). These factors result in leaders who assume a personal interest in the welfare and development of followers and who emphasize group harmony and smooth, conflict-free interpersonal relations (Steers et al., 1989). While harmony *(inhwa)* is desirable, it is based on inequality among those of differing rank, power, and prestige (Alston, 1989). Thus, followers' responsiveness to their leaders is heavily reinforced by strong Confucian mandates of respect and obedience to leaders who maintain and care for their followers. Combining these values with generally vague job descriptions and training results in leaders with considerable power to direct activities. Based on these observations, we predict *supportive and directive leadership* to be highly impactful in South Korea.

Centralized planning and control and strong directiveness are clearly evident in the *chaebols,* which are large diversified companies, primarily owned and managed by founders and/or family members, which dominate South Korean business. Perhaps because of highly centralized and formalized organizational structures, key information is normally concentrated at the top organizational levels in South Korea. Top-down decision making style is typical with subordinates taking a passive role in communications (Chen, 1995). Although a recent survey reported South Korean executives expressing the importance of an "environment for voluntary participation," subordinates have difficulty in expressing views contrary to those of their supervisors. We predict, therefore, that *participative leadership* will have little or no impact in South Korea.

There is a clear emphasis on collective, rather than individual, achievement in South Korea (Hofstede, 1980; Steers et al., 1989) and differentiating rewards among individuals is believed to disturb the needed harmony. These factors argue against leader contingent reward behavior in South Korea. However, the contingent reward scale used in this study measures social rewards only (e.g., compliments and recognition). A survey of executives showed that South Koreans prefer recognition to tangible rewards (Hayashi, 1988), and leader contingent reward behaviors have been found impactful in other cultures characterized by Confucianism (Fahr et al., 1987). We therefore expect *leaders' contingent reward behavior* to have a positive impact in South Korea. In contrast, because negative feedback may undermine harmonious relations, managers often evaluate subordinates leniently and will temper criticism if the individual puts forth reasonable effort (Chen, 1995). The

combination of trying to preserve the internal peace and harmony of others *(kibun)* and not conveying bad news or news someone does not wish to hear leads us to predict that *leaders' contingent punishment behavior* will have no impact in South Korea.

South Korean corporations are highly entrepreneurial in spirit. Successful South Korean entrepreneurs enunciate a clear and convincing vision of their business goals to obtain government-assisted loans and, like Chairman Kim of Daewoo, they aggressively pursue their vision. The charisma of Chairman Chung of Hyundai was evident when he personally inspired subordinates to believe in their new (and eventually successful) shipbuilding venture, in spite of expert opinion that it would fail. Family ownership, importance of personal loyalty, and combined ownership/management of South Korean companies suggest that charismatic leadership should be impactful in South Korea. We offer the following summary hypothesis for South Korea:

> **Hypothesis 2.** In South Korea, directive, supportive, charismatic, and contingent reward leader behaviors will positively affect mediators and/or outcome measures; contingent punishment and participative leader behaviors will have no significant impacts.

LEADERSHIP IN TAIWAN

Taiwan reflects the prosperous "overseas" Chinese culture found in many areas of the Pacific Rim. Hofstede (1980) also reported the Chinese to be very high on collectivism and Dorfman and Howell (1988) found them high on both collectivism and paternalism. The Confucian norm of deference to rank *(wu-lun)* is strong, with followers preferring clear-cut directions from kind, "human-hearted" leaders *(jen)* who care about followers (Redding, 1990; Hsu, 1982). Most overseas Chinese business and management practices are based on the family business model—even large-scale business operations usually follow this cultural norm. According to Redding (1990), the managerial philosophy can be summarized by the word "patromonialism"—indicating themes such as paternalism, hierarchy, familialism, mutual obligation, personalism, and connections. Ingratiation of leaders (providing compliments, conformity in opinions and behavior, gift-giving) is common by followers and is called *enhancing others' face.* Hsu (1982) found that Chinese subordinates prefer a leadership style where the leader maintains a harmonious considerate relationship with followers while being directive. Hsu (1982) found that leader initiating structure correlated positively with Chinese followers' job satisfaction and that subordinates preferred leaders who define clear-cut tasks for each member of the group. We therefore expect *supportive and directive leadership* to be highly impactful among the Taiwanese workers sampled.

In a comparative study of beliefs about management behavior, Redding and Casey (1976) found Chinese managers distinctly more authoritarian and autocratic than Western managers, especially regarding sharing information with subordinates and allowing them to participate in decision making. Open discussion about decision-making processes tends to be viewed as a challenge to the leader's authority and is therefore not done (Redding & Casey, 1976). Subordinates typically assume the leader has considered all relevant factors prior to making a decision. A large power distance is maintained by the boss (Chen, 1995). One Chinese executive pointed out a weakness in Chinese organizations that very little input is obtained from employees. We therefore expect *participative leadership* to have no positive impact in Taiwan.

In Chinese organizations, control is achieved through conformity, nepotism, and obligation networks *(guanxi),* not through performance contingent rewards and punishments (Redding & Wong, 1986). Judgment of a person's worth is based on loyalty rather than ability or performance against objective criteria (Chen, 1995). Chinese culture urges avoidance of confrontation which is sometimes considered uncivilized behavior. Preserving others' face in social encounters is important so supervisors usually do not point out others' mistakes directly. They typically use vague or moderate language to protect the face of those being criticized. Fahr, Podsakoff, and Cheng (1987) found that punishment behavior of any kind has significant dysfunctional effects on subordinate performance in Taiwan. In contrast to punishing behaviors, recent studies of overseas Chinese (Fahr, Podsakoff, & Cheng, 1987) indicate that performance contingent rewards may play a positive role in Chinese organizations. We therefore expect *leaders' contingent punishment behavior* to have a negative impact in our Taiwanese sample, but *leaders' contingent reward behavior* will have a positive impact.

Redding (1990) has pointed out that managerial leadership among overseas Chinese is primarily transactional, not charismatic. Subordinates are expected to exhibit loyalty, diligence, conformity, and behaviors that enhance the superiors' face. This psychological contract governing the superior–subordinate relationship is a direct reflection of the Confucian family social structure which is based on filial piety *(hsiao).* The loyalty and devotion of subordinates derives from cultural dictates, not from an inspirational, charismatic leader. However, leaders at the very top of an organization may create a vision that inspires followers. One example was Mao Tse-tung, who also endeavored to replace the Confucian social structure with a socialistic structure, but overseas Chinese have not generally accepted the socialistic structure. And the individuals in our Taiwanese sample are supervisors, middle managers, and professional workers—not top level managers. We therefore expect that *charismatic leadership* will have no significant impact on followers in the Taiwanese sample. The following hypothesis summarizes our predictions for Taiwan:

> **Hypothesis 3.** In Taiwan, directive, supportive, and contingent reward leader behaviors will positively affect mediators and/or outcome measures; contingent punishment will have a negative impact on mediators and/or outcome measures. Participative and charismatic leader behaviors will have no significant effects.

LEADERSHIP IN MEXICO

Mexico's high collectivism, paternalism, power distance, and masculinity seems to resemble the Asian culture cluster more than its neighbor the United States (Dorfman & Howell, 1988; Hofstede, 1991). Its Spanish/Indian history of authoritarian and omnipotent leaders has been enacted via the autocratic *patrón* and compliant follower roles which pervade Mexican society (Riding, 1985). Mexican society today still functions through relationships of power where status differences predominate. Mexico is also highly paternalistic (Dorfman & Howell, 1988; Farmer & Richman, 1965), and the compliant role of subordinates reinforces the strong directive leader. High collectivism and paternalism in Mexico encourages a caring, supportive type of leadership. Kakar (1971) and Ayman and Chemers (1983) found supportive leadership to have positive impacts on the attitudes of Mexican workers. We thus expect both *directive and supportive leadership* to be highly impactful in Mexico.

The authoritarian tradition in Mexico still resists incursions of Western liberalism, including seeking input from all levels for decision making. Participative leadership, as practiced in Western Europe and North America, requires individualistic followers, trusting relationships between managers and followers, and a firm structure for participation (Hofstede, 1980; Riding, 1985). None of these conditions are present in Mexican culture which is highly collectivist, nontrusting, and elitist without a history or framework for wide participation in organizational processes. Marrow (1964) reported that participative leaders in Latin America were viewed as weak and caused increased turnover as followers deserted a leader they deemed destined to fail. We therefore predict that *participative leadership* will not be impactful in Mexico.

Leaders' contingent reward and punishment behaviors seem well suited for individualistic cultures like the United States, not collectivist cultures like Mexico. However, recall that Mexican society functions through relationships of power and influence. In organizations, control of rewards and punishments are major reflections of one's power. Bass (1990) concluded that leaders' contingent punishment behavior was impactful in high power distance cultures. However, qualitative research with focus groups in Mexico (conducted as part of GLOBE leadership project; House et al., 1994) revealed that the prototypical "good leader" will not offend or embarrass others but will maintain respect and interact with others in a culturally sensitive manner *(simpatico)*. These limited, and somewhat contradictory observations, lead us to expect leaders' *contingent reward behavior* to have positive impacts but *contingent punishment behaviors* to have no significant impact on followers in Mexico.

Mexican history is filled with revolutionary charismatic leaders whose names are continuously honored and celebrated. Current political leaders often adopt key Mexican charismatics from the past as "spiritual" advisors (Riding, 1985). These historical figures are strongly masculine and possess a high degree of power. Bass (1990) predicted that charismatic leadership would be especially impactful in collectivist cultures. We therefore expect *charismatic leadership* to have a strong impact on Mexican followers. The following hypothesis is based on the information presented above:

> **Hypothesis 4.** In Mexico, directive, supportive, contingent reward, and charismatic leader behaviors will positively affect mediators and/or outcome measures. Participative leadership and contingent punishment will have no significant effects.

LEADERSHIP IN THE UNITED STATES

The United States is culturally unique in comparison to the other countries sampled in this study. Hofstede (1980) described the United States as highly individualistic, low on power distance and uncertainty avoidance, and medium on masculinity. Dorfman and Howell (1988) reported the United States as medium on paternalism. These cultural factors make the expected leadership impacts somewhat distinct for the U.S. sample. Also, in contrast to the other cultures sampled for this study, there are clearer lines of leadership research in the United States from which to make predictions.

Supportive leadership has shown consistently strong positive relationships with followers' satisfaction and organizational commitment as well as moderate to strong relationships with followers' role ambiguity and performance in the United States (Indvik, 1986). These findings may reflect the moderate masculinity and low power distance scores for the U.S. culture. Directive leadership has also been important in U.S. organizations, with meta-analyses reporting strong positive relationships with measures of follower satisfaction and role ambiguity and moderate positive relationships with follower performance (Podsakoff, Tudor, & Schuler, 1983). Yet, these impacts are heavily moderated by many organizational and individual follower characteristics (Yukl, 1994). Kerr and Jermier (1978) suggested that workers who are highly experienced, educated, and professional will have less need for traditional directive leader behaviors in carrying our their job tasks. This may be particularly true of the managerial/ professional sample in this study. Smith and Peterson (1988) and Hofstede (1980) pointed out that the extremely high individualism in the United States strongly supports participative management processes. For these reasons, we expect *supportive and participative leadership* to have a high degree of impact, but *directive leadership* to have no significant impact on followers in the U.S. sample.

Rewards and punishments contingent on individual performance also reflect the high individualism and high achievement motivation that characterizes U.S. workers (McClelland & Boyatzis, 1982). Podsakoff and his associates (1992) have consistently demonstrated positive effects for contingent reward behavior in the United States. Leaders' contingent punishment behavior has also demonstrated positive impacts on follower attitudes in several U.S. samples. *Leader contingent reward and punishment behaviors* are therefore expected to have positive impacts in the U.S. sample, although contingent reward behavior will likely have the strongest impact.

Much of the leadership research conducted in the United States in the last decade has focused on charismatic leadership. Numerous books and empirical studies have demonstrated its importance and prevalence at all levels in U.S. organizations (Bass, 1990). The high achievement orientation of U.S. workers, especially managers and professionals, will also likely cause followers to respond well to charismatic leader behaviors. We thus expect *charismatic leader behavior* to be highly impactful in the U.S. sample. The following hypothesis summarizes our predictions for the United States.

> **Hypothesis 5.** In the United States, supportive, contingent reward, contingent punishment, participative, and charismatic leadership will positively affect mediators and/or outcome measures. Directive leadership will have no significant effects. . . .

METHOD

Field studies were conducted in each of the five countries to test the hypotheses. The research samples consisted of a total of 1,598 managers and professionals of large multinational or national companies located in the United States, Mexico, and the Asian-Pacific Basin. The United States, Mexican, and Taiwanese samples consisted entirely of managers and professionals working in electronics manufacturing operations. Large manufacturing organizations were studied because they represent the primary avenue for economic growth for the Asian-Pacific countries, and they provide intense market competition for U.S. manufacturers. Focusing on managers and professionals allowed us to provide some control for job duties and responsibilities across the cultures. The organizations were matched closely in terms of technological sophistication, organizational goals, and structure. The majority of the Japanese and South Korean samples were also engaged in complex manufacturing operations. All respondents were highly skilled and educated, with the majority of each sample having college degrees. . . .

MEASURES

Predictors—Leadership Behaviors

The following six patterns of leadership behavior were measured:

1. Directive—Clarifying performance expectations and assigning tasks. This was a modified version of the scale developed by Schriesheim (1978) for use in path-goal theory testing.

2. Supportive—Indicating a concern for the welfare of subordinates; showing warmth, respect, and trust. This scale was also developed by Schriesheim (1978).

3. Contingent reward—Developed by Podsakoff and Skov (1980), this scale assesses the degree to which leaders provide praise, positive feedback, and recognition contingent on high performance.

4. Contingent punishment—Voicing displeasure and providing negative feedback contingent on poor performance. This scale was also developed by Podsakoff and Skov (1980).

5. Charisma—Inspiring and developing confidence among followers, setting challenging goals, and encouraging high expectations. This scale was modified from scales developed by House (personal communication, 1987) and Yukl (1982) to encompass many of the dimensions in current models of charismatic leadership.

6. Participation—Consulting with, asking for suggestions, and obtaining information from subordinates for important decisions. This scale was also modified from scales developed by Yukl and House and reflects common interpretations of participative leadership in the management literature. . . .

Results in Japan

Two of the four predictions of significant positive effects were supported—*supportive leadership* increased satisfaction with supervision and satisfaction with work; *contingent reward behavior* increased satisfaction with supervision and organizational commitment. Also as predicted, *contingent punishment* had a negative impact on satisfaction with supervision. *Participative and direct leadership* were not impactful in the Japanese sample (counter to our predictions). Also counter to our prediction, *charismatic leadership* did significantly reduce subordinates' role ambiguity. Note that supportive leadership and contingent reward behaviors both had multiple significant paths and strong effect sizes. . . .

Results in South Korea

Hypothesis 2 for South Korea was supported for three of four predictions of significant effects.

Contingent reward behavior improved satisfaction with work; *supportive leadership* increased satisfaction with supervision and reduced role ambiguity. *Charismatic leadership* improved satisfaction with supervision and organizational commitment. Also as predicted, *contingent punishment* had no effects. Counter to our predictions, *participative leadership* slightly improved satisfaction with work and *directive leadership* had no effects. Charismatic and supportive leadership both had multiple significant paths and strong effect sizes.

Results in Taiwan

All six leader behaviors had significant effects in Taiwan, although the three leader behaviors predicted to be significant in Hypothesis 3 were among the strongest impacts. *Leader directiveness* increased satisfaction with supervision and organizational commitment and decreased role ambiguity; *contingent reward behavior* increased satisfaction with work and supervision; and *supportive leadership* increased satisfaction with supervision and organizational commitment. Although *contingent punishment* had a negative impact on satisfaction with supervision (as predicted), it had a positive effect on organizational commitment (not as predicted). Contrary to expectations, *charismatic leadership* increased satisfaction with work and supervision and decreased role ambiguity. The effect of *participative leadership* was most interesting as it had a significant *negative* impact on organizational commitment. Perhaps also noteworthy, Taiwan was the only country where all leader behaviors were impactful.

Results in Mexico

Results in Mexico supported predictions for the leader behaviors expected to have a positive effect. *Directive leadership* increased organizational commitment and decreased role ambiguity; *contingent reward behavior* increased organizational commitment; *supportive leadership* increased satisfaction with supervision, organizational commitment, and decreased role ambiguity. *Charismatic leadership* increased satisfaction with supervision. Directive and supportive leadership had strong impacts as did charismatic leadership and contingent reward. The effect of *participative leadership* was nonsignificant as predicted. *Contingent punishment* yielded a significant negative effect (on satisfaction with supervision) when we predicted no effect. Hypothesis 4 was thus supported for 5 of the 6 leader behaviors.

Results in the United States

The predictions for hypothesis 5 were supported for five of the six leader behaviors, providing strong support for this hypothesis in the United States. *Contingent reward behavior* increased organizational commitment and satisfaction with work and supervision; *contingent punishment behavior* decreased role ambiguity; *supportive leadership* increased satisfaction with supervision and decreased role ambiguity; and *charismatic leadership* increased satisfaction with supervision. As expected, *directive leadership* had no impact. *Participative leadership* also had no impact, contrary to predictions. Supportive, charismatic, contingent reward, and leaders' contingent punishment all had strong effects. Note that contingent punishment significantly decreased subordinates' role ambiguity without the negative effects found in several other countries. . . .

DISCUSSION

LEADERSHIP ACROSS CULTURES

The results of this study in two Western and three Asian cultures support Bass's (1990) contention regarding the validity of both the "universal" and the "culture-specific" perspectives in the study of leadership across cultures. *Of six leader behaviors derived from popular contingency-based leadership theories, three behaviors (leader supportiveness, contingent reward, and charismatic) showed universally positive impacts in all five cultures; and three leader behaviors (participativeness, directiveness, and contingent punishment) had positive impacts in only two cultures.* The impact of contingent punishment was most unique among leader behaviors as it had a completely desirable effect only in the United States, but equivocal or undesirable effects in other countries. Overall, results from the independent and simultaneous tests supported our original "syncretic leadership model" which guided this study of individuals in different cultures.

The universality of leader supportiveness and contingent reward behavior are not surprising when one considers their specific content. Supportive leaders show concern for followers and are considerate and available to listen to followers' problems. Contingent rewarding leaders show appreciation for followers' good performance and provide recognition and compliments. The correlation between these two behaviors was .65 or above in all five cultures (leaders who are concerned and considerate are also often seen as appreciative and complimentary), and there was overlap between these two behavior patterns in the factor analyses for the three Asian cultures. A leader who demonstrates supportive kindness and concern for followers is clearly valued and impactful in all the cultures (Bennett, 1977; Misumi & Peterson, 1985A; Yukl, 1994). Reward systems in collectivist cultures are usually described as group-oriented (Hofstede, 1980; Bond & Hwang, 1986), but apparently performance contingent social rewards by the leader are individualized even in collectivist cultures with very positive results. These findings support the results by Fahr, Podsakoff, and Cheng (1987) that leader contingent reward behavior is a highly culture-free leadership pattern.

The universality of charismatic leadership was not expected. This leader behavior is emotional in nature and had its most consistent effects on subordinate satisfaction measures across cultures. It appears that charismatic leadership results in positive subordinate attitudes among midlevel managers and professionals in all the cultures studied. We should note that charismatic leadership *did not* affect follower performance in the three countries where performance data was available.

The impacts of leaders' directive, participative, and contingent punishment behaviors were culture-specific. Directive leadership had no impact in the United States, Japan, and South Korea. We expected the extremely high individualism and low/medium power distance of the U.S. culture, combined with the participative climate common among highly educated professionals and managers in U.S. organizations, to at least partially *neutralize* the effects of leaders' directiveness. This apparently occurred, making directiveness the only leader behavior that was not impactful in the U.S. sample. Although the lack of impact of leader directiveness in Japan is not consistent with findings by Misumi and Peterson (1985b), it might be explained by tendencies of Japanese managers to outline general objectives and to allow subordinates to use their own approaches to achieve those objectives. We have no explanation for the lack of impact of directiveness in South Korea. For Taiwan, the results showing a high impact of directive leadership . . . are mirrored when examining the high *level* of directive leadership displayed. This leader behavior had the highest level of all leader behaviors (i.e., mean scale score) in Taiwan, and it was considerably higher than in any other country in our sample. These findings are consistent with the review of leader-

ship studies in Taiwan by Bond and Hwang (1986). As expected, leader directiveness was a very important leader behavior in the status conscious and high power distance culture of Mexico.

Participative leadership had positive effects in the United States and South Korea. Our participation scale included items such as asking followers for suggestions, giving consideration to followers' inputs, and modifying proposals in light of follower objections. These items resulted in predictable positive responses in the United States. In fact, participative leadership in the U.S. sample was the strongest predictor of follower performance in the entire study. In addition, the *level* of participation displayed by supervisors in the United States was the highest of all samples. Although not predicted, a positive impact of participation on subordinate satisfaction was found in South Korea. This may be explained by the increasing tendency of South Korean managers to make decisions with the consultation of subordinates (Chen, 1995). This process involves informal consensus formation *(sajeonhyupui)* and is similar to *nemawashi* in Japan. We should note, however, that openly sharing information and expressing opinions in a work environment is difficult for many South Koreans.

Participation was also predicted to have no positive impacts in Taiwan and Mexico due to their military histories emphasizing strong central leadership and their low individualism (high collectivism) which discourages individual desires to impact organizational processes. These predictions were supported. Taiwanese managers tend to carefully control information, use authoritarian decision styles, and maintain power distances with their subordinates. In Mexico, the lack of a firm structure for participation, high collectivism, and lack of trust make participative leadership ineffective.

We did predict participation to be impactful in Japan which is known for high worker involvement *(nemawashi)* and group decision making *(ringi seido)* (Chen, 1995; Ronen, 1986). In hindsight, perhaps we should have expected that, because the type of worker involvement practiced in Japan is different from the type of participative leadership practiced in the United States, results would also differ. In our discussions with Japanese managers, they pointed out that in Japan managers turn problems over to their groups and let the group solve them. The leader will ask to hear the group's solution before implementation, but the problem belongs to the group. The leader facilitates the group's efforts. In the

United States, problems are typically the responsibility of a manager who may solicit input and suggestions from followers to help him/her solve it. In the United States, the group's input may be used at the discretion of the leader; in Japan the leader's input may be used at the discretion of the group. We believe these widely different cultural perspectives on worker involvement are responsible for the nonsignificant finding for our participation measure in Japan. Not only did our measure of leader participation have no impact on worker attitudes or perceptions in Japan, the *level* of participative leader behaviors shown by Japanese managers was also low. We expect that this topic of participation/worker involvement will be a particularly interesting area for cross-cultural management research in the future. The Vroom-Yetton-Jago model of participative decision making (Vroom & Jago, 1988) may be a useful theoretic approach to guide an exploration of different styles of participative leadership in Western and Asian cultures.

The significant positive impact of leaders' contingent punishment behavior was predicted in the United States, where giving feedback to individual followers (positive and negative) is emphasized in management training. The negative impact of this leader behavior on subordinate satisfaction in Mexico and Japan gives empirical support to Riding's (1985) opinion that Mexicans are more Asian than Western in philosophy—Mexico's high collectivism is comparable to that of many Asian cultures (Hofstede, 1980). The negative effect of contingent punishment also conforms to what we expected in Japan. In Japanese organizations, individualized negative feedback is usually withheld or done with much subtlety to maintain group harmony and face saving. Japanese managers describe "by the window people" who are slowly shunted toward increasingly menial tasks if they continue to perform poorly. The Japanese stood out in their low *level* of contingent punishment behavior—the lowest of all samples and the lowest of all leader behaviors in Japan. . . .

CROSS-CULTURAL ISSUES FOR THEORY BUILDING

In comparing the impacts of leadership behaviors in Asian versus Western culture clusters, one is struck by the fact that the United States is as different from Mexico as it is from the Asian cultures. *While there clearly are universal leader behavior patterns found in this study, the United States is unique in two respects.* It is the *only* culture where

participative leadership had a positive effect on subordinate performance, and it is the *only* culture where leaders' contingent punishment behavior had a uniformly positive effect on subordinates. The following factors likely contributed toward the culturally unique results regarding leadership behaviors in the United States: uniquely high individualism (Dorfman & Howell, 1988; Hofstede, 1991), egalitarian management climate, changing attitudes towards formal authority, movements toward increased professionalism, team processes, and employee empowerment (Yukl, 1994). These national and cultural characteristics may play important roles in cross-cultural models of leadership. . . .

References

Adler, N. J. (1991). *International dimensions of organizational behavior,* 2nd ed. Boston: PWS-KENT.

Al-Gattan, A. R. A. (1985). Test of the path-goal theory of leadership in the multi-national domain. *Group and Organization Studies,* 10(4), 429–445.

Alston, J. P. (1989). *Wa, Guanxi* and *Inhwa*: Managerial principles in Japan, China, and Korea. *Business Horizons, March–April,* 26–31.

Ayman, R. (1993). Leadership perception: The role of gender and culture. In M. M. Chemers & R. Ayman (Eds.), *Leadership theory and research* (pp. 137–166). San Diego: Academic Press.

Ayman, R., & Chemers, M. M. (1983). Relationship of supervisory behavior ratings to work group effectiveness and subordinate satisfaction among Iranian managers. *Journal of Applied Psychology,* 68(2), 338–341.

Bass, B. M. (1985). *Leadership and performance beyond expectations.* New York: Free Press.

Bass, B. M. (1990). *Bass and Stogdill's handbook of leadership: Theory, research and managerial applications,* 3rd ed. New York: Free Press.

Bass, B. M., & Avolio, B. J. (1993). Transformational leadership: A response to critiques. In M. M. Chemers & R. Ayman (Eds.), *Leadership theory and research* (pp. 49–80). San Diego: Academic Press.

Bass, B. M., Burger, P. C., Doktor, R., & Barrett, G. V. (1979). *Assessment of managers: An international comparison.* New York: Free Press.

Bass, B. M., & Yokochi, N. (1991). Charisma among senior executives and the special case of Japanese CEOs. *Consulting Psychology Bulletin, 1 (Winter/Spring),* 31–38.

Behling, O., & McFillan, J. (1993). A syncretical model of charismatic leadership. Paper presented at the Pan-Pacific Conference, Beijing.

Bennett, M. (1977). Testing management theories cross-culturally. *Journal of Applied Psychology, 62,* 578–581.

Bentler, P. M., & Bonnett, D. G. (1980). Significance tests and goodness of fit in the analysis of covariance structures. *Psychological Bulletin, 88,* 588–606.

Berry, J. W. (1980). Social and cultural change. *Handbook of Cross-Cultural Psychology, 5,* 211–279.

Bond, M., & Hwang, K. (1986). The social psychology of Chinese people. In M. H. Bond (Ed.), *The psychology of the Chinese people* (pp. 213–237). Hong Kong: Oxford University Press.

Bond, M. H., & Smith, P. B. (1996). Cross-cultural social and organizational psychology. *Annual Review of Psychology, 47,* 205–235.

Boyacigiller, N., & Adler, N. (1991). A parochial dinosaur: Organizational science in a global context. *Academy of Management Review, 16,* 262–290.

Chen, M. (1995). *Asian management systems: Chinese, Japanese, and Korean styles of business.* London: Routledge.

Dorfman, P. W. (1996). International and cross-cultural leadership research. In B. J. Punnett & O. Shenkar (Eds.), *Handbook for international management research* (pp. 267–349). Oxford, UK: Blackwell.

Dorfman, P. W., & Howell, J. P. (1988). Dimensions of national culture and effective leadership patterns: Hofstede revisited. In E. G. McGoun (Ed.), *Advances in international comparative management* (vol. 3, pp. 127–149). Greenwich, CT: JAI Press.

Dorfman, P. W., & Howell, J. P. (1994). *The construct validity of Hofstede's culture scales: Replication and extension to individualized measures.* [Research colloquium]. New Mexico State University.

Dorfman, P. W., & Ronen, S. (1991). The universality of leadership theories: Challenges and paradoxes. Paper presented at the National Academy of Management annual meeting, Miami, FL.

Earley, P. C., & Mosakowski, E. (1996). Experimental international management research. In B. J. Punnett & Shenkar (Eds.), *Handbook for international management research* (pp. 83–114). Oxford, UK: Blackwell.

Earley, P. C., & Singh, H. (1995). International and intercultural management research: What's next? *Academy of Management Journal, 38,* 327–340.

Fahr, J. L., Podsakoff, P. M., & Cheng, B. S. (1987). Culture-free leadership effectiveness versus moderators of leadership behaviors: An extension and test of Kerr and Jermier's "substitutes for leadership" model in Taiwan. *Journal of International Business Studies, 18,* 43–60.

Farmer, R., & Richman, B. M. (1965). *Comparative management and economic progress.* Homewood, IL: Irwin.

Fiedler, F. E., & Garcia, J. E. (1987). *New approaches to effective leadership: Cognitive resources and organizational performance.* New York: Wiley.

Fiedler, F. E., & House, R. J. (1988). Leadership: A report of progress. In C. L. Cooper (Ed.), *International review of industrial and organizational psychology.* Greenwich, CT: JAI Press.

Ganster, D. C., Hennessey, H. W., & Luthans, F. (1983). Social desirability response effects: Three alternative methods. *Academy of Management Journal, 36,* 321–331.

Gioia, D. A., & Sims, H. P. (1985). On avoiding the influence of implicit leadership theories in leader behavior descriptions. *Educational and Psychological Measurement, 45,* 217–232.

Gomez-Mejia, L. R., & Balkin, D. B. (1992). Determinants of faculty pay: An agency theory perspective. *Academy of Management Journal, 35*(5), 921–955.

Hayashi, S. (1988). *Culture and management in Japan.* University of Tokyo Press.

Hofstede, G. (1980). *Culture's consequences: International differences in work-related values.* Beverly Hills, CA: Sage.

Hofstede, G. (1991). Culture and organizations: *The software of the mind.* New York: McGraw-Hill.

Hofstede, G. (1993). Cultural constraints in management theories. *Academy of Management Executive, 7*(1), 81–94.

House, R. J. (1971). A path-goal theory of leader effectiveness. *Administrative Science Quarterly, 16,* 321–338.

House, R. J. (1991). Charismatic leadership across cultures. Paper presented at the Academy of Management Annual Meeting, Miami, FL.

House, R. J., Hanges, P., Agar, M., & Ruiz-Quintanilla, A. (1994). Conference on Global Leadership and Organizational Behavior (GLOBE). Calgary, Canada.

Hsu, F. L. K. (1982). *American and Chinese: Passage to differences.* Honolulu: University of Hawaii Press.

Iaffaldono, J. T., & Muchinsky, P. M. (1985). Job satisfaction and job performance: A meta-analysis. *Psychological Bulletin, 97*(2), 251–273.

Indvik, J. (1986). Path-goal theory of leadership: A meta-analysis. In Proceedings of the Academy of Management Annual Meeting (pp. 189–192). Chicago: AMA.

Indvik, J. (1988). A more complete testing of path-goal theory. Paper presented at the Academy of Management Annual Meeting, Anaheim, CA.

Jackofsky, E. F., Slocum, J. W., Jr., & McQuaid, S. J. (1988). Cultural values and the CEO: Alluring companions? *Academy of Management Executive, 2*(1), 39–49.

James, L. R., Mulaik, S. A., & Brett, J. M. (1982). *Causal analysis: Assumptions, models and data.* Beverly Hills, CA: Sage.

Janssens, M., Brett, J. M., & Smith, F. (1995). Confirmatory cross-cultural research: Testing the viability of a corporation-wide safety policy. *Academy of Management Journal, 2,* 364–382.

Jöreskog, K. G., & Sorbom, D. (1989). *LISREL VII: Analysis of linear structural relationships by the method of maximum likelihood.* Mooresville, IN: Scientific Software.

Jöreskog, K. G., & Sorbom, D. (1993). *LISREL 8 user's reference guide.* Chicago, IL: Scientific Software International.

Kakar, S. (1971). Authority patterns and subordinate behavior in Indian organizations. *Administrative Science Quarterly, 16,* 298–307.

Kerr, S., & Jermier, J. (1978). Substitutes for leadership: Their meaning and measurement. *Organizational Behavior and Human Performance, 22,* 374–403.

Lord, R., & Maher, K. J. (1991). *Leadership and information processing: Linking perceptions and performance.* Boston: Unwin-Everyman.

Marrow, A. J. (1964). Risks and uncertainties in action research. *Journal of Social Issues, 20,* 5–20.

McClelland, D., & Boyatzis, R. E. (1982). Leadership motive pattern and long term success in management. *Journal of Applied Psychology, 67(6),* 737–743.

Medsker, G. J., Williams, L. J., & Holohan, P. J. (1994). A review of current practices for evaluating causal models in organizational behavior and human resources management research. *Journal of Management, 20,* 439–464.

Misumi, J., & Peterson, M. F. (1985a). *The behavioral science of leadership: An interdisciplinary Japanese research program.* Ann Arbor, MI: University of Michigan Press.

Misumi, J., & Peterson, M. F. (1985b). The performance-maintenance theory of leadership: Review of a Japanese research program. *Administrative Science Quarterly, 30,* 198–223.

Morgan, J. C., & Morgan, J. J. (1991). *Cracking the Japanese market: Strategies for success in the new global market.* New York: The Free Press.

Mulaik, S. A., James, L. R., Van Alstine, J., Bennett, N., Lind, S., & Stillwell, C. D. (1989). An evaluation of goodness-of-fit indices for structural equation models. *Psychological Bulletin, 105,* 430–445.

Negandhi, A. R., & Prasad, S. B. (1971). *Comparative management.* New York: Appleton-Century-Croft.

Ostroff, C. (1992). The relationship between satisfaction, attitudes, and performance: An organizational level analysis. *Journal of Applied Psychology, 77,* 963–974.

Peng, T. K., Peterson, M. F., & Shyi, Y. P. (1991). Quantitative methods in cross-national organizational research: Trends and equivalence issues. *Journal of Organizational Behavior, 12,* 87–108.

Podsakoff, P. M., & Skov, R. (1980). Leader reward and punishment behavior scales. Unpublished research, Indiana University: Bloomington, IN.

Podsakoff, P. M., Tudor, W. D., & Schuler, R. S. (1983). Leader expertise as a moderator of the effects of instru-mental and supportive leader behavior. *Journal of Management, 9(2),* 173–185.

Podsakoff, P. M., Niehoff, B. P., MacKenzie, S. B., & Williams, M. L. (1992). Do substitutes for leadership really substitute for leadership? An empirical examination of Kerr and Jermier's situational leadership model. *Organizational Behavior and Human Decision Processes, 54,* 1–44.

Porter, L. W., & Smith, F. J. (1970). The etiology of organizational commitment: A progress report. Unpublished manuscript, University of California, Irvine.

Randall, D. M., Huo, Y. P., & Pawelk, P. (1993). Social desirability bias in cross-cultural ethics research. *International Journal of Organizational Analysis, 1* (April), 185–202.

Redding, S. G. (1990). *The spirit of Chinese Capitalism.* New York: deGruyter.

Redding, S. G., & Casey, T. W. (1976). Managerial beliefs among Asian managers. In R. L. Taylor, M. J. O'Connell, R. A. Zawacki, & D. D. Warwick (Eds.), *Proceedings of the Academy of Management 36th Annual Meeting* (pp. 351–356). Kansas City: Academy of Management.

Redding, S. G., & Wong, G. Y. (1986). The psychology of Chinese organizational behavior. In M. H. Bond (Ed.), *The psychology of the Chinese people* (pp. 267–295). Hong Kong: Oxford University Press.

Riding, A. (1985). *Distant neighbors: A portrait of the Mexicans.* New York: Random House.

Riordan, C. M., & Vandenberg, R. J. (1994). A central question in cross-cultural research: Do employees of different cultures interpret work-related measures in an equivalent manner? *Journal of Management, 20(3),* 643–671.

Rizzo, J. R., House, R. J., & Lirtzman, S. I. (1970). Role conflict and ambiguity in complex organizations. *Administrative Science Quarterly, 15,* 150–163.

Ronen, S. (1986). *Comparative and international management.* New York: Wiley.

Ronen, S., & Shenkar, O. (1985). Clustering countries on attitudinal dimensions: A review and synthesis. *Academy of Management Review, 10,* 435–454.

Schaubroeck, J., Cotton, J. L., & Jennings, K. R. (1989). Antecedents and consequences of role stress: A covariance structure analysis. *Journal of Organizational Behavior, 10,* 35–58.

Schriesheim, C. A. (1978). *Development, validation and application of the new leader behavior and expectancy research instruments.* Unpublished doctoral dissertation, Ohio State University, Columbus, OH.

Schumacher, R. E., & Lomax, R. G. (1996). *A beginner's guide to structural equation modeling.* Mahwah, NJ: Lawrence Erlbaum.

Singh, J. (1995). Measurement issues in cross-national research. *Journal of International Business Studies,* 3rd quarter, 597–619.

Sinha, J. B. P. (1980). *The nurturant task leader*. New Delhi: Concept.

Smith, P. C., Kendall, L. M., & Hulin, C. L. (1969). *The measurement of satisfaction in work and retirement*. Chicago: Rand-McNally.

Smith, P. B., & Peterson, M. F. (1988). *Leadership, organizations and culture: An event management model*. Beverly Hills, CA: Sage.

Smith, P. B., Peterson, M. F., Bond, M., & Misumi, J. (1992). Leader style and leader behavior in individualist and collectivist cultures. In S. Iwawaki, Y. Kashima, & K. Leung (Eds.), *Innovations in cross-cultural psychology: Selected papers from the tenth international conference of the International Association for Cross-Cultural Psychology* (pp. 76–85). Amsterdam: Swets Zeitlinger.

Smith, P. B., Peterson, M. F., Misumi, J., & Tayeb, M. (1989). Testing leadership theory cross culturally. *Recent advances in social psychology: An international* perspective (pp. 383–391). Amsterdam: North-Holland.

Steers, R. M., Shin, Y. K., & Ungson, G. R. (1989). *The Chaebol: Korea's new industrial might*. New York: Harper.

Thurstone, L. L. (1947). *Multiple factor analysis*. Chicago: University of Chicago Press.

Triandis, H. C. (1993a). Cross-cultural industrial and organizational psychology. In M. Dunnette & L. Hough (Eds.), *Handbook of Industrial and Organizational Psychology*, 4, 103–172. Palo Alto, CA: Consulting Psychologists Press.

Triandis, H. C. (1993b). The contingency model in cross-cultural perspective. In M. Chemers & R. Ayman (Eds.), *Leadership theory and research: Perspectives and directions* (pp. 167–188). San Diego: Academic Press.

Vroom, V., & Jago, A. G. (1988). *The new leadership: Managing participation in organizations*. Englewood Cliffs, NJ: Prentice-Hall.

Wakabayashi, M., & Graen, G. (1984). The Japanese career progress study: A seven year follow-up. *Journal of Applied Psychology, 69,* 603–614.

Whitehall, A. M., & S. Takezawa (1968). *The other worker*. Honolulu: East-West Center Press.

Williams, L., & Hazer, J. T. (1986). Antecedents and consequences of satisfaction and commitment in turnover models: A reanalysis using latent variable structure equation methods. *Journal of Applied Psychology, 71,* 219–231.

Yukl, G. (1982). Managerial behavior survey. Questionnaire for assessing patterns of managers' leadership behavior.

Yukl, G. (1994). *Leadership in organizations*, 3rd ed. Englewood Cliffs, NJ: Prentice-Hall.

Yukl, G., & Van Fleet, D. D. (1992). Theory and research on leadership in organizations. In M. Dunnette & L. M. Hough (Eds.), *Handbook of industrial and organizational psychology,* 2nd ed. (pp. 147–197). Palo Alto, CA: Consulting Psychologists Press.

Reading 26

Comparing Leadership Practices Between the United States, Nigeria, and Slovenia: Does Culture Matter?

Hugo Zagorsek and Marko Jaklic
University of Ljubjana, Slovenia

Stanley J. Stough
Southeast Missouri State

INTRODUCTION

In this era of rapid globalization and the increasing interdependence of the world's economies, national culture is paradoxically becoming more, rather than less, important. As Doug Ivestor, the former CEO of the Coca-Cola Corporation pointed out, "as economic borders come down, cultural barriers go up, presenting new challenges and opportunities in business" (Javidan & House, 2001). If a few decades ago leaders could operate in the relative isolation of their home countries, today they are increasingly exposed to various cultures with different lifestyles, and different management and leadership practices. The situations that global leaders and would-be leaders must face are highly complex, constantly changing, and difficult to interpret. Even local leaders from developing countries and countries in transition are being affected by globalization forces. Those from dynamic enterprises are facing new leadership challenges as they penetrate Western and Eastern markets, acquire companies, and build new facilities abroad. Those that endure are increasingly integrated into the managerial networks of global companies. And all of them are uncertain about the applicability of various leadership theories promoted by foreign or domestic consultants and academics in their specific circumstances, institutions, and cultures.

. . . House & Aditya (1997) note that "almost all of the prevailing theories of leadership and about 98% of empirical evidence at hand are distinctly American in character: individualistic rather than collectivistic, stressing follower responsibilities rather than rights, assuming hedonism rather than commitment to duty or altruistic motivation, assuming centrality of work and democratic value orientation and emphasizing assumptions of rationality rather than asceticism, religion, or superstition."

There is mounting evidence that cultures vary to the extent that they employ and value specific leadership behaviors (Hofstede, 2001; Den Hartog, House, Hanges, Ruiz-Quintanilla & Dorfman, 1999; Peterson & Hunt, 1997). This study aims to compare the usage of leadership practices found to be effective in a Western setting in three nations in culturally and economically different regions: the United States, Nigeria, and Slovenia. The first is one of the most advanced and competitive nations in the world. It is the home of almost all major theories of leadership. It has more than 280 million inhabitants from a wide variety of ethnic backgrounds. The main religions are Protestant denominations (56%), followed by Roman Catholicism (28%), and Judaism (2%).

Nigeria is the most populous African nation, with around 130 million inhabitants. It is situated in West Africa, bordering Benin, Cameroon, Chad, and Niger. It was ruled by the military for 16 years until a new constitution was adopted in 1999 and a peaceful transition to civilian government was completed. It consists of more than 250 ethnic groups and is fraught with ethnic and religious tensions. The main religions are Islam (50%), Christianity (40%), and indigenous beliefs (10%).

Slovenia is a small central European country, with only two million inhabitants. It borders Italy, Austria, Hungary, and Croatia. It was part of socialist Yugoslavia, but seceded from it in 1991 and is now scheduled to join the European Union in May 2004. The majority of people are Roman Catholics (70.8%).

Apart from having different cultures, the countries selected also differ in their level of development. Nigeria is an undeveloped country with a per capita GDP of only $840 (estimated by purchasing power parity in 2001). Slovenia has a rapidly developing transitional economy with a

Source: Edited and reprinted with permission from *Cross Cultural Management*, 2004, 11, 2, 16–34. Copyright Emerald Group Publishing, 2004.

per capita GDP of almost $16,000 (PPP, 2001). The United States has the largest and most technologically powerful economy in the world, with a per capita GDP of $36,300 (World Bank, 2002).

LEADERSHIP PRACTICES

There are many theories of leadership, each contributing some insights into the nature of the phenomenon. In recent years "neocharismatic leadership theories" such as transformational leadership theory (Burns, 1978; Bass, 1985) and visionary leadership theory (Bennis & Nanus, 1985; Kouzes & Posner, 1987; Sashkin, 1988) have gained widespread acceptance, both with scholars and practitioners alike. House and Aditya (1997) note that these theories are all of a common type and have several common characteristics. First, they all "attempt to explain how leaders are able to lead organizations to attain outstanding accomplishments. . . . Second, these theories also attempt to explain how certain leaders are able to achieve extraordinary levels of follower motivation, admiration, respect, trust, commitment, dedication, loyalty, and performance. Third, they stress symbolic and emotionally appealing leader behaviors, such as visionary, frame alignment, empowering, role modeling, image building, exceptional, risk taking, and supportive behaviors, as well as cognitively oriented behavior, such as adapting, showing versatility and environmental sensitivity, and intellectual stimulation. Finally, the leader effects specified in these theories include follower self-esteem, motive arousal and emotions, and identification with the leader's vision, values, and the collective, as well as the traditional dependent variables of earlier leadership theories: follower satisfaction and performance" (House & Aditya, 1997).

Kouzes and Posner's (1987) visionary or practices leadership theory belongs to this group. They analyzed more than 1,200 "personal best leadership experiences" of managers and executives from various industries in the United States. Based on extensive case studies and interviews, they have identified five practices that are common to successful leaders:

- *Challenging the Process (CP):* Searching for challenging opportunities, questioning the status quo, experimenting, and taking risks.

- *Inspiring a Shared Vision (ISV):* Envisioning an exciting future and enlisting others to pursue that future.

- *Enabling Others to Act (EOA):* Fostering collaboration, and empowering and strengthening others.

- *Modeling the Way (MW):* Consistently practicing one's own espoused values, setting the example, planning small wins.

- *Encouraging the Heart (EH):* Giving positive feedback, recognizing individual contributions, and celebrating team accomplishments. . . .

CULTURE AND ITS IMPACT ON LEADERSHIP PRACTICES

Culture refers to those learned behaviors characterizing the total way of life of members within any given society (Hughes, Ginnett & Curphy, 1999). Hofstede (1980) defines culture as "collective programming of the mind that distinguishes the members of one group or category of people from another." The GLOBE research program (House *et al.*, 1999) provides comprehensive interpretation of culture as "shared motives, values, beliefs, identities, and interpretations or meanings of significant events that result from common experiences of members of collectives and are transmitted across age generations."

Hofstede (1980) has identified four core dimensions of culture:

- *Power distance (PD):* The extent to which people accept inequality in power among institutions, organizations, and people.

- *Uncertainty avoidance (UA):* The extent to which members of a society feel uncomfortable with unstructured situations, uncertainty, and ambiguity.

- *Individualism vs. collectivism (IND):* The degree to which individuals are supposed to look after themselves or remain integrated in groups, usually centered on the family. Collectivism means a preference for a tightly knit social framework in which individuals look after one another and organizations protect their members' interests.

- *Masculinity vs. femininity (MAS):* The degree to which people prefer achievement, heroism, assertiveness, work centrality (with resulting high stress), and material success as opposed to relationships, cooperation, group decision-making, and quality of life.

Hofstede (2001) later added a fifth dimension: *Long-term vs. short-term orientation,* which refers

TABLE 1   **Hofstede's Country Culture Scores for Selected Countries**

Country	PD	UA	IND	MAS
US	40	46	91	62
Nigeria (West Africa)	77	54	20	46
Slovenia	71	88	27	19

to the extent to which a culture programs its members to accept delayed gratification of their material, social, and emotional needs.

Hofstede's culture scores for the countries studied are presented in Table 1. Because there is no culture score available for Nigeria, scores from the West African region (Nigeria, Ghana & Sierra Leone) were used instead. . . .

There are great differences between the cultures of the three countries. Slovenia is a highly collectivistic, feminine society, characterized by high uncertainty avoidance and power distance. The United States is quite the opposite: very individualistic, quite masculine, and a little below average on uncertainty avoidance and power distance.

Nigeria scores the strongest for power distance and collectivism, even more than Slovenia. It is moderately feminine and is characterized by moderate uncertainty avoidance, similar to the United States. Somewhat counterintuitively, it appears that Slovenia and Nigeria are culturally more similar to each other than to the United States. If absolute differences in the country culture scores on all four dimensions are summed up, cultural distance between the United States and Nigeria appears to be 132, between the United States and Slovenia 180, and between Slovenia and Nigeria only 74.

Many cross-cultural studies suggest that culture can influence leadership concepts, styles, and practices (Hofstede, 2001; House & Aditya, 1997; Gerstner & Day, 1994). As House *et al.* (1999) suggest, "what is expected of leadership, what leaders may or not may do, and the status and influence bestowed upon them vary considerably as a result of the cultural forces in the countries or regions in which the leaders function." In some cultures, one might need to take strong decisive action in order to be an effective leader, whereas in another culture consultation and a democratic approach may be a prerequisite. Jung, Bass, and Sosik (1995) argue that transformational leadership emerges more easily and is more effective in collectivistic cultures than in individualistic cultures. According to them, the centrality of work in life and the high level of group orientation among followers should promote transformational leadership, and the

high respect for authority and the obedience in collectivistic cultures should enhance transformational processes. Den Hartog *et al.* (1999) suggest that in high power distance societies there should exist a less negative attitude towards authoritarian leadership. Dominance and ostentatious displays of power might thus be appropriate for leaders in such societies. Additionally, Smith, Peterson, and Misumi (1994) show that managers in high power distance societies report more use of rules and procedures than do managers from low power distance countries. Because the countries studied differ considerably in their cultures, it is expected that the extent to which respondents from selected countries would engage in certain leadership practices would differ among them. *Proposition 1 (P1): There will exist differences in the leadership practices of respondents from the United States, Nigeria, and Slovenia.*

Koopman *et al.* (1999) argue that high uncertainty avoidance cultures, with their resulting emphasis on rules and procedures, may place other demands on leaders than do low uncertainty avoidance cultures, with the resulting attitude of tolerance of ambiguity and innovative behavior. Therefore, it could be expected that respondents from countries that are high on uncertainty avoidance will not *Challenge the Process* as much as respondents from low uncertainty avoidance. *P2: Respondents from Slovenia will engage less in the leadership practice Challenging the Process than respondents from the United States.*

In highly feminine cultures, people strive for high quality of life, maintain relationships, and care for their co-workers more than in highly masculine cultures. Therefore, it can be expected that leaders from those cultures would *Encourage the Heart* more. *P3: Respondents from Slovenia will engage in the leadership practice Encouraging the Heart more than respondents from Nigeria or the United States.*

It seems that collectivism fosters collaborative, considerate, and empowering leadership practices. On the other hand, high power distance allows for strong, authoritarian, and directive leaders. Therefore, it can be expected that leaders from collectivistic but low power distance cultures would *Enable Others to Act* more than leaders from individualistic or high power distance cultures. Unfortunately, Slovenia and Nigeria have high power distance and are collectivistic at the same time, whereas the United States is exactly the opposite. Thus it is hard to predict which effect would prevail and which country's respondents would *Enable Others to Act* more.

Leaders that *Model the Way* are clear about their business values and beliefs. They set an example, and focus on key priorities by making plans and breaking down big projects into achievable steps. Therefore, this leadership practice would be most supported in high power distance, high uncertainty avoidance cultures. *P4: Respondents from Slovenia and Nigeria will engage in the leadership practice Modeling the Way more than respondents from the United States. . . .*

METHODOLOGY

The Leadership Practices Inventory (LPI) (Kouzes & Posner, 1993) was administered to 110 MBA students from the United States (Southeast Missouri State University), 105 MBA students from Nigeria (Nugu State University of Science & Technology, Lagos) and 134 MBA and master's degree students from Slovenia (University of Ljubljana). . . .

RESULTS

AGGREGATE

The usage of the five leadership practices in the three countries was compared using ANOVA. Levene's test for equality of variances showed that they are sufficiently equal for the ANOVA procedure to be used. Contrary to expectations and propositions, the LPI (Leadership Practices Inventory) scores of MBA students in the United States, Nigeria, and Slovenia were relatively similar. Significant differences were found for only two leadership practices: *Enabling Others to Act* and *Modeling the Way*. Respondents from the United States engage in the practice *Enabling Others to Act* substantially less than their counterparts from the other two countries (M for the US = 25.36, M for Nigeria = 24.75, M for Slovenia = 24.57). Respondents from Nigeria perceive themselves as *Modeling the Way* to a greater degree than respondents from the United States or Slovenia. Overall, American MBA students scored lowest on all five leadership practices, while their counterparts from Nigeria scored highest on the three middle leadership practices (however, most of these distinctions were not statistically significant).

Rank order for the LPI scores did not substantially differ among MBA students from the three countries (it was identical for Slovenia and the United States). *Enabling Others to Act* was rated highest in all of them. *Inspiring the Shared Vision* and *Challenging the Process* were rated last and next to last everywhere. *Modeling the Way* and *Encouraging the Heart* were rated second and third for Nigerians and the other way around for Americans and Slovenians.

Enabling Others to Act appears to have the smallest variability (i.e. standard deviation), while *Challenging the Process* has the highest variability across all three countries.

Scores for the American sample are similar to those obtained by Kouzes & Posner (1993) when surveying more than 36,000 managers and their subordinates. The only exception is the practice *Encouraging the Heart,* which respondents from our sample use much more frequently than the respondents from Kouzes & Posner's sample. However, this difference may be due to the higher proportion of females in our sample compared to Kouzes & Posner's sample, because in both samples females score higher than males on this practice. . . .

Judging from the mean values for the selected behaviors, it appears that Nigerian respondents most frequently—and much more than respondents from the other two countries—take time to celebrate accomplishments and make certain that people adhere to the values that have been agreed on. American respondents are much more clear about their own philosophy of leadership than others, but do not create an atmosphere of mutual trust like the others do. Slovenian respondents seek out challenging opportunities more than their Nigerian or American counterparts.

DISCUSSION

In the aggregate, the LPI scores of students from the United States, Nigeria, and Slovenia were very similar. Proposition 1 was only partially supported, with statistically significant differences appearing only for the practices *Enabling Others to Act* and *Modeling the Way*. Propositions 2 and 3 were not confirmed by the data. Proposition 4 was partially supported, with Nigerian respondents engaging in the practice *Modeling the Way* more than Slovenian respondents, and both of these more than American respondents (though only the

TABLE 6 **Specific Behaviors from the LPI Questionnaire That Discriminate Most Between the Countries Studied**

Item number	Specific Behavior	US	Mean values Nigeria	Slovenia
5	Take time to celebrate accomplishments when project milestones are reached	3.85	4.22	3.83
4	Clear about own philosophy of leadership	3.63	3.16	3.50
14	Spend time and energy on making certain that people adhere to the values that have been agreed on	3.44	4.03	3.51
23	Create atmosphere of mutual trust (in the projects I lead)	3.92	4.30	4.35
1	Seek out challenging opportunities (that test my skills and abilities)	3.65	3.68	4.06

difference between Nigerian respondents and respondents from the other two countries was statistically significant).

Our research suggests that there may be some leadership behaviors that are universally endorsed. MBA students from the three countries engage in visionary, inspirational, and risk-taking leadership behaviors with equal frequency. All these behaviors are components of "(neo) charismatic" leadership, as defined, for example, by House and Aditya (1997). This suggests that charismatic leadership may as well be a universal phenomenon. Although our study did not examine the impact of various leadership practices on performance, it has shown that leaders from culturally different countries use many leadership practices in similar ways and with similar frequency. This at least implicitly suggests that they view these practices as effective.

Our results can be compared with findings from the GLOBE research program (Den Hartog *et al.*, 1999), which has studied culture and leadership behaviors in 62 cultures. The research found that there exist several attributes reflecting charismatic/transformational leadership that are universally endorsed as contributing to outstanding leadership. These are referred to as *motive arouser*, foresight, *encouraging*, communicative, trustworthy, *dynamic, positive, confidence builder, and motivational*. Those in italics are included in leadership practices scales for *Challenging the Process, Inspiring the Shared Vision*, and *Encouraging the Heart*. This may explain the similarity of responses.

Data from this study suggest that the impact of cultural differences on management and leadership practices across countries may be decreasing. However, several factors that may have led to such results should be noted. First, the present study investigates only "etic" leadership behaviors. House *et al.* (1999) note that "etic" phenomena are common to all cultures, or at least to all cultures studied to date. A phenomenon is etic if all cultures can be assessed in terms of a common metric with respect to the phenomena. Thus cultures can be compared in terms of etic phenomena. In contrast to etic phenomena, emic phenomena are culture specific phenomena that occur in only a subset of cultures." Because "emic" phenomena were not studied, some dissimilarities between leadership practices in the three nations were neglected.

Second, it should be noted that the LPI questionnaire captures only a small fraction of the total range of leadership behaviors that may occur in the countries studied. It examines leadership practices that were deemed important and effective for good performance by American managers in American culture. The questionnaire was developed, pretested, and operationalized in the United States by American researchers. It is questionable whether this five-factor structure applies to other countries, especially Nigeria. As such, the LPI may not be able to detect many of the differences in leadership behaviors that exist among respondents in the three countries.

Third, the characteristics of the sample may contribute to the uniformity of responses as well. MBA students in all three countries, and especially in Nigeria and Slovenia, are more educated, more ambitious, and younger than average middle managers. They are more exposed to global (or

American) influences and even study from similar, if not the same, textbooks. Therefore, their behavior and reasoning might be more uniform (that is, similar to American) than it would be in the case of a broader sample of managers from local companies. Due to these characteristics of the sample, it is probable that the differences between respondents in the leadership practices *Enabling Others to Act* and *Modeling the Way* are conservative estimates of real differences in the population of managers. . . .

Culture does matter. But its impact is not as strong as is commonly thought. Maybe the world is actually becoming a "global village" after all.

References

Bass, B. M. (1985). *Leadership and Performance Beyond Expectations*. New York: Free Press.

Bennett, M. (1977). "Response Characteristics of Bilingual Managers to Organizational Questionnaires." *Personnel Psychology*, 30, pp. 29–36.

Bennis, W., & Nanus, B. (1986). *Leaders: The Strategies for Taking Charge*. New York: Harper & Row.

Bond, M. H., & Cheung, M. K., (1984). "Experimenter Language Choice and Ethnic Affirmation of Chinese Trilinguals in Hong Kong." *International Journal of Intercultural Relations*, 8, pp. 347–356.

Burns, J. M. (1978). *Leadership*. New York: Harper & Row.

Carless, S. A. (2000). "Assessing the Discriminant Validity of the Leadership Practices Inventory." *Journal of Occupational and Organizational Psychology*, 74, pp. 233–239.

Den Hartog, D. N., House, R. J., Hanges, P. J., Ruiz-Quintanilla, A. S., & Dorfman, P. W. (1999). "Culture Specific and Cross-culturally Generalizable Implicit Leadership Theories: Are Attributes of Charismatic/ Transformational Leadership Universally Endorsed." *Leadership Quarterly*, 10(2), pp. 219–238.

Eagly, A. H., & Johnson, B. T. (1990). "Gender and Leadership Style: A Meta-analysis." *Psychological Bulletin*, 108(2), pp. 233–257.

Gerstner, C. R., & Day, D. V. (1994). "Cross-cultural Comparison of Leadership Prototypes." *Leadership Quarterly*, 5, pp. 121–134.

Gibson, C. B. (1995). "An Investigation of Gender Differences in Leadership Across Four Countries." *Journal of International Business Studies*, 26(2), pp. 255–280.

Hartman, L. (1999). "A Psychological Analysis of Leadership Effectiveness." *Strategy & Leadership*, 27(6), pp. 30–33.

Hofstede, G. (1980). *Culture's Consequences: International Differences in Work-related Values*. Beverly Hills, CA: Sage.

Hofstede, G. (1993). "Cultural Constraints in Management Theories." *Academy of Management Executive*, 7(1), pp. 81–94.

Hofstede, G. (2001). *Culture's Consequences: Comparing Values, Behaviors, Institutions and Organizations Across Nations*. Thousand Oaks, CA: Sage.

House, R. J., & Aditya, R. N. (1997). "The Social Scientific Study of Leadership: Quo Vadis?" *Journal of Management*, 23(3), pp. 409–474.

House, R. J., Hanges, P. J., Ruiz-Quintanilla, A. S., Dorfman, P. W., Javidan, M., Dickson, M. W., et al. (1999). "Cultural Influences in Leadership and Organizations: Project GLOBE." In W. H. Mobley, M. J. Gessner and V. Arnold (Eds.), *Advances in Global Leadership*, Vol. 1, pp. 171–233. Stamford, CT: JAI Press.

Hughes, R. L., Ginnett, R. C., & Curphy, G. J. (1999). *Leadership: Enhancing the Lessons of Experience* (3rd ed.). Boston: Irwin/McGraw Hill.

Javidan, M., & House, R. J. (2001). "Cultural Acumen for the Global Manager: Lessons from Project GLOBE." *Organizational Dynamics*, 29(4), pp. 289–305.

Jung, D. I., Bass, B. M., & Sosik, J. J. (1995). "Bridging Leadership and Culture: A Theoretical Consideration of Transformational Leadership and Collectivistic Cultures." *Journal of Leadership Studies*, 2, pp. 3–18.

Kanter, R. M. (1977). *Men and Women of the Corporation*. New York: Basic Books.

Koopman, P. L., Den Hartog, D. N., Konrad, E., & GLOBE Research Team (1999). "National Culture and Leadership Profiles in Europe: Some Results from the GLOBE Study." *European Journal of Work and Organizational Psychology*, 8(4), pp. 503–520.

Kouzes, J. M., & Posner, B. Z. (1987). *The Leadership Challenge: How to Get Extraordinary Things Done in Organizations*. San Francisco: Jossey-Bass.

Kouzes, J. M., & Posner, B. Z. (1993). *Psychometric Properties of the Leadership Practices Inventory*. San Diego: Pfeifer.

Opeke, O. (2002). *Women and Work in Nigeria: Problems and Prospects*. Paper presented at the World's Women Congress 2002, Nigeria.

Peterson, M. F., & Hunt, J. G. (1997). "International Perspectives on International Leadership." *Leadership Quarterly*, 8(3), pp. 203–232.

Posner, B. Z., & Kouzes, J. M. (1990). "Leadership Practices: An Alternative to the Psychological Perspective." In K. E. Clark & M. B. Clark (Eds.) *Measures of Leadership*, pp. 205–217. Greensboro, NC: Center for Creative Leadership.

Rosner, J. B. (1990). "Ways Women Lead." *Harvard Business Review*. November–December, pp. 119–125.

Sashkin, M. (1988). "The Visionary Leader." In J. A. Conger & R. A. Kanungo (Eds.), *Charismatic Leadership: The Elusive Factor in Organizational Effectiveness*, pp. 122–160. San Francisco: Jossey-Bass.

Sharma, S. (1996). *Applied Multivariate Techniques*. New York: Wiley.

Smith, P. B., Peterson, M. F., & Misumi, J. (1994). "Event Management and Work Team Effectiveness in Japan, Britain and the USA." *Journal of Occupational and Organizational Psychology,* 67, pp. 33–43.

Triandis, H. C. (1995). *Individualism and Collectivism*. Boulder, CO: Westview Press.

World Bank (2002). *World Development Indicators*. Washington DC: World Bank.

Followers and the Leadership Process

While it is trite to say that leadership and followership go hand in hand, and that without followers there would be no need for leaders, it is important to note that the study of leadership has to a very large extent been leader-centric. The study of leadership from the perspective of the follower (or followership) and the study of the follower and followership have been largely ignored. To the extent that followers enter into the study of leadership, they have most commonly been treated as the dependent variable, where the effects of leadership (i.e., the effects of leader traits, leader behavior and style, leader vision and sacrifice) have been observed. Reacting to this reality, Heller and Van Til (1982)[1] remind us that "leadership and followership are linked concepts, neither of which can be comprehended without the other" (p. 405), and thus it is important to study the interaction between the two. Hollander (1993)[2] made a similar point when he said, "Without followers there are plainly no leaders or leadership" (p. 29). Thus, leadership should be seen both as a process and as a relational phenomenon.

Heller and Van Til (1982) suggest that "leadership and followership are best seen as roles in relationship" (p. 406). Smircich and Morgan (1982) highlight this observation when they state, "While individuals may look to a leader to frame and concretize their reality, they may also react against, reject, or change the reality thus defined" (p. 259). If we are to understand leadership, we need to understand the two roles and the dynamics of the relationship that links and sustains that relationship as there is forward movement toward goal attainment. Commenting on this dynamic relationship, Heller and Van Til (1982) leave us with three propositions: (1) "The leader must lead, and do it well to retain leadership, the follower must follow, and do it well to retain followership," (2) "Good leadership enhances followers, just as good followership enhances leaders," and (3) "In many cases, the follower is a potential leader who chooses not to become active in a given situation" (pp. 406–408).

Lord and Maher (1991)[3] also focus our attention on the follower in our study of leadership. They define "leadership as the process of being perceived by others as a leader" (p. 11). In effect, an individual's possession of all the right traits, skills, and abilities and engagement in the right behaviors does not make that individual a leader unless he or she is also *perceived* as a leader. This notion of the evaluations that people (e.g., followers) make about leaders (i.e., being perceived as a leader) is a central part of their implicit leadership theory.

[1] T. Heller & J. Van Til, "Leadership and Followership: Some Summary Propositions," *Journal of Applied Behavioral Science* 18, 3 (1982), pp. 405–414.
[2] E. P. Hollander, "Legitimacy, Power and Influence: A Perspective on Relational Features of Leadership." In M. M. Chemers & R. Ayman (eds.), *Leadership Theory and Research: Perspectives and Directions* (San Diego, CA: Academic Press, 1993), pp. 29–48.
[3] R. G. Lord & K. L. Maher, "*Leadership and Information Processing: Linking Perception and Performance*" (Boston: Unwin Hyman, 1991).

Implicit leadership theory assumes that people develop a prototype, a mental model, that reflects and defines for them who a leader is and what leadership entails. Some writers (e.g., Hartog, Deanne, House, Hanges, Ruiz-Quintanilla, Dorfman, et al., 1999)[4] believe that these prototypes have a strong cultural anchoring. For example, employing Hofstede's (1980) cultural typology, one might propose that when followers have a low power distance value set, they will prefer and accept (follow) egalitarian leadership, while followers with high power distance values prefer and accept as their leaders those who are more authoritarian and directive (less participative) in their approach to leadership. Thus, from the perspective of implicit leadership theory, leadership is dependent upon follower perceptions. At this point in the development of our understanding of the follower and the leadership process, we need an understanding of how these implicit models are constructed and who constructs what type of model. The GLOBE[5] project is attempting to answer some of these questions from a cross-cultural perspective.

The readings in this chapter address the role of the follower in the leadership process. Two major questions have been addressed in the leadership literature. First, what are the attributes of the follower that serve to moderate the leader behavior–outcome (e.g., satisfaction, performance) relationship? Some scholarship has also been directed toward the second question: How does the follower affect or influence the leader and the nature of the leader–follower relationship?

As we have seen thus far, students of leadership have sought to understand leadership and the leadership process by focusing primarily on the leader and on how his or her behaviors influence, for example, follower attitudes, motivation, behavior, and group effectiveness. In the first reading in this chapter Charles N. Greene (1975) calls attention to the fact that the causal arrow between leader behavior and followers may run in the opposite direction, suggesting that *follower performance may shape the amount of consideration and initiating structure behavior exhibited by the leader.* Even if this is true, this observation does not negate the impact that leader behavior (e.g., initiating structure and consideration) has on subordinate attitudes and performance, but it highlights the notion that *the relationship between leader and follower is a reciprocal relationship.* The idea of a reciprocal relationship (i.e., a two-way influence process) reinforces Murphy's (1941) suggestion that leadership is an interactive and dynamic process, whereby the leader influences the follower, the follower influences the leader, and both are influenced by the context surrounding this leader–follower relationship. Greene's arguments and observation of the causal arrow running from follower to leader is consistent with Hollander's (1964) notion that followers choose their leaders through their assignment of idiosyncrasy credits, and predictions from LMX theory (see Scandura, 1999) suggesting that follower compliance behavior strongly influences who will emerge in the leader's in- and out-groups.

In the second reading Fillmore H. Sanford (1952) observes that attributes of the follower serve to influence the leadership process. He calls our attention to the personality traits that the followers carry into the leadership context, suggesting that the followers' personalities shape their reactions to the leader's behaviors.

According to Sanford, leadership can be seen as a relationship between a leader and follower. Therefore, it is important to understand the role of the follower in this relationship if one hopes to understand the total process. Sanford suggests that *the*

[4] D. Hartog, N. Deanne, R. J. House, P. J. Hanges, S. A. Ruiz-Quintanilla, P. W. Dorfman, et al., "Culture Specific and Cross-culturally Generalizable Implicit Leadership Theories: Are Attributes of Charismatic/Transformational Leadership Universally Endorsed?" *Leadership Quarterly* 10, 2 (1999), pp. 219–256.
[5] The Global Leadership and Organizational Behavior Effectiveness (GLOBE) research program was launched in the early 1990s by Professor R. J. House, from the Wharton School at the University of Pennsylvania, and is hosted by Thunderbird's Garvin School of International Management. The project involves a network of approximately 170 social scientists from 61 cultures/countries from around the world who are working on a variety of cross-cultural leadership and organizational effectiveness questions and theories.

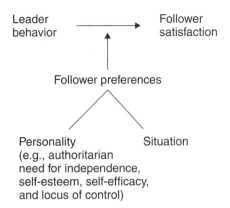

FIGURE 10.1
**The Leader
Behavior–Follower
Satisfaction
Relationship**

follower's own unique personality (e.g., needs, abilities, and attitudes) *defines his or her "readiness for leadership."* When the follower's personality is placed into a leadership situation, these factors combine to determine the follower's receptivity to a particular leader and his or her personality and leadership style. Those followers with an authoritarian personality tend, for example, to accept leaders who exhibit a strong and directive style of leadership, while those with more of an equalitarian personality tend to accept leaders who exhibit a democratic style of leadership.

Gary Yukl (1971)[6] explores the role of the follower's personality in the leadership equation as he presents a behavioral theory of leadership. As a part of this process, Yukl identifies the conditions under which three different dimensions of leader behavior (i.e., initiating structure, consideration, and decision centralization) are associated with members' satisfaction with the leader and their level of productivity.

Yukl carefully presents these three leader behaviors as separate and distinct dimensions and suggests that variation in one dimension does not imply variation in the next. His observation parallels earlier contentions that a production and people emphasis, or initiating structure and consideration behaviors, are not opposite ends of the same continuum. Instead, these behaviors are independent of one another, and it is therefore possible for a leader to display either one or both behaviors.

In Yukl's behavioral theory of leadership, consideration and initiating structure stem from the leadership work conducted at The Ohio State University. *Consideration* refers to the degree to which a leader expresses a positive, indifferent, or negative attitude toward a subordinate. A leader high in consideration is friendly, supportive, and considerate. *Initiating structure* is a task-oriented behavior reflecting the leader's concern for productivity (e.g., goal orientation), making sure that task decisions are made, and exhibiting behaviors that are directed toward making sure that directives are carried out. *Decision centralization* builds upon Lewin, Lippitt, and White's work with democratic, autocratic, and laissez-faire leaders. Specifically, decision centralization refers to the manner in which decisions are made, highlighting the amount of influence exercised by the leader and followers. Thus, decision centralization can range from high subordinate influence to complete leader influence over decisions affecting the group.

The degree to which a particular leader behavior produces follower satisfaction is shaped by the follower's personal preferences for that behavior (see Figure 10.1). This statement suggests that not all followers will necessarily like or dislike any particular leader behavior (e.g., initiating structure, decision centralization). Instead, the relationship between leader behavior and follower satisfaction with the leader will be influenced (moderated) by the follower's preferences.

[6] G. Yukl, "Toward a Behavioral Theory of Leadership," *Organizational Behavior and Human Performance* 6 (1971), pp. 414–440; and an expanded version in *Leadership in Organizations* (Englewood Cliffs, NJ Prentice-Hall, 1994).

FIGURE 10.2
The Leader Behavior–Follower Performance Relationship*

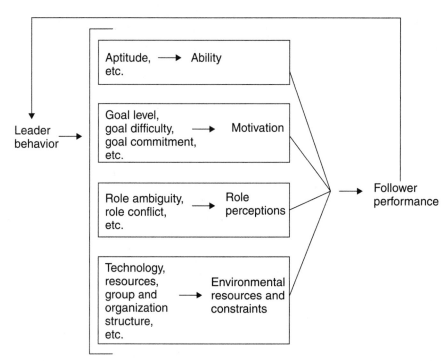

* This model depicts many of the arguments made by Wofford and Spinivaser (1983) in their leader-environment-follower theory of leadership. J. C. Wofford and T. N. Spinivaser, "Experimental Tests of the Leader-Environment-Follower Interaction Theory of Leadership," *Organizational Behavior and Human Performance* 32 (1983), pp. 35–54.

Subordinate preferences tend to be shaped by their own personalities, the situation in which they find themselves, and what they believe their leader should be doing at a particular point in time.

Yukl's work, along with that of Vroom (1964),[7] suggests that leader behavior is unlikely to have a direct impact on follower performance. Instead, if a leader's behavior is going to have an impact on performance, it must lead to an increase in one or more of the following intermediate (mediating) conditions: the skills and abilities that the follower brings to task performance; follower task motivation (i.e., the effort put forth toward task performance); the accuracy of the perceptions that the followers have in terms of their role requirements; and/or by providing the group with needed information, resources, and cooperation from individuals or groups outside of the work group (see Figure 10.2).

The concepts of social exchange (Blau, 1964)[8] and norms of reciprocity (Gouldner, 1960)[9] provide us with insight into the motivational forces encouraging followers to respond by giving something back when their leaders initiate transactional relationships. One of these leader–follower exchange relationships has been highlighted in leader–member exchange (LMX) theory. As noted in the introduction to Chapter 2, LMX theory, as presented by George Graen and his colleagues (cf., Dansereau, Graen, & Haga, 1975;[10] Graen & Cashman, 1975),[11] examines the follower–leader working relationship from a transactional perspective. Transactional models of leadership suggest that leaders employ resources that

[7] V. H. Vroom, *Work and Motivation* (New York: Wiley, 1964).
[8] P. Blau, *Exchange and Power in Social Life* (New York: Wiley, 1964).
[9] A. W. Gouldner, "The Norm of Reciprocity," *American Sociological Review* 25 (1960), pp. 165–167.
[10] F. Dansereau, G. Graen, & W. J. Haga, "A Vertical Dyad Linkage Approach to Leadership within Formal Organizations," *Organizational Behavior and Human Performance* 13 (1975), pp. 46–78.
[11] G. B. Graen & J. Cashman, "A Role-making Model of Leadership in Formal Organizations: A Developmental Approach." In J. G. Hunt and L. L. Larson (eds.), *Leadership Frontiers* (Kent, OH: Kent State University Press, 1975), pp. 143–165.

they have access to (i.e., their position of power) to develop different types of exchange relationships with their followers. The model might be seen as a quid pro quo approach to leadership, where a leader offers X to one follower in exchange for Z, while offering W to another follower in exchange for Y. Thus, different relationships are developed with different followers.

According to LMX, some of these relationships may become high-quality relationships characterized by respect and mutual trust, whereas other relationships may be of low quality and based strictly on a calculation of the value of that which is being exchanged. When a high-level (quality) leader–member exchange relationship exists, followers perceive themselves as having a good working relationship with their leader. High leader–member exchange relationships have been associated with follower satisfaction and productivity (Graen, Novak, & Sommerkamp, 1982),[12] maintenance of group membership (Ferris, 1985),[13] and citizenship and in-role behavior (Setton, Bennett, & Liden, 1996).[14]

The LMX model suggests that we should not think strictly in terms of what the leader does, as though there is a single behavior or relationship that develops with his or her group. In fact, *there may be many different behaviors engaged in by a leader, with different behaviors directed toward different followers*. The model also suggests that we need to look at the follower's personality and perceptions, as they will play an important role in explaining the leader–follower working relationship.

In the third reading, Edwin P. Hollander provides a perspective on leadership that is based on the follower's role in reacting to leader qualities. He suggests that the leader–follower relationship is strongly affected by the "perceptions, misperceptions, and self-oriented biases" brought to the relationship by both the leader and the follower.

In summary, the literature focused on followers within the leadership context generates several observations that enhance our understanding of this dynamic and complex mosaic called the leadership process (see Figure 10.3). A view of the followers in a leadership model reveals that they take on several different roles (see Figure 10.4). First and most frequently, we see the follower treated as the dependent variable whereby leaders influence followers (e.g., leader consideration behavior has a positive and causal relationship with follower satisfaction). Second, and as is noted in the first reading in this chapter by Greene (1975), the follower is positioned as the independent variable whereby the follower influences the leader (e.g., follower performance causes leaders to exercise consideration behavior). Third, on more than one occasion, we have been reminded that followers bring to the leadership situation their personalities, skills and abilities, motives (e.g., needs, wants, preferences, expectations), biases, and personal histories. These follower attributes, in part, influence the effectiveness of a leader's influence attempts. Thus, the follower has been positioned as a moderating (i.e., situational) variable. For example, House and Mitchell (1976), in the path-goal theory of leadership, suggest that leader participatory behavior is satisfying for followers with a nonauthoritarian personality, while the directive style of leadership is satisfying for those followers with an authoritarian personality. Finally, the follower has been positioned as the mediating variable. Van Knippenberg and his colleagues[15] examined the literature focused on the role

[12] G. B. Graen, M. Novak, & P. Sommerkamp, "The Effects of Leader–Member Exchange and Job Design on Productivity and Job Satisfaction: Testing a Dual Attachment Model," *Organizational Behavior and Human Performance* 30 (1982), pp. 109–131.

[13] G. R. Ferris, "Role of Leadership in the Employee Withdrawal Process: A Constructive Replication," *Journal of Applied Psychology* 70 (1985), pp. 777–781.

[14] R. P. Setton, N. Bennett, & R. C. Liden, "Social Exchange in Organizations: Perceived Organizational Support, Leader–Member Exchange, and Employee Reciprocity," *Journal of Applied Psychology* 81 (1996), pp. 219–227.

[15] D. van Knippenberg, B. van Knippenberg, D. De Cremer, & M. A. Hogg. "Leadership, Self, and Identity: A Review and Research Agenda," *Leadership Quarterly* 15 (2004), pp. 825–867.

FIGURE 10.3
The Leadership
Process: Followers

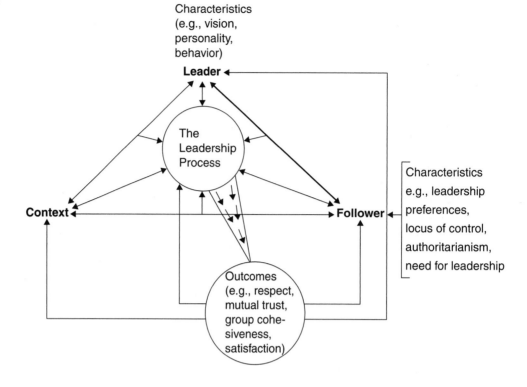

played by the follower's self-concept within the leadership context. They conclude by noting that (a) leader behavior affects follower performance, (b) leader behavior may affect the follower's state (versus trait) self-efficacy, (c) follower self-efficacy positively affects their level of performance, and (d) *leader behavior (e.g., transformational leadership behavior) may affect follower performance by working through its effects on the follower's efficacy beliefs.*

FIGURE 10.4
Follower in the
Leadership Model

Follower as the Dependent Variable

   Leader consideration behavior → Follower satisfaction

Follower as the Independent Variable

   Follower performance → Leader consideration behavior

Follower as the Moderating Variable

   Leader participatory behavior → Follower motivation and satisfaction
                                      ↑
                     Follower's authoritarian personality

Follower as the Mediating Variable

   Transformational leadership → Follower's state self-efficacy → Follower's performance

Reading 27

The Reciprocal Nature of Influence between Leader and Subordinate

Charles N. Greene
Indiana University

Researchers and practitioners would agree that leader behavior is an important variable related to organizational effectiveness. Much of the empirical evidence on organizational leadership has come from the numerous field studies investigating the relationships between leadership styles (e.g., initiating structure and consideration) and subordinate performance and satisfaction (see Fleishman, 1973b). The majority of these studies have employed static correlational techniques or have contrasted the leader behavior of high- and low-productivity groups, which do not allow inferences of the direction of causality. To what extent does the leader influence the subordinate? To what extent does the subordinate influence the leader's behavior? Further, to what extent are there reciprocal effects? There is a need for more studies investigating such directional relationships between leader and group behavior (see e.g. Fleishman, 1973a).

Most often, the importance attributed to leader behavior stems from the presumed effect of the leader's behavior on his subordinates' performance and job satisfaction (Likert, 1961). There is evidence that leadership style affects subordinate performance and attitudes. For example, Day and Hamblin (1964) found subordinate performance varied according to the leader's use of punishment and closeness of supervision. More recently, Dawson, Messe, and Phillips (1972) have shown that experimental variation in the leader's consideration and structure produces changes in group behavior, and Jones, Gergen, Gumpert, and Thibaut (1965) have shown that leader attitudes do get translated into group attitudes.

Other studies investigating the possible effects of subordinate performance on leadership style have had mixed results. Jackson (1953) found that supervisors' leadership styles remained unchanged even though the performance charac-

teristics of the different groups they managed varied substantially—thus indicating that subordinate performance did not affect subsequent leader behavior. In contrast, however, Hawthorne, Couch, Haefner, Langham, and Carter (1956), Lowin and Craig (1968), Farris and Lim (1969), and Crowe, Bochner, and Clark (1972) provided evidence that subordinate performance caused changes in leader behavior. . . .

There are sound theoretical bases (a number of which are reviewed by Lowin and Craig, 1968) from which one can argue that subordinate performance and, in addition, subordinate satisfaction can cause the leader to vary his style of leadership. For example, Katz and Stotland (1959) in their "functional view of attitudes" postulate that a person will develop positive attitudes toward objects which are instrumental to the satisfaction of his needs. This proposition can be applied to leader–subordinate relationships to the degree that the organization makes rewards bestowed on the leader contingent upon his subordinates' performance; in such an organization, the leader may develop more positive attitudes toward his high-performing subordinates. The expectation is that the person whose behavior causes another to be positively reinforced will in return be rewarded by the other. A further expectation is that low performance by a subordinate will cause the leader to restrict or to further specify the subordinate's work activities (both are forms of increased initiating structure) in attempting to improve his performance and, further, to express disapproval (a form of reduced consideration). Conversely, the leader would be expected to see little need for structure and thus engage in less structuring behavior with the high-performing subordinate and, further, to show greater approval and concern for the subordinate's own interests (both are forms of increased consideration). Similar predictions can be made about the influence of subordinate satisfaction on leader behavior to the extent that a subordinate's expression of satisfaction with work is perceived as reinforcing to the leader.

Of the few studies which have examined such causality questions, none were designed to examine the extent to which causation may be reciprocal. When longitudinal data are obtained, as an alternative to experimental designs, there are means for inferring the strength and direction of causality, without requiring the actual manipulation of variables. Two methods for longitudinal data collection are the cross-lagged panel correlational technique and dynamic correlational analysis.

The purpose of this research was to assess, by means of these two techniques, questions of the direction of causal influence in relationships between leader and follower variables. Does a manager's leadership style (in particular, consideration and structure) have greater effect on his subordinate's performance and satisfaction, or is the opposite direction of causality stronger? Further, to what extent are the relationships reciprocal?

METHOD

SAMPLE

The data were collected from 103 first-line managers and, for each manager, two of his immediate subordinates. The sample of first-line managers included: 42 department heads employed at either the corporate headquarters or a regional office of an insurance company; 31 project managers representing the research and engineering functions of a manufacturer of industrial and electronics equipment; and 30 first-line managers employed in the financial and marketing divisions of a chemical products firm. . . .

RESULTS

CONSIDERATION AND SATISFACTION

. . . The "consideration-causes-subordinate satisfaction" coefficients were relatively strong (.40, .34, and .45, for the three respective time periods; all p's < .001) and considerably stronger than the S → C cross-lagged coefficients. . . .

In addition, the significant but rather *moderate* dynamic correlations (r's extended from .42 to .50, all p's < .001) indicate that a third variable and, more likely, several additional variables may have contributed to the covariance between consideration and satisfaction. This particular finding is not surprising, however, since there are other known causes of satisfaction with work.

Thus, one interpretation that can be made from these results is that leader emphasis on consideration constitutes one of several likely causes of subordinate satisfaction.

CONSIDERATION AND PERFORMANCE

The coefficients provided rather strong indications that subordinate performance *causes* leader emphasis on consideration. The only significant correlations were the P → C cross-lagged coefficients: r's = .37, .45, and .33, respectively; all p's < .001. All of the remaining correlations, including the C → P cross-lagged coefficients, were low and did not approach significance. These results help confirm the findings of Lowin and Craig's (1968) experiment and, further, can be interpreted as supporting the theoretical proposition that the leader's attitude toward his subordinates, and its expression, is contingent upon their performance. The leader may be expected, for example, to support and show his approval of those subordinates who have positively reinforced him by their good performance and to be less considerate of subordinates who negatively reinforce him by their low performance. . . .

INITIATING STRUCTURE AND SATISFACTION

The correlations testing the relationships between leader initiating structure and subordinate work satisfaction . . . provide little evidence of causality. . . .

INITIATING STRUCTURE AND PERFORMANCE

The only significant correlations obtained in the cross-lagged analysis of relationships between leader initiating structure and subordinate satisfaction were the moderate, though significant, P → IS cross-lagged coefficients (−.33, −.37, and −.36). Consistent with the theory discussed earlier, the most apparent explanation of these findings (given the negative signs of all of the coefficients) is that low performance by a subordinate caused the leader to engage in more structuring behavior. High subordinate performance, on the other hand, would appear to lead to reduced emphasis on initiating structure. The dynamic coefficients were significant but, as before, too low to exclude the possibility of additional variables affecting the relationships found.

The results concerning the proposition about the moderating effects of consideration were suggested earlier by Fleishman and Harris (1962) who did provide evidence of one such "additional variable." This earlier work by Fleishman and Harris demonstrated that leadership styles may interact so that high emphasis on consideration allows the leader to initiate more structure to achieve organizational objectives. Thus, high turnover and grievances were related to low consideration and high structure. However, supervisors with high consideration could increase structure without adverse effects on grievances and turnover. Supervisors with low structure had high turnover and grievances regardless. Thus, Fleishman and Harris (1962) found consideration to be an important moderator variable of the leader structure-group performance relationship. Cummins (1971) later replicated these results using "quality" as a group output measure. . . .

For leaders perceived to be high on consideration, the "initiating structure-causes-subordinate performance" cross-lagged coefficients were positive, significant, and substantially higher than the corresponding P → IS coefficients. Conversely, significant results in exactly the opposite direction were obtained when the leader was perceived as not emphasizing a high degree of consideration. Here, all of the correlations were negative and the patterns of coefficients rather strongly indicated that performance caused initiating structure, particularly in the low consideration group. While of substantially lesser magnitudes, the negative signs of the IS → P cross-lagged coefficients in the low consideration group are supportive of the contention that high emphasis on structure may be counterproductive when the leader shows little consideration. . . .

Summary

The results of this investigation have provided indications that consideration causes subordinate satisfaction and, conversely, that subordinate performance causes both leader consideration and structure across conditions. However, when the relationship between initiating structure and subordinate performance was moderated by consideration, there was evidence of reciprocal causation. In particular, the results indicate how a leader might positively affect subordinate performance by increased emphasis on both consideration and structure. . . .

References

Campbell, D. T. From description to experimentation: Interpreting trends as quasi-experiments. In C. W. Harris (Ed.), *Problems in measuring change.* Madison: University of Wisconsin Press, 1963.

Crowe, B. J., Bochner, S., & Clark, A. W. The effects of subordinates' behavior on managerial style. *Human Relations,* 1972, 25, 215–237.

Cummins, R. C. Relationship of initiating structures and job performance as moderated by consideration. *Journal of Applied Psychology,* 1971, 55, 489–490.

Dawson, J. E., Messe, L. A., & Phillips, J. L. Effect of instructor-leader behavior on student performance. *Journal of Applied Psychology,* 1972, 56, 369–376.

Day, R. C., & Hamblin, R. L. Some effects of close and punitive styles of supervision. *American Journal of Sociology,* 1964, 69, 499–510.

Farris, G. F., & Lim, G. F., Jr. Effects of performance on leadership cohesiveness, influence, satisfaction and subsequent performance. *Journal of Applied Psychology,* 1969, 53, 490–497.

Fleishman, E. A. Overview. In E. A. Fleishman & J. G. Hunt (Eds.), *Current developments in the study of leadership.* Carbondale: Southern Illinois University Press, 1973. (a)

Fleishman, E. A. Twenty years of consideration and structure. In E. A. Fleishman & J. G. Hunt (Eds.), *Current developments in the study of leadership.* Carbondale: Southern Illinois University Press, 1973. (b)

Fleishman, E. A., & Harris, E. F. Patterns of leadership related to employee grievances and turnover. *Personnel Psychology,* 1962, 15, 43–56.

Greene, C. N. Causal connections among managers' merit pay, satisfaction, and performance. *Journal of Applied Psychology,* 1973, 58, 95–100.

Hawthorne, W. W., Couch, A., Haefner, D., Langham, P., & Carter, L. F. The effects of varying combinations of authoritarian and equalitarian leaders and followers. *Journal of Personality and Social Psychology,* 1956, 53, 210–219.

Jackson, J. M. The effect of changing the leadership of small work groups. *Human Relations,* 1953, 6, 25–44.

Jones, E. E., Gergen, K. J., Gumpert, P., & Thibaut, J. W. Some conditions affecting the use of ingratiation to influence performance evaluation. *Journal of Personality and Social Psychology,* 1965, 1, 613–625.

Katz, D., & Stotland, E. A preliminary statement to a theory of attitude structure and change. In S. Koch (Ed.), *Psychology: A study of science* (Vol. 3). New York: McGraw-Hill, 1959.

Lawler, E. E., & Suttle, J. L. A causal correlational test of the need hierarchy concept. *Organizational Behavior and Human Performance,* 1972, 3, 265–287.

Likert, R. *New patterns of management.* New York: McGraw-Hill, 1961.

Lowin, A., & Craig, J. R. The influence of level of performance on managerial style: An experimental object lesson in the ambiguity of correlational data. *Organizational Behavior and Human Performance,* 1968, 3, 441–458.

Pelz, D. C., & Andrews, F. M. Detecting causal priorities in panel study data. *American Sociological Review,* 1964, 29, 836–848.

Simon, H. A. Spurious correlation: A causal interpretation. *Journal of the American Statistical Association,* 1954, 49, 467–479.

Stogdill, R. M. *Manual for job description and job expectation questionnaire—Form XII.* Columbus: Ohio State University, Bureau of Business Research, 1965. (a)

Stogdill, R. M. *Manual for job description and job expectation questionnaire.* Columbus: Ohio State University, College of Administrative Science, Program for Research in Leadership and Organization, 1965. (b)

Vroom, V. H. A comparison of static and dynamic correlation methods in the study of organizations. *Organizational Behavior and Human Performance,* 1966, 1, 55–70.

Yee, A. H., & Gage, N. L. Techniques for estimating the source and direction of causal influence in panel data. *Psychological Bulletin,* 1968, 2, 115–126.

Reading 28
The Follower's Role in Leadership Phenomena

Fillmore H. Sanford

Most psychological researches on leadership have been concerned with the traits of leaders. Psychologists, traditionally, have dealt with the characteristics of individuals and have made available many instruments, such as personality tests, to facilitate thinking in terms of traits. The search for "leadership traits," however, has not been very rewarding. Stogdill's review[1] strongly suggests that some new approach is needed if we are going to make sense out of leadership phenomena. The literature leads us to think either (a) that there are no general "leadership traits" or (b) that if there are, they do not come in such a form as to be properly described in terms of those personality variables which we now can most easily measure.

The present study departs rather drastically from the search for leadership traits. It looks instead at the follower. It starts off with the idea that leadership is a *relation* between leader and follower, as marriage is a relation between husband and wife and friendship a relation between two people. If we want to learn about marriage, we do not study only husbands or only wives. We have to study the relation that exists between them. The same thing holds for friendship or enmity or partnership or leadership. The present study, while based on the notion that leadership is

a relation between leader and follower, does not succeed in studying the relation directly. It seeks to learn about the relation by looking at the follower— the heretofore neglected follower—and his role in the relationship.

The follower is always there when leadership occurs. It is he who accepts or rejects leadership. It is he who follows reluctantly or enthusiastically, obediently or creatively. In any situation where leadership occurs, he is there with all his psychological attributes. He brings with him his habits, attitudes, preferences, biases, and deep-lying psychological needs. If we know something about these psychological attributes, we know something about the follower's "readiness for leadership." We know something about the sort of relations he will be inclined to establish with what sort of leaders.

It is probably true, our general notion says, that every individual has his own unique pattern of readiness for leadership. He has learned both general and specific attitudes toward authority and the ways it is exercised. Perhaps he has learned to like strong and directive leadership, exercised by people with all the accoutrements of conventional status. Perhaps he dislikes leaders who are less than six feet tall and has a great antipathy for any female who tries to assume a leadership role. Another individual may have learned, by contrast, to reject any form of autocratic or directive leadership, preferring his leaders to be more human, more sympathetic, and more responsive to the follower.

In any group or in any society we may expect to find a wide variety of learned readinesses for leadership. But any group may have a modal pattern of readinesses that sets it off from other groups. Eventually we may be able to describe the southern or the middle class or the Jewish or the Protestant or the educated or uneducated orientation to leadership. Or we may be able to trace out the American as contrasted with the German or the Samoan pattern of attitudes toward authority in its various forms.

The present paper presents first some specimen data on what may be roughly called the American orientation to leadership. It analyzes followers' responses to some interview items designed to elicit general attitudes about leadership, and it goes on

Source: Excerpts from "The Follower's Role in Leadership Phenomena," from *Readings in Social Psychology* by E. L. Hartley, Theodore M. Newcomb, and G. E. Swenson. 1958. Reprinted by permission of Wadsworth, a division of Thomson Learning: www.thomsonrights.com. Fax 800-730-2215.

The present paper reports on some of the results from a large-scale study of leadership conducted at The Institute for Research in Human Relations. More detailed accounts appear in the author's book *Authoritarianism and Leadership* (Philadelphia: The Institute for Research in Human Relations, 1950), and in his report "Public Orientation to Roosevelt," *Public Opinion Quarterly* XV (1951), 189–216. Permission to reprint certain materials from these sources has been given by The Institute for Research in Human Relations and by Princeton University Press.

The project was supported by the Office of Naval Research, but the publication of assertions growing out of the study does not imply their endorsement by any branch of the Naval Service. John N. Patterson, Barney Korchin, Harry J. Older, Emily L. Ehle, Irwin Rosenstock, Doris M. Barnett, F. Loyal Greer, and Douglas Courtney were collaborators in the overall project and were direct or indirect contributors to the present report.

to examine the public's orientation to F. D. Roosevelt as a leader. Then the paper talks about one personality factor in the individual which has something to do with his readiness to follow. . . .

THE FOLLOWER'S PERSONALITY AS A FACTOR IN LEADERSHIP

The foregoing data bear on what we may eventually be able to describe as the "typical" American way of reacting to leadership. We have been working under the general background hypothesis that psychological needs or predispositions of the follower have an important hand in determining both how a leader is perceived and the degree to which he is accepted. The data so far presented tend to fall in line with this hypothesis and lead to tentative statements about some follower needs that are involved in the leader–follower relation. But we can come to closer grips with such matters if we can deal with the psychology of the individual follower rather than the psychology of masses of followers.

The plan of the project called for the intensive study of one personality variable which, on the basis of theory, ought to have a great deal to do with the individuals' reactions to leadership. The variable chosen was authoritarianism, and the instrument used to study it was an authoritarian–equalitarian (A–E) scale.[2] . . .

On the basis of theory and existing evidence, we expect that the people who score toward the authoritarian end of the A–E scale will want strong and directive leadership and will accept leadership that "pays off" in material terms. The authoritarian's "bargaining" orientation to authority, his respect for the strong and scorn for the weak, should lead him to accept Roosevelt as a good leader because Roosevelt was strong and because he produced.

The low scorers, on the other hand, tending toward a warmer—and perhaps more rational—relation with people and with authority, should emphasize Roosevelt's humanity or humanitarianism and should take a reasonably objective view of his ability to do his job. Being less deeply concerned with authority relationships, they should not be concerned with the strength-weakness dimension, unless they perceive strength as necessary for the achievement of a social goal, and should judge Roosevelt against a relatively "democratic" frame of reference.

In order to test such hypotheses, the procedure was:

1. To select from our population 80 individuals who were in the B economic group ($5,000 to $10,000 annual income) and who had completed at least a high-school education.

2. To split the 80 into two groups with respect to A–E scores—40 "highs" and 40 "lows."

3. To classify the responses of all 80 individuals with respect to psychologically conceived variables.

4. To examine the tendency, if any, of "highs" and "lows" to respond in accordance with theoretical expectations.

The selection of 80 individuals of approximately the same income group and educational level should succeed in holding relatively constant these demographic variables so that personality variables can show through clearly.

Each response of these 80 individuals was classified according to the following variables:

1. *Emphasis on function.* The tendency of the respondent to think of Roosevelt's functioning as a leader of a democratic country. "Was an excellent administrator," "chose good advisers."

2. *Material dependency.* The respondent's emphasis on Roosevelt's "payoff," the material benefits he brought to his followers. "Looked out for the average man," "saved us from depression."

3. *Emphasis on power.* The emphasis on power and strength of the man; the suggestion that the follower wanted a powerful leader to keep him safe. "He was a pillar of strength in time of need."

4. *Personal warmth.* The emphasis on FDR's responsiveness to and fondness for people. "He liked people," "he was a great humanitarian."

The procedure was for three judges, two of whom were trained in psychology, to examine all 80 responses, to discuss each one, then to put in one pile all those agreed upon as clearly expressing the quality under consideration. This was done, of course, in ignorance of the A–E scores of the respondents. By this method all the 80 responses agreed upon as expressing a *concern with function* were separated out. Then the total 80 were shuffled, and those agreed upon as showing *material dependency* were separated, and so on for each of the four variables. It was then possible to compare with chance expectation the frequency of high scorers and low scorers in each pile.

Of the 80 responses, 25 were agreed upon as showing *concern with function.* Theory dictates that those who demonstate this relatively objective concern for the leader's function should be low scorers. The results showed 19 out of the 25 answers in this category were made by people in the low-scoring group. This result is different from chance expectation at the 2-percent level of significance. (The C.R. by the sign test is 2.40.)

Only 6 of these 80 respondents gave responses that were agreed upon as showing clear *material dependency*. (These 80 were all middle- or upper-middle-class people.) We expect from theory that high scorers will give this sort of response. The fact is that five out of the six expressing material dependency are high scorers. This difference is suggestive but by no means conclusive since the N is so small.

Thirty-one of the respondents gave responses agreed upon as *emphasizing the leader's power*. We would expect, theoretically, that our high scorers, with their respect for power, would be the ones responding in this category. Eighteen out of the 31 respondents here were high, 13 were low. This result does not differ significantly from chance. One gets the impression, however, that this may be because the low scorers, in a way consistent with personality structure, are regarding Roosevelt's strength as a *means* rather than as an end in itself. In time of stress the equalitarian is perfectly willing to accept the powerful leader whose emergency function is clear. There is reason to believe that while the equalitarian can take power or leave it alone, the authoritarian *needs* it—almost to a neurotic degree. In the reaction to Roosevelt, the low scorers may be expressing admiration for strength when strength was functionally necessary—during a war and a depression when democracy was threatened. The authoritarian may be admiring strength for its own sweet savor. But our present data cannot be used to test these hypotheses.

There were 13 of the 80 responses agreed upon by three judges as expressing admiration for Roosevelt's *warmth and humanitarian qualities*. We would expect our low scorers to predominate in this area. Twelve out of the 13 responses in this category were made by our equalitarians—a result that differs significantly (at better than the 1-percent level) from chance expectation.

These results show with reasonable clarity that personality factors in the follower play a role in determining the orientation to a leader. While authoritarians and equalitarians, as classified by the A–E scale, are almost equal in the frequency with which they express admiration for Roosevelt, they clearly differ in the reasons they give for accepting him as a leader. Authoritarians do not think of him in terms of his social function or in terms of his humanity and warmth. They tend to emphasize his materially beneficial accomplishments. The low scorers on the A–E scale—the so-called "equalitarians"—clearly see FDR's concern for people, observe his successful functioning, and show little concern for how he "paid off" in terms of beneficial accomplishments.

DISCUSSION

The study of the follower and an emphasis on the leader–follower relation lead to a way of thinking about leadership that may overcome some of the limitations inherent in a trait approach and that someday may develop into a systematic theory of leadership. It may be worthwhile here to look at a summary sketch of this way of thinking.

Leadership is a relation. Psychological factors in the follower as well as psychological factors in the leader help determine this relation. The individual follower has his own unique pattern of needs and attitudes that constitute his readiness for leadership. He has problems which the leader must solve. He has learned certain standards whereby he judges the leader's effectiveness. All these factors are there in determining what sort of relation will be established with what sort of leader.

Because all Americans have more-or-less common learning experiences, American followers can be expected to have a more-or-less "typical" way of reacting to authority. And because the relevant learning differs somewhat from one group to another within American society, we might expect the ways of reacting to authority to differ somewhat from one demographic segment of the population to another.

In a concrete leadership situation, the follower's deep-lying attitudes and needs are present as background determiners of his reaction to the leader, but there are also *situationally determined needs* that arise. The need to achieve a group goal or the need to adjust to here-and-now demands is imposed on the more persistent patterns of needs, making new demands on the leader. In a life-or-death situation, the follower's need for warm approval is likely to be less important than his need to survive. He will thus be less likely to accept the "nice guy" as a leader, more likely to follow the man who appears able to help solve the immediate and pressing problem. It is possible to state this sort of observation as a definite hypothesis: The more psychologically significant the group goal, the greater the follower's emphasis on the leader's competence to assist in achieving that goal. A corollary to the hypothesis is as follows:

The more *clearly perceived* the goal, and the more visible is progress toward it, the more follower emphasis there will be on the functional competence of the leader. The converse of each of these hypotheses will also be of interest. In groups where the goal is (*a*) not very important, and (*b*) not very visible, there will be a preference for leaders who meet those persistent psychological needs that are relatively independent of the immediate situation—e.g., the need for warm approval. Certainly in many everyday groups (fraternities, clubs, neighborhood or church organizations, etc.) the preferred leader often seems to be the one who is good at giving psychological structure and satisfaction to garden-variety individuals with standard American social needs. It sometimes happens in these groups, that "nice guy" leaders are bypassed or thrown out when the group comes down with a desire to do a specific and challenging job. Sometimes in such groups we also see "leadership by default." Where the role of the leader is neither very functionally significant nor clearly defined, the individual who desperately wants to be leader is allowed to assume the mantle, whether or not he is a "nice guy."

These are examples of the sort of hypotheses—testable hypotheses—that grow out of the present approach to leadership phenomena.

We can, with profit, start to think about leadership in terms of the follower's needs or problems and their variations from situation to situation. But we still cannot understand leadership without paying close attention to the leader and *his* problems. The leader is as much of an individual as is the follower. His needs, his abilities, obviously are involved in the leader–follower relation. We have built up a picture here of follower's needs creating a demand for leadership of a certain sort. In any situation there will be a pressure to put into the leader's role a person who fits the demand. Formal or informal candidates for the leader's role have their own pressures to exert also. Some people want to be leaders, sometimes desperately so. Some of these will be able, because of their own pattern of needs, to play the leader's role with only one style. Some people are very chronic "nice guys" and cannot meet situational demands for strong and directive authority. Others are chronic authoritarians who may desperately want to dominate others and would be a severe handicap to a group with a strong need for individual initiative and freedom of expression. There are individuals who seek responsibility but who clearly lack the abilities necessary to advance specific group goals. Others will have requisite abilities but do not particularly like to assume responsibility.

Who will become leader will depend on (*a*) the pattern of follower needs and (*b*) the pattern of leader needs and abilities. The leader–follower relation most likely to become established in a free situation—and most likely to persist in either a free situation or one in which leadership is determined from outside—is the relation that is reciprocally rewarding to both follower and leader.

Notes

1. R. M. Stogdill, "Personal Factors Associated with Leadership: A Survey of the Literature," *J. Psychol.*, 1948, XXV, 35–71.

2. The most extensive studies of the variable are contained in W. Adorno, E. Frenkel-Brunswik, D. Levinson, and R. N. Sanford, *The Authoritarian Personality* (New York: Harpers, 1950). The A–E scale used in the present study is an adaptation of the F scale described in that volume.

Reading 29

Leadership, Followership, Self, and Others

Edwin P. Hollander
City University of New York Baruch College and University Graduate Center

Attempts to understand leadership as a function of leader qualities still represent a challenge in the field (see e.g., Kenny & Zaccaro, 1983; Lord, DeVader, & Alliger, 1986; Kirkpatrick & Locke, 1991). As a starting place, that venerable approach gained credence if only because the leader is usually seen as the major actor in leadership. It is easier to focus on one individual as the center of action, influence, and power than many in making attributions.

Another practical reason for attention to the leader is that leader action or inaction can have multiple effects on other people, not only in the success of the enterprise, but also in the "social health" of a group, organization, or larger entity, including a nation. Indeed, a reasonable question, not asked enough, is what are the *costs* of putting this person in a position of authority *and* responsibility? Another might be, how does he or she respond to disconfirming information from subordinates?

Despite the understandable focus on the leader, the concepts of leader and leadership do not exist in isolation. To be viable, both depend upon followership (see Hollander & Offermann, 1990a,b). Accordingly, this paper takes a relational approach to leader qualities, whose significance lies in how they are perceived and responded to by followers within the situation experienced with the leader. As Gibb (1947) long ago indicated, "Leadership is a concept applied to the personality-environment relation" (p. 267).

Although leaders are usually directors of activity, all initiatives need not come from the leader. Followers also have the potential for making significant contributions to successful leadership. Indeed, at every level in organizations, leaders are called upon to be responsive also as followers. Not least is the reality that leaders typically rise from among those who have shown ability in the follower role, and are thereby given a boost.

President Dwight D. Eisenhower's career presents a dramatic case in point. Long a junior staff officer before World War II, he was mentored by Generals MacArthur and Marshall. Promoted to colonel near the onset of war, 26 years after graduating from West Point, he was made a major general and commander of U.S. forces in Europe the very next year, elevated over 366 eligible officers. What were the qualities he displayed as a follower that eventually advanced him to supreme commander of Allied Forces and beyond? Without knowing them in detail, it is reasonable to surmise that they fit the task demands of the situation and that not just desire, nor geniality coupled with keen intelligence, could account alone for his dramatic rise and evident success.

LEADER QUALITIES BY STAGES

Maccoby (1987) is among those who have made the essential point that the style that gets the leadership position is not the same as what is required for effectiveness later. There are even more distinctions, however, in addressing leader qualities needed at successive stages (cf., e.g., Howard & Bray, 1988; Kraut et al., 1989). Moreover, there are the more fundamental questions of who seeks the leader role? What motivates that quest? What features of leader style go with which motives?

Viewed sequentially, at least four distinctive, if partially overlapping, stages can be identified where certain qualities are more likely to be seen. Put briefly, these stages are definable as *wanting, getting, doing,* and *maintaining the job.* Motivational elements in seeking a leader role obviously take precedence, including needs for personalized power, achievement, and affiliation (see McClelland, 1975), as well as self-efficacy (Bandura, 1977), to touch on only some.

At the next stage come the qualities perceived to be important in securing it, such as self-presentation skills directed at seeming to fit legitimators' prototypes and perhaps serving their needs, which may involve self-monitoring (Snyder, 1979). Finally come those qualities involved in succeeding in leadership and maintaining the leader role, assessed by various, often indeterminant, performance criteria. As noted, the latter stages may call forth

Source: Reprinted from Leadership Quarterly 3, 1, 43–54. Copyright 1992, with permission from Elsevier.

manipulative skills aimed at impression management to achieve favorable outcomes for one's self, often at the expense of others and the broader enterprise (see e.g., Conger, 1990, on John DeLorean). In any case, leader qualities are more likely perceived by followers relevant to the present and future, in the context of the situation, rather than as desirable absolutely (see Hollander & Julian, 1968; Hollander, 1985, p. 493).

An illustration of this is provided by the characteristic known as Machiavellianism (Christie & Geis, 1970). Those high on this measure see the world in manipulative and power-oriented terms and look for situations where he or she can gain control, especially where there is low or less structure. An experiment by Gleason, Seaman, and Hollander (1978) was directed to precisely this point. Sixteen four-man task groups were constructed composed of one Hi Mach, one Lo Mach, and two middle Machs, based on pretesting introductory psychology students with the Machiavellianism Scale. As expected, the Hi Machs were observed to show greater ascendance than the others, especially under the low structure condition. Even more relevant in revealing the followers' perspective, their post-interaction ratings of those preferred as future leaders of the group showed the Middle Machs to be significantly more desired for the leader role than either the Hi's or Lo's. Without knowing precisely why these others were different, follower preferences clearly avoided those who scored at the extremes.

As leaders move through the stages of getting, to doing and maintaining the job, qualities like empathy, creativity, and flexibility loom larger as mediators of performance, beyond the drive to get the position. In general, this helps to account in part for why qualities that seemed appropriate at the wanting and getting stages fail to be satisfactory in the doing and maintaining stages. An obvious instance occurs when high expectations are created at the getting stage which are not sustained in doing the job. This phenomenon of heightened follower perceptions and expectations, which are disconfirmed, has been called "anticipointment."

FOLLOWER PERCEPTIONS AND EXPECTATIONS

Recent developments in the study of leadership have made evident the practical importance of follower perceptions on the leader–follower relationship. The nature of this linkage increasingly is recognized as central to affecting the success or failure of leadership (Hollander & Offermann, 1990a,b). One instance of this is shown in the work on "derailment" (McCall, Lombardo, & Morrison, 1988), with 400 promising managers, seen to be on a fast track. Those failing to reach their expected potential were often perceived to lack interpersonal skills.

Other research by Kouzes and Posner (1987), with a sample of 2,600 top level managers, dealt with qualities they admired in their leaders. Among the most frequently chosen qualities were being honest and inspiring, in addition to being competent and forward looking. Again, the interpersonal or relational realm was perceived to play a significant role. Clearly, the followers' perspective is useful as an avenue to understanding leadership.

Hollander and Kelly (1990) gathered critical incidents and ratings of good and bad leadership from 81 respondents (40 men and 41 women) with organizational work experience, preponderantly of two years or more. Content analyses of the rewards in the situation described indicated that sensitivity to followers, support, and praise dominated good but were absent or negative in bad leadership. Respondents in good leadership reported increased participation/productivity, satisfaction, and a sense of being valued. This effect has been confirmed now with 120 more respondents.

LEADER–FOLLOWER RELATIONSHIPS

This newer approach considers leadership to involve a set of relationships which includes the leader, follower, and their situation, most notably the task or function at hand. Especially now, the emergence of a diverse work force demands more attention to the complex interrelationships in the workplace that are vital to what comes out of the process. This reflects a growing recognition of leadership as a process, and not just a person.

The functions performed by leadership include the obvious one of directing activity, but also decision-making, goal-setting, communicating, adjudicating conflict, and otherwise maintaining the enterprise, among others. These dispersed functions often need some delegation to followers, which reveals the interlocking system of relationships between leaders and followers, and their commonly desired characteristics (Hollander & Webb, 1955; Kouzes & Posner, 1987).

Leadership also operates within constraints and opportunities that are presented by followers (Stewart, 1982). The constraints include the expectations and perceptions of followers which can influence leaders (Hollander, 1985, 1986; Lord & Maher, 1990). One early exponent of this general view, Fillmore Sanford (1950), asserted the proposition that followers are crucial to any leadership event. In addition, the repeated finding that follower behavior is affected by leader behavior is also shown to be reciprocal. Followers affect leaders in a variety of ways, not least as an audience to which leaders orient and address themselves (Hollander & Offermann, 1990a).

Given their need for mutual responsiveness, leadership and followership can be considered to be reciprocal systems requiring synchronization. Leadership is usually seen as the more active system, but followership can be proactive, not only reactive, as seen especially in social movements. Empowerment in some sectors of activity would be another instance of giving followership a more proactive role, as an accompaniment to leadership in the traditional directive mode.

ROLE OF FOLLOWER ATTRIBUTIONS ABOUT LEADERS

Follower attributions about leaders affect followers' responses to and relations with their leader. These are affected by the leader's perceived attributes, including his or her competence, motivation, and personality characteristics, as related to followers and the prevailing situation. Lord and Maher (1990) consider these perceptions to be checked against prototypes held by followers of leader attributes, such as intelligence and expectations of how leaders should perform. In this feature of leadership, follower perceptions are seen as the key linking past performance and future performance, as part of the greater attention now to cognitive elements in leader–follower relations. This development is well represented by follower "implicit leadership theories" (ILTs), among other concepts (see Calder, 1977; Lord, DeVader, & Alliger, 1986; Rush, Thomas, & Lord, 1977). A precursor of this was the relating of followers' expectancies of leader attributes to perceptions of leader behavior (Hollander, 1964).

Indeed, the link between perceptions and behavior is the essence of the interest now in leader attributes *as perceived by followers,* and the response that ensues. For example, Calder (1977) and Pfeffer (1977) are among the proponents of a perceptual/attributional perspective which says that leaders are credited or blamed for outcomes over which they alone had little effect. Because positive or negative outcomes are more likely to be attributed to the leader, he or she is more readily faulted and even removed as a symbol when things go wrong, rather than firing the whole staff or team.

SELF AND OTHER: DOMINANCE AND IDENTIFICATION MOTIFS

Fundamental to the leadership process is the way the leader perceives his or her social self relative to followers. A traditional view of the leader role associates it with authority as the basis for using power, which puts distance between the leader and followers (see Kipnis, 1976). Such a view sees followers as essentially compliant and manipulable, within a dominance motif. One expression of this is a quote from a corporate CEO that "leadership is confirmed when the ability to inflict pain is demonstrated" (Menzies, 1980).

An alternative view, more in keeping with a participative ethos, sees the leader–follower relationship within a mutual identification motif. This includes the prospect of two-way influence, and the perception and counterperception of leader and followers. Cantril (1958) has said that the leader must be able to perceive the reality worlds of followers and have sensitivity to guide intuitions, if a common consensus and mutual trust rather than "mere power, force, or cunning" are to develop and prevail (p. 129). In practical political terms, Kellerman (1984) has observed that presidential leadership has to be accomplished from "within the world of other people."

The identification with the leader motif is exemplified in Freud's (1921) concept of the leader as a shared "ego-ideal" with whom members of a group mutually identify. Fromm (1941) extended this contention in personality terms by writing that "the psychology of the leader and that of his followers, are, of course, closely linked with each other" (p. 65). Erikson (1975) made an associated point about this linkage in asserting that followers "join a leader and are joined together by him" (p. 153).

A good part of the imbalance in treating the leader–follower relationship arises from the lingering mythology that leaders simply exercise authority and power. Cowley (1928) called this "headship," rather than leadership, which by contrast engages followers in a concerted program of action. More recently, Kipnis (1976) has shown that assertions of power effectively undermine the goals of authentic leadership. Such assertions also are limited in creating positive identifications.

LEGITIMACY AS A BASIS OF AUTHORITY

Followers' perceptions and identification with the leader begin with how he or she attained the role. This is the leader's basis of authority, which is the issue of legitimacy. Such perceptions also are a function of follower expectations, and of persisting "implicit theories" about leaders and how they are perceived to act or should act.

Election and appointment are two contrasting instances of legitimacy, which have been found to produce different effects on followers, insofar as they generate varying commitments to the leader. Election creates a heightened psychological identification with the leader, but also more vulnerability to criticism and the withdrawal of support by followers. The evidence indicates that a leader's legitimacy has a considerable effect in shaping followers' perceptions (e.g., Ben-Yoav, Hollander, & Carnevale, 1983), and on group performance and the leader's perception of followers (cf., Green & Mitchell, 1979).

The election case is, of course, a more obvious instance of leader emergence with the consent of followers. In that regard, election gives followers a greater sense of responsibility for and investment in the leader. But they also may have been found to have higher expectations about the leader, at least initially. Elected leaders who fail to perform to expectations have been found to be more vulnerable to criticism than appointed leaders, particularly if they were seen to be competent in the first place (Hollander & Julian, 1970, 1978). While election and appointment create different psychological climates between leaders and followers, organizational leaders *can* attain a "following" by doing more than exercising authority, as Katz and Kahn (1978) have observed.

One effect of the current attributional view is to make even more explicit the significance of followers' and others' perceptions of the leader as a constraint of check on leader behavior. There also are the related expectations about such leader characteristics as their requisite level of competence and motivation. The reverse perspective of the leader's perception of followers also is of significance (see Mitchell, Green, & Wood, 1981).

This is illustrated in the findings of an experiment by Elgie, Hollander, and Rice (1988). Leader evaluations were studied of four types of followers, who provided either positive or negative feedback with either high or low task activity. The outcome measure was a score made up of their ratings of each follower on 10 semantic differential scales. An overall result showed that elected leaders gave more positive ratings generally than appointed leaders in ratings of their followers. A specific finding of interest was that elected and appointed leaders responded differently to high and low activity followers under the negative feedback condition, but similarly under the positive feedback condition. With the lower ratings they assigned, appointed leaders evidently viewed such negative feedback more critically, possibly as a greater threat to their status.

TRANSACTIONAL MODELS OF LEADERSHIP

Process-oriented "transactional" models of leadership developed initially out of a social exchange perspective, emphasizing the implicit social exchange or transaction that exists between leader and followers as a feature of effectiveness (see Hollander, 1964, 1978; Hollander & Julian, 1969; Homans, 1961). In the transactional view, the leader gives benefits to followers, such as a definition of the situation and direction, which is reciprocated by followers in heightened esteem for and responsiveness to the leader. This transactional approach is part of the current organizational theme emphasizing a more active role for followers, and the potential for two-way influence (see Hollander & Offermann, 1990a). It also conveys the sense of the leader earning or deserving a following.

Followers' perceptions of and expectations about the leader's actions and motives are generated in accordance with an attributional process. Such interpersonal perceptions are seen in Heider's (1958) distinction between "can" and "will." When a leader is perceived to be able to achieve a favorable outcome, but does not because of a perceived failure of will, this causes a greater loss of following than the reverse, that is, an inability to achieve something desirable but still with an apparent try.

IDIOSYNCRASY CREDIT

This attributional analysis is related to a social exchange concept, the "idiosyncrasy credit" (IC) model of innovative leadership (Hollander, 1958, 1964). The model deals with the latitude a leader has to bring about change as a function of followers' perceptions of that leader's competence and signs of loyalty that engender trust.

Credit is a term in common usage which emphasizes an interpersonal process long recognized. We give credit, take credit, and are discredited, as examples. It has its root in the word creed, referring to the belief, confidence, trust, and faith we have in another. In leadership it applies to attributions of a leader's intentions, and expectations of action, and likely consequences. An essential virtue of the credit perspective is to make plain the leader's need to establish himself or herself with followers as perceivers and evaluators who give or withhold credit.

In the IC model, leadership is viewed as a dynamic process of interpersonal evaluation in which credits are earned in the eyes of followers. These credits provide latitude for deviations that would be unacceptable for those without such credit. Credits come from perceived competence and conformity to group norms, as a sign of loyalty, and then can be used to take innovative actions expected as part of the leader's role.

Other factors may contribute to the accumulation of credits. Seniority is one of these that operates widely, though obviously not with uniform impact. A person may also benefit by having "derivative credit," in the form of a favorable reputation from another group, or from the society at large, as seen for example in high socioeconomic status. Most usually, however, a new member of a group is in a poor position to assert influence, especially in the direction of change, unless he or she has a unique qualification, such as an idea that helps deal with a major group problem, or a badly needed skill. In these circumstances their credit is gained by maximizing on the competence factor.

A benefit may also result from calling attention to oneself in a figure-ground sense, if the outcome for the group is positive. This is verified in the research by Sorrentino and Boutillier (1975) who found that initial quantity of participation in a group was viewed by others as a positive sign of a group member's motivation, while later participation was evaluated more as to quality. Relatedly, Ridgeway (1981) has contended that nonconformity may be a greater initial score of influence and has presented experimental evidence that appears contradictory to the IC model. Certainly it is true that within a brief time a person may call attention to himself or herself by manifest nonconformity to prevailing norms. However, this will be evaluated in due course by the standard of the task contribution made, and a point of dysfunctionality may be reached where rejection may result.

An experiment pertinent to the expenditure of credits was conducted by Hollander, Julian, and Sorrentino (1969). They studied the effects on appointed or elected leaders of disagreements with their followers. Elected leaders who had been told they had strong group support in attaining that position were significantly more likely to make total reversals of their group's decision—indeed on about half the critical trials—than were those in the other conditions. In addition, elected leaders with strong support showed lower conciliation in their responses to group judgments, based on a content analysis of their messages to the group. Evidently, the elected leader in this condition felt freer to challenge group judgments, as a likely function of idiosyncrasy credit.

Unused credits can be lost by failing to fulfill follower expectations for that role, including inaction in the face of need. Also, the leader's self-serving and other negatively viewed behaviors can drain credits, as can perceptions of weak motivation, incompetence, and the responsibility for failure (see Alvarez, 1968).

Perceiving how and when credit is earned and expended therefore seems to be an essential interpersonal task. On the earning end, as one example, Porter (1985) says, "Managers are reluctant to spend the time and resources on interrelationship projects if they are uncertain to receive credit for them" (p. 389). On the expending end, situations may be perceived by a leader as risky to his or her status, and thereby cause restraint in taking action, especially for fear of a loss of personal power (see McClelland, 1975).

SOCIAL SELF, SOCIAL PERCEPTIVENESS, AND SELF-MONITORING

As already noted, the study of leadership requires attention to the leader's self-concept. More pointedly, it is the social self that is pivotal to understanding the leader-follower relationship. If the leader's self-perception is inaccurate with respect to others' perceptions, the relationship is likely to be affected adversely. Misperception of others' perceptions and desires becomes magnified as a problem in leadership. It also accounts for a failure to know whether and when to use credit, as exemplified when a leader takes no action in the face of manifest need.

One quality that has been postulated as a significant ingredient in gaining and doing leadership successfully is social perceptiveness, that is, alertness to the surrounding environment and understanding of situations (see Stogdill, 1948;

Hollander & Julian, 1968). A related feature of this quality is "self-monitoring," which Snyder (1979) identified as the ability to monitor and control one's expressive behaviors. Among the three characteristics included within this quality is "sensitivity to social cues." Recent research by Zaccaro, Foti, and Kenny (1991), using a rotation design, found that self-monitoring was stable as a characteristic correlating significantly with overall leader ranking.

SELF-SERVING BIASES

More than the usual tendency, leaders may be given to self-serving biases that exist in many relationships. This is revealed in such everyday comments as "You are stubborn, but I am acting out of principle," or "I am only doing this for your own good." The role of leader may enhance this tendency, even in the absence of power over others, but especially with it (Kipnis, 1976). This brings about self-absorption and self-deception, which may readily be fed by followers, and result in what is commonly called an "ego-trip." More significantly, in executive suites, it can lead to calamitous results for the organizations involved (see, e.g., Conger, 1990; Byrne et al., 1991).

In an analysis of some psychological elements involved, Greenwald (1985) has presented an interpretation of how the leader's ego or self incorporates several distinctive cognitive biases. These include the self as the focus of knowledge, "beneffectance" as the perception of responsibility for desired, but not undesired, outcomes, and resistance to change.

A necessary corrective is to be aware of the perception, motives, and more about others. But the narcissism associated with leaders who draw on the affection of followers, as in "charismatic leadership," deprives them of this corrective (see Post, 1986). Followers, also, may be vulnerable to perceptual distortions as a feature of the self-serving bias and identification with the leader that can serve a need to bolster the self.

CHARISMATIC AND TRANSFORMATIONAL LEADERSHIP

The concept of the "charismatic leader" (Weber, 1921) deals with leaders who have considerable emotional appeal to followers and a great hold over them through an identification process. While charisma refers to a quality usually seen to be possessed by a leader, it manifests itself in followers who accord it. Without their responsiveness, charisma is hollow.

More recently, from a political science perspective, Burns (1978) proposed a related concept of the "transformational leader." Burns' idea of the leader as an agent who may transform the outlook and behavior of followers has been applied to organizational leadership by Bass (1985) and Bennis and Nanus (1985). Their main point is that such leaders strive to go beyond the bounds of the usual to bring about a change in followers that will create a climate for exceptional performance (see Fiedler & House, 1988).

In one view, transformational leadership can be seen as an *extension* of transactional leadership, with greater leader intensity and follower arousal (Hollander & Offermann, 1990a). Research by Bass (1985) and Yammarino and Bass (1988) on transformational leadership in fact involves a measure with two transactional factors in addition to charisma, intellectual stimulation, and individual attention to followers. However, charisma also may be negative when primarily directed to the leader's self-serving ends, not least the manipulation of others primarily for the leader's ego gratification, as well as for other dubious causes, that can have disastrous effects for the broader good.

The potential for damage from a leader with charismatic appeal is evident. Such a leader is "mirror hungry" and has narcissistic needs for continual approval from others (Post, 1986). Coupled with personalized power needs, a charismatic appeal also can be destructive, as Hogan, Raskin, and Fazzini (1990) have observed in writing about "the dark side of charisma." Moreover, the charismatic leader fosters an atmosphere where imagery substitutes for, or is elevated above, performance (see Drucker, 1988).

All charismatic-transformational leaders do not provide problems in these ways, but their potential for affecting large numbers of others adversely requires attention, if only because appeals based on emotional arousal provide ample opportunities for abuse. It is not enough to say, for instance, that charismatic-transformational leaders transmit a vision—as if they were the only kind of leader who did so—without examining that vision and its probable or known consequences.

CONCLUSIONS

Granted that the study of leadership has usually assumed the existence of followers, their role nonetheless has been seen as mainly passive. This is so despite the truth that followers are more likely to see and know the reality of the leader's day-to-day approach to leadership. Recent models and applications have increasingly sought to integrate followers more fully into the understanding of leadership phenomena. Building on the foundation provided by newer conceptions of leadership, such as the operation of attribution processes, leader-follower relations now have been examined with heightened attention.

A major implication of what has been presented here is to accord a more active role for those considered followers. In this newer view, leaders and their qualities are important particularly as they engage followers toward productive ends. Central to this process are the self–other perceptions, and misperceptions including self-serving biases, that can exist in leader–follower relations. The impact of these transcends the usual way of viewing leader qualities as personal possessions. Leader "charisma," for instance, needs to be seen as essentially interpersonal, since it depends upon the followers' recognizing the leader's special attributes. An essential question, therefore, is what leader qualities elicit a favorable response from particular followers, as well as generally. Some suggestions in that direction have been offered within a relational conception of leadership.

References

Alvarez, R. (1968). Informal reactions to deviance in simulated work organizations: A laboratory experiment. *American Sociological Review, 33,* 895–912.

Bandura, A. (1977). *Social learning theory.* Englewood Cliffs, NJ: Prentice-Hall.

Bass, B. M. (1985). *Leadership and performance beyond expectations.* New York: Free Press.

Bennis, W. G., & Nanus, B. (1985). *Leaders.* New York: Harper & Row.

Ben-Yoav, O., Hollander, E. P., & Carnevale, P. J. D. (1983). Leader legitimacy, leader-follower interaction, and followers' ratings of the leader. *Journal of Social Psychology, 121,* 111–115.

Burns, J. M. (1978). *Leadership.* New York: Harper & Row.

Byrne, J. A., Symonds, W. C., & Siler, J. F. (1991). CEO Disease. *Business Week,* April 1, 52–60.

Calder, B. J. (1977). An attribution theory of leadership. In B. M. Staw & G. R. Salancik (Eds.), *New directions in organizational behavior.* Chicago: St. Clair Press.

Cantril, H. (1958). Effective democratic leadership: A psychological interpretation. *Journal of Individual Psychology, 14,* 128–138.

Christie, R., & Geis, F. L. (1970). *Studies in Machiavellianism.* New York: Academic Press.

Conger, J. A. (1990). The dark side of leadership. *Organizational Dynamics, 19*(2), 44–55.

Cowley, W. H. (1928). Three distinctions in the study of leaders. *Journal of Abnormal and Social Psychology, 23,* 144–157.

Drucker, P. F. (1988). Leadership: More doing than dash. *Wall Street Journal,* January, 6, p. 14.

Elgie, D. M., Hollander, E. P., & Rice, R. W. (1988). Appointed and elected leader responses to favorableness of feedback and level of task activity from followers. *Journal of Applied Social Psychology, 18,* 1361–1370.

Erikson, E. H. (1975). *Life history and the historical moment.* New York: W.W. Norton.

Fiedler, F. E., & House, R. J. (1988). Leadership theory and research: A report of progress. In C. L. Cooper & I. Roberston (Eds.), *International review of industrial and organizational psychology* (pp. 73–92). London: Wiley.

Freud, S. ([1921]1960). *Group psychology and the analysis of the ego.* New York: Bantam. (Originally published in German in 1921.)

Fromm, E. (1941). *Escape from freedom.* New York: Rinehart.

Gibb, C. A. (1947). The principles and traits of leadership. *Journal of Abnormal and Social Psychology, 42,* 267–284.

Gleason, J. M., Seaman, F. J., & Hollander, E. P. (1978). Emergent leadership processes as a function of task structure and Machiavellianism. *Social Behavior and Personality, 6,* 33–36.

Green, S. G., & Mitchell T. R. (1979). Attributional processes of leaders in leader-member interactions. *Organizational Behavior and Human Performance, 23,* 429–458.

Greenwald, A. (1985). Totalitarian egos in the personalities of democratic leaders. Symposium Paper, International Society of Political Psychology Annual Meeting, Washington, DC, June 20.

Heider, F. (1958). *The psychology of interpersonal relations.* New York: Wiley.

Hogan, R., Raskin, R., & Fazzini, D. (1990). The dark side of charisma. In K. E. Clark & M. B. Clark, (Eds.), *Measures of leadership.* West Orange, NJ: Leadership Library of America.

Hollander, E. P. (1958). Conformity, status, and idiosyncrasy credit. *Psychological Review, 65,* 117–127.

Hollander, E. P. (1964). *Leaders, groups, and influence.* New York: Oxford University Press.

Hollander, E. P. (1978). *Leadership dynamics: A practical guide to effective relationships.* New York: Free Press/Macmillan.

Hollander, E. P. (1985). Leadership and power. In G. Lindzey & E. Aronson (Eds.), *The handbook of social psychology* (3rd edition, pp. 485–537). New York: Random House.

Hollander, E. P. (1986). On the central role of leadership processes. *International Review of Applied Psychology,* 35, 39–52.

Hollander, E. P., & J. W. Julian. (1968). Leadership. In E. F. Borgatta & W. W. Lambert (Eds.), *Handbook of personality theory and research* (pp. 890–899). Chicago: Rand McNally.

Hollander, E. P., & Julian, J. W. (1969). Contemporary trends in the analysis of leadership processes. *Psychological Bulletin,* 71, 387–397.

Hollander, E. P., & Julian, J. W. (1970). Studies in leader legitimacy, influence, and innovation. In L. L. Berkowitz (Ed.), *Advances in experimental social psychology* (Volume 5, pp. 33–69). New York: Academic Press.

Hollander, E. P., & Julian J. W. (1978). A further look at leader legitimacy, influence, and innovation. In L. Berkowitz (Ed.), *Group processes* (pp. 153–165). New York: Academic Press.

Hollander, E. P., Julian, J. W., & Sorrentino, R. M. (1969). The leader's sense of legitimacy as a source of constructive deviation. *ONR Technical Report No. 12.* Department of Psychology, State University of New York at Buffalo.

Hollander, E. P., & Kelly, D. R. (1990). Rewards from leaders as perceived by followers: Further use of critical incidents and rating scales. Eastern Psychological Association Annual Meeting, Philadelphia, March 30.

Hollander, E. P., & Offermann, L. (1990a). Power and leadership in organizations: Relationships in transition. *American Psychologist,* 45, 179–189.

Hollander, E. P., & Offermann, L. (1990b). Relational features of organizational leadership and followership. In K. E. Clark & M. B. Clark, (Eds.), *Measures of leadership* (pp. 83–97). West Orange, NJ: Leadership Library of America.

Hollander, E. P., & Webb, W. B. (1955). Leadership, followership, and friendship: An analysis of peer nominations. *Journal of Abnormal and Social Psychology,* 50, 163–167.

Homans, G. C. (1961). *Social behavior: Its elementary forms.* New York: Harcourt, Brace and World.

Howard, A., & Bray D. (1988). *Managerial lives in transition: Advancing age and changing times.* New York: Dorsey.

Katz, D., & Kahn R. L. (1978). *The social psychology of organizations* (2nd edition). New York: Wiley.

Kenny, D. A., & Zaccaro, S. J. (1983). An estimate of variance due to traits in leadership. *Journal of Applied Psychology,* 68, 678–685.

Kipnis, D. (1976). *The powerholders.* Chicago: University of Chicago Press.

Kirkpatrick, S. A., & Locke, E. A. (1991). Leadership: Do traits matter? *Academy of Management Executive,* 5(2), 48–60.

Kouzes, J. M., & Posner, B. Z., (1987). *The leadership challenge: How to get extraordinary things done in organizations.* San Francisco: Jossey-Bass.

Kraut, A. I., Bedigo, P. R. McKenna, D. D., & Dunnette. M. D. (1989). The role of the manager: What's really important in different management jobs. *Academy of Management Executive,* 3, 286–293.

Lord, R. G., & Maher, K. J. (1990). Leadership perceptions and leadership performance: Two distinct but interdependent processes. In J. Carroll (Ed.), *Advances in applied social psychology: Business settings* (Volume 4), pp. 129–154. Hillsdale, NJ: Erlbaum.

Lord, R. G., DeVader, C. L., & Alliger, G. M. (1986). A meta-analysis of the relation between personality traits and leadership perceptions: An application of validity generalization procedures. *Journal of Applied Psychology,* 71, 402–409.

Maccoby, M. (1989). Leadership for our time. In L. Atwater & R. Penn (Eds.), *Military leadership: Traditions and future trends* (pp. 41–46). Annapolis: U.S. Naval Academy.

McCall, M. W., Lombardo, M. M., & Morrison, A. M. (1988). *The lessons of experience.* Lexington, MA: Lexington Books.

McClelland, D. (1975). *Power: The inner experience.* New York: Irvington.

Menzies, H. D. (1980). The ten toughest bosses. *Fortune,* 101, 62–69.

Mitchell, T. R., Green, S. G., & Wood, R. E. (1981). An attributional model of leadership and the poor-performing subordinate: Development and validation. In B. Shaw and L. Cummings (Eds.), *Research in organizational behavior* (Volume 3, pp. 197–234). Greenwich, CT: JAI Press.

Pfeffer, J. (1977). The ambiguity of leadership. In M. W. McCall, Jr., & M. M. Lombardo (Eds.), *Leadership: Where else can we go?* Durham, NC: Duke University Press.

Porter, M. E. (1985). *Competitive advantage.* New York: Free Press.

Post, J. M. (1986). Narcissism and the charismatic leader–follower relationship. *Political Psychology,* 7, 675–688.

Rush, M. C., Thomas, J. C., & Lord, R. G. (1977). Implicit leadership theory: A potential threat to the internal validity of leader behavior questionnaires. *Organizational Behavior and Human Performance,* 20, 93–110.

Sanford, F. (1950). *Authoritarianism and leadership.* Philadelphia, PA: Institute for Research in Human Relations.

Snyder, M. (1979). Self-monitoring processes. In L. Berkowitz (Ed.), *Advances in Experimental Social Psychology,* 12 (pp. 86–128). New York: Academic Press.

Sorrentino, R. M., & Boutillier, R. G. (1975). The effect of quantity and quality of verbal interaction on ratings of leadership ability. *Journal of Experimental Social Psychology,* 11, 403–411.

Stewart, R. (1982). *Choices for the manager.* Englewood Cliffs, NJ: Prentice-Hall.

Stogdill, R. M. (1948). Personal factors associated with leadership. *Journal of Psychology,* 25, 35–71.

Weber, M. (1921). The sociology of charismatic authority. Republished in translation (1946) in H. H. Gerth, & C. W. Mills (Trans. and Eds.), *From Max Weber: Essays in Sociology* (pp. 245–252). New York: Oxford University Press.

Yammarino, R., & Bass, B. M. (1988). Long term forecasting of transformational leadership and its effects among Naval Officers: Some preliminary findings. In K. E. & M. B. Clark (Eds.), *Measures of leadership* (pp. 151–169). West Orange, NJ: Leadership Library of America.

Zaccaro, S. J., Foti, R. J., & Kenny, D. A. (1991). Self-monitoring and trait-based variance in leadership: An investigation across multiple group situations. *Journal of Applied Psychology,* 76, 308–315.

Participative Leadership

The classic study of leader behavior, conducted during 1939 and 1940 at the University of Michigan by Kurt Lewin and his students Ronald Lippitt and Ralph K. White, stimulated an interest in looking at the relative effectiveness of three leadership styles—authoritarian, democratic, and laissez-faire—on group and individual behavior. Among the results from their investigation was the suggestion that leader behavior has a number of different effects on member reactions. Among their major observations are the following: (a) laissez-faire and democratic leadership are not the same; (b) democratic leadership can be efficient; (c) greater hostility, aggression, and discontent arise under autocratic than under democratic leadership; (d) autocratic leadership produces more dependence and less individuality; (e) there is more group-mindedness and more friendliness under democratic leadership; and (f) groups with democratic leaders are more productive even when the leader is not present.[1]

Following the Hawthorne studies (1927–1933), the work of Lewin and his associates, Eric Trist and Fred Emery's work with sociotechnical systems, the onset of the human relations movement, and the development of the human resource model, there emerged a strong interest in participative leadership practices. This interest is evident in numerous participative management theories, a myriad of research investigations, the development of a number of employee-involvement strategies, and organizational efforts to create high-involvement organizations (cf. Lawler, 1992).[2]

The work of Lewin and his students contributed to our thinking about *leadership style* as it pertains to the use and location of power within the group. Different perspectives have been offered regarding leadership styles. One perspective positions the laissez-faire leadership style (i.e., do whatever you want) at one end of a continuum that becomes increasingly directive; laissez-faire leadership is followed by consensus, participative, consultative, benevolent autocratic, and, finally, autocratic (i.e., I will tell you what we are going to do because I am the leader/boss). This perspective has been contrasted with the use of a power (i.e., autocratic versus democratic) and involvement (i.e., active versus passive) orientation to differentiate between leadership styles.[3] Accompanying this typology, the laissez-faire leader is positioned outside the framework and is seen as employing a passive style of leadership (i.e., he or she is seen as not leading *per se*). In the first reading, Stephen M. Sales (1966) provides a review of the theory and empirical observations of the effects associated with authoritarian and democratic dimensions of leader behavior. Sales's observations, when coupled with those stemming from Lewin, Lippitt, and White's work, suggest that

---

[1] R. White & R. Lippitt, "Leader Behavior and Member Reaction in Three 'Social Climates.'" In D. Cartwright & A. Zander (eds.), *Group Dynamics: Research and Theory* (New York: Harper & Row, 1968), pp. 318–335.
[2] E. E. Lawler III, *The Ultimate Advantage: Creating the High-Involvement Organization* (San Francisco: Jossey-Bass, 1992).
[3] G. L. Steward & C. C. Manz, "Leadership for Self-managing Work Teams: A Typology and Integrative Model," *Organizational Dynamics* 19, 4 (1995), pp. 18–35.

absenteeism and turnover may be higher under autocratic leaders than their democratic counterparts, and, as a result, productivity may be lower.

It has been suggested that leader behavior is determined by an interaction between attributes of the leader and characteristics of the situation in which the leadership process unfolds. Scholars recognizing the role of situational differences and their impact upon the leadership process often raise the question about when democratic or participative practices should be employed within the organizational context. In an earlier chapter, House and Mitchell (1974) provided insight into the appropriate conditions for participative management in their path-goal theory of leadership.

Fueled by Frederick Herzberg's and Douglas McGregor's criticisms of scientific management, a number of different schools of thought (e.g., human relations, human resource) and theoretical models (e.g., cognitive, affective, contingency) have articulated the processes associated with efficacious participatory practices. While numerous empirical studies have examined participation, questions as to the effectiveness of participation remain.

In the face of the uncertainty surrounding the effectiveness of participative leadership practices (see the reviews conducted by Locke & Schweiger, 1979; Dachler &Wilpert, 1978; Strauss, 1982),[4] Cotton (1993) observes that the past several decades have been characterized by the adoption of a number of different employee involvement systems (e.g., employee ownership, self-directed work teams, job enrichment, representative participation, quality circles, and quality of work life programs).[5] These involvement systems reflect organizational experimentation with different *forms* of participative leadership at different organizational *levels*—some operating at the team and department level, and others reflecting a top-management orientation toward organizational leadership.

In the second reading in this chapter, Katherine I. Miller and Peter R. Monge (1988) discuss the relationship of participation with satisfaction and productivity. They highlight three theoretical models—contingency, affective, and cognitive—to articulate how and why participation might have a favorable relationship with both of these outcomes. Miller and Monge conducted a statistical meta-analytic review of the participation literature, providing a test for each of the three models. They report finding strong support for the affective model, some support for the cognitive model, and no support for the contingency model. They suggest (see Figure 11.1) that "participation fulfills needs, fulfilled needs lead to satisfaction, satisfaction strengthens motivation, and increased motivation improves workers' productivity" (Miller & Monge, p. 731).

The third, and final, reading in this chapter highlights the appropriateness and efficacy of participative leadership under certain circumstances. The research findings reported by Seokhwa Yun, Samer Faraj, and Henry P. Sims, Jr. (2004) are consistent with Vroom's (2000) normative theory of leadership and with the observations reported by House and Mitchell (1974), both of which suggest that participative forms of leadership are congruent with certain types of tasks (e.g., task structure is discussed by Fiedler [1972] and by House and Mitchell [1974]). Figure 11.2, identifies task structure as a critical situation variable calling for participating leadership. It is, therefore, incumbent upon a leader to be capable of *diagnosing the* situation to ascertain the type (style) of leadership that is

[4] H. P. Dachler & B. Wilpert, "Conceptual Dimensions and Boundaries of Participation in Organizations," *Administrative Science Quarterly* 23 (1978), pp. 1–39; E. A. Locke & D. M. Schweiger, "Participation in Decision Making: One More Look," *Research in Organizational Behavior* 1 (1979), pp. 265–339; G. Strauss, "Workers' Participation in Management: An International Perspective," *Research in Organizational Behavior* 4 (1982), pp. 173–265.

[5] J. L. Cotton, *Employee Involvement: Methods for Improving Performance and Work Attitudes* (Newbury Park, CA: Sage, 1993).

FIGURE 11.1   Affective Participation Model

Participation ⟶ Higher-order Need Fulfillment ⟶ Satisfaction ⟶ Motivation ⟶ Productivity

most appropriate and to have the 'behavioral *flexibility* to move comfortably from one style (e.g., participative) to another (e.g., directive).

Yun and colleagues examined the team effectiveness of empowering and directive leadership under two variations in team member experience (i.e., experienced and inexperienced relative to the task at hand) and environmental velocity (i.e., high and low velocity, wherein velocity refers to an environment that requires fast decision making often under conditions of rapid change, high uncertainty, and risk). They created experimental manipulations (severely injured versus not-severely injured patient; experienced versus inexperienced team; and directive versus empowering leadership) at a level I trauma center of a major mid-Atlantic medical center in the United States. Their findings revealed that directive leadership was more effective than empowering leadership when trauma severity and velocity were high (i.e., with a severely injured patient) and when team experience was low. Empowering leadership, on the other hand, was most effective when the team was treating not-severely injured patients and when team experience was high. They also concluded that more learning opportunities stem from an empowering leadership style.

The self-assessment presented at the end of this chapter opener can provide you with insight into your human resource–human relations (i.e., Theory Y versus Theory X) orientation. Individuals with a strong Theory Y orientation are more predisposed to, and comfortable with, a participatory leadership orientation.

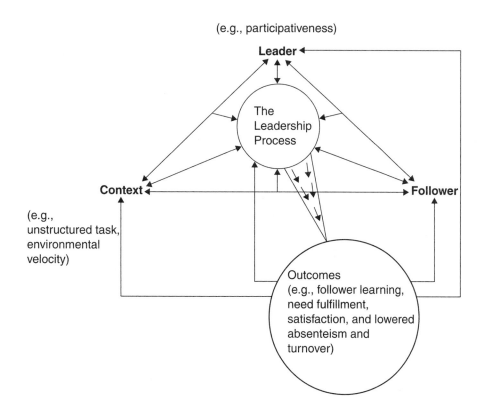

FIGURE 11.2
The Leadership Process: Participation

EXERCISE	**Participatory Leadership Attitudes**
Self-Assessment	**Instructions:** In the section below, you will see a series of statements. Please indicate your agreement or disagreement. Use the scale below for each statement. For example: It is easier to work in cool weather than in hot.

: _____	: _____	: _____	: _____	: _____
Strongly Agree	Agree	Undecided	Disagree	Strongly Disagree

If you think it is easier to work in cool weather, put an (X) above "agree"; if you think it is much easier to work in cool weather, put a mark above "strongly agree." If you think it doesn't matter, put a mark over "undecided" and so on. Put your mark in a space, not on the boundaries.

There is no right or wrong answer. It is only your opinion about the statements that follow that matters.

1. The average human being prefers to be directed, wishes to avoid responsibility, and has relatively little ambition.

: _____	: ___✓___	: _____	: _____	: _____
Strongly Agree	Agree	Undecided	Disagree	Strongly Disagree

2. Leadership skills can be acquired by most people regardless of their particular inborn traits and abilities.

: _____	: ___✓___	: _____	: _____	: _____
Strongly Agree	Agree	Undecided	Disagree	Strongly Disagree

3. The use of rewards (pay, promotion, etc.) and punishment (failure to promote, etc.) is not the best way to get subordinates to do their work.

: _____	: _____	: _____	: ___✓___	: _____
Strongly Agree	Agree	Undecided	Disagree	Strongly Disagree

4. In a work situation, if the subordinates cannot influence me, then I lose some influence on them.

: _____	: ___✓___	: _____	: _____	: _____
Strongly Agree	Agree	Undecided	Disagree	Strongly Disagree

5. A good leader should give detailed and complete instructions to his or her subordinates rather than merely giving them general directions and depending upon their initiative to work out the details.

: ___✓___	: _____	: _____	: _____	: _____
Strongly Agree	Agree	Undecided	Disagree	Strongly Disagree

6. Group goal setting offers advantages that cannot be obtained by individual goal setting.

: _____	: ___✓___	: _____	: _____	: _____
Strongly Agree	Agree	Undecided	Disagree	Strongly Disagree

7. A superior should give his or her subordinates only that information which is needed for them to do their immediate tasks.

: _____	: _____	: _____	: _____	: ___✓___
Strongly Agree	Agree	Undecided	Disagree	Strongly Disagree

8. The superior's authority over his or her subordinates in an organization is primarily economic.

: _____	: _____	: _____	: ___✓___	: _____
Strongly Agree	Agree	Undecided	Disagree	Strongly Disagree

Scoring: Four attitudes are being assessed by these 8 questions: (1) attitudes toward the average person's capacities (questions 1 and 2); (2) attitudes toward sharing information (questions 5 and 7); (3) attitudes toward participation (questions 4 and 6); and (4) attitudes toward the nature of supervisory controls (questions 3 and 8).

For each of the 8 questions, assign:

5 points for "strongly agree"
4 points for "agree"
3 points for "undecided"
2 points for "disagree"
1 point for "strongly disagree"

1. Rescore your answer to questions 1, 5, 7, and 8 by subtracting your score from 6.

2. Next, sum your scores for questions 1 and 2, and divide by 2.

3. Sum your scores for questions 5 and 7, and divide by 2.

4. Sum your scores for questions 4 and 6, and divide by 2.

5. Sum your scores for questions 3 and 8, and divide by 2.

6. Finally, sum your final scores as produced in steps 2, 3, 4, and 5 above and divide by 4.

My participatory attitude scores are:

My *Person's Capacity* (i.e., belief that people have the ability to learn, take on leadership roles, and exercise self-direction and self-control) score_____.

My *Information Sharing* (i.e., belief that a leader should provide his/her followers with a full understanding of the situation, and allow them to exercise personal initiative in carrying out the task at hand) score_____.

My *Participation* (i.e., belief that followers should be able to get involved and exercise influence) score _____.

My *Control* (i.e., belief that the use of extrinsic rewards is not the best way to influence/control one's followers) score_____.

My *Overall Participatory Leadership Attitude* score _____.

Interpretation: These questions on leadership, according to Haire, Ghiselli, and Porter (1966), are focused on attitudes that pertain to a somewhat unilateral, autocratic approach to management at one extreme and a more group-oriented, team, participatory approach at the other. The questions are intended to capture beliefs in "the capacity of subordinates," and views on "the efficacy of participation, of sharing information, and of providing opportunities for internal self-control on the job" (p. 3).

A high score (4 and greater) for each of the four attitudes and in the aggregate would reflect a "favorable" disposition toward subordinates (followers), their capacities, and their involvement in organizational activities. A score of 2 and less might reflect a hesitancy toward the full and active involvement of followers in the leadership context (i.e., a propensity toward leader control as opposed to a participatory style of leadership). The high score might be reflective of McGregor's vision of the Theory Y leader, while the low score is reflective of Theory X.

Source: M. Haire, E. E. Ghiselli, and L. W. Porter, *Managerial Thinking: An International Study* (New York: John Wiley & Sons, 1966). Reprinted with permission.

Reading 30

Supervisory Style and Productivity

Review and Theory[1]

Stephen M. Sales
University of Michigan

It is widely assumed that employees will work harder for supervisors who employ given styles of supervision than they will for supervisors who use other styles. This supposition clearly underlies much of supervisory training; it is a basic tenet of the writings of Morse (1953), Likert (1961), and many others. However, the theoretical underpinnings of this assumption are often unclearly stated (when they are stated at all); furthermore, the wide variety of studies investigating the validity of this position are rarely fully described. The present article will sketch a theory which accounts for the predicted differential in productivity and will review and evaluate the literature relevant to this theory.

AUTHORITARIANISM AND DEMOCRACY

The styles to be discussed are the authoritarian and democratic dimensions. The distinction between these orientations has often been made in the literature; it will not be extensively elaborated here. Rather, we shall discuss only the major differences between these styles.

Authoritarian supervision, in general, is characterized by the relatively high degree of power wielded by the supervisor over the work group. As contrasted with democratic supervision, both power and all decision-making functions are absolutely concentrated in the person of the authoritarian. Democratic supervision, on the other hand, is characterized by a sharing of power and by participative decision making. Under democratic supervision, the work group becomes in some ways co-equal with the supervisor; responsibility is spread rather than concentrated.

DIFFERENTIAL EFFECTIVENESS

It is commonly assumed that, with other conditions held constant, employees will produce more

Source: Edited and reprinted with permission from *Personnel Psychology* 19 (1966), pp. 275–86.

under democratic supervision than they would have produced under autocratic supervision. (Such an assumption, of course, lies behind the entire human relations movement.) There is at least one good reason for this prediction. Specifically, the reinforcing value of work performed under democratic supervision should be higher than that of work performed under autocratic supervision.

It is a basic tenet of experimental psychology that high levels of performance will be obtained in situations in which the reinforcement is large, whereas low performance levels will occur in those in which the reinforcement is small. In terms of industrial situations, the more reinforcement an employee receives for production, the higher his production should be. (This is, of course, the assumption which underlies incentive systems, although reinforcement is rather narrowly defined in such programs.) Vroom (1962, pp. 26–43) in particular has explored the ramifications of this argument.

The importance of this point for the present consideration is that production is attended by two different levels of need-satisfaction under the two styles of supervision sketched above. Democratic supervision, by allowing subordinates freedom in determining the specific form and content of their work, implicates the personalities of the employees in the tasks they perform. This means that production, under democratic supervision, becomes a means for satisfying the employees' ego-esteem and self-actualization needs (see Maslow, 1954; Argyris, 1957). That is, the "greater opportunity for regulating and controlling their own activities [provided by democratic supervision] . . . should increase the degree to which individuals could express their various and diverse needs and could move in the direction of fully exploiting their potential while on the job" (Morse & Reimer, 1956). Authoritarian supervision, inasmuch as it makes work merely the carrying out of the supervisor's will, reduces the degree to which such need-satisfaction can be derived from production. Therefore, since productivity is less satisfying under autocratic than under democratic supervision, one would expect that workers would be less productive in the former condition than in the latter. (This effect, of course, should be accentuated for those individuals for whom the needs in question are most important.)

It should be noted that the above considerations do not involve between-style differences which rest upon uncontrolled factors (even when such factors might themselves follow from the style variation). For instance, if turnover were higher under one supervisory style than under the other, one would expect that the method resulting in higher turnover would be accompanied by the lower productivity rate (because of lowered effectiveness during learning periods). Factors of this sort would lead to productivity differences between the supervisory styles; however, such differences would not truly bear upon the question of effectiveness as usually posed. That is, statements about supervisory style center in general about the proposition that employees will work harder for some supervisors than for others. This statement cannot be supported by dependent variable differences which may be shown to result from between-condition variations other than that of supervisory style. The present discussion is concerned solely with productivity differences which follow *directly* from the style of supervision. . . .

EXPERIMENTAL INVESTIGATIONS

The original and best known study in this area is the experiment of Lewin, Lippitt, and White (e.g., Lippitt & White, 1958, pp. 496–510; White & Lippitt, 1962). These investigators employed as subjects 30 10-year-old boys who met in six groups which ostensibly were recreational clubs. These groups were supervised by adults who had been trained to act in either a democratic, autocratic, or laissez-faire manner. (The last condition is not considered in the present discussion.) Each club was exposed to each of the three styles for six weeks.

The results of this experiment, in terms of productivity, are extremely difficult to establish. When exposed to autocratic supervision[2] the boys spent more time at work than they did under democratic supervision (74 percent of the total time as opposed to 50 percent under democratic supervision). However, the "work-mindedness" of the democratically supervised boys appeared to be somewhat higher since under democratic supervision the groups engaged in a slightly larger amount of "work-minded conversation." (There were 63 work-minded remarks per child under the democratic condition, whereas in the autocratic condition this figure fell to 52.) However, *no objective measure of productivity is reported by the authors, and therefore it is impossible to determine accurately which of the two styles evoked the higher production* (a factor often overlooked by reviewers of this study).

McCurdy and Eber (1953) examined supervisory style in an investigation on group problem-solving. In this experiment, three-man groups participated in a task in which the group determined the proper setting of three switches. In the authoritarian condition one subject was given the power to order the others at will, making him an "absolute" supervisor. The other subjects were instructed merely to obey orders. In the democratic condition the instructions emphasized equalitarianism, specifying that each subject could offer suggestions and that no individual could order the others in any way. No differences whatever appeared between the two conditions on a productivity criterion.

Shaw (1955), working with communication networks, also used problem-solving as a dependent variable in an investigation of supervisory style effects. Employing three different "nets," he instructed the subjects assigned to the position with the highest independence score within each structure[3] to behave either in an autocratic manner (e.g., by giving orders) or in a democratic manner (e.g., by making suggestions). Shaw found that the autocratically-supervised subjects (*a*) required less time to solve the problems, regardless of the communication net in which they were placed, and (*b*) made fewer errors.

Day and Hamblin (1964) trained a female student to employ "close" and "general" supervisory styles in leading groups of female subjects in an assembly-line task. These researchers found that subjects exposed to close supervision produced less than did subjects exposed to general supervision.

Sales (1964), like Day and Hamblin, replicated an industrial assembly-line setting in the laboratory. In Sales's experiment two male supervisors played democratic and autocratic roles over male and female groups. (Both role and sex of the subordinates were fully counterbalanced in this experiment.) Sales reports no differential effectiveness whatever between the two styles; the productivity means for the two conditions were virtually identical.

Spector and Suttell (1957) report a relevant laboratory study with naval trainees as subjects. These authors trained supervisors to use either "single leadership" or "leadership sharing" styles, patterns which seem to parallel the democratic–autocratic distinction. The task consisted of problems in which team members cooperated in receiving, processing, and recording information. No differences were detected in the productivity of the groups under the two styles.

In the most extensive of the investigations reported in this area, Morse and Reimer (1956) created groups exposed either to democratic or to autocratic supervision by altering the style of supervision used in an on-going industrial setting. In two divisions ("participative treatment") an attempt was made to push down the level of decision making. Supervisors were trained to employ more democratic supervisory methods, and they were given greater freedom of action than previously had been allowed. In two other divisions an "hierarchically controlled treatment" was established by an increase in the closeness of supervision and a movement upward in the level at which decisions were made. The treatments were administered for a year's time to approximately 500 employees.

Morse and Reimer found that both programs resulted in a significant increase in productivity. This increase was slightly higher for the hierarchically controlled divisions; however, the actual difference between the treatments was quite small.

On balance, then, the experimental studies reviewed above show no consistent superiority of one style over the other in terms of a productivity criterion. Of the six studies for which objective production data are available, one (Day & Hamblin, 1964) reports democratic supervision to be more effective and one (Shaw, 1955) reports authoritarian supervision to be more effective. The other four investigations note no differences of consequence between the two styles.

SURVEY INVESTIGATIONS

Survey researches applied to the problem discussed herein follow a standard methodology. The supervisory style which exists in each of the work groups in the situation is determined (usually by means of questionnaires administered to the employees), and this variable is then related to productivity. Researchers using this methodology generally have found a clear relationship between style of supervision and work group productivity.

The extensive investigations performed by the Survey Research Center at the University of Michigan during the early 1950s (Katz, Maccoby, & Morse, 1950; Katz, Maccoby, Gurin, & Floor, 1951; Katz & Kahn, 1951, pp. 146–171) are representative of this approach. In a wide variety of industrial situations (including railway maintenance crews,

insurance office staffs, and heavy industry production lines), these authors found (1) that general supervision was associated with high productivity whereas close supervision was associated with low productivity, and (2) that "employee-oriented" attitudes in the supervisor were associated with high productivity whereas "job-oriented" attitudes were associated with low productivity. It is unclear exactly what relationship these independent variables have to the democratic–autocratic dimension; however, it can certainly be assumed that employee-oriented attitudes and general supervision will tend to be associated with democracy (as here used) whereas job-oriented attitudes and close supervision will tend to be associated with authoritarianism. The data of Morse (1953) and Argyle, Gardner, and Cioffi (1957) support these assumptions.

Argyle et al. (1958) performed a successful replication of these earlier investigations in a British industrial situation. The authors report that foremen of high-producing work groups tended to use general rather than close supervision and were relatively more democratic in their behavior than were foremen of less productive work groups. Further, the attitudes of the more effective foremen tended to be more "employee-oriented" than those of the less effective foremen. In contrast to experimental findings, therefore, these survey data clearly seem to support the hypothesis that democratic supervision leads to higher production than does authoritarian supervision.

DISCUSSION

The usual explanations offered for the failure of the experimental method to replicate survey findings rest upon either (*a*) the brevity of the experimental sessions or (*b*) the peripheral nature of the experimental tasks. It seems to the present author, however, that these explanations are respectively (*a*) too facile and (*b*) inadequately elaborated for proper handling of the problem.

Of the two, the "brevity" argument is the more open to attack. Experimental sessions are, of course, of relatively short duration. However, the entire science of experimental social psychology rests upon the assumption that experimental periods are sufficiently lengthy for treatments to "take," an assumption which is supported in every significant finding obtained in an experimental laboratory. To argue that the experiments reviewed here failed to demonstrate predicted productivity differences because of inadequate time periods (especially when these same time periods are sufficient to evoke morale differences—favoring the democratic supervisor—between the groups exposed to the two styles) seems somehow an unscientific and unsatisfactory way of explaining the findings. Furthermore, such an explanation fails to account for the quite small productivity differential which existed between the conditions created by Morse and Reimer in an experiment which continued over the course of an entire year.

It appears to the author that, rather than looking to brevity, one may best explain the equal experimental effectiveness of the two supervisory styles by concentrating upon the nature of the tasks involved. (This is, of course, the approach incompletely hinted at in the "peripheral nature" argument.) Specifically, it seems that no differences in effectiveness have been found between the two styles *because the tasks employed wholly fail to meet the conditions under which differential productivity was predicted.*

Democratic supervision, it will be remembered, was expected to be the more effective style because of the greater extent to which it makes productivity a means to need-satisfaction. This prediction rests upon the assumption that democratic supervision allows productivity to be a path to the satisfaction of self-actualization and ego-esteem needs, whereas autocratic supervision does not serve such a purpose.

These conditions do not seem to have been generated by the experimental investigations reported above. Democratic supervision, in these experiments, can hardly be seen as allowing the subjects to see production on the task involved as a path to self-actualization. *The thought is virtually absurd.* Regardless of the intent of the investigators, the decisions allowed by the democratic supervisors (e.g., suggesting possible solutions to simple problems) do not seem to implicate the unique personalities of the subjects in their tasks. This seems to have been true even in the Morse and Reimer investigation, for the authors report that "both groups of clerks indicated that their jobs throughout the course of the experiment did not give them a very high degree of self-actualization." To the extent that experimental studies fail to make productivity under democratic supervision a path to significantly greater need-satisfaction than it would be under autocratic supervision, there is no reason to suspect that they should demonstrate democratic supervision to be more effective. Such investigations simply fail to provide the conditions necessary for a test of the hypothesis in question.

It should not be inferred, however, that survey investigations provide a more adequate test of the hypothesis that workers will work harder for democratic supervisors, in spite of the satisfying direction of the findings. There are at least two reasons for approaching the results of these studies with caution, both of which rest upon the fact that spurious variables which clearly affect work group productivity accompany both these styles. To the extent that the effects of such variables cannot be discounted, survey methodology is incapable of offering convincing evidence concerning the relative effort expended by workers exposed to the styles in question.

In the first place, the supervisory styles discussed herein are accompanied by differential turnover and absenteeism (e.g., Mann & Baumgartel, 1953; Morse & Reimer, 1956; Argyle et al., 1958). These effects do contribute to productivity differences between groups exposed to these styles, since the higher absenteeism and turnover evoked by autocratic supervision would lead to a productivity difference favoring democratic supervision. However, such a difference would be irrelevant to the hypothesis that democratic supervision leads directly to more concerted effort on the part of the employees involved. The effects of absenteeism and/or turnover could be removed from the analysis by means of simple statistical techniques, although no survey research known to the author has as yet attempted to do so.

A second consideration lies in the fact that supervisors who naturally affect a democratic style of supervision cannot be assumed to be otherwise similar to those who affect an authoritarian style. In particular, the author feels that democratically oriented supervisors can be expected to be more intelligent than are autocratically oriented supervisors. There are no direct data drawn from industry which bear on this statement. However, the fact that intelligence has clearly been shown to be negatively correlated with measured (F-scale) authoritarianism (e.g., Titus & Hollander, 1957), which in turn has been shown to be highly correlated with authoritarian behavior (McGee, 1955), seems sufficient to make the point.

It may be assumed that the intelligence of the supervisor should be of some importance in determining the productivity of the employees under him. The more intelligent supervisor might be expected to diagnose production difficulties more quickly than the less intelligent supervisor, and he might also be expected to take more effective remedial action. Therefore, inasmuch as authoritarian and democratic supervisors are differentiated on intelligence, one might expect them to be differentiated on their skill in dealing with day-to-day production problems. The advantage, of course, would go to the democratic supervisors.

The effect of this predicted difference between the two supervisory populations would be to make the work groups under democratic supervision more productive than those under autocratic supervision. However, as in the case of the different levels of turnover evoked by the two styles, such a finding would *not* necessarily imply that employees worked harder for supervisors affecting the democratic style. Like the effect of absenteeism, the effect of supervisory intelligence could be removed from the analysis by means of proper statistical techniques, but again there has been no survey research which has done so.

Therefore, in neither experimental studies nor survey investigations has an adequate test of the theory sketched above been made. Experimental studies have not created the conditions necessary for such a test; survey research has introduced at least two contaminating variables which render proper interpretation of the observed relationship extremely difficult. Such studies have not *disproved* the theory in question. They simply have not offered the unambiguous evidence administrative science must have in order to evaluate plans of action (e.g., supervisory training) tacitly based on this theory.

This should not be interpreted to mean that such a test cannot be made. Experimental investigations of the sort attempted by Morse and Reimer (1956), *using a technology in which self-actualization could occur under democratic supervision,* would provide an adequate test, as would survey investigations in which the intelligence of the supervisors and the turnover (and/or absenteeism) levels existing in the various work groups were assessed and partialled out of the correlation between the style of the supervisor and the productivity of the subordinates. (Research now in progress is directed toward this latter objective.) Without such conditions, however, the hypothesis that democratic supervision will evoke greater effort from employees than will autocratic supervision cannot truly be either supported or rejected.

Notes

1. The author wishes to express his appreciation to Dr. Ned A. Rosen of the New York State School of Industrial and Labor Relations, Cornell Unviversity, for his constant assistance and encouragement. A grant from the Foundation for Research on Human Behavior, Ann Arbor, Michigan, provided the time necessary for the preparation of this article.

2. Only the "submissive reaction" to autocracy will be here considered; the "aggressive reaction" is felt to be a function of the subjects and the situation employed by the investigators.

3. The research of Leavitt (1951) clearly suggests that these positions are the ones from which leadership is exercised.

References

Argyle, Michael, Gardner, Godfrey, & Cioffi, Frank. "The Measurement of Supervisory Methods." *Human Relations,* X (1957), 295–313.

Argyle, Michael, Gardner, Godfrey, & Cioffi, Frank. "Supervisory Methods Related to Productivity, Absenteeism, and Labour Turnover." *Human Relations,* XI (1958), 23–40.

Argyris, Chris. *Personality and Organization.* New York: Harper & Brothers, 1957.

Coch, L., & French, J. R. P., Jr. "Overcoming Resistance to Change." *Human Relations,* I (1948), 512–532.

Day, R. C., & Hamblin, R. L. "Some Effects of Close and Punitive Styles of Supervision." *American Journal of Sociology,* LXIX (1964), 499–510.

Katz, D., & Kahn, R. L. "Human Organization and Worker Motivation." In Tripp, L. Reed (Ed.), *Industrial Productivity.* Madison, Wisconsin: Industrial Relations Research Association, 1951.

Katz, D., Maccoby, N., Gurin, G., & Floor, Lucretia. *Productivity, Supervision, and Morale among Railroad Workers.* Ann Arbor, Michigan: Institute for Social Research, 1951.

Katz, D., Maccoby, N., & Morse, Nancy C. *Productivity, Supervision and Morale in an Office Situation.* Part 1. Ann Arbor, Michigan: Institute for Social Research, 1950.

Leavitt, Harold. "Some Effects of Certain Communication Patterns on Group Performance." *Journal of Abnormal and Social Psychology,* XLVI (1951), 16–30.

Likert, Rensis. *New Patterns of Management.* New York: McGraw-Hill, 1961.

Lippitt, R., & White, R. K. "An Experimental Study of Leadership and Group Life." In Maccoby, E. E., Newcomb, T. N., & Hartley, E. L. (Eds.), *Readings in Social Psychology,* Third Edition. New York: Holt, Rinehart, & Winston, 1958.

Mann, F. C., & Baumgartel, H. D. "Absences and Employee Attitudes in an Electric Power Company." Ann Arbor, Michigan: Institute for Social Research, 1953.

Maslow, A. H. *Motivation and Personality.* New York: Harper & Brothers, 1954.

McCurdy, H. G., & Eber, H. W. "Democratic Versus Authoritarian: A Further Investigation of Group

Problem-Solving." *Journal of Personality,* XXII (1953), 258–269.

McGee, H. M. "Measurement of Authoritarianism and Its Relation to Teacher Classroom Behavior." *Genetic Psychological Monographs,* LII (1955), 89–146.

Morse, Nancy C. *Satisfactions in the White-Collar Job.* Ann Arbor, Michigan: Institute for Social Research, 1953.

Morse, Nancy C., & Reimer, E. "The Experimental Change of a Major Organizational Variable." *Journal of Abnormal and Social Psychology,* LI (1956), 120–129.

Sales, Stephen M. "A Laboratory Investigation of the Effectiveness of Two Industrial Supervisory Dimensions." Unpublished MS Thesis, Cornell University, 1964.

Shaw, M. E. "A Comparison of Two Types of Leadership in Various Communication Nets." *Journal of Abnormal and Social Psychology,* L (1955), 127–134.

Spector, Paul, & Suttell, Barbara. *An Experimental Comparison of the Effectiveness of Three Patterns of Leadership Behavior.* Washington, DC: American Institute for Research, 1957.

Titus, H. E., & Hollander, E. P. "The California *F*-Scale in Psychological Research: 1950–1955." *Psychological Bulletin,* LIV (1957), 47–65.

Vroom, V. H. "Human Relations Research in Industry: Some Things Learned." In Baristow, Frances (Ed.), *Research Frontiers in Industrial Relations Today.* Montreal: Industrial Relations Centre, 1962.

White, Ralph, & Lippitt, R. "Leader Behavior and Member Reaction in Three 'Social Climates.'" In Cartwright, Dorin, & Zander, Alvin (Eds.), *Group Dynamics, Research & Theory,* Second Edition. Evanston, Illinois: Row, Peterson, 1962.

Reading 31

Participation, Satisfaction, and Productivity: A Meta-analytic Review

Katherine I. Miller
Michigan State University

Peter R. Monge
University of Southern California

I would not think of making a decision by going around the table and then deciding on the basis of how everyone felt. Of course, I like to hear everyone, but then I go off alone and decide. The decisions that are important must be made alone.

—*Richard M. Nixon (Schecter, 1972:18–19)*

Like Mr. Nixon, most people have strong feelings about the best way to make decisions. However, individuals often disagree about the proper decision-making procedure. Should subordinates be included in decision-making processes, or should managers stand alone as decision makers? Far from being limited to high national offices, the debate over the efficacy of participation in decision making exists throughout government, business, and many academic fields.

There are several reasons for the continuing disagreement on this topic. Moral reasoning regarding participation is often confounded with practical reasoning. Locke and Schweiger (1979) provided several examples of managers and academicians advocating the use of participation on moral grounds, regardless of whether or not it works. In addition, conflicting models of the mechanisms at work in the process of participation lead to confusion over the interpretation of research findings. Finally, in spite of the plethora of empirical research studies investigating participation, when reviewers of the literature draw conclusions on its effectiveness, they invariably still state that "it depends" (Locke & Schweiger; Lowin, 1968; Singer, 1974). Unfortunately, the question of what it depends on has never been clearly answered. To begin to answer this question, we carried out a meta-analytic review of past

research on the effects of participation in decision making on satisfaction and productivity.

"ONE MORE LOOK" REVISITED

In recent years, several sets of scholars have done wide-ranging reviews of thinking and research on participation in the workplace. For example, Strauss (1982) took an international perspective on workers' participation, and Dachler and Wilpert (1978) looked at the dimensions and boundaries of the participation process. Perhaps the most comprehensive review of empirical research to date, however, is Locke and Schweiger's (1979) "one more look" at participation in decision making, which considered both moral and practical arguments for participation. They reviewed laboratory studies, correlational studies, multivariate field studies, and univariate field studies in which satisfaction and productivity were criterion variables. Locke and Schweiger concluded that little could be said about the effects of participation from multivariate field studies because too many other variables—differences in training, reward systems, education, and so forth—could account for effects often attributed to participation. They did, however, make generalizations based on correlational, laboratory, and univariate field studies.

Locke and Schweiger classified the conclusions of studies as "participation superior," "participation inferior," or "no difference or contextual" (1979: 317). Having found that the results in laboratory, correlational, and univariate field studies were remarkably consistent, they finally concluded:

(1) With respect to the productivity criterion, there is no trend in favor of participative leadership as compared to more directive styles; and (2) with respect to satisfaction, the results generally favor participative over directive methods, although nearly 40 percent of the studies did not

Source: Edited and reprinted with permission from *Academy of Management Journal* 29 (1986), pp. 727–53. Copyright (1986) *Academy of Management Journal.*

find participation to be superior (Locke & Schweiger, 1979: 316).

Although Locke and Schweiger's review considered well over 50 empirical research reports on participation, their final conclusions seem somewhat anticlimatic—probably for several reasons. First, they used a very gross classification system in considering effects of participation. The categories of superior, inferior, and contextual, though certainly useful, tell us nothing about the strength of participation's effects on satisfaction and productivity. Second, many studies fell into the contextual category, 56 percent for the productivity criterion and 30 percent for the satisfaction criterion. They suggested a number of contextual factors to account for the effectiveness of participation, including two individual factors, knowledge and motivation, and several organizational factors, such as task attributes, group characteristics, and leaders' attributes, but did not go back to the studies reviewed to systematically sort out these contextual effects. Finally, no attempt was made to consider systematic patterns differentiating the studies concluding that participation was superior from those concluding that participation was inferior.

Meta-analysis (Hunter, Schmidt, & Jackson, 1982) can be employed to refine and extend Locke and Schweiger's findings. This method of cumulating results over studies allowed us to summarize numerically the effects of participation on satisfaction and productivity and to take into account artifactual and substantive sources of variance in the individual estimates of effects. Meta-analysis is an improvement over the review methods used by Locke and Schweiger on several counts. It considers the strength of effects between two variables rather than simply counting significant results or levels of probability, thus providing a more accurate representation of cumulated relationships between variables and eliminating the problem of giving a study with a strong effect the same consideration as one with a barely significant effect. Meta-analysis also provides methods for correcting for such systematic, artifactual sources of variance in the estimates of effects as measurement error and restriction in range. Finally, meta-analysis allows for the consideration of both substantive and methodological moderator variables that could account for unexplained variance in estimates of effects. . . .

Thus, we decided that a meta-analysis of this literature would be useful in resolving several of the problems of earlier reviews. In the next section, we discuss the relationships of participation with satisfaction and productivity through the presentation of cognitive, affective, and contingency models of participation. Meta-analysis does not allow for direct tests of these models, but the models enable identification of substantive and methodological variables that could moderate the relationships of participation with satisfaction and productivity.

PARTICIPATION, SATISFACTION, AND PRODUCTIVITY

Theorists have advanced a variety of models to account for participation's influence on satisfaction and productivity; each proposes mechanisms through which participation has its effects. We used three types of models—cognitive, affective, and contingency—to highlight differences in these propositions. Each of the three types emphasizes a different explanatory mechanism. The three are not mutually exclusive, however, as many theorists have proposed that cognitive, affect, and contingency variables all play important roles in the participative process.

COGNITIVE MODELS OF PARTICIPATIVE EFFECTS

Cognitive models of participative effects suggest that participation in decision making is a viable strategy because it enhances the flow and use of important information in organizations. Theorists supporting such models (Anthony, 1978; Frost, Wakely, & Ruh, 1974) propose that workers typically have more complete knowledge of their work than management; hence, if workers participate in decision making, decisions will be made with better pools of information. In addition, cognitive models suggest that if employees participate in decision making, they will know more about implementing work procedures after decisions have been made (Maier, 1963; Melcher, 1976). Other scholars (Miles & Ritchie, 1971; Ritchie & Miles, 1970), designating cognitive models as the "human resources" theory of participation, note that such a model is "primarily concerned with the meaningful utilization of subordinates' capabilities and views satisfaction as a by-product of their participation in important organizational decisions" (Ritchie & Miles, 1970: 348).

Cognitive models predict a definite pattern of results in empirical research investigating participation, satisfaction, and productivity. First, because these models consider information to be crucial, increases in productivity are expected to be stronger where workers have good information about decisions to be made. For instance, such models would predict a stronger effect for participation in job design than for participation in companywide policy decisions or experimental discussions. Second, such models do not predict immediate increases in satisfaction as a result of participation in decision making, as it is essentially a knowledge of results that is hypothesized to lead to eventual increases in satisfaction. Third, they do not predict increases in workers' productivity and satisfaction simply from their working in participative work climates or for nondirective leaders. According to cognitive models, increases in productivity and satisfaction are attributable to specific inputs from subordinates on issues in which they are interested and knowledgeable.

AFFECTIVE MODELS OF PARTICIPATIVE EFFECTS

There are several models linking participation to productivity and satisfaction through affective mechanisms. Followers of the "human relations"[1] school of management (Blake & Mouton, 1964; Likert, 1967; McGregor, 1960) adamantly espouse these models, in which the most crucial link is that between participation and workers' satisfaction. These theorists propose that participation will lead to greater attainment of high-order needs, such as self-expression, respect, independence, and equality, which will in turn increase morale and satisfaction. Ritchie and Miles stated that "managers who hold the human relations theory of participation believe simply in involvement for the sake of involvement, arguing that as long as subordinates feel they are participating and are being consulted, their ego needs will be satisfied and they will be more cooperative" (1970: 348).

The link between participation and productivity in affective models is less straightforward than that between participation and satisfaction. Essentially, this school proposes that participation will enhance productivity through intervening motivational processes: participation fulfills needs, fulfilled needs lead to satisfaction, satisfaction strengthens motivation, and increased motivation improves workers' productivity. According to French, Israel, and As (1960):

> One effect of a high degree of participation by workers in decisions concerning their own work will be to strengthen their motivation to carry out these decisions. This is the major rationale for expecting a relation between participation and production. When management accords the workers participation in any important decision,

it implies that workers are intelligent, competent, and valued partners. Thus, participation directly affects such aspects of worker-management relations as the perception of being valued, the perception of common goals, and cooperation. It satisfies such important social needs as the need for recognition and appreciation and the need for independence. These satisfactions and, in addition, the improvements in their jobs that are introduced through participation lead to higher job satisfaction (1960: 5).

Although several theorists (Locke & Schweiger, 1979; Ritchie & Miles, 1970) feel strongly that scholarly and practical emphasis should be placed on the cognitive effects of participation, researchers in the tradition of McGregor (1960), Likert (1967), and Coch and French (1948) still hold strongly to the importance of participation in providing affective changes in workers. Thus, it is important to consider the predictions of affective models as to the effects of participation on satisfaction and productivity. First, they predict that participation will affect satisfaction in a wide variety of situations. Participation need not be centered on issues of which employees are particularly knowledgeable, for it is the act, not the informational content, of participation that is the crucial mechanism. Second, such models do not predict increases in productivity without initial increases in workers' satisfaction. Finally, affective models suggest that participation will more strongly influence lower-level employees, because managers' higher-order ego needs may well be fulfilled by other aspects of their work.

CONTINGENCY MODELS OF PARTICIPATIVE EFFECTS

Several theorists suggest that it is not possible to develop models of participative effects that will hold across a wide variety of individuals and situations. Rather, they suggest that participation will affect satisfaction and productivity differently for different people and situations. Scholars have offered a variety of contingency theories centering on personality, particular decision situations, relationships between superiors and subordinates, job levels, and values.

Vroom (1960) was the first to propose that personality might mediate the effects of participation on satisfaction and productivity. Specifically, he suggested that participation will positively influence only employees having personalities with low authoritarianism and high needs for independence. Vroom found some support for his hypotheses, and his work has stimulated other research. However, further studies have provided mixed support for his hypotheses (Abdel-Halim, 1983; Tosi, 1970; Vroom & Mann, 1960).

Vroom was also involved in the major theoretical statement of situational influences on the participation process. Vroom and Yetton (1973), building on the work of Tannenbaum and Schmidt (1958), considered different decision situations and provided rules for deciding the optimal level of participation in decision making. They proposed both rules to protect the quality of decisions and rules to protect their acceptance. Most of the research on this model has been descriptive, drawing on self-reports about how managers behave in different decision situations. However, several normative tests (Vroom & Jago, 1978) have indicated that decisions made within participative modes specified by these rules were more effective than other decisions. Vroom and Yetton's work moves toward an integration of cognitive and affective models of participation. Their contingency rules for protecting the quality of decisions deal with the cognitive portion of participation, and their rules for protecting the acceptance of decisions address its affective components.

Several other theorists have proposed additional variables as intervening in the process of participation. For example, Vroom and Deci (1960) suggested that the types of problems dealt with at various organizational levels influence the appropriateness of participation; it may be less appropriate at low levels, where jobs are routine, and more appropriate at high levels, where jobs involve addressing complex problems. Several scholars (Hulin, 1971; Singer, 1974) have suggested that values mediate the relationship between participation and outcomes, specifically, that many workers may not value participation to the extent that academicians do. Singer further commented, "While the necessity for determining a 'one best' leadership style for the 'composite worker' is understandable from a financial and expediency standpoint, to assume that *all* workers desire participation opportunities is to lack sensitivity to *individual* needs—the antithesis of the humanization that ardent proponents of participation advocate" (1974: 359). Thus, these scholars predicted that participation may only be effective for employees in certain types of organizations—such as research or service organizations, rather than manufacturing organizations—or only for middle- or upper-level employees.

OVERVIEW

In sum, *cognitive* models of participation propose that participation leads to increases in productivity through bringing high-quality information to

decisions and through increasing knowledge at times of implementation. Such models predict that: (1) The effects of participation on an individual's productivity will be the strongest for decisions that draw on the individual's expertise; (2) There will not be a direct influence of participation on job satisfaction. Rather, the effect of participation on productivity will mediate this effect. (3) Participation in specific decisions is necessary for increases in productivity and satisfaction; working in a participative climate is not adequate.

Affective models suggest that participation will satisfy higher-order needs of workers and that, as these needs are satisfied, workers will be more satisfied with their jobs. Such models predict that: (1) Working in a participative climate is adequate for increasing workers' productivity. It is not necessary that workers participate in decisions on which they have special knowledge. (2) There is no direct link between participation and productivity. Rather, improved attitudes reduce resistance to change and increase motivation through the satisfaction of needs. (3) Participation may provide more noticeable increases in satisfaction for employees who are not having higher-order needs fulfilled from other aspects of their jobs.

Contingency models of participation suggest that no single model of participation is appropriate for all employees in all organizations. Instead, various contingency models predict that: (1) Employees with high needs for independence and personalities with low authoritarianism will be the most positively influenced by participation. (2) Some decisions are more appropriate for participation than others. Appropriateness depends on requirements for the quality or acceptance of a decision (Vroom & Yetton, 1973), or on its complexity. (3) Employees who value participation will be the most positively influenced by it, and these are likely to be higher-level employees, or individuals working in research or service industries. . . .

METHODS

Our literature search for relevant research on the effects of participation on satisfaction and productivity included journals in the areas of social psychology, management, organizational behavior, and communication, and several relevant social citation indices. We restricted it to the published literature and to English language journals and books, excluding dissertations and other unpublished research. It is possible that this led us to include more studies with significant results and fewer with nonsignificant results. However, Hunter, Schmidt, and Jackson (1982) did not see this as a serious problem, noting that it is likely that nonsignificant dissertation results may well be attenuated owing to methodological problems. They further stated that, typically, only a very large number of lost studies will make a substantive difference in a meta-analysis.

This literature search identified 106 articles and book chapters on participation. However, many of these were not appropriate for meta-analysis. We eliminated literature reviews and essays that were not based on data (12 articles), 13 data-based articles without quantifiable effect sizes, 5 studies in which participation was the dependent variable, 6 studies whose dependent variables were not appropriate for this meta-analysis, 15 studies lacking clear measures of participation, and 7 studies in which methodological problems[2] posed serious questions about an estimation of effects or whose data came from another study included in the meta-analysis. . . .

RESULTS

SATISFACTION

Forty-one estimates of the relationship between participation and satisfaction were considered. After cumulation of estimates of effects, the weighted mean correlation was .34, and the true variance was .0301. A chi-square test showed this variance to be statistically different from 0 ($x^2 = 244.27$, $df = 40$, $p < .01$), indicating that moderator variables would reduce the variance in estimates. We first looked at substantive moderators like organizational type, job level, and type of decision. None of these subgroupings proved useful in reducing variance or in differentiating among effect sizes. Hence, we considered methodological moderators. . . .

The organizational studies were divided into those that measured actual participation and those that measured perceived participation. The mean weighted correlation for studies of actual participation was .16; the variance among these estimates was .0035, which is not significantly different from 0 ($x^2 = 8.19$, $df = 10$, $p > .05$). However, the variance in studies investigating perceived participation was still significant. We considered one additional moderator to eliminate the remaining variance: whether perceived participation was in reference to specific issues, such as goals, pay plans, or job redesign, or in reference to multiple issues or a general participative climate,

evaluated by a question like "In general, how much do you participate in decision making on your job?" The mean weighted correlation for studies concerned with specific issues was .21; the variance among these estimates was .0009. This variance was not significant ($x^2 = .78$, $df = 4$, $p > .05$). The mean weighted correlation for studies concerned with multiple issues was .46. The variance among these effect size estimates was .0156. This variance is still significant ($x^2 = 88.5$, $df = 19$, $p < .01$). Several other variables (measurement, job level, and organizational type) were considered for further reducing the variance among effect sizes. However, no other moderator variables reduced the variance within subgroups, so the analysis of studies in which satisfaction was the dependent variable ended at this point.

. . . The satisfaction subgroups in which variance was reduced to the greatest extent possible . . . include (1) nonorganizational studies, (2) studies of actual participation, (3) studies of perceived participation in relation to specific issues, and (4) studies of perceived participation in relation to multiple issues. . . . Figure 1 is a tree diagram of analyses performed with satisfaction as the dependent variable.

All of the subgroup estimates for satisfaction differ significantly from 0, but there is substantial variation in the magnitudes of effects. The strongest effects of participation on satisfaction are found in studies of perceived participation focusing on multiple issues and in the nonorganizational studies. Much smaller effects are found in the studies of perceived participation focusing on

FIGURE 1 Tree Diagram of Studies in the Meta-analysis for Satisfaction as Dependent Variable

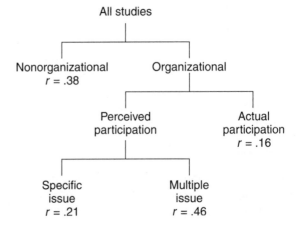

single issues and in the studies of actual participation. In three out of four subgroups, the variance has been reduced to what would be expected from sampling error. Because of the reduction in variance and the sharp differences among subgroups in sizes of effects, it appears that the analyses were successful in partitioning the studies into appropriate subgroups.

PRODUCTIVITY

Twenty-five studies containing estimates of the relationship between participation and productivity were analyzed. After cumulation of effect estimates the weighted mean correlation was .15, and the true variance was .0334. A chi-square test showed this variance differed significantly from 0 ($x^2 = 69.47$, $df = 25$, $p < .01$), so we considered moderator variables. Again, substantive moderator variables were considered first. Of these variables, the objects of participation proved to be useful for subgroup analysis. Seven studies investigated the effects of participation in goal setting on productivity. The cumulated mean weighted correlation for studies of goal setting was .11, and the variance among these estimates was 0. However, the variance among other studies was still significant, so we sought additional moderators. Because other substantive moderators did not prove useful, we evaluated methodological moderators. The first methodological moderator used was research setting. The mean weighted correlation for the nine field studies was .27; the variance among these estimates was 0. Hence, no further analyses were necessary on this subgroup. The variance among estimates for the laboratory studies was significant, so we analyzed these further.

The final moderator considered for studies in which productivity was the dependent variable was the manipulation used in the laboratory studies. Four of the studies manipulated leadership style; a research assistant or member of the experimental group had been instructed to be leader and to behave in an authoritarian or democratic style. The correlation between participation and productivity in the studies manipulating leadership style was −.33 the variance among these estimates was .014. This variance was not significant ($x^2 = 3.73$, $df = 3$, $p > .05$). The other four studies manipulated the nature of the tasks the groups performed, by placing subjects in assigned or participative task groups. The correlation between participation and productivity in these studies was −.01; the variance among the estimates was 0. . . .

The subgroups of studies investigating productivity in which variance was reduced to the great-

FIGURE 2 Tree Diagram of Studies in the Meta-analysis for Productivity as Dependent Variable

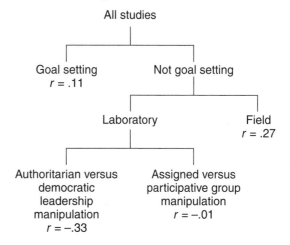

est extent possible . . . are (1) studies concerned with participation in goal setting, (2) field studies, (3) laboratory studies in which leadership style was manipulated, and (4) laboratory studies in which the nature of a task was manipulated. . . . Figure 2 is a tree diagram of subgroup analyses performed with productivity as the dependent variable.

As with the satisfaction studies, the mean weighted correlations of the different subgroups differ substantially. The laboratory studies that manipulated the nature of a task show essentially no correlation, and the studies concerned with goal setting exhibit a significant, but small, positive correlation. The field studies show a relatively strong positive correlation, and the studies of leadership style exhibit a relatively strong negative correlation. The variance among estimates in these subgroups has been reduced to that attributable to sampling error. The substantially different effect sizes and the reduction in subgroup variance suggest that our partitioning efforts were appropriate and successful.

DISCUSSION

CONTINGENCY MODELS OF PARTICIPATION

This meta-analysis provided no support for any of the contingency predictions discussed. We considered both job type and organizational type as possible moderator variables at all stages of analysis, but there was no reduction of variance in effect sizes through subgroupings on the basis of these variables. Thus, it does not appear that participation is more effective for managers than for lower-level employees, or vice versa. There is also no evidence that research, service, and manufacturing organizations differ in terms of the effectiveness of participation. It was not possible to provide a test of contingency predictions referring to personality, because very few studies provided subgroup analyses considering individuals with different personality types. As mentioned earlier, studies that have considered authoritarianism and need for independence have provided conflicting conclusions.

Finally, it should be noted that the variance in studies of participation in goal setting was reduced to that accountable to sampling error. The correlation between participation in goal setting and productivity was significant, but small ($r = .11$). This result should come as little surprise to those researching goal setting, most of whom have now concluded (e.g., Latham & Marshall, 1982; Latham & Steele, 1983) that participation may have an effect on the levels of goals set, but that it has no effect on productivity if the levels of goals stay the same. Cumulating these results over a variety of research settings adds credence to the generalizability of this conclusion.

COGNITIVE VERSUS AFFECTIVE MODELS OF PARTICIPATION

This meta-analysis provided several tests of the efficacy of cognitive and affective models of participation. First, the findings can be considered in terms of contrasting the effects of participation on satisfaction with the effects of participation on productivity. Affective models predict that participation will have a stronger effect on satisfaction than on productivity, and cognitive models predict the opposite. Second, cognitive models predict that participation will have a stronger influence on productivity and satisfaction for decisions about which employees have specific knowledge. In contrast, affective models predict that working in a participative climate will have the most beneficial effects on workers' attitudes and productivity.

The studies investigating effects of participation other than goal setting on *productivity* exhibited a stronger influence of participation ($r = .27$) than the studies of satisfaction investigating actual participation ($r = .16$) or perceived participation for a single variable ($r = .21$). Of course, comparisons of these effects for different dependent variables should be made with caution, and the differences here are not substantial. However, even the fact that there is a moderately strong effect size for field studies investigating the influence of

participation on productivity indicates that cognitive models have some plausibility. Further, the relatively low, but significant, correlations between actual participation and satisfaction and between participation and satisfaction in studies of single issues might lessen confidence in affective models of participation.

However, the data seem more consistent with an affective explanation when we consider studies of participation involving multiple issues. These studies investigated perceived participation and typically used such items as "In general, how participative is your workplace?" or "How much do you generally share in decision making with your supervisor?" After subgroup analysis, some unexplained variance remained in this subgroup, but the mean weighted effect size was .46, much larger than the average correlations in other subgroups of field studies. It appears that working in a participative climate is strongly related to satisfaction at work. This result is in keeping with the human relations school of organizational behavior and with current interest in work climates. In particular, it supports the idea that microclimates (Schneider, 1981), such as a climate for variety, a climate for innovation, or a climate for participation, are related to individual attitudes. However, it is important to consider the structure of this relationship. Does a participative climate cause workers' satisfaction? Does workers' satisfaction help develop a participative climate? Or are these two variables redundant indicators of the same concept? LaFollette and Sims (1975), discussing Johannesson (1973), summarized this dilemma well:

> If it appears as if perceptual climate research is converging upon any domain, job satisfaction seems the likely candidate. Indeed it is hard to imagine how this possibly could have been avoided. Even if researchers had taken the pains to create new items and had adopted different item formats (which they have not) there remains the psychological problem of divorcing description from feelings. Since descriptions of work situations have been operationally defined as indices of job satisfaction it seems redundant at best to also term such descriptions organizational climate (1975: 257).

Climate has traditionally been defined as a descriptive construct and satisfaction as an affective construct. However, these definitions get muddied operationally if satisfaction is measured through descriptors, as it is in the Job Descriptive Index (JDI), or if scales measuring climate include items on attitude. This problem probably is not crucial for the studies in this meta-analysis, because participation involves a specific microclimate, rather than omnibus organizational climate. Thus, it is not likely that measures of participative climate and overall work satisfaction are redundant. In addition, all of these studies considered descriptions of participation rather than attitudes toward participation as the independent variable. Finally, with the exception of studies using the JDI, measures of satisfaction were purely affective. Moreover, results of studies using the JDI were not systematically different from those of studies using other measures of satisfaction.

The question of causality remains: Does participation cause satisfaction or does satisfaction cause participation? All of the studies in the multiple-issue subgrouping were correlational, so we cannot answer this question with full confidence. However, we can bring evidence from the literature on climate to bear on this issue. Laboratory research investigating experimentally created social climates (Litwin & Stringer, 1968) found that manipulated climate had an effect on satisfaction. Hand, Richards, and Slocum (1973) found a positive relationship between initial perceptions of climate and subsequent acceptance of self and others. Taylor and Bowers's (1972)[3] cross-lagged panel study of over 284 work groups in 15 different organizations found that "organization climate shows evidence of being more the cause of, than caused by, satisfaction" (1972: 89).

Several concluding comments about the comparison between cognitive, affective, and contingency models of participation are in order. First, there was little support for contingency models of participation, though the lack of measures for several contingency variables could have affected findings. Second, this meta-analysis did not allow for a complete test of the models presented, as we lacked data on several intervening variables in these models, such as upward and downward sharing of information and satisfaction of higher-order ego needs. We would encourage researchers to measure these variables in future investigations of participation. Despite this limitation, some evidence to support both cognitive and affective models of participation emerged. The relatively large correlation between participation and productivity in field studies somewhat supports cognitive models. However, the largest subgroup correlation, between perceived participation and satisfaction, provides greater support for affective models of participation.

Estimates of the effect of participation on *both* satisfaction and productivity appeared in 13 stud-

ies. An examination of these studies sheds some light on the relative efficacy of cognitive and affective models: (1) the relationship between participation and satisfaction was stronger than that between participation and productivity in four studies (Katzell, Miller, Rotter, & Venet, 1970; Schuler & Kim, 1978; Shaw, 1955; and Vroom, 1960), (2) the relationship between participation and productivity was stronger in one study (Ivancevich, 1977), and (3) no significant difference emerged in the other eight studies. These studies provide somewhat stronger evidence for the relationship between participation and satisfaction than for that between participation and productivity. However, the large number of insignificant differences in this subset precludes our suggesting that this comparison provides strong evidence for either cognitive or affective models.

RESEARCH SETTING AS A MODERATOR

Several of the strongest moderators were methodological variables; in particular, research setting and type of subject played important roles. For the studies concerned with satisfaction, the variance was zero among investigations involving nonorganizational subjects, all but one of which (Veen, 1972) had a laboratory setting. The weighted correlation for these studies was relatively high ($r = .38$). This effect size was considerably higher than that in studies involving actual participation in organizations ($r = .16$) or perceived participation in reference to a specific issue ($r = .21$).

There are two clear explanations for these results. First, an explanation in terms of internal validity suggests that the high degree of control in laboratories over extraneous variables would make the higher correlation a better indicator of the true relationship between participation and satisfaction. However, an explanation in terms of external validity suggests that college students and laboratory tasks have little in common with real organizational life; hence, field estimates of the effect between participation and satisfaction would be more meaningful. Both arguments undoubtedly have merit. This meta-analysis seems to indicate that there is a relatively high pure effect of participation on satisfaction, but that a host of other organizational influences dilute this effect in field studies investigating actual participation or perceived participation in relation to specific issues.

The effect of research setting in the productivity studies is also striking. Among studies not investigating goal setting, field studies showed a moderately high positive correlation ($r = .27$), and laboratory studies yielded either no correlation (assigned versus participative task manipulation, $r = -.01$) or negative correlations (authoritarian versus democratic leadership manipulation, $r = -.33$). The points of interest here are the sharp differences between laboratory and field studies and the differences in effect sizes for different manipulations.

The substantial difference between field and laboratory studies can probably be attributed to the tasks typically performed in these settings. The laboratory studies typically involved a simple and well-defined manipulated task like turning switches on a control panel or a game of 20 questions; the field studies typically involved participation in naturally occurring, more complex activities, such as pay incentive plans or job design, or participation over a wide gamut of organizational issues. In the laboratory, there usually was a correct answer; there are rarely such guarantees in organizations. Finally, organizational members in field studies had more at stake in the decisions that were made than students in a laboratory.

All of these factors contributed to a higher level of complexity for the organizational participative tasks than for the laboratory participative tasks. Research on small group behavior (Cartwright & Zander, 1960) has suggested that different types of leadership and structure are appropriate for different types of tasks; specifically, that authoritarian leadership and centralized group structure are most appropriate for simple tasks. The studies in this meta-analysis investigating leadership behavior bear this out. Most of the tasks were simple, and authoritarian leadership was more effective in eliciting high levels of productivity. In contrast, the field studies involving complex problems benefited more from participative processes. The lack of effects in the laboratory studies that manipulated the nature of a task is more difficult to interpret. It could be that in laboratory groups without defined leaders, such typical manipulations as assigned or participative groups are not strong enough to elicit effects on productivity. . . .

CONCLUSIONS AND FUTURE DIRECTIONS

In spite of these limitations, this research supports some current wisdom about the effects of participation and extends our knowledge of the participative process in organizations in important ways. First, the meta-analysis provides some support for the conclusions reached by Locke and Schweiger (1979). Participation has an effect on both satisfaction and productivity, and its effect on satisfaction is somewhat stronger than its effect on productivity. This meta-analysis allowed us to be more explicit about these effects. As Figures 1 and 2 demonstrate, we can now make quite precise statements about the *magnitude* of the effect of participation on satisfaction and productivity. In addition, strong evidence exists for a consistent and substantial effect of research setting in these studies, because consideration of this methodological variable considerably reduces the variance among studies. Finally, our analysis indicates specific organizational factors that may enhance or constrain the effect of participation. For example, there is evidence that participative climate has a more substantial effect on workers' satisfaction than participation in specific decisions, and it appears that participation in goal setting does not have a strong effect on productivity.

These conclusions provide some clear avenues for future research. It is important for organizational scholars to conduct research that can specifically test the relationships in the cognitive and affective models. For instance, research contrasting the effects of both participative climate and participation in relation to specific issues on both satisfaction and productivity could lead to an important clarification of the cognitive and the affective processes at work in participative situations. Researchers should also extend our consideration of contingency variables to areas this meta-analysis highlights. For example, the contrast between studies of participative climate and studies of participation in relation to specific issues suggests that organizations with formal systems of participation may differ greatly from organizations in which participativeness is an informal managerial norm. Our investigation (Miller & Monge, 1986) of the Scanlon plan of participative management suggests that this might be the case. Future research could also usefully consider the development of participative systems and norms in organizations over time. Longitudinal research of this nature could help clarify the causal structure of the relationships among participation, satisfaction, and productivity. Finally, the meta-analytic procedure itself could be usefully extended to allow for the testing of relationships that go beyond the simple bivariate level.

Notes

1. Ritchie and Miles (1970: 348) coined this term in regard to participation in decision making.

2. The category of methodological problems included a number of studies in which confounding variables or unusual methods made accurate estimation of effects impossible. For instance, the overtime study of Lawler and Hackman (1969) included an outlying data point that made interpretation difficult. In addition, the non-participative group in this study had much lower attendance than the participative group to begin with, limiting our confidence in the results. A second example of a methodological problem is Ivancevich's (1976) investigation of goal setting in which both participative and assigned groups went through extensive and active training sessions. In all ways except the actual goal setting, both groups had high levels of participation.

3. LaFollette and Sims (1975) cited this study.

References

Abdel-Halim, A. A. 1983. Effects of task and personality characteristics on subordinate responses to participative decision making. *Academy of Management Journal,* 26, 477–484.

Abdel-Halim, A. A., & Rowland, K. M. 1976. Some personality determinants in the effects of participation: A further investigation. *Personnel Psychology,* 29, 41–55.

Alutto, J. A., & Acito, F. 1974. Decisional participation and sources of job satisfaction: A study of manufacturing personnel. *Academy of Management Journal,* 17, 160–167.

Alutto, J. A., & Vrenenburgh, D. J. 1977. Characteristics of decisional participation by nurses. *Academy of Management Journal,* 20, 341–347.

Anthony, W. P. 1978. *Participative management.* Reading, Mass.: Addison-Wesley.

Bartlem, C. S., & Locke, E. A. 1981. The Coch and French study: A critique and reinterpretation. *Human Relations,* 34, 555–566.

Baumgartel, H. 1956. Leadership, motivations, and attitudes in research laboratories. *Journal of Social Issues,* 12, 24–31.

Blake, R. R., & Mouton, J. S. 1964. *The managerial grid.* Houston: Gulf.

Carey, A. 1967. The Hawthorne studies: A radical criticism. *American Sociological Review,* 32, 403–416.

Cartwright, D., & Zander, A. 1960. *Group dynamics: Research and theory* (2nd ed.). Evanston, Ill.: Row, Peterson.

Coch, L., & French, J. R. P. 1948. Overcoming resistance to change. *Human Relations,* 1, 512–532.

Dachler, H. P., & Wilpert, B. 1978. Conceptual dimensions and boundaries of participation in organizations. *Administrative Science Quarterly,* 23, 1–39.

Dossett, D. L., Latham, G. P., & Mitchell, T. R. 1979. Effects of assigned versus participatively set goals, knowledge of results, and individual differences on employee behavior when goal difficulty is held constant. *Journal of Applied Psychology,* 64, 291–298.

Falcione, R. L. 1974. Credibility: Qualifier of subordinate participation. *Journal of Business Communication,* 11 (3), 43–54.

Fiman, B. G. 1973. An investigation of the relationships among supervisory attitudes, behaviors, and outputs: An examination of McGregor's Theory Y. *Personnel Psychology,* 26, 95–105.

Fox, W. M. 1957. Group reactions to two types of conference leadership. *Human Relations,* 10, 279–289.

French, J. R. P., Israel, J., & As, D. 1960. An experiment in a Norwegian factory: Interpersonal dimensions in decision-making. *Human Relations,* 13, 3–19.

French, J. R. P., Kay, E., & Meyer, H. H. 1966. Participation and the appraisal system. *Human Relations,* 19, 3–20.

Frost, C. H., Wakely, J. H., & Ruh, R. A. 1974. *The Scanlon Plan for organization development: Identity, participation, and equity.* East Lansing: Michigan State University Press.

Gibb, C. A. 1951. An experimental approach to the study of leadership. *Occupational Psychology,* 25, 233–248.

Glass, G. V., McGaw, B., & Smith, M. L. 1981. *Meta-analysis in social research.* Beverly Hills, Calif.: Sage Publications.

Hand, H. H., Richards, M. D., & Slocum, J. W. 1973. Organizational climate and the effectiveness of a human relations training program. *Academy of Management Journal,* 16, 185–195.

House, R. J., & Dessler, G. 1974. The path-goal theory of leadership: Some post hoc and a priori tests. In J. Hunt & L. Larson (Eds.), *Contingency approaches to leadership,* 29–55. Carbondale, IL.: Southern Illinois University Press.

Hulin, C. L. 1971. Individual differences and job enrichment: The case against general treatment. In J. R. Maher (Ed.), *New perspectives in job enrichment:* 159–191. New York: Van Nostrand Reinhold Co.

Hunter, J. W., Schmidt, F. L., & Jackson, G. B. 1982. *Meta-analysis: Cumulating research findings across studies.* Beverly Hills, Calif.: Sage Publications.

Ivancevich, J. M. 1974. A study of a cognitive training program: Trainer styles and group development. *Academy of Management Journal,* 17, 428–439.

Ivancevich, J. M. 1976. Effects of goal setting on performance and job satisfaction. *Journal of Applied Psychology,* 61, 605–612.

Ivancevich, J. M. 1977. Different goal setting treatments and their effects on performance and job satisfaction. *Academy of Management Journal,* 20, 406–419.

Jenkins, G. D., & Lawler, E. E. 1981. Impact of employee participation in pay plan development. *Organizational Behavior and Human Performance,* 28, 111–128.

Johannesson, R. E. 1973. Some problems in the measurement of organizational climate. *Organizational Behavior and Human Performance,* 10: 118–144.

Katzell, R. A., Miller, C. E., Rotter, N. G., & Venet, T. G. 1970. Effects of leadership and other inputs on group processes and outputs. *Journal of Social Psychology,* 80, 157–169.

LaFollette, W. R., & Sims, H. P. 1975. Is satisfaction redundant with organizational climate? *Organizational Behavior and Human Performance,* 13, 257–278.

Lanzetta, J. T., & Roby, T. 1960. The relationship between certain group process variables and group problem-solving efficiency. *Journal of Social Psychology,* 52, 135–148.

Latham, G. P., & Marshall, H. A. 1982. The effects of self-set, participatively set, and assigned goals on the performance of government employees. *Personnel Psychology,* 35, 399–404.

Latham, G. P., Mitchell, T. R., & Dossett, D. L. 1978. Importance of participative goal setting and anticipated rewards on goal difficulty and job performance. *Journal of Applied Psychology,* 63, 163–171.

Latham, G. P., & Saari, L. M. 1979. The effects of holding goal difficulty constant on assigned and participatively set goals. *Academy of Management Journal,* 22, 163–168.

Latham, G. P., & Steele, T. P. 1983. The motivational effects of participation versus goal setting on performance. *Academy of Management Journal,* 26, 406–417.

Latham, G. P., & Yukl, G. A. 1976. Effects of assigned and participative goal setting on performance and job satisfaction. *Journal of Applied Psychology,* 61, 166–171.

Lawler, E. E. 1975. Pay, participation and organizational change. In E. L. Cass & F. G. Zimmer (Eds.), *Man and work in society:* 137–149. New York: Van Nostrand Reinhold Co.

Lawler, E. E., & Hackman, J. R. 1969. Impact of employee participation in the development of pay-incentive plans: A field experiment. *Journal of Applied Psychology,* 53, 467–471.

Likert, R. L. 1967. *The human organization.* New York: McGraw-Hill Book Co.

Lischeron, J., & Wall, T. D. 1974. Attitudes towards participating among local authority employees. *Human Relations,* 28, 499–517.

Lischeron, J., & Wall, T. D. 1975. Employee participation: An experimental field study. *Human Relations,* 28, 863–884.

Litwin, G. H., & Stringer, R. A., Jr. 1968. *Motivation and organizational climate.* Boston: Harvard Business School, Division of Research.

Locke, E. A., & Schweiger, D. M. 1979. Participation in decision-making: One more look. *Research in Organizational Behavior,* 1, 265–339.

Lowin, A. 1968. Participative decision making: A model, literature critique, and prescriptions for research. *Organizational Behavior and Human Performance,* 3, 68–106.

Maier, N. R. F. 1963. *Problem solving discussions and conferences: Leadership methods and skills.* New York: McGraw-Hill Book Co.

McCurdy, H. G., & Lambert, W. E. 1952. The efficiency of small human groups in the solution of problems requiring genuine cooperation. *Journal of Personality,* 20, 478–494.

McGregor, D. 1960. *The human side of enterprise.* New York: McGraw-Hill Book Co.

Melcher, A. J. 1976. Participation: A critical review of research findings. *Human Resource Management,* 15 (2), 12–21.

Miles, R. E., & Ritchie, J. B. 1971. Participative management: Quality vs. quantity. *California Management Review,* 13 (4), 48–56.

Miller, K. I., & Monge, P. R. 1986. The development and test of a system of organizational participation and allocation. In M. McLaughlin (Ed.), *Communication yearbook* 10: in press. Beverly Hills, Calif.: Sage Publications.

Mitchell, T. R., Smyser, C. M., & Weed, S. E. 1975. Locus of control: Supervision and work satisfaction. *Academy of Management Journal,* 18, 623–631.

Morse, N. C., & Reimer, E. 1956. The experimental change of a major organizational variable. *Journal of Abnormal and Social Psychology,* 52, 120–129.

Neider, L. L. 1980. An experimental field investigation utilizing an expectancy theory view of participation. *Organizational Behavior and Human Performance,* 26, 425–442.

Obradovic, J. 1970. Participation and work attitudes in Yugoslavia. *Industrial Relations,* 9, 161–169.

Obradovic, J., French, J. R. P., & Rodgers, W. 1970. Workers' councils in Yugoslavia. *Human Relations,* 23, 459–471.

Ritchie, J. B., & Miles, R. E. 1970. An analysis of quantity and quality of participation as mediating variables in the participative decision making process. *Personnel Psychology,* 23, 347–359.

Roberts, K. H., Blankenship, L. V., & Miles, R. E. 1968. Organizational leadership, satisfaction, and productivity. *Academy of Management Journal,* 11, 401–422.

Roethlisberger, F. J., & Dickson, W. J. 1939. *Management and the worker.* Cambridge, Mass.: Harvard University Press.

Runyon, K. E. 1973. Some interactions between personality variables and management styles. *Journal of Applied Psychology,* 57, 288–294.

Schecter, J. 1972. The private world of Richard Nixon. *Time,* 99 (1), 18–19.

Schneider, B. 1981. *Work climates: An interactionist perspective.* Research report No. 81-2, Department of Psychology, Michigan State University, East Lansing.

Schuler, R. S. 1976. Participation with supervisor and subordinate authoritarianism: A path-goal theory reconciliation. *Administrative Science Quarterly,* 21, 320–325.

Schuler, R. S. 1980. A role and expectancy perception model of participation in decision making. *Academy of Management Journal,* 23, 331–340.

Schuler, R. S., & Kim, J. S. 1978. Employees' expectancy perceptions as explanatory variables for effectiveness of participation in decision making. *Psychological Reports,* 43, 651–656.

Schweiger, D. M., & Leana, C. R. 1986. Participation in decision making. In E. A. Locke (Ed.), *Generalizing from laboratory to field settings:* 147–166. Lexington, Mass.: D. C. Heath Co.

Seeborg, I. S. 1978. The influence of employee participation in job redesign. *Journal of Applied Behavioral Science,* 14, 87–98.

Shaw, M. E. 1955. A comparison of two types of leadership in various communication nets. *Journal of Abnormal and Social Psychology,* 50, 127–134.

Singer, J. N. 1974. Participative decision-making about work: An overdue look at variables which mediate its effects. *Sociology of Work and Occupations,* 1, 347–371.

Smith, M. L., & Glass, G. V. 1977. Meta-analyses of psychotherapy outcome studies. *American Psychologist,* 32, 752–760.

Smith, P. C., Kendall, M., & Hulin, C. L. 1969. *The measurement of satisfaction in work and retirement.* Chicago: Rand McNally & Co.

Strauss, G. 1982. Workers' participation in management: An international perspective. *Research in Organizational Behavior,* 4, 173–265.

Tannenbaum, R., & Schmidt, W. 1958. How to choose a leadership pattern. *Harvard Business Review,* 36 (2), 95–101.

Taylor, J. C., & Bowers, D. G. 1972. *Survey of organizations: A machine-scored standardized questionnaire instrument.* Ann Arbor, Mich.: Institute for Social Research.

Torrance, E. P. 1953. Methods of conducting critiques of group problem-solving performance. *Journal of Applied Psychology,* 37, 394–398.

Tosi, H. 1970. A reexamination of personality as a determinant of the effect of participation. *Personnel Psychology,* 23, 91–99.

Veen, P. 1972. Effects of participative decision-making in field hockey training: A field experiment. *Organizational Behavior and Human Performance,* 7, 288–307.

Vroom, V. H. 1960. *Some personality determinants of the effects of participation.* Englewood Cliffs, N.J.: Prentice-Hall.

Vroom, V. H., & Deci, E. L. (Eds.). 1960. *Management and motivation.* Baltimore: Penguin Books.

Vroom, V. H., & Jago, A. G. 1978. On the validity of the Vroom/Yetton model. *Journal of Applied Psychology,* 63, 151–162.

Vroom, V. H., & Mann, F. C. 1960. Leader authoritarianism and employee attitudes. *Personnel Psychology,* 13, 125–140.

Vroom, V. H., & Yetton, P. W. 1973. *Leadership and decision-making.* Pittsburgh, Pa.: University of Pittsburgh Press.

Wexley, K. E., Singh, J. P., & Yukl, G. A. 1973. Subordinate personality as a moderator of the effects of participation in three types of appraisal interviews. *Journal of Applied Psychology,* 58, 54–59.

Yukl, G. A., & Kanuk, L. 1979. Leadership behavior and the effectiveness of beauty salon managers. *Personnel Psychology,* 32, 663–675.

Reading 32

Contingent Leadership and Effectiveness of Trauma Resuscitation Teams

Seokhwa Yun
Montclair State University

Samer Faraj and Henry P. Sims Jr.
University of Maryland

Teams have emerged as a critical organizing structure (e.g., Guzzo & Dickson, 1996; LePine, Erez, & Johnson, 2002) to deal with today's high-velocity environments, which are dramatically changing, uncertain, and high risk (Riolli-Saltzman & Luthans, 2001). These environments require fast decision making on the basis of information that is often inaccurate, unavailable, or equivocal (e.g., Riolli-Saltzman & Luthans, 2001). In these situations, teams are used to integrate disparate expertise and to coordinate effort under demanding circumstances. Yet, little is known about how leader behaviors influence the effectiveness of teams operating in high-velocity settings. In this research, we extend our understanding of leadership by investigating leadership of trauma resuscitation teams, a particular type of team that operates in a high-velocity environment. . . .

TRAUMA RESUSCITATION TEAMS

A trauma team provides medical care to a patient who has experienced a trauma such as a gun shot. A new trauma team is constituted each time a patient arrives for treatment, and then the team dissolves after providing patient care. The team typically exists for only a very short period of time, from less than a half an hour to several hours. The first 60 min. following trauma are considered a "golden hour" in that the patient may go into shock and die from complications. Because much of that hour is spent transporting the patient to the hospital, often little time remains for the trauma team to prevent shock.

A trauma team is a cross-functional and multidisciplinary knowledge-based action team. It includes a number of specialists such as surgeons, anesthesiologists, nurses, technicians (or nurse extenders), and resident physicians. Team membership is fluid, and new members are integrated into the treatment task, depending on the needs of the patient. Often, the trauma resuscitation unit has several admissions within 1 hr. (as many as six admissions in 1.5 hr. were observed), which may require some team members to cross over between different teams.

A trauma team accomplishes its task under a severe information shortage. The patient is often brought in unconscious and with little information beyond what the transporting paramedic has reported (e.g., "White male, 40 years of age, fell two stories, found unconscious by a passerby"). Frequently, the patient is unable to communicate crucial information such as medical history, existing allergies, or circumstances of injury. In essence, the team must often find a balance between "action" and seeking more information.

The attending surgeon is the formal leader who is responsible for supervising and coordinating team members' activities and the team's performance (Cicala & Murphy, 1993). He or she has final authority and can override other team members' decisions. Without his or her permission, the team members cannot run the resuscitation or provide trauma treatment to the patient. Therefore, this study focuses on the attending surgeon's behaviors during resuscitation.

The trauma teams have two main responsibilities. Primarily, trauma teams exist to serve the emergency medical needs of trauma patients. Second, the trauma teams also facilitate learning the specialized practice of trauma care. These two objectives are closely intertwined as the team leader (i.e., the attending surgeon) strives to provide learning opportunities without jeopardizing the quality of patient care. Therefore, these two outcomes were conceptualized as main dimensions of team effectiveness in this study.

Source: Edited and reprinted with permission. *Journal of Applied Psychology*, 2005, 90, 6, 1288–1296. Copyright American Psychological Association, 2005.

EMPOWERING AND DIRECTIVE LEADERSHIP

Our ethnographic investigation found that attending surgeons had unique patterns of leadership and differed on the basis of the directive–empowering dimension. Follower participation during trauma resuscitation can be ordered along a continuum ranging from none to very active participation, even approaching almost total control over the trauma resuscitation. At one extreme, some attending surgeons develop and finalize the patient care plan with little consultation with other team members, provide detailed instructions to the team members, and expect team members to follow their instructions and carry out their care plan without discussion. These behaviors are called *directive* in this study, which is similar to autocratic leadership in Vroom and Jago's (1988) theory and directive leadership in path-goal theory (e.g., House, 1971). Under a directive leader, trauma team members have little opportunity to express their opinions. They follow the directive leader's orders and instructions and carry out the care plan the attending surgeon formulates.

Other leaders encourage the team members to actively participate in decision making and task management. Such leaders consult with the team members and encourage them to express their opinions and ideas. They delegate responsibility and authority to team members and provide opportunities for team members to take initiative (e.g., House, 1971; Vroom & Jago, 1988). This type of leader is called *empowering* in this study. In a trauma resuscitation team, an empowering leader is one who consults with team members (consultation) and encourages team members to actively participate in developing and implementing the patient care plan (joint decision making). In addition, in the extreme case, an empowering attending surgeon might delegate virtually the entire responsibility for resuscitation to a team (delegation). Our ethnographic evidence showed that an empowering attending surgeon engages in all three behaviors to some degree. Thus, we did not distinguish between these three activities, although we do recognize the differences between them.

HYPOTHESES DEVELOPMENT. . .

LEADERSHIP AND QUALITY HEALTH CARE

Drawing on our own ethnographic investigation, we proposed a contingency form of leadership in which the effects of leadership on care differ depending on two important situational elements: (a) severity of patient trauma and (b) level of team experience. As a patient's condition becomes increasingly severe, a trauma team has less time to treat the patient, and a higher level of expertise may be necessary to diagnose a severely injured patient, to develop a comprehensive care plan, and to implement treatment. If the team leader displays empowering leadership in this situation, the decision making and the treatment may take longer. Further, some team members may not have sufficient expertise to treat the patient without direction from the leader—and if they are asked to do so, it may endanger the patient. Moreover, when a patient is severely injured, less experienced team members may be overwhelmed, which can make it difficult for them to make decisions and fully use their cognitive capabilities. Thus, the most skillful and experienced team member, typically the attending surgeon, needs to personally take charge of the resuscitation to provide the highest level of treatment. As an attending surgeon interviewed in our ethnographic investigation said,

> It is depending on how critical the patient is. I think if the patient doesn't seem to be critical, you will see the attending kind of roll out of the picture, act as a backup and allowing team members kind of to carry things on. But if it gets escalated and the patient gets more critical, such as hypertension, you will tend to see the attending at the bedside, probably you will see the attending makes all the calls.

This view also had some support in previous literature. For example, Khetarpal et al. (1999) found that resuscitation was more effective for severely injured patients in the presence of a trauma surgeon. Similarly, Vroom (2000), in his normative model of leader actions, emphasized situations in which timing of decisions is critical. Under such circumstances, a leader should make decisions that at other times would be delegated to team members.

However, when a patient is not severely injured, the team has some flexibility and more time to treat the patient. Moreover, the procedures required are likely to be less complicated, sophisticated, and difficult, and team members are more likely to possess the expertise needed to treat the patient. Team members may need to follow only well-rehearsed protocols. Therefore, under these conditions, they can be empowered to do the resuscitation.

Hypothesis 1: The relationship between leadership and team effectiveness is moderated by the severity of patient trauma. Specifically, directive leaders provide better quality of care when a patient is very severely injured, but empowering leaders provide better quality of care when a patient is not severely injured.

The effectiveness of leadership may also depend on the level of team experience. Inexperienced teams may not have sufficient knowledge or expertise to successfully undertake resuscitation on their own. When the attending surgeon empowers an inexperienced team, the patient is exposed to a higher level of risk, which may cause a serious problem. Thus, a leader needs to be more directive when he or she leads an inexperienced team. One trauma nurse interviewed in our ethnographic investigation said,

> Actually, [it depends on] even what period in the rotation the team is in. If they are brand new, all of them [attending surgeons] tend to have a little bit less participation [from other team members] until they feel like the process has been, at least, about some kind of routine. And then they do tend to step back and more allow the team to run it.

Existing research suggests that directive leadership is less useful when followers are more experienced as recognized in the path-goal theory of leadership (e.g., House, 1971), the substitutes for leadership research (Howell, Bowen, Dorfman, Kerr, & Podsakoff, 1996), and the situational leadership model (e.g., Hersey, Blanchard, & Johnson, 1996). Vroom and his colleagues' theory (e.g., Vroom & Jago, 1988) also suggests that subordinate participation and joint decision making are more appropriate when subordinates possess the information required to complete the task.

Hypothesis 2: The relationship between leadership and team effectiveness is moderated by the degree of team experience. Specifically, directive leaders provide better quality of care when a trauma resuscitation team is inexperienced, but empowering leaders provide better quality of care when a trauma team is experienced.

LEADERSHIP AND LEARNING OPPORTUNITIES

We propose that an empowering leader provides more learning opportunities than does a directive leader. An empowering leader is one who consults with and delegates responsibility to the team members. These kinds of leaders give team members opportunities to think, apply their knowledge to the actual situation, and learn by doing. When

an attending surgeon empowers team members, team members have chances to develop and implement a care plan—in essence, to practice medicine. This is a crucial learning tool for team members, most of whom have already accumulated some degree of knowledge through formal education.

In contrast, directive leaders make virtually all decisions themselves, give orders to team members, and run the resuscitation themselves. They expect team members to carry out their orders and commands without expressing opinions, while often failing to explain the logic of their own decisions. In this situation, the team members have limited opportunities to increase their professional expertise. As an attending surgeon interviewed in our ethnographic investigation said,

> A perfect attending gives [the team] the opportunity to think; you've empowered them to decide, to struggle with the choice. Can't decide for them or they learn that the ultimate therapeutic tool is the telephone. They are just secretaries if he tells them what to do.

Yukl and Fu (1999) have provided useful insights regarding the relationship between leadership and providing learning opportunities. They investigated what determines manager's choice of delegation and consultation strategies, concluding that one of the main reasons for delegation is to develop subordinates' skills. Their findings suggest that managers should use empowerment as a way to develop followers' skills. Attending surgeons can use an empowering approach to help team members develop their skills. It follows that team members under empowering leaders will have more learning opportunities than will those under directive leaders. Also, Vroom and Jago (1988) suggested that participative leadership, including consultation and joint decision making, is suitable for achieving subordinate development.

Hypothesis 3: An empowering leader provides more learning opportunities than does a directive leader.

METHOD

RESEARCH SITE AND PARTICIPANTS

This research was conducted at a Level I trauma center (TC) of a major mid-Atlantic medical center in the United States. A TC is an organization that provides emergency care to patients who have experienced a major trauma event and require immediate intensive care. Our research was mainly conducted in the trauma resuscitation unit (TRU), a type of specialized emergency room where trauma patients are brought for initial treatment and stabilization. . . .

RESEARCH DESIGN

This study used a 2 (severely injured vs. not-severely injured patient) × 2 (experienced vs. inexperienced team) × 2 (directive vs. empowering leadership) design. . . .

DISCUSSION

This research investigated leadership in knowledge teams operating in a high-reliability setting, specifically in trauma resuscitation teams. Overall, the results support a contingency model. The results suggested that the influence of leadership varies, depending on the situation and the goal (i.e., quality health care or education) that a leader pursues. Our findings supported a contingency view of leadership in which the relationship between leadership and team effectiveness was moderated by specific situational elements. Specifically, directive leadership was more effective when trauma severity was high, whereas empowering leadership was more effective when trauma severity was low. In addition, when team experience was high, empowering leadership was more effective. However, directive leadership was more effective when an inexperienced team treated a severely injured patient, whereas empowering leadership was more effective when an inexperienced team treated a not-severely injured patient. Also, the results demonstrated that an empowering leader provided team members more learning opportunities than did a directive leader.

THEORETICAL AND PRACTICAL IMPLICATIONS

Contingency theory, as a broad class of more specific theories, has a long history in leadership research and has widespread intuitive appeal. Yet, empirical support for contingency theories has been mixed. Podsakoff, MacKenzie, Ahearne, and Bommer (1995), for example, stated that research on situational factors had "unfortunately, over the years, not received much empirical support" (p. 464). They characterized the empirical identification of moderators of leadership as "searching for a needle in a haystack" (p. 422). . . .

Our findings extend the work of Yukl and Fu (1999), who found that leaders use more delegation when they perceive their subordinates to have high competence and a longer tenure working under their authority. We extend these previous findings by adding patient severity (a particular type of urgency or time limitation) and team experience into the theoretical mix. We also expanded their study to the team level. Moreover, our research investigated team effectiveness as an outcome and clarified the circumstances under which empowering leader behavior was likely to be effective.

Our findings support parts of Vroom and Jago's (1988) theory. That is, when followers have sufficient information or knowledge, joint decision making (see GII in Vroom & Jago, 1988) is more appropriate than autocratic decision making, but autocratic leadership is more effective when timing is critical. Both of these statements are consistent with our results. Vroom and Jago also gave greater prominence to follower development as an important outcome. They suggested that leadership should tend to be more follower-centric when development is important, which was strongly supported by our research, which concluded that empowering leadership was superior in promoting team learning.

Our study advances theory on leadership in several ways. First, our study is among the first to empirically examine leadership in a high-velocity setting. On the basis of our own ethnographic work and the literature, we developed and tested a contingency model of leadership. Second, related to the first, our study advances the understanding of high-velocity organizations. Many authors researching high-velocity organizations have previously concluded that the source of error-free operations is a culture of reliability (e.g., La Porte, 1996; Weick & Roberts, 1993). Our findings shed some light on this broad conclusion by describing how leaders play a crucial role. Our study found that in such settings leaders need to display different leadership styles depending on the situation to avoid a severe failure and deliver highly reliable team performance. Moreover, our findings imply that a leader's capability to diagnose the situation is critically important in providing reliable performance across situations. Organizations aiming for reliable operation need to train managers to adjust their leadership in accordance with changing circumstances. Future research should examine the process through which leadership influences team performance in high-velocity settings. For instance, a leader can influence the culture, communication, and coordination practices, which in turn can determine the performance of the team in a high-velocity setting.

Third, our findings, along with the characteristics of trauma teams, imply the importance of leader adaptability, although we did not directly examine leader adaptability (e.g., Hall, Workman, & Marchioro, 1998). In our trauma setting, team leaders and their teams work in an uncertain and time-constrained environment. They cannot anticipate when they will admit a new patient or how many and what type of patients they will admit. They often do not know with accuracy such essential information as a patient's medical history. Still, teams need different forms of leadership contingent on the situations. Different forms of leadership might be attained through at least two methods: by changing the leader (a between-leader approach) or by a leader changing his or her own leadership style depending on the situation (a within-leader approach). In the TC, the urgency of the situation makes it extremely difficult to change leaders in a timely manner to fit the situation. Therefore, effective leaders should be able to adjust their own behaviors to better influence team outcomes. That is, leader adaptability becomes more important in uncertain and urgent situations.

In many high-velocity settings, organizations select leaders on the basis of their medical or technical knowledge, skill, and experience. They should also consider candidates' ability to analyze the situation and adapt their leadership behaviors to the situation. Simulations may be used as a useful selection method for this purpose. Another approach can be training. For example, TCs might develop a training program to help attending surgeons improve their leadership. These programs could start with a discussion of appropriate leadership styles during trauma resuscitation. It is necessary to emphasize the situational factors that influence the choice of leadership style. These training programs should stress the importance of adaptability as well. In addition, medical schools could offer leadership courses especially for students who major in surgery, emergency medicine, or traumatology. These programs could help medical students understand and develop appropriate leadership skills before entering practice. . . .

References

Campbell, J. P. (1977). The cutting edge of leadership: An overview. In J. G. Hunt & L. L. Larson (Eds.), *Leadership: The cutting edge* (pp. 221–234). Carbondale: Southern Illinois University Press.

Cicala, R. S., & Murphy, M. T. (1993). Trauma centers, systems, and plans. In C. M. Grande (Ed.), *Textbook of trauma anesthesia and critical care* (pp. 56–70). St. Louis, MO: Mosby.

Guzzo, R. A., & Dickson, M. W. (1996). Teams in organizations: Recent research on performance and effectiveness. *Annual Review of Psychology, 47,* 307–338.

Hall, R. J., Workman, J. W., & Marchioro, C. A. (1998). Sex, task, and behavioral flexibility effects on leadership perceptions. *Organizational Behavior and Human Decision Processes, 74,* 1–32.

Hersey, P., Blanchard, K., & Johnson, D. (1996). *Management of organizational behavior.* Upper Saddle River. NJ: Prentice Hall.

House, R. J. (1971). A path goal theory of leader effectiveness. *Administrative Science Quarterly, 16,* 321–338.

Howell, J. P., Bowen, D. E., Dorfman, P. W., Kerr, S., & Podsakoff, P. M. (1996). Substitutes for leadership: Effective alternatives to ineffective leadership. In R. M. Steers, L. W. Porter, & G. A. Bigley (Eds.), *Motivation and leadership at work* (pp. 672–686). Boston: McGraw-Hill.

Khetarpal, S., Steinbrunn, B. S., McGonigal, M. D., Stafford, R., Ney, A. L., Kalb, D. C., et al. (1999). Trauma faculty and trauma team activation: Impact on trauma system function and patient outcome. *Journal of Trauma, Injury, Infection, and Critical Care, 47,* 576–581.

Kirk, R. E (1995). *Experimental design: Procedures for the behavioral sciences* (3rd ed.). Pacific Grove, CA: Brooks/Cole.

La Porte, T. R. (1996). High reliability organizations: Unlikely, demanding and at risk. *Journal of Contingencies and Crisis Management, 4,* 60–71.

LePine, J. A., Erez, A., & Johnson, D. E. (2002). The nature and dimensionality of organizational citizenship behavior: A critical review and meta-analysis. *Journal of Applied Psychology, 87,* 52–65.

Mims, B. C. (1990). *Case Studies in critical care nursing.* Baltimore: Williams &Wilkins.

Pearce, C. L., & Sims, H. P., Jr. (2002). Vertical vs. shared leadership as predictors of the effectiveness of change management teams: An examination of aversive, directive, transactional, transformational, and empowering behaviors. *Group Dynamics, 7,* 172–197.

Podsakoff, P. M., MacKenzie, S. B., Ahearne, M., & Bommer, W. H. (1995). Searching for a needle in a haystack: Trying to identify the elusive moderators of leadership behaviors. *Journal of Management, 21,* 422–470.

Riolli-Saltzman, L., & Luthans, F. (2001). After the bubble burst: How small high-tech firms can keep in front of the wave. *Academy of Management Executive, 15,* 114–124.

Vroom, V. H. (2000). Leadership and the decision-making process. *Organizational Dynamics, 28,* 82–94.

Vroom, V. H., & Jago. A. G. (1988). *The new leadership: Managing participation in organizations.* Englewood Cliffs. NJ: Prentice Hall.

Weick, C., & Roberts, K. (1993). Collective mind in organizations, heedful interrelating on flight decks. *Administrative Science Quarterly,* 38, 357–381.

Yauch, C. A., & Studel, H. J. (2003). Complementary use of qualitative and quantitative cultural assessment methods. *Organizational Research Methods,* 6, 465–581.

Yukl, G. A. (2002). *Leadership in organizations* (5th ed.). Upper Saddle River, NJ: Prentice Hall.

Yukl, G., & Fu, P. P. (1999). Determinants of delegation and consultation by managers. *Journal of Organizational Behavior,* 20, 219–232.

Yun, S., Faraj, S., Xiao, Y., & Sims. H. P., Jr. (2003). Team leadership and coordination in trauma resuscitation. *Advances in Interdisciplinary Study of Work Teams: Team-Based Organizing,* 9, 189–214.

Substitutes for Leadership

The question posed in this chapter is, Are there viable substitutes for leader-based (centered) leadership? For many, this question is often difficult to take seriously and to understand. Alternatively, we might ask, When do leaders matter the most, and why? When and where do leaders matter least, and why? Is there something about reward systems, the work people perform, the structure of the organization, for example, that reduces the role and importance of leader-based leadership? To answer these questions, we should start by asking ourselves, What is leadership and what do leaders do? We can then proceed to the question, Are there viable substitutes for those roles and actions?

The previous two chapters suggested that the leadership-outcome relationship is not a simple and direct relationship. The path-goal (House & Mitchell, 1974), behavioral (Yukl, 1971), and contingency (Fiedler, 1974) theories of leadership, for example, suggest that there are a variety of situational factors that serve to mediate and moderate the leader-outcome relationship. As a consequence, the effectiveness of a particular leader behavior is influenced, for example, by characteristics of the task and the followers.

Influenced by his 1974[1] review of the literature on leader initiating structure and consideration, Steven Kerr concludes that existing evidence does not necessarily support a hypothesis that was implicitly embedded in most situational theories of leadership—namely, that in every situation some form of leadership will be effective. Instead, Kerr (1977) argues that there are many individual, task, and organizational factors that may serve as either *substitutes for* or *neutralizers of* a leader's behavior in terms of its impact on follower satisfaction and performance.

There are two readings in this chapter. Both readings—the first, by Steven Kerr and John M. Jermier (1978), and the second, by Philip M. Podsakoff and his colleagues Scott B. MacKenzie and William H. Bommer (1996)—provide insight into the task, follower, and organizational factors that serve as substitutes and neutralizers of leadership. Both readings provide insight into these somewhat startling questions: Is leadership necessary? Is leader-based leadership necessary?

The concept of a substitute for leadership suggests that *there are factors in the work environment that can take the place of the behavior of a leader.* Attributes of the organization, technology, task, and follower can provide the motivation, guidance, reward, and satisfaction needed for effective performance to such a degree that the behaviors of the leader are rendered unimportant. The concept of a neutralizer of leadership suggests that certain work environment factors *prevent*

[1] S. Kerr, C. Schriesheim, C. Murphy, & R. Stogdill, "Toward a Contingency Theory of Leadership Based upon the Consideration and Initiating Structure Literature," *Organizational Behavior and Human Performance* 12 (1974), pp. 62–82.

leaders from acting as they wish or neutralize the effects of certain acts of leadership. (The first self-assessment at the end of this chapter opener provides you with an opportunity to assess the extent to which factors in your work environment act as substitutes for leadership within your job.)

The organization literature suggests that a number of different forces within the work environment structure the behavior and thinking of organizational members, as well as serve as sources of member motivation and satisfaction. For example, social system design (e.g., organization and work unit), technology, job design, and leader-initiating structure represent four sources of environmental structuring to which group and organizational members are exposed. Looking at the relative contributions of each of these sources of structure on employee attitudes (e.g., satisfaction, job involvement, identification), intrinsic motivation, and behaviors (e.g., performance and absenteeism), Pierce, Dunham, and Cummings (1984)[2] find that technology, job design, and work unit structure are possible substitutes for leader-initiating structure. Leader structure has little unique association with employee reactions except when the other sources of environmental structure are weak. In general, the most powerful correlate is found in the design of the member's job.

A study by Podsakoff and his associates (1993) reveals that the effects of a number of substitutes (i.e., subordinate, task, and organizational characteristics) have a substantial impact on employee attitudes, perceptions, and performance.[3] Commenting on their findings, they note: "The results of the present research provide strong support for Kerr and Jermier's (1978) suggestion that one reason why leader behaviors account for little variance in employee attitudes, perceptions, and behaviors is that the leader's context, defined in terms of subordinate, task, and organizational characteristics, also has an impact on such criterion measures" (p. 36). Based on the findings of Podsakoff et al., three conclusions can be tentatively drawn: (1) the substitutes are more important than leader behavior in the determination of job satisfaction, commitment, and role ambiguity; (2) leader behaviors seem to be more important than the substitutes in terms of employee performance; (3) for role conflict, altruism, attendance, and conscientiousness, the substitutes and leader behaviors are equally influential. At the conclusion of their meta-analysis, Podsakoff and his colleagues state that "more than 20 years of research on the substitutes model has generally failed to support the model's hypothesis" (p. 396). That said, the notion of substitutes for leadership remains intriguing and has enough tangential support that the authors call for (a) longitudinal tests of this longitudinal model and (b) more conceptual (theoretical) work detailing which substitute is a replacement for which leader behavior in relation to which follower attitude, motivational, and behavioral responses. It remains clear that in many instances such substitutes as job design, technology, or organization structure account for more variance in follower attitudes, motivation, and behavior than is accounted for by such behaviors as leader initiating structure.

Since Kerr and Jermier (1978) introduced the substitutes for leadership idea, there have been many empirical tests of the model. Podsakoff and MacKenzie (1997)[4] note that many of the early empirical tests failed to provide robust support for the model. More recent research has attempted to overcome some of the measurement problems that characterized the early studies.

[2] J. L. Pierce, R. B. Dunham, & L. L. Cummings, "Sources of Environmental Structuring and Participant Responses," *Organizational Behavior and Human Performance* 33 (1984), pp. 214–242.
[3] P. M. Podsakoff, B. P. Niehoff, S. B. MacKenzie, & M. L. Williams, "Do Substitutes for Leadership Really Substitute for Leadership? An Empirical Examination of Kerr and Jermier's Situational Leadership Model," *Organizational Behavior and Human Decision Processes* 54 (1993), pp. 1–44.
[4] P. M. Podsakoff & S. B. MacKenzie, "Kerr and Jermier's Substitutes for Leadership Model: Background, Empirical Assessment, and Suggestions for Future Research," *Leadership Quarterly* 8, 2 (1997), pp. 117–125.

In the second reading, Podsakoff and his colleagues MacKenzie and Bommer (1996) report the results of their meta-analytic review of the empirical research that has been conducted to test the substitutes for leadership model. Their review of the literature provides basic support for Kerr and Jermier's (1978) thesis. Their findings reveal that "on average, substitutes for leadership uniquely account for more variance in criterion variables than do the leader behaviors" (p. 395). Across 10 employee response outcomes, the substitutes for leadership accounted for an average of 20.2 percent of the criterion variance. This is compared with the 7.2 percent accounted for by the leader behaviors. Podsakoff et al.[5] (1996) note that this is not to suggest that leader behavior is unimportant, as it does influence follower attitudes, role perceptions, and behaviors.

Howell, Bowen, Dorfman, Kerr, and Podsakoff (1990)[6] suggest that certain attributes of the organization, task, and follower actually serve to *enhance* (magnify) the leader and leadership effects. The concept of leadership enhancers is similar to Fiedler's (1974) notion of situation favorableness. For example, directive leader behavior, coming from a relatively weak leader in a highly cohesive work group, is likely to be able to benefit from the presence of peer support, work facilitation, and clan control. (The second self-assessment at the end of this chapter opener provides you with an opportunity to assess the level of cohesiveness within a work group with which you are associated.)

Charles C. Manz (1986) introduces the concept of self-leadership. The follower (subordinate) who exhibits self-leadership (e.g., self-direction and self-control) engages in behaviors that may render unnecessary the same behaviors stemming from the leader.[7] Building on the work of Manz, we might hypothesize that individuals with a strong sense of self (i.e., organization-based self-esteem and generalized self-efficacy) are more likely to have the capacity for self-leadership and serve as substitutes for directive leader behavior. (You can profile yourself with regard to the strength of your own organization-based self-esteem by turning to the third self-assessment at the end of this chapter opener.)

The substitutes for leadership notion has, for the most part, been treated at the leader–follower level of analysis as opposed to the leader–group of followers level. In closing, it is at this level of analysis that we want to comment on the question, Is leader-based leadership necessary for effective group functioning, or are there viable substitutes at this level as well? Recall that Bowers and Seashore (1966) (see Chapter 7) suggest that there are certain behaviors that are important to effective group (team) functioning. In some instances, these behaviors (e.g., support, work and interaction facilitation, goal emphasis) need to be supplied by the leader. They go on to note, however, that it is not necessary that the leader *supply* these behaviors. These behaviors may find their substitute in one's peers or one's self, as well as features of the organization, its technology, and the design of the job.

Bowers and Seashore's observation of leadership emanating from the group as opposed to coming from an individual occupying a leadership role is illustrated by Orpheus. Orpheus, one of the world's great chamber orchestras, has operated for several decades *without* a formal conductor. Julian Fifer, the founder, says Orpheus has 26 conductors instead of just 1. Each one is given the opportunity to have input into the specific pieces of music and the interpretation of music that will be played. Although an organization like that used by Orpheus may not work and work well in all circumstances, it has clearly demonstrated that a

[5] P. M. Podsakoff, S. B. MacKenzie, & W. H. Bommer, "Meta-analysis of the Relationships between Kerr and Jermier's Substitutes for Leadership and Employee Job Attitudes, Role Perceptions, and Performance," *Journal of Applied Psychology* 81 (1996), pp. 380–399.

[6] J. P. Howell, D. E. Bowen, P. W. Dorfman, S. Kerr, & P. M. Podsakoff, "Substitutes for Leadership: Effective Alternatives to Ineffective Leadership," *Organizational Dynamics* 19, 1 (1990), pp. 21–38.

[7] C. C. Manz, "Self-leadership: Toward an Expanded Theory of Self-influence Processes in Organizations," *Academy of Management Review* 11 (1986), pp. 585–600.

FIGURE 12.1
The Role of the Leadership Process: Substitutes, Neutralizers, and Enhancers

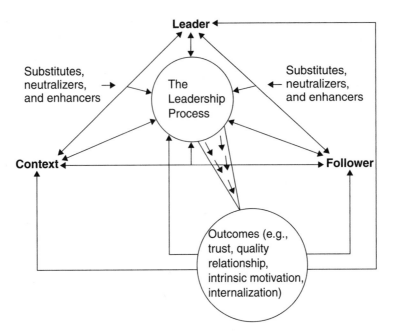

group of individuals can create the systems needed to successfully lead themselves, with leadership coming from one another instead of being imposed on them by a vertical leader in a top-down hierarchical fashion. Pearce (2004) refers to this as horizontal leadership. *Horizontal leadership* (shared leadership) "entails a simultaneous, ongoing, mutual influence process within a team" (p. 48).[8] Orpheus exemplifies the sharing of leadership, enabling the members to be a leaderless group. Such an approach, according to Julian Fifer, brings out the talents, creative ideas, and passion of all orchestra members as they are empowered and their roles are transformed from passive to active participantes in this democratic social system. Figure 12.1 provides an expanded view of the leadership process, reflecting the potential note of substitutes, neutralizers, and enhancers.

[8] C. L. Pearce, "The Future of Leadership: Combining Vertical and Shared Leadership to Transform Knowledge Work," *Academy of Management Executive* 18, 1 (2004), pp. 47–57.

Substitutes for Leadership

Instructions: Turn to Table 2 in the reading by Kerr and Jermier (1978), "Substitutes for Leadership: Their Meaning and Measurement." Thinking in terms of your current job, answer each of the questions posed in Table 2 by employing the following response scale:

5 = Almost always true, or almost completely true.
4 = Usually true, or true to a large extent.
3 = Sometimes true, sometimes untrue, or true to some extent.
2 = Usually untrue, or untrue to a large extent.
1 = Almost always untrue, or almost completely untrue.

Scoring: For each of the questions in Table 2 with an (R) following the items, subtract your response (i.e., 1–5) from 6. Next, sum your score to each of the items in category 1 and divide by 3. Following this procedure, move to the next category of questions, sum your score to each item and divide by the number of questions in that category. Complete this process for each of the 10 categories.

Interpretation: A high score (4 and greater) indicates your perception of a relatively strong presence of that "category" (e.g., ability, experience, training, and knowledge; professional orientation; indifference toward organizational rewards; unambiguous, routine, and methodologically invariant tasks; and so on) acting as a substitute for leadership within your job. A low score reflects your perception of the relative absence of that attribute's ability to possibly serve as a substitute.

EXERCISE *Self-Assessment*	**Group Cohesiveness**
	Instructions: This questionnaire is concerned with work groups in an organization. Please think of your "work group" as the set of people with whom you work most closely on a day-to-day basis. If you are a member of only one work group, these questions will be easy to answer.

If you are not a member of a work group, think about the individual or set of individuals you deal with most frequently in the performance of your job.

If you are a member of two or more different groups, you will need to decide which one group is most important (for example, that you deal with most frequently). Think about one and only one group while answering these questions.

The following statements may or may not describe your work group. How much do you AGREE or DISAGREE with each statement?

	Strongly Disagree	Disagree	Slightly Disagree	Neither Agree nor Disagree	Slightly Agree	Agree	Strongly Agree
1. I feel I am really part of my work group.	1	2	3	4	5	6	(7)
2. There is confidence and trust among members of my work group.	1	2	3	4	5	6	(7)
3. This group is extremely attractive to me.	1	2	3	4	5	(6)	7
4. I look forward to being with the members of my work group each day.	1	2	3	4	5	(6)	7
5. There is a strong bond holding members of this group together.	1	2	3	4	5	6	(7)
6. There is a high level of tension among certain members of my work group.	(1)	2	3	4	5	6	7

Scoring: Subtract your numeric answer to question 6 from 8. Next, add this adjusted score to your responses to questions 1 through 5, divide the total by 6, and enter your score here: _6.5_

Interpretation: A high score (6 and greater) suggests that you perceive a relatively high degree of group cohesiveness. A low score (2 and less) is indicative of a relatively low degree of group cohesiveness. As might be hypothesized from the material covered in this chapter, cohesive work groups are extremely likely to provide their members with personal and task support, thereby reducing the importance of (need for) certain leader behaviors.

Source: These are illustrative group cohesiveness items, constructed for this self-assessment. There is no prior validation evidence available.

Organization-Based Self-Esteem (OBSE)

EXERCISE

Self-Assessment

Instructions: The following questions ask about you and your relationship with an organization.

Please indicate the extent to which you believe in each of the following statements by expressing the level of your agreement or disagreement.

I BELIEVE that:	Strongly Disagree	Disagree	Neither Agree nor Disagree	Agree	Strongly Agree
1. I COUNT around here.	1	2	3	4	(5)
2. I am TAKEN SERIOUSLY around here.	1	2	3	4	(5)
3. There is FAITH IN ME around here.	1	2	3	4	(5)
4. I am TRUSTED around here.	1	2	3	4	(5)
5. I am HELPFUL around here.	1	2	3	4	(5)
6. I am a VALUABLE PART of this place.	1	2	3	4	(5)
7. I am EFFICIENT around here.	1	2	3	4	(5)
8. I am an IMPORTANT PART of this place.	1	2	3	4	(5)
9. I MAKE A DIFFERENCE around here.	1	2	3	4	(5)
10. I am COOPERATIVE around here.	1	2	3	4	(5)

50

Scoring: Sum your scores to each of the 10 statements and then divide by 10.

My OBSE score is: _5_.

Interpretation: A high score (4 and greater) suggests that you have a relatively high level of organization-based self-esteem. A low score (2 and less) suggests a relatively weak organization-based self-esteem.

It has been suggested that individuals who have a strong and positive sense of "self," as might be reflected by a high level of organization-based self-esteem and a strong generalized self-efficacy (see your self-efficacy assessment from the Prologue), are more capable of functioning with less leadership support and direction than individuals whose sense of self within the work environment is relatively weak. This becomes particularly true as role conditions become increasingly difficult, conflict-laden, ambiguous, nonsupportive, and overloaded.

Source: Reprinted with permission from J. L. Pierce, D. G. Gardner, L. L. Cummings, and R. B. Dunham, "Organization-Based Self-Esteem: Construct Definition, Measurement, and Validation," *Academy of Management Journal* 32 (1989), pp. 622–48.

Reading 33

Substitutes for Leadership: Their Meaning and Measurement

Steven Kerr
University of Southern California

John M. Jermier
The Ohio State University

A number of theories and models of leadership exist, each seeking to most clearly identify and best explain the presumedly powerful effects of leader behavior or personality attributes upon the satisfaction and performance of hierarchical subordinates. These theories and models fail to agree in many respects, but have in common the fact that none of them systematically accounts for very much criterion variance. It is certainly true that data indicating strong superior–subordinate relationships have sometimes been reported. In numerous studies, however, conclusions have had to be based on statistical rather than practical significance, and hypothesis support has rested upon the researcher's ability to show that the trivially low correlations obtained were not the result of chance.

Current theories and models of leadership have something else in common: a conviction that hierarchical leadership is always important. Even situational approaches to leadership share the assumption that while the *style* of leadership likely to be effective will vary according to the situation, *some* leadership style will *always* be effective *regardless* of the situation. Of course, the extent to which this assumption is explicated varies greatly, as does the degree to which each theory is dependent upon the assumption. Fairly explicit is the vertical dyad linkage model developed by Graen and his associates (Graen, Dansereau, & Minami, 1972; Dansereau, Cashman, & Graen, 1973), which attributes importance to hierarchical leadership without concern for the situation. The Fiedler (1964, 1967) contingency model also makes the general assumption that hierarchical leadership is important in situations of low, medium, and high favorableness, though predictions about relationships between LPC [least preferred co-worker] and performance in Octants VI and VII are qualified (Fiedler & Chemers, 1974, p. 82). Most models of

Source: This article was published in *Organizational Behavior and Human Performance*, 22, Kerr et al., Substitutes for Leadership, 375–403. Copyright Elsevier 1978. Edited and reprinted with permission from Elsevier.

decision-centralization (e.g., Tannenbaum & Schmidt, 1958; Heller & Yukl, 1969; Vroom & Yetton, 1973; Bass & Valenzi, 1974) include among their leader decision-style alternatives one whereby subordinates attempt a solution by themselves, with minimal participation by the hierarchical superior. Even in such cases, however, the leader is responsible for initiating the method through delegation of the problem and is usually described as providing (structuring) information.

The approach to leadership which is least dependent upon the assumption articulated above, and which comes closest to the conceptualization to be proposed in this paper, is the path-goal theory (House, 1971; House & Mitchell, 1974). Under circumstances when both goals and paths to goals may be clear, House and Mitchell (1974) point out that "attempts by the leader to clarify paths and goals will be both redundant and seen by subordinates as imposing unnecessary close control." They go on to predict that "although such control may increase performance by preventing soldiering or malingering, it will also result in decreased satisfaction."

This prediction is supported in part by conclusions drawn by Kerr, Schriesheim, Murphy, and Stog-dill (1974) from their review of the consideration-initiating structure literature and is at least somewhat consistent with results from a few recent studies. A most interesting and pertinent premise of the theory, however, is that even unnecessary and redundant leader behaviors will have an impact upon leadership satisfaction, morale, motivation, performance, and acceptance of the leader (House & Mitchell, 1974; House & Dessler, 1974). While leader attempts to clarify paths and goals are therefore recognized by path-goal theory to be unnecessary and redundant in certain situations, in no situation are they explicitly hypothesized by path-goal (or any other leadership theory) to be irrelevant.

This lack of recognition is unfortunate. As has already been mentioned, data from numerous studies collectively demonstrate that in many situations these leader behaviors *are* irrelevant, and hierarchical leadership (as operationalized in these studies) per se does not seem to matter. In fact, leadership variables so often account for very little criterion variance that a few writers have begun to argue that the leadership construct is sterile altogether, that "the concept of leadership itself has outlived its usefulness" (Miner, 1975, p. 200). This view is also unfortunate, however, and fails to take note of accurate predictions by leadership theorists even as such theorists fail to conceptually reconcile their inaccurate predictions.

What is clearly needed to resolve this dilemma is a conceptualization adequate to explain both the occasional successes and frequent failures of the various theories and models of leadership.

SUBSTITUTES FOR LEADERSHIP

A wide variety of individual, task, and organizational characteristics have been found to influence relationships between leader behavior and subordinate satisfaction, morale, and performance. Some of these variables (for example, job pressure and subordinate expectations of leader behavior) act primarily to influence which leadership style will best permit the hierarchical superior to motivate, direct, and control subordinates. The effect of others, however, is to act as "substitutes for leadership," tending to negate the leader's ability to either improve or impair subordinate satisfaction and performance.

Substitutes for leadership are apparently prominent in many different organizational settings, but their existence is not explicated in any of the dominant leadership theories. As a result, data describing formal superior–subordinate relationships are often obtained in situations where important substitutes exist. These data logically ought to be, and usually are, insignificant and are useful primarily as a reminder that when leadership styles are studied in circumstances where the choice of style is irrelevant, the effect is to replace the potential power of the leadership construct with the unintentional comedy of the law of the instrument.[1]

What is needed, then, is a taxonomy of situations where we should not be studying "leadership" (in the formal hierarchical sense) at all. Development of such a taxonomy is still at an early stage, but Woodward (1973) and Miner (1975) have laid important groundwork through their classifications of control, and some effects of

nonleader sources of clarity have been considered by Hunt (Note 2) and Hunt and Osborn (1975). Reviews of the leadership literature by House and Mitchell (1974) and Kerr et al. (1974) have also proved pertinent in this regard and suggest that individual, task, and organizational characteristics of the kind outlined in Table 1 will help to determine whether or not hierarchical leadership is likely to matter.

CONCEPTUAL DOMAIN OF SUBSTITUTES FOR LEADERSHIP

Since Table 1 is derived from previously conducted studies, substitutes are only suggested for the two leader behavior styles which dominate the research literature. The substitutes construct probably has much wider applicability, however, perhaps to hierarchical leadership in general.

It is probably useful to clarify some of the characteristics listed in Table 1. "Professional orientation" is considered a potential substitute for leadership because employees with such an orientation typically cultivate horizontal rather than vertical relationships, give greater credence to peer review processes, however informal, than to hierarchical evaluations, and tend to develop important referents external to the employing organization (Filley, House, & Kerr, 1976). Clearly, such attitudes and behaviors can sharply reduce the influence of the hierarchical superior.

"Methodologically invariant" tasks may result from serial interdependence, from machine-paced operations, or from work methods which are highly standardized. In one study (House, Filley, & Kerr, 1971, p. 26), invariance was found to derive from a network of government contracts which "specified not only the performance requirements of the end product, but also many of the management practices and control techniques that the company must follow in carrying out the contract."

Invariant methodology relates to what Miner (1975) describes as the "push" of work. Tasks which are "intrinsically satisfying" (another potential substitute listed in Table 1) contribute in turn to the "pull" of work. Miner believes that for "task control" to be effective, a force comprised of both the push and pull of work must be developed. At least in theory, however, either type alone may act as a substitute for hierarchical leadership.

Performance feedback provided by the work itself is another characteristic of the task which potentially functions in place of the formal leader. It has been reported that employees with high growth need strength in particular derive

TABLE 1 Substitutes for Leadership

	Will Tend to Neutralize	
Characteristic	**Relationship-Oriented, Supportive, People-Centered Leadership: Consideration, Support, and Interaction Facilitation**	**Task-Oriented, Instrumental, Job-Centered Leadership: Initiating Structure, Goal Emphasis, and Work Facilitation**
Of the Subordinate		
1. Ability, experience, training, knowledge.		X
2. Need for independence.	X	X
3. Professional orientation.	X	X
4. Indifference toward organizational rewards.	X	X
Of the Task		
5. Unambiguous and routine.		X
6. Methodologically invariant.		X
7. Provides its own feedback concerning accomplishment.		X
8. Intrinsically satisfying.	X	
Of the Organization		
9. Formalization (explicit plans, goals, and areas of responsibility).		X
10. Inflexibility (rigid, unbending rules and procedures).		X
11. Highly-specified and active advisory and staff functions.		X
12. Closely-knit, cohesive work groups.	X	X
13. Organizational rewards not within the leader's control.	X	X
14. Spatial distance between superior and subordinates.	X	X

beneficial psychological states (internal motivation, general satisfaction, work effectiveness) from clear and direct knowledge of the results of performance (Hackman & Oldham, 1976; Oldham, 1976). Task-provided feedback is often: (1) the most immediate source of feedback given the infrequency of performance appraisal sessions (Hall & Lawler, 1969); (2) the most accurate source of feedback given the problems of measuring the performance of others (Campbell, Dunnette, Lawler, & Weick, 1970); and (3) the most self-evaluation evoking and intrinsically motivating source of feedback given the controlling and informational aspects of feedback from others (DeCharms, 1968; Deci, 1972, 1975; Greller & Herold, 1975). For these reasons, the formal leader's function as a provider of role structure through performance feedback may be insignificant by comparison.

Cohesive, interdependent work groups and active advisory and staff personnel also have the ability to render the formal leader's performance feedback function inconsequential. Inherent in mature group structures are stable performance norms and positional differentiation (Bales & Strodtbeck, 1951; Borgatta & Bales, 1953; Stogdill, 1959; Lott & Lott, 1965; Zander, 1968). Task-relevant guidance and feedback from others may be provided directly by the formal leader, indirectly by the formal leader through the primary work group members, directly by the primary work group members, by staff personnel, or by the client. If the latter four instances prevail, the formal leader's role may be quite trivial. Cohesive work groups are, of course, important sources of affiliative need satisfaction.

Programming through impersonal modes has been reported to be the most frequent type of coordination strategy employed under conditions of low-to-medium task uncertainty and low task interdependence (Van de Ven, Delbecq, & Koenig, 1976). Thus, the existence of written work goals, guidelines, and ground rules (organizational formalization) and rigid rules and procedures (organizational inflexibility) may serve as substitutes for leader-provided coordination under certain conditions. Personal and group coordination modes involving the formal leader may become important only when less costly impersonal strategies are not suitable. . . .

ELABORATION OF THE CONSTRUCT

Table 1 was designed to capsulize our present knowledge with respect to possible substitutes for hierarchical leadership. Since present knowledge is the product of past research, and since past research was primarily unconcerned with the topic, the table is probably oversimplified and incomplete in a number of respects. Rigorous elaboration of the substitutes construct must necessarily await additional research, but we would speculate that such research would show the following refinements to be important.

DISTINGUISHING BETWEEN "SUBSTITUTES" AND "NEUTRALIZERS"

A "neutralizer" is defined by Webster's as something which is able to "paralyze, destroy, or counteract the effectiveness of" something else. In the context of leadership, this term may be applied to characteristics which make it effectively *impossible* for relationship and/or task-oriented leadership to make a difference. Neutralizers are a type of moderator variable when uncorrelated with both predictors and the criterion and act as suppressor variables when correlated with predictors but not the criterion (Zedeck, 1971; Wherry, 1946).

A "substitute" is defined to be "a person or thing acting or used in place of another." In context, this term may be used to describe characteristics which render relationship and/or task-oriented leadership not only impossible but also *unnecessary*.[2] Substitutes may be correlated with both predictors and the criterion, but tend to improve the validity coefficient when included in the predictor set. That is, they will not only tend to affect which leader behaviors (if any) are influential, but will also tend to impact upon the criterion variable.

The consequences of neutralizers and substitutes for previous research have probably been similar, since both act to reduce the impact of leader behaviors upon subordinate attitudes and performance. For this reason it is not too important that such summaries of previous research as Table 1 distinguish between them. Nevertheless, an important theoretical distinction does exist. It is that substitutes do, but neutralizers do not, provide a "person or thing acting or used in place of" the formal leader's negated influence. The effect of neutralizers is therefore to create an "influence vacuum" from which a variety of dysfunctions may emerge.

As an illustration of this point, look again at the characteristics outlined in Table 1. Since each characteristic has the capacity to counteract leader influence, all 14 may clearly be termed neutralizers. It is *not* clear, however, that all 14 are substitutes. For example, subordinates' perceived "ability, experience, training, and knowledge" tend to impair the leader's influence, but may or may not act as substitutes for leadership. It is known that individuals who are high in task-related self-esteem place high value upon nonhierarchical control systems which are consistent with a belief in the competence of people (Korman, 1970). The problem is that subordinate perceptions concerning ability and knowledge may not be accurate. Actual ability and knowledge may therefore act as a substitute, while false perceptions of competence and unfounded self-esteem may produce simply a neutralizing effect.

"Spatial distance," "subordinate indifference toward organizational rewards," and "organizational rewards not within the leader's control" are other examples of characteristics which do not render formal leadership unnecessary, but merely create circumstances in which effective leadership may be impossible. If rewards are clearly within the control of some other person, this other person can probably act as a substitute for the formal leader, and no adverse consequences (except probably to the leader's morale) need result. When no one knows where control over rewards lies, however, or when rewards are linked rigidly to seniority or to other factors beyond anyone's control, or when rewards are perceived to be unattractive altogether, the resulting influence vacuum would almost inevitably be dysfunctional.

DISTINGUISHING BETWEEN DIRECT AND INDIRECT LEADER BEHAVIOR EFFECTS

It is possible to conceptualize a *direct effect* of leadership as one which occurs when a subordinate is influenced by some leader behavior *in and of itself*. An *indirect effect* may be said to result when the subordinate is influenced by the *implications* of the behavior for some future consequence. Attempts by the leader to influence subordinates must always produce direct and/or indirect effects or, when strong substitutes for leadership exist, no effect.

This distinction between direct and indirect effects of leader behavior has received very little attention, but its importance to any discussion of leadership substitutes is considerable. For example, in their review of path-goal theory, House and

TABLE 2 **Questionnaire Items for the Measurement of Substitutes for Leadership**

(1) Ability, Experience, Training, and Knowledge
—Because of my ability, experience, training, or job knowledge, I have the competence to act independently of my immediate superior in performing my day-to-day duties.
—Because of my ability, experience, training, or job knowledge, I have the competence to act independently of my immediate superior in performing unusual and unexpected job duties.
—Due to my lack of experience and training, I must depend upon my immediate superior to provide me with necessary data, information, and advice. (R)

(2) Professional Orientation
—For feedback about how well I am performing, I rely on people in my occupational specialty, whether or not they are members of my work unit or organization.
—I receive very useful information and guidance from people who share my occupational specialty, but who are not members of my employing organization.
—My job satisfaction depends to a considerable extent on people in my occupational specialty who are not members of my employing organization.

(3) Indifference toward Organizational Rewards
—I cannot get enthusiastic about the rewards offered in this organization, or about the opportunities available.
—This organization offers attractive payoffs to people it values. (R)
—In general, most of the things I seek and value in this world cannot be obtained from my job or my employing organization.

(4) Unambiguous, Routine, and Methodologically Invariant Tasks
—Because of the nature of the tasks I perform on my job, there is little doubt about the best way to get the work done.
—Because of the nature of the work I do, I am often required to perform nonroutine tasks. (R)
—Because of the nature of my work, at the beginning of each work day, I can predict with near certainty exactly what activities I will be performing that day.
—There is really only one correct way to perform most of my tasks.
—My job duties are so simple that almost anyone could perform them after a little bit of instruction and practice.
—It is so hard to figure out the correct approach to most of my work problems that second-guessers would have a field day. (R)

(5) Task-provided Feedback Concerning Accomplishment
—After I've done something on my job, I can tell right away from the results I get whether I've done it correctly.
—My job is the kind where you can make a mistake or an error and not be able to see that you've made it. (R)

—Because of the nature of the tasks I perform, it is easy for me to see when I've done something exceptionally well.

(6) Intrinsically Satisfying Tasks
—I get a great deal of personal satisfaction from the work I do.
—It is hard to imagine that anyone could enjoy performing the tasks that I perform on my job. (R)
—My job satisfaction depends to a considerable extent on the nature of the actual tasks I perform on the job.

(7) Organizational Formalization
—Clear, written goals and objectives exist for my job.
—My job responsibilities are clearly specified in writing.
—In this organization, performance appraisals are based on written standards.
—Written schedules, programs, and work specifications are available to guide me on my job.
—My duties, authority, and accountability are documented in policies, procedures, and job descriptions.
—Written rules and guidelines exist to direct work efforts.
—Written documents (such as budgets, schedules, and plans) are used as an essential part of my job.
—There are contradictions and inconsistencies among the written statements of goals and objectives. (R)
—There are contradictions and inconsistencies among the written guidelines and ground rules. (R)

(8) Organizational Inflexibility
—In this organization, the written rules are treated as a bible and are never violated.
—People in this organization consider the rulebooks and policy manuals as general guidelines, not as rigid and unbending. (R)
—In this organization, anytime there is a policy in writing that fits some situation, everybody has to follow that policy very strictly.

(9) Advisory and Staff Functions
—For feedback about how well I am performing, I rely on staff personnel inside the organization, based outside my work unit or department.
—In my job I must depend on staff personnel located outside of my work unit or department to provide me with data, reports, and informal advice necessary for my job performance.
—I receive very useful information and guidance from staff personnel who are based outside my work unit or department.

(10) Closely Knit, Cohesive, Interdependent Work Groups
—For feedback about how well I am performing, I rely on members of my work group other than my superior.
—The quantity of work I turn out depends largely on the performance of members of my work group other than my superior.

—I receive very useful information and advice from members of my work group other than my superior.

—I am dependent on members of my work group other than my superior for important organizational rewards.

—My job satisfaction depends to a considerable extent on members of my work group other than my superior.

(11) Organizational Rewards Not within the Leader's Control

—On my job I must depend on my immediate superior to provide the necessary financial resources (such as budget and expense money). (R)

—On my job I must depend on my immediate superior to provide the necessary nonfinancial resources (such as file space and equipment). (R)

—My chances for a promotion depend on my immediate superior's recommendation. (R)

—My chances for a pay raise depend on my immediate superior's recommendation. (R)

—My immediate superior has little say or influence over which of his or her subordinates receives organizational rewards.

—The only performance feedback that matters to me is that given me by my immediate superior. (R)

—I am dependent on my immediate superior for important organizational rewards. (R)

(12) Spatial Distance between Superior and Subordinates

—The nature of my job is such that my immediate superior is seldom around me when I'm working.

—On my job my most important tasks take place away from where my immediate superior is located.

—My immediate superior and I are seldom in actual contact or direct sight of one another.

(13) Subordinate Need for Independence

—I like it when the person in charge of a group I am in tells me what to do. (R)

—When I have a problem, I like to think it through myself without help from others.

—It is important for me to be able to feel that I can run my life without depending on people older and more experienced than myself.

Dessler (1974, p. 31) state that "subordinates with high needs for affiliation and social approval would see friendly, considerate leader behavior as an immediate source of satisfaction" (direct effect). As Table 2 suggests, it is conceivable that fellow group members could supply such subordinates with enough affiliation and social approval to eliminate dependence on the leader. With other subordinates, however, the key "may be not so much in terms of what the leader does but may be in terms of how it is *interpreted* by his members" (Graen et al., 1972, p. 235). Graen et al. concluded from their data that "consideration is interpreted as the leader's evaluation of the member's role behavior . . ." (p. 233). For these subordinates, therefore, consideration seems to have been influential primarily because of its perceived implications for the likelihood of receiving future rewards. In this case the effect is an indirect one, for which group member approval and affiliation probably cannot substitute.

In the same vein, we are told by House and Dessler (1974, pp. 31–32) that:

> Subordinates with high needs for achievement would be predicted to view leader behavior that clarifies path-goal relationships and provides goal-oriented feedback as satisfying. Subordinates with high needs for extrinsic rewards would be predicted to see leader directiveness or coaching behavior as instrumental to their satisfaction if

such behavior helped them perform in such a manner as to gain recognition, promotion, security, or pay increases.

It is apparent from House and Dessler's remarks that the distinction between direct and indirect effects need not be limited to relationship-oriented behaviors. Such characteristics of the task as the fact that it "provides its own feedback" (listed in Table 2 as a potential substitute for task-oriented behavior) may provide achievement-oriented subordinates with immediate satisfaction (direct effect), but fail to negate the superior's ability to help subordinates perform so as to obtain future rewards (indirect effect). Conversely, subordinate experience and training may act as substitutes for the indirect effects of task-oriented leadership by preventing the leader from improving subordinate performance, but may not offset the direct effects.

IDENTIFYING OTHER CHARACTERISTICS AND OTHER LEADER BEHAVIORS

Any elaboration of the substitutes construct must necessarily include the specification of other leader behaviors, and other characteristics which may act as substitutes for leader behaviors. As was mentioned earlier, most previous studies of leadership were concerned with only two of its

TABLE 3   Substitutes for Leadership: A Theoretical Extension

	Will Act as a Substitute for					
	Relationship-Oriented, Supportive, People-Centered Leadership (Consideration, Support, and Interaction Facilitation):		Task-Oriented, Instrumental, Job-Centered Leadership (Initiating Structure, Goal Emphasis, and Work Facilitation):		(Other Leader Behaviors . . .)	
Characteristic*	Directly	Indirectly	Directly	Indirectly	Directly	Indirectly
Substitutes						
of the subordinate						
1. ability				X	?	?
3. "professional" orientation	X	X	X	X	?	?
of the task						
5. unambiguous and routine			X	X	?	?
7. provides its own feedback concerning accomplishment			X		?	?
8. intrinsically satisfying	X				?	?
of the organization						
12. closely-knit, cohesive work groups	X		X	X	?	?
Neutralizers						
4. indifference toward organizational rewards		X		X	?	?
13. organizational rewards not within the leader's control		X		X	?	?

* Note: Identifying numbers for characteristics refer to item numbers in Table 1.

dimensions. This approach is intuitively indefensible. Richer conceptualizations of the leadership process already exist and almost inevitably underscore the importance of additional leader activities. As these activities are delineated in future research, it is likely that substitutes for them will also be identified.

Table 3 is offered as a guide to research. It portrays a state of increased sophistication of the substitutes construct, assuming future development along lines suggested in this section. Substitutes would be differentiated from neutralizers, and direct effects of leadership empirically distinguished from indirect effects. The columns on the right are intended to represent as-yet-unexplored leader behaviors . . .

DISTINGUISHING BETWEEN CAUSE AND EFFECT IN LEADER BEHAVIOR

Another area where the substitutes construct appears to have implications for leadership research concerns the question of causality. It is now evident from a variety of laboratory experiments and longitudinal field studies that leader behavior may result from as well as cause subordinate attitudes and performance. It is possible to speculate upon the effect that leadership substitutes would have on the relative causal strength of superior- and subordinate-related variables. This paper has tried to show that such substitutes act to reduce changes in subordinates' attitudes and performance which are *caused* by leader behaviors. On the other hand, there seems no reason why leadership substitutes should prevent changes in leader behavior which *result* from different levels of subordinate performance, satisfaction, and morale. The substitutes for leadership construct may therefore help to explain why the direction of causality is sometimes predominantly from leader behavior to subordinate outcomes, while at other times the reverse is true.

SPECIFICATION OF INTERACTION EFFECTS AMONG SUBSTITUTES AND NEUTRALIZERS

From the limited data obtained thus far, it is not possible to differentiate at all among leadership substitutes and neutralizers in terms of relative strength and predictive capability. We have received some indication that the strength of a substitute, as measured by its mean level, is not strongly related to its predictive power. Substitutes for leadership as theoretically important as intrinsic satisfaction, for example, apparently need only be present in moderate amounts . . . to have potent substituting effects. . . . Other, less important substitutes and neutralizers might have to be present to a tremendous degree before their effects might be felt. Clearly, the data reported in this study are insufficient to determine at what point a particular substitute becomes important, or at what point several substitutes, each fairly weak by itself, might combine to collectively impair hierarchical leader influence. Multiplicative functions involving information on the strength and predictive power of substitutes for leadership should be able to be specified as evidence accumulates.

CONCLUSIONS

The research literature provides abundant evidence that for organization members to maximize organizational and personal outcomes, they must be able to obtain both guidance and good feelings from their work settings. Guidance is usually offered in the form of role or task structuring, while good feelings may stem from "stroking" behaviors,[3] or may be derived from intrinsic satisfaction associated with the task itself.

The research literature does *not* suggest that guidance and good feelings must be provided by the hierarchical superior; it is only necessary that they somehow be provided. Certainly the formal leader represents a potential source of structuring and stroking behaviors, but many other organization members do too, and impersonal equivalents also exist. To the extent that other potential sources are deficient, the hierarchical superior is clearly in a position to play a dominant role. In these situations the opportunity for leader downward influence is great, and formal leadership ought to be important. To the extent that other sources provide structure and stroking in abundance, the hierarchical leader will have little chance to exert downward influence. In such cases it is of small value to gain entree to the organization, distribute leader behavior questionnaires to anything that moves, and later debate about which leadership theory best accounts for the pitifully small percentage of variance explained, while remaining uncurious about the large percentage unexplained.

Of course, few organizations would be expected to have leadership substitutes so strong as to totally overwhelm the leader, or so weak as to require subordinates to rely entirely on him. In most organizations it is likely that, as was true here, substitutes exist for some leader activities but not for others. Effective leadership might therefore be described as the ability to supply subordinates with needed guidance and good feelings which are not being supplied by other sources. From this viewpoint it is inaccurate to inform leaders (say, in management development programs) that they are incompetent if they do not personally provide these things regardless of the situation. While it may (or may not) be necessary that the organization as a whole function in a "9–9" manner (Blake & Mouton, 1964), it clearly is unnecessary for the manager to behave in such a manner unless no substitutes for leader-provided guidance and good feelings exist.

Dubin (1976, p. 33) draws a nice distinction between "proving" and "improving" a theory and points out that "if the purpose is to prove the adequacy of the theoretical model . . . data are likely to be collected for values on only those units incorporated in the theoretical model. This usually means that, either experimentally or by discarding data, attention in the empirical research is focused solely upon values measured on units incorporated in the theory."

In Dubin's terms, if we are really interested in improving rather than proving our various theories and models of leadership, a logical first step is that we stop assuming what really needs to be demonstrated empirically. The criticality of the leader's role in supplying necessary structure and stroking should be evaluated in the broader organizational context. Data pertaining to both leadership and possible substitutes for leadership (Table 1) should be obtained, and both main and interaction effects examined. A somewhat different use of information about substitutes for leadership would be a "prescreen," to assess the appropriateness of a potential sample for a hierarchical leadership study.

What this all adds up to is that, if we really want to know more about the sources and consequences of guidance and good feelings in organizations, we should be prepared to study these things *whether or not* they happen to be provided through hierarchical leadership. For those not so catholic, whose interest lies in the derivation and refinement of theories of formal leadership, a commitment should be made to the importance of developing and operationalizing a *true* situational theory of leadership, one which will explicitly limit its propositions and restrict its predictions *to those situations* where hierarchical leadership theoretically ought to make a difference.

Notes

1. Abraham Kaplan (1964, p. 28) has observed, "Give a small boy a hammer, and he will find that everything he encounters needs pounding."

2. This potentially important distinction was first pointed out by M. A. Von Glinow in a doctoral seminar.

3. "Stroking" is used here, as in transactional analysis, to describe "any type of physical, oral, or visual recognition of one person by another" (Huse, 1975, p. 288).

References

Bales, R., & Strodtbeck, F. Phases in group problem solving. *Journal of Abnormal and Social Psychology,* 1951, 46, 485–495.

Bass, B., & Valenzi, E. Contingent aspects of effective management styles. In J. G. Hunt & L. L. Larson (Eds.), *Contingency approaches to leadership.* Carbondale: Southern Illinois Press, 1974.

Blake, R., & Mouton, J. *The managerial grid.* Houston: Gulf, 1964.

Bordua, D., & Reiss, A. Command, control, and charisma: Reflections on police bureaucracy. *American Journal of Sociology,* 1966, 72, 68–76.

Borgatta, E., & Bales, R. Task and accumulation of experience as factors in the interaction of small groups. *Sociometry,* 1953, 16, 239–252.

Campbell, J., Dunnette, E., Lawler, E., & Weick, K. *Managerial behavior, performance and effectiveness.* New York: McGraw-Hill, 1970.

Dansereau, F., Cashman, J., & Graen, G. Instrumentality theory and equity theory as complementary approaches in predicting the relationship of leadership and turnover among managers. *Organizational Behavior and Human Performance,* 1973, 10, 184–200.

DeCharms, R. *Personal causation.* New York: Academic Press, 1968.

Deci, E. Intrinsic motivation, extrinsic reinforcement, and inequity. *Journal of Personality and Social Psychology,* 1972, 22, 113–120.

Deci, E. *Intrinsic motivation.* New York: Plenum, 1975.

Dubin, R. Theory building in applied areas. In M. Dunnette (Ed.), *Handbook of industrial and organizational psychology.* Chicago: Rand-McNally, 1976.

Fiedler, F. E. A contingency model of leadership effectiveness. In L. Berkowitz (Ed.), *Advances in experimental social psychology.* New York: Academic Press, 1964.

Fiedler, F. E. *A theory of leadership effectiveness.* New York: McGraw-Hill, 1967.

Fiedler, F. E., & Chemers, M. M. *Leadership and effective management.* Glenview, IL: Scott, Foresman, 1974.

Filley, A. C., House, R. J., & Kerr, S. *Managerial process and organizational behavior* (2nd ed.). Glenview, IL: Scott, Foresman, 1976.

Graen, G., Dansereau, F., Jr., & Minami, T. Dysfunctional leadership styles. *Organizational Behavior and Human Performance,* 1972, 7, 216–236.

Greller, M., & Herold, D. Sources of feedback: A preliminary investigation. *Organizational Behavior and Human Performance,* 1975, 13, 244–256.

Hackman, R., & Oldham, G. Motivation through the design of work: Test of a theory. *Organizational Behavior and Human Performance,* 1976, 16, 250–279.

Hall, D., & Lawler, E. Unused potential in R and D labs. *Research Management,* 1969, 12, 339–354.

Heller, F. A., & Yukl, G. Participation, managerial decision-making, and situational variables. *Organizational Behavior and Human Performance,* 1969, 4, 227–234.

House, R. J. A path-goal theory of leader effectiveness. *Administrative Science Quarterly,* 1971, 16, 321–338.

House, R. J., & Dessler, G. The path-goal theory of leadership: Some post hoc and a priori tests. In J. G. Hunt & L. L. Larson (Eds.), *Contingency approaches to leadership.* Carbondale: Southern Illinois University Press, 1974.

House, R. J., Filley, A. C., & Kerr, S. Relation of leader consideration and initiating structure to R and D subordinates' satisfaction. *Administrative Science Quarterly,* 1971, 16, 19–30.

House, R. J., & Mitchell, T. R. Path-goal theory of leadership. *Journal of Contemporary Business,* 1974, 3, 81–97.

House, R. J., & Rizzo, J. R. Toward the measurement of organizational practices: Scale development and validation. *Journal of Applied Psychology,* 1972, 56, 288–296.

Hunt, J. G., & Osborn, R. N. An adaptive-reactive theory of leadership: The role of macro variables in leadership research. In J. G. Hunt & L. L. Larson (Eds.), *Leadership frontiers.* Carbondale: Southern Illinois University Press, 1975.

Huse, E. F. *Organization development and change.* St. Paul: West, 1975.

Kaplan, Abraham. *The conduct of inquiry.* San Francisco: Chandler, 1964.

Kerr, S., Schriesheim, C., Murphy, C. J., & Stogdill, R. M. Toward a contingency theory of leadership based upon the consideration and initiating structure literature. *Organizational Behavior and Human Performance,* 1974, 12, 62–82.

Korman, A. Toward a hypothesis of work behavior. *Journal of Applied Psychology,* 1970, 54, 31–41.

Lott, A., & Lott, B. Group cohesiveness as interpersonal attraction: A review of relationships with antecedent and consequent variables. *Psychological Bulletin,* 1965, 64, 259–302.

McNamara, J. Uncertainties in police work: The relevance of police recruits' backgrounds and training. In

D. Bordua (Ed.), *The police: Six sociological essays.* New York: Wiley, 1967.

Miner, J. The uncertain future of the leadership concept: An overview. In J. G. Hunt & L. L. Larson (Eds.), *Leadership frontiers.* Carbondale: Southern Illinois Press, 1975.

Oldham, G. Job characteristics and internal motivation: The moderating effect of interpersonal and individual variables. *Human Relations,* 1976, 29, 559–570.

Ouchi, W. The relationship between organizational structure and organizational control. *Administrative Science Quarterly,* 1977, 22, 95–113.

Porter, L., Steers, R., Mowday, R., & Boulian, P. Organizational commitment, job satisfaction, and turnover among psychiatric technicians. *Journal of Applied Psychology,* 1974, 59, 603–609.

Rizzo, J. R., House, R. J., & Lirtzman, S. I. Role conflict and ambiguity in complex organizations. *Administrative Science Quarterly,* 1970, 15, 150–163.

Schuler, R., Aldag, R., & Brief, A. Role conflict and ambiguity: A scale analysis. *Organizational Behavior and Human Performance,* 1977, 20, 111–128.

Stogdill, R. *Individual behavior and group achievement.* New York: Oxford University Press, 1959.

Tannenbaum, R., & Schmidt, W. How to choose a leadership pattern. *Harvard Business Review,* 1958, 36, 95–101.

Van de Ven, A., Delbecq, A., & Koenig, R. Determinants of coordination modes within organizations. *American Sociological Review,* 1976, 41, 322–338.

Vroom, V., & Yetton, P. *Leadership and decision making.* Pittsburgh: University of Pittsburgh Press, 1973.

Wherry, R. Test selection and suppressor variables. *Psychometrika,* 1946, 11, 239–247.

Wilson, O., & McLaren, R. *Police administration* (3rd ed.). New York: McGraw-Hill, 1972.

Woodward, J. Technology, material control, and organizational behavior. In A. Negandhi (Ed.), *Modern organization theory.* Kent: Kent State University, 1973.

Zander, A. Group aspirations. In D. Cartwright & A. Zander (Eds.), *Group dynamics: Research and theory* (3rd ed.). New York: Harper & Row, 1968.

Zedeck, S. Problems with the use of "moderator" variables. *Psychological Bulletin,* 1971, 76, 295–310.

Reference Note

[1] Hunt, J. Paper presented at the Eastern Academy of Management Conference, 1975.

Reading 34

Meta-Analysis of the Relationships between Kerr and Jermier's Substitutes for Leadership and Employee Job Attitudes, Role Perceptions, and Performance

Philip M. Podsakoff and Scott B. MacKenzie
Indiana University Bloomington

William H. Bommer
Southern Illinois University at Edwardsville

Since its introduction more than a decade and a half ago, Kerr and Jermier's (1978) substitutes for leadership model has generated a considerable amount of interest among leadership researchers in fields as diverse as organizational behavior (cf. Howell & Dorfman, 1981, 1986; Jermier & Berkes, 1979; Kerr & Slocum, 1981; Podsakoff, MacKenzie, & Bommer, 1996; Podsakoff, MacKenzie, & Fetter, 1993; Podsakoff, Niehoff, MacKenzie, & Williams, 1993; Podsakoff, Todor, Grover, & Huber, 1984; Tosi, 1991), education (cf. Brandt, 1992; Freeston, 1987; Pitner, 1986; Pitner & Charters, 1987–88; Sergiovanni, 1992a, 1992b), marketing (cf. Childers, Dubinsky, & Gencturk, 1986; Childers, Dubinsky, & Skinner, 1990), cross-cultural comparative management (cf. Farh, Podsakoff, & Cheng, 1987; Podsakoff, Dorfman, Howell, & Todor, 1986), and the management of professional employees (cf. Kerr, 1977; Howell & Dorfman, 1986). Indeed, Kerr and Jermier's original presentation of the theory is considered by many to be a leadership classic that is discussed in virtually every organizational behavior and leadership text currently on the market.

Essentially, the substitutes for leadership model (Howell, Dorfman, & Kerr, 1986; Kerr, 1977; Kerr & Jermier, 1978) posits that there are a variety of situational variables that can substitute for, neutralize, or enhance the effects of a leader's behavior. Thus they can diminish or amplify the leader's ability to influence the performance and job attitudes of subordinates. Kerr and Jermier (1978) defined leadership *neutralizers* as variables that "paralyze, destroy, or counteract the effectiveness of something else. In the context of leadership this term may be applied to characteristics which make it effectively impossible

for . . . leadership to make a difference" (p. 395). They defined leadership *substitutes* as "a person or thing acting or used in place of another . . . [that renders] . . . leadership not only impossible but also unnecessary" (p. 395). Thus, a *substitute* is something that reduces leaders' ability to influence subordinate criterion variables and, in effect, replaces leader influence. In contrast, neutralizers do not replace the leader's behavior and, as a result, may be said to produce an *influence vacuum*. In addition to substitutes and neutralizers, Howell et al. (1986) posited that things in a leader's environment may also serve to enhance the relationships between particular leader behaviors and subordinate criterion variables.

Despite widespread intuitive appeal, empirical support for the substitutes model has not been encouraging. As noted by Kerr and colleagues (see p. 92 of Howell et al., 1986), the only appropriate way to test the notion that the substitutes variables will change or replace the influence of leader behavior is to examine whether the substitutes variables moderate relationships between leader behavior and subordinate criterion variables. Unfortunately, when the model has been tested in this manner, results have not been very supportive (cf. Farh et al., 1987; Howell & Dorfman, 1981, 1986; Kerr & Jermier, 1978; Pitner, 1986; Pitner & Charters, 1987–88; Podsakoff et al., 1984; Podsakoff et al., 1986; Podsakoff, Niehoff, et al., 1993; Podsakoff, MacKenzie, et al., 1993; Podsakoff, MacKenzie, & Bommer, in press). Indeed, a recent review (Podsakoff, MacKenzie, Ahearne, & Bommer, 1995) of the research testing the moderating effects of the substitutes variables indicated few moderating effects on the relationships between leader behaviors and subordinate criterion variables. Moreover, moderating effects that were observed were not consistent across studies. Besides not providing much evidence of moderating effects, this research can be

Source: Edited and reprinted with permission. *Journal of Applied Psychology*, 1996, 81, 4, 380–399. Copyright American Psychological Association, 1996.

criticized for relying on cross-sectional research methods without examining the direction of causality through use of longitudinal or experimental research designs and failing to use ratio-scaled measures of the substitutes for leadership variables. The latter is essential for rigorously testing whether the form of the observed interactions are consistent with the particular substitute, neutralizer, and enhancer patterns predicted by the substitutes for leadership model (cf. Bobko, 1995; Cohen & Cohen, 1983). Thus, although the notion that subordinate, task, and organizational characteristics moderate the effect of a leader's behavior seems intuitively appealing, the weight of the empirical evidence has not supported it.

Interestingly, some researchers (e.g., Howell & Dorfman, 1981; Kerr & Jermier, 1978; Shoultz, 1991) attempted to test the substitutes model by looking only at main effects of the leader behaviors and substitutes variables. . . .

Although main effects tests have not captured the fundamental notion that substitute variables change (moderate) the influence of leader behavior on subordinate criterion variables, this research nevertheless has made an important contribution to the field by drawing attention to the strong relationships between the substitutes variables and employee role perceptions, job attitudes, and performance. Over the past two decades, empirical evidence has indicated subordinate, task, and organizational characteristics in the substitutes model substantially increase the proportion of variance accounted for in employee role perceptions, job attitudes, and performance; and often they are more strongly related to the criterion variables than the leader behaviors. This pattern of effects suggests that substitutes for leadership variables are key contextual factors worthy of study in their own right. Thus, the purpose of the present research was to meta-analyze relationships between leader behaviors, substitutes, and subordinate criterion variables. It is hoped that aggregating the results of a wide range of studies will give a clearer picture of the relative importance of these variables and that leadership researchers and managers will gain a better understanding of the key determinants of employee role perceptions, job attitudes, and performance.

METHOD

LITERATURE SEARCH

To obtain the broadest sample possible, we conducted a search for studies that included empirical findings involving substitutes for leadership. . . from January 1977 through December 1993. . . .

Overall, our literature search identified 164 published studies, dissertations, or book chapters that included citations of the substitutes for leadership model. However, many articles were not appropriate for inclusion in this meta-analysis. First, the vast majority of these publications were not empirical. Second, the selection of studies was limited to studies using Kerr and Jermier's (1978) original substitutes for leadership scales or recent adaptations of these scales (e.g., Podsakoff & MacKenzie, 1994; Podsakoff, MacKenzie, et al., 1993; Podsakoff, Niehoff, et al., 1993). To our knowledge, these scales are the only ones that are based on Kerr and Jermier's original conceptualization of the substitutes constructs.

. . . Thus, 36 independent samples were available for the final meta-analysis.

The 36 samples reported relationships between 13 substitutes for leadership, seven leader behaviors, and 10 subordinate criterion variables. This resulted in 435 relationships for our meta-analysis. . . .

RESULTS AND DISCUSSION

META-ANALYTIC FINDINGS

. . . The average true correlation among the leader behaviors was .31. Some of these were quite large. For example, leader clarification was fairly strongly correlated (average true $r = .45$) with all but one of the other leader dimensions (i.e., noncontingent reward behavior); supportive leader behavior was highly correlated with both contingent reward behavior (true $r = .76$) and noncontingent punishment behavior (true $r = -.74$); and noncontingent punishment was highly correlated with contingent reward behavior (true $r = -.60$). These findings suggest that on average, the leader behaviors have approximately 9% of their variance in common, with the range extending from 0% to as high as 50%. . . .

Aggregate effects. When conducting the aggregate analyses, we divided leader behaviors and substitutes into the following groups: (a) leader behaviors pertaining to the administration of rewards and punishments, (b) supportive and instrumental leader behaviors (path–goal dimensions), (c) subordinate characteristics, (d) task characteristics, and (e) organizational characteristics. These categories are consistent with the substitutes for leadership model and prior theoretical and empirical work in the leadership domain (cf. Howell & Dorfman, 1981, 1986; Howell et al., 1986; Kerr, 1977; Kerr & Jermier, 1978; Kerr & Slocum, 1981; Podsakoff et al., 1984; Podsakoff et al., 1986; Podsakoff, Niehoff, et al., 1993). . . .

Results of the aggregate analyses described above reveal a number of interesting patterns. First, the amount of variance explained in general satisfaction (83%), organizational commitment (67%), role ambiguity (72%), and role conflict (47%) by leader behaviors and substitutes for leadership is quite large when contrasted with prior research that has examined the same criterion variables (cf. Jackson & Schuler, 1985; Mowday, Steers, & Porter, 1979; Rizzo, House, & Lirtzman, 1970). Some of the variance explained in these self-report criterion variables may be attributable to common method variance (Bagozzi, Yi, & Phillips, 1991; Cote & Buckley, 1987; Podsakoff & Organ, 1986). However, variance explained in the behavioral measures, which are not subject to any same-source bias, is two to four times higher (with an average of approximately 21%) than the 5% to 9% generally reported in the leadership literature.

The data also indicate that leadership substitutes generally have a considerably stronger relationship than leader behaviors with employee attitudes, role perceptions, and behaviors (except for role conflict and in-role performance). Specifically, leadership substitutes accounted for more unique variance than leadership behaviors in the case of employee satisfaction (40% vs. 17%), commitment (50% vs. 2%), role ambiguity (29% vs. 9%), altruism (13% vs. 6%), conscientiousness (11% vs. 6%), sportsmanship (10% vs. 6%), courtesy (11% vs. 3%), and civic virtue (20% vs. 2%), and about the same variance in role conflict (15% vs. 14%). Leader behaviors explained more unique variance only in the case of in-role performance (3% vs. 7%).

Finally, examining the variance explained in the criterion variables shared by both groups of leader behaviors and all three categories of leadership substitutes makes it possible to see the importance of simultaneously examining the effects of leader behaviors and substitutes for leadership. This is especially true for attitude, role perception, and in-role performance criterion variables. Indeed, the variance jointly explained by the leader behaviors and substitutes for leadership was approximately 35% of the total variance explained in employee attitudes and perceptions and 33% of the variance in in-role performance. The average proportion of shared variance (19%) was lower, but still substantial for the extra-role (OCB) performance measures.

INDIVIDUAL EFFECTS

We also examined the relationships between each of the seven leader behaviors and 13 substitutes for leadership and the 10 criterion variables. . . .

Supportive leader behavior was related to the greatest number of criterion variables (seven), followed closely by contingent reward and contingent punishment behaviors (six each). The most important substitutes for leadership variables in terms of the number of significant relationships were task feedback, task routinization, and group cohesiveness (eight each) followed by organizational formalization and inflexibility (seven each).

General satisfaction. The results suggest that task characteristics were more strongly related to employee satisfaction than the other criterion variables. Overall, task characteristics uniquely accounted for 13% of the variance in employee satisfaction, which is more than any other leader behavior or substitute for leadership category. This finding is supportive of Hackman and Oldham's (1980) and Scott's (1966) suggestion that task variables are key predictors of employee satisfaction. It is also consistent with a great deal of prior empirical research (cf. Hackman & Oldham, 1980) and suggests that among the most important things that can be done to enhance employee satisfaction is to design tasks that provide ample feedback, are intrinsically interesting, and are not overly routine.

In addition, group cohesiveness, indifference to rewards, supportive leader behavior, and leader clarification also had important relationships with employee satisfaction. Findings indicate that satisfied employees (a) have supportive leaders who clarify job expectations, (b) work in cohesive groups, and (c) value organizational rewards. Somewhat surprisingly, the findings also show employees are more satisfied when leaders do not administer rewards and punishments contingent upon the employees' performance. . . .

Commitment. The results suggest that subordinate characteristics were more strongly related to organizational commitment than the other types of leader behaviors or substitute variables. Indeed, subordinate characteristics uniquely accounted for 23% of the variance in organizational commitment. This is four times the variance uniquely accounted for by all of the other predictors combined. The most critical subordinate characteristic is indifference to organizational rewards, which has a strong negative relationship with commitment. This suggests that individuals who value rewards in their organization are more likely to be committed than those who do not value rewards. It also underscores the importance of understanding what types of rewards employees value and structuring the reward systems so that employees receive them. . . .

Role ambiguity. Jackson and Schuler (1985) noted:

> Most theoretical formulations of role theory assert that the organizational environment is the primary determinant of employees' experienced role ambiguity and conflict. However, some have argued that personal characteristics may lead to differences in the way individuals exposed to the same organizational context perceive and/or react to the situation. (pp. 34–35)

The current results suggest organizational characteristics are more important than individual characteristics, or at least the particular subordinate characteristics included in our meta-analysis. Overall, organizational characteristics (10%), task characteristics (9%), and the path–goal leadership dimensions (7%) uniquely accounted for the greatest amount of the variance in employee perceptions of role ambiguity.

Specifically, role ambiguity is lower when (a) organizations adopt formalized rules and procedures; (b) employees work in highly cohesive groups; (c) tasks are structured to provide adequate feedback; and (d) leaders clarify expectations. With the exception of group cohesiveness, which they did not study, the above findings are consistent with the meta-analytic results of Jackson and Schuler (1985). However, our analysis permitted an examination of the strengths of the relationships between each of these variables and role ambiguity while controlling for relationships between other variables and role ambiguity. Jackson and Schuler (1985) examined only the zero-order correlations between each of these variables and role ambiguity.

Contingent reward behavior again had an unanticipated positive relationship with role ambiguity, contradicting the negative zero-order correlation. This could have occurred because the zero-order correlation failed to control for the relationships between role ambiguity and the other predictors or to a potential suppression effect. Subsequent analyses indicated the correlations met the conditions for a suppression effect (Cohen & Cohen, 1983), inasmuch as the correlation between contingent reward and role ambiguity ($r = -.43$) was less than the product of the correlations between noncontingent reward and role ambiguity ($r = .00$) and contingent and noncontingent rewards ($r = .23$). Thus, it appears that the relationship between contingent reward behavior and

role ambiguity is more complex than previously thought and deserves more attention in future research.

Role conflict. In contrast to other criteria, role conflict was almost equally related to leader behaviors and substitutes for leadership. Leader reward and punishment behaviors had the strongest relationships with role conflict. Of the substitutes for leadership, the organizational characteristics were the most strongly related to conflict. As expected, role conflict was negatively related to leader clarification, organizational formalization and inflexibility, and group cohesiveness. It was positively related to noncontingent punishment, indifference to rewards, advisory/staff support, and spatial distance. . . .

In-role performance. In-role performance is the only criterion variable where leader behaviors accounted for more variance than substitutes for leadership. Contingent reward behavior was positively related to in-role performance. Leader specification of procedures, task routinization, and spatial distance were all negatively related to in-role performance. Furthermore, the relationship between contingent reward behavior and in-role performance accounts for the most unique variance.

Altruism. The substitutes for leadership had stronger relationships with employee altruism. Only one leader behavior (noncontingent reward behavior) had a significant (positive) relationship with altruism. The results indicated that employees engage in more altruism when (a) they are not professionally oriented; (b) their tasks provide a lot of feedback, are intrinsically satisfying, and are not highly routinized; and (c) they work in cohesive groups in less highly formalized organizations where leaders work nearby the employees they supervise and are perceived to control rewards. . . .

Conscientiousness. As in the case of employee altruism, task characteristics had the most important relationships with conscientiousness. Employees exhibited conscientiousness when they performed tasks that provided feedback and were low in routinization. This finding is largely consistent with suggestions in the total quality management literature about the contextual determinants of work performance. However, it may be somewhat surprising that task rather than subordinate characteristics have the strongest relationships with conscientiousness. After all, conscientiousness is widely recognized as one of the Big Five personality characteristics presumed to account for consistencies in behavior across situations. Moorman (1990) found this trait to be one of the main predictors of conscientious behavior. Perhaps the reason subordinate characteristics were not more strongly related to conscientiousness is that the set of subordinate characteristics identified by Kerr and Jermier (1978) did not capture a very broad range of specific personality traits. This suggests that identifying a broader set of subordinate substitutes might be an important priority for future research. In the interim, those concerned with employee conscientiousness may want to focus on understanding the relationship between conscientiousness and the design of tasks that employees perform.

Sportsmanship. According to Organ (1988), *sportsmanship* is defined as a willingness on the part of an employee to tolerate less than ideal circumstances without "complaining, . . . railing against real or imagined slights, and making federal cases out of small potatoes" (p. 11). Subordinate and organizational characteristics had the most substantial relationships with employee sportsmanship. Employees who tend to exhibit more sportsmanship are not professionally oriented, exhibit low levels of ability, experience, training, and knowledge, value organizational rewards, and work in cohesive groups for inflexible organizations that are not highly formalized. These findings are consistent with observations made from the literature. . . .

Courtesy. Task and organizational characteristics had the strongest relationships with employee courtesy. Most important were task feedback, task routinization, and group cohesiveness. Employees tended to be more courteous when they receive ample amounts of task feedback and work in cohesive groups on tasks that are not highly routine. As previously noted, high levels of feedback and low levels of routinization may enhance the meaningfulness of work, encouraging employees to take greater responsibility and to enhance the overall effectiveness of the organization through various forms of citizenship behavior. Similarly, group cohesiveness may enhance mutual interdependence and thereby encourage employees to "touch base" with each other more frequently and to avoid creating problems for one another, both of which are forms of courtesy.

Civic virtue. Task characteristics had the strongest relationships with employee civic virtue. Employees are more likely to exhibit civic virtue when tasks provide ample feedback without being overly routinized or intrinsically satisfying. This was somewhat surprising, but it led us to conclude that employees who perform interesting and enjoyable tasks may prefer to devote as much time as possible to them instead of exhibiting civic virtue (e.g., participating in the governance of the organization or attending outside functions that enhance the organization's image).

GENERAL DISCUSSION

Several conclusions are warranted from the meta-analytic results. First, the results indicated that on average, the combination of leader behaviors and substitutes for leadership accounted for the majority of the variance in employee attitudes (75%) and role perceptions (60%) and a substantial proportion of the variance in performance (21%). This suggests the addition of the substitutes variables substantially improves our ability to explain the variance in a wide range of employee criterion variables. . . .

The results also suggest that on average, substitutes for leadership uniquely account for more variance in criterion variables than do the leader behaviors. Indeed, across the 10 criterion variables, substitutes for leadership account for an average of 20.2% of criterion variance. This is approximately three times the variance accounted for by leader behaviors (7.2%). However, we have not concluded that leader behaviors are unimportant because leaders influence employee attitudes, role perceptions, and behaviors in two ways: directly through traditional forms of leader behavior and indirectly by shaping the contexts in which employees work. That is, the actions of leaders influence the substitutes through employee selection, task design, work group assignment, and the design of organizational systems. Therefore, the results suggest that the substitutes have very important effects but do not diminish the role of the leader.

Furthermore, the results also indicate that on average, almost one third (31%) of the variance explained in the subordinate criterion variables can be accounted for by either the leader behaviors or the substitutes for leadership variables. . . .

SUGGESTIONS FOR FUTURE RESEARCH

Even though substitutes for leadership variables account for substantial proportions of the variance in subordinate criterion variables, it is important to keep in mind that they are supposed to serve as moderators of the leader behavior-subordinate criterion variable relationships. However, as noted earlier, the existing empirical evidence (cf. Farh et al., 1987; Howell & Dorfman, 1981, 1986; Kerr & Jermier, 1978; Pitner, 1987–1988; Podsakoff et al., 1984; Podsakoff et al., 1986; Podsakoff; MacKenzie, & Bommer, 1995; Podsakoff, MacKenzie, et al., 1993; Podsakoff, Niehoff, et al., 1993) suggests (a) few substitutes actually moderate leader behavior and subordinate criterion variable relationships; (b) in those cases in which a substitute variable has a moderating effect, it does not account for much of the variance in the criterion measure; and (c) there is no consistent pattern of moderating effects across studies. Thus, more than 20 years of research on the substitutes model has generally failed to support the model's hypotheses. . . .

Finally, it is essential for future research to improve our understanding of the theoretical mechanisms through which substitute variables have their effects. In contrast to the leader behaviors, which have received a considerable amount of research attention over the past several decades, the substitutes variables have received far less attention. Indeed, some of the substitutes (e.g., indifference to organizational rewards, organizational formalization, organizational inflexibility, rewards outside the leader's control, and spatial distance) that have some of the strongest relationships with the subordinate criterion variables have been virtually ignored outside the substitutes for leadership context. Thus, a priority for future research should be the development of a more detailed rationale explaining why each substitute variable influences the subordinate criterion variables.

References

The asterisk (*) indicates studies included in the meta-analysis.

Allen, N., & Meyer, J. (1990). The measurement and antecedents of affective, continuance, and normative commitment. *Journal of Occupational Psychology, 63,* 1–18.

Bagozzi, R. P., Yi, Y., & Phillips, L. W. (1991). Assessing construct validity in organizational research. *Administrative Science Quarterly, 36,* 421–458.

Bobko, P. (1995). *Correlation and regression: Principles and applications for industrial/organizational psychology and management.* New York: McGraw-Hill.

Brandt, R. (1992). On rethinking leadership: A conversation with Tom Sergiovanni. *Educational Leadership, 49,* 46–49.

Brown, S. P., & Peterson, R. A. (1993). Antecedents and consequences of salesperson job satisfaction: Meta-analysis and assessment of causal effects. *Journal of Marketing Research, 30,* 63–77.

Childers, T. L., Dubinsky, A. J., & Gencturk, E. (1986). On the psychometric properties of a scale to measure leadership substitutes. *Psychological Reports, 59,* 1215–1226.

*Childers, T. L., Dubinsky, A. J., & Skinner, S. J. (1990). Leadership substitutes as moderators of sales supervisory behavior. *Journal of Business Research, 21,* 363–382.

Cohen, J., & Cohen, P. (1983). *Applied multiple regression/correlation analysis for the behavioral sciences* (2nd ed.). Hillsdale, NJ: Erlbaum.

Cote, J. A., & Buckley, R. (1987). Estimating trait, method, and error variance: Generalizing across 70 construct validation studies. *Journal of Marketing Research, 24,* 315–318.

*Esquivel-Olson, T. R. (1986). *Head nurse leadership impact: A study of head nurse self-perceptions of leadership, environmental substitutes for leadership.* Unpublished doctoral dissertation, University of Houston.

*Farh, J. L., Podsakoff, P. M., & Cheng, B. S. (1987). Culture-free leadership effectiveness versus moderators of leadership behavior: An extension and test of Kerr and Jermier's "substitutes for leadership" model in Taiwan. *Journal of International Business Studies, 18,* 43–60.

Farh, J. L., Podsakoff, P. M., & Organ, D. W. (1990). Accounting for organizational citizenship behavior: Leader fairness and task scope versus satisfaction. *Journal of Management, 16,* 705–721.

*Federie, M. O., & Maloney, W. F. (1992). Substitutes for leadership and unionized construction carpenters. *Journal of Construction Management, 118,* 332–349.

*Ford, J. K. (1981). Departmental context and formal structure as constraints on leader behavior. *Academy of Management Journal, 24,* 274–288.

*Freese, G. A. (1989). *Staff nurse's perceptions of job satisfaction and work environment in community hospitals.* Unpublished master's thesis, Texas Woman's University.

*Freeston, K. R. (1987). Leader substitutes in educational organizations. *Educational Administration Quarterly, 23,* 45–59.

Hackman, J. R., & Oldham, G. R. (1980). *Work redesign.* Reading, MA: Addison-Wesley.

*Hadaway, F. J. (1990). *Substitutes for leadership and their effects upon industrial sales personnel.* Unpublished doctoral dissertation, Texas Tech University.

Howell, J. M., & Frost, P. J. (1989). A laboratory study of charismatic leadership. *Organizational Behavior and Human Decision Processes, 43,* 243–269.

*Howell, J. P., & Dorfman, P. W. (1981). Substitutes for leadership: Test of a construct. *Academy of Management Journal, 24,* 714–728.

*Howell, J. P., & Dorfman, P. W. (1986). Leadership and substitutes for leadership among professional and non-professional workers. *Journal of Applied Behavioral Science, 22,* 29–46.

Howell, J. P., Dorfman, P. W., & Kerr, S. (1986). Moderator variables in leadership research. *Academy of Management Review, 11,* 88–102.

Hunter, J. E., & Schmidt, F. L. (1990). *Methods in meta-analysis.* Newbury Park, CA: Sage.

Jackson, S. E., & Schuler, R. S. (1985). A meta-analysis and conceptual critique of research on role ambiguity and role conflict in work settings. *Organizational Behavior and Human Decision Processes, 36,* 16–78.

*Jermier, J. M., & Berkes, L. J. (1979). Leader behavior in a police command bureaucracy: A closer look at a quasi-military model. *Administrative Science Quarterly, 24,* 1–23.

*Jernigan, I. (1989). *Communication competence and substitutes for leadership: Extension of a construct.* Unpublished doctoral dissertation, Memphis State University.

Jöreskog, K. G., & Sörbom, D. (1982). Recent developments in structural equation modeling. *Journal of Marketing Research, 19,* 404–416.

Jöreskog, K. G., & Sörbom, D. (1993). *LISREL 8: Analysis of linear structural relationships by maximum likelihood, instrumental variables and least squares methods* (8th ed.). Mooresville, IN: Scientific Software.

Kerr, S. (1977). Substitutes for leadership: Some implications for organizational design. *Organization and Administrative Sciences, 8,* 135–146.

*Kerr, S., & Jermier, J. M. (1978). Substitutes for leadership: Their meaning and measurement. *Organizational Behavior and Human Performance, 22,* 375–403.

Kerr, S., & Slocum, J. W., Jr. (1981). Controlling the performances of people in organizations. In P. C. Nystrom & W. H. Starbuck (Eds.), *Handbook of organizational design* (pp. 116–134). New York: Oxford University Press.

Kirkpatrick, S. A., & Locke, E. A. (1996). Direct and indirect effects of three core charismatic leadership components on performance and attitudes. *Journal of Applied Psychology, 81,* 36–51.

Lord, R. G. (1985). An information processing approach to social perceptions, leadership and behavioral measurement in organizations. In L. L. Cummings & B. M. Staw (Eds.), *Research in organizational behavior* (Vol. 7, pp. 87–128). Greenwich, CT: JAI Press.

Lord, R. G., Foti, R. J., & Rush, M. C. (1980). A test of leadership categorization. In J. G. Hunt, U. Sekaran, & C. Schriesheim (Eds.), *Leadership: Beyond establishment views* (pp. 104–121). Carbondale: Southern Illinois University Press.

Meindl, J. R. (1990). On leadership: An alternative to conventional wisdom. In B. M. Staw & L. L. Cummings (Eds.), *Research in organizational behavior* (Vol. 12, pp. 159–204). Greenwich, CT: JAI Press.

Meyer, J., & Allen, N. (1991). A three-component conceptualization of organizational commitment. *Human Resources Management Review, 1,* 64–98.

Moorman, R. H. (1990). *The role of cognition and disposition as predictors of organizational citizenship behaviors: A study of personality and perceived fairness.* Unpublished doctoral dissertation, Indiana University at Bloomington.

Mowday, R. T, Steers, R. M., & Porter, L. W. (1979). The measurement of organizational commitment. *Journal of Vocational Behavior, 14,* 224–247.

*Nugent, A. H. (1991). *The relationship of substitutes for leadership and effective school characteristics.* Unpublished doctoral dissertation, Fordham University.

Organ, D. W. (1988). *Organizational citizenship behavior: The good soldier syndrome.* Lexington, MA: Lexington Books.

Pitner, N. (1986). Substitutes for principal leader behavior: An exploratory study. *Educational Administration Quarterly, 22,* 23–43.

*Pitner, N., Charters, W. W. (1987–1988). Principal influence on teacher commitment: Substitutes for leadership. *Educational Research Quarterly, 12,* 25–36.

Podsakoff, P. M., Dorfman, P. W., Howell, J. P., & Todor, W. D. (1986). Leader reward and punishment behaviors: A preliminary test of a culture-free style of leadership effectiveness. In R. N. Farmer (Ed.), *Advances in international comparative management* (Vol. 2, pp. 95–138). Greenwich, CT: JAI Press.

Podsakoff, P. M., & MacKenzie, S. B. (1994). An examination of the psychometric properties and nomological validity of some revised and reduced "substitutes for leadership" scales. *Journal of Applied Psychology, 79,* 702–713.

*Podsakoff, P. M., & MacKenzie, S. B. (1995). An empirical examination of the effects of leader behaviors and substitutes for leadership at the individual-level and group-level of analysis. *The Leadership Quarterly, 6,* 289–328.

Podsakoff, P. M., MacKenzie, S. B., Ahearne, M., & Bommer, W. H. (1995). Searching for a needle in a haystack: Trying to identify the illusive moderators of leader behavior. *Journal of Management, 21,* 422–470.

Podsakoff, P. M., MacKenzie, S. B., & Bommer, W. H. (1996). Transformational leader behaviors and substitutes for leadership as determinants of employee satisfaction, commitment, trust, and organizational citizenship behaviors. *Journal of Management, 22,* 259–298.

*Podsakoff, P. M., MacKenzie, S. B., & Fetter, R. (1993). Substitutes for leadership and the management of professionals. *The Leadership Quarterly, 4,* 1–44.

*Podsakoff, P. M., Niehoff, B. P., MacKenzie, S. B., & Williams, M. L. (1993). Do substitutes for leadership really substitute for leadership? An empirical examination of Kerr and Jermier's situational leadership model. *Organizational Behavior and Human Decision Processes, 54,* 1–44.

Podsakoff, P. M., & Organ, D. W. (1986). Self-reports in organizational research: Problems and prospects. *Journal of Management,* 12, 531–544.

*Podsakoff, P. M., Todor, W. D., Grover, R. A., & Huber, V. L. (1984). Situational moderators of leader reward and punishment behavior: Fact or fiction? *Organizational Behavior and Human Performance,* 34, 21–63.

Rizzo, J. R., House, R. J., & Lirtzman, S. I. (1970). Role conflict and ambiguity in complex organizations. *Administrative Science Quarterly,* 15, 150–163.

Scott, W. E., Jr. (1966). Activation theory and task design. *Organizational Behavior and Human Performance,* 1, 3–30.

Sergiovanni, T. J. (1992a). *Moral leadership: Getting to the heart of school improvement.* San Francisco: Jossey-Bass.

Sergiovanni, T. J. (1992b). Why we should seek substitutes for leadership. *Educational Leadership,* 49, 41–45.

Sheridan, J. E., Vredenburgh, D. J., & Abelson, M. A. (1984). Contextual model of leadership influence in hospital units. *Academy of Management Journal,* 27, 57–78.

*Shoultz, D. C. (1991). *"Substitutes for leadership" in a manufacturing support environment.* Unpublished doctoral dissertation, University of South Florida.

Tosi, H. L., Jr. (1991). The organization as a context for leadership theory: A multilevel approach. *The Leadership Quarterly,* 2, 205–228.

Von Glinow, M. A. (1988). *The new professionals: Managing today's high-tech employees.* Cambridge, MA: Ballinger.

*Wendler, E. R. (1984). *The role of the work group in paralleling hierarchical leadership functions: Supplements, substitutes, neutralizers, and enhancers.* Unpublished doctoral dissertation, University of Southern California.

Williams, M. L., & Podsakoff, P. M. (1988). A meta-analysis of attitudinal and behavioral correlates of leader reward and punishment behaviors. *Southern Management Association Proceedings,* 161–163.

Williams, M. L., Podsakoff, P. M., Todor, W. D., Huber, V. L., Howell, J., & Dorfman, P. W. (1988). A preliminary analysis of the construct validity of Kerr and Jermier's "substitutes for leadership" scales. *Journal of Occupational Psychology,* 61, 307–333.

Wofford, J. C., & Liska, L. Z. (1993). Path-goal theories of leadership: A meta-analysis. *Journal of Management,* 19, 857–876.

Charismatic Leadership

This chapter, "Charismatic Leadership," and the next chapter, "Transformational Leadership," are intimately related. Some leadership scholars treat charismatic and transformational leadership as essentially the same; others, while acknowledging many similarities, draw distinctions between them. The last two decades of the twentieth and now the early part of the twenty-first century presented organizations with unparalleled levels of uncertainty, turbulence, rapid change, and intense competition. Many organizations are struggling with the need to manage chaos, to undergo internal cultural change, to reinvent their businesses, to restructure their organizations, to adopt or invent new technologies, to empower organizational members, to reduce organizational boundaries, to discover the path to continuous improvement, to globalize their operations, and to invent high involvement organization and management systems. In the face of such challenges, the transformational and charismatic leader (sometimes referred to as the visionary or inspirational leader) represents a style of leadership that may be capable of navigating organizations through the chaos of the twenty-first century.

The current interest in charismatic leaders brings us back, in part, to a focus on the leader. It provides another perspective on traits of the leader and the "things" that leaders do. Yet, *charisma is relational* in nature. It is not something found solely in the leader as a psychological phenomenon, nor is it totally situationally determined. Instead, charisma is found in the interplay between the leader (his or her traits and behaviors) and the follower (his or her needs, beliefs, values, and perceptions).

As previously noted, the study of leadership has been very leader-centric, largely excluding the important role of the follower. Hollander (1993) reminds us that without followers, there are no leaders nor is there leadership.[1] It has also been noted on several occasions that leadership is a relational phenomenon and that to fully understand it, one needs to understand each of its components–the leader, the situation, the followers, and the dynamic interaction (e.g., exchange) that goes on between each of them (cf. Murphy, 1941).

In this chapter we will focus on the charismatic leader and charismatic leadership. The famous German sociologist, Max Weber, described the charismatic leader as one who reveals "a transcendent mission or course of action that may not be in itself appealing to the potential followers, but which is acted on because the followers believe their leader is extraordinarily gifted." Charismatic leaders are often described as "supernatural, superhuman or exceptional."[2] The *charismatic leader* is described as someone who by the sheer force of personality is capable of having profound effects upon followers. Charismatic leaders generate extremely intense loyalty, passion, and devotion. Followers are inspired and

---

[1] E. P. Hollander, "Legitimacy, Power and Influence: A Perspective on Relational Features of Leadership." In M. M. Chemers & R. Ayman (eds.), *Leadership Theory and Research: Perspectives and Directions* (San Diego: Academic Press, 1993), pp. 29–48.

[2] M. Weber, *The Theory of Social and Economic Organization,* A. M. Henderson & T. Parsons, eds. and trans. (New York: Oxford University Press, 1947), p. 358.

seem to enthusiastically and unquestionably give "blind" obedience to the leader, heeding his or her word almost without hesitation. Their relationship is extremely emotional in nature, producing a profound effect upon the follower's commitment, motivation, and performance.

Charismatic leadership is seen not only in terms of the leader–follower relationship and its effects, but also with regard to the traits such leaders possess and the behaviors they engage in. Among the most defining characteristics of those leaders who have charisma are a strong sense of self-confidence, a strong conviction of the rightness of their own beliefs and ideals, and dominance (i.e., a strong need for power with a reliance upon referent power as their primary power base). In terms of behaviors, charismatic leaders role-model a set of values and beliefs that they want their followers to internalize, they set high goals and have demanding expectations, they demonstrate confidence in their followers' abilities, and they articulate exciting visions of the future.[3]

In the first two readings in this chapter, Robert J. House (1977), and Jay A. Conger and Rabindra N. Kanungo (1987) provide their perspectives into charismatic leadership within the organizational context. House provides a theoretical explanation of charisma from a psychological perspective. His work gives us insight into how charismatic leadership emerges, and its effects in organizations. Building upon the assumption that charismatic leadership emerges from the behavior of the leader, Conger and Kanungo pursue the question, "What are the behavioral components that produce the experiences of a charismatic leader?"

While much of the literature on charismatic leadership demonstrates that such leadership has profound effects—especially in crisis situations—the processes involved are less clear. The next reading addresses the question, How are these effects produced? Boas Shamir, Robert J. House, and Michael B. Arthur (1993) offer a self-concept-based motivational theory to explain the process by which charismatic behavior causes profound effects on followers. In essence, they theorize that charismatic leadership produces its effects through an engagement of the followers' self-concept in the interest of the leader's vision.

Charismatic leadership is clearly relational in nature. Some people will experience a particular person as a charismatic leader, while others may not. As a consequence, to understand charismatic leadership one also needs to understand the role of the follower in the charismatic leadership process. In the fourth, and final, reading in this chapter Jane M. Howell and Boas Shamir (2005) present a theoretical analysis of the follower's role within the context of charismatic leadership.

The readings in this chapter provide yet another piece of understanding of the leadership phenomenon (see Figure 13.1). They remind the reader of the interactive nature of leadership and that a part of the leadership process is relational in nature. Followers see leaders as individuals and experience their acts of leadership. In some instances attributions are made, and some individuals emerge as charismatic leaders for some followers. In addition, some acts of leadership are extremely emotional in nature—powerful experiences—that tend to lift and energize followers, propelling them forward toward the achievement of some potentially tremendous feats. The results are not always positive, as might be witnessed through the acts of Adolf Hitler, James Jones, and, more recently, David Koresh. Each has been described as a leader with charismatic qualities but misguided values.

---

[3] R. J. House, "A 1976 Theory of Charismatic Leadership." In J. G. Hunt and K. Rowland (eds.), *The Cutting Edge of Leadership* (Carbondale, IL.: Southern Illinois University Press, 1976), pp.189–207.

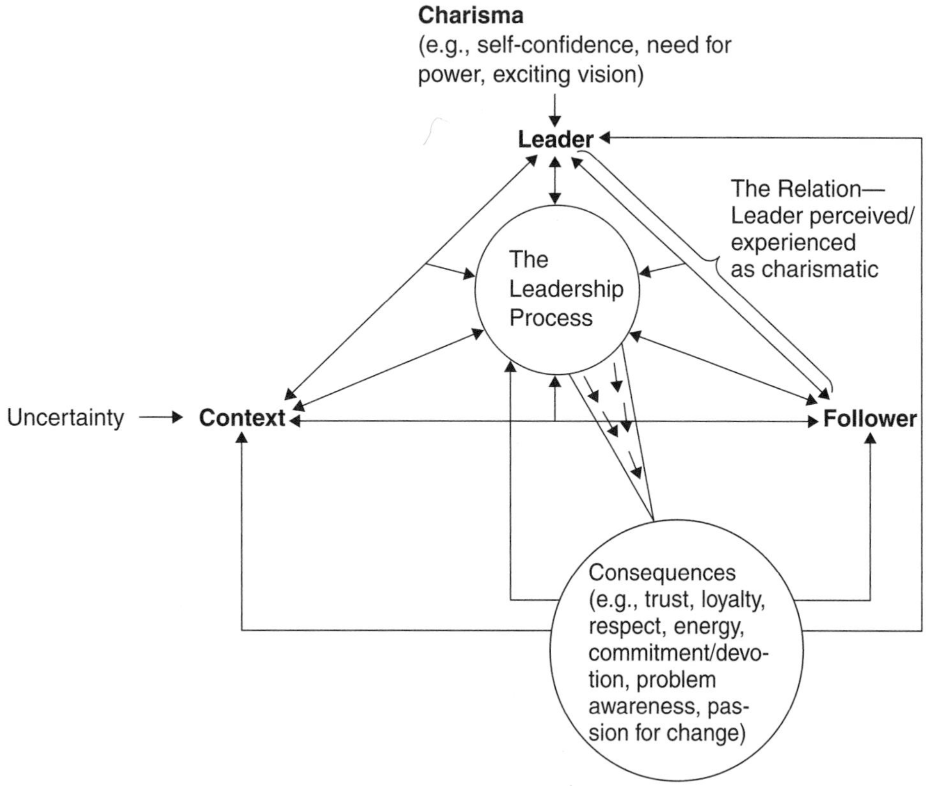

Charisma
(e.g., self-confidence, need for power, exciting vision)

FIGURE 13.1
Charismatic Leadership

Leader

The Leadership Process

The Relation—
Leader perceived/
experienced
as charismatic

Uncertainty → **Context**

Follower

Consequences
(e.g., trust, loyalty, respect, energy, commitment/devotion, problem awareness, passion for change)

Reading 35

A 1976 Theory of Charismatic Leadership

Robert J. House
University of Toronto

Charisma is the term commonly used in the sociological and political science literature to describe leaders who by force of their personal abilities are capable of having profound and extraordinary effects on followers.[1] These effects include commanding loyalty and devotion to the leader and inspiring followers to accept and execute the will of the leader without hesitation or question or regard to one's self-interest. The term *charisma,* whose initial meaning was "gift," is usually reserved for leaders who by their influence are able to cause followers to accomplish outstanding feats. Frequently, such leaders represent a break with the established order, and through their leadership major social changes are accomplished.

Most writers concerned with charisma or charismatic leadership begin their discussion with Max Weber's conception of charisma. Weber describes as charismatic those leaders who "reveal a transcendent mission or course of action which may be in itself appealing to the potential followers, but which is acted on because the followers believe their leader is extraordinarily gifted" (Weber, 1947, p. 358). Transcendence is attributed implicitly to both the qualities of the leader and the content of his mission, the former being variously described as "supernatural, superhuman, or exceptional (Weber, 1947, p. 358).

Shils (1965) points out that Weber conceived of charismatic leadership as one of the processes through which routinized social processes, norms, and legal rules are changed. Weber distinguished innovators and creators from maintainers and attributed the "gift" of charisma in part to the creative or innovative quality of the leader's goals.

Several writers contend that charismatic leadership can and does exist in formal complex organizations (Dow, 1969; Oberg, 1972; Runciman, 1963; Shils, 1965). Yet despite the profound effects that charismatic leaders are presumed to have on followers' commitment, motivation, and performance, discussions of charisma have been speculative in nature and almost exclusively theoretical. To the knowledge of this writer none of the theoretical notions in the sociological or political science literature have been subjected to empirical test, despite the fact that many of these notions are implicitly testable.

In this chapter the sociological and political science literature on charisma will be reviewed and, where possible, the major assertions in this literature will be restated as propositions in an attempt to make them testable. In addition, selected literature from the discipline of social psychology will be reviewed and propositions which the writer believes are relevant to the concept of charisma will be inferred from the literature.

The outcome of this analysis is a speculative theoretical explanation of charisma from a psychological perspective rather than from a sociological or political science perspective. Hopefully, such an explanation will help us to have greater insight into how charismatic leadership emerges and its effects in modern organizations. Further, it is hoped that such an explanation will provide testable propositions with which to further leadership research.

In the remainder of this presentation the concept of charisma will be examined under the following topics: charismatic effects, characteristics of charismatic leaders, behavior of charismatic leaders, and situational factors associated with the emergence and effectiveness of charismatic leaders. While these topics will be addressed separately, they are necessarily intertwined. Thus, at times a discussion of one topic will have implications for the other topics, and reference will be made to such implications.

THE EFFECTS OF CHARISMATIC LEADERSHIP

In the current literature the term charismatic leadership is generally defined and described in terms of the effects of the leader on followers, or in terms of the relationship between leaders and followers. For example, Oberg (1972) states that "the test for charisma . . . is the degree of devotion and

Source: Edited and reprinted with permission from J. G. Hunt and K. Rowland (eds.), *The Cutting Edge of Leadership* (Carbondale, IL: Southern University Press).

trust the object (charismatic leader) inspires and the degree to which it enables the individual to transcend his own finiteness and alienation and feel made whole" (p. 22). Tucker (1968) refers to both "charismatic following" and the "charismatic relationship":

> Often times, the relationship of the followers to the charismatic leader is that of disciples to a master, and in any event he is revered by them. They do not follow him out of fear or monetary inducement, but out of love, passionate devotion, enthusiasm. They are not as a rule concerned with career, promotion, salary, or benefice. The charismatic following is a nonbureaucratic group (p. 735).

It appears that most, if not all, writers agree that the effects of charismatic leadership are more emotional than calculative in that the follower is inspired enthusiastically to give unquestioned obedience, loyalty, commitment, and devotion to the leader and to the cause that the leader represents.

The charismatic leader is also implicitly assumed to be an object of identification by which the followers emulate the leader's values, goals, and behavior. Thus, one of the effects of the charismatic leader is to cause followers to model their behavior, feelings, and cognitions after the leader (Friedrich, 1961). Through the articulation of a transcendent goal the leader is assumed to clarify or specify a mission for the followers. By the leader's expression of self-confidence, and through the exhibition of confidence in followers, the leader is also assumed to inspire self-confidence in the followers. Thus the charismatic leader is asserted to clarify followers' goals, cause them to set or accept higher goals, and have greater confidence in their ability to contribute to the attainment of such goals.

Finally, according to the political science and sociological literature on charisma, the charismatic leader is assumed to have the effect of bringing about rather radical change by virtue of beliefs and values that are different from the established order. Thus Oberg (1972) speaks of the "change agent" function of the charismatic leader.

The above review of the effects of charismatic leadership suggests several dependent variables for a theory of charisma. Some of these effects are: follower trust in the correctness of the leader's beliefs, similarity of followers' beliefs to those of the leader, unquestioning acceptance of the leader, affection for the leader, willing obedience to the leader, identification with and emulation of the leader, emotional involvement of the follower in the mission, heightened goals of the follower, and the feeling on the part of followers that they will be able to accomplish, or contribute to the accomplishment of, the mission. This large number of charismatic effects is consistent with Etzioni's definition of charisma as "the ability of an actor to exercise diffuse and intensive influence over the normative (ideological) orientations of other actors" (Etzioni, 1961, p. 203).

The charismatic effects listed above constitute an *initial* list of variables that can be used as preliminary dependent variables for a theory of charisma. While this number of variables lacks parsimony as the defining criteria of a charismatic leader, this list of presumed "charismatic effects" provides a starting point for empiric research on charisma. If one were to identify a number of persons in a population (say military or industrial leaders in a given population) who informed observers (such as superiors or peers) could agree on as being clearly charismatic, it would be possible to identify these leaders' effects by measuring the degree to which their followers' responses to them were different from responses of followers of other leaders randomly selected from the same population. The major differences in follower responses could then be clustered into primary groups and scaled. The scores of the followers in these groups could then serve as the basis for a more accurate, complete, and parsimonious operational definition of charismatic effects. Leaders who have such effects on followers could be identified in subsequent samples. Such leaders could then be classified as charismatic leaders. Their personality characteristics and behaviors could be compared with those of other leaders (who do not have such effects) to identify characteristics and behaviors which differentiate the charismatic leaders from others. This process of operationally defining charismatic leadership permits one to identify leaders in a population who have the charismatic effects described in the political science and sociological literature and thereby specify an operational set of dependent variables for a theory of leadership.

Some of the above effects have also been the dependent variables in social-psychological research. Specifically, the ability of one person to arouse needs and enhance self-esteem of others, and the ability of one person to serve successfully as a behavioral model for another have been the subject of substantial empirical investigation by psychologists. Later in this chapter we will review this research in an attempt to identify and describe the specific situational factors and leader behaviors that result in such "charismatic" effects.

Defining charismatic leadership in terms of its effects permits one to identify charismatic leaders only after they have had an impact on followers. Such a definition says nothing about the personal characteristics, behaviors, or situational factors that bring about the charismatic effects. This is the scientific challenge that must be addressed if the mysterious quality of charismatic leadership is to be explained and charismatic effects are to be made predictable. We now turn to a discussion of these issues.

DEFINITION OF CHARISMATIC LEADERSHIP

Throughout this chapter the term charismatic leadership will be used to refer to any leader who has the above "charismatic effects" on followers to an unusually high degree.[2] The operational definition of a given charismatic leader awaits research which will allow one to scale the above specific "charismatic effects." While it is not likely that all charismatic leaders have all of the above "charismatic effects," there are many possibilities that can be examined. For example, such effects may be present in a complex interacting manner. Alternatively, it may be the sum of, or some absolute level of, selected effects that do indeed differentiate charismatic leaders from others.

CHARACTERISTICS OF THE CHARISMATIC LEADER

Both the literature concerning charismatic leadership and the opinion of laymen seem to agree that the charismatic leader can be described by a specific set of personal characteristics. According to Weber (1947), the charismatic leader is accepted by followers because both the leader and the follower perceive the leader as possessing a certain extraordinary gift. This "gift" of charisma is seldom specified and generally held to be some mysterious quality that defies definition. In actuality the "gift" is likely to be a complex interaction of personal characteristics, the behavior the leader employs, characteristics of followers, and certain situational factors prevailing at the time of the assumption of the leadership role.

The literature on charismatic leadership repeatedly attributes three personal characteristics to leaders who have charismatic effects, namely extremely high levels of self-confidence, dominance, and a strong conviction in the moral righteousness of his/her beliefs.[3] It is interesting to note that three of these characteristics are also attributed to charismatic leaders by laymen as well as by scholars. As a classroom exercise I have on three occasions asked students to form into small groups and to discuss the characteristics of some charismatic leader that they have personally known or to whom they have been exposed. These groups repeatedly described the charismatic leaders that they selected for discussion as possessing dominance, self-confidence, and a strong conviction in their beliefs and ideals.

While the consensus of political science and sociological writers and the results of my own informal experiment are not evidence that leaders who have charismatic effects do indeed possess these characteristics, the argument is certainly subject to an empiric test with self-report measures of personality traits, beliefs, and values.

In addition to the characteristics discussed above it is hypothesized here that leaders who have charismatic effects have a high need to have influence over others. Such a need seems intuitively likely to characterize leaders who have such effects because without such a need they are unlikely to have developed the necessary persuasive skills to influence others and also are unlikely to obtain satisfaction from the leadership role. Uleman (1972) has developed a measure of the need for influence that can be used to test the above hypotheses.

The following proposition summarizes the above discussion:

Proposition 1. Characteristics that differentiate leaders who have charismatic effects on subordinates from leaders who do not have such charismatic effects are dominance and self-confidence, need for influence, and a strong conviction in the moral righteousness of their beliefs.[4]

BEHAVIOR OF CHARISMATIC LEADERS

The sociological and political science literature offer some hints about the behavior of charismatic leaders.

ROLE MODELING

First it is suggested that leaders who have charismatic effects express, by their actions, a set of values and beliefs to which they want their followers to subscribe. That is, the leader "role models" a value system for the followers. Gandhi constitutes an outstanding example of such systematic and intentional role modeling. He preached self-sacrifice, brotherly love, and nonviolent resistance to British rule. Repeatedly he engaged in self-sacrificing behaviors, such as giving up his lucrative law practice to live the life of a peasant, engaging in civil disobedience, fasting, and refusing to accept the ordinary conveniences offered to him by others.

The importance of the role modeling as a leadership strategy is illustrated by Gandhi's proposed leadership policies for the self-governance of India. "Most important for Gandhi was the example that leaders set for their followers . . . 'No leader of an independent India will hesitate to give an example by cleaning out his own toilet box'" (Collins & LaPierre, 1975, 234–35).

Concerning role modeling, a study by Joestling and Joestling (1972) is suggestive of the effects that a high status role model can have on the self-esteem of observers. Male and female students were asked to rate the value of being a woman. Half of the students were enrolled in the class taught by a qualified female instructor. Twenty-six percent of the women subjects in the class taught by a male thought there was nothing good about being a woman. In contrast only five percent of the women subjects in the class taught by a qualified female had similar negative attitudes toward being a woman.

While role modeling often proves successful, success does not always occur. The question then is what permits a leader to be a successful role model, i.e., to be emulated by the followers.

There is substantial evidence that a person is more likely to be modeled to the extent that that person is perceived as nurturant (i.e., helpful, sympathic, approving) and as being successful or possessing competence.

There is evidence that role modeling can have profound effects. Behavior resulting from modeling may be very specific such that the individual can be said to imitate or mimic the behavior of the model. Or, the behavior may be more general, taking the form of innovative behavior, generalized behavior orientations, and applications of principles for generating novel combinations of responses (Bandura, 1968).

Bandura (1968) reviews a substantial body of experimental evidence that shows that: (a) model's emotional responses to rewards or punishments elicit similar emotional responses in observers (p. 240); (b) stable changes in the valences (a measure of attractiveness) subjects assign to outcomes and changes in long-standing attitudes often result

from the role modeling (pp. 243–44); and (c) modeling is capable of developing generalized conceptual and behavioral properties of observers such as moral judgment orientations and delay-of-gratification patterns of behavior (p. 252).

Of particular significance for the study of leadership are the diverse kinds of attitudes, feelings, and behavior and the diversity of subjects involved in prior studies. Role modeling has been shown to influence the degree to which: (a) undergraduate females learn assertive behavior in assertiveness training programs (Young, Rimm & Kennedy, 1973); (b) mentally disturbed patients assume independence in their personal life (Goldstein, Martins, Hubben, Van Belle, Schaaf, Wiersma, & Goedhart, 1973); (c) undergraduates are willing to disclose unfavorable or favorable anxiety-related information to others (Sarason, Ganzer & Singer, 1972); (d) personal changes and learning outcomes result from adult t-groups (Pers, 1973); (e) individuals are willing to induce punishment (electric shock) to others (Baron, 1971); (f) nurses experience fear of tuberculosis (DeWolfe, 1967); and (g) subjects adopt biased attitudes toward minority ethnic groups (Kelman, 1958; Stotland and Patchen, 1961).

Many of the subjects in the above studies were either college students or adults. Thus, the findings are not limited to young children but are also relevant to persons in full-time occupations. Further, the dependent variables are all of significance for effective organizational or group performance. Feelings of fear, willingness to administer punishment, prejudicial attitudes, learning of interpersonal skills, and learning independence are relevant to interpersonal relations within organizations. Similarly, these cognitions and behaviors are relevant to the establishment of trust, to adequacy of communication, and to experiences that are satisfying in organizational life.

Thus it is argued here that role modeling is one of the processes by which leaders bring about charismatic effects. Furthermore, it is likely that the feelings, cognitions, and behavior that are modeled frequently determine subordinates' adjustment to organizational life, their job satisfaction, and their motivation to work. With respect to motivation, the above findings suggest that leaders can have an effect on the values (or valences) subordinates attach to the outcomes of their effort as well as their expectations. And, as will be discussed below, leaders can also have an effect on subordinates' self-esteem and their goal levels. Based on the above review of the literature concerned with role modeling, the following proposition is advanced:

Proposition 2. The more favorable the perceptions of the potential follower toward a leader, the more the follower will model: (*a*) the valences of the leader; (*b*) the expectations of the leader that effective performance will result in desired or undesired outcomes for the follower; (*c*) the emotional responses of the leader to work-related stimuli; and (*d*) the attitudes of the leader toward work and toward the organization. Here "favorable perceptions" is defined as the perceptions of the leader as attractive, nurturant, successful, or competent.

IMAGE BUILDING

If proposition 2 is valid, then it can be speculated that leaders who have charismatic effects not only model the values and beliefs they want followers to adopt, but also that such leaders take actions consciously designed to be viewed favorably by followers. This speculation leads to the following proposition:

Proposition 3. Leaders who have charismatic effects are more likely to engage in behaviors designed to create the impression of competence and success than leaders who do not have such effects.

This proposition is consistent with the traditional literature on charismatic leadership. Weber (1947) speaks of the necessity of the charismatic leader to "prove" his extraordinary powers to the followers. Only as long as he can do so will he be recognized. While Weber and others have argued that such "proof" lies in actual accomplishments, the above proposition stresses the *appearance* of accomplishments and asserts that charismatic leaders engage in behaviors to gain such an appearance.

GOAL ARTICULATION

In the traditional literature on charisma it is frequently asserted that charismatic leaders articulate a "transcendent" goal which becomes the basis of a movement or a cause. Such a goal is ideological rather than pragmatic and is laden with moral overtones. Alternatively, if a movement is already in effect, one behavior of the emergent leader is the articulation of the goal of the movement with conviction and exhortation of the moral rightness of the goal (Tucker, 1968, p. 738).

Examples of such goals are Martin Luther King's "I have a dream," Hitler's "Thousand-year Reich" and his "lebensraum," or Gandhi's vision of an India in which Hindus and Moslems would live in brotherly love independent from British rule.

Berlew (1974, p. 269) states:

> The first requirement for . . . charismatic leadership is a common or shared vision for what the future *could be*. To provide meaning and generate excitement, such a common vision must reflect goals or a future state of affairs that is valued by the organization's members and thus important to them to bring about. . . . All inspirational speeches or writings have the common element of some vision or dream of a better existence which will inspire or excite those who share the author's values. This basic wisdom too often has been ignored by managers.

Thus the following proposition is advanced:

Proposition 4. Leaders who have charismatic effects are more likely to articulate ideological goals than leaders who do not have such effects.

EXHIBITING HIGH EXPECTATIONS AND SHOWING CONFIDENCE

Leaders who communicate high performance expectations for subordinates and exhibit confidence in their ability to meet such expectations are hypothesized to enhance subordinates' self-esteem and to affect the goals subordinates accept or set for themselves. Some examples of this kind of charismatic leader behavior are Churchill's statement that England's air defense in World War II was "England's finest hour," Hitler's claim that Aryans were "the master race," black leaders' exhortation that "Black is beautiful," and Martin Luther King's prediction that "We shall overcome." All of these statements imply high expectations and confidence in the followers.

There is substantial evidence that the expectation that one can accomplish one's goals is positively related to motivation and goal attainment. Persons with high self-esteem are more likely than persons with low self-esteem to seek higher personal rewards for performance (Pepitone, 1964) and to choose occupations that are congruent with self-perceived traits (Korman, 1966) and self-perceived ability level (Korman, 1967). Further, Korman (1968) has shown experimentally that for high self-esteem subjects there is a positive relationship between task performance and satisfaction, but that no such relationship exists for low self-esteem subjects. Raben and Klimoski (1973) have also shown experimentally that high self-esteem subjects are more likely than low self-esteem subjects to rise to the challenge of doing a task for which they believe they are not qualified. Thus, it is argued here that, to the extent the leader can affect the self-esteem of subordinates, leader behavior will have an effect on the kinds of rewards subordinates seek, their satisfaction with the rewards they obtain, and their motivation to perform effectively.

The effect of leader behavior on subordinate self-esteem has been given little attention in the leadership literature.[5] The assertion that leaders can affect subordinates' self-esteem is derived from two lines of research: research concerning the role-modeling effects and research concerned with reality testing.

We have already argued that through role modeling leaders can have a rather profound effect on subordinates' beliefs. One of these beliefs is self-esteem, which is defined by Lawler (1971, p. 107) as the belief that subordinates have with respect to their own general level of ability to cope with and control their environment. It is argued here that subordinates' self-perceptions are likely to be modeled after the leader's perceptions of the subordinates.[6] Thus if the leader communicates high performance expectations and shows confidence in subordinates, they will in turn set or accept a higher goal for themselves and have greater confidence in themselves.[7]

The second line of research suggesting that leaders affect subordinates' self-esteem is that research concerned with "reality testing." In social situations where interpersonal evaluation is highly subjective, individuals tend to "reality test," i.e., to test their notions of reality against the opinions of others (Deutsch & Gerard, 1955; Festinger, 1950). Consequently, to the extent that the leader shows followers that he/she believes them to be competent and personally responsible, the followers are hypothesized also to perceive themselves as competent. This self-perception is hypothesized to enhance motivation, performance, and satisfaction. Some indirect evidence in support of this line of reasoning is found in the results of studies by Berlew and Hall (1966), Stedry and Kay (1966), Korman (1971), Rosenthal and Jacobson (1968), Seaver (1973), and Meichenbaum, Bowers, and Ross (1969). Berlew and Hall (1966) and Stedry and Kay (1966) in field studies both found that individual performance increased as a function of the level of expectation superiors communicated to the individuals. Similarly, Korman (1971) showed in a laboratory study that the performance of students on creative tasks was a direct positive function of the expectations that other college students had for the laboratory subjects. Korman (1971) also showed that ratings of subordinates' performance in two field settings

and self-ratings of motivation in three field settings were all significantly correlated with the degree to which subordinates perceived their leaders' practices to reflect confidence in the subordinates.

These findings are consistent with those conducted in educational settings in which the expectations of teachers have been shown to be reflected in the performance of students (Meichenbaum, et al., 1969; Rosenthal & Jacobson, 1968; Seaver, 1973). In these studies teachers were induced to believe that certain students were more competent than others. This belief, or expectancy, on the part of the teacher was shown to be associated with higher student performance. However, there are also studies conducted in educational settings which have failed to demonstrate an effect of teachers' expectancies of students' performance (Anderson & Rosenthal, 1968; Collins, 1969; Conn, Edwards, Rosenthal, & Crowne, 1968; Evans & Rosenthal, 1969; Fiedler, Cohen & Finney, 1971). Seaver (1973) points out that in all of these disconfirming studies and also in the Rosenthal and Jacobson study, which is the subject of much controversy, the means of inducing teacher expectations were weak and thus "failure to find expectancy effects may be attributable solely to their failure to induce the desired expectancy in teachers" (p. 341).

If it is assumed that the leader's expectation of subordinates affects the subordinates' self-esteem and their self-esteem in turn affects their performance, then the above studies all provide indirect support for the assertion that leaders' expectations affect subordinates' performance.

The *combination* of a leader's confidence and high expectations, rather than high expectations alone, should be emphasized here. It is possible that leaders might set high performance standards, thus implying high expectations of subordinates, while at the same time showing low confidence in the subordinates' ability to meet such expectations. An example of this would be the leader who scores high on such questionnaire items as "he needles foremen for production."[8] While such leader behavior may motivate subordinates to strive for high performance in order to avoid punishment, it is also likely to induce fear of failure. Such a state in turn will likely be accompanied by efforts to avoid accountability on the part of the subordinates, strong feelings of dissatisfaction, low acceptance of the leader, and resistance to the leader's influence attempts in the long run.

Thus, while leader expectations are considered to have a significant effect on the reactions of subordinates, high expectations are hypothesized to have a positive effect *only* when subordinates perceive the superior to also have confidence in their (the subordinates') ability to meet such expectations.

EFFECT ON FOLLOWERS' GOALS

In addition to affecting the self-esteem of subordinates, leader expectations and confidence are also hypothesized to affect several important characteristics of the subordinates' goals. In the following paragraphs we review the research concerned with goal characteristics.

In a series of laboratory studies, Locke and his associates (Bryan & Locke, 1967a, 1967b; Locke & Bryan, 1966a, 1966b) have demonstrated that when subjects are given specific goals by the experimenter they perform at significantly higher levels than those given the instruction to "do your best." Two field studies (Mace, 1935; Mendleson, 1971) also offer support for the generalizability of these laboratory findings to natural field settings. Thus, it is argued here that, if laboratory experimenters can influence the goal characteristics of experimental subjects, it seems reasonable that leaders can have similar influence on the goal characteristics of subordinates.

Specific and high expectations of leaders are hypothesized to clarify subordinates' performance goals. Further, it is hypothesized that the more the leader shows confidence in the subordinates' ability to meet goals, the more subordinates are likely to accept them as realistic and attainable.

Specific and high leader expectations are likely to provide a standard against which subordinates can evaluate their own performance. Accordingly, it is hypothesized here that leaders' expectations also serve as a basis on which subordinates may derive feedback. Finally, it is hypothesized that, when the leader's expectations are both high and clear to the subordinate and when the leader shows confidence in the subordinate's ability to meet such expectations, the subordinates will set and/or accept higher goals for themselves than would otherwise be the case, and will have more confidence that they will be able to meet the goals.

The above hypotheses concerning the leader's effect on followers' self-esteem and goals can be summarized in the following proposition:

Proposition 5. Leaders who simultaneously communicate high expectations of, and confidence in, followers are more likely to have followers who accept the goals of the leader and believe that they can contribute to goal accomplishment and are more likely to have followers who strive to meet specific and challenging performance standards.

MOTIVE AROUSAL LEADER BEHAVIOR

One explanation for the emotional appeal of the charismatic leader may be the specific content of the messages he communicates to followers. It is speculated here that charismatic leaders communicate messages that arouse motives that are especially relevant to mission accomplishment. For example, Gandhi's exhortations of love and acceptance of one's fellow man likely aroused the need for affiliation, a need (or motive) especially relevant to the goal of uniting Hindus, Moslems, and Christians.

Military leaders often employ symbols of authoritarianism and evoke the image of the enemy, thus arousing the power motive, a motive especially relevant to effective combat performance. For example, Patton, when addressing infantry recruits, would do so against the background of a large American flag, dressed with medals of his accomplishments, and wearing a shining helmet displaying the four stars indicating the status of general.

Miner's research is relevant to defining some of the conditions under which the arousal of the need for power is associated with successful performance. Miner found that individuals who were high on a projective (sentence completion) measure of the power need were more likely to be successful in hierarchical bureaucratic organizations than individuals low on the power need. These findings did not hold true in egalitarian nonbureaucratic organizations, however (Miner, 1965).

Industrial leaders and leaders of scientists frequently stress excellence of performance as a measure of one's worth, thus arousing the need for achievement, a motive especially relevant to the assumption of personal responsibility, persistence, and pride in high-quality work performance. Varga (1975) has shown that the need for achievement is positively associated with economic and technical performance among research and development project leaders. He has also shown that the need for power is a strong factor contributing to such success when in conjunction with the need for achievement, but a factor making for failure when possessed by leaders low on the need for achievement.

There is some evidence that formally appointed leaders in a laboratory situation are capable of arousing subordinates' need for achievement (Litwin & Stringer, 1968). There is also a substantial amount of evidence that the achievement, affiliation, and power needs can be aroused from experimental inductions. For example the need for achievement has been aroused for males by suggesting to subjects that the experimental task is a measure of personal competence, or that the task is a standard against which one can measure his general level of ability (Heckhausen, 1967; McClelland, 1953; McClelland, Clarke, Roby, & Atkinson, 1958; Raynor, 1974).

The need for affiliation has been aroused by having fraternity members rate one another, while all were present, on a sociometric friendship index (Shipley & Veroff, 1952) while at the same time requiring each brother to stand and be rated by the other members of the fraternity on a list of trait adjectives.

The power need has been aroused experimentally by (*a*) evoking the image of, or reminding one of, an enemy, (*b*) having subjects observe the exercise of power by one person over another, or (*c*) allowing subjects to exercise power over another (Winter, 1973). Thus it is hypothesized that needs can be, and often are, similarly aroused by leaders in natural settings. By stressing the challenging aspects of tasks, making group members' acceptance of each other salient to performance appraisal, or talking about competition from others, it is hypothesized that leaders can and frequently do arouse the needs for achievement, affiliation, and power. Further it is hypothesized that, to the extent that such motives are associated with task-required performance, the arousal of these motives will result in increased effectiveness on the part of subordinates. Thus the performance consequence of motive arousal is contingent on the task contingencies. For example, when task demands of subordinates require assumption of calculated risks, achievement-oriented initiative, assumption of personal responsibility, and persistence toward challenging goals, the arousal of the need for achievement will facilitate task accomplishment. Further, there is evidence that when subordinates' need for achievement is high, task accomplishment will lead to satisfaction. When subordinates' need for achievement is low, task accomplishment will not be related to satisfaction (Steers, 1975).

When the task demands of subordinates require them to be persuasive, assert influence over or exercise control of others, or be highly competitive or combative, the arousal of the power motive is hypothesized to be related to effective performance and satisfaction. For example, on competitive tasks, or tasks requiring persuasion or aggression, the arousal of the power motive is hypothesized to lead to effective performance.

Finally, when task demands require affiliate behavior, as in the case of tasks requiring cohesiveness, team work, and peer support, the arousal of the affiliative motive becomes highly relevant to performance and satisfaction. An example of such tasks would be tasks that are enriched by assignment of major work goals to groups rather than individuals (Trist & Bamforth, 1951).

These speculations are summarized with the following proposition:

Proposition 6. Leaders who have charismatic effects are more likely to engage in behaviors that arouse motives relevant to the accomplishment of the mission than are leaders who do not have charismatic effects.[9]

SOCIAL DETERMINANTS OF CHARISMATIC LEADERSHIP

The sociological literature (Weber, 1947) stresses that charismatic leadership is born out of stressful situations. It is argued that such leaders express sentiments deeply held by followers. These sentiments are different from the established order and thus their expression is likely to be hazardous to the leader (Friedland, 1964). Since their expression is hazardous, the leader is perceived as courageous. Because of other "gifts" attributed to the leader, such as extraordinary competence, the followers believe that the leader will bring about social change and will thus deliver them from their plight.

Thus it can be hypothesized that a strong feeling of distress on the part of followers is one situational factor that interacts with the characteristics and behavior of leaders to result in charismatic effects.

However Shils (1965) argues that charisma need not be born out of distress. Rather, according to Shils, charisma is dispersed throughout the formal institutions of society. Accordingly, persons holding positions of great power will be perceived as charismatic because of the "awe-inspiring" quality of power. Shils's only requirement is that the expression of power must appear to be integrated with a transcendent goal.

The above controversy suggests the hypothesis that leaders are more likely to have charismatic effects in situations stressful for followers than in nonstressful situations. Further it can be hypothesized that persons with the characteristics of dominance, self-confidence, need for influence, and strong convictions will be more likely to emerge as leaders under stressful conditions. Whether or not follower distress is a necessary condition for leaders to have charismatic effects or for persons with such characteristics to emerge as leaders is an empirical question that remains to be tested.

While there is lack of agreement as to whether or not leaders can have charismatic effects under nonstressful situations, all writers do seem to agree that charisma must be based on the articulation of an ideological goal. Opportunity to articulate such a goal, whether in stressful or nonstressful situations, thus can be hypothesized as one of the situational requirements for a person to have charismatic effects. This hypothesis suggests that, whenever the roles of followers can be defined as contributing to ideological values held by the follower, a leader can have some degree of charismatic effect by stressing such values and engaging in the specific behaviors described in the above propositions.

The question then is under what circumstances are roles definable in terms of ideological values. Clearly the roles of followers in political or religious movements can be defined in terms of ideological values. In addition, Berlew (1974) argues that since man seeks meaning in work there are many such ideological values to be stressed in modern formal organizations. Specifically he argues that any of the value-related opportunities [such as a chance to do something well, and a chance to do something good] can have a charismatic effect.

There are some work roles in society which do not lend themselves to ideological value orientation. These are generally the roles requiring highly routine, nonthinking effort in institutions directed exclusively to economic ends. It is hard to conceive of clerks or assembly-line workers in profit-making firms as perceiving their roles as ideologically oriented. However the same work when directed toward an ideological goal could lend itself to charismatic leadership. For example, in World War II, "Rosie the Riveter" expressed the ideological contribution of an assembly-line worker. And such menial efforts as stuffing envelopes frequently are directed toward ideological goals in political or religious organizations. The following proposition summarizes the above argument:

Proposition 7. A necessary condition for a leader to have charismatic effects is that the role of followers be definable in ideological terms that appeal to the follower.

SUMMARY AND OVERVIEW

Figure 1 presents a diagrammatic overview of the theory presented above. It is hypothesized that leaders who have charismatic effects are differentiated from others by some combination (possibly additive and possibly interactive) of the four personal characteristics shown in the upper right box: dominance, self-confidence, need for influence, and a strong conviction in the moral righteousness of his or her beliefs. Charismatic leaders are hypothesized to employ these characteristics with the following specific behaviors: goal articulation, role modeling, personal image-building, demonstration of confidence and high expectations for followers, and motive arousal behaviors. Goal articulation and personal image-building are hypothesized to result in favorable perceptions of the leader by followers. These favorable perceptions are asserted to enhance followers' trust, loyalty, and obedience to the leader and also to moderate the relationships between the remaining leader behaviors and the follower responses to the leader. The follower responses are hypothesized to result in effective performance if the aroused behavior is appropriate for their task demands.

CONCLUSION—WHY A 1976 THEORY

This chapter presents a "1976" theory of charismatic leadership. The date 1976 is attached to the title to reflect the philosophy of science of the writer. The theory is advanced for the purpose of guiding future research and not as a conclusive explanation of the charismatic phenomenon. As such it includes a set of propositions that are hopefully testable. Admittedly tests of the theory will require the development and valuation of several new scales. However it is hoped that the propositions are at least presently testable in principle. "A theory that can not be mortally endangered cannot be alive" (cited in Platt, 1964, from personal communication by W. A. H. Rustin).

The results of empiric tests of the theory will undoubtedly require revision of the theory. It is believed by the writer that theories, no matter how good at explaining a set of phenomena, are ultimately incorrect and consequently will undergo modification over time. Thus as MacKenzie and House (1975) have stated, "the fate of the better theories is to become explanations that hold for some phenomena in some limited condition." Or, as Hebb (1969, p. 21) asserts, "A good theory is one that holds together long enough to get you to a better theory."

FIGURE 1 A Model of Charismatic Leadership (Dotted Lines Indicate That Favorable Perceptions Moderate the Relationship Between Leader and Follower Responses)

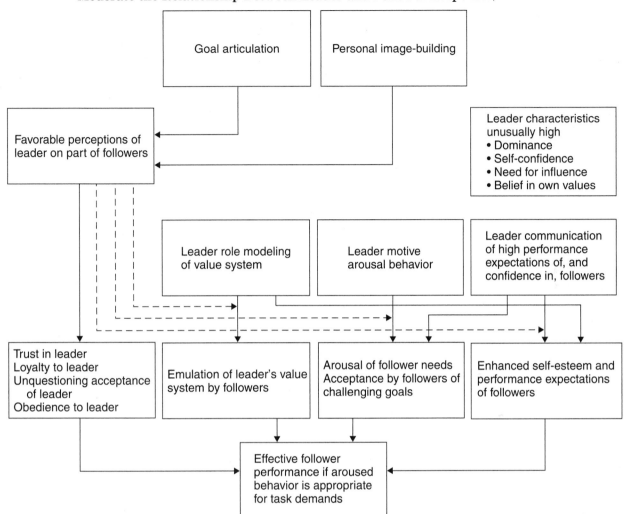

Hopefully at some future date this theory will have led to a better theory.

Notes

1. The author is indebted to Hugh J. Arnold, Martin G. Evans, Harvey Kolodny, Stephan J. Motowidlo, John A. Dearness, and William Cooper for their helpful critiques of this chapter. The literature review on which this chapter is based was conducted while the author was visiting professor at Florida International University, April–July, 1975.

2. This definition would be tautological if the "charismatic effects" were not operationally discovered using two independent operations. However, since the discovery of the "charismatic effects" involves having charismatic leaders identified by one set of observers (peers or superiors) and specification of their effects by an independent set of observers (namely their followers), such a definition avoids the tautological problem.

3. It is entirely possible that charismatic leaders present themselves as highly confident and as having a strong conviction in the moral righteousness of their beliefs but do not indeed believe in either themselves or their beliefs. Some leaders may thus have charismatic effects because of their ability to *act as though* they have such confidence and convictions. The writer is indebted to Ed Locke for pointing out this alternative hypothesis.

4. Sashkin, in his commentary on the present chapter, points out that earlier research has shown eminent leaders possess the traits of "intellectual fortitude and integrity of character" and speech fluency (or "capacity for ready communication"). While these traits were not specified in the earlier version of this presentation which Professor Sashkin reviewed, they are not in contradiction to the earlier literature on charismatic leadership and rather consistent with the general description of the charismatic personality advanced in this literature. Thus I would accept these characteristics, along with those in proposition 1, as

possible characteristics that differentiate leaders who have charismatic effects from other leaders.

5. The argument that the enhancement of subordinate self-esteem is an important charismatic effect grew out of earlier conversations between the writer and David E. Berlew. See Berlew (1974) for further elaboration of this argument.

6. Such modeling, of course, will be a function of the degree to which the subordinate holds favorable perceptions of the leader, as specified in proposition 2.

7. It is possible that such leader behavior will have a positive effect on subordinates' task-related self-esteem only (i.e., on the subordinates' confidence in their ability to accomplish task goals). It is also possible that such leader behavior will result in enhanced chronic and generalized self-esteem of subordinates. Whether leaders can indeed have such a powerful effect on subordinates' self-perceptions is, of course, a question that requires empiric investigation.

8. Fleishman, E. A. *Manual for the Supervisory Behavior Description Questionnaire.* Washington, DC: American Institutes for Research, 1972.

9. The ability of the leader to arouse motives of subordinates is hypothesized to be a function of the degree to which subordinates hold favorable perceptions of the leader, as specified in proposition 2.

Reading 36

Toward a Behavioral Theory of Charismatic Leadership in Organizational Settings

Jay A. Conger and Rabindra N. Kanungo
McGill University

Charismatic leadership has been largely overlooked by organizational theorists. In part, the problem can be attributed to the lack of a systematic conceptual framework. Drawing from political science, sociology, and social psychology, this paper addresses the problem by proposing a model linking organizational contexts to charismatic leadership. A series of research hypotheses is offered.

The term *charisma* often is used in political science and sociology to describe a subset of leaders who "by the force of their personal abilities are capable of having profound and extraordinary effects on followers" (House & Baetz, 1979, p. 399). Followers perceive the charismatic leader as one who possesses superhuman qualities and accept unconditionally the leader's mission and directives for action (Willner, 1984). These leaders represent revolutionary social forces, and they are responsible for significant social transformations (House & Baetz, 1979).

Certain writers contend that charismatic leaders can be found in business firms and other complex formal organizations (Bass, 1985; Berlew, 1974; Berger, 1963; Conger, 1985; Dow, 1969; Etzioni, 1961; House, 1977; Katz & Kahn, 1978; Oberg, 1972; Runciman, 1963; Shils, 1965; Zaleznik & Kets de Vries, 1975). Yet while examples of charismatic business leaders such as John DeLorean and Lee Iacocca are well documented in the press and popular journals (Baker, 1983; Nicholson, 1983; Wright, 1979), they have received little attention as a subject of serious study. For example, only 12 of 5,000 citations reported in Bass's revision of *Stogdill's Handbook of Leadership* (1981) deal with charismatic leadership.

Several reasons are possible for the topic's conspicuous absence from the research literature. First, researchers have shied away from studying charismatic leadership because of its elusive

nature and the mystical connotation of the term. Second, without a systematic conceptual framework, researchers often have found it difficult to define and operationalize charisma and to identify the variables that influence its development (Willner, 1984). Third, it is difficult to obtain access to charismatic business leaders.

This paper addresses the second of these problems, and by doing so, alleviates the first. It presents a model linking organizational contexts to charismatic leadership drawing upon research and theory from political science, sociology, social psychology, and existing theories of organizational leadership.

THE LITERATURE

Charisma is a Greek word meaning gift. It is used in two letters of St. Paul—Romans, Chapter 12, and 1 Corinthians, Chapter 12—in the Christian Bible to describe the Holy Spirit. Prophecy, ruling, teaching, ministry, wisdom, and healing are among the charismatic gifts described. However, over time the word also came to signify the basis of ecclesiastical organization for the Church itself. The various roles played by members of the Church were determined by gifts of God, rather than by a set of rules or procedures designed by man.

Influenced by this use of charisma to describe a basis for legitimacy, the sociologist Max Weber expanded the concept to include any authority that derives its legitimacy not from rules, positions, or traditions, but from a "devotion to the specific and exceptional sanctity, heroism, or exemplary character of an individual person, and of the normative patterns or order revealed or ordained by him" (Eisenstadt, 1968, p. 46). In addition, Weber ascribed a revolutionary and counternormative quality to charismatic authority: "its attitude is revolutionary and transvalues everything; it makes a sovereign break with all traditional and rational norms" (Eisenstadt, 1968, p. 24).

Source: Edited and reprinted with permission from *Academy of Management Review* 12, 4 (1987), pp. 637–47.

Weber's conceptualization of charismatic authority, however, is limited by its lack of specificity. For example, he used only generalities to describe a leader's qualities: "[they] comprise especially magical abilities, revelations of heroism, power of the mind and speech" (Etzioni, 1961, p. 12). He identified few behavioral dimensions that might distinguish these individuals from other leaders. Although he described charisma as "a certain quality of an individual personality," he also appears to acknowledge a relational basis for charisma: "It is recognition on the part of those subject to authority which is decisive for the validity of charisma" (Weber, 1947, p. 359).

Political scientists and sociologists have spent several decades examining the phenomenon. Although several have identified specific charismatic attributes such as a transcendent vision and/or ideology (Blau, 1963; Dow, 1969; Marcus, 1961; Willner, 1984), acts of heroism (Willner, 1984), an ability to inspire and build confidence (Dow, 1969; Friedrich, 1961; Marcus, 1961; Willner, 1984), the expression of revolutionary and often "hazardous" ideals (Berger, 1963; Dow, 1969; Friedland, 1964; Marcus, 1961), rhetorical ability (Willner, 1984), and a "powerful aura" (Willner, 1984), much of their work centered on determining the locus of charismatic leadership.

Some (Blau, 1963; Chinoy, 1961; Friedland, 1964; Wolpe, 1968) argued that social and historical contexts were the critical elements in the emergence of charismatic leadership, whereas others (Dow, 1969; Marcus, 1961; Willner, 1984) argued that attributes and relational dynamics between leaders and followers were responsible for the emergence of charisma:

> It involves a distinct social relationship between the leader and follower, in which the leader presents a revolutionary idea, a transcendent image or ideal which goes beyond the immediate . . . or the reasonable; while the follower accepts this course of action not because of its rational likelihood of success . . . but because of an effective belief in the extraordinary qualities of the leader (Dow, 1969, p. 315).

From in-depth case studies, Willner (1984) concluded that charismatic leadership was neither personality-based nor contextually-determined, but rather the phenomenon was largely relational and perceptual: "It is not what the leader is but what people see the leader as that counts in generating the charismatic relationship" (Willner, 1984, p. 14). Dow (1969) and Willner (1984) found that variations in individual personalities were too great to discern a single charismatic personality type and that the existence of a crisis—previously argued to be necessary for the emergence of charismatic leadership (Chinoy, 1961; Devereux, 1955; Downtown, 1973; Hummel, 1975; Schiffer, 1973)—was "neither a necessary nor a sufficient cause" (Willner, 1984, p. 60).

Among organizational theorists, the topic of charismatic leadership was largely overlooked. Only a handful of theories of charismatic leadership in organizational or business settings have been proposed (Bass, 1985; Bennis & Nanus, 1985; Berlew, 1974; Conger, 1985; Etzioni, 1961; House, 1977; House & Baetz, 1979; Katz & Kahn, 1978; Zaleznik, 1977; Zaleznik & Kets de Vries, 1975). Generally these efforts have been conceptually less sophisticated than their counterparts in political science.

In addition to theoretical works, empirical studies of charismatic (and/or transformational) leadership have been reported by Avolio and Bass (1985), Bass (1985), Conger (1985), House (1985), Howell (1985), Smith (1982), Waldman, Bass, and Einstein (1985), and Yukl and Van Fleet (1982). These studies emphasized the behavioral and psychological attributes of charismatic leadership. Certain personal attributes of charismatic leaders that are identified consistently throughout this literature include vision or appealing ideological goals (Bass, 1985; Berlew, 1974; Conger, 1985; Katz & Kahn, 1978; House, 1977; Zaleznik & Kets de Vries, 1975), behavior that instills confidence (Bass, 1985; Berlew, 1974; House, 1977), an ability to inspire and/or create inspirational activities (Bass, 1985; Berlew, 1974; Conger, 1985; Zaleznik & Kets de Vries, 1975), self-confidence (Bass, 1985; House, 1977; Zaleznik & Kets de Vries, 1975), dominance (House, 1977; Zaleznik & Kets de Vries, 1975), a need for influence (House, 1977), rhetorical or articulation ability (Conger, 1985), and unconventional and/or counternormative behavior (Conger, 1985; Martin & Siehl, 1983).

In addition, House and Baetz (1979, p. 399) postulated a set of behavioral dimensions that distinguished the followers of charismatic leaders from others. These characteristics include an unquestioning acceptance of the leader by followers, followers' trust in the leader's beliefs, affection for the leader, willing obedience to the leader, emulation of and identification with the leader, similarity of followers' beliefs to those of the leader, emotional involvement of followers in the mission, heightened goals of the followers, and feelings on the part of the followers that they are able to accomplish or contribute to the leader's mission.

Unlike the political science and sociological literature, there appears to be little disagreement over the locus of charismatic leadership; a relational basis for charismatic leadership is widely accepted (Bass, 1985; Berlew, 1974; Conger, 1985; House, 1977; House & Baetz, 1979; Katz & Kahn, 1978; Zaleznik & Kets de Vries, 1975). It is believed that charisma per se is not found solely in the leader and his/her personal qualities but rather is found in the interplay between the leader's attributes and the needs, beliefs, values, and perceptions of his/her followers. Both Katz and Kahn (1978) and House and Baetz (1979) further contended that both the leader and his/her followers must share basic beliefs and values in order to validate the leader's charisma.

Unfortunately, a more unified conceptual framework for understanding the behavioral dimensions of the phenomenon has yet to be presented by organizational theorists. Instead, the literature provides a set of overlapping attributes that identify pieces of the puzzle but lack a structure to explain their relationships. Equally important, there is little or no empirical evidence to support conclusions.

A BEHAVIORAL FRAMEWORK FOR STUDYING CHARISMA

If a deeper understanding of charismatic leadership within organizations is to be obtained, it is important to strip the aura of mysticism from charisma and to deal with it strictly as a behavioral process. Charismatic leadership, like any other form of leadership, should be considered to be an observable behavioral process that can be described and analyzed in terms of a formal model.

The model presented here builds on the idea that charisma is an attributional phenomenon. When members of a group work together to attain group objectives, observations of the influence process within the group help them determine their status. One who exerts maximum influence over other members is perceived as a leader. This role is consensually validated when followers recognize and identify the leader on the basis of interaction with him or her. Charismatic leadership is no exception to this process. Like other kinds of leadership, charisma must be viewed as an attribution made by followers who observe certain behaviors on the part of the leader within organizational contexts. The roles played by a person not only make the person, in the eyes of the followers, a task leader or a social leader, but they also make him or her a charismatic leader or a noncharismatic leader. The leader's observed behavior within the organization can be interpreted by his/her followers as expressions of charismatic qualities. Such dispositional attributes are inferred from the leader's observed behavior in the same way that many personal styles of leadership have been observed previously (Blake & Mouton, 1964; Fiedler, 1967; Hersey & Blanchard, 1977; House, 1971). In this sense, charisma can be considered to be an additional inferred dimension of leadership behavior. As such, it is not an attribution made about an individual because of his or her rank in the organization, but rather it is an attribution made because of the behavior he or she exhibits. Charismatic disposition or leadership style should be subjected to the same empirical and behavioral analysis as participative, task, or people dimensions of leadership have been subjected to in the past.

BEHAVIORAL COMPONENTS OF CHARISMA

If the follower's attribution of charisma depends on observed behavior of the leader, then what are the behavioral components responsible for such attributions? Can these attributions be identified and operationalized in order to develop charismatic qualities among organizational leaders? Table 1 includes a hypothesized description of what the present authors believe to be the essential and distinguishable behavioral components of charismatic leadership.

It is assumed that these components are interrelated and that they differ in presence and intensity among charismatic leaders. These ideas are represented in the following hypothesis.

Hypothesis 1: *The behavioral components of charismatic leadership are interrelated, and as such they form a constellation of components.*

Although all leadership roles involve charting a clear path for group members to achieve a common goal, attribution of charisma to leaders is believed to depend on four variables: the degree of discrepancy between the status quo and the future goal or vision advocated by the leader; the use of innovative and unconventional means for achieving the desired change; a realistic assessment of environmental resources and constraints for bringing about such change; and the nature of articulation and impression management employed to inspire subordinates in the pursuit of the vision. The role of these variables in the development of charisma is discussed on the next page.

TABLE 1   **Behavioral Components of Charismatic and Noncharismatic Leaders**

	Noncharismatic Leader	Charismatic Leader
Relation to status quo	Essentially agrees with status quo and strives to maintain it.	Essentially opposed to status quo and strives to change it.
Future goal	Goal not too discrepant from status quo.	Idealized vision which is highly discrepant from status quo.
Likeableness	Shared perspective makes him/her likable.	Shared perspective and idealized vision makes him/her a likeable and honorable hero worthy of identification and imitation.
Trustworthiness	Disinterested advocacy in persuasion attempts.	Disinterested advocacy by incurring great personal risk and cost.
Expertise	Expert in using available means to achieve goals within the framework of the existing order.	Expert in using unconventional means to transcend the existing order.
Behavior	Conventional, conforming to existing norms.	Unconventional or counternormative.
Environmental sensitivity	Low need for environmental sensitivity to maintain status quo.	High need for environmental sensitivity for changing the status quo.
Articulation	Weak articulation of goals and motivation to lead.	Strong articulation of future vision and motivation to lead.
Power base	Position power and personal power (based on reward, expertise, and liking for a friend who is a similar other).	Personal power (based on expertise, respect, and admiration for a unique hero).
Leader–follower relationship	Egalitarian, consensus-seeking, or directive; nudges or orders people to share his/her views.	Elitist, entrepreneur, and exemplary; transforms people to share the radical changes advocated.

Charisma and the Future Vision

Many theorists see vision as a component of charismatic leadership (Bass, 1985; Berlew, 1974; Blau, 1963; Conger, 1985; Dow, 1969; Katz & Kahn, 1978; House, 1977; Marcus, 1961; Willner, 1984; Zaleznik & Kets de Vries, 1975). Here the word *vision* refers to some idealized goal that the leader wants the organization to achieve in the future. In this paper, it is hypothesized that the nature, formulation, articulation, and means of achieving this goal can be distinguished from those advocated by other kinds of leaders.

The more idealized or utopian the goal advocated by the leader, the more discrepant it is relative to the status quo. And, the greater the discrepancy of the goal from the status quo, the more likely followers will attribute extraordinary vision to the leader. By presenting an idealized goal to followers, a leader provides a challenge and a motivating force for change. The literature on change in attitude suggests that a maximum discrepant position within the latitude of acceptance puts the greatest amount of pressure on the followers to change their attitudes (Hovland & Pritzker, 1957; Petty & Cacioppo, 1981). Since the idealized goal represents a perspective shared by the followers and promises

to meet their hopes and aspirations, it tends to be within the latitude of acceptance in spite of the extreme discrepancy. A leader becomes charismatic when he/she succeeds in changing his/her followers' attitudes to accept the advocated vision. In religion, charisma stems from prophecy; in organizations, charisma stems from advocacy for the future. Failure of either prophecy or advocacy may change the attribution from charisma to madness.

What attributes of charismatic leaders make them successful advocates of their discrepant vision? Research on persuasive communication suggests that in order to be a successful advocate, one needs to be a credible communicator. A leader's credibility could result from projecting an image of being likable, trustworthy, and knowledgeable (Hovland, Janis, & Kelley, 1953; Sears, Freedman, & Peplau, 1985).

It is the shared perspective of the charismatic leader's idealized vision and its potential for satisfying followers' needs that makes the leader likable. Both the perceived similarity between followers and their leader and the perceived potential of the leader to satisfy followers' needs form the basis of their interpersonal attraction (Byrne, 1977; Rubin, 1973). Through this idealized (and therefore discrepant) version of their vision, followers respect their leader and find him or her worthy of identifying with and imitating. Charismatic leaders are not just similar others who are generally liked (as one would find with popular, consensus-seeking leaders), but they are also holders of an idealized vision. Thus, the following hypothesis is advanced.

Hypothesis 2: *Leaders are charismatic when their vision is highly discrepant from the status quo yet remains within a latitude of acceptance for their followers.*

It is important for leaders to be trusted. Generally leaders are trusted when they advocate their position in a disinterested manner and demonstrate a concern for followers' needs rather than their own self-interest (Walster, Aronson, & Abrahams, 1966). However, charismatic leaders make these qualities appear extraordinary. They transform their concern for followers' needs into total dedication and commitment to the common cause they share with followers in a disinterested and selfless manner. They engage in exemplary acts that followers perceive as involving great personal risk, cost, and energy (Friedland, 1964). These personal risks might include: possible loss of finances or career success; the withdrawal of organizational resources; the potential for being fired or demoted; and the loss of formal or informal status, power, authority, and credibility. Lee Iacocca's reduction of his salary to one dollar during his first year at Chrysler (Iacocca & Novak, 1984) and John DeLorean's confrontations with senior management at GM (Martin & Siehl, 1983) are examples of personal risk. The higher the personal cost or sacrifice for the common good, the greater is the trustworthiness of leaders. The more leaders demonstrate that they are prepared to take high personal risks or incur high personal costs for achieving the shared vision, the more they are charismatic in the sense of being worthy of complete trust. This leads to the next hypothesis.

Hypothesis 3: *Charismatic leaders may take on high personal risks, incur high costs, and engage in self-sacrifice to achieve a shared vision.*

Finally, charismatic leaders appear to be experts in their area of influence. Past success may be a condition for the attribution of charisma (Weber, 1947)—for example, Iacocca's responsibility for the Ford Mustang. The attribution of charisma generally is influenced by leaders'

expertise in two areas. First, charismatic leaders demonstrate the inadequacy of the traditional technology, rules, and regulations of the status quo as a means of achieving the shared vision (Weber, 1947). Second, the leaders devise effective but unconventional strategies and plans of action (Conger, 1985). Leaders are perceived as charismatic when they demonstrate expertise in transcending the existing order through the use of unconventional means. Iacocca's use of government-backed loans, money-back guarantees on cars, union representation on the board of directors, and advertisements featuring himself are examples of unconventional strategic actions in the automobile industry. Such phenomena lead to the following hypothesis.

Hypothesis 4: *Charismatic leaders demonstrate expertise in transcending the existing order through the use of unconventional or extraordinary means.*

Charisma and Unconventional Behavior

Attribution of charisma to leaders depends on followers' perception of their revolutionary and unconventional qualities (Berger, 1963; Conger, 1985; Dow, 1969; Friedland, 1964; Marcus, 1961). The revolutionary qualities of leaders are manifested in part in their discrepant idealized visions. More important, charismatic leaders engage in innovative behaviors that run counter to the established norms of their organizations, industries, and/or societies while leading their followers toward the realization of their visions. Martin and Siehl (1983) demonstrated this in their analysis of John DeLorean's counternormative behavior at GM. Charismatic leaders are not group facilitators like consensual leaders, but they are active innovators. Their plans and the strategies they use to achieve change, their exemplary acts of heroism involving personal risks, and their self-sacrificing behaviors must be novel, unconventional, and out of the ordinary. Such behavior, when successful, evokes surprise and admiration in followers. Such uncommon behavior also leads to an attribution of charisma in the sense of the possession of super-human abilities. Thus the following hypothesis is advanced.

Hypothesis 5: *Charismatic leaders engage in behaviors that are novel, unconventional, and counternormative, and as such, involve high personal risk or high probability of harming their own self-interest.*

CHARISMA AND SENSITIVITY TO THE ENVIRONMENT

When a leader loses sight of reality and his or her unconventional behavior fails to achieve its objective, the leader may be degraded from charismatic to ineffective (Friedland, 1964). The knowledge, experience, and expertise of the leader become critical. Charismatic leaders realistically assess environmental resources and constraints affecting their ability to bring about change within their organizations. They are sensitive to both the abilities and emotional needs of followers, and they understand the resources and constraints of the physical and social environments in which they operate. Their innovative strategies and unconventional actions are based on realistic appraisals of environmental conditions. Instead of launching a course of action as soon as a vision is formulated, often leaders prepare the ground or will wait for an appropriate time, place, and the availability of resources. Charisma often fades due to a lack of sensitivity for the environment. The following hypothesis captures this idea.

Hypothesis 6: *Charismatic leaders engage in realistic assessments of the environmental resources and constraints affecting the realization of their visions. They implement innovative strategies when the environmental resource-constraint ratio is favorable to them.*

Charisma and Articulation

Charismatic leaders articulate their visions and strategies for action through two processes. First, they articulate the context including: (*a*) the nature of the status quo; (*b*) the nature of the future vision; (*c*) the manner through which these future visions, if realized, remove sources of discontent and provide fulfillment of hopes and aspirations of the followers; and (*d*) plans of action for realizing the vision. In articulating the context, leaders' verbal messages paint positive pictures of the future vision and negative ones of the status quo. The status quo often is presented as intolerable, whereas the vision is presented as the most attractive and attainable alternative in clear, specific terms.

Second, charismatic leaders also communicate their own motivation to lead their followers. Through expressive modes of action, both verbal and nonverbal, the leaders communicate their convictions, self-confidence, and dedication in order to give credibility to what they advocate. Expression of high energy and persistence, unconventional and risky behavior, heroic deeds and personal sacrifices, all communicate the leaders' high motivation and enthusiasm, which then become contagious with their followers. In articulating their motivation to lead, charismatic leaders use a number of impression management techniques. For instance, they use rhetoric by selecting words to reflect assertiveness, confidence, expertise, and concern for followers' needs. These same qualities are also expressed through their dress, appearance, and other forms of body language. Unconventionality in the use of rhetoric and nonverbal forms of communication creates conditions for a dispositional attribution of charisma. These ideas about charismatic leaders' articulation of context and motivation are contained in the following two hypotheses.

Hypothesis 7: *Charismatic leaders portray the status quo as negative or intolerable and the future vision as the most attractive and attainable alternative.*

Hypothesis 8: *Charismatic leaders articulate their motivation to lead through assertive behavior and expression of self-confidence, expertise, unconventionality, and concern for followers' needs.*

Charisma and the Use of Personal Power

Influence over followers can stem from different bases of power (French & Raven, 1968). Charismatic influence, however, stems from leaders' personal idiosyncratic power (referent and expert powers) rather than their position power (legal, coercive, and reward powers) legitimated by organizational rules and regulations. Participative consensual leaders also use personal power through consensus seeking. Some nonparticipative organizational leaders also use personal power through their benevolent but directive behavior. However, charismatic leaders differ from both consensual and directive leaders in the use of their personal power. Charismatic personal power stems from the elitist idealized vision, the entrepreneurial advocacy of radical changes, and the depth of knowledge and expertise to help achieve desired objectives. All these personal qualities appear extraordinary to their followers, and they form the basis of charisma. The following two hypotheses state this aspect of charismatic leadership.

Hypothesis 9: *Charismatic leaders' influence on their followers stems from the use of their personal idiosyncratic power (expert and referent) rather than the use of their position power (legal, coercive, and reward) within the organization.*

Hypothesis 10: *Charismatic leaders exert idiosyncratic personal power over their followers through elitist, entrepreneurial, and exemplary behavior rather than through consensus-seeking or directive behavior.*

Charisma and the Reformer Role

A charismatic leader is seen as an organizational reformer. As Weber (1947) pointed out, charismatic authority is essentially unstable and transitory. Once a new order is institutionalized, charisma fades (Eisenstadt, 1968). Thus charisma is seen in leaders only when they act as agents bringing about radical changes. The attribution is made simply on the basis of actions taken to bring about change or reform. It is not a post facto attribution made after the outcomes of changes are known. Outcomes may, however, reinforce or diminish existing attributions.

From the perspective of change management, leaders should be distinguished from administrators (Zaleznik, 1977). Administrators act as caretakers responsible for the maintenance of the status quo. They influence others through their position power as legitimated by the organization. Leaders, as posed to administrators, direct or nudge their followers in the direction of an established goal. Charismatic leaders, however, transform their followers (instead of nudging them) and seek radical reforms in them in order to achieve the idealized goal. Thus, charisma can never be perceived either in an administrator (caretaker) role or in a leadership role designed only to nudge the system. This idea is contained in the following hypothesis.

Hypothesis 11: *Charismatic leaders act as reformers or agents of radical changes, and their charisma fades when they act as administrators (caretaker role) or managers (nudging role).*

The Context for Emergence of Charisma

The preceding discussion implies that a need for major transition or change triggers the emergence of a charismatic leader. Sometimes contextual factors are so overwhelmingly in favor of a change that leaders take advantage of them. For instance, when a system is dysfunctional or when it faces a crisis, leaders find it to their advantage to advocate radical change, thereby creating a charismatic image for themselves. In periods of relative tranquility, leaders play a major role in creating the need for change in their followers. They anticipate future change and induce supportive conditions. In any case, context must be viewed as a

precipitating factor, sometimes facilitating the emergence of certain behavior in leaders that forms the basis of charisma. As Willner (1984) pointed out regarding political leadership, "preconditions of exogeneous social crisis and psychic distress are conducive to the emergence of charismatic political leadership, but they are not necessary" (p. 52). From the point of view of the leader, however, sensitivity to contextual factors is important if he or she is to develop appropriate strategies for change. The following two hypotheses deal with the role of context in the emergence of charisma.

Hypothesis 12: *Contextual factors that cause potential followers to be disenchanted with the prevailing social order, or that cause followers to experience psychological distress, although not a necessary condition for the emergence of charismatic leaders, facilitate such emergence.*

Hypothesis 13: *Under conditions of relative social tranquility and lack of psychological distress among followers, the actions by a leader that foster or support an attribution of charisma facilitate the emergence of that leader as a charismatic leader.*

IMPLICATIONS

In order to demystify charisma, these tentative hypotheses for future testing have been presented. Existing evidence forms the basis of the model, but the specific predictions should be tested.

In the model, charisma is viewed both as a set of dispositional attributions by followers and as a set of leaders' manifest behaviors. The two are linked in the sense that the leaders' behaviors form the basis of followers' attributions. To validate such a framework, two steps are necessary. First, the behavioral and dispositional attributes of charismatic leaders suggested in this framework require independent empirical confirmation. To determine if convergent and discriminant validity exist, a behavioral attribute checklist or questionnaire could be developed including the attributes believed to characterize charismatic leaders as well as those cited in the literature for other forms of leadership. A group of test subjects could identify leaders they perceive as charismatic and as noncharismatic. Respondents then could describe the distinguishing attributes of charismatic and noncharismatic leaders using the checklist. With this format, it would be possible to test whether an attribution of charisma is associated with the attributes described. Second, the discriminant validity of the charismatic leadership construct as described in this paper could be tested by demonstrating that a dependent variable (e.g., followers' trust) is related to charisma in a different way than other leadership constructs.

The model also has direct implications for management. Specifically, if the behavioral components of charismatic leadership can be isolated, it may be possible to develop these attributes in managers. Assuming that charismatic leadership is important for organizational reforms, organizations may wish to select managers on the basis of charismatic characteristics that have been identified. Certain tests such as those already developed to test sensitivity to the environment (Kenny & Zaccaro, 1983) could be administered to potential managerial candidates. The need for such selection procedures may be particularly important for developing countries, where greater levels of organizational change would be necessary in order to adopt new technologies and to transform traditional ways of operating.

References

Avolio, B. J., & Bass, B. M. (1985). *Charisma and beyond.* Paper presented at the annual meeting of the Academy of Management, San Diego.

Baker, R. (1983, March 27). Peripatetic pitchman. *New York Times Magazine,* p. 26.

Bass, B. M. (1981). *Stogdill's handbook of leadership.* New York: Free Press.

Bass, B. M. (1985). *Leadership performance beyond expectations.* New York: Academic Press.

Bennis, W. G., & Nanus, G. (1985). *Leaders.* New York: Harper & Row.

Berger, P. L. (1963). Charisma and religious innovation: The social location of Israelite prophecy. *American Sociological Review, 28,* 940–950.

Berlew, D. E. (1974). Leadership and organizational excitement. *California Management Review, 17*(2), 21–30.

Blake, R. R., & Mouton, J. S. (1964). *The managerial grid.* Houston: Gulf.

Blau, P. (1963). Critical remarks on Weber's theory of authority. *American Political Science Review, 57,* 305–315.

Byrne, D. (1977). *The attraction paradigm.* New York: Academic Press.

Chinoy, E. (1961). *Society.* New York: Random House.

Conger, J. (1985). *Charismatic leadership in business: An exploratory study.* Unpublished doctoral dissertation, Harvard Business School, Boston.

Devereux, G. (1955). Charismatic leadership and crisis. In W. Muensterberger & S. Axelrod (Eds.), *Psychoanalysis and the social sciences* (Vol. 4, pp.145–157). New York: International University Press.

Dow, T. E., Jr. (1969). The theory of charisma. *Sociological Quarterly,* 10, 306–318.

Downtown, J. V., Jr. (1973). *Rebel leadership.* New York: Free Press.

Eisenstadt, S. N. (1968). *Max Weber: On charisma and institution building.* Chicago: University of Chicago Press.

Etzioni, A. (1961). *A comparative analysis of complex organizations.* New York: Free Press.

Fiedler, F. F. (1967). *A theory of leadership effectiveness.* New York: McGraw-Hill.

French, J. R., Jr., & Raven, B. H. (1968). The bases of social power. In D. Cartwright & A. Zander (Eds.), *Group dynamics* (pp.259–269.) New York: Harper & Row.

Friedland, W. H. (1964). For a sociological concept of charisma. *Social Forces,* 43, 18–26.

Friedrich, C. J. (1961). Political leadership and the problem of the charismatic power. *Journal of Politics,* 23, 3–24.

Hersey, P., & Blanchard, K. H. (1977). *Management of organizational behavior: Utilizing human resources* (4th ed.). Englewood Cliffs, NJ: Prentice-Hall.

House, R. J. (1971). A path-goal theory of leadership effectiveness. *Administrative Science Quarterly,* 321–332.

House, R. J. (1977). A 1976 theory of charismatic leadership. In J. G. Hunt & L. L. Larson (Eds.), *Leadership: The cutting edge* (pp. 189–207). Carbondale, IL: Southern Illinois University press.

House, R. J. (1985). *Research contrasting the behavior and effects of reputed charismatic versus reputed noncharismatic.* Paper presented at the annual meeting of the Administrative Science Association, Montreal.

House, R. J., & Baetz, M. L. (1979). Leadership: Some empirical generalizations and new research directions. In B. M. Staw (Ed.), *Research in organizational behavior* (Vol. 1, pp. 399–401). Greenwich, CT: JAI Press.

Hovland, C. I., Janis, I. L., & Kelley, H. H. (1953). *Communication and persuasion.* New Haven, CT: Yale University Press.

Hovland, C. I., & Pritzker, H. A. (1957). Extent of opinion change as a function of amount of change advocated. *Journal of Abnormal Psychology,* 54, 257–261.

Howell, J. M. (1985). *A laboratory study of charismatic leadership.* Paper presented at the annual meeting of the Academy of Management, San Diego.

Hummel, R. P. (1975). Psychology of charismatic followers. *Psychological Reports,* 37, 759–770.

Iacocca, L., & Novak, W. (1984). *Iacocca.* New York: Bantam Books.

Katz, D., & Kahn, R. L. (1978). *The social psychology of organizations.* New York: Wiley.

Kenny, D. A., & Zacarro, S. J. (1983). An estimate of variance due to traits in leadership. *Journal of Applied Psychology, 68,* 678–685.

Marcus, J. T. (1961). March Transcendence and charisma. *Western Political Quarterly, 14,* 236–241.

Martin, J., & Siehl, C. (1983). Organizational culture and counterculture: An uneasy symbiosis. *Organizational Dynamics, 12*(2), 52–64.

Nicholson, T. (1983, February 14). Iacocca shifts into high. *Newsweek,* pp. 101, 64.

Oberg, W. (1972). Charisma, commitment, and contemporary organization theory. *Business Topics, 20*(2), 18–32.

Petty, R. E., & Cacioppo, J. T. (1981). *Attitudes and persuasion: Classic and contemporary approaches.* Dubuque, IA: Brown.

Rubin, Z. (1973). *Liking and loving: An invitation to social psychology.* New York: Holt, Rinehart, & Winston.

Runciman, W. G. (1963). Charismatic legitimacy and one-party rule in Ghana. *Archives Eupreenes de Sociologie, 4,* 148–165.

Schiffer, I. (1973). *Charisma: A psychoanalytic look at mass society.* Toronto: University of Toronto Press.

Sears, D. O., Freedman, L., & Peplau, L. A. (1985). *Social psychology* (5th ed.). Englewood Cliffs, NJ: Prentice-Hall.

Shils, E. A. (1965). Charisma, order, and status. *American Sociological Review, 30,* 199–213.

Smith, B. J. (1982). *An initial test of a theory of charismatic leadership based on responses of subordinates.* Unpublished doctoral dissertation, University of Toronto.

Tucker, R. C. (1968). The theory of charismatic leadership. *Daedalus, 97,* 731–756.

Waldman, D. A., Bass, B. M., & Einstein, W. O. (1985). *Effort, performance and transformational leadership in industrial and military settings* (Working Paper 85-80). State University of New York at Binghamton, School of Management.

Walster, E., Aronson, D., & Abrahams, D. (1966). On increasing the persuasiveness of a low prestige communicator. *Journal of Experimental Social Psychology, 2,* 325–342.

Weber, M. (1947). *The theory of social and economic organization* (A. M. Henderson & T. Parsons, Trans.). New York: Oxford University Press.

Willner, A. R. (1968). *Charismatic political leadership: A theory.* Princeton, NJ: Princeton University, Center of International Studies.

Willner, A. R. (1984). *The spellbinders: Charismatic political leadership.* New Haven, CT: Yale University Press.

Wolpe, H. (1968). A critical analysis of some aspects of charisma. *Sociological Review, 16,* 305–318.

Wright, P. J. (1979). *On a clear day you can see General Motors.* New York: Avon Books.

Yukl, G. A. (1981). *Leadership in organizations.* Englewood Cliffs, NJ: Prentice-Hall.

Yukl, G. A., & Van Fleet, D. D. (1982). Cross-situational multimethod research on military leader effectiveness. *Organizational Behavior and Human Performance, 30,* 87–108.

Zaleznik, A. (1977). Managers and leaders: Are they different? *Harvard Business Review, 55*(3), 67–78.

Zaleznik, A., & Kets de Vries, M. F. R. (1975). *Power and the corporate mind.* Boston: Houghton Mifflin.

Reading 37

The Motivational Effects of Charismatic Leadership: A Self-concept Based Theory

Boas Shamir
The Hebrew University

Robert J. House
University of Pennsylvania

Michael B. Arthur
Suffolk University

INTRODUCTION

In the past 15 years a new genre of leadership theory, alternatively referred to as "charismatic," "transformational," "visionary," or "inspirational," has emerged in the organizational literature (House, 1977; Burns, 1978; Bass, 1985; Bennis & Nanus, 1985; Tichy & Devanna, 1986; Boal & Bryson, 1988; Conger & Kanungo, 1987; Kuhnert & Lewis, 1987; Sashkin, 1988).

These theories focus on exceptional leaders who have extraordinary effects on their followers and eventually on social systems. According to this new genre of leadership theory, such leaders transform the needs, values, preferences, and aspirations of followers from self-interests to collective interests. Further, they cause followers to become highly committed to the leader's mission, to make significant personal sacrifices in the interest of the mission, and to perform above and beyond the call of duty. We refer to this new genre of theories as charismatic because charisma is a central concept in all of them, either explicitly or implicitly.

Theories of charismatic leadership highlight such effects as emotional attachment to the leader on the part of the followers; emotional and motivational arousal of the followers; enhancement of follower valences with respect to the mission articulated by the leader; follower self-esteem, trust, and confidence in the leader; follower values; and follower intrinsic motivation.

The leader behavior specified by charismatic theories is different from the behavior emphasized in earlier theories of organizational leadership. The earlier theories describe leader behavior in terms of leader/follower exchange relationships (Hollander, 1964; Graen & Cashman, 1975), providing direction and support (Evans, 1970; House, 1971), and reinforcement behaviors (Ashour, 1982; Podsakoff, Todor, & Skov, 1982). In contrast, the new leadership theories emphasize symbolic leader behavior, visionary and inspirational messages, nonverbal communication, appeal to ideological values, intellectual stimulation of followers by the leader, display of confidence in self and followers, and leader expectations for follower self-sacrifice and for performance beyond the call of duty. Such leadership is seen as giving meaningfulness to work by infusing work and organizations with moral purpose and commitment rather than by affecting the task environment of followers, or by offering material incentives and the threat of punishment.

Research based on these theories has yielded an impressive set of findings concerning the effects of charismatic leaders on follower attitudes, satisfaction, and performance. However, there is no motivational explanation to account for the profound effects of such leaders, some of which are difficult to explain within currently dominant models of motivation. The purpose of this paper is to offer a motivational theory to account for the effects of charismatic leaders on their followers.

EMPIRICAL EVIDENCE

In the last decade, at least 35 empirical investigations of charismatic leadership in organizations have been conducted. . . .

Source: Edited and reprinted with permission from *Organization Science* 4, 4 (1993), pp. 577–594. Copyright 1993 Institute for Operations Research and the Management Sciences (INFORMS).

These studies were conducted across a wide variety of samples. . . .

Space limitations prevent a detailed review of the findings of these studies (for reviews see Bass, 1990; House, Howell, Shamir, Smith, & Spangler, 1991). While the studies were not guided by a unified theoretical perspective, there is a considerable convergence of the findings from studies concerned with charismatic leadership and those concerned with transformational and visionary leadership. Collectively, these findings indicate that leaders who engage in the theoretical charismatic behaviors produce the theoretical charismatic effects. In addition, they receive higher performance ratings, have more satisfied and more highly motivated followers, and are viewed as more effective leaders by their superiors and followers than others in positions of leadership. Further, the effect size of charismatic leader behavior on follower satisfaction and performance is consistently higher than prior field study findings concerning other leader behavior, generally ranging well below 0.01 probability of error due to chance, with correlations frequently ranging in the neighborhood of 0.50 or better.

THE PROBLEM

Unfortunately, the literature on charismatic leadership does not provide an explanation of the process by which charismatic leadership has its profound effects. No motivational explanations are provided to explain how charismatic leaders bring about changes in followers' values, goals, needs, and aspirations.

Three types of changes that have been emphasized by previous theories present a particular theoretical challenge. First, Burns (1978) and Bass (1985) suggested that transformational or charismatic leaders are able to elevate followers' needs from lower to higher levels in the Maslow hierarchy. Second, Burns (1978) claimed that such

FIGURE 1 An Outline of the Theory

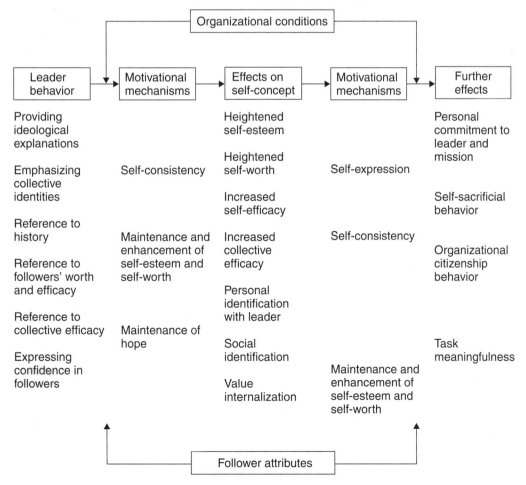

leaders raise followers to higher levels of morality, to "more principled levels of judgment" (p. 455). Third, House (1977), Burns (1978), and Bass (1985) proposed that such leaders are successful in motivating followers to transcend their own self-interests for the sake of the team, the organization, or the larger polity. We shall refer to these effects as "the transformational effects of charismatic leadership." . . .

In the following sections of this paper, we first present some assumptions about the motivational significance of the self-concept. We then show how charismatic leaders activate self-concept related motivations, and how these motivations can explain the effects that are not well explained by current theories. Following, we specify leader behaviors that are likely to activate these processes. We derive from our motivational analysis testable propositions about the effects of these behaviors on followers' self-concepts, and their further effects on followers. We then discuss some follower attributes that moderate the hypothesized relationships. Finally, we specify organizational conditions under which charismatic leadership is likely to emerge and be effective. . . .

THE THEORY

Our assumptions about the self-concept and its motivational implications allow us to propose a theory to explain the transformational effects of charismatic leadership. The theory has four main parts: (*a*) leader behaviors; (*b*) effects on followers' self-concepts; (*c*) further effects on followers; and (*d*) the motivational processes by which the leader behaviors produce the charismatic effects. These processes link the leader behaviors to their effects on followers' self-concepts, and the effects on followers' self-concepts to further effects on followers. The theory is outlined in Figure 1.

At the heart of our theory are five processes by which charismatic leaders motivate followers through implicating their self-concepts. These processes are presented first. We then derive from our motivational analysis a set of empirically observable leader behaviors that are hypothesized to activate the self-implicating processes, a set of effects on followers' self-concepts that are triggered by the leader behaviors, and a set of further effects on followers that are mediated by the self-concept effects.

We do not view the variables specified within each set as constituting exhaustive sets. Nor can we rule out the possibility that the variables

within each set are intercorrelated and constitute syndromes (Meindl, 1990). At this stage, our propositions refer to the relationships between the sets of variables. Hopefully, empirical research guided by these propositions will enable a more parsimonious and more exact formulation of the relationships implied by the theory.

THE SELF-IMPLICATING EFFECTS OF CHARISMATIC LEADERSHIP[1]

We suggest that charismatic leaders motivate their followers in the following manner:

(a) Increasing the Intrinsic Valence of Effort

This is accomplished by emphasizing the symbolic and expressive aspects of the effort—the fact that the effort itself reflects important values—that by making the effort, one makes a moral statement. Charismatic leadership is presumed to strengthen followers' belief in the necessity and propriety of "standing up and being counted."

The intrinsic valence of the effort may also be increased by making participation in the effort an expression of a collective identity, thus making the effort more meaningful for the follower. This implicates the self-concept of followers by increasing the salience of that identity in the follower's self-concept, thus increasing the likelihood of efforts and behaviors representing that identity. Charismatic leaders may use existing identities and emphasize their uniqueness or superiority

---

[1] In the analysis that follows, we do not distinguish between "good" or "moral" and "evil" or "immoral" charismatic leadership. Indeed, our analysis suggests that the psychological mechanisms relied upon by the "Hitlers" and the "Gandhis" may be similar in certain respects. This means that the risks involved in following charismatic leaders are at least as large as the promises. The motivational processes and the creation of personal commitment described in this paper can lead to blind fanaticism in the service of megalomaniacs and dangerous values, no less than to heroic self-sacrifice in the service of a beneficial cause. An awareness of these risks is missing from most of the current literature on organizational charismatic or transformational leadership. We believe that these risks should not be neglected, but rather that we need more studies of the nature and effects of charismatic leadership and the conditions under which it produces harmful versus beneficial effects for followers and collectives. "Beware Charisma! . . . But to beware does not necessarily mean or entail 'Avoid!' . . . Be aware! Then choose" (Hodgkinson, 1983). We hope that the analysis presented here will help lead to the awareness called for by Hodgkinson (1983). However, we do not endorse charismatic leadership as necessarily good or bad. For a theory that differentiates personalized authoritarian and exploitive charismatics from collective, egalitarian, and not exploitive, see House and Howell (1992).

("Black is beautiful"), or they may create "new" desirable social categories for the followers ("the master race"). In both cases, the self-concepts of the followers are clearly engaged.

Meindl and Lerner (1983) have suggested that the salience of a shared identity can increase the "heroic motive" and the likelihood that self-interest oriented pursuits will voluntarily be abandoned for more altruistic or collectivistic endeavors. It follows that, when charismatic leaders increase the salience of collective identities in their followers' self-concepts, they also increase the likelihood of self-sacrificial, collective-oriented behavior on the part of followers.

It is important to note that, once followers choose to make the effort and through that effort identify themselves with certain values and with the leader and the collective, they are subject to considerable social and psychological forces that are likely to increase their commitment to that effort (Kanter, 1967; Salancik, 1977). We will return to this point in our discussion of personal commitment.

(b) Increasing Effort-Accomplishment Expectancies

Charismatic leaders increase effort-accomplishment expectancies by enhancing the followers' self-esteem and self-worth. They enhance self-esteem by expressing high expectations of the followers and confidence in the followers' ability to meet such expectations (Yukl, 1989; Eden, 1990). By so doing, they enhance followers' perceived self-efficacy, defined as a judgment of one's capability to accomplish a certain level of performance. Self-efficacy is a strong source of motivation (Bandura, 1986, p. 351).

Charismatic leaders also increase followers' self-worth through emphasizing the relationships between efforts and important values. A general sense of self-worth increases general self-efficacy; a sense of moral correctness is a source of strength and confidence. Having complete faith in the moral correctness of one's convictions gives one the strength and confidence to behave accordingly.

Another aspect of charismatic leadership that is likely to increase effort-accomplishment expectancies is its emphasis on collective efficacy. "Perceived collective efficacy will influence what people choose to do as a group, how much effort they put into it, and their staying power when group efforts fail to produce results" (Bandura, 1986, p. 449). Thus, being a member of an efficacious collective enhances one's self-efficacy.

(c) Increasing the Intrinsic Valence of Goal Accomplishment

This is one of the most import motivational mechanisms of charismatic leadership. Articulation of a vision and a mission by charismatic leaders presents goals in terms of the values they represent. Doing so makes action oriented toward the accomplishment of these goals more meaningful to the follower in the sense of being consistent with his or her self-concept.

Charismatic leadership also increases the meaningfulness of goals and related actions by showing how these goals are consistent with the collective past and its future and thus creating the sense of "evolving" which is central for self-consistency and a sense of meaningfulness (McHugh, 1968). In addition, such leadership stresses the importance of the goal as a basis for group identity and for distinguishing the group or collective from other groups. This brings meaning to the followers' lives and efforts by connecting them to larger entities and to concerns that transcend their own limited existence (Jahoda, 1981). By these leadership actions, certain identities are evoked and made more salient and therefore more likely to be implicated in action.

(d) Instilling Faith in a Better Future

The "rewards" involved in the charismatic leadership process involve self-expression, self-efficacy, self-worth, and self-consistency, which emerge from the process and cannot be exchanged. In most cases, charismatic leadership de-emphasizes extrinsic rewards and their related expectancies in order to emphasize the intrinsic aspects of the effort. Refraining from providing pragmatic extrinsic justification for the required behavior increases the chances that followers will attribute their behavior to internal self-related causes and thus adds to followers' commitment to that course of action.

Note that while noncharismatic leadership emphasizes proximal, specific goals and increases the subjective likelihood that goal attainment would lead to specific outcomes (Locke & Latham, 1990; House, 1971), charismatic leadership tends to emphasize vague and distal goals and utopian outcomes. It is here that Bass refers to charismatic leaders' use of "symbolism, mysticism, imaging, and fantasy" (1985, p. 6). In order to understand the motivational impact of such messages (that contradict current motivational models which stress goal specificity and proximity), we have to resort to our assumption that having faith in a better future is a satisfying condition in itself. People would therefore follow leaders who provide hope (a vision) for a better future and faith in its attainment, even if such faith cannot be translated into specific proximal goals whose attainment is highly probable.

(e) Creating Personal Commitment

Another important aspect of charismatic motivational influence is the creation of a high level of commitment on the part of the leader and the followers to a common vision, mission, or transcendent goal (Bennis & Nanus, 1985; House, 1977). "Their art is to manufacture ethics to give life through commitment to the spirit of the organization" (Hodgkinson, 1983, p. 218).

When we speak about commitment in the context of charismatic leadership, we refer to unconditional commitment—internalized "personal" or "moral" commitment (Johnson, 1982). This is a motivational disposition to continue a relationship, a role, or a course of action and to invest efforts regardless of the balance of external costs and benefits and their immediate gratifying properties.

We propose that such commitment is achieved when the relationship or role under consideration becomes a component of the individual's self-concept and when the course of action related to that relationship or role is consistent with and expressive of the individual's self-concept; in other words, when "action is not merely a means of doing but a way of being" (Strauss, 1969, p. 3).

Such a concept of commitment fits very well into our analysis of charismatic leadership. By recruiting the self-concept of followers, increasing the salience of certain identities and values, and linking behaviors and goals to those identities and values and to a mission that reflects them, charismatic leadership motivates followers through the creation of personal commitments.

These processes are self-reinforcing because the behavioral manifestations of such a commitment are likely to further bind the self-concept of the individual to the leader and the mission. Faced with their own voluntary and public action on behalf of the leader, the collective, or the mission, individuals are likely to integrate these relationships and values even further into their self-concepts as a result of self-attribution and self-justification processes and the need to reduce or avoid cognitive dissonance (Salancik, 1977; Staw, 1980). When the self is engaged in a situation, the need for self-justification and dissonance reduction is particularly strong.

Generated and reinforced in these ways, personal commitment is perhaps the most intrinsic of all intrinsic motivators since in the final analysis it is a commitment to one's own self-concept and evaluative standards, "to a conception of (oneself) as a certain kind or kinds of person who is expected and expects to act in a certain way in certain situations" (Strauss, 1969, p. 3).[2]

Summary

To recapitulate, we have suggested that charismatic leaders achieve transformational effects through implicating the self-concept of followers. More specifically, we have argued that such leaders increase the intrinsic value of efforts and goals by linking them to valued aspects of the follower's self-concept, thus harnessing the motivational forces of self-expression, self-consistency, self-esteem, and self-worth. We have further argued that charismatic leaders change the salience hierarchy of values and identities within the follower's self-concept, thus increasing the probability that these values and identities will be implicated in action. Since values and identities are socially based, their control of behavior is likely to represent a shift from the instrumental to the moral and from concern with individual gains to concern with contributions to a collective. Finally, we have argued that charismatic leaders increase self-efficacy and collective efficacy through expressing positive evaluations, communicating higher performance expectations of followers, showing confidence in followers' ability to meet such expectations, and emphasizing the individual's ties to the collective. The differences between these processes and the motivational processes implied by more traditional leadership theories are outlined in Table 1.

LEADER BEHAVIOR

The motivational processes described above are activated by two classes of leader behavior: (*a*) role modeling, and (*b*) frame alignment.

---

[2]From an organizational perspective, however, commitment is a double-edged sword. To the extent that the leader's goals and values are congruent with the goals and values of the organization, charismatic leadership is likely to provide a strong link between organizational goals and member commitment to such goals. To the extent that the leader's goals and values are in conflict with those of the organization, such as when leaders represent a challenge to the status quo, charismatic leadership is likely to induce negative attitudes toward the organization and resistance to directives from management by organizational members. Thus, charismatic leadership represents a strong force for *or against* member commitment to organizational goals.

TABLE 1 Summary of the Motivational Effects of Traditional and Charismatic Leadership Processes

Motivational Charismatic Component Processes	Traditional Leadership Processes	Charismatic Leadership
Intrinsic value of behavior	Making the task more interesting, varied, enjoyable, challenging, as in job enrichment	Linking behavior to followers' self-concepts, internalized values and cherished identities
Behavior-accomplishment expectancy	Coaching, training; providing material, instrumental and emotional support; clarifying goals	Increasing general self-efficacy (through increasing self-worth and communicating confidence and high expectations). Emphasizing collective efficacy
Intrinsic value of goal accomplishment	Setting goals, increasing task identity, providing feedback	Linking goals to the past and the present and to values in a framework of a "mission" which serves as a basis for identification
Accomplishment-reward expectancies	Establishing clear performance evaluation and tying rewards to performance	Generating faith by connecting behaviors and goals to a "dream" or a utopian ideal vision of a better future.
Valence of extrinsic rewards	Taken into consideration in rewarding performance	Not addressed

(a) Role Modeling

Vicarious learning occurs when the relevant messages are inferred by followers from observation of leaders' behavior, life style, emotional reactions, values, aspirations, preferences, and the like. The leader becomes a "representative character" (Bellah et al., 1985)—a symbol which brings together in one concentrated image the way people in a given social environment organize and give meaning and direction to their lives. He or she becomes an image that helps define for the followers just what kinds of traits, values, beliefs, and behaviors it is good and legitimate to develop. Thus, the leader provides an ideal, a point of reference and focus for followers' emulation and vicarious learning.

This is sometimes exemplified by leaders' display of self-sacrificial behavior in the interest of the mission. By taking risks, making personal sacrifices, and engaging in unconventional ideological behavior (Conger and Kanungo, 1987; Sashkin, 1988), charismatic leaders demonstrate their own courage and conviction in the mission and thus both earn credibility and serve as a role model of the values of the vision and the mission.

(b) Frame Alignment

[This term] (Snow et al., 1986) refers to the linkage of individual and leader interpretive orientations, such that some set of followers' interests, values, and beliefs and the leader's activities, goals, and ideology become congruent and complementary. The term "frame" denotes "schemata of interpretation" (Goffman, 1974) that enables individuals to locate, perceive, and label occurrences within their life and the world at large. By rendering events or occurrences meaningful, frames function to organize experience and guide action, whether individual or collective (see also Boal and Bryson, 1988).

Charismatic leaders engage in communicative processes that affect frame alignment and "mobilize" followers to action. They interpret the present and past. They link present behaviors to past events by citing historical examples (Willner, 1984). They articulate an ideology clearly, often using labels and slogans. They provide a vivid image of the future. Further, they amplify certain values and identities and suggest linkages between expected behaviors, amplified values and identities, and their vision of the future.

By articulating an ideological vision and recruiting a number of followers who share the values of the vision, charismatic leaders provide for followers a sense of identity with the collectivity and a sense of efficacy resulting from membership in the collectivity. Articulation of high performance expectations, together with display of confidence in followers, results in enhancing both follower self-esteem and self-worth.

By relating the vision to significant historical events and projecting it into the future, charismatic leaders provide for followers a sense of continuity.

These general behavioral principles can be translated into more specific and observable behaviors.

Proposition 1. *In order to implicate the followers' self-concepts, compared to noncharismatic leaders, the deliberate and nondeliberate messages of charismatic leaders will contain:*

(a) More references to values and moral justifications.

(b) More references to the collective and to collective identity.

(c) More references to history.

(d) More positive references to followers' worth and efficacy as individuals and as a collective.

(e) More expressions of high expectations from followers.

(f) More references to distal goals and less reference to proximal goals.

EFFECTS ON FOLLOWERS' SELF-CONCEPT

Several effects on the followers' self-concept evolve directly from our preceding discussion. These are specified in the following proposition:

Proposition 2. *The more leaders exhibit the behaviors specified above, the more followers will have:*

(a) A high salience of the collective identity in their self-concept.

(b) A sense of consistency between their self-concept and their actions on behalf of the leader and the collective.

(c) A high level of self-esteem and self-worth.

(d) A similarity between their self-concept and their perception of the leader.

(e) A high sense of collective efficacy.

These effects on the self-concept represent three common processes of psychological attachment: personal identification, social identification, and value internalization. . . .

SELF-CONCEPT AS AN INTERVENING VARIABLE AND FURTHER EFFECTS ON FOLLOWERS

The theory suggests that the above specified effects on followers' self-concepts mediate other effects of charismatic leaders on the followers. The changes in followers' self-concepts will produce these effects through the motivational mechanisms of self-expression, self-consistency, and the maintenance and enhancement of self-esteem and self-worth. These further effects are observable manifestations of the transformational effects of charismatic leadership.

First, it is proposed that the linkage formed by charismatic leaders between followers' self-concepts and the leader's mission will be evidenced by increased personal commitment of the followers to the leader and the mission. Second, increased social identification and value internalization will lead to a high willingness among followers to make personal sacrifices for the collective mission as articulated by the leader, and a high level of "extra role," organizational citizenship behaviors (O'Reilly & Chatman, 1986; Organ, 1988; Podsakoff et al., 1990). Such behaviors are of particular interest because they are the voluntary behavioral manifestations of performance beyond expectations—exertion of effort and self-sacrifice in the interest of the work team or the larger organization.

In addition, followers of charismatic leaders are expected to have a high sense of "meaningfulness" associated with the task. Such meaningfulness stems from a high sense of consistency between their self-concepts and their actions on behalf of the leader and the collective, and from the implications of these actions for their self-esteem and self-worth. Thus,

Proposition 3. *The more leaders exhibit the behaviors specified in the theory the more followers will demonstrate:*

(a) Personal commitment to the leader and the mission.

(b) A willingness to make sacrifices for the collective mission.

(c) Organizational citizenship behavior.

(d) Meaningfulness in their work and lives.

It is further proposed that the increased self-efficacy and collective efficacy, together with the high personal commitment to the mission and the sense of "meaningfulness" associated with the tasks, will produce heightened performance motivation among followers, which will in turn result in higher levels of performance. These final effects are not specified in our propositions because they are not unique to the proposed theory and may be produced by other leader behaviors triggering other motivational mechanisms. They are reinforced, however, by the self-processes outlined in our model.

FOLLOWER ATTRIBUTES

Our theory implies that charismatic leaders will not have similar effects on all followers. We now turn to a discussion of some follower characteristics that may moderate the hypothesized relationships between leader behaviors and effects on followers.

FOLLOWER VALUES AND IDENTITIES

The theory presented here implies that the leader, in order to have the transformational effects specified in the theory, must appeal to existing elements of the followers' self-concepts—namely, their values and identities. . . .

This line of reasoning leads to the following proposition:

Proposition 4. *A necessary condition for a leader's messages to have charismatic effects is that the message is congruent with the existing values and identities held by potential followers.*

FOLLOWER ORIENTATIONS

Other follower characteristics may moderate the transformational effects of charismatic leadership. Organization members are known to differ on the dimension of having an "instrumental" or "expressive" orientation to work (Goldthorpe et al., 1968). Since charismatic leadership arouses expressive motivations, it can be hypothesized that it will have a higher appeal to people with an expressive orientation to work.

In addition, people differ in the extent to which they conceive of themselves as either pragmatic or principled in their relations with others (Snyder, 1979). We propose that people with a more principled orientation to social relations will be more susceptible to leadership messages that link their behaviors and actions to ideological values.

These considerations suggest the following propositions:

Proposition 5. *The more the potential followers have an expressive orientation toward work and life. the more susceptible they will be to the influence of charismatic leaders.*

Proposition 6. *The more the potential followers have a principled orientation to social relations, the more susceptible they will be to the influence of charismatic leaders.*

ORGANIZATIONAL CONDITIONS FOR CHARISMATIC LEADERSHIP

Current enthusiasm about charismatic and transformational leadership in the organizational literature tends to give the impression that this type of leadership is equally applicable to all organizational situations. Our analysis leads us to qualify this enthusiasm and to theoretically specify the conditions under which charismatic leadership is more likely to emerge and to be effective.

First, the organizational task is a relevant consideration. Recall that charismatic leadership gives meaning to efforts and goals by connecting them to followers' values. These values are likely to reflect, at least in part, the dominant values of society or of the subculture of potential followers. Thus, it follows that charismatic leadership is more likely to emerge and be effective when the organizational task is closely related to dominant social values to which potential followers are exposed than when it is unrelated to such values or contradicts them. In the former case, it is easier to translate followers' dominant values into a mission.

To take an obvious example, at this time in the United States, charismatic leadership is more likely to emerge in high technology industries whose tasks can be easily linked to values such as scientific and economic progress and national pride, than in the production of tobacco, which may be perceived to contradict the dominant value of health. In other words, the situation has to offer at least some opportunities for "moral" involvement. Otherwise, charismatic leadership cannot emerge.

Second, charismatic leadership is more likely to be relevant under conditions that do not favor leadership based on the use of extrinsic rewards and punishments. The use of extrinsic incentives requires certain organizational conditions to be effective, among them the ability of the leader to specify and clarify goals, considerable available knowledge about the means for achieving them, objective or highly consensual ways of measuring performance, and a high degree of discretion in the allocation of rewards on the basis of performance. Under such conditions, the utilitarian and calculative logic of a leader who uses extrinsic motivation can be clarified to the followers and adhered to by the leader (House, 1971). We propose that charismatic leadership is more likely to emerge when performance goals cannot be easily specified and measured, and when leaders cannot link extrinsic rewards to individual performance.

Mischel (1973) describes such conditions as "weak psychological situations," which are not uniformly construed in the same way by all observers, do not generate uniform expectancies concerning desired behavior, do not provide sufficient performance incentives, or fail to provide the learning conditions required for successful construction of behavior. In such "weak" situations, followers' self-concepts, values, and identities can be more readily appealed to and engaged. Furthermore, in the absence of clear extrinsic justifications for behavior, followers are more likely to look for self-related justifications for their efforts (Bem 1982) and thus become more prone to the influence of charismatic leadership.

Third, charismatic leadership may be more appropriate under exceptional conditions, such as those requiring nonroutine and unusually high performance, in order to prevail and be effective, such as crises of high levels of uncertainty. When conditions change or when the situation requires exceptional efforts, behaviors, and sacrifices, extrinsically motivated leadership is not likely to be effective, since it is by definition "conditional" and these situations require "unconditional" commitment. Furthermore, in unstable conditions or when a new organization is being formed, there is more ambiguity and anxiety and a greater need for orientation on the part of organizational members. Under such conditions, members are more likely to look for charismatic leaders and to accept their definitions of the organization's identity and its mission.

Three related points are worth noting. First, exceptional circumstances are not a necessary condition for the emergence of charismatic leadership. Our analysis does not rule out the possibility of charismatic leadership in nonexceptional situations. For instance, members may be alienated from the existing organizational order under routine situations, and charismatic leadership may emerge to lead a movement to alleviate such alienating conditions (Boal & Bryson, 1988). Second, exceptional conditions do not necessarily imply crisis situations. They may include situations of exceptional opportunities as well. Crises are not necessary for the emergence of charismatic leaders (Willner, 1984; Conger & Kanungo, 1987). Third, when crisis-handling leaders have charismatic effects, these effects will be short-term

unless the leader can relate the handling of the crisis to a higher purpose that has intrinsic validity for the actors (Boal and Bryson, 1988, p. 17).

Based on the above reasoning, we suggest the following proposition:

Proposition 7. *The emergence and effectiveness of charismatic leaders will be facilitated to the extent to which:*

(a) There is an opportunity for substantial moral involvement on the part of the leader and the followers.

(b) Performance goals cannot be easily specified and measured.

(c) Extrinsic rewards cannot be made clearly contingent on individual performance.

(d) There are few situational cues, constraints and reinforcers to guide behavior and provide incentives for specific performance.

(e) Exceptional effort, behavior, and sacrifices are required of both the leaders and followers.

CONCLUSION

In this paper, we have focused on certain fundamental effects of charismatic leaders on followers. We have argued that these effects are produced by leadership actions that implicate the self-concept of the followers, and engage the related motivations for self-expression, self-esteem, self-worth, and self-consistency. Our argument has resulted in a theory that links leader behavior and follower effects through follower self-concepts. According to this theory, leader behaviors activate self-concepts which in turn affect further motivational mechanisms. These intervening variables and processes in turn have a strong positive impact on the behaviors and psychological states of followers. Hopefully, our explanation helps to provide greater insights concerning the charismatic leadership phenomenon.

The outcome of our analysis is a theoretical extension of current theories of charismatic and transformational leadership. We recognize that the theory is speculative. However, we believe such speculation is warranted because it provides an explanation and accounts for the rather profound effects of charismatic leader behaviors demonstrated in prior research.

Some scholars have voiced skepticism concerning whether or not leaders can make a difference in organizational performance (Pfeffer, 1977;

Salancik & Pfeffer, 1977; Meindl, Ehrlich, & Dukerich, 1985). This skepticism reflects the argument that people are biased toward over-attributing to leaders influence on events which are complex and difficult to understand. As a result, leadership in general, and charismatic leadership in particular, could be dismissed as an exaggerated perception on the part of the followers which does not have strong substantive effects on organizational outcomes, and is therefore not worthy of much attention by students of organizations.

Others, notably Meindl (1990), have criticized charismatic leadership theories for being much too "leader-centered." Meindl has offered a "follower-oriented" approach as an alternative to the conventional theories. In his view, the charismatic effects are a function of social psychological forces operating among followers, subordinates, and observers, rather than arising directly out of the interactions between followers and leaders. According to Meindl, these social-psychological forces are functionally autonomous from the traits and behaviors of the leaders per se. Therefore, according to this radical perspective, leader behavior and leader traits should be deleted from explanations of charismatic leadership.

Obviously, we do not accept this extreme position. We believe that the evidence for the effects of charismatic leadership is too strong to be dismissed. We view Meindl's (1990) ideas as complementary, rather than contradictory, to the theory presented here. The self-processes we have described can be influenced by inter-follower processes as well as by leader behaviors. Followers' self-concepts and the related motivations can be engaged by informal role models and other social influence processes that occur among peers. This does not rule out, however, the potentiality for self-engagement as a result of charismatic leader behaviors, nor does it rule out the possibility that leaders will be instrumental in the initiation or orchestration of such inter-follower processes.

We have presented our arguments in the form of testable propositions. The theory presented here also suggests the ways in which follower attributes and organizational conditions can moderate the charismatic leadership process. Our assumptions and theoretical propositions do not contradict existing models of motivation; rather, they suggest the existence of additional motivational mechanisms without which the transformational effects of charismatic leadership cannot be explained. Hopefully, the theory advanced here will be pruned, modified, and extended as a result of future empirical testing.

References

Ashforth, B. E., & Mael, F. (1989). "Social Identity Theory and the Organization," *Academy of Management Review,* 14, 1, 20–39.

Ashour, A. S. (1982). "A Framework for a Cognitive Behavioral Theory of Leader Influence and Effectiveness," *Organizational Behavior and Human Performance,* 30, 407–430.

Avolio, B. J., & Bass, B. M. (1987). "Charisma and Beyond," in J. G. Hunt, B. R. Baliga, H. P. Dachler, & C. A. Schreisheim (Eds.), *Emerging Leadership Vistas,* Lexington: MA: D.C. Heath and Company.

——, Waldman, D. A., & Einstein, W. O. (1988). "Transformational Leadership in Management Game Simulation," *Group and Organization Studies,* 13, 1, 59–80.

Bandura, A. (1986). *Social Foundations of Thought and Action: A Social Cognitive Theory,* Englewood Cliffs, NJ: Prentice-Hall.

Bass, B. M. (1985). *Leadership and Performance Beyond Expectations,* New York: The Free Press.

——, (1990). *Bass & Stogdill's Handbook of Leadership,* 3rd ed., New York: The Free Press.

——, Avolio, B. J., & Goodheim, L. (1987). "Biographical Assessment of Transformational Leadership at the World-Class Level," *Journal of Management,* 13, 7–19.

—— and Yammarino, F. J. (1988). "Long Term Forecasting of Transformational Leadership and Its Effects among Naval Officers: Some Preliminary Findings," *Technical Report No. ONR-TR-2,* Arlington, VA: Office of Naval Research.

Bellah, R. N., Madsen, R., Sullivan, W. M., Swidler, A., & Tipton, S. M. (1985). *Habits of the Heart: Individualism and Commitment in American Life,* New York: Harper & Row.

Bem, D. J. (1982). "Self-Perception Theory," in L. Berkowitz (Ed.), *Advances in Experimental Social Psychology,* Vol. 6, New York: Academic Press.

Bennis, W., & Nanus, B. (1985). *Leaders: The Strategies for Taking Charge,* New York: Harper & Row.

Boal, K. B., & Bryson, J. M. (1988). "Charismatic Leadership: A Phenomenological and Structural Approach," in J. G. Hunt, B. R. Baliga, H. P. Dachler, & C. A. Schriesheim (Eds.), *Charismatic Leadership,* San Francisco: Jossey-Bass, 11–28.

Burns, J. M. (1978). *Leadership,* New York: Harper & Row.

Callero, P. J. (1985). "Role Identity Salience," *Social Psychology Quarterly,* 48, 3, 203–215.

Conger, J. A., & Kanungo, R. A. (1987). "Towards a Behavioral Theory of Charismatic Leadership in Organizational Settings," *Academy of Management Review,* 12, 637–647.

Csikszentmihalyi, M., & Rochberg-Halton, E. (1981). *The Meaning of Things: Domestic Symbols and the Self,* New York: Cambridge University Press.

Curphy, G. J. (1990). "An Empirical Study of Bass" (1985) *Theory of Transformational and Transactional Leadership,* Unpublished Doctoral Dissertation, The University of Minnesota.

Eden, D. (1990). *Pygmalion in Management,* Lexington, MA: D. C. Heath and Co.

Evans, G. (1970). "The Effects of Supervisory Behavior on the Path-Goal Relationship," *Organizational and Human Performance,* 5, 277–298.

Gecas, V. (1982). "The Self Concept," *Annual Review of Sociology,* 8, 1–33.

Goffman, E. (1974). *Frame Analysis,* Cambridge: Harvard University Press.

Goldthorpe, J. G., Lockwood, D. Beechofer F., & Platt, J. (1968). *The Affluent Worker: Industrial Attitudes and Behavior,* Cambridge: Cambridge University Press.

Graen, G., & Cashman, J. F. (1975). "A Role-Making Model of Leadership in Formal Organizations: A Developmental Approach," in J. G. Hunt, & L. L. Larson (Eds.), *Leadership Frontiers,* Kent, OH: Kent State University Press, 143–165.

Hater, J. J., & Bass, B. M., (1988). "Supervisor's Evaluations and Subordinates' Perceptions of Transformational Leadership," *Journal of Applied Psychology,* 73, 695–702.

Hodgkinson, C. (1983). *The Philosophy of Leadership,* New York: St. Martin's Press.

Hollander, E. P. (1964). *Leaders, Groups, and Influence,* New York: Oxford University Press.

House, R. J. (1971). "A Path Goal Theory of Leader Effectiveness," *Administrative Science Quarterly,* 16, 3, 321–338.

——, (1977). "A 1976 Theory of Charismatic Leadership," in J. G. Hunt & L. L. Larson (Eds.), *Leadership: The Cutting Edge,* Carbondale: Southern Illinois University Press.

——, Howell, J. M., Shamir, B., Smith, B. J., & Spangler, W. D. (1991). "A 1991 Theory of Charismatic Leadership," Graduate School of Business Administration, University of Western Ontario, London, Ontario, Canada.

——, Spangler, W. D., & Woycke, J. (1991). Personality and Charisma in the U.S. Presidency: A Psychological Theory of Leadership Effectiveness, *Administrative Science Quarterly* (in press).

Howell, J. M. (1988). "Two Faces of Charisma: Socialized and Personalized Leadership in Organizations," in J. A. Conger and R. N. Kanungo (Eds.), *Charismatic Leadership,* 213–236, San Francisco: Jossey-Bass.

—— & Frost, P. J. (1989). "A Laboratory Study of Charismatic Leadership," *Organizational Behavior and Human Decision Process,* 43, 2, 243–269.

—— and Higgins C. (1990). "Champions of Technological Innovation," *Administrative Science Quarterly,* 35, 317–341.

Jahoda, M. (1981). "Work Employment and Unemployment: Values, Theories and Approaches in Social Research," *American Psychologist,* 36, 184–191.

Johnson, M. P. (1982). "Social and Cognitive Features of the Dissolution of a Commitment to a Relationship," in S. Duch (Ed.), *Personal Relationships,* London: Academic Press.

Kanter, R. M. (1967). "Commitment and Social Organization: A Study of Commitment Mechanisms in Utopian Communities," *American Sociological Review,* 33, 4, 499–517.

Kelman, H. C. (1958). "Compliance, Identification and Internalization: Three Processes of Attitude Change," *Journal of Conflict Resolution,* 2, 51–60.

Kinder, D. R., & Sears, D. O. (1985), "Public Opinion and Political Action, in and G. Lindsey & E. Aronson (Eds.), *Handbook of Social Psychology,* 3rd ed., New York: Random House.

Kuhnert, K. W., & Lewis, P. (1987). "Transactional and Transformational Leadership: A Constructive/Developmental Analysis," *Academy of Management Review,* 12, 648–657.

McCall, G. H., & Simmons, J. T. (1978). *Identities and Interaction,* revised ed., New York: Free Press.

McHugh, P. (1968). *Defining the Situation: The Organization of Meaning in Social Interaction,* Indianapolis: Bobbs-Merril.

Meindl, J. R. (1990). "On Leadership: An Alternative to the Conventional Wisdom," in B. M. Straw & L. L. Cummings (Eds.), *Research in Organizational Behavior,* 12, Greenwich, CT: JAI Press, 159–203.

——, Ehrlich, S. B., & Dukerich, J. M. (1985). "The Romance of Leadership," *Administrative Science Quarterly,* 30, 78–102.

—— and Lerner, M. J. (1983). "The Heroic Motive: Some Experimental Demonstrations," *Journal of Experimental Social Psychology,* 19, 1–20.

Mischel, W. (1973). "Toward a Cognitive Social Learning Reconceptulization of Personality," *Psychological Review,* 80, 200–213.

O'Reilly & Chatman, J. (1986). "Organizational Commitment and Psychological Attachment: The Effects of Compliance, Identification and Internalization on Prosocial Behavior," *Journal of Applied Psychology,* 71, 3, 492–499.

Organ, D. W. (1988). *Organizational Citizenship Behavior,* Lexington, MA: Lexington Books.

Pereria, D. (1987). "Factors Associated with Transformational Leadership in an Indian Engineering Firm," Paper Presented at Administrative Science Association of Canada.

Pfeffer, J. (1977). "The Ambiguity of Leadership," *Academy of Management Review,* 2, 104–112.

Podsakoff, P. M., Mackenzie, S. B., Moorman, R. H., & Fetter, R. (1990). "Transformational Leader Behaviors and Their Effects on Followers' Trust in Leader, Satisfaction, and Organizational Citizenship Behaviors," *Leadership Quarterly,* 1, 2, 107–142.

Podsakoff, P. M., Todor W. D. & Skov R. (1982). "Effects of Leader Performance Contingent and Non-Contingent Reward and Punishment Behaviors on Subordinate Performance and Satisfaction," *Academy of Management Journal,* 25, 812–821.

Prentice, D. A. (1987). "Psychological Correspondence of Possessions, Attitudes and Values," *Journal of Personality and Social Psychology,* 53, 6, 993–1003.

Puffer, S. M. (1990). "Attributions of Charismatic Leadership: The Impact of Decision Style, Outcome, and Observer Characteristics," *Leadership Quarterly,* 1, 3, 177–192.

Roberts, N. (1985). "Transforming Leadership: A Process of Collective Action," *Human Relations,* 38, 1023–46.

Roberts, N. C., & Bradley, R. T. (1988). "The Limits of Charisma," in J. A. Conger & R. N. Kanungo (Eds.), *Charismatic Leadership: The Elusive Factor in Organizational Effectiveness,* San Francisco: Jossey-Bass.

Salancik, G. R. (1977). "Commitment and the Control of Organizational Behavior and Belief," in B. M. Staw & G. R. Salancik, (Eds.), *New Directions in Organizational Behavior,* Chicago: St. Clair, 1–54.

—— and Pfeffer, J. (1977). "Constraints on Administrators' Discretion: The Limited Influence of Mayors on City Budgets," *Urban Affairs Quarterly,* June.

Santee, R., & Jackson, S. (1979). "Commitment to Self-Identification: A Sociopsychological Approach to Personality," *Human Relations,* 32, 141–158.

Sashkin, M. (1988). "The Visionary Leader," in J. A. Conger and R. A. Kanungo (Eds.), *Charismatic Leadership: The Elusive Factor in Organizational Effectiveness,* San Francisco: Jossey-Bass, 122–160.

Schlenker, B. R. (1985). "Identity and Self-Identification," in B. R. Schlenker (Ed.), *The Self and Social Life,* New York: McGraw-Hill.

Shamir, B. (1991). "Meaning, Self and Motivation in Organizations," *Organization Studies,* 12, 405–424.

Smith, B. J. (1982). *An Initial Test of a Theory of Charismatic Leadership Based on the Responses of Subordinates,* Unpublished Doctoral Dissertation, University of Toronto, Canada.

Snow, D. A., Rochford, E. B., Worden, S. K., & Benford, R. D. (1986). "Frame Alignment Processes, Micromobilization and Movement Participation," *American Sociological Review,* 51, August, 464–481.

Snyder, M. (1979). "Self Monitoring Processes," in L. Berkowitz (Ed.), *Advances in Experimental Social Psychology,* 12, New York: Academic Press, 85–128.

—— and Ickes, W. (1985). "Personality and Social Behavior," in G. Lindzey, and E. Aronson, *Handbook of Social Psychology,* 3rd ed., New York: Random House.

Staw, B. M. (1980). "Rationality and Justification in Organizational Life," in B. M. Staw, and L. L. Cummings (Eds.), *Research in Organizational Behavior,* 2, Greenwich, CT: JAI Press, 45–80.

Strauss, A. L. (1969). *Mirrors and Masks,* London: M. Robertson.

Stryker, S. (1980). *Symbolic Interactionism: A Social Structural Version,* Menlo Park, CA: The Benjamin/Cummings Publishing Company.

Tajfel, H., & Turner, J. C. (1985). "Social Identity Theory and Intergroup Behavior," in S. Worchel & W. G. Austin (Eds.), *Psychology of Intergroup Relations,* 2nd ed., Chicago: Nelson-Hall, 7–24.

Tichy, N. M., & Devanna, M. A. (1986), *The Transformational Leader,* New York: Wiley.

Trice, H. M., & Beyer, J. M. (1986). "Charisma and Its Routinization in Two Social Movement Organizations," in B. M. Staw & L. L. Cummings (Eds.), *Research in Organizational Behavior,* Greenwich, CT: JAI Press, 113–164.

Turner, R. H. (1968). "The Self Conception in Social Interaction," in G. Gordon and R. Gergen (Eds.), *The Self in Social Interaction,* New York: Wiley.

Waldman, D. A., Bass, B. M., & Einstein, W. O. (1987), "Leadership and Outcomes of Performance Appraisal Processes," *Journal of Occupational Psychology,* 60, 177–186.

Willner, A. R. (1984). *The Spellbinders: Charismatic Political Leadership,* New Haven, CT: Yale University Press.

Yukl, G. A. (1989). *Leadership in Organizations.* 2nd ed., Englewood Cliffs, NJ: Prentice-Hall.

—— and Van Fleet, D. D. (1982). "Cross-Situational, Multimethod Research on Military Leader Effectiveness." *Organizational Behavior and Human Performance,* 30, 87–108.

References Added in Proof

House, R. J., & Howell, J. M. (1992). "Personality and Charismatic Leadership," *Leadership Quarterly,* 3, 2, 81–108.

Howell, J. M., & Avolio, B. J. (1993). "Transformational Leadership, Transactional Leadership, Locus of Control and Support for Innovation: Key Predictors of Consolidated-business-unit Performance," *Journal of American Psychology,* 78, 6, in press.

Keller, R. T. (in press). "Transformational Leadership and the Performance of Research and Development Project Groups," *Journal of Management.*

Kirkpatrick, S. A. (1992). "Decomposing Charismatic Leadership: The Effects of Leader Content and Process on Follower Performance, Attitudes, and Perceptions," Unpublished Doctoral Dissertation, University of Maryland, College Park.

Koene, H., Pennings, H., & Schreuder, M. (1991). "Leadership, Culture, and Organizational Effectiveness," Paper Presented at the Center for Creative Leadership Conference, Boulder, Colorado.

Koh, W. L., Terborg, J. R., & Steers, R. M. (1991). "The Impact of Transformational Leaders on Organization Commitment, Organizational Citizenship Behavior, Teacher Satisfaction and Student Performance in Singapore," Academy of Management Meetings, August, 1991, Miami, FL.

Locke, E. A., & Latham, G. P. (1990), *A Theory of Goal Setting and Task Performance,* Englewood Cliffs, NJ: Prentice-Hall.

Waldman, D. A., & Ramirez (1992), "CEO Leadership and Organizational Performance: The Moderating Effect of Environmental Uncertainty," Concordia University Working Paper 92-10-37, p. 59.

Reading 38

The Role of Followers in the Charismatic Leadership Process: Relationships and Their Consequences

Jane M. Howell
The University of Western Ontario

Boas Shamir
The Hebrew University of Jerusalem

Without followers, there are plainly no leaders or leadership (Hollander, 1993: 29).

> We must know much more about the hitherto nameless persons who comprise the followers of leaders if we are to develop adequate understanding of the reciprocal relationship (Burns, 1978; 61).

Many writers (e.g., Graen & Uhl-Bien, 1995; Hollander, 1993; Jermier, 1993; Klein & House, 1995; Yukl & Van Fleet, 1992) agree that leadership is a relationship that is jointly produced by leaders and followers. Furthermore, these writers and others (e.g., Meindl, 1990, 1995) criticize extant leadership theories for being too "leader centric," in the sense that they focus almost exclusively on the impact of leader traits and behaviors on followers' attitudes and behaviors. However, beyond paying lip service to the importance of followers, few scholars have attempted to theoretically specify and empirically assess the role of followers in the leadership process. As Yukl and Van Fleet conclude, after reviewing the literature, "Most of the prevailing leadership theories have been simple, unidirectional models of what a leader does to subordinates" (1992: 186). And as Lord, Brown, and Freiberg more recently have asserted, "The follower remains an under-explored source of variance in understanding leadership processes" (1999: 167).

This state of affairs is especially noticeable in the case of charismatic leadership. Theories of charismatic leadership have been accused of promoting a "heroic leadership" stereotype (Beyer, 1999; Yukl, 1998), which depicts leaders as heroic figures that are single-handedly capable of determining the fate and fortunes of groups and organizations. In this heroic conception the leader is omnipotent, and followers are submissive to the leader's will and demands. Although this view of charismatic leadership is oversimplified and exaggerated, it is true that currently prominent theories of charismatic leadership (e.g., Conger & Kanungo, 1998; House, 1977) are leader centered, in the sense that they attribute both the positive and negative consequences of charismatic leadership mainly to the leader's personality or behavior.

We believe this leader-centric perspective of charismatic leadership relies too heavily on the influence of leader characteristics and behaviors in producing followers' motivation, attitudes, and behaviors. In this article we attempt to correct the heroic image of charismatic leadership by showing that the role of followers in leadership processes is broader than the role previously given them in leadership theories. Most theories, to the extent they consider the followers at all, have only attended to their characteristics as potential moderators of the impact of the leader's behaviors. We think this role is important but believe that followers also play a more active role in constructing the leadership relationship, empowering the leader and influencing his or her behavior, and ultimately determining the consequences of the leadership relationship. We offer a theoretical analysis of the ways in which followers influence the charismatic leadership process.

Articulating the role of followers in the charismatic leadership process is of theoretical *and* practical importance with respect to the following questions: How can followers amplify charismatic leaders' strengths and modulate their weaknesses so that both serve the common purpose? How do followers shape charismatic leaders' behavior and contribute to leaders' development? How can followers counteract the pitfalls of charismatic leadership, such as the abuse of power? Given the accumulating evidence that demonstrates both the positive and negative outcomes of charismatic leadership (e.g., Conger & Kanungo, 1998; O'Connor, Mumford, Clifton, Gessner, & Connelly, 1995), we believe it is important to explore how followers can foster the charismatic relationship in an attempt to start addressing these questions.

Following other writers (Lord et al., 1999; Shamir, House, & Arthur, 1993), we suggest that followers' self-concepts are powerful determinants of their behavior and their reactions to the leader. Specifically, we distinguish between two types of charismatic relationships—personalized and socialized—and argue that followers' self-concepts play a crucial role in determining the type of relationship they develop with the leader. The type of charismatic relationship followers form with the leader has many consequences: it is reflected in the type of leader the followers select or endorse, the attributions they make to the leader, their susceptibility to the leader's influence, and their dependence on the leader. These consequences, together with the active role followers play in empowering the leader, may determine the ultimate outcomes of the charismatic relationship.

We begin with a brief examination of the role of followers in other (noncharismatic) leadership theories, followed by a description of the uniqueness of the charismatic leader-follower relationship and our definitions of charismatic leadership and followership. We then articulate the distinction between the two types of charismatic relationships—personalized and socialized—and present general propositions about the impact of followers' self-concepts on the type of relationship they develop with the leader. On the basis of these general propositions, we develop a series of more specific propositions about the followers' role in various stages of the charismatic leadership process, starting with the susceptibility of followers to charismatic influence and ending with its consequences. We conclude with the implications of our propositions regarding followers' responsibility for the consequences of charismatic leadership and some suggestions for theoretical extensions.

THE ROLE OF FOLLOWERS IN NONCHARISMATIC LEADERSHIP THEORIES

The idea that followers' characteristics influence the impact of leadership is not new in the litera-

ture (Dvir, 1998). For instance, Fiedler's (1967) contingency model specifies group atmosphere, which includes followers' loyalty, support, and cooperation with the leader, as an important situational determinant of the effectiveness of people-oriented versus task-oriented leaders. Similarly, Hersey and Blanchard (1977) refer to follower maturity level and House (1971), in his path-goal theory, to followers' experience, skills, and confidence as factors influencing the appropriateness of various leadership styles. Vroom and Yetton (1973) include various follower characteristics in their model of decision-making styles, and Kerr and Jermier's (1978) leadership substitutes theory includes follower experience, ability, training, and professional orientation as factors that can negate the need for leadership or moderate its impact on various outcomes.

These theories, however, focus on leader behaviors, such as the structuring of tasks, consideration and support of followers, and the inclusion of followers in leader decision making. They conceive of the role of followers from the point of view of their susceptibility to certain leader behaviors or styles. None of them address the charismatic leadership processes we examine in this article, nor do they consider the more active role followers often play in the leadership process.

An important exception is the leader-member exchange (LMX) approach developed by Graen (1976) and extended by Graen and Uhl-Bien (1995). Unlike most leadership theories, this theory acknowledges the importance of the role of followers in leadership processes, and it emphasizes that both leader and follower mutually determine the quality of the relationship. Graen and Uhl-Bien (1995) classify leadership theories into three domains: the leader, the follower, and the relationship. While LMX theory emphasizes the importance of all three domains, its main contribution has been to shift the focus from the leadership domain to the relationship domain. Indeed, Graen and Uhl-Bien title their article "Relationship-Based Approach to Leadership" and state that "the centroid concept of the theory is that effective leadership processes occur when leaders and followers are able to develop mature leadership relationships (partnerships) and thus gain access to the many benefits these relationships bring" (1995: 225).

Our approach here is consistent with some of the basic tenets of LMX theory but extends it in some important ways. First, the follower domain has remained relatively underdeveloped and less researched in LMX theory, as explicitly acknowledged by Graen and Uhl-Bien (1995: 239). LMX theory suggests that followers' motivation and abilities contribute to the quality of the leader-member relationship, but it does not fully articulate the manner in which followers influence the nature of the relationship. We believe that elaborating on the followers' role in the charismatic leadership process would stimulate more research on the follower domain as advocated by Graen and Uhl-Bien (1995).

Second, as a dyadic approach to leadership, LMX theory focuses on the development of different dyadic relationships between leaders and individual followers. While Graen and Uhl-Bien suggest that the theory can be extended to the group and organization levels, this extension is based on the idea that group and system properties evolve from different combinations of dyadic relationships. In its present form, the LMX model de-emphasizes the relationship between the leader and his or her followers as a group and does not consider the possibility that the followers as a group may influence the leader and the relationship. Charismatic leadership theories, in contrast, consider the possibility that a leader will develop a relationship with his or her followers as a group, and they contain the implied possibility that the followers will react to the leader and influence the leader and the relationship as members of a group—not only as individuals (e.g., Klein & House, 1995; Shamir et al., 1993).

Third, LMX is a gradual leadership-making model that describes the development of the leader-member relationship over time. According to LMX theory, the exchange between leader and member is limited at first to material transactions and only gradually includes more and more social and psychological benefits. Only in the third and final stage of the model does the leader-member relationship reach maturity. At this stage it is characterized by some features that also characterize a charismatic relationship, like a high level of trust between leader and followers and a transformation in the followers' orientation from self-interests to collective interests. Charismatic relationships, however, do not always develop in such a gradual manner and typically are not built on a foundation of material transactions (e.g., Conger & Kanungo, 1998; Klein & House, 1995). Therefore, there is a need to examine the role of followers in such relationships as well. For all of these reasons, we believe there is a need to complement the LMX emphasis on the follower and extend it to charismatic leadership.

THE CHARISMATIC LEADER-FOLLOWER RELATIONSHIP

Over the past twenty years, a new genre of organizational leadership theories, variously termed *charismatic, inspirational,* or *transformational,* has been developed to emphasize exceptional leadership that has profound effects on followers, organizations, and societies. Given the theoretical overlap and convergence of empirical findings, following Shamir and his colleagues (1993), we call this genre of leadership theories "charismatic leadership."

We view charisma as residing in the relationship between leaders who exhibit certain charismatic qualities and behaviors and those followers who have certain perceptions, emotions, and attitudes toward the leader, the group led by the leader, and the vision advocated by the leader (Gardner & Avolio, 1998; House, Spangler, & Woycke, 1991; Klein & House, 1995). We view the follower as "a person who acknowledges the focal leader as a continuing source of guidance and inspiration, regardless of whether there is any formal reporting relationship" (Yukl, 1998: 6).

Many scholars have emphasized that traditional leader-follower relationships can be distinguished from charismatic leader-follower relationships (e.g., Bass, 1985; Burns, 1978; Conger & Kanungo, 1998; House et al., 1991; Kuhnert & Lewis, 1987; Shamir et al., 1993). Followers who share a charismatic relationship with a leader are willing to transcend self-interests for the sake of the collective (team or organization), to engage in self-sacrifice in the interest of the mission, to identify with the vision articulated by the leader, to show strong emotional attachment to the leader, to internalize the leader's values and goals, and to demonstrate strong personal or moral (as opposed to calculative) commitment to those values or goals (e.g., Bass, 1985; House & Shamir, 1993; House et al., 1991). A charismatic relationship is defined by these follower reactions.

We define the charismatic leadership process as the process through which the charismatic relationship is created and maintained. Most theories and studies of charismatic leadership have focused on the leaders' qualities and behaviors that contribute to this process. Specifically, the personal characteristics of charismatic leaders that contribute to the formation of a charismatic relationship include self-confidence, need for influence, moral conviction, and prosocial assertiveness (Bass, 1985; Conger & Kanungo, 1998; House et al., 1991). Charismatic leader behaviors that give the leader the potential for developing a charismatic relationship with followers include communicating an ideological vision that is discrepant from the status quo, intellectually stimulating followers to think in new and different directions, communicating high expectations and confidence in followers, referring to followers' worth and efficacy as individuals and as a collective, and engaging in exemplary and symbolic behavior and role modeling (e.g., Bass, 1985; Conger & Kanungo, 1998; House & Shamir, 1993; Shamir et al., 1993).

Only a few writers have noted that followers may play a role in developing and maintaining charismatic relationships. For instance, Burns (1978) states that transforming leadership is a process of mutual influence between leader and followers, but his analysis of such leadership, like that of Bass (1985), focuses mainly on the leader. Klein and House (1995) use a fire metaphor to suggest that charismatic leadership requires three components: a spark (the leader), flammable material (the followers), and oxygen (a conducive environment). However, by viewing followers as "flammable material" waiting to be ignited by the leader, these scholars portray followers in a limited and passive role. With few exceptions—most notably Weierter's (1997) work, which we discuss below—the role of followers in the charismatic leadership process has not been developed much further. Thus, there is a need to complement charismatic leadership theories in this regard, and we do so in the following sections.

TWO TYPES OF CHARISMATIC RELATIONSHIPS

Our basic argument is that, depending on their self-concepts, followers may develop two different types of charismatic relationships with the leader—personalized or socialized—and these relationships are likely to result in different consequences. Our argument is based on the theoretical foundations laid by Shamir et al. (1993) and Howell (1988; House & Howell, 1992), as recently extended and developed by Kark and Shamir (2002) and Weierter (1997).

According to Shamir et al. (1993), the essence of the charismatic relationship is strong links between followers' self-concepts and the leader, the collectivity (group, organization, movement) led by the leader, and the collective mission. When a charismatic relationship exists, followers identify with the leader, the group, and the collective mission and regard them as expressing important aspects of their self-concepts.

Kark and Shamir (2002) have recently refined Shamir et al.'s theory by integrating it with theoretical work on different levels of self-concept (Brewer & Gardner, 1996; Lord et al., 1999). Brewer and Gardner (1996) contend that the self-concept is multifaceted, consisting of three loci of self: the self as an individual, as an interpersonal being, and as a group member. These three loci of self-definitions represent distinct orientations of identity, each with its own social motivation, sources of self-worth, and types of significant self-knowledge (Brewer & Gardner, 1996: 83).

Kark and Shamir (2002) maintain that of the three self-identity levels suggested by Brewer and Gardner, the relational and collective levels, which link the individual to the leader and the organization, may be central to understanding the charismatic leadership process. The relational self is derived from interpersonal connections and role relationships with specific others (e.g., follower–leader). At this level, individuals conceive of themselves predominantly in terms of their roles in relation to significant others, and their self-worth is derived from appropriate role behavior, as conveyed through reflected appraisals of the other person involved in the relationship. Their primary motivation is to enhance the relationship partner's well-being and derive mutual benefits (Brewer & Gardner, 1996).

The collective self, however, is based on membership in larger, more impersonal collectives or social categories (e.g., work team or organization). At this level of self-identity, individuals use the group prototype as a basis for intergroup comparisons and self-definition and evaluate their self-worth by comparing their group to an outgroup (Brewer & Gardner, 1996). Therefore, their primary motivation is to enhance their group's status and achievements.

Drawing on Brewer and Gardner's work and its extension to the domain of leadership by Lord et al. (1999), Kark and Shamir (2002) propose that there are two types of charismatic relationships; one in which the relational self is activated and the primary mechanism of influence is followers' personal identification with the charismatic leader, and one in which the collective self is activated and the primary mechanism of influence is followers' social identification with the group or the organization. Personal identification is characterized by the attribution of desirable qualities to the leader, a definition of self in terms of the relationship with the leader, and a desire to become like the leader. Social identification is characterized by self-definition in terms of group membership and a perception of group successes and failures as personal successes and failures (Ashforth & Mael, 1989). The two types of identification are not unrelated, and followers often identify with both the leader and the group. However, following Shamir et al. (1993), Kark and Shamir (2002) suggest that when the collective self is activated, the followers identify with the leader not on the basis of the personal qualities they attribute to the leader but, rather, because they see the leader as a representative character or a prototypical member (Hogg, 2001) who embodies a unit's identity and values.

Weierter (1997, 1998) also suggests that there are two types of charismatic relationships, following Howell's (1988; House & Howell, 1992) distinction between two types of charismatic leadership: personalized and socialized. Weierter's distinction, which is supported by some empirical evidence, is based on the nature of the needs that the relationship fulfills for followers.

In the personalized relationship, followers are confused and disoriented before joining the relationship, and the relationship provides them with a clearer sense of self and greater self-confidence. This type of relationship is based mainly on followers' personal identification with the leader, rather than on their identification with or acceptance of the leader's message. Lacking a strong internal reference point from which to judge the leader's messages and influence attempts, followers in this type of relationship are dependent on and vulnerable to the leader.

In the socialized relationship, followers have a clear sense of self and a clear set of values, and the charismatic relationship provides them with a means for expressing their important values within the framework of a collective action. Followers in this type of relationship derive their sense of direction and self-expression not from personal identification with the leader but from the leader's message. In this relationship followers place constraints on the leader's influence, play an active role in determining the values expressed by the leader, are less dependent on the leader, and are less open to manipulation by the leader.

To conclude, following the authors whose work we discuss in this section, we define the personalized charismatic relationship as a relationship between followers and a charismatic leader in which followers' relational level of self is activated. This relationship is based primarily on followers' personal identification with the leader. We define the socialized charismatic relationship as a

relationship between followers and a charismatic leader in which followers' collective level of self is activated. This relationship is based primarily on followers' social identification with the group or organization.

FOLLOWERS' SELF-CONCEPTS AND THE FORMATION OF CHARISMATIC RELATIONSHIPS

The work discussed in the previous section suggests that two characteristics of followers' self-concepts may determine the nature of the charismatic relationship followers form with the leader: their self-concept clarity and their core level of self-identity, relational or collective. In this section we first offer general propositions about the relationships between these self-concept characteristics and the nature of the charismatic relationship. In the following sections we derive from these propositions more specific propositions concerning various stages of the charismatic leadership process: followers' susceptibility to the influence of the leader, followers' responses to the leader, followers' empowerment of the leader, and the consequences of the leadership process.

Campbell (1990) defines the construct of self-concept clarity as the extent to which the contents of the individual's self-concept are clearly and confidently defined, internally consistent, and temporally stable. This construct is related to, but not identical with, self-esteem, which is the evaluative component of the self-concept or the degree to which people perceive their identities and characteristics as good or desirable (Gecas, 1982). Both self-concept clarity and self-esteem are at least partially stable characteristics of individuals. People with high self-esteem are also characterized by high self-concept clarity. People with low self-esteem, however, are typically not characterized by a well-defined negative view of themselves but, rather, by a high level of uncertainty, instability, and inconsistency of their self-concept (Campbell et al., 1996).

Traditionally, the charismatic leadership literature has implied that followers with low self-esteem and low self-concept clarity are more susceptible to the influence of charismatic political and religious leaders (e.g., Freemesser & Kaplan, 1976; Galanter, 1982). For instance, Freemesser and Kaplan (1976) have observed, on the basis of interviews, that those who join a charismatic religious cult have lower self-esteem than a comparable set of others. Similarly, Erikson (1980) has suggested that individuals with identity diffusion (a notion very similar to low self-concept clarity) are particularly susceptible to the influence of ideologies and charismatic leaders. It has also been argued that, in times of stress, anxiety, or ambiguity, followers are more susceptible to domination attempts and persuasive communications by charismatic leaders (e.g., Fromm, 1971). These theories have focused only on "weak" followers' susceptibility to charismatic leadership. The possibility that charismatic leadership may also appeal to "strong" followers and the possibility that followers play an active role in the charismatic relationship have not been considered in these theories.

In contrast with traditional theories, our dual conceptualization of the charismatic relationship does not imply that charismatic leadership appeals only to individuals with chronically low self-concept clarity but, rather, that the level of self-concept clarity will determine the nature of the relationship formed with the leader. People with low self-concept clarity do not have a clear and consistent self-concept that can guide their behavior. Such people are characterized by high self-plasticity, which means they are highly susceptible to self-relevant social cues, especially when such cues come from attractive or powerful others (Brockner. 1988). Since they need self-direction, these people are likely to look for charismatic leaders, identify strongly with such leaders, and gain a sense of self-direction from this identification. The charismatic relationship they form with the leader is likely to be personalized.

In contrast, individuals with high self-concept clarity are likely to have a high motivation for self-expression and to attach a high importance to self-consistency. They are also likely to be motivated to protect and enhance their already high self-esteem. Therefore, they may respond to leaders who link goals and required behaviors to valued components of their self-concepts, particularly their values and social identities. These individuals' relationships with the leader will be based on the extent to which the leader embodies and advocates their salient identities and values and shows how the mission reflects these identities and values. Therefore, such relationships are likely to be socialized.

These arguments suggest that charismatic leadership may be applicable both to weak and vulnerable potential followers and to strong and confident followers, but there will be differences in the nature of the relationship formed between leader and follower and in the primary mechanism of influence: personal or social identification. The conclusions from this discussion are captured in the following propositions.

> *Proposition 1a: Followers with low self-concept clarity will form a personalized charismatic relationship with the leader.*

> *Proposition 1b: Followers with high self-concept clarity will form a socialized charismatic relationship with the leader.*

Another aspect of followers' self-concept that is likely to affect the type of charismatic relationship they form with the leader is their self-identity orientation: relational or collective. Lord et al. (1999) and Kark and Shamir (2002) have focused on the leader's influence on followers' self-identity level, and therefore on the malleable aspects of the self-concept. However, implied in their work is that followers' more stable identity orientations also affect the leadership process. Thus, Lord et al. propose that leaders will be effective to the extent that their actions match the identity level of followers, and they further assert that "followers' self-concepts are powerful determinants of follower behavior and reactions to leaders" (1999: 167).

There are reasons to believe that the self-identity levels identified by Brewer and Gardner (1996) exist as stable properties of the self-concept and not only as transient cognitive states. Brewer and Gardner's categorization is an extension of the individualism-collectivism dimension. This dimension has several meanings and has come under criticism on these grounds (Earley & Gibson, 1998). Brewer and Gardner's work refers to a specific meaning of this dimension—namely, differences in self-construal. According to Markus and Kitayama (1991), individualists define themselves in terms of their personal characteristics, whereas collectivists define themselves in terms of the groups to which they belong. Individualists view the self as autonomous and independent from groups, whereas collectivists view the self as interdependent with others. While this dimension was initially suggested as a variable that distinguishes among cultures, subsequent findings have revealed considerable within-culture variation on this factor (Earley & Gibson, 1998). Both cross-cultural and within-culture approaches to this dimension view independent and interdependent self-construal as relatively stable orientations.

Brewer and Gardner (1996) added a third identity level orientation to this basic distinction. Their work suggests that, in addition to individualists, who define themselves primarily in terms of their individual characteristics and attainments, and collectivists, who define themselves primarily in terms of the groups to which they belong and with which they identify, there are people who define themselves primarily in terms of interpersonal relationships with significant others. Research following Brewer and Gardner's framework reflects the belief that these self-definitions are, at least to some extent, stable (Gabriel & Gardner, 1999).

Based on this differentiation of self-identity levels, we can expect individualists to be less likely to form a charismatic relationship with a leader than people having either a relational or a collectivistic identity orientation. Because individualists focus on personal interests (Erez & Earley, 1993) and are typically motivated by calculative self-centered considerations, they are more likely to be motivated by the creation of strong links between rewards and performance, which characterize noncharismatic exchange-based leadership. Charismatic relationships offer rewards that stem either from the relationship with the leader or from the relationship with the group. Therefore, such relationships are likely to appeal primarily to people with a relational or a collective identity orientation.

People with a relational identity orientation define themselves in terms of their relationships with significant others. They seek direction, self-validation, and satisfaction from personal relationships. Therefore, they are likely to be drawn to attractive or powerful individuals and to form charismatic relationships that will be based on personal identification with the leader. In contrast, the collective identity and values of the group are salient in the self-concept of people with a collective identity orientation, whose self-esteem and satisfaction are based on group achievements and comparisons with other groups. Therefore, collectivists are likely to form a charismatic relationship with a leader who advocates, embodies, and represents the identity and values of the group. This relationship will be based primarily on social identification with the group.

These considerations lead to the following propositions.

Proposition 2a: Followers with a relational identity orientation will form a personalized charismatic relationship with the leader.

Proposition 2b: Followers with a collective identity orientation will form a socialized charismatic relationship with the leader.

FOLLOWERS' SUSCEPTIBILITY TO CHARISMATIC INFLUENCE

Leader-centered theories of charismatic leadership (e.g., Bass, 1985; Conger & Kanungo, 1998; House, 1977) attribute the emergence of such leadership mainly to the traits and/or behaviors of the leader. In contrast, Meindl (1990, 1995) presents a follower-oriented view, according to which charismatic leadership emerges as a result of social psychological forces operating among followers, subordinates, and observers, rather than arising from the traits or behaviors of leaders or out of the interactions between followers and leaders. Meindl advances two explanations: the romance of leadership and social contagion, according to which the source of charismatic leadership is in the followers, not in the leaders. According to this rather radical perspective, it does not matter who occupies the leadership position. Leaders are irrelevant and interchangeable, and their behavior and traits should be removed from the explanation of charismatic leadership.

In contrast with both the dominant leader-centric view and Meindl's follower-centric view, we maintain that the charismatic relationship emerges as a result of the interaction between leaders who display certain traits and behaviors and followers who have different levels of self-concept clarity and identity level orientations. We agree with Meindl that followers play a crucial role in the emergence of charismatic leadership, but we submit that this role centers on the type of leader they are likely to form a charismatic relationship with and on the type of relationship that develops.

The arguments presented in the previous section imply that followers with low self-concept clarity or a relational orientation will be susceptible to a different type of charismatic leader than followers with high self-concept clarity or a collective orientation. Followers with low self-concept clarity or a relational orientation will be more susceptible to the type of leader Howell (1988) calls "personalized"—namely, a leader who is motivated by a need to accumulate personal power and who employs tactics designed to increase followers' identification with him or her. Such a leader is likely to be rejected by followers with high self-concept clarity or a collective orientation. These followers are likely to be susceptible to a socialized leader who seeks power for social purposes and emphasizes collective identity and collective values. In this section we refine and further articulate the rationale behind this expectation.

Followers with low self-concept clarity or a relational identity orientation seek direction and self-validation from their relationship with the leader. Such individuals are likely to be drawn to leaders who appear to be powerful or attractive, because a relationship with such leaders promises to provide them with a higher sense of clarity and self-esteem. Lord's leader categorization theory is potentially relevant to the explanation of the emergence of charismatic leadership in the case of such individuals. According to this theory (Lord, 1985; Lord, Foti, & De Vader, 1984), most people from the same culture have a common set of categories that fit the image of what the typical leader is like. These categories describe the "prototypical" leader. Individuals store leadership prototypes inside their heads and use them to select and evaluate information about a particular leader. When they observe acts of a salient individual, they note particular salient characteristics and compare them against their own leadership prototypes. If there is a match between a small number of observed acts or perceived traits of the salient person and the prototype, the entire prototype is activated, and the person is more likely to be seen as "a leader." It has further been suggested that leaders who match individuals' leadership prototypes are perceived as more powerful and are given more credit for work outcomes (Lord et al., 1984).

It can be assumed that, in order to find clarity and direction in a relationship with a leader, individuals with low self-concept clarity or a relational identity orientation do not just project "a charismatic personality" on any leader. Rather, they seek a relationship with a salient person who displays some traits and behaviors that match their prototype of "a charismatic leader." One implication of this assumption is that such individuals are likely to be drawn to a leader who actively displays prototypical charismatic attributes, such as self-confidence or a high level of energy. In other words, they are likely to be susceptible to image-building efforts that emphasize the personal qualities of the leader and to "fall" for a leader who appears to be charismatic in the prototypical sense of the word.

Another implication is that once such individuals notice several traits or behaviors that match their prototype, they will activate the entire prototype and construct an entire "charismatic personality" for that leader. In other words, they will attribute to that person other traits and behaviors that are included in their prototype of a charismatic leader. This process is likely to lead to an idealized or "romanticized" view of the leader—namely, to the overattribution of positive qualities and a high level of influence to the leader.

Susceptibility to charismatic leadership is likely to be different in the case of followers with high self-concept clarity or with a collective identity orientation. In the case of followers with high self-concept clarity, in order for a charismatic relationship to emerge, the leader needs to appeal to existing elements of the followers' self-concepts—namely, their values and identities. Such followers may actively choose a leader and decide to follow him or her, based on the extent to which the leader is perceived to represent their values and identities. Because values and identities have a social basis, these followers' attraction to the leader is likely to be more social than personal (Hogg, 2001).

Social attraction as the basis for susceptibility to charismatic leadership is likely to be particularly relevant in the case of followers with a collective orientation, especially followers who are already strongly identified with the group, unit, or organization to which they belong. While charismatic leaders engage in verbal and symbolic behaviors in the attempt to raise the collective identity in followers' self-concepts and to link it to the organizational mission and followers' tasks (Shamir et al., 1993), identification with the group may exist prior to the emergence of charismatic leadership and may affect its emergence. According to Hogg's (2001) social identity theory of leadership, which is supported by a series of empirical studies, when group membership is salient in members' self-concepts, members are likely to be attracted to the most prototypical member of the group—the one who embodies the aspirations, attitudes, and identity of the group. This individual will be endorsed by the group and imbued with prestige and status, eventually leading to the construction of a charismatic relationship.

To summarize the arguments presented in this section, we offer the following propositions.

Proposition 3: Followers with low self-concept clarity or a relational identity orientation will form a charismatic relationship with a leader on the basis of the personal attributes of the leader and the match between these attributes and the followers' prototype of a charismatic leader.

Proposition 4: Followers with low self-concept clarity or a relational identity orientation will be more susceptible than followers with high self-concept clarity or a collective identity orientation to image-building efforts, on the part of the leader, that emphasize the leader's power and desirable personal attributes.

Proposition 5: Followers with low self-concept clarity or a relational identity orientation will have a higher tendency than followers with high self-concept clarity or a collective identity orientation to idealize or romanticize the leader, in the sense of overattributing to the leader desirable qualities and a high level of influence.

Proposition 6: Followers with high self-concept clarity or a high collective identity orientation will form a charismatic relationship with the leader on the basis of social attraction.

Proposition 6a: Followers with high self-concept clarity will form a charismatic relationship with a leader on the basis of the extent to which the leader and his/her messages match the followers' values and identities.

Proposition 6b: Followers with a high collective identity orientation will form a charismatic relationship with a leader on the basis of the match between the leader's traits and behaviors and the group identity.

FOLLOWER RESPONSES TO CHARISMATIC LEADERSHIP

Once personalized or socialized charismatic relationships are formed, they have different consequences, in terms of followers' responses to the leader's influence attempts. Since a personalized relationship is formed by followers with low self-concept clarity, and because such a relationship includes idealization and romanticization of the leader, followers who form this type of relationship are likely to be prone to "blind" faith in the leader and to "hypercompliance" (Zablocki, 1999) and unquestioning obedience to the leader. Furthermore, because a personalized relationship is based on personal identification with the leader, it is likely to lead to dependency on the leader, in the sense that the absence or departure of the leader will seriously decrease followers' motivation and commitment to the leader's mission (Kark & Shamir, 2002).

In contrast, because a socialized charismatic relationship is formed by people with high self-concept clarity and does not include over-attribution of positive qualities and influence of the leader, such a relationship will not lead to blind faith and unquestioning obedience to the leader. Followers in this type of relationship are not susceptible to the leader's influence because he or she is perceived to possess unusual qualities. Rather, they are responsive to the values and identities emphasized by the leader's vision and other forms of behavior. Such

followers are likely to be more discriminating in their responses to the leader and to exercise greater independent judgment and critical thinking. They will follow a leader to the extent that he or she appeals to substantive aspects of their self-concepts—namely, their identities and values. For such individuals, obedience to the leader is not automatic but depends on the extent to which the leader embodies the followers' salient identities and values and shows how the mission reflects these identities and values. Furthermore, because their relationship with the leader is based on social rather than personal identification, these followers are less likely to become dependent on the leader. Rather, they are more likely to manifest self-reliance and autonomy. Their commitment to the mission and ability to work toward its achievement are less likely to be affected by the leader's absence or departure than in the case of personalized relationships.

Proposition 7: Followers who form a personalized charismatic relationship with a leader are more prone to blind faith and unquestioning obedience to the leader than followers who form a socialized charismatic relationship with the leader.

Proposition 8: Followers who form a personalized charismatic relationship with a leader are more likely to become dependent on the leader than followers who form a socialized charismatic relationship with the leader.

FOLLOWERS' EMPOWERMENT OF THE CHARISMATIC LEADER

Followers' impact on the charismatic leadership process is not only limited to their role in the emergence of the charismatic relationship and to their selective and differential responses to the leader's influence attempts. A third way in which followers play a role in the charismatic leadership process is through their impact on the leader. Some writers have described charismatic leaders as puppets who are controlled by their followers. For instance, Hodgkinson quotes the Comte de Mirabeau, who said, "There goes the mob, and I must follow them, for I am their leader" (according to one story, he said so while sitting in a cafe and suddenly hearing a disturbance outside; 1983: 163). Hodgkinson then quotes Speer, who wrote about Goebbels and Hitler being

> molded by the mob itself, guided by its yearning and daydreams. Of course, Goebbels and Hitler knew how to penetrate through to the instincts of their audience; but in a deeper sense they derived

their whole existence from the audience. Certainly the masses roared to the beat set by Hitler and Goebbels' baton; yet they were not the true conductors. The mob determined the theme (Speer, 1970: 19–20; cited in Hodgkinson, 1983; 163).

We do not accept this extreme view as applied to the entire phenomenon of charismatic leadership. It may not even apply to the leaders discussed by Speer, who overlooked the fact that Hitler developed his ambitions and vision long before he was popular or had an audience he could follow. Charismatic leadership requires that the leader display a strong sense of commitment to the mission, a high level of self-confidence, and a willingness to take risks for the achievement of the collective mission. Charismatic leaders do not just wish to identify group preferences and represent or reflect them. They have their own agenda and are often willing to enter into conflicts in order to promote it. Their actions do not necessarily depend on wide consensus and wide approval, at least not initially. Their self-confidence is often higher than the confidence of most group or organizational members. Indeed, it is the ability to transcend currently popular views and the current level of confidence among potential followers that often makes a leader charismatic.

This does not mean, however, that even charismatic leaders can maintain their sense of mission and self-confidence without followers' support. Followers may endorse leaders, vote for leaders, and give them the power necessary to carry out their role. Thus, followers' responses are necessary in order to sustain charismatic leaders. Their support may increase leaders' self-confidence and their willingness to continue to self-sacrifice and invest energy in the collectivity and mission. In short, followers' actions may empower leaders.

In recent years, scholars have paid much attention to the concept of empowerment. However, this attention has focused only on the empowerment of followers or subordinates by their leaders or managers. Empowerment by the leader has been regarded as one way in which followers can be given a more practice role in the leadership process (Hollander, 1992). We suggest that followers can empower their leaders no less than leaders can empower their followers and that the development of charismatic leadership may depend on such empowerment.

Conger and Kanungo (1988) defined empowerment in terms of increasing the self-efficacy of others. Thomas and Velthouse (1990) then broadened this definition, arguing that empowerment means increasing both the capacity of an individual to perform his or her role and the energy the individual devotes to the role. These authors define empowerment as intrinsic motivation manifested in four cognitions reflecting an individual's orientation to his or her work role: meaning, competence, self-determination, and impact. Meaning involves a fit between the requirements of the role and an individual's beliefs, values, and behaviors. Competence refers to self-efficacy specific to the role and is analogous to agency beliefs, personal mastery, and effort-performance expectancy. Self-determination is a sense of choice in initiating and regulating actions. Impact is the degree to which an individual can influence strategic, administrative, and operating outcomes at work.

Thus, empowered individuals (1) find meaning in their role involvement, (2) feel efficacious with respect to their ability and capacity to perform, (3) have a sense of determination regarding specific means to achieve a desired outcome within their role, and (4) believe that they have control over desired outcomes and can have an impact on the environment. These states or characteristics can be seen as necessary conditions for the exercise of charismatic leadership. Individuals have to find meaning in their role, feel self-efficacious, have a sense of self-determination, and feel they have an impact in order to be charismatic leaders (Gardner & Avolio, 1998; House, 1977).

The leader's self-concept is also relevant to the charismatic process (Sosik & Dworakivsky, 1998). In the majority of cases, for a leader to be able to lead in a charismatic manner, he or she must have a high sense of self-worth, self-esteem, self-consistency, and self-efficacy. Since self-concepts are determined in part by the reflected appraisals of others (Cooley, 1902; Marsh, Barnes, & Hocevar, 1985; Miyamoto & Dornbusch, 1956), followers' approval and support, together with their attribution of special qualities to the leader, are likely to increase these self-perceptions.

According to Spreitzer (1995), one of the factors contributing to empowerment is sociopolitical support: endorsement and support from or legitimacy granted by organizational constituencies. An important constituency, and therefore an important source of empowerment, is the individual's subordinates or followers. Spreitzer also argues that access to resources increases the level of empowerment of an individual. Followers may be viewed as the main resource needed for the leader to promote his or her mission (Conger & Kanungo, 1988). They often control many resources needed by the leader: information, expertise, cooperation, and legitimacy. Followers' acceptance and approval of the leader, support for the leader, and cooperation with the leader increase the availability of these resources for the leader and, thus, empower him or her.

Followers also serve as a main source of feedback for the leader. Their agreement with the leader and their respect and admiration for the leader affirm the correctness of his or her beliefs and validate the direction in which he or she tries to lead. Followers also provide legitimacy for that person's leadership and affirm his or her status.

Furthermore, many studies of the Pygmalion effect (Eden, 1990) have shown that significant others' positive expectations increase the self-efficacy of people and, ultimately, their performance. All Pygmalion studies, however, have focused on superiors' expectations of their subordinates. We hypothesize that similar Pygmalion effects will be found in the other direction as well. Followers' positive expectations of their leader may increase the leader's self-efficacy and confidence and, thus, his or her ability to display charismatic behaviors, such as developing an even more challenging vision of the future. Such positive expectations may exist prior to followers' exposure to leader behaviors and stem from followers' need for orientation or from the leader's reputation, may develop out of first impressions of the leader and the degree to which these impressions fit followers' prototype of a charismatic leader, or may develop later as responses to the leader's behaviors. Dvir and Shamir (2002) recently found that direct followers' relatedness to the leader, as measured by satisfaction with the leader, perceived leader effectiveness, similarity to the leader, and willingness to exert extra effort, predicted charismatic leadership.

Proposition 9: The more followers accept the leader, approve of the leader, show the leader respect and admiration, cooperate with the leader, and provide the leader with resources, the more the leader will feel empowered, in the sense of having greater role involvement and meaningfulness, higher self-efficacy, and a greater sense of determination and control over means and outcomes.

Proposition 10: The more the leader feels empowered, the more he or she will engage in charismatic behaviors, such as displaying self-confidence and presenting a challenging vision. This, in turn, will increase the charismatic leader's influence on followers.

CONSEQUENCES OF CHARISMATIC RELATIONSHIPS

The empowerment of the charismatic leader by followers may have positive or negative consequences, depending on both leader and followers. In the case of personalized charismatic leaders (Howell, 1988), followers' support and admiration may feed both the leader's desire for absolute personal power and his or her delusions of omnipotence. But even if the leader initially does not seek self-aggrandizement or personal power, personalized charismatic relationships may "overempower" the leader, because such relationships include adoration, idolization, and unquestioning obedience to the leader. The leader may internalize the exaggerated reflected appraisals of followers and eventually develop an illusion of omnipotence. This, in turn, may lead to the abandonment of ethical and other restraints on the use of power.

Socialized charismatic relationships may also empower the leader. However, since such relationships do not include idolization and unquestioning obedience to the leader, they are not likely to reinforce or create a delusion of omnipotence on the part of the leader. In such relationships, followers' acceptance, support, and approval of the leader are accompanied by their exercise of independent judgment and their ethical standards. Therefore, the leader will be empowered only as long as he or she exercises restraints on the use of power, conforms to ethical standards, and pursues the collective goal.

A major implication of this discussion is that followers may be no less responsible than the leader for the consequences of charismatic leadership. Previous writing about the "dark side" of charisma (Conger, 1990; House & Howell, 1992; Howell & Avolio, 1992; Sankowsky, 1995) have tended to attribute the negative consequences mainly to the traits and behaviors of the leader. Here we suggest that the "blame" for such consequences may be with followers as well. Blind adoration and unquestioning obedience to the leader not only remove potential obstacles from the leader's path but also may empower the leader with a personalized power motivation to pursue his or her misguided and potentially harmful goals. Acceptance, support, and approval of the leader, when they are accompanied by the exercise of independent judgment and ethical standards by followers, may disempower the leader with a personalized power motive and empower the leader with a socialized need for power.

Proposition 11: Personalized charismatic relationships are more likely than socialized charismatic relationships to lead to harmful consequences for the organization and its members.

IMPLICATIONS AND OPPORTUNITIES FOR THEORETICAL EXTENSION

Leaders and followers both play an active role in shaping their mutual relationships, and therefore in shaping organizational outcomes (Dvir, 1998; Graen & Uhl-Bien, 1995). In our theoretical analysis we have attempted to correct the heroic bias in current charismatic leadership theories by focusing on the followers' role in the charismatic leadership process. We integrated self-identity theory with two types of charismatic relationships—socialized and personalized—and derived propositions about how followers' self-concepts influence the type of relationship they form with the leader. We then examined how followers may affect various stages of the charismatic relationship process, including susceptibility to charismatic leadership, responses to charismatic influence, empowerment of the leader, and consequences of the charismatic relationship for individuals and organizations. The research propositions advanced in this paper need to be tested empirically.

We have rejected a unidirectional explanation of charismatic leadership. We do not believe that charisma is either totally leader produced or totally follower produced. Rather, we have defined charisma as a relationship that is jointly produced by leaders and followers. At the same time, our theoretical analysis gives followers a much more central role than they have had traditionally in theory and research on organizational leadership in general and charismatic leadership in particular. Previous writings have placed the responsibility for the development and outcomes of personalized and socialized charismatic relationships squarely on the shoulders of the leader. We have argued that the nature of these relationships and their impact rest on the follower as well.

Our analysis explicitly acknowledges that the formation of different types of charismatic relationships operates within the constraints and opportunities presented by followers. These constraints and opportunities include followers' self-concept clarity, self-identity orientation, attribution tendencies, leadership prototypes, and social attraction. Furthermore, our theoretical analysis acknowledges that the nature of the charismatic relationship produces selective and differential follower responses to leaders' influence attempts. Our discussion of follower empowerment of a leader distinguishes between "personalized empowerment," in which followers' submissive behaviors and unquestioning

obedience reinforce the self-aggrandizing views of the leader, and "socialized empowerment," in which followers accept the leader conditionally, reinforce some of his or her behaviors, and challenge him or her intellectually and ideologically. The latter type of empowerment may create changes in the leader, which, according to Burns (1978), is part of the transformational leadership process.

Both the academic and management literature are replete with compelling examples of the abuse of power by leaders, especially charismatic leaders, in business, education, and politics (e.g., Bedeian, 2002; Gardner, 1990; Khurana, 2002; Maccoby, 2000). A fundamental question is how can the pitfalls of charismatic leadership, such as the abuse of power, be counteracted? While some scholars have claimed that charismatic leaders need to engage in self-reflection, self-monitoring, and feedback seeking in order to recognize the deleterious impact of their actions and change their behavior accordingly (e.g., Sankowsky, 1995), we believe this recommendation may be naïve. It is unlikely that leaders involved in personalized charismatic relationships will engage in the necessary self-monitoring and correction to stem their abuse of power. Rather, our model suggests that followers may play a powerful role in shaping charismatic leader behaviors by virtue of their differential responses to the leader. Follower obedience and loyal submission, as well as uncritical acceptance and endorsement of a misguided course of action, may reinforce the personalized leader's belief in his or her invincibility and the belief that follower behavior is not self-controlled but controlled by the leader (Kipnis, 1976). In contrast, follower initiative and independent thinking may encourage the socialized leader to govern in an egalitarian way, to recognize followers' needs, and to encourage followers' divergent views.

To amplify charismatic leaders' strengths and to modulate their weaknesses, our analysis suggests that actions need to be taken at the organizational level. Senior managers need to monitor the type of leader–follower relationships that develop in their units and to intervene in order to prevent the formation of personalized relationships in various ways. Howell and House (1995) recommend several strategies to support followers in their efforts to curb the abuse of power by leaders, including giving followers periodic opportunities to provide anonymous feedback concerning their superiors to higher-level managers and providing the means by which followers can report flagrantly unethical behaviors to higher-level managers without fear of reprisal from their leaders, such as the use of "hotlines."

Another strategy is for organizations to have a well-developed organizational ideology and a socialization process that emphasizes the values underlying the ideology. In order to minimize the occurrence of personalized charismatic relationships, organizations need to attend constantly to the development, maintenance, and enforcement of norms of trust, collaboration, openness, integrity, and respect for expertise. Organizational policies and actions that increase social identification might reduce the risk of leader-follower relationships that are based primarily on personal identification.

Our theoretical analysis can be extended in several ways. First, here we have focused mainly on the individual level of analysis—that followers influence the charismatic leadership process as a collection of individuals with certain attributes. Our model could also be extended to the group level of analysis by outlining the group processes and the characteristics and actions of followers as a group that influence the charismatic leadership process. Specifically, there are two ways in which followers' collective characteristics may influence the charismatic leadership process: (1) certain group or collective characteristics, such as group culture, norms, and cohesiveness, may make the group, as a group, more or less receptive to charismatic leadership: (2) different members of the same group or organization may have different relationships with the same leader. Thus, there may be considerable intra-group variance in both the strength of the charismatic relationship with the leader and the type of charismatic relationship (Weierter, 1997). This is the issue of the homogeneity of charismatic relationships within a group or organization that was first raised by Klein and House (1995).

Second, the present analysis distinguishes between two types of charismatic relationships—personalized and socialized—which may represent an oversimplification of the complexities and dynamics of the leader-follower relationship. It is possible that the charismatic relationship may involve a mix of personalized and socialized elements, and further elaboration of the individual and group characteristics and processes and contextual factors that influence the nature of this "mixed" relationship is needed.

Third, our model of the follower's role in the charismatic leadership process could be further extended to include contextual variables. For instance, times of instability, crisis, and turmoil increase the likelihood that people will feel helpless, threatened, and anxious and will therefore be more susceptible to the influence of a personalized charismatic leader who appears uniquely qualified to lead them out of their distress. Under conditions of acute follower distress, the personalized charismatic leader's influence is more likely to induce suspension of independent assessment of reality on the part of followers and blind obedience to the leader. It is also possible that potential followers' need for orientation, and therefore their susceptibility to frame-alignment influence by the leader, may exist in other unique or ambiguous situations that are not necessarily characterized by psychological distress—for instance, when followers face particularly difficult and challenging tasks (Shamir & Howell, 1999).

Fourth, our analysis can be further refined by including other follower characteristics that influence followers' receptivity to personalized or socialized charismatic relationships, such as their level of moral development or their values. For instance, Kelman and Hamilton (1989) studied the individual differences involved in people's readiness to challenge the legitimacy of authoritative demands and to disobey leaders' orders that appeared unlawful or immoral. They reported that role-oriented individuals were motivated by the obligation to obey, arising from identification with the leader that fostered a tendency to obey without question and to deny personal responsibility for actions taken under the leader's orders. In contrast, value-oriented individuals were motivated by an internalized commitment to societal rules necessary to fulfill collective, shared values, which encouraged a questioning attitude toward leaders and the assertion of personal responsibility for actions taken under the leaders' orders.

We have attempted to show that it is not necessary to dismiss the leader in order to make more room for followers in the explanation of charismatic leadership (Meindl, 1990). Our analysis does not reduce the leader's responsibility for the consequences of charismatic relationships. However, the emphasis on followers enlightens us about the active role followers assume in determining the deleterious and beneficial consequences of charismatic leadership. We hope that scholars and practitioners alike will focus the spotlight on the development of effective followers, as well as effective leaders. In our view, understanding followers is as important as understanding leaders.

References

Ashforth, B. E., & Mael, F. 1989. Social identity theory and the organization. *Academy of Management Review,* 14, 20–39.

Bass, B. M. 1985. *Leadership and performance beyond expectations.* New York: Free Press.

Bedeian, A. G. 2002. The dean's disease: How the darker side of power manifests itself in the office of the dean. *Learning and Education*, 1, 164–173.

Beyer, J. M. 1999. Taming and promoting charisma to change organizations. *Leadership Quarterly,* 10, 307–330.

Brewer, M. B., & Gardner, W. L. 1996. Who is this "we"? Levels of collective identity and self-representations. *Journal of Personality and Social Psychology,* 50, 543–549.

Brockner, J. 1988. *Self esteem at work: Research, theory and practice.* Lexington, MA: Lexington Books.

Burns, J. M. 1978. *Leadership.* New York: Harper & Row.

Campbell, J. D. 1990. Self-esteem and clarity of the self-concept. *Journal of Personality and Social Psychology,* 59, 538–549.

Campbell, J. D., Trapnell, P. D., Heine, S. J., Katz, I. M., Lavallee, L. F., & Lehman, D. R. 1996. Self-concept clarity: Measurement, personality correlates, and cultural boundaries. *Journal of Personality and Social Psychology,* 70, 141–156.

Conger, J. A. 1990. The dark side of leadership. *Organizational Dynamics,* 19(2), 44–55.

Conger, J. A., & Kanungo, R. N. 1988. The empowerment process: Integrating theory and practice. *Academy of Management Review,* 13, 471–482.

Conger, J. A., & Kanungo, R. N. 1998. *Charismatic leadership in organizations.* Thousand Oaks, CA: Sage.

Cooley, C. H. 1902. *Humane nature and the social order.* New York: Scribner.

Dvir, T. 1988. *Impact of transformational leadership training on follower development and performance: A field experiment.* Unpublished doctoral dissertation. Faculty of Management Tel-Aviv University, Israel.

Dvir, T., & Shamir, B. 2002. *Transformational followership: A longitudinal study of follower group characteristics as predictors of leadership.* Working paper, Faculty of Management, Tel-Aviv University, Israel.

Earley, P. C., & Gibson, C. B. 1998. Taking stock in our progress on individualism-collectivism: 100 years of solidarity and community. *Journal of Management,* 24, 265–304.

Eden, D. 1990. *Pygmalion in management.* Lexington, MA: Heath.

Erez, M., & Earley, P. C. 1993. *Culture, self-identity and work.* New York: Oxford University Press.

Fiedler, F. E. 1967. *A theory of leadership effectiveness.* New York: McGraw-Hill.

Freemesser, G. F., & Kaplan, H. B. 1976. Self-attitudes and deviant behavior: The case of the charismatic religious movement. *Journal of Youth and Adolescence,* 5(1), 1–9.

Fromm, E. 1971. *Escape from freedom.* New York: Avon.

Gabriel, S., & Gardner, W. L. 1999. Are there "his" and "hers" types of interdependence? The implications of gender differences in collective vs. relational interdependence for affect, behavior and cognition. *Journal of Personality and Social Psychology,* 77, 642–645.

Galanter, M. 1982. Charismatic religious sects and psychiatry: An overview. *Journal of Psychiatry,* 139, 1539–1548.

Gardner, J. W. 1990. *On leadership.* New York: Free Press.

Gardner, W. L., & Avolio, B. J. 1998. The charismatic relationship: A dramaturgical perspective. *Academy of Management Review,* 23, 32–58.

Gecas, V. 1982. The self-concept. *Annual Review of Sociology,* 8, 1–33.

Graen, G. B. 1976. Role making processes within complex organizations. In M. D. Dunnette (Ed.), *Handbook of industrial and organizational psychology:* 1201–1245. Chicago: Rand-McNally.

Graen, G. B., & Uhl-Bien, M. 1995. Relationship-based approach to leadership: Development of leader-member-exchange (LMX) theory over 25 years: Applying a multi-level multi-domain perspective. *Leadership Quarterly,* 6, 219–247.

Hersey, P., & Blanchard, K. H. 1977. *The management of organizational behavior* (3rd ed.). Englewood Cliffs, NJ: Prentice-Hall.

Hodgkinson, C. 1983. *The philosophy of leadership.* New York: St. Martin's Press.

Hogg, M. A. 2001. A social identity theory of leadership. *Personality and Social Psychology Review,* 5, 184–200.

Hollander, E. P. 1992. Leadership, followership, self, and others. *Leadership Quarterly,* 3, 43–54.

Hollander, E. P. 1992. Legitimacy, power and influence: A perspective on relational features of leadership. In M. M. Chemers & R. Ayman (Eds.), *Leadership theory and research: Perspectives and directions:* 29–48. San Diego: Academic Press.

House, R. J., 1971. A path-goal theory of leader effectiveness. *Administrative Science Quarterly,* 16, 321–339.

House, R. J. 1977. A 1976 theory of charismatic leadership. In J. G. Hunt & L. L. Larson (Eds.), *Leadership: The cutting edge:* 189–207. Carbondale, IL.: Southern Illinois University Press.

House, R. J., & Howell, J. M. 1992. Personality and charismatic leadership. *Leadership Quarterly,* 3, 81–108.

House, R. J., & Shamir, B. 1993. Toward the integration of charismatic, visionary and transformational leadership theories. In M. M. Chemers & R. Ayman (Eds.), *Leadership theory and research: Perspectives and directions:* 81–107. San Diego: Academic Press.

House, R. J., Spangler, W. D., & Woycke, J. 1991. Personality and charisma in the U.S. presidency: A psychological theory of leadership effectiveness. *Administrative Science Quarterly, 36,* 374–396.

Howell, J. M. 1988. Two faces of charisma: Socialized and personalized leadership in organizations. In J. A. Conger, R. N. Kanungo, & Associates (Eds.), *Charismatic leadership: The elusive factor in organizational effectiveness:* 213–236. San Francisco: Jossey-Bass.

Howell, J. M, & Avolio, B. J. 1992. The ethics of charismatic leadership: Submission or liberation? *Academy of Management Executive,* 6(2), 43–54.

Howell, J. M., & House, R. J. 1995. *The bright and dark sides of charismatic leadership.* Paper presented at the annual Society of Industrial and Organizational Psychology Conference, Orlando, FL.

Jermier, J. M. 1993. Introduction: Charismatic leadership: Neo-Weberian perspectives. *Leadership Quarterly,* 4, 217–234.

Kark, R., & Shamir, B. 2002. The dual effect of transformational leadership: Priming relational and collective selves and further effects on followers. In B. J. Avolio & F. J. Yammarino (Eds.), *Transformational and charismatic leadership: The road ahead:* 67–91. Oxford: Elsevier Science.

Kelman, H. C., & Hamilton, V. L. 1989. *Crimes of obedience: Towards social psychology of authority and responsibility.* New Haven, CT: Yale University Press.

Kerr, S., & Jermier, J. M. 1978. Substitutes for leadership: Their meaning and measurement. *Organizational Behavior and Human Performance,* 22, 375–403.

Khurana, R. 2002. *Searching for a corporate savior: The irrational quest for charismatic CEOs.* Princeton, NJ: Princeton University Press.

Kipnis, D. 1976. *The powerholders.* Chicago: University of Chicago Press.

Klein, K. J., & House, R. J. 1995. On fire: Charismatic leadership and levels of analysis. *Leadership Quarterly,* 6, 183–198.

Kuhnert, K. W., & Levis, P. 1987. Transactional and transformational leadership: A constructive/developmental analysis. *Academy of Management Review,* 12, 648–657.

Lord, R. G. 1985. An information processing approach to social perception, leadership perceptions and behavioral measurement in organizational settings. *Research in Organizational Behavior,* 7, 87–128.

Lord, R. G., Brown, D. J., & Freiberg, S. J. 1999. Understanding the dynamics of leadership: The role of follower self-concepts in the leader/follower relationship. *Organizational Behavior and Human Decision Processes,* 78, 167–203.

Lord, R. G., Foti, R. J., & De Vader, D. L. 1984. A test of cognitive categorization theory: Internal structure, information processing and leadership perceptions. *Organizational Behavior and Human Performance,* 34, 343–378.

MaCcoby, M. 2000. Narcissistic leaders: The incredible pros, the inevitable cons. *Harvard Business Review,* 78(1), 69–77.

Markus, H., & Kitayama, S. 1991. Culture and the self: Implications for cognitions, emotion and motivation. *Psychological Review,* 98, 224–252.

Marsh, H. W., Barnes, J., & Hocaevar, D. 1985. Self-other agreement on multidimensional self-concept rating: Factor analysis and multitrait-multimethod analysis. *Journal of Personality and Social Psychology,* 49, 1360–1377.

Meindl, J. R. 1990. On leadership: An alternative to the conventional wisdom. *Research in Organizational Behavior,* 12, 159–203.

Meindl, J. R. 1995. The romance of leadership as a follower-centric theory: A social constructionist approach. *Leadership Quarterly,* 6, 329–341.

Miyamoto, S. F., & Dornbusch, S. 1956. A test of interactionist hypothesis of self-perception. *American Journal of Sociology,* 61, 399–403.

O'Connor, J., Mumford, M. D., Clifton, T. C., Gessner, T. L., & Connelly, M. S. 1995. Charismatic leaders and destructiveness: An historimetric study. *Leadership Quarterly,* 6, 529–555.

Sankowsky, D. 1995. The charismatic leader as narcissist: Understanding the abuse of power. *Organizational Dynamics,* 23(4), 57–71.

Shamir, B., House, R. J., & Arthur, M. B. 1993. The motivational effects of charismatic leadership: A self-concept based theory. *Organization Science,* 4, 577–594.

Shamir, B., & Howell, J. M. 1999. Organizational and contextual influences on the emergence and effectiveness of charismatic relationship. *Leadership Quarterly,* 10, 257–283.

Sosik, J. J., & Dworakivsky, A. C. 1998. Self-concept based aspects of the charismatic leader: More than meets the eye. *Leadership Quarterly,* 9, 503–526.

Speer, A. 1970. *Inside the Third Reich.* New York: Macmillan.

Spreitzer, G. M. 1995. Individual empowerment in the workplace: Dimensions, measurement, validation. *Academy of Management Journal,* 38, 1442–1465.

Thomas, K. W., & Velthouse, B. A. 1990. Cognitive elements of empowerment: An interpretive model of intrinsic task motivation. *Academy of Management Review,* 15, 666–681.

Vroom, V. H., & Yetton, P. W. 1973. *Leadership and decision making.* Pittsburgh: University of Pittsburgh Press.

Weierter, S. J. M. 1997. Who want to play "follow the leader"? A theory of charismatic relationships based on routinized charisma and followers characteristics. *Leadership Quarterly,* 8, 171–194.

Weierter, S. J. M. 1998. *Charismatic relationships between leaders and followers.* Unpublished doctoral dissertation, Graduate School of Management, University of Queensland, Australia.

Yukl, G. 1998. *Leadership in organizations* (4th ed.). Upper Saddle River, NJ: Prentice-Hall.

Yukl, G., & Van Fleet, D. D. 1992. Theory and research on leadership in organizations. In M. D. Dunnette & L. M. Hough (Eds.), *Handbook of industrial and organizational psychology* (2nd ed.): 147–197. Palo Alto, CA: Consulting Psychologists Press.

Zablocki, B. D. 1999. Hyper-compliance in charismatic groups. In D. D. Franks & T. S. Thomas (Eds.), *Mind, brain, and society: Toward a neurosociology of emotion:* 287–310. Stamford, CT: JAI Press.

Transformational Leadership

As noted at the outset of the previous chapter, charismatic and transformational leadership are often intertwined. Instead of treating them the same, yet recognizing their close connection they are presented here in sequential order starting with charismatic leadership as it appeared in the literature first (cf. Max Weber's writings in 'The theory of social and economic organization,' 1947).

While the focus on the charismatic and transformational leader, in part, encourages a look at the person, his/her behaviors, and the context out of which this type of leadership is born, the dominant paradigm in the study of leadership had shifted in the 1960s from the study of leader traits, behaviors, and situational forces toward a focus on transactions (i.e, exchanges) that occur between the leader and his or her followers (Bass, 1990).[1] In 1978 James Burns presented a leadership model introducing the transformational leader, differentiating that approach to leadership from the transactional leader (one who, for example, offers rewards in exchange for individual and group effort directed toward goal attainment.).[2] Since the publication of Burns's book *Leadership,* the past two decades have witnessed a great deal of scholarship focused on advancing our understanding of the transformational leader and transformational leadership.

Both transformational and charismatic forms of leadership are commonly discussed in terms of the effects that the leader has upon his or her followers and in terms of the relationship that exists between leader and followers. It has been suggested that transformational leaders move and change (fix) things in a big way, not by offering inducements but by inspiring others. Transformational leadership motivates followers to transcend their self-interests for a collective purpose. Transformational leaders use their personal values, vision, commitment to a mission, and passion to energize and move others (Burns, 1978). This form of leadership produces an admiration of and trust in the leader that results in followers' going above and beyond expectation and accomplishing the extraordinary. According to Bass (1990) there have been many great transformational leaders; among them he includes Abraham Lincoln, Franklin Delano Roosevelt, and John F. Kennedy.

The distinction between the charismatic and the transformational leader will not always be readily apparent. Some leadership scholars make no distinction between the two (using the terms interchangeably), while others conceptualize charisma as one of several attributes that may define the transformational leader. Charismatic leaders are often those who bring about major changes, and

[1] B. M. Bass, *Bass and Stogdill's Handbook of Leadership: Theory, Research, and Managerial Implications* (New York: Free Press, 1990).
[2] J. M. Burns, *Leadership* (New York: Harper & Row, 1978).

thus they might also be defined as transformational leaders. Those who make a distinction suggest that not all transformational leaders achieve their transforming effects through the charismatic effects produced by their personalities and the relationship inspired with their followers.

Bernard M. Bass has studied and written extensively about leaders and the leadership process. He contrasts the transactional leader (i.e., that leadership style whereby something is offered by the leader in exchange for something wanted from the follower) with the transformational leader. Similar to the charismatic leader, the transformational leader is one who engages in a particular set of behaviors—he or she is a model of integrity and fairness, sets clear goals, has high expectations, encourages, provides support and recognition, stirs the emotions and passions of people, and gets people to look beyond their self-interests and to reach for the improbable. As with the charismatic leader, Bass sees trust, loyalty, and respect as common by-products of this form of leadership. Transformational leaders achieve their results in one or more ways. They may inspire their followers through charisma, they may meet the emotional needs of their followers through individualized consideration, and/or they may intellectually stimulate their followers by stirring within them an awareness of problems, insights into solutions, and the passion to bring about resolution.[3] Transformational leaders produce their effects by transforming the attitudes, beliefs, and values of their followers instead of gaining compliance through quid pro quo transactions.

The research on transformational leaders and transformational leadership has had several different foci. Some scholars have attempted to define transformational leadership and to differentiate it from transactional leadership. This work commonly focuses on the behaviors that characterize each style and the means by which the leaders influence their followers. In addition, there have been attempts to define *who* is the transformational leader, asking whether or not she or he tends to possess certain personality characteristics. There has also been an extensive amount of research focused on the effects of transformational leadership, both in terms of what these leaders do to their followers (e.g., inspire, motivate behavior that transcends self-interest) and their overall level of effectiveness. There has also been scholarship directed toward the development of an understanding of *how* transformational leadership produces its effects, research aimed at answering the question, What is the process through which this approach to leadership operates?

The readings contained in this chapter will provide insight into the following questions: What is transformational leadership? What are the different dimensions of transformational leadership? What individual and group outcomes stem from transformational leadership? How do transformational leaders produce their effects? Regarding the attempt to define who is the transformational leader, Bono and Judge (2004)[4] conducted a meta-analysis of this literature. They report that personality traits were related to three transformational leader behaviors—individualized consideration, intellectual stimulation, and idealized influence (inspirational motivation, also referred to as charisma.) The personality dimension of extroversion emerged as the strongest and most consistent correlate of transformational leadership.

In the first reading in this chapter, Alannah E. Rafferty and Mark A. Griffin (2004) review the literature on defining transformational leadership through a

---

[3] B. M. Bass, "Leadership: Good, Better, Best," *Organizational Dynamics* 13 (1985), pp. 26–40.
[4] J. E. Bono & T. A. Judge, "Personality and Transformational and Transactional Leadership: A Meta-analysis," *Journal of Applied Psychology* 89 (2004), pp. 901–910; see also B. C. Lim & R. E. Ployhart, "Transformational Leadership: Relations to the Five-Factor Model and Team Performance in Typical and Maximum Contexts," *Journal of Applied Psychology* 89 (2004), pp. 610–621.

focus on its major dimensions. This work provides insight into transformational leadership from the perspective of what it is that transformational leaders do. Rafferty and Griffin also hypothesize a number of outcomes (e.g., affective commitment, self-efficacy, turnover intentions, helping behaviors) that are associated with this approach to leadership. Each of the remaining readings focuses on other outcomes (effects) produced by transformational leadership and provides insight into the processes through which the effects (e.g., trust, satisfaction, efficacy) are produced.

In the second reading, Fred O. Walumbwa and his colleagues Peng Wang, John Lawler, and Kan Shi (2004) see transformational leadership producing its outcomes through a group-level effect. More specifically, they demonstrate that transformational leadership leads to an increase in the strength of the collective efficacy (i.e., a team member's assessment of his or her group's collective capability to perform job-related behaviors) among the transformational leader's followers.

In both the third and fourth readings, the authors see transformational leadership working through special effects that this style of leadership has at the individual level (e.g., through the quality of the leader–member exchange relationship, trust, and follower satisfaction). In the third reading, Philip W. Podsakoff, Scott B. MacKenzie, Robert H. Moorman, and Richard Fetter (1990) provide empirical insight into transformational leaders, their behaviors, and the effects that they produce. Specifically, they identify and look at several consequences produced by six transformational leader behaviors—articulating a vision, providing an appropriate model, fostering acceptance of group goals, expressing high performance expectations, providing individualized support, and promoting intellectual stimulation. Follower trust and satisfaction are seen as playing key roles linking transformational leadership with followers' citizenship behaviors.

Finally, the reading by Hui Wang, Kenneth S. Law, Rick D. Hackett, Duanzi Wang, and Zhen Xiong Chen (2005) employs leader–member exchange (LMX) theory to provide insight into the relationship between transformational leadership and follower performance and citizenship behaviors. The self-assessment presented at the end of this chapter opener gives you the opportunity to profile yourself on several behavioral dimensions associated with transformational and transactional leader behaviors. Which type of leader are *you* most inclined to be?

Other models provide us with insight into the causal path linking transformational leadership with both its individual follower–level and group-level effects. Kark, Shamir, and Chen (2003)[5] suggest that the transformational leader generates a strong level of follower identification with the leader and the group and that it is through this identification that the transformational leader is able to orchestrate extraordinary effects. Psychological empowerment,[6] task design characteristics, intrinsic motivation, and goal commitment[7] are examples of other possible linkages in this complex causal chain.

[5] R. Kark, B. Shamir, & G. Chen, "The Two Faces of Transformational Leadership: Empowerment and Dependency," *Journal of Applied Psychology*, 88 (2003), pp. 246–255.
[6] B. J. Avolio, W. Zhu, W. Koh, & P. Bhatia, "Transformational Leadership and Organizational Commitment: Mediating Role of Psychological Empowerment, and Moderating Role of Structural Distance," *Journal of Organizational Behavior* 25 (2004), pp. 951–968.
[7] R. F. Piccolo & J. A. Colquitt, "Transformational Leadership and Job Behaviors: The Mediating Role of Core Job Characteristics," *Academy of Management Journal* 49 (2006), pp. 327–340.

EXERCISE	**Transformational Leadership**
Self-Assessment	**Instructions:** Think about a situation in which you either assumed or were given a leadership role. Think about your own behaviors within this context. To what extent does each of the following statements characterize your leadership orientation?

	Very Little 1	2	3	A Moderate Amount 4	5	6	Very Much 7
1. Have a clear understanding of where we are going.	1	2	3	4	5	6	7
2. Paint an interesting picture of the future for my group.	1	2	3	4	5	6	7
3. Am always seeking new opportunities for the organization/group.	1	2	3	4	5	6	7
4. Inspire others with my plans for the future.	1	2	3	4	5	6	7
5. Am able to get others to be committed to my dreams.	1	2	3	4	5	6	7
6. Lead by "doing," rather than simply by "telling."	1	2	3	4	5	6	7
7. Provide a good model for others to follow.	1	2	3	4	5	6	7
8. Lead by example.	1	2	3	4	5	6	7
9. Foster collaboration among group members.	1	2	3	4	5	6	7
10. Encourage employees to be "team players."	1	2	3	4	5	6	7
11. Get the group to work together for the same goal.	1	2	3	4	5	6	7
12. Develop a team attitude and spirit among employees.	1	2	3	4	5	6	7
13. Show that I expect a lot from others.	1	2	3	4	5	6	7
14. Insist on only the best performance.	1	2	3	4	5	6	7
15. Will not settle for second best.	1	2	3	4	5	6	7
16. Act without considering the feelings of others.	1	2	3	4	5	6	7
17. Show respect for the personal feelings of others.	1	2	3	4	5	6	7
18. Behave in a manner thoughtful of the personal needs of others.	1	2	3	4	5	6	7
19. Treat others without considering their personal feelings.	1	2	3	4	5	6	7
20. Challenge others to think about old problems in new ways.	1	2	3	4	5	6	7
21. Ask questions that prompt others to think.	1	2	3	4	5	6	7
22. Stimulate others to rethink the way they do things.	1	2	3	4	5	6	7
23. Have ideas that challenge others to reexamine some of their basic assumptions about work.	1	2	3	4	5	6	7
24. Always give positive feedback when others perform well.	1	2	3	4	5	6	7
25. Give special recognition when others' work is very good.	1	2	3	4	5	6	7
26. Commend others when they do a better-than-average job.	1	2	3	4	5	6	7
27. Personally compliment others when they do outstanding work.	1	2	3	4	5	6	7
28. Frequently do not acknowledge the good performance of others.	1	2	3	4	5	6	7

Scoring: Subtract your responses to questions 16, 19, and 28 from 8. There are seven dimension scores to be computed. *Articulate vision*—Sum your response to questions 1 through 5 and divide by 5. *Provide appropriate model*—Sum your responses to questions 6 through 8 and divide by 3. *Foster acceptance of goals*—Sum your responses to questions 9 through 12 and divide by 4. *High-performance expectations*—Sum your responses to questions 13 through 15 and divide by 3. *Individual support*—Sum your responses to questions 16 through 19 and divide by 4. *Intellectual stimulation*—Sum your responses to questions 20 through 23 and divide by 4. *Transactional leader behaviors*—Sum your responses to questions 24 through 28 and divide by 5.

My scores are:
  Articulate vision _____.
  Role model _____.
  Foster goal acceptance _____.
  Performance expectations _____.
  Individual support _____.
  Intellectual stimulation _____.
  Transactional leader behavior _____.

Interpretation: Six basic dimensions of the *transformational* leader are profiled by this self-assessment: articulate vision, provide appropriate model, foster acceptance of goals, high-performance expectations, individual support, and intellectual stimulation. A high score (6 and greater) reflects a high behavioral orientation to engage in each of these behaviors. The seventh leadership dimension profiled here reflects your tendency to engage in behaviors characteristic of the transactional leader. A high score (6 and greater) reflects a strong behavioral orientation to give something to your followers in *exchange* for their giving something to you that as a leader you want (expect). A low score of 2 or less for the first six behaviors reflects an unlikelihood of your engaging in these behaviors. A low score of 2 or less on the seventh behavior reflects an unlikelihood to engage in behaviors characteristic of a transactional leader.

Source: Reprinted with permission. P. M. Podsakoff, S. B. MacKenzie, R. H. Moorman, and R. Fetter, "Transformational Leader Behaviors and Their Effects on Followers' Trust in Leader, Satisfaction, and Organizational Citizenship Behaviors," *Leadership Quarterly* 1, no. 2 (1990), pp. 107–42. Copyright Elsevier Science 1990.

Reading 39

Dimensions of Transformational Leadership: Conceptual and Empirical Extensions

Alannah E. Rafferty and Mark A. Griffin
Queensland University of Technology

1. INTRODUCTION

Bass' (1985) model of transformational leadership has been embraced by scholars and practitioners alike as one way in which organizations can encourage employees to perform beyond expectations. . . .

1.1. TRANSFORMATIONAL LEADERSHIP THEORY

Burns (1978) was the first author to contrast "transforming" and transactional leadership. Transactional leadership involves an exchange relationship between leaders and followers such that followers receive wages or prestige for complying with a leader's wishes. Transactional leadership encompasses contingent reward and management-by-exception.

In contrast, transformational leaders motivate followers to achieve performance beyond expectations by transforming followers' attitudes, beliefs, and values as opposed to simply gaining compliance (Bass, 1985; Yukl, 1999a, 1999b). Bass identified a number of subdimensions of transformational leadership including charisma (which was later renamed idealized influence), inspirational motivation, intellectual stimulation, and individualized consideration. . . .

1.2. EMPIRICAL SUPPORT FOR THE TRANSFORMATIONAL LEADERSHIP MODEL

Research has not provided convincing evidence in support of the transformational leadership model (Bycio et al., 1995; Tepper & Percy, 1994). Conflicting evidence has been reported concerning the factor structure of the model, and very strong relationships have been reported among the leadership factors (Avolio et al., 1999; Carless, 1998; Tejeda, Scandura, & Pillai, 2001). . . .

. . . We re-examine the theoretical model developed by Bass (1985) to identify five subdimensions of transformational leadership that will demonstrate discriminant validity with each other and with outcomes.

1.3. VISION

We identify vision as an important leadership dimension encompassed by the more general construct of charisma. Bass (1985) argued that the most general and important component of transformational leadership is charisma. Empirical findings support this statement, with meta-analytic results indicating that charisma is most strongly associated with measures of effectiveness such as satisfaction with the leader (Lowe, Kroeck, & Sivasubramaniam, 1996).

Authors have been critical of the way in which charisma has been defined (Barbuto, 1997; Beyer, 1999). Beyer argued that the essential components of charisma have been dramatically downplayed or ignored. Weber (1968) stated that charisma involves five components including an extraordinarily gifted person; a social crisis; a set of ideas providing a radical solution to a problem; a set of followers who are attracted to the exceptional person and believe that the leader is linked to transcendent powers; and the validation of the leader's extraordinary gifts through repeated success.

Charisma, as discussed in the transformational model, does not incorporate all of these components. The contribution of the situation surrounding leaders and followers, the personal qualities linked with charisma, and the association that followers make between a charismatic leader and transcendent powers are not explored.

A common theme when discussing charisma is the importance of articulating a vision. Weber (1968) identified vision as one of the five elements that contribute to charisma, and House (1977) stated that charismatic leaders demonstrate a number of behaviors including articulating an ideology that enhances goal clarity, task focus, and value congruence.

The current study focuses on vision as opposed to the broader construct of charisma or idealized influence proposed by Bass and his colleagues. House (1977) defined vision as a transcendent ideal that represents shared values, and which is ideological in nature. McClelland (1975) suggested that vision results in the internalization of organizational values and goals, which encourages individuals to adopt behaviors because of the attractiveness of the behavior itself as opposed to the attractiveness of a given leader. In this study, we define vision as:

The expression of an idealized picture of the future based around organizational values.

1.4. INSPIRATIONAL COMMUNICATION

Although inspirational motivation has been identified as an important component of transformational leadership, this construct has been variously defined (Barbuto, 1997). Bass (1985) stated that charismatic leaders use inspirational appeals and emotional talks to arouse follower motivations to transcend self-interest for the good of the team.

At a later date, Bass (1999) stated that both charisma *and* inspirational motivation are displayed when a leader envisions a desirable future, articulates how it can be reached, sets an example to be followed, sets high standards of performance, and shows determination and confidence. This description suggests vision and inspirational motivation might be combined into a single construct. However, other researchers have argued that it is useful to maintain a distinction between vision and inspirational motivation (e.g., Barbuto, 1997; McClelland, 1975). Below, we present a theoretical rationale for making a distinction between the constructs of inspirational leadership and the vision component of charisma.

Downton (1973) defined inspiration as the action or power of moving the intellect or emotions. In contrast, Bass (1985) restricted the use of the term inspirational leadership to instances when a leader employs or adds nonintellectual, emotional qualities to the influence process. He stated that inspirational leaders add affective qualities to the influence process through the use of inspirational talks and emotional appeals. Similarly, Yukl (1981, p. 121) suggested that inspiration refers to "the extent to which a leader stimulates enthusiasm among subordinates for the work of the group and says things to build subordinate confidence in their ability to perform assignments successfully and attain group objectives."

A recurring element within existing definitions of inspirational leadership is the use of oral communication to motivate and arouse followers' emotions. As a result, we focus on inspirational communication, or the use of appeals and emotion-laden statements to arouse followers' emotions and motivation, as opposed to the broader construct of inspirational motivation proposed by Bass and his colleagues. In this study, we suggest that inspirational communication is a distinct construct, defined as:

The expression of positive and encouraging messages about the organization and statements that build motivation and confidence.

1.5. SUPPORTIVE LEADERSHIP

One factor that distinguishes transformational leadership from other New Leadership theories is the inclusion of individualized consideration. Bass (1985) initially stated that individualized consideration occurs when a leader has a developmental orientation towards staff and displays individualized attention to followers and responds appropriately to their personal needs.

More recently, discussions of individualized consideration have focused on one component of this construct, supportive leadership. For example, Avolio and Bass (1995, p. 202) stated "the leader displays more frequent individualized consideration by showing general support for the efforts of followers." Other authors in the transformational leadership field have also focused on supportive leadership as opposed to the broader construct of individualized attention. Podsakoff et al. (1990) examined individualized support, which was defined as behavior on the part of a leader that indicates that he or she respects his or her followers and is concerned with followers' feelings and needs.

We focus on supportive leadership here, and use the extensive research that has been conducted on this topic to guide our discussion. Supportive leadership is a key aspect of effective leadership in path–goal theory (House, 1971). House (1996, p. 327) defined supportive leader behavior as "behavior directed toward the satisfaction of subordinates' needs and preferences, such as displaying concern for subordinates' welfare and creating a friendly and psychologically supportive work environment." We define supportive leadership as:

Expressing concern for followers and taking account of their individual needs.

1.6. INTELLECTUAL STIMULATION

The most underdeveloped component of transformational leadership is intellectual stimulation (Lowe et al., 1996). This leadership factor encompasses behaviors that increase followers' interest in and awareness of problems, and that develop their ability and propensity to think about problems in new ways (Bass, 1985). The effects of intellectual stimulation are seen in increases in followers' abilities to conceptualize, comprehend, and analyze problems and in the improved quality of solutions that they generate (Bass & Avolio, 1990).

While this leadership factor has not been the subject of extensive research, this construct encompasses a more focused, and internally consistent set of behaviors than the other subdimensions of transformational leadership. As a result, the definition of intellectual stimulation adopted by Bass and his colleagues is retained in this study. Based on the work of Bass (1985), we define intellectual stimulation as:

Enhancing employees' interest in, and awareness of problems, and increasing their ability to think about problems in new ways.

1.7. PERSONAL RECOGNITION

Our fifth dimension is based on the body of research that has found a strong link between transactional leadership and the subdimensions of transformational leadership. Transactional leadership encompasses contingent reward and management-by-exception. Contingent reward involves rewarding followers for attaining specified performance levels. Bass (1985) suggested that praise for work well done, recommendations for pay increases and promotions, and commendations for excellent effort are all examples of contingent reward behaviors.

Empirical evidence indicates that contingent reward is highly positively correlated with transformational leadership, and displays a similar pattern of relationships to outcomes as the transformational subdimensions (e.g., Den Hartog, Van Muijen, & Koopman, 1997; Tepper & Percy, 1994). A number of reasons have been proposed to explain these strong relationships.

Goodwin et al. (2001) hypothesized that the contingent reward scale, as assessed by the MLQ-5X, captures behaviors associated with the *negotiation* of rewards for good performance and behaviors associated with the *provision* of rewards based on performance. These authors argued that the negotiation of rewards for good performance represents a form of transactional leadership. However, rewarding followers based on their performance was argued to represent a transformational process as followers and leaders in a transformational relationship have a personal investment in the vision. As a result, followers assume that performance consistent with the vision will be rewarded.

Goodwin et al. (2001) found support for a two-factor solution for contingent reward using confirmatory factor analysis (CFA). These authors interpreted their findings as providing support for the argument that contingent reward encompasses both transactional and transformational processes. This interpretation is consistent with models of high-performance work systems (e.g., Arthur, 1994; Becker & Gerhart, 1996; Vandenberg, Richardson, & Eastman, 1999), which distinguish between reward as a control mechanism and reward as a component of a system designed to increase employee commitment.

In the current study, we use the term "personal recognition" to capture that aspect of contingent reward that is conceptually related to transformational leadership. Personal recognition occurs when a leader indicates that he or she values individuals' efforts and rewards the achievement of outcomes consistent with the vision through praise [*sic*] the acknowledgment of followers' efforts. We define personal recognition as:

The provision of rewards such as praise and acknowledgement of effort for achievement of specified goals.

In summary, the above review identified a set of more focused subdimensions of transformational leadership including articulating a vision, inspirational communication, supportive leadership, intellectual stimulation, and personal recognition. An important aim of the current study is to determine whether individuals differentiate between these subdimensions when describing their leader's behavior. In addition, we examine whether the subdimensions demonstrate discriminant validity with each other. Below, a nomological network, relating the leadership subdimensions identified in this study with a range of theoretically selected outcomes, is developed.

1.8. THE NOMOLOGICAL NETWORK

When studying the effects of transformational leadership, researchers have focused on outcomes such as satisfaction, follower extra effort, and ratings of leader effectiveness (e.g., Lowe et al., 1996). However, theorists have also proposed that transformational leaders have a powerful influence on a range of other outcomes including motivation and attachment to the organization (e.g., Bass, 1985; Shamir, House, & Arthur, 1993).

We develop a series of hypotheses suggesting that certain subdimensions of transformational leadership are uniquely associated with a number of outcomes including affective and continuance commitment, role breadth self-efficacy (RBSE), interpersonal helping behaviors, and intentions to turnover.

1.8.1. Affective Commitment

Affective commitment refers to the extent to which followers identify with, are involved in, and are emotionally attached to an organization (Meyer & Allen, 1997). Researchers have found that all of the subdimensions of transformational leadership and contingent reward are strongly positively associated with affective commitment (Bycio et al., 1995). We propose, however, that only vision and inspirational communication will be uniquely positively associated with affective commitment. The reasoning behind this hypothesis is presented below.

H1. Vision and inspirational communication have a unique positive relationship with affective commitment to the organization.

Empirical research suggests that vision has a positive impact on affective commitment. Podsakoff, MacKenzie, and Bommer (1996) examined the influence of six subdimensions of transformational leadership and a range of substitutes for leadership (Kerr & Jermier, 1978) on affective commitment to the organization. Results indicated that only one of the leadership factors, articulating a vision, was significantly positively associated with affective commitment. . . .

Very few researchers have examined inspirational leadership separate from charisma. As a result, there is little empirical evidence regarding the influence of inspirational leadership on employees' attitudes and behaviors. We suggest, however, that inspirational communication will display a unique positive relationship with affective commitment. In particular, we propose that expressing positive and encouraging messages will increase the attractiveness of the organization to individuals, which will positively impact on the extent to which individuals identify with, and feel attached to the organization as a whole.

1.8.2. Continuance Commitment

Continuance commitment refers to an employee's awareness that there are costs associated with leaving an organization. Employees who report strong continuance commitment stay with an organization because they feel that they have to (Allen & Meyer, 1990; Meyer & Allen, 1997). Bycio et al. (1995) examined relationships among the subdimensions of transformational and transactional leadership and continuance commitment. These authors hypothesized that contingent reward would be significantly positively associated with continuance commitment. Contrary to expectations, however, the only leadership factor that was associated with continuance commitment was management-by-exception. . . .

We . . . propose that when leaders reward followers by recognizing their efforts, then followers' sense of investment in an organization will increase. As a result it is proposed that:

H2. Personal recognition has a unique positive relationship with continuance commitment.

1.8.3. Role Breadth Self-efficacy

Shamir et al. (1993) argued that transformational leaders increase followers' self-efficacy, which refers to individuals' beliefs in their capabilities to organize and execute actions required to produce given attainments (Bandura, 1997). Self-efficacy is an important motivational construct that influences individuals' choices, goals, emotional reactions, and their effort, coping, and persistence (Bandura, 1997; Gist & Mitchell, 1992).

This study focuses on one particular type of self-efficacy, RBSE, which refers to the extent to which people feel confident that they are capable of carrying out a range of proactive integrative tasks beyond prescribed technical requirements (Parker, 1998, 2000). Examples of proactive tasks include solving long-term problems, designing improved procedures, setting goals, and resolving conflicts. . . .

We argue that inspirational communication is a form of verbal persuasion that will increase RBSE. When leaders communicate positive and encouraging messages, then it is likely that people will feel more capable of carrying out a range of proactive integrative tasks beyond prescribed technical requirements. Specifically, it is proposed that:

H3. Inspirational communication has a unique positive relationship with RBSE.

1.8.4. Interpersonal Helping Behavior

Podsakoff et al. (1990) stated that the real essence of transformational leadership is that these leaders cause followers to do more than they originally expected to do. As a result, the most important effect of transformational leadership is on extra-role performance or organizational citizenship behaviors (OCBs) rather than on in-role performance. OCB refers to "individual behavior that is discretionary, not directly or explicitly recognized by the formal reward system, and that in the aggregate promotes the effective functioning of the organization" (Organ, 1988, p. 4).

We focus on interpersonal helping behaviors, which occur when people voluntarily help others with, or prevent the occurrence of work-related problems (Podsakoff, MacKenzie, Paine, & Bachrach, 2000). Empirical research indicates that a number of subdimensions of transformational leadership and contingent reward are positively associated with helping behaviors. . . .

In summary, research has provided evidence to suggest that supportive leadership will be strongly positively associated with interpersonal helping behaviors after taking account of the effects of the other leadership subdimensions. As a result of these findings it is proposed that:

H4. Supportive leadership has a unique positive relationship with interpersonal helping behaviors.

1.8.5. Turnover Intentions

Researchers have concentrated on the influence of affective variables such as commitment and satisfaction on turnover intentions (Mathieu & Zajac, 1990; Williams & Hazer, 1986). However, Bycio et al. (1995) reported that all of the transformational leadership behaviors and contingent reward were significantly negatively associated with intentions to leave the job. Charisma displayed the strongest relationship with intention to leave the job and intention to leave the profession. . . .

Some empirical evidence does suggest that vision has a strong influence on turnover intentions. In particular, authors have examined the effects of goal congruence between leaders and followers (e.g., Vancouver, Millsap, & Peters, 1994; Vancouver & Schmitt, 1991). Vancouver and Schmitt proposed that agreement among organizational members in schools regarding the goals of the school was related to the attitudes of its members. These authors focused on nonoperational goals, which do not define measurable outcomes, and as such reflect a leader's vision.

Vancouver and Schmitt (1991) found that both between-constituency and within-constituency goal congruence were significantly associated with intentions to turnover. That is, when individuals in different hierarchical positions agreed on nonoperational goals, and when there was agreement between an individual and all the other individuals in a group on nonoperational

goals, intentions to turnover decreased. These results suggest that articulation of a vision has a powerful influence on turnover intentions. On the basis of the above findings, it is proposed that:

H5. Articulating a vision has a unique negative relationship with turnover intentions.

2. METHOD

2.1. PROCEDURE AND PARTICIPANTS

Three thousand three hundred and seven surveys were distributed across an Australian public sector organization, and 1398 employees responded (response rate 42.2%). . . .

3. RESULTS

. . . Table 2 displays the means, standard deviations, and zero-order correlations among the leadership factors, the outcome variables, and bureaucracy, the marker variable used in this study.

4. DISCUSSION

Our study provided support for the five-factor leadership model that distinguishes between vision, inspirational communication, intellectual stimulation, supportive leadership, and personal recognition. . . .

4.1. VISION

One of the most interesting set of findings obtained in this study involves the relationships among articulation of a vision and outcomes. First, vision displayed a unique negative association with continuance commitment. This relationship was evident in both the zero-order relationships and in the structural model. This finding was not hypothesized, and conflicts with the general wisdom in the leadership field. However, a number of alternate expectations regarding the relationship between vision and continuance commitment could be conceived.

On the one hand, it could be hypothesized that vision is likely to be positively associated with continuance commitment, as articulating an idealized picture of the future increases people's investment in the future of an organization. On the other hand, it could be argued that articulating a vision will expand people's awareness of the possibilities inherent in their environment. If this is the case, then vision may be associated with a decrease in

TABLE 2 Zero-order Correlations Between the Study Variables

Scale	Mean	SD	1	2	3	4	5	6	7	8	9	10	11
1. Vision	3.37	1.04	(.82)										
2. IS[a]	2.94	0.99	.57***	(.84)									
3. Inspiration	2.94	1.06	.67***	.63***	(.88)								
4. Support	2.90	1.20	.59***	.56***	.75***	(.95)							
5. Recognition	2.91	1.23	.59***	.59***	.74***	.78***	(.96)						
6. RBSE	3.67	0.95	.11***	.12***	.19***	.16***	.17***	(.87)					
7. AC[b]	2.80	1.02	.25***	.30***	.34***	.29***	.28***	.14***	(.80)				
8. CC[c]	2.91	0.29	-.13***	.00	-.09**	-.08**	-.11***	-.13***	.17***	(.76)			
9. TO[d]	2.30	1.10	-.21***	-.19***	-.22***	-.20***	-.18***	.03	-.32***	-.16***	(.75)		
10. Helping	4.15	0.61	.07**	.09**	.10***	.08**	.06*	.29***	.15***	-.01	-.03	(.76)	
11. Bureaucracy	3.76	0.91	-.08**	-.14***	-.21***	-.18***	-.17***	-.02	-.03	.12***	.07*	.15***	(.71)

Cronbach's alphas are reported on the diagonal. N ranges from 1357 to 1398.

[a]IS = Intellectual stimulation.

[b]AC = Affective commitment.

[c]CC = Continuance commitment.

[d]TO = Turnover intentions.

*$p < .05$.

**$p < .01$.

***$p < .001$.

continuance commitment by empowering people and positively influencing their perceptions of the opportunities available to them.

At present, we are unable to select between the alternatives proposed above. There is a clear need for more attention to be devoted to understanding the theoretical nature of the relationship between vision and continuance commitment. In addition, it is also important to replicate the relationship reported in this study as very few authors have examined the construct of continuance commitment in relation to transformational leadership.

Vision also displayed a significant negative relationship with RBSE. Post hoc exploration of this result suggested that the relationship between vision and RBSE was negative only after controlling for the relationship between inspirational communication and RBSE. This suggests that in the absence of inspirational communication, expression of a vision is associated with a reduction in followers' confidence. However, this result needs to be interpreted cautiously as there was a positive zero-order correlation between vision and RBSE.

The findings of this study raise the possibility that articulating a vision does not always have a positive influence on followers. Some previous work conducted by Shamir, Zakay, Breinin, and Popper (1998) in the Israeli Defense Forces provides support for this idea. In particular, Shamir et al. reported that leader behaviors designed to link employees' self-concepts with the organizational mission such as adopting an ideological approach or setting a personal example, were either unrelated or negatively related to followers' perceptions of and attitudes toward the leader and the unit. There is a need for researchers to explore the conditions under which articulation of a vision positively impacts on followers and those conditions under which vision has a negative impact on followers.

4.2. INSPIRATIONAL COMMUNICATION

Our study also revealed that inspirational communication was significantly positively associated with RBSE, affective commitment, and interpersonal helping. Expressing positive and encouraging messages about the organization was positively associated with emotional attachment to a firm, individuals' confidence in their capacity to carry out a range of proactive and integrative tasks, and the extent to which people voluntarily helped others with or prevented the occurrence of work-related problems.

It is interesting to contrast the relationships between vision and inspirational communication and follower outcomes. Inspirational communica-

tion was strongly positively associated with three of the five outcomes examined, while vision was negatively associated with two of the five outcomes studied. These results support the importance of distinguishing between vision and inspirational leadership, and highlight the need for future research to further address the distinction between these constructs.

4.3. INTELLECTUAL STIMULATION

Intellectual stimulation displayed a unique positive relationship with affective commitment to the organization and with continuance commitment to the organization. The positive relationship between affective commitment and intellectual stimulation contrasts with past research findings that have reported that intellectual stimulation has a negative impact on employees (e.g. Podsakoff et al., 1990).

Podsakoff et al. (1990) reported that intellectual stimulation was negatively associated with a number of employee attitudes including trust in the leader and satisfaction. These authors explained their findings by suggesting that intellectual stimulation is associated with higher levels of role ambiguity, conflict, and stress in the workplace. We suggest that while intellectual stimulation may enhance ambiguity and conflict in the workplace, employees may also feel valued when they are encouraged to actively engage in a firm.

Eisenberger, Huntington, Hutchinson, and Sowa (1986) discuss perceived organizational support, which refers to employee' global beliefs concerning the extent to which an organization values their contributions and cares about their well-being. These authors suggested that to the extent that perceived support meets needs for approval and praise, individuals incorporate organizational membership into their self-identity and thus, develop a positive emotional bond to the organization. Intellectual stimulation may be one way in which leaders indicate to employees that their firm values their contribution, which increases affective commitment to the organization.

Intellectual stimulation was also significantly positively associated with continuance commitment. One explanation for this result is that when leaders encourage followers to consider problems in new ways and to actively engage in the workplace, employees experience an increased sense of investment in an organization based on the increased effort they are exerting. This increased sense of investment increases continuance commitment.

4.4. PERSONAL RECOGNITION

We proposed that when people received recognition for their work then they would feel an increased sense of investment in an organization. Contrary to expectations, personal recognition was significantly negatively associated with continuance commitment. This unexpected result might be explained by considering the additional aspect of continuance commitment assessed in measures of this construct. That is, authors have suggested that the continuance commitment scale assesses investments and perceptions of alternative employment options (McGee & Ford, 1987).

To the extent that personal recognition provides information about individuals' worth, they might perceive a greater ability to move to new opportunities. Alternatively, when the only rewards that are available for use by leaders are verbal encouragement or rewards of a personal nature, this may result in follower frustration as people do not feel that they are being adequately rewarded for performance. Increased frustration may lead individuals to evaluate alternative opportunities more positively, reducing continuance commitment to the organization.

4.5. SUPPORTIVE LEADERSHIP

Finally, supportive leadership did not display any significant unique relationships with the outcome variables after statistically controlling for the influence of the other leadership factors and CMV Analyses supported the distinction between supportive leadership and the other leadership constructs. However, the lack of a unique relationship between supportive leadership and the outcome measures raises some questions about the meaning of this distinction.

Results of this study suggest that further attention should be directed towards examining whether supportive leadership is truly "transformational" as determined by its relationships with followers' motivation, needs, and values (Shamir et al., 1993). Research on the path–goal theory (e.g., House, 1996) has suggested that supportive leadership is primarily associated with satisfaction and not motivational outcomes or attachment to the organization. If this is the case, there may be a need to reconsider existing definitions of the construct of individualized consideration, which currently encompass supportive leadership.

4.6. PRACTICAL IMPLICATIONS

There are a number of important practical implications that arise from the findings of this study.

Most importantly, results suggest that it will be useful to evaluate the different component of leadership identified in this study for purposes such as performance appraisal, training and development, and succession planning. The constructs represent distinct attributes that should be considered when organizations seek to select and train leaders.

In addition, our analysis indicates managers can have a powerful positive effect on employees by expressing positive and encouraging messages to staff. Inspirational communication seems to be particularly important when expressing a vision for the future. In the absence of encouragement and confidence building efforts, articulating a vision may have a neutral or even negative influence on employees.

Another practical implication concerns intellectual stimulation. This leadership factor displayed a range of different relationships with outcomes. Specifically, intellectual stimulation was positively associated with affective attachment to an organization and attachment based on a recognition of the costs associated with leaving an organization. Leaders who engage in intellectual stimulation may need to consider that while they are increasing emotional attachment to a firm, they are also enhancing followers' sense that they are "tied" to the organization. Research suggests that individuals that have strong continuance commitment to an organization are less likely to make positive contributions to a firm (Meyer & Allen, 1997). . . .

References

Allen, N. J., & Meyer, J. P. (1990). The measurement and antecedents of affective, continuance, normative commitment to the organization. *Journal of Occupational and Organizational Psychology, 63*(1), 1–18.

Anderson, J. C., & Gerbing, D. W. (1988). Structural equation modeling in practice: A review and recommended two-step approach. *Psychological Bulletin, 103*(3), 411–423.

Arthur, J. A. (1994). Effects of human resource systems on manufacturing performance and turnover. *Academy of Management Journal, 37*(3), 670–687.

Avolio, B. J., & Bass, B. M. (1995). Individual consideration viewed at multiple levels of analysis: A multilevel framework for examining the influence of transformational leadership. *The Leadership Quarterly, 6,* 199–218.

Avolio, B. J., Bass, B. M., & Jung, D. L. (1999). Re-examining the components of transformational and transactional leadership using the Multifactor Leadership Questionnaire. *Journal of Occupational and Organizational Psychology, 72,* 441–462.

Awamleh, R., & Gardner, W. M. (1999). Perceptions of leader charisma and effectiveness: The effects of vision content, delivery, organizational performance. *The Leadership Quarterly,* 10(3), 345–373.

Bandura, A. (1986). *Social foundations of thought and action: A social cognitive theory.* Englewood Cliffs, NJ: Prentice-Hall.

Bandura, A. (1997). *Self-efficacy: The exercise of control.* New York: W.H. Freeman.

Barbuto, J. E. (1997). Taking the charisma out of transformational leadership. *Journal of Social Behavior and Personality,* 12 (3), 689–697.

Bass, B. (1985). *Leadership and performance beyond expectations.* New York: The Free Press.

Bass, B. M. (1999). Two decades of research and development in transformational leadership. *European Journal of Work and Organizational Psychology,* 8(1), 9–32.

Bass, B. M., & Avolio, B. J. (1990). The implications of transactional and transformational leadership for individual, team, organizational development. *Research in Organizational Change and development,* 4, 231–272.

Becker, B., & Gerhart, B. (1996). The impact of human resource management on organizational performance: Progress and prospects. *Academy of Management Journal,* 39(4), 779–801.

Berson, Y., Shamir, B., Avolio, B. J., & Popper, M. (2001). The relationship between vision strength, leadership style, context. *The Leadership Quarterly,* 12, 53–73.

Beyer, J. M. (1999). Taming and promoting charisma to change organizations. *The Leadership Quarterly,* 10(2), 307–330.

Bryman, A. (1992). *Charisma and leadership in organizations.* London: Sage Publications.

Burns, J. M. (1978). *Leadership.* New York: Harper & Row.

Bycio, P., Hackett, R. D., & Allen, J. S. (1995). Further assessments of Bass' 1985 conceptualization of transactional and transformational leadership. *Journal of Applied Psychology,* 80(4), 468–478.

Carless, S. A. (1998). Assessing the discriminant validity of transformational leadership behaviour as measured by the MLQ. *Journal of Occupational and Organizational Psychology,* 71, 353–358.

Den Hartog, D. N., Van Mujjen, J. J., & Koopman, P. L. (1997). Transactional versus transformational leadership: An analysis of the MLQ. *Journal of Occupational and Organizational Psychology,* 70, 19–34.

Dvir, T., Eden, D., Avolio, B. J., & Shamir, B. (2002). Impact of transformational leadership on follower development and performance: A field experiment. *Academy of Management Journal,* 45(4), 735–744.

Dvir, T., & Shamir, B. (2003). Follower developmental characteristics as predicting transformational leadership:

A longitudinal field study. *The Leadership Quarterly,* 14, 327–344.

Downton, J. V. (1973). *Rebel leadership: Commitment and charisma in the revolutionary process.* New York: The Free Press.

Eisenberger, R., Huntington, R., Hutchinnson, S., & Sowa, D. (1986). Perceived organizational support. *Journal of Applied Psychology,* 71, 500–507.

Gist, M., & Mitchell, T. R. (1992). Self-efficacy: A theoretical analysis of its determinants and malleability. *Academy of Management Review,* 17(2), 183–211.

Goodwin, V. L., Wofford, J. C., & Whittington, J. L. (2001). A theoretical and empirical extension to the transformational leadership construct. *Journal of Organizational Behavior,* 22, 759–774.

Hage, J., & Aiken, M. (1967). Relationship of centralization to other structural properties. *Administrative Science Quarterly,* 12, 72–92.

House, R. J. (1971). A path–goal theory of leader effectiveness. *Administrative Science Quarterly,* 16, 321–339.

House, R. J. (1977). A 1976 theory of charismatic leadership. In J. G. Hunt, & L. L. Lawson (Eds.), *Leadership: The cutting edge* (pp. 189–207). Carbondale: Southern Illinois University Press.

House, R. J. (1996). Path–goal theory of leadership: Lessons, legacy, a reformulated theory. *The Leadership Quarterly,* 7(3), 323–353.

House, R. J. (1998). Appendix: Measures and assessments for the charismatic leadership approach: Scales, latent constructs, loadings, Cronbach alphas, interclass correlations. In F. Dansereau, & F. J. Yammarino (Eds.), *Leadership: The multiple-level approaches contemporary and alternative* (24, Part B, pp. 23–30). London: JAI Press.

Jöreskog, K. G., & Sorbom, D. (1996). *LISREL 8: User's reference guide.* Chicago, IL: Scientific Software International.

Jung, D. I., & Sosik, J. J. (2002). Transformational leadership in work groups: The role of empowerment, cohesiveness, collective efficacy on perceived group performance. *Small Group Research,* 33(3), 313–336.

Kerr, S., & Jermier, J. M. (1978). Substitutes for leadership: Their meaning and measurement. *Organizational Behavior and Human Performance,* 22, 375–403.

Kirkpatrick, S. A., & Locke, E. A. (1996). Direct and indirect effects of three core charismatic leadership components on performance and attitudes. *Journal of Applied Psychology,* 81(1), 36–51.

Lindell, M. K., & Whitney, D. J. (2001). Accounting for common method variance in cross-sectional research designs. *Journal of Applied Psychology,* 86(1), 114–121.

Lowe, K. B., Kroeck, K. G., & Sivasubramaniam, N. (1996). Effectiveness correlates of transformational and transactional leadership: A meta-analytic review of the MLQ literature. *The Leadership Quarterly,* 7(3), 385–425.

Mathieu, J. E., & Zajac, D. M. (1990). A review and meta-analysis of the antecedents, correlates, consequences of organizational commitment. *Psychological Bulletin,* 108(2), 171–194.

McClelland, D. C. (1975). *Power: The inner experience.* New York: Irvington Publishers.

McGee, G. W., & Ford, R. C. (1987). Two (or more?) dimensions of organizational commitment: Re-examination of the affective and continuance scales. *Journal of Applied Psychology,* 72(4), 638–642.

Meyer, J. P., & Allen, N. J. (1997). *Commitment in the workplace: Theory, research, application.* Thousand Oaks: Sage Publications.

Meyer, J. P., Allen, N. J., & Smith, C. A. (1993). Commitment to organizations and occupations: Extension and test of a three component conceptualization. *Journal of Applied Psychology,* 78, 538–551.

Moorman, R. H., & Blakely, G. L. (1995). Individualism–collectivism as an individual difference predictor of organizational citizenship behavior. *Journal of Organizational Behavior,* 16, 127–142.

Organ, D. W. (1988). *Organizational citizenship behavior: The good soldier syndrome.* Lexington, MA: Lexington Books.

Organ, D. W., & Ryan, K. (1995). A meta-analytic review of attitudinal and dispositional predictors of organizational citizenship behavior. *Personnel Psychology,* 48, 775–802.

Parker, S. K. (1998). Enhancing role breadth self-efficacy: The roles of job enrichment and other organizational interventions. *Journal of Applied Psychology,* 83(6), 835–852.

Parker, S. K. (2000). From passive to proactive motivation: The importance of flexible role orientations and role breadth self-efficacy. *Applied Psychology: An International Review,* 49(3), 447–469.

Pillai, R., Schriesheim, C. A., & Williams, E. S. (1999). Fairness perceptions and trust as mediators for transformational and transactional leadership: A two-sample study. *Journal of Management,* 25(6), 897–933.

Podsakoff, P. M., & Organ, D. M. (1986). Self-reports in organizational research: Problems and prospects. *Journal of Management,* 12(4), 531–544.

Podsakoff, P. M., MacKenzie, S. B., Moorman, R. H., & Fetter, R. (1990). Transformational leader behaviors and their effects on followers' trust in leader, satisfaction, organizational citizenship behaviors. *The Leadership Quarterly,* 1(2), 107–142.

Podsakoff, P. M., MacKenzie, S. B., & Bommer, W. H. (1996). Transformational leadership behaviors and substitutes for leadership as determinants of employee satisfaction, commitment, trust, organizational citizenship behaviors. *Journal of Management,* 22(2), 259–298.

Podsakoff, P. M., MacKenzie, S. B., Paine, J. B., & Bachrach, D. G. (2000). Organizational citizenship behaviors: a critical review of the theoretical and empirical literature and suggestions for future research. *Journal of Management,* 26(3), 513–563.

Richardson, H. A., Simmering, M. J., & Roman, P. M. (2003). A comparison of statistical corrections for common method variance. *Paper presented at the Southern Management Association meeting in Clearwater, Florida.*

Shamir, B., House, R. J., & Arthur, M. A. (1993). The motivational effects of charismatic leadership: A self-concept based theory. *Organization Science,* 4(4), 577–594.

Shamir, B., Zakay, E., Breinin, E., & Popper, M. (1998). Correlates of charismatic leader behavior in military units: Subordinates' attitudes, unit characteristics, superiors' appraisals of leader performance. *Academy of Management Journal,* 41(4), 387–409.

Tejeda, M. J., Scandura, T. A., & Pillai, R. (2001). The MLQ revisited: Psychometric properties and recommendations. *The Leadership Quarterly,* 12, 31–52.

Tepper, B. J., & Percy, P. M. (1994). Structural validity of the Multifactor Leadership Questionnaire. *Educational and Psychological Measurement,* 54(3), 734–744.

Vancouver, J. B., & Schmitt, N. W. (1991). An exploratory examination of person–organization fit: Organizational goal congruence. *Personnel Psychology,* 44, 333–352.

Vancouver, J. B., Millsap, R. E., & Peters, P. A. (1994). Multilevel analysis of organizational goal congruence. *Journal of Applied Psychology,* 79(5), 666–679.

Vandenberg, R. J., Richardson, H. A., & Eastman, L. A. (1999). The impact of high involvement work processes on organizational effectiveness: A second-order latent variable approach. *Group and Organization Management,* 24(3), 300–339.

Weber, M. (1968). *On charisma and institution building.* Chicago: University of Chicago Press.

Williams, L. J., & Anderson, S. E. (1994). An alternative approach to method effects by using latent-variable models: Applications in organizational behavior research. *Journal of Applied Psychology,* 79(3), 323–331.

Williams, L. L., & Harz, J. A. (1986). Antecedents and consequences of satisfaction and commitment in turnover models: A reanalysis using structural equation models. *Journal of Applied Psychology,* 71(2), 219–231.

Yukl, G. A. (1981) *Leadership in organizations.* Englewood Cliffs, NJ: Prentice-Hall.

Yukl, G. (1999a). An evaluation of conceptual weaknesses in transformational and charismatic leadership. *The Leadership Quarterly,* 10(2), 285–305.

Yukl, G. (1999b). An evaluative essay on current conceptions of effective leadership. *European Journal of Work and Organizational Psychology,* 8(1), 33–48.

Reading 40

The Role of Collective Efficacy in the Relations between Transformational Leadership and Work Outcomes

Fred O. Walumbwa
University of Nebraska

Peng Wang and John J. Lawler
University of Illinois at Urbana–Champaign

Kan Shi
Chinese Academy of Sciences

Research studies have consistently revealed that transformational leadership is positively related to work outcomes (Dumdum, Lowe, & Avolio, 2002; Fuller, Patterson, Hester, & Sringer, 1996; Lowe, Kroeck, & Sivasubramaniam, 1996). However, the question of what are the underlying processes and mechanisms by which transformational leaders exert their influence on followers and ultimately on performance has not fully been explored (Kark & Shamir, 2002; Kark, Shamir, & Chen, 2003). Bass (1999) notes, "much more explanation is needed about the inner workings of transformational leadership' (p. 24). Therefore, research on these processes is needed in order to gain better understanding of transformational leadership and why followers of transformational leaders demonstrate high level of commitment, job satisfaction and less withdrawal behaviours (Kark & Shamir, 2002). In this study, we explored the role of collective efficacy in mediating the relations between transformational leadership and followers' work-related outcomes using data collected from Chinese and Indian financial firms.

Collective efficacy refers to each individual's assessment of his or her group's collective capability to perform job-related behaviours (Riggs, Warka, Babasa, Betancourt, & Hooker, 1994). Although Bandura (1986) originally defined efficacy belief as occurring at the individual level, recent conceptualization suggests that efficacy beliefs can also occur at the collective level (Bandura, 1997, 2000; Maddux, 2002). Specifically, Bandura (1997) argues that efficacy beliefs play an important role in both individual and group motivation because people have to rely, at least to some extent, on others to accomplish their tasks.

Because collective efficacy appears to account for important organizational outcomes, better understanding of how organizations could boost collective efficacy is important (Chen & Bliese, 2002). Unfortunately, research on collective efficacy has mainly focused on its outcomes, whereas relatively little is known about the situational antecedents of collective efficacy. We believe that to understand the role of collective efficacy in organizations better, it is important to examine not only how collective efficacy affects organizational outcomes, but also how it is affected by other variables. Given the dominant role of leadership in the workplace, one key situational factor that may have substantial impact on collective efficacy is leadership. The goal of this study is to address this important yet relatively unstudied issue.

TRANSFORMATIONAL LEADERSHIP, COLLECTIVE EFFICACY AND WORK OUTCOMES

TRANSFORMATIONAL LEADERSHIP AND WORK OUTCOMES

As already noted, the link between transformational leadership and work outcomes, such as organizational commitment and job satisfaction, is well established (Bass, 1998). According to Bass (1985), transformational leaders motivate their followers to transcend their own self-interests for the sake of the group. As a consequence, such leaders are able to bring a deeper understanding and appreciation of input from each member. Bass (1985) further argued that such leaders encourage followers to think critically and to

Source: Edited and reprinted with permission. *Journal of Occupational and Organizational Psychology.* 2004, 77, 515–530.
Copyright: The British Psychological Society, 2004.

seek new ways to approach their jobs. This charge to seek new ways to approach problems and challenges motivates followers to become more involved in their duties, resulting in an increase in the levels of satisfaction with their work and commitment to the organization. This position has received support empirically. For instance, work by Dvir, Eden, Avolio, and Shamir (2002) demonstrated that transformational leaders had direct effects on followers' motivation, morality and empowerment. Barling, Weber, and Kelloway (1996) in another experimental study reported a significant effect of transformational leadership on followers' organizational commitment and unit-level financial performance. Other studies (e.g., Bycio, Hackett, & Allen, 1995; Koh, Steers, & Terborg, 1995), including three meta-analytic reviews (e.g., Dumdum *et al.*, 2002; Fuller *et al.*, 1996; Lowe *et al.*, 1996) have also shown transformational leadership positively related to work-related outcomes such as satisfaction, commitment, and performance. It is possible that by encouraging followers to go beyond their immediate needs to address the long-term interests of their organizations, transformational leaders are able to mobilize higher levels of commitment from their followers for a common good of the organization (Avolio & Bass, 1988).

Although there is a theoretical basis to expect transformational leadership behaviour will influence perceptions of withdrawal behaviours, this area of research has received less research attention. According to Bass (1998), transformational leaders show respect and confidence, and they motivate their followers to work hard to improve organizational effectiveness (Bass & Avolio, 1994). By showing respect and confidence in their followers, transformational leaders are able to bring a high degree of trust and loyalty on the part of followers to the extent that followers are willing to identify with the leader and the organization. As a result, followers trust in and emotionally identify with the leader, such that they are willing to stay with the organization—even under very difficult circumstances. Others (e.g., Avolio, 1999; Bass, 1998) have argued that transformational leaders cause followers to become attached to their organization and work toward group goals leading to undesired behaviours. For instance, by encouraging followers to think more deeply about the obstacles confronting them in their jobs, transformational leaders are able to help followers develop a better understanding of what needs to be done to be successful, resulting in reduced withdrawal behaviours. Indeed, research findings have shown that transformational leadership is negatively related to withdrawal behaviours (Sosik & Godshalk, 2000; Walumbwa & Lawler, 2003).

TRANSFORMATIONAL LEADERSHIP AND COLLECTIVE EFFICACY

There is reason to believe the transformational leaders can influence collective efficacy. Shamir (1990) argued that one of the most important characteristics of transformational leadership is its ability to heighten followers' collective motivation. To explain how this process might occur, we draw on two interrelated theories. First, we turn to social identification theory—defined as a process whereby an individual's belief about a group or organization becomes self-referential or self-defining (Pratt, 1988), Transformational leaders are able to influence their followers by connecting followers' self-concept to the mission of the group, 'such that followers' behavior for the sake of group becomes self-expressive' (Kark & Shamir, 2000, p. 7). Indeed, empirical findings suggest that leaders who raise followers' identification with the group increase followers' willingness to contribute to group objectives (Shamir, Zakay, Breinin, & Popper, 1998, 2000).

Transformational leaders also can enhance collective efficacy by providing emotional and ideological explanations that link followers' individual identities to the collective identity of their organization (Kark & Shamir, 2002). For example, through individualized consideration, transformational leaders are able to help their followers' recognize their (followers') capabilities, which then provides a basis for elevating each follower's needs and performance to higher than expected levels (Shamir, House, & Arthur, 1993). Avolio, Kahai, Dumdum, and Sivasubramanian (2001) argued that transformational leaders influence perceptions of team members' ability, benevolence, integrity and information exchange (and by extension group effectiveness) by highlighting the importance of cooperation in performing collective tasks. Further, by emphasizing the group mission, stressing shared values and ideology, connecting followers' individual and group interests, transformational leaders provide followers with more opportunities to appreciate group accomplishments and other group members' contributions, resulting in collective identities (Kark & Shamir, 2002). Work by Jung and Sosik (2002), using 47 groups drawn from four Korean firms, demonstrated that transformational leadership was positively related to group cohesiveness and group effectiveness. It is possible that by encouraging followers to take greater responsibility for their own development as well as the development of others, transformational leaders are able to build greater collective identification in what's important for the group to consider and accomplish successfully (Kark & Shamir, 2002; Kark *et al.*, 2003). Such leaders are able to build followers' collective efficacy by raising their awareness of other group members' contribution and by emphasizing the value of self-sacrifice for the good of the group (Avolio, 1999; Bass, 1998).

Another important theoretical framework that can help explain how transformational leadership influences collective efficacy, is the self-concept theory (Brewer & Gardner, 1996). According to this theory, group norm is the yardstick for measuring individual self-worth in relation to other out-group members (Brewer & Gardner, 1996). This theory suggests increasing followers' self-efficacy and facilitating followers' self-identification with the group as mechanisms through which transformational leaders motivate followers. We argue that by emphasizing similarities among group members, transformational leaders can increase activation of collective efficacy by shaping the context of work and linking followers' values and ideologies to the mission of the group (Kark & Shamir, 2002; Shamir *et al.*, 1998). Such leaders work to raise their followers; confidence and expand their needs in line with what they have come to identify with in terms of groups' collective mission (Sosik, Avolio, & Kahai, 1997). By building followers' confidence, such leaders are expected to have a strong, positive influence over time on followers' level of collective identification and motivation (Shamir *et al.*, 1993).

COLLECTIVE EFFICACY AND FOLLOWERS' WORK-RELATED OUTCOMES

Collective efficacy can influence followers' work-related outcomes in a number of ways. Bandura (2000) argued that when faced with obstacles, groups with higher levels of collective efficacy are more likely to persist in trying to solve such problems. Bandura (1986, 1997) further argued that efficacy beliefs influence what people choose to do as a group, how much effort they put into it and their staying power when collective efforts fail to produce results. Thus, it is possible that employees with lower efficacy are likely to call in sick rather than face another day of frustration on a job they feel unable to perform. On the other hand, employees higher on efficacy may exhibit fewer withdrawal behaviours, as they are likely to

expend more effort and persistence in task performance (Bandura, 1986). These views have received support empirically. For instance, Hochwarter, Kiewitz, Castro, Perrewe, and Ferris (2003) reported that individuals with low perceived collective efficacy were less satisfied with their jobs when levels of 'go-along-to-get-along' politics increased. Jex and colleagues (e.g., Jex & Bliese, 1999); Jex & Thomas, 2003), using military personnel samples, found collective efficacy related to job-related stressors and strains (i.e., job satisfaction, commitment). Specifically, Jex and Bliese (1999) found collective efficacy significantly related to average levels of job satisfaction and organizational commitment. Mulvey and Klein (1998), in testing the impact of perceived loafing and collective efficacy on group goal process and performance, found collective efficacy positively related to group goal commitment. Zellars, Hochwarter, Perrewe, Miles, and Kiewitz (2001), using a sample of 188 nurses, found that collective efficacy was associated with lower levels of turnover intentions and higher levels of job satisfaction, even after controlling for age, gender and self-efficacy. Two recent meta-analytic reviews also reached similar conclusions regarding the validity of collective efficacy in predicting work-related outcomes (Gully, Incalcaterra, Joshi, & Beaubien, 2002; Stajkovic & Lee, 2001). Taken together, we advance the following hypotheses.

> *Hypothesis 1:* Transformational leadership will be positively associated with collective efficacy.

> *Hypothesis 2a:* Collective efficacy will mediate the relations between transformational leadership and organizational commitment.

> *Hypothesis 2b:* Collective efficacy will mediate the relations between transformational leadership and job satisfaction (i.e., satisfaction with supervisor and with work in general).

> *Hypothesis 3:* Collective efficacy will mediate the relations between transformational leadership and withdrawal behaviours (i.e., job and work withdrawal). . . .

RESULTS

Table 1 summarizes the means, standard deviations, coefficient alphas and correlations for all measures.

TESTS OF HYPOTHESES

To test the direct and indirect effect of transformational leadership, we followed the procedure

TABLE 1   Means, Standard Deviations, Coefficient Alphas and Correlations of Study Variables

Variables	M	SD	α	1	2	3	4	5	6
1. Transformational leadership	3.04	.72	.92	—					
2. Collective efficacy	4.31	.88	.74	.28**	—				
3. Organizational commitment	3.43	.69	.85	.42**	.39**	—			
4. Supervisor satisfaction	2.50	.49	.82	.58**	.37**	.36**	—		
5. Work satisfaction general	2.23	.60	.87	.47**	.27**	.52**	.27**	—	
6. Job withdrawal	2.55	.67	.72	−.09	−.22**	−.40**	−.28**	−.20**	—
7. Work withdrawal	1.46	.34	.84	.00	−.12**	−.17**	−.17**	−.01	.28**

**Correlation is significant at the .01 level (two-tailed).
Note. Collective efficacy variable is group mean from 33 groups assigned back to individuals; α = coefficient alpha.

described by Kenny, Kashy, and Bolger (1998) using hierarchical multiple regression. However, before conducting our analyses, we examined the residual plots and confirmed that regression assumptions were not violated. . . .

As shown in step 1 . . . , transformational leadership made a significant contribution to collective efficacy ($\beta = .36$, $p < .001$). Results in step 2 indicate that transformational leadership made significant contributions to all outcomes (organizational commitment, $\beta = .36$, $p < .001$; satisfaction with supervisor, $\beta = .67$, $p < .001$; satisfaction with work in general, $\beta = .40$, $p < .001$; job withdrawal, $\beta = -.14$, $p < .01$; and work withdrawal, $\beta = -.11$, $p < .05$). As indicated in step 3, collective efficacy significantly predicted work-related outcomes (organizational commitments, $\beta = .34$, $p < .011$; satisfaction with supervisor, $\beta = .36$, $p < .001$; satisfaction with work in general, $\beta = .29$, $p < .001$; job withdrawal, $\beta = -.23$, $p < .001$; and work withdrawal, $\beta = -.16$, $p < .01$). The decreased, but still significant, coefficient for transformational leadership at step 4 (column 13 and 14) indicates that collective efficacy *partially* mediates the contribution of transformational leadership to organizational commitment, satisfaction with supervisor, and with work in general. . . . However, [findings] indicate that collective efficacy completely mediates the relationship between the transformational leadership and withdrawal behaviours. Thus, these results fully support Hypotheses 1 and 3, and partially Hypothesis 2.

DISCUSSION

Research on transformational leadership has been criticized for providing little information about the possible mechanisms through which transformational leadership behaviour influences work-related outcomes (Podsakoff, MaKenzie, Paine, & Bachrach, 2000; Yukl, 1999). Thus, the present study was intended to enhance our understanding on leadership processes by explaining how transformational leaders motivate their followers (Kark & Shamir, 2002).

The finding that collective efficacy fully or partially mediated the relations between transformational leadership and work outcomes is a step forward in uncovering the process through which transformational leadership influences work-related outcomes, and more importantly, why followers of transformational leaders demonstrate high levels of job satisfaction and commitment, and less withdrawal intentions. Specifically, we found that collective efficacy completely mediated the effect of transformational leadership on followers' withdrawal behaviours, but only partially on work attitudes. The finding that collective efficacy partially mediated the relationship between transformational leadership and work-related attitudes suggests that transformational leadership may influence work-related attitudes through multiple mechanisms. Ajzen and Fishbein (1980) suggested that two constructs must correspond in terms of their levels of specificity in order to have strong relationship. Job satisfaction and organizational commitment are relatively general attitudes while collective efficacy is a task-specific belief in this study. Thus, it is reasonable to expect factors other than collective efficacy may mediate the relationship between transformational leadership and work attitudes. Moreover, because transformational leaders are able to encourage followers to think critically and to seek new ways to approach their job, this may directly strengthen followers' job involvement and intrinsic motivation, resulting in more desirable work-related attitudes. This is an important area for future research.

The results of this study are also in line with results of Chen and Bliese (2002) which suggested that leadership may be a good predictor of collective efficacy. Specifically, the pattern of results support prior research which highlights the importance of transformational leadership in raising followers' confidence and their groups' collective mission (Sosik *et al.*, 1997). Many leadership researchers have argued the importance of collective efficacy in the transformational leadership process. For example, Shamir and colleagues (e.g., Shamir *et al.*, 1993; Shamir *et al.*, 1998) argued that transformational leadership can increase the salience of collective identity of followers by highlighting their membership in the unit and simultaneously emphasize the identity of the unit, by stressing its uniqueness from other units. Bass and Avolio (1994) take a similar position, suggesting that transformational leaders increase group members' motivation, confidence and performance by elevating the salience of the group and its capabilities while also supporting followers in achieving the collective goals. Finally, our findings also suggest that by developing collective efficacy through transformational leadership, withdrawal behaviours can be greatly minimized. That is, high collective efficacy may lower the rates of undesired behaviours (i.e., reporting late to work or calling in sick when they are actually not), e.g., by providing group members with emotional support (Cohen & Wills, 1985). . . .

References

Ajzen, I., & Fishbein, M. (1980). *Understanding attitudes and predicting social behavior.* Englewood Cliffs, NJ: Prentice-Hall.

Antonakis, J., Avolio, B. J., & Sivasubramaniam, N. (2003). Context and leadership: An examination of the nine full-range leadership theory using the multifactor leadership questionnaire. *Leadership Quarterly, 14,* 261–295.

Arbuckle, J. L., & Wothke, W. (1999). *AMOS 4.0 user's guide.* Chicago, Il.: Smallwaters.

Avolio, B. J. (1999). *Full leadership development: Building the vital forces in organizations.* Newbury Park. CA: Sage.

Avolio, B. A., & Bass, B. M. (1988). Transformational leadership, charisma and beyond. In J. G. Hunt, B. R. Balaga, H. P. Bachler, & C. Schriesheim (Eds.), *Emerging leadership vista* (pp. 29–50). Elmsford, NY: Pergamon Press.

Avolio, B. J., Bass, B. M., & Jung, D. I. (1999). Re-examining the components of transformational and transactional leadership using the multifactor leadership questionnaire. *Journal of Occupational and Organizational Psychology, 72,* 441–462.

Avolio, B. J., Kahai, S., Dumdum, R., & Sivasubramaniam, N. (2001). Virtual teams: Implications e-leadership and team development. In M. London (Ed.), *How people evaluate others in organizations* (pp. 337–358). Mahwah, NJ: Erlbaum.

Bandura, A. (1986). *Social foundations of thought and action: A social cognitive view.* Englewood Cliffs, NJ: Prentice Hall.

Bandura, A. (1997). *Self-efficacy: The exercise of control.* New York: Freeman.

Bandura, A. (2000). Exercise of human agency through collective efficacy. *Current Directions in Psychological Science, 9,* 75–78.

Barling, J., Weber, T., & Kelloway, E. K. (1986). Effects of transformational leadership training on attitudinal and financial outcomes: A field experiment. *Journal of Applied Psychology, 81,* 827–832.

Bass, B. M. (1985). *Leadership and performance beyond expectations.* New York: Free Press.

Bass, B. M. (1998). *Transformational leadership: Industry, military, and educational impact.* Mahwah, NJ: Erlbaum.

Bass, B. M. (1999). Two decades of research in transformational leadership. *European Journal of Works and Organizational Psychology, 10,* 9–32.

Bass, B. M., & Avolio, B. J. (1994). *Improving organizational effectiveness through transformational leadership.* Thousand Oaks. CA: Sage.

Bass, B. M., & Avolio, B. J. (1985). *Multifactor leadership questionnaire: Manual leader form, rater, and scoring key for MLQ* (Form 5x-Short). Redwood City, CA: Mind Garden.

Bliese, P. D. (2000). Within-group agreement, non-independence, and reliability: Implications for data aggregation and analysis. In K. J. Klein & S. W. J. Kozlowski, (Eds.), *Multilevel theory, research and methods in organizations: Foundations, extensions, and new directions* (pp. 349–381). San Francisco. CA: Jossey-Bass.

Brislin, R. W. (1980). Translation and content analysis of oral and written materials. In H. C. Triandis & J. W. Berry (Eds.), *Handbook of cross-cultural psychology* (Vol. 2, pp. 389–444). Boston, MA: Allyn and bacon.

Brewer, M. B., & Gardner, W. (1996). Who is this "we"? Levels of collective identity and self representations. *Journal of Personality and Social Psychology, 71,* 83–93.

Bycio, P., Hackett, R. D., & Allen, J. S. (1995). Further assessment of Bass's (1985) conceptualization of transactional and transformational leadership. *Journal of Applied Psychology, 80,* 468–478.

Chen, M. (1995). *Asian management systems: Chinese, Japanese, and Korean styles of business.* London: International Thomson.

Chen, G., & Bliese, P. D. (2002). The role of different levels of leadership in predicting self and collective efficacy: Evidence for discontinuity. *Journal of Applied Psychology,* 87, 549–556.

Crampton, S. M., & Wagner, III, J. A. (1994). Percept-percept in microorganization research: An investigation of prevalence and effect. *Journal of Applied Psychology,* 79, 67–76.

Cohen, S., & Wills, T. A. (1985). Stress social report, and the buffering hypothesis. *Psychological Bulletin,* 98, 310–357.

Donner, A. (1982). The relative effectiveness of procedures commonly used in multiple regression analysis for dealing with missing values. *American Statistician,* 36, 378–381.

Dumdum, U. R., Lowe, K. B., & Avolio, B. J. (2002). A meta-analysis of transformational and transactional leadership correlates of effectiveness and satisfaction: An update and extension. In B. J. Avolio & F. J. Yammarino (Eds.), *Transformational and charismatic leadership: The road ahead* (Vol. 2, pp. 36–66). Oxford: Elsevier Science.

Dvir, T., Eden, D., Avolio, B. J., & Shamir, B. (2002). Impact of transformational leadership on follower development and performance: A field experiment. *Academy of Management Journal,* 45, 735–744.

Farh, J. L., & Cheng, B. S. (2000). A cultural analysis of paternalistic leadership in Chinese organizations. In J. T. Li, A. S., Tsui, & E. Weldon (Eds.), *Management and organizations in the Chinese context* (pp. 84–127). London: Macmillan.

Fuller, J. B., Peterson, C. E., Hester, K., & Stringer, D. Y. (1996). A quantitative review of research on charismatic leadership. *Psychological Reports,* 78, 271–287.

Gully, S. M., Incalcaterra, K. A., Joshi, A., & Beaubien, J. M. (2002). A meta-analysis of team-efficacy, potency, and performance: Interdependence and level of analysis as moderators of observed relationships. *Journal of Applied Psychology,* 87, 819–832.

Harman, H. H. (1967). *Modern factor analysis.* Chicago, IL: University of Chicago Press.

Hanisch, K. A., & Hulin, C. L. (1991). General attitudes and organizational withdrawal: An evaluation of a causal model. *Journal of Vocational Behavior,* 39, 110–128.

Hochwarter, W. A., Kiewitz, C., Castro, S. L., Perrewe, P. L., & Ferris, G. R. (2003). Positive affectivity and collective efficacy as moderators of the relationship between perceived politics and job satisfaction. *Journal of Applied Social Psychology,* 33, 1009–1035.

Hofstede, G. (1980). *Culture's consequences: International differences in work-related values.* Thousand Oak, CA: Sage.

Hwang, K. K. (2001). The deep structure of Confucianism: A social psychological approach. *Asian Philosophy,* 11, 179–204.

Jex, S. M., & Bliese, P. D. (1999). Efficacy beliefs as a moderator of the impact of work-related stressors: A multilevel study. *Journal of Applied Psychology,* 84, 349–361.

Jex, S. M., & Thomas, J. L. (2003). Relations between stressors and group perceptions: Main and mediating effects. *Work and Stress,* 17, 158–170.

Jung, D. I., & Sosik, J. J. (2002). Transformational leadership in work groups: The role of empowerment, cohesiveness, and collective-efficacy on perceived group performance. *Small Group Research,* 33, 313–336.

Kark, R., & Shamir, B. (2002). The dual effect of transformational leadership: Priming relational and collective selves and further effects on followers. In B. J. Avolio & F. J. Yammarino (Eds.), *Transformational and charismatic leadership: The road ahead* (pp. 67–91). Oxford, UK: Elsevier Science.

Kark, R., & Shamir, B., & Chen, G. (2003). The two faces of transformational leadership: Empowerment and dependency. *Journal of Applied Psychology,* 88, 246–255.

Kenny, D. A., Kashy, D. A., & Bolger, N. (1998). Data analysis in social psychology. In D. T. Gilbert, S. T. Fiske, & G. Lindzey (Eds.), *The handbook of social psychology* (4th. ed., pp. 233–265). Boston, MA: McGraw-Hill.

Koh, W. L., Steers, R. M., & Terborg, J. R. (1995). The effects of transformational leadership on teacher attitudes and student performance in Singapore. *Journal of Organizational Behavior,* 16, 319–333.

Lowe, K. B., Kroeck, K. G., & Sivasubramaniam, N. (1996). Effectiveness correlates of transformational and transactional leadership: A meta-analysis review of the MLQ literature. *Leadership Quarterly,* 7, 385–425.

Maddux, J. E. (2002). Self-efficacy. In C. R. Snyder & S. J. Lopez (Eds.), *Handbook of positive psychology* (pp. 277–287). Oxford: Oxford University Press.

Mohrman, S. A., Cohen, S. G., & Mohrman, A. M. (1995). *Designing team-based organizations: New forms for knowledge work.* San Francisco. CA: Jossey-Bass.

Morgeson, F. P., & Hofmann, D. A. (1999). The structure and function of collective constructs. Implications for multilevel research and theory development. *Academy of Management Review,* 24, 249–265.

Mowday, R. T., Steers, R. M., & Porter, L. W. (1979). The measurement of organizational commitment. *Journal of Vocational Behavior,* 14, 224–247.

Mulvey, P. W., & Klein, H. J. (1998). The impact of perceived loafing and collective efficacy on group goal process and group performance. *Organizational Behavior and Human Decision Processes,* 74, 62–87.

Podsakoff, P. M., MacKenzie, S. B., Paine, J. B., & Bachrach, D. G. (2000). Organizational citizenship behaviours: A critical review the theoretical and empirical literature and suggestions for future research. *Journal of Management,* 26, 513–563.

Podsakoff, P., MacKenzie, S., Lee, J., & Podsakoff, N. (2003). Common method biases in behavioral research:

A critical review of the literature and recommendation remedies. *Journal of Applied Psychology, 88,* 879–903.

Podsakoff, P. M., & Organ, D. W. (1986). Self-reports in organizational research: Problems and prospects. *Journal of Management,* 12, 531–544.

Pratt, M. G. (1998). To be or not to be: Central questions in organizational identification. In D. A. Whetten & P. C. Godfrey (Eds.), *Identity in organizations: Building theory through conversation* (pp. 171–207). Thousand Oaks, CA: Sage.

Raju, N. S., Laffitte, L. J., & Byrne, B. M. (2002). Measurement equivalence: A comparison of methods on confirmatory factor analysis and item response theory. *Journal of Applied Psychology,* 87, 517–529.

Riggs, M. L., Warka, J., Babasa, B., Betancourt, R., & Hooker, S. 1994. Development and validation of self-efficacy and outcome expectancy scales for job-related applications. *Educational and Psychological Measurement,* 58, 1017–1034.

Schriesheim, C. A. (1979). The similarity of individual directed and group directed leader behavior descriptions. *Academy of Management Journal,* 22, 345–455.

Shamir, B. (1990). Calculations, values, identities: The sources of collectivistic work motivation. *Human Relations,* 43, 313–332.

Shamir, B., House, R. J., & Arthur, M. B. (1993). The motivational effect of charismatic leadership: A self-concept based theory. *Organization Science,* 4, 577–594.

Shamir, B., Zakay, E., Breinin, E., & Popper, M. (1998). Correlates of charismatic leader behavior in military units: Subordinates attitudes, unit characteristics and superiors' appraisals of leader performance. *Academy of Management Journal,* 41, 387–409.

Shamir, B., Zakay, E., Breinin, E., & Popper, M. (2000). Leadership and social identification in military units. *Journal of Applied Social Psychology,* 30, 612–640.

Sinha, J. B. P. (1997). A cultural perspective on organizational behavior in India. In P. C. Earley and M. Erez (Eds.), *New Perspectives on international industrial/organizational psychology* (pp. 53–74). San Francisco, CA: New Lexington.

Smith, P. C., Kendall, L. M., & Hulin, C. L. (1969). *The measurement of satisfaction in work and retirement.* Chicago, IL: Rand-McNally.

Sosik, J. J., Avolio, B. J., & Kahai, S. S. (1997). Effects of leadership style and anonymity and group potency and effectiveness in a group decision support system environment. *Journal of Applied Psychology,* 82, 89–103.

Sosik, J. J., & Godshalk, V. (2000). Leadership styles, mentoring functions received, and job-related stress: A conceptual model and preliminary study. *Journal of Organizational Behavior,* 21, 365–390.

Stajkovic, A. D., & Lee, D. S. (2001). *A meta-analysis of the relationship between collective efficacy and group performance.* Paper presented at the National Academy of Management meeting. Washington, DC, USA.

Walumbwa, F. O. (1999). Rethinking the issues of international technology transfer. *Journal of Technology Studies,* 25, 51–54.

Walumbwa, F. O., & Lawler, J. J. (2003). Building effective organizations: Transformational leadership, collectivist orientation, work-related attitudes, and withdrawal behaviours in three emerging economies. *International Journal of Human Resource Management,* 14, 1083–1101.

Yukl, G. (1999). An evaluation of conceptual weaknesses in transformational and charismatic leadership theories. *Leadership Quarterly,* 10, 285–305.

Zellars, K. L., Hochwarter, W. A., Perrewe, P. L., Miles, A. K., & Kiewitz, C. (2001). Beyond self-efficacy: Interactive effects of role conflict and perceived collective efficacy. *Journal of Managerial Issues,* 13, 483–499.

Reading 41

Transformational Leader Behaviors and Their Effects on Followers' Trust in Leader, Satisfaction, and Organizational Citizenship Behaviors

Philip M. Podsakoff and Scott B. Mackenzie
Indiana University

Robert H. Moorman
West Virginia University

Richard Fetter
Indiana University

The search for and identification of those behaviors that increase a leader's effectiveness has been a major concern of practicing managers and leadership researchers alike for the past several decades (cf. Bass, 1981; House, 1971, 1988; House & Baetz, 1979; Stogdill, 1974; Yukl, 1989a, 1989b). Traditional views of leadership effectiveness have focused primarily, although not exclusively, on what Burns (1978) and Bass (1985) have called *transactional* leader behaviors. According to Burns (1978), transactional behaviors are founded on an exchange process in which the leader provides rewards in return for the subordinate's effort.

More recently, however, the focus of leadership research has shifted from one of examining the effects of transactional leadership to the identification and examination of those behaviors exhibited by the leader that make followers more aware of the importance and values of task outcomes, activate their higher-order needs, and induce them to transcend self-interests for the sake of the organization (Bass, 1985; Yukl, 1989a, 1989b). These *transformational* or *charismatic* behaviors[1] are believed to *augment* the impact of transactional leader behaviors on employee outcome variables, because "followers feel trust and respect toward the leader and they are motivated to do more than they are expected to do" (Yukl, 1989b, p. 272). Examples of this new focus on leadership include the work of House, Bass, and others (e.g., Avolio & Bass, 1988; Bass, 1985; Bass, Avolio, & Goodheim, 1987; Bass, Waldman, Avolio, & Bebb,

1987; Bennis & Nanus, 1985; Boal & Bryson, 1988; House, 1977; House, Spangler, & Woycke, 1989; House, Woycke, & Fodor, 1988; Howell & Frost, 1989; Conger & Kanungo, 1987; Shamir, House, & Arthur, 1988; Tichy & DeVanna, 1986). While each of these approaches differs somewhat in the specific behaviors they associate with transformational leadership, all of them share the common perspective that effective leaders transform or change the basic values, beliefs, and attitudes of followers so that they are willing to perform beyond the minimum levels specified by the organization.

Preliminary research on transformational leadership has been rather promising. Some of this research (Bass, 1985; Bennis & Nanns, 1985; Boal & Bryson, 1988; Conger & Kanungo, 1987; House, 1977; House, Woycke, & Fodor, 1988; Howell & Frost, 1989; Kouzes & Posner, 1987; Tichy & DeVanna, 1986) has been primarily conceptual in nature, focusing on the identification of the key transformational behaviors, and the development of theories of their antecedents and consequences. The remainder of this research has focused on empirically testing these conceptual frameworks. Generally speaking, the empirical results have verified the impact of transformational leader behaviors on employee attitudes, effort, and "in-role" performance. For example, Bass (1985) cites a variety of field studies demonstrating that transformational leader behaviors are positively related to employees' satisfaction, self-reported effort, and job performance. Similar results have been reported by Howell and Frost (1989). They manipulated the behavior of leaders in a laboratory setting and found that charismatic leader behaviors produced better performance, greater

Source: Edited and reprinted from the *Leadership Quarterly* 1, 2, 107–142. Copyright 1990, with permission from Elsevier.

satisfaction, and enhanced role perceptions (less role conflict) than directive leader behaviors.

Despite these encouraging results, it is important to note that the majority of the empirical research in this area has focused on the impact of transformational leader behaviors on in-role performance and follower satisfaction, rather than "extra-role" performance. While the effects of transformational behaviors on employee in-role performance are interesting, they do not capture the most important effects of transformational leader behaviors. The real essence of transformational leadership is that these leaders "lift ordinary people to extraordinary heights" (Boal & Bryson, 1988, p. 11) and cause followers to "do more than they are expected to do" (Yukl, 1989a, p. 272) and "perform beyond the level of expectations" (Bass, 1985). In other words, as noted by Graham (1988), the most important effects of transformational leaders should be on extra-role performance, rather than in-role performance. Transformational leaders should motivate followers to perform at a level "over and above mechanical compliance with the routine directives of the organization" (Katz & Kahn, 1978, p. 528).

Also surprising, given the theoretical discussions of Bennis and Nanus (1985), Boal and Bryson (1988), and Yukl (1989a, 1989b), is that a follower's *trust* in his or her leader has not been given more attention in empirical research as a potential mediator of the effects of transformational leader behaviors on criterion variables. Bennis and Nanus (1985), for example, have suggested that effective leaders are ones that earn the trust of their followers. Similarly, trust in and loyalty to the leader play a critical role in the transformational leadership model of Boal and Bryson (1988). Finally, as noted by Yukl (1989b), one of the key reasons why followers are motivated by transformational leaders to perform beyond expectations is that followers trust and respect them. Indeed, Kouzes and Posner (1987) cite several studies, all of which indicate that the leader characteristics most valued by followers are honesty, integrity, and truthfulness. Thus, trust is viewed as playing an important mediating role in the transformational leadership process.

Another potential mediator of the impact of transformational leader behaviors on extra-role performance, in addition to trust, is employee satisfaction. Organ (1988a, 1988b, in press) has reviewed empirical research which demonstrates that employee job satisfaction is an important determinant of extra-role (e.g., "organizational citizenship") behavior. Moreover, virtually all models of transformational leadership postulate that transformational leaders enhance followers' work attitudes and satisfaction. Thus, when Organ's research on the antecedents of organizational citizenship behaviors (OCBs) is combined with models of the effects of transformational leadership, satisfaction emerges as a potential mediator of the impact of transformational leader behavior on the extra-role performance of followers.

In summary, previous theoretical and empirical research suggests that there is good reason to believe that transformational leader behaviors influence extra-role or organizational citizenship behaviors. There are, however, several potential ways in which this might happen. As shown in Figure 1, one way is for transformational leader behaviors to *directly* influence organizational citizenship behaviors, much in the same way that transactional leader behaviors have been shown to influence in-role performance (e.g., Podsakoff, Todor, & Skov, 1982; Podsakoff, Todor, Grover, & Huber, 1984; Sims & Szilagyi, 1975). This is consistent with Smith, Organ, and Near's (1983) finding that a leader's individualized support behavior, one of the transformational leader behaviors identified by Bass (Avolio & Bass, 1988; Bass, 1985), has a direct effect on some forms of employee citizenship behavior (i.e., conscientiousness).

Another possibility, also depicted in Figure 1, is that transformational leader behaviors influence organizational citizenship behaviors *only indirectly*, through their effects on mediators like *followers' trust in their leaders and satisfaction*. For example, in addition to documenting the direct effects of leader supportiveness on conscientiousness, Smith et al. (1983) also found that employee satisfaction *mediated* the impact of leader supportiveness on employee altruism. Followers' trust in and loyalty to the leader also has been accorded a similar role in several recent discussions of the transformational leadership process (e.g., Boal & Bryson, 1988; Kouzes & Posner, 1987; Yukl, 1989b). Thus, both followers' trust and satisfaction have been identified as potential mediators of the impact of transformational leader behaviors on followers' citizenship behaviors.

Finally, it is possible that transformational leader behaviors influence followers' citizenship behaviors *both directly* and *indirectly*. Their total effects may, in other words, be due to a combination of direct (unmediated) effects, and indirect effects working through mediators like trust and satisfaction.

The purpose of the present study, therefore, is to examine the effects of transformational leader

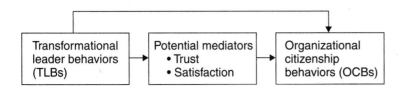

FIGURE 1
**Conceptual
Relationship
Between
Transformational
Leader Behaviors,
Potential Mediators,
and Organizational
Citizenship
Behaviors**

behaviors on organizational citizenship behaviors, and the potential mediating roles of trust and satisfaction in that process. Measures of transformational leader behaviors, trust, and satisfaction were obtained from 988 exempt employees of a large petrochemical company, and measures of these employees' citizenship behaviors were obtained from their leaders. Structural equation modeling then was used to examine the direct and indirect effects of these behaviors on trust, satisfaction, and citizenship behavior. Moreover, because Bass (Avolio & Bass, 1988; Bass, 1985) argues that the effects of transformational leadership behaviors *augment* or *supplement* the effects of transactional leadership behaviors, we examined the effects of the transformational behaviors in the empirical context of the effects of the principal transactional leader behavior identified by him—contingent reward behavior. . . .

MEASURES

TRANSFORMATIONAL LEADER BEHAVIORS

Although broadly speaking, the topic of transformational leadership has received a great deal of attention in recent years, our understanding of what is involved in transformational leadership still is somewhat unclear. The one thing that is clear, however, is that transformational leadership is multidimensional in nature. Our review of the extant literature suggests that there are at least six key behaviors associated with transformational leaders:

- *Identifying and articulating a vision*—Behavior on the part of the leader aimed at identifying new opportunities for his or her unit/division/company, and developing, articulating, and inspiring others with his or her vision of the future.

- *Providing an appropriate model*—Behavior on the part of the leader that sets an example for

employees to follow that is consistent with the values the leader espouses.

- *Fostering the acceptance of group goals*—Behavior on the part of the leader aimed at promoting cooperation among employees and getting them to work together toward a common goal.

- *High performance expectations*—Behavior that demonstrates the leader's expectations for excellence, quality, and/or high performance on that part of followers.

- *Providing individualized support*—Behavior on the part of the leader that indicates that he/she respects followers and is concerned about their personal feelings and needs.

- *Intellectual stimulation*—Behavior on the part of the leader that challenges followers to re-examine some of their assumptions about their work and rethink how it can be performed.

As shown in Table 1, each of these behaviors has been identified as an important element of the transformational leadership process. There is a great deal of consensus among the researchers on some of these behaviors, but not on others. For example, identifying and articulating a vision has been identified by virtually all of the authors as an important component of the transformational leadership process. Similarly, facilitating the acceptance of group goals and providing an appropriate model were identified by at least four different authors as elements of transformational leadership. In contrast, only Bass and his colleagues (Avolio & Bass, 1988; Bass, 1985) argue that intellectual stimulation should be considered an aspect of transformational leadership. However, in order to make certain that the domain of transformational leader behaviors was adequately tapped, and that our test of the impact of these behaviors was comprehensive, we chose to include all six of the categories identified above in the present study. . . .

TABLE 1 **Behavioral Components of Existing Models of Transformational Leadership**

Behavioral Components	House (1977)	Bradford and Cohen (1984)	Bass (1985)	Bennis and Nanus (1985)	Tichy and DeVanna (1986)	Conger and Kanungo (1987)	Kouzes and Posner (1987)
Identify and articulate a vision	Provide an appealing vision	Determine and build a common vision	Charismatic leader behavior	Management of attention through vision	Recognize a need for change and create a new vision	Advocate an appealing yet unconventional vision	Challenge the process and inspire a shared vision
Provide an appropriate model	Set an example for followers to imitate		Charismatic leader behavior			Take a high personal risk to support the vision	Model the way
Foster the acceptance of group goals		Build a shared responsibility team		Work to develop commitment and trust	Team build to gain support for new vision		Enable others to act
High performance expectations		Communicate high expectations of follower performance	Inspirational leader behavior				
Provide individualized support			Individualized consideration			Be sensitive to the needs of the followers	
Recognize accomplishments						Behave with confidence and enthusiasm	Encourage the heart
Intellectual stimulation			Intellectual stimulation				
Other	Behave to arouse individual motives	Continuously develop the skills of individuals	Charismatic leader behavior*				

Note: *Bass's (1985) conceptualization of charismatic leadership includes leader vision, as well as respect for the leader and the inspiration and encouragement provided by his or her presence.

AGGREGATE EFFECTS OF LEADER BEHAVIORS ON OCBS

An examination of the aggregate effects of the set of transformational leader behaviors on the set of organizational citizenship behaviors indicates that the effects of these leader behaviors on OCBs are *indirect,* rather than *direct,* in that they are mediated by followers, trust in their leaders. More specifically, our findings generally showed that: (*a*) transformational leader behaviors has no direct effects on OCBs, (*b*) transformational leader behaviors influenced both employee trust and satisfaction, and (*c*) trust influenced OCBs, but employee satisfaction did not. Moreover, it is important to note that these findings are completely independent of the effects of transactional leader behaviors, and also were relatively robust in comparison to the effects of common method biases.

In contrast, the effects of the transactional leader behavior (contingent rewards) on OCBs produced a markedly different pattern. Unlike the transformational leader behaviors, contingent reward behavior had a direct positive impact on both altruism and sportsmanship, but no effect at all on either trust or employee satisfaction. Thus, in contrast to the transformational behaviors, transactional leader behavior influenced OCBs *directly,* rather than indirectly. The fact that these two types of leader behavior appear to influence extra-role performance in very different ways emphasizes the importance of the distinction between transactional and transformational leader behaviors.

One possible explanation for why transactional leader behaviors have direct rather than indirect effects may have to do with the nature of the behaviors themselves. Transactional leader behaviors are ones which are founded on some sort of exchange, or give and take, between the leader and the subordinate. If, as shown by Jackson, Keith, and Schlacter (1983), managers consider both in-role and extra-role behaviors when evaluating employee performance, they may also recognize accomplishments in both of these areas as well. This may cause employees to see the performance of OCBs as a means of obtaining recognition and other forms of rewards, thus motivating them to engage in organizational citizenship behavior.

INDIVIDUAL EFFECTS OF LEADER BEHAVIORS ON OCBs

An examination of the individual level results produced some interesting findings. The standardized estimates suggest that the "core" transformational leader behaviors, individualized support, and intellectual stimulation, were the key derminants of both trust and satisfaction. The "core" transformational behaviors and individualized support both had positive effects, as expected. However, intellectual stimulation was found to have a negative impact on both trust and satisfaction.

One possible explanation for this surprising finding may have to do with the effect of intellectual stimulation on role ambiguity, conflict, and stress. Although intellectual stimulation may produce desirable effects in the long run, it may be that in the short run, leaders who continually urge or exhort followers to search for new and better methods of doing things create ambiguity, conflict, or other forms of stress in the minds of those followers. If the increased task demands produced by a leader's intellectual stimulation behavior increase stress, ambiguity, and conflict, we might expect that followers will express less trust in the leader and engage in fewer OCBs. Indeed, this is consistent with recent research (cf. Cohen, 1980; Motowidlo, Packard, & Manning, 1986) that suggests that stress induced by increased task demands decreases interpersonal sensitivity and helping behavior.

Another possible reason why intellectual stimulation may reduce follower trust and satisfaction may have to do with the destabilizing nature of intellectual stimulation itself. According to Avolio and Bass (1988), intellectual stimulation causes a "cognitive reappraisal of current circumstances," thus possibly reversing an individual's "figure-ground" and leading to a questioning of "old" and perhaps comfortable assumptions.[2] It may be that this process is dissatisfying, and that leaders who continually do this are trusted less because they are perceived as being less predictable and/or dependable.

One additional finding of note is that high performance expectations reduced employee trust. Although it is not immediately obvious why this occurred, it may have to do with the way in which we measured high performance expectations. House (1977) suggests that two aspects of high performance expectations are important. One is that the leader must communicate those expectations to his/her subordinates. The other is that the leader must let them know that he/she is confident they can meet these expectations. In retrospect, our measure seems to do a good job of tapping the former component, but not the latter. It may be natural for an employee to distrust a leader who continually demands high levels of performance without ever expressing any confidence in the employee's ability to achieve those expectations. . . .

Notes

1. Although there are differences between transformational and charismatic leader behaviors, they are similar in many respects. The principal reason we chose to use the term transformational leadership is that it is broader in the sense that it includes a wider variety of leader behaviors. Thus, unless otherwise indicated in our discussion, we will use the term transformational leadership throughout the paper.

2. We would like to thank one anonymous reviewer for pointing out this possibility.

References

Alexander, S., & Ruderman, M. (1987). The role of procedural and distributive justice in organizational behavior. *Social Justice Research,* 1, 177–198.

Avolio, B. J., & Bass, B. M. (1988). Transformational leadership, charisma, and beyond. In J. G. Hunt, B. R. Baliga, H. P. Dachler, & C. A. Schriesheim (Eds.), *Emerging leadership vistas* (pp. 29–49). Lexington, MA: Lexington Books.

Bagozzi, R. P. (1978). The construct validity of the affective, behavioral, and cognitive components of attitude by analysis of covariance structures. *Multivariate Behavioral Research,* 13, 9–31.

Bagozzi, R. P. (1980). *Causal models in marketing.* New York: Wiley.

Bass, B. M. (1981). *Stogdill's handbook of leadership* (rev. ed.). New York: Free Press.

Bass, B. M. (1985). *Leadership and performance beyond expectations.* New York: Free Press.

Bass, B. M., Avolio, B. J., & Goodheim, L. (1987). Biography and the assessment of transformational leadership at the world class level. *Journal of Management,* 13, 7–19.

Bass, B. M., Waldman, D. A., Avolio, B. J., & Bebb, M. (1987). Transformational leadership and the falling dominoes effect. *Group and Organization Studies,* 12, 73–87.

Batesman, T. S., & Organ, D. W. (1983). Job satisfaction and the good soldier: The relationship between affect and employee "citizenship." *Academy of Management Journal,* 26, 587–595.

Bennis, W., & Nanus, B. (1985). *Leaders: The strategies for taking charge.* New York: Harper & Row.

Bentler, P. M., & Bont, D. G. (1980). Significance tests and goodness of fit in the analysis of covariance structures. *Psychological Bulletin,* 88, 588–606.

Boal, K. B., & Bryson, J. M. (1988). Charismatic leadership: A phenomenological and structural approach. In J. G. Hunt, B. R. Baliga, H. P. Dachler, & C. A. Schriesheim (Eds.), *Emerging Leadership Vistas* (pp. 5–28). Lexington, MA: Lexington Books.

Bradford, D. L., & Cohen, A. R. (1984). *Managing for excellence: The guide to developing high performance in contemporary organizations.* New York: Wiley.

Burnkrant, R. E., & Page, T. J., Jr. (1982). An examination of the convergent, discriminant, and predictive validity of Fishbein's behavioral intention model. *Journal of Marketing Research,* 19, 550–561.

Burns, J. M. (1978). *Leadership.* New York: Harper & Row.

Churchill, G. A., Jr. (1979). A paradigm for developing better measures of marketing constructs. *Journal of Marketing Research,* 16, 64–73.

Cohen, S. (1980). Aftereffects of stress on human performance and social behavior: A review of research and theory. *Psychological Bulletin,* 88, 82–108.

Conger, J. A., & Kanungo, R. N. (1987). Toward a behavioral theory of charismatic leadership in organizational settings. *Academy of Management Review,* 12, 637–647.

Cook, J., & Wall, T. (1980). New work attitude measures of trust, organizational commitment and personal need non-fulfillment. *Journal of Occupational Psychology,* 53, 39–52.

Dansereau, F., Jr., Graen, G., & Haga, W. J. (1975). A vertical dyad linkage approach to leadership within formal organizations: A longitudinal investigation of the role-making process. *Organizational Behavior and Human Performance,* 13, 46–78.

Dunham, R. B., Smith, F. J., & Blackburn, R. S. (1977). Validation of the index of organizational reactions with the JDI, the MSQ, and the faces scales. *Academy of Management Journal,* 20, 420–432.

Folger, R. (1977). Distributive and procedural justice: Combined impact of "voice" and improvement on experienced inequity. *Journal of Personality and Psychology,* 35, 108–119.

Folger, R. (1986). Rethinking equity theory. In H. W. Bierhof, R. L. Cohen, & J. Greenberg, (Eds.), *Justice in Social Relations* (pp. 145–162). New York: Plenum.

Folger, R. (1987). Distributive and procedural justice in the workplace. *Social Justice Research,* 1, 143–159.

Folger, R., & Konovsky, M. A. (1989). Effects of procedural and distributive justice on reactions to pay raise decisions. *Academy of Management Journal,* 32, 115–130.

Giffin, K. (1967). The contribution of studies of source credibility to a theory of interpersonal trust in the communication process. *Psychological Bulletin,* 68, 104–120.

Gillet, B., & Schwab, D. P. (1975). Convergent and discriminant validities of corresponding Job Descriptive Index and Minnesota Satisfaction Questionnaire scales. *Journal of Applied Psychology,* 60, 629–631.

Graen, G. (1976). Role making processes within complex organizations. In M. D. Dunnette (Ed.), *Handbook of Industrial and Organizational Psychology* (pp. 1201–1245). Chicago: Rand McNally.

Graen, G., & Cashman, J. (1975). A role-making model of leadership in formal organizations: A developmental approach. J. G. Hunt & L. L. Larson (Eds.), *Leadership frontiers* (pp. 143–166). Kent, OH: Kent State University Press.

Graen, G., & Scandura, T. A. (1987). Toward a psychology of dynamic organizing. L. L. Cummings & B. M. Staw (Eds.), *Research in Organizational Behavior* (Vol. 9, pp. 175–208). Greenwich, CT: JAI.

Graham, J. W. (1988). Chapter 3 commentary: Transformational leadership: Fostering follower autonomy, not automatic followership. In J. G. Hunt, B. R. Baliga, H. P. Dachler, & C. A. Schriesheim (Eds.), *Emerging leadership vistas* (pp. 73–79). Lexington, MA: Lexington Books.

House, R. J. (1971). A path-goal theory of leader effectiveness. *Administrative Science Quarterly,* 16, 321–338.

House, R. J. (1977). A 1976 theory of charismatic leadership. In J. G. Hunt & L. L. Larson (Eds.), *Leadership: The cutting edge.* Carbondale, IL: Southern Illinois University Press.

House, R. J. (1988). Leadership research: Some forgotten, ignored, or overlooked findings. In J. G. Hunt, B. R. Baliga, H. P. Dachler, & C. A. Schriesheim (Eds.), *Emerging leadership vistas.* Lexington, MA: Lexington.

House, R. J., & Baetz, M. L. (1979). Leadership: Some empirical generalizations and new research directions. In B. M. Staw (Ed.), *Research in Organizational Behavior* (Vol. 1, pp. 341–423). Greenwich, CT: JAI Press.

House, R. J., Spangler, W. D., & Woycke, J. (1989). *Personality and charisma in the U.S. presidency: A psychological theory of leadership effectiveness.* Working paper, Wharton Business School, University of Pennsylvania.

House, R. J., Woycke, J., & Fodor, E. M. (1988). Perceived behavior and effectiveness of charismatic and non-charismatic U.S. presidents. In J. Conger, & R. Kanungo, (Eds.), *Charismatic Leadership and Management.* San Francisco: Jossey-Bass.

Howell, J. M., & Frost, P. J. (1989). A laboratory study of charismatic leadership. *Organizational Behavior and Human Decision Processes, 43,* 243–269.

Jackson, D. W., Keith, J. E., & Schlacter, J. L. (1983). Evaluation of selling performance: A study of current practices. *Journal of Personal Selling and Sales Management, 3,* 43–51.

Joreskog, K. G., & Sorbom, D. (1986). *LISREL IV: Analysis of linear structural relationships by maximum likelihood, instrumental variables and least squares methods* (4th ed.). Mooresville, IN: Scientific Software.

Katz, D., & Kahn, R. L. (1978). *The social psychology of organizations* (2nd ed.). New York: Wiley.

Kouzes, J. M., & Posner, B. Z. (1987). *The Leadership Challenge.* San Francisco: Jossey-Bass.

Kuhnert, K. W., & Lewis, P. (1987). Transactional and transformational leadership: A constructive/developmental analysis. *Academy of Management Review, 12,* 648–657.

Lord, R. G. (1985). An information processing approach to social perceptions, leadership and behavioral measurement in organizations. In L. L. Cummings & B. M. Staw (Eds.), *Research in Organizational Behavior* (Vol. 7, pp. 87–128). Greenwich, CT: JAI Press.

Lord, R. G., Binning, J. F., Rush, M. C., & Thomas, J. C. (1978). The effect of performance cues and leader behavior on questionnaire ratings of leadership behavior. *Organizational Behavior and Human Performance, 21,* 27–39.

Marsh, H. W., Balla, J. R., & McDonald, R. P. (1988). Goodness-of-fit indexes in confirmatory factor analysis: The effect of sample size. *Psychological Bulletin, 103,* 391–410.

McCrae, R. R., & Costa, P. T. (1987). Validation of the five-factor model of personality across instruments and observers. *Journal of Personality and Social Psychology, 52,* 81–90.

Motowidlo, S. J. (1984). Does job satisfaction lead to consideration and personal sensitivity? *Academy of Management Journal, 27,* 910–915.

Motowidlo, S. J., Packard, J. S., & Manning, M. R. (1986). Occupational stress: Its causes and consequences for job performance. *Journal of Applied Psychology, 71,* 618–629.

Nunnally, J. C. (1978). *Psychometric theory* (2nd ed.). New York: McGraw-Hill.

Organ, D. W. (1988a). *Organizational citizenship behavior: The good soldier syndrome.* Lexington, MA: Lexington Books.

Organ, D. W. (1988b). A restatement of the satisfaction-performance hypothesis. *Journal of Management, 14,* 547–557.

Organ, D. W. (in press). The motivational basis of organizational citizenship behavior. In B. M. Staw, & L. L. Cummings, (Eds.), *Research in organizational behavior* (Vol. 12). Greenwich, CT: JAI Press.

Phillips, J. S., & Lord, R. G. (1986). Notes on the practical and theoretical consequences of implicit leadership theories for the future of leadership measurement. *Journal of Management, 12,* 31–41.

Podsakoff, P. M., & Organ, D. W. (1986). Self-reports in organizational research: Problems and prospects. *Journal of Management, 13,* 419–441.

Podsakoff, P. M., Todor, W. D., Grover, R. A., & Huber, V. L. (1984). Situational moderators of leader reward and punishment behavior: Fact or fiction? *Organizational Behavior and Human Performance, 34,* 21–63.

Podsakoff, P. M., Todor, W. D., & Skov, R. (1982). Effects of leader performance contingent and noncontingent reward and punishment behaviors on subordinate performance and satisfaction. *Academy of Management Journal, 25,* 812–821.

Puffer, S. M. (1987). Prosocial behavior, noncompliant behavior, and work performance among commission salespeople. *Journal of Applied Psychology, 72,* 615–621.

Rotter, J. B. (1967). A new scale for the measurement of interpersonal trust. *Journal of Personality, 35,* 651–665.

Schmitt, N., & Stults, D. M. (1986). Methodology review: Analysis of multitrait-multimethod matrices. *Applied Psychological Measurement, 10,* 1–22.

Schwab, D. P. (1980). Construct validity in organizational behavior. In L. L. Cummings & B. M. Staw (Eds.), *Research in Organizational Behavior* (Vol. 2, pp. 3–43). Greenwich, CT: JAI Press.

Shamir, B., House, R. J., & Arthur, M. B. (1988). *The transformational effects of charismatic leadership: A motivational theory.* Unpublished Working Paper, The Hebrew University, Jerusalem.

Sims, H. P., Jr., & Szilagyi, A. D. (1975). Leader reward behavior and subordinate satisfaction and performance. *Organizational Behavior and Human Performance, 14,* 426–437.

Smith, C. A., Organ, D. W., & Near, J. P. (1983). Organizational citizenship behavior: Its nature and antecedents. *Journal of Applied Psychology, 68,* 653–663.

Stogdill, R. M. (1974). *Handbook of leadership.* New York: Free press.

Tichy, N., & DeVanna, M. (1986). *The transformational leader*. New York: Wiley.

Tucker, L. R., & Lewis, C. (1973). The reliability coefficient for maximum likelihood factor analysis. *Psychometrika,* 38, 1–10.

Weiss, D. J., Dawis, R. V., England, G. W., & Lofquist, L. H. (1967). *Manual for the Minnesota Satisfaction Questionnaire* (Minnesota Studies in Vocational Rehabilitation: XXII). Minneapolis: University of Minnesota, Industrial Relations Canter Work Adjustment Project.

Widaman, K. F. (1985). Hierarchically nested covariance structure models for multitrait-multimethod data. *Applied Psychological Measurement,* 9, 1–26.

Yukl, G. A. (1989a). *Leadership in organizations* (2nd ed.). Englewood Cliffs, NJ: Prentice-Hall.

Yukl, G. A. (1989b), Managerial leadership: A review of theory and research. *Yearly Review of Management,* 15, 251–289.

Reading 42

Leader-Member Exchange as a Mediator of the Relationship Between Transformational Leadership and Followers' Performance and Organizational Citizenship Behavior

Hui Wang
Peking University

Kenneth S. Law
Hong Kong University of Science and Technology

Rick D. Hackett
McMaster University

Duanxu Wang
Zhejiang University

Zhen Xiong Chen
University of Canberra

Two contrasting perspectives on leadership in organizations are prevalent in the academic and applied literatures. The first is leader-focused and attempts to explain individual, group, and organizational performance outcomes by identifying and examining specific leader *behaviors* directly related to them. This viewpoint is exemplified by theories of transformational leadership (e.g., Bass, 1985). The second perspective is more relationship-based, focusing explicitly on how one-on-one reciprocal social exchanges between leader and follower evolve, nurture, and sustain the dyadic relationship. This approach is best exemplified by leader-member exchange (LMX) theory (Graen & Uhl-Bien, 1995). Although transformational leadership approaches concentrate predominantly on leader behaviors unilaterally directed toward subordinates, the mainstay of LMX research has been studying two-way, reciprocal exchanges between leader and follower.

There have been several calls for a theoretical integration of the transformational leadership and LMX literatures (Avolio, Sosik, Jung, & Berson, 2003; Gerstner & Day, 1997; Graen & Uhl-Bien, 1995; Howell & Hall-Merenda, 1999). In this study, we attempted such integration. Howell and Hall-Merenda (1999) contended that in leadership

research, a relationship of some sort between leader and follower is assumed, and it is further assumed that the nature and quality of that relationship are fundamental to linking leader behavior to follower response. Stated alternatively, the assumption has been that it is the quality of the leader-follower relationship through which transformational leadership behaviors influence follower performance. Consistently with this reasoning, we developed and tested a structural model in which LMX mediates between perceived transformational leadership behavior and follower performance (task performance and reported organizational citizenship behavior).

THEORY AND HYPOTHESES

TRANSFORMATIONAL LEADERSHIP

The behaviors most commonly associated with transformational leadership include articulating a compelling vision of the future of an organization; offering a model consistent with that vision; fostering the acceptance of group goals; and providing individualized support, intellectual stimulation, and high performance expectations. Positive relationships have been consistently reported between individual, group, and organizational performance and the ratings followers give their leaders on these transformational leadership behaviors. Typically, these findings have been explained as showing that leader behaviors cause

Source: Republished with permission of The Academy of Management Review. From *Academy of Management Journal*, Wang et al., 2005, 48:3, 420–432. Permission conveyed through Copyright Clearance Center, Inc.

basic values, beliefs, and attitudes of followers to align with organizational collective interests (Podsakoff, MacKenzie, Moorman, & Fetter, 1990).

Transformational leadership and task performance. One theoretical basis for expecting positive associations between transformational leadership and task performance is Kelman's (1958) typology of social influence processes. *Personal identification* and *internalization* are two of them. Specifically, when followers attribute exceptionally strong positive qualities, such as the ability to articulate visions, to a transformational leader, personal identification has occurred. They internalize their leader's values and beliefs and behave consistently with them, including putting collective interests over self-interests. In so doing, they receive leader praise and recognition. These in turn nourish the follower's sense of self-worth and felt obligation to reciprocate, thereby motivating behaviors that serve this obligation (e.g., Bass, 1985; Yukl, 2002). An alternative, but closely related, reason to expect positive associations between transformational leadership and task performance is the process of social identification. By means of social identification, which derives from followers taking pride in being part of a group or organization, followers come to view their individual efforts and work roles as contributing to a larger collective cause. This perspective enhances the personal meaningfulness and importance of their work. By emphasizing the ideological importance of an inspirational and unifying vision, and by linking the followers' self-concepts to this vision, transformational leaders build the social identification and self-concepts of their followers.

Internalization of the beliefs and values of a leader in such an instance is driven less by a desire to emulate the leader and more by the desire to identify with a collective cause (Shamir, House, & Arthur, 1993). Behaving in ways that express the values and beliefs of this social entity enhances a follower's self-concept. The self-efficacy of followers is strengthened when transformational leaders express confidence in their abilities and celebrate their accomplishments. A positive association between transformational leadership and followers' task performance has received considerable empirical support (cf. Lowe, Kroeck, & Sivasubramaniam, 1996).

Transformational leadership and OCB. Organizational citizenship behavior (OCB) is behavior, largely discretionary, and seldom included in formal job descriptions, that supports task performance by enhancing a social and psychological work environment. Transformational leaders motivate followers by getting them to internalize and prioritize a larger collective cause over individual interests. Individuals who are intrinsically motivated to fulfill a collective vision without expecting immediate personal and tangible gains may be inclined to contribute toward achieving the shared workplace goal in ways that their roles do not prescribe. These individuals make these contributions because their senses of self-worth and/or self-concepts are enhanced in making these contributions. Individuals for whom this link between the interests of self and others has not been established are less likely to make largely discretionary, nontangibly rewarded contributions. A positive association between transformational leadership and OCB is expected and has been supported empirically (e.g., Podsakoff et al., 1990).

LEADER-MEMBER EXCHANGE

LMX theory is premised on notions of role making (Graen, 1976), social exchange, reciprocity, and equity (Deluga, 1994). Leaders convey role expectations to their followers and provide tangible and intangible rewards to followers who satisfy these expectations. Likewise, followers hold role expectations of their leaders, with respect to how they are to be treated and the rewards they are to receive for meeting leader expectations. Followers are not passive "role recipients"; they may either reject, embrace, or renegotiate roles prescribed by their leaders. There is a reciprocal process in the dyadic exchanges between leader and follower, wherein each party brings to the relationship different kinds of resources for exchange. Role negotiation occurs over time, defining the quality and maturity of a leader-member exchange, and leaders develop relationships of varying quality with different followers over time (Graen, 1976; Graen & Uhl-Bien, 1995).

LMX and task performance. Leaders exercising formal authority and allocating standard benefits in return for standard job performance characterize low-quality exchanges. The exchanges underlying these relationships are predominantly quid pro quo and "contractual." In high-quality LMX relationships, however, social exchange is moved to a higher level, nourished by *mutual trust, respect,* and *obligation* (Graen & Uhl-Bien, 1995). In return for exemplary performance contributions (e.g., consistently volunteering to work extra hours to meet project deadlines), followers receive special privileges (e.g., access to key personnel or information), career-enhancing opportunities (e.g., special work assignments), and increasing levels of discretion in doing their jobs. Accordingly, task performance is a form of currency in the social exchange between leader and follower, and a means of fulfilling obligations for reciprocity. Specifically, the positive affect, respect, loyalty, and felt obligation characteristic of high-quality LMX, according to Liden and Maslyn (1998), build as a result of favorable treatment by the leader, and are expressed by high task performance, which fulfils reciprocity expectations. Gerstner and Day (1997) reported meta-analytically derived correlations of .31 between LMX and supervisory ratings of performance and of .11 between LMX and objective measures of employee performance.

Leader-member exchange and organizational citizenship behavior. In high-quality LMX relationships, obligations are often diffuse and unspecified, and no standard or value against which gifts, favors, or contributions can be measured is present (Blau, 1964). A positive association between LMX and OCB is expected because OCB helps fulfill the reciprocity obligations of followers, and represents an exchange currency that is diffuse, unspecified, and weakly time-bound. Moreover, in high-quality exchange, leaders appeal to the higher-order social needs of followers by getting them to place collective interests over short-term personal gratification (Graen & Uhl-Bien, 1995). An individual's being a "good citizen" promotes the welfare of the larger collective. Accordingly, LMX is expected to correlate positively with OCB. Support for this relationship was provided by Hackett, Farh, Song, and Lapierre (2003), who reported a meta-analytic mean correlation of .32 between LMX and overall OCB, leading them to conclude that OCB plays a key role in the reciprocal social exchange process of LMX.

STUDIES OF BOTH TRANSFORMATIONAL LEADERSHIP AND LEADER-MEMBER EXCHANGE

Only three published studies have included measures of both transformational leadership and LMX (see Basu & Green, 1997; Deluga, 1992; Howell & Hall-Merenda, 1999). Deluga (1992) argued that a transformational leader "catalyzes" conventional social exchanges, stimulating subordinates to surpass initial performance goals and self-interests. More specifically, he provided empirical data suggesting that the heightened outcomes associated with transformational leadership *result from* the individualized dyadic relationship between a given subordinate and leader. Deluga noted that

"transformational leaders may foster the formation of high quality relationships and a sense of a common fate with individual subordinates; while in a social-exchange process, subordinates strengthen and encourage the leader" (1992: 245). Reporting regression analyses of data from 145 U.S. Navy offices, Deluga (1992) wrote that individualized consideration and charisma were the only two transformational leadership factors that predicted LMX. These results suggest that it is a leader's charisma and individualized consideration—both of which have been considered dyad-level influences (Seltzer & Bass, 1990)—that cause subordinates to behave in ways (such as making extra efforts) that strengthen relational ties with the leader.

Basu and Green (1997) studied employees of a Fortune 500 manufacturing facility and factor-analyzed the employees' responses to an 8-item measure of LMX and a 28-item measure of transformational leadership. Their analysis failed to distinguish LMX from intellectual stimulation and individualized consideration, which they interpreted to be consistent with viewing these two dimensions as intangible rewards (currency) within a dyadic social exchange.

Howell and Hall-Merenda (1999) studied 109 community-banking managers. They collected subordinates' ratings of these managers on both transformational leadership and leader-member exchange. The managers provided performance measures of subordinates approximately six months after the LMX measures were taken. Partial least squares analysis showed that within a predictor set consisting of LMX, transformational leadership, and three transactional leadership dimension scores, LMX was a significant predictor of follower performance, whereas transformational leadership was not. Specifically, the path from transformational leadership to performance failed to reach statistical significance when other leader behaviors and LMX were included in the model. These authors also found that of a predictor set consisting of transformational leadership and the three transactional leadership dimension scores, all were significant predictors of LMX, but the strongest was transformational leadership, followed by contingent rewards. Together, these results suggested a temporal path from transformational leadership to LMX and from LMX to follower performance.

None of the three cited studies showed how transformational leadership and LMX are related to each other and to work performance. Transformational leadership theories are still at early stages of specifying the developmental mediating processes between leader behavior and performance (Dvir, Eden, Avolio, & Shamir, 2002). Our contribution in this study lies in explicitly testing a structural model that positions LMX as a *mediator* between transformational leadership and task performance/organizational citizenship behavior. Although transformational leadership and LMX appear to overlap conceptually, we contend that transformational leadership comprises a set of leader behaviors that directly influence the development and maintenance of leader-member exchange relationships.

THE MEDIATING ROLE OF LEADER-MEMBER EXCHANGE

The mediating role of LMX in the relationship between transformational leadership and task performance/OCB is premised on the notion that a high-quality LMX relationship reflects an affective bonding accompanied by largely unstated mutual expectations of reciprocity. Such a relationship evolves from a predominantly transactional exchange into a social exchange as mutual trust, respect, and loyalty are earned (Graen & Uhl-Bien, 1995). We argue that transformational leadership builds and nourishes high-quality LMX. Findings by Dvir and coauthors (2002) suggest that follower development and the accompanying social bonding mediate the effects of transformational leadership behaviors on follower performance. They suggested this: "Perhaps a critical level of interaction with a transformational leader is indispensable for the impact of follower development to emerge" (Dvir et al., 2002: 742). Deluga (1992) argued that the heightened outcomes associated with transformational leadership result from the individualized dyadic relationship between a given subordinate and leader.

LMX is said to develop through three sequential stages, "stranger," "acquaintance," and "partner," each of which relies successively less on instrumental transactional exchange and more on social exchanges of a "transformational" kind (Graen & Uhl-Bien, 1995). In the stranger stage, the leader "offers" modestly expanded role responsibilities and assesses whether the follower successfully fulfills them. Greater responsibilities, discretion, and benefits are given as the follower meets these successively expanded role responsibilities. The transformation characteristic of mature LMX relationships occurs when there is a shift in the motivation of followers from a desire to satisfy immediate self-interests via a quid pro quo transactional exchange to a desire to satisfy

longer-term and broader collective interests of the work unit.

Moreover, transformational leaders, because of their charismatic appeal, are more effective than their purely transactional counterparts in enhancing follower receptivity to social exchange offers and thereby building higher-quality LMX. Transformational leaders are particularly effective in eliciting personal identification from their followers and getting them to accept offers of expanded role responsibilities. Followers with strong personal identification with their leaders enhance their sense of self-worth by internalizing their leaders' values and beliefs and by behaving in accordance with them. In so doing, followers garner praise, recognition, and enriched role responsibilities, and these result in a higher quality of social exchange with their leaders. This process is consistent with the finding that transformational leadership encompasses an element of higher-order transactional leadership, reflecting leaders' and followers' internalized expectations of mutual trust and their reciprocal exchange obligations (Goodwin, Wofford, & Whittington, 2001). Most successful leaders effectively use transformational behaviors to create long-term loyalty and organizational commitment (Graen & Uhl-Bien, 1995).

We also believe that transformational leadership is "personalized" through LMX. Graen (1976) noted the importance of leadership behaviors in the role-making process of LMX, emphasizing the need for leaders to convey compelling and unifying organizational missions to get followers to identify their vocations within the ideologies of their organizations. It is through establishing high-quality relationships that leaders, by example and by treatment, convince followers that an organization deserves their commitment (Graen, 1976). Accordingly, transformational leaders may provide the broader cultural framework and facilitating conditions within which leader-member relationships are personalized in the LMX relationship-building process. As Avolio and his coauthors noted, "To 'make sense' of each follower's future requires the leader to develop a relationship, whereby followers come to identify with the leader's vision" (2003: 280). The leader-member exchange process provides for this relationship building.

The preceding text suggests the following:

Hypothesis 1. Transformational leadership is positively related to the task performance and organizational citizenship behaviors of followers.

Hypothesis 2. Leader-member exchange relates positively to the task performance and organizational citizenship behaviors of followers.

We hypothesized that OCB is also related to task performance. OCB is largely discretionary and typically not compensated. Individuals performing OCB tend also to show altruism, organizational commitment, and conscientiousness (LePine, Erez, & Johnson, 2002), variables positively related to task performance. Accordingly, it is reasonable to expect a positive correlation between OCB and task performance. OCB appears to have a significant influence on the in-role performance of employees, especially managers' ratings of employee performance (Allen & Rush, 1998; Werner, 1994). Therefore, following an approach similar to that of Wayne, Shore, Bommer, and Tetrick (2002), we added a structural path from OCB to task performance to our model.

Hypothesis 3. Leader-member exchange mediates the relationship between transformational leadership and followers' task performance and organizational citizenship behavior. . . .

DESCRIPTIVE STATISTICS

Table 3 presents the means, standard deviations, reliability coefficients, and zero-order correlations of all the studied variables. Transformational leadership correlated significantly ($p < .05$) with task performance and OCB ($r = .20$ and .18, respectively), and LMX correlated significantly ($p < .01$) with these same two variables ($r = .38$ and .29, respectively).

HYPOTHESIS TESTS

The univariate correlations between transformational leadership and task performance ($r = .20$, $p < .01$) and OCB ($r = .18$, $p < .01$) provided preliminary evidence to support Hypothesis 1, which states that transformational leadership has positive relationships with task performance and OCB. Supporting Hypothesis 2, LMX had positive

correlations with those variables as well (task performance, $r = .38$, $p < .01$; OCB. $r = .29$, $p < .01$).

Hypothesis 3, which predicts that LMX mediates the relationship between transformational leadership and followers' performance and citizenship behavior, was tested through a series of nested model comparisons. . . .

In summary, the results support Hypothesis 3: leader-member exchange mediates the relationship between transformational leadership and performance (task performance and OCB). Figure 1 shows that the coefficient of the path from transformational leadership to LMX was significant ($\beta = .80$, $p < .01$), as were the coefficients of the paths from LMX to task performance ($\beta = .16$, $p < .05$) and OCB ($\beta = .32$, $p < .01$).

In support of Hypothesis 2, we found statistically significant and positive coefficients for the paths from LMX to both task performance and OCB. Finally, the substantial path between OCB and task performance ($\beta = .77$) suggested that OCB influences supervisory ratings of employee task performance.

DISCUSSION

This study was a response to calls to investigate the conceptual and empirical links between transformational leadership and leader-member exchange and thereby theoretically integrate transformational and exchange models of leadership (Gerstner & Day, 1997; Graen & Uhl-Bien, 1995). The literature on transformational leadership has linked leader behaviors directly to performance outcomes, whereas the LMX literature has given only marginal attention to behaviors, focusing primarily on the quality of the social exchange relationship between dyadic partners. Our study suggests that LMX mediates between transformational leadership and performance (task and OCB).

TABLE 3   Means, Standard Deviations, and Correlations[a]

Variables	Mean	s.d.	1	2	3	4
1. Transformational leadership	3.86	0.45	(.93)			
2. Leader-member exchange[b]	3.81	0.58	.71**	(.21)		
3. Task performance	3.55	0.79	.20*	.38**	(.89)	
4. Organizational citizenship behavior	3.47	0.52	.18*	.29**	.58**	(.80)

[a]$n = 162$: reliability coefficients for the scales are in parentheses along the diagonal.
[b]LMX-MDM was the measure.
*$p < .05$
**$p < .01$

FIGURE 1
Results of
Structural Equation
Modeling on the
Mediating Effect of
LMX

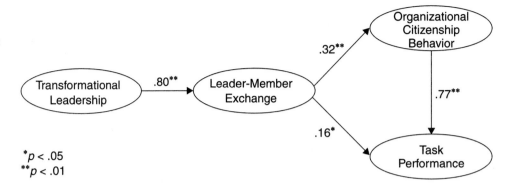

*p < .05
**p < .01

These findings are consistent with the notions that: (1) transformational leadership behaviors are social currency, nourishing high-quality LMX; (2) transformational leadership is associated positively with task performance and OCB: (3) transformational leaders enhance follower receptivity to role-expanding offers and extrarole behaviors, through processes of personal and/or social identification; and (4) LMX makes transformational leadership more personally meaningful.

Our findings also suggest that the effect of transformational leadership on follower performance and OCB is based on how each follower personally experiences and interprets these behaviors (Dasborough & Ashkanasy, 2002). Social bonding between leader and follower is important, and a critical level of interaction with a transformational leader may be essential for follower development and social bonding to emerge (Dvir et al., 2002).

GENERALIZABILITY OF RESULTS

Although our findings are based on samples drawn from mainland China, we have no reason to expect different results were the same study to be conducted in the West. Although some have questioned whether Western leadership models are applicable to "high-power-distance" (authoritarian), collectivist cultures such as mainland China, research has shown remarkably consistent results across cultures (cf. Chen & Farh, 1999; Hackett et al., 2003; Hui, Law, & Chen, 1999). Our study joins a growing body of literature that shows basic relationships between leadership and performance established in the West hold up in China, thereby increasing the generalizability of previous findings from Western samples. Because this study is the first to have shown LMX as mediating between transformational leadership and performance, future research should attempt a replication of our results using samples from other national cultures. . . .

PRACTICAL IMPLICATIONS

Overall, our findings suggest that effective leaders express their transformational behaviors within a personal, dynamic relational exchange context. They fulfill the psychological contract implicit in their social exchange relationships with followers. They are sensitive to follower contributions to the exchanges and reciprocate in way, that build follower self-worth and/or self-concept. Effective leaders link achievement of organizational goals to follower fulfillment of self-development goals, with the former advancing the latter. We are advocating a socially interactive and dynamic model of leadership, where the influence of transformational leadership on performance is through a social exchange between leader and follower. . . .

Additionally, our findings provide insights into how high-quality leader-member exchange relationships can be developed. The LMX literature focuses strongly on the outcomes of high-quality leader-member exchange, giving less attention to how leaders can build high-quality exchange relationships with their followers. The transformational leadership literature has a primary focus on performance-enhancing leader behaviors. Our findings suggest that transformational leadership behaviors are instrumental to developing high-quality LMX relationships. It follows that the effectiveness of leadership programs aimed at developing the quality of leader-follower dyadic relationships can be enhanced by incorporating training in transformational leadership skills.

References

Allen, T. D., & Rush, M. C. 1998. The effects of organizational citizenship on performance judgments: A field study and a laboratory experiment. *Journal of Applied Psychology, 83,* 247–260.

Anderson, J. C., & Gerbing, D. W. 1988. Structural equation modeling in practice: A review and recommended two-step approach. *Psychological Bulletin,* 103, 411–423.

Avolio, B. J., Sosik, J. J., Jung, D. I., & Berson, Y. 2003. Leadership models, methods and applications. In W. Borman, D. Ilgen, & R. Klimoski (Eds.), *Handbook of psychology, vol. 12—Industrial and organizational psychology,* 277–307. New York: Wiley.

Bass, B. M. 1985. *Leadership and performance beyond expectation.* New York: Free Press.

Basu, R., & Green, S. G. 1997. Leader-member exchange and transformational leadership: an empirical examination of innovative behaviors in leader-member dyads. *Journal of Applied Social Psychology,* 27, 477–499.

Blau, P. M. 1964. *Exchange and power in social life.* New York: Jossey-Bass.

Brislin, R. W. 1980. Translation and content analysis of oral and written material. In H. C. Triandis & J. W. Berry (Eds.), *Handbook of cross-cultural psychology, vol. 2—Methodology,* 349–444. Boston: Allyn & Bacon.

Campion, M. A. 1988. Interdisciplinary approaches to job design: A constructive replication with extensions. *Journal of Applied Psychology,* 73, 467–481.

Chen, X., & Farh, J. L. 1999. *The effectiveness of transactional and transformational leader behaviors in Chinese organizations: Evidence from Taiwan.* Paper presented at the annual meeting of the Academy of Management, Chicago.

Cohen, J., & Cohen, P. 1983. *Applied multiple regression/correlation analysis for the behavioral sciences* (2nd ed.). Hillsdale, NJ: Erlbaum.

Dasborough, M. T., & Ashkanasy, N. M. 2002. Emotion and attribution of intentionality in leader-member relationships. *Leadership Quarterly,* 13, 615–634.

Deluga, R. J. 1992. The relationship of leader-member exchanges with laissez-faire, transactional, and transformational leadership. In K. E. Clark, M. B. Clark, & D. R. Campbell (Eds.), *Impact of leadership,* 237–247. Greensboro, NC: Center for Creative Leadership.

Deluga, R. J. 1994. Supervisor trust building, leader-member exchange and organizational citizenship behavior. *Journal of Occupational and Organizational Psychology,* 67, 315–326.

Dvir, T., Eden, D., Avolio, B. J., & Shamir, B. 2002. Impact of transformational leadership on follower development and performance: A field experiment. *Academy of Management Journal,* 45, 735–744.

Fornell, C., & Larcker, D. F. 1981. Evaluating structural equation models with unobservable variables and measurement error. *Journal of Marketing Research,* 18, 39–50.

Gerstner, C. R., & Day, D. V. 1997. Meta-analysis review of leader-member exchange theory: Correlation and construct issues. *Journal of Applied Psychology,* 82, 827–844.

Goodwin, V. L., Wofford, J. C., & Whittington, J. L. 2001. A theoretical and empirical extension of transformational leadership construct. *Journal of Organizational Behavior,* 22, 759–776.

Grean, G. B. 1976. Role making processes within complex organization. In M. D. Dunnette (Ed.), *Handbook of industrial and organizational psychology,* 1201–1245. Chicago: Rand-McNally.

Grean, G. B., & Uhl-Bien, M. 1995. Development of leader-member exchange (LMX) theory of leadership over 25 years. Applying a multi-level multi-domain perspective. *Leadership Quarterly,* 6, 219–247.

Hackett, R. D., Farh, J. -L., Song, L. J., & Lapierre, L. M. 2003. LMX and organizational citizenship behavior: Examining the links within and across Western and Chinese samples. In G. Graen (Ed.), *Dealing with diversity: LMX leadership—The series,* vol. 1: 219–263. Greenwich. CT: Information Age.

House, R. J., & Aditya, R. N. 1997. The social scientific study of leadership: Quo vadis? *Journal of Management,* 23, 409–473.

Howell, J. M., & Hall-Merenda, K. E. 1999. The ties that bind: The impact of leader-member exchange, transformational leadership and transactional leadership, and distance on predicting follower performance. *Journal of Applied Psychology,* 84, 680–694.

Hui, C., Law, K. S., & Chen, Z. X. 1999. A structural equation model of the effects of negative affectivity, leader-member exchange, and perceived job mobility on in-role and extra-role performance: A Chinese case. *Organizational Behavior and Human Decision Processes,* 77, 3–21.

Jöreskog, K. G., & Sörbom, D. 2001. *LISREL 8.50.* Scientific Software International.

Kelman, H. C. 1958. Compliance, identification, and internalization: Three processes of attitude change. *Journal of Conflict Resolution,* 2, 51–56.

Lam, S. S. K., Hui, C., & Law, K. S. 1999. Organizational citizenship behavior: Comparing perspectives of supervisors and subordinated across four international samples. *Journal of Applied Psychology,* 84, 594–601.

LePine, J. A., Erez, A., & Johnson, D. E. 2002. The nature and dimensionality of organizational citizenship behavior: A critical review and meta-analysis. *Journal of Applied Psychology,* 87, 52–65.

Liden, R. C., & Maslyn, J. M. 1998. Multi-dimensionality of leader-member exchange: An empirical assessment through scale development. *Journal of Management,* 24, 43–72.

Lowe, K. B., Kroeck, K. G., & Sivasubramaniam, N. 1996. Effectiveness correlates of transformational and transactional leadership: A meta-analytic review of the MLQ literature. *Leadership Quarterly,* 7, 385–425.

Medsker, G. J., Williams, L. J., & Holahan, P. J. 1994. A review of current practice for evaluating causal models in organizational behavior and human resources management research. *Journal of Management,* 20, 439–464.

Netemeyer, R. G., Johnston, M. W., & Burton, S. 1990. Analysis of role conflict and role ambiguity in a structural equation framework. *Journal of Applied Psychology,* 75, 148–157.

Podsakoff, P. M., Mackenzie, S. B., Lee, J.-Y., & Podsakoff, N. P. 2003. Common method biased in behavioral research: A critical review of the literature and recommended remedies. *Journal of Applied Psychology,* 85, 879–903.

Podsakoff, P. M., MacKenzie, S. B., Moorman, R. H., & Fetter, R. 1990. Transformational leader behaviors and their effects on followers' trust in leader, satisfaction, and organizational citizenship behavior. *Leadership Quarterly,* 1, 107–142.

Scandura, T. A., & Graen, G. B. 1984. Moderating effects of initial leader-member exchange status on the effects of a leadership intervention. *Journal of Applied Psychology,* 69, 428–436.

Seltzer, J., & Bass, B. M. 1990. Transformational leadership: Beyond initiation and consideration. *Journal of Management,* 16, 693–703.

Shamir, B., House, R. J., & Arthur, M. B. 1993. The motivational effects of charismatic leadership: A self-concept theory. *Organizational Science,* 4, 1–17.

Tsui, A. S., Pearce, J. L., Porter, L. W., & Tripoli, A. M. 1997. Alternative approaches to the employee-organization relationship: Does investment in employees pay off? *Academy of Management Journal,* 40, 1089–1121.

Wayne, S. J., Shore, L. M., Bommer, W. H., & Tetrick, L. E. 2002. The role of fair treatment and rewards in perceptions of organizational support and leader-member exchange. *Journal of Applied Psychology,* 87, 590–598.

Werner, J. M. 1994. Dimensions that make a difference: Examining the impact of in-role and extra-role behaviors on supervisory ratings. *Journal of Applied Psychology,* 79, 98–107.

Wong, C. S., & Campion, M. A. 1991. Development and test of a task level model of motivational job design. *Journal of Applied Psychology,* 76, 825–837.

Yukl, G. 2002. *Leadership in organizations* (5th ed.). Upper Saddle River, NJ: Prentice-Hall.

Chapter **Fifteen**

The Dark Side of Leadership

It is common to think positively in terms of leaders and take for granted the positive (or presumed positive) effects associated with leadership. Examples include Lee Iacocca's turnaround of Chrysler, Steve Jobs's creation of Apple and the MacIntosh, Jack Welch's "reinvention" of General Electric, Norman Schwarzkopf and Colin Powell's victorious strategies during Operation Desert Storm, George Mitchell's negotiated settlement in Northern Ireland, Richard Holbrooke's similar achievement in Bosnia, and Coach Mike Krzyzewski's success in building a basketball powerhouse at Duke University. However, not all of our leadership stories are positive in nature. David Koresh's standoff with state and federal authorities at the Davidian compound in Waco, Texas; Adolf Hitler's leadership of Germany in World War II and his widespread slaughter of the Jewish people; James Jones's leading of several hundred to commit mass suicide; Marshall Applewhite's similar encouragement of mass suicide among the members of Heaven's Gate; and Serbia's Slobodan Milosevic's ethnic cleansing of Kosovo serve to remind us that there can also be a negative (dysfunctional) side to leadership. At one extreme, some leaders' behaviors even become pathological (e.g., Saddam Hussein) once positions of power have been attained. Other leaders succumb to self-importance and indulgence (greed). Examples include those involved in the corporate scandals (e.g., Enron, Tyco) of the late twentieth and early twenty-first centuries.

In the first reading of this chapter, Christine Clements and John B. Washbush encourage us to recognize that there is a dark side to leader–follower dynamics. Influenced by the spiritual writings of Parker Palmer,[1] the authors remind us of the numerous occasions when there is bad decision making, dysfunctional organization, wasted resources, deception, ruined careers, organizational decline and dissolution, and failed planning or the absence of planning to simply illustrate that *not all leadership acts are positive, effective, and ethical* in nature. Clements and Washbush call attention to the elements that make up the negative face of both leaders and followers.

In the second reading in this chapter, Jay A. Conger (1990) also addresses the dark side of leadership. He suggests that there are leaders who have lost touch with reality and who use their positions of leadership for their own personal gain. In both instances, negative consequences for the group and/or organization are common by-products. In this reading, Conger explores the dual question, How do leaders produce such negative outcomes, and why? Conger takes the position that leadership can make a significant difference. Unfortunately, this difference is not always positive.

---

[1] P. J. Palmer, "Leading from Within: Out of the Shadows, into the Light," in J. A. Conger, (Ed.), *Spirit at Work: Discovering the Spirituality in Leadership* (San Francisco: Jossey-Bass, 1994), 19–40.

FIGURE 15.1
Dysfunctional
Leadership Effects

Source: R. B. Dunham and
J. L. Pierce, *Management*
(Glenview, IL: Scott, Foresman,
1989), p. 556.

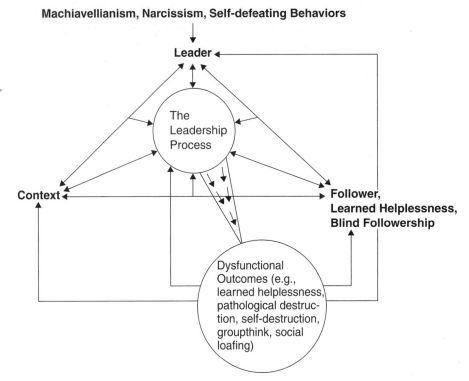

In the third reading, Manfred F. R. Kets de Vries and Danny Miller (1985) note that *leaders can be either extremely inspiring or pathologically destructive.* They ask the question, What is it about leaders themselves that makes it so? In this reading, Kets de Vries and Miller explore the narcissistic personality and suggest that narcissism plays a central role in the personality of the pathologically destructive leader. Individuals whose personalities are characterized by a high degree of narcissism are driven by intense needs for power and prestige, leading them to seek out and attain leadership positions.

Machiavellianism reflects a person's general strategy for dealing with people. Individuals who have a strong Machiavellian orientation (Figure 15.1) feel that people are manipulable in interpersonal situations; as leaders, these individuals tend to employ manipulation techniques (and sometimes cunning, deception, and expediency) as an influence tactic. The self-assessment exercise presented at the end of this chapter opener provides you with an opportunity to construct your own Machiavellian profile.

In one of our early readings, Smircich and Morgan (1982) alerted us to the fact that the leader–follower relationship can result in *learned helplessness*—that condition in which individuals become dependent on others to deal with uncertainty and ambiguity and are nearly incapable of problem solving on their own.

In another article, Manfred F. R. Kets de Vries (1989) has written about leaders who self-destruct:[2] He suggests that the leadership position can be associated with loneliness and a disconnectedness that often results in self-defeating (destructive) behaviors. In addition to providing additional insight into how leaders sometimes unconsciously take steps that lead to their failure, he also offers a perspective on what might cure this problem.

[2] Manfred F. R. Kets de Vries, "Leaders Who Self-destruct: The Causes and Cures," *Organizational Dynamics* 17, 4 (1989), pp. 4–17.

The leadership dysfunctions identified in this chapter are by no means an exhaustive catalogue of the dark side of leadership. Small-group scholars, for example, have alerted us to a number of maladies that can have an impact on groups, each of which can be related to the presence of a leader and each of which poses a challenge to leader effectiveness. Among the maladies are (*a*) *groupthink,* the condition in which a group has illusions of invulnerability and engages in single-minded thinking; (*b*) *risky shift (polarization),* the "presumed" tendency for a group to take a more extreme position than its members would have taken if acting alone; (*c*) *social loafing,* wherein group members fail to put forth their best efforts in the belief that their contributions (involvements) will essentially get lost in the group effort; and (*d*) *diffusion of responsibility,* a group dynamic or group process through which individuals fail to act in the belief or expectation that it is the job of others to act, or because the presence of others reduces feelings of accountability. Similar to groupthink, charismatic leadership may well result in followers unquestioningly going along as a result of their emotional and passionate bond with their leader and his or her cause. Leaders concerned about the effectiveness of their groups will want to attempt to minimize the dysfunctional effects that stem from these group behaviors.

EXERCISE
Self-Assessment

Machiavellianism

Instructions: Listed below are a number of statements. Each represents a commonly held opinion and there are no right or wrong answers. You will probably disagree with some items and agree with others. We are interested in the extent to which you *agree* or *disagree* with such matters of opinion.

    Read each statement carefully. Then indicate the extent to which you agree or disagree by circling the number after each statement. The numbers and their meaning are indicated below.

    If you *agree strongly*, circle +3.
    If you *agree somewhat*, circle +2.
    If you *agree slightly*, circle +1.

    If you *disagree slightly*, circle −1.
    If you *disagree somewhat*, circle −2.
    If you *disagree strongly*, circle −3.

    First impressions are usually best in such matters. Read each statement, decide if you agree or disagree and the strength of your opinion, and then circle the appropriate number after the statement. Give your opinion on every statement.

    If you find that the numbers do not adequately indicate your own opinion, use the one which is closest to the way you feel.

	Agree Strongly	Agree Somewhat	Agree Slightly	Disagree Slightly	Disagree Somewhat	Disagree Strongly
1. Never tell anyone the real reason you did something unless it is useful to do so.	+3	+2	+1	−1	−2	−3
2. The best way to handle people is to tell them what they want to hear.	+3	+2	+1	−1	−2	−3
3. One should take action only when sure it is morally right.	+3	+2	+1	−1	−2	−3
4. Most people are basically good and kind.	+3	+2	+1	−1	−2	−3
5. It is safest to assume that all people have a vicious streak and it will come out when they are given a chance.	+3	+2	+1	−1	−2	−3
6. Honesty is the best policy in all cases.	+3	+2	+1	−1	−2	−3
7. There is no excuse for lying to someone else.	+3	+2	+1	−1	−2	−3
8. Generally speaking, men won't work hard unless they're forced to do so.	+3	+2	+1	−1	−2	−3
9. All in all, it is better to be humble and honest than to be important and dishonest.	+3	+2	+1	−1	−2	−3
10. When you ask someone to do something for you, it is best to give the real reasons for wanting it rather than giving reasons which carry more weight.	+3	+2	+1	−1	−2	−3
11. Most people who get ahead in the world lead clean, moral lives.	+3	+2	+1	−1	−2	−3
12. Anyone who completely trusts anyone else is asking for trouble.	+3	+2	+1	−1	−2	−3
13. The biggest difference between most criminals and other people is that the criminals are stupid enough to get caught.	+3	+2	+1	−1	−2	−3

14. Most men are brave.	+3	+2	+1	−1	−2	−3
15. It is wise to flatter important people.	+3	+2	+1	−1	−2	−3
16. It is possible to be good in all respects.	+3	+2	+1	−1	−2	−3
17. Barnum was wrong when he said that there's a sucker born every minute.	+3	+2	+1	−1	−2	−3
18. It is hard to get ahead without cutting corners here and there.	+3	+2	+1	−1	−2	−3
19. People suffering from incurable diseases should have the choice of being put painlessly to death.	+3	+2	+1	−1	−2	−3
20. Most men forget more easily the death of their father than the loss of their property.	+3	+2	+1	−1	−2	−3

Scoring:

If you *agree strongly*, circling +3, give yourself 7 points.
If you *agree somewhat,* circling +2, give yourself 6 points.
If you *agree slightly,* circling +1, give yourself 5 points.

If you *disagree slightly,* circling −1, give yourself 3 points.
If you *disagree somewhat,* circling −2, give yourself 2 points.
If you *disagree strongly,* circling −3, give yourself 1 point.

Next, for each of the following questions (3, 4, 6, 7, 9, 10, 11, 14, 16, and 17) subtract your score from 8.

Now sum your scores across all of the 20 questions and add 20 points to that score.

My Machiavellian (Mach IV) score is: _____.

Interpretation: One hundred (100) points is normed as the neutral point. Your score will range between a low of 40 and a high of 160. The instrument is scaled such that the higher the score the stronger the Machiavellianism; the lower the score the weaker the Machiavellianism. A high Mach score might be reflected by 140 and more points, while a low Mach score might be reflected by 60 and fewer points.

According to Christie (1969), the Machiavellianism assessment attempts to tap into a person's general strategy for dealing with people. Machiavellianism reflects the degree to which an individual feels that other people are manipulable in interpersonal situations. Christie also notes that high Machs have a "'cool detachment,' which makes them less emotionally involved with other people, with sensitive issues, or with saving face in embarrassing situations."

An experimental study by Drory and Gluskinos (1980)[1] focusing on Machiavellianism and leadership reveals no performance differences between high Mach and low Mach groups. High Mach leaders did, however, give more orders and were less involved in reducing tension than their low Mach leader counterparts. Gemmill and Heisler (1972)[2] report that Machiavellianism was negatively related to job satisfaction and positively associated with job strain.

Source: Reprinted from R. Christie, *Studies in Machiavellianism,* Copyright © 1970, with permission from Elsevier.

[1] A. Drory and U. M. Gluskinos, "Machiavellianism and Leadership," *Journal of Applied Psychology* 65 (1980), pp. 81–86.
[2] G. R. Gemmill and W. J. Heisler, "Machiavellianism as a Factor in Managerial Job Strain, Job Satisfaction, and Upward Mobility," *Academy of Management Journal* 15 (1972), pp. 51–62.

Reading 43

The Two Faces of Leadership: Considering the Dark Side of Leader–Follower Dynamics

Christine Clements and John B. Washbush
University of Wisconsin–Whitewater

LEADERSHIP'S POSITIVE FACE

A common feature of modern perceptions of leadership is that leadership is a good and positive thing. In the modern era, Burns (1978) cast leadership as action uniting leaders and followers in the pursuit of significant and morally desirable change. Bennis and Nanus (1985) proposed that leaders are people who "do the right thing," and Bass (1990) used the term transformational leadership to describe inspirational leadership wherein followers are elevated and empowered. Two themes emerge from this body of theory. The over-riding theme is that leadership necessarily involves moral purpose—the positive face of leadership. Proof of the power of this imagery was provided by Palmer (1994, p. 25) who commented:

> Many books on leadership seem to be about the power of positive thinking. I fear they feed a common delusion among leaders that their efforts are always well intended, their power always benign.

Palmer's words suggest that leadership can show a dark side.

The second implication of popular leadership models is that followers play a rather passive role. Transformational models define leadership in terms of the effect on followers. That is, followers experience a sense of significance, motivation and commitment to leader ideals. But if there is a dark side to leadership, followers must surely carry some responsibility in recognizing and addressing these darker issues. And if there is a dark side to leadership, isn't it also likely that there is a dark side to followership, as well? Failure to acknowledge and examine the "dark side" of leadership and influence can distort efforts to learn about the leadership process and may encourage a blind eye approach to examining the results of influence attempts. Authentic understanding of leadership requires a balanced discussion.

Source: Edited and reprinted with permission from *Journal of Workplace Learning*. Vol. 11, No. 5, 1999, pp. 170–175. © MCB University Press.

The positive face of leadership strongly reflects the concept of social power as discussed by McClelland (1970, 1976). Individuals high in social power are institution-oriented, aspire to office, want to serve others and foster an effective work climate. Contrasted to this is the concept of self-aggrandizing personal power that seeks to use position, and often charisma, for personal gain. Common wisdom would suggest that people who employ personal power see followers as utilitarian tools, incapable of independent thought, and captured by the magnetism of an overwhelming personality. However, McClelland (1970) has illustrated how even the most villainous personalities often arouse social-power responses in their followers, who see themselves as elevated and empowered. These responses are the same as those that would be predicted by the proponents of transforming (transformational, inspirational) leadership.

It is clear that effective leadership can be instrumental in promoting social good, but what should be equally clear is that effective leadership can also be instrumental in promoting social disaster. The positive face dominates leadership theory, discussion, and education, but as Palmer has noted (1994), this feeds a costly delusion. We need to identify and deal with the shadow aspects of leadership, especially in leadership education and training.

LEADERSHIP'S NEGATIVE FACE

There are many effects of this failure: bad decision making, frustration, dysfunctional organizations, unintended consequences, wasted resources, ruined careers, organizational decline or dissolution, and scores of other negative. These outcomes are not accidents. How are they caused, and how does leadership contribute? Some authors have begun to address these important issues.

A FAILURE TO LOOK INSIDE

Palmer (1994, pp. 25–6) has asserted that:

> A leader must take special responsibility for what's going on inside his or her own self, inside

his or her consciousness, lest the act of leadership create more harm than good. . . . I suggest that the challenge is to examine our consciousness for those ways in which we leaders may project more shadow that light. . . . The problem is that people rise to leadership in our society by a tendency toward extroversion, which too often means ignoring what's going on inside themselves. . . . I have looked at some training programs for leaders, and I am discouraged by how often they focus on the development of skills to manipulate the external world rather than the skills necessary to go within and make the spiritual journey. . . . It feeds a dangerous syndrome among leaders who already tend to deny their inner world.

MIRRORING

Kets de Vries (1993) has identified several of those shadows that leaders fail to recognize. One of these is mirroring, or the tendency to see themselves as they are perceived by their followers and to feel they must act to satisfy the projections or fantasies of followers. A certain amount of mirroring is part of human existence. Our understanding of the world will always reflect some shared perceptions of what is real. But, in a crisis, even the best of us is likely to engage in distorted mirroring. The impact is most serious when leaders use their authority and power to initiate actions that have serious, negative consequences for the organization.

NARCISSISM

A second problem identified by Kets de Vries is narcissism, a distorted view of self. Narcissists need power, prestige, drama and enjoy manipulation of others. These qualities draw them to positions of leadership, but at extreme levels of narcissism, the results can be disastrous. Narcissists can become intolerant of criticism, unwilling to compromise, and frequently surround themselves with sycophants. While narcissists often "appear" to be ideal choices for leadership positions, they may fall victim to the distortions of their narcissistic tendencies that are reinforced by their position.

EMOTIONAL ILLITERACY

A third problem discussed by Kets de Vries is an inability to differentiate and verbalize emotion, known as emotional illiteracy (or "alexithymia"). These individuals do not respond to their emotions, and are easy prey for the distortions of others. "In the case of these individuals, the general human tendency toward mirroring . . . seems to have been carried ad absurdum" (Kets de Vries, 1993, p. 68). Emotional illiterates closely resemble the stereotyped bureaucrat of Whyte's *Organization Man*

(1956). They may be viewed within certain organizations as ideal candidates for leadership positions. While they are controlled, structured and dispassionate, they lack the emotional abilities to empathize, energize, foster creativity and respond appropriately to conflict. They contribute to mediocrity which, in turn, drives out excellence.

UNWILLINGNESS TO LET GO

Kets de Vries (1993) has also identified several sources of dysfunction that arise within individuals who, knowing they no longer fit the demands of the job, nevertheless cannot let go. The cause may be strong ego identification with a leadership position. In this case, the loss of position and power suggests a condition of nothingness, which is countered by intensity, single-mindedness and persistence. Another factor contributing to the fear of letting go is the "Talion Principle," the fear of reprisals. While in leadership positions, individuals are at times forced to make decisions that have unpleasant consequences for others' lives. People who give vent to the paranoid fear of retaliation hang on to power and even resort to preemptive action against others. Finally, the fear of nothingness can lead to the "Ediface Complex," the fear that their legacy will be destroyed, which encourages them to hold on to power as long as possible. This dysfunction may also be expressed in generational envy resulting in blocking younger people's careers.

FOLLOWERSHIP'S NEGATIVE FACE

Not all these counterproductive behaviors emanate from the leader. Contrary to what might be suggested by transformational leadership theory, inspired and empowered followers can take actions that produce decidedly negative consequences for the leader. Some of these actions stem from purposeful attempts to gain personal benefit and others result simply from personal characteristics having an inadvertent negative impact on the leader-follower relationship. There is a dearth of research addressing followership and almost none addresses the negative face of follower behavior. Followers are collaborators in the influence process no matter what leadership model is employed. They are not just lemmings being led into the sea. This is a fact well addressed by Chester Barnard (1938) in the acceptance theory of authority (a bottom up phenomenon, not top down). If dysfunctional aspects of personality can affect leaders, then they can affect followers as well. Authentic discussion of all that can go wrong in the leadership process requires that we take a hard look at follower participation in unhealthy influence processes.

There are at least two ways in which followers can affect leader-follower dynamics. The first is through the personal traits that followers carry into the influence process, and the second is the synergy that emerges through leaders and follower interaction. A few personal traits have been studied with respect to preferred leadership style. We know from past research that an individual with an internal locus of control prefers a participative leadership style and one with an external locus of control prefers a more autocratic or directive style (Burger, 1986). We also know that authoritarianism relates specifically to an individual's response to authority, and that whether one is high or low in authoritarianism again affects the preferred leadership style when an individual is the object of influence behaviors. But very little has been done to examine differences in follower behavior across a number of potentially relevant individual traits, and much more could be done to identify differences in perceptions of leader behavior.

THE SEARCH FOR EXEMPLARY FOLLOWERS

Kelly (1992) is one of few leadership researchers to focus on follower behavior. Kelly's model (Figure 1) categorizes follower behaviors using a two-dimensional taxonomy:

From these two dimensions, Kelly classifies followers into five styles:

1. *exemplary* (active and independent, critical thinking);

2. *conformist* (active and dependent, uncritical thinking);

3. *passive* (passive and dependent, uncritical thinking);

4. *alienated* (passive and independent, critical thinking); and

5. *pragmatist* (medium on both dimensions).

Although incomplete, these styles are helpful in pointing out to leaders possible problems with

FIGURE 1 **Follower Behavior Using a Two-Dimensional Taxonomy**

Independent, critical thinking ⎣— — — — — — — — — — — — — — — — — ⎦ Dependent, uncritical thinking

Active ⎣— — — — — — — — — — — — — — — ⎦ Passive

Source: Kelly (1992)

follower behavior. But Kelly operates on the assumption that leaders will seek to develop "exemplary followers," something many leaders have little interest in nor know how to do. He also assumes that follower behaviors are relatively superficial and related to organizational objectives in some way. Realistically, followers are not always forthcoming about (or even aware of) their shadow sides and may have a strong hidden agenda they seek to gratify. The model places no burden on followers to go within themselves and identify the darker sides of their behavior, and take responsibility for how their behavior interacts with the shadow aspects of leadership. Thus, Kelly's leader is solely responsible for maintaining healthy leader-follower relations.

Another recent work on leader-follower dynamics is Hirschhorn (1997), *Rethinking Authority*. Hirschhorn addresses the impact of system-induced feelings of vulnerability on relationships between leaders and followers. His discussions of dependency, envy and abdication in these interactions go further in addressing shadow aspects in relationships. However, his main point is that factors in postmodern systems have created negative feelings which must then be responded to in a particular way by the leader (i.e through openness in relationships). The sense of personal responsibility for self-knowledge and understanding beyond the imposed vulnerability is never discussed, and, here again, the message is intended for leaders, not followers.

FOLLOWER SYNDROMES

Kets de Vries (1989), whose psychoanalytic background more readily draws him to shadow aspects of personality, is again among those few who consider the dark side of the difficult and basic relationship between leader and follower. In his discussion of personality syndromes, he has identified dispositions that, at a relatively pathological level, can have serious consequences for the health of leader-follower relationships.

One of these is the controlling disposition. The controller is very similar to the authoritarian personality and the *Organization Man*. It is quite common for this type to end up in a position of leadership, but they are also frequently followers. They tend to see relationships in terms of superior-inferior, dominant-submissive, and their behavior is defined by their position in the pecking order. As a follower they are likely to do whatever they are told by superiors, and can be very deferential and ingratiating when interacting with those in higher level positions of leadership.

A second disposition that may result in dysfunctional follower behavior is the histrionic. Histrionics have a desperate need to attract attention at all costs. They are over reactive to external stimuli and allow their behaviors to be defined by the moods and desires of others. Like controllers, they have a tendency to respond positively to anyone with strong authority. They are also highly impressionable, and may be particularly likely to provide unquestioning loyalty to charismatic or transformational leaders.

. . . Individual[s] with a passive-aggressive disposition can appear acquiescent, making it difficult for a superior to confront them. But their pessimism, resentment and covert resistance make them poor followers. Because at the surface their behavior is cordial and appears compliant, it may take leaders some time to recognize the negative impact they can have on achieving outcomes.

Persons with the dependent dispositions, whose dependency needs have not been met, are likely to form extremely intense, over-powering connections with the individual who satisfies those needs. Dependency needs (or the need for direction) are universal, and followers may be willing to sacrifice anything, including reality, to have them met. People of this disposition will go out of their way to place themselves in dependent situations and so are extremely likely to be followers. A transformational leader surrounded by followers with strong dependency needs may find it very difficult to get objective or realistic feedback even when actively seeking it.

Lastly, there is the masochistic disposition. Masochists encourage others to take advantage of them, accept blame for things for which they are not responsible and find positive reinforcement in their misfortune. As with most of other types discussed above, they are unlikely to offer to leaders critical, objective feedback with any conviction.

THE NEED FOR RESEARCH AND SOME SUGGESTIONS

All these personality attributes lie on continua ranging from normal to pathological. While we would not normally expect organizations to be overrun with pathological members, the interaction between more moderate levels of pathology in followers and pathological inclinations of leaders may have devastating effects. Exacerbating the problem is the fact that these dispositions are not easily assessed or recognized, nor are they commonly discussed in leadership research or education. Clearly, studies examining correlations between leader styles and follower dispositions are needed. Additionally, there is a host of other better known and more easily measured

individual characteristics that have not even been identified in the leader-follower relationship. These are traits that may not exist at pathological levels, but can nevertheless indicate potential concerns in long term leader-follower relationships. For the most part, leadership research focuses on global subordinate characteristics (Path-Goal Theory is the most notable exception) or on outcomes in terms of relative effectiveness.

Among the traits that deserve to be considered in the followership process is Machiavellianism (Christie and Geis, 1970). High Mach personalities may be possessed by sycophants, who deprive leaders of critical feedback for the purpose of self-enhancement. The desire to satisfy their need for power may cause them a create situations that set up current leaders for failure. The process is based heavily in a context promoted for political considerations rather than for the purpose of defining an objective reality.

In the same vein, no research has considered the impact of strong follower power needs, social or personal, in the leadership process. It is possible that the more interested individuals are in obtaining their own leadership positions, the greater the temptation to contaminate the current influence process by distorting leader perceptions of reality.

Other follower traits that could have a damaging impact on both the leader-follower relationship and leader perceptions of reality are self-esteem, self-efficacy, risk aversion, conflict avoidance and tolerance for ambiguity. Again, it is not just the traits themselves that bring about negative results, but the effect the traits have when combined with mirroring, narcissism, emotional illiteracy or other shadow aspects of leader personality.

Interactions between leaders and followers can become arenas for creating distortion. In his psychoanalytic examination of leadership, Kets de Vries (1989) discussed a phenomenon known as "*folie a deux*," or shared madness. *Folie a deux* is the sharing of a delusional system by a least two individuals. It involves:

> . . . shifts of delusions and unusual behavior patterns form the originator of the activities to one or more others who were closely associated with him. These associates not only took an active part but also frequently enhanced and elaborated on these delusions. (p. 119)

It is clear that shadow aspects of both leaders and followers can combine to produce a negative effect. If the dark side of leadership can alone produce serious personal and organizational outcomes, then inclusion of the dark side of followership can surely add to the devastating impact.

RETHINKING LEADER-FOLLOWER RELATIONS

The implications of the dark sides of leadership and followership are clear. Leaders, themselves, can misperceive and act in inappropriate ways. Also, followers may, with good or bad intentions, contribute significantly to those misperceptions and misguided actions. Therefore, authentic leadership education must give ample weight to these realities. No actual or intended leader is immune from taking actions, whether or not well-intentioned, that can lead to the worst of consequences and no follower is immune from being an active participant in the process.

IMPLICATIONS FOR ACTION

We need to de-mythologize the word "leadership." Leadership needs to be treated as influence, reflecting power over others. However, we must strip it of the concept of moral rectitude. Effective leaders can promote terrible things.

We have to define not only the positive side of leadership, but we must take pains to illuminate the characteristics of the negative side and present them with equal weight. This will require some courage because we have been conditioned to emphasize positives and euphemize negatives.

At the same time, we must begin to look at the potential negatives contributed by followers. This cannot be done until we accept the significance of follower behavior in influence processes and outcomes. We must be willing to assume responsibility for outcomes when we are not holding positions of authority, and we must be willing to go within ourselves and look at how the dark sides of who we are can play themselves out in manipulating and covert ways.

As active participants in influence processes, leaders and followers need, in the words of Hillman (1996, p. 243), to grow down:

> Growing down shifts the focus of the personality form . . . single-minded egocentricity . . . into common humanity, twisting the call to transcend toward extension into the world and its claims.

This implies that leaders and followers need to work at understanding themselves, both the good and the bad, understanding their own personalities, and being open to all forms of information and feedback. Additionally and importantly, leaders need to be sensitive to what follower behaviors are really saying. Finally, leaders need to help followers become leaders in their own right. There are obvious implications for research focusing on the dynamics of leader-follower dispositions and interactions. . . .

The implications for leadership theorists and educators are challenging and important. Only recently have leadership scholars begun to talk openly about the dark side of leadership which is in us. As Palmer (1994, p. 28) has said:

> Why must we go in and down? Because as we do so, we will meet the violence and terror that we carry within ourselves. If we do not confront these things inwardly, we will project them outward onto other people. When we have not understood that the enemy is within ourselves, we will find a thousand ways of making someone "out there" into the enemy. . . .

References

Bamard, C. I. (1938). *The Functions of the Executive,* Harvard University Press, Cambridge, MA.

Bass, B. M. (1990). *Bass & Stogdill's Handbook of Leadership: Theory, Research & Managerial Applications,* The Free Press, New York, NY.

Bennis, W., & Nanus, B. (1985). *Leaders: The Strategies for Taking Charge,* Harper & Row, New York, NY.

Burger, J. M. (1986). *Personality: Theory and Research,* Wadsworth, Belmont, CA.

Burns, J. M. (1978). *Leadership,* Harper & Row, New York, NY.

Christine R., & Geis, F. L. (1970). *Studies in Machiavellianism,* Academic Press, New York, NY.

Hillman, J. (1996). *The Soul's Code: In Search of Character and Calling,* Random House, New York, NY.

Hirschhorn, L. (1997). *Reworking Authority: Leading and Following in the Post-Modern Organization,* MIT Press, Cambridge, MA.

Kelly, R. E. (1992). *The Power of Followership,* Doubleday Currency, New York, NY.

Kets de Vries, M. F. R. (1989). *Prisoners of Leadership,* Wiley & Sons, New York, NY.

Kets de Vries, M. F. R. (1993). *Leaders, Fools and Imposters: Essays on the Psychology of Leadership,* Jossey-Bass, San Francisco, CA.

McClelland, D. C. (1970). "The two faces of power," *Journal of International Affairs,* pp. 29–47.

McClelland, D. C. (1976). "Power is the great motivator," *Harvard Business Review,* March-April, pp. 100–10.

Palmer, P. J. (1994). "Leading from within: out of the shadows, into the light," in Conger, J. A. (Ed.), *Spirit at Work: Discovering the Spirituality in Leadership,* Jossey-Bass, San Francisco, CA.

Whyte, W. H. (1956). *The Organization Man,* Simon & Schuster, New York, NY.

Reading 44

The Dark Side of Leadership

Jay A. Conger
McGill University

In recent years, business leaders have gained great popularity: Lee Iacocca and Steven Jobs, for example, have stepped into the limelight as agents of change and entrepreneurship. But though we tend to think of the positive outcomes associated with leaders, certain risks or liabilities are also entailed. The very behaviors that distinguish leaders from managers also have the potential to produce problematic or even disastrous outcomes for their organizations. For example, when a leader's behaviors become exaggerated, lose touch with reality, or become vehicles for purely personal gain, they may harm the leader and the organization.

How do leaders produce such negative outcomes—and why? Three particular skill areas can contribute to such problems. These include leaders' strategic vision, their communications and impression-management skills, and their general management practices. We will examine each to discover its darker side.

PROBLEMS WITH THE VISIONARY LEADER

As we know, the 1970s and 1980s brought tremendous changes in the world's competitive business environment. Previously successful organizations that had grown huge and bureaucratic were suddenly faced with pressures to innovate and alter their ways. Out of these turbulent times came a new breed of business leader: the strategic visionary. These men and women, like Ross Perot of Electronic Data Systems and Mary Kay Ash of Mary Kay Cosmetics, possessed a twofold ability: to foresee market opportunities and to craft organizational strategies that captured these opportunities in ways that were personally meaningful to employees. When their success stories spread, "vision" became the byword of the 1980s. Yet though many of these leaders led their organizations on to great successes, others led their organizations on to great failures. The very qualities

Source: Edited and reprinted from *Organizational Dynamics*, 19:2, pp. 44–55. Copyright 1990 with permission from Elsevier.

that distinguished the visionary leader contained the potential for disaster.

Generally speaking, unsuccessful strategic visions can often be traced to the inclusion of the leaders' personal aims that did not match their constituents' needs. For example, leaders might substitute personal goals for what should be shared organizational goals. They might construct an organizational vision that is essentially a monument to themselves and therefore something quite different from the actual wishes of their organizations or customers.

Moreover, the blind drive to create this very personal vision could result in an inability to see problems and opportunities in the environment. Thomas Edison, for example, so passionately believed in the future of direct electrical current (DC) for urban power grids that he failed to see the more rapid acceptance of alternating power (AC) systems by America's then-emerging utility companies. Thus the company started by Edison to produce DC power stations was soon doomed to failure. He became so enamoured of his own ideas that he failed to see competing and, ultimately, more successful ideas.

In addition, such personal visions encourage the leader to expend enormous amounts of energy, passion, and resources on getting them off the ground. The higher their commitment, the less willing they are to see the viability of competing approaches. Because of the leader's commitment, the organization's investment is also likely to be far greater in such cases. Failure therefore will have more serious consequences.

Fundamental errors in the leader's perceptions can also lead to a failed vision. Common problems include (1) an inability to detect important changes in markets (e.g., competitive, technological, or consumer needs); (2) a failure to accurately assess and obtain the necessary resources for the vision's accomplishment; and (3) a misreading or exaggerated sense of the needs of markets or constituents. For example, with a few exceptions like the Chrysler minivan, Lee Iacocca inaccurately believed that automobile style rather than engineering was the primary concern of automotive buyers. At Chrysler, he relied on new body styles

TABLE 1 **The Sources of Failed Vision**

> The vision reflects the internal needs of leaders rather than those of the market or constituents.
>
> The resources needed to achieve the vision have been seriously miscalculated.
>
> An unrealistic assessment or distorted perception of market and constituent needs holds sway.
>
> A failure to recognize environmental changes prevents redirection of the vision.

and his charisma to market cars built on an aging chassis (the K car) developed in the late 1970s. The end result was that, after several initial years of successful sales, Chrysler's sales plunged 22.8 percent in 1987. Today, the future of Chrysler looks equally cloudy.

Ultimately, then, the success of a leader's strategic vision depends on a realistic assessment of both the opportunities and the constraints in the organization's environment and a sensitivity to constituents' needs. If the leader loses sight of reality or loses touch with constituents, the vision becomes a liability. Visions may fail for a wide variety of reasons; Table 1 outlines some of the more significant ones. We will examine several of these categories and illustrate them with the experiences of some prominent business leaders.

MAKING THE LEADER'S PERSONAL NEEDS PARAMOUNT

As mentioned, one of the most serious liabilities of a visionary leader occurs when he or she projects purely personal needs and beliefs onto those of constituents. A common example is the inventor with a pet idea who acquires sufficient resources to initiate a venture that fails to meet the market's needs. When a leader's needs and wishes diverge from those of constituents, the consequences can be quite costly. . . .

BECOMING A "PYRRHIC VICTOR"

In the quest to achieve a vision, a leader may be so driven as to ignore the costly implications of his strategic aims. Ambition and the miscalculation of necessary resources can lead to a "Pyrrhic victory" for the leader. The term "Pyrrhic victory" comes from an incident in Ancient Greece: Pyrrhus, the King of Epirus, sustained such heavy losses in defeating the Romans that despite his numerous victories over them, his entire empire was ultimately undermined. Thus the costs of a "Pyrrhic"

victory deplete the resources that are needed for future success.

In this scenario, the leader is usually driven by a desire to expand or accelerate the realization of his vision. The initial vision appears correct, and early successes essentially delude or weaken the leader's ability to realistically assess his resources and marketplace realities. The costs that must be paid for acquisitions or market share ultimately become unsustainable and threaten the long-term viability of the leader's organization. . . .

CHASING A VISION BEFORE ITS TIME

Sometimes a leader's perceptions of the market are so exaggerated or so significantly ahead of their time that the marketplace fails to sustain the leader's venture. The organization's resources are mobilized and spent on a mission that ultimately fails to produce the expected results. In this case, the leader is perhaps too visionary or too idealistic. He or she is unable to see that the time is not ripe, so the vision goes on to failure or, at best, a long dormancy. . . .

Two other factors may play important roles. In their own excitement over an idea, leaders may fail to adequately test-market a new product or service or fail to hear naysayers or overlook contrary signs from the environment. Again, because of successes in other projects . . . , they may delude themselves into believing they know their markets more accurately than they actually do. Or their spell-binding ability to lead may not be backed up by an adequate understanding of marketplace trends.

HOW LEADERS COME TO DENY FLAWS IN THEIR VISIONS

All three of these cases share certain characteristics that cause leaders to deny the flaws in their visions. Often, for example, leaders will perceive that their course of action is producing negative results, yet they persist. Why this happens can be explained by a process called "cognitive dissonance," which prevents the leader from changing his course. Simply put, individuals act to keep the commitments they have made because failing to do so would damage their favorable perceptions of themselves. For example, studies have found that executives will sometimes persist in an ineffective course of action simply because they feel they have committed themselves to the decision. This same process, I suspect, occurs with leaders.

Others in the organization who tend to become dependent on a visionary leader may perpetuate the problem through their own actions. They may idealize their leader excessively and thus ignore negative aspects and exaggerate the good qualities. As a result, they may carry out their leader's orders unquestioningly—and leaders may in certain cases encourage such behavior because of their needs to dominate and be admired. The resulting sense of omnipotence encourages denial of market and organizational realities. The danger is that leaders will surround themselves with "yes people" and thus fail to receive information that might be important but challenging to the mission. Their excessive confidence and the desire for heroic recognition encourages them to undertake large, risky ventures—but because of their overreliance on themselves and their cadre of "yes people," strategic errors go unnoticed. Bold but poorly thought-out strategies will be designed and implemented. The leader's vision, in essence, becomes a vehicle for his or her own needs for attention and visibility.

Finally, problems with "group-think" can occur where the leader's advisors delude themselves into agreement with the leader or dominant others. In such a case, decision making becomes distorted, and a more thorough and objective review of possible alternatives to a problem are all but precluded. This is especially true of groups that are very cohesive, highly committed to their success, under pressure, and possessing favorable opinions of themselves—common characteristics in the organizations of powerful and charismatic leaders. When group-think occurs, the opinions of the leader and advisors with closely allied views come to dominate decision making. Doubts that others might have are kept hidden for fear of disapproval. It is more important "to go along to get along" rather than to consider contrary viewpoints. . . .

MANIPULATION THROUGH IMPRESSION

MANAGEMENT AND COMMUNICATION SKILLS
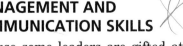

Because some leaders are gifted at communicating, it may be quite easy for them to misuse this ability. For instance, they may present information that makes their visions appear more realistic or more appealing than the visions actually are. They may also use their language skills to screen out problems in the larger environment or

TABLE 2 Potential Liabilities in the Leader's Communications and Impression Management Skills

Exaggerated self-descriptions.

Exaggerated claims for the vision.

A technique of fulfilling stereotypes and images of uniqueness to manipulate audiences.

A habit of gaining commitment by restricting negative information and maximizing positive information.

Use of anecdotes to distract attention away from negative statistical information.

Creation of an illusion of control through affirming information and attributing negative outcomes to external causes.

to foster an illusion of control when, in reality, things are out of control. Table 2 highlights a number of these possible problem areas. . . .

When leaders rely greatly on their impression management skills in communicating, they do themselves a disservice. For instance, research in impression management indicates not only that one's self-descriptions are effective in deceiving an audience, but also that they may deceive the presenter as well. This is especially true when an audience reinforces and approves of the individual's image. Such positive responses encourage leaders to internalize their own self-enhancing descriptions. Especially when exaggeration is only moderate, leaders tend to internalize and believe such claims. . . .

Considerable research has also been performed on people who are ingratiators—people who play to their audiences by telling them what they want to hear. Two particular tactics that I suspect charismatic leaders use to ingratiate themselves with their audiences are to (1) fulfill stereotypes and (2) create an image of uniqueness.

Research shows that if individuals behave in ways that fulfill the positive stereotypes of an audience they are more likely to interact successfully with them. This can be achieved by espousing the beliefs, values, and behaviors associated with the stereotype and appearing as the stereotype is expected to look. . . .

Anecdotal information may be used by the leader not only to influence decision makers' choices, but also to increase their confidence in a choice. The sheer amount of information the leader provides may act to build overconfidence. Various studies of decision making indicate that more information apparently permits people to generate more reasons for justifying their decisions and, in turn, increases the confidence of others in the decisions. Leaders might also create an illusion of control by selectively providing information that affirms they are in control and attribute failures or problems to external causes. All of these tactics may be used by leaders to mislead their direct reports and their investors.

MANAGEMENT PRACTICES THAT BECOME LIABILITIES

The managerial practices of leaders also have certain inherent liabilities. Some leaders are known for their excessively impulsive, autocratic management style. Others become so disruptive through their unconventional behavior that their organizations mobilize against them. Moreover, leaders can at times be poor at managing their superiors and peers. In general, some of the very management practices that make leaders unique may also lead to their downfall.

Leaders' liabilities fall into several categories: (1) the way they manage relations with important others, (2) their management style with direct reports, and (3) their thoroughness and attention to certain administrative detail. Typical problems associated with each of these categories are shown in Table 3. We will start with the first category: managing relations with important others.

TABLE 3   Potential Liabilities of a Leader's Management Practices

Poor management of people networks, especially superiors and peers.

Unconventional behavior that alienates.

Creation of disruptive "in-group/out-group" rivalries.

An autocratic, controlling management style.

An informal/impulsive style that is disruptive and dysfunctional.

Alternation between idealizing and devaluing others, particularly direct reports.

Creation of excessive dependence in others.

Failure to manage details and effectively act as an administrator.

Attention to the superficial.

Absence from operations.

Failure to develop successors of equal ability.

MANAGING UPWARDS AND SIDEWAYS

Some leaders—particularly charismatic leaders in large organizations—seem to be very poor at managing upwards and sideways. Because they are usually unconventional advocates of radical reform, they may often alienate others in the organization, including their own bosses. The charismatic leader's unconventional actions may trigger the ire of forces within the organization which then act to immobilize him or her. Leaders' aggressive style may also alienate many potential supporters and ultimately leave them without sufficient political support for their ambitious plans. This problem is common when charismatic leaders are brought in from the outside; their radically different values and approaches may alienate the rest of the organization.

This kind of situation occurred at General Motors when Ross Perot was made a board member. Once on the board, Perot became one of the company's most outspoken critics. As an entrepreneur, he was quite naturally accustomed to running his own show, and after his company, Electronic Data Systems (EDS), merged with GM, he insisted that any changes made in EDS procedures be cleared through him. His style and outspokenness were so much at odds with the General Motors culture that the company offered Perot $700 million in stock to step down from the board—an offer he finally accepted.

A second problem related to managing relations within large organizations is the tendency of certain leaders to cultivate a feeling of being "special" among members of their operating units. This practice is often accompanied by a corresponding depreciation of other parts of the corporation. In short, the leader creates an "us versus them" attitude. Although this heightens the motivation of the leader's group, it further alienates other groups that may be important for resources or political support. Steven Jobs did this with the MacIntosh division at Apple Computer. Even though the company's Apple II Computer provided the profits, Jobs consistently downplayed that division's importance. He essentially divided the company into two rivals. He was fond of telling people in the MacIntosh division, "This is the cream of Apple. This is the future of Apple." He even went so far as telling marketing managers for Apple II that they worked for an outdated, clumsy organization. Jobs's later departure from Apple stemmed in part from morale problems he created within the company by using this tactic.

In another case, the charismatic president of a division in a large corporation used as his group's emblem a mascot symbol of the TV cartoon character Roadrunner. (In the cartoons, Roadrunner was particularly adept at outwitting a wily coyote.) To him, his division managers were the "roadrunners" who were smarter and faster than the corporate "coyotes" who laid roadblocks in their path. He also had a habit of ignoring corporate staff requests for reports or information, and he returned their reports with "STUPID IDEA" stamped on the front cover. Although such behaviors and tactics fostered a sense of camaraderie and aggressiveness within the charismatic leader's division, they were ultimately detrimental both to the leader and to the organization. In this case, the executive eventually stepped down from the organization.

RELATIONSHIPS WITH SUBORDINATES

Highly directive and visionary leaders are often described as autocratic. Jobs, for example, has been described as dictatorial. I suspect that in many cases the vision is such a personification of the leader that he or she becomes obsessed about its perfection or implementation. Leaders' natural impatience with the pace of the vision's achievement exacerbates the problem and encourages them to be more hands-on, more controlling.

There also appears to be, at times, an impulsive dynamic at work in the way leaders manage—and at such times they will override subordinates' suggestions or insights. Again, this occurs especially in relation to accomplishing the vision. DeLorean is described as increasing his production of the DeLorean car by 50 percent in the belief that his product would become an overnight sensation. Production went to an annual rate of 30,000 cars. This was done in spite of market research that showed total annual sales of between 4,000 and 10,000 cars. A company executive lamented, "Our figures showed that this was a viable company with half the production. If the extravagance had been cut out of New York, we could have broken even making just 6,000 cars a year. But that wasn't fast enough for John. First he had to build his paper empire in the stock market. A creditable success was not enough for him" (ibid., pg. 282).

Steven Jobs is known to have darted in and out of operations causing havoc: "He would leap-frog back and forth among various projects, dictating designs, with little or no knowledge of whether or not the technology even existed to make his ideas

work" (L. Butcher, *Accidental Millionaire,* Paragon House, 1988, pp. 140–141).

Another potential problem can arise from a style of informality when managing the hierarchy of an organization—this is especially true of charismatic leaders. Advantages of this style are that leaders are highly visible, approachable, and able to react quickly to issues and problems. The drawback is that they often violate the chain of command by going around direct reports and thus undercut their direct reports' authority. If a particular project or idea interests them, they do not hesitate to become involved, sometimes to the detriment of the project managers' responsibilities. DeLorean would drop in on his engineers to suggest what seemed trivial ideas. One company engineer said: "He came in one day to say we should hook into the cooling system and make a little ice-box for a six-pack of beer behind the driver's seat. Or, another time, he told us to work on a sixty-watt radio speaker that could be detached and hung outside the car for picnics" (H. Levin, ibid., pg. 267).

ADMINISTRATIVE SKILLS

Some visionary leaders are so absorbed by the "big picture" that they fail to understand essential details—except for "pet" projects in which they become excessively involved. Iacocca, for instance, turned over most of the day-to-day operations to others as he became increasingly famous. As a result, he lost touch with new model planning. He himself admitted: "If I made one mistake, it was delegating all the product development and not going to a single meeting" (ibid., pg. 267). A DeLorean executive complained "He [John DeLorean] just didn't have time for the details of the project. But attention to detail is everything" (ibid., p. 267). Then, too, leaders may get so caught up in corporate stardom that they become absentee leaders. Again, Iacocca is an example. His success at Chrysler led to his becoming a best-selling author, a U.S. presidential prospect, and the head of the $277 million fund-raising campaign for the Statue of Liberty—all of which distracted him from the important task of leading Chrysler.

Because these individuals are often excited by ideas, they may at times be poor implementors. Once an idea begins to appear as a tangible reality, I suspect they feel the need to move on to the next challenge, thereby leaving subordinates scrambling to pick up the pieces. Furthermore, because some leaders have high needs for visibility, they gravitate toward activities that afford them high people contact and recognition. Such activities are generally not performed at a desk while paying careful attention to the details.

SUCCESSION PROBLEMS

A true leader is usually a strong figure and, as noted, often one upon whom subordinates develop dependencies. Thus it is difficult for others with leadership potential to develop fully in the shadow of such leaders. For while they may actively coach their subordinates, I suspect that it is extremely difficult for them to develop others to be leaders *of equal power*. Leaders simply enjoy the limelight too much to share it, so when they ultimately depart, a leadership vacuum is created. Moreover, under charismatic leadership authority may be highly centralized around the leader—and this is an arrangement that, unfortunately, weakens the authority structures that are normally dispersed throughout an organization.

It's clear that many of the qualities of a strong leader have both a positive and a negative face. That's why the presence of leaders entails risks for their direct reports, their organizations, and at times their societies. They must be managed with care. The negatives, however, must always be weighed in light of the positives. For companies and society, the need for organizational change and strategic vision may be so great that the risks of confrontation, unconventionality, and so on may seem a small price to pay. It is also possible that organizations and educational institutions can train, socialize, and manage future leaders in ways that will minimize their negative qualities.

Selected Bibliography

For an in-depth look at the psychological dynamics of the dark side of leaders, we recommend *The Neurotic Organization* (Jossey-Bass, 1984) by Manfred Kets de Vries and Danny Miller and "Personality, Culture, and Organization" (*The Academy of Management Review,* April 1986), also by Manfred Kets de Vries and Danny Miller.

Works that provide an informative treatment on the topic of impression management include *The Presentation of Self in Everyday Life* (Doubleday-Anchor, 1959) by Erving Goffman and *Impression Management* (Brooks/Cole, 1980) by B. R. Schlenker. Books and articles that deal more systematically with the issue of commitment to a course of action as well as communicating information are *A Theory of Cognitive Dissonance* (Row, Peterson, 1957) by L. Festinger; Charles R. Schwenk's "Information, Cognitive Bias, and Commitment to a Course of Action" (*The Academy of Management Review,* April 1986); Barry Staw's "Knee Deep in the Big Muddy: A Study of Escalating Commitment to a Chosen Course of Action" (*Organizational Behavior and Human Performance,* June 1976); and "The Escalation of Commitment to a Course of Action" (*The Academy of Management Review,* October 1981). The definitive work on group-think is *Victims of Group Think* (Houghton Mifflin, 1972), by I. L. Janis.

Readers wishing more depth on the individual case studies of leaders should consult the following sources. P. C. Wensberg's *Land's Polaroid* (Houghton Mifflin, 1987). Two interesting sources on John DeLorean are Michael Daly's "The Real DeLorean Story" (*New York,* Nov. 8, 1982) and Hill Levin's *Grand Delusions* (Viking Press, 1983). *Accidental Millionaire* (Paragon House, 1988) by Lee Butcher presents a darker-side view of Steven Jobs.

Reading 45

Narcissism and Leadership: An Object Relations Perspective

Manfred F. R. Kets de Vries
European Institute of Business Administration (INSEAD), France

Danny Miller
École des Hautes Études Commerciales, Montreal and McGill University

If each of us were to confess his most secret desire, the one that inspires all his deeds and designs, he would say, "I want to be praised." Yet none will bring himself to do so, for it is less dishonorable to commit a crime than to announce such a pitiful and humiliating weakness arising from a sense of loneliness and insecurity, a feeling that afflicts both the fortunate and the unfortunate with equal intensity. No one is sure of who he is, or certain of what he does. Full as we may be of our own worth, we are gnawed by anxiety and, to overcome it, ask only to be mistaken in our doubt, to receive approval from no matter where or no matter whom . . .

—*Corian, Desir et honneur de la gloire*

INTRODUCTION

When we think of leaders and leadership, a wide array of images comes to mind, often conveying emotional reactions. Some leaders elicit thoughts of strength, power, and care, others recall the forces of terror, malevolence, and destructiveness. Our ubiquitous judgments of a leader's degree of "goodness" or evil are reflected in epithets such as Akbar the Great or Ivan the Terrible. We shall attempt in this paper to show that leadership effectiveness and dysfunction can often be explained by the narcissistic dispositions of the leader. We shall discuss and contrast three types of leaders and probe the etiology and consequences of their narcissistic orientations. The task will be to show the relationships between the intrapsychic development of the leader (using an object relations perspective), his subsequent narcissistic orientation, and the concrete manifestations of this orientation in his leadership behavior. In no sense will our method be positivistic. We draw upon our experiences as practicing psychoanalysts, professors of management, and management consultants to demonstrate the linkages between early developmental experiences, types of narcissism, and leader behavior (Kets de Vries, 1980). The framework we shall employ is based on our clinical experiences with individuals who play a leadership role. It therefore goes without saying that our conclusions are to be viewed more as hypotheses than findings.

LEADERS AND FOLLOWERS

The dynamics of leadership have remained very much a puzzle. We still know little about what makes a good leader. . . .

What most leaders seem to have in common is the ability to reawaken primitive emotions in their followers. Leaders, particularly those who are charismatic, are masters at manipulating certain symbols. Followers, when under the "spell" of certain types of leaders, often feel powerfully grandiose and proud, or helpless and acutely dependent. Max Weber (1947) used the term *charisma* to elucidate this strange influence of some leaders over followers which, for him, consisted of:

> a certain quality of an individual personality by virtue of which he is set apart from ordinary men and treated as endowed with supernatural, superhuman, or at least specifically exceptional powers or qualities. These are such as are not accessible to the ordinary person, but are regarded as of divine origin or as exemplary, and on the basis of them, the individual concerned is treated as a leader (pp. 358–359).

We don't have to go so far as Weber, but whatever strange "quality" leaders possess, some have

Source: Edited and reprinted with permission from *Human Relations* 38, 6 (1985), pp. 583–601. Copyright 1985, Sage Publications, Inc.

the power to induce regressive behavior among their followers. They have the uncanny ability to exploit, not necessarily in full awareness, the unconscious feelings of their subordinates. In this process, some followers may try to embrace an idealized, "omnipotent" leader, one who will fulfill their dependency needs. This may lead to the destructive suspension of their own rational faculties. The mesmerizing influence of some leaders may also cause the common good to be sacrificed for personal folly. Rituals of adulation can supplant task-related activity. Form tends to dominate substance, as the followers become pawns to be manipulated, like the gullible spectators in Andersen's "The Emperor's New Clothes." Thus, functional requirements pertaining to common purposes or ideals may be neglected in favor of fleeting narcissistic gratifications.

In spite of the regressive potential of some leaders, there are others who transcend petty concerns, who are able to create a climate of constructiveness, involvement, and care, who engender initiative, and spur creative endeavors. This is the kind of person Zaleznik (1977) had in mind when he said:

> One often hears leaders referred to in adjectives rich in emotional content. Leaders attract strong feelings of identity and difference, or of love and hate. Human relations in leader-dominated structures often appear turbulent, intense, and at times even disorganized. Such an atmosphere intensifies individual motivation and often produces unanticipated outcomes. (p. 74)

James MacGregor Burns (1978) probably had similar thoughts when he compared transactional with transforming leadership. While the first type of leader motivates followers by exchanging rewards for services rendered, whether economic, political, or psychological, the latter type of leader recognizes and exploits an existing need or demand of a potential follower. But, beyond that, the successful transforming leader looks for potential motives in followers, seeks to satisfy their higher needs, and engages their full potential. The result of the most adept transforming leadership is a relationship of mutual stimulation and elevation that converts followers into leaders and leaders into moral agents (Burns, 1978, p. 4).

To conclude, leadership can be pathologically destructive or most inspiring. But what is it about the leaders themselves that makes it so? What differentiates styles of leadership? Our theme will be that the degree of narcissism, and its genesis, stand central.

THE NARCISSISTIC DISPOSITION

In studying leaders, we soon recognized that one critical component of their orientation is the quality and intensity of their narcissistic development. If there is one personality constellation to which leaders tend to gravitate it is the narcissistic one. Freud (1921, pp. 123–124), in his study of the relationship between leaders and followers already confirmed this, stating that "the leader himself need love no one else, he may be of a masterful nature, absolutely narcissistic, self-confident and independent." Later, he introduced a narcissistic libidinal personality, an individual whose main interest is self-preservation, who is independent and impossible to intimidate. Significant aggressiveness is possible, which sometimes manifests itself in a constant readiness for activity. People belonging to this type impress others as being strong personalities. They are especially suited to act as moral ideological bastions for others, in short, as true leaders (Freud, 1931, p. 21).

In a similar context, Wilhelm Reich referred to a phallic-narcissistic character which he portrayed as being "self-confident, often arrogant, elastic, vigorous and often impressive. . . . The outspoken types tend to achieve leading positions in life and resent subordination. . . . If their vanity is hurt, they react either with cold reserve, deep depression or lively aggression" (Reich, 1949, p. 201).

Narcissism became a particularly important topic for study when new developments in psychoanalytic theory occurred. The introduction of object relations theory and self-psychology was especially fruitful. The most important revisions concerning narcissism were formulated by clinicians such as Otto Kernberg (1975) and Heinz Kohut (1971).

For the purpose of this paper, we will not dwell on the theoretical controversies about whether narcissism is a result mainly of developmental arrest or regression, or whether it possesses its own developmental lines. Our aim is to explore the relationships between narcissism and leadership, a connection recognized by both Kernberg and Kohut. For example, Kernberg states that "because narcissistic personalities are often driven by intense needs for power and prestige to assume positions of authority and leadership, individuals with such characteristics are found rather frequently in top leadership positions" (Kernberg, 1979, p. 33). Kohut, in focusing on leaders as objects of identification, mentions that "certain types of narcissistically fixated personalities with their apparently absolute self-confidence and certainty lend themselves specifically to this role" (Kohut, 1971, p. 316).

Narcissism is often the driving force behind the desire to obtain a leadership position. Perhaps individuals with strong narcissistic personality features are more willing to undertake the arduous process of attaining a position of power. A central theme of our discussion will be that the kind of behavior we encounter in a leader will be likely to reflect the nature and degree of his narcissistic tendencies.

Although the narcissistic type of personality has long been recognized, only recently has it come under critical scrutiny. For example, the latest version of the Diagnostic and Statistical Manual of Mental Disorders (DSM III, American Psychiatric Association, 1980), lists a large number of criteria to describe narcissistic personality disorders. There are overtones of mental illness and impairment of functioning: symptoms include extremes of grandiosity, exploitativeness, exhibitionism, and so on. Many of these characteristics are also applicable, albeit in smaller measure, to narcissistic individuals who adopt a more "normal" mode of functioning.

Narcissists feel they must rely on themselves rather than on others for the gratification of life's needs. They live with the assumption that they cannot reliably depend on anyone's love or loyalty. They pretend to be self-sufficient, but in the depth of their beings they experience a sense of deprivation and emptiness. To cope with these feelings and, perhaps, as a cover for their insecurity, narcissists become preoccupied with establishing their adequacy, power, beauty, status, prestige, and superiority. At the same time, narcissists expect others to accept the high esteem in which they hold themselves, and to cater to their needs. What is striking in the behavior of these people is their interpersonal exploitativeness. Narcissists live under the illusion that they are entitled to be served, that their own wishes take precedence over those of others. They think that they deserve special consideration in life.

It must be emphasized, however, that these characteristics occur with different degrees of intensity. A certain dose of narcissism is necessary to function effectively. We all show signs of narcissistic behavior. Among individuals who possess only limited narcissistic tendencies, we find those who are very talented and capable of making great contributions to society. Those who gravitate toward the extremes, however, give narcissism its pejorative reputation. Here we find excesses of rigidity, narrowness, resistance, and discomfort in dealing with the external environment.

The managerial implications of narcissism can be both dramatic and crucial.

THREE TYPES OF NARCISSISM: ETIOLOGY, DEFENSES, AND MANIFESTATIONS

We shall proceed to discuss three types of narcissistic orientations beginning with the most pernicious or pathological and proceeding toward the more adaptive or functional: these we shall call *reactive, self-deceptive,* and *constructive.* We will first discuss the general etiology and common defenses of these types, using an object relations perspective. We shall then present a discussion of the behavioral manifestations of the types in a leadership situation. Each type is based on examples from our clinical experiences which confirm how executives with different formative backgrounds manifest narcissistic behavior in various leadership situations. Table 1 summarizes our major findings for each of the three types.

OBJECT RELATIONS AND THE ETIOLOGY OF NARCISSISM

Leaders may be said to occupy different positions on a spectrum ranging from healthy narcissism to pathology. We are by no means dealing with distinct categories. The factors that distinguish between health and dysfunction are the intrapsychic and interpersonal dynamics of the leader.

Over time, most people develop relatively stable ways of representing the experiences of themselves and others. These psychic representations in one's private inner world are known as *internal objects;* they are accumulated perceptions. They are composed of fantasies, ideals, thoughts, and images which create a kind of cognitive map of the world (Klein, 1948; Fairbairn, 1952; Jacobson, 1964; Guntrip, 1969; Mahler, Pine, & Bergman, 1975; Kernberg, 1976). The term "object relations" thus refers to theories, or aspects of theories, concerned with exploring the relationships between real, external people, the mental images retained of these people, and the significance of these mental residues for psychic functioning (Greenberg & Mitchell, 1983). Our interactions with actual people depend not only on how we view them, but also on our views of internal others. These psychic representations profoundly influence our affective states as well as our behavior. Good internal objects have a generative and restorative function, and serve as a source of sustenance in dealing with life's adversities. They constitute the underpinnings of

TABLE 1   **"Ideal" Varieties of Narcissism**

Reactive	Self-deceptive	Constructive
Early object relations (etiology)	Overburdening parenting	"Good enough" care
Rejecting, unresponsive parenting	Absence of secure attachment	Sense of acceptance
Absence of secure attachment		
Defensive reactions		
(splitting, projective identification,		
idealization/devaluation)		
Pervasive	Manifestation, frequency, and	Rare
Severe	intensity varies	Mild
Frequent		Infrequent
	Exploitativeness	Manipulation
Symptomatology		
Exhibitionism	Lack of empathy	Sense of humor
Grandiosity	Machiavellianism	Creativity
Ruthlessness	Fear of failure	Self-confidence
Coldness	"Ideal-hungry"	Ambition
Entitlement	Preoccupation	Energy
(want to dominate)	with own needs	Stubbornness
	(want to be loved)	Pride (want to achieve)
Manifestation in organizational		
functioning		
1. Leadership		
Transforming orientation	Transactional orientation	Transforming/transactional orientation
Expelling mode	Binding mode	Reciprocal mode
Tolerate only sycophants	Prefer noncritical subordinates	Meritocratic
Cruel taskmaster	Diplomatic	Inspirational
Ignore subordinates' needs	Instrumental consideration	Mentor role
	of subordinates	
Enraged by criticism	Hurt by criticism	Learns from criticism
2. Decision-making		
Major, risk-laden, spectacular	Conservative, risk-averse,	Consultative in information-
projects	overcautious	gathering, independent in
		decision-making
Consults no one	Consults too many	Inner-directed
Crushes opponents	Lacks resolve	
Uses scapegoats		
Never admits defeat		

healthy functioning. But in the absence of good internal objects, various dysfunctions accrue. Therein lies the genesis of pathological narcissism. Naturally, the earliest "objects" are the parents whose nurturing gives rise to different kinds of "internal worlds." Since parents are not always consistent in dealing with their children, this world can be highly complex and turbulent. We shall proceed to discuss the etiology or early object relations of three types of narcissistic leaders.

Reactive Narcissism

In describing messianic and charismatic leaders, Kohut (1971) argues that such leaders suffer from a pathology of narcissistic development. He attributes it to their failure during early childhood to integrate two important spheres of the self, namely, *the grandiose self* and *the idealized parental image* (Kohut, 1978, p. 826). The first construct refers to early feelings of grandiose omnipotence, when a child wishes to display his evolving capabilities and wants to be admired for it. The second construct applies to the equally illusory wishes about the idealized powers attributed to the parents, the desire to experience a sense of merger with an idealized person. Typically, the child's "I am perfect and you admire me," gradually changes into "you are perfect and I am part of you."

Clinical studies indicate that these early experiences which are a part of everyone's maturation, become mitigated and neutralized through phase-appropriate development (Winnicott, 1975). By this process, the child is gradually able to reduce frustration from the inevitable failures of parents to live up to his or her archaic expectations, and through experience, comes gradually to understand the difference between the ideal of perfection and just being good enough. He or she learns that the parent is neither completely good nor completely bad. A more balanced and integrated image of the parent is internalized to make for a more realistic appreciation. This fusion of originally split "good and bad" objects is said to be essential for the development of trust in the permanence, "constancy," or reliability of the parental figures (Klein, 1948). In turn, this early success in creating secure interpersonal attachments makes for confident self-esteem and for stable relationships. Kohut (1971) calls this a process of "transmuting internalization." He believes it to be the basis of the development of a permanent and durable psychic structure.

Unfortunately, phase-appropriate development does not always occur. Parental behavior may be experienced as cold and unempathic, even at the earliest stage of development. Parents might not be sufficiently sensitive to the needs of the growing child. In these cases, children acquire a defective sense of self and are unable to maintain a stable level of self-esteem. Consequently, childhood needs are not modified or neutralized, but continue to prevail. This, in turn, results in a persistent longing and a search for narcissistic recognition throughout adulthood. The stage is thus set for "reactive" narcissism. In a classic article, Kohut and Wolf (1978) refer to the understimulated and fragmented self that results from too few stimulating and integrating parental responses during childhood.

The legacy for the child of such deficient interactions may be a lingering sense of inadequacy. To cope with such feelings some individuals create for themselves a self-image of "specialness." This can be viewed as a compensatory, reactive refuge against an ever-present feeling of never having been loved by the parent. The illusion of uniqueness will vitally affect how the individual deals with his external environment. Any discrepancies between capacities and wants are likely to contribute to anxiety and to impaired reality testing, the inability to distinguish wish from perception or, in other words, "inside" from "outside." Individuals with this "reactive" kind of orientation will frequently distort outside events to manage anxiety and to prevent a sense of loss and disappointment. If they are in a position of leadership this can have grave consequences. Reactive narcissism caused

by emotionally unresponsive, rejecting parents is the severest type. This will become obvious from our discussion of defenses and symptoms.

In making these inferences, we should bear in mind that early experiences in themselves rarely have a direct impact on adult functioning. There are many mediating experiences during one's life. Early experiences do, however, play a substantial role in shaping the core personality which influences the kind of environment sought out by the individual. This has an effect on experience and, in turn, will influence personality. We are thus talking about an interactive cycle of personality, behavior, and situation (Erikson, 1963; McKinley Runyan, 1982).

Self-deceptive Narcissism

We often find a second type of narcissistic leader with a very different type of early childhood development. These individuals were once led by one or both parents to believe that they were completely lovable and perfect, regardless of their actions and in spite of any basis in reality. Such self-deceptive leaders probably suffer from what Kohut and Wolf (1978) describe as an overstimulated or overburdened self. Because the responses of the figures of early childhood were inappropriate given the children's age, the latter never learn to moderate their grandiose self-images or their idealized parental images. Ideals of perfection have been too demanding to allow them to internalize soothing, stabilizing internal objects. These children become the proxies of their parents, entrusted with the mission to fulfill many unrealized parental hopes. What may appear as indulgence on the part of the parents is, in fact, exactly the opposite. The parents use their children to take care of their own needs, overburdening them with their implicit desires. When parents impose their unrealistic hopes onto their children, they engender delusions. They confuse the children about their true abilities.

Such unrealistic beliefs may sometimes be the original impetus which differentiates these individuals from others and makes them successful. Perhaps Freud (1917, p. 156) had this in mind when he noted that "if a man has been his mother's undisputed darling, he retains throughout life the triumphant feeling, the confidence in success, which not seldom brings actual success along with it." In those rare instances when such encouragements work out, the child may be sufficiently talented to live up to the parents' exaggerated expectations. A person who in more normal circumstances might have led an ordinary life, has used the expectations imposed on him as a child as a basis for excellence.

In general, however, the self-delusory quality of the unrealistic beliefs created by the parents will lead to problems. An exalted self-image is usually difficult to sustain in the light of external circumstances such as disappointment and failure. Thus, even though the early internalized objects are benign, disturbing interpersonal encounters when the child ventures forth from the protective family environment will give them an element of instability, of frailty. The overvalued image of the self that was garnered from an idealizing parent becomes more realistic after interactions with more honest and critical peers. Still, the traumas of early disappointments may have left a somewhat fragile and distorted concept of self. Self-deceiving narcissists are likely to suffer from interpersonal difficulties due to their desire to live up to the now internalized parental illusions of self-worth. They tend to demonstrate emotional superficiality and poverty of affect. Their behavior has an "ideal-hungry" quality resulting from difficulties in identity formation.

Conceptually, we have to be able to differentiate between the etiology of the reactive and self-defective modes of narcissism. In practice, however, a distinction is more difficult to make. Parents might each have responded differently toward the developing child. One parent might have taken a cold, hostile, rejecting attitude, while the other might have been supportive. Thus could have been created different gradations of benign and vicious internal objects, which accounts for mixtures of narcissistic styles. In addition, instead of being frustrated when ambitious parental expectations are incongruent with external reality, the child can sometimes strive successfully to bring his abilities up to his perceived capacity, as Freud notes so poignantly. Moreover, as we have pointed out, learning experiences later in life may also have buffering or mitigating effects.

Constructive Narcissism

Miller (1981), in describing the childhood object relations of healthy or constructive narcissists, stated:

> Aggressive impulses [were] neutralized because they did not upset the confidence and self-esteem of the parents.
>
> Strivings toward autonomy were not experienced [by parents] as an attack.
>
> The child was allowed to experience and express "ordinary" impulses (such as jealousy, rage, defiance) because his parents did not require him to be "special," for instance, to represent their own ethical attitudes.
>
> There was no need to please anybody (under optimal conditions), and the child could develop and exhibit whatever was active in him during each developmental phase. . . .
>
> Because the child was able to display ambivalent feelings, he could learn to regard both himself and the subject [the other] as "both good and bad," and did not need to split off the "good" from the "bad" object. (pp. 33–34)

The constructive narcissists do not behave in a reactive or self-deceptive manner. They do not feel the same need to distort reality to deal with life's frustrations. Nor are they so prone to anxiety. They make less frequent use of primitive defenses, and are less estranged from their feelings, wishes, or thoughts. In fact, they often generate a sense of positive vitality that derives from confidence about their personal worth. Such people have internalized relatively stable and benign objects, which sustain them in the face of life's adversities. They are willing to express their wants and to stand behind their actions, irrespective of the reactions of others. When disappointed, they do not act spitefully, but are able to engage in reparative action. That is, they have the patience to wait, to search out the moment when their talents will be needed (Erikson, 1978). Boldness in action, introspection, and thoughtfulness are common.

DEFENSE SYSTEMS

How do these three types of narcissistic leaders use their defensive systems? What struck us most in observing their behavior was how primitive the defenses of the first two types tend to be (Kernberg, 1975). At the core of the defensive systems is a mental process called *splitting*. All other defenses can be seen as derivatives of this very primitive mechanism.

What we mean by splitting is the tendency to see everything as either ideal (all good) or persecutory (all bad). When the individual has not sufficiently integrated or synthesized the opposite qualities of internal objects, these representations are kept separate to avoid contamination of "good" with "bad." Individuals with a tendency toward splitting possess affective and cognitive representations of themselves and others that are dramatically oversimplified. They fail to appreciate the real complexity and ambiguity of human relationships. Relationships are polarized between unbridled hatred, fear, or aggression on the one hand, and those of omnipotence and overidealization on the other. Splitting thus avoids conflicts and preserves an illusory sense of being good. All evil is ascribed unto others. The price of maintaining this illusory sense of goodness is, of course, an impaired conception of reality.

Closely related to this defense are primitive *idealization* and *devaluation*. First, there is a need to create unrealistic, all-good, all-powerful representations of others. This process can be viewed as a protection against persecutory objects. A sense of intense helplessness and insignificance creates the need for all-powerful protectors. In the long run, however, no one can sustain these exaggerated expectations. A vengeful devaluation of the idealized figure then occurs when needs are not met.

Other derivatives of splitting are *projection* and *projective identification* (Ogden, 1982). These defense mechanisms serve to defend against persecution by bad internal objects. The person tries to get rid of unwanted aspects of the self. Consequently, internal representations of self and others are externalized and attributed (projected) to others. Blame is always placed on someone or something else. Never is there any sense of personal responsibility. Again, all this is associated with distortions of reality.

As we can see from Table 1, the frequency, severity, and intensity of these defensive mechanisms vary among the types of narcissism. The reactive type shows the highest frequency and intensity, the constructive type, the lowest.

SYMPTOMS OF NARCISSISM

The most extreme symptoms of this developmental legacy and these defenses are summarized in the DSM III (American Psychiatric Association, 1980, p. 317), which lists the following diagnostic criteria for narcissistic personality disorders:

A. Grandiose sense of self-importance or uniqueness, for example, exaggeration of achievements and talents, focus on the special nature of one's problems.
B. Preoccupation with fantasies of unlimited success, power, brilliance, beauty, or ideal love.
C. Exhibitionism: the person requires constant attention and admiration.
D. Cool indifference or marked feelings of rage, inferiority, shame, humiliation, or emptiness in response to criticism, indifference of others, or defeat.
E. At least two of the following characteristics of disturbances in interpersonal relationships:
  1. Entitlement: expectation of special favors without assuming reciprocal responsibilities,

for example, surprise and anger that people will not do what one wants.
  2. Interpersonal exploitativeness: taking advantage of others to indulge one's own desires or for self-aggrandizement, disregard for the personal integrity and rights of others.
  3. Relationships that characteristically alternate between the extremes of over-idealization and devaluation.
  4. Lack of empathy: inability to recognize how others feel, for example, one may be unable to appreciate the distress of someone who is seriously ill.

It is important once again to realize that particularly the first two types of narcissistic leaders will show many of these clinical indications, but each to a different extent. In our experience, reactive narcissists will be cold, ruthless, grandiose, and exhibitionistic. They will show a desire to dominate and control and will be extremely exploitative. Self-deceptive narcissists will be milder, they want to be liked and are much less tyrannical. Still, they lack empathy, are obsessed mainly with their own needs, and are given to being discreetly Machiavellian. Their behavior has an "as if" quality, because they lack a strong sense of inner conviction and identity (Deutsch, 1965). Finally, constructive narcissistic leaders are also quite ambitious and can be manipulative and hypersensitive to criticism. But they have enough self-confidence, adaptability, and humor to stress real achievements. They get on well with others because of their insights into relationships.

ORGANIZATIONAL FUNCTIONING

THE REACTIVE LEADER

We shall describe two managerial situations in which we have seen the reactive narcissistic (RN) personality in operation. The first is in *leadership* or interpersonal relations. The second relates to their efforts at *environmental scanning, analysis,* and *decision making.* The reactive narcissist can be an extremely demanding taskmaster. His grandiosity and exhibitionism cause him to gravitate toward subordinates who are sycophants. The arguments of others are ignored if they run counter to the ideas of the boss. Solicitous subordinates seem to be the only ones who are tolerated by a reactive narcissist, all others are "expelled." A strong Machiavellian streak runs through these situations: The leader cares little about hurting and exploiting others in the pursuit of his own advancement. The followers play politics simply to survive. The RN leader surpasses all other types in his total lack of empathy. He completely ignores the needs of subordinates and peers alike, reserving his attention to matters that concern him and him alone. The fluctuations in attitude toward his people will be extreme. Consequently, the level of employee turnover tends to be very high. Projects that require teamwork or subordinate initiative are seriously jeopardized.

The RN leader exhibits characteristic dysfunctions in making important decisions for his organization. He tends to do very little scanning or analysis of the internal and external environment before making decisions. The RN leader feels that he can manipulate and act upon his environment so that he need not study it very closely. The environment is somehow "beneath him," it is assumed to pose no challenges that cannot easily be met. The RN's grandiosity, exhibitionism, and preoccupation with fantasies of unlimited success cause him to undertake extremely bold and venturesome projects. The quality of his leadership style is transforming rather than transactional. He wishes to attract the attention of an invisible audience, to demonstrate his mastery and brilliance. Projects are undertaken on a grand scale, but they are often doomed to fail. First, their overblown scale reflects the desires of the leader more than the realities of the situation; too many resources are placed at risk for too little reason. Second, the leader doesn't listen to his advisors, peers, or subordinates. He feels that only he is sufficiently informed to make judgments. A potentially crucial forum is thereby lost. Third, even when it is clear that things are not going well with the project, the RN leader is reluctant to admit the evidence. He will not own up to having made any errors and he becomes especially rigid and sensitive to criticism. Thus, he initiates a momentum that is difficult to reverse (Miller & Friesen, 1980, 1984). When the leader finally realizes how fast the situation is deteriorating, his penchant for splitting causes him to blame others. He never sees himself as being responsible for anything that is at all negative.

THE SELF-DECEPTIVE LEADER

These individuals have many of the traits of the reactive executives, but these are less evident in a managerial situation. We can again explore the categories of leadership, environmental scanning, and decision making. As leaders, self-deceptive (SD) executives are much more approachable than their RN counterparts. They care more about

their subordinates, are more given to listening to the opinions of others, and are not nearly as exploitative as the RNs. However, they also show a hypersensitivity to criticism, extreme insecurity, and a strong need to be loved. SD leaders will be more tolerant of dissenting opinions in that they may seem to react sympathetically when the opinions are expressed. But they will tend to carry a grudge, to be less available to habitual critics and to promote weaker-willed subordinates over their vocal peers.

While the SD leader will often express interest in his subordinate's preoccupations, it will be out of a desire to appear sympathetic rather than out of a genuine sense of concern. He will want to do the right thing, but does not feel very enthusiastic about it. An exception to this pattern occurs in cases where the leader becomes attached to a subordinate that he has come to idealize. He will do all in his power to "bind" this person, to develop and bring him along in his own image. It is not surprising of course that this treasured subordinate generally idolizes the boss and is not usually a very strong or opinionated individual. If the subordinate were to show personal initiative, it would be interpreted as treason. The leader's idealization would then quickly change into devaluation, with predictable results for the subordinate's future in the organization.

The SD leader, in contrast to his RN counterpart, may be very eager to discover opportunities, and particularly threats, in his environment. He is insecure and therefore does a great deal of scanning of the internal and external environment to make sure that he will be able to neutralize threats and avoid costly mistakes. Competitors are watched, customers are interviewed, and information systems are established. A good deal of analysis and assessment takes place, so much so that it might sometimes paralyze action.

In making strategic decisions, the SD leader has a degree of performance anxiety. He wants to do the best job he possibly can so that he will be respected and admired, but he worries about his ability to do so. He is afraid of failure. This tends to make him much more conservative than the reactive executive. The SD executive studies the situation very thoroughly and solicits the opinions of others. Decision making is done in response to exchanges of various types, quite in contrast to the pernicious transforming style of the reactive leader. The SD leader's orientation is thus predominantly of a transactional nature. Of course, conservative (like-minded) managers are much more likely to get a receptive hearing than the more venturesome ones. They have a general tendency to procrastinate, to put things off just a bit too long, and their perfectionism and hesitancy can give rise to organizational stagnation. Note that the RN narcissist was working to impress the broader political or business community, to be revered, to fulfill bold, impossible, visionary dreams. The SD narcissist just wants to be loved and admired by the people he interacts with. Also his symptoms will wax and wane according to his degree of anxiety to a greater extent than those of the RN leader.

THE CONSTRUCTIVE LEADER

These leaders are no strangers to manipulation and are not beyond occasional acts of opportunism. But they generally are able to get on fairly well with their subordinates. Constructive narcissists possess a high degree of confidence in their abilities and are highly task and goal oriented. Thus they may sometimes come across as lacking in warmth or consideration.

Although constructive leaders (CLs) enjoy being admired, they have a realistic appreciation of their abilities and limitations. Their attitude is one of give and take, and they recognize the competence of others. Constructive leaders are good listeners and appreciate the opinions of their subordinates, even though they are content to assume the ultimate responsibility for collective actions. They are willing to take a stand and stick to their decisions. This attitude may cause subordinates to complain that CLs are unsociable or uncooperative. In fact, constructive leaders sometimes do lack true empathy and may be prone to using others as mere instruments to accomplish their own objectives.

These leaders possess a sense of inner direction and self-determination that makes them confident. They have the ability to inspire others and to create a common cause, thereby transcending petty self-interests. Their inner directedness, however, can also be reflected by coldness, arrogance, or a stubborn insensitivity to the needs of others. Abstract concerns, such as "the good of the company" or "helping the worker," may replace reciprocity in interpersonal relations and the building of a team. In general, however, constructive narcissists have a sense of humor that makes it possible for them to put things in perspective. Their independence can make for the creativity and vision necessary to energize subordinates to engage in ambitious endeavors. Since it lacks the rigidity of the other two types, the dominant leadership style has both a transforming and transactional quality.

The constructive leaders vary a good deal in their decision-making styles which are more reflections of the situation facing the firm than the personal foibles of the executive. Their flexibility allows them to do a good deal of analysis, environmental scanning, and consultation before making strategic decisions of far-reaching consequences. But it also enables them to handle more routine situations with dispatch, entrusting matters to subordinates. They also tend to avoid extremes of boldness and conservatism, operating more in "the middle range."

ORGANIZATIONAL THERAPY

Constructive narcissistic leaders pose few organizational problems. But what can a firm's healthy managers do about the two more dysfunctional types of leaders? Where the organization is centralized and the narcissistic leader is dominant, poor performance and subsequent dismissal by a strong board of directors may be the only effective catalysts for change. And even these mutative influences are ruled out when a leader has strong financial control. But the outlook is much brighter where organizational power is more broadly distributed or where the narcissist occupies a less elevated position (Kets de Vries & Miller, 1984).

In fact, there are a number of organizational measures that can be taken to minimize the damage done by *lower level* narcissistic leaders. The first might be to try to become aware of their existence. In this pursuit, it may be useful to bear in mind that single indicators of each of the neurotic types are not sufficient to warrant a diagnosis of narcissism. But when these combine to form a syndrome this may indicate trouble.

It is very difficult to change a narcissist's personality. The primary emphasis must be to transfer the individual out of harm's way or to reduce his influence. A number of structural devices may be used to accomplish the latter. For example, power can be more broadly distributed in the organization so that many people get involved in strategic decisions, and lower level managers are induced to take responsibility for more routine concerns. Cross-functional committees, task forces, and executive committees can provide a useful forum in which a multitude of managers can express their viewpoint, providing opportunities for the narcissistic leaders (and especially their subordinates) to learn from and have their influence mitigated by others. Monolithic and unrealistic perspectives are thereby discouraged.

Regular leader appraisals in which subordinates have a chance to express their opinions to a third party about their boss may also be useful. Where a consensus of dissatisfaction emerges, particularly if it coincides with poor unit performance, it might be time to transfer or release the leader. Such an appraisal policy might inhibit overtly narcissistic exploitation.

When the top decision makers in an organization become aware of the narcissistic proclivities of some of the organization's managers, they can use this information in carrying out personnel policy. This is especially true when assigning subordinates to a narcissistic leader. One of the greatest dangers is to engage insecure, inexperienced managers to work for the narcissist. These employees will have too little strength or resolve to be able to cope, and still less potential to act as useful counterbalancing forces. In contrast, it might be useful to assign strong, confident, and secure personalities to work with the narcissistically inclined executive, those who are not afraid to express their opinions and can help to introduce more "reality" into the decision-making process.

It is particularly important, also, to look for signs of excessive narcissism in recruiting and making promotions. Psychological tests by trained clinicians and interviews with a candidate's previous superiors and subordinates might flag a narcissistic leader. There is no doubt that the easiest way to deal with these managers is to avoid hiring them, or failing that, to refrain from giving them much power.

References

American Psychiatric Association. *DSM III: Diagnostic and statistical manual of mental disorders* (3rd ed.). Washington, 1980.

Bass, B. B. *Stogdill's handbook of leadership.* New York: The Free Press, 1981.

Burns, J. M. *Leadership.* New York: Harper and Row, 1978.

Deutsch, H. *Neuroses and character types.* New York: International Universities Press, 1965.

Erikson, E. H. *Childhood and society.* New York: W. W. Norton and Co., 1963.

Erikson, E. H. *Life history and the historical moment.* New York: W. W. Norton and Co., 1978.

Fairbairn, W. R. D. *An object-relations theory of personality.* New York: Basic Books, 1952.

Freud, S. *A childhood recollection from Dichtung und Wahrheit. The standard edition of the complete psychological works of Sigmund Freud* (Vol. XVII). London: The Hogarth Press and the Institute of Psychoanalysis, 1917.

Freud, S. *Group psychology and the analysis of the ego. The standard edition of the complete psychological works of Sigmund Freud* (Vol. XVIII). London: The Hogarth Press and the Institute of Psychoanalysis, 1921.

Freud, S. *Libidinal types, The standard edition of the complete psychological works of Sigmund Freud* (Vol. XXI). London: The Hogarth Press and the Institute of Psychoanalysis, 1931.

Greenberg, J. R., & Mitchell, S. A. *Object relations in psychoanalytic theory.* Cambridge, Massachusetts: Harvard University Press, 1983.

Guntrip, H. *Schizoid phenomena, object relations and the self.* New York: International Universities Press, 1969.

House, R. J., & Baetz, M. L. Leadership: Some empirical generalizations and new research directions. *Research in Organizational Behavior,* 1979, 1, 341–423.

Jacobson, E. *The self and the object world.* New York: International Universities Press, 1964.

Kernberg, O. *Borderline conditions and pathological narcissism.* New York: Jason Aronson, 1975.

Kernberg, O. *Object relations theory and clinical psychoanalysis.* New York: Jason Aronson, 1976.

Kernberg, O. Regression in organizational leadership. *Psychiatry,* 1979, 42, 29–39.

Kets de Vries, M. F. R. Leadership in a narcissistic age. Faculty of Management, *McGill University Working Paper,* 1980.

Kets de Vries, M. F. R., & Miller, D. *The neurotic organization: Diagnosing and changing counterproductive styles of management.* San Francisco: Jossey Bass, 1984.

Klein, M. *Contributions to psychoanalysis, 1921–1945.* London: The Hogarth Press, 1948.

Kohut, H. *The analysis of the self.* New York: International Universities Press, 1971.

Kohut, H. Creativeness, charisma, group psychology. In Paul H. Ornstein (Ed.), *The search for the self* (Vol. 2). New York: International Universities Press, 1978.

Kohut, H., & Wolf, E. S. The disorders of the self and their treatment: An outline. *The International Journal of Psychoanalysis,* 1978, 59, 413–426.

Mahler, M. S., Pine, F., & Bergman, A. *The psychological birth of the human infant.* New York: Basic Books, 1975.

McKinley Runyan, W. *Life histories and psychobiography.* New York: Oxford University Press, 1982.

Miller, A. *Prisoners of childhood.* New York: Basic Books, 1981.

Miller, D., & Friesen, P. H. Momentum and revolution in organizational adaptation. *Academy of Management Journal,* 1980, 24, 591–614.

Miller, D., & Friesen, P. H. *Organizations: A quantum view.* Englewood Cliffs, NJ: Prentice-Hall, 1984.

Mintzberg, H. If you're not serving Bill and Barbara, then you're not serving leadership. In J. G. Hunt, U. Sekaran, & C. A. Schriesheim (Eds.), *Leadership: Beyond establishment views.* Carbondale, Illinois: Southern Illinois University Press, 1981.

Ogden, T. H. *Projective identification and psychotherapeutic technique.* New York: Jason Aronson, 1982.

Reich, W. *Characteranalysis.* New York: Farrar, Strauss and Giroux, 1949.

Weber, M. *The theory of social and economic organizations.* New York: Oxford University Press, 1947.

Winnicott, D. W. *Through paediatrics to psychoanalysis.* New York: Basic Books, 1975.

Zaleznik, A. Managers and leaders: Are they different? *Harvard Business Review,* 1977, 55, 67–78.

Zaleznik, A., & Kets de Vries, M. F. R. *Power and the corporate mind.* Boston: Houghton Mifflin, 1975.

Does Leader-Imposed Leadership Really Make a Difference?

Jon L. Pierce
John W. Newstrom
University of Minnesota Duluth

There are few management and organization topics that have generated more interest and research activity, spanning five decades, than the focus on leadership. Thousands of pages in academic books and journals have been devoted to the topic. During the past several years, the popular press has published and sold millions of copies of several dozen books written on the topic of leaders and leadership. Organizations frantically search for that magical leader who can pull the firm together and place it back onto the competitive path. We frequently hear stories about important historical leaders, we attribute organizational successes and failures to the things that our leaders did or failed to do, and at the national level we commonly resurrect dreams of the way it was when certain charismatic leaders were at the nation's helm.

Embedded in and reinforced by this attention is the implicit assumption that leadership is important, that leaders make a difference, and that positive group and organizational effects are produced by leaders and the leadership process. Our preoccupation with leaders and the leadership process makes the following question appear to hinge upon the absurd—Does leadership really make a difference?

However, not everyone agrees on the answer to this question. Instead, it has produced a debate among a number of leadership scholars. James R. Meindl and his colleagues (Sanford B. Ehrlich & Janet M. Dukerich, 1985) have argued that as a society we have developed romantic notions about leaders and leadership.[1] In the process, observers make attributions that suggest that the successful turnaround was due to the new CEO and that the losing season was due to the coach's inability to bring out the talent of his or her team.

Joining the leadership debate are the contextualists and constructionists. The contextualists (e.g., Richard Hall, 1977; Jeffrey Pfeffer & Gerald R. Salancik, 1978) argue that situations generally place such strong constraints upon organizational leaders that it is virtually impossible for them to be able to significantly affect the behavior of the organization and its final level of performance.[2] The

[1] J. R. Meindl, S. B. Ehrlich, & J. M. Dukerich, "The Romance of Leadership," *Administrative Science Quarterly* 30 (1985), pp. 78–102.
[2] R. H. Hall, *Organizations: Structure and Process*, 2nd ed. (Englewood Cliffs, NJ: Prentice-Hall 1977); J. Pfeffer & G. R. Salancik, *The External Control of Organizations: A Resource Dependence Perspective* (New York: Harper & Row, 1978).

social constructionists (e.g., Calder, 1977; Meindl, Ehrlich, & Dukerich, 1985; Meindl, 1990) contend that much of our understanding about leaders and leadership stems from socially provided information.[3] Echoing this debate, James Meindl and his colleagues note that "as observers of and as participants in organizations, we may have developed highly romanticized, heroic views of leadership" (p. 79). These heroic views paint unrealistic pictures about what leaders do, what they are able to accomplish, and the general effects they have on our lives.

Along with Chao C. Chen, Meindl (1991) has argued that much of what people have come to believe about leaders and leadership is the result of what others have told them. This romantic love affair with leaders results in stories that make *effective leadership a socially constructed reality.*[4] While these socially constructed and heroic views of leadership may be dramatically overestimated and removed from what is reality, Meindl and his colleagues note that this romantic relationship may be very important by helping to sustain followership—a phenomenon that produces significant contributions to the needs and goals of social systems, without which they would surely wither and die.

In an attempt to provide support for the argument that leadership does *not* make a difference, several scholars have looked at the leadership succession literature to see if changes in organizational leadership are associated with significant gains (losses) in organizational performance. Two studies are frequently drawn upon in an attempt to support the view that leadership does not make a significant difference in terms of organizational performance. Stanley Lieberson and James F. O'Connor (1972) compare the impact of leadership relative to environmental and organizational influences in 167 organizations operating in 13 different industries. They conclude their study by suggesting that organizational performance was influenced more significantly by environmental factors than by those in top organizational leadership roles.[5] In addition, Gerald Salancik and Jeffrey Pfeffer (1977), in their study of the performance of city governments, concludes that changes from mayor to mayor were minor and unlikely to bring about major organizational changes.[6]

Others take the position that leadership *does* make a difference (e.g., Robert J. House, 1988; Day & Lord, 1988).[7] Summarizing evidence from field-based longitudinal studies of the effects of lower organizational leadership and those conducted in the laboratory setting, House (1988) notes that there is an abundance of evidence demonstrating significant leadership effects in the areas of level of effort expended, adaptability to change, performance under change conditions, level of group turnover, absenteeism, group member performance, decision acceptance, quality of decisions made, and the amount of follower learning from leadership training efforts (p. 347).

Very few scientific investigations have been conducted with a focus on the leadership effects produced by middle-level and upper-level organizational leaders even though House cites evidence of leaders producing changes in organizational structure. In addition, House's interpretation of the evidence from the

[3] B. J. Calder, "An Attribution Theory of Leadership," in B. M. Staw and G. R. Salancik (Eds.), *New Directions in Organizational Behavior* (Chicago: St. Clair, 1977), pp. 179–204; J. R. Meindl, "On Leadership: An Alternative to the Conventional Wisdom," *Research in Organizational Behavior* 12 (1990), pp. 159–203.

[4] C. C. Chen & J. R. Meindl, "The Construction of Leadership Images in the Popular Press: The Case of Donald Burr and People Express," *Administrative Science Quarterly* 36 (1991), pp. 521–51.

[5] S. Lieberson & J. F. O'Connor, "Leadership and Organizational Performance: A Study of Large Corporations," *American Sociological Review* 37 (1972), pp. 117–30.

[6] G. R. Salancik & J. Pfeffer, "Constraints on Administrator Discretion: The Limited Influence of Mayors on City Budgets," *Urban Affairs Quarterly* 12 (1977), pp. 475–98.

[7] R. J. House, "Leadership Research: Some Forgotten, Ignored, or Overlooked Findings," in J. G. Hunt, B. R. Baglia, H. P. Dachaler, and C. A. Schriesheim (Eds.), *Emerging Leadership Vistas* (Lexington, MA: D.C. Heath 1988); D. V. Day & R. G. Lord, "Executive Leadership and Organizational Performance: Suggestions for a New Theory and Methodology," *Journal of Management* 14 (1988), pp. 453–464.

Lieberson and O'Connor study suggests that 31 percent of the variance in organizational net profit on sales over a 20-year time period could be directly attributed to changes in the top leadership of the companies participating in this study (pp. 347–348).

According to House, the research evidence, "when viewed collectively, demonstrates unequivocally that leadership can potentially influence significant variables related to organizational effectiveness and individual member satisfaction. However, there have also been longitudinal and experimental studies that show that leader behavior has little or no effect on subordinates' performance. Further, there are several studies that show that leader behavior is *caused* by the performance of subordinates" (p. 348).

POINT–COUNTERPOINT

At this stage, we encourage you to reflect upon the readings that have appeared in this collection and to construct two arguments. The first argument that we invite you to make states: Leader-imposed leadership *does not* make a difference (presumed leader effects are merely an illusion, an attribution misplaced). While this argument may be more difficult to make, in part because of our own biases (an issue worth thinking about in and of itself), the literature that you have read does provide you with some of the grist (e.g., think about the strength of many empirical observations; think about Orpheus; think about the notion of substitutes for leadership) that is needed for the construction of this argument. The second argument that we would like you to address is: Leader-imposed leadership *does* make a difference. Employing the works of the authors (i.e., both the conceptual/theoretical arguments and empirical observations) that you have now read, construct an essay that addresses this proposition.

Having a conversation (i.e., point–counterpoint argument) with one or more of your student colleagues may be engaging, will provide a good review of the literature that you have now read, and should be of value as you develop your thoughts in support of these two propositions: (a) Leader-imposed leadership does not make (much of) a difference, and (b) leadership does make a difference.

POINT: LEADERSHIP IS BUT A MIRAGE—IT REALLY *DOES NOT* MAKE A DIFFERENCE

Jeffrey Pfeffer (1977) questions the implicit assumption that leadership is causally related to the performance of organizations.[8] He challenges common thinking about leadership by raising several significant questions. First, Pfeffer raises issues regarding the definition of leadership. He contends that there remains a great deal of ambiguity surrounding the meaning that is attached to the term, and that the concept of leadership is essentially redundant with other important organizational constructs such as influence, social power, and authority. As a result, it is difficult to know whether leadership is needed and whether it is leadership or other factors that account for the differences in organizational performance. Pfeffer also calls attention to the fact that there remains a considerable amount of confusion regarding the behaviors that leaders actually engage in and whether or not these behaviors have any significant and meaningful relationship with other organizational outcomes.

While Pfeffer's first question focuses on the ambiguity of the leadership construct, his second question is concerned with whether or not leadership has any discernible effects on organizational outcomes. He suggests that there is very

[8] J. Pfeffer. "The Ambiguity of Leadership," *Academy of Management Review* 2, 1 (1977), pp. 104–112.

little evidence that the effects attributable to leadership are large in nature. He also argues that there are so many organizational constraints placed upon the behavior of all leaders that it should not be surprising that they are rendered incapable of producing any profound organizational effects. Third, Pfeffer argues that leadership is perceived to be an important and powerful force because we generally like to have a focus for the assignment of causal attributions. It is difficult, for example, to assign the functions of leadership—task accomplishment and group maintenance—to a large number of individuals whose interactions and relationships are left to chance. Instead, comfort is found in reducing causal uncertainty by directing cause and effect attributions toward a single point of focus—a leader. Thus, *leaders are important social constructions*. They are symbols, and hence targets for our attributions. They serve as scapegoats for our failures and heroes around which members of a group can rally in celebration of their collective accomplishments.

COUNTERPOINT: LEADERSHIP REALLY *DOES* MAKE A DIFFERENCE

Consistent with most of our thinking, as noted by Pfeffer (1977), leadership is generally cast as making a difference. In the previous chapter, Conger (1990) provided insight into problems that can be associated with leadership. Now we turn to the positive difference that leadership can make in terms of organizational performance.

David V. Day and Robert G. Lord (1988) argue that there is ample evidence to indicate that top-level leadership is significantly related to organizational performance. There are instances where leadership has accounted for 45 percent of the variance in organizational performance. In one study of 167 corporations in 13 industries over a two-year time period, it was found that top-level leadership accounted for 7.5 percent of the variance in net income. While 7.5 percent might be seen as a relatively small proportion, 7.5 percent of several hundreds of millions of dollars translates into a very significant amount of money.

The effects of executive leadership may be *direct* in their impact upon both the external and internal environments of the organization. In addition, many of the effects of leadership are *indirect* in nature. In many instances, for example, top-level leaders create the culture of the organization, which in turn impacts the strength of commitment displayed by members throughout the organization. The philosophical orientation of top-level management has also been seen as indirectly affecting the success of employee involvement programs (e.g., management by objectives) and the degree to which employee ownership systems have resulted in the creation of psychological ownership and employee performance (e.g., citizenship) behaviors.[9]

In sum, a review and analysis of the research literature asking whether leadership makes a difference to organizational performance led Alan Berkeley Thomas (1988) to conclude that "it is evident that it will require very considerable additional research before we can offer a general assessment of the impact of leadership on organizational performance" (p. 399).[10] In addition, the observations

[9] R. Rodgers & J. E. Hunter, "Impact of Management by Objectives on Organizational Productivity," *Journal of Applied Psychology* 76 (1991), pp. 322–336; L. Van Dyne, J. L. Pierce, & L. L. Cummings, "Employee Ownership: Empirical Support for Mediated Relationships." Presented at the eighth annual conference of the Society for Industrial and Organizational Psychology, Symposium on Psychological Ownership: Individual and Organizational Consequences, San Francisco, 1993.
[10] A. B. Thomas, "Does Leadership Make a Difference to Organizational Performance?" *Administrative Science Quarterly* 33 (1988), pp. 388–400.

offered by House (1988) suggest that the contingency models of leadership best represent our understanding of whether or not leadership really makes a significant difference. It is clear that at times the answer to this question may well be yes—leaders and the leadership process make a difference (directly or indirectly). At other times the effects of leadership may be neutralized or substituted for by other forces operating within the organization (group) and/or its environment. Finally, it should be noted that the effects of leadership, when produced, are *not* always positive in nature.

Reading the Scientific Literature: A Tutorial

Jon L. Pierce
John W. Newstrom[1]
University of Minnesota Duluth

Many students approach the task of reading a scientific journal article much like they would a piece of prose. They start at the beginning and read it word for word until they arrive at the end—often bewildered, overwhelmed, and wondering, What was it that I just read? This confusion, if typical among students, begs for a better approach. The purpose of this tutorial is to help you read, understand, and even critique such articles more effectively.

We believe that a bit of background on journal articles will be helpful to you. There are three different types of scientific literature—empirical studies, theoretical pieces, and literature reviews—that you are likely to be exposed to as a student of management and organizational studies. Articles reporting *empirical studies* present research findings conducted by the author(s) of the article. Empirical research unfolds in the field (real world) or in the research laboratory. These types of articles are likely to be the most challenging to read and comprehend. In addition, there are articles that present a *theory*. A theory is a generalized explanation (i.e., something akin to a story) of some phenomenon that provides us with insight into that phenomenon, why and when it exists, what it is related to, and what effects that it produces. Finally, there are articles that are *literature reviews*. In these articles the author attempts to summarize the theory and empirical work that has focused on a particular phenomenon. The primary purpose of literature reviews is to provide an up-to-date summary of an existing body of knowledge.

Each type of scientific literature has an underlying structure to it. For example, empirical studies often contain a title, an abstract, and an introduction; a discussion of hypotheses, study design and participants, variables and their measurement, analyses, and results; along with discussion and conclusion sections. You will find that some portions of these journal articles will be easier to read and comprehend than others. We believe that there are three key tasks for you to master: (1) knowing how to cut through the peripheral details, (2) learning how to interpret sophisticated statistics, and (3) establishing how to identify the central ideas of an article. Once you achieve some capability in doing these three things, your job as a student will be easier, richer, and more rewarding.

In this tutorial, we will provide you with a road map for reading each of these three types of literature. We believe that this "user's guide" to the scientific literature will prove useful to you in both the short and long terms.

---

[1] We appreciate the constructive contributions made to this document by Dr. Geoffrey G. Bell.

READING EMPIRICAL ARTICLES

Some articles report the results of various forms of empirical studies. These research articles are based on observation, experimentation, data collection, and analyses. They typically include quantitative and, on occasion, qualitative data, which may be primary (gathered directly) or secondary (derived from preexisting sources) in nature. When examining an empirical study, you should understand both who the author is and where the work was published.

BACKGROUND

Author[2]

Who is saying it (who is the author)?

Why is the author saying what is being said (does she or he have an "ax to grind" or a preexisting point of view to confirm)?

What are the author's credentials relative to what is being said? (For example, is she a qualified researcher? Is he affiliated with any special cause? Has she conducted and published prior research? What was his field of study?)

Journal[3]

Recognize that journals differ markedly in their reputation, often as a function of the quality of articles that have appeared in the past, as well as the reputation, skills, and commitment of the editor and members of his or her editorial review board. Therefore, it is important that you find answers for these questions:

What is the reputation of the journal?

Is there a review board, or are articles screened only by paid editorial staff members?

Are articles submitted by authors, published by invitation, or provided by paid writers?

Note that there are substantial differences in the quality of journals in which empirical articles may appear. The same is true for literature reviews and articles

---

[2] Although learning about an author may be difficult, there are several places to look that may provide you with information about the author and his or her professional reputation. First, you can go to a credible academic site, such as Google Scholar, and enter the author's name. Second, you can visit the author's institution's Web site. This site should enable you to identify an author's rank and possibly give you access to either the vita or a biographical sketch. Third, you can go to a major literature search engine (e.g., ABI/INFORM Business Source Premier, JSTOR, PsycINFO, or Web of Science) and type in the author's name. This should reveal works published by that author. In addition, some search engines, such as Business Source Premier, will show how many times an author's work has been cited. The general rule of thumb is that the more times a given work has been cited, the more influential it has been.

[3] It is similarly difficult to find information about a particular journal. If you have access to the hard copy of the journal, look inside the front (or back) cover. Generally appearing inside the cover is the name and institutional affiliation of the editor and members of the editorial review board. By using Google, you can also locate the home page for most journals, which provides some information about the journal (e.g., mission, editor, members of the editorial review board and their institutional affiliations). On occasion, journals will publish an annual report, providing information on the number of submissions, acceptances, and rejections. *Cabell's Dictionary of Publishing Opportunities in Management* provides important information, such as aim and scope of the journal, acceptance rates, as well as information about the review process (e.g., number of reviewers, whether the reviewers are internal or external to the journal, whether they conduct blind reviews). A reference librarian or a professor within the discipline may be able to provide you with information that identifies whether a journal is judged to be a Tier One, Tier Two, and so on journal. At a minimum, talk to one of the professors within the discipline that you are studying. We are reasonably confident that he or she will be able to offer a professional (informed, we hope) judgment as to the credibility of a particular journal. Ask two or more professors the same question to see whether you get a convergence (or a divergence) of opinion.

presenting theory. Many of these differences stem from two factors: (a) the percentage of articles submitted that are ultimately accepted for publication versus those that are rejected (a lower acceptance rate implies greater selectivity and hence, presumably higher quality), and (b) whether the article is blind reviewed (with the authors remaining anonymous to the reviewers) by an independent review panel whose independent judgments to publish or reject are the primary determining factor in the publication of the manuscript.

SUGGESTIONS FOR YOUR READING PROCESS

• Read the *title* of the article first. Try to establish for yourself what the article is about.

• Read the *abstract* of the article second. This will set the tone for the article, briefly introduce the underlying theory tested, and provide an overview of the conclusions reached.

• Read the *introduction* third. This will help you develop a feeling for the background of the study, the issue being explored, the research question(s) being asked, and the hypotheses being tested. Make sure that you have a firm grasp on the conceptual definition (i.e., how the variable is defined with other words) for each of the constructs (variables) in the research question and hypothesis. Then dig for the logic, rationale, and reasoning that justify the hypotheses (i.e., What is the theory that is involved? Does it appear to be internally consistent in its reasoning?).

• Read the section of the *variables and their measurement* next. Make sure that you have a good understanding of both the conceptual and operational definitions (i.e., how the variable was measured or manipulated) for variables being investigated.

• Read the *discussion* and *conclusion* sections fifth. It is here that you are generally provided with an an overview to the study—its purpose, questions, hypotheses, and important findings and their interpretation and implications. Just like the abstract, this is an extremely useful summary of the study and its highlights.

• Read the *method* and *results* sections next. These two sections may be the most difficult to read and understand, and possibly the least interesting, as it is here that the complete research design of the study is explained, the population studied described, and the statistical findings and results presented.

Depending on your statistical skills, you can begin to get a feel for the research findings by following these steps:

1. Look at the mean and standard deviation for each variable. Examine the mean relative to the response scale that was employed to measure the variable (e.g., a mean of 4.2 on job satisfaction that was measured on a 5-point Likert scale gives you a feel for how job satisfied or dissatisfied this group of employees is). The standard deviation gives you a feel for how much spread (variance) there is among the respondents. This variance is on that specific and unique measure, and for the specific group of employees studied.

2. Look at the alpha coefficient reported for each variable (coefficient alpha is a measure of the *reliability* of the data employed in the study). An alpha coefficient less than .70 should be looked upon with extreme caution. Note that without reliable data, it is impossible to have valid research findings.

3. Next look at the correlations among the study variables. This will give you a feel for *what is related to what,* the *strength* and the *direction* of the relationship among the variables.

4. Look at the 'p' statistic that accompanies each correlation. The *p* statistic tells you the likelihood of observing this size of a correlation between the two variables in question (given this sample size) by chance alone (e.g., a $p < .05$ means that given the sample size employed, the observed correlation could be this strong less than 5 times out of a 100 by chance alone; a $p < .01$ would mean less than 1 time out of a 100 by chance alone). Generally, we employ a *decision rule* of $p \leq .05$ to report a statistically significant relationship. Beyond this, your statistical education may help you understand some of the analyses employed, or it may be somewhat limiting. No matter which is the case, you can read the author's words and they will most likely tell you what findings are significant and what findings support or fail to support the hypotheses that were presented earlier.

• *Reread the discussion* section (especially the first few paragraphs) and the *abstract*. As you read these sections, try answering several questions:

What conclusions (statements of fact) can be drawn from the study?

Does the study help resolve the problem or question(s) raised at the beginning?

What are the theoretical implications of the findings?

Do the results contradict or support past findings? If there is a contradiction, how does the author explain the discrepancy?

What are the practical implications of the findings?

EVALUATION

Next should come *your* interpretation of the study and its findings. Use these questions to guide your evaluation:

What is the answer to the research question(s) asked?

Were the hypotheses supported?

What meaning do you give to the findings?

What are the shortcomings of the present study? (Note that the authors will most likely comment on the shortcomings in their discussion section.)

What other shortcomings do *you* see?

Finally, place the study into the context that prompted your reading the article. What is the question that you are working on, and how does this study fit? From the context of why you read the article in the first place, what new questions do you now have?

CAUTIONARY NOTES

1. The results section of an empirical paper is often intimidating to the reader, especially when it is laden with statistics. Take heart, you are not alone. Many academics (this textbook's authors included) often find such material difficult to fully absorb and comprehend. Strive to get *something* of value from your efforts, however. Be persistent.

Throughout this section, you will most likely find comments noting whether a particular hypothesis was supported or not, and comments on what the findings mean. *This* is the important stuff. Look at the tables and graphs, and pay attention to the means, standard deviations, and correlations, as you are most likely familiar with these. When reading good academic journals (those with a strong reputation for quality), you can usually rely on the fact that members of the editorial review board have already looked very carefully at the statistics employed and made sure they were applied appropriately.

2. Most of the authors whose articles you will read are quite passionate about their work; they believe strongly in the importance of it and that their measures are the best available. They are not always disinterested parties, and as a result, they will want to sell you on the correctness or soundness of their ideas, hypotheses, and theories, as well as on the logic of the "story" that they depict in detailing the relationships under investigation.

3. While reading an article, you may find it extremely difficult to avoid simultaneously evaluating and judging the work. We encourage you to suspend your initial judgment, which can come very easily and quickly. As consumers of information, we should have as our objective to try to understand the researcher's story. (Understanding does not mean blindly accepting however.) Try to understand the rationale for the hypotheses, try to understand previous findings, try to understand the facts, try to understand the findings and how they were obtained, and try to understand the researcher's interpretation. After all, in all likelihood she or he has been a student of this subject for a substantial period of time. We just might be able to learn something from her or him. This is especially true of those works that we find published in reputable outlets, by individuals who have the credentials that qualify them to reflect on the phenomenon in question.

Assuming that you have succeeded and that you understand what it is that the author has to say, it is your turn. It is at this stage you may decide to take the researcher to task by critiquing the work, but you should do this only after you understand what it is that the researcher has done and what it is that he or she has had to say. In short *hear the author out before passing judgment.*

The exciting thing about science is that "it progresses by people taking off on one another's work" (Aronson, 1995, p. 5). They build on each other's foundation. "Science is indeed a cumulative enterprise, and each new study builds on what has (or sometimes, has not) gone before it" (Jordon & Zanna, 1999, p. 464). This is why the context for a study, as well as previous research on related issues and questions, is so important.

READING ARTICLES THAT ARE LITERATURE REVIEWS

Some articles, rather than being data-based and narrow in focus, take a broader perspective. After identifying a theme or topic that has been rather widely researched, the authors engage in a comprehensive review of all (or many) of the major studies to identify trends and major conclusions that are supported by the bulk of the research evidence. Literature reviews are intended to present us with a state of understanding of the phenomenon under review. They provide us with the best possible current answer to the research question that drove this particular literature review.

There are two types of reviews: One is narrative and one is quantitative in nature. The former is best characterized by the author's reading, interpreting, and summarizing for us what it is that the literature tells him or her about a particular topic. As an example of this traditional literature review, the author may be interested in answering the question, What do we now know about the determinants and consequences of self-esteem in the work and organizational context? The second type of review is quantitative in nature. Starting during the decade of the 1990s the use of a statistical technique called *meta-analysis* has been employed to provide a more objective summarization of existing empirically based research findings. In a meta-analysis, the author uses the statistics (e.g., sample sizes, correlations among the variables of interest) reported in previously published studies to calculate, for example, the average strength of the relationship between variables. Through this statistical analysis, he or she draws conclusions about a particular body of knowledge.

Reading literature reviews should proceed according to the type of review that has been conducted. If the article is a narrative-based review, we suggest employing the process that we detail below. If the literature review is a meta-analysis, we suggest that you employ the reading process presented previously in our discussion on reading empirical literature.

BACKGROUND

Just as with empirical articles (and somewhat overlapping the process used for them), you should seek information regarding the author and where the work was published.

Author

Who is saying it (who is the author)?

Why is the author saying what is being said?

What are the author's credentials relative to what is being said?

Journal

Where does the article appear?

What is the reputation of the outlet?

Is there a review board, or are articles published by invitation?

THE READING PROCESS

- Read the title first.

- Read the abstract second.

- Read the body of the paper third. Identify the domain of the review in the article. Determine the basis for the organization of the review. Is it organized:

  a. Chronologically (e. g., from earliest study to most recent)?

  b. Around the dependent variables (i.e., around the "so what?" question that examines what was affected by the independent variable)?

  c. Around the independent variables?

  d. Around problems with the area of research? What suggestions are offered on needed future work and how it might be done?

- Read the discussion and conclusion sections last.

READING ARTICLES THAT PRESENT A THEORY

"Theory," according to Dubin (1976), "tries to make sense out of the observable world by ordering the relationships among elements that constitute the theorist's focus of attention in the real world" (p. 26). Theory has an important role to play in our understanding of that world, and also in guiding our actions to be taken in that world. Social psychologist Kurt Lewin expressed it well when he stated that "nothing is so practical as a good theory" (1945, p. 129). Ultimately, theory should point us in the direction of effective and systematic behavior. Theory, when coupled with sound empirical evidence, should provide us with a powerful basis for our practice of evidence-based management.

WHAT IS GOOD THEORY?

You may already realize that not all theory is equally good. According to Klein and Zedeck (2004), good theory:

1. Offers *novel insights*. It provides a "sense of discovery and illumination."

2. Is *interesting*. It is more than a ho-hum documentation of the obvious.

3. Is *focused and cohesive*. "Good theory illuminates and clarifies, often by organizing, and thus simplifying, a set of previously unorganized and scattered observations"; it "renders real-world processes and phenomena clear and coherent by simplifying and structuring our inchoate understanding of them. This is only possible if the theory itself is clear and coherent" (p. 932).

They go on to note that good theory:

4. Is *grounded in the relevant literature*, but offers more than a review or integration of this literature.

5. Presents *clearly defined constructs* and offers clear, thorough, and thoughtful *explanations of how and why the constructs in the model are linked*. "If clearly defined constructs are the building blocks of good theory, then thorough and thoughtful propositions linking the constructs—explaining what constructs lead to what, when, how, and why—provide the mortar" (p. 932).

Finally, they indicate that good theory:

6. Is *testable*. The constructs are clear and precise; how the constructs are to be measured and how key ideas are to be tested are clearly articulated.

7. In many fields, a theory has *practical implications*. For example, good organization theory is theory that can be used to address organizational problems (e.g., the causes and consequences of job satisfaction).

8. Is *well written*. The work presents a clear and logical flow, while it is simultaneously "clear, focused and interesting" (p. 933).

Employing these eight factors, ask yourself: How well does the theory you are currently reading about meet Klein and Zedeck's (2004) criteria for good theory?

BACKGROUND

As with other types of scientific articles, look for information regarding the author and where the work was published.

Author

Who is saying it (who is the author)?

Why is the author saying what is being said?

What are the author's credentials relative to what is being said?

Journal

Where does the article appear?

What is the reputation of the outlet?

Is there a review board, or are articles published by invitation?

THE READING PROCESS

- Read the title first.

- Read the abstract second.

- Read the body of the paper third.

    Is it internally valid? (Is there a logical structure to the ideas and arguments that are being presented?)

    Is it innovative? (Is there something new here?)

    Is it provocative? (Does it elicit an emotional response from the reader?)

    Is it elegant? (Is the product a work of art?)

    Does it exhibit parsimony? (Is it tight and devoid of extraneous material?)

    Is it presented in a straightforward manner? (Is it easy and logical to follow?)

    Does it build upon existing science (empirical evidence)? Alternatively, is it a philosophical or ideological statement grounded primarily in faith or in the author's personal experience?

- Read the discussion and conclusion sections last.

A NOTE ON CASE ANALYSES

Many students are familiar with case studies. The case study will not be treated here as a type of scientific literature. *Case studies* are best seen as an educational tool (i.e., an instructional vehicle employed by many of your professors as a way of facilitating your learning a particular subject matter). Case studies typically represent an in-depth (intensive) examination of a single unit of analysis (e.g., person, group, or some organizational phenomenon such as a merger).

Case research, on the other hand, is an important subset of theoretical research. In case research, the scholar selects one or more cases (e.g., person, group, organizational phenomenon), which are designed to highlight important elements of a topic under study. The goal of case research is to strategically choose samples which will allow the researcher to understand issues in the topic of interest (see Eisenhardt, 1989; Yin, 1994). Data are frequently collected by a researcher employing multiple data collection means (e.g., interviews, organizational memos, and financial records) of the phenomenon under investigation and within its natural setting. There is no attempt to employ exact variable measurement, experimentation coupled with the use of control groups, and the statistical testing of relationships among variables. As a scientific tool, case research is particularly well suited for the generation of hypotheses and theory construction. It is less rigorous and less well suited for the testing of hypotheses and the making of generalizations to other settings. Consequently, both its internal and external validity are extremely limited.

CAUTIONARY NOTES

1. Most of the authors whose articles you will read are quite passionate about their work—especially when they are developing new theory or trying to dispel old theory. These authors are not always disinterested parties, and as a result, they will want to sell you on the correctness or soundness of their ideas, hypotheses, and theories, as well as on the logic of the story that they depict in detailing the relationships under investigation.

2. While reading a theoretical article, you are likely to find it extremely tempting to simultaneously evaluate and judge the work. We would like to

encourage you to suspend judgment, which can come very easily and quickly. As consumers of information, we should have as our objective to try to understand the theory being discussed. (Understanding does not mean blindly accepting.) Try to understand the rationale for the hypotheses, try to understand previous findings, try to understand the existing evidence, try to understand how this evidence is being woven into the theory, and try to understand the arguments for the new or revised theory.

CONCLUSION

We would like to encourage you to make the regular consumption of the management and organizational sciences literature a part of your formal education experience, as well as a part of your lifelong educational activities. Contemporary history has quite clearly demonstrated that education is a good investment in yourself, and that investment should not be completed upon receipt of your formal degree.

One important part of this education should consist of your regular reading of the top-level journals in your discipline. This will consist of your reading theory, literature reviews, and empirical investigations. The end to which all of this is aimed is your personal enlightenment and the ability to make your professional career one that is driven and characterized by evidence-based practices.

REFERENCES

Aronson, E. 1995. *Reading about the social animal.* New York: Bedford, Freeman, & Worth.

Dubin, R. 1976. Theory building in applied areas. In M. Dunnette (Ed.), *Handbook of industrial and organizational psychology* (pp. 17–39). Chicago: Rand McNally.

Eisenhardt, K. M. 1989. Building theories from case study research. *Academy of Management Review,* 14:4, 532–550.

Jordon, C. H., & Zanna, M. P. 1999. How to read a journal article in social psychology. In R. F. Baumeister (Ed.), *The self in social psychology* (pp. 461–470). Philadelphia. Psychology Press.

Klein, K. J., & Zedeck, S. 2004. Theory in applied psychology: Lessons (re)learned. *Journal of Applied Psychology,* 87, 931–933.

Lewin, K. 1945. The Research Center for Group Dynamics at Massachusetts Institute of Technology.

Yin, R. K. 1994. *Case study research: Design and methods.* Thousand Oaks CA: Sage.

Beyond the Theory and Empiricism and into the Practice of Leadership

The first 15 chapters have been devoted to a historical sampling of the empirical and conceptual literature on leadership and the leadership process. However, there are many other sources of learning about leadership, and these should not be overlooked. In particular, this section provides a glimpse into three domains that can be viewed as practitioner reflections and reports, analytical opportunities, and experiential exercises.

PRACTITIONER REFLECTIONS AND REPORTS

A wide range of leaders (especially CEOs) have taken the time and initiative to think about what they believe made them successful and report their insights in book form. Examples include Bill George at Medtronic, Rudolph Giuliani at New York City, Jack Welch at GE, Andy Grove at Intel, Steven Jobs at NeXt and Apple, and Max DePree at Herman Miller. In other cases, writers have attempted to capture the presumed leadership beliefs and actions of historic or mythical figures, such as General George Patton, Mahatma Gandhi, Eleanor Roosevelt, Abraham Lincoln, Chief Sitting Bull, Sir Ernest Shackleton, General Colin Powell, the Sopranos, or Santa Claus (!). More recently, scholars (such as Warren Bennis, Noel Tichy, John Kotter, and Daniel Goleman) and consultants (such as William Byham and Stephen Covey) have observed leaders in action and shared their observations and conclusions in the form of books written for the practitioner market. These portraits are often rich in anecdotal information and contemporary illustrations, although invariably lacking the broader data basis of well-designed studies.

We encourage you to explore some of these "contemporary and popular" leadership books because they can provide a different perspective on leading and the leadership phenomenon. A sampling of some of the more recent publications that you might find of interest includes:

Badaracco, *Leading Quietly*

Bennis, *On Becoming a Leader*

Bennis and Goldsmith, *Learning to Lead*

Bennis and Thomas, *Geeks and Geezers*

Blanchard, *Heart of a Leader*

Blanchard, *Servant Leader*

Charan, *The Leadership Pipeline*

Cottrell, *Monday Morning Leadership*

Hybels, *Courageous Leadership*

George, *True North*

Giuliani and Kurson, *Leadership*

Goleman et al., *Primal Leadership*

Greenleaf, *Servant Leadership*

Iacocca, *Where Have All the Leaders Gone?*

Kellerman, *Bad Leadership*

Kouzes, *The Leadership Challenge*

Kriegbaum, *Leadership Prayers*

Lipman-Blumen, *The Allure of Toxic Leaders*

Maccoby, *The Productive Narcissist*

McIntosh and Rima, *Overcoming the Dark Side of Leadership*

Nielsen, *The Myth of Leadership*

Tichy and Cardwell, *The Cycle of Leadership*

Ulrich, *Results-Based Leadership*

Useem, *The Leadership Moment*

ANALYTICAL OPPORTUNITIES

It is a well-established fact that people learn in different ways. One fruitful approach is through the analysis of cases and (shorter) incidents. These provide opportunities to sift through information, identify key issues, determine the applicability of relevant theories, and suggest appropriate action plans. Cases and incidents, properly guided by a discussion leader, make it possible for the analyst to engage in both deductive (application of principles) and inductive (development of tentative generalizations) thinking. Also, because they are drawn from actual circumstances, they provide a sense of realism to the study of the leadership process. A number of cases and incidents are included to provide an opportunity for learning through the analysis and application of concepts.

EXPERIENTIAL EXERCISES

An oft-quoted phrase (attributed to Confucius and others) suggests that "I hear and I forget, I see and I remember, I do and I understand." This forms the basic rationale for learning some things through experience. Structured experiential exercises typically involve the participants either in a physical activity or in generating some relevant individual or group data. The group is then invited to engage in a retrospective discussion of what took place or what the "data" mean (in the context of leadership theories). The process of active involvement serves as a powerful incentive to "see" abstract concepts take on meaning and shape realistic personal agendas for the future. Again, we have included a sample of experiential exercises to facilitate such personalized learning.

Case Studies and Experiential Exercises

Case

Sam Perkins

Dr. Sam Perkins, a graduate of the Harvard University College of Medicine, was engaged in the private practice of internal medicine for 12 years. Fourteen months ago, he was persuaded by the governor to give up private practice to be director of the State Division of Human Services.

After one year as director, Perkins recognized he had made little progress in reducing the considerable inefficiency in the Division of Human Services. Employee morale and effectiveness seemed even lower than when he assumed the position. He realized his past training and experiences were of a clinical nature with little exposure to effective leadership techniques. Perkins decided to research literature published on the subject of leadership available to him at a local university.

Perkins soon realized that management scholars are divided on the question of what constitutes effective leadership. Some feel that leaders are born with certain identifiable personality traits that make them effective leaders. Others feel a leader can learn to be effective by treating subordinates with a personal and considerate approach and by giving particular attention to the subordinate's need for good working conditions. Still others emphasize the importance of developing a style of leadership characterized by either authoritarian, democratic, or laissez-faire approaches. Perkins was confused further when he learned there are a growing number of scholars who advocate that effective leadership is contingent on the situation, and a proper response to the question of what

constitutes effective leadership is that it "depends on the situation."

Since a state university was located nearby, Perkins contacted its College of Business Administration dean. The dean referred him to the director of the college's Management Center, Professor Joel McCann. Discussions between Perkins and McCann resulted in a tentative agreement that the Management Center would organize a series of leadership training sessions for the State Division of Human Services. Before agreeing on the price tag for the leadership conference, Perkins asked McCann to prepare a proposal reflecting his thoughts on the following:

QUESTIONS

1. How will the question of what constitutes effective leadership be answered during the conference?

2. How will the lack of congruence among leadership researchers be resolved or reconciled?

3. What will be the specific subject content of the conference?

4. Who will the instructors be?

5. What will be the conference's duration?

6. How can the conference's effectiveness be evaluated?

7. What policies should the State Division of Human Services adopt regarding who the conference participants should be and how they should be selected? How can these policies be best implemented?

Source: Reprinted with permission from Champion/James, "Effective Leadership," *Critical Incidents in Management* (Homewood, IL: Richard D. Irwin, Inc.).

Case

A Different Style of Leadership

In my new position as Systems Engineer with BBG Industries, my initial assignment was in the Glass Research and Development Automations Section. My immediate supervisor, Al Sirroco, was given the mission of providing computer services for laboratory personnel and production, thus bridging the gap between data processing and process control. With a background in chemical engineering and computer sciences, Al was instrumental in pioneering the powerful and beneficial use of the computer as an aid to scientists and engineers. Utilizing a rented time-shared terminal, results were obtained that maximized calculation thruput and accuracy, thus providing concise historical records so vital in the research environment. Upper management was very impressed by Al's initial success in the realm of automation. The formation of the automation section was concrete evidence that management encouraged further growth in this field for BBG Industries.

Al faced the basic problem of obtaining group cohesiveness and coordination in order to build it into an effective organization. People in our group had diverse backgrounds, including a PhD in mathematics, computer operators with high-school diplomas, electrical engineers, and operations research personnel.

To overcome possible communications barriers among members of such a diverse unit, informal group meetings were held once a month. During such meetings each member could openly expound upon any problems requiring clarification, without any fear of retaliation. These staff meetings created an air of openness and relaxation of the status differences caused by differences in rank in our group. Each member had ample opportunity to make an informal presentation of what he or she was contributing to the group effort. Talk about work often spilled over to talk about personal life; the net effect was to produce a feeling of togetherness. After awhile one got the impression that any group member would help any other member with any kind of problem. One weekend, five of us helped bail out Tim, a computer operator, whose basement flooded in a rainstorm.

Our group obtained its first real surprise about Al's approach to managing people following a once-in-a-lifetime incident. An unfortunate situation occurred at the computer center which required the immediate dismissal of a key senior analyst. Although quiet and seemingly introverted, the analyst was held in high esteem because of his diligence and his record of accomplishment. Everyone in the group wondered what violation necessitated such drastic action on Al's part.

Rumors spread that perhaps the systems analyst had been engaged in sabotage, physical attack upon a fellow worker, criminal activity, drug abuse, or maybe a combination of several of these. The day after the incident, Al summoned the group into his office for an important announcement. He informed us that the extreme dedication to job performance shown by this systems analyst had caused him to suffer a nervous breakdown. Al maintained that it was necessary for his safety and the safety of the group for this man to be immediately separated from the company.

Evidence to corroborate Al's explanation was discovered when the individual's desk was cleaned out. A note was found buried beneath some papers in one of the drawers. His writings reflected several approaches to suicide. Al instigated efforts and received approval for the analyst to undergo psychiatric help immediately at the company's expense. In addition, severance pay of six month's salary was granted to him, and the company agreed to help him find future employment once his condition improved.

Al's explanation and the suicide note seemed to satisfy everyone's curiosity. However, several weeks later the real cause for the dismissal of the systems analyst surfaced via the company grapevine. One night when the analyst was working late, the only other employee in the building was a female computer operator. While she was walking down the aisle between the office and the computer equipment, he unzipped his pants, exposing himself. Upset by the incident, the computer operator reported the analyst's exhibitionism to her father, a manager in the laboratory. The father demanded retaliation and subsequent criminal prosecution.

Al's handling of the situation was unique and the termination of the systems analyst placated the father. By firing the analyst, the operator was

Source: Reprinted with permission from Andrew J. DuBrin (Robert E. Gmitter researched and wrote this case, with the exception of several editorial changes); *Casebook of Organizational Behavior,* 1977, Pergamon Press.

spared the embarrassment of confronting him again at work. Yet, a couple of people in the group felt that Al's handling of the situation was bizarre. Irv, a mathematician, expressed it this way:

"Al sure is cool under pressure, but he's also quite a moralist. Sure, the poor guy exposed himself once that we know of. We cannot estimate the probability that he would expose himself again given the same circumstances. Maybe the father who complained so bitterly was really just jealous of the systems analyst. Worst of all, I question the value of Al making up a phony story just to bury the incident. If we fired everybody in this company who displayed a little deviant behavior once in their lives, we would probably have a pretty thin work force."

Al's approach to leadership can also be understood in his handling of overtime work. Many times crucial projects required extended periods of late hours in order to meet critical deadlines. For exempt professionals, the lab rule stipulated that no compensation would be given, regardless of the time expended in discharging one's responsibilities.

Al informally modified the rule for his group. The term "E-Time," for earned time, could be accumulated by each member for extra hours worked. This was an honor system with responsibility left entirely to the individual. Earned time could be cashed in by trading it for time off with pay when the project load lessened. Al's policy minimized the long, arduous hours of extended toil and promoted excellent group morale.

Al strived constantly to support individual accomplishments and to foster creativity in the glass industry. The director of research required a monthly meeting to discuss his group's progress, concepts, improvements, and future goals. Although key projects were mandatory in the agenda, voluntary participation and the initiation of topics were allowed at these important meetings. Each member of the group was encouraged by Al to make his contribution.

Al's impact upon people can be illustrated in his dealings with Kiwabi, a senior mathematician in the group. Kiwabi was advised to present a radical technique for the regression analysis of process data which reduced the time and amount of data, yet maintained qualitative accuracy. His brief presentation in the limelight impressed upper management and paved the way toward Kiwabi obtaining a fully paid leave of absence to obtain his PhD.

A study I had made of various computer systems for process control, as to their power and cost, was scheduled by Al for one of these meetings. My presentation led to future study of this same topic, which verified my findings. Not only was my career as a systems engineer brightened because of it, but the company benefited by obtaining more efficient computer systems with the latest technology at the maximum return upon investment. I honestly believe that without Al's prodding and guidance this study would not have come to fruition.

Supplementing our exposure at meetings, Al would circulate, via interlab memos, accomplishments and proposals of his personnel. By this mechanism, all pertinent managers and head scientists were made aware of the existence of group members. It also provided a first-rate opportunity for interface with groups requiring our supportive capabilities in the field of automation.

Al also scheduled trips to the plants to introduce us, explain our function, and relate our specialties. Plant associates could depend upon our expertise to assist them with problems. One such problem solved by our group was the correct depositing of raw materials, such as sand and dolomite, into holding bins. Predetermined amounts of raw material are required for each raw batch composition of glass before heating. The existing manual method had caused production upset due to the wrong ingredients in the bins. An automated, batch unloading protection system was designed, developed, and implemented by our group.

You can understand Al's comprehensive approach to managing people only by sampling the kind of things he did for people. Al would arrange trips for us to other companies, such as Mead Paper, to exchange technological applications and broaden our knowledge of automation. Al also encouraged a few of us to write articles for trade journals, and even provided help in this area. On the basis of these efforts a couple of us have achieved some national recognition.

Al had a keen sense of the ever-persistent technological changes taking place in the world of automation. To maintain the group's expertise, Al would submit a list of appropriate courses relevant to each individual's background. Participation and attendance at symposia and conferences were integrated into the work schedule. One of Al's pet projects was to get us involved in the Process Control Workshop at Purdue University. The workshop consisted of international representation dedicated to standardization of the principles of process control automation.

For my money, Al is a top manager. But not everybody agrees with me. One of the skeptics in our groups said, "If Al walked into my office at 4:30 and reminded me to brush my teeth because it was good for me, I wouldn't be surprised. It would fit his leadership style."

QUESTIONS

1. Evaluate Al Sirroco's handling of the systems analyst problem. What would you have done if you were the supervisor?

2. What style of leadership do you prefer? Would you want a leader like Al? Discuss the pros and cons.

Case
Donny Is My Leader

BREAKING IN HARVEY

The first day I joined the team, Donny asked me how far I was going to run. The team had a goal of running two miles every Monday, Wednesday, and Friday morning, at a fair pace—about eight minutes a mile—on an inside track with 18 laps to the mile. I said I'd try for one mile and a half, a distance I had occasionally managed to complete jogging by myself. I ran at the tail end of the team and did, in fact, run the mile and a half. At the end of a mile and a half, Donny turned and shouted back to me from his place at the front of the group, "OK, Harvey, that's enough!" And I stopped.

When the others finished, Donny came over and congratulated me. He told me I'd run well. He suggested I try adding three more laps next time, stay at that level for a while, and then add another three until I reached the 36 laps or two-mile objective of the team.

The "team" is a very informal collection of people with no formally appointed leader. Donny, however, is referred to as the coach. The team has existed for a while with a small, hard core and with others who come and go. The regulars comprise Donny, who always runs on the right side of the "pacer," who is almost always "Choc," and Herb, who runs about fourth and takes over as leader when Donny is away. Barrie generally runs third and sometimes sets the pace but is sort of an irregular regular since he occasionally forsakes the group for a squash game or gets in late after a hard night. Harry and Larry are two recent regulars.

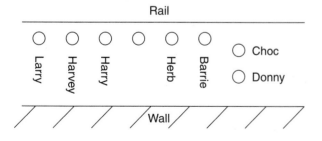

Source: Kolodny, H. F. & House, R. J., "Donny Is My Leader: A case Study of Leadership," *The Organizational Behavior Teaching Journal* VI, 2 (1981), pp. 51–56. Copyright 1981 The Organizational Behavior Teaching Society. Reprinted by permission of Sage Publications, Inc..

Larry always runs last and Harry runs just ahead of me. There are three or four others who occasionally join us. On some mornings we are as few as four running. On other mornings there are nine running.

My second day was a beautiful, warm morning and we ran outside. I quit after a mile and a quarter. Harry quit after a mile. No one said anything to us about the running—neither good nor bad.

My third day and my big mistake! I vowed to run one mile and 12 laps to myself, 3 better than my previous inside run. At the end of the 11th lap of the second mile, since I still had a little left in me, I sprinted the last lap, passing everyone. I'd noticed that all the finishers usually sprinted for the last one or two laps. However, when he was done, Donny came over and severely castigated me. How could I possibly have sprinted? If I could sprint, I must have had some strength left in me and therefore I could have gone for several more laps; in fact, I might even have been able to finish the two miles. He verbally lashed out at me several times both on the track and back down in the locker room. The others joined in, though in a more teasing mode. They said that next time I was not only going to run the two miles, but they would make me set the pace.

Soon after this occurrence, Harry became the culprit and the victim of Donny's wrath. We did each lap in about 28 seconds. Donny was the time-keeper. He shouted out the time for the first lap and for the first mile, and he counted out every second lap each time we passed the starting point (where a wall clock was mounted). Donny constantly encouraged us to keep going. Herb and Larry did so too. They called out milestones, "Three-quarters done!" or "Two-thirds done!" or "Five laps to go!" Near the end of the run, they kept up a steady stream of comments to urge those of us who were struggling to keep going and to try to finish the distance. On this particular day, at the end of the first lap, Harry said, "Hey, we're going too fast! We did it in 20 seconds." It was a bad day. Quite a few of us didn't finish. Donny was angry. He took it out on Harry repeatedly. He said that Harry's statement was incorrect and, furthermore, it had discouraged several of the team members, making them—including me—quit. He carried on all the way down to the locker room, in the showers, and even into the next running day.

WEIGH-IN

Once a month, Donny had us weigh in. At that time, we set our objectives for how much weight we would lose by the next weigh-in. He made a big occasion out of it, talking about it several days before, advising us to begin to fast a few days before, and culminating with a rather ceremonious act on the day of the weigh-in.

Stepping out to the scale, he asked each person to announce his objective, then weighed him and made a large fanfare about those who had achieved their objective and those who hadn't. We were put into two groupings: those who'd reached target and those who had not. Each one who didn't was publicly castigated, in humour, and asked to reset goals for the next weigh-in. The successful ones were not pressed.

The next running day after the weigh-in, there was a great ceremony. Herb received a jersey on which was printed "Doctor D's Track Team." Choc had had them made up and kept them in his locker waiting for the appropriate occasion to have one handed out. Herb was the only one to be awarded. He had not only consistently run the distance, but he had also made his weight target. Donny let us all know that he wasn't going to be generous about giving the others out—even though they were all ready and printed. Only consistent demonstrations of performance across several fronts would merit a "Doctor D's Track Team" jersey.

CHALLENGING THE LEADER

Larry usually ran in last place with the team. One summer he broke his ankle playing baseball, and he didn't run with us for most of the year. Then he started running again, sometimes joining us for short periods, sometimes running before or after us, sometimes faster for short spurts, though usually slower. He was slowly getting back in top shape.

Then one day he took his usual position at the rear as we were starting. After the first few laps, Donny had not called out the number of laps, and Larry chose to call them out loudly. Someone kibitzed and said that wasn't his job. I chipped in jokingly and said that I liked it when Larry called the laps. It was like old times again, I said, having Larry back. Larry kept calling the laps out as we completed them, and Donny, up front, said nothing.

Then Larry lost count somewhere around the eighth or ninth lap. I shouted to Donny, up front, to tell us where we were but he wouldn't answer. Because I feel lost when I don't know what I've run, I asked a few more times, "Would someone please say where we are?" Donny didn't answer. Then, after a while, in a loud voice, he said, "Strictly for Harvey, that was one mile we just passed." The next mile, he gave us two counts, one at the half mile and one at the end of the second mile. Normally he would count out every two laps (i.e., nine times a mile). In the third mile, he gave us three counts.

At the end of the run, he muttered something about "Teaching you guys respect the hard way."

EXERCISE
Feeling and
Expressing
Emotions
at Work

Task:	Class members reflect back on four different emotions that they have experienced at work; they complete a brief questionnaire in advance of the class discussion.
Group Size:	Discussion can take place in a total-class setting, or class members can break into small groups (e.g., 5 persons).
Materials Needed:	Newsprint (flip chart pages) and masking tape for each group; Excel software for the instructor.
Time Required:	Approximately one hour in class.
Procedure:	1. Ask class members to think about some powerful emotional experiences that they have had at work (or at school, or interpersonally). Make sure that each class member selects four situations that resulted in these four emotions—happiness/joy, anger/irritation, liking/trusting others, and being anxious/fearful.
	2. Ask each class member to complete a copy of the questionnaire below—a day or two in advance of the actual discussion. Collect these, tabulate them, and insert the results on a chart showing the average class score (between 1 and 7) on each of the four dimensions.
	3. Have the class, either in its entirety or in small groups, discuss the questions below.
Discussion Questions:	1. From a descriptive standpoint, what do the data shown on the chart reveal?
	2. What *questions* do the data stimulate you to ask?
	3. What does this exercise demonstrate about the role of emotions from a leader–subordinate perspective?0
	4. Is there a difference between the degree to which we *feel* emotions versus *express* emotions at work? If so, why? In what ways might a leader create a climate for the appropriate expression of an array of feelings at work?
	5. What types of circumstances or events *caused* each of the four emotions you experienced? Visually diagram the major causal relationships.
	6. What were the major consequences of each situation that you have described? Were these positive or negative?
	7. Are there organizational norms (implicit or explicit) that have been imposed by leaders to limit emotional expression and thus prevent people from being authentic?
	8. What action principles does this exercise generate for leaders?
	9. What effect would a leader with high emotional intelligence ("the ability to monitor one's own and others' feelings and emotions, to discriminate among them, and to use this information to guide one's thinking and action") have on the open and appropriate expression of emotions in a work group?

TABLE 1   Emotions at Work

Think about a time when you experienced each of four strong emotions at work. For each emotion listed below, indicate your response to the four scales.

Happiness/Joy

How *strongly* did you feel this emotion?

1	2	3	4	5	6	7
Not at all			Moderately			Very strongly

To what degree did you *express* your emotion to the person(s) who caused it?

1	2	3	4	5	6	7
Not at all			Moderately			Very strongly

How *appropriate* is it to express this emotion in your organization or work group?

1	2	3	4	5	6	7
Not at all appropriate			Moderately appropriate			Clearly appropriate

In the situation you are thinking of, to what degree were the consequences of the episode *positive or negative*?

1	2	3	4	5	6	7
Primarily negative			Neutral			Primarily positive

Anger/Irritation

How *strongly* did you feel this emotion?

1	2	3	4	5	6	7
Not at all			Moderately			Very strongly

To what degree did you *express* your emotion to the person(s) who caused it?

1	2	3	4	5	6	7
Not at all			Moderately			Very strongly

How *appropriate* is it to express this emotion in your organization or work group?

1	2	3	4	5	6	7
Not at all appropriate			Moderately appropriate			Clearly appropriate

In the situation you are thinking of, to what degree were the consequences of the episode *positive or negative*?

1	2	3	4	5	6	7
Primarily negative			Neutral			Primarily positive

Liking/Trusting Others

How *strongly* did you feel this emotion?

1	2	3	4	5	6	7
Not at all			Moderately			Very strongly

To what degree did you *express* your emotion to the person(s) who caused it?

1	2	3	4	5	6	7
Not at all			Moderately			Very strongly

How *appropriate* is it to express this emotion in your organization or work group?

1	2	3	4	5	6	7
Not at all appropriate			Moderately appropriate			Clearly appropriate

In the situation you are thinking of, to what degree were the consequences of the episode *positive or negative*?

1	2	3	4	5	6	7
Primarily negative			Neutral			Primarily positive

Being Anxious/Fearful

How *strongly* did you feel this emotion?

1	2	3	4	5	6	7
Not at all			Moderately			Very strongly

To what degree did you *express* your emotion to the person(s) who caused it?

1	2	3	4	5	6	7
Not at all			Moderately			Very strongly

How *appropriate* is it to express this emotion in your organization or work group?

1	2	3	4	5	6	7
Not at all appropriate			Moderately appropriate			Clearly appropriate

In the situation you are thinking of, to what degree were the consequences of the episode *positive or negative*?

1	2	3	4	5	6	7
Primarily negative			Neutral			Primarily positive

Source: Adapted from Donald E. Gibson, "Emotional Episodes at Work: An Experiential Exercise in Feeling and Expressing Emotions," *Journal of Management Education* 30, 3 (June 2006), pp. 477–500.

EXERCISE
Exploring Leadership Beliefs

Task:	Class members reflect back on the accumulation of explicit and implicit messages they have accumulated about the nature of effective leadership as well as the probable origins of these beliefs.
Group Size:	Class members break into small groups (e.g., 3 to 5 persons).
Materials Needed:	Newsprint (flip chart pages) for each group; masking tape.
Time Required:	Approximately one hour in class.
Procedure:	Break the class into small groups (e.g., 3 to 5 persons). Ask them to brainstorm all the things that they "know" about leadership (e.g., "Leaders are born, not made.") from earlier course-work, life experiences, and work situations. Have each group list these on a page of newsprint. In a separate column, ask them to code each statement to indicate its likely source, such as W.E. (work experience), S.E. (social experience), F.L. (family life), P.C. (prior coursework), P.R. (popular reading), or O. (other). After about 20 minutes, ask the groups to report their results to the larger class. Using a show of hands, ask class members to indicate whether they basically agree with each of the statements.
Discussion Questions:	1. What are the common beliefs about leadership that appear in more than one group's report?
	2. By scanning the coded origins of leadership beliefs held by the class members, from where do most of them originate?
	3. How valid are each of these beliefs about leadership? What is their source?
	4. Assuming that these beliefs are not derived from substantive research, what can we do to help ourselves and others "let go" of these beliefs during this course?

TABLE 1 **Beliefs about Leadership**

	Belief Statement	Origin
1.	_____	____
2.	_____	____
3.	_____	____
4.	_____	____
5.	_____	____
6.	_____	____
7.	_____	____
8.	_____	____
9.	_____	____
10.	_____	____

EXERCISE
What You See Is (Not Necessarily) What You Get: Connecting Observations of Leadership Figures to Inferences[1]

Task

Class members, divided into three groups, are given one of three different objects (representing applicants for a top leadership position) to observe, touch, and assess.

Group Size

Any number, as long as the group members can comfortably interact with each other (e.g., up to 10 or 15).

Materials Needed

A ball of clay, a fancy bottle, and a Tinkertoy figure

Time Required

Approximately 45 minutes.

Procedure

1. Divide the class into three groups, and present each group (preferably without the other groups seeing it) one of the three objects. Tell them that their object represents a candidate for a leadership position in a for-profit firm.
2. Ask them to develop a comprehensive—but defensible—list of all the characteristics they can observe in their object.
3. After approximately 10 minutes, ask them to switch the focus of their efforts to generating a second list, which is an associated set of inferences about the leadership qualities (both positive and negative) that can be inferred from each characteristic.
4. Ask each group to briefly report (possibly using an overhead projector, flip chart paper, or the chalkboard), their group's conclusions (both lists).

Discussion Questions

1. What similarities or differences do you see across the three candidates/objects?
2. Which "candidate" is most qualified for the position?
3. Under what conditions might the rejected candidates be effective in another context? Would it make any difference if the context was a not-for-profit organization?
4. What are the risks of relying on visual impressions and subsequent inferences to ascertain leadership traits? What other methods exist to identify leadership traits?
5. Which of the inferences made by another group are less defensible than others?
6. Which of the leader characteristics identified could be viewed as exactly the opposite in nature (desirable or undesirable)? Is this one of the "paradoxes" of leadership—that desirable leadership is in the eye of the beholder?
7. To what degree do we project our own characteristics (or valued characteristics) onto leadership "candidates"?
8. How does this exercise relate to the text's readings on "traits"?
9. If the groups now exchanged objects, would their observations of characteristics and the associated inferences be any different? If so, why?

[1] An interesting reading for reference in conjunction with this exercise is Robert Cunningham, "Meet Dr. Clay and Dr. Glass: A Leadership Exercise," *Journal of Management Education* (May 1997), pp. 262–64.

EXERCISE
Tinkertoy Construction

Task: A sighted group leader instructs blindfolded subordinates in putting together a Tinkertoy structure.

Group Size: Groups of 4 to 6 persons.

Materials Needed: One set of basic Tinkertoys for each group (or only one, if a demonstration group is to be used). One blindfold for each participant. One picture of the structure to be built for each leader.

Time Required: Approximately one hour.

Procedure: Divide the class into groups. Ask each group to designate a leader for the exercise. All other members—the subordinates—are then asked to put on blindfolds. Once all subordinates are blindfolded, a picture of the structure to be built is handed to the leader of each group (see Figure 1). Leaders are told that they may do anything they wish to get their subordinates to build the structure, except remove the blindfolds or touch the Tinkertoys themselves.

FIGURE 1
Structure for Blindfold Leadership Exercise

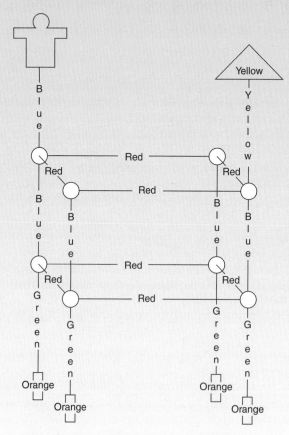

Discussion Questions:
1. Does the structure look like you expected it to look? How is it different?
2. What did your leader do that was helpful?
3. What did your leader do that was not helpful?
4. What feelings did you have during, or following, this exercise?
5. What lessons for leadership can you derive from this experience?
6. What are the implications of, and relevant insights from, your readings about leadership?

Source: Cindy P. Lindsay and Cathy A. Enz, "Resource Control and Visionary Leadership: Two Exercises," *Journal of Management Education* 15, no.1 (February 1991), pp. 127–35.

Class members select a leader and examine that person's life, significant contributing events, and leadership behaviors.	**Task**
Members work as individuals initially, then combine their efforts in a group and all-class discussion.	**Group Size**
None.	**Materials Needed**
Approximately one hour in class.	**Time Required**
Assign class members this task: "Examine the life of an individual whom you believe exemplifies the role of leader. This can be anyone, famous or not, past or present, industry or government, public or private, known to you personally or through the media. Some attention ought to be devoted to the chronology of events in the person's life. However, the bulk of your work should be directed at producing in-depth sociopsychological understanding. Pay attention to *how* the events and circumstances of the person's life affected the ultimate leadership self."	**Procedure**

1. Did your choice of leader come from:
   a. Public figures (current or historical)?
   b. Persons known from work?
   c. Family members?
   d. Personal acquaintances?
2. What factors do you think account for the class's observed distribution of choice from question 1?
3. Explore, in small groups, the leaders selected. What leadership qualities and characteristics are consistently represented there?
4. What can you learn about yourself as a leader from your choice of a leader to write about?
	Discussion Questions

Source: David I. Sommers, "The Choice of a Leader to Write About Is Not a Random Event," *Journal of Management Education* (August 1991), pp. 359–61.

EXERCISE

Characteristics of Superior Leaders

Task: Rank-order a set of leader characteristics on an individual and group basis, comparing the results to those from a broad sample of top-level managers.

Group Size: Groups of 3 to 5 persons.

Materials Needed: One ranking sheet for each member.

Time Required: Approximately one hour.

Procedure: Distribute copies of the "Leader Characteristics" form to each class member (see Table 1). Ask them to rank-order the items from 1 to 10 according to which traits they most admire in leaders (1 being highest) and record their responses in column 2. Then form them into small discussion groups and have them develop a group-based ranking of the items from 1 to 10 and record their responses in column 4. Finally, allow them to score themselves (both individually and as a group) against the responses of 2,600 top-level managers (to be inserted in column 3). Subtract each column 2 score from the corresponding number in column 3 (without regard to arithmetic sign) and enter it in column 1. Similarly, subtract each column 4 score from the corresponding number in column 3 (without regard to arithmetic sign) and enter it in column 5. Use these results to help answer Question 4 below.

Discussion Questions:
1. Which characteristics of leaders seem to be most admired by class members? Why?
2. What traits seem to be missing from this list?
3. How do these results compare to the research literature on leadership traits?
4. Why might your individual ranking differ from that of the top-level managers?
5. In a later book, Kouzes and Posner make a compelling argument that a leader's credibility is the most important ingredient contributing to his or her success (in the eyes of subordinates). Which factors in the list of 10 might be components of credibility?

Source: Data drawn from James M. Kouzes and Barry Z. Posner, *The Leadership Challenge* (San Francisco: Jossey-Bass, 1988), p. 17.

TABLE 1   Leader Characteristics

Trait	Columns				
	1	2 (Ind.)	3	4 (Grp.)	5
Ambitious	_____	_____	_____	_____	_____
Caring	_____	_____	_____	_____	_____
Competent	_____	_____	_____	_____	_____
Determined	_____	_____	_____	_____	_____
Forward-looking	_____	_____	_____	_____	_____
Honest	_____	_____	_____	_____	_____
Imaginative	_____	_____	_____	_____	_____
Inspiring	_____	_____	_____	_____	_____
Loyal	_____	_____	_____	_____	_____
Self-controlled	_____	_____	_____	_____	_____

Source: Data drawn from James M. Kouzes and Barry Z. Posner, *The Leadership Challenge* (San Francisco: Jossey-Bass, 1988), p. 17.

Teaching Note: Characteristics of Superior Leaders

1. Make sure that all participants first complete the *individuals* ranking process, placing their answers in column 2 of their forms.
2. Form class members into groups of 3–5, and instruct them that they must reach a *group* consensus on their rankings (column 4).
3. Share the "key" with them (column 3). Instruct them to derive an index of their individual accuracy by computing the absolute mathematical difference between their individual ranking for each item and the key (e.g., $8 - 4 = 4$; $6 - 9 = 3$), and then adding up the sum of all the 10 differences. Repeat this process for their group ranking. A low difference score indicates a closer match with the survey results provided by Kouzes and Posner.
4. Then lead the class in a discussion of the questions provided in the exercise itself.

Participants complete the LSF questionnaire, share and tabulate results, and discuss their implications. **Task**

Groups of 3 to 5 persons. **Group Size**

One copy of the questionnaire for each participant (see Table 1). One transparency master for tabulating results (see Table 2). **Materials Needed**

Minimum of one hour, depending on depth of discussion desired. **Time Required**

Distribute a copy of the LSF questionnaire to each participant and allow a few minutes for its completion. Using a show of hands for each question and response category, tabulate the results (preferably using a visual display, such as the chalkboard or a transparency). Then lead the group in a discussion of the following questions. **Procedure**

Discussion Questions

1. What does *friendship* mean to you?
2. Can leaders and subordinates be friends on the job and still maintain an effective work environment?
3. What skills contribute to friendships?
4. What are the risks of these friendships?
5. Can LSFs substitute for other leader behaviors?
6. How friendly should a leader be with followers?
7. What are the organizationally desirable consequences of leader–subordinate friendships?
8. Is it possible that LSFs would prevent objective appraisal of subordinate performance?
9. How can one obtain the benefits of LSFs without incurring the drawbacks?
10. How does LSF relate to a leader's source of power?

TABLE 1   **Leader–Subordinate Friendship Questionnaire**

Please respond to the following statements according to your level of agreement: SA—Strongly agree; A—Agree; N—Neutral; D—Disagree; SD—Strongly disagree. Circle the appropriate letters.

1. Managers should not try to maintain friendships with subordinates. SA A N D SD
2. It is possible to maintain friendships with subordinates without damaging one's effectiveness as a leader. SA A N D SD
3. As for myself, it works best if I do not try to be friends with my subordinates. SA A N D SD
4. Maintaining friendships with subordinates actually can make one a better leader. SA A N D SD
5. There is a certain skill associated with maintaining leader–subordinate friendships and still being an effective leader: Some managers have it and some don't. SA A N D SD
6. Friendships between leaders and subordinates are a natural consequence growing out of close physical proximity and considerable interpersonal contact. SA A N D SD
7. If a manager wants to maintain a friendship with one subordinate, then he or she must try to maintain friendship relationships with all subordinates. SA A N D SD
8. If a manager is going to maintain friendship relationships with subordinates at all, it might be a good idea to tie those relationships to performance (i.e., the better the performer, the more you encourage a friendship relationship with that subordinate). SA A N D SD
9. Maintaining friendships with subordinates gives a manager more information on which to base business decisions. SA A N D SD
10. Maintaining friendships with subordinates facilitates a manager's ability to motivate subordinates. SA A N D SD
11. The closer the leader–subordinate friendship, the greater the likelihood the subordinate will feel free to disagree with the boss. SA A N D SD
12. Maintaining leader–subordinate friendships gives the subordinate more power to influence the leader. SA A N D SD
13. It is generally not a good idea for subordinates to have the power to influence their bosses. SA A N D SD
14. The closer the friendship relationship between leader and subordinate, the greater the likelihood that the leader will feel free to give the negative performance feedback when a subordinate is doing poorly. SA A N D SD
15. The closer the leader–subordinate friendship, the less likely it is that a leader will give a subordinate a negative mark on a formal performance appraisal. SA A N D SD
16. Being a considerate manager or leader is the same as maintaining a friendship relationship with subordinates. SA A N D SD
17. It is easier for staff-area managers to maintain leader–subordinate friendships than it is for production or line-area managers. SA A N D SD
18. It is easier for an upper-level manager (a vice president for instance) to maintain leader–subordinate friendships with his or her immediate subordinates than it is for a lower-level manager or supervisor. SA A N D SD
19. What do you see as the major benefits, if any, of a manager maintaining friendships with subordinates?

    1.

    2.

    3.

    4.

20. What do you see as the major drawbacks, if any, of a manager maintaining friendships with subordinates?

    1.

    2.

    3.

    4.

21. In general, the benefits of maintaining leader–subordinate friendships outweigh the drawbacks. SA A N D SD

TABLE 2 Leader–Subordinate Friendship Tally

Question	Responses				
	SA	A	N	D	SD
1. ______					
2. ______					
3. ______					
4. ______					
5. ______					
6. ______					
7. ______					
8. ______					
9. ______					
10. ______					
11. ______					
12. ______					
13. ______					
14. ______					
15. ______					
16. ______					
17. ______					
18. ______					
21. ______					

Source: Robert R. Taylor, Susan C. Hanlon, and Nancy G. Boyd, "Can Leaders and Subordinates Be Friends? A Classroom Approach for Addressing an Important Managerial Dilemma," *Journal of Management Education* (February 1992), pp. 39–55.

EXERCISE
Leadership
(Locker-room)
Talks

Task:	Class members are assigned a topic (see Table 1). Each member prepares and delivers a concise talk on the assigned topic, followed by class and instructor critiques of the effectiveness of the talk and the leadership dimensions demonstrated. The objective is to demonstrate the importance of, and develop, each student's confidence, willingness, and readiness to play an inspirational leadership role.
Group Size:	Any number (overlapping assignments to topics are possible).
Time Required:	Two minutes per student, plus critique time.
Procedure:	1. Explain the objectives of the exercise to the class.
	2. Indicate the types of locker-room talk topics and how they fit into the classification scheme.
	3. Assign topics and dates of presentations.
	4. Cue the class members to act as real audiences, reacting as they might to the situation and the comments made by the speaker.
	5. Call for two-minute talks, using a student timekeeper to cue the speaker when 15 seconds remain.
	6. Call for comments from the class about the quality and effectiveness of the speeches, as well as the various dimensions of leadership displayed.
Discussion Questions:	1. What are the primary objectives of locker-room talks by leaders?
	2. What are the primary abilities that need to be demonstrated by each speaker in these settings?
	3. What characteristics of feedback to the speakers are most constructive?
	4. How do you handle hostility? Distrust? Apathy?

(continued)

TABLE 1 Topics for the Leadership Talks and a Classification of Each

Topic Number	Topic Description
1.	Taking charge of an established group. The speaker is a manager newly assigned to a group that has worked together under other managers for some time.
2.	Announcing a new project. The speaker is announcing a new undertaking to members of his or her department and is calling on all to rally behind the effort.
3.	Calling for better customer service. The speaker is motivating all employees to be as attentive and responsive to the customer as possible.
4.	Calling for excellence and high-quality work. The speaker is motivating all employees to perform their jobs with a commitment to meeting the highest possible standards.
5.	Announcing the need for cost reductions. The speaker is requesting that everyone look for ways to cut expenditures and immediately begin slashing spending.
6.	Commending for a job well done. The speaker is extolling a group of people who have worked very hard for an extended period to produce outstanding results.

Topic Number	Topic Description
7.	Reprimanding unacceptable behavior. The speaker is calling to task certain individuals who have failed to perform up to required levels.
8.	Calming a frightened group of people. The speaker is endeavoring to restore peace and confidence to those who now panic in the face of distressing business developments.
9.	Addressing a challenging opposition. The speaker is presenting some heartfelt belief to a critical, even hostile, audience.
10.	Mediating opposing parties. The speaker is calling for reconciliation between two groups bitterly opposed on some key issue.
11.	Taking responsibility for error. The speaker is the figurehead spokesman for an institution that has produced some unfortunate result affecting the audience.
12.	Petitioning for special allowances. The speaker is presenting the case for an institution seeking certain rights that must be authorized by some external body.

	Individual	Group	Institution
Task-oriented	Taking responsibility: Taking charge of an established group; Introducing a new project; Taking responsibility for error.[a]	Shaping behavior: Commending for a job well done; Reprimanding unacceptable behavior.	Forging a direction: Calling for better customer service; Calling for excellence and high-quality work; Announcing the need for cost reductions.
Emotional-/values-oriented	Taking a stand: Addressing a challenging opposition.	Building cohesion: Calming a frightened group of people; Mediating opposing parties.	Representing the firm: Taking responsibility for error;[a] Petitioning for special allowances.

[a] This topic is suitable for both "taking responsibility" and "representing the firm."
Source: Richard G. Linowes, "Filling a Gap in Management Education: Giving Leadership Talks in the Classroom," *Journal of Management Education* (1992), pp. 6–24.

EXERCISE
Follow the Leader

Task:	Students are assigned to read biographical materials on well-known leaders and identify their relationship with their followers.
Group Size:	Any number.
Time Required:	Approximately one class session per leader studied.
Procedure:	Divide the class into study groups. Following prior reading, lecture, or discussion on "follower-ship" factors in leader effectiveness, assign (or allow choice in selection) one major leader (e.g., Lee Iacocca, Martin Luther King, Jr., Adolph Hitler, Eleanor Roosevelt, Carly Fiorina) per group. Provide the group with appropriate references documenting the leaders' lives, from which they may draw their analyses. Ask each group to identify:

1. The ways in which the leader they studied influenced his/her followers.
2. The influence of the followers on the leader studied.
3. How characteristics of their own and their followers' personalities affected the leader's success.

Discussion Questions:	

1. Was your chosen leader successful?
2. Would you have willingly followed that leader?
3. What kinds of facts about the leader studied did you use to make your argument?
4. What kinds of facts about the leader studied did you omit in making your argument?
5. What leadership theories are relevant to your understanding of this leader, and how?
6. What characteristics of their followers' personalities (e.g., skills/abilities, needs, wants, preferences, expectations, biases, and personal histories) affected the leader's success?

Suggested Leader References

Burrows, P., *Backfire: Carly Fiorina's High-Stakes Battle for the Soul of Hewlett-Packard.* New Jersey: John Wiley & Sons, Inc., 2003.

Garrow, D. J. *Bearing the Cross: Martin Luther King, Jr., and the Southern Christian Leadership Conference.* New York: William Morrow, 1986.

Hitler, A. *Mein Kampf.* Boston: Houghton Mifflin, 1927.

Iacocca, L., with W. Novak. *Iacocca: An Autobiography.* New York: Bantam, 1984.

Lacey, R. *Ford: The Men and the Machine.* Boston: Little, Brown, 1986.

Langer, W. C. *The Mind of Adolf Hitler.* New York: New American Library, 1972.

Roosevelt, E. *The Autobiography of Eleanor Roosevelt.* Boston: G. K. Hall, 1984.

Sloan, A. *The Bendix–Martin Marietta War.* New York: Dow-Jones, 1977.

Youngs, J. W. T. *Eleanor Roosevelt: A Personal and Public Life.* Boston: Little Brown, 1985.

Source: Clayton P. Alderfer, "Teaching Personality and Leadership: A Course on Followership," *OBTR* 12, 4 (1987–88), pp. 12–33.

EXERCISE

Probing Metaphors for Their Leadership Lessons

Class members examine a variety of metaphors and explore their relevance and implications for the study of leadership.

Task

Small groups (e.g., 3 to 5 persons).

Group Size

Newsprint (flip chart pages) for each group, masking tape.

Materials Needed

Approximately one hour in class.

Time Required

Break the class into small groups (e.g., 3 to 5 persons). Ask them to select one of the metaphors from the list below (no duplicate selections within the class) and identify the ways in which that metaphor helps them understand and explain the leadership process. They should record their major conclusions on the flip chart paper under the heading of their chosen metaphor. After about 30 minutes, ask the groups to report their results to the larger class. After their brief presentations, ask class members to indicate, via a show of hands, the degree (5 = Very useful, 4 = Quite useful, 3 = Moderately useful, 2 = Somewhat useful, 1 = Not at all useful) to which they found each metaphor useful. Tabulate the results in Table 1.

Procedure

1. Which of the metaphors was richest in its implications for leadership? Why?
2. Looking beyond the sample metaphors listed in Table 1, what other metaphors would be useful to analyze?
3. What are the potential risks in borrowing and adapting metaphors such as these to the leadership process?
4. What are the potential benefits from borrowing and adapting metaphors such as these to the leadership process?

Discussion Questions

TABLE 1   **Metaphors Possibly Relevant to Leadership**

Metaphor	Degree of Usefulness				
	5	4	3	2	1
1. Chess	——	——	——	——	——
2. Snowboarding	——	——	——	——	——
3. Conducting musical groups	——	——	——	——	——
4. Jet plane piloting	——	——	——	——	——
5. Texas Hold 'Em (poker)	——	——	——	——	——
6. Bartending	——	——	——	——	——
7. Beekeeping	——	——	——	——	——
8. Parenting	——	——	——	——	——
9. Carpentry/woodworking	——	——	——	——	——
10. NASCAR racing	——	——	——	——	——

Source: Simulated by and loosely patterned after an exercise in Cynthia Wagner Weick, "Out of Context: Using Metaphor to Encourage Creative Thinking in Strategic Management Courses," *Journal of Management Education* 27, 3 (June 2003), pp. 323–343.

EXERCISE
Leadership Through Film: Power and Influence

Task:	Students view a "popular" film (full-length movie) and analyze it for illustrations of various sources and applications of power. This draws on Bandura's concept of vicarious (observational) learning.
Group Size:	Assignments can be made at three levels: total class, small group, or individual.
Materials Needed:	VCR/TV and selected video or DVD, if a single, common stimulus is desired for total-class discussion.
Time Required:	Approximately two hours to view an entire film, plus subsequent discussion time.
Procedure:	1. Choose a film that is rich in demonstration of a leader's use of power and influence. Many prime examples exist, such as *Dead Poets' Society, Watership Down, Aliens, A Few Good Men,* and *The Magnificent Seven.* 2. Show the film to the class. (Alternatively, allow each class member to select the film of his or her choice and prepare a report.) 3. Ask each member to prepare a written paper that thoroughly discusses leadership and power.
Discussion Questions:	1. *Who* has power in the film, *why* do they have that power, and *how* did they acquire it? 2. What was the *source* of that power (e.g., expert, legitimate, referent)? 3. How did they *use* their power (e.g., to make a legitimate request, to gain compliance, to persuade or inspire)? 4. What were the positive/negative *effects* of that power on the followers? 5. Alternatively, how could they have influenced their followers?

Sources: Adapted from various reports by Timothy Serey, Claudia Harris, Kermith V. Harrington, and Ricky W. Griffin.

EXERCISE
Deriving Leadership Lessons from The Lion King

Provide meaningful text-based responses to a variety of discussion questions.

Task

Groups of 3–5 students.

Group Size

Video or DVD of Disney's *The Lion King.*

Materials Needed

Approximately one hour, plus viewing time.

Time Required

Divide the class into small groups. Show the video to them (it's the story of Simba, heir to the throne of Pride Rock, who makes a bad decision and sends himself into exile as punishment. His power-crazed Uncle Scar ascends to the throne as king, but eventually Simba is persuaded by friends Timon, Pumbaa, and Nala to forget his past and return to save his homeland). Assign them the first set of questions and give them 20 minutes to develop responses to them. Reconvene as a full class and facilitate a large-group discussion for 10 minutes. Repeat the process with the second set of questions in both small-group and large-group discussion.

Procedure

1. According to French and Raven (1959), individuals have five sources of power by which they can induce others to behave in accordance with their wishes. Give examples of characters in *The Lion King* that have (a) reward power, (b) coercive power, (c) legitimate power, (d) expert power, and (e) referent power.
2. Katz (1955) discussed technical, human, and conceptual skills. Which of these three kinds of skills does an effective leader need? How do leaders acquire and develop these skills? Give examples from the movie.
3. Kirkpatrick and Locke (1991) asserted that certain key traits predispose individuals to lead effectively. Explain how each of the following affect the leadership of the three lion kings: (a) a personalized versus socialized power drive, (b) honesty and integrity, and (c) self-confidence.
4. How do the behaviors of the three lion kings contribute to their effectiveness as leaders?
5. How did Timon and Pumbaa help their friend Simba become an effective leader? How did their motto "hakuna matata" impede Simba's development as a leader?
6. Compared with Scar, Mufasa and Simba shone as leaders. Nonetheless, neither one was perfect. Identify each one's leadership flaw.

Discussion Questions (1)

1. How can a leader's enemies undermine the leader's effectiveness? How should an organizational leader view and deal with his or her enemies?
2. Simba took a personal physical risk when he battled Scar to reclaim Pride Rock. What risks do organizational leaders take when contending with their enemies?
3. What are the consequences, for both a leader and his or her group, of the leader's running away from a problem instead of confronting it?
4. Management educators have recently recognized the usefulness of the notion of spirituality (e.g., Bolman & Deal, 1995; Ferris, 1998; Neal, 1997). Rafiki persuaded Simba to reclaim the throne by helping him communicate with the spirit of his father, Mufasa. How can organizational leaders who do not necessarily subscribe to religion or to the supernatural use spirituality to lead more effectively?
5. It is not uncommon for organizational leaders to experience fear while facing stressful situations (Ferris, 1998). Simba had to confront his feelings of sadness, shame, guilt, and inadequacy before he could reclaim the throne. What lesson may be generalized to organizational leaders from Simba's process of overcoming his negative feelings about himself?
6. In the movie, effective leadership was associated with plentiful resources and a balanced ecosystem. Ineffective leadership was associated with depleted resources and a dysfunctional system. What analogous outcomes are associated with effective and ineffective leadership in business organizations?

Discussion Questions (2)

(continued)

7. Identify a leader from history or fiction (or religious texts, which some view as history and others view as fiction) who faced experiences comparable to those Simba encountered. Elaborate on the parallels between this leader and Simba.
8. Before Simba reclaimed his throne, the inhabitants of the Pride Lands were in dire straits. Had Simba not returned to battle Scar, what, if anything, would the lionesses and other animals have done? Why do group members tend to look to a leader to rescue them from their problems? How can overdependence on a leader harm group members?

Source: Adapted from Debra R. Comer, "Not Just a Mickey Mouse Exercise: Using Disney's *The Lion King* to Teach Leadership," *Journal of Management Education* 25, 4, pp. 430–436, copyright 2001 by Sage Publications. Reprinted by permission of Sage Publications, Inc.

EXERCISE

Exploring Leadership Beliefs

Task

Class members reflect back on the results of their brainstorming early in the course regarding the beliefs they had previously accumulated about the nature of effective leadership as well as the probable origins of these beliefs.

Group Size

Total class discussion.

Materials Needed

Transparency (or printed copy for distribution) of the combined results of the class's brainstorming from the "Exploring Leadership Beliefs" experiential exercise.

Time Required

Approximately one hour in class.

Procedure

Present the summary of class-generated beliefs about leadership to the class. Ask them to review each statement for consistency with the research on leaders and the leadership process, as they have studied it in this book. Using a show of hands, ask class members to indicate the degree (5 = Very high, 4 = High, 3 = Moderate, 2 = Low, 1 = Very low) to which they now agree with each of the statements.

Discussion Questions

1. Have some of the previous class beliefs about leadership been exploded (i.e., exposed as myths)? Which ones, in particular?
2. What can you now conclude about the validity of "street knowledge" about leadership, in general?
3. What lessons does this hold for your future accumulation of knowledge about leadership?
4. How can you go about convincing others (e.g., managers in work organizations) that they, too, should be exploring the research literature on leadership—both past and future?

TABLE 1 Beliefs about Leadership

Belief Statement	Degree of Agreement				
	5	4	3	2	1
1. _____	___	___	___	___	___
2. _____	___	___	___	___	___
3. _____	___	___	___	___	___
4. _____	___	___	___	___	___
5. _____	___	___	___	___	___
6. _____	___	___	___	___	___
7. _____	___	___	___	___	___
8. _____	___	___	___	___	___
9. _____	___	___	___	___	___
10. _____	___	___	___	___	___

EXERCISE
*Identifying
Causal
Connections*

Task: Class members review the readings in this book (and other sources available to them) and develop a composite visual model of likely causal connections (antecedents and consequences of leadership).

Group Size: Class members break into small groups (e.g., 3 to 5 persons).

Materials Needed: Newsprint (flip chart pages) for each group, masking tape.

Time Required: Approximately one hour in class.

Procedure: Divide the class into small groups, and ask each of the groups to create a comprehensive visual model of leadership, drawing upon all of their prior readings. This model should identify, at a minimum, contributing factors to successful leadership (antecedents) and documented outcomes (consequences). Ideally, it would also specify mediating or moderating variables. When all groups are finished, ask each of them to briefly present their model to the entire class, and invite comments and feedback.

Discussion Questions:
1. What does your model (and the models of others) tell us about the complexity of the leadership process?
2. What conflicting conclusions did you discover in your readings that made it difficult to include in your model?
3. What differences do you see among the leadership models? Why do they exist, given the common sources of information?
4. What value lies in the creation (and future updating) of an overall conceptual model of the leadership process?
5. How can you go about convincing others (e.g., managers in work organizations) that they should be aware of, and be guided by, a (research-based) personal model for their leadership behavior?

Source: Simulated by and loosely patterned after an exercise in Jeffrey A. Mello, "Profiles in Leadership: Enhancing Learning through Model and Theory Building," *Journal of Management Education* 27, 3 (June 2003), pp. 344–361.

EXERCISE
Generating
Leadership
Lessons

Class members reflect back on, and make explicit, the practical implications of the knowledge that they have accumulated about the nature of effective leadership. | **Task**

Class members break into small groups (e.g., 3 to 5 persons). | **Group Size**

Newsprint (flip chart pages) for each group, masking tape. | **Materials Needed**

Approximately one hour in class. | **Time Required**

Break the class into small groups (e.g., 3 to 5 persons). Ask them to brainstorm a comprehensive set of the ten most important action prescriptions for leaders to use, based on the leadership studies they have examined in this book. Have each group list these on a page of newsprint. After about 30 minutes, ask the groups to report their results to the larger class. Using a show of hands, ask class members to indicate the degree to which they agree (5 = Very high, 4 = High, 3 = Moderate, 2 = Low, 1 = Very low) with each of the action prescriptions. | **Procedure**

1. What are the common action prescriptions about leadership that appear in more than one group's report? | **Discussion Questions**
2. Which of these prescriptions are likely to be the most controversial among leaders? Which might be the most difficult for leaders to implement? Which of these are likely to be commonly used already by leaders today?
3. How useful are each of these prescriptions for leadership?
4. Do any of these prescriptions contradict each other? If so, how do you reconcile them?
5. For those action prescriptions with a low degree of agreement from the class, indicate what could be done to improve the statement to make it more actionable.

TABLE 1

Action Prescription	Degree of Agreement				
	5	4	3	2	1
1. _____	___	___	___	___	___
2. _____	___	___	___	___	___
3. _____	___	___	___	___	___
4. _____	___	___	___	___	___
5. _____	___	___	___	___	___
6. _____	___	___	___	___	___
7. _____	___	___	___	___	___
8. _____	___	___	___	___	___
9. _____	___	___	___	___	___
10._____	___	___	___	___	___

Index